Guatemala
Belize & Yucatán

La Ruta Maya

Tom Brosnahan
Nancy Keller

Guatemala, Belize & Yucatán

3rd edition

Published by
Lonely Planet Publications
Head Office: PO Box 617, Hawthorn, Vic 3122, Australia
Branches: 155 Filbert St, Suite 251, Oakland, CA 94607, USA
               10 Barley Mow Passage, Chiswick, London W4 4PH, UK
               71 bis rue du Cardinal Lemoine, 75005 Paris, France

Printed by
SNP Printing Pte Ltd, Singapore

Photographs by

Jeffrey Becom (JB)	Mario Gallotta (MG)	Richard Nebesky (RN)
Tom Brosnahan (TB)	James Lyon (JL)	Kevin Schafer (KS)
Mark Downey (MD)	Yoshi Makino (YM)	Paul Wentford (PW)
Greg Elms (GE)		

Front cover: Tikal, Guatemala, Harold Pfeiffer, Tony Stone Images

First Published
October 1991

This Edition
November 1997

Although the author and publisher have tried to make the information as accurate as possible, they accept no responsibility for any loss, injury or inconvenience sustained by any person using this book.

National Library of Australia Cataloguing in Publication Data

Brosnahan, Tom.
Guatemala, Belize & Yucatán.

3rd ed.
Includes index.
ISBN 0 86442 424 8.

1. Yucatán Peninsula – Guidebooks. 2. Guatemala – Guidebooks. 3. Belize – Guidebooks.
I. Brosnahan, Tom. Guatemala, Belize & Yucatán, la Ruta Maya. II. Title.
III. Title: Guatemala, Belize & Yucatán, la Ruta Maya.

917.28

text & maps © Lonely Planet 1997
photos © photographers as indicated 1997
climate charts compiled from information supplied by Patrick J Tyson, © Patrick J Tyson, 1997

Tom Brosnahan

Tom Brosnahan was born and raised in Pennsylvania, went to college in Boston, then set out on the road. After traveling in Europe he joined the Peace Corps and saw Mexico for the first time as part of the Peace Corps training program. A short term of teaching English in a Mexico City school whetted his appetite for more exploration. After graduate school he traveled throughout Mexico, Guatemala and Belize, writing travel articles and guidebooks for various publishers, and in the past two decades his 20 books covering numerous destinations have sold over two million copies in twelve languages.

Ever since he first saw Yucatán, Guatemala and Belize, Tom had a dream of returning to follow in the footsteps of John L Stephens and write an authoritative guidebook to the Mayan lands. This guide is the fulfillment of that dream.

This book is for Lydia Celestia, who's Mayan, in a way.

Nancy Keller

Born and raised in Northern California, Nancy worked in the alternative press for several years, doing every aspect of newspaper work from editorial and reporting to delivering the papers. She returned to university to earn a master's degree in journalism, finally graduating in 1986 after many breaks for extended stays on the west coast of Mexico. Since then she's been traveling and writing in Mexico, Israel, Egypt, Europe, various South Pacific islands, New Zealand and Central America. Nancy is author or co-author of several Lonely Planet books, including those to California & Nevada, Mexico, New Zealand and Rarotonga & the Cook Islands.

From the Authors

From Tom I know of no more fascinating places, or better places to explore, than southern Mexico, Guatemala and Belize. Though their fascination is eternal, their exchange rates and economies are not. Nancy and I have done our best to provide detailed, exact and complete information on accommodations, meals, transportation, etc. But a swing in the world price of oil or an economic policy decision made in Mexico City, Guatemala City or Belize City can change all of our carefully recorded information in a day. If this happens, please rest assured that the establishments recommended will still offer the best value for the price, whether that price is higher or lower than noted in this guide.

When you return from your journey through the region, I'm sure you'll have suggestions, recommendations and perhaps even criticisms. Please write and let me know about them so that I can improve the next edition of this guide. You'll be helping many thousands of faithful

Lonely Planet readers to enjoy Guatemala, Belize and southern Mexico as you have. I'm very grateful for letters – I read each one and I reply if I can. The names of the travelers who have written are listed on page 567.

A surer way to get a quick reply is to send me electronic mail. Contact me on the Internet at tbros@infoexchange.com. For updates to this guide, access my website at www.infoexchange.com. Also check out Lonely Planet's award-winning website at www.lonelyplanet.com.

If you have problems with any establishment mentioned in this guide, please write to me so that I can reassess it or remove it and save future travelers from similar problems. Establishments recommended in this guide must provide you, the reader, with good, honest, courteous service at fair prices, or they do not warrant a recommendation.

From Nancy In Guatemala, thanks to the national tourist office (INGUAT) for their helpfulness. Thanks also to Real Desrosiers of the Adventure Travel Center, the folks at the Rainbow Reading Room and to Juan Francisco Sic (all of Antigua), David and Flori of the Desarrollo del Pueblo Spanish school (Quetzaltenango), Ashley de Acuña and family (Cobán), Carole DeVine (Poptún), Ricardo Pocorny, Alexandra and Carlos (Flores), Eugene at Hacienda Tijax (Río Dulce), María 'La Mexicana' and Julio Raúl Chew (Lívingston) and Antonio 'Maharishi' (San Pedro La Laguna). Thanks also to travelers met along the way who made the journey brighter, especially Tara Ryan.

Thanks also to TACA airline and Rosa Castro and María Ng of Central America Corp for their assistance.

At Lonely Planet, thanks to editors Kate Hoffman, Michelle Gagne and Don Gates; to Alex Guilbert and the cartographic crew; and to Caroline Liou for much helpfulness throughout the project. And, as always, boundless gratitude to Tom.

From the Publisher
This edition of *La Ruta Maya* saw the light in Lonely Planet's office in Oakland, California. Don Gates was the coordinating editor, with ample assistance from Carolyn Hubbard. Michelle Gagné-Ballard, Kate Hoffman and Laini Taylor edited text and maps, and Laura Harger and Jacqueline Volin both proofed text and edited maps. Rini Keagy was in charge of mapping and layout, under the guidance of Alex Guilbert and Scott Summers. Alex, Hayden Foell, Cyndy Johnsen, Henia Miedzinski, Beca Lafore, Diana Nankin and Scott Noren also created maps for this edition. Illustrations were drawn by Hayden, Rini and Hugh D'Andrade, who also created the cover.

Extra thanks to Caroline Liou, Carolyn and Kate for editorial expertise and support along the way.

This Book
The 1st and 2nd editions of this book were researched and written by Tom Brosnahan. The Guatemala section of this 3rd edition was updated by Nancy Keller, all the rest was updated by Tom.

Warning & Request
Things change – prices go up, schedules change, good places go bad and bad places go bankrupt – nothing stays the same. So, if you find things better or worse, recently opened or long since closed, please tell us and help make the next edition even more accurate and useful.

We value all of the feedback we receive from travelers. A small team reads and acknowledges every letter, postcard and email and ensures that every morsel of information finds its way to the appropriate authors, editors and publishers. Everyone who writes to us will find their name in the next edition of the appropriate guide and will also receive a free subscription to our quarterly newsletter, *Planet Talk*. The very best contributions will be rewarded with a free Lonely Planet guide.

Excerpts from your correspondence may appear in updates (which we add to the end pages of reprints); new editions of this guide; in our newsletter; or in the Postcards section of our website – so please let us know if you don't want your letter published or your name acknowledged.

Contents

BELIZE

YUCATÁN

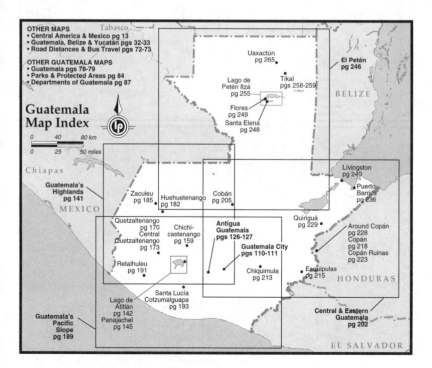

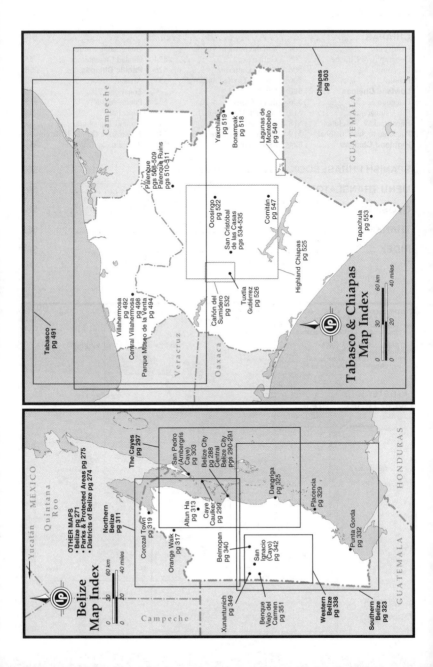

Belize Map Index

MEXICO

Yucatán

Quintana Roo

OTHER MAPS
• Belize pg 271
• Parks & Protected Areas pg 275
• Districts of Belize pg 274

The Cayes pg 297

San Pedro (Ambergris Caye) pg 303

Belize City pg 288
Central Belize City pgs 290-291

Northern Belize pg 311

Altun Ha pg 313

Caye Caulker pg 299

Corozal Town pg 319

Orange Walk pg 317

Dangriga pg 325

Belmopan pg 340

San Ignacio (Cayo) pg 342

Placencia pg 329

Punta Gorda pg 332

Xunantunich pg 349

Benque del Carmen pg 351

Western Belize pg 338

Southern Belize pg 323

GUATEMALA

HONDURAS

Campeche

0   30   60 km
0   20   40 miles

Tabasco & Chiapas Map Index

Campeche

Chiapas pg 503

Palenque pgs 508-509
Palenque Ruins pgs 510-511

Villahermosa pg 492

Central Villahermosa pg 498

Parque Museo de la Venta pg 494

Veracruz

Oaxaca

Tabasco pg 491

Yaxchilán pg 519

Bonampak pg 518

Lagunas de Montebello pg 549

Ocosingo pg 522

San Cristóbal de las Casas pgs 534-535

Comitán pg 547

Tapachula pg 553

GUATEMALA

Cañón del Sumidero pg 532

Tuxtla Gutiérrez pg 526

Highland Chiapas pg 525

0   30   60 km
0   20   40 miles

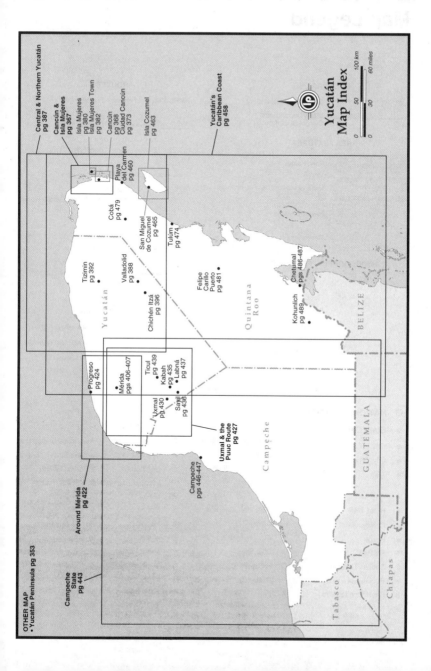

OTHER MAP
• Yucatán Peninsula pg 353

Campeche State pg 443

Around Mérida pg 422

Central & Northern Yucatán pg 387

Cancún & Isla Mujeres pg 367
Isla Mujeres pg 380
Isla Mujeres Town pg 382
Cancún pg 368
Ciudad Cancún pg 373
Isla Cozumel pg 463

Yucatán's Caribbean Coast pg 458

Progreso pg 424

Mérida pgs 406-407

Uxmal pg 430

Ticul pg 439

Kabah pg 435

Labná pg 437

Sayil pg 438

Uxmal & the Puuc Route pg 427

Campeche pgs 446-447

Tizimín pg 392

Valladolid pg 388

Chichén Itzá pg 396

Cobá pg 479

Playa del Carmen pg 460

San Miguel de Cozumel pg 465

Tulum pg 474

Felipe Carillo Puerto pg 481

Kohunlich pg 489

Chetumal pgs 486-487

Yucatán

Quintana Roo

Campeche

BELIZE

GUATEMALA

Tabasco

Chiapas

Yucatán Map Index

0   50   100 km
0   30   60 miles

Map Legend

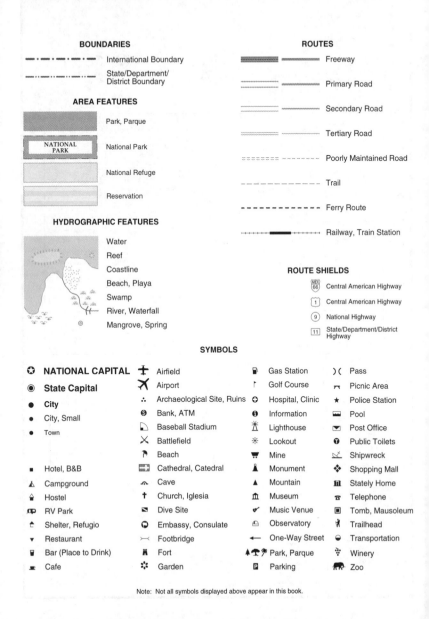

BOUNDARIES

— · — · — · — International Boundary

— ·· — ·· — ·· State/Department/District Boundary

AREA FEATURES

Park, Parque

NATIONAL PARK — National Park

National Refuge

Reservation

HYDROGRAPHIC FEATURES

Water
Reef
Coastline
Beach, Playa
Swamp
River, Waterfall
Mangrove, Spring

ROUTES

Freeway

Primary Road

Secondary Road

Tertiary Road

Poorly Maintained Road

Trail

Ferry Route

Railway, Train Station

ROUTE SHIELDS

MEX 66 Central American Highway

1 Central American Highway

9 National Highway

11 State/Department/District Highway

SYMBOLS

✪ NATIONAL CAPITAL
◉ State Capital
● City
● City, Small
● Town

■ Hotel, B&B
▲ Campground
⌂ Hostel
⊡ RV Park
⌂ Shelter, Refugio
▼ Restaurant
🍸 Bar (Place to Drink)
☕ Cafe

✠ Airfield
✈ Airport
∴ Archaeological Site, Ruins
⑤ Bank, ATM
⟐ Baseball Stadium
✕ Battlefield
⚓ Beach
⊟ Cathedral, Catedral
⌒ Cave
✝ Church, Iglesia
⬟ Dive Site
◗ Embassy, Consulate
⌣ Footbridge
⛫ Fort
✺ Garden

⛽ Gas Station
⚑ Golf Course
✚ Hospital, Clinic
ℹ Information
⛴ Lighthouse
✳ Lookout
⛏ Mine
⚐ Monument
▲ Mountain
⛪ Museum
♪ Music Venue
⌂ Observatory
← One-Way Street
▲⚑♣ Park, Parque
🅿 Parking

)(Pass
⌐ Picnic Area
★ Police Station
⊂⊃ Pool
▼ Post Office
⊕ Public Toilets
⌐ Shipwreck
❖ Shopping Mall
▥ Stately Home
☎ Telephone
◼ Tomb, Mausoleum
⚑ Trailhead
◖ Transportation
☘ Winery
🐗 Zoo

Note: Not all symbols displayed above appear in this book.

Introduction

The Mayan lands of Guatemala, Belize and southern Mexico were home to the Western Hemisphere's greatest ancient civilization. Travelers to this region today come to see the huge pyramids and temples, the great stelae covered in hieroglyphic inscriptions and the broad ball courts where mysterious athletic contests were held.

But Mayan lore is more than the forgotten culture of a long-dead empire. As you travel here, the Maya are all around you. Modern descendants of the ancient Maya drive your bus, catch the fish you dine upon, work in the bank where you change money and greet you as you trudge up the side of a smoking volcano. The Mayan kingdoms may be dead, but the Maya – some two million of them – are very much alive in their ancient land.

The land is varied, from the flat limestone shelf of Yucatán to the cool pine-clad mountains of Chiapas and Guatemala, from the steamy jungles of El Petén, rich with tropical birdlife, to the swamps and fens of northern Belize. It is also threatened. Pressured by rapid population growth, development and exploitation, it is in danger of overuse and consequent ecological destruction. The dense tropical forest is disappearing at an alarming rate as farmers and ranchers, responding to personal need and world market conditions, slash and burn to carve out new fields for subsistence farming or pasture land for high-profit herds of beef cattle.

The rich heritage of Mayan civilization and its environment has its defenders, however. Both governments and private organizations are instituting programs to preserve and protect both the Mayan heritage and its natural setting. Tourism is one of the most important forces in these plans.

LA RUTA MAYA

La Ruta Maya (The Mayan Route) was a plan conceived and championed by Wilbur E Garrett, former editor of the US *National Geographic* magazine. The concept of La

Ruta Maya provides for carefully controlled touristic development with minimal adverse impact on the land, the people and the Maya's heritage. Income from increased tourism may be used to preserve and protect Mayan archaeological sites and jungle biosphere reserves; it may also offer an alternative source of income to those now destroying the forests. The governments of Mexico, Guatemala, Belize, Honduras and El Salvador have subscribed to the plan and have established an intergovernmental organization called El Mundo Maya to make tourism work to the benefit of the Maya and their land.

The purpose of these plans is to highlight the cultural, ecological and archaeological significance of the Mayan lands, to provide direction and resources for protection and conservation and to help the Maya preserve their ancient culture while improving the conditions under which they live.

The plan envisions not one but many travel routes and circuits throughout the region, encompassing seaside resorts such as Cancún and Cozumel; jungle preserves in Chiapas, Quintana Roo, El Petén and Belize; Spanish colonial cities; and most archaeological sites, excavated and unexcavated.

This guidebook, while emphasizing Mayan culture both ancient and modern, also gives complete information for those going to Mexico's Caribbean coast or to Belize's offshore islands for sun, sand, surf and snorkeling, and for those interested in Mérida's beautiful colonial architecture, Campeche's pirate history and climbable volcanoes in Guatemala. In short, it is a complete guide to the lands of the Maya.

Facts about the Region

HISTORY
Archaic Period (20,000 to 2000 BC)

The great glaciers that blanketed northern Europe, Asia and North America in the Pleistocene Epoch robbed earth's oceans of a lot of water, lowering the sea level. The receding waters exposed enough land so that wandering bands of Asiatic men and women could find their way on dry land from Siberia to Alaska, and then southwards through the Western Hemisphere.

They made this journey perhaps as early as 23,000 years ago and soon found their way to every part of North and South America down to the Straits of Magellan. When the glaciers melted (about 7000 BC) and the sea level rose, the land bridge over which they crossed was submerged beneath what is now the Bering Strait.

The early inhabitants hunted mammoths, fished and gathered wild foods. After the Ice Age came a hot, dry period in which the mammoths' natural pastureland disappeared and the wild harvests of nuts and berries became scarce. The primitive inhabitants had to find some other way to get by, so they sought out favorable microclimates and invented agriculture.

Beans, tomatoes and squash (marrow) were cultivated, but these took second place to maize (corn), which was nurtured, by hybridization, from a wild grass into the Mayan staff of life, a status that it enjoys to this day. Baskets were woven to carry in the crops, and turkeys and dogs were domesticated for food. These early homebodies used crude stone tools and primitive pottery and shaped simple clay fertility figurines.

Early Preclassic Period (2000 to 800 BC)

The improvement in the food supply led to an increase in population, a higher standard of living and more time to fool around with such things as decorating pots and growing ever-plumper ears of corn. Even at the beginning of the Early Preclassic period, people here spoke an early form of the Mayan language. These early Maya also decided that living in caves and under palm fronds was old-fashioned, so they invented the *na*, or thatched Mayan hut, which is still used today, some 4000 years later, throughout much of the region. Where spring floods were a problem, a family would build its na on a mound of earth. When a family member died, burial took place right there in the living room, and the Dear Departed attained the rank of honored ancestor.

The Copán Valley (in present-day Honduras) had its first proto-Mayan settlers by about 1100 BC, and a century later the settlements on the Pacific coast of what is now Guatemala were developing a hierarchical society.

Olmecs Without question, the most significant happening of the Early Preclassic period took place about 1000 BC, not in the traditional Mayan lands, but in nearby Tabasco and Veracruz (both in modern Mexico). The mysterious Olmec people developed a writing system of hieroglyphics, perhaps based on knowledge borrowed from the Zapotecs of Oaxaca. They also developed what is known as the Vague Year calendar of 365 days (see the Mayan Calendar System section at the end of this chapter).

The Olmecs' jaguar god art became widespread through Mesoamerica ('middle America'). Their huge, mysterious basalt-carved heads weighing up to 60 tons were sculpted with characteristic 'jaguar mouths' and Negroid features. How the heads were hewn without metal tools and moved some 100 km from basalt quarries to the Olmecs' capital city of La Venta remains a mystery to this day.

It's assumed that the Olmecs were trampled by waves of invaders, but aspects of their culture lived on among their neighbors, paving the way for the later accomplishments of Mayan art, architecture and science.

Middle Preclassic Period (800 to 300 BC)

By this time there were rich villages in Honduras's Copán Valley and settlers had founded villages at Tikal. Trade routes developed, with coastal peoples exchanging salt for highland tribes' tool-grade obsidian. Everybody happily traded pots.

Late Preclassic Period (300 BC to 250 AD)

As the Maya got better at agriculture they got richer and could then afford such luxuries as a class of scribes and nobility and all the extravagances that these classes demand. Among the luxuries demanded were temples consisting of raised platforms of earth topped by a thatch-roofed shelter very much like a normal na. Pyramid E-VII-sub, of the Chicanel culture at Uaxactún, is a good example of this; others are found at Tikal, El Mirador and Lamanai, sites flourishing in this period. As with a na, the local potentate was buried beneath the shelter. In the lowlands, where limestone was abundant, they began to build platform temples from stone. As each succeeding local potentate had to have a bigger temple, more and larger platforms were put over other platforms, forming huge step pyramids with a na-style shelter on top.

Timeline

The history of the Maya and their predecessors stretches back over 4000 years. The following timeline may help you to keep track of what was happening when and where. The division of historical periods for Mayan civilization is that used by Professor Michael D Coe (author of *The Maya*). I've added notes in parentheses on contemporary historical events in the Old World so you can compare developments.

20,000 to 2000 BC: Archaic Period Hunting and gathering for food. After the end of the Ice Age (7500 BC), primitive agriculture begins.

2000 to 800 BC: Early Preclassic Period In a few Mayan regions, formation of fishing and farming villages producing primitive crops. Early Olmec civilization flourishes (1200 to 900 BC) at San Lorenzo, Veracruz; Teotihuacán culture flourishes in central Mexico. (Old Testament times of Abraham, Isaac and Jacob; Israelites escape from Egypt and cross Jordan into the Promised Land; reigns of King David, King Solomon, Tutankhamen and Nefertiti. Invention of the alphabet.)

800 to 300 BC: Middle Preclassic Period Larger towns, Olmec civilization reaches its height at La Venta, Tabasco. Great increase in Mayan population. (Flowering of classical Hellenic culture and art around the Aegean Sea.)

300 BC to 250 AD: Late Preclassic Period Mayan cities have large but simple temples and pyramids; pottery and decoration become elaborate. (Alexander the Great's conquests; Ptolemy dynasty in Egypt; Roman republic and early empire; life of Jesus.)

250 to 600: Early Classic Period Use of the Long Count calendar. In the highlands of Guatemala and Chiapas, great temples are built around spacious plazas; Mayan art is technically excellent. (Founding of Constantinople and building of Hagia

The potentate was buried deep within the stack of platforms. Sometimes the pyramids were decorated with huge stylized masks.

More and more pyramids were built around large plazas, much as the common people clustered their thatched houses in family compounds facing a common open space. The stage was set for the flourishing of classic Mayan civilization.

Early Classic Period (250 to 600)

Armies from Teotihuacán (near modern Mexico City) invaded the Mayan highlands, conquered the Maya and imposed their rule and their culture for a time, but were finally absorbed into Mayan daily life. The so-called Esperanza culture, a blend of Mexican and Mayan elements, was born of this conquest.

The great ceremonial centers at Copán, Tikal, Yaxchilán, Palenque and especially Kaminaljuyú (near present-day Guatemala City) flourished during this time. Mayan astronomers used the elaborate Long Count calendar to date all of human history.

Late Classic Period (600 to 900)

At its height, the Mayan lands were ruled not as an empire but as a collection of independent but also interdependent city-states. Each city-state had its noble house, headed by a king who was the social, political and religious focus of the city's life. The king propitiated the gods by shedding his blood in ceremonies where he pierced his tongue

---

Sophia; Huns invade Europe; Vandals sack Rome, beginning of Middle (or Dark) Ages in Europe; Saxons invade Britain.)

600 to 900: Late Classic Period High Mayan civilization moves from the western highlands to the lowlands of Petén and Yucatán. Mayan art at its most sensitive and refined. (Life of Mohammed; rise of the Arab Empire; Dome of the Rock built in Jerusalem; Harun al-Rashid sends an ambassador to the court of Charlemagne.)

900 to 1200: Early Postclassic Period Population growth, food shortages, decline in trade, military campaigns, revolutions and migrations cause the swift collapse of Classic Mayan culture. In central Mexico, Toltecs flourish at Tula, later abandon it and invade Yucatán, establishing their capital at Chichén Itzá. (Europe's Dark Ages continue; Norman invasion of Britain; Crusades.)

1200 to 1530: Late Postclassic Period Toltec civilization collapses mysteriously, and the Itzaes move from Campeche to El Petén, then to Belize, and finally dominate northern Yucatán. (Magna Carta; Mongol invasion of Eastern Europe under Genghis Khan; Gothic architecture; fall of Constantinople; reigns of Süleyman the Magnificent, Henry VIII, Charles V; European Renaissance; rise of the Inca Empire in Peru.)

1530 to 1821: Colonial Period Francisco de Montejo conquers Yucatán, and Pedro de Alvarado subdues Chiapas and Guatemala, but harsh colonial rule leads to frequent Mayan rebellions.

1821 to Present: Independence Period Yucatán declares independence from Spain and soon after joins the Mexican union. United Provinces of Central America proclaims independence, later divides into separate countries. ■

and/or penis with a sharp instrument. He also led his city's soldiers into battle against rival cities, capturing prisoners for use in human sacrifices. Many a king perished in a battle he was too old to fight; but the king, as sacred head of the community, was required to lead in battle for religious as well as military reasons.

King Pacal ruled at Palenque and King Bird-Jaguar at Yaxchilán during the early part of this period, marking the height of civilization and power in these two cities. Mayan civilization in Tikal was also at its height during the Late Classic period. By the end of the period, however, the great Mayan cities of Tikal, Yaxchilán, Copán, Quiriguá, Piedras Negras and Caracol had reverted to little more than minor towns, or even villages. The focus of Mayan civilization then shifted to northern Yucatán, where a new civilization developed at Chichén Itzá, Uxmal and Labná, giving us the artistic styles known as Maya-Toltec, Puuc, Chenes and Río Bec.

Early Postclassic Period (900 to 1200)

The collapse of classic Mayan civilization is as surprising as it was sudden. It seems as though the upper classes demanded ever more servants, acolytes and laborers, and though the Mayan population was growing rapidly, it did not furnish enough farmers to feed everyone. Thus weakened, the Maya were prey to the next wave of invaders from central Mexico.

The Toltecs of Tula (near Mexico City) conquered Teotihuacán, then marched and sailed eastwards to Yucatán. They were an extremely warlike people, and human sacrifice was a regular practice. The Toltecs were led by a fair-haired, bearded king named Quetzalcóatl (Plumed Serpent), who established himself in Yucatán at Uucil-abnal (Chichén Itzá). He left behind in Mexico, and then in Yucatán, a legend that he would one day return from the direction of the rising sun. The culture at Uucil-abnal flourished after the late 9th century, when all of the great buildings were constructed, but by 1200 the city was abandoned.

Late Postclassic Period (1200 to 1530)

Itzaes After the abandonment of Toltec Uucil-abnal, the site was occupied by a people called the Itzaes. Probably of Mayan race, the Itzaes had lived among the Putun Maya near Champoton in Tabasco until the early 13th century. Forced by other invaders to leave their traditional homeland, they headed southeast into El Petén to the lake that became known as Petén Itzá after their arrival. Some continued to Belize, later making their way north along the coast and into northern Yucatán, where they settled at Uucil-abnal. The Itzá leader styled himself Kukulcán, as had the city's Toltec founder, and recycled lots of other Toltec lore as well. But the Itzaes strengthened the belief in sacred cenotes (the natural limestone caves that provided the Maya with their water supply on the riverless plains of the northern Yucatán Peninsula), and they even named their new home Chichén Itzá (At the Mouth of the Well of the Itzaes).

From Chichén Itzá, the ruling Itzaes traveled westwards and founded a new capital city at Mayapán (built 1263-83), which dominated the political life of northern Yucatán for several centuries. The Cocom lineage of the Itzaes ruled a fractious collection of Yucatecan city-states from Mayapán until the mid-15th century, when a subject people called the Xiú, from Uxmal, revolted and overthrew Cocom power. Mayapán was pillaged, ruined and never repopulated. For the next century, until the coming of the conquistadors, northern Yucatán was alive with battles and power struggles among its city-states.

The Coming of the Spaniards The Spaniards had been in the Caribbean since Christopher Columbus arrived in 1492, with their main bases on the islands of Santo Domingo (modern Haiti and the Dominican Republic) and Cuba. Realizing that they had not reached the East Indies, they began looking for a passage through the land mass to their west but were distracted by tales of gold, silver and a rich empire. Trading, slaving and exploring expeditions from Cuba were led by Francisco Hernández de Córdoba in 1517 and Juan de Grijalva in 1518 but didn't penetrate inland from Mexico's Gulf coast, where they were driven back by hostile natives.

In 1518 the governor of Cuba, Diego Velásquez, asked Hernán Cortés to lead a new expedition westward. As Cortés gathered ships and men, Velásquez became uneasy about the costs of the venture and about Cortés's questionable loyalty, so he canceled the expedition. Cortés ignored the governor and set sail on February 15, 1519 with 11 ships, 550 men and 16 horses.

At this time, Central Mexico was dominated by the Aztec Empire, ruled from Mexico City. The story of the confrontation between Spaniards and Aztecs is one of the most bizarre in history. Aztec legends predicted the 'return' of fair-skinned gods from the east at just about the time of Cortés's arrival. Thrown off guard by these legends, the rulers of the mighty Aztec empire were toppled by the small Spanish expeditionary force. A detailed first-hand account may be found in the *True History of the Conquest of New Spain* by one of Cortés's soldiers, Bernal Díaz del Castillo.

Landing first at Cozumel off Yucatán, the Spaniards were joined by Jerónimo de Aguilar, a Spaniard who had been shipwrecked there several years earlier. With Aguilar acting as translator and guide, Cortés's force moved west along the coast to Tabasco. There they defeated some hostile Indians, and Cortés delivered the first of many lectures to the Indians on the importance of Christianity and the greatness of King Carlos V of Spain. Cortés went on to conquer central Mexico, after which he turned his attentions – and his armies – to Yucatán.

The Cocoms and the Xiús were still battling when the conquistadors arrived. Yucatán's Maya could not present a united front to the invaders, and the invaders triumphed. In less than a century after the fall of Mayapán, the conquistadors conquered the Aztec capital of Tenochtitlán (1521; it's now Mexico City), founded Guatemala

Hernán Cortés (1485-1547)

City (1527) and Mérida (1542), and controlled most of the formerly Mayan lands.

Colonial Period (1530 to 1821)

Yucatán Despite the political infighting among the Yucatecan Maya, conquest by the Spaniards was not easy. The Spanish monarch commissioned Francisco de Montejo (El Adelantado, the Pioneer) with the task, and he set out from Spain in 1527 accompanied by his son, also named Francisco de Montejo. Landing first at Cozumel on the Caribbean coast, then at Xel-ha on the mainland, the Montejos discovered (perhaps not to their surprise) that the local people wanted nothing to do with them. The Maya made it quite clear that they should go conquer somewhere else.

Montejo *père et fils* then sailed around the peninsula, conquered Tabasco (1530) and established their base near Campeche, which could be easily supplied with necessities, arms and new troops from New Spain (central Mexico). They pushed inland to conquer, but after four long, difficult years were forced to retreat and to return to Mexico City in defeat.

The younger Montejo (El Mozo, the Lad) took up the cause again, with his

d to
guess
e two
id with
ves with
eating the
converts to

baptized, he
n name, so he
chose⌋ ⌊eared to him to
be the mos⌋ ⌊ie of the entire
16th century an⌋ ⌊ne Francisco de
Montejo Xiú.

The Montejos founded Mérida in 1542 and within four years had almost all of Yucatán subjugated to Spanish rule. The once proud and independent Maya became peons, working for Spanish masters without hope of deliverance except in heaven. The attitude of the conquerors toward the indigenous peoples is graphically depicted in the reliefs on the facade of the Montejo mansion in Mérida: in one scene, armor-clad conquistadors are shown with their feet holding down ugly, hairy, club-wielding savages.

Chiapas & Guatemala The conquest of Chiapas and Guatemala fell to Pedro de Alvarado (1485-1541), a clever but cruel soldier who had been Cortés's lieutenant at the conquest of Aztec Tenochtitlán. Several towns in highland Guatemala had sent embassies to Cortés, offering to submit to his control and protection. In response, Cortés dispatched Alvarado in 1523, and his armies roared through Chiapas and the highland kingdoms of the Quiché and Cakchiquel Maya, crushing them. The Mayan lands were divided into large estates or *encomiendas*, and the Maya living on the lands were mercilessly exploited by the landowning *encomenderos*.

With the coming of Dominican Friar Bartolomé de las Casas and groups of Franciscan and Augustinian friars, things got a bit better for the Maya. However, while in many cases the friars were able to protect the local people from the worst abuses, exploitation was still the rule.

The capital city of the Captaincy-General of Guatemala was founded as Santiago de los Caballeros de Guatemala at the site now called Ciudad Vieja, near Antigua (also known as Antigua Guatemala), in 1527. Destroyed by a mudslide less than two decades later, the capital was then moved to Antigua (1543). After a devastating earthquake (1773), the capital was moved to the present site of Guatemala City.

Friar Diego de Landa The Maya recorded lots of information about their history, customs and ceremonies in beautiful 'painted books' made of beaten-bark paper coated with fine lime. These 'codices' must have numbered in the hundreds when the conquistadors and missionary friars first arrived in the Mayan lands. But because the ancient rites of the Maya were seen as a threat to their adoption and retention of Christianity, the priceless books were destroyed upon the orders of the Franciscans. Only a handful of painted books survive, but these provide much insight into ancient Mayan life.

Among those Franciscans directly responsible for the burning of the Mayan books was Friar Diego de Landa, who, in July of 1562 at Maní (near present-day Ticul in Yucatán), ordered the destruction of 27 'hieroglyphic rolls' and 5000 idols. Landa went on to become Bishop of Mérida from 1573 until his death in 1579.

Ironically, it was Friar Diego de Landa, the great destroyer of Mayan cultural records, who wrote the most important book on Mayan customs and practices, the source for very much of what we know about the Maya. Landa's book, *Relación de las Cosas de Yucatán*, was written about 1565. It covers virtually every aspect of Mayan life as it was in the 1560s, from the climate, Mayan houses, food and drink, wedding and funeral customs, to the calendar and the counting system. In a way, Landa atoned for the cultural destruction for which he was responsible.

Landa's book is available in English as *Yucatán Before and After the Conquest*; see the Books section of Facts for the Visitor.

You can buy it in a number of bookstores and shops at archaeological sites in Yucatán and Guatemala.

The Last Mayan Kingdom The last region of Mayan sovereignty was the city-state of Tayasal in Guatemala's department of El Petén. Making their way south after being driven out of Chichén Itzá, a group of Itzaes settled on an island in Lago Petén Itzá, at what is now the town of Flores. They founded a city named Tayasal and enjoyed independence for over a century after the fall of Yucatán. The intrepid Cortés visited Tayasal in 1524, while on his way to conquer Honduras, but did not make war against King Canek, who greeted him peacefully. Only in the latter years of the 17th century did the Spanish decide that this last surviving Mayan state must be brought within the Spanish Empire, and in 1697 Tayasal fell to the latter-day conquistadors, some 2000 years after the founding of the first important Mayan city-states in the Late Preclassic period.

It's interesting to consider that the last independent Mayan king went down to defeat only a decade before the union of England and Scotland (1707) and at a time when Boston, New York and Philadelphia were small but thriving seaport towns.

Independence Period
During the colonial period, society in Spain's New World colonies was rigidly and precisely stratified, with Spanish natives at the very top; next were the creoles, people born in the New World of Spanish stock; below them were the *ladinos* or *mestizos*, people of mixed Spanish and Indian blood; and at the bottom were the Indians and blacks of pure race. Only the native Spaniards had real power, a fact deeply resented by the creoles.

The harshness of Spanish rule resulted in frequent revolts, none of them successful for very long. Mexico's Miguel Hidalgo y Costilla gave the Grito de Dolores, the 'Cry (of Independence) at Dolores', at his church near Guanajuato in 1810, inciting his parishioners to revolt. With his lieu-tenant, a mestizo priest named José María Morelos, he brought large areas of central Mexico under his control. But this rebellion, like earlier ones, failed. The power of Spain was too great.

Napoleon's conquests in Europe changed all that, destabilizing the Spanish Empire to its very foundations. When the French emperor deposed Spain's King Ferdinand VII and put his brother Joseph Bonaparte on the throne of Spain (1808), creoles in many New World colonies took the opportunity to rise in revolt. By 1821 both Mexico and Guatemala had proclaimed their independence. As with the American Revolution of 1776, the Latin American movements were conservative in nature, preserving control of politics, the economy and the military for the upper classes of European blood but native birth.

Independent Mexico urged the peoples of Yucatán, Chiapas and Central America to join it in the formation of one large new state. At first Yucatán and Chiapas refused and Guatemala accepted, but all later changed their minds. Yucatán and Chiapas joined the Mexican union, and Guatemala led the formation of the United Provinces of Central America (July 1, 1823), with El Salvador, Nicaragua, Honduras and Costa Rica. Their union, torn by civil strife from the beginning, lasted only until 1840 before breaking up into its constituent states.

Central American independence has been marred from the beginning by civil war and conflicts among the various countries of the region, a condition that persists today.

Though independence brought new prosperity to the creoles, it worsened the lot of the Maya. The end of Spanish rule meant that the Crown's few liberal safeguards, which had afforded the Indians minimal protection from the most extreme forms of exploitation, were abandoned. Mayan claims to ancestral lands were largely ignored and huge plantations were created for the cultivation of tobacco, sugar cane and henequen (agave rope fiber). The Maya, though legally free, were enslaved by debt peonage to the great landowners.

Modern Nations

Following independence from Spanish colonial rule, each of the countries in the region went its own way. For the histories of these modern nations, see the beginning of each country's section in this guide.

CLIMATE

The hottest month in the region is April, the coolest is February. The most rain falls in June. Hurricane season in the Caribbean, including Cancún, Cozumel, Isla Mujeres, Mexico's Caribbean coast and all of the Belizean coast and its cayes, is from July to November, with most of the activity from mid-August to mid-September. Normally, there are at least a few tropical storms in the area, which may or may not affect your travel plans.

About once every decade, somebody gets clobbered, as Cancún was by Hurricane Gilbert in 1988. If there's a full-blown hurricane predicted for where you are, go somewhere else – fast! Sitting out a hurricane may look exciting in the movies, but hurricanes are always followed by lack of housing, transportation, electricity, water, food, medicine, etc, which can be very unpleasant – even unphotogenic – not to mention perilous.

For more detailed climate information, see the section on each country.

ECOLOGY & ENVIRONMENT

Tropical forests have been called the 'lungs of the planet', converting carbon dioxide into oxygen, purifying and enriching the air we breathe. Besides acting as the planet's lungs, tropical forests are storehouses of chemical and biological substances and gene materials that have yet to be extensively explored. The thousands of organisms in the forest may contain the materials needed to cure dreaded diseases and develop new forms of life. But if the forests disappear – and they are disappearing at an alarming rate worldwide – humankind will lose this great storehouse and may not be able to breathe.

The bad news is that the destruction of tropical forests throughout the region is progressing at an alarming rate. One visit to the countryside around Palenque will confirm this. Huge tracts of land still smolder from the fires that clear the forest for the farmer's plow and the herder's cattle.

The good news is that preliminary steps have been taken to preserve vast tracts of tropical forest. *Biotopos*, or biosphere reserves, have been established in Mexico, Guatemala and Belize. The restrictions in these reserves vary, but in general the cutting or burning of forest and the hunting of animals is forbidden or controlled.

Of the many biosphere reserves, the most impressive is the vast multinational reserve formed by the juxtaposing of three large national reserves along the joint borders of Mexico, Guatemala and Belize. The large Calakmul reserve in the southern part of the Yucatán peninsula adjoins the enormous Maya biosphere reserve that covers all of the northern Petén in Guatemala. Adjoining to the east is Belize's Río Bravo Conservation Area, over 1000 sq km of tropical forests, rivers, ponds and Mayan archaeological sites.

FLORA & FAUNA

As you might expect, the lush jungles of Chiapas, Guatemala and Belize are teeming with fascinating animals and plants. But the drier forests of Yucatán also provide habitats for a surprising number and variety of beasts.

The Maya call Yucatán 'The Land of the Pheasant and the Deer'. These two animals formed the basis for countless legends – and delicious meals – among the ancient Maya. The legends are still alive, and the animals are still on the menu today.

Birds

As you might imagine, birds are numerous and varied throughout the region. In fact, bird-watching in itself is enough reason to plan an extended stay here. In addition to the more well-known species listed below, the region's habitats harbor such ornithological wonders as the acorn woodpecker and keel-billed toucan, the endangered horned guan and an abundance of macaws, parrots, forest songbirds and aquatic birds – there are 500 recorded species on the Yucatán Peninsula alone, though habitat destruction is taking its steady toll. In Guatemala, for instance, the giant pie-billed grebe once endemic to the shores of Lago de Atitlán is now believed to be extinct.

Turkey The 'pheasant' of Mayan lore is actually the ocellated turkey, a beautiful bird that reminds one of a peacock. Originally, turkeys were native to New England and the Middle Atlantic states in the USA and to Yucatán, not to Turkey. The birds got their odd Middle Eastern name when they were shipped from New England and Yucatán to the West Indies in the Triangle Trade, from where they then continued their journey to Europe. They were transshipped at Genoa onto English merchant ships returned from the Ottoman Empire; because they arrived in England aboard the 'Turkey boats' they were known as Turkey-birds. In Turkey, by the way, they're called *hindi* (Indian bird), because they came from the (West) Indies; the French name *dinde* (from India) derives from the same source.

Flamingo These long, lanky but graceful birds inhabit certain areas of northern Yucatán, principally the wetlands near the towns of Río Lagartos (northeastern Yucatán) and Celestun (northwestern Yucatán). Flamingoes can be white, pink or salmon-colored. It's the pink and salmon ones that draw the oohs and ahhs. Look for them when the rainy season begins in late May.

In addition to the flamingo, other long-legged birds such as the heron, snowy egret and white ibis often visit Yucatán and Belize. The egrets are especially easy to see in cattle pastures.

Quetzal The gorgeous quetzal, its long, curving tailfeathers iridescent with blue and green (the colors associated with the Mayan world-tree), was highly valued by the ancient Maya for its incomparably beautiful plumage: quetzal feathers were important to the costumes of Mayan royalty. The quetzal is the national bird of Guatemala. It is also nearly extinct.

As the quetzal becomes scarcer, its value rises; and as the rainforests are slashed and burned, its habitat disappears. Still, there are quetzals to be seen, and you may be lucky enough to see one if you work at it. The places to look are in the jungles of Chiapas, in the highlands of Guatemala, or at Tikal National Park. The Guatemalans have established a special quetzal forest reserve (Biotopo del Quetzal) on the road to Cobán, capital of the department of Alta Verapaz. But the bird is shy and elusive, and establishing a reserve does not guarantee that there will be birds in abundance for you to see.

Cats

Mayan culture, and that of the Olmecs which preceded it, could hardly get along without the jaguar, symbol of power, stealth, determination – and bloodletting. Jaguars still roam the forests of the Mayan lands. You are unlikely to see one except in a cage, but that won't change your opinion of it. You'll realize at once that the jaguar is an animal worthy of respect.

The jaguar lives on deer, peccary and tapir, which may explain why the tapir, when attacked, runs blindly in any direction – anything to get away.

The ocelot and puma also live in the jungles here, but are just as rare as the jaguar these days. Other seldom-seen cat species include the jaguarundi and the margay.

Deer

Deer are plentiful enough in Yucatán for deer hunting to be still popular both as sport and as a way of getting a cheap dinner. Venison appears on many restaurant menus in the tourist resorts (those that serve more than hamburgers or steak and lobster). Deer multiply rapidly, love eating corn and don't seem to be in danger of depopulation.

Reptiles

Iguana One animal you can see at any Yucatecan archaeological site is the iguana, a harmless lizard of fearsome appearance. There are many different kinds of iguanas, but most are green with black bands encircling the body. Iguanas can grow to one meter in length, including their long, flat tails, though most of the ones you'll see will be shorter than 15 cm (about one foot). Iguanas love to bask in the sun on the warm rocks of old Mayan temples, but they'll shoot away from their comfy perches and hide if you approach them.

Sea Turtle Giant sea turtles are found in the waters off Yucatán and Belize. They're protected by law, especially during mating and nesting seasons. Though there are legal methods for hunting small numbers of the turtles, most of the casualties come as the result of poaching and of egg-hunting, as sea turtle eggs are believed by the uninformed to be an aphrodisiac. You may see turtle on a menu. It may have been taken legally. Then again, who knows? My feeling is that it's best to discourage trade in any endangered species, even 'controlled' trade.

Other Reptiles Yucatán is home to several varieties of snakes, including the very deadly coral snakes, the fer-de-lance and tropical rattlesnakes. These beasts do not look for trouble and will slither away from you if they can. It's unlikely that you'll meet one, and if you do, it's unlikely that you'll do something to anger it, and if you do, it's unlikely that you'll get bitten. But if you do, you'll need help quickly as they are deadly poisonous. Watch where you step.

Another dangerous reptile is the caymansn, a sort of crocodile, found mostly near the town of Río Lagartos on the northern coast of Yucatán. These beasts are fascinating to look at but unpleasant, even deadly, to meet up close. Keep your distance.

Armadillos & Anteaters

Armadillos are creatures about 25 to 30 cm long with prominent ears, snouts and tails, and hard bony coverings for protection. Though they look fearsome, they are dangerous only to insects, which is what they live on. Their sharp claws help them to dig for fat, tasty grubs and to hollow out the underground burrows where they live. You might see armadillos in northern Yucatán – unfortunately, most likely as road kill.

The anteater is a cousin of the armadillo, though it's difficult to see the resemblance. There are several species, all with very long, flexible snouts and sharp-clawed, shovel-like front paws, the two tools needed to seek out and enjoy ants and other insects. Unlike the armadillo, the anteater is covered in hair, with a long bushy tail. Its slow gait and poor eyesight makes it another common road-kill victim.

Tapirs & Peccaries

Short of leg and tail, stout of build, small of eye, ear and intelligence, the tapir eats plants, bathes daily and runs like mad when approached. If you're wandering the leafy paths of Tikal and you hear something crashing through the underbrush nearby, you've probably frightened a tapir. Or it could have been a peccary, a sort of wild pig that can grow to 30 kg (66 lbs) or more in weight. If the crashing has been particularly noisy, it's probably peccaries as they tend to travel in groups.

POPULATION & PEOPLE

Many of the Maya you meet today are the direct descendants of the people who built the marvelous temples and pyramids. To confirm this, all you need to do is compare their appearance with that of the ancient Maya shown in inscriptions and drawings. For information on the people of each part of the region, see the introduction to each country's section.

Popular Attitudes

With only a few exceptions, the people you encounter throughout the region will be friendly, good-humored and willing to help. Language difficulties can obscure this fact. Some people are shy or will ignore you because they haven't encountered foreigners before and don't imagine a conversation is possible. But just a few words of Spanish will often bring you smiles and warmth, not to mention lots of questions. Then someone who speaks a few words of English will pluck up the courage to try them out on you, and conversation is under way.

Some Indian peoples adopt a cool attitude to visitors; they have learned to mistrust outsiders after five centuries of exploitation by Spaniards and mestizos. They don't like being gaped at by crowds of tourists and can be sensitive about cameras, particularly in churches and at religious festivals.

If you have white skin and speak a foreign language, you'll be referred to as a *gringo* or *gringa*, depending upon whether you're male or female, and you'll be assumed to be a citizen of the USA. Your presence may provoke any reaction from curiosity or wonder to reticence or, occasionally, hostility. If you're not a citizen of the USA and you make it known, you may get little reaction at all, or you may be treated as an even greater curiosity, perhaps even as a freak of nature.

The classic Mexican attitude to the USA is a combination of the envy and resentment that a poorer, weaker neighbor feels for a richer, more powerful one. The *norteamericanos* have also committed the sin of sending their soldiers into Mexican territory three times.

Any hostility towards individual Americans usually evaporates as soon as you show that you're human too. And while 'gringo' isn't exactly a compliment, it can also be used with a brusque friendliness.

In Guatemala and Belize, however, it's Mexico that's the richer, more powerful 'neighbor to the north'. Guatemalan and Belizean attitudes towards North Americans are usually more intensely friendly when they're friendly, and more intensely hostile when they're hostile.

ARCHITECTURE & ARCHAEOLOGY

Mayan architecture is amazing for its achievements, but perhaps even more amazing because of what it did not achieve. Mayan architects never seem to have understood or to have used the true arch (a rounded arch with a keystone), and they never thought to put wheels on boxes and use them as wagons to move the thousands of tons of construction materials needed in their tasks. They had no metal tools – they were technically in a Stone Age culture – yet they could build breathtaking temple complexes and align them so precisely that windows and doors were used as celestial observatories of great accuracy.

The arch used in most Mayan buildings is the corbelled vault (or corbelled arch), which consists of large flat stones on either side set at an angle inward and topped by capstones. This arch served the purpose, but limited severely the amount of open space beneath. In effect, Mayan architects were limited to long, narrow vaulted rooms. True (Roman) arches and Gothic-style vaulting would have allowed them to build stone roofs above far larger halls.

Another important element lacking to them was draught animals (horses, donkeys, mules, oxen). All the work had to be done by humans, on their feet, with their arms and with their backs, without wagons or even wheelbarrows.

The Celestial Plan

In Mayan architecture there was always a celestial plan. Temples were aligned in such a manner as to enhance celestial observation, whether of the sun, moon or certain stars, especially Venus. The alignment might not be apparent except at certain conjunctions of the celestial bodies (ie at Venus Rising, or at an eclipse), but the Maya knew each building was properly 'placed' and that this enhanced its sacred character.

Temples usually had other features that linked them to the stars. The doors and windows might be aligned in order to sight a celestial body at a certain exact point in its course on a certain day of a certain year. This is the case with the Governor's Palace at Uxmal, which is aligned in such a way that, from the main doorway, Venus would have been visible exactly on top of a small mound some 3.5 km away, in the year 750 AD. You may notice when you visit Uxmal that all the buildings at the site are aligned on the same pattern except for the Governor's Palace. The reason is that the palace is aligned so that the planet Venus is visible in a certain way on a certain day each year.

At Chichén Itzá the observatory building called El Caracol was aligned in order to sight Venus exactly in the year 1000 AD.

Furthermore, the main door to a temple might be decorated to resemble a huge mouth, signifying entry to Xibalba (the secret world or underworld). Other features might have significance in terms of the numbers of the Calendar Round, as at Chichén Itzá's El Castillo. This pyramid has 364 stairs to the top; with the top platform this makes 365, the number of days in the Mayan Vague Year. On the sides of the pyramid are 52 panels, signifying the 52-year cycle of the Calendar Round. The terraces on each side of each stairway total 18 (nine on either side), signifying the 18 'months' of the solar Vague Year. The alignment of El Castillo catches the sun and turns it into a sacred sky-serpent descending into the earth on the vernal equinox (March 21) each year. The serpent is formed perfectly only on that day, and descends during a short period of only 34 minutes.

As mentioned in the section on Religion, Mayan temples were often built on top of smaller, older temples. This increased their sacredness and preserved the temple complex's alignment.

Mayan Architectural Styles

Mayan architecture's 1500-year history has seen a fascinating progression of styles. The style of architecture changed not just with the times, but with the particular geographic area of Mesoamerica in which the architects worked.

Late Preclassic Late Preclassic architecture is perhaps best exhibited at Uaxactún, north of Tikal in Guatemala's Petén department. At Uaxactún, Pyramid E-VII-sub is a fine example of how the architects of what is known as the Chicanel culture designed their pyramid-temples in the time from

around 100 BC to 250 AD. E-VII-sub is a square stepped-platform pyramid with central stairways on each of the four sides, each stairway flanked by large jaguar masks. The entire platform was covered in fine white stucco. The top platform is flat, and probably bore a temple *na* made of wooden poles topped with palm thatch. This temple was well preserved because others had been built on top of it; these later structures were ruined by the ages, and were cleared away to reveal E-VII-sub. Chicanel-style temples similar to this one were built at Tikal, El Mirador and Lamanai (in Belize) as well.

By the end of the Late Preclassic period, simple temples such as E-VII-sub were being aligned and arranged around plazas, and all was prepared for the next phase of Mayan architecture.

Early Classic The Esperanza culture typifies this phase. In Esperanza-style temples, the king was buried in a wooden chamber beneath the main staircase of the temple; successive kings were buried in similar places in the pyramids built on top of the first one. Among the largest Early Classic Esperanza sites is Kaminaljuyú in Guatemala City; unfortunately, most of the site was destroyed by construction crews or covered by their buildings, and urban sprawl engulfed the site before archaeologists could complete their work.

Of the surviving Early Classic pyramids, perhaps the best example is the step-pyramid at Acanceh, a few km south of Mérida.

Late Classic The most important Classic sites flourished during the latter part of the period, the so-called Late Classic. By this time the Mayan temple-pyramid had a masonry building on top, replacing the na of wood poles and thatch. Numbers of pyramids were built close together, sometimes forming contiguous or even continuous structures. Near them, different structures now called palaces were built. These palaces sat on lower platforms and held many more rooms, perhaps a dozen or more.

In addition to pyramids and palaces, Classic sites have carved stelae and round 'altar-stones' set in the plaza in front of the pyramid. Another feature of the Classic and later periods is the ball court, with sloping playing surfaces of stone covered in stucco. Among the purest of the Classic sites is Copán in Honduras, which can be reached on a day's excursion from Guatemala's Motagua Valley. Along the eastern reaches of the Motagua is Quiriguá (Guatemala), where the pyramids are unremarkable but the towering stelae and mysterious zoomorphs are unique.

Of all the Classic sites, however, Tikal is the grandest yet uncovered and restored. Here the pyramids reached their most impressive heights, and were topped by superstructures (called roofcombs by archaeologists) that made them even taller. As in earlier times, these monumental structures were used as the burial places of kings.

If Tikal is the most impressive Classic Mayan city, Palenque (Chiapas) is certainly the most beautiful. Mansard roofs and large relief murals characterize the great palace, with its unique watchtower, and the harmonious Temple of the Inscriptions. Palenque exhibits the perfection of the elements of the Classic Mayan architectural style. The great stairways, the small sanctuaries on top of pyramids, the lofty roofcombs were all brought to their finest proportions here. The tomb of King Pacal in the Temple of the Inscriptions, reached by a buried staircase, is unique in its Egyptian-like qualities: a secret chamber accessible without dismantling the pyramid, and a great carved slab covering the sarcophagus.

Puuc, Chenes & Río Bec Among the most distinctive of the Late Classic Mayan architectural styles are those that flourished in the western and southern regions of the Yucatán Peninsula. These styles valued exuberant display and architectural bravado more than they did proportion and harmony.

The Puuc style, named for the low Puuc Hills near Uxmal, used facings of thin limestone 'tiles' to cover the rough stone walls of buildings. The tiles were worked into geometric designs and stylized figures of monsters and serpents. Minoan-style columns and rows of engaged columns (half-round cylinders) were also a prominent feature of the style, and were used to good effect on facades of buildings at Uxmal and at the Puuc Route sites of Kabah, Sayil, Xlapak and Labná. Puuc architects were crazy about Chac, the rain god, and stuck his grotesque face on every temple, many times. At Kabah, the facade of the Codz Pop temple is completely covered in Chac masks.

The Chenes style, prevalent in areas to the south of the Puuc Hills in Campeche, is very similar to the Puuc style, but Chenes architects seem to have enjoyed putting huge masks as well as smaller ones on their facades.

The Río Bec style, epitomized in the richly decorated temples at the Río Bec archaeological site on the highway between Escárcega and Chetumal, used lavish decoration as in the Puuc and Chenes styles, but added huge towers to the corners of its low buildings, just for show. Río Bec buildings look like a combination of the Governor's Palace of Uxmal and Temple I at Tikal.

Early Postclassic The collapse of Classic Mayan civilization created a power vacuum that was filled by the invasion of the Toltecs from central Mexico. The Toltecs brought with them their own architectural ideas, and in the process of conquest these ideas were assimilated and merged with those of the Puuc style.

The foremost example of what might be called the Toltec-Maya style is Chichén Itzá. Elements of Puuc style – the large masks and decorative friezes – coexist with Toltec Atlantean warriors and *chac-mools*, the odd reclining statues that are purely Toltec, and have nothing to do with Mayan art. Platform pyramids with very broad bases and spacious top platforms, such as the Temple of the Warriors, look as though they might have been imported from the ancient Toltec capital of Tula (near Mexico

City), or by way of Teotihuacán, with its broad-based pyramids of the sun and moon. Because Quetzalcóatl (called Kukulcán in Mayan) was so important to the Toltecs, feathered serpents are used quite extensively as architectural decoration.

Late Postclassic After the Toltecs came the Itzaes, who established their capital at Mayapán, south of Mérida, and ruled a confederation of Yucatecan states. After the golden age of Tikal and Palenque, even after the martial architecture of Chichén Itzá, the architecture of Mayapán is a disappointment. The pyramids and temples are small and crude compared to the glorious Classic structures. Mayapán's only architectural distinction comes from its vast defensive city wall, one of the few such walls ever discovered in a Mayan city. The fact that the wall exists testifies to the weakness of the Itzá rulers and the unhappiness of their subject peoples.

Tulum, another walled city, is also a product of this time. The columns of the Puuc style are used here, and the painted decoration on the temples must have been colorful, but there is nothing to rival the Classic age.

Cobá has the finest architecture of this otherwise decadent period. The stately pyramids here had new little temples built atop them in the style of Tulum, the walled seaport town on the coast east of Cobá.

In Guatemala, the finest and best preserved Late Postclassic sites are: Mixco Viejo, north of Guatemala City; Utatlán (or K'umarcaaj), the old Quiché Maya capital on the outskirts of Santa Cruz del Quiché; and Iximché, the last Cakchiquel capital on the Panamericana near Tecpan. All of these sites show pronounced central Mexican influences in their twin temple complexes, which probably descend from similar structures at Teotihuacán.

Spanish Colonial Architecture
The conquistadors, Franciscans and Dominicans brought with them the architecture of their native Spain and adapted it to the conditions they met in the Mayan

lands. Churches in the largest cities were decorated with baroque elements, but in general the churches are simple and fortress-like. The exploitation of the Maya by the Spaniards led to frequent rebellions, and the strong, high stone walls of the churches worked well in protecting the upper classes from the wrath of the indigenous people.

As you travel through the region, you'll be surprised to find so many very plain churches – plain outside and plain inside. The crude and simple borrowings from Spanish architecture are eclipsed by the richness of the religious pageantry that takes place inside the buildings: such as the half-Mayan, half-Catholic processions, decorations and costumes in the churches of Yucatán or the crowds of the faithful sitting among hundreds of lighted candles on the floor of the small church of Santo Tomás in Chichicastenango, Guatemala, inhaling the thick incense and scattering flower petals in offering to their ancestral spirits.

TRADITIONAL CULTURE
Traditional Dress
One of the most intriguing aspects of Indian life throughout the Mayan lands is the colorful, usually handmade traditional clothing. This comes in infinite and exotic variety, often differing dramatically from village to village. Under the onslaught of modernity, such clothing is less common in everyday use than a few decades ago, but in some areas – notably around San Cristóbal in Chiapas – it's actually becoming more popular as Mayan pride reasserts itself and the commercial potential of handicrafts is developed. In general, Mayan women have kept to traditional dress longer than men.

Some styles still in common use go back to precolonial times. Among these (all worn by women) are the *huipil*, a long, sleeveless tunic; the *quechquémitl*, a shoulder cape; and the *enredo*, a wraparound skirt. Blouses are colonial innovations. Mayan men's garments owe more to Spanish influence; nudity was discouraged by the church, so shirts, hats and *calzones*, long baggy shorts, were introduced.

The most eye-catching feature of these costumes is their colorful embroidery – often entire garments are covered in a multicolored web of stylized animal, human, plant and mythological shapes that can take months to complete. Each garment identifies the group and village from which its wearer comes. *Fajas*, waist sashes, which bind the garments and also hold what we would put in pockets, are also important in this respect.

The designs often have multiple religious or magical meanings. In some cases the exact significance has been forgotten, but in others the traditional associations are still alive. To the Mayan weavers of Chiapas, diamond shapes represent the universe (the ancient Maya believed the earth was a cube), while wearing a garment with saint figures on it is a form of prayer.

Materials and techniques are changing but the pre-Hispanic backstrap loom is still widely used. The warp (long) threads are stretched between two horizontal bars, one of which is fixed to a post or tree, while the other is attached to a strap that goes round the weaver's lower back. The weft (cross) threads are then woven in.

Yarn is hand-spun in many villages. Vegetable dyes are not yet totally out of use, and natural indigo is employed in several areas. Red dye from cochineal insects and purple dye from sea snails are used by some groups. Modern luminescent dyes go down very well with the Maya, who are happily addicted to bright colors, as you will see.

The variety of techniques, materials, styles and designs is bewildering. (For more on clothing and other handicrafts, see Things to Buy in the introductory Facts for the Visitor chapter.)

Music & Dance

You're likely to hear live music at any time on streets, plazas or even buses. The musicians are playing for their living and range from marimba teams (with big wooden 'xylophones') and mariachi bands (violinists, trumpeters, guitarists and a singer, all dressed in 'cowboy' costume) to ragged

Colorful huipiles are always in vogue.

lone buskers with out-of-tune guitars and hoarse voices. Marimbas are particularly popular in Guatemala's highlands and on Mexico's Gulf coast.

Music and traditional dances are important parts of the many colorful festivals on the Mayan calendar. Performances honor Christian saints, but in many cases they have pre-Hispanic roots and retain traces of ancient ritual. There are hundreds of traditional dances: some are popular in many parts of the country, others can be seen only in a single town or village. Nearly all of them feature special costumes, often including masks. Some dances tell stories of clear Spanish or colonial origin. Moros y Cristianos is a fairly widespread one that re-enacts the victory of Christians over Moors in medieval Spain.

Ancient Mayan Customs

Personal Beauty Friar Diego de Landa wrote that the Maya of the 16th century, just as in the Classic period, flattened the foreheads of their children by tying boards tightly to them, a flat forehead being a mark of beauty. Crossed eyes were another mark of beauty, and to encourage it parents would tie a bead of wax so as to dangle between the child's eyes. Young boys had scalding-hot cloths placed on their faces to discourage the growth of beards, which were considered ugly by the Maya.

Both men and women made cuts in their skin so as to get much-desired scar markings, and both were enthusiastic about tattoos. Women sharpened their teeth to points, another mark of beauty, which, for all we know, may have helped them to keep the men in line. And both men and women dyed their bodies red, though women refrained from dyeing their faces.

Clothing As for clothing, in the old days the men wrapped long cloths around their loins, with the ends hanging in front and back; a square cape was worn on the shoulders, and leather sandals on the feet. Though this sort of clothing has long since disappeared, the men in many Guatemalan highland villages still wrap cloths around them to make a sort of skirt; they wear trousers underneath. Everybody still wears sandals or goes barefoot.

The women wore huipiles, embroidered dresses that must have looked very much like the huipiles that are still worn by Mayan women in Yucatán, Chiapas and Guatemala today.

Food & Drink Landa tells us that the Maya loved to give banquets for one another, offering roast meat, stews with vegetables, corn cakes (perhaps tortillas or tamales) and cocoa, not to mention lots of alcoholic beverages. The lords got so drunk at these banquets that their wives had to come and drag them home, a condition that still exists. The 'banquets' today are cantinas, and the 'lords' are workmen, but the dragging remains the same. The attitude of the drinkers is aptly expressed in the name of a bar in Acanceh, south of Mérida: *Aqui me quedo*, 'Here I stay'.

Sport The recreation most favored by the Maya was hip-ball. Using a hard rubber ball on stone courts, players tried to stop the ball from hitting the ground, keeping it airborne by batting it with any part of their body other than their hands, head or feet. A wooden bat may have been used. In some regions, a team was victorious if one of its players hit the ball through stone rings with holes little larger than the ball itself.

The ball game was taken quite seriously and was often used to settle disputes between tribes. On occasion, it is thought that the captain of the losing team was punished by the forfeiture of his life.

Do & Don'ts
The traditional Maya are wonderfully welcoming to strangers, even though most foreigners are from that race that has caused them such discomfort in the past. Even so, you should take care to be sensitive to local cultural norms.

The most serious conflict arises over photography. Although many local people don't mind being captured on film or video, by some people and in some villages it is seen as highly offensive. The solution is simple: ask before you shoot. Sign language – pointing at your camera, then at the subject – will usually suffice. Abide by the response.

RELIGION
World-Tree & Xibalba
For the Maya, the world, the heavens and the mysterious 'unseen world' or underworld called Xibalba (shee-bahl-BAH) were all one great, unified structure that operated according to the laws of astrology and ancestor worship. The towering ceiba tree was considered sacred, for it symbolized the Whack Chan, or world-tree, which united the 13 heavens, the surface of the earth and the nine levels of the underworld of Xibalba. The world-tree had a sort of cruciform shape and was associated with the color blue-green. In the 16th century, when the Franciscans friars came bearing a cross and required the Indians to venerate it, the symbolism meshed easily with established Maya beliefs.

Points of the Compass
In Mayan cosmology, each point of the compass had special religious significance. East was most important, as it was where the sun was reborn each day; its color was red. West was black because it was where the sun disappeared. North was white and was the direction from which the all-important rains came, beginning in May. South was yellow because it was the 'sunniest' point of the compass.

Everything in the Mayan world was seen in relation to these cardinal points, with the world-tree at the center; but the cardinal points were only the starting point for the all-important astronomical and astrological observations that determined fate. (See The Mayan Calendar System later in this section for more on Mayan astrology.)

Bloodletting & Human Sacrifice

Humans had certain roles to play within this great system. Just as the great cosmic dragon shed its blood, which fell as rain to the earth, so humans had to shed blood to link themselves with Xibalba.

Bloodletting ceremonies were the most important religious ceremonies, and the blood of kings was seen as the most acceptable for these rituals. Thus when the friars said that the blood of Jesus, the King of the Jews, had been spilled for the common people, the Maya could easily understand the symbolism.

Sacred Places

Mayan ceremonies were performed in natural sacred places as well as their human-made equivalents. Mountains, caves, lakes, cenotes (natural limestone cavern pools), rivers and fields were all sacred and had special importance in the scheme of things. Pyramids and temples were thought of as stylized mountains; sometimes these had secret chambers within them, like the caves in a mountain. A cave was the mouth of the creature that represented Xibalba, and to enter it was to enter the spirit of the secret world. This is why some Mayan temples have doorways surrounded by huge masks: as you enter the door of this 'cave' you are entering the mouth of Xibalba.

The plazas around which the pyramids were placed symbolized the open fields or the flat land of the tropical forest. What we call stelae were to the Maya 'tree-stones', that is, sacred tree-effigies echoing the sacredness of the world-tree. These tree-stones were often carved with the figures of great Mayan kings, for the king was the world-tree of Mayan society.

As these places were sacred, it made sense for succeeding Mayan kings to build new and ever grander temples directly over

older temples, as this enhanced the sacred character of the spot. The temple being covered over was not seen as mere rubble to be exploited as building material, but as a sacred artifact to be preserved. Certain features of these older temples, such as the large masks on the facade, were carefully padded and protected before the new construction was placed over them.

Ancestor worship and genealogy were very important to the Maya, and when they buried a king beneath a pyramid, or a commoner beneath the floor or courtyard of his na, the sacredness of the location was increased.

The Mayan 'Bible'

Of the painted books destroyed by Friar Landa and other Franciscans, no doubt some of them were books of sacred legends and stories similar to the Bible. Such sacred histories and legends provide a world-view to believers and guidance in belief and daily action.

One such Mayan book, the *Popol Vuh*, survived not as a painted book but as a transcription into the Latin alphabet of a Mayan narrative text; that is, it was written in Quiché Maya, but in Latin characters, not hieroglyphs. The *Popol Vuh* was apparently written by Quiché Maya Indians of Guatemala who had learned Spanish and the Latin alphabet from the Dominican friars. The authors showed their book to Francisco Ximénez, a Dominican who lived and worked in Chichicastenango from 1701 to 1703. Friar Ximénez copied the Indians' book word for word, then translated it into Spanish. Both his copy and the Spanish translation survive, but the Indian original has been lost.

For a translation of the Spanish version into English, see *Popol Vuh: Ancient Stories of the Quiche Indians of Guatemala*, by Albertina Saravia E (Guatemala City: Editorial Piedra Santa, 1987), on sale in many bookshops in Guatemala for about US$4.

According to the *Popol Vuh*, the great god K'ucumatz created humankind first from earth (mud), but these 'earthlings' were weak and dissolved in water. He/She

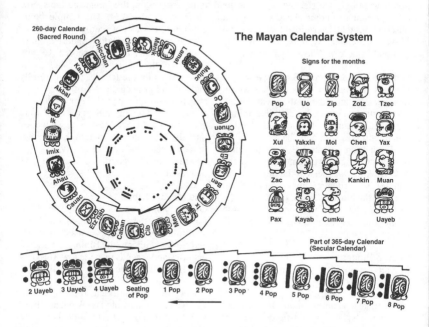

260-day Calendar (Sacred Round)

The Mayan Calendar System

Signs for the months

Pop Uo Zip Zotz Tzec

Xul Yakxin Mol Chen Yax

Zac Ceh Mac Kankin Muan

Pax Kayab Cumku Uayeb

Part of 365-day Calendar (Secular Calendar)

2 Uayeb 3 Uayeb 4 Uayeb Seating of Pop 1 Pop 2 Pop 3 Pop 4 Pop 5 Pop 6 Pop 7 Pop 8 Pop

tried again using wood. The wood people had no hearts or minds and could not praise their Creator. These too were destroyed, all except the monkeys who live in the forest, who are the descendants of the wood people. The Creator tried once again, this time successfully, using substances recommended by four animals – the grey fox, the coyote, the parrot and the crow. The substance was white and yellow corn, ground into meal to form the flesh and stirred into water to make the blood.

After the devastating earthquake of 1976 in Guatemala, the government rebuilding program included the printing and distribution of posters bearing a picture of an ear of corn and the words *Hombre de maíz, ¡levántate!* (Man of corn, arise!)

The *Popol Vuh* legends include some elements that made it easier for the Maya to understand certain aspects of Christian belief, including virgin birth and sacrificial death followed by a return to life.

Shamanism & Catholicism

The ceiba tree's cruciform shape was not the only correspondence the Maya found between their animist beliefs and Christianity. Both traditional Mayan animism and Catholicism have rites of baptism and confession, days of fasting and other forms of abstinence, religious partaking of alcoholic beverages, burning of incense and the use of altars.

Today, the Mayan practice of Catholicism is a fascinating fusion of shamanist-animist and Christian ritual. The traditional religious ways are so important that often a Maya will try to recover from a malady by seeking the advice of a religious shaman rather than a medical doctor. Use of folk remedies linked with animist tradition is widespread in Mayan areas.

MAYAN CALENDAR SYSTEM

In some ways, the ancient Mayan calendar is more accurate than the Gregorian calen-

Top: Elderly Mayan Indian, Guatemala (MD)
Bottom Left: Traditional family, Zunil, Guatemala (JB)
Center Right: Restaurant decor, San Pedro de Jesús (YM)
Bottom Right: Mayan Indian girl (MD)

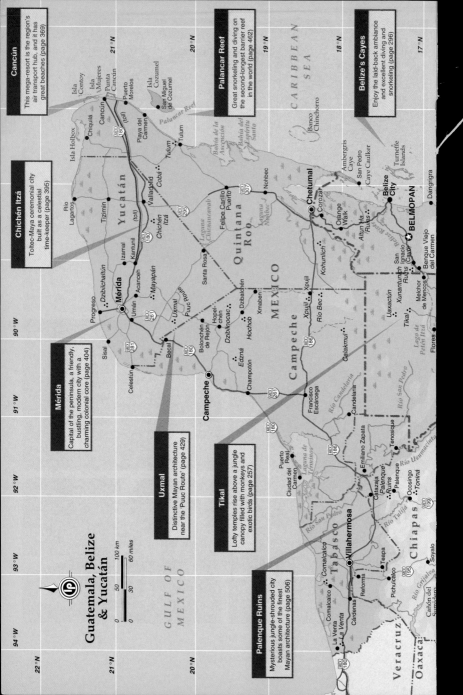

Guatemala, Belize & Yucatán

Cancún
This mega-resort is the region's air transport hub, and it has great beaches (page 369)

Chichén Itzá
Toltec-Maya ceremonial city built as a celestial time-keeper (page 395)

Palancar Reef
Great snorkeling and diving on the second-longest barrier reef in the world (page 462)

Belize's Cayes
Enjoy the laid-back ambiance and excellent diving and snorkeling (page 296)

Mérida
Capital of the peninsula, a friendly, bustling, modern city with a charming colonial core (page 404)

Uxmal
Distinctive Mayan architecture near the Puuc Route (page 429)

Tikal
Lofty temples rise above a jungle canopy filled with monkeys and exotic birds (page 257)

Palenque Ruins
Mysterious jungle-shrouded city boasts some of the finest Mayan architecture (page 506)

CARIBBEAN SEA

GULF OF MEXICO

0 50 100 km
0 30 60 miles

MEXICO

Yucatán

Quintana Roo

Campeche

Tabasco

Chiapas

Veracruz

Oaxaca

BELIZE

BELMOPAN

Belize City

Chetumal

Mérida

Campeche

Cancún

Villahermosa

Flores

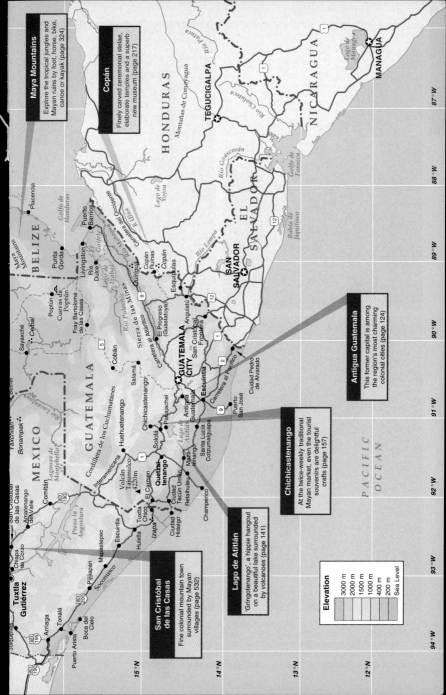

Maya Mountains

Explore the tropical jungles and Mayan ruins by foot, horse, bike, canoe or kayak (page 324)

Copán

Finely carved ceremonial stelae, elaborate temples and a superb new museum (page 217)

Antigua Guatemala

This former capital is among the region's most charming colonial cities (page 124)

Chichicastenango

At the twice-weekly traditional Mayan market, even the tourist souvenirs are delightful crafts (page 157)

Lago de Atitlán

'Gringotenango', a hippie hangout on a beautiful lake surrounded by volcanoes (page 141)

San Cristóbal de las Casas

Fine colonial mountain town surrounded by Mayan villages (page 532)

Elevation

| 3000 m |
| 2000 m |
| 1500 m |
| 1000 m |
| 400 m |
| 200 m |
| Sea Level |

Top Left: Temple roofcombs tower above the jungle canopy, Tikal (KS)
Bottom Left: Serpent motif on El Castillo, Chichén Itzá (RN)
Top Right: Templo del Sol (Temple of the Sun), Palenque (MG)
Center Right: Chac-mool (reclining god) statue, Chichén Itzá (RN)
Bottom Right: Pirámide del Adivino (Pyramid of the Magician), Uxmal (MG)

dar we use today. Without sophisticated technology, Mayan astronomers were able to ascertain the length of the solar year, the lunar month and the Venus year. Their calculations enabled them to pinpoint eclipses with uncanny accuracy, their lunar cycle was a mere seven minutes off today's sophisticated technological calculations and their Venus cycle errs by only two hours for periods covering 500 years.

Time and the calendar, in fact, were the basis of the Mayan religion, which resembled modern astrology in some respects. Astronomical observations played such a pivotal role in Mayan life that astronomy and religion were linked and the sun and moon were worshipped. Most Mayan cities were constructed in strict accordance with celestial movements (see Architecture & Archaeology, above).

How the Calendar Worked
Perhaps the best analogue to the Mayan calendar is in the gears of a mechanical watch, where small wheels mesh with larger wheels, which in turn mesh with other sets of wheels to record the passage of time.

Tonalamatl or Tzolkin The two smallest wheels in this Mayan calendar 'watch' were two cycles of 13 days and 20 days. Each of the 13 days bore a number from one to 13; each of the 20 days bore a name

such as Imix, Ik, Akbal or Xan. As these two 'wheels' meshed, the passing days received unique names. For example, Day 1 of the 13-day cycle meshed with the day named Imix in the 20-day cycle to produce the day named 1 Imix. Next came 2 Ik, then 3 Akbal, 4 Xan, etc. After 13 days, the first cycle began again at one, even though the 20-day name cycle still had seven days to run, so the 14th day was 1 Ix, then 2 Men, 3 Cib, etc. When the 20-day name cycle was finished, it began again with 8 Imix, 9 Ik, 10 Akbal, 11 Xan, etc. The permutations continued for a total of 260 days, ending on 13 Ahau, before beginning again on 1 Imix.

The two small 'wheels' of 13 and 20 days thus created a larger 'wheel' of 260 days, called a *tonalamatl* or *tzolkin*. Let's leave the 13-day and 20-day 'wheels' and the larger 260-day wheel whirling as we look at another set of gears in the watch.

Vague Year (Haab) Another set of wheels in the Mayan calendar watch comprised the 18 'months' of 20 days each, which formed the basis of the Mayan solar Vague Year calendar, or *haab*. Each month had a name – Pop, Uo, Zip, Zotz, Tzec, etc, and each day had a number from zero (the first day, or 'seating', of the month) to 19, much as our Gregorian solar calendar does. There was 0 Pop (the 'seating' of the month Pop),

Mayan Time Divisions			
Unit	Same as	Days	Gregorian Years*
Kin	–	1	–
Uinal	20 kins	20	–
Tun	20 uinals	360	0.99
Katun	20 tuns	7200	19.7
Baktun	20 katuns	14,000	394
(Great Cycle)	13 baktuns	1.872 million	5125
Pictun	20 baktuns	2.88 million	7885
Calabtun	20 pictuns	57.6 million	157,705
Kinchiltun	20 calabtuns	1.152 billion	3,154,091
Alautun	20 kinchiltuns	23.04 billion	63,081,809

* Approximate

1 Pop, 2 Pop, etc to 19 Pop, then 0 Uo, 1 Uo and so forth.

Eighteen months, each of 20 days, equals 360 days; the Maya added a special omen-filled five-day period called the *uayeb* at the end of this cycle in order to produce a solar calendar of 365 days. Anthropologists today call this the Vague Year, its vagueness coming from the fact that the solar year is actually 365.24 days long. To account for this extra quarter-day, we add an extra day to our Gregorian calendars every four years in Leap Year. The Maya did not do this.

Calendar Round The huge wheels of the tzolkin and the haab also meshed, so that each day actually had two names and two numbers, a tzolkin name-number and a haab name-number, used together: 1 Imix 5 Pop, 2 Ik 6 Pop, 3 Akbal 7 Pop, and so on. By the time the huge 260-day wheel of the tzolkin and 365-day wheel of the Vague Year had meshed completely, exhausting all the 18,980 day-name permutations, a period of 52 solar years had passed.

This bewilderingly complex meshing of the tzolkin and the haab is called the Calendar Round, and it was the dating system used throughout Mesoamerica by the Olmecs, the Aztecs, the Zapotecs and the Maya. In fact, it is still in use in some traditional mountain villages of Chiapas and highland Guatemala.

Though fascinating in its complexity, the Calendar Round has its limitations, the greatest being that it only goes for 52 years. After that, it starts again, and it provides no way for Maya ceremony planners (or modern historians) to distinguish a day named 1 Imix 5 Pop in this 52-year Calendar Round cycle from the identically named day in the next cycle, or in the cycle after that, or a dozen cycles later. Thus the need for the Long Count.

Long Count As Mayan civilization developed, Mayan scientists recognized the limits of a calendar system that could not run more than 52 solar years without starting over, so they developed the so-called Long Count or Great Cycle, a system of distinguishing the 52-year Calendar Round cycles from one another. The Long Count came into use during the Classic period of Mayan civilization.

The Long Count system modified the Vague Year solar mechanism, then added yet another set of wheels to the already complex mechanism of Mayan time.

In place of the Vague Year of 365 days, the Long Count uses the *tun*, the 18 months of 20 days each, and ignores the final five-day period. In Long Count terminology, a day was a *kin* (meaning 'sun'). A 20-kin 'month' is called a *uinal*, and 18 uinals make a tun. Thus the 360-day tun replaced the Vague Year in the Long Count system.

The time wheels added by the Long Count were huge. The names of all the time divisions are shown in the table on the previous page.

In practice, the gigantic units above baktun (pictun, calabtun, etc) were not used except for grandiose effect, as when a very self-important king wanted to note exactly when his extremely important reign took place in the awesome expanse of time. The largest unit in use in monument inscriptions was usually the baktun. There were 13 baktuns (1,872,000 days, or 5125 Gregorian solar years) in a Great Cycle.

When a Great Cycle was completed a new one would begin, but for the Maya of the Classic period this was unimportant as Classic Mayan civilization died out long before the end of the first Great Cycle. For them, the Great Cycle began on August 11, 3114 BC (some authorities say August 13), and it will end on December 23, 2012 AD. The end of a Great Cycle was a time fraught with great significance – usually fearsome. Keep that date in mind, and let's see how this Great Cycle finishes up!

Even the awesome alautun was not the largest unit used in the Long Count. In order to date everything in proper cosmic style, one date found at Cobá is equivalent to 41,341,050,000,000,000,000,000,000,000 of our years! (In comparison, the Big Bang that is said to have formed our universe is estimated to be a mere 15,000,000,000 years ago.)

It's important to remember that to the Maya, time was not a continuum but a cycle, and even this incomprehensibly large cycle of years would be repeated, over and over, infinitely, in infinitely larger cycles. In effect, the Mayan 'watch' had an unlimited number of gear wheels, and they kept ticking around and around forever.

Mayan Counting System

The Mayan counting system was elegantly simple: dots were used to count from one to four; a horizontal bar signified five; a bar with one dot above it was six, with two dots was seven, etc. Two bars signified 10, three bars 15. Nineteen, the highest common number, was three bars stacked up and topped by four dots.

To signify larger numbers the Maya used positional numbers, a fairly sophisticated system similar to the one we use today, and much more advanced than the crude additive numbers used in the Roman Empire.

In positional numbers, the position of a sign as well as the sign's value determine the number. For example, in our decimal system the number '23' is made up of two signs: a '2' in the 'tens' position and a '3' in the 'ones' position: two tens plus three ones equals 23.

The Maya used not a decimal system (base 10) but a vigesimal system, that is, a system with base 20; and positions of increasing value went not right to left (as ours do) but from bottom to top. So the bottom position showed values from one to 19, the next position up showed values from 20 to 380. The bottom and upper positions together could show up to 19 twenties plus 19 ones (ie 399). The third position up showed values from one 400 to 19 four hundreds (ie 7600). The three positions together could signify numbers up to 7999. By adding more positions one could count as high as needed.

Such positional numbers depend upon the concept of zero, a concept the Romans never developed but which the Maya did. The zero in Mayan numbering was represented by a stylized picture of a shell or some other object – anything except a bar or a dot.

The Mayan counting system was used by merchants and others who had to add up many things, but its most important use – and the one you will encounter during your travels – was in writing calendar dates.

MAYAN LANGUAGE

During the Classic period, the Mayan lands were divided into two linguistic areas. In the Yucatán Peninsula and Belize, people spoke Yucatecan, and in the highlands and Motagua Valley of Guatemala they spoke a related language called Cholan. People in El Petén were likely to speak both languages, as this was where the linguistic regions overlapped. Yucatec and Chol were quite similar – about as similar as Spanish and Italian – a fact which facilitated trade and cultural exchange.

In addition, both Yucatecan and Cholan were written using the same hieroglyphic system, so a written document or inscription could be understood by literate members of either language group.

The written language of the Classic Maya was very complex: glyphs could signify a whole word, or just a syllable, and the same glyph could be drawn in a variety of ways. Sometimes extra symbols were appended to a glyph to help indicate pronunciation. To read ancient Mayan inscriptions and texts accurately takes a great deal of training and experience. In fact, many aspects of the written language are not fully understood even by the experts. In Classic Mayan times it was the same way, as only the nobility would have been able to understand the inscriptions and codices completely.

Facts for the Visitor

PLANNING
When to Go
You can travel the region at any time of year; there is no off season. The Caribbean's pellucid waters are always invitingly warm, the beaches always good for sunning. But the topography of the region is varied, from low-lying Yucatán to the lofty volcanoes of Chiapas and Guatemala, so you will encounter a variety of climatic conditions whenever you go.

The height of the tourist season is in winter, from Christmas to the end of March; the other high-season month is August. During these times you should reserve middle and top-end hotel rooms in advance for Mérida, Uxmal, Cancún, Cozumel, Isla Mujeres, Belize's cayes and the resorts of Mexico's Caribbean coast. For bottom-end rooms, try to get to your destination as early in the day as possible so you can nail down a room at the price you want.

What to Bring
Clothing Local people of the Mayan lands tend to dress informally but conservatively. Most men of all classes, from taxi drivers to business executives, wear long trousers and sports shirts or *guayaberas*, the fancy shirts decorated with tucks and worn outside the belt, which substitute for jacket and tie in this warm climate. Women dress traditionally, in long white Mayan dresses with embroidered collars or bodices, or stylishly in dresses or blouses and skirts. The local people do not expect you to dress in the same manner. They allow for foreign ways, but you should know that shorts and T-shirt are the mark of the tourist.

In lowland areas, both men and women should always have a hat, sunglasses and sunblock cream. If your complexion is particularly fair or if you burn easily, consider wearing light cotton shirts with long sleeves and light cotton slacks. Otherwise, men can wear light cotton trousers or shorts, tennis shoes or sandals and T-shirts, although more conservative wear is in order when visiting churches. Women can dress similarly except off the beaten track in villages unaccustomed to tourists. In general, it is better for women to dress somewhat more conservatively when in town – no shorts, tank tops, etc. Cancún is the exception; in Cancún, wear whatever you like. Bring a light sweater or jacket for evening boat rides. Denim is uncomfortably heavy in these warm, humid areas.

In the highlands of Chiapas and Guatemala you will need warmer clothing – a pair of slacks or jeans for sure – plus a sweater or jacket, perhaps both if you plan to be out for long periods in the evening or early morning. A light rain jacket, preferably a loose-fitting poncho, is good to have from October to May and is a necessity from May to October.

Other Items Toiletries such as shampoo, soap, toothpaste, toilet paper, razors and shaving cream are readily available in all but the smallest villages. You should bring your own contact lens solution, tampons, contraceptives and deodorant.

Don't forget the all-important insect repellent containing DEET (see the Health section), which may be easier to find at home. Besides, if you buy it before you leave home, you'll have it when you need it.

Other items you might find useful are a flashlight (torch) for exploring caves, pyramids and your hotel room when the electricity fails, disposable lighter (for the same reasons), pocket knife, two to three meters of cord, diving or snorkeling equipment, fishing equipment, a small sewing kit, money belt or pouch, lip balm and a small Spanish-English dictionary.

Maps
International Travel Maps, a division of ITMB Publishing Ltd, PO Box 2290, Van-

couver, BC V6B 3W5, Canada, publishes a series of Traveler's Reference Maps. Titles include *Guatemala-El Salvador* (1:500,000), which also covers neighboring portions of Chiapas, Tabasco, Belize and Honduras; *Yucatán Peninsula* (1:1 million), which includes Tabasco, Chiapas, Guatemala's Petén and Belize; and *Belize* (1:350,000). They're available from many travel book and map stores, including World Wide Books & Maps (☎ (604) 687-3320, fax 687-5925), 736A Granville St, Vancouver, BC, Canada V6Z1G3.

For motorists in Mexico, the best road atlas is generally reckoned to be the *Pemex Atlas de Carreteras*, available from some Pemex stations. Mexico's Secretaría de Comunicaciones y Transportes (SCT) also publishes a line of maps, including individual state maps at 1:350,000. They're sold in some bookstores in tourist areas.

A letter to the Instituto Guatemalteco de Turismo (INGUAT), 7 Avenida 1-17, Zona 4, Guatemala City, sent well in advance of your departure, will yield a useful map of the country with city street plans, but the scale is fairly small. The same map, called the *Mapa Vial Turístico*, may be bought in Guatemala at shops or from street vendors for several dollars (you can bargain with vendors).

For Belize, the various British Ordnance Survey maps (1:750,000 to 1:1000) are the most detailed and accurate of Belize. Contact the OS (☎ (44-170) 379 2000, fax 379 2234), Romsey Rd, Southampton, UK SO16 4GU. In North America, order them from OMNI Resources (☎ (910) 227-8300, fax 227-8374), PO Box 2096, Burlington, NC 27216; or Map Link (☎ (805) 692-6777, fax 692-6787), 30 South La Patera Lane, Unit 5, Santa Barbara, CA 93117.

More readily accessible in Belize is the *Belize Facilities Map* issued by the Belize Tourist Board, PO Box 325, Belize City. Derived from the Ordnance Survey maps, it has plans of all major towns in Belize, a road map, plans of the archaeological sites at Altun-ha and Xunantunich and a list of facts about Belize. If you write to the Board in advance you may be able to get one for free; in Belizean shops the map is sold for US$4.

SUGGESTED ITINERARIES

Most travelers arrive at Cancún, as that resort city has the busiest airport and the most frequent, far-reaching and cheap air services. Other possible approaches are via Mexico City, Guatemala City or Belize City. See the introductory Getting There & Away chapter.

The Top Sights in a Week

Spend your first night in Cancún or Isla Mujeres, changing money, getting used to Mexico and enjoying the beaches. Start for Chichén Itzá on the morning of the second day, visit the ancient city and spend the night in the nearby town of Piste. On the third day return to the ruins in the relative cool of the morning, then drive to Mérida for the afternoon and overnight. On the fourth day visit Uxmal, south of Mérida, either staying overnight at the ruins or returning to Mérida. On the fifth day head back towards Cancún, via Valladolid or via Felipe Carrillo Puerto and Tulum; spend the night in either of these cities, or in Cancún. On the sixth or seventh day, take a flight from Cancún to Tikal, Guatemala, for a visit to the most magnificent of Mayan cities; stay overnight in nearby Flores, returning to Cancún the following day.

This itinerary is rushed, and you may want to go by rented car rather than by bus to make it more comfortable. The rented car and the flights make it quite expensive, but it does allow you to see the top sights – Cancún, Chichén Itzá, Mérida, Uxmal, Tulum, Tikal – and a good deal of the countryside in the shortest possible time.

It is also possible to see the top archaeological sites – Chichén Itzá, Uxmal and Tikal – on day trips or overnight excursions by air from Cancún. If you're addicted to the beaches, or if you've signed up for a package vacation that provides a hotel in Cancún, you may want to see them that way.

Two Weeks

This itinerary gives you a good look at the Mayan sites in Mexico, the highlands of Guatemala, the fabulous ruins of Tikal and a glimpse of Belize, all in 14 or 15 days. It includes one or two flights, but the rest can be done by bus. If you have 15 or 16 days, or if you move at a slightly faster pace, you can do it all by bus, which brings the cost down considerably.

Day 1 – Cancún or Isla Mujeres, arrive and find your hotel

Day 2 – Ride to Chichén Itzá, visit the ruins and stay overnight.

Day 3 – To Mérida and overnight

Day 4 – Spend another day in Mérida if you like, or take a day trip to Dzibilchaltún and Progreso, or head south to Mayapán, Ticul and Uxmal.

Day 5 – Uxmal; overnight near the ruins

Day 6 – Visit Kabah on the Puuc Route and perhaps Sayil, then on to Campeche for the night; or, if you like, go directly to Palenque.

Day 7 – To Palenque and overnight

Day 8 – Visit the ruins at Palenque, then onwards to San Cristóbal de las Casas.

Day 9 – From San Cristóbal, cross the border into Guatemala and get as far as Huehuetenango or, preferably, Quetzaltenango.

Day 10 – If it's Wednesday or Saturday, go to Chichicastenango and find a hotel room in preparation for the market (Thursday and Sunday). If it's Tuesday or Friday. go to Sololá and catch the market there before continuing to Panajachel on Lago de Atitlán for the night.

Day 11 – Depending upon market days, visit Chichicastenango, Sololá, or Antigua (markets every day, but especially Monday, Thursday and Saturday).

Day 12 – Start early from Antigua to the airport at Guatemala City for a flight to Flores, then on to Tikal.

Day 13 – Visit Tikal. Return to Flores for the night, or head to Guatemala City.

Day 14 – From Flores, fly to Guatemala City or to Belize City for a flight back to Cancún, or fly directly home.

Day 15 – If you have an extra day, go by bus from Flores to Belize City on Day 14, then from Belize City to Chetumal and back to Cancún on Day 15. This is a lot of bus time, but it saves the cost of a flight and gives you a look at Belize.

Three Weeks

An itinerary of three weeks would follow the same general course as the one for two weeks but would include more time in several spots. You'd have time to see all the Puuc Route sites, including Kabah, Sayil, Labná, Xlapak and the Grutas de Loltún, and you could take a detour to Villahermosa to visit the Parque Museo La Venta. You would also have time for visits to Quiriguá, on Guatemala's Carretera al Atlántico, and to Copán (in Honduras), as well as more time in Belize. Three weeks also gives you an extra day or two at the beach, whether on the Belizean cayes, Mexico's Caribbean coast, Cozumel or Cancún.

Four Weeks

A month is enough time to include interesting but seldom-visited places in your itinerary, such as Toniná, near Ocosingo in Chiapas; Cobá, inland from Tulum; Kohunlich near Chetumal; Lago de Bacalar, the gorgeous and virtually untouristed lake just north of Chetumal; Mountain Pine Ridge in Belize, as well as the southern part of that country. You'd have lots of time for treks on horseback into the forests surrounding San Cristóbal de las Casas, time to look for pink flamingoes at Río Lagartos in northern Yucatán, and time to relax in a cabaña on the beach south of Tulum. In fact, one could easily spend months traveling the lands of the Maya.

HIGHLIGHTS

The top sights of La Ruta Maya are among the most fascinating on the planet, but some of the most enjoyable and memorable travel experiences happen in small towns and villages off the beaten track – places like Cobán (Guatemala), San Ignacio (Belize) or Xpujil, in Campeche. Just because these lesser known spots are not mentioned below does not mean they are unworthy of your time.

Cities & Towns

The first rank for charm, ambiance and interesting things to do includes Mérida, San Cristóbal de las Casas and Antigua Guatemala (usually just called Antigua).

They are, however, on the tourist track. Should you want to get off it, spend a few days in the city of Campeche, an attractive, authentic, very untouristy place with a rich history, beautiful architecture and low prices. Another good choice would be Valladolid, on the highway between Cancún and Chichén Itzá.

Pleasant small towns? First has to be Panajachel, on Guatemala's Lago de Atitlán, in the highlands. It's very touristy, and for good reason: the lake is breathtakingly beautiful, and the villages on its shores offer fascinating possibilities for meeting and getting to know the modern Maya. In Belize, the most pleasant place to spend a few days – apart from the wonderful cayes – is San Ignacio, on the banks of a peaceful river in the forests of the Maya Mountains.

Mayan Archaeological Sites
Without a doubt the top four sites are Chichén Itzá and Uxmal in Yucatán; Palenque, near the city of Villahermosa in Chiapas; and Tikal in Guatemala. These sites have the tallest pyramids, the most buildings, the boldest architecture and the best restoration. Tulum, on the coast south of Cancún, is not particularly impressive. It is heavily visited simply because it is close to Cancún.

If you enjoy having archaeological sites more or less to yourself, consider my favorites among the 'second rank': Kabah, Sayil and Xlapak on the Puuc Route south of Uxmal; Cobá, inland from Tulum; Edzná, near Campeche; Uaxactún, north of Tikal; and Quiriguá off Guatemala's Carretera al Atlántico. Copán, just across the border from Guatemala in Honduras, is among the most important Mayan sites and falls somewhere in between the first and second rank.

Museums
As for museums, the only top-class museums are the ones in Guatemala City and Villahermosa, Tabasco.

For Olmec lore – including the enormous basalt heads – the Parque Museo La Venta is worth the detour if you get as far as Palenque, only an hour or so east of Villahermosa by bus. And while you're in Villahermosa, take a tour through the good Museo Regional de Antropología Carlos Pellicer Cámara, which offers a competent introduction to Olmec and Mayan culture.

In Guatemala City, don't miss the Museo Popol Vuh, a superb private collection of pre-Columbian and colonial artifacts given to the university; also the Museo Ixchel, famous for its displays of exquisite traditional hand-woven textiles and other crafts still thriving in Guatemala.

VISAS & DOCUMENTS
See the individual country sections for information on passports and visas. If you are traveling the region by private car, you will need motor vehicle insurance and a valid import permit. See the Getting There & Away chapter for details.

Student & Hostel Cards
If you have a student card, you may find it useful for reductions in admission fees at a few museums, but not for much else.

Hostel cards are even less useful along La Ruta Maya. The hostels – found only in Mexico – tend to cost at least as much as cheap hotels and usually do not require hostel membership in any case.

EMBASSIES & CONSULATES
For lists of embassies and consulates, see each country's Facts for the Visitor section.

An embassy is a mission from one government to another. A consulate is a mission in a foreign country that promotes the home country's business interests and protects its citizens. If you need help from your home government while in a foreign country, call upon your nearest consulate or the consular section of your embassy.

If you're in trouble while abroad, most consulates can help you by contacting relatives or friends, by suggesting reliable doctors or clinics, etc. Consulates do not normally provide emergency funds or airline tickets home. However, good-hearted diplomats at some posts have been known to contribute private funds to informal loan banks from which travelers in distress may be permitted to draw with the understanding that the loan must be repaid as soon as possible.

If you plan to travel in unstable areas or to stay in a country longer than a month or two, it's a good idea to register with your consulate so that they can warn you of dangers if necessary.

CUSTOMS

Customs officers only get angry and excited about a few things: drugs, weapons, large amounts of currency, automobiles and other expensive items that might be sold while you're in the country. Don't take illegal drugs or any sort of firearm across these borders. If you want to take a hunting rifle across a border, get a permit from the country's diplomatic mission in advance.

Luggage Inspection

Normally the customs officer will not look seriously in your luggage and may not look at all. At some border points the amount of search is inversely proportional to the amount of 'tip' you have provided; that is, big tip no search, no tip big search. As for valuable items, if you have an expensive camera, electronic gizmo or jewelry, there is a risk that they may be seen as leverage or be deemed as liable for duty at Customs' discretion. Be prepared and be firm but flexible. (See the section on Crossing Borders in the Getting There & Away chapter for more information.)

Whatever you do, keep it all formal and polite. Anger, surliness or impoliteness can get you thrown out of the country or into jail, or worse.

MONEY
Costs

See Facts for the Visitor in each country section. At the time of writing, Mexico is the cheapest country in the region, followed by Guatemala, with Belize being substantially overpriced.

Carrying Money

As pickpockets and robbers are not uncommon in the cities of this region, it's important to carry your money, passport and other valuables in a pouch or belt underneath your clothing. A neck pouch is preferable to a money belt as a neck pouch can be retrieved and the contents extracted without disrobing in public.

Cash

For details on the currency of Guatemala, Belize and Mexico, see Money in the Facts for the Visitor chapter of each country.

Carry your money in US dollars or US dollar travelers' checks. Though you should be able to change other sorts of currency (especially Canadian dollars) in major banks in large cities and resorts (ie, Cancún), it can require some time-consuming hassles and may be supremely difficult in smaller cities and towns. In many parts of the region (especially Mexico) it can take a lot of time in a bank just to change US dollars, let alone some currency that is, to a local bank teller, highly exotic.

Travelers' Checks

It is often difficult or impossible to exchange travelers' checks on weekends. Friday should be one of your routine money changing days so that you'll be supplied with cash for the weekend.

ATMs

Automated teller machines can now be found in many cities along La Ruta Maya, especially in Mexico (but not yet in Belize). They often provide instructions in English as well as in Spanish and issue local currency debited against your home cash-card account or credit card. They offer fast, hassle-free service at exchange rates better than at most banks or casas de cambio.

Don't depend on ATMs to supply all your local-cash needs. Have travelers' checks and/or a credit card for backup.

Currency Exchange

There is no black market to speak of in this region, as currencies are freely convertible. The best rates of exchange are often from freelance moneychangers at border crossing points – but for US dollars only. However, I'd avoid the street moneychangers in the cities because when you deal with them you're showing them where you keep your money and how much you have. They might end up with it all.

Banks exchange foreign currencies, but often only at very limited hours, sometimes at disadvantageous rates, and subject to fees and commissions. Casas de cambio (exchange offices) often have lower rates of exchange, but may not charge commissions, and offer fast, hassle-free service.

Cross-Border Exchange

Try to spend all of your local currency before you cross a border because the exchange rates between countries are often terrible. For example, if you exchange pesos for quetzals in Guatemala the rate will be very low; the same thing happens if you exchange quetzals for pesos in Mexico, and ditto for quetzals or pesos to Belizean dollars.

Tipping

In general, staff in the smaller, cheaper places don't expect much in the way of tips, while those in the expensive resort establishments expect you to be lavish in your largesse. Tipping in Cancún and Cozumel is up to US standards of 15% to 20%; elsewhere, 10% is usually sufficient; in a small eatery you needn't tip.

Bargaining

Though you can attempt to haggle down the price of a hotel room, these rates are usually set and fairly firm, especially during the busy winter season. Off-season price reductions are sometimes negotiable.

For handicrafts and other souvenirs, and for anything in an open-air market, bargaining is the rule, and you may pay many times the going price if you pay the first price quoted. The exception to this rule comes when you buy handicrafts from some Chiapan and Guatemalan artisans' cooperatives, which use fixed prices.

Taxes & Refunds

European-style VAT refund plans are not available.

POST & COMMUNICATIONS
Sending & Receiving Mail

Almost every city and town (but not villages) in the region has a post office where you can buy postage stamps and send or receive mail.

If you are sending something by air mail from Mexico or Guatemala, be sure to clearly mark it with the words 'Por Avión'. An airmail letter sent from this part of the world to Canada or the USA may take anywhere from four to 14 days. Airmail letters to Europe can take anywhere from one to three weeks.

If you can arrange for a private address to receive mail, do so. There's less chance of your mail getting put aside, lost or returned to the sender if you're late in picking it up.

See each country's individual Post & Communications section for details on the post office.

Telephone

Local calls are cheap. International calls are generally very expensive. Don't go to the post office looking for telephones, as telephone companies in these countries are quasi-independent corporations separate from the post office. For details on calling from each country, see that country's section.

To call establishments listed in this guide from your home, follow the international calling procedures for your home telephone company, which will include dialing an access code for international service, then the country code, the area or city code, and then the local number. City codes are given for most telephone numbers in this guide. Country codes are (52) for Mexico, (502) for Guatemala and (501) for Belize.

Fax

Many middle-range and most top-end hotels have facsimile machines, as do airlines, car rental companies, tourist offices and other businesses. When making reservations or asking for information, a fax is often the cheapest and most efficient way of going about it. The recipient will get written instructions, which makes translations easier and minimizes the chance for errors. Also, faxes usually take less time than voice calls, saving you money on telephone tolls.

Email
The very few public email offices in the region are mentioned in the text.

CompuServe has 28,800 bps nodes (access numbers) in Guadalajara, León, Mexico City and Puebla, and also a nationwide toll-free number (modem (91-800) 7-20-00); they have no nodes in Belize or Guatemala. In practice, it's often difficult to get a line from Yucatán to other parts of Mexico, so getting online can be problematic.

America Online has AOL GlobalNet nodes in Cancún (modem (98) 84-12-12), Guadalajara (modem (3) 827-0590), Guatemala City (modem 230-0931), Mexico City (modem (5) 628-9393) and Monterrey (modem (8) 340-3724). The Cancún node is at 9600 bps, the others at 28,800 bps.

BOOKS
Many aspects of Mayan life and culture remain shrouded in mystery. New discoveries are being made every year by Mayanists and released to the world in books and magazine articles. The University of Okla-

---

ONLINE SERVICES
The following are some websites that you might find helpful.

Useful Organizations
Mundo Maya Organization
www.wotw.com/mundomaya

US Department of Health, Centers for Disease Control & Prevention
www.cdc.gov/travel/travel.html

US Department of State, Bureau of Consular Affairs
travel.state.gov

Transportation
Explore Worldwide Ltd
www.explore.co.uk

Journey Latin America
www.journeylatinamerica.co.uk

Guatemala
Guatemala Weekly
www.pronet.net.gt/gweekly/

The Siglo News
www.sigloxxi.com

Belize
For a small country with a primitive telephone system, Belize has embraced the Internet with surprising speed and success. Many Belizean businesses are reachable by email (often in the format *businessname*@btl.net), and there are several useful websites, including:

www.belize.com
www.belizeit.com
www.belizenet.com

Ambergris Caye
www.ambergriscaye.com

El Pilar archaeological reserve near San Ignacio, Cayo
alishaw.sscf.ucsb.edu/~ford/index.html

Maya Research Project excavations, Blue Creek
www.qvision.com/MRP

Yucatán
Aquamarina Beach Hotel, Zona Hotelera, Cancún
www.mextnet.com/mexico.htm

Autonomous University of Chiapas
www.unach.mx

Howard Johnson Hotel, Villahermosa
www.hojo.com.mx

Mexican Secretariat of Tourism
www.mexico-travel.com ■

homa Press, Norman, OK 73019-0445, USA, has a particularly strong Meso-american list.

Lonely Planet

Lonely Planet's encyclopedic *Mexico* guidebook covers the entire country in great detail. *Central America on a shoe-string* is your guide if you're traveling through the rest of the region on a tight budget. Lonely Planet's *Costa Rica* provides full information on that other top Central American destination.

Mayan Life & Culture

In preparation for your journey, find a copy of *Maya: The Riddle and Rediscovery of a Lost Civilization* by Charles Gallenkamp, the best general introduction to Mayan life and culture. Equally good but more scholarly is *The Maya* by the eminent Mayanist Michael D Coe.

Prehistoric Mesoamerica by Richard EW Adams is a scholarly survey of the history, culture and peoples of Mesoamerica. Another entertaining and academically accurate book is *A Forest of Kings: The Untold Story of the Ancient Maya* by Linda Schele & David Freidel (Morrow, 1990), a much more detailed look at Mayan history and beliefs.

Much of what we know about Mayan life and culture is derived from Friar Diego de Landa's book, translated as *Yucatan Before and After the Conquest* (Dover Publications, 1978). You can find this in numerous bookshops within the region, or you can order it from your bookshop at home or directly from the publisher, Dover Publications, 31 East 2nd St, Mineola, NY 11501-3582, USA.

If you have access to back issues of *National Geographic*, get hold of 'La Ruta Maya', Volume 176, No 4 (October 1989), pp 424-505, for the best short introduction to the concept of La Ruta Maya. Other *National Geographic* articles worth reading are 'Jade, Stone of Heaven' and 'Exploring a Vast Maya City, El Mirador', Volume 172, No 3 (September 1987), pp 282-339.

Travel Guides

We've worked hard to provide you with all of the information you'll need on a normal trip along La Ruta Maya, but your particular interests may demand more.

For an exhaustive survey of archaeological sites in the region, get hold of Joyce Kelly's comprehensive and authoritative paperbacks: *An Archaeological Guide to Mexico's Yuc-atán Peninsula* (1993) and/or *An Archaeo-logical Guide to Northern Central America: Belize, Guatemala, Honduras and El Sal-vador* (1996). Unfortunately, there is not yet a comparable handbook for the ruins of Tabasco or Chiapas.

Tikal: A Handbook of the Ancient Maya Ruins by William R Coe is available at Tikal but may be cheaper if you buy it at home before you leave. If you expect to spend several days exploring Tikal, you'll want William Coe's excellent guide.

Backpacking in Central America by Tim Burford (Bradt Publications, 1996) is a fine book with maps and descriptions for hikes both short and long in all the Central American countries except Belize.

Travelogues

Most important of all are the delightful travel books written more than a century and a half ago by John L Stephens and beautifully illustrated by Frederick Cather-wood. Stephens, a New York lawyer, sometime diplomat and amateur archaeol-ogist, and Catherwood, a patient and skilled draftsman, traveled extensively in the Mayan lands in the mid-19th century. The descriptions of their journeys, pub-lished soon after their return, were instant transatlantic best-sellers, entertaining readers throughout North America and Britain. More than just travelogues, their discoveries and painstaking explorations produced the first extensive and serious look at many Mayan archaeological sites. Their detailed descriptions and drawings are now the only evidence we have for some features of the sites that have been lost, destroyed or stolen.

The books *Incidents of Travel in Central America, Chiapas and Yucatan*, in two volumes (1969 and later reprints of the original 1841 edition), and *Incidents of Travel in Yucatan*, in two volumes (1963 and later reprints of the 1843 edition), are available in paperback at some bookshops in the region, from many bookshops in the USA and elsewhere with good selections of travel literature, and also directly from the publisher, Dover Publications, 31 E 2nd St, Mineola, NY 11501-3582, USA.

Aldous Huxley traveled through Mexico, too; *Beyond the Mexique Bay*, first published in 1934, has interesting observations on the Maya. Equally interesting is Graham Greene's *The Lawless Roads*, chronicling the writer's travels through Chiapas and Tabasco in 1938.

Contemporary writers have also found the lands of the Maya to be inspiring. *Sweet Waist of America* by Anthony Daniels (Arrow/Hutchinson, 1990) is a fine book telling about the author's travels, mostly in Guatemala but also in Honduras, El Salvador and Nicaragua.

So Far from God: A Journey to Central America by Patrick Marnham was the winner of the 1985 Thomas Cook Travel Book Award. It's an insightful and often amusing account of a leisurely meander from Texas down to Mexico City and on through Oaxaca and San Cristóbal de las Casas into Central America.

Around the Edge, otherwise entitled *Tekkin a Waalk* (Viking Penguin, 1991; Flamingo, 1993) is by Peter Ford, who traveled by foot and boat along the Caribbean coast from Belize to Panama.

Time Among the Maya: Travels in Belize, Guatemala, and Mexico by Ronald Wright is a thoughtful account of numerous journeys made in recent years among the descendants of the ancient Maya and will certainly help you to 'feel' Mayan culture as you travel the region.

History

Atlas of Ancient America by Michael Coe, Dean Snow & Elizabeth Benson (Facts on File, New York and Oxford, 1986) covers North, South and the rest of Central America as well as Mexico. It's too big to carry in a backpack but is a fascinating, superbly illustrated book.

Ambivalent Conquests: Maya and Spaniard in Yucatan, 1517-1570 by Inga Clendinnen covers the formative years of the relationship between the Maya and their Spanish overlords, years that set the tone of Indian-Hispanic relations for the rest of Yucatecan history.

The multi-volume *Handbook of Middle American Indians* edited by Robert Wauchope is an encyclopedic work that covers both the pre-Hispanic and more recent stages of Indian history and culture in great detail.

Culture, Art & Architecture

The basic text of Mayan religion is the *Popol Vuh*, which recounts the Mayan creation myths. A version easily available in Guatemala is *Popol Vuh: Ancient Stories of the Quiche Indians of Guatemala* by Albertina Saravia E.

The Flayed God: The Mythology of Mesoamerica by Roberta H Markman and Peter T Markman is a fascinating exploration of the religious and cultural myths of the Maya from the earliest times to the present day.

Maya Missions: Exploring the Spanish Colonial Churches of Yucatan by Richard and Rosalind Perry is an excellent guide to the more prominent fortress-like churches of Yucatán. Order it through your bookstore or from the publisher, Esplanada Press, PO Box 31067, Santa Barbara, CA 93130, USA.

The Blood of Kings: Dynasty & Ritual in Maya Art by Linda Schele & Mary Ellen Miller is a heavily illustrated guide to the art and culture of the Mayan period with particular emphasis on sacrifices, bloodletting, torture of captives, the ball game and other macabre aspects of Mayan culture. The illustrated analyses of Mayan art are fascinating.

The incredibly complex and portentous Mayan calendrical system makes a fascinating study. *The Book of the Year: Middle American Calendrical Systems* by Munro S Edmonson is an excellent but fairly expensive book.

NEWSPAPERS & MAGAZINES

Some major US newspapers such as *USA Today*, the *Miami Herald* and the *Los Angeles Times* are sold in luxury-hotel newsstands and some big-city and airport bookshops in the region. *Newsweek* and *Time* magazines are also sometimes available, along with *The New York Times* and the *Wall Street Journal*. The better hotel shops also have good selections of European newspapers and magazines in French, German, Italian and Spanish.

RADIO & TV

Local radio broadcasting, both AM and FM, is all in Spanish except in Belize and for a few hours of English programming each day in Cancún. In the evening you may be able to pick up US stations on the AM (medium wave) band.

Many middle-range hotel rooms in Yucatán have TV sets, often with satellite hookups that can receive some US stations. Most popular are ESPN (the sports channel) and UNO (the Spanish-language US network). Local Spanish-language programming includes hours and hours of talk shows and soap operas, some sports and reruns of old US movies dubbed in Spanish. The situation is similar in Guatemala.

In Belize, the local station is in English, so you can easily understand the news programs and you needn't read subtitles while watching the old movies.

PHOTOGRAPHY & VIDEO

In general, you are allowed to bring in no more than one camera and 12 rolls of film. I have never heard of this mandate being enforced. Camera stores, pharmacies and hotels are the most common outlets for buying film. Be suspicious of film that is being sold at prices lower than what you might pay elsewhere in North America – it is often outdated.

Print film, both B&W and color, is easily found, though you may not find the brand you like without a search. Processing is not particularly expensive and can be done in a day or two, even quicker in the large cities.

Print film prices are US$1 or US$2 higher than in the USA.

Slide (transparency) film may be more difficult to find in Mexico, especially in smaller locales. Kodachrome is not sold in these countries because they have no facilities to process it, though you may find some of the various E-6 process films (Ektachrome, Velvia, etc) at premium prices.

Most people in the region do not mind having their photographs taken. Indeed, the children may joyously pester you to take theirs. Of course one must use common sense and decency: ask permission before snapping away at anything military, religious or close-up personal. And keep in mind that there are a few locations – the village of San Juan Chamula outside San Cristóbal de las Casas, other villages nearby, the church of Santo Tomás in Chichicastenango – where photography is forbidden. If local people make any sign of being offended, you should put your camera away and apologize immediately, both out of decency and for your own safety.

TIME

North American Central Standard Time (GMT/UTC minus six hours) is the basis of time throughout the region. Daylight saving (or 'summer') time is not used in the region. Here's the time in some other cities when it's noon in Cancún, Mérida, Guatemala or Belize:

City	Summer	Winter
Paris, Rome	8 pm	7 pm
London	7 pm	6 pm
GMT/UTC	6 pm	6 pm
New York, Toronto	2 pm	1 pm
Chicago, New Orleans	1 pm	noon
San Francisco, LA	11 am	10 am
Perth, Hong Kong	3 am*	2 am*
Sydney, Melbourne	5 am*	4 am*
Auckland	6 am*	7 am*
*next day		

ELECTRICITY

Electrical current, flat-pronged plugs and sockets (points) are the same as in the USA and Canada: 115 to 125 V, 60 Hz.

WEIGHTS & MEASURES

Guatemala and Mexico use the metric system. For conversion information, see the inside back cover of this book. Because of the great commercial influence of the USA, you may find that ounces *(onzas)*, pounds *(libras)*, feet *(pies)*, miles *(millas)* and US gallons *(galones)* are used informally, at village markets for instance. Officially, however, everything's metric.

In Belize, both systems are used – and confused. For example, your rental car odometer and speedometer will be in kilometers and kilometers per hour, but the few road signs indicate distances in miles. When you see quarts and gallons, they are the American measure, not the old British Imperial measure.

LAUNDRY

The largest cities have laundries and dry-cleaning shops where you can leave your clothes to be cleaned. Often you can have your laundry back in a day; dry cleaning usually takes at least overnight. Addresses of convenient laundries are given in this guidebook for each city that has them.

HEALTH
Predeparture Preparations

Ideally, you should make sure you're as healthy as possible before you start traveling. If you're going for more than a couple of weeks, make sure your teeth are OK; there are lots of places in the region where a visit to the dentist would be the last thing you'd want to do. If you wear glasses, take a spare pair and your prescription.

Health Insurance A travel insurance policy to cover theft, loss and medical problems is a wise idea. Travel agencies sell them; STA Travel and other student travel organizations usually offer good value.

Some policies specifically exclude 'dangerous activities', which can include scuba diving, motorcycling, even trekking. If such activities are on your agenda, you don't want that sort of policy.

Medical Kit Take a small first-aid kit with adhesive bandages, a sterilized gauze bandage, cotton, a fever thermometer, tweezers and scissors.

Consider taking these: an antiseptic agent (Dettol or Betadine), burn cream (Caladryl is good for sunburn, minor burns and itchy bites), aspirin or ibuprofen or acetaminophen for pain or fever, and insect repellent containing DEET. Antihistamine (such as Benadryl) is useful for colds and allergies, also to ease the itch from insect bites and stings or to help prevent motion sickness. A rehydration mixture for treatment of severe diarrhea is particularly important if you're traveling with children.

Don't forget a full supply of any medication you're already taking; the prescription might be difficult to match abroad. If you're traveling off the beaten track, it may be wise to include anti-malarial medication and antibiotics, which must be prescribed – make sure you carry the prescription with you.

Illness Prevention Specific immunizations are not normally required for travel anywhere in Guatemala, Mexico or Belize. All the same, it's a good idea to be up to date on your tetanus, typhoid-paratyphoid and polio immunizations; if you were born after 1957 you should also make sure that you're immune to measles (ask your doctor). If you plan to stay for more than a few weeks in the region and you're adventurous in your eating, an immune globulin shot and/or Havrix are also recommended for protection against infectious hepatitis. You only need a yellow fever certificate to enter the country if, within the last six months, you have been to a country where yellow fever is present.

Food spoils easily in the tropics, mosquitoes roam freely and sanitation is not always the best, so you must take special care to protect yourself from illness. The most important steps you can take are to be careful about what you eat and drink, to stay away from mosquitoes (or at least make them stay away from you) and to practice safe sex. These measures are particularly important for adventurous travelers who enjoy getting off the beaten track, mingling with the locals and trekking into remote areas.

Before I begin on this somewhat disturbing catalogue of potential illnesses, let me say that after dozens of journeys in every region of these countries in every season of the year, climbing pyramids in remote jungle sites, camping out, staying in cheap hotels and eating in all sorts of markets and restaurants, I have never had anything more serious than traveler's diarrhea (but I've gotten that frequently!). I have rarely taken medicines to help get rid of diarrhea, instead preferring to let my body heal itself. I have not taken malaria prevention medicine or immune globulin, and I have not come down with malaria or hepatitis. Thus I believe that travel in the region is not a particularly perilous activity. But I have known people who have got dengue fever and typhoid fever, so I know that it can happen.

If you come down with a serious illness, be very careful to find a competent doctor and don't be afraid to get second opinions. You may want to telephone your doctor at home for consultation as well. In some cases it may be best to end your trip and fly home for treatment, difficult as this may be. A friend of mine who contracted typhoid fever in Mexico went to the local hospital where a sympathetic doctor strongly recommended that she and her husband fly home to the USA and go to the hospital there, which she did. Medical practice in the region is not always the exact science it should be.

Basic Rules

Food & Water Food can be contaminated by bacteria, viruses and/or parasites when it is harvested, shipped, handled, washed (if the water is contaminated) or prepared. Cooking, peeling and/or washing food in pure water is the way to get rid of the germs. To avoid gastrointestinal diseases, avoid salads, uncooked vegetables and unpasteurized milk or milk products (including cheese). Make sure the food you eat has been freshly cooked and is still hot.

Do not eat raw or rare meat, fish or shellfish. Peel fruit yourself with clean hands and a clean knife.

As for beverages, don't trust any water except that which has been boiled for 20 minutes or treated with purifiers or comes in an unopened bottle labeled *agua purificada*. Most hotels have large bottles of purified water from which you can fill your carafe or canteen; some will put smaller capped bottles of purified water in your room. Local people may drink the water from the tap or the well, or rainwater from the cistern, and their systems may be used to it; or they may have chronic gastric diseases! Cancún supposedly has purified tap water safe to drink. All the same, I drink bottled water there, as I do everywhere else in the region. Purified water and ice are available from supermarkets, small grocery stores *(tiendas)* and liquor stores *(licorerías* or *vinos y licores)*.

Use only pure water for drinking, washing food, brushing your teeth and making ice. Tea, coffee and other hot beverages should be made with boiled water. If the waiter swears that the ice in your drink is made from agua purificada, you may feel you can take a chance with it.

Canned or bottled carbonated beverages, including carbonated water, are usually safe, as are beer, wine and liquor. If you plan to travel off the main roads and into the middle of nowhere, a water purification system is recommended as bottled water may not be readily available outside of touristed areas. Your water purification method might be one of these:

- Tincture of iodine 2% *(yodo)* sold in pharmacies: add about seven drops per liter of clear water; strain cloudy water through a clean cloth first, then add 14 drops of iodine per liter.
- Water purification drops or tablets containing tetraglycine hydroperiodide or hydroclonazone, sold under brand names such as Globaline, Potable-Agua or Coughlan's in pharmacies and sporting goods stores in the USA. Within the region, ask for *gotas* (drops) or *pastillas* (tablets) *para purificar agua*, sold in pharmacies and supermarkets.

- Boiled water: bringing it to a rolling boil will kill most germs, but you must boil it for at least 20 minutes to kill parasites.
- A portable water filter that eliminates bacteria: compact units are available from major camping supply stores in the USA such as Recreational Equipment, Inc (REI; ☎ (206) 431-5804), PO Box C-88126, Seattle, WA 98188, and Mountain Equipment, Inc (MEI; ☎ (800) 344-7422), 1636 South 2nd St, Fresno, CA 93702, and through outfitters such as Eddie Bauer and LL Bean.

Protection Against Mosquitoes Many serious tropical diseases are spread by infected mosquitoes. If you protect yourself against mosquito bites, your travels will be both safer and more enjoyable.

Some mosquitoes feed during the day, others at night. In general, they're most bothersome when the sun is not too hot, in the evening and early morning, and on overcast days. There are many more mosquitoes in lowland and coastal regions and in the countryside than there are in cities or in highland areas, and many more during the rainy season (May to October) than during the dry (October to May). Avoid going to mosquito-infested places during these times and seasons if you can.

Mosquitoes seem to be attracted more to dark colors than to light, so in mosquito-infested areas wear light-colored long trousers, socks, a long-sleeved shirt and a hat. Clothing should be loose-fitting, as mosquitoes can drill right through the weave of a tight T-shirt. Mosquitoes also seem to be attracted by scents such as those in perfume, cologne, lotions, hair spray, etc, so avoid using these cosmetics if possible. Sleep in screened rooms or beneath mosquito netting after you have disposed of the little suckers who have somehow got in there with you. Check to make sure screens are intact, and that all openings to the outside are either screened or blocked.

Use insect repellent that has at least a 20% but no more than a 30% concentration of DEET (N,N diethyl-metatoluamide) on clothing and exposed skin. Repellents with higher concentrations of DEET work longer, but are also more likely to cause allergic reactions.

It's best to buy repellent before leaving home as repellents bought in Mexico, Guatemala or Belize may or may not have this most effective ingredient. To avoid reactions to the repellent, apply it sparingly only to exposed skin or to clothing, don't inhale the stuff or get it in your eyes or mouth or on broken or irritated skin, and wash it off soon after you enter a mosquito-free area.

Be particularly careful with children: don't apply it to infants or young children; don't put it on hands, which may be put in the mouth or eyes; use as little as possible; and wash it off just as soon as you're in a mosquito-free area.

Medical Problems & Treatment
Traveler's Diarrhea The food and water in a different country has different bacteria from what your digestive system is used to – germs that your immune system may not be prepared to combat. If you plunge right into the local culture and eat lots of food with high concentrations of these different bacteria, your body's natural defenses will be overwhelmed and you may get sick.

Travelers to many less developed countries suffer from what is known medically as traveler's diarrhea (TD) and informally as Montezuma's revenge, *turista* or the trots, a condition defined as having twice (or more) unformed bowel movements as normal; typically one has four or five watery stools per day.

Symptoms In addition to frequent watery stools, other possible symptoms include abdominal cramps, nausea, fever, malaise, a bloated feeling and urgency of bowel movements. The disease usually hits within the first week of travel, but it may hit at any time and may hit more than once during a trip. A bout of TD typically lasts three or four days, but may be shorter or longer. It seems to affect younger travelers more than older ones, which may be due to lack of caution among the young, or acquired immunity among the old.

Prevention Epidemiologists recommend that you *do not* take medicines for TD prophylaxis; that is, don't take any medicine just in the hope that it will prevent a case of the disease. Taking prophylactic medicines such as antibiotics, bismuth subsalicylate (Pepto-Bismol) or difenoxine (Lomotil) can actually make it *easier* for you to get the disease later on by killing off the benign digestive bacteria that help to protect you from the 'foreign' bacteria. These strong drugs can also cause side effects (some of them serious) such as photosensitivity, a condition in which your skin is temporarily oversensitive to sunlight (in the sunny tropics!).

Instead, observe the rules of safe eating and drinking, and don't overdo it early in your trip. For the first week after arrival, be extremely careful and conservative in your eating habits, avoid overeating or eating heavy or spicy food, don't get overtired and don't drink lots of alcoholic beverages or coffee.

Treatment If you come down with a case of TD, take it easy, with no physical exertion; stay in bed if you can. Be especially careful to replace fluids and electrolytes (potassium, sodium, etc) by drinking caffeine-free soft drinks or glasses of fruit juice (high in potassium) with honey and a pinch of salt added, plus a glass of pure water with a quarter teaspoon of sodium bicarbonate (baking soda) added; weak tea, preferably unsweetened and without milk, is all right. Avoid dairy products. Eat only salted crackers or dry toast for a day or so. After that, eat easily digested foods that are not fatty or overly acid. Yogurt with live cultures is particularly good as it helps to repopulate the bowel with benign digestive organisms. When you feel better, be particularly careful about what you eat and drink from then on.

- As for medications, it's best if you cure yourself without them. If you must have some chemical help, go to a doctor, who may recommend one of the following treatments as described in the US Public Health Service's book, *Health Information for International Travel*. Treatments and dosages should be determined by a competent medical doctor who can tell you about side effects and contraindications; those noted here are the normal ones for otherwise healthy adults *(not* children) and are for information only.

- Bismuth subsalicylate (Pepto-Bismol) – One ounce of liquid or the equivalent in tablets every half-hour for four hours. This treatment is not recommended if symptoms last more than more than 48 hours, or if you have high fever, blood in the stool, kidney problems or are allergic to salicylates. Children under the age of two should not be given this medicine. Your tongue may turn black after taking Pepto-Bismol. This is a harmless, though frightening, side effect.

- Diphenoxylate and loperamide (Lomotil, Imodium) – These are antimotility agents made from synthetic opiate derivatives. They temporarily slow down the diarrhea but do not cure it, they increase the risk of getting TD again, and they can make you sluggish or sleepy. They should not be used if you have a high fever, or blood in the stool, or are driving a motor vehicle or operating machinery (your alertness is impaired). In any case, don't use them for longer than two full days.

- Doxycycline (100 mg twice daily); or trimethoprim (200 mg twice daily); or trimethoprim (160 mg)/sulfamethoxazole (800 mg, once daily), known as TMP/SMX and sold in Mexico as Bactrim F (Roche) – These are antibiotics that may be required if there are three or more loose stools in an eight-hour period, especially with nausea, vomiting, abdominal cramps and fever.

It bears repeating: traveler's diarrhea is self-limiting, and you're usually better off if you can get through it without taking strong drugs. If you feel that you need medicine, go to a doctor. Make sure that you have TD and not some other gastrointestinal ailment for which the treatment may be very different.

Medicines Not to Take You can walk into a pharmacy in Mexico, Guatemala or Belize and buy medicines – often without a prescription – which might be banned for good reason in your home country. Well-meaning but incompetent doctors or pharmacists might recommend such medicines for gastrointestinal ailments, but such medicines may be worse than no medicine at all. Though they may bring some relief from the symptoms of TD, they may cause other sorts of harm such as neurological damage. Medicines called halogenated hydroxyquinoline derivatives are among these, and may bear the chemical names clioquinol or iodoquinol, or brand names EnteroVioform, Mexaform or Intestopan, or something similar. It's best not to take these medicines without consulting a trusted physician, preferably your regular doctor at home.

Heatstroke Only slightly less common than traveler's diarrhea are the illnesses caused by excessive heat and dehydration. These are more dangerous because they display fewer symptoms.

Symptoms If you exercise excessively in hot regions such as Yucatán, Belize and the low-lying regions of Guatemala, or if you fail to replace lost fluids and electrolytes (salt, potassium, etc), you can suffer from dizziness, weakness, headaches, nausea and greater susceptibility to other illnesses such as traveler's diarrhea. This is heat exhaustion, heat prostration or, in severe cases, heatstroke. In this last case, exposure to intense heat can cause convulsions and coma.

Prevention Protect yourself against heat-related diseases by taking special care to drink lots of fluids. If you urinate infrequently and in small amounts, you're not drinking enough fluids. If you feel tired and have a headache, you're not drinking enough fluids. Don't just drink when you're thirsty; make it a habit to drink frequently, whether you're thirsty or not. It's so easy to prevent dehydration that you should feel foolish if you succumb to it.

Alcohol, coffee and tea are diuretics – they make you urinate and lose fluids. They are not a cure for dehydration, they're part of the problem. Drink pure water, fruit juices and soft drinks instead; go easy on the beer. Salty food is good to eat in hot climates as the salt helps your body to retain fluids.

Other measures to take against the heat: don't overdo it. Take it easy climbing pyramids and trekking through the jungle. Wear light cotton clothing that breathes and cools you; wear a hat and sunglasses. Allow yourself frequent rest breaks in the shade, and give your body a chance to balance itself. Use sunblock to prevent bad sunburn. Be doubly cautious if you spend time near or on the water, as the sun's glare from sand and water can double your exposure. You may want to swim or go boating wearing a T-shirt and hat.

Fungal Infections Hot weather fungal infections are most likely to occur on the scalp, between the toes or fingers (athlete's foot), in the groin (jock itch or crotch rot) and on the body (ringworm). You get ringworm (which is a fungal infection, not a worm) from infected animals or by walking on damp areas, like shower floors.

Other Illnesses

Though you're unlikely to contract anything more than an unpleasant bout of traveler's diarrhea, you should be informed about the symptoms and treatments of these other diseases just in case.

Cholera This serious disease now seems endemic in Mexico and Central America. Like dysentery, it is a disease of poor sanitation and spreads quickly in areas, urban and rural, where sewage and water supplies are rudimentary. It can also be spread in foods that are uncooked or parcooked, such as the popular *ceviche*, which is made from marinaded raw fish, as well as salads and raw vegetables.

The disease is characterized by a sudden onset of acute diarrhea with 'rice water' stools, vomiting, muscular cramps and extreme weakness. You need medical help – but first treat for dehydration, which can be extreme, and if there is an appreciable delay in getting to the hospital, then begin taking tetracycline (adults one 250 mg capsule four times a day, children half this dose; if they are under eight, one third). The disease does respond to treatment if caught early.

Dengue Fever Symptoms include the fast onset of high fever, severe frontal headache and pain in muscles and joints; there may be nausea and vomiting, and a skin rash may develop about three to five days after the first symptoms, spreading from the torso to arms, legs and face. It is possible to have subclinical dengue (that is, a 'mild' case of it) and also to contract dengue hemorrhagic fever (DHF), a very serious and potentially fatal disease.

Dengue is spread by mosquitoes. Risk of contraction, though low for the average traveler, is highest during the summer (July to September), several hours after daybreak and before dusk, and on overcast days. There are four different dengue viruses, but no medicines to combat them.

There is no effective treatment for dengue. The disease is usually self-limiting, which means that the body cures itself. If you are generally healthy and have a healthy immune system, the disease may be unpleasant but it is rarely serious. To prevent against getting dengue, see the section on Protection against Mosquitoes, above.

Dysentery There are two types of dysentery, both of which are characterized by diarrhea containing blood and/or mucus. You require a stool test to determine which type you have.

Bacillary dysentery, the most common variety, is short, sharp and nasty but rarely persistent. It hits suddenly and lays you out with fever, nausea, cramps and diarrhea, but it is self-limiting. Treatment is the same as for traveler's diarrhea; as it's caused by bacteria, the disease responds well to antibiotics if needed.

Amebic dysentery is caused by amebic parasites and is more dangerous. It builds up slowly, cannot be starved out and if untreated will get worse and can permanently damage your intestines. Do not have anyone other than a doctor diagnose your symptoms and administer treatment.

Giardiasis This is caused by a parasite named *Giardia lamblia*, contracted by eating fecally contaminated food or beverages or by contact with a surface that has been similarly contaminated. Symptoms usually last for more than five days (perhaps months!), may be mild or serious, and may include diarrhea, abdominal cramps, fatigue, weight loss, flatulence, loss of appetite and/or nausea. If you have gastrointestinal gripes for a length of time, talk to a doctor and have a stool sample analyzed for giardia.

Hepatitis Hepatitis A (formerly called infectious hepatitis) is the most common travel-acquired illness that can be prevented by vaccination. Protection can be provided in two ways either with the antibody immune globulin or with a vaccine called Havrix.

Havrix provides long-term immunity (possibly more than 10 years) after an initial course of two injections and a booster at one year. It may be more expensive than immune globulin (IG, also called gammaglobulin) but certainly has many advantages, including length of protection and ease of administration. Finish your shots at least three weeks before your trip if you want full protection when you arrive.

Immune globulin is not a vaccination but a ready-made antibody that has proven very successful in reducing the chances of hepatitis infection. Because it may interfere with the development of immunity, it should not be given until at least 10 days after administration of the last vaccine needed; it should also be given as close as possible to departure because it is at its most effective in the first few weeks after administration and the effectiveness tapers off gradually between three and six months.

The risk is only moderate in Mexico, Guatemala and Belize, and is low for the average, careful traveler. But with good water and adequate sewage disposal in most industrialized countries since the 1940s, very few young Western adults now have any natural immunity and must be protected.

Hepatitis is spread by contaminated food or water. The symptoms are fever, chills, headache, fatigue, feelings of weakness and aches and pains, followed by loss of appetite, nausea, vomiting, abdominal pain, dark urine, light colored feces, jaundiced skin and the whites of the eyes may turn yellow. In some cases you may feel unwell, tired, have no appetite, experience aches and pains and be jaundiced. You should seek medical advice, but in general there is not much you can do apart from rest, drink lots of fluids, eat lightly and avoid fatty foods. People who have had hepatitis must forego alcohol for six months after the illness, as hepatitis attacks the liver and it needs that amount of time to recover.

Hepatitis B, which used to be called serum hepatitis, is spread through contact with infected blood, blood products or bodily fluids, for example through sexual contact, unsterilized needles and blood transfusions. Other risk situations include having a shave or tattoo in a local shop, or having your ears pierced. The symptoms of type B are much the same as type A except that they are more severe and may lead to irreparable liver damage or even liver cancer.

Although there is no treatment for hepatitis B, an effective prophylactic vaccine is readily available in most countries. The immunization schedule requires two injections at least a month apart followed by a third dose five months after the second. Persons who should receive a hepatitis B vaccination include anyone who anticipates contact with blood or other bodily secretions, either as a health care worker or through sexual contact with the local population, particularly those who intend to stay in the country for a long period of time.

Hepatitis Non-A Non-B is a blanket term formerly used for several different strains of hepatitis, which have now been separately identified. Hepatitis C is similar to B but is less common. Hepatitis D (the 'delta particle') is also similar to B and always occurs in concert with it; its occurrence is currently limited to IV-drug users. Hepatitis E, however, is similar to A and is spread in the same manner, through water or food contamination.

Tests are available for these strands, but are very expensive. Travelers shouldn't be too paranoid about this apparent proliferation of hepatitis strains; they are fairly rare (so far) and following the same precautions as for A and B should be all that's necessary to avoid them.

Sexually Transmitted Diseases Sexual contact with an infected sexual partner spreads these diseases. While abstinence is the only 100% preventative, using condoms and otherwise observing safe-sex procedures is usually effective.

Gonorrhea and syphilis are the most common of these diseases: sores, blisters or rashes around the genitals, discharges or pain when urinating are common symptoms. Symptoms may be less marked or not observed at all in women.

Syphilis symptoms eventually disappear completely but the disease continues and can cause severe problems in later years. The treatment of gonorrhea and syphilis is by antibiotics.

There are numerous other sexually transmitted diseases, for most of which effective treatment is available. However, there is no cure for herpes and there is also no cure for AIDS. Abstinence is the only effective preventive; using condoms is next best.

AIDS can be spread through infected blood transfusions; most developing countries cannot afford to screen blood for transfusions properly. AIDS can also be spread by dirty needles – vaccinations, acupuncture and tattooing can potentially be as dangerous as intravenous drug use if the equipment is not clean. If you do need an injection it may be a good idea to buy a new syringe from a pharmacy and ask the doctor to use it.

Malaria This is the one disease that everyone fears and the one about which you must make an important decision.

Symptoms may include jaundice (a yellow cast to the skin and/or eyes), general malaise, headaches, fever and chills, bed sweats and anemia. Symptoms of the disease may appear as early as eight days after infection, or as late as several months after you return from your trip. You can contract malaria even if you've taken medicines to protect yourself.

Malaria is spread by mosquitoes, which bite mostly between dusk and dawn. Risk of infection is low in the major resort areas and in the highlands and lower in the dry season (October to May) than in the rainy season (May to October). But it is fair to say that somewhere in the region you will encounter mosquitoes. They may or may not carry infectious diseases. Mexico, Guatemala and Belize have no chloroquine-resistant strains of *Anopheles* mosquitoes, so chloroquine medicines can help to prevent infection.

The best way to protect yourself against malaria is to protect yourself against mosquito bites (see that section). You can also take medicines to protect against malarial infection, usually chloroquine phosphate (Aralen) or hydroxychloroquine sulfate (Plaquenil), though other medicines may be indicated for specific individuals. You must consult a doctor on the use of these medicines, and get a prescription to buy them. Begin taking the medicine *one or two weeks before you arrive* in a malarial area, continue taking it while you're there, and also for a month after you leave the area, according to your doctor's instructions. Taking medicine does not absolutely guarantee that you will not contract malaria, though.

The choice you must make is whether or not to take preventive medicine. As an adventurous traveler, you are more at risk than a person who buys a package tour to Cancún. Although most visitors to Mexico, Guatemala and Belize do not take malaria medicine, and most do not get malaria, you must decide for yourself.

Talk to your doctor. Call a hospital or clinic that specializes in tropical diseases. In the USA, call the Centers for Disease Control's toll-free telephone information system (☎ (800) 526-6367) or the CDC Malaria Hotline (☎ (404) 332-4555); in the UK, the Medical Advisory Service for Travellers Abroad (MASTA) of the London School of Hygeine and Tropical Medicine

(☎ (0891) 224100); in Australia, the Traveller's Medicine and Vaccination Centre in Sydney (☎ (02) 9221-7133). Check out the very good information and guidance on the CDC's useful World Wide Web site at www.cdc.gov/travel/travel.html. Whether or not you take medicine, do be careful to protect yourself against mosquito bites.

Rabies The rabies virus is spread through bites by infected animals, or (rarely) through broken skin (scratches, licks) or the mucous membranes (as from breathing rabid-bat-contaminated air in a cave, for instance). Typical signs of a rabid animal are mad or uncontrolled behavior, inability to eat, biting at anything and everything and frothing at the mouth.

If any animal (but especially a dog) bites you, assume you have been exposed to rabies until you are certain this is not the case – there are no second chances. First, immediately wash the wound with lots of soap and water – this is very important! If it is possible and safe to do so, try to capture the animal alive, and give it to local health officials who can determine whether or not it's rabid. Begin rabies immunization shots as soon as possible; if you are taking antimalarial medicine, be sure to mention this to the doctor because antimalarial medicines can interfere with the effectiveness of rabies vaccine. Rabies is a potentially fatal disease, but it can be cured by prompt and proper treatment.

Schistosomiasis This parasitic worm makes its way into the bodies of certain tiny freshwater snails and then into humans swimming, wading or otherwise touching the infected fresh water in pools, ponds or cenotes. Two or three weeks after your dip you may experience fever, weakness, headache, loss of appetite, loss of weight, pain in the gut and/or pain in the joints and muscles. You may have nausea and/or coughing. Six to eight weeks after infection, evidence of the worm can be found in the stools.

After this very unpleasant month or two, diagnosis can correctly identify schistosomiasis as the culprit, and you can get rid of it quickly and effectively by taking an inexpensive medicine. To guard against the illness, don't swim in fresh water that may be infected by sewage or other pollution. If you expose your skin to schistosomiasis-infected water, rub the skin vigorously with a towel and/or rub alcohol on it.

Typhoid Fever This serious disease is spread by contaminated food and beverages and has symptoms similar to those of traveler's diarrhea. If you get it, you should have close supervision by a competent doctor for awhile and perhaps spend a short time in the hospital. Inoculation can give you some protection but is not 100% effective. If diagnosed and treated early, typhoid can be treated effectively.

Typhus If you go to a mountain town and get head lice, be aware that they can give you typhus; otherwise, risk is extremely low. Typhus is treated by taking antibiotics.

Hospitals & Clinics
Almost every town and city now has either a hospital or medical clinic and Red Cross (Cruz Roja) emergency facilities, all of which are indicated by road signs that show a red cross. Hospitals are generally inexpensive for typical ailments (diarrhea, dysentery) and minor surgery (stitches, sprains). Clinics are often too understaffed and overburdened with local problems to be of much help, but they are linked by a government radio network to emergency services.

If you must use these services, try to ascertain the competence of the staff treating you. Compare their diagnoses and prescriptions to the information in this section. If you have questions, call your embassy and get a referral for a doctor, or call home and have your doctor advise you.

By the way, Guatemalans and Belizeans with serious illnesses often go to Mexican cities (Chetumal, Mérida, Cancún, Villahermosa or even Mexico City) for treatment in better medical facilities. People from all three countries look upon Miami, New Orleans and Houston as the medical centers of last resort.

Women's Health
Gynecological problems, poor diet, lowered resistance due to the use of antibiotics for stomach upsets and even contraceptive pills can lead to vaginal infections when traveling in hot climates. Wearing skirts or loose-fitting trousers and cotton underwear will help to prevent infections.

Yeast infections, characterized by a rash, itch and discharge, can be treated with a vinegar or even lemon-juice douche or with yogurt. Nystatin suppositories are the usual medical prescription. Trichomonas is a more serious infection; symptoms are a discharge and a burning sensation when urinating. Male sexual partners must also be treated, and if a vinegar-water douche is not effective, medical attention should be sought. Flagyl is the prescribed drug.

Pregnancy Most miscarriages occur during the first three months of pregnancy, so this is the most risky time to travel. The last three months should also be spent within reasonable distance of good medical care, as quite serious problems can develop at this time. Pregnant women should avoid all unnecessary medication, but vaccinations and malarial prophylactics should still be taken where possible. Additional care should be taken to prevent illness and particular attention should be paid to diet and nutrition.

TOILETS
In a hot climate, where your body loses lots of moisture through perspiration, you have less frequent need of toilets. This is good, as public toilets are virtually nonexistent. Use the ones in cafes, restaurants, your hotel and at archaeological sites.

Luxury Mexican buses are equipped with toilets. The first one to use it gets a clean toilet, and it goes downhill after that. Bus station toilets range can be indecent.

WOMEN TRAVELERS
In general, the local men aren't great believers in the equality of the sexes (what would you expect from the home of machismo?), and women alone have to

expect numerous attempts to chat them up. It's commonly believed that foreign women without male companions are easy game for local men. This can get tiresome at times; the best discouragement is a cool, unsmiling but polite initial response and a consistent firm 'No'.

Avoid situations in which you might find yourself alone with one or more strange men, at remote archaeological sites, on empty city streets or on secluded stretches of beach.

GAY & LESBIAN TRAVELERS

Anything goes in Cancún, but throughout the rest of the region machismo rules, and the quiet, private enjoyment of your preference is the best policy.

Gay and lesbian travelers may want to contact the International Gay Travelers Association (☎ (800) 448-8550, Box 4974, Key West, FL 33041, USA) to locate a travel agent familiar with gay and gay-friendly tours and lodgings.

DISABLED TRAVELERS

Much of Cancún can be negotiated by wheelchair, and sidewalk ramps are found in central Mérida, but in general the unstandardized sidewalks, streets and colonial buildings make access difficult.

SENIOR TRAVELERS

Senior travelers pay particular heed to the medical advice given above on the dangers of dehydration and exposure to excessive heat and sun.

TRAVEL WITH CHILDREN

Children are highly regarded throughout the region and can often break down the barriers and open the doors to local hospitality. For a wealth of good ideas, pick up a copy of Lonely Planet's *Travel with Children* by Maureen Wheeler (1995).

DANGERS & ANNOYANCES
Safety

Guatemala, and to a lesser extent, Belize and Mexico, demand caution. Up-to-date travel advisories are available from the US Department of State's website (see Online Services, earlier in the chapter). If you do not have Internet access, US citizens can telephone the Department of State's Citizens Emergency Center (☎ (202) 647-5225); British subjects can contact the UK Foreign Office's Travel Advisory Service (☎ (071) 270-3000).

The 36-year-long guerrilla war in Guatemala is supposedly over, but this danger has been replaced by an alarming rise in the general crime rate. There have been incidents of rape, robbery, car-jacking and even murder of foreign tourists. These incidents occur at random and are not predictable. See the Guatemala chapter for specific warnings.

Will you run into trouble? No one can say. Tens of thousands of foreign visitors enjoy the incomparable beauties of the region and the friendliness of its people every year, the huge majority without untoward incidents of any kind. But then there are the unlucky few.

Your best defenses against trouble are up-to-date information and reasonable caution. You should take the trouble to contact your government and inquire about current conditions and trouble spots and follow the advice offered.

If you plan to travel by road in the Guatemalan Highlands or El Petén, you should also ask as many other travelers as possible about current conditions. Don't rely on local newspapers, governmental officials or business people as your sole sources of information, as they often cover up 'unpleasant' incidents that might result in the loss of tourist revenues. If you speak Spanish, ask local children, who will not be as reticent as their parents to pass on 'bad' news. Your home country's government, however, is the most reliable source as it has an interest in safeguarding your well-being.

In past years there have been a few bizarre incidents in which foreign visitors have been unjustly suspected of kidnapping Guatemalan children in order to use their organs in transplant operations. One innocent woman taking photographs of children in a town on Guatemala's Pacific Slope was nearly murdered by a hysterical crowd. Be careful not to put yourself in any situation that might be thus misinterpreted.

In Belize, the problem is mostly petty theft and robbery in Belize City. See that section for details.

Generally, Mexico is quite safe, though you must take normal precautions against pickpockets, purse snatchers and thieves. Special caution is necessary when traveling in eastern and southern Campeche state, especially on the road east from Escárcega, which has been the scene of repeated robberies of buses, mostly at night though also in daylight. The road between Palenque and San Cristóbal de las Casas via Ocosingo has also been subject to roadblocks by bandits who say they are guerrillas resisting the government. They make you pay a 'tax', which may be small or may equal all of your valuables. Your best bet here is to travel these roads in the morning with a major bus company.

Robbery & Theft

Robbery is a danger in Guatemala City, Antigua, Chichicastenango and Belize City. Theft, particularly pocket picking and purse snatching, is also not unusual in cities such as Mérida and Antigua, and in beach areas. Foreign tourists are particularly singled out for theft as they are presumed to be 'wealthy' and to be carrying valuables.

To protect yourself, take these common-sense precautions:

- Unless you have immediate need of them, leave most of your cash, travelers' checks, passport, jewelry (earrings, necklaces, bracelets), airline tickets, credit cards, expensive watch, etc (and perhaps your camera) in a sealed, signed envelope in your hotel's safe; obtain a receipt for the envelope. Virtually all hotels except the very cheapest provide safe-keeping for guests' valuables. You may have to provide the envelope (buy some at a *papelería*, or stationer's shop). Your signature on the envelope and a receipt from the hotel clerk will help to insure that hotel staff won't pilfer your things.

- Leaving valuable items in a locked suitcase in your hotel room is often safer than carrying them with you on the streets of Guatemala City.

- Have a money belt or a pouch on a string around your neck, place your remaining valuables in it and wear it *underneath your clothing*. You can carry a small amount of ready money in a pocket or bag.

- Be aware that any purse or bag in plain sight may be slashed or grabbed. Often two thieves work together, one cutting the strap, the other grabbing the bag in a lunge past you, even as you walk along a street or stand at a bus stop. At ticket counters in airports and bus stations, keep your bag between your feet, particularly when you're busy talking to a ticket agent.

- Do not wander alone in empty city streets or isolated areas, particularly at night.

- Do not leave any valuables visible in your vehicle when you park it in a city, unless it is in a guarded parking lot.

- On beaches and in the countryside, do not camp overnight in lonely places unless you can be sure it's safe.

Reporting a Robbery or Theft There's little point in going to the police after a robbery unless your loss is insured, in which case you'll need a statement from the police to present to your insurance company. You'll probably have to communicate with them in Spanish, so if your own is poor take a more fluent speaker along. Say, *Yo quisiera poner una acta de un robo* (I'd like to report a robbery). This should make it clear that you merely want a piece of paper and aren't going to ask the police to do anything inconvenient like look for the thieves or attempt to recover your goods. With luck you should get the required piece of paper without too much trouble. You may have to write it up yourself, then present it for official stamp and signature.

LEGAL MATTERS

Police officers in these countries are sometimes (if not often) part of the problem rather than of the solution. The less you have to do with the law, the better.

Whatever you do, *don't* get involved in any way with illegal drugs: don't buy or sell, use or carry, or associate with people who do – even if the locals seem to do so freely. As a foreigner, you are at a distinct disadvantage, and may be set up by others. Drug laws in all of these countries are strict, and though enforcement may be uneven, penalties are severe.

PUBLIC HOLIDAYS & SPECIAL EVENTS

You will notice that Sunday is indeed a day of rest. Local people put on their best clothes, go to church, then spend the afternoon relaxing in the parks or strolling along the streets. Most businesses are closed, though some towns and villages have Sunday markets. Bus services may be curtailed. In the big resorts (Cancún, Cozumel, Isla Mujeres), Sundays are not observed so strictly.

The big national holidays are dictated by the Roman Catholic Church calendar. Christmas and Holy Week (Semana Santa), leading up to Easter, are the most important, though the celebrations are often as much Mayan shamanist in spirit as Christian. Hotels and buses are very busy in Mexico and packed throughout Guatemala during Holy Week, especially in the towns that have particularly elaborate and colorful celebrations, such as Antigua.

January

Though the first two weeks of January see somewhat fewer hordes of tourists flocking to Cancún after the Christmas rush, the busy winter sun-and-fun season begins in earnest by mid-January. The weather is dry.

January 1 – *New Year's Day* is a legal holiday in Mexico, Guatemala and Belize.

January 6 – *Día de los Reyes Magos*, or Day of the Three Wise Men. Mexicans exchange Christmas presents on this day, in memory of the kings who brought gifts to baby Jesus.

Last Sunday in January – *Día de la Inmaculada Concepción*, or Festival of the Immaculate Conception. In Yucatán, nine days of devotions lead up to a secular festival including a dance that features a pig's head decorated with offerings of flowers, ribbons, bread, liquor and cigarettes. The traditional Yucatecan *jaranas* dances are usually performed as well.

February

Height of the tourist season, with most hotel rooms filled, most rental cars rented and most other activities in full swing.

Religious Holidays – Late February or early March is when *Carnival* comes, preceding Lent, the start of which is determined by the date of Easter. Carnival festivities are important throughout the region and include parades with fantastic floats, folk dancing, athletic competitions and everybody dressing up in costumes. Carnival begins in earnest on the weekend preceding the beginning of Lent. The final day of Carnival is often called *Mardi Gras* (Fat Tuesday), the last day on which observant Catholics are allowed to eat meat. Fat Tuesday is followed by *Ash Wednesday*, first of the 40 days of Lent leading up to Easter. On Ash Wednesday the Carnival party is over; fasting and prayers are the rule. Fat Tuesday is February 23, 1999.

February 5 – *Constitution Day* is a legal holiday in Mexico.

March

The tourist season continues at its height.

Religious Holidays – *Carnival* (see February) usually falls in late February and early March, ending on Fat Tuesday, which is March 3, 1998; March 14, 2000; and March 6, 2001.

March 9 – *Baron Bliss Day* is a legal holiday in Belize. It honors the English nobleman who dropped anchor in Belizean waters in the 1920s, fell in love with the place and willed his considerable fortune (several million dollars) to the people of Belize. His bequest, held in trust and earning interest, has been funding worthwhile projects such as roads, schools, market halls, etc ever since.

March 21 – *Birthday of Benito Juárez*, a legal holiday in Mexico, celebrates the plucky Indian president who fought off the French intervention headed by Emperor Maximilian of Hapsburg in the 1860s. Also on March 20 or 21 is the vernal equinox, celebrated at Chichén Itzá as the sun strikes the 'serpent' on the stairway of El Castillo (see the section on Chichén Itzá for details).

April

The rainy season may start by late April. The few weeks before it does are often the hottest of the year. Everyone and everything swelters in the lowlands, while up in the mountains the weather is delightful.

Religious Holidays – During *Holy Week*, the week before Easter Sunday, things are especially busy in the lands of the Maya, particularly in the towns of highland Guatemala. Holy Week begins on *Palm Sunday*, the Sunday before Easter, which is April 5, 1998; March 28, 1999; April 16, 2000; and April 8, 2001. *Good Friday, Holy Saturday* and *Easter Sunday* are official holidays in all three countries. *Holy Thursday* is a holiday in Guatemala; *Easter Monday* is a holiday in Belize.

April 21 – *Queen's Birthday* is a legal holiday in Belize.

May

The rainy season begins in earnest, with heavy rains during the first few weeks after the season begins. No place escapes the rains, though they are heaviest to the west, in Chiapas and in Guatemala's highlands. In Yucatán the rains may be limited to an hour's downpour in the afternoon.

May 1 – *Labor Day* is a legal holiday in Mexico, Guatemala and Belize.

May 5 – *Cinco de Mayo* is a legal holiday in Mexico commemorating the Battle of Puebla (1862), when Juárez's forces defeated French armies of Maximilian of Hapsburg decisively, ending the European-sponsored occupation of Mexico.

24 May – *Commonwealth Day* is a legal holiday in Belize.

June

Rains may continue to be heavy during June.

June 30 – *Army Day* and commemoration of the revolution of 1871 is a legal holiday in Guatemala.

July

Rains are less bothersome, and the summer tourist season is in full swing. The hurricane season officially begins in July, though historically there are few storms this month. Summer visitors are usually more interested in archaeology and local culture than the sun-and-sea crowd that comes in winter.

August

The summer tourist season peaks, and rooms in some places may be difficult to find. Hurricane season comes to the Caribbean; this is one of the most active months for tropical storms.

August 15 – *Festival of Guatemala* in Guatemala City; offices and shops close for the day.

August 29 – *Postal Workers' Holiday*; all post offices closed in Guatemala.

September

The summer crowd thins out, but it's still quite hot and humid. Hurricane season continues, another active month for tropical storms.

Religious Holidays – *El Señor de las Ampollas*, a festival in Mérida celebrating the 'Christ of the Blisters' in the cathedral, runs from the end of September into mid-October.

September 1 – *President's Message to Congress* (Mexico).

September 10 – *Belize National Day* is a legal holiday in Belize. It commemorates the Battle of St George's Caye fought in 1798 between British buccaneers and Spanish naval forces. The victory prize was Belize itself. The British won. Celebrations begin today, and continue until Independence Day on the 21st.

September 15 – *Independence Day* is a legal holiday in Guatemala.

September 16 – *Independence Day* is a legal holiday in Mexico.

September 21 – *Independence Day* is a legal holiday in Belize. The colony of British Honduras gained its independence from the UK in 1981.

October

The rains cease sometime during October, as does most danger of hurricanes. The number of visitors drops off, facilities are less crowded and there are many bargains to be had. It's a great time to travel here.

Religious Holidays – The festival of *las Ampollas* continues in Mérida (see September). In late October (18 to 28) Izamal (east of Mérida) is the place to be. The *Día del Cristo de Sitilpech* is celebrated as a venerated statue of Christ comes in procession from the village of Sitilpech to the great monastic church in Izamal. On the evenings of October 25 and 28, *jaranas* (Yucatecan dances) are performed in the plazas.

October 12 – *Day of the Race* (Mexico); *Columbus Day* is a legal holiday in Belize.

October 20 – Commemoration of the revolution of 1944 (Guatemala).

October 31 – On the eve of *Todos Santos* (All Saints' Day) in Mexico, visitors place flowers on graves of the deceased and light candles in their memory.

November
A low season for travel, it's wonderful for the person who wants uncrowded beaches, empty hotels, quiet restaurants, an unhurried pace and discount travel-service prices. Hurricane season officially comes to an end.

November 1 – *Todos Santos*, or All Saints' Day (Guatemala). In Mexico, celebrations and observances continue on November 2, the Day of the Dead.

November 2 – *Día de los Muertos,* or Day of the Dead (Mexico). Every cemetery in the country comes alive with festive visitors.

November 19 – *Garifuna Settlement Day* (Belize) commemorates the Garinagus (Black Caribs) arrival to settle in Belize in 1823.

November 20 – *Anniversary of the Mexican Revolution* (Mexico).

December
Until the Christmas rush to the resorts begins, December is an excellent month to visit, with little rain, good temperatures, low prices and uncrowded facilities. The crowds begin to arrive – and prices rise substantially – after December 15.

December 8 – *Feast of the Immaculate Conception* takes place in many towns of Mexico and Guatemala. The festivities in Izamal, Yucatán, are particularly lively.

December 11 to 12 – *Day of the Virgin of Guadalupe*, Mexico's patron saint is a legal holiday in Mexico.

December 24 to 25 – *Christmas Eve* is a holiday in the afternoon in Mexico and Guatemala; *Christmas Day* is a holiday in all three countries.

December 26 – *Boxing Day* is a legal holiday in Belize.

December 31 – *New Year's Eve* afternoon is a holiday in Guatemala.

ACTIVITIES
Mayan culture, art and archaeology are of prime interest, and anyone visiting this area would want to spend some time exploring these.

Archaeology
Dozens of great sites are in this region. Seeing many of them entails a good deal of walking and climbing (Cobá springs to mind) or a trek deep into the jungle (Tikal and Caracol).

Swimming
The Caribbean coast from Cancún and Isla Mujeres in the north to the Belizean cayes in the south is a paradise for water sports, including swimming, snorkeling, scuba diving, fishing, sailing and sailboarding.

Guatemala's Pacific coast is relatively undeveloped, and water sports possibilities are not nearly as attractive as they are along the Caribbean. Likewise, the beaches and waters along Mexico's Gulf coast often leave something to be desired (usually cleanliness). The north coast of the Yucatán peninsula has some beaches, most notably at Progreso, but it also has mangrove swamps, shallow waters and – in certain places – crocodile-like beasts called caymans.

Diving & Snorkeling
Cancún has the most water-sports facilities, but Cozumel and the Belizean cayes have the barrier reef and thus the best diving to look at tropical fish, coral and undersea flora. If you plan to dive, bring evidence of your certification to show the dive shop people, and check the rental equipment over carefully before you dive.

Hiking & Climbing
Much of the region is flat, flat, flat, and tropical jungle to boot, not the most interesting trekking country. The exceptions are the highlands of Chiapas and Guatemala, which have excellent hiking possibilities and many picturesque volcanoes to climb. The best base for hikes into the forests and jungles of Chiapas is San Cristóbal de las Casas. Treks on horseback may be organized here as well. In Guatemala you can climb the volcanoes bordering Lago de Atitlán, though caution is in order as rural areas hereabouts harbor guerrillas and robbers. The volcanoes near Antigua in

Guatemala also offer excellent possibilities, but see the warning in the Guatemala's Highlands chapter for information on how to find out whether or not it is currently safe to climb.

Cycling
See the Bicycling section in the Getting Around chapter. Highway robbers have beset several cyclists, so you must use caution.

COURSES
Spanish-language courses are popular in Antigua and Quetzaltenango, Guatemala, and to a lesser extent in San Cristóbal de las Casas, Chiapas, Mexico. See those sections for details.

WORK
According to law you must have a work permit to work in any of these countries. In practice you may get paid under the table, or through some bureaucratic loophole, if you can find suitable work. The most plentiful work for native English speakers is of course teaching their language. Consult the classified advertisements in local newspapers (both English- and Spanish-language), owse the bulletin boards in spots where gringos gather, and ask around. Big cities offer the best possibilities, of course. Pay may be very low, but it's better than a negative cash flow.

More lucrative teaching is to tutor business and bank executives. It takes a while to establish a network of contacts and referrals, so you should not plan to tutor for just a month or two. If you get a good reputation, however, it can pay quite well as your students are among the commercial elite.

ACCOMMODATIONS
Accommodations range from luxury resort hotels, tourist vacation hotels, budget hotels and motels to *casas de huéspedes* (guesthouses) and *albergues de la juventud* (youth hostels).

Hotels & Motels
The luxury resort hotels are mainly found in Cancún, though there are upper-class hostelries in Villahermosa, Guatemala City and Belize City as well. Some of the resorts on the Belizean cayes are positively sybaritic, with prices to match. They are all expensive but most offer excellent value for what you get compared to establishments of a similar class at home. Double room rates start at about US$80 per night and go beyond US$250. Most of the guests at these palatial places do not pay these 'rack rates', however, but are booked on package tours that offer far better value.

In the middle range are comfortable hotels and motels, some with appealing colonial ambiance, others quite modern with green lawns, tropical flowers and swimming pools shaded by palm trees; still others are urban high-rise buildings with many services and comforts. These range in price from US$25 to US$80 or so, the higher prices being charged in the major cities.

Budget lodgings, those costing US$6 to US$25 a double, come in many varieties and degrees of comfort and cleanliness. Guatemala has the cheapest and simplest budget hotels and pensions, although as the country becomes more popular prices are rising; Belize has the most expensive ones, with quality not much higher than the Guatemalan ones. Mexico has a good range of options in all price ranges.

Casas de Huéspedes
The next cheapest option is the casa de huéspedes ('guesthouse'), a home converted into simple guest lodgings. A double can cost anywhere from US$5 to US$20 with or without meals.

Youth Hostels
Mexico's albergues de la juventud, formerly organized by the federal government, are now mostly run by local or state governments or youth groups. The charge per night for two dormitory beds often equals or even exceeds the cost of a simple double room in a hotel or pension. As hostels are often located away from the town center, you may find a cheap hotel the

better option. Guatemala and Belize do not really have any usable official hostels.

Camping

You can camp for free on most beaches, though you must be careful to pick a safe place far from thieves. Wherever facilities are available for campers, though, expect to pay from US$3 to US$15 per night, depending upon the facilities and the choiceness of the location. Most equipped campgrounds are trailer parks designed for campers or travel trailers.

Cabañas & Hammocks

These are the two cheapest forms of accommodations, usually found in low-key beach spots. Cabañas are palm-thatched huts with wooden walls, sometimes with a dirt floor and nothing inside but a bed, other times more solidly built with electric light, mosquito nets, fans, even a hot plate. Prices range from US$5 up to US$20 or even more for the most luxurious in the choicest spots.

You can rent a hammock and a place to hang it for less than US$3 in some beach places – usually under a thatched roof outside a small casa de huéspedes or a fishing family's hut. If you bring your own hammock the cost may be even less. It's easy enough to buy hammocks in Mexico; Mérida has many shops specializing in them, and they are widely available in other towns throughout Yucatán as well.

FOOD

There are similarities among the cuisines throughout the region but there are also differences. Traditional Yucatecan cuisine is quite different from what is served in the rest of Mexico, with several distinctive ingredients such as turkey and venison. Guatemalan cooking, though derived from the same roots as Mexican, has regional specialties and variations. Belizean cooking tends to the rough and ready, reflecting its roots.

There are three meals a day: breakfast *(el desayuno)*, lunch *(la comida)* and supper *(la cena)*. Each includes one or more of three traditional staples:

Tortillas are thin round patties of pressed corn (maize) dough cooked on griddles. Tortillas may be wrapped around or topped with various foods. Fresh handmade tortillas are best, followed by fresh machine-made ones bought at a *tortillería*. Usually what one finds are fairly fresh ones kept warm in a hot, moist cloth. These are all right, but they take on a rubbery quality. Worst are old tortillas left to dry out; their edges curl and dry out while the center could be used to patch a tire. But don't confuse old tortillas with toasted, thoroughly dried, crisp tortillas, which are another thing altogether, and very good.

Frijoles are beans eaten boiled, fried, refried, in soups, spread on tortillas or with eggs. If you simply order frijoles they may come in a bowl swimming in their own dark sauce, as a runny mass on a plate, or as a thick and almost black paste. No matter how they come, they're usually delicious and very nutritious. The only bad ones are refried beans that have been fried using too much or low-quality fat.

Chiles (peppers) come in many varieties and are consumed in hundreds of ways. Some chiles such as the *habanero* and *serrano* are always spicy-hot while others such as the *poblano* vary in spiciness according to when they were picked. If you are unsure about your tolerance for hot chiles, ask if the chile is *picante* (spicy-hot) or *muy picante* (very spicy-hot).

For full lists of menu items with translations, see the Menu Translator at the back of this book.

Meals

Breakfast This can be either continental or US-style. A light, continental-style breakfast can be made of sweet rolls *(pan dulce)* or toast and coffee. In Mexico a basket of pan dulce may be placed on your breakfast table when your coffee is served. When the time comes to pay, you tell the clerk how many you have eaten.

US-style breakfasts are always available: bacon or sausage and eggs, hot cakes (called just that – *hot cakes* – in Mexico, *panqueques* in Guatemala), cold cereal such as corn flakes or hot cereal such as oatmeal, cream of wheat, fruit juice and coffee. You may order eggs in a variety of ways (see the Menu Translator).

Lunch This, the biggest meal of the day, is served about 1 or 2 pm. In restaurants that do not cater primarily to tourists, menus might change every day, every week or not at all. Meals might be ordered á la carte or table d'hôte. A fixed-price meal of several courses called a *comida corrida* (the bargain or daily special meal) is sometimes offered, and may include from one to five or six courses; choices and price are often displayed near the front door of the restaurant. Simple comidas corridas may consist of a plain soup or pasta, a garnished main course plate and coffee; more expensive versions may have a fancy soup or ceviche, a choice main course such as steak or fish, salad, dessert and coffee.

Supper La cena is a lighter version of lunch served about 7:30 pm. In beach resorts the evening meal tends to be the big one, as everyone is out at the beach during the day, and they hardly want to drag themselves inside for a big meal.

Local Cuisine
For details on each country's cuisine, see under Food in the Facts for the Visitor chapter of each country.

DRINKS
Because of the hot climate in many parts of the region, you will find yourself drinking lots of fluids. Indeed, you must remember to drink even if you don't feel particularly thirsty in order to prevent dehydration and heat exhaustion (see the Health section in this chapter).

Water & Soft Drinks
Bottled or purified water is widely available in hotels and shops (see Food & Water in the Health section). You can also order safe-to-drink fizzy mineral water by saying 'soda'.

Besides the easily recognizable and internationally known brands of *refrescos* (soft drinks) such as Coca-Cola, Pepsi and Seven-Up, you will find interesting local flavors. Orange *(naranja)* flavored soda is very popular, and grapefruit *(toronja)* is even better, though less readily available. Squirt (pronounced SKWEERT) is a brand of lemon-flavored soda that is a bit drier than Seven-Up. Also in Mexico, try the two apple-flavored drinks named Sidral and Manzanita.

Coffee, Tea & Cocoa
The Soconusco region along the Pacific slope of Chiapas and Guatemala has many large coffee plantations that produce excellent beans, including those typed as Guatemalan Antigua and Maragogipes. Some hotels in Antigua have coffee bushes growing right on their grounds (no pun intended). Coffee is available everywhere, strong and flavorful in Mexico, surprisingly weak and sugary in parts of Guatemala.

Black tea *(té negro)*, usually made from bags (often locally produced Lipton), tends to be a disappointment to devoted tea drinkers. It's best to bring your own supply of loose tea and a tea infuser, then just order *una taza de agua caliente* (a cup of hot water) and brew your own.

Herbal teas are much better. Camomile tea *(té de manzanilla)*, a common item on restaurant and café menus, is a specific remedy for queasy stomach and gripy gut.

Hot chocolate or cocoa was the royal stimulant during the Classic period of Mayan civilization, being drunk on ceremonial occasions by the kings and nobility. Their version was unsweetened and dreadfully bitter. Today it's sweetened and, if not authentic, at least more palatable.

Fruit & Vegetable Juices
Fresh fruit and vegetable juices *(jugos)*, milkshakes *(licuados)* and flavored waters *(aguas frescas)* are popular drinks, particu-

larly in Mexico. Almost every town has a stand serving one or more of these, and Mérida seems to have one every few blocks. All of the fruits and a few of the squeezable vegetables are used either individually (as in jugos or aguas frescas) or in some combination (as in licuados).

The basic licuado is a blend of fruit or juice with water and sugar. Other items can be added or substituted: raw egg, milk, ice, flavorings such as vanilla or nutmeg. The delicious combinations are practically limitless.

Aguas frescas are made by mixing fruit juice or a syrup made from mashed grains or seeds with sugar and water. You will usually see them in big glass jars on the counters of juice stands. Try the *agua fresca de arroz* (literally rice water), which has a sweet nutty taste.

Alcohol

Supermarkets, grocery stores and liquor stores stock both beer and wine, both imported and locally made. Some of the local stuff is quite good. You certainly won't go thirsty, and drinking won't bust your budget. But remember that excessive alcohol intake is a very efficient way to become dehydrated in the hot climate of the region. If you want to get drunk, make sure you take in plenty of non-alcoholic fluids as well.

Beer Breweries were first established in Mexico and Guatemala by German immigrants in the late 19th century. European techniques and technology have been used ever since the beginning, which may explain why Mexico has so many delicious beers, both light and dark. Most beers *(cervezas)* are light lagers, served cold from bottles or cans, but there are also a few flavorful dark beers such as Modelo Negro (Mexico) and Moza (Guatemala).

Mexico's breweries now produce more than 25 brands of beer, including major labels such as Modelo, Superior, Corona, Bohemia and Carta Blanca. Local beers made in Yucatán include the lagers Carta

Clara and Montejo, and the dark León Negro.

Guatemala's two nationally distributed beers are Gallo (GAH-yoh, rooster) and Cabro (goat). The distribution prize goes to Gallo – you'll find it everywhere.

In Belize, Belikin virtually owns the beer market. Belikin Export, their premium version, comes in a larger bottle, is much tastier, costs more and is worth it. When you get sick of Belikin you can readily find US and European beers (Heineken, Löwenbrau, etc), but they cost considerably more.

In restaurants and bars unaccustomed to tourists, beer is sometimes served at room temperature. If you want to be sure of getting a cold beer, ask for *una cerveza fría*. Sometimes the waiter or bartender will hand you the bottle or can and let you feel it for proper coldness. This usually means it's not very cold, and your choice is then the dismal one of 'this beer or no beer at all'.

Wine Wine is not the local drink of choice. That distinction goes to beer and liquor made from sugar cane, by far. But as foreign wine lovers spread through the region, so does the availability of wine.

Mexico has three big wineries producing very drinkable vintages: Industrias Vinicolas Domecq, Formex-Ybarra and Bodegas de Santo Tomás.

Domecq is renowned in Mexico for its Los Reyes table wines. Formex has more than 800 acres of vineyards in the Valle de Guadalupe and is known for its Terrasola table wine. Santo Tomás hopes eventually to produce wines that can compete with California's, including varietal wines such as Pinot Noir, Chardonnay and Cabernet Sauvignon.

The situation in Guatemala and Belize is much worse. Local wines are no thrill to drink, and imported wines are fairly expensive, but at least they're available. In all but the best places you may have to specify that you want your red wine at room temperature and your white wine chilled.

Spirits The traditional Mayan ardent spirit in Yucatán is *xtabentún* (SHTAH-behn-TOON), an anise-flavored brandy, which, when authentic, is made by fermenting honey. The modern version has a goodly proportion of grain neutral spirits, however. It is made to be either dry *(seco)* or sweet *(crema)*. The seco tastes much like the Greek ouzo or French pastis; the crema is like the sweeter Italian Sambuca. It is served in some restaurants as an after-dinner drink; you can find it readily in many liquor shops in Mérida, Cancún and other Yucatecan towns.

Many other famous liquors, liqueurs and brandies are made in Mexico: Bacardi rum, Pedro Domecq brandy, Controy (orange liqueur, a knock-off Cointreau), Kahlúa (coffee-flavored liqueur) and Oso Negro vodka. All are of good quality and inexpensive. Tequila and mezcal, made from the maguey plant, come from 'mainland' Mexico.

Rum and *aguardiente* (sugar cane liquor) are the favorite strong drinks in Guatemala and Belize as well, and though most are of low price and matching quality, some local products are exceptionally fine. Zacapa Centenario is a smooth aged Guatemalan rum made in Zacapa, off the Carretera al Atlántico. It should be sipped slowly, neat, like fine cognac. Cheaper rums and brandies are often mixed with soft drinks to make potent but cooling drinks like the *Cuba libre* of rum and Coke.

Other drinks include gin, mixed with tonic water, ice and lime juice to make what many consider the perfect drink for the hot tropics, and whisky, mostly from the USA.

ENTERTAINMENT
Cancún offers lots of nightclubs, bars, dancing places, spectacles, booze cruises and razzmatazz, all slickly packaged and marketed to the one-week tour crowd. Prices are high (for Mexico), but most people feel they get their money's worth, because the staff is certainly experienced at what it does. Some of the middle-range restaurants in Ciudad Cancún also provide entertainment – a pair of troubadours, a trio of mariachis, a lasso twirler – at no extra cost.

The only other place in the entire region with good nightclubs is Guatemala City. In smaller cities and towns it is not unusual to find a strolling guitarist or other musician(s) entertaining in the better restaurants.

Cinemas are located in the larger cities. Except in Belize, virtually all movies are in Spanish.

THINGS TO BUY
Most *artesanías* (handicrafts) originated in objects made for everyday use or for specific occasions such as festivals. Today many objects are made simply to sell as 'folk art' – some purely decorative, others with a useful function – but that doesn't necessarily reduce their quality. Although traditional materials, particularly textiles, are rarer than they used to be, some artisans have used the opportunity to develop their artistic talents to high levels.

The places where crafts are made aren't always the best places to buy them. There's wide trade in artesanías and you'll often find a better selection in shops and markets in towns and cities than in the original villages. Nor do prices necessarily get much higher in the bigger centers. Indeed, the artisans who make these crafts have learned that the real markets for their wares are in cities such as Mérida, San Cristóbal de las Casas, Panajachel and Antigua Guatemala where there are lots of appreciative tourists interested in buying.

You can get a good overview of the best that's available and an idea of prices by looking round some of the city stores devoted to these products. Buying in these places also saves the time and effort of seeking out the sometimes remote towns and villages where items are made. The government-run shops in several cities usually have good ranges of high-quality stock at decent prices.

Hammocks

Whether or not you plan to follow the Yucatecan custom of bedding down in a hammock, you should plan to take one home for lazy summer afternoons. Yucatecan hammocks are woven of fine cotton string, natural in tone or dyed in pale colors. With their hundreds of strings they are supremely comfortable and cool, and very cheap. For details, refer to the Mérida chapter, as that city is the center of the hammock trade.

Textiles

Colorful hand-woven and embroidered Indian costumes come in a number of basic shapes and as many designs as there are weavers. Chiapas and the Guatemalan highland towns have the best work and the widest selection. Some of the finest huipiles are made in the villages around Lago de Atitlán and in the villages near Antigua. Cheaper than the fairly pricey huipiles are the colorful *fajas* (waist sashes).

Other Woven Goods

Many goods are woven all over the country from palm, straw, reeds or sisal (rope made from the henequen plant). Mérida is a center for sisal mats, hammocks, bags and hats.

Pottery

Pottery comes in a huge variety of local forms. There are basically two types – unglazed earthenware and sturdier, Spanish-influenced, often highly decorated glazed ware. You can pick up attractive items for a couple of dollars or less in many places. The village of Amatenango del Valle turns out earthenware jugs, vases and animals, fired not in kilns but in open fires and painted in pleasing 'natural' colors.

Wooden Masks

Ceremonial masks are fascinating, eye-catching and still in regular use. You'll see them in the markets in San Cristóbal de las Casas, Panajachel, Chichicastenango, Sololá and Antigua.

Getting There & Away

The easiest approach to the region, and the one most travelers use, is by air. The region's major international airports are at Cancún and Guatemala City, with a small amount of international traffic heading for Belize City. Mexico City also receives a large number of flights from all parts of the world, with connecting flights to Cancún, Chetumal, Guatemala City, Mérida, Palenque, Tuxtla Gutiérrez and Villahermosa.

Approaches by road from Mexico and Central America (El Salvador and Honduras) are easy, with fairly good roads, and frequent service in comfortable (though not luxurious) buses.

Amtrak and Southern Railways trains approach the US-Mexican border along the Rio Grande, and there are some good Mexican trains from border towns southward to Mexico City. But beyond the Isthmus of Tehuantepec train service is slow, unreliable, uncomfortable and often unsafe. There is no passenger train service connecting Guatemala with the rest of Central America, and no trains in Belize.

There is no regular car or passenger ferry service between the region and the USA.

AIR
Routes

International air routes are structured so that virtually all flights into the region from the rest of the world pass through half a dozen 'hub' cities: Dallas/Fort Worth, Houston, Los Angeles, Miami, Mexico City or San Salvador. You may have to change planes in one of these cities.

Mayan Route Tickets

The national airlines of the Central American countries, including Aviateca, COPA, LACSA, NICA and TACA, have formed a marketing organization named America Central Corporation that offers special Mayan Route fare plans. Such fares allow you to fly from a gateway (usually Miami, New Orleans or Houston) to the region, make stops in several places, then fly home. Call the airlines or your travel agent for details on current pricing.

North America

American, Continental, Delta, Northwest and United are the US airlines with the most service to La Ruta Maya. Aeromexico, Aeronica, Aeroquetzal, Aviateca, COPA, LACSA, Mexicana and TACA are the Latin American airlines with flights to the USA.

You can fly nonstop on a major scheduled airline to Cancún from any of these North American cities: Atlanta, Chicago, Dallas/Fort Worth, Houston, Los Angeles, Miami, New Orleans, New York, San Francisco and Tampa/St Petersburg.

Fares There are dozens of airfares that apply to any given air route. They vary with each company, class of service, season of the year, length of stay, dates of travel, date of purchase and reservation. Your ticket may cost more or less depending upon the flexibility you are allowed in changing your plans. The price of the ticket is even affected by how you buy it and from whom.

Travel agents are the first people to consult about fares and routes. Once you've discovered the basics of the airlines flying, the routes taken and the various discounted tickets available, you can consult your favorite bucket shop, consolidator or charter airline to see if their fares are better. Here are some sample fixed-date roundtrip fares (also called excursion fares) from various cities to Cancún:

Chicago	US$427
Dallas/Fort Worth	US$350
Los Angeles	US$350
Miami	US$229
New York	US$446
Toronto	US$399

Besides these excursion fares, there are many package tours from the USA that typically provide a roundtrip airfare, transfers and accommodation for a few days or a week. These are by far the most economical way to visit Cancún. Some of these tour packages allow you to extend your stay in order to tour the region on your own.

These package tours change in price and features as the seasons change. For a cheap flight to Cancún, read the advertisements in the travel section of your local newspaper and call a package tour operator, or a travel agent who sells such tours, and ask if you can buy 'air only' (just the roundtrip air transportation, not the hotel or other features). Often this is possible, and usually it is cheaper than buying a discounted excursion ticket. Sometimes, though, the difference between air-only and a tour package with hotels is so small that it makes sense just to accept the hotel along with the flight. To a limited extent, this is also true of package tours to Guatemala and Belize.

Consolidators (called bucket shops in Europe) are organizations that buy bulk seats from airlines at considerable discounts and then resell them to the public, often through travel agents, sometimes directly through newspaper and magazine ads. Though there are some shady dealers, many consolidators are legitimate. Ask your travel agent about buying a consolidator ticket, or look for the consolidator ads in the travel section of the newspaper (they're the ones with tables of destinations and fares and a toll-free number to call).

Cancún is easy to reach cheaply; it's a bit more difficult to find air-only fares to Guatemala City and Belize.

Caribbean, Central & South America

America Central Corporation airlines (see Mayan Route Tickets, above) predominate in the region. Mexicana and Cubana fly between Cancún and Havana.

Europe

The cheapest fares are on charter flights to Cancún, such as those run by Air Europa from Spain and Martinair from Amsterdam. Most of the scheduled airlines' routes take you to one of the US hub cities, where you change to a plane of a US, Mexican, Guatemalan or other Central American airline. Your flight then continues to Cancún, Chetumal, Cozumel, Guatemala City, Mérida, Tuxtla Gutiérrez or Villahermosa.

UK For cheap tickets from London, pick up a copy of *City Limits, Time Out, TNT* or any of the other magazines that advertise discount (bucket shop) flights, and check out a few of the advertisers. The magazine *Business Traveller* also has a great deal of good advice on airfare bargains. Most bucket shops are trustworthy and reliable, but the occasional sharp operator appears – *Time Out* and *Business Traveller* give some useful advice on precautions to take.

Agents offering cheap fares to Mexico include Journey Latin America (☎ (0181) 747-3108) at 16 Devonshire Rd, Chiswick, London W4 2HD (this company also has an information service for its customers and runs some small-group tours to Mexico); STA Travel (☎ (0171) 937-9962) at 86 Old Brompton Rd, London SW7 3LQ, and 117 Euston Rd, London NW1 2SX; and London Student Travel (☎ (0171) 730-3402) at 52 Grosvenor Gardens, London SW1.

A typical fixed-date return (excursion) fare from London to Cancún at the time of writing was UK£555.

Elsewhere in Europe Discount tickets are available at prices similar to London's in several European cities. Amsterdam, Paris and Frankfurt are among the main cheap flight centers. Air France, KLM, Iberia and the Colombian airline Avianca are some of the airlines whose tickets are handled by discount agents.

Here are some typical fixed-date return (excursion) fares to Cancún valid at the time of writing:

Amsterdam	NLG 1300
Frankfurt	DM 1300
Paris	FFr 4000

Australasia

There are no direct flights from Australia to the region. The cheapest way of getting there is via the USA – often Los Angeles. Discount returns from Sydney to Los Angeles cost from A$1200. Cheap flights from the USA to the region are hard to find in Australia. The cheapest Los Angeles-Cancún fares are US$350 return (see North America, above).

If you want to combine a visit to the Mayan region with South America, the cheapest roundtrip tickets from Sydney to Lima or Rio de Janeiro are about A$2100. Santiago and Buenos Aires are a little cheaper at about A$1800. If you want to fly into South America and out of the USA, or vice-versa, the best option is to get a roundtrip ticket to South America on an airline such as United, which flies to South America via the USA, and simply don't use one of the legs you have paid for. Fortunately, at the time of writing, United's fares for this route were much the same as those of airlines that go directly to South America – discount returns via the USA from Sydney to Buenos Aires, Lima, Santiago or Rio de Janeiro were all available at around A$2130.

Round-the-world tickets with a Mexico/Guatemala option are sometimes available in Australia. STA Travel, with 40 offices around the country, is one of the most popular discount travel agents in Australia. It also has sales offices or agents all over the world.

Fixed-date return (excursion) fares to Cancún from Sydney, via Los Angeles, valid at the time of writing, are around A$2100. To Cancún via Los Angeles one way is A$1100.

A fixed-date return fare from Auckland, New Zealand, to South America stopping in Los Angeles, Mexico, Buenos Aires, Lima and Santiago, is around NZ$4516.

Departure Tax

A departure tax equivalent to approximately US$10 or US$12 is levied in each of these countries for travelers departing by air for foreign destinations. Exit tax at Belizean land border crossing points is BZ$1 (US$0.50).

LAND
Bus & Train

For details of buses and trains, see the Getting There & Away chapter for each country.

Car

For US and Canadian visitors, taking your own vehicle across the USA/Mexico border is a practical and convenient option. The most apparent difficulty in driving your own vehicle is that most North American cars now have catalytic converters, which require unleaded fuel. Unleaded fuel, called Magna Sin, is available in most cities and large towns in Mexico, but you cannot expect to find it at every fuel station. In Guatemala and Belize it is not yet available. You can arrange to have your catalytic converter disconnected, and replaced with a straight piece of exhaust pipe soon after you cross into Mexico (it's illegal to have it done in the USA). Save the converter and have it replaced before recrossing the border into the USA.

Another consideration is that in Guatemala and Belize it may be difficult to find mechanics and parts for newer-model US and Canadian cars with sophisticated electronics and pollution-control systems. If your vehicle breaks down and needs parts, they may have to be sent from the USA or Canada.

Coming from overseas, you may want to buy a used car or van in the USA, where they're relatively cheap, drive through the USA to Mexico and travel the entire Ruta Maya.

Importing Motor Vehicles To take a motor vehicle (car, motorcycle, boat, etc) into Mexico, Guatemala or Belize you will need: the car's current valid registration; proof that you own it (if the registration is in a different name) or, if you don't own it, a notarized affidavit of authorization from the car's owner stating that you are allowed to take the car out of the USA; your current valid driver's license; and a temporary import permit from the Mexican authorities.

Temporary import permits are normally issued for free at the border when you enter, but the issuance of a permit may require prior purchase of liability insurance (see below). In Mexico the permits are normally valid for 90 days; in Guatemala and Belize it's 30 days.

You must have a permit for each vehicle that you bring into Mexico. For example, if you have a motorcycle attached to your car, you must also have a permit for the motorcycle, but there is a catch: one person cannot have more than one permit even if that person owns both vehicles. Consequently, another person traveling with you must obtain the second permit. As with all rules of this sort, though, they are not written in stone.

Another rule for drivers intending to travel in Mexico: you cannot leave the country without your vehicle even if it breaks down, unless you obtain permission from either the Registro Federal de Vehículos (Federal Registry of Vehicles) in Mexico City or a Hacienda (Treasury Department) office in another city or town. Similar rules apply for Guatemala and Belize.

Don't drive someone else's car across the border. The car will be registered on your tourist card or in your passport, and you will not be permitted to leave the country without taking the car or paying a huge customs import duty. If you drive into Mexico, officials will take your tourist card and issue you a single document that serves as both motor vehicle permit and tourist card; both you and the car must leave Mexico at the same time, surrendering the document as you leave.

Motor Vehicle Insurance US and Canadian motor vehicle liability insurance policies are not yet recognized as valid by the governments of Mexico, Guatemala or Belize, though the provisions of the North American Free Trade Agreement (NAFTA) may change this soon. For now, you must still buy local insurance; thus if you drive your vehicle into all three countries, you will have to buy three separate policies. See each country for details.

CROSSING BORDERS

Most of the time and at most entry points, this is a breeze. If you fly into any of these countries you should have few, if any, hassles. If you cross at border points, you may run into other situations. There are a few things that you ought to know.

For more details on land border crossings, see the Getting There & Around sections for each country.

La Mordida

Border officials in Latin American countries sometimes request small 'tips' or unofficial 'fees' from travelers at the border. Usually *la mordida*, the 'bite', is put on you in an official tone of voice: the officer will scribble something on your tourist card or in a ledger, stamp your passport or do some other little action, then say, 'Too dallah'. When crossing from one Latin American country to another, the officials on both sides of the border may play this little game, causing you to part with a quantity of cash before you're finally through the formalities. There are several things you can do to avoid paying.

The first is to look very important by dressing in a business suit or other such intimidating clothing. Wearing dark sunglasses can help.

The second is to scowl quietly and act cosmopolitan. Scowl all you want, but whatever you do, keep everything formal. Never *ever* raise your voice, mumble a curse, get angry or verbally confront a Latin American official. This will get you nowhere – except into deep trouble. Act quietly superior and unruffled at all times.

The third thing is to ask for a receipt, *un recibo*. Some fees are official and legitimate. If the fee is legitimate, you'll be given an official-looking receipt; often the official will show you the receipt booklet when he makes the request, to prove to you that the fee is legitimate. If you don't get a receipt, you've succumbed to the mordida, a tip or bribe.

The fourth thing is to offer some weird currency such as Thai baht or even Norwegian kroner or Dutch guilders or Australian dollars – anything but US dollars or the currency of either of the countries at the border. Border officials are usually used to seeing only US dollars (and some Canadian ones), Mexican pesos, Belizean dollars, Honduran lempiras and Guatemalan quetzals. At the sight of strange money the officer will probably drop the request. If he doesn't, or if the fee turns out to be legitimate, 'search' for several minutes in your belongings and come up with the dollars you need. In the unlikely event that the official will accept the unusual currency, inflate its value, declaring that a nearly worthless note is actually worth big bucks.

WARNING

The information in this chapter is particularly vulnerable to change and must serve only as a general indication of possibilities. Airfares in particular are complicated and ever-changing. Do as much research as possible on fares and restrictions, and make sure you understand how a fare (and ticket you may buy) works.

Getting Around

Bus travel has always been the most dependable means of travel within the region, but air routes are expanding, allowing travelers with more money than time to get to the major sights quickly.

Unfortunately, car rental companies have yet to join this 'easy access' campaign. Rental cars are expensive in Yucatán, more expensive in Guatemala and very expensive in Belize. In most cases you may not drive a rental car outside the national territory of the country in which you rented it (that is, you cannot drive it across a border). In those cases where you may drive across borders, you usually need permission in writing from the car rental company. Thus a plan to tour most of the region by rental car often involves different rentals in three countries and bus or plane in between.

AIR

You can avoid some long, hot and even dangerous bus trips by taking a plane between these points:

Palenque/Villahermosa-Mérida	US$90
Cancún-Chetumal	US$55
Chetumal-Villahermosa	US$75
Belize City-Flores (Tikal)	US$75
Guatemala City-Flores (Tikal)	US$59 to US$91

BUS

The prevalent means of transport is bus. You can travel on a bus to 95% of the sites described in this book (the other 5% can be reached by boat or on foot). Bus travel can be luxurious or very uncomfortable, but it is usually cheap.

In general, bus traffic is most intense in the morning (beginning as early as 4 or 5 am), tapering off by mid- or late afternoon. In many places within the region there are no buses in the late afternoon or evening.

Routes to remote towns and villages are run for the convenience of villagers going to market in larger market towns. This often means that the only bus departs from the village early in the morning and returns from the larger market town by mid-afternoon. If you want to visit the village, you may find that you must take this late afternoon bus and stay the night in the village, catching the bus back to the market town the next morning. Remote villages rarely have hotels, so you should be prepared to camp.

For details on getting around by bus, see each country's section.

TRAIN

Trains connect Mérida with Campeche, Palenque, Veracruz and other points in Mexico. They also run from Veracruz to Juchitan and along the Soconusco (Pacific coast of Chiapas) to Tapachula. From Ciudad Tecún Umán, across the border from Tapachula in Guatemala, trains run to Guatemala City.

All of these trains are very cheap, all are slow and unreliable, most are quite uncomfortable. Some are unsafe, as sneak thieves and robbers work with train crew members to relieve foreign tourists of wallets and cameras. Trains in this region are more a means of high adventure than a means of comfortable, safe transport. Avoid them.

CAR

Private car, camper van or trailer/caravan is perhaps the best way to travel the region. You can go at your own pace and easily reach many areas not served by frequent public transport. The major roads and many of the minor roads are easily passable by any sort of car, and border crossings are fairly easy. But you need private motor vehicle insurance, an import permit and you may need a car which uses leaded fuel or has had its unleaded-fuel catalytic converter removed. See the previous chapter (Getting There & Away) for details on bringing vehicles into the region.

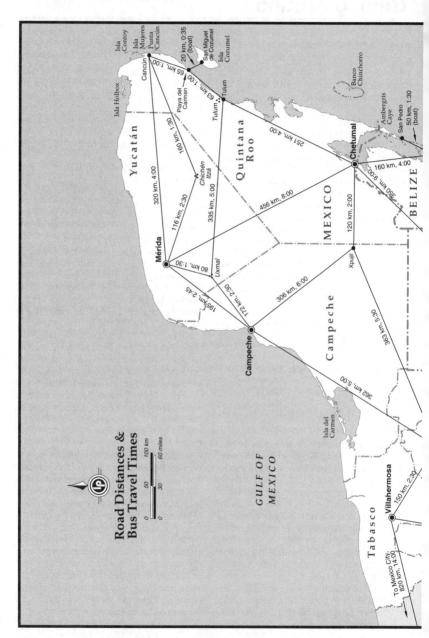

Road Distances & Bus Travel Times

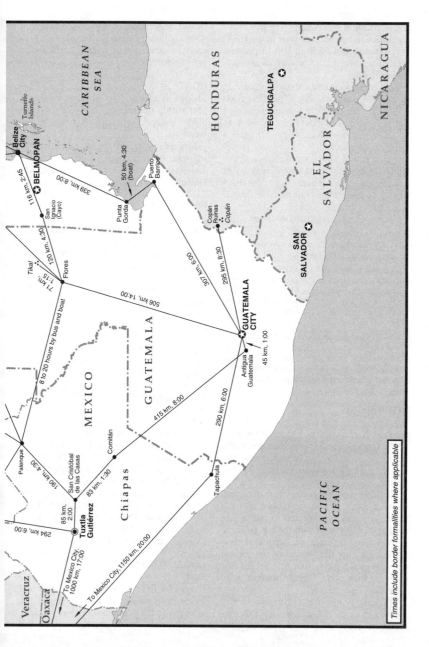

Times include border formalities where applicable

Car rental is more expensive in Guatemala, Belize and Mexico than in the USA, averaging about US$30 to US$45 per day, all in, for a very basic car such as a Volkswagen Beetle.

Fuel in Mexico costs about the same as in the USA – about US$1.30 per US gallon (US$0.35 per liter). In Guatemala and Belize, fuel costs almost twice as much as in USA – about US$2.50 per US gallon (US$0.67 per liter).

When you buy fuel, many station attendants – especially in Mexico – may try to overcharge you. There are numerous scams. To avoid them, follow these steps:

1. Get out of your car and stand by the gas pump.

2. Learn to estimate how much fuel you'll need *in pesos*, and ask for so-and-so many pesos' worth of fuel. (Don't just say 'fill it up').

3. Watch to be sure that the attendant resets the pump to zero before pumping, then note the amount immediately when he stops pumping. (He or another attendant may try to reset the pump immediately so you can't check the final amount.)

4. Pay in exact change if you can. If not, tell him out loud the amount of money you're offering as you hand it to him. (This prevents them from claiming you gave them 50 pesos when in fact you gave them a 100-peso bill.)

HITCHHIKING

Hitching is done at a few places, such as the Puuc Route south of Uxmal in Yucatán, where transportation is very infrequent. But hitching in Mexico can be dangerous, and it's very dangerous in Guatemala and Belize.

Hitching is not necessarily free transport. In most cases, if you are picked up by a truck, you will be expected to pay a fare similar to that charged on the bus (if there is one). In some areas, pickup and flatbed stake trucks *are* the 'buses' of the region, and every rider pays. Your best bet for free rides is with other foreign tourists who have their own vehicles.

Hitching is never entirely safe in any country in the world, and we don't recommend it. Travelers who decide to hitch should understand that they are taking a potentially serious risk. People who do choose to hitch will be safer if they travel in pairs or groups.

BOAT

Though there is no long-distance sea transport within the region, boats are used for public transport in a surprising number of locations.

Motor launches are the favored means of transport on Guatemala's Lago de Atitlán, and dugout canoes take you up the Río Dulce and El Golfete to Lago de Izabal for a look at the wildlife. Dugouts are also used for excursions on Lago Petén Itzá around Flores (near Tikal).

Belize has the most transport by sea. Fast motor launches connect Belize City, Caye Chapel, Caye Caulker and Ambergris Caye several times daily. Other boats go to the many other cayes several times a week on scheduled services or by charter. There is boat service connecting Punta Gorda, in southern Belize, with Lívingston and Puerto Barrios in Guatemala, and Puerto Cortés in Honduras. In western Belize, boat, canoe or kayak trips along the rivers of Mountain Pine Ridge are mostly for fun, but also sometimes for transport when the rainy season has turned the unpaved roads to sloughs of mud.

In Mexico, ferryboats and hydrofoils connect the island of Cozumel to the mainland, and ferries run to Isla Mujeres as well. Charter boats and hired fishing boats take you to Isla Holbox and other small uninhabited islands off Yucatán's coast. In Chiapas, you can take a boatride through the stupendous Cañon del Sumidero. Boats also transport adventurous travelers down rivers on the route between Palenque (Mexico) and Flores (Guatemala).

LOCAL TRANSPORT
Bus

Except for Belize City, all major cities and towns have public bus service. Buses are always the US schoolbus type of vehicle, usually rattly and uncomfortable, but always cheap, ranging from US$1 in Cancún to US$0.25 in Guatemala City. In many places the buses are insufficient to meet demand, and thus they tend to be packed solid at rush hours and perhaps at other times as well.

Jitney

Guatemala City has an extensive jitney cab network that becomes important at night after the city buses have ceased to run. Jitneys also run some popular tourist routes, such as from Tulum to Cobá and Belize City to San Ignacio, offering the comfort and speed of a car at only slightly more than bus fare.

Taxi

Taxis are quite expensive, charging rates equal to or exceeding those in places like New York City. None have meters, so it's necessary to determine the price of the trip before setting out. Rates are set, but drivers will often try to rip you off by quoting a higher price. This means that you must usually resort to bargaining or asking several drivers.

Bicycle

Sport bicycling is not yet popular. Roads are often not the smoothest, the sun can be relentless and one may have to travel long distances between towns. Often there's not much to look at except the walls of jungle which hem in the road. Insects – both those that hit you in the face and those that eat you for lunch – are another disincentive.

This having been said, certain areas are beautiful for biking. The Guatemalan highlands have light traffic, decent roads and manageable distances between towns, but they also present the danger from robbers. Highland Chiapas is similar. Unless you like pedaling in the rain, though, it's wise to plan your trip for the dry season (from October to May).

Horse

Horseback riding is not so much a means of transport as a means of pleasure, though in the back country of western Belize it is also eminently practical. Treks on horseback are possible in many places, including San Cristóbal de las Casas, Lake Atitlán, Flores and Mountain Pine Ridge.

Facts about Guatemala

Guatemala is the heart of the Mayan world, a beautiful, fertile land with a tragic history.

The Maya who live in the highlands amid breathtaking mountain scenery guard jealously their ancient customs and way of life. Holidays and ceremonies are filled with ancient pageantry, and the weekly markets are ablaze with the vivid colors of traditional handmade costumes.

At the same time, the modern world is penetrating Mayan culture, bringing good things and bad. Money from tourism is helping the Maya to improve their quality of life, education and health, but it is luring the younger generation away from their traditions and toward the raucous, bustling cities.

The distinction between indigenous and 'European' blood, between the traditional and the 'modern', culture and commerce, has been felt strongly here since the days of the Conquistadores. Today the distinction divides Guatemalan society in two and has often led to oppression and bloody conflict.

Traditional life and modern values also clash when local farmers and ranchers clear the rainforest to provide for their families. The need is for a livelihood; the method is the traditional one of slash-and-burn; the result is ecological disaster.

The paradoxes of Guatemala are part of its fascination.

HISTORY

The history of the country since independence has been one of rivalry and struggle between the forces of left and right. The Liberals have historically wanted to turn backward Guatemala into an enlightened republic of political, social and economic progress. The Conservatives hoped to preserve the traditional verities of colonial rule, with a strong Church and a strong government. Their motto might have been 'power must be held by those with merit, virtue and property'. Historically, both movements have benefited the social and economic elites and disenfranchised the people of the countryside, mostly Maya.

Morazán & the Liberals

The Liberals, the first to advocate independence, opposed the vested interests of the elite Conservatives, who had the Church and the large landowners on their side.

During the short existence of the United Provinces of Central America, Liberal President Francisco Morazán (1830-39) instituted reforms aimed at correcting three persistent problems: the great economic, political and social power of the Church; the division of society into a Hispanic upper class and an Indian lower class; and the region's powerlessness in world markets. This Liberal program was echoed by Guatemalan Chief of State Mariano Gálvez (1831-38).

But unpopular economic policies, heavy taxes and a cholera epidemic in 1837 led to an Indian uprising that brought a Conservative pig farmer, Rafael Carrera, to power. Carrera held power until 1865 and undid much of what Morazán and Gálvez had achieved. The Carrera government allowed Great Britain to take control of Belize in exchange for construction of a road between Guatemala City and Belize City. The road called for in the treaty was never built, and Guatemala's claims for compensation were never resolved.

Liberal Reforms of Rufino Barrios

The Liberals came to power again in the 1870s, first under Miguel García Granados, next under Justo Rufino Barrios, a rich young coffee *finca* (plantation) owner who held the title of president and ruled as a dictator (1873-79). With Rufino Barrios at its head the country made great strides toward modernization, with construction of roads, railways, schools and a modern banking system. To boost the economy, everything possible was done to encourage coffee production. Peasants in good coffee-growing areas (up to 1400 meters altitude on the Pacific Slope) were forced off their lands to make way for new coffee fincas, and those living above 1400 meters (mostly Indians) were forced to contribute seasonal labor on the fincas, as on plantations during colonial times. Idealistic Liberal policies, championed by the British and often meant to benefit the common people, ended up oppressing them. Most of the policies of the Liberal reform movement benefited the finca owners and the traders in the cities.

Succeeding governments generally pursued the same policies. Economic control of the country was in the hands of a small group of land-owning and commercial families; foreign companies were given generous concessions; opponents of the government were censored, imprisoned or exiled by the extensive police force; and the government apparatus remained subservient to economic interests despite a liberal constitution.

Estrada Cabrera & Minerva

Manuel Estrada Cabrera ruled from 1898 to 1920, and his dictatorial style, while bringing progress in technical matters, placed a heavy burden on all but the ruling oligarchy. He fancied himself a bringer of light and culture to a backward land, styling himself the 'Teacher and Protector of Guatemalan Youth'.

He sponsored Fiestas de Minerva (Festivals of Minerva) in the cities, inspired by the Roman goddess of wisdom, invention and technology, and ordered construction of temples to Minerva, some of which still exist (as in Quetzaltenango). Guatemala was to become a 'tropical Athens'. At the same time, however, he looted the treasury, ignored the schools and spent millions on the armed forces.

Jorge Ubico

When Estrada Cabrera was overthrown, Guatemala entered a period of instability that ended in 1931 with the election of General Jorge Ubico as president. Ubico ruled as Estrada Cabrera had, but more effi-

ciently. Though his word was law, he insisted on honesty in government, and he modernized the country's health and social welfare infrastructure. Debt peonage was outlawed, releasing the Indians from this servitude, but a new servitude of labor contributions to the government road-building program was established in its place. Other public works projects included the construction of the vast presidential palace on the main plaza in Guatemala City.

In the 1940s Ubico dispossessed and exiled the great German coffee finca owners and otherwise assumed a pro-Allied stance during the war, but at the same time he openly admired Spain's Generalissimo Francisco Franco. In 1944 he was forced to resign and go into exile.

Arévalo & Arbenz Guzmán

Just when it appeared that Guatemalan politics was doomed to become a succession of well-intentioned but harsh dictators, the elections of 1945 brought a philosopher – Juan José Arévalo – to power. Arévalo, in power from 1945 to 1951, established the nation's social security system, a government bureau to look after Indian concerns, a modern public health system and liberal labor laws. During his six years as president there were 25 coup attempts by conservative military forces – an average of one coup attempt every three months or less.

Arévalo was succeeded by Colonel Jacobo Arbenz Guzmán in 1951. Arbenz continued the policies of Arévalo, instituting an agrarian reform law that was meant to break up the large estates and foster high productivity on small individually owned farms. He also expropriated vast lands conceded to the United Fruit Company during the Estrada and Ubico years, but now held fallow. Compensation was paid at the value that they had declared for tax purposes, which was below its actual value, and he announced that the lands were to be distributed to peasants and put into cultivation for food. But the expropriation, supported by the Guatemalan Communist Party, set off alarms in Washington, who supported the interests of United Fruit. In 1954 the

GUATEMALA

USA orchestrated an invasion from Honduras led by two exiled Guatemalan military officers, and Arbenz was forced to step down. The land reform never took place.

After Arbenz, the country had a succession of military presidents elected with the support of the officers' corps, business leaders, compliant political parties and the Church. Violence became a staple of political life. Opponents of the government regularly turned up dead. The land reform measures were reversed, voting was made dependent on literacy (which disenfranchised around 75% of the population), the secret police force was revived and military repression was common.

The poor majority was not happy, and there was no way their grievances could be addressed within the system. In 1960 guerrilla groups began to form.

The 1960s & 1970s

During the 1960s and '70s, Guatemalan industry developed at a fast pace. Most profits from the boom flowed upwards, labor union organization put more stresses on the political fabric, and migration from the countryside to the cities, especially the capital, produced urban sprawl and slums.

As the pressures in society increased so did the violence of protest and repression, which led to the total politicization of society. Everyone took sides, usually the poorer classes in the countryside versus the power elite in the cities. By 1979, Amnesty International estimated that 50,000 to 60,000 people had been killed during the political violence of the 1970s.

A severe earthquake in 1976 killed about 22,000 people and left about a million people homeless. Most of the aid sent to help the people in need never reached them.

The 1980s

In the early 1980s the military suppression of antigovernment elements in the countryside reached a peak, especially under the presidency of General José Efraín Ríos Montt, an evangelical Christian who came to power in a coup in March 1982. Alarming numbers of people, mostly Indian men,

were killed in the name of anti-insurgency, stabilization and anticommunism.

The policy behind these killings was known as 'scorched earth'. The government did not know the identities of the rebels but did know which areas were bases of rebel activity; the government decided to exterminate the general populations of those areas to kill off the rebels. The government also hoped such tactics would dissuade the peasantry from joining or supporting the guerrillas. Over 400 villages were razed, and most of their inhabitants massacred (often tortured as well). The survivors were herded into remote, newly constructed 'model villages' surrounded by army encampments. It was later estimated that 15,000 civilian deaths occurred as a result of counter-insurgency operations during Ríos Montt's term of office.

Despite these heavy-handed tactics, perhaps half a million people, mostly peasants in the western and central highlands and in the northern El Petén region, actively supported the guerrilla movement. In February 1982 four powerful guerrilla organizations united to form the URNG (Guatemalan National Revolutionary Unity).

As the civil war dragged on and atrocities were committed on both sides, the lines between them blurred. Many peasants and rural people did support the guerrilla movement but perhaps even more came to feel caught in the crossfire.

In August 1983 Ríos Montt was deposed by a coup led by General Oscar Humberto Mejía Victores, but the abuses continued. It was estimated that over 100 political assassinations and 40 abductions occurred every month under his rule. The bloodbath led to a cutoff of US military assistance to the Guatemalan government, which led in turn to the 1985 election of a civilian president, Marco Vinicio Cerezo Arévalo, the candidate of the Christian Democratic Party.

Before turning over power to the civilians, the military ensured that its earlier activities would not be examined or prosecuted, and it established formal mechanisms for the military control of the countryside. There was hope that Cerezo

Arévalo's administration would temper the excesses of the power elite and the military and establish a basis for true democracy. When Cerezo Arévalo's term ended in 1990, however, many people wondered if any real progress had been made.

The Early 1990s

President Cerezo Arévalo was succeeded by Jorge Serrano Elías (1990-93), an evangelical Christian who ran as the candidate of the conservative Movimiento de Acción Solidaria (Solidarity Action Movement). Serrano reopened a dialogue with the URNG, hoping to bring the decades-long civil war to an end. When the talks collapsed, the mediator from the Catholic Church blamed both sides for intransigence.

As Serrano's popularity declined, he came to depend more on the army for support. On May 25, 1993, Serrano carried out an *autogolpe* (auto-coup), supported by the military. After a tense few days Serrano was forced to flee into exile. Congress elected Ramiro de León Carpio, the Solicitor for Human Rights and an outspoken critic of the army's strongarm tactics, as the country's new president, to complete Serrano's term, which was scheduled to end in January 1996.

In March 1995 the USA announced it was suspending aid to Guatemala yet again due to the government's failure to investigate the murder or disappearance of US citizens in Guatemala. These cases included the 1990 murder of Michael Devine, who had operated Finca Ixobel in Poptún, and URNG leader Efraín Bámaca Velásquez, whose wife, US attorney Jennifer Harbury, had been conducting a protest (covered in the international media) since his disappearance in 1992. (Eventually it was revealed that he had been murdered.) Charges were made that the CIA had been instrumental in the murders, but the US government investigated the claims and determined they were unfounded.

At the presidential elections held on November 12, 1995, no candidate won a majority of the vote, so a runoff election was held on January 7, 1996. It was won by

Álvaro Enrique Arzú Irigoyen of the middle-right PAN (Partido de Avanzada Nacional) party, who took office on January 14.

Negotiations continued between the government and the URNG, and finally, in December of that year, the two parties came to agreement and peace accords were signed.

The Signing of the Peace Accords

The peace accords, signed at the National Palace in Guatemala City on December 29, 1996, put an end to the 36 year civil war. During that period an estimated 200,000 Guatemalans had been killed, a million made homeless and untold thousands had 'disappeared.' The accords contain provisions calling for accountability for the human rights violations perpetrated by the armed forces during the war and the resettlement of Guatemala's one million displaced people. The accords also address the identity and rights of indigenous peoples, health care, education and other basic social services, women's rights, the abolition of obligatory military service and the incorporation of the ex-guerrillas into civilian life.

Guatemala Today

The greatest challenge to a lasting peace stems from great inequities in the basic social and economic power structure of Guatemalan society. It's estimated that 70% of cultivable land is owned by less than 3% of the population. According to a United Nations report, the top 20% of the population has an income 30 times (that's 3000%) greater than the bottom 20%. Discrimination against the indigenous people, which has been deeply ingrained in the society for five centuries, manifests in poverty and misery for a large percentage of the population. The desire for an improvement in economic and social conditions, basic social services, land reform and labor rights has been the motivation for much of the revolutionary movement. How these needs are met may be the most important factor in creating a true and lasting peace.

Both sides acknowledged that the signing of the peace accords was not a conclusion but a beginning. As one guerrilla representative told us, 'The peace accords will be signed on December 29. Our most challenging work will begin on December 30'.

GEOGRAPHY

Guatemala covers an area of 109,000 sq km with mountainous forest highlands and jungle plains.

The western highlands linked by the Interamericana are the continuation of Chiapas' Sierra Madre and include 30 volcanoes reaching heights of 3800 meters in the Cuchumatanes range northwest of Huehuetenango. Land that has not been cleared for Mayan *milpas* (cornfields) is covered in pine forests. Many of the volcanoes are active, which signals that this is an earthquake area as well. Major quakes struck in 1773, 1917 and 1976.

The Pacific Slope of Guatemala is the continuation of Chiapas' Soconusco, with rich coffee, cacao, fruit and sugar plantations along the Carretera al Pacífico. Down along the shore the volcanic slope meets the sea, yielding vast beaches of black volcanic sand in a sweltering climate that is difficult to bear. Grass grows profusely in this climate, and it's fed to cattle.

South and east along the Interamericana the altitude decreases to about 1500 meters at Guatemala City.

North of Guatemala City the highlands of Alta Verapaz gradually decline to the lowland of El Petén, which is the continuation of southern Yucatán. Petén's climate and topography is like that of Yucatán, hot and humid or hot and dry, depending upon the season. To the southeast of Petén is the valley of the Río Motagua, dry in some areas, moist in others. Bananas thrive in the Motagua Valley.

CLIMATE

In the Guatemalan highlands, temperatures can get down to freezing at night in the mountains. Days can be dank and chill during the rainy season, but in the dry season from October to May they're warm

GUATEMALA

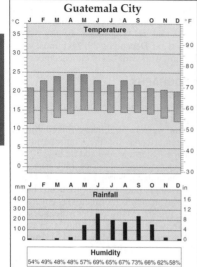

and delightful. Guatemala's coasts are tropical, rainy, hot and humid, with temperatures often reaching 32°C to 38°C (90°F to 100°F) and almost constant high humidity, abating only slightly in the dry season. While the rainy and dry seasons are distinct on the Pacific coast and in the highlands, on the Caribbean side rain is possible anytime. Cobán has only about one month of dry weather (in April).

The vast jungle lowland of El Petén has a climate and topography like that of Yucatán: seasonally hot and humid or hot and dry. December and January are the coolest months; March and April are the hottest.

ECOLOGY & ENVIRONMENT
As elsewhere in Central American, deforestation is a problem in Guatemala, especially in the Petén region, where jungle is being felled at an alarming rate to make way for cattle ranches. Only a few years ago, the government required anyone buying tracts of land in the Petén to clear a certain portion of it – presumably in the name of 'progress'.

Most of the Petén region is now officially designated as a protected area; in addition to the 575-sq-km Tikal national park, there's the nearly two-million-hectare Maya biosphere reserve, which includes most of the northern Petén region. Though these parks signify advances in conservation, the forest is still being ravaged by people illegally harvesting timber on a massive scale. While the government has so far not acted, conservation organizations are trying to document offenses.

On the Pacific side of the country, where most of the population of Guatemala lives, the land is mostly agricultural.

The following organizations in Guatemala City are good resources for finding out more about Guatemala's natural and protected areas:

Centro de Estudios Conservacionistas de la Universidad de San Carlos (CECON), Avenida La Reforma 0-63, Zona 10 (☎ 331-0904, 334-6064, 334-7662)

Comisión Nacional del Medio Ambiente (CONAMA), 5a Avenida 8-07, Zona 10 (☎ 334-1708, 331-2723)

Consejo Nacional de Areas Protegidas (CONAP), 8a Avenida 3-72, Zona 1 (☎ 253-7612, 253-7061)

Fundación Defensores de la Naturaleza (Defensores), Avenida Las Américas 20-21, Zona 14 (☎ 337-3897, 337-0319)

Fundación para el Ecodesarrollo y la Conservación (FUNDAECO), 7a Calle A 20-53, Zona 11, Colonia El Mirador (☎ 472-4268)

FLORA & FAUNA
Flora
Guatemala has over 8000 species of plants in 19 different ecosystems ranging from the mangrove forests on both coasts to the pine forests of the mountainous interior to the cloud forests at higher altitudes.

The national flower, the *monja blanca* or white nun orchid, is said to have been picked so much that it's now rarely seen in the wild; nevertheless, with around 600 species of orchid (one-third of these species endemic to Guatemala), you shouldn't have any trouble finding some. (If you're interested in orchids and you're in Cobán, check out the orchid nursery there.)

Fauna

With its 19 ecosystems, Guatemala also has an abundance of animals. So far, estimates point to 250 species of mammals, 600 species of birds, 200 species of reptiles and amphibians and many species of butterflies and other insects.

The national bird, the resplendent quetzal, is often used to symbolize Central America as well. (The national monetary unit, the quetzal, is named for the bird.) It's a small but exceptionally beautiful bird, with a bright red breast, a brilliant blue-green neck, head, back and wings, a spot of bright white on the underside of the tail, and a blue-green tail several times as long as the bird's body, which stands only around six inches tall.

Other interesting birds in Guatemala include toucans, macaws and parrots. If you visit Tikal, you will probably see the ocellated turkey, also called the Petén turkey, a large, impressive, multicolored bird reminiscent of a peacock. There are also large white herons, hawks, woodpeckers, hummingbirds, harpy eagles (rare), waterfowl and a plethora or other resident and migratory birds.

Notable mammals include the jaguar, ocelot, puma, howler and spider monkeys, tapirs, kinkajous, koatimundis, pizotes, tepezcuintles, white-tailed deer, armadillos and manatees. Reptiles and amphibians include at least three species of sea turtles (the leatherback, the olive Ridley and the *tortuga negra)* and at least two species of crocodile (one found in the Petén, the other in the Río Dulce).

Parks & Protected Areas

Guatemala has more than 30 protected areas, including *parques nacionales* (national parks) and *biotopos* (biological reserves). Over 40 more areas have been proposed for protection. Many of the protected areas are remote; the ones mentioned here are some of the most easily accessible and interesting to visitors.

Pizote

Reserva de la Biosfera Maya – Covering the northern half of the Petén region, this 1,844,900-hectare reserve is Guatemala's largest protected area. Within its boundaries are a number of important Mayan archaeological sites, including Tikal, Uaxactún, El Mirador and El Zotz.

Reserva de la Biosfera de Sierra de Las Minas – In the eastern part of the country, Guatemala's most important cloud forest reserve protects a mountainous area ranging in elevation from 150 to over 3000 meters above sea level. Before entering, visitors must obtain permission from the Fundación Defensores de la Naturaleza (see Ecology & Environment, above) in Guatemala City.

Parque Nacional Tikal – One of Guatemala's principal tourist attractions, this park within the larger Maya biosphere reserve contains the magnificent Tikal archaeological site as well as 57,600 hectares of pristine jungle. It's also one of the easiest places to observe wildlife in Guatemala.

Parque Nacional Río Dulce – In eastern Guatemala, between Lago de Izabal and the Caribbean, this 7200-hectare reserve protects the canyon of the Río Dulce, one of the country's most beautiful rivers. Boat trips on the river can be taken from either Lívingston or Río Dulce.

Parque Nacional Lachuá – In the northeast of the department of Alta Verapaz, this 10,000-hectare park contains a beautiful, circular,

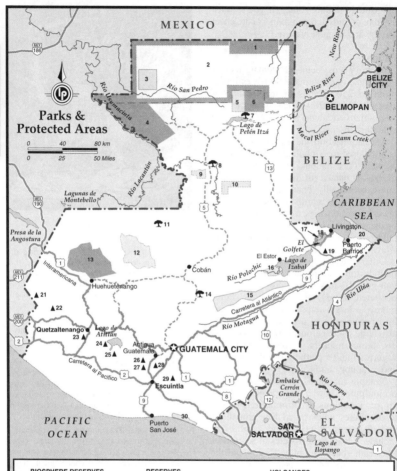

Parks & Protected Areas

BIOSPHERE RESERVES
2 Reserva de la Biosfera Maya
15 Reserva de la Biosfera de
    Sierra de Las Minas

NATIONAL PARKS
1 Parque Nacional-Mirador-
   Dos Lagunas-Río Azul
4 Parque Nacional Sierra
   del Lacandón
6 Parque Nacional Tikal
8 Parque Nacional Ceibal
11 Parque Nacional Lachuá
13 Parque Nacional los
    Cuchumatanes
18 Parque Nacional Río Dulce

RESERVES
9 Reserva Aguateca-Dos Pilas
10 Reserva Machaquilá
12 Reserva Natural Cerro Bisís

BIOLOGICAL RESERVES
3 Biotopo Laguna del Tigre-
   Río Escondido
5 Biotopo San Miguel-
   La Pelotada-El Zotz
7 Biotopo Cerro Cahuí
14 Biotopo del Quetzal
    (Biotopo Mario Dary Rivera)
17 Biotopo Chocón-Machacas
20 Biotopo Punta de Manabique
30 Biotopo Monterrico-Hawaii

VOLCANOES
21 Volcán Tacaná (4093m)
22 Volcán Tajumulco (4220m)
23 Volcán Santa María (3772m)
24 Volcán San Pedro (3020m)
25 Volcán Atitlán (3537m)
26 Volcán Acatenango (3976m)
27 Volcán Fuego (3763m)
28 Volcán Agua (3766m)
29 Volcán Pacaya (2552m)

WILDLIFE REFUGES
16 Bocas del Polochic
19 Cerro San Gil

turquoise-colored lake that is only five km in surface area but over 220 meters deep, with a great variety of fish. It has hiking trails, a camping area and visitors' center.

Parque Nacional Sierra del Lacandón – In the western Petén region, this large park includes the southern portion of the Sierra del Lacandón mountains and abuts the Río Usumacinta, which forms part of the border between Guatemala and Mexico. It's accessible from El Naranjo or by boat along the Río Usumacinta.

Biological reserves *(biotopos protegidos)* include the following:

Biotopo del Quetzal – This 1000-hectare cloud forest reserve, also called the Biotopo Mario Dary Rivera, was established for the protection of quetzals. Well-maintained trails snake through a lush, cool forest of broad-leaf and coniferous trees, climbing plants, ferns, mosses, orchids and bromeliads. This reserve is one of the easiest of access of all Guatemalan reserves.

Biotopo Cerro Cahuí – On the northeast shore of Lago Petén Itzá, this 650-hectare reserve has hiking trails with fine views.

Biotopo Chocón Machacas – This 7600-hectare reserve is within the Río Dulce national park on the north bank of the river.

Biotopo Punta de Manabique – This 50,000-hectare reserve is on the Caribbean. The only access is by boat, which can be arranged from the piers at either Puerto Barrios or Lívingston.

Biotopo San Miguel-La Pelotada-El Zotz – Part of the Maya biosphere reserve, this is west of and contiguous with Tikal national park. It protects a dense forest, bat caves (*zotz* means 'bat' in many Maya languages) and the archaeological site El Zotz.

Biotopo Laguna del Tigre/Río Escondido – Situated within the Maya biosphere reserve in the northwest of the Petén, this 46,300-hectare reserve is one of Guatemala's most remote protected areas. It conserves the largest freshwater wetlands in Central America, a refuge for countless bird species. Boat trips can be arranged at El Naranjo, where the administration office is situated, with prior permission from the Centro de Estudios Conservacionistas de la Universidad de San Carlos (CECON) in Guatemala City.

Wildlife refuges include the following:

Bocas del Polochic – On the western side of Lago de Izabal, the Río Polochic forms a marshy delta where it empties into the lake; this is Guatemala's second-largest freshwater wetland area. It's especially attractive for bird watchers, with a great abundance and variety of birds, especially during migrations. It's accessible only by water; boats can be arranged at El Estor or Mariscos.

Cerro San Gil – On the south side of El Golfete, east of Lago de Izabal, this refuge occupies the highest part of the Montañas del Mico, the continuation of the Sierra de las Minas. It has many endemic species and great biodiversity. Two parts of the refuge are open to the public.

Natural and cultural monuments include the following:

Quiriguá – This Mayan archaeological site, two km off the Carretera al Atlántico and easily accessible, is famous for its giant stelae, the tallest in the Maya world.

Iximché – Capital of the Cakchiquel Maya at the time of the Spanish conquest, this is one of the few archaeological sites with a documented history. The site is easily accessible, two km from Tecpán.

Ceibal y Aguateca-Dos Pilas – This monument protects several important archaeological sites and the forest around them. It's in the Río La Pasión valley, in the southwest of the Petén, in the municipality of Sayaxché. It's accessible from Sayaxché or by tour from Flores/Santa Elena.

Semuc-Champey – On the Río Cahabón in the municipality of Lanquín, Alta Verapaz, Semuc-Champey is a series of pristine pools surrounded by rainforest. It's accessible by 4WD vehicle or by tour from Cobán.

GOVERNMENT & POLITICS

Guatemala is a republic with 22 departments. Executive power is held by a president who is elected by direct universal adult suffrage to a term of four years. He is assisted by a vice president and an appointed cabinet. The unicameral national congress consists of 80 members (64 departmental representatives and 16 national seats) also elected to four-year terms. Judicial power rests in a Supreme Court and associated courts.

Government in Guatemala has traditionally been one of beautiful theory and brutal reality. Always a constitutional democracy in form, Guatemala has been ruled by a succession of military strongmen ever since Pedro de Alvarado came and conquered the Maya in the 16th century. With a few notable exceptions, such as the administrations of Juan José Arévalo and Jacobo Arbenz Guzmán, Guatemala's government has been controlled for the benefit of the commercial, military, landowning and bureaucratic classes of society. While the niceties of democracy are observed, real government often takes place by means of intimidation and secret military activities (see History, above).

One Guatemalan writer summed up his society this way: a bourgeoisie that doesn't invest in its country, but rather stashes its capital abroad; an incompetent, inept and corrupt political class; a left-leaning intellectual class that keeps to the realm of theory and refuses to participate in politics because it equates politics with corruption; a political left wing that won't make peace or participate in the mainstream because it knows it has little chance of popular approval; a military class, divided into factions more or less rightist, that sees civil peace and democracy as endangering its claims to impunity, privilege and economic benefits; and a demoralized people who believe in neither their leaders nor the political process as means to make their country prosper.

ECONOMY

The Guatemalan highlands are given over to agriculture, particularly corn, with some mining and light industry around the larger cities. The Pacific Slope has large coffee, citrus and sugar cane plantations worked by migrant labor from the highlands, and the Pacific coast has cattle ranches and some fishing villages. Coffee is the country's biggest export crop, followed by beef, cotton, cocoa, corn, beans, bananas, sugar cane, vegetables, flowers and fruits.

Guatemala City is the industrial and commercial center of the country, a copy in miniature of Mexico City, its great sister to the north. Like Mexico City, Guatemala City has problems of immigration, pollution, congestion and street crime arising from its near-monopoly on the commercial life of the country.

Guatemala's Motagua Valley has some mining, but agriculture is most important here, with vast banana plantations. In the lush green hills of Alta Verapaz there are dairy farms, cardamom plantations and forests for timber.

El Petén depends upon tourism and farming for its livelihood. The rapid growth of agriculture and cattle farming is a serious threat to the ecology of Petén, a threat that will have to be controlled if the forests of this vast jungle province are to survive. Tourism, on the other hand, is a positive factor here, providing alternative sources of income in jobs that depend upon the preservation of the ecology for success.

POPULATION & PEOPLE

In Guatemala's population of 10 million people, the division between Mayan and Spanish descent is much stricter than in Mexico. Under Spanish rule, most of highland Guatemala was administered by the friars who came to convert the Maya. The friars did a great deal to protect the indigenous people from exploitation by the government authorities and to preserve traditional Mayan society (though not Mayan religion). But the region around Guatemala City was directly administered by the colonial government without the softening effect of the friars' intervention, and the traditional life of the Maya was largely replaced by a hybrid culture that was neither Mayan nor strictly Hispanic. Interrelations produced a mestizo population, known as *ladinos*, who had abandoned their Mayan traditions to adopt the Spanish ways but were not accepted into white Spanish society.

Today, ladinos fill in the middle ground between the old guard Hispanic, European and North American elite and the

GUATEMALA

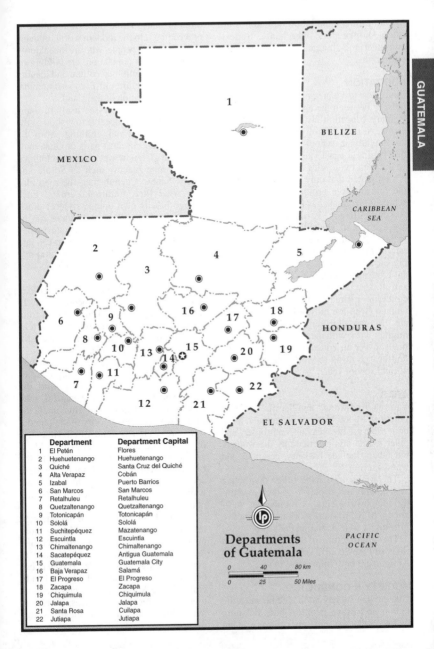

	Department	Department Capital
1	El Petén	Flores
2	Huehuetenango	Huehuetenango
3	Quiché	Santa Cruz del Quiché
4	Alta Verapaz	Cobán
5	Izabal	Puerto Barrios
6	San Marcos	San Marcos
7	Retalhuleu	Retalhuleu
8	Quetzaltenango	Quetzaltenango
9	Totonicapán	Totonicapán
10	Sololá	Sololá
11	Suchitepéquez	Mazatenango
12	Escuintla	Escuintla
13	Chimaltenango	Chimaltenango
14	Sacatepéquez	Antigua Guatemala
15	Guatemala	Guatemala City
16	Baja Verapaz	Salamá
17	El Progreso	El Progreso
18	Zacapa	Zacapa
19	Chiquimula	Chiquimula
20	Jalapa	Jalapa
21	Santa Rosa	Cuilapa
22	Jutiapa	Jutiapa

**Departments
of Guatemala**

0   40   80 km

0   25   50 Miles

Mayan farmers and laborers. Ladinos are often shopkeepers, merchants, traders, administrators, bureaucrats and especially politicians.

EDUCATION

Education in Guatemala is free and compulsory between the ages of seven and 14. Primary education lasts for six years; it's estimated that 79% of children of this age are actually in school. Secondary education begins at age 13 and lasts for up to six years, with two cycles of three years each; it's estimated that only 23% of children of the relevant age group are in secondary school. Guatemala has five universities.

Adult literacy is around 65%. The average rate of adult illiteracy is 37% for males, 53% for females, the second highest rate in the western hemisphere. There's a big variation in literacy rates among different groups, however. A Guatemalan organization specializing in Mayan women's concerns estimates that 95% of rural women (who are mostly Maya) are illiterate. Mayan children who do seasonal migrant work with their families find it difficult to get an education, as the time the families go away to work falls during the normal school year.

ARTS

Various traditional handicrafts are still practiced by the Maya of Guatemala. Most noticeable are the weaving, embroidery and other textile arts practiced by the women, but others include basketry, ceramics and wood carving.

The Maya also have other distinctive arts, notably music played on their own traditional instruments. A number of well-known Maya painters work in a distinctive primitivist style depicting daily life.

The architecture of the ancient Maya ruins and the Spanish colonial structures in Antigua are both impressive to see.

SOCIETY & CONDUCT

Guatemalan society is divided between the ladino and Maya peoples, both pursuing pathways that are sometimes convergent but often at odds. While the ladino culture is proceeding into the modern world, in many ways the Maya people, who are the majority of Guatemala's population, are holding on tight to their traditional culture and identity despite five centuries of European domination and occupation of their land.

Maya culture expresses itself in many ways. The most noticeable to visitors is the beautiful traditional clothing worn by Maya women. In most parts of Guatemala the Maya men now wear western clothing, but in some places, such as Sololá and Todos Santos Cuchumatán, the men also still wear their traditional *trajes*. Each village has its own unique style of dress, and within the village style there can be variations according to social status; when all of the different variations are taken into account, there are something like 500 distinctive forms of design, each with its own significance.

Mayan languages are still the everyday language of most Mayan people, with 21 different languages spoken by Maya from different regions of the country. Maya religion, firmly based in nature, is also still practiced by Maya people.

Today the Maya are being pushed further and further into the background of society. Travelers, who often find the Maya and their traditions beautiful, may be surprised to learn that in Guatemala the Maya (who are the majority of the population) are viciously (and often violently) discriminated against. While some Maya are going to universities, working in the business world and joining modern society, those continuing the traditional way of life are the poorest sector of Guatemalan society.

The plight of these people has attracted international attention. Many non-governmental organizations from around the world are working in Guatemala to assist the indigenous people. Travelers can help by buying traditional Mayan handicrafts. If the Maya can sell their wares to tourists and receive fair prices, it helps to make their craft an economically viable occupation.

Dos & Don'ts

Politeness is a very important aspect of social interaction in Guatemala, as it is everywhere in this part of the world. When beginning to talk to someone, even in such routine situations as in a store or on the bus, it's polite to preface your conversation with a greeting to the other person – a simple 'Buenos días' or 'Buenas tardes' and a smile, answered by a similar greeting on the other person's part, gets a conversation off to a positive start. When you enter a room, even a public place such as a restaurant or waiting room, it's polite to make a general greeting to everyone in the room – a simple 'Buenos días' or 'Buenas tardes' will do. Handshakes are another friendly gesture and are used frequently.

Note that many Mayan children speak only their indigenous language. Where this is the case, it's futile to try to engage them in conversation in Spanish. In recent years, stories circulated through Guatemala that some foreign visitors were kidnapping Maya children, perhaps for the grisly purpose of selling their bodily organs. Do be aware that some people are extremely suspicious of foreigners who make friendly overtures towards local children.

Many Mayan women prefer to avoid contact with foreign men; in their culture, talking with strange men is not something that a virtuous woman does.

Pay attention to your appearance when traveling. Latin Americans on the whole are very conscious of appearance, grooming and dress; it's difficult for them to understand why a foreign traveler, who is naturally assumed to be rich, would go around looking scruffy when even poor people in Latin America do their best to look neat. Try to present as clean an appearance as possible, especially if you're dealing with officialdom (police, border officials, immigration officers, etc); in such cases it's a good idea to look not only clean, but also as conservative and respectable as possible.

An interesting paradox is that while Mayan women are extremely eager to sell their traditional clothing to foreign visitors, especially the beautiful embroidered *huip-iles* (blouses), it is considered very bad form for a visitor to wear these things in Guatemala.

Standards of modesty in dress are becoming more relaxed in recent years; you may see women wearing mini-skirts, where just a few years ago this would have been unthinkable. Nevertheless, not everyone appreciates this type of dressing, and many locals still find it offensive. Take particular care not to offend local people with your attire.

Dress modestly when entering churches, as this shows respect for local people and their culture. Some churches in heavily touristed areas will post signs at the door asking that shorts and tank tops (singlets) not be worn in church, but in most places such knowledge is assumed.

Shorts are usually worn by both sexes only at the beach and in coastal towns, or where there are plenty of foreign tourists. (See the Women Travelers section in the following chapter for further tips specifically for women travelers.)

Also think about safety in connection with your appearance. Particularly in the capital, locals will warn you against wearing even cheap imitation jewelry: you could be mugged for it. If you have any wealth, take care not to flaunt it. See the Dangers & Annoyances section earlier in this book for other basic rules of travel safety.

RELIGION

Roman Catholicism is the predominant religion in Guatemala, but it is not the only religion. Since the 1980s, evangelical Protestant sects, around 75% of them Pentecostal, have surged in popularity and now it is estimated that about 30% of Guatemalans are of this faith.

When Catholicism was instituted in Guatemala it did not wipe out the traditional Mayan religion, and it still has not today. Many aspects of Catholicism easily blended with Mayan beliefs (see the Facts about the Region chapter), and Mayas still worship at a number of places where they have worshipped since ancient times, bringing offerings and making sacrifices to gods that predate the arrival of the Spanish.

Various Catholic saints hold a double meaning for the Maya people; often the Catholic identity of the saint was superimposed over a deity or saint the Maya people already had when the Spanish arrived. Mayas also have some of their own saints, which are quite independent of the Catholic church: two of these are Maximón (venerated in Santiago Atitlán) and San Simón (venerated in Zunil).

LANGUAGE

Spanish is the official national language, but in practice 23 different languages are spoken in Guatemala, including Spanish, Garifuna and 21 Mayan languages. Many Mayan people speak Spanish, but you can't assume for sure that they do; many Mayan women and children do not. Mayan children often start to learn Spanish only after they start school.

Facts for the Visitor

PLANNING
When to Go
The busy tourist season in Guatemala is from around mid-December until April. This coincides with the dry season, which lasts from around October to May. Another flurry of tourism takes place during July and August, the northern hemisphere summer holiday months. If you can pick any time of year, the beginning and end of the dry season would probably be the most ideal, with perfect weather and not too many tourists around.

Maps
International Travel Maps publishes a good 1:500,000 scale map of Guatemala. INGUAT, the Guatemalan national tourist office, publishes a tourist map with the country on one side and street maps of the larger cities and towns on the other. Pick it up for US$1 from any INGUAT office.

In Guatemala, the Instituto Geográfico Militar, Avenida Las Américas 5-76, Zona 13, Guatemala City (☎ 332-2611) publishes a number of useful maps, including a series of 1:50,000 maps. You can buy them there at the Institute. In Antigua, you may be able to find some of their maps at the Casa Andinista bookstore.

TOURIST OFFICES
The main office of Instituto Guatemalteco de Turismo (INGUAT), the national tourist office, is in Guatemala City. Branch offices are in Antigua, Panajachel, Quetzaltenango and at the international airports in Guatemala City and Flores/Santa Elena.

VISAS & DOCUMENTS
Visa regulations were changed in October 1996, and citizens of many countries can now enter Guatemala without a visa. Regulations do change, so it's best to check with a Guatemalan consulate before heading there. If you need a visa and arrive at the border without one, you will be turned back; if you're flying into Guatemala, you probably won't be allowed to board the plane without having the visa you need for entry.

As of late 1996, citizens of the following countries need no visa or tourist card and receive 90 days in Guatemala upon arrival: Andorra, Argentina, Austria, Belgium, Chile, Denmark, Finland, Germany, Israel, Italy, Japan, Liechtenstein, Luxembourg, Monaco, Norway, the Netherlands, Sweden, Switzerland, Uruguay and the USA.

Citizens of the following countries do not need a visa or tourist card and receive 30 days in Guatemala upon arrival: Australia, Belize, Brazil, Canada, Costa Rica, El Salvador, France, Greece, Honduras, Ireland, Mexico, Nicaragua, New Zealand, Panama, Paraguay, Portugal, San Marino, Spain, Taiwan, the UK, the Vatican and Venezuela.

Citizens of the following countries can enter either with a visa or a tourist card, which can be obtained at the time of entry: Bahrain, Czech Republic, Iceland, Kuwait, the Philippines, Poland, Saudi Arabia, Slovakia and South Africa.

Citizens of all other countries must obtain a visa from a Guatemalan consulate.

If you want to extend your visit, contact an immigration office within Guatemala for current requirements.

If you have a tourist card and you want to cross into Honduras on a day pass to visit Copán, the Guatemalan Migración official will usually allow you to return to Guatemala and continue your journey using the same Guatemalan tourist card. For information on this, refer to the section on Copán.

Minors Traveling Alone
If you are under 18 years of age and traveling alone, technically you must have a letter of permission signed by both your parents and witnessed by a Guatemalan consular official in order to enter Guatemala.

EMBASSIES & CONSULATES
Guatemalan Embassies & Consulates Abroad

Some of the consulates mentioned here are actually honorary consuls or consular agencies. These posts can issue tourist cards and visas, but they refer more complicated matters to the nearest full consulate or to the embassy's consular section. All the listings are for embassies unless noted.

Australia
   Guatemala does not maintain an embassy in Australia; contact the Guatemalan Embassy in Tokyo

Belize
   See Belize City

Canada
   130 Albert St, Suite 1010, Ottawa, Ontario K1P 5G4 (☎ (613) 233-7188, 233-7237, fax (613) 233-0135)
   Consulate in Toronto

Costa Rica
   100 meters north, 50 meters east of Pizza Hut de Plaza del Sol, Curridabat (☎ 224-5721, 283-2555, fax 283-2556)

El Salvador
   15 Avenida Norte 135, San Salvador (☎ 271-2225)

France
   73 rue de Courcelles, 75008 Paris (☎ (01) 42-27-78-63, fax (01) 47-54-02-06)
   Consulates in Ajaccio, Bordeaux, Le Havre, Strasbourg and Marseilles

Germany
   Zietenstrasse 16, 53173 Bonn (☎ (228) 35-15-79, fax (228) 35-49-40)
   Consulates in Dusseldorf, Hamburg and Munich

Honduras
   Embassy, 4a Calle & Avenida Juan Lindo, No 2421, Colonia Las Minitas, Tegucigalpa (☎ 32-9704, 32-1543, fax 31-5655)
   Consulate, 8a Calle between 5a & 6a Avenida NO, No 38, Barrio Guamilito, San Pedro Sula (☎ 53-3560, fax 33-1242)

Israel
   74 Hei Belyar St, Kikar Ha-Medina, Tel Aviv (☎ (3) 57-45-94, fax (3) 546-73-17)

Italy
   Via Dei Colli Della Farnesina 128, I-00194 Roma (☎ (6) 36-30-73-92, fax (6) 329-1639)
   Consulates in Genoa, Milano, Napoli, Trieste and Turin

Japan
   38 Kowa Bldg, Room 905, 4-12-24 Nichi-Azabu, Tokyo 106 (☎ (3) 3400-1830, fax (3) 3400-1820)
   Consulate in Osaka

Mexico
   Embassy, Avenida Explanada 1025, Lomas de Chapultepec, 11000 México 4, DF (☎ (5) 540-7520, fax (5) 202-1142)
   Consulate, Calle Héroes de Chapultepec No 354 at Cecilio Chi, Chetumal, Q Roo (☎ (983) 2-85-85)
   Consulate, 3 Calle Poniente & 10 Avenida Norte, Ciudad Hidalgo, Chiapas (☎ (962) 8-01-84, fax (962) 8-01-93)
   Consulate, Avenida 2 Pte Sur at Calle 1 Sur Pte, Comitán, Chiapas (☎ (963) 2-26-69)
   Consulate, Mango 1440, Colonia del Fresno, Guadalajara (☎ (36) 11-15-03, fax (36) 10-12-46)
   Consulate, Luis G Urbina 1208, Colonia Terminal, Monterrey (☎ (8) 372-8648, fax (8) 374-4722)
   Consulate, 2 Calle Oriente No 33, Tapachula, Chiapas (☎ (962) 6-12-52)

Netherlands
   2e Beukelaan 3, 7313 Apeldoorn (☎ (55) 55-74-21)

Nicaragua
   Km 11.5, Carretera a Masaya, Managua (☎ 279-9609)

Panama
   Avenida Federico Boyd & Calle 48, Bella Vista district, over the Colossal store (☎ 269-3475)

South Africa
   Greenmarket Place, Greenmarket Square 54, Shortmarket St, 5th floor, Cape Town 8001 (☎ (21) 22-57-86, fax (21) 418-1280)

Spain
   Calle Rafael Salgado 3, 4o Izquierda, 28036 Madrid (☎ (1) 344-1417, fax (1) 458-7894)
   Consulates in Alicante, Barcelona, Las Palmas, Santander, Valencia and Zaragoza

Sweden
   Wittstocksgatan 30, 115 27 Stockholm (☎ (8) 660-5229, fax (8) 660-4229)
   Consulates in Göteborg and Malmo

Switzerland
   10 bis, rue du Vieux Collége 1204, Geneva
   (☎ (22) 311-4022, fax (22) 311-7459)
   Consulates in Lausanne and Zurich

UK
   13 Fawcett St, London SW 10
   (☎ (0171) 351-3042, fax (0171) 376-5708)

USA
   Embassy, 2220 R St NW, Washington DC
   (☎ (202) 745-4952, fax (202) 745-1908)
   Consulates in Atlanta, Baltimore, Chicago,
   Houston, Fort Lauderdale, Leavenworth,
   Los Angeles, Memphis, Miami,
   Minneapolis, Montgomery, New Orleans,
   New York, Philadelphia, Pittsburgh,
   Providence, San Antonio, San Diego,
   San Francisco and Seattle

Embassies & Consulates in Guatemala

Foreign embassies are in Guatemala City; see that section.

CUSTOMS

Customs limits are the usual two cartons of cigarettes and three liters of alcohol. Tourists are allowed an exemption of US$100 in customs duty.

MONEY
Costs

Prices here are among the best in the region. Beds in little pensions may cost US$6 per person in a double, and camping places charge less. Elaborate markets sell fruits and snacks for pennies, cheap eateries called *comedores* offer one-plate meals for US$2 or less, and bus trips cost less than US$1 per hour. If you want a bit more comfort, you can readily move up to rooms with private showers and meals in nicer restaurants, and still pay only US$25 per day for room and two – or even three – meals.

Credit Cards & ATMs

Visa and MasterCard are accepted at all airline and car rental companies and at the larger hotels and restaurants. American Express cards are often accepted at the fancier and larger places and at some smaller ones.

ATMs (automatic teller machines, called *cajeros automáticos*) are appearing in the major cities, usually on bank premises. Many banks give cash advances on Visa cards, fewer on MasterCard. Credomatic branches in Guatemala City and Quetzaltenango give cash advances on both.

Currency

The Guatemalan quetzal (Q) is named for the country's gorgeous but rare national bird; the quetzal is divided into 100 centavos. There are coins of one, five, 10 and 25 centavos and bills (notes) of 50 centavos, one, five, 10, 20, 50 and 100 quetzals.

Currency Exchange

Currency exchange rates at the time of writing were:

Foreign	Guatemala	Honduras
A$1	Q5	L10.35
C$1	Q4.35	L8.25
DM1	Q3.50	L8.65
NZ$1	Q4.50	L9.35
UK£1	Q9.45	L18.40
US$1	Q6	L12.50

Changing Money

US dollars are the currency to bring to Guatemala. Any other currency – even the currencies of Honduras, El Salvador and Mexico, Guatemala's neighboring countries – will probably prove impossible to exchange. The bank exchange desks at the airports in Guatemala City and Flores/ Santa Elena are among the few places that exchange other currencies.

Many establishments accept cash dollars instead of quetzals, usually at the bank exchange rate, or even better, but sometimes worse. Even so, you'll need quetzals because shopkeepers, restaurateurs and hotel desk clerks may not want to deplete their supplies of ready quetzals and take on dollars, which they must then take to the bank.

Black Market

There's a healthy unofficial exchange market for dollars, but it pays only about the same as the bank rate. The national hotbed of this activity is around the main post office in Guatemala City. At most border crossing

GUATEMALA

points you may find yourself buying quetzals unofficially as there are no banks; at the airports, the bank exchange desks are open only during certain hours, and you may find yourself buying your first quetzals (or your last, to pay the US$10-equivalent departure tax) at a shop in the terminal.

Tipping & Bargaining

A 10% tip is expected at restaurants. In small *comedores* tipping is optional, but it's still polite to leave at least a little spare change.

Bargaining is essential in some situations and not done in others. Bargaining is standard practice at handicrafts markets or any other time you're buying handicrafts; the first price you're told will often be double or triple what the seller really expects. Remember that bargaining is not a fight to the death; the object is to arrive at a price agreeable to both you and the seller. Be friendly about it, keep your sense of humor and have patience.

You can sometimes bargain for better rates at hotels and guest houses, especially at times when business is slow. Often you can get a discount off the nightly rate if you take the room for a few days or a week; ask about this at the time you take the room.

Taxes

Guatemala's IVA is 10%, and there's also a 10% tax on hotel rooms to pay for the activities of the Guatemala Tourist Commission (INGUAT), so a total tax of 20% will be added to your hotel bill. (In this book, we have included the tax in the prices we quote.) The very cheapest places usually charge no tax.

A departure tax equivalent to about US$10 is levied on travelers departing Guatemala by air.

POST & COMMUNICATIONS
Sending & Receiving Mail

The Guatemalan postal system is notoriously unreliable – mail coming into the country, or even going out, disappears so frequently that it's practically the norm.

Many Guatemalans rely on private courier services for important mail. You'll see the offices of these courier services (which often have the word 'express' in their names) in many towns. Some are trustworthy, some are not. EMS (Express Mail Service) is more reliable than the regular post; it often has an office in or near the regular post office. The big international express services such as Federal Express, DHL and United Parcel Service (UPS) have offices in Guatemala City and Antigua. Or if you know someone leaving the country and going somewhere that the mail system is more reliable, you might want to send mail out with them.

Otherwise, you can try trusting the mail system for non-urgent mail. (We sent postcards to many countries when we were in Guatemala, and they all got through.) If you are sending something by airmail from Guatemala, be sure to clearly mark it with the words 'Por Avión'. An airmail letter sent to Canada or the USA may take anywhere from four to 14 days. Airmail letters to Europe can take anywhere from one to three weeks. It costs only a few cents to send mail anywhere in the world, US$0.03 to the USA, for example.

To receive mail, have it addressed to you care of Poste Restante, and take along your passport when you pick it up.

Telephone

Guatel, the Guatemalan telephone company, offers domestic and international telephone, fax, telex and telegraph services. There's a Guatel office in virtually every city and town. Often the Guatel office is open long hours, from around 7 am to 10 pm or so, but it varies. Coin phones are usually situated outside the Guatel office (see below).

Local and domestic long-distance calls are very cheap; international calls are extraordinarily expensive.

In August 1996, every telephone number in Guatemala was changed. Now all telephone numbers have seven digits, and city codes have been abolished. Guatel offices have a handy conversion chart to help you find the new number.

If you are calling from outside the country, Guatemala's country code is 502.

International Calls Guatel's international tolls are frightfully expensive. Your best bet, as in Mexico, is to make a short call, inform the other person of a time and telephone number at which you may be reached, and end the call.

Guatel charges for a minimum of three minutes, whether or not you talk that long. Interestingly, though, they don't do so with faxes, so it costs much less to send a fax than to phone. For example, while a telephone call to the USA costs US$9 with Guatel, it costs only US$1.56 per page to send a fax.

In places where there are plenty of tourists, private businesses offer telephone and fax services, and some also offer email and Internet connections. It often works out cheaper to telephone with these services than with Guatel, since they do not charge a three-minute minimum.

Collect/reverse-charge calls may be made from Guatemala *only* to the following countries and regions: Central America, Mexico, USA, Canada, Japan, Italy, Spain and Switzerland.

To place an international direct call, dial the international prefix '00' (zero zero), then the country code, area or city code, and local number. Calls are more expensive at some times of day than others, with the less expensive time varying according to which country you're calling. A full rate schedule is published in the introductory section of the Guatemalan telephone directory.

For semi-automatic (operator-assisted) calls, dial 171. The minimum call period is three minutes, and thus the minimum charge to the USA or Canada is about US$9; to countries overseas (ie, outside the western hemisphere), the minimum charge is about US$22.50.

There are also numerous 'direct line' services, such as AT&T's *USADirect*: dial 190 and you will be connected with an AT&T operator in the USA who will complete your collect or credit card call. Below are the direct line numbers.

National Police	120
Intercity Long Distance Calls	121
Fire	123
Directory Assistance	124
Red Cross	125
Correct Time	126
Ambulance	128
International Calls (by Operator)	171
MCI Call USA	189
USADirect (AT&T)	190
España Directo	191
Italia Directo	193
Sprint Express	195
Costa Rica Directo	196
Canada Directo	198

Coin Phones Coin phones *(teléfonos monederos)* accept coins of 10 or 25 centavos. Each coin gives you only so much time, which varies according to the place you're calling to; local calls cost 10 centavos per minute, places in other parts of the country can cost twice that. When making a call from a coin phone, it's best to start out with more coins than you think you will need; once your time is up, you'll be given a short warning tone and then if you don't insert another coin in time, your call will be cut off. Some coin phones have a slanted slot so that you can put in several coins, which will drop one by one as your time requires. On phones without this, you must insert another coin every time you hear the warning tone.

Some telephones have a button on the face of the phone, underneath the handset. On this type of phone, when the person you're calling to answers, you must press the button in order for them to start hearing you.

BOOKS

I, Rigoberta Menchú: An Indian Woman in Guatemala, by 1992 Nobel Peace Prize laureate Rigoberta Menchú, tells the story of her life among the highland Maya people and the birth of her social consciousness. Menchú brought the plight of Guatemala's Mayan Indians to the attention of the world. In Guatemala, where the position of the Maya in society is a continuing issue, both she and the book, which clearly conveys the point of view of a highland Quiché Maya, are controversial. Highly recommended. The same book is published in Spanish as *Me Llamo Rigoberta Menchú y Así Me Nació La Conciencia* (Siglo XXI, 1985).

Rigoberta Menchú Tum

Rigoberta Menchú was born in 1959 in Guatemala's southern highlands and lived the life of a typical young Mayan woman until the early 1980s, when the country's internal turmoil affected her tragically. By 1981 she had lost her father, mother and brother, who were killed in the course of the rampages carried out by the Guatemalan military in the name of 'pacification' of the countryside and the repression of guerrilla movements.

Menchú fled to exile in Mexico, where she wrote her story, *I, Rigoberta Menchú*, which was translated and published throughout the world. While in Mexico and after returning to Guatemala, she worked tirelessly in defense of the rights of indigenous peoples throughout Latin America.

In 1992, Rigoberta Menchú was awarded the Nobel Prize for Peace, which provided her and her cause with international stature and support.

Guatemalans were proud that one of their own had been recognized by the Nobel committee. In the circles of power, however, Menchú's renown was unwelcome, as she is seen as a 'troublemaker'. But among the indigenous people of Guatemala, she is the hero who brought worldwide recognition of their plight. ∎

Unfinished Conquest: The Guatemalan Tragedy by Victor Perera explores the current situation of the Maya in their homeland and the long history that led to it. *Between Two Armies* by David Stoll shows the position that the Maya people have often felt themselves in, caught between the government army on one side and the guerrilla army on the other.

Jennifer Harbury's *Searching for Everardo: A Story of Love, War and the CIA in Guatemala* tells how she attracted the attention of the world when she conducted three hunger strikes, two in front of Guatemala's National Palace and one in front of the White House in Washington, DC, asking for information on her husband, a URNG commander, who disappeared mysteriously in 1992. Her earlier book, *Bridge of Courage: Life Stories of the Guatemalan Compañeros and Compañeras* (Common Courage Press) focuses on a number of people who fought in the Guatemalan guerrilla movement.

Time and the Highland Maya by Barbara Tedlock is an anthropological book about Momostenango and the Quiché Maya people who live there.

Bird of Life, Bird of Death by Jonathan Evan Maslow, subtitled 'A naturalist's journey through a land of political turmoil', tells of the author's travels in Guatemala, where he went to see the resplendent quetzal (the 'bird of life'). What he found was the quetzal becoming increasingly endangered, while the *zopilote* (vulture), the 'bird of death', was flourishing.

Birds of Guatemala by Hugh C Land (Livingston, 1970) is a field guide to bird watching in Guatemala. Other more localized field guides for bird watching, with bird checklists, are available at Tikal and at the Biotopo del Quetzal.

Guatemala Handbuch by Barbara Honner is a German-language guidebook in the Reise Know-How series.

NEWSPAPERS & MAGAZINES

Guatemala has many daily newspapers to choose from, including the *Prensa Libre*, *El Gráfico*, *La República*, *Siglo Veintiuno*, *El Periódico* and *Al Día*. The *Prensa Libre* is the most widely read. There's also a weekly paper, *El Regional*, written in both Spanish and Maya languages; it's read by many Maya people.

Newspapers in English include the *Guatemala Weekly* and *The Siglo News*, both free weekly papers published in Guatemala City and distributed in major hotels and tourist spots around the country. The *Revue* is Guatemala's English-language magazine, published monthly. Subscriptions are available by mail, and the two newspapers also have websites. Contact:

Guatemala Weekly, 14 Calle 3-27, Zona 10,
Local 8, Guatemala City (☎ 337-1061,
fax 337-1076, gweekly@pronet.net.gt);
in the USA, PO Box 591999-F-69,
Miami, FL 33159-1999

Revue, 4a Calle Oriente No 23,
Antigua Guatemala
(☎ /fax 832-0767, revue@guate.net)

The Siglo News, 11 Calle 0-65, Zona 10,
Edificio Vizcaya, 4th floor, Guatemala City
(☎ 332-8101/2/3, fax 332-8119,
sales@sigloxxi.com); in the USA,
NotiNET SA, Worldbox Gu-0147,
PO Box 379012, Miami, FL 33137-9012
(☎ (888) 287-4921)

Several other publications focus on making news about Guatemala available internationally.

CERIGUA is an independent Guatemalan news agency providing alternative news and analysis about Guatemala in English and Spanish. In English, they produce the Weekly Briefs, comprehensive news and analysis covering human rights, labor, politics, popular organizing, the economy, the environment and more. For subscriptions to the Weekly Briefs, contact ANI, PO Box 578191, Chicago, IL 60657-8191, USA. For services in English and Spanish, contact their Guatemala City office at 9a Calle A 3-49, Zona 1 (☎ /fax 232-5519, cerigua@guate.net).

Central America Report is the English-language publication of Inforpress Centroamericana, providing weekly news analysis on the Central America region, with the greatest emphasis on Guatemala. In Guatemala City, you can find them at 7a Avenida 2-05, Zona 1 (☎ /fax 232-9034, inforpre@guate.net). Foreign correspondence or checks should be sent to Inforpress Centroamericana, Section 23, PO Box 52-7270, Miami, FL 33152-7270, USA.

The Guatemala News and Information Bureau (GNIB) publishes *Report On Guatemala*, the quarterly publication of the Network in Solidarity with the People of Guatemala (NISGUA). Contact GNIB at PO Box 28594, Oakland CA 94604, USA (☎ /fax (510) 835-0810, gnib@igc.apc.org).

RADIO & TV
Guatemala has 11 radio stations and five TV stations. A number of stations from the USA, including CNN news, come in by cable. Not all hotels have TV, but when they do have it, it's usually cable TV.

LAUNDRY
Laundries are everywhere in Guatemala, offering wash, dry and fold service for around US$2 per load; drop it off and pick it up a few hours later. Cheaper lodgings usually have a *lavadero*, where you can wash your clothes by hand, and a line where you can hang them.

HEALTH
Tap water is not safe to drink in Guatemala, so you must either purify water yourself or drink bottled water. Bottled water is widely available; it's what most locals drink.

Malaria is present in Guatemala, especially in lowland rural areas, but there is no malaria risk in the central highlands. Chloroquine is the recommended anti-malarial. Dengue fever is also present, as is cholera. See the Health section in the introductory Facts for the Visitor chapter for more about protecting your health while traveling.

WOMEN TRAVELERS
Women should encounter no special problems traveling in Guatemala. The primary thing you can do to make it easy for yourself while traveling here is to dress modestly; most Guatemalan women do. Modesty in dress is regarded highly here, and if you practice it you will usually be treated with respect.

Specifically, shorts should be worn only at the beach, not in town, and especially not in the highlands. Skirts should be at or below the knee. Be sure to wear a bra, as not doing so is regarded as provocative. Many local women swim with T-shirts over their swimming suits; in places where they do this, you may want to do the same, to avoid stares.

Women traveling alone can expect plenty of attempts by men to chat them up. It's up to you, how you react to it – there's no need to be intimidated. You can have some very interesting conversations with locals. Just don't put yourself in a compromising situation.

The catcalls, hisses and the like that are so frequently directed at women in some other parts of the region seem to be less common in Guatemala. Still, it can happen; it's a fact of life that in some parts of Latin America, this is what men do when they see a female. Do what the local women do – ignore it completely.

While there's no need to be paranoid, you must be aware that the possibility of rape, mugging, etc does exist. It happens more in some places than others. Use your normal traveler's caution – avoid walking alone in isolated places, or through city streets late at night, avoid hitchhiking, don't camp alone, etc.

See Society & Conduct in Facts about Guatemala for more on conduct that will help to smooth your way while you travel in Guatemala. Take special note of what it says about wearing traditional Guatemalan women's dress.

GAY & LESBIAN TRAVELERS

Guatemala is still very much in the closet. The only specifically gay place we heard about in Guatemala is *Pandora's*, a bar in Guatemala City, which is said to have been there for years and to be 'the' place for gay people to meet.

DANGERS & ANNOYANCES

See the Facts for the Visitor chapter for general comments on theft and other crimes.

The greatest danger is from armed thieves who roam the highlands and the streets of Guatemala City. Don't wander around in Guatemala City late at night. Avoid empty streets in Antigua at night, and don't wander to the outskirts of that town except in a large group. Avoid stopping by the roadside in lonely places in the highlands. In general, ask around for information on where it is safe to go.

If you are threatened by armed bandits, it's usually best to give up your belongings (and your vehicle) without a struggle, as most do not hesitate to use their weapons.

There have been incidents of purse-snatching and car-jacking in Guatemala City. If you drive in the city, keep valuables (purses, jewelry, etc) out of sight, and keep the car windows rolled at least half way up at all times. (This discourages thieves from lunging through the window to grab a purse, watch or necklace.) If you are approached by armed car-jackers, embassies suggest that you give up your vehicle without resistance, rather than risk injury or worse.

Guatemala has been the scene of antigovernment insurgent activity for a century or so. The signing of the peace accord in December 1996 is expected to stop guerrilla activity.

BUSINESS HOURS

Banks are generally open from 8:30 or 9 am to around 6 pm on weekdays (until 7 or 8 pm in some places), and on Saturdays from around 9 am to 1 pm. Shops open about 9 am and close for lunch around 12:30 or 1 pm, reopening an hour or so later and remaining open till about 6 pm, Monday to Friday; on Saturday many shops close for the day at 12:30 or 1 pm. Government office hours are officially Monday to Friday from 8 am to 4 pm, though there's some absenteeism around lunchtime.

PUBLIC HOLIDAYS & SPECIAL EVENTS

The following are public holidays:

January 1 – *New Year's Day*

March/April – *Holy Thursday, Holy Friday* and *Easter Sunday*

May 1 – *Labor Day*

June 30 – *Army Day*

August 15 – *Guatemala City*
September 15 – *Independence Day*
October 20 – *Revolution of 1944*
November 1 – *All Saints' Day*
December 24 – *Christmas Eve*
December 25 – *Christmas Day*
December 31 – *New Year's Eve*

A number of special events throughout the year are worth attending. Semana Santa (Holy Week, the week before Easter) in Antigua is an unforgettable spectacle. Intricate, colorful carpets made of dyed sawdust are created in the street where later on, a solemn procession of Christ on the cross, borne on a large, heavy litter by a robed *cofradía* (religious brotherhood), bears the image over the carpet, accompanied by swinging incense burners and music. The events leading up to Christ's crucifixion and resurrection are re-enacted in impressive ceremonies.

Semana Santa is celebrated in other places, too – each of the indigenous peoples have their own religious and folkloric traditions. Huehuetenango and Totonicapán also have processions and enactments of the passion of Christ, held on Wednesday through Easter Sunday.

Traditional celebrations also take place on All Saints' Day (November 1) and All Souls' Day (November 2). Since it's believed that this is the time of the year when the souls of the dead are nearest, throughout Guatemala people in every city, village and town spruce up the graveyards in preparation for this time, pulling weeds and painting the tombs. On November 1 and 2, families bring flowers and a picnic to the tombs of their loved ones and spend the day there. It's not a sad occasion – it's the one time in the year when they can visit with those they miss.

On November 1, giant, colorful *barriletes* (kites) are flown in the cemetery at Santiago Sacatepéquez, 24 km from Antigua. Traditionally, it's believed that the kites rising into the atmosphere provide communication with dead loved ones. Thousands of visitors come to witness the

spectacle, and food, especially the traditional *fiambre*, is sold under tents.

On the same day, in Todos Santos Cuchumatán, local men dressed in traditional costumes hurtle through the town in a festive horse race – the culmination of a week of festivities (October 21 through November 1) and usually an all-night drinking spree the night before. Traditional foods are served throughout the day.

Each town celebrates the day of its patron saint with fiestas including social, cultural and sporting events. A famous fiesta is the one in Chichicastenango, celebrated from December 13 to 21, honoring the town's patron saint, Santo Tomás. The fiesta begins with traditional celebrations, including a *palo volador*, in which a very tall pole is set up in the plaza and costumed *voladores* (flyers) swing around the top of it.

Perhaps the most impressive festival of Indian traditions takes place in Cobán, where there's the folkloric festival of Rabin Ajau, with its traditional dance of the Paabanc. It's celebrated throughout the region by the Kekchi Indians, who wear traditional costumes and eat traditional foods. It takes place in the latter part of July, approximately July 21 to 26.

ACTIVITIES

There are many possibilities for hiking in Guatemala. Climbing volcanoes is a highlight of many a traveler's trip. People climb volcanoes around Antigua, Lago de Atitlán and Quetzaltenango; see those sections for details. Mountain bikes can be rented in Panajachel and Antigua; a place in Panajachel also rents off-road motorcycles.

Swimming is popular in the sea and in rivers and lakes. In Lago de Atitlán you can also go diving, with a diving company based in Santa Cruz La Laguna. Whitewater rafting is practiced all year round by a rafting company based in Antigua.

Bird watching is good in Tikal national park, on the Río Ixpop that flows into Lago Petén Itzá near El Remate, at Santiago Atitlán on Lago de Atitlán, along the Río Dulce, in Monterrico and in many other places.

COURSES
Language Studies

Many people from around the world come to study Spanish in Guatemala. Antigua has had a high reputation for its many language schools for many years. Nowadays, Quetzaltenango's schools are also gaining a reputation. Other places with a school or two include Panajachel, San Pedro La Laguna (on Lago de Atitlán), San Andrés (on Lago Petén Itzá), Huehuetenango, Todos Santos Cuchumatán, Monterrico, Lívingston, Guatemala City and Copán (Honduras).

In Momostenango schools offer classes in the Quiché language and Maya calendar and culture. One school in Quetzaltenango offers courses in the Quiché and Mam languages, as well as in Spanish. *K'iche'*, by Kermit Frazier, who lives in Momostenango, is a Quiché Maya language kit that includes a phrasebook, an English/Quiché cassette tape and a Mayan calendar booklet, all for US$20 (Happy Camper Publications, 1997). To order one, contact Kermit in Momostenango through the Kuinik Ta'ik Language School (☎ 736-5036, momos @guate.net).

Virtually all language schools offer the option of homestays with local families, typically costing around US$50 per week for your own private room and three meals a day. This 'total immersion' is an excellent way to learn the language.

Diving

ATI Divers in Santa Cruz La Laguna, on Lago de Atitlán, offers diving courses, including the four-day PADI open water diving course and advanced courses including a high altitude diving course.

Weaving

Weaving courses are offered in Quetzaltenango and Zunil; see those sections.

WORK

Guatemala is a poor country, and work is hard to come by. You might find work teaching English, but don't count on it. Even if you do, wages will not be high. However, volunteer opportunities in Guatemala are legion.

INGUAT, the national tourist office, may be able to help you find a volunteer program to work with, if you have a specific interest. For example, there's an international group that works with street children in Guatemala City.

ADIFAM provides education for working Quiché children in 46 communities within the municipality of Momostenango. The teachers, who instruct the children in their own Quiché language, are all volunteers and receive around US$14 a month. Volunteers can also help the children with 'extra-curricular' activities; also, anyone in the medical, veterinary, organic gardening, computer and various other technical fields can likely find some task for themselves here. Some knowledge of Spanish or Quiché is practically essential (there's a Quiché language school in Momostenango). Contact ADIFAM, Hotel Ixchel, 1a Calle 4-15, Zona 1, Momostenango (☎ 736-5036, momos@guate.net).

Quetzaltenango has several social organizations working with the local Quiché Maya people; you could ask them about volunteering (see Quetzaltenango for more details).

Casa Guatemala (☎ 232-5517), 14a Calle 10-63, Zona 1, Guatemala City, helps abandoned, orphaned and malnourished children. In Guatemala City it has a clinic and food distribution program. It also has an orphanage on the Río Dulce, in eastern Guatemala.

Proyecto Ak' Tenamit, working with the Kek'chi Maya people of eastern Guatemala, has a medical volunteer project, a school, potable water projects and a women's cooperative. Contact Proyecto Ak' Tenamit (☎ /fax 251-1136), Apdo Postal 2675, Guatemala City, or in the USA, the Guatemalan Tomorrow Fund (☎ (407) 747-9790, fax (407) 747-0901), PO Box 3636, Tequesta, FL 33469.

ARCAS (Asociación de Rescate y Conservación de Vida Silvestre, the Wildlife Rescue and Conservation Association), operates two wildlife rescue stations. One is a wildlife rescue center near Flores; the other is a sea turtle hatchery east of Monterrico. See the Monterrico and Flores sections for details. ARCAS also has other volunteer projects you can participate in, including education and health projects. Contact ARCAS, 1a Calle 50-37, Zona 11, Colonia Molino de las Flores, Guatemala City (☎ /fax 591-4731, arcas@pronet.net.gt). Their mailing address is in the USA: ARCAS, Section 717, PO Box 52-7270, Miami, FL 33152-7270.

The Guatemala News and Information Bureau (GNIB), based in California, has information on long-term volunteer work in Guatemala (over three months; see Magazines & Newspapers, above, for contact information).

ACCOMMODATIONS

All levels of accommodations are available in Guatemala, from simple, very basic hotels and pensions up to luxury four- and five-star hotels and resorts. If you'll be studying Spanish, you may prefer a homestay with a local family, which costs less than a hotel; virtually all Spanish language schools offer this option.

FOOD

When it comes to cuisine, Guatemala is the poorer cousin to the more elaborate cuisines of Mexico, the USA and Europe. You can find a few Mexican standards such as *enchiladas* (tortillas topped with beans, meat or cheese), *guacamole* (a salad of mashed or chopped avocados, onions and tomatoes) and *tamales* (steamed corn dough rolls, perhaps with a meat or other stuffing).

But mostly you will encounter *bistec* (tough grilled or fried beef), *pollo asado* (grilled chicken), *chuletas de puerco* (pork chops) and lighter fare such as *hamburguesas* (hamburgers) and *salchichas* (sausages similar to hot dogs). Of the simpler food, *frijoles con arroz* (beans and rice) is cheapest and often best.

One of the unexpected and surprising things about Guatemala, however, is the omnipresence of Chinese restaurants. All the cities and some large towns have at least one Chinese eatery, usually small and not overly authentic, but cheap and good for a change of scene.

DRINKS

Guatemalan coffee is savored all around the world, and not surprisingly, it's one of the delights of traveling in Guatemala. Restaurants that cater to international travelers tend to serve magnificently rich coffee. In more out-of-the-way places, though, the coffee may not be as tasty. This is because the internationally oriented restaurants serve top-quality, export-grade coffee, which is more expensive than your common, garden-variety bean.

As elsewhere throughout the region, sweetened fruit juice mixed with water is a popular and refreshing beverage. It's usually made with purified water – but ask before you drink it! All the usual brands of soft drinks are available *everywhere*.

Gallo is Guatemala's most popular light beer. *Moza*, a dark beer, is what some travelers prefer. *Dorado* is lighter than Gallo.

Guatemala grows plenty of sugar cane, and rum is also made here. *Ron Zacapa Centenario*, a dark rum that comes in a bottle with a wicker basket around it, is said to be the best. *Ron Botrán Añejo*, another dark rum, is also good. Then there's *Quetzalteca*, a white firewater made of sugar cane that comes in a tiny bottle.

THINGS TO BUY

Guatemalan handicrafts, especially the brilliantly colorful weavings and textiles, are world famous. Weaving is a traditional art of the Mayan people throughout Guatemala. Wall hangings, clothing (especially the beautiful embroidered *huipiles* (blouses) and the *cortes* (skirts) of the Mayan women), purses, belts, sashes, friendship bracelets, tablecloths, bedspreads and many other woven items are almost irresistible.

Other notable handicrafts include the blankets made in Momostenango, the wood carvings of El Remate and the ceramics of Antigua.

The largest handicrafts markets are the Thursday and Sunday markets in Chichicastenango and the permanent market in Panajachel. If you're serious about buying handicrafts, it's worth a trip to one of these places. Many fine handicrafts are also available in Antigua, but the prices are higher.

Each village also has market days, which may or may not include handicrafts; often the village markets for locals are full of more mundane items like vegetables and household goods, but sometimes you can find worthwhile things.

When buying handicrafts, it's normal practice to bargain until buyer and seller arrive at a mutually agreeable price. (See the Money section, earlier on, for more about bargaining.)

Getting There & Around

Getting There & Away

AIR

Guatemala has two places served by major airrlines: Guatemala City (Aeropeurto Internacional La Aurora) and Flores, near Tikal in El Petén. See the Guatemala City and El Petén chapters for details.

LAND

There are two highway routes and three road-and-river routes going from Chiapas (Mexico) to Guatemala, one road and one sea route from Belize and numerous routes to and from Honduras and El Salvador.

For the road routes from Chiapas, refer to the Highland and Pacific sections of the Chiapas chapter in Yucatán; for the road-and-river routes, see the El Petén chapter in Guatemala; for the routes from Belize, see the Western Belize and Southern Belize chapters in Belize.

There's a remote crossing between El Cinchado (eastern Guatemala) and Corinto (Honduras) and an even more remote overland route that some travelers take between Puerto Barrios (eastern Guatemala) and Omoa or Puerto Cortés (Honduras), via Finca La Inca (Guatemala), El Límite (on the Río Motagua) and Cuyamelito (Honduras). This latter route is covered in the Central & Eastern Guatemala chapter. It isn't an official border crossing, but people do go this way.

Bus

Several Guatemalan lines run comfortable passenger buses on long-distance routes between Guatemala City and the Mexican and Salvadoran borders, and to Puerto Barrios on the Gulf of Honduras.

For bus-travel information on most of Guatemala, see Getting There & Away in the Guatemala City chapter.

For details on the direct bus between Flores, Petén and Chetumal (Mexico), see Flores in the El Petén chapter.

RIVER & SEA

There are three routes between Palenque (in Chiapas) and Flores (in El Petén) through the jungle. Most travel is by road, but each route entails a boat ride on the Río Usumacinta. For details, see the El Petén chapter.

There are regular boat services between the Guatemalan town of Puerto Barrios on the Gulf of Honduras and the southern Belizean town of Punta Gorda. There's a twice-weekly route between Lívingston and Punta Gorda and another between Li\vingston and Omoa (Honduras). There's also a sailboat that makes a trip from Utila (one of Honduras' Bay Islands) to Lívingston twice a month or so. See these towns' sections for details.

Be sure to get your exit and entry stamps at the immigration offices at both ends of the journey if you're arriving or departing the country by water.

Getting Around

AIR

Daily flights between Guatemala City and Flores save you from a torturous 15-hour bus ride. See those sections for details.

BUS

By far the most popular sort of bus used by Guatemala's many private bus companies is the second-hand American school bus, often with the original seats that allow room enough for school children but are very cramped for adults of European or North American stature. Fares are very cheap and buses plentiful, but most bus activity dies down by late afternoon.

GUATEMALA

Shuttle Minibus

Realizing that normal bus transport poses challenges to foreigners, various companies offer tourist minibus services on the main tourist routes (Guatemala City-Aeropuerto La Aurora-Antigua-Panajachel-Chichicastenango). Shuttle minibuses depart from La Aurora International Airport every hour or so, bound for Antigua; the same buses offer door-to-door transport between Antigua and Guatemala City. Other shuttles operate between Guatemala City, Panajachel and Chichicastenango.

Most of these operators have their offices in Antigua; check that section for contact information. TURANSA has an office in Guatemala City (☎ 595-3574, fax 595-3583) in the Supercentro Metro, Carretera Roosevelt Km 15, Zona 11, Local 68-69.

CAR

Traffic in Guatemala City is very heavy. Major roads in the highlands are free of heavy traffic. The Carretera al Atlántico has a moderate amount of heavy vehicle traffic.

You will need to buy a Guatemalan liability policy when you reach Guatemala. Policies are on sale at border posts and in the major towns near the borders.

If you see the branch of a tree, bushes or some other unusual object in the road, slow down – this is the signal that something unexpected is just ahead, whether a broken-down vehicle or a washout in the road.

Because of these and many other hazards, including armed bandits who stop vehicles and rob the occupants under cover of darkness, many drivers in Guatemala never drive at night.

Rental

Rental cars are available in Guatemala. Most companies offer several types of vehicles, including 4WD vehicles and minivans. Most of the rental companies have offices in Guatemala City, many both in town and at the airport; a few have offices in other cities as well.

Cost is high for renting a vehicle, about US$60 to US$95 per day total (including rental charges, insurance, charges per km

and fuel) for even the cheapest car. Insurance does not protect you from all losses by collision or theft. You will usually be liable for $600 to $1500 or more of damage, after which the insurance covers any loss. Drive safely and park in a secure area at night.

You must show your passport, driver's license and a major credit card when you rent, and you must normally be 25 years or older. If you do not have a valid credit card for the rental, a very large cash deposit may be required; check in advance to avoid disappointment.

As Guatemala grows in popularity as a tourist destination, rental cars become scarcer during the busy times of year. Reserve a car ahead of time if possible. Sometimes you'll get a better deal if you reserve from your home country.

Note that if you wish to drive a Guatemalan rental car to Copán in Honduras, you must obtain an official letter of permission from the rental agency to give to the Guatemalan customs official at the border. Without such a letter, you must leave the car at the border and proceed by public transport.

BICYCLE

Bicycling can be a way to get around in Guatemala, if you don't mind the hills or the bandits. Mountain bikes can be rented in several places, notably in Antigua and Panajachel.

HITCHHIKING

It's extremely unusual to see people hitching a ride in Guatemala. It's not safe.

WALKING

Unfortunately, long walking trips are not recommended due to the threat from robbers.

BOAT

Passenger boats run frequently between Lívingston and Puerto Barrios, and along the Río Dulce between Río Dulce village and Lívingston. Boats also form the major way to get around on some lakes, notably Lago de Atitlán and to a lesser extent on Lago de Izabal and Lago Petén Itzá.

A few of Guatemala's natural parks and reserves and archaeological sites are accessible only – or preferably – by water (see Parks & Protected Areas in Facts about Guatemala).

LOCAL TRANSPORT

Local buses in larger cities and towns provide inexpensive transportation in town and to the nearby suburbs and villages. Most routes operate very frequently and cost very little.

With only a couple of exceptions, taxis in Guatemala are not metered, so it's important to agree on a fare before you climb into the cab.

ORGANIZED TOURS

Organized tours are a good way to get to certain places. As noted in the section on Tikal, if you want to stay in a hotel there, your best bet may be to come with a package tour that includes accommodations, some meals, a guided tour of the ruins and airfare. Tours may be the best way to reach certain remote places in the El Petén region and around Cobán. Tours in Antigua will take you to some interesting places in the area that you probably would never find on your own, and they are a must for climbing many of Guatemala's volcanoes. Specialized tours may include horseback riding, bicycling, white-water rafting and more.

In the Guatemala chapters, tours are mentioned in all the following sections: Antigua Guatemala, Panajachel, Chichicastenango, Quetzaltenango, Totonicapán, Cobán, Copán (Honduras), Lívingston, Flores, Santa Elena, El Remate and Tikal.

GUATEMALA

Guatemala City

Population 2 million

Guatemala's capital city, the largest urban agglomeration in Central America, sprawls across a range of flattened mountains (altitude 1500 meters), scored by deep ravines.

At first, this city may remind you of Mexico City, its great Latin sister to the north. But the superficial resemblance soon gives way to purely Guatemalan impressions. There's the huge and chaotic market, typically colorful and disorganized. There are the ramshackle city buses that trundle citizens about with surprising efficiency, though hardly in comfort. And there are the thousands of guards in blue clothing carrying very effective-looking firearms. Wherever there's money or status – banks, offices, private clubs, even McDonald's – there are armed guards.

Guatemala City today has few colonial buildings to beautify its aggressive urban sprawl. The colonial buildings are all in nearby Antigua Guatemala, the former capital. Buildings are mostly concrete, but at least they're generally only five or six stories high, allowing light to flood the narrow streets.

The few interesting sights in Guatemala City may be seen in a day or two. Nowadays many travelers are avoiding the city altogether, preferring to make Antigua their base. Still, you may need to know your way around the capital because this is the hub of the country, where all transportation lines meet and where all services are available.

HISTORY

Many cities in this part of the world have seen their histories end with an earthquake, but for Guatemala City, the terrible *temblor* of July 29, 1773, resulted in its founding. Prior to that earthquake the Spanish capital of Central America was at La Ciudad de Santiago de los Caballeros de Guatemala, known today as Antigua Guatemala, in the Panchoy valley. The earthquake destroyed much of the colonial capital, and the government decided to move its headquarters to La Ermita valley, the present site of Guatemala City, hoping to escape any further such terrible destruction. On September 27, 1775, King Carlos III of Spain signed a royal charter for the founding of La Nueva Guatemala de la Asunción, and Guatemala City was officially born.

Hopes for a quakeless future were shaken in 1917, 1918 and 1976 as temblors did major damage to buildings in the capital – as well as in Antigua. The city's comparatively recent founding and its history of earthquakes have left little to see in the way of grand churches, palaces, mansions or quaint old neighborhoods.

ORIENTATION
Street Grid System

Guatemala City, like all Guatemalan towns, is laid out according to a street grid system that is logical and easy to use. Avenidas run north-south; calles run east-west. Streets are usually numbered from north and west (lowest) to south and east (highest); building numbers run in the same directions, with odd numbers on the left-hand side and even on the right as you head south or east. In smaller Guatemalan cities and towns this street grid system allows you to pinpoint destinations effortlessly. However, Guatemala City is divided into 15 *zonas*; each zona has its own separate version of this grid system. Thus 14a Calle in Zona 10 is a completely different street several miles distant from 14a Calle in Zona 1, though major thoroughfares such as 6a Avenida and 7a Avenida cross through several zones maintaining the same name.

Addresses are given in this form: '9a Avenida 15-12, Zona 1', which means '9th Avenue above 15th Street, No 12, in Zone 1'. The building you're looking for (in this case the Hotel Excel), will be on 9th Avenue between 15th and 16th Streets, on the right-hand side as you walk south. Guatemala City's street grid has a number of other anomalies: diagonal streets called *rutas* and *vías*, wandering boulevards called *diagonales*.

Short streets may be numbered 'A', as in 14a Calle A, a short street running between 14a Calle and 15a Calle.

Landmarks

The ceremonial center of Guatemala City is the Plaza Mayor (sometimes called the Parque Central) at the heart of Zona 1, surrounded by the Palacio Nacional, the Catedral Metropolitana and the Portal del Comercio. Beside the Plaza Mayor to the west is the large Parque Centenario, the city's central park. Zona 1 is also the retail commercial district, with shops selling clothing, crafts, film and a myriad of other things. The Mercado Central, a market selling lots of crafts, is behind the cathedral. Most of the city's good cheap and middle-range hotels are in Zona 1. 6a Avenida running south and 7a Avenida running north are the major thoroughfares that connect Zona 1 with other zonas.

Zona 4, south of Zona 1, holds the modern Centro Cívico (Civic Center) with various government buildings. In southwestern Zona 4 is the city's major market district and chaotic bus terminals.

Zona 9 (west of Avenida La Reforma) and Zona 10 (east of Avenida La Reforma) are south of Zona 4; Avenida La Reforma is the southerly extension of 10a Avenida. These are the fancier residential areas of the city, also boasting several of the most interesting small museums. Zona 10 is the poshest, with the Zona Viva (Lively Zone) arrayed around the deluxe Camino Real Guatemala and Guatemala Fiesta hotels. The Zona Viva holds many of the city's better restaurants and nightclubs. In Zona 9, convenient landmarks are the mini-Eiffel Tower called the Torre del Reformador at 7a Avenida and 2a Calle and the Plazuela España traffic roundabout at 7a Avenida and 12a Calle.

Zona 13, just south of Zona 9, has the large Parque Aurora, several museums and the Aeropuerto Internacional La Aurora.

Maps

The INGUAT tourist office (see below) sells a useful tourist map for US$1, with the country on one side and the cities and towns on the other. It has a map of greater Guatemala City, as well as a close-up of the downtown area.

INFORMATION
Tourist Offices

The tourist office is in the lobby of the INGUAT headquarters (Guatemalan Tourist Commission; ☎ 331-1333, fax 331-8893, 332-2881), 7a Avenida 1-17, Centro Cívico, Zona 4. Look for the blue-and-white sign with the letter 'i' on the east side of the street, next to a flight of stairs a few meters south of the railway viaduct that crosses above 7a Avenida. Hours are Monday to Friday from 8 am to 4 pm, Saturday 8 am to 1 pm, closed Sunday. Staff members are friendly and helpful.

INGUAT's office at La Aurora International Airport (☎ 331-8392) is open every day from 6 am to 9 pm.

Embassies & Consulates

There are many more embassies and consulates than are listed here. You can find them in the blue section of the Guatemalan telephone directory, along with their working hours. Remember that embassies *(embajadas)* and their consular sections *(consulados)* often have strange, short working hours, so call ahead. Unless otherwise noted, the places listed below are embassies.

Belize
    Avenida La Reforma 1-50, Zona 9,
    Edificio El Reformador, Office 803
    (☎ 334-5531, 331-1137, fax 334-5536)

Canada
    Embassy & Consulate, 13a Calle 8-44,
    Zona 10, Edificio Plaza Edyma (8th floor)
    (☎ 333-6102, 363-4348)

Costa Rica
    Embassy & Consulate, Avenida La Reforma
    8-60, Zona 9, Edificio Galerías Reforma,
    Office 702 (☎ 331-9604, ☎ /fax 332-1522)

GUATEMALA

El Salvador
Embassy & Consulate,
18a Calle 14-30, Zona 13
(☎ 334-3942, 334-8196, fax 360-1312)

France
Embassy & Consulate, 16a Calle 4-53,
Zona 10, Edificio Marbella
(☎ 337-3639, 337-4080)

Germany
Embassy & Consulate, 20a Calle 6-20, Zona
10, Edificio Plaza Marítima (☎ 337-0028)

Honduras
Embassy & Consulate, 13a Calle 12-33,
Zona 10, Colonia Oakland
(☎ 337-4337, ☎ /fax 337-4344)

Mexico
Embassy, 15a Calle 3-20, Zona 10,
Edificio Centro Ejecutivo (7th floor)
(☎ 333-7254 to 333-7258)
Consulate, 13a Calle 7-30, Zona 9
(☎ 331-8165, 331-9573)

Nicaragua
Embassy & Consulate, 10a Avenida 14-72,
Zona 10 (☎ 368-0785, fax 337-4264)

Panama
Embassy & Consulate, 5a Avenida 15-45,
Zona 10, Edificio Centro Empresarial,
Torre II, Offices 708 & 709
(☎ 333-7182/3, 337-2445, fax 337-2446)

South Africa
Consulate, 10a Avenida 30-57,
Zona 5 (CIDEA)
(☎ 332-6890, 334-1531, fax 332-7291)

Spain
Embassy & Consulate, 6a Calle 6-48,
Zona 9 (☎ 334-3757, fax 332-2456)

Switzerland
4a Calle 7-73, Zona 9, Edificio Seguros
Universales, (5th floor)
(☎ 331-3725/6, 334-0743, fax 331-8524)

UK
Embassy & Consulate, 7a Avenida 5-10,
Zona 4, Edificio Centro Financiero, Torre II
(7th floor) (☎ 332-1601/2/4, fax 334-1904)

USA
Embassy & Consulate, Avenida La Reforma
7-01, Zona 10 (☎ 331-1541 to 331-1555)

Immigration

If you need to extend your visa or tourist card for a longer stay, contact the Dirección General de Migración (☎ 475-1302, 475-1404, fax 475-1289), 41a Calle 17-36, Zona 8, one block off Avenida Castellana. It's open Monday to Friday, 8 am to 4 pm.

Money

Banco del Agro (☎ 230-5506), on the south side of Parque Centenario, changes US dollars cash and travelers' checks; it's open Monday to Friday from 9 am to 8 pm, Saturday 10 am to 2 pm. ATMs are also beginning to appear.

Credomatic (☎ 251-4185), in the tall building at the corner of 5a Avenida and 11a Calle, Zona 1, gives cash advances on Visa and MasterCard. It's open Monday to Friday from 8 am to 7 pm, Saturday 9 am to 1 pm. Inside, you can withdraw a maximum of US$500; their 24-hour ATM gives a maximum of US$100 per transaction, but there's no limit to the number of transactions.

The airport terminal office of Banco del Quetzal is open Monday to Friday from 7 am to 8 pm, Saturday and Sunday 8 am to 6 pm. Here you can change US dollars cash or travelers' checks into quetzales, change European currencies into US dollars and buy US-dollar travelers' checks.

American Express is represented in Guatemala by Banco del Café (☎ 331-1311), in the Edificio Torre del País, Avenida La Reforma 9-30, Zona 9, 1st floor. It's open Monday to Friday, 8:30 am to 4:30 pm.

Post & Communications

The city's main post office is at 7a Avenida 12-11, Zona 1, in the huge pink building – by the racks of postcards shall ye know it. It's open from 8 am to 7 pm on weekdays, 8 am to 4:30 pm on Saturday, closed Sunday. The Philatelic Department is open Monday to Friday, 9 am to 5:30 pm.

EMS (Express Mail Service), in the rear of the post office building, is open weekdays, 9 am to 5 pm.

Guatel's main office is on the corner of 12a Calle & 8a Avenida, Zona 1, a block from the main post office. Services are available every day from 7 am to midnight. Several smaller Guatel branches are found around the city.

At La Aurora International Airport there's a post office (open Monday to Friday from 7 am to 3 pm) and a Guatel office (open every day, 7 am to 7 pm).

Bookstores
The Arnel bookstore is at No 108 in the Edificio El Centro, at the corner of 9a Calle & 7a Avenida, Zona 1, a block from Parque Central. It has a variety of books in English and French, including general fiction, Latin American literature in translation, travel guides, books about the region, Maya civilization and Spanish language learning.

Geminis Bookshop (☎ 366-1031, fax 366-1034) in the Edificio Casa Alta at 3a Avenida 17-05, Zona 14, has a good selection of international books, but it's farther from the center. The Europa bar/restaurant (see Places to Eat) has a shelf of used books in English for sale or trade.

Libraries
The Biblioteca Nacional (National Library; ☎ 232-2443), on the west side of Parque Centenario, is open Monday to Friday, 9 am to 6 pm.

Medical Services
This city has many private hospitals and clinics. One is the Hospital Centro Médico (☎ 332-3555, 334-2157) at 6a Avenida 3-47, Zona 10; another is Hospital Herrera Llerandi, (☎ 334-5959, emergencies 334-5955), 6a Avenida 8-71, Zona 10, which is also called Amedesgua. The Guatemalan Red Cross (☎ 125) is at 3a Calle 8-40, Zona 1.

Guatemala City uses a duty-chemist *(farmacia de turno)* system with designated pharmacies remaining open at night and weekends. Ask at your hotel for the nearest farmacia de turno, or consult the farmacia de turno sign in the window of the closest chemist/pharmacy. The Farmacia del Ejecutivo, on 7a Avenida at the corner of 15a Calle, Zona 1, is open 24 hours; it accepts Visa and MasterCard.

Emergency
Emergency telephone numbers are:

Ambulance	125, 128
Fire	122, 123
Police	120, 137, 138

Dangers & Annoyances
Street crime is increasing in downtown Guatemala City. Use sensible caution – don't walk down the street with your wallet hanging out of the back pocket of your jeans, and avoid walking downtown late at night. It's safe to walk downtown in early evening, as long as you stick to streets with plenty of lighting and people. 18a Calle in Zona 1, an area with many bus stations, etc, is notoriously dangerous at night; if you are arriving by bus at night or must go someplace on 18a Calle at night, take a taxi.

The more affluent sections of the city – Zona 9 and Zona 10, for example – are much safer.

ZONA 1
Plaza Mayor
Most of what you'll want to see is in Zona 1 near the Plaza Mayor, bounded by 6a and 8a Calles and 6a and 7a Avenidas.

According to the standard Spanish colonial town-planning scheme, every town in the New World had to have a large plaza for military exercises, reviews and ceremonies. On the north side of the plaza was to be the *palacio de gobierno*, or colonial government headquarters. On another side, preferably the east, there was a church (if the town was large enough to merit a bishop, it was a cathedral). On the other sides of the square there could be other civic buildings, or the large and imposing mansions of wealthy citizens. Guatemala's Plaza Mayor is a good example of the classic town plan.

To appreciate the Plaza Mayor, you've got to visit it on a Sunday when it's thronged with thousands of citizens who have come to stroll, lick ice cream cones, play in the fountains, take the air, smooch on a bench, listen to *salsa* music on boomboxes and ignore the hundreds of trinket vendors. If you can't make it on a Sunday, try for lunchtime or late afternoon.

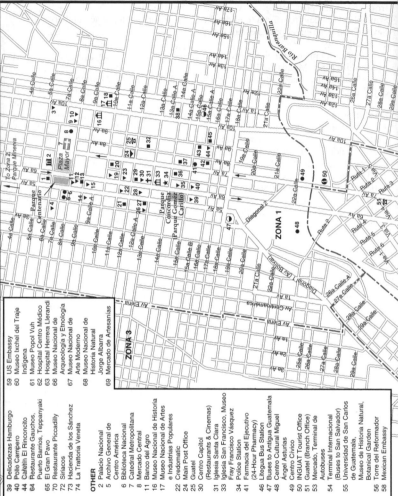

PLACES TO STAY
1 Hotel Centenario
13 Hotel Pan American
18 Pensión Meza
20 Hotel Ritz Continental
21 Hotel Lessing House
27 Hotel del Centro
29 Hotel-Apartamentos
    Guatemala Internacional
32 Spring Hotel
36 Chalet Suizo
37 Hotel Colonial
38 Posada Belén
42 Hotel Ajau
43 Hotel Excel
45 Hotel Capri
52 Hotel Plaza
54 Hotel del Istmo
57 Hotel Cortijo Reforma
71 Hotel Princess Reforma
72 Radisson Suites Villa
    Magna
75 Hotel Camino Real
    Guatemala
76 Hotel El Dorado
77 Hotel Posada de los
    Proceres

PLACES TO EAT
3 Restaurante Tao
4 Restaurante Long Wah
9 McDonald's
10 Pollo Campero
11 Restaurante Vegetariano
    Rey Sol
14 Pollo Campero
15 Pastelería Las Américas
19 Cafetería El Roble
20 Restaurante Bologna,
    Dunkin' Donuts
23 Restaurante/Bar Europa
23 Restaurante Piccadilly
26 El Gran Pavo
27 Hotel del Centro
28 Restaurante Altuna
30 Centro Capitol
    (Restaurants & Cinemas)
35 McDonald's

39 Delicadezas Hamburgo
40 Pollo Campero
44 Cafetín El Rinconcito
64 Restaurante Gauchos,
    Puerto Barrios, Teppanyaki
65 El Gran Pavo
70 Restaurante Piccadilly
72 Siriacos
73 Hacienda de los Sánchez
74 La Trattoria Veneta

OTHER
2 Palacio Nacional
5 Archivo General de
    Centro América
6 Biblioteca Nacional
7 Catedral Metropolitana
8 Mercado Central
11 Banco del Agro
16 Museo Nacional de Historia
17 Museo Nacional de Artes
    e Industrias Populares
22 Credomatic
24 Main Post Office
25 Guatel
30 Centro Capitol
    (Restaurants & Cinemas)
31 Iglesia Santa Clara
33 Iglesia San Francisco, Museo
    Fray Francisco Vásquez
34 Police Station
41 Farmacia del Ejecutivo
    (24-Hour Pharmacy)
46 Litegua Bus Station
47 Buses to Antigua Guatemala
48 Centro Cultural Miguel
    Angel Asturias
49 Centro Cívico
50 INGUAT Tourist Office
51 Guatel (Branch Office)
53 Mercado, Terminal de
    Autobuses
54 Terminal Internacional
    (Buses to San Salvador)
55 Universidad de San Carlos
    de Guatemala,
    Museo de Historia Natural,
    Botanical Garden
56 Torre del Reformador
58 Mexican Embassy

59 US Embassy
60 Museo Ixchel del Traje
    Indígena
61 Museo Popol Vuh
62 Hospital Centro Médico
63 Hospital Herrera Llerandi
66 Museo Nacional de
    Arqueología y Etnología
67 Museo Nacional de
    Arte Moderno
68 Museo Nacional de
    Historia Natural
    Jorge Albarra
69 Mercado de Artesanías

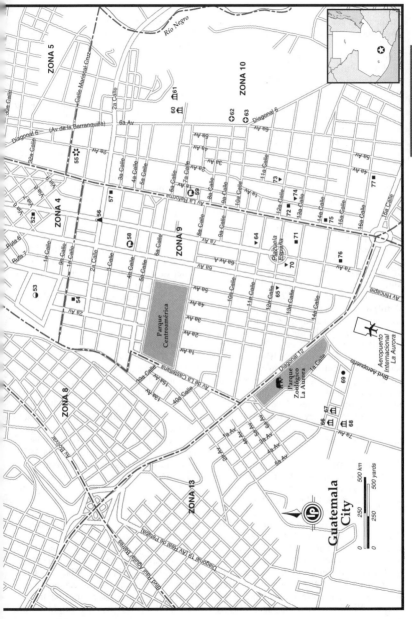

GUATEMALA

Palacio Nacional

On the north side of the Plaza Mayor is the magnificent Palacio Nacional, built during the dictatorial presidency of General Jorge Ubico (1931-44) at enormous cost. It's the third palace to stand here.

The Palacio Nacional is being restored and will house a museum of the history of Guatemala. (The national government offices, which have been here till now, are being decentralized throughout the city.)

Free tours are given Monday to Friday from 9 am to 5:30 pm, Saturday and Sunday 9 am to 3 pm. The tour takes you through a labyrinth of gleaming brass, polished wood, carved stone and frescoed arches painted by Alberto Gálvez Suárez. Notable features include the two-ton gold, bronze and Bohemian-crystal chandelier in the reception salon and the two Arabic-style inner courtyards.

Catedral Metropolitana

Built between 1782 and 1809 (the towers were finished later, in 1867), the Catedral Metropolitana has survived earthquake and fire (much better than the site of the Palacio Nacional), though the quake of 1917 did a lot of damage and that of 1976 did even more. All has been restored. It's not a particularly beautiful building, inside or out. Heavy proportions and spare ornamentation make it look severe, though it does have a certain stateliness. The cathedral is supposedly open every day from 8 am to 7 pm, though you may find it closed, especially at siesta time.

Mercado Central

Until it was destroyed by the quake of 1976, the central market on 9a Avenida between 6a and 8a Calles behind the cathedral was a place to buy food and other necessities. Reconstructed in the late 1970s, the modern market specializes in tourist-oriented items such as cloth (hand-woven and machine-woven), carved wood, worked leather and metal, basketry and other handicrafts. Necessities have been moved aside to the streets surrounding the market. When you visit the Plaza Mayor,

you should take a stroll through here, though there are better places to buy crafts. Market hours are 6 am to 6 pm Monday to Saturday, 9 am to noon Sunday.

The city's true 'central' food market is in Zona 4.

Museums

Museums in Zona 1 include **Museo Fray Francisco Vasquez** (☎ 232-3625), Iglesia San Francisco, corner 6a Avenida & 13a Calle. It houses the belongings of this Franciscan friar. The museum is open every day, 9 am to noon and 3 to 6 pm.

The **Museo Nacional de Artes e Industrias Populares** (☎ 238-0334),10a Avenida 10-72, is the national popular arts museum, with paintings, ceramics, masks, musical instruments, metalwork and gourds. It's open Monday to Friday, 9 am to 5 pm.

The collection of the **Museo Nacional de Historia** (☎ 253-6149), 9a Calle 9-70, corner of 10a Avenida, is a jumble of historical relics. It's open every day, 10 am to 4 pm. This museum may be moved to the Palacio Nacional after it's restored.

ZONA 2
Parque Minerva

Zona 2 is north of Zona 1. Though mostly a middle-class residential district, its northern end holds the large Parque Minerva, itself surrounded by golf courses, the rod-and-gun club, sports grounds and the buildings of the Universidad Mariano Gálvez.

Minerva, goddess of wisdom, technical skill and invention, was a favorite of President Manuel Estrada Cabrera (1898-1920, see History in Facts about Guatemala).

The Parque Minerva is a pretty place, good for relaxing, strolling among the eucalyptus trees and sipping a soft drink. Be on the alert for pickpockets, purse-snatchers and other such types, who look especially for tourists.

The prime sight in Zona 2 is the Relief Map of Guatemala, called simply the **Mapa En Relieve** in Parque Minerva. Constructed in 1904 under the direction of Francisco Vela, the map shows the country at a scale of 1:10,000, but the height of the

Top: The commercial centre of Guatemala City, Guatemala (TB)
Bottom: Antigua Guatemala, Guatemala (PW)

   Top: Palacio Nacional, Guatemala City, Guatemala (TB)
Middle: A hotel courtyard, Antigua Guatemala, Guatemala (TB)
Bottom: Lake Atitlán and Tolimán Volcano, Guatemala (TB)

mountainous terrain has been exaggerated to 1:2000 for dramatic effect. Little signs indicate major towns and topographical features. Viewing towers afford a panoramic view. This place is odd but fun, and costs only a few centavos for admission; hours are 8 am to 5 pm every day. Nearby are carnival rides and games for children.

The Mapa En Relieve and Parque Minerva are two km north of the Plaza Mayor along 6a Avenida, but that street is one-way heading south. Catch a northbound bus (No 1, 45 or 46) on 5a Avenida in Zona 1 and take it to the end of the line.

ZONA 4

Pride of Zona 4 is the Centro Cívico, constructed during the 1950s and '60s. (The complex of buildings actually stretches into Zona 1 and Zona 5 as well.) Here you'll find the Palace of Justice, the headquarters of the Guatemalan Institute of Social Security (IGSS), the Banco del Quetzal, city hall and the headquarters of INGUAT. The Banco del Quetzal building bears high-relief murals by Dagoberto Vásquez depicting the history of his homeland; in the city hall is a huge mosaic by Carlos Mérida completed in 1959.

Behind INGUAT is the Ciudad Olímpica sports grounds, and across the street from the Centro Cívico on a hilltop are the Centro Cultural Miguel Ángel Asturias (the national theater, chamber theater, open-air theater and a small museum of old armaments).

Zona 4 is known mostly for its mercados and its bus stations, all thrown together in the chaotic southwestern corner of the zona near the railway.

ZONA 10

East of Avenida La Reforma, Zona 10 is the upscale district of posh villas, luxury hotels, embassies and two of the city's most important museums.

The **Museo Ixchel del Traje Indígena** (☎ 331-3638, 331-3739) is named for Ixchel, wife of Mayan sky god Itzamná and goddess of the moon, women, reproduction and textiles, among other things. Photographs and exhibits of Indian costumes,

textiles and other village crafts show the incredible richness of traditional arts in Guatemala's highland towns. If you enjoy seeing Guatemalan textiles at all, you must make a visit to the Museo Ixchel.

Behind this is the **Museo Popol Vuh**, where well-chosen polychrome pottery, figurines, incense burners, burial urns, carved wooden masks and traditional textiles fill several exhibit rooms. Others hold colonial paintings, gilded wood and silver objects. A faithful copy of the Dresden Codex, one of the precious 'painted books' of the Maya, is among the most interesting pieces. If you're at all interested in Mayan and Spanish colonial art, you must make a visit to this museum.

Both museums are in large, new buildings at the Universidad Francisco Marroquín, on the east end of 6a Calle in Zona 10, about six blocks east of Avenida La Reforma. They're open Monday to Friday from 8 am to 6 pm, Saturday 9 am to 1 pm; admission is US$1.65.

The biology department at the Universidad de San Carlos de Guatemala (☎ 476-2010) at Calle Mariscal Cruz 1-56 has a natural history museum and a large botanical garden open to the public Monday to Friday from 8 am to 4 pm.

ZONA 13

The major attraction in the southern reaches of the city is the Parque Aurora, with its zoo, children's playground, fairgrounds and several museums.

The Moorish-looking **Museo Nacional de Arqueología y Etnología** (☎ 472-0489) has a collection of Mayan archaeological finds from all over Guatemala, including stone carvings, jade, ceramics, statues, stelae, a tomb and models of the ruins at Tikal and Zaculeu. Exhibits in the ethnology section show the distribution of all the various indigenous peoples and languages throughout Guatemala, with exhibits on their traditional costumes, dances and implements of daily life.

Facing the Museo Nacional de Arqueología y Etnología is the **Museo Nacional de Arte Moderno** (☎ 472-0467), with a

GUATEMALA

collection of 20th-century Guatemalan art, especially painting and sculpture.

Hours at these museums are Tuesday to Friday from 9 am to 4 pm, Saturday and Sunday from 9 to noon and 1:30 to 4 pm (closed Monday). Admission is free.

Several hundred meters east of the museums is the city's official handicrafts market, the **Mercado de Artesanías** (☎ 472-0208), on 11a Avenida, just off the access road to the airport. Like most official handicrafts markets it's a sleepy place in which shopkeepers display the same items available in hotel gift shops. It's open 9 am to 6 pm Monday to Saturday, 9 am to 1 pm Sunday.

The pleasant **Zoológico La Aurora** (☎ 472-0507) is open Tuesday to Sunday from 9 am to 5 pm. Admission is US$0.85 for adults, half price for children.

KAMINALJUYÚ

Several kilometers west of the center lie the extensive ruins of Kaminaljuyú (☎ 253-1570, 232-5948), a Late Preclassic/Early Classic Mayan site displaying both Mexican and Mayan influences.

Unfortunately, much of Kaminaljuyú, located in Colonia Kaminaljuyú, Zona 7, has been covered by urban sprawl. Though you can visit from 9 am to 4 pm daily, your time would be better spent looking at the artifacts recovered here that are on display in the city's museums. Buses No 35 and 37 come here from 4a Avenida, Zona 1.

PLACES TO STAY

Guatemala City has a good range of lodgings in all price ranges. Those at the very bottom end of the price scale, as well as those at the very top, often fill up, but there are usually plenty of rooms to be had at prices in-between. Taxes are included in the quoted prices.

Places to Stay – budget

Perhaps the greatest concentration of low-budget hotels in the city is about eight blocks south of the Plaza Mayor near the Policia Nacional (National Police Head-

quarters) and the Correos (Post Office), in the area bounded by 6a Avenida A and 9a Avenida and 14a and 16a Calles. There are at least a dozen decent hotels to choose from and several handy little restaurants as well. It's very important to keep street noise in mind as you search for a budget room. All the places listed below are in Zona 1.

Spring Hotel (☎ 230-2858, 230-2958, fax 232-0107), 8a Avenida 12-65, is a clean and pleasant old hotel that's often *completo* (full) because the location is good, the 43 rooms presentable, the courtyard sunny and the price right. Singles/doubles with shared bath are US$10/14.50, rooms with private bath and color cable TV are US$14.50/19 and fancier rooms in the new *anexo* are US$22/28. A cafeteria serves meals from 7 am to 2 pm.

Hotel Lessing House (☎ 251-3891), 12a Calle 4-35, offers eight tidy rooms, all with private bath. Rooms can accommodate one (US$8), two (US$14), three (US$20) or four (US$28).

Hotel Ajau (☎ 232-0488, 251-3008, fax 251-8097; hotajau@gua.gbm.net), 8a Avenida 15-62, is fairly clean, somewhat cheaper and quite a bit quieter than many 9a Avenida hotels. Singles/doubles are US$7/9 with shared bath, US$12/14 with private bath. All rooms come with color cable TV. Laundry service and coffee are available, and guests are welcome to use the email.

Hotel Chalet Suizo (☎ 251-3786, 230-2930), 14a Calle 6-82, has been a favorite of adventurous travelers for decades. The 47 rooms around plant-filled courtyards are pleasant and exceptionally clean. Rates are US$14/17 a single/double with shared bath, or US$24/30 with private bath. Book in advance.

Hotel Excel (☎ 253-2709, 230-0140, fax 238-4071), 9a Avenida 15-12, is a bright, modern place with 17 rooms on three levels around an L-shaped courtyard used as a car park. It has a 2nd-floor cafeteria. Rooms with bath and cable TV are US$20/25/30 a single/double/triple. In the same block are several cheaper hotels, including the *Capri*, the *España* and the *Gran Central*.

Pensión Meza (☎ 232-3177, 253-4576), 10a Calle 10-17, is drab and beat-up but busy with international budget travelers who like the sunny courtyard, the camaraderie, the helpful proprietor and the low prices. With shared bath, singles/doubles are US$5.50/6 with one bed, US$7.50 with two beds, or US$2.50 per person in a dormitory. One room with private bath costs US$9 for one to three people. The restaurant serves cheap meals.

If you're arriving by bus from San Salvador, the *Hotel del Istmo* (☎ 332-4389) at the Terminal Internacional bus terminal, 3a Avenida 1-38, Zona 9, is clean, comfortable and convenient. Rooms with private hot bath are US$11/14 a single/double, and there's an inexpensive cafeteria.

Places to Stay – middle
Guatemala City's midrange lodgings are good values. All are comfortable, some quite charming. All these places are in Zona 1, except for the Hotel Plaza and the Hotel Posada de los Proceres.

Posada Belén (☎ 232-9226, 253-4530, fax 251-3478), 13a Calle A 10-30, is on a quiet side street. A converted colonial home, the Belén is a charming hostelry with 11 rooms-with-bath, a dining room serving all meals and laundry service. Rooms accommodate one (US$36), two (US$43), three (US$48) or four (US$53) people.

Hotel Pan American (☎ 232-6807/8/9, 253-5991, fax 232-6402), 9a Calle 5-63, was this city's luxury hotel before WWII. It still attracts many faithful return visitors who like its faded charm. The 55 rooms, all Art Deco and Biedermeier, are pleasant and comfortable, with cable TV, telephone, private bath (with tub) and fan. Avoid rooms facing the noisy street. Rates are US$65/74/82 a single/double/triple, and there's a restaurant serving all meals.

Hotel del Centro (☎ 232-5547, 232-5980, fax 230-0208), 13a Calle 4-55, is a good, solid hotel, dependable for decades. The 55 large, comfortable rooms come with shiny baths, color cable TV and often with two double beds; there's a bit of street

noise in some. Singles/doubles are US$46/52. There's also a restaurant, a bar with music on Friday nights and a rooftop terrace garden.

Hotel Colonial (☎ 232-6722, 232-2955, fax 232-8671), 7a Avenida 14-19, is a large old city house converted to a hotel with heavy colonial decor. The covered interior court is pleasant, the 42 rooms clean. Singles/doubles in four rooms with general bath are US$18/24; the rest, all with private bath, are US$24/32.50. A restaurant serves meals from 6:30 am to 2 pm.

Hotel-Apartamentos Guatemala Internacional (☎ 238-4441/2/3/4/5), 6a Avenida 12-21, offers 27 furnished units, each with fully-equipped kitchen, TV and telephone. The location is convenient, and the prices are good. Studios are US$22/25 for singles/doubles; larger one- or two-bedroom apartments are US$30/36 single, US$36/42 double and US$42/48 triple or quad. Some larger apartments can sleep six.

Hotel Centenario (☎ 238-0381/2/3, fax 238-2039), 6a Calle 5-33, on the north side of the Parque Centenario, has 42 rooms, many with a double and a single bed, plus well-worn but clean showers. Prices for this central location are US$25/30 a single/double.

Hotel Plaza (☎ 331-6173, 331-0396, fax 331-6824), Vía 7, No 6-16, Zona 4, with colonial appointments, is one km south of the Centro Cívico and a 15-minute walk east of the market and bus station area. The 64 ample rooms, each with private bath, telephone and color cable TV, go for US$55/61 per single/double.

Hotel Posada de los Proceres (☎ /fax 363-0744/46, 363-4423), 16a Calle 2-40, is in a pleasant residential district in the up-market Zona 10 near Los Proceres shopping center. Singles/doubles/triples are US$49/59/69. Most other hotels in this district are much more expensive; this one is a find.

Places to Stay – top end
Most luxurious of this city's hotels is the *Hotel Camino Real Guatemala* (☎ 333-4633, fax 337-4313, in the USA (800) 228-3000), Avenida La Reforma at 14a

Calle, Zona 10, in the middle of the Zona Viva. This is the capital's international-class hotel, with 400 rooms and five-star comforts, including swimming pools and lush gardens. Rates for singles/doubles are US$168/192.

Another excellent luxury hotel in the Zona Viva is the four-star, 100-suite *Radisson Suites Villa Magna* (☎ 332-9769, 332-9797, fax 332-9772, in the USA (800) 333-3333), 1a Avenida 12-46, Zona 10. The upper-floor suites have beautiful views from full-wall windows. A buffet breakfast is included in the rates of US$126/138.

Hotel Princess Reforma (☎ 334-4545, fax 334-4546), 13a Calle 7-65, Zona 9, is just across Reforma from the Zona Viva on a quiet street. The four-star, 90-room Reforma is an excellent European-style business hotel, without the extensive grounds but with style and everything you need, including a small swimming pool, sauna, gym, restaurant and bar; its 108 rooms go for US$132.

The modern, five-star *Hotel El Dorado* (☎ 331-7777, fax 332-1877), 7a Avenida 15-45, Zona 9, has 250 rooms for US$96/102 single/double, breakfast included.

Several hundred meters north of the Zona Viva stands the *Hotel Cortijo Reforma* (☎ 332-0712, fax 331-8876), Avenida La Reforma 2-18, Zona 9. The 120 suites feature a bedroom, living room, minibar, tiled bathroom with tub and shower, space for a kitchenette and a tiny balcony. Singles/doubles are a good value at US$64/70.

Downtown, the four-star *Hotel Ritz Continental* (☎ 238-1671, 238-1871, fax 232-4659), 6a Avenida A 10-13, Zona 1, has recently been renovated. The 106 rooms are US$78/84, including breakfast; there's a swimming pool. The location, three blocks south of the Plaza Mayor, is quiet and convenient.

Farther from the center, one of the newer of the city's luxury hotels is the five-star *Hotel Gran Plaza Las Américas* (☎ 339-0666, fax 339-0690), Avenida Las Américas 9-08, Zona 13, operated by Holiday Inn, with rooms for US$120.

PLACES TO EAT
Places to Eat – budget

It is not difficult to find cheap eats. Fast-food and snack shops abound. But to really save money, head for Parque Concordia, bound by 5a and 6a Avenidas and 14a and 15a Calles in Zona 1. The west side of the park is lined with little open-air food stalls serving sandwiches and snacks at rock-bottom prices from early morning to late evening. A meal for US$2 is the rule here.

Delicadezas Hamburgo, 15a Calle 5-34, Zona 1, on the south side of Parque Concordia, provides a long list of sandwiches at lunch and dinner. It's open from 7 am to 9:30 pm every day.

Restaurante Cantón (☎ 251-6331), 6a Avenida 14-29, Zona 1, facing the park on its east side, is the place to go for Chinese food, at US$5 to US$8 per platter; it's open every day from 9 am to 9:30 pm.

There are numerous other Chinese restaurants near the corner of 6a Avenida and 14a Calle, Zona 1. The city's other rich concentration of Chinese restaurants is in the blocks west of the Parque Centenario along 6a Calle, where you'll find the *Restaurante Long Wah* (☎ 232-6611), 6a Calle 3-70, Zona 1, along with several other places such as the *Palacio Real, Palacio Dorado* and the *Jou Jou*.

6a Avenida between 10a and 15a Calles has dozens of restaurants and fast-food shops of all types: hamburgers, pizzas, pasta, Chinese, fried chicken. You'll have no trouble eating well for US$3 to US$4. The *Pastelería Las Américas*, 6a Avenida 8-52, half a block south of Plaza Mayor, is pleasant place to stop for a coffee and a European-style pastry or cake while you're out sightseeing.

9a Avenida between 15a and 16a Calles, in the midst of the cheap hotel area, has several good little restaurants. There's the *Cafetín El Rinconcito*, 9a Avenida 15-74, facing the Hotel Capri, which is good for tacos and sandwiches, where breakfast, lunch and dinner each cost around US$1.50 to US$2. The restaurant in the Hotel Capri itself, 9a Avenida 15-63, Zona 1, serves more substantial meals.

You might also want to try the *Cafetería El Roble*, 9a Calle 5-46, Zona 1, facing the entrance to the Hotel Pan American. This clean little cafe is very popular with local office workers for lunch (US$1. 65) as well as for breakfast and dinner (US$1.15).

Europa (☎ 253-4929), 11a Calle 5-16, next door to Credomatic, is a comfortable restaurant, bar and gathering place for locals and foreigners alike. A sign on the door says 'English spoken, but not understood.' It has international cable TV, a book exchange and good, inexpensive food; it's open Monday to Saturday, 8 am to 1 am.

Pollo Campero (Country Chicken) is the name of Guatemala's KFC clone. You can find branches of the chain on the corner of 9a Calle and 5a Avenida, at 6a Avenida and 15a Calle and at 8a Calle 9-29, all in Zona 1. Two pieces of chicken, French fries (chips) and a soft drink or coffee costs US$2.50.

Many branches of American fast-food chains like *McDonald's, Wendy's, Burger King* and *Pizza Hut* are all around the city. They're open long hours, often from 7 am to 10 pm. Pizza Hut offers free delivery (☎ 230-3490 in Zona 1, 332-0939 in Zona 9).

The *Restaurante Vegetariano Rey Sol*, 8a Calle 5-36, on the south side of Parque Centenario, has a long cafeteria line with a good selection where you can walk along and order what you like: whole grain breads and baked goods, sandwiches, soya products, fruit and vegetable salads, hot foods and more. It's open Monday to Saturday, 7:15 am to 8:45 pm.

Places to Eat – middle
Most middle-range hotels in Zona 1 offer excellent set-price lunches for US$6 to US$10. Try the *Hotel Del Centro, Hotel Pan American* and *Hotel Ritz Continental*. My favorite for ambiance is definitely the Pan American, 9a Calle 5-63, Zona 1.

Restaurante Altuna (☎ 232-0669, 251-7185), 5a Avenida 12-31, Zona 1, is a large restaurant with the atmosphere of a private club, located just a few steps north of the Hotel del Centro. Specialties are seafood

and Spanish dishes, with meals about US$7 to US$14 per person. It's open Tuesday to Saturday from noon to 11 pm, Sunday from noon to 4:30 pm, closed Monday.

Restaurante Bologna (☎ 251-1167), 10a Calle 6-20, Zona 1, just around the corner from the Hotel Ritz Continental, is very small but attractive, serving tasty pizza and pasta dishes for US$3 to US$4 per plate. It's open every day but Tuesday, 10 am to 9:30 pm.

Several other good restaurants have their main establishments in Zona 1 and their branches in Zona 9 or 10.

El Gran Pavo (The Big Turkey, ☎ 232-9912), 13a Calle 4-41, Zona 1, is a big place just to the left (west) of the Hotel del Centro's entrance. The menu seems to include every Mexican dish imaginable. The birria, a spicy-hot soup of meat, onions, peppers and cilantro, served with tortillas, is a meal in itself for US$3.75. The Big Turkey is open seven days a week from 10 am to midnight, with mariachi music on Friday and Saturday nights starting around 10 pm. There's another branch (☎ 331-3976) at 12a Calle 5-54, Zona 9, and a few others around town.

Restaurante Piccadilly (☎ 230-2866, 253-9223), 6a Avenida 11-01, Zona 1, is among the capital's most popular eateries, with a multinational menu that might have come from the United Nations cafeteria. Most main courses cost US$3 or less. There's another branch of the Piccadilly on the Plazuela España, 7a Avenida 12-00, Zona 9.

Places to Eat – top end
The most elegant dining in the city is to be found in the Zona Viva, the several blocks near the Hotel Camino Real Guatemala.

La Trattoria Veneta (☎ 331-0612, 334-3718), 13a Calle 1-55, Zona 10, is the place to go for good Italian specialties. Service is attentive. Expect to spend US$12 to US$15 per person for dinner with wine.

Hacienda de los Sánchez (☎ 331-6240, 334-8448), 12a Calle 2-25, Zona 10, is where Guatemalan meat-eaters come to pig out. The ambiance is aggressively *ranchero*.

Steaks and ribs are priced about US$11 to US$12.50. The parking lot is full of shiny American pickup trucks. It's open every day from noon to midnight.

Puerto Barrios (☎ 334-1302), 7a Avenida 10-65, Zona 9, is awash in a nautical themes: waiters in knee breeches and frogged coats, oil paintings of buccaneers, portholes for windows and a big compass by the door. You can easily spend US$16 to US$30 per person here. Come aboard any day from 11 am to 3 pm or 7 to 11 pm.

In the same little complex, open the same hours, are *Restaurante Gauchos* (☎ 334-1302), an Argentinean steak-and-seafood restaurant, and *Restaurante Teppanyaki* (☎ 332-4646), with Japanese cuisine.

Siriacos (☎ 334-6316), 1a Avenida 12-12, Zona 10, very near the Radisson Suites Villa Magna, is flashy but informal, with a sunken dining room and bar, a skylighted patio courtyard and a menu of continental specialties. Expect to spend US$15 or so per person for dinner. It's open for lunch Monday to Friday, dinner Monday to Saturday, closed Sunday.

ENTERTAINMENT

Wining and dining the night away in the Zona Viva is what many visitors do. If that's beyond your budget, take in a movie at one of the cinemas along 6a Avenida between the Plaza Mayor and Parque Concordia. Tickets sell for about US$1.50. Or check out the cultural events at the Centro Cultural Miguel Ángel Asturias (☎ 232-4041/2/3/4/5, 253-1743) in Zona 4.

GETTING THERE & AWAY
Air

International air routes to Guatemala arrive and depart from the La Aurora International Airport in Guatemala City and from the international airport at Flores/Santa Elena, near Tikal.

International flights serving Guatemala City usually go through Houston, Los Angeles, Miami, San Francisco, Washington DC, Mexico City or San Salvador. If you begin your trip in any other city, you will probably find yourself stopping in one of these 'hub' cities. The few exceptions are mostly flights from cities in the region operated by smaller local airlines. The following is a list of the cities with direct and nonstop flights to and from Guatemala City, plus a couple of useful connecting routes, and the airlines that fly them.

Amsterdam – KLM has flights five times a week, via Mexico City.

Belize City – TACA has daily flights via El Salvador. Tikal Jets flies five days a week via Flores. Aerovías flies three times a week via Flores.

Cancún – Aerocaribe and Aviateca each have direct flights three times a week.

Chetumal (Mexico) – Aeroméxico has flights four times weekly via Flores.

Flores, El Petén (for Tikal) – Mayan World has three flights daily. Tikal Jets has daily flights. Aviateca has four flights weekly. All are direct flights.

Havana – Aviateca has direct flights twice a week.

Houston – Continental has direct flights daily. Aviateca has three direct flights per week. TACA has daily flights via El Salvador and Belize City.

Huatulco – Mexicana has direct flights three times a week.

Los Angeles – Aviateca, United and TACA all have daily direct flights. Mexicana has daily flights via Mexico City.

Madrid – Iberia has one flight per week via Miami.

Mexico City – Mexicana and Aviateca have daily nonstop flights. KLM has direct flights five times a week.

Mérida – Aviateca has a morning flight three days per week.

Miami – American has two direct flights weekly. Aviateca and Iberia each have one direct flight per week. TACA has daily flights via El Salvador.

New Orleans – TACA has flights four times weekly via El Salvador.

New York – TACA has flights daily via Washington DC.

San José (Costa Rica) – United and COPA have direct flights every day. SAM has direct flights four times weekly. TACA, Aviateca and LACSA have daily flights, making one stop on the way. Avianca has a flight going Guatemala City-San José-San Andrés Island-Bogotá.

San Francisco (California, USA) – TACA has direct flights four times weekly.

San Salvador – Daily nonstops by TACA, COPA and Aviateca.

Washington DC – TACA has daily flights.

Here is how to contact the airlines:

Aerocaribe – see Mexicana

Aeroflot, 5a Avenida 13-21, Zona 9
  (☎ 331-4265)

Aerolíneas Argentinas, 10a Calle 3-17,
  Zona 10 (☎ 331-1567)

Aeroméxico – see Mexicana

Aerovías – La Aurora International Airport
  (☎ 332-7470, 361-5703, fax 334-7935)

Air France – Avenida La Reforma 9-00,
  Zona 9, Edificio Plaza Panamericana,
  8th floor (☎ 331-1952, fax 332-0286)

Alitalia – 10a Calle 3-17, Zona 10
  (☎ 331-1276)

American Airlines – Hotel El Dorado,
  7a Avenida 15-45, Zona 9 (☎ 334-7379)

Avianca – Avenida La Reforma 13-89, Local 1,
  Zona 10 (☎ 334-6801/2/9, tel/fax 334-6797)

Aviateca – see TACA

British Airways – 1a Avenida 10-81,
  Zona 10, Edificio Inexsa, 6th floor
  (☎ 332-7402/3/4, fax 332-7401)

Continental Airlines – 12a Calle 1-25, Zona 10,
  Edificio Géminis 10, Torre Norte, 12th
  floor, office 1210 (☎ 335-3341, fax 335-
  3444); La Aurora International Airport
  (☎ 331-2051/2/3/4, fax 331-2055)

COPA (Compañía Panameña de Aviación) –
  1a Avenida 10-17, Zona 10
  (☎ 361-1567/1607, fax 331-8314)

Delta Airlines – 15a Calle 3-20, Zona 10,
  2nd floor (☎ 337-0642/70, fax 337-0588)

El Al – 10a Calle 6-21A, Zona 9,
  3rd floor (☎ 334-3314)

Iberia – Avenida La Reforma 8-60, Zona 9,
  Edificio Galerías Reforma, Local 204
  (☎ 332-0911/1012, fax 334-3715); also,
  La Aurora International Airport
  (☎ 332-5517/8, fax 332-3634)

Japan Air Lines – 7a Avenida 15-45, Zona 9
  (☎ 331-8531/97)

KLM Royal Dutch Airlines – 6a Avenida 20-25,
  Zona 10, Edificio Plaza Marítima
  (☎ 337-0222/3/4/5/6, fax 337-0227)

Korean Air – 6a Avenida 20-25, Zona 10,
  Edificio Plaza Marítima, 5th floor, office 5-5
  (☎ 333-5755/6, fax 337-0109)

LACSA (Líneas Aereas Costariquenses) – see
  TACA

Ladeco – Avenida La Reforma 12-81, Zona 10
  (☎ 331-8564, 334-6238)

Lufthansa German Airlines – Diagonal 6 10-01,
  Zona 10, Centro Gerencial Las Margaritas,
  Torre II, 8th floor
  (☎ 336-5526, fax 339-2995)

LTU International Airways – 6a Avenida 20-25,
  Zona 10 (☎ 337-0107/8, fax 337-0109)

Mayan World – 7a Avenida 6-53, Zona 4,
  Edificio El Triángulo, 2nd floor
  (☎ 334-2070/77)

Mexicana – 13a Calle 8-44, Zona 10 (☎ 333-
  6048); La Aurora International Airport
  (☎ 332-1924, 331-3291)

Nica – see TACA

SAM – see Avianca

TACA – reservations ☎ 334-7722; main office,
  Avenida Hincapie 12-22, Zona 13 (☎ 331-
  8222, fax 334-2775); Centro de Servicio,
  7 Avenida 14-35, Zona 9 (☎ 332-
  2360/4640); Hotel Ritz Continental, 6a
  Avenida A 10-13, Zona 1 (☎ 238-1415,
  238-1479); La Aurora International Airport
  (☎ 361-5784); Plaza Biltmore, 14 Calle 0-
  20, Zona 10 (☎ 331-2520, 337-3462)

Tapsa – La Aurora International Airport
  (☎ 331-4860/9180, fax 334-5572)

Tikal Jets – La Aurora International Airport
  (☎ 334-5631, 334-5568, fax 334-5631)

TWA (Trans World Airlines) – Avenida La
  Reforma 12-81, Zona 10
  (☎ 334-6240, 331-6333)

United Airlines – Avenida La Reforma 1-50,
  Zona 9, Edificio El Reformador, 2nd floor
  (☎ 332-2995, fax 332-3903);
  La Aurora International Airport
  (☎ 332-1994/5, fax 332-2795)

Varig – Avenida La Reforma 9-00, Zona 9,
  Edificio Plaza Panamericana, 8th floor
  (☎ 331-1952, fax 332-0286)

Bus

Guatemala City has no central bus terminal, though many Guatemalans will refer you to the Terminal de Autobuses in Zona 4. Ticket offices and departure points are different for each company. Many are near the huge, chaotic market in Zona 4. If the bus you want is one of these, go to the market and ask until you find it.

The following is route information for most of Guatemala.

Amatitlán – 25 km, 30 minutes, US$0.30; buses depart from 20a Calle & 2a Avenida, Zona 1; every half-hour from 7 am to 7 pm. Also see Puerto San José.

Antigua – 45 km, one hour, US$0.50; Transportes Unidos makes the trip every half-hour from 7 am to 7 pm, stopping in San Lucas Sacatepéquez. 15 Calle 3-65, Zona 1 (☎ 232-4949, 253-6929). Other buses depart more frequently, every 15 minutes from around 4 am to 7 pm, from the corner of 18a Calle and 4a Avenida, Zona 1. Several shuttle minibus companies also offer services; see that section below.

Autosafari Chapin – 88 km, 1½ hours, US$1; Delta y Tropical, 1a Calle & 2a Avenida, Zona 4; buses every 30 minutes via Escuintla.

Biotopo del Quetzal – 160 km, three hours, US$2.20; Escobar y Monja Blanda, 8a Avenida 15-16, Zona 1; hourly buses, 4 am to 5 pm via El Rancho and Purulhá. (Any bus heading for Cobán will stop here.)

Chichicastenango – 146 km, 3½ hours, US$1.70; Veloz Quichelense, Terminal de Buses, Zona 4, runs buses every half-hour from 5 am to 6 pm, stopping in San Lucas, Chimaltenango and Los Encuentros.

Chiquimula – 169 km, three hours, US$3; Rutas Orientales (☎ 253-6714, 251-2160), 19 Calle 8-18, Zona 1, runs buses via El Rancho, Río Hondo and Zacapa to Chiquimula every 30 minutes from 5 am to 6 pm. If you're heading for Copán, Honduras, change buses at Chiquimula to continue to the border. See El Florido.

Cobán – 219 km, four hours; Escobar Monja Blanca (☎ 238-1409), 8a Avenida 15-16, Zona 1, has buses hourly from 4 am to 5 pm, stopping at El Rancho, the Biotopo del Quetzal, Purulhá, Tactic and San Cristóbal.

Copán (Honduras) – see El Florido

El Carmen/Talismán (Mexican border) – 278 km, five to six hours, US$6; Transportes Galgos (☎ 232-3661, 253-4868), 7a Avenida 19-44, Zona 1, runs direct buses along the Pacific Slope road to this border-crossing point, stopping at Escuintla (change for Santa Lucía Cotzumalguapa), Mazatenango, Retalhuleu and Coatepeque, at 5:30 and 10 am, 3 and 4:30 pm. They also operate buses going all the way to Tapachula (Mexico); see Tapachula.

El Florido/Copán (Honduras) – Bus to Chiquimula, where you change buses to continue on to the border at El Florido, a remaining 58 km, 2½-hour trip via Jocotán and Camotán.

Escuintla – 57 km, one hour, US$1.15; see Autosafari Chapin, El Carmen/Talismán, La Democracia, Monterrico, Puerto San José and Tecún Umán.

Esquipulas – 222 km, four hours, US$3.50; Rutas Orientales (☎ 253-7882/6714, 251-2160), 19a Calle 8-18, Zona 1, has buses departing every half-hour from 4 am to 6 pm, with stops at El Rancho, Río Hondo, Zacapa and Chiquimula.

Flores (Petén) – 506 km, 12 hours, US$12; Fuentes del Norte (☎ 238-3894, 251-3817), 17a Calle 8-46, Zona 1, runs buses departing from the capital at 7:30 and 11 am, noon, 1, 3, 5 and 10 pm. Máxima (☎ 232-2495, 238-4032), 9a Avenida 17-28, Zona 1, has buses departing at 6:30 pm and 8 pm. La Petenera (☎ 232-9658), 16a Calle 10-55, Zona 1, operates one luxury bus daily, the Linea Dorada, departing at 7:30 pm and arriving at 7 am (US$22.50). Buses make stops at El Rancho, Teculután, Río Hondo, Los Amates, Quiriguá, Morales, Río Dulce, San Luis and Poptún. Buses usually leave Guatemala City and Santa Elena full; anyone getting on midway stands or rides on the roof.

Huehuetenango – 270 km, five hours, US$4; Los Halcones, 7a Avenida 15-27, Zona 1, runs two buses a day (7 am and 2 pm) up the Interamericana to Huehue, stopping at Chimaltenango, Patzicía, Tecpán, Los Encuentros, San Cristobal and Totonicapán. Buses to La Mesilla also stop here; see La Mesilla.

La Democracia – 92 km, two hours, US$1; Chatia Gomerana, Muelle Central, Terminal de Autobuses, Zona 4, has buses every half-hour from 6 am to 4:30 pm, stopping at Escuintla, Siquinalá (change for Santa Lucía Cotzumalguapa), La Democracia, La Gomera and Sipacate.

La Mesilla/Ciudad Cuauhtémoc (Mexican border) – 380 km, seven hours, US$4.50; Transportes Velásquez, 20a Calle & 2a Avenida, Zona 1, has buses going to La Mesilla, on the Interamericana at the border with Mexico, hourly from 8 am to 4 pm. Stops are at Los Encuentros, Totonicapán and Huehuetenango.

Monterrico – 124 km, 4½ hours, US$1.50; Transportes Cubanita, Muelle Central, Terminal de Buses, Zona 4, has buses departing at 10:30 am, 12:30 and 2:30 pm, stopping at Escuintla, Taxisco and La Avellana.

Panajachel – 147 km, three hours, US$1.70; Transportes Rébuli (☎ 230-2748, 251-3521), 21a Calle 1-34, Zona 1, departs for Lake Atitlán and Panajachel hourly from 6 am to 4 pm, stopping at Chimaltenango, Patzicía, Tecpán Guatemala (for the ruins at Iximché), Los Encuentros and Sololá.

Puerto Barrios – 307 km, five hours, US$6; Transportes Litegua (☎ 232-7578, 253-8169), 15a Calle 10-40, Zona 1, has *especial* (direct) buses at 6:30, 7:30, 10 and 10:30 am, 12:30, 2, 4, 4:30 and 5 pm, with stops at El Rancho, Teculután, Río Hondo, Los Amates and Quiriguá. Regular buses take longer, around six to nine hours.

Puerto San José – 58 km, one hour; Transportes Esmeralda, Trebol, Zona 12, operates buses every 10 minutes from 5 am to 8 pm, stopping at Amatitlán, Palín and Escuintla.

Quetzaltenango – 206 km, four hours, US$4.20; Transportes Alamo (☎ 253-2105), 21a Calle 1-14, Zona 1, has buses at 8 am, 3 and 5:45 pm. Líneas América (☎ 232-1432), 2a Avenida 18-47, Zona 1, has buses departing at 5 and 9 am, noon, 3:15, 4:40 and 7:30 pm. Transportes Galgos (☎ 253-4868, 232-3661), 7a Avenida 19-44, Zona 1, makes this run at 5:30, 8:30 and 11 am, and 2:30, 5 and 7 pm. All of these buses stop at Chimaltenango, Los Encuentros and San Cristobal.

Quiriguá – see Puerto Barrios

Retalhuleu – 186 km, three hours, US$3.65; see El Carmen and Tecún Umán

Río Dulce – 220 km, five hours; see Flores

Río Hondo – see Chiquimula, Esquipulas and Puerto Barrios

San Pedro La Laguna, on Lago de Atitlán – 170 km, three to four hours, US$2.65; Ruta Méndez, 21a Calle & 5a Avenida, Zona 1, operates buses at 10 and 11 am, noon and 1 pm.

San Salvador (El Salvador) – 268 km, five hours; Melva Internacional (☎ 331-0874/6323), 3a Avenida 1-38, Zona 9, runs buses from Guatemala City via Cuilapa, Oratorio and Jalpatagua to the Salvadoran border at Valle Nuevo and onward to San Salvador hourly from 5 am to 4 pm (US$6.65).

Tica Bus (☎ 361-1773, 331-4279), 11a Calle 2-72, Zona 9, has a bus leaving daily at 12:30 pm (US$8.50 one-way, US$17 roundtrip). From San Salvador, buses continue to all the other Central American capitals except Belize City.

Comfort Lines (☎ 361-2516/2493), based at the Hotel Gran Plaza Las Américas, Avenida Las Américas 9-08, Zona 13, has luxury buses departing daily at 8 am and 2 pm (US$15 one-way, US$25 roundtrip). From the same place, King Quality luxury buses depart at 6:30 am and 3:30 pm (US$20 one-way, US$35 roundtrip).

Pulmantur (☎ 332-9797) has one luxury bus daily, departing at 3:15 pm from the Radisson Suites Villa Magna hotel, 1a Avenida 12-43, Zona 10 (US$23 one way, US$45 roundtrip).

Santa Elena – see Flores

Santa Lucía Cotzumalguapa – see El Carmen, La Democracia and Tecún Umán

Tapachula (Mexico) – 295 km, five hours, US$19; Transportes Galgos, (☎ 253-4868, 232-3661), 7a Avenida 19-44, Zona 1, has direct buses from Guatemala City to Tapachula at 7:30 am and 1:30 pm. (From Tapachula they depart for Guatemala City at 9:30 am and 1:30 pm.) These buses cross the border at El Carmen/Talismán and go into Mexico as far as Tapachula, where they connect with Mexican buses.

Tecún Umán/Ciudad Hidalgo (Mexican border) – 253 km, five hours, US$5; Transportes Fortaleza (☎ 230-3390, 220-6372), 19 Calle 8-70, Zona 1, has hourly buses from 1:30 am to 6 pm, stopping at Escuintla (change for Santa Lucía Cotzumalguapa), Mazatenango, Retalhuleu and Coatepeque.

Tikal – see Flores

Shuttle Minibus

Minibus companies capitalize on the difficulty most travelers have navigating the bus system. While their routes are very limited, they do serve the airport and connect Guatemala City and Antigua. See Getting Around, below, for more details.

GUATEMALA

Car

Major international rental companies have offices both at La Aurora International Airport and in the city center (see Rental in Guatemala's Getting Around section). Rental offices in Guatemala City include:

Ahorrent – Boulevard Liberación 4-83, Zona 9 (☎ 332-0544/7515, 361-5661, fax 361-5621); Hotel Cortijo Reforma, Avenida La Reforma 2-18, Zona 9 (☎ 332-0712, ext 180); La Aurora International Airport (☎ 332-6491/2/3/4/5, ext 115)

Avis – 12a Calle 2-73, Zona 9 (☎ 331-2750, fax 332-1263); La Aurora International Airport (☎ 331-0017, 361-5620)

Budget – Avenida La Reforma 15-00, Zona 9 (☎ 331-6546/2788, fax 331-2807); Hotel El Dorado, 7a Avenida 15-45, Zona 9 (☎ 360-9725); La Aurora International Airport (☎ 331-0273, 361-5613)

Dollar – Hotel Ritz Continental, 6a Avenida A 10-13, Zona 1 (☎ 232-3446); La Aurora International Airport (☎ 331-7185)

Guatemala – 19a Calle 16-91, Zona 12, Avenida Petapa (☎ 473-1330/2703, fax 473-1420); La Aurora International Airport (☎ 473-1330)

Hertz – 7a Avenida 14-76, Zona 9 (☎ 331-5374, 332-2242, fax 331-7924); Hotels Camino Real and Princess Reforma; La Aurora International Airport (☎ 331-1711)

National (Interrent-Europcar-Tilden) – 14a Calle 1-42, Zona 10 (☎ 366-4670, 368-0175, fax 337-0221); La Aurora International Airport (☎ 331-8218/8365)

Tabarini – 2a Calle A 7-30, Zona 10 (☎ 331-9814, 334-5907, fax 334-1925); La Aurora International Airport (☎ 331-4755)

Tally – 7a Avenida 14-60, Zona 1 (☎ 232-0421/3327, fax 253-1749); La Aurora International Airport (☎ 332-6063, fax 334-5925)

Thrifty – Avenida La Reforma & 11a Calle, Zona 9 (☎ 332-1130/1220, fax 332-1207); La Aurora International Airport (☎ 332-1306/1230, fax 332-1273)

Tikal – 2a Calle 6-56, Zona 10 (☎ 232-4721, 361-0247)

GETTING AROUND
To/From the Airport

La Aurora International Airport (☎ 334-7680, 331-7241/3, 334-7689) is in Zona 13, the southern part of the city, 10 to 15 minutes from Zona 1 by taxi, half an hour by bus. Car rental offices and taxi ranks are outside, down the stairs from the arrivals level.

For the city bus, go upstairs to the departures level and walk across the airport parking lot to the bus stop. Bus No 83 comes by every 15 minutes, 6 am to 9 pm, costs US$0.15 and will take you through Zonas 9 and 4 to Zona 1. Going from town to the airport, No 83 goes south through Zona 1 on 10a Avenida, through Zona 9 on 6a Avenida, passes by the zoo and the museums on 7a Avenida and stops right in front of the international terminal.

Taxi fares to various points in the center are supposedly set rates but are actually negotiable, though quite high: from the airport to Zona 9 or 10, US$5; to Zona 1, US$7. A tip is expected. Be sure to establish the destination and price before getting into the taxi (see also Taxi, below).

Several companies offer direct shuttle service between the airport and Antigua, with door-to-door service on the Antigua end. They depart from the airport every hour or so, take an hour to reach Antigua and cost around US$10. Coming from Antigua to the airport, competition among the many shuttle services keeps prices a little lower, around US$7.

Bus & Jitney

Guatemala City buses are cheap, frequent and, though often very crowded, useful. They are, however, not always safe. Theft and robbery are not unusual; there have even been incidents of rape. *Preferencial* buses are newer, safer, not as crowded and more expensive at about US$0.20 per ride. Ordinary buses cost US$0.15 per ride.

6a Avenida (southbound) and 7a Avenida (northbound) in Zona 9 are loaded with buses traversing the city; in Zona 1 these buses tend to swing away from the commercial district and travel along 4a, 5a, 9a and 10a Avenidas. The most useful north-south routes are buses No 2, 5 and 14. Note that modified numbers (such as 2A or 5-Bolívar) follow different routes and may not get you where you expect to go. Any bus with 'Terminal' in the front window stops at the Terminal de Autobuses in Zona 4.

City buses stop running at about 9 pm, and *ruteleros* (jitneys) begin to run up and down the main avenues. The jitneys run all night, until the buses resume their rattling rides at 5 am. Hold up your hand as the signal to stop a jitney or bus.

Taxi

Taxis are quite expensive, around US$5 for a normal ride – even a short one – within the city. Be sure to agree on the fare before entering the cab, as most taxis do not have meters.

In Guatemala City you will rarely see taxis cruising. Rather you'll probably have to phone for one. Taxi Amarilla (☎ 332-1515) charges about half the price of most of the other taxi companies, and their taxis are metered.

GUATEMALA

Antigua Guatemala

Population 30,000

Antigua Guatemala (1530 meters) is among the oldest and most beautiful cities in the Americas. Its setting is superb, between three magnificent volcanoes: Agua, Fuego and Acatenango. Fuego (Fire) is easily recognizable by its plume of smoke and – at night – by the red glow it projects against the sky. Experienced Guatemala travelers spend as little time in Guatemala City as possible, preferring to make Antigua their base.

On weekends a long stream of cars and buses brings the citizens of Guatemala City up the serpentine route into the mountains for a day of strolling, shopping and sipping in the former capital. On Sunday evening, traffic jams Antigua's cobbled streets as the day trippers head home.

If you have the opportunity to be in Antigua during Holy Week – especially on Good Friday – seize it, but make your hotel reservations months in advance – this is the busiest week of the year for tourism. Other busy tourist months are July and August; from November to April there's a steady flow; May/June and September/October are much quieter. In winter, Antigua can be cold after sunset, so bring warm clothes; you might even consider bringing a sleeping bag or buying a blanket or two.

Residents of Antigua are known by the nickname *panza verde* (green belly), as they are said to eat lots of avocados, which grow abundantly here.

HISTORY

Antigua was founded on March 10, 1543, as La muy Noble y muy Leal Ciudad de Santiago de los Caballeros de Goathemala, after the capital at what is now called Ciudad Vieja, on the flanks of Volcán Agua, was flooded in 1541 (see Around Antigua Guatemala, later in the chapter). The capital was moved to Antigua's present site in the Valle de Panchoy in 1543 and remained here for 233 years. The capital was transferred again, to present-day Guatemala City, in 1776, after the great earthquake of July 29, 1773, destroyed the city, which had already suffered considerable damage from earlier earthquakes.

After the 1773 earthquake, Antigua was repopulated, very slowly, without losing its traditional character, architecture and cobblestoned streets. In 1799 the city was renamed La Antigua Guatemala (the Old Guatemala). In 1944 the Legislative Assembly declared Antigua a national monument, and in 1979 UNESCO declared it a World Heritage Site.

Most of Antigua's buildings were constructed during the 17th and 18th centuries, when the city was a rich Spanish colonial capital, and it seems no expense was spared in the city's magnificent architecture. Many handsome, sturdy colonial buildings remain, and several impressive ruins have been preserved and are open to the public.

ORIENTATION

Volcán Agua is southeast of the city and visible from most points within it, Volcán Fuego is southwest and Volcán Acatenango is to the west. These three volcanoes (which appear on the city's coat of arms) provide easy reference points.

Antigua's street grid uses a modified version of the Guatemala City numbering system. (For details on that system, see Orientation under Guatemala City.) In Antigua, compass points are added to the avenidas and calles. The central point is the northeast corner of the city's main plaza, the Parque Central. Calles run east-west, so 4a Calle west of the Parque Central is 4a Calle Poniente; avenidas run north-south, so 3a Avenida north of the Parque Central is 3a Avenida Norte. The city is thus divided into quadrants by 4a Avenida and 4a Calle.

The old headquarters of the Spanish colonial government, called the Palacio de los Capitanes, is on the south side of the plaza; you'll know it by its double (two-story) arcade. On the east side is the cathedral, on the north side is the Palacio del Ayuntamiento (Town Hall) and on the west side are banks and shops.

The Arco de Santa Catarina (Arch of St Catharine), spanning 5a Avenida Norte between 1a Calle and 2a Calle, is another famous Antigua landmark.

Intercity buses arrive at the Terminal de Buses, a large open lot just west of the mercado, four blocks west of the Parque Central along 4a Calle Poniente. Buses serving towns and villages in the vicinity leave from the terminal as well, or from other points around the mercado.

INFORMATION
Tourist Offices
Antigua's INGUAT tourist office is next door to the cathedral, on the east side of the Parque Central. (If you don't find it there, check in the Palacio de los Capitanes.) It's open from 8 am to 6 pm, seven days a week. They offer free city maps and plenty of helpful advice. You can pick up a schedule of Semana Santa events here.

Visitors should look for the informative little book *Antigua Guatemala: An illustrated history of the city and its monuments* by Elizabeth Bell and Trevor Long.

Other useful sources of information are the *Revue* monthly magazine, the *Guatemala Weekly* newspaper and the bulletin boards at the Doña Luisa Xicotencatl restaurant, the Rainbow Reading Room & Cafe and the Casa Andinista bookstore, all described below.

Money
Several banks around Parque Central change US dollars cash and travelers' checks. Banco Occidental, on 4a Calle Poniente just off the northwest corner of the plaza, changes both and also gives cash

advances on Visa cards; it's open weekdays from 8:30 am to 7 pm, Saturday 9 am to 2 pm. Banco Industrial, on 5a Avenida Sur next to the Guatel office, just off the plaza, is open weekdays from 8 am to 7 pm, Saturday 8 am to 5 pm, and has an ATM for cash advances on Visa cards 24 hours a day.

Post & Communications
The post office is at 4a Calle Poniente and Alameda de Santa Lucía, west of the Parque Central near the mercado.

The Guatel telephone office is just off the southwest corner of the Parque Central, at the intersection of 5a Calle Poniente and 5a Avenida Sur. It's open every day and offers fax service.

Conexion (☎ 832-3768, fax 832-0082, 832-0602) at 4a Calle Oriente 14, inside La Fuente courtyard, will send and/or receive phone, fax, electronic mail and telex messages for you. Prices for sending are fairly high; receiving is cheap. They're open every day. International telephone and fax services are also available at WC, 1a Calle Poniente 9, opposite La Merced church, and at Maya Communications in the Hotel Villa San Francisco, 1a Avenida Sur 15.

Travel Agencies
Everywhere you turn in Antigua, you'll see travel agencies offering tours to places in Guatemala, international flights, shuttle buses to the airport and to the most popular tourist destinations, and more. Reputable agencies include the following:

Adventure Travel Center, 5a Avenida Norte No 25-B, near the arch (☎ /fax 832-0162, viareal@guate.net)

Agencia de Viajes Tivoli, upstairs over the Un Poco de Todo bookshop on the west side of Parque Central (☎ /fax 832-3041, 832-0892)

Servicios Turísticos Atitlán, 6a Avenida Sur No 7 (☎ 832-0648, or 832-3311 after 8 pm)

TURANSA, 9a Calle and Salida a Ciudad Vieja, in the Hotel Radisson Villa Antigua (☎ /fax 832-2928); 5a Calle Poniente No 11-B (☎ /fax 832-3316)

GUATEMALA

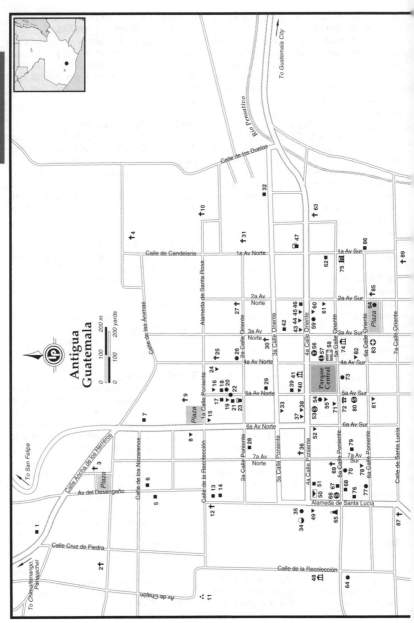

Antigua
Guatemala

0   100   200 m
0   100   200 yards

To San Felipe

To Chimaltenango,
Panajachel

To Guatemala City

Río Pensativo

Calle de los Duelos

Calle de Candelaria

1a Av Norte

1a Av Sur

1a Av Sur

Alameda de Santa Rosa

Calle de las Ánimas

2a Av
Norte

2a Av Sur

2a Calle Oriente

3a Av
Norte

3a Calle Oriente

3a Av Oriente

3a Av Sur

4a Calle Oriente

Parque
Central

4a Av Sur

5a Calle Oriente

5a Av Norte

5a Av Sur

6a Av Norte

6a Av Sur

6a Calle Oriente

7a Calle Oriente

1a Calle Poniente

Plaza

2a Calle
Norte

3a Calle Poniente

Calle de la Recolección

4a Calle Poniente

5a Calle Poniente

6a Calle Poniente

7a Calle
Norte

7a Av
Sur

Alameda de Santa Lucía

Calle de Santa Lucía

Calle Ancha de los Herreros

Av del Desengaño

Calle de los Nazarenos

Calle Cruz de Piedra

Av de Chajón

Plaza

Plaza

Plaza

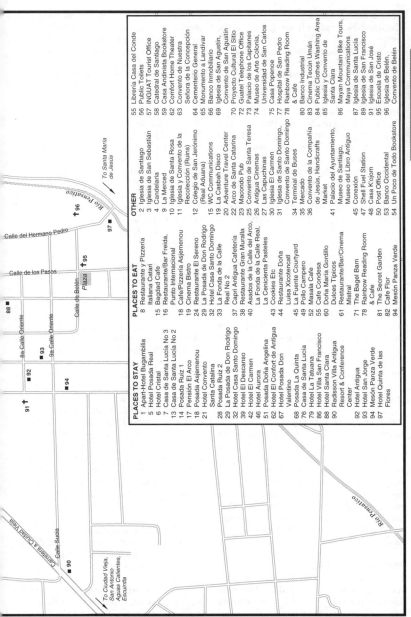

GUATEMALA

PLACES TO STAY
1 Apart-Hotel Bugambilia
5 Hotel Posada Real
6 Hotel Cristal
7 Casa de Santa Lucia No 3
13 Casa de Santa Lucia No 2
14 Posada Ruiz 1
17 Pensión El Arco
18 Posada Asjemenou
21 Hotel Convento
   Santa Catalina
28 Posada Ruiz 2
29 La Posada de Don Rodrigo
32 Hotel Casa Santo Domingo
39 Hotel El Descanso
42 Hotel El Carmen
46 Hotel Aurora
51 Posada Doña Angelina
62 Hotel El Confort de Antigua
67 Hotel Posada Don
   Valentino
68 Posada La Quinta
76 Casa de Santa Lucia
79 Hotel La Tatuana
86 Hotel Villa San Francisco
88 Hotel Santa Clara
90 Radisson Villa Antigua
   Resort & Conference
   Center
92 Hotel Antigua
93 Hotel San Jorge
94 Mesón Panza Verde
97 Hotel Quinta de las
   Flores

PLACES TO EAT
8 Restaurante y Pizzeria
   Italiana Catari
15 Bagdad Cafe
16 Restaurante/Bar Freida,
   Punto Internacional
18 Cafe/Pizzeria Asjemenou
19 Cinema Bistro
24 Restaurante El Sereno
29 La Posada de Don Rodrigo
32 Hotel Casa Santo Domingo
33 La Fonda de la Calle
   Real No 2
37 Capri Antigua Cafeteria
38 Restaurante Gran Muralla
40 Asados de la Calle del Arco,
   La Fonda de la Calle Real,
   La Cenicienta Pasteles
43 Cookies Etc
44 Restaurante Doña
   Luisa Xicotencatl
45 La Fuente Courtyard
49 Pollo Campero
52 Masala Cafe
55 Cafe Condesa
60 Doña Maria Gordillo
   Dulces Tipicos
61 Restaurante/Bar/Cinema
   Mistral
71 The Bagel Barn
78 Rainbow Reading Room
   & Cafe
81 The Secret Garden
82 Cafe Flor
94 Mesón Panza Verde

OTHER
2 Iglesia de Santiago
3 Iglesia de San Sebastián
4 Candelaria
9 La Merced
10 Iglesia de Santa Rosa
11 Iglesia y Convento de la
   Recolección (Ruins)
12 Colegio de San Jerónimo
   (Real Aduana)
15 WC Communications
19 La Casbah Disco
20 Adventure Travel Center
22 Arco de Santa Catarina
23 Macondo Pub
25 Convento de Santa Teresa
26 Antigua Cinemas
27 Las Capuchinas
30 Iglesia El Carmen
31 Iglesia de Santo Domingo,
   Convento de Santo Domingo
34 Terminal de Buses
35 Mercado
36 Convento de la Compañía
   de Jesus, Handicrafts
   Market
41 Palacio del Ayuntamiento,
   Museo de Santiago,
   Museo del Libro Antiguo
45 Conexion
47 Shell Fuel Station
48 Casa K'ojom
50 Post Office
53 Banco Occidental
54 Un Poco de Todo Bookstore
55 Libreria Casa del Conde
56 Public Toilets
57 INGUAT Tourist Office
58 Catedral de Santiago
59 Casa Andinista Bookstore
62 Comfort Home Theater
63 Convento de Nuestra
   Señora de la Concepción
64 Cementerio General
65 Monumento a Landivar
66 Banco Inmobiliario
69 Iglesia de San Agustín,
   Convento de San Agustín
70 Proyecto Cultural El Sitio
72 Guatel Telephone Office
73 Palacio de los Capitanes
74 Museo de Arte Colonia,
   Universidad de San Carlos
75 Casa Popenoe
77 Hospital de San Pedro
78 Rainbow Reading Room
   & Cafe
80 Banco Industrial
83 Cinema Tecún Umán
84 Public Clothes Washing Area
85 Iglesia y Convento de
   Santa Clara
86 Mayan Mountain Bike Tours,
   Maya Communications
87 Iglesia de Santa Lucia
89 Iglesia de San Francisco
91 Iglesia de San José
95 Escuela de Cristo
96 Iglesia de Belén,
   Convento de Belén

Bookstores & Library

The Rainbow Reading Room & Cafe, at the corner of 7a Avenida Sur and 6a Calle Poniente, has thousands of used books in English and Spanish for sale, rent or trade. Un Poco de Todo and the Librería Casa del Conde, both on the west side of Parque Central, and the Casa Andinista at 4a Calle Oriente No 5, opposite the Doña Luisa Xicotencatl restaurant, are other excellent bookstores. All carry both new and used books in several languages, and all are open every day.

La Biblioteca Internacional de Antigua (The International Library of Antigua), 5a Calle Poniente 15 in the Proyecto Cultural El Sitio building, has a good collection of books, with temporary or long-term memberships available.

Laundry

Laundries are everywhere. They all seem to charge the same price – US$1.65 for wash, dry and fold of seven pieces of laundry.

Medical Services

Hospital de San Pedro (☎ 832-0301) is at 3a Avenida Sur and 6a Calle Oriente.

Toilets

Public toilets are on 4a Calle Oriente near the corner of 4a Avenida Norte, near the northeast corner of Parque Central.

Dangers & Annoyances

Antigua seems like such a tranquil town that you wouldn't think any misfortune could ever befall you. Not so. Though you probably will never have a problem, be wary of walking the deserted streets late at night, as robberies have been known to take place. Armed robberies (and even murder) have also occurred on Cerro de la Cruz and on Volcán Pacaya (see Around Antigua Guatemala, below).

PARQUE CENTRAL

This plaza is the gathering place for citizens and foreign visitors alike. On most days the periphery is lined with villagers who have brought their handicrafts to sell

to tourists; on Sunday it's mobbed with marketers, and the streets on the east and west sides of the park are closed to traffic in order to give them room. The best prices are to be had late on Sunday afternoon, when the mercado is winding down.

The plaza's famous fountain was built in 1738.

Palacio de los Capitanes

Built in 1543, the Palacio de los Capitanes has a stately double arcade on its facade, which marches proudly across the southern extent of the park. The facade is original, but most of the rest of the building was reconstructed a century ago. From 1543 to 1773, this building was the governmental center of all Central America, in command of Chiapas, Guatemala, Honduras and Nicaragua.

Catedral de Santiago

The Catedral de Santiago, on the east side of the park, was founded in 1542, damaged by earthquakes many times, badly ruined in 1773, and only partially rebuilt between 1780 and 1820. In the 16th and early 17th centuries, Antigua's churches had lavish baroque interiors, but most lost this richness when they were rebuilt after the earthquakes. The present cathedral, stripped of its expensive decoration, occupies what was the narthex of the original edifice. In a crypt lie the bones of Bernal Díaz del Castillo, historian of the Spanish conquest, who died in 1581. Restoration work is being carried out on other parts of the cathedral, but it will never regain its former grandeur. If the front entrance is not open, you can enter from other entrances in the rear of the building and on the south side.

Palacio del Ayuntamiento

On the north side of the park stands the Palacio del Ayuntamiento, Antigua's town hall, which dates mostly from 1743. In addition to town offices, it houses the **Museo de Santiago**, which exhibits a collection of colonial furnishings, artifacts and weapons. Hours are 9 am to 4 pm Tuesday

Top: 'Mayan Relics' shop, Panajachel, Guatemala (TB)
Bottom: Chichicastenango, Guatemala (PW)

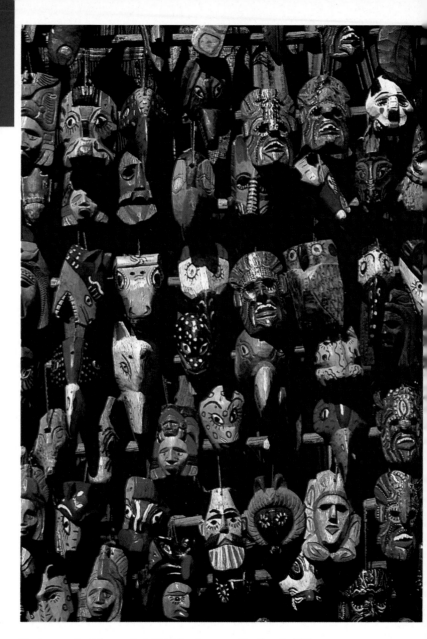

Masks on sale at the market, Chichicastenango, Guatemala (TB)

to Friday, and 9 am to noon and 2 to 4 pm on Saturday and Sunday (closed Monday); admission costs US$0.05.

Next door (and with the same hours) is the **Museo del Libro Antiguo** (Old Book Museum), which has exhibits of colonial printing and binding, and the colonial prison.

Universidad de San Carlos

The Universidad de San Carlos was founded in 1676; its main building (built in 1763), 5a Calle Oriente No 5 half a block east of the park, now houses the **Museo de Arte Colonial** (same hours as the Museo de Santiago).

CASA K'OJOM

In 1984, Samuel Franco Arce began photographing Maya ceremonies and festivals, and recording their music on audio tape. By 1987 he had enough to found Casa K'ojom ('House of Music'), a museum of Mayan music and the ceremonies in which it was used.

Some visitors to Guatemalan towns and villages are lucky enough to witness a parade of the *cofradías*, or some other age-old ceremony. But lucky or not, you can experience some of the fascination of the culture in a visit to Casa K'ojom. Besides the fine collection of photographs, Franco has amassed musical instruments, tools, masks and figures. These have been arranged to show scenes of traditional Maya life; recordings of the music play softly in the background. Be sure to see the exhibit featuring Maximón, the evil folk-god venerated by the people of several highland towns.

The museum is at Calle de Recoletos 55, a block west of the bus station. It's open Monday to Friday from 9:30 am to 12:30 pm and 2 to 5 pm (till 4 pm on Saturday), and is closed on Sunday. Admission costs US$0.85, including an audiovisual show.

CHURCHES

Once glorious in their gilded baroque finery, Antigua's churches have suffered indignities from both nature and humankind. Rebuilding after earthquakes

gave the churches thicker walls, lower towers and belfries and unembellished interiors, and moving the capital to Guatemala City deprived Antigua of the population needed to maintain the churches in their traditional richness. Still, they are impressive. Most are open daily 9 am to 5 pm; entrance costs under US$2. In addition to those churches noted below, you'll find many others scattered around town.

La Merced

From the park, walk three long blocks up 5a Avenida Norte, passing beneath the Arco de Santa Catarina, built in 1694 and rebuilt in the 19th century. At the northern end of 5a Avenida is the Iglesia y Convento de Nuestra Señora de La Merced, known simply as La Merced – Antigua's most striking colonial church.

La Merced's construction began in 1548. Improvements continued to be made until 1717, when the church was ruined by earthquakes. Reconstruction was completed in 1767, but in 1773 earthquake struck again and the convent was destroyed. Repairs to the church were made from 1850 to 1855; its baroque facade dates from this period. Inside the ruins of the convent is a fountain said to be the largest in Central America; entering the convent costs US$0.05 and is well worth it.

San Francisco

The next most notable church is the Iglesia de San Francisco, 7a Calle Oriente and 1a Avenida Sur. It dates from the mid-16th century, but little of the original building remains. Rebuilding and restoration over the centuries has produced a handsome structure; reinforced concrete added in 1961 protected the church from serious damage in the 1976 earthquake. All that remains of the original church is the Chapel of Hermano Pedro, resting place of Hermano Pedro de San José Betancourt, a Franciscan monk who founded a hospital for the poor and earned the gratitude of generations. He died here in 1667; his intercession is still sought by the ill, who pray fervently by his casket.

Las Capuchinas

The Iglesia y Convento de Nuestra Señora del Pilar de Zaragoza, usually called simply Las Capuchinas, 2a Avenida Norte and 2a Calle Oriente, was a convent founded in 1736 by nuns from Madrid. Destroyed repeatedly by earthquakes, it is now a museum, with exhibits of the religious life in colonial times. The building has many unusual features, including a circular building of 18 concentric nuns' cells around a circular patio. Guided tours are available.

La Recolección

The Iglesia y Convento de la Recolección, a massive ruin at the west end of 1a Calle Poniente, is among Antigua's most impressive monuments. Built between 1701 and 1708, the church was inaugurated in 1717, but suffered considerable damage from earthquake in that same year. The buildings were destroyed in the earthquake of 1773.

Colegio de San Jerónimo (Real Aduana)

Near La Recolección, at the corner of Alameda de Santa Lucía and 1a Calle Poniente, this church was built in 1757 by friars of the Merced order. However, because it did not have royal authorization, it was taken over by Spain's Carlos III in 1761. In 1765 it was designated for use as the Real Aduana (Royal Customs House) but was destroyed in the earthquake of 1773. The construction includes the hermitage of San Jerónimo. Guided tours are available for around US$8.

Santa Clara

The Iglesia y Convento de Santa Clara, 2a Avenida Sur 27, at the corner of 6a Calle Oriente, was built in 1715 and destroyed by earthquake two years later. The present construction was inaugurated in 1734 but was destroyed by the earthquake of 1773. The dome of the church, which survived the 1773 quake, was destroyed by another in 1874.

In front of the church is a public washing area, where Indian women still come today to do their wash, spreading their laundry out on the lawn to dry.

CASA POPENOE

At the corner of 5a Calle Oriente and 1a Avenida Sur stands this beautiful mansion built in 1636 by Don Luis de las Infantas Mendoza y Venegas. Ruined by the earthquake of 1773, the house stood desolate for $1\frac{1}{2}$ centuries until it was bought in 1931 by Dr and Mrs Popenoe. The Popenoes' painstaking and authentic restoration yields a fascinating glimpse of how the family of a royal official (Don Luis) lived in Antigua in the 17th century. The house is open Monday to Saturday from 2 to 4 pm; the guided tour costs US$0.85.

MONUMENT TO LANDÍVAR

At the western end of 5a Calle Poniente is the Monumento a Landívar, a structure of five colonial-style arches set in a little park. Rafael Landívar, an 18th-century Jesuit priest and poet, lived and wrote in Antigua for some time. Landívar's poetry is esteemed as the best of the colonial period, even though much of it was written in Italy after the Jesuits were expelled from Guatemala. Landívar's Antigua house was nearby on 5a Calle Poniente.

MARKET

At the west end of 4a Calle Oriente, on the west side of Alameda de Santa Lucía, sprawls the mercado – chaotic, colorful and always busy. Morning, when all the village people from the vicinity are actively buying and selling, is the best time to come. (See also Things to Buy, below.)

CEMETERY

Take the opportunity to stroll through Antigua's large Cementerio General, west of the market and bus terminal. Hints of ancient Mayan beliefs are revealed in the lavishly decorated tombs, many of which also have homey touches, including fresh flowers and other evidence of frequent visits.

ACTIVITIES
Horseback Riding

Several stables in Antigua rent horses and arrange for day or overnight tours into the countryside. Establo Santiago has been recommended; contact them through the Adventure Travel Center (see Travel Agencies, above).

Several readers have recommended the Ravenscroft Riding Stables, at 2a Avenida Sur No 3, San Juan del Obispo, 3.2 km south of Antigua, on the road to Santa María de Jesús (buses leave every half-hour from the bus station behind the mercado). They do English-style riding, with scenic rides of three, four or five hours in the valleys and hills around Antigua. Reservations and information are available through the Hotel San Jorge (☎ 832-3132), 4a Avenida Sur No 13.

R Rolando Pérez (☎ 832-2809), San Pedro El Panorama No 28, also offers horseback riding.

Bicycling

Bicycles can be rented at several places in Antigua, including:

Alquiler de Bicicletas San Vicente, 6a Avenida Sur No 6 (☎ /fax 832-3311)

Aviatur, 5a Avenida Norte No 27, just north of the arch (☎ /fax 832-2642)

Servicios Turísticos San Vicente, 6a Calle Poniente No 28 (☎ /fax 832-3311)

Prices are around US$1.35 an hour, US$4.15 a half-day, US$6 to US$8.35 a day, US$25 a week or US$35 for two weeks. Prices vary, so it pays to shop around.

Mayan Mountain Bike Tours (☎ 832-3383), 1a Avenida Sur No 15, offers a variety of mountain bike tours of different levels around the area. Tours usually last around four or five hours and cost around US$19, including all gear. They also do hike/bike tours to volcanoes Agua (10 hours, US$25) and Acatenango (12 hours, US$39). They also rent bicycles, and can arrange longer tours for up to 15 days.

White-Water Rafting

Area Verde Expeditions (☎ /fax 832-3863, in the USA ☎ /fax (719) 539-7102), 4a Avenida Sur No 8, offers a variety of white-water rafting tours lasting from one to five days. Different rivers are rafted at different times of year, making it possible to raft all year round.

COURSES

Antigua is famous for its Spanish language schools, which attract students from around the world. There are many schools from which to choose – around 70 at last count.

Price, quality of teaching and satisfaction of students varies greatly from one school to another. Often the quality of the instruction depends upon the particular instructor, and thus may vary even within a single school. Visit several schools before you choose one. If possible, ask for references and talk to someone who has studied at your chosen school recently – you'll have no trouble running into lots of Spanish students in Antigua. The INGUAT tourist office also has a list of reputable schools. They include:

Academia de Español Sevilla, 1a Avenida Sur No 8 (☎ /fax 832-0442)

Academia de Español Tecún Umán, 6a Calle Poniente No 34 (☎ /fax 832-2792)

AmeriSpan Guatemala, 6a Avenida Norte No 40 (☎ /fax 832-0164); in the USA, AmeriSpan USA, PO Box 40513, Philadelphia PA, 19106 (☎ (215) 985-4522, fax 985-4524, (800) 879-6640)

Centro de Español Don Pedro de Alvarado, 1a Calle Poniente No 24 (☎ /fax 832-4180)

Centro Lingüístico Maya, 5a Calle Poniente No 20 (☎ 832-0656)

Christian Spanish Academy (CSA), 6a Avenida Norte No 15 (☎ 832-3922, fax 832-3760)

Don Quijote Spanish Academy, Portal del Ayuntamiento No 6, in the Museo del Libro Antiguo, on the north side of Parque Central (☎ 832-2868)

Escuela de Español San José el Viejo, 5a Avenida Sur No 34 (☎ 832-3028, fax 832-3029)

Proyecto Lingüístico Francisco Marroquín, 4a Avenida Sur No 4 (☎ /fax 832-0406)

Classes start every Monday at most schools, though you can usually be placed with a teacher any day of the week. Cost for four hours of classes daily, five days a week, ranges from around US$45 to US$95 per week, usually for one-to-one instruction; you can also sign up for up to seven hours a day of instruction. Most schools offer to arrange room and board with local families for around US$40 to US$60 per week, giving you the chance for total immersion in the language.

Some students have reported that the main difficulty with studying Spanish in Antigua is the number of foreigners in town, making it a temptation to socialize in your native language rather than sticking to Spanish!

ORGANIZED TOURS

Elizabeth Bell, author of books on Antigua, offers cultural tours of the town (in English and/or Spanish) on Mondays, Tuesdays, Wednesdays, Fridays and Saturdays. The walking tours take two hours and cost US$12. Information is available at the Adventure Travel Center (see Travel Agencies under Information, earlier), where her books are also sold. (See Entertainment, below, for information on her weekly slide shows.)

A variety of tours take you further afield. The Adventure Travel Center offers an interesting three-hour Villages & Farm Tour for US$25.

Numerous travel agencies offer tours to many places further afield, including Tikal, Copán-Quiriguá-Río Dulce, Monterrico, Chichicastenango and Panajachel.

SPECIAL EVENTS
Semana Santa

By far the most interesting time to be in Antigua is during the Semana Santa (Holy Week) celebrations, when hundreds of people dress in deep purple robes to accompany daily religious processions in remembrance of the Crucifixion. Streets are covered in breathtakingly elaborate and colorful *alfombras* (carpets) of colored sawdust and flower petals. These beautiful but fragile works of art are destroyed as the processions shuffle through them, but are recreated the next morning for another day.

Traditionally, the most interesting days are Palm Sunday, when a procession departs from La Merced (see Churches, above) in mid-afternoon; Holy Thursday, when a late afternoon procession departs from the Iglesia de San Francisco; and Good Friday, when an early morning procession departs from La Merced, and a late afternoon one from the Escuela de Cristo. Have ironclad hotel reservations well in advance of these dates, or plan to stay in another town or in Guatemala City and commute to the festivities.

The booklet *Lent and Easter Week in Antigua* by Elizabeth Bell gives explanations and a day-by-day schedule of processions, *velaciones* (vigils) and other events taking place throughout the Lenten season, the 40 days before Easter.

Warning On a secular note, beware of pickpockets. It seems that Guatemala City's entire population of pickpockets (numbering perhaps in the hundreds) decamps to Antigua for Semana Santa. In the press of the emotion-filled crowds lining the processional routes, they target foreign tourists especially.

PLACES TO STAY
Places to Stay – budget

When checking a pension or small hotel, look at several rooms, as some are much better than others.

Posada Ruiz 2, 2a Calle Poniente 25, is a good deal for the price, with small singles/doubles for US$2.85/5, all with shared bath, opening onto a central courtyard. Lots of young international travelers stay here, congregating in the courtyard in the evening.

Pensión El Arco (☎ 832-2701), 5a Avenida Norte 32, just north of the Santa Catarina arch, is clean, friendly and small, and the smiling señora makes you feel safe and welcome. Singles/doubles are US$4/6 with shared bath, US$10 with private bath. The only drawback is the Disco El Casbah, two doors away, which is incredibly loud on Friday and Saturday nights.

Not as attractive, but acceptable for the price, *Posada La Quinta*, 5a Calle Poniente 19 near the bus station, is a basic place with rooms for US$8.35/10 with shared/private bath. The *Posada Doña Angelina*, nearby at 4a Calle Poniente 33, has singles/doubles for US$4/7 with shared bath, US$9/14 with private bath.

The *Hotel Cristal* (☎ 832-4177), Avenida El Desengaño 25, is great for the price, with 10 clean rooms around a beautiful central garden. Singles/doubles are US$6/8.35 with shared bath, US$8.35/12.50 with private bath. Discounts are given for students, and for stays of five days or more. Meals are available.

Hotel Villa San Francisco (☎ 832-3383), 1a Avenida Sur No 15 at the corner of 6a Calle Oriente, is simple but pleasant. Singles/doubles are US$7/9.50 with shared bath, US$10/12.50 with private bath. An upstairs terrace, a courtyard garden, a telephone and fax service, and bicycle rental are all here.

Casa de Santa Lucía, Alameda de Santa Lucía No 9, between 5a and 6a Calles Poniente, has dark rooms with pseudo-colonial atmosphere for US$10/12 a single/double with private bath; ring the bell to the left of the door. There's parking.

More attractive are the two newer establishments operated by the same people. They are the *Casa de Santa Lucía No 2*, Alameda de Santa Lucía Norte 21, and *Casa de Santa Lucía No 3*, 6a Avenida Norte 43-A, near La Merced church. Both have clean, pleasant, attractive rooms with ample windows and private hot bath for US$10/12 a night, rooftop terraces with views of Antigua, and parking. Neither place has a sign.

Hotel La Tatuana (☎ 832-0537), 7a Avenida Sur No 3, has good, clean rooms with private bath for US$10/17 for singles/doubles.

A step up in quality, *Hotel Posada Don Valentino* (☎ 832-0384), 5a Calle Poniente No 28, has a nice patio and garden, with bright and clean rooms for US$10/15 a single/double with shared bath, US$12/20 with private bath. They have a parking lot one block away.

Hotel El Confort de Antigua (☎ 832-0566), 1a Avenida Norte No 2, is clean and beautifully kept. The five rooms share two baths, and cost US$15/20/25 a single/double/triple, including continental breakfast.

Posada Asjemenou (☎ 832-2670), 5a Avenida Norte No 31, just north of the arch, is a beautifully renovated house built around a grassy courtyard with a fountain. Its prices of US$13/19/26 for single/double/triple rooms with shared bath, US$19/25/29 with private bath, make it the best value for money in town. The Cafe/Pizzería Asjemenou is also here, and there's a pay parking lot nearby.

Apart-Hotel Bugambilia (☎ 832-2732, 832-7767), Calle Ancha de los Herreros 27, has 10 apartments, each with fully equipped kitchen, two or three double beds, cable TV and private hot bath. Daily rates are US$20 (US$24 with three beds, US$120 per week, or US$420 per month). It has sitting areas, a beautiful patio garden, a fountain and a rooftop terrace.

Places to Stay – middle

Antigua's mid-range hotels allow you to wallow in the city's colonial charms for a very moderate outlay of cash.

Hotel El Descanso (☎ 832-0142), 5a Avenida Norte 9, '50 steps from the central parque' in the building facing the restaurant called Café Café, is clean and convenient. Its five rooms are US$20/24/30/40 for one to four people with shared bath, or US$20/24 for singles/doubles with private bath. There's a private upstairs terrace in the rear.

Hotel Santa Clara (☎ 832-0342), 2a Avenida Sur No 20, is quiet, proper and clean, with a pleasant garden and some large rooms with two double beds. Singles/doubles with bath are US$21/25, less in low season.

Hotel Posada Real (☎ 832-3396), Avenida El Desengaño 24, is a beautiful colonial homey hotel new in 1996. Its 10 rooms and suites, all with private bath, are lovely, and many have fireplaces. Singles/doubles/triples are US$25/35/42.

Hotel San Jorge (☎ /fax 832-3132), 4a Avenida Sur No 13, is in a modern building where all 14 rooms have fireplace, cable TV and private bath with tub. Parking and laundry are also here, and the guests (mostly older couples from the USA) may use the swimming pool and room service facilities of the posh Hotel Antigua nearby. Rooms are US$30/35/40 a single/double/ triple, with possible discounts in low season. Credit cards are accepted.

Hotel Convento Santa Catalina (☎ 832-3080, fax 832-3079), 5a Avenida Norte No 28, just south of the arch, is a nicely reno-vated convent around a courtyard. Large singles/doubles with bath are reasonably priced at US$25/30 most of the year, US$35/45 from November to April.

Hotel El Carmen (☎ 832-3850, fax 832-3847), 3a Avenida Norte No 9, is very tidy and quiet despite its location only 1½ blocks from the square. Twelve pleasant rooms with cable TV, telephone, private bath and continental breakfast are US$35/40/45/50 for one to four beds, and there's a courtyard sitting area, a Jacuzzi and a rooftop terrace with a fine view.

The beautiful *Hotel Aurora* (☎ 832-0217), 4a Calle Oriente 16, has a grassy courtyard graced by a fountain and many flowers. Its 17 old-fashioned rooms with bath are US$38/46/51 for singles/doubles/ triples, including continental breakfast. There's a private car park.

Mesón Panza Verde (☎ /fax 832-2925), 5a Avenida Sur No 19, four blocks south of the park, is an elegant American-owned guesthouse and restaurant with comfy, quiet rooms, each with its own private garden, for US$48, and suites with fire-place for US$84. The restaurant here is one of the best in Antigua.

Places to Stay – top end

The *Hotel Quinta de las Flores* (☎ 832-3721, fax 832-3726), Calle del Hermano Pedro No 6, is a very special place. The spacious grounds have beautiful gardens and fountains, a children's play area, swim-ming pool, sitting areas and a restaurant. The eight large, luxurious rooms, most with fireplace, are US$54/66 for singles/ doubles. Five houses, each with two bed-rooms, two stories, a kitchen and living room, are US$102 for five people. Consid-

erable discounts are offered if you stay by the week.

Hotel Casa Santo Domingo (☎ 832-0140, 832-2628, fax 832-0102), 3a Calle Oriente No 28, is a wonderful luxury hotel set in the partially restored convent of Santo Domingo (1642), which takes up an entire city block. Rooms are of an international five-star stan-dard, but the public spaces are wonderfully colonial and include a swimming pool. The Dominican friars never had it so good. Rates are US$97/105/118/126 a single/double/ triple/suite, tax included. Two cheaper rooms are US$54/66.

Hotel Antigua (☎ 832-0331, 832-0288, fax 832-0807, in the USA (800) 223-6764), 8a Calle Poniente No 1, is a large Spanish colonial country club. The 60 rooms have private baths and fireplaces, and many have two double beds. Rates are US$120/132/144 a single/double/triple, tax included.

The five-star *Radisson Villa Antigua Resort & Conference Center* (☎ 832-0011, fax 832-0237, in the USA (800) 333-3333), 9a Calle Poniente and Carretera a Ciudad Vieja, is the largest and most modern hotel in town, with 139 rooms and 45 suites. Rooms have balconies, fireplaces, modern baths, and the complex has every amenity. Singles/ doubles are US$144/159, tax included.

La Posada de Don Rodrigo (☎ 832-0291, 832-0387), 5a Avenida Norte 17, is a maze of rooms and restaurants around colonial courtyards. The restaurant/bar is the scene of free marimba concerts each afternoon and evening. Some of the 35 rooms are charming, if old-fashioned; others are just drab. A few have fireplaces. Rooms with bath are US$72/82/91 a single/double/ triple, which is too much for what you get. The hotel's restaurants and public areas are much better than its rooms.

PLACES TO EAT
Places to Eat – budget

Eating cheaply is easy, even in touristy Antigua.

Probably the cheapest food in town is the good, clean, tasty food served from stands set up under the arches on the west side of the Parque Central every day from around

11:30 am to 7:30 pm. You can also eat cheaply and well at the mercado.

Capri Antigua Cafetería, 4a Calle Poniente 24, near the corner of 6a Avenida Norte, is a simple, modern place that's very popular with younger diners and budget travelers. They usually fill its little wooden benches and tables, ordering soup for US$0.70, sandwiches for US$1.35 to US$2.65, or *platos fuertes* (substantial platters of meat or chicken served with salad and fries) for US$1.65 to US$3. Nearby, *Restaurante Gran Muralla*, 4a Calle Poniente 18, is a simple, inexpensive place serving a Guatemalan highland version of Chinese food.

Antigua's best known restaurant is probably the *Restaurant Doña Luisa Xicotencatl*, 4a Calle Oriente No 12, 1½ blocks east of Parque Central. A small central courtyard is set with dining tables, with more dining rooms on the upper level. The menu lists a dozen sandwiches made with bread baked on the premises, as well as yogurt, chili, burgers, stuffed potatoes, cakes and pies, all priced under US$4. Alcohol is served, as is excellent Antigua coffee. The restaurant is open every day, 7 am to 9:30 pm, and it is usually busy. The bakery here sells many kinds of breads, including whole grain.

Rainbow Reading Room & Cafe, 7a Avenida Sur and 6a Calle Poniente, is a lending library, bookstore, travelers' club and restaurant all in one. Healthy vegetarian dishes are a specialty, as is close camaraderie. The cafe is open every day from 9 am to 11 pm.

Cafe Condesa, in an opulent courtyard on the west side of the plaza (walk through the Librería Case del Conde book shop to the courtyard in the rear) is a beautiful restaurant in the patio of an opulent Spanish mansion built in 1549. On the menu are excellent breakfasts, coffee, light meals and snacks. The Sunday buffet from 10 am to 2 pm, a lavish spread for US$6, is an Antigua institution. It's open every day.

La Fuente, 4a Calle Oriente No 14, is another beautiful restaurant, in the courtyard of a beautiful old Spanish home. It has lots of vegetarian selections, good coffee

and desserts. It's open every day, 7 am to 7 pm. The *Bagdad Cafe*, 1a Calle Poniente No 9, opposite La Merced church at the corner of 6a Avenida Norte, is a smaller, simpler, inexpensive patio restaurant.

A rich concentration of restaurants is on 5a Avenida Norte, north of Parque Central. *Asados de la Calle del Arco*, just off the Parque Central on the right, has a simple but beautiful atmosphere, with candlelight in the evening and tables both inside and in the rear patio. It serves grilled meats and Tex-Mex food, though portions are small. It's open every day, 7 am to 10 pm.

La Fonda de la Calle Real, 5a Avenida Norte No 5, appears to have no room for diners, but that's because all the tables are upstairs. The menu is good and varied. The house specialty is *caldo real*, a hearty chicken soup that for US$3.50 makes a good lunch. Grilled chicken and meats, *queso fundido* (melted cheese), *chiles rellenos* (stuffed peppers) and nachos are priced from US$3 to US$8. It's open every day, 7 am to 10 pm. Around the corner at 3a Calle Poniente No 7, *La Fonda de la Calle Real No 2* has the same menu and is open every day from noon to 10 pm.

La Cenicienta Pasteles, next door at 5a Avenida Norte 7, serves mostly cakes, pastries, pies and coffee, but the blackboard menu often features quiche Lorraine and quiche chapín (Guatemalan-style), yogurt and fruit as well. A slice of something and a hot beverage cost less than US$2. It's open every day. *Cookies Etc*, 3a Avenida Norte at the corner of 4a Calle Oriente, is another good place for a sweet; it's open every day. *The Bagel Barn*, on 5a Calle Poniente just off the Parque Central, is popular for bagels, soups, candies and coffee.

Also on 5a Avenida Norte, at No 29 near the arch, *Restaurante/Bar Freida* serves good Mexican and is a popular gathering spot in the evening, sometimes with live music. Nearby at No 35, the *Punto Internacional* has been recommended by readers.

Cafe Flor, 4a Avenida Sur No 1, serves huge portions of delicious food including Thai, Indonesian, Chinese and Indian dishes, each for around US$5, which can easily feed two people. They also offer take-out. It's open Tuesday to Saturday, noon to 2:30 pm and 6 to 9 pm. The *Masala Cafe*, 6a Calle Norte 14, near the corner of 4a Calle Poniente, has been recommended by readers for its Thai and Japanese food. It's open every day except Wednesday.

The Secret Garden, a block south of Parque Central at the corner of 5a Avenida Sur and 6a Avenida Poniente, is a good vegetarian restaurant. Also here are a gym, sauna, massage, table tennis and natural therapies.

For Italian food there's the *Restaurante y Pizzería Italiana Catari*, 6a Avenida Norte 52, opposite La Merced church, run by well-known chef Martedino Castrovinci. From noon to 4 pm the enormous lunch special including beverage is US$3. It's open daily.

Mistral, a restaurant/bar upstairs at 2a Avenida Norte 6-B between 4a and 5a Calle Oriente, serves a good selection main dishes from US$2.35 to US$6. The bar is a popular gathering place. News and sports in English are shown on satellite TV, and downstairs is a video cinema with movies in English.

Places to Eat – middle

The dining room in the *Posada de Don Rodrigo* (☎ 832-0291, 832-0387), 5a Avenida Norte 17, is one of the city's most pleasant and popular places for lunch or dinner. Order the house favorite, the Plato Chapín, a platter of Guatemalan specialties for US$11. A marimba band plays every day from noon to 4 pm and 7 to 9 pm.

Mesón Panza Verde (☎ 832-2925), 5a Avenida Sur No 19, provides excellent Continental cuisine in an appealing Antiguan atmosphere. The Italian chef is from Bergamo, the food is very good and the prices are moderate – about US$18 per person for a full dinner.

Doña María Gordillo Dulces Típicos, 4a Calle Oriente 11, across the street from the Hotel Aurora, is filled with traditional Guatemalan sweets for take-out, and there's often a crowd of antigüeños lined up to do just that. Local handicrafts are for sale here as well.

Places to Eat – top end

El Sereno (☎ 832-0501), 4a Avenida Norte 16, is Antigua's most exclusive restaurant. A colonial home has been nicely restored and modernized somewhat to provide a traditional wooden bar, plant-filled court and several small dining rooms hung with oil paintings. Cuisine is international, leaning heavily on French dishes; the menu changes every week. The short wine list is good but expensive. Expect to pay US$17 to US$30 per person for dinner, when reservations are a good idea. It's open noon to 10 pm every day but Tuesday.

The restaurant at the luxurious *Hotel Casa Santo Domingo* (see Places to Stay) is another beautiful spot for a splurge, with tables inside and out in the garden.

ENTERTAINMENT

Elizabeth Bell gives fascinating slide shows about the town on Tuesdays from 6 to 7 pm at the Christian Spanish Academy (see Courses, above); admission costs US$2.50.

Proyecto Cultural El Sitio (☎ 832-3037), 5a Calle Poniente No 15, presents a variety of cultural events including live theater, concerts, video films and art exhibitions. Stop by to check the schedule, or look in the *Revue* monthly magazine.

Bars for music and dancing open and close frequently. The *Macondo Pub*, 5a Avenida Norte at 2a Calle Poniente, just south of the arch, is a trendy favorite. In the same block, *La Casbah Disco* is popular, though it can get rough on weekends.

The *Rainbow Reading Room & Cafe* and *Mistral* (see Places to Eat) are popular spots to congregate in the evening.

One of Antigua's most pleasant forms of entertainment is video-watching at cinema houses, where you can see a wide variety of international films. Included are:

Antigua Cinemas, 2a Calle Oriente No 2 at the corner of 4a Avenida Norte

Cinema Bistro, 5a Avenida Norte 28

Cinema Tecún Umán, 6a Calle Poniente 34-A

Comfort Home Theater, 1a Avenida Norte No 2

Mistral, 2a Avenida Norte 6-B

Proyecto Cultural El Sitio, 5a Calle Poniente
   No 15

Most show several films daily, with the films changing daily, and admission is around US$1.50. Check their posted schedules at the door, or look for schedules posted around town.

THINGS TO BUY

Lots of vendors come to cater to tourists' desires for colorful Guatemalan woven goods and other handicrafts. Wherever there is an open space to spread their wares, you'll find villagers selling. The mercado, on the west side of town by the bus station, has plenty to choose from. A number of shops are on 4a Calle Poniente, in the blocks between the Parque Central and the mercado. Also look for outdoor markets at the corner of 6a Calle Oriente and 2a Avenida Sur, and at 4a Calle Poniente at 7a Avenida Norte. Vendors may also approach you in the Parque Central.

Be aware, though, that prices for handicrafts tend to be much higher in Antigua than elsewhere in Guatemala. If you will be traveling to other regions, you might want to wait; prices will be cheaper, for example, at the markets in Chichicastenango, Panajachel and even Guatemala City. Whenever buying handicrafts, be sure to bargain for a decent price.

In 1958 an ancient Mayan jade quarry near Nebaj, Guatemala, was rediscovered. When it was shown to yield true jadeite equal in quality to Chinese stone, the mine was reopened. Today it produces jade (pronounced HAH-deh) both for gemstone use and for carving.

Beautiful well-carved stones can cost US$100 or much more. Look for translucency, purity and intensity of color and absence of flaws. Ask the merchant if you can scratch the stone with a pocket knife; if it scratches, it's not true jadeite but an inferior stone.

Antigua has two shops specializing in jade: La Casa de Jade, 4a Calle Oriente 3, and Jades, SA, 4a Calle Oriente 34. At both places you can have a free tour of the jade factories in the rear of the showrooms. Jades, SA has interesting exhibits about jade. Both places are open every day.

Galería El Sitio, 5a Calle Poniente 15 at the Proyecto Cultural El Sitio, specializes in paintings by modern Guatemalan artists. Ring the bell on the gate for admission. A number of other interesting galleries are along 4a Calle Oriente, in the blocks east of the Parque Central.

Kashlan Pot, a shop in the La Fuente courtyard at 4a Calle Oriente 14, is worth a visit to see its dozens of top-quality huipiles, the embroidered women's blouses made in distinctive designs for each region of Guatemala.

GETTING THERE & AWAY
Bus

Buses arrive and depart from a large open lot to the west of the market, on the west side of town. Bus connections with Guatemala City are frequent, and there's one direct bus daily to Panajachel. To reach other highland towns such as Chichicastenango, Quetzaltenango and Huehuetenango, or Panajachel at any other time of day, take one of the frequent buses to Chimaltenango, on the Interamericana, and catch an onward bus from there. Or take a bus heading towards Guatemala City, get off at San Lucas Sacatepéquez and change buses there – this takes a little more time, but it's a good road and since you'll be boarding the bus closer to the capital you're more likely to get a seat (important if you want to avoid the possibility of standing for several hours).

Buses to outlying villages such as Santa María de Jesús (half hour, US$0.25) and San Antonio Aguas Calientes (25 minutes, US$0.20) also depart from the bus area west of the market. It's best to make your outward trip early in the morning and your return trip by mid-afternoon, as bus services drop off dramatically as late afternoon approaches.

Chimaltenango – 19 km, one hour, US$0.30; buses every 15 minutes, 5:30 am to 6 pm

Escuintla – 102 km, 2½ hours, US$0.85; two buses daily, 7 am and 1 pm

Guatemala City – 45 km, one hour, US$0.50; buses every 15 minutes, 4 am to 7 pm, stopping in San Lucas Sacatepéquez

Panajachel – 80 km, two hours, US$2.85; one bus daily, 7:15 am. Or, take a bus to Chimaltenango and change buses there, taking a bus bound for Los Encuentros, Sololá or Panajachel. One of these buses passes by Chimaltenango every 20 minutes or so.

Shuttle Minibuses

Numerous travel agencies and tourist minibus operators offer frequent and convenient shuttle services to places tourists go, including Guatemala City, La Aurora International Airport, Panajachel and Chichicastenango. They also go less frequently (usually on weekends) to places further afield such as Río Dulce, Copán Ruinas (Honduras) and Monterrico. These services cost a lot more than ordinary buses (for example, from US$5 to US$10 to Guatemala City, as opposed to US$0.50 on a normal bus), but they are comfortable and convenient, with door-to-door service on both ends.

It seems there are dozens of these agencies in Antigua; you certainly won't have any trouble finding one. For recommendations, see Travel Agencies, earlier in the chapter.

Car

Rental car companies in Antigua include:

Ahorrent, La Fuente, 4a Calle Oriente No 14 (☎ 832-3768)

Avis, 5a Avenida Norte No 22 (☎ 832-2692)

Tabarini, 2a Calle Poniente 19-A (☎ 832-3091)

GETTING AROUND

Several shops rent bicycles (see Activities, above). Taxi stands are at the bus station and on the east side of Parque Central. A ride in town costs US$1.65.

AROUND ANTIGUA GUATEMALA
Cerro de la Cruz

Overlooking Antigua on the northeast side of town is a hill called Cerro de la Cruz (Hill of the Cross). The fine view over town looks south towards Volcán Agua. However, we urge you not to go there, as this hill is famous for lurking muggers, waiting to prey on unsuspecting visitors. Accounts of armed robberies on Cerro de la Cruz have been so numerous that few people go there, yet in 1996 a large group of Spanish students and their teachers decided there was safety in numbers. When they were robbed by a group of armed bandits, one of their party was shot and killed. Don't go.

Ciudad Vieja &
San Antonio Aguas Calientes

Six and a half km southwest of Antigua along the Escuintla road (the one that passes the Radisson Villa Antigua Resort) is Ciudad Vieja (Old City), site of the first capital of the Captaincy General of Guatemala. Founded in 1527, it was destroyed in 1541 when the aptly named Volcán Agua loosed a flood of water penned-up in its crater. Cascading down the steep volcano's side, the water carried tons of rock and mud over the city, leaving only a few ruins of the Church of La Concepción. There is little to see today.

Past Ciudad Vieja, turn right at a large cemetery on the right-hand side; the unmarked road takes you through San Miguel Dueñas to San Antonio Aguas Calientes. In San Miguel Dueñas, take the first street on the right – between two houses – after coming to the concrete-block paving; this, too, is unmarked. If you come to the Texaco station in the center of San Miguel, you've missed the road.

The road winds through coffee fincas, little fields of vegetables and hamlets of farmers to San Antonio Aguas Calientes, 14 km from Antigua. As you enter San Antonio's plaza, you will see why the village is noted for its weaving. Market stalls in the plaza sell local woven and embroidered goods, as do shops on side streets (walk to the left of the church to find them). Bargaining is expected.

Volcanoes

Climbing the volcanoes around Antigua is exciting in more ways than one. In recent years robbers have intercepted groups of foreigners from time to time on Volcán Pacaya, relieving them of all their goods (including clothing). There have been incidents of rape and murder as well. Still, many visitors take their chances in return for the exhilaration and the beauty of the view.

Because Pacaya is the only volcano near Antigua that is active, it's the one that attracts the most tourists and, consequently, the bandits that prey on them. The volcanoes nearer Antigua (Agua, Fuego and Acatenango) are not active, so they attract fewer tourists and, consequently, haven't been attracting bandits (as of this writing). Climbing one of these won't let you see the glow, but the volcanoes are still very impressive and offer magnificent views.

Get reliable advice about safety before you climb. Check with your embassy in Guatemala City, or with the tourist office in Antigua, or with some of Antigua's reputable tourist and travel agencies. If you do decide to go, make sure you go with reputable guides, through an established agency. (Some 'freelancers' may be in cahoots with the robbers!)

Take sensible precautions. Bring adequate footwear, warm clothing (it's colder up there) and, in the rainy season, some sort of rain gear. Carry a flashlight, partly because you may be climbing down after dark, and also in case the weather changes; it can get as dark as night when it rains on the mountain. Don't neglect to take water and snacks.

Various agencies operate tours up **Volcán Pacaya** (about US$15 per person), including a 1½-hour bus ride to the trailhead followed by a two-hour trek to the summit.

Volcán Agua is the large volcano looming over Antigua, on the south side of town. To get there, follow 2a Avenida Sur or Calle de los Pasos south toward El Calvario (two km), then continue onward via San Juan del Obispo (another three km) to Santa María de Jesús, nine km south of Antigua. This is the jumping-off point for treks up the slopes of Volcán Agua (3766 meters), which rises dramatically right behind the village.

Santa María (2080 meters, population 11,000) is a village of unpaved streets and bamboo fences. The main plaza is also the bus terminal. *Comedor & Hospedaje El Oasis*, a tidy little pension, offers a meal or a bed for the night.

Various outfitters in Antigua can furnish details about the Volcán Agua climb.

You could also climb the other two volcanoes near Antigua, **Volcán Acatenango** and **Volcán Fuego**. Various companies offer guided tours on Acatenango, and Mayan Mountain Bike Tours (see the Activities section, earlier) does hike/bike tours on Acatenango and Agua.

Chimaltenango

The road westward from Antigua makes its way 17 km up to the ridge of the Continental Divide, where it meets the Interamericana at Chimaltenango, capital of the department of Chimaltenango. This was an old town to the Cakchiquel Maya when the conquistadores arrived in 1526; today, it's mostly just a place to change buses, with little to detain you.

Guatemala's Highlands

The highlands, stretching from Antigua to the Mexican border northwest of Huehuetenango, are Guatemala's most beautiful region. The verdant hills are clad in carpets of emerald-green grass, fields of tawny maize (corn) and towering stands of pine. All of this lushness comes from the abundant rain that falls between May and October. If you visit during the rainy season, be prepared for some dreary, chilly, damp days. But when the sun comes out, this land is glorious.

Highlights of the region include Antigua, Guatemala's most beautiful colonial city; Lago de Atitlán, a perfect mirror of blue surrounded by Fuji-like volcanoes; Chichicastenango, where traditional Maya religious rites blend with Catholic ones; Quetzaltenango, the commercial and market center of the southwest; and Huehuetenango, jumping-off place for the cross-border journey to Comitán and San Cristóbal de las Casas in Chiapas, Mexico.

Every town and village in the highlands has a story to tell, which usually begins more than a thousand years ago. Most towns here were already populated by the Maya when the Spanish arrived. The traditional values and ways of life of Guatemala's indigenous peoples are strongest in the highlands. Mayan is the first language, Spanish a distant second.

The age-old culture based on maize is still alive; a sturdy cottage set in the midst of a thriving *milpa* (field of maize) is a common sight, one as old as Maya culture itself. On every road one sees men and women carrying loads of *leña* (firewood) to be used for heating and cooking.

Each highland town has its own market and festival days. Life in a highland town can be *muy triste* (sad, boring) when there's not a market or festival going on, so you should try to visit on those special days.

If you have only three or four days to spend in the highlands, spend them in Antigua, Panajachel and Chichicastenango. With more time you can make your way to Quetzaltenango and the sights in its vicinity, such as Zunil, Fuentes Georginas, San Francisco El Alto, Momostenango and Totonicapán.

Huehuetenango and the ruins nearby at Zaculeu are worth a visit only if you're passing through or if you have lots of time; the towns and villages high in the Cuchumatanes mountains north of Huehuetenango offer wonderful scenery and adventures for intrepid travelers.

Warning

Though most visitors never experience any trouble, there have been some incidents of robbery, rape and murder of tourists in the highlands. These have occurred on trails up the volcanoes, on the outskirts of Antigua and Chichicastenango and at lonely spots along country roads. Attacks happen at random. If you use caution and common sense and don't do much roaming or driving at night, you should have a fine time in this beautiful region.

Before traveling in the highlands, contact your embassy or consulate in Guatemala City for information on the current situation and advice on how and where to travel. Don't rely on local authorities for safety advice, as they may downplay the dangers. For a list of embassy phone numbers, see the Guatemala City chapter.

Getting Around

Guatemala City and the Guatemalan/Mexican border station at La Mesilla are connected by the Interamericana, which is also known as Centroamérica 1 (CA-1). It is a curvy mountain road that must be traveled slowly in many places. Driving the 266 km between Guatemala City and Huehuetenango can take five hours, but the time passes pleasantly amid the beautiful scenery. (The Carretera al Pacífico, CA-2,

Guatemala's Highlands

0   15   30 km
0   10   20 miles

MEXICO

Reserva Biosfera
Selva Lacandona

Río Lacantún

Parque Nacional
Lagunas de
Montebello
Lagunas de
Montebello

Gracías a Diós

Playa
Grande

Parque
Nacional
Lachuá

Sierra de Chamá

San Mateo
Ixtatán   Barillas

Nantón

San
Miguel
Acatán   Santa Eulalia

Soloma

San Juan Ixcoy

Reserva
Natural
Cerro Bisís

Ciudad
Cuauhtémoc
La Mesilla

Todos Santos
Cuchumatán

Parque Nacional
Los Cuchumatanes

Chajul

Cordillera de los Cuchumatanes   Cobán

San Juan Cotzal

Mozintla   Cuilco

Chiantla   Aguacatán   Nebaj

Zaculeu

Huehuetenango   Sacapulas

Uspantán

Volcán
Tacaná
▲4093m

Volcán
Tajumulco
▲4220m

San Pedro
Jocopilas

Cubulco

Santa Cruz
del Quiché   Chinique   Zacualpa

Rabinal

Tuxtla
Chico   El Carmen   San
Marcos San Pedro

San Francisco
El Alto

Momostenango

Joyabaj   El Chol

Granados

Tapachula

Cuatro Caminos   Totonicapán   Chichicastenango

Sierra de Chuacús

Los Encuentros

San Martín
Jilotepeque

San Juan
Sacatepéquez

Quetzaltenango

Tecpán
Guatemala

Ciudad
Tecún
Umán

Zunil

Sololá Iximché

Panajachel

Chimaltenango

GUATEMALA
CITY

Ciudad
Hidalgo

Volcán
Santa María
▲3772m

Volcán
San Pedro
▲3020m

Lago de
Atitlán

Patzicía

Patzún

Carretera al Pacífico

Abaj
Takalik

Maza-
tenango

Santiago
Atitlán

San Lucas
Tolimán

Antigua
Guatemala

Volcán
Agua
▲3766m

Lago de
Amatitlán

Ocós

PACIFIC
OCEAN

Retalhuleu Cuye-
tenango

Volcán
Atitlán ▲
3537m

Volcán
Acatenango
3976m ▲

Volcán Fuego
3763m ▲

To Cocales, Santa Lucía
Cotzumalguapa

Río Naranjo

Interamericana

Río Lacantún

via Escuintla and Retalhuleu is straighter and faster, and it's the better route to take if your goal is to reach Mexico as quickly as possible.)

Many buses rumble up and down the highway; refer to specific destinations under Getting There & Away in the Guatemala City chapter. As most of the places you'll want to reach are some distance off the Interamericana, you may find yourself waiting at major highway junctions such as Los Encuentros and Cuatro Caminos to connect with the right bus. Travel is easiest on market days and in the morning. By mid- or late afternoon, buses may be diffi-

cult to find, and all short-distance local traffic stops by dinner time. You should follow suit.

Lago de Atitlán

Westward 32 km along the highway from Chimaltenango, you pass the turnoff for the back road to Lago de Atitlán via Patzicía and Patzún. The area around these two towns has been notable for high levels of guerrilla activity in recent years, and the road is often in poor condition, so it's advisable to stay on the Interamericana to Tecpán Guatemala, the starting point for a visit to the ruined Cakchiquel capital city of Iximché.

If you travel another 40 km westward along the Interamericana from Tecpán, you come to the highway junction of **Los Encuentros**. There is a nascent town here, based on the presence of a lot of people waiting to catch buses. The road to the right heads north to Chichicastenango and Santa Cruz del Quiché. From the Interamericana a road to the left descends 12 km to Sololá, capital of the department of the same name, and then eight km more to Panajachel, on the shores of Lago de Atitlán.

If you are not on a direct bus to these places, you can always get off at Los Encuentros and catch another bus or minibus, or even hitch a ride, from here down to Panajachel or up to Chichicastenango; it's a half-hour ride to either place.

The road from Sololá descends more than 500 meters through pine forests in its eight-km course to Panajachel. All the sights and views are on your right, so try to get a seat on the right-hand side of the bus.

Along the way the road passes Sololá's colorful cemetery and a Guatemalan army base. The guardpost by the main gate is in the shape of a huge helmet resting upon a

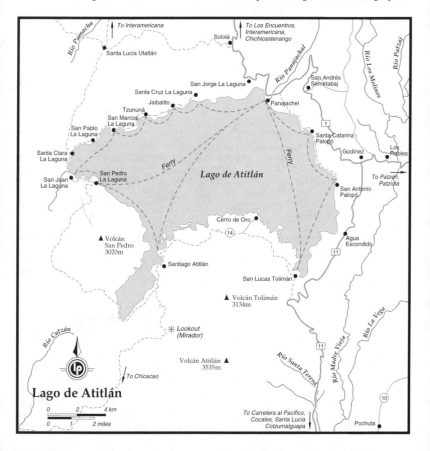

Lago de Atitlán

pair of soldier's boots. Soon the road turns to snake its way down the mountainside to the lakeshore, offering breathtaking views of the lake and its surrounding volcanoes.

TECPÁN GUATEMALA

Founded as the Spanish military headquarters during the conquest, Tecpán Guatemala today is a small, somewhat dusty town with numerous handicrafts shops, two small hotels and, not far away, the ruins of the Cakchiquel Maya capital of Iximché.

Tecpán's market day is Thursday. The annual festival in honor of the town's patron saint, Francis of Assisi, is held in the first week of October.

Iximché

Set on a flat promontory surrounded by steep cliffs, Iximché (founded in the late 15th century) was well sited to be the capital city of the Cakchiquel Maya. The Cakchiquel were at war with the Quiché Maya, and the city's natural defenses served them well.

When the conquistadors arrived in 1524, the Cakchiquel formed an alliance with them against their enemies the Quiché and the Tzutuhils. The Spaniards set up their headquarters right next door to the Cakchiquel capital at Tecpán Guatemala, but Spanish demands for gold and other loot soon put an end to the alliance, and in the ensuing battles, the Cakchiquel were defeated.

As you enter Tecpán you will see signs pointing to the unpaved road leading through fields and pine forests to Iximché, less than six km to the south. You can walk the distance in about an hour, see the ruins and rest (another hour), then walk back to Tecpán – a total of three hours. If you're going to walk, it's best to do it in the morning so that you can get back to the highway by early afternoon, as bus traffic dwindles by late afternoon.

After you enter the archaeological site and pass the small museum on the right, you come to four ceremonial plazas surrounded by grass-covered temple structures and ball courts. Some of the structures have been cleaned and maintained; on a few the original plaster coating is still in place, and there are even some traces of the original paint.

The site is open daily from 9 am to 4 pm.

Places to Stay & Eat

Should you need to stay the night in Tecpán, *Hotel Iximché*, 1a Avenida 1-38, Zona 2, will put you up in basic rooms for US$3 per person, as will *Pensión Doña Ester*, 2a Calle 1-09, Zona 3. There are various small eateries.

Getting There & Away

Transportes Poaquileña runs buses to Guatemala City (87 km, 1½ hours) every half hour from 3 am to 5 pm. From Guatemala City to Tecpán, buses run from 5 am to 7:30 pm just as frequently.

SOLOLÁ
Population 9000

Though the Spaniards founded Sololá (2110 meters) in 1547, there was a Cakchiquel town (called Tzoloyá) here before they came. Sololá's importance comes from its geographic position on trade routes between the *tierra caliente* (hot lands of the Pacific Slope) and *tierra fría* (the chilly highlands). All the traders meet here, and Sololá's Friday market is one of the best in the highlands.

On market days, the plaza next to the cathedral is ablaze with the colorful costumes of people from a dozen surrounding villages and towns. Displays of meat, vegetables and fruit, housewares and clothing are neatly arranged in every available space, with tides of buyers ebbing and flowing along the spaces in between. Several elaborate stands are well stocked with brightly colored yarn and sewing notions for making the traditional costumes you see all around you. This is a market serving locals, not tourists.

Every Sunday morning the officers of the traditional religious brotherhoods *(cofradías)* parade ceremoniously to the cathedral for their devotions. On other days, Sololá sleeps.

You can make a very pleasant walk from Sololá down to the lake, whether walking on the highway to Panajachel or on the walking track to Santa Cruz La Laguna.

Places to Stay

Virtually everyone stays in Panajachel, but if you need a bed in Sololá, try the six-room *Posada del Viajero*, 7a Avenida 10-45, Zona 2, or the *Hotel Tzolojya* (☎ 762-1266), 11a Calle 7-70, Zona 2. *Hotel Santa Ana*, 150 meters uphill from the church tower on the road that comes into town from Los Encuentros, is even simpler.

PANAJACHEL

Population 5000

Nicknamed Gringotenango (Place of the Foreigners) by locals and foreigners alike, Pana has long been known to tourists. In the hippie heyday of the 1960s and '70s, it was crowded with laid-back travelers in semi-permanent exile. When the civil war of the late '70s and early '80s made Panajachel a dangerous – or at least unpleasant – place to be, many moved on. But in recent years the town's tourist industry has boomed again.

There is no notable colonial architecture in this town, which is a small and not particularly attractive place that has developed haphazardly according to the demands of the tourist trade. The reflections of volcanoes and clouds on the lake surface may help you ignore the village lad strolling along the lakeshore with an armful of newspapers shouting 'Miami Herald! Miami Herald!'

Lago de Atitlán is often still and beautiful early in the day, which is the best time for swimming. By noon the Xocomil, a southeasterly wind, may have risen to ruffle the lake's surface. Note that the lake is a caldera (collapsed volcanic cone) and is more than 320 meters deep. The land drops off sharply very near the shore. Surrounding the lake are three volcanoes: Volcán Tolimán (3158 meters), due south of Panajachel; Volcán Atitlán (3537 meters), also to the south; and Volcán San Pedro (2995 meters), to the southwest.

Six different cultures mingle on the dusty streets of Panajachel: The ladino citizens operate the levers of its tourist industry. The Cakchiquel and Tzutuhil Maya from surrounding villages come to sell their handicrafts to tourists. The lakeside villa owners drive up on weekends from Guatemala City. Group tourists descend on the town from buses for a few hours, a day or an overnight. And there are the 'traditional' hippies with long hair, beards, bare feet, local dress and Volkswagen minibuses.

Orientation

As you near the bottom of the long hill descending from Sololá, a road on the right leads to the Hotel Visión Azul, Hotel Atitlán and those obtrusive white high-rise buildings. The main road then bears left and becomes the Calle Real (also called Calle Principal), Panajachel's main street.

The geographic center of town, and the closest thing it has to a bus station, is the intersection of Calle Real and Calle Santander, where you will see the Banco Agricola Mercantil (BAM). Calle Santander is the main road to the beach. All kinds of tourist services line Calle Santander in the few blocks from the bus stop and bank at the top of the street down to the lake.

Northeast along Calle Real are more hotels, restaurants and shops; finally, at the northeastern end of town you come to the town's civic center, with the post and telegraph offices, church, town hall, police station and market (busiest on Sunday and Thursday, but with some activity on other days, from 9 am to noon).

Calle Rancho Grande is the other main road to the beach; it's parallel to, and east of, Calle Santander.

A beautiful green park stretches along the lakeside between Calle Santander and Calle Rancho Grande. It's a wonderful place for strolling, day and night.

The area east of the Río Panajachel is known as Jucanyá (Across the River).

Information

Tourist Offices The INGUAT tourist office (☎ 762-1392) is in the Edificio Rincón Sai on Calle Santander. It's open every day from 8 am to 1 pm and from 2 to 5 pm. Bus and boat schedules are posted on the door.

GUATEMALA

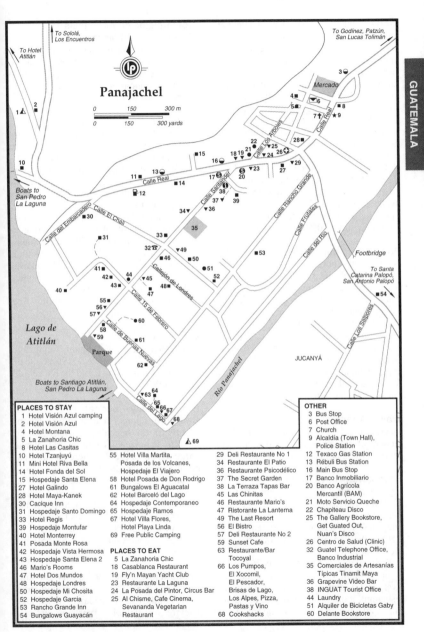

Panajachel

0   150   300 m
0   150   300 yards

To Sololá, Los Encuentros

To Hotel Atitlán

To Godínez, Patzún, San Lucas Tolimán

Mercado

Calle Real

Calle Los Árboles

Calle Rancho Grande

Calle Santander

Calle Real

Boats to San Pedro La Laguna

Calle del Embarcadero

Calle El Chalí

Calle Frutales

Calle del Río

Footbridge

To Santa Catarina Palopó, San Antonio Palopó

Callejón de Londres

Calle 15 de Febrero

Lago de Atitlán

Calle de Buenas Nuevas

Parque

JUCANYÁ

Calle Los Sapotes

Río Panajachel

Boats to Santiago Atitlán, San Pedro La Laguna

Calle del Lago

PLACES TO STAY
1 Hotel Visión Azul camping
2 Hotel Visión Azul
4 Hotel Montana
5 La Zanahoria Chic
8 Hotel Las Casitas
10 Hotel Tzanjuyú
11 Mini Hotel Riva Bella
14 Hotel Fonda del Sol
15 Hospedaje Santa Elena
27 Hotel Galindo
28 Hotel Maya-Kanek
30 Cacique Inn
31 Hospedaje Santo Domingo
33 Hotel Regis
39 Hospedaje Montufar
40 Hotel Monterrey
41 Posada Monte Rosa
42 Hospedaje Vista Hermosa
43 Hospedaje Santa Elena 2
46 Mario's Rooms
47 Hotel Dos Mundos
48 Hospedaje Londres
49 Hospedaje Mi Chosita
52 Hospedaje Garcia
53 Rancho Grande Inn
54 Bungalows Guayacán

55 Hotel Villa Martita, Posada de los Volcanes, Hospedaje El Viajero
58 Hotel Posada de Don Rodrigo
61 Bungalows El Aguacatal
62 Hotel Barceló del Lago
64 Hospedaje Contemporaneo
65 Hospedaje Ramos
67 Hotel Villa Flores, Hotel Playa Linda
69 Free Public Camping

PLACES TO EAT
5 La Zanahoria Chic
18 Casablanca Restaurant
19 Fly'n Mayan Yacht Club
23 Restaurante La Laguna
24 La Posada del Pintor, Circus Bar
25 Al Chisme, Cafe Cinema, Sevananda Vegetarian Restaurant

29 Deli Restaurante No 1
34 Restaurante El Patio
36 Restaurante Psicodélico
37 The Secret Garden
38 La Terraza Tapas Bar
45 Las Chinitas
46 Restaurante Mario's
47 Ristorante La Lanterna
49 The Last Resort
56 El Bistro
57 Deli Restaurante No 2
59 Sunset Cafe
63 Restaurante/Bar Tocoyal
66 Los Pumpos, El Xocomil, El Pescador, Brisas de Lago, Los Alpes, Pizza, Pastas y Vino
68 Cookshacks

OTHER
3 Bus Stop
6 Post Office
7 Church
9 Alcaldía (Town Hall), Police Station
12 Texaco Gas Station
13 Rébuli Bus Station
16 Main Bus Stop
17 Banco Inmobiliario
20 Banco Agrícola Mercantil (BAM)
21 Moto Servicio Queche
22 Chapiteau Disco
25 The Gallery Bookstore, Get Guated Out, Nuan's Disco
26 Centro de Salud (Clinic)
32 Guatel Telephone Office, Banco Industrial
35 Comerciales de Artesanías Típicas Tinamit Maya
36 Grapevine Video Bar
38 INGUAT Tourist Office
44 Laundry
51 Alquiler de Bicicletas Gaby
60 Delante Bookstore

Money Banco Industrial on Calle Santander changes US dollars cash and travelers' checks, gives cash advances on Visa cards and has a 24-hour ATM. Banco Inmobiliario on the corner of Calle Santander and Calle Real also changes money, and it's open longer hours. BAM, on the same corner, changes money and is an agent for Western Union.

Apart from the banks, several other businesses offer financial services. You can change cash and travelers' checks at the INGUAT tourist office and at the Hotel Regis, both on Calle Santander. Cash advances on Visa and MasterCard are available from the Hotel Regis and from Servicios Turísticos Atitlán, both on Calle Santander, for a 10% commission.

Post & Communications The post office is next to the church.

The Guatel office on Calle Santander is open every day. Many other places along Calle Santander offer the same services.

Get Guated Out (☎ /fax 762-2015), at the Gallery Bookstore in the Centro Comercial on Avenida Los Arboles, can ship your important letters and parcels by air freight or international courier. They will also buy handicrafts for you and ship them for export – handy if you can't come to Panajachel yourself.

Travel Agencies There are many full-service travel agencies along Calle Santander, offering trips, tours and shuttle bus services to other places around Guatemala.

Bookstores The Delante Bookstore, down a pathway off Calle de Buenas Nuevas (follow the signs), has an excellent collection of used books in English and other languages. They sell, trade and rent books (rental US$0.15 per day), and they have six rooms for rent.

The Gallery Bookstore (☎ /fax 762-2015) is upstairs in the Centro Comercial on Avenida Los Arboles, next to Al Chisme restaurant. It offers new and used books for sale, a telephone/fax service and travel and ticket sales.

Comerciales de Artesanías Típicas Tinamit Maya

This is one of Guatemala's most extensive handicrafts markets, with dozens of stalls. You can get good buys here if you bargain and take your time. The market is open every day from 7 am to 7 pm.

Activities

Various lakeside villages, reachable by foot, bicycle, bus or passenger boat, are interesting to visit. The most popular destination for day trips is Santiago Atitlán, directly across the lake south of Panajachel, but there are others. Most of the villages have places to stay overnight.

You can walk from Panajachel to Santa Catarina in about an hour, continuing to San Antonio in about another hour; it takes only half as long on bicycle (see Getting Around for bike rental). Or take the bike by boat to Santiago, San Pedro or another village to start a tour of the lake.

Boat tours are another possibility (see Getting There & Away, below).

Courses

Panajachel has two Spanish-language schools: Panatitlán (fax 762-1196), Calle de la Navidad 0-40, Zona 1, and the Escuela de Español Panajachel (fax 762-1196).

Places to Stay – budget

Camping There's a free public campground on the beach on the east side of the Río Panajachel's mouth in Jucanyá. Safety can be a problem here. A safer but more expensive alternative is the campground on the spacious lakeside lawn at the Hotel Visión Azul (☎ /fax 762-1426), on the western outskirts of town. It has electrical and water hookups for campers and caravans; cost is US$1.65 per person, plus US$5 per tent, plus US$2.50 per vehicle.

Hospedajes & Hotels Luckily for low-budget travelers, Panajachel has numerous little family-run hospedajes (pensions). They're very simple – perhaps just two rough beds, a bedside table and a light bulb in a room of bare boards – but quite cheap. Most provide clean toilets and hot showers.

The first place to look for hospedajes is along Calle Santander midway between Calle Real and the beach. Follow signs along the main street for the various hospedajes down narrow side streets and alleys.

The cheapest place in town is the *Hospedaje Londres*, down one of these pathways, Callejón de Londres (follow the sign). It's very basic, with six rooms around a covered courtyard sharing a hot bath; cost is US$1.50/1.85/2.50 for a single/double/triple. The owner speaks English and Spanish.

Hospedaje Santa Elena 2, Calle 15 de Febrero 3-06, off Calle Santander on the road to the Hotel Monterrey, is tidy and typical of Pana's hospedajes. Singles/doubles with shared bath are US$3/4. The original *Hospedaje Santa Elena* is down a pathway off Calle Real, farther from the lake; it's a simple family-run place, where rooms that share cold showers go for US$2.40/3.65/4.35.

Hospedaje Vista Hermosa, Calle 15 de Febrero 3-55, is a friendly place with simple rooms on two levels around a small, pretty courtyard. There are hot showers in the daytime only, with very little water at night. Rooms with general bath are US$2.50 per person, or US$6.65 for two people with private bath. Next door, *Posada Monte Rosa* is a pleasant new hotel with five comfortable single/double rooms for US$11/20.

Hospedaje Santo Domingo is a step up in quality but a few steps off the street; follow the road toward the Hotel Monterrey, then follow signs along a shady path. It's well away from the noise on Calle Santander. Rooms with general bath are US$2.50/4.50 for simple wooden rooms, or US$7.50 for more attractive upstairs rooms. Singles/doubles with private bath are US$9.15/13.35.

Mario's Rooms (☎ 762-1313) on Calle Santander is popular with young, adventurous travelers. Singles/doubles with shared hot bath are US$5.50/6.50; with private cold bath they are US$9.15/12. The restaurant at Mario's serves economical meals.

Hospedaje Mi Chosita, on Calle El Chali (turn at Mario's Rooms), is tidy, quiet and costs US$4.15/5.15/6.15 for a single/double/triple with shared bath. *Hospedaje García* (☎ 762-2187), 4a Calle 2-24, Zona 2, farther east along the same street toward Calle Rancho Grande, charges US$5.25/6/7.50 for a single/double/triple.

Hotel Villa Martita, on Calle Santander half a block from the lake, is a friendly family-run place with singles/doubles with general bath for US$6/8.35. The rooms are around a quiet courtyard, set back from the street. Next door, the more upmarket *Posada de los Volcanes* (☎ /fax 762-2367), Calle Santander 5-51, is a beautiful new place where all the rooms have private bath and cable TV; rooms are US$20/25.

Next door again, *Hospedaje El Viajero* is perhaps the best value for money in town. It's a new place, pleasant and clean, with just five rooms with private bath set about 40 meters back from the street. It's quiet and peaceful, yet you're near everything, including the lake. Singles/doubles are US$9/12, and there's laundry service and parking.

Another clean, new place is the *Hospedaje Montufar*, down a pathway off Calle Santander. Rooms with shared bath are US$7/12/12/19 for one/two/three/four people.

La Zanahoria Chic (☎ 762-1249, fax 762-2138), Avenida Los Arboles 0-46, has seven clean rooms opening onto a communal upstairs sitting area with two shared baths. The rooms are simple but comfortable, and the whole place has a cozy, friendly feeling. Downstairs is the pleasant La Zanahoria Chic video-cafe. Singles/doubles/triples are US$4.15/6/8.35.

Near the beach and the Hotel Playa Linda are several more places. *Hospedaje Ramos* has simple rooms with private bath for US$6/10. Fifty meters behind it, the *Hospedaje Contemporaneo* (☎ 762-2214) is a newer place with simple but clean rooms with private bath for US$7.50/12. Also along here, the *Hotel Villa Flores* (☎ 762-2193), next door to the Hotel Playa Linda, is even newer. Many restaurants along here are convenient for meals.

Moving up in comfort, *Hotel Las Casitas* (☎ 762-1224), opposite the market near the church and town hall, rents little brick bungalows with private bath and tile roofs for US$6.65/13.35/15 for a single/double/triple.

Hotel Fonda del Sol (☎ 762-1162), Calle Real 1-74, Zona 2, is a two-story building on the main street, west of the intersection with Calle Santander. The 25 simple rooms on the upper floor are well used but fairly decently kept; they cost US$6/11 with shared bath, US$11/17 with private bath. Larger, nicer rooms are more expensive, at US$16/23 for a single/double. Downstairs is a restaurant.

Hotel Maya-Kanek (☎ 762-1104), Calle Real just down from the church, is a motel-style hostelry. Rooms face a cobbled court with a small garden; the court doubles as a secure car park. The 20 rooms, though simple, are a bit more comfortable than at a hospedaje, and they cost US$7/11 with shared cold bath or US$10/15 with private hot bath. It's quiet here.

Hotel Galindo (☎ /fax 762-1168), on Calle Real northeast of the Banco Agricola Mercantil, has a surprisingly lush garden surrounded by modest rooms that rent for US$12 for smaller rooms, US$14 for larger rooms (some with fireplace), US$20 for triple rooms with fireplace. Look at the room before you rent.

Down an alleyway in front of the church, the *Hotel Montana* (☎ /fax 762-2180) has 15 clean, bright, single/double rooms with private bath, cable TV and parking for US$15/27.

The *Delante Bookstore* (see Bookshops above) has six pleasant rooms for rent around a tranquil, quiet courtyard. The room rate includes use of the communal kitchen and having your laundry and dishes washed. You can also read all the books in the bookstore for free. Such a deal!

Places to Stay – middle
Midrange lodgings are busiest at weekends. From Sunday to Thursday you may get a discount. All of these lodgings provide private hot showers in their rooms.

Rancho Grande Inn (☎ 762-1554, 762-2255, fax 762-22-47), Calle Rancho Grande, has 12 perfectly maintained German country-style villas in a tropical Guatemalan setting amid emerald-green lawns. Some bungalows sleep up to five persons. Marlita Hannstein, the congenial proprietor, charges a very reasonable US$30/40 to 60 for a single/double, including tax and a full delicious breakfast. This is perhaps Pana's best place to stay. It's a good idea to reserve in advance.

Bungalows El Aguacatal (☎ 762-1482), Calle de Buenas Nuevas, is aimed at weekenders from the capital. Each modern bungalow has two bedrooms, equipped kitchen, bath and salon, and costs US$42 for one to four people Sunday to Thursday, US$52 on Friday and Saturday. Bungalows without kitchen are cheaper, at US$10 per person Sunday to Thursday, US$45 on weekends.

Mini Hotel Riva Bella (☎ 762-1348, 762-1177, fax 762-1353), Calle Real, is a collection of neat two-room bungalows, each with its own parking place, set around pleasant gardens. The location is convenient, and the price is US$27/32 for a single/double. The same owners also operate *Bungalows Guayacán*, just across the river, with six apartments, each with kitchenette, one bedroom, living room and garden, for US$42 for up to three people.

Hotel Dos Mundos (☎ /fax 762-2078), Calle Santander 4-72, is an attractive place with 16 bungalows, all with cable TV and nice decor, in a walled compound of tropical gardens for US$30/40/50 for a single/double/triple. The compound is set well back from the street. Also here are a swimming pool and a good Italian restaurant.

Hotel Regis (☎ 762-1149, fax 762-1152), Calle Santander, is a group of colonial-style villas set back from the street across a lush lawn shaded by palms. The 25 comfortable guestrooms are set around the ample grounds, which have a small swimming pool, a children's playground and an open-air mineral hot springs for guests only. Rooms are US$45/55/65 for a single/double/triple.

Hotel Monterrey (☎ /fax 762-1126), Calle 15 de Febrero, down an unpaved road going west from Calle Santander (look for the sign), is a blue-and-white, two-story motel-style building facing the lake across lawns and gardens that extend down to the beach. The Monterrey offers 29 clean and cheerful single/double rooms opening onto a terrace with a beautiful lake view for US$30/40.

Hotel Playa Linda (☎ /fax 762-1159, akennedy@gua.gbm.net), facing the beach at Calle del Lago 0-70, has an assortment of rooms, a few with nice views of the lake. Rooms 1 to 5 have large private balconies with tables, chairs and wonderful lake views, rooms 6 to 15 do not; all have private bath, all but two have fireplaces and some have TV with satellite programs. Singles/doubles are US$35/40 with balcony and view, US$25/30 without.

Cacique Inn (☎ /fax 762-1205), Calle del Embarcadero, off Calle Real at the western edge of town, is an assemblage of pseudo-rustic red-tile-roofed buildings arranged around verdant gardens and a swimming pool. The 34 large, comfortable rooms have double beds, fireplaces and locally made blankets. Rates are US$52/59/66 for a single/double/triple, tax included.

Hotel Visión Azul (☎ /fax 762-1426), on the Hotel Atitlán road, is built into a hillside in a quiet location looking toward the lake through a grove of trees. The big, bright rooms in the main building have spacious terraces festooned with bougainvillea and ivy. Modern bungalows a few steps away provide more privacy for families. There's a swimming pool. Prices are US$38/50/56 for a single/double/triple.

Along the same road, *Hotel Tzanjuyú* (☎ 762-1318) has large garden grounds on a private beach on a beautiful cove. All the rooms open onto small balconies with a great lake view. They may be overpriced at US$40/45/50, but the setting is wonderful. There's a swimming pool and restaurant.

Places to Stay – top end

The nicest hotel in town is the *Hotel Atitlán* (☎ /fax 762-1416/29/41), on the lakeshore two km west of the town center. Spacious gardens surround this rambling three-story colonial-style hotel. Inside are gleaming tile floors, antique wood carvings and exquisite handicraft decorations. The patio

has views across the heated swimming pools to the lake. The 65 rooms with private bath and lake-view balconies are US$84/96/118 for a single/double/triple.

At the lake end of Calle Santander, *Hotel Posada de Don Rodrigo* (☎ 762-2326, 762-2329) is another beautiful luxury hotel, with a lakeside swimming pool terrace and many other amenities. Rooms are US$84/94/103 for a single/double/triple.

Hotel Barceló del Lago (☎ /fax 762-1555 to 1560, in Guatemala City ☎ /fax 334-7633), at the beach end of Calle Rancho Grande, is a modern six-story building that seems out of place in low-rise, laid-back Panajachel. Besides the beach, the hotel has two swimming pools (one for children) set in nice gardens. Each of its 100 rooms has two double beds and costs US$85/112 single/double, including all meals.

Places to Eat – budget

The cheapest places to eat are down by the beach at the mouth of the Río Panajachel. Right by the river's mouth are crude cook-shacks with very low prices. The food stands around the car park cost only a bit more. Then there are the little restaurants just inland from the car park, with names such as *Los Pumpos, El Xocomil, El Pescador, Brisas de Lago* and *Los Alpes*. Not only is the food inexpensive (US$4 for a fill-up), but the view of the lake is a priceless bonus. *Pizza, Pastas y Vino* along here is open 24 hours.

At the lake end of Calle Santander, the open-air *Sunset Cafe* has a great view of the lake. Meat or vegetarian meals are US$3 to US$5, snacks are less, and there's a bar and live music on weekends. It's open every day from 11 am to 10 pm.

Nearby on Calle Santander, the *Deli Restaurante 2* is a tranquil garden restaurant serving a good variety of whole, healthy, inexpensive foods to the strains of soft classical music. It's open every day except Tuesday from 7 am to 5:45 pm; breakfast is served all day. *Deli Restaurante No 1*, on Calle Real next to the Hotel Galindo, has the same menu and hours; it closes on Thursday.

El Bistro, on Calle Santander half a block from the lake, is another lovely, relaxing restaurant with tables both inside and out in the garden. There's candlelight in the evening and sometimes live music. It's open every day from 7 am to 10 pm.

Las Chinitas, on Calle Santander very near the Hotel Dos Mundos, is a tiny outdoor restaurant with delicious, inexpensive Chinese food. Ling, the friendly owner, is from Malaysia via New York and has been in Panajachel for many years. *Restaurante Mario's*, on Calle Santander beside Mario's Rooms, is another good spot for economical meals.

Restaurante Psicodélico, on Calle Santander, is a pleasant open-air restaurant with candlelight in the evening. Meals are ample and economical: Grilled meat or chicken (US$3.35) and fish or shrimp (US$5) come with soup, guacamole, French fries, salad and dessert. Alcohol is served, and the Grapevine Video Bar is upstairs.

The Last Resort restaurant/bar, just off Calle Santander on Calle El Chali, is small, pleasant and famous for its good, economical food. A buffet breakfast is served for US$2; a good variety of meals, all served with soup, salad, bread and coffee, are US$3.35 to US$5. Alcohol is served, there's table tennis in the rear, and on cool evenings the fireplace is a welcome treat. It's open every day.

Al Chisme (The Gossip), on Avenida Los Arboles, is a favorite with regular Pana foreign visitors and residents, with its shady streetside patio. Breakfasts of English muffins, Belgian waffles and omelettes cost US$2 to US$4. For lunch and dinner, Al Chisme offers a variety of meat and vegetarian dishes, including Tex-Mex specialties and 'death by chocolate'. It's open every day except Wednesday. *Cafe Cinema* is upstairs in the rear.

Next door in the Centro Comercial complex on Los Arboles is *Sevananda Vegetarian Restaurant*, offering sandwiches and vegetable plates for US$2 to US$4. It's open every day except Sunday. *The Secret Garden*, down a pathway off Calle Santander, is another good vegetarian restaurant, with tables set around a beautiful, quiet garden. It's open every day from 10 am to 3 pm for brunch and lunch. Follow the signs from Calle Santander, just on the north side of the INGUAT tourist office building.

La Posada del Pintor and its *Circus Bar*, on Avenida Los Arboles, is a restaurant, pizzería and bar with walls hung with old circus posters and a vast selection of items on the menu. There's live music every night from 8 pm on; it's open every day, noon to midnight. This is one of Pana's most popular places.

Restaurante La Laguna, on Calle Real at the intersection of Avenida Los Arboles, has a pretty front patio and garden with umbrella-covered tables. There's live music in the garden Tuesday to Sunday nights.

At the *Fly'n Mayan Yacht Club*, near the intersection of Calle Real and Calle Santander, the pizzas (US$3.50 to US$6.50) have a good reputation. It's open daily except Thursday.

Restaurante/Bar Tocoyal, opposite the big Hotel Barceló del Lago, at the beach end of Calle Rancho Grande, is a tidy, modern thatch-roofed place serving good, moderately priced meals (including fish) for about US$8.

Places to Eat – middle

Ristorante La Lanterna at the Hotel Dos Mundos, set back from the street on Calle Santander, is a good, authentic Italian restaurant with both inside and garden tables; you're welcome to use the swimming pool if you come to eat here. It's open every day, 7 am to 3 pm and 6 to 10 pm.

Upstairs in the same building with the INGUAT tourist office, *La Terraza Tapas Bar* is a lovely, upmarket open-air restaurant that's open every day. *Restaurant El Patio*, also on Calle Santander, is another good but more expensive place, as is the *Casablanca Restaurant* (☎ 762-1015), at the intersection of Calle Santander and Calle Real.

The luxury *Hotel Barceló del Lago* offers lavish Sunday breakfast and dinner buffets when the hotel is fully occupied, which usually happens on weekends and holidays. The breakfast/dinner buffets cost US$7/13.

The even more luxurious *Hotel Atitlán* has a beautiful restaurant with tables inside and out on the patio and magnificent lake views. If you come to eat here, you can use the swimming pool, gardens, beach and so on, all for free. Lunch or dinner buffets (US$11) are offered when occupancy is high and usually on Thursday afternoons; call ahead. Otherwise, there's an ample four-course set meal for the same price, as well as other selections on the menu.

Entertainment

Strolling along the path at the lakeside park, greeting the dawn or watching the sun set behind the volcanoes are unsurpassable entertainment. The colors of the lake, the sky, the volcanoes and mountains constantly change from dawn to sunset, and at night the sky over the lake is alive with stars.

Live music is presented at the *La Posada del Pintor/Circus Bar*, *Restaurante La Laguna*, *Sunset Cafe* and *El Bistro* (see Places to Eat).

Pana's two discos, *Chapiteau* and *Noan's*, both on Avenida Los Arboles, open around 9 or 10 pm.

Video films in English and Spanish are shown at the *Grapevine Video Bar*, on Calle Santander upstairs from the Restaurante Psicodélico, and at *Cafe Cinema*, on Avenida Los Arboles upstairs in the rear from Al Chisme; both show several films nightly and have schedules posted out front. At *La Zanahoria Chic* video cafe on Avenida Los Arboles, you can choose from a list of over a hundred films. All of these are pleasant places with food and drink available.

Getting There & Away

Bus The town's main bus stop is where Calle Santander meets Calle Real, across from the Mayan Palace Hotel and the Banco Agrícola Mercantil. Rébuli buses depart from the Rébuli office on Calle Real (see map).

Antigua – 80 km, three hours, US$2; Rébuli runs one direct bus every day *except Sunday* at 11 am. Or take any bus heading for Guatemala City and change buses at Chimaltenango.

Chichicastenango – 29 km, 1½ hours, US$1.65; nine buses daily, 7 am to 4 pm. (These buses may run only on Thursday and Sunday, Chichi's market days.) Or take any bus heading to Los Encuentros and change buses there.

Cocales (Carretera al Pacífico) – 56 km, 2½ hours, US$1

El Carmen/Talismán (Mexican border) – via the Pacific route, bus to Cocales and change buses there. Via the highland route, bus to Quetzaltenango and change buses there.

Guatemala City – 147 km, three hours, US$2; Rébuli has buses departing from its office on Calle Real nine times daily, 5 am to 2:30 pm. Or take a bus to Los Encuentros and change there.

Huehuetenango – 159 km, 3½ hours; bus to Los Encuentros and wait there for a bus bound for Huehue or La Mesilla (see Getting There & Away in the Guatemala City section for a schedule of these buses). Or catch a bus heading to Quetzaltenango, get out at Cuatro Caminos and change buses there.

La Mesilla, Mexican border – 241 km, seven hours; see Huehuetenango

Los Encuentros – 20 km, 35 minutes, US$0.50; take any bus heading toward Guatemala City, Chichicastenango, Quetzaltenango or the Interamericana.

Quetzaltenango – 99 km, two hours, US$2; four buses daily, 5:30, 6:15 and 7:30 am and 2 pm. Or take a bus to Los Encuentros and change there.

San Antonio Palopó – nine km, one hour, US$0.50; daily buses, via Santa Catarina Palopó

San Lucas Tolimán – 24 km, 1½ hours, US$1; two buses daily, 6:45 am and 4 pm. Or, take any bus heading for Cocales, get off at the crossroads to San Lucas and walk about one km into town.

Santa Catarina Palopó – four km, 30 minutes, US$0.50; daily buses

Sololá – eight km, 10 minutes, US$0.15; frequent direct local buses. Or take any bus heading to Guatemala City, Chichicastenango, Quetzaltenango or Los Encuentros.

Shuttle Minibus A number of travel agencies on Calle Santander offer convenient shuttle buses to popular tourist destinations, including Guatemala City, Antigua, Chichicastenango, Quetzaltenango and the Mexican border.

Car & Motorcycle Dalton Rent A Car (☎ / fax 762-1275, 762-2251) has an office on Avenida Los Arboles. Moto Servicio Queche (☎ 762-2089), at the intersection of Avenida Los Arboles and Calle Real, rents bicycles and off-road motorcycles.

Boat Passenger boats depart from the public beach at the foot of Calle Rancho Grande in Panajachel. The boat schedule is posted outside the door of the INGUAT tourist office in Panajachel, or stop by the dock to see when boats are leaving. You usually don't have to wait long for a boat.

The trip to Santiago Atitlán takes about an hour (or a little longer, depending upon the winds) and costs US$1.25 each way.

Another boat route heads to Santa Catarina Palopó (US$1.25)/San Antonio Palopó (US$2.50)/San Lucas Tolimán (US$3.35), returning to Panajachel.

Another route connects Panajachel and San Pedro (1¼ hours); departing from Panajachel, these boats stop (in order) at Santa Cruz La Laguna (20 minutes), Jaibalito, Tzununá, San Marcos La Laguna (one hour) and San Juan La Laguna. They depart Panajachel from the Calle Rancho Grande docks and then stop at another dock at the foot of Calle del Embarcadero before heading out of town (vice versa, when arriving at Panajachel). Fare is US$1.25 for any destination for tourists, US$0.50 for locals.

Another option is to take a boat tour of the lake, which includes various towns. For example, the INGUAT tourist office in Panajachel makes bookings for a boat tour departing Panajachel at 8:30 am, visiting San Pedro (one hour), Santiago (1½ hours) and San Antonio (one hour) for US$6.65, arriving back in Panajachel at 3:30 pm. Advance booking is suggested.

Getting Around
Several places along Calle Santander rent bicycles, as do Moto Servicio Queche (see Car & Motorcycle, above) and Alquiler de Bicicletas Gaby, on Calle 14 de Febrero between Calle Santander and Calle Rancho Grande.

SANTA CATARINA PALOPÓ & SAN ANTONIO PALOPÓ
Four km east of Panajachel along a winding, unpaved road lies the village of Santa Catarina Palopó. Narrow streets paved in stone blocks, adobe houses with roofs of thatch or corrugated tin, huddled around a gleaming white church: that's Santa Catarina. Chickens cackle, dogs bark and the villagers go about their business dressed in their beautiful traditional costumes. Except for exploring village life and enjoying views of the lake and the volcanoes, there's little in the way of sightseeing. For refreshments, there are several little comedores on the main plaza, one of which advertises 'Cold beer sold here'.

If your budget allows, a drink or a meal at the village's best hotel is pleasant. The *Villa Santa Catarina* (☎ 762-1291, in Guatemala City 334-8136 to 39, fax 334-8134) has 30 comfortable rooms with bath and views of the lake. Rooms 24, 25, 26 and 27 (partly) face west and have fine views of Volcán San Pedro; all overlook the pretty swimming pool and grounds right on the shore. The dining room provides moderately priced table d'hôte meals. Accommodations cost US$60/70/80 for a single/double/triple.

The road continues past Santa Catarina five km to San Antonio Palopó, a larger but similar village. Three km along the way you pass the *Hotel Bella Vista* (☎ 762-1566), eight km from Panajachel. Fourteen little bungalows, each with TV, private bath and lake view, share gardens with a swimming pool and a restaurant. The bungalows are US$45/48/50 a single/double/triple. In San Antonio there's also the *Hotel Terrazas del Lago*, a beautiful place with a lovely lake view and singles/doubles/triples for US$20/26/32.

Getting There & Away

See the Panajachel section for details on buses and passenger or tour boats. From Panajachel, you can also walk to Santa Catarina in about an hour, continuing to San Antonio in about another hour.

SAN LUCAS TOLIMÁN

Farther around the lake from San Antonio, and reached by a different road, San Lucas Tolimán is busier and more commercial than most lakeside villages. Set at the foot of the dramatic Volcán Tolimán, San Lucas is a coffee-growing town and a transport point on the route between the Interamericana and the Carretera al Pacífico. Market days are Monday, Tuesday, Thursday and Friday. From San Lucas, a rough, badly maintained road goes west around Volcán Tolimán to Santiago Atitlán, then around Volcán San Pedro to San Pedro La Laguna.

See Getting There & Away under Panajachel for details on buses and passenger boats.

SANTIAGO ATITLÁN

South across the lake from Panajachel, on the shore of a lagoon squeezed between the towering volcanoes of Tolimán and San Pedro, lies the small town of Santiago Atitlán. Though it is the most visited village outside Panajachel, it clings to the traditional lifestyle of the Tzutuhil Maya. The women of the town still weave and wear huipiles with brilliantly colored flocks of birds and bouquets of flowers embroidered on them. The best day to visit is market day (Friday and Sunday, with a lesser market on Tuesday), but in fact any day will do.

Santiago is also a curiosity because of its reverence for Maximón (MAH-shee-MOHN), a local deity who is probably a blend of ancient Maya gods, Pedro de Alvarado (the fierce conquistador of Guatemala) and the biblical Judas. Despised in other highland towns, Maximón is revered in Santiago Atitlán, and his effigy with wooden mask and huge cigar is paraded triumphantly during Semana Santa processions (see Holidays & Festivals in the Facts for the Visitor chapter for the dates of Holy Week). The rest of the time, Maximón resides in a different house every year, receiving offerings of candles, beer and rum. Local children will offer to take you to see him for a small tip.

Children from Santiago greet you as you disembark at the dock, selling clay whistles and little embroidered strips of cloth. They'll be right behind, alongside and in front of you during much of your stay here.

Orientation & Information

Walk to the left from the dock along the shore to reach the street into town, which is the main commercial street. Every tourist walks up and down it between the dock and the town, so it's lined with shops selling woven cloth and other handicrafts and souvenirs.

Near the dock is the office of the Grupo Guías de Turismo Rilaj Maam, a tourist guide cooperative offering trips to many nearby places, including the Atitlán, Tolimán and San Pedro volcanoes, the Chutinamit archaeological site and other places. The office is open every day from 8 am to 5 pm.

Santiago has a post office, a Guatel telephone/fax office and a bank where you can change US dollars cash and travelers' checks.

Things to See & Do

At the top of the slope is the main square, with the town office and huge **church**, which dates from the time, several centuries ago, when Santiago was an important commercial town. Within the stark, echoing church are some surprising sights. Along the walls are wooden statues of the saints, each of whom gets new clothes made by local women every year. On the carved wooden pulpit, note the figures of corn (from which humans were formed, according to Maya religion), of a quetzal bird reading a book and of Yum-Kax, the Maya god of corn. There is similar carving on the back of the priest's chair.

The walls of the church bear paintings, now covered by a thin layer of plaster. A memorial plaque at the back of the church commemorates Father Stanley Francis Rother, a missionary priest from Oklahoma; beloved by the local people, he was despised by ultra-rightist 'death squads', who murdered him right here in the church during the troubled year of 1981.

There's a bird refuge near Santiago; the Posada de Santiago (☎ 702-8462) can give you directions.

Places to Stay & Eat

Near the dock, the *Hotel Chi-Nim-Yá* (☎ 721-7131) is a pleasant, simple hotel with 22 rooms around a central courtyard. Clean singles/doubles with shared bath are US$3.35/6.65; with private bath they're US$8.35/10. The nicest room in the place is No 106, large and airy, with lots of windows and excellent lake views. Nearby, the *Restaurante Regiomontano* is open every day from 6:30 or 7 am to 7 pm.

Hotel y Restaurante Tzutuhil (☎ 721-7174), about three blocks uphill on the road coming up from the dock, is a modern five-story building, an anomaly in this little town. Many of the rooms have large windows to the outside, with fine views, and some have cable TV. Clean rooms are US$2.50 per person with shared hot bath, US$4.15 per person with private bath. It's a good place and a great deal for the price. Go up on the rooftop for a fine view. The restaurant here is open every day from 6 am to 10:30 pm.

Restaurant Santa Rita, a few steps from the northeast corner of the plaza past Distribuidor El Buen Precio, boasts *deliciosos pays* (delicious pies).

One of the most charming hotels around the lake, or in all Guatemala for that matter, is the *Posada de Santiago* (☎ 702-8462, posdesantiago@guate.net). Half a dozen free-standing bungalows and two suites, all with stone walls, fireplaces, porches and hammocks, are set around beautiful gardens stretching up the hill from the lake. Rates are US$30/40/50/66/80 for a single/double/triple/quad/suite. It's one km from the town center; to get there, walk out of town on the road past the Hospedaje Rosita, and keep walking along the lakeside road.

The restaurant at the Posada de Santiago is special, too, with famous gourmet food and a very pleasant ambiance.

Getting There & Away

Boats between Santiago and San Pedro La Laguna take about 45 minutes to make the crossing.

SAN PEDRO LA LAGUNA

Perhaps the next most popular lakeside town to visit, after Santiago, is San Pedro La Laguna. Its number-two ranking means that fewer flocks of *muchachos* will swirl around you as you stroll the narrow cobblestone streets and wander to the outskirts for a dip in the lake.

When you arrive by boat from Panajachel, boys will greet you, asking if you want a guide to ascend the San Pedro volcano, by hiking or horseback. It's worth it to go with a guide; cost is US$2.50 per person for the whole trip by hiking, or US$1.65 per hour on horseback.

Coffee is grown in San Pedro. You'll see coffee being picked and spread out to dry on wide platforms at the beginning of the dry season.

Orientation & Information

San Pedro has two docks. The one on the south side of town serves boats going to/from Santiago Atitlán. Another dock, around on the east side of town, serves boats going to/from Panajachel. At either dock, walk straight ahead a few blocks on the road leading uphill from the dock to reach the center of town.

San Pedro has a post office, a Guatel telephone/fax office and a casa de cambio where you can change US dollars cash and travelers' checks.

None of the hotels, restaurants or other businesses here have private telephones. To reach them, you can phone to the community telephone at Guatel (☎ 762-2486) and give them a time you expect to call back; the business will send someone over to receive your return call.

Thermal Waters

Thermal Waters has open-air solar-heated pools right on the lakeshore between the two docks; there's a great view. Come in the afternoon or evening, after the water has had a chance to warm up; a reservation is a good idea, as it's a popular spot. Cost is US$3.35 for the first person, US$1.65 for each additional person. Antonio from California, the eccentric horticulturist inventor who built and operates Thermal Waters, also has an organic vegetarian restaurant here and an underground solar steam sauna. Health retreats are offered each weekend.

Courses

Casa Rosario, a Spanish-language school, is operated by Professor Samuel Cumes, a well-known San Pedro teacher. It's more economical than most Spanish schools at US$45 per week for instruction and lodging (food not available).

Places to Stay & Eat

When you arrive at the dock serving boats to/from Panajachel, turn right and walk along the lake for about 75 meters to reach the *Hotel & Restaurante Valle Azul*, right on the lakeshore. It's a new, beautiful, simple hostelry, supremely relaxing and tranquil, with hammocks on balconies, a great view across the lake and a pleasant, small lakeside restaurant. Rooms with shared bath are US$1.65 per person (plus US$0.50 per shower); singles/doubles with private bath are US$3.35/5. The restaurant is a great, inexpensive little place; it's open every day, 7 am to 10 pm.

Several other little restaurants are also near here, including the *Restaurante El Viajero*, right beside the dock, and the *Restaurante/Bar El Mesón* and *Restaurante El Fondeadero* to the right of it.

Hospedaje Casa Elena, on the lakeshore fifty meters to the left of the dock, is a pleasant, simple family-run pension; singles/doubles with shared bath are US$2.50/3.35.

Over by the dock serving boats to/from Santiago are several more places to stay. *Ti Kaaj*, on the lakeside road near the dock, is popular and inexpensive, with hammocks around the gardens and single/double/triple rooms with shared bath for US$1.65/3/4.35. There is a restaurant, disco and bar, and *cayucos* (canoes) are available for rent. Next door, the *Comedor Ranchón* is an open-air restaurant known for its good food.

Along and just off the road leading uphill from the Santiago dock are several more good places to stay. *Hospedaje Villa Sol*, with 45 simple rooms around a grassy courtyard, charges US$5/6 per room with shared/private bath. Next door, *Hotel San Pedro* also has rooms around a courtyard; singles/doubles are US$6.65 with shared bath or US$4.50/8.35 with private bath.

Just off this road, *Hospedaje San Francisco* is a pleasant, new place up on the hill. The rooms have small outdoor kitchens, a great view of the lake from their tiny patios and hammocks in the garden. Rooms with general bath are US$3.35 per person, and rooms with private bath are being built. Nearby, *Hospedaje El Balneario* is the cheapest place in town, with 14 basic rooms, each opening onto a balcony with a lake view; single/double rooms with shared bath are US$1.33/2.50.

Cafe Arte, on the road leading uphill from the Santiago dock, is a good, inexpensive cafe serving meat, fish and vegetarian dishes. It's operated by the family of internationally known primitivist artist Pedro Rafael González Chavajay; his paintings, and those of many of his students, are exhibited at the cafe. It's open every day from 7 am to 11 pm.

If you have a chance, check out the organic vegetarian restaurant at *Thermal Waters*, on the lakeshore road between the two docks. Choose from the extensive menu, and Antonio will run out to the garden to gather the ingredients. Next door, *Kolibrí Pizza* is another good little lakeside restaurant.

Getting There & Away

Land The rough road from San Lucas Tolimán to Santiago Atitlán continues 18 km to San Pedro, making its way around the lagoon and the back side of Volcán San Pedro.

GUATEMALA

A rough road connects San Pedro with the Interamericana; the turnoff is at Km 148. The road meets the lake at Santa Clara La Laguna and turns right to San Marcos. From San Pedro it continues to Santiago Atitlán and San Lucas Tolimán. From San Marcos it continues to Tzununá, but beyond that it's a walking trail only, which continues to Santa Cruz La Laguna. Buses to Guatemala City depart from San Pedro at 3, 3:30 4, 4:30 and 5 am; see the Guatemala City section for return buses. The trip takes three to four hours and costs US$2.65.

Unless you want to bring a vehicle, it's easier to reach San Pedro by boat.

Boat Passenger boats come here from Panajachel (see that section for details) and from Santiago.

SAN MARCOS LA LAGUNA

San Marcos is a very peaceful little place, with houses set among shady coffee plants near the lakeshore. The lakeshore is beautiful here, with several little docks you can swim from.

San Marcos' greatest claim to fame is **Las Pirámides** meditation center (fax 762-2080), on the path heading inland from Posada Schumann. A one-month spiritual course called the Curso Lunar de Meditación (lunar meditation course for spiritual and human development) begins every full moon. It covers four elements of human development (physical, mental, emotional and spiritual), with one week for each. If you can stay for a month to do the whole course, come in time for full moon. If you can only stay a week, the week just before full moon is best, when there's a special meditation retreat program. Or come for the channeling sessions, held on the new and full moon.

Other things done here include yoga, aura work, Tarot readings and regression.

Every structure on the property is built in the shape of pyramids and oriented to the four cardinal points. Accommodations are available in pyramid-shaped little houses for US$8.35/7.50/6.65 per day by the day/

week/month. Included in this price is the meditation course, use of the kitchen and sauna, and access to a fascinating library with books in several languages.

Places to Stay & Eat

There are several places to stay in San Marcos. *Posada Schumann* is 400 meters to the left of the dock, walking along the lakeside path. When you reach Posada Schumann, turn inland and walk up the pathway to reach all the rest of the places listed here.

Right on the lakeside, Posada Schumann has three stone bungalows, each with kitchen and private bath; there's also a restaurant and sauna. Singles/doubles are US$9/17, cheaper by the week or month. For reservations, contact them in Guatemala City (☎ 360-4049, 339-2683, fax 473-1326).

Hotel Paco Real (fax 762-1196) has beautiful gardens and rooms that are simple but beautiful and tastefully decorated; all in all it's a very artistic place. Rooms with shared bath are US$6/10/14 for a single/ double/triple. Also here is a pleasant restaurant, open every day from 7 am to 9 pm.

Hotel La Paz (☎ 702-9168) has three beautiful little bungalows, each with sleeping loft and private bath; cost is US$17 for one to four people. There's also a vegetarian restaurant and a sauna. Camping is allowed.

Unicornio Rooms is another attractive place, with beautiful gardens, a sauna and a communal kitchen (but no electricity). Three small, thatch-roofed, A-frame bungalows with shared cold bath are US$2.50/3.65 for a single/double. One large two-story bungalow with private kitchen and bath is US$6.65 per day for one or two people, US$10 for three.

Hotel San Marcos is another option here; it's not as beautiful as the other places. Rooms with shared cold bath are US$3.35 per person.

Getting There & Away

You can drive to San Marcos from the Interamericana, where there's a turnoff at Km 148. See the San Pedro section.

See under Panajachel for information on passenger boats.

SANTA CRUZ LA LAGUNA

Santa Cruz La Laguna is another peaceful little village beside the lake. The main part of the village is up the hill from the dock; the hotels are on the lakeside, right beside the dock.

Diving

ATI Divers (fax 762-1196) operates a diving school and does underwater archaeology dives and special projects. A four-day PADI open-water diving certification course costs US$150; they also offer a PADI high-altitude advanced diving course and fun dives. It's based at La Iguana Perdida hotel.

Hiking

You can take some good walks starting at Santa Cruz. A beautiful option is the lakeside walking track between Santa Cruz and San Marcos; it takes about 2½ hours one way. Or you can walk up the hill to Sololá, a three- to 3½-hour walk one way.

Places to Stay & Eat

Three pleasant lakeside hotels, all right beside the dock, provide accommodations and meals. While there's electricity up the hill in town, there's none at the hotels. In the evening guests eat by candlelight and lantern-light.

None of these hotels has a telephone, but you can fax them (fax 762-1196). It can take a few days to hear back from them.

Arca de Noé has been known for its excellent food and friendly managers, but the management has recently changed.

La Iguana Perdida also has a restaurant and a variety of accommodations. The cost is US$2.50 per person for a dorm bed, US$3.35/5 for a single/double in the 'massage room', or US$6/8 for single/double rooms with shared bath. Here, too, meals are served family-style, with everyone eating together; dinner is US$5. There's also a sauna. The friendly managers, Deedle Denman (from the UK) and

Mike Kiersgard (from Greenland), also operate ATI Divers.

The *Posada Abaj Hotel*, also here on the lakefront, is a nice, big place that also has a restaurant. Rooms with shared bath are US$8.35/12/15 for a single/double/triple; bungalows with private bath are US$20 for up to three people. Spanish classes are offered here.

Getting There & Away

See Panajachel for details on passenger boats.

Quiché

The Departamento del Quiché is famous mostly for the town of Chichicastenango, with its bustling markets on Thursday and Sunday. Beyond Chichi to the north is Santa Cruz del Quiché, the capital of the department. On its outskirts lie the ruins of K'umarcaaj (or Gumarcaah), also called Utatlán, the last capital city of the Quiché Maya.

The road to Quiché leaves the Interamericana at Los Encuentros, winding its way through pine forests and cornfields, down into a steep valley and up the other side. Women sit in front of their little roadside cottages weaving yet another gorgeous piece of cloth on their simple backstrap looms. From Los Encuentros, it takes half an hour to travel to Chichicastnango, 17 km to the north.

CHICHICASTENANGO

Population 8000

Surrounded by valleys, with nearby mountains looming overhead, Chichicastenango (2030 meters) seems isolated from the rest of Guatemala. When its narrow cobbled streets and red-tiled roofs are enveloped in mists, as they often are, it can seem magical. Chichi is a beautiful, interesting place; not the many shiny tour buses parked near the market nor even the gaggles of camera-toting tour groups can change that. If you have a choice of days, come for the Sunday market rather than the Thursday

Traditional Clothing

Anyone visiting the Highlands can delight in the beautiful *traje indígena* (traditional clothing) of the local people. The styles, patterns and colors used by each village are unique, and each garment is the creation of its weaver, with subtle differences from the others.

The basic elements of the traditional wardrobe are the *tocoyal* (head-covering), *huipil* (blouse), *córte* or *refago* (skirt), *calzones* (trousers), *tzut* or *kaperraj* (cloth), *paz* or *faja* (sash) and *caítes* or *xajáp* (sandals).

Women's head-coverings are beautiful and elaborate bands of cloth up to several metres in length, wound about the head and decorated with tassels, pompoms and silver ornaments. In recent years they have been worn only on ceremonial occasions and for tourist photos.

Women's huipiles, however, are worn proudly every day. Though some machine-made fabrics are now being used, most huipiles are made completely by hand. The white blouse is woven on a backstrap loom, then decorated with appliqué and embroidery designs and motifs common to the weaver's village. Many of the motifs are traditional symbols. No doubt all had religious or historical significance at one time, though today that meaning may be lost to memory.

Córtes (refajos) are pieces of cloth seven to 10 yards long that are wrapped around the body. Traditionally, girls wear theirs above the knee, married women at the knee and old women below the knee, though the style can differ markedly from region to region.

Both men and women wear fajas, long strips of backloom-woven cloth wrapped around the midriff as belts. Wrapped with folds upward like a cummerbund, the folds serve as pockets.

Tzutes (male) or kaperraj (female) are the all-purpose cloths carried by local people and used as head-coverings, baby-slings, produce sacks, basket covers and shawls. There are also shawls for women called *perraj*, probably a contraction of kaperraj.

Before the coming of the Spaniards, it was most common for simple leather thong sandals (caítes, xajáp) to be worn only by men. Even today, many Highland women and children go barefoot, while others have thongs, more elaborate huarache-style sandals or modern shoes. ■

one, as the cofradías (religious brotherhoods) often hold processions on Sunday.

Though isolated, Chichi has always been an important market town. Villagers from throughout the region would walk for many hours carrying their wares to participate in the commerce here – and that was in the days before good roads.

Today, though many traders come by bus, others still arrive on foot. When they reach Chichi's main square on the night before the market, they lay down their loads, spread out a blanket and go to sleep in one of the arcades that surround the square. At dawn on Thursday and Sunday they spread out their vegetables, fruits, chunks of chalk (ground to a powder, mixed with water and used to soften dried maize), balls of wax, handmade harnesses and other wares and wait for customers.

Many ladino business types also set up fairly touristy stalls in the Sunday and Thursday markets. Somehow they end up adding to the color and fascination, not detracting from it.

Besides the famous market, Masheños (citizens of Chichicastenango) are famous for their adherence to pre-Christian religious beliefs and ceremonies. You can readily see versions of these old rites in and around the church of Santo Tomás and at the shrine of Pascual Abaj on the outskirts of town.

Government

Chichi has two religious and governmental establishments. The Catholic Church and the Republic of Guatemala appoint priests and town officials to manage their interests, but the local people elect their own religious and civil officers to deal with local matters.

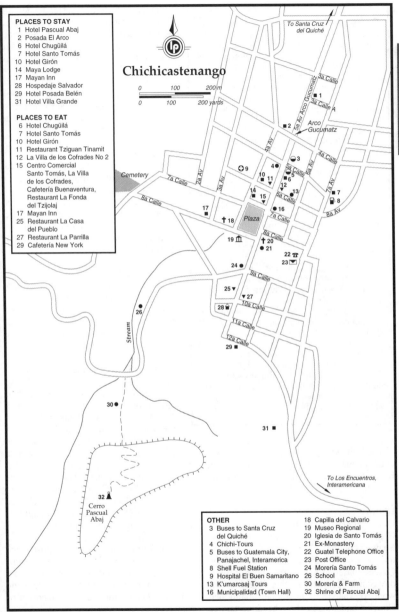

Chichicastenango

PLACES TO STAY
1 Hotel Pascual Abaj
2 Posada El Arco
6 Hotel Chugüilá
7 Hotel Santo Tomás
10 Hotel Girón
14 Maya Lodge
17 Mayan Inn
28 Hospedaje Salvador
29 Hotel Posada Belén
31 Hotel Villa Grande

PLACES TO EAT
6 Hotel Chugüilá
7 Hotel Santo Tomás
10 Hotel Girón
11 Restaurant Tziguan Tinamit
12 La Villa de los Cofrades No 2
15 Centro Comercial
     Santo Tomás, La Villa
     de los Cofrades,
     Cafetería Buenaventura,
     Restaurant La Fonda
     del Tzijolaj
17 Mayan Inn
25 Restaurant La Casa
     del Pueblo
27 Restaurant La Parrilla
29 Cafetería New York

OTHER
3 Buses to Santa Cruz
    del Quiché
4 Chichi-Tours
5 Buses to Guatemala City,
    Panajachel, Interamerica
8 Shell Fuel Station
9 Hospital El Buen Samaritano
13 K'umarcaaj Tours
16 Municipalidad (Town Hall)
18 Capilla del Calvario
19 Museo Regional
20 Iglesia de Santo Tomás
21 Ex-Monastery
22 Guatel Telephone Office
23 Post Office
24 Morería Santo Tomás
26 School
30 Morería & Farm
32 Shrine of Pascual Abaj

To Santa Cruz del Quiché

Arco Gucumatz

Cemetery

Plaza

Stream

Cerro Pascual Abaj

To Los Encuentros, Interamericana

GUATEMALA

Cofradías

Chichi's religious life is centered in traditional religious brotherhoods known as cofradías. Membership in the brotherhood is an honorable civic duty; leadership is the greatest honor. Leaders are elected periodically, and the man who receives the honor of being elected must provide banquets and pay for festivities for the cofradía throughout his term. Though it is very expensive, a *cofrade* (member of the brotherhood) happily accepts the burden, even going into debt if necessary.

Each of Chichi's 14 cofradías has a patron saint. Most notable is the cofradía of Santo Tomás, Chichicastenango's patron saint. The cofradías march in procession to church every Sunday morning and during religious festivals, the officers dressed in costumes showing their rank. Before them is carried a ceremonial staff topped by a silver crucifix or sun-badge that signifies the cofradía's patron saint. Indian drum and flute, and perhaps a few more modern instruments such as a trumpet, may accompany the procession, as do fireworks.

During major church festivals, effigies of the saints are brought out and carried in grand processions, and richly costumed dancers wearing the traditional carved wooden masks act out legends of the ancient Maya and of the Spanish conquest. For the rest of the year, these masks and costumes are kept in storehouses called *morerías*; you'll see them, marked by signs, around the town. ∎

The Indian town government has its own council, mayor and deputy mayor, and it has a court that decides cases involving local Indians exclusively.

History

Once called Chaviar, this was an important Cakchiquel trading town long before the Spanish conquest. Not long before the conquistadors arrived, the Cakchiquel and the Quiché (based at K'umarcaaj near present-day Santa Cruz del Quiché, 20 km north) went to war. The Cakchiquel abandoned Chaviar and moved their headquarters to Iximché, which was easier to defend. The conquistadors came and conquered K'umarcaaj, and many of its residents fled to Chaviar, which they renamed Chugüilá (Above the Nettles) and Tziguan Tinamit (Surrounded by Canyons). These are the names still used by the Quiché Maya, although everyone else calls the place Chichicastenango, a foreign name given by the conquistadors' Mexican allies.

Orientation

Though supposedly laid out as a typical Spanish colonial street grid, Chichi's hilly topography defeats the logic of the plan, and lack of street signs often keeps you wondering where you are. Use our map, identify some landmarks, and you should have little trouble, as Chichi is fairly small.

Information

Tourist Offices There is no official tourist information office in Chichi. Ask your questions at the museum on the main square or at one of the hotels. The Mayan Inn is perhaps the most helpful and best informed.

Money Since Sunday is Chichi's biggest day of commerce, all the banks here are open on Sunday, taking their day off on some other day of the week (the day varies from bank to bank, so you can always find some bank open). Most banks change US dollars cash and travelers' checks; Bancafé, on 5a Avenida between 6a and 7a Calle, gives cash advances on Visa cards. (There's no place in town for MasterCard.) The Hotel Santo Tomás (see Places to Stay) will change travelers' checks for guests and nonguests alike, at the same rate as the banks.

Post & Communications The post office is at 7a Avenida 8-47, two blocks south of the Hotel Santo Tomás on the road into town. Very near it is the Guatel telephone office, at 7a Avenida 8-21, on the corner of 8a Calle.

GUATEMALA

Market

Years ago, intrepid travelers made their way to this mountain-bound fastness to witness Chichi's main square packed with Indian traders attending one of Guatemala's largest indigenous markets. Today the market has stalls aimed directly at tourists, as well as those for local people.

On Wednesday and Saturday evenings you'll see men carrying bundles of long poles up the narrow cobbled streets to the square, then stacking them out of the way. In the evening the arcades around the square are alive with families cooking supper and arranging their bedding for a night's sleep out of doors.

Between dawn and about 8 or 9 am on Sunday and Thursday, the stacks of poles are erected into stalls, hung with cloth, furnished with tables and piled with goods for sale. In general, the tourist-oriented stalls selling carved wooden masks, lengths of embroidered cloth and garments are around the outer edges of the market in the most visible areas. Behind them, the center of the square is devoted to things that the villagers want and need: vegetables and fruit, baked goods, macaroni, soap, clothing, spices, sewing notions and toys. Cheap cookshops provide lunch for buyers and sellers alike.

Most of the stalls are taken down by late afternoon. Prices are best just before the market breaks up, as traders would rather sell than carry goods away with them.

You may want to arrive in town the day before market day to pin down a room and a bed and to be up early for the market. One traveler wrote to say it's worth being here on Saturday night to attend the Saturday night mass. Otherwise, you can always come by bus on market day itself, or by shuttle bus: market day shuttle buses come over from Antigua, Panajachel and Guatemala City, returning in late afternoon. The market starts winding down around 3 or 4 pm.

Iglesia de Santo Tomás

Though dedicated to the Catholic rite, this simple church, dating from about 1540, is more often the scene of rituals that are only slightly Catholic and more highly Mayan.

The front steps of the church serve much the same purpose as did the great flights of stairs leading up to Maya pyramids. For much of the day (especially on Sunday), the steps smolder with incense of copal resin, while indigenous prayer leaders called *chuchkajaues* (mother-fathers) swing censers (usually tin cans poked with holes) containing *estoraque* incense and chant magic words in honor of the ancient Maya calendar and of their ancestors.

It's customary for the front steps and door of the church to be used only by important church officials and by the chuchkajaues, so you should go around to the right and enter by the side door.

Inside, the floor of the church may be spread with pine boughs and dotted with offerings of maize kernels, bouquets of flowers, bottles of liquor wrapped in corn husks and candles – candles everywhere. Many local families can trace their lineages back centuries, some even to the ancient kings of Quiché. The candles and offerings on the floor are in remembrance of the ancestors, many of whom are buried beneath the church floor just as Maya kings were buried beneath pyramids.

On the west side of the plaza is another little whitewashed church, the Capilla del Calvario, which is similar in form and function to Santo Tomás, but smaller.

Museo Regional

In the arcade facing the south side of the square is the Museo Regional. Inside you can see ancient clay pots and figurines, arrowheads and spearheads of flint and obsidian, copper ax-heads and *metates* (grindstones for maize).

The museum also holds the Rossbach jade collection, with several beautiful necklaces, figurines and other objects. Ildefonso Rossbach served as Chichi's Catholic priest for many years until his death in 1944.

The museum is open every day but Tuesday, from 8 am to noon and 2 to 5 pm.

Shrine of Pascual Abaj

Before you have been in Chichi very long, some village lad will offer to guide you (for a tip) to a hilltop on the outskirts to have a look at Pascual Abaj (Sacrifice Stone), which is the local shrine to Huyup Tak'ah (Mountain Plain), the Mayan earth god. Said to be hundreds – perhaps thousands – of years old, the stone-faced idol has suffered numerous indignities at the hands of outsiders, but local people still revere it. Chuchkajaues come here regularly to offer incense, food, cigarettes, flowers, liquor and Coca-Cola to the earth god, and perhaps even to sacrifice a chicken. The offerings are in thanks and hope for the earth's continuing fertility.

Sacrifices do not take place at regular hours. If you're in luck, you can witness one. The worshipers will not mind if you watch, and some (but not all!) won't mind if you take photographs, though they may ask if you want to make an offering (of a few quetzals) yourself. If there is no ceremony, you can still see the idol and enjoy the walk up to the pine-clad hilltop and the views of the town and valley.

There have been some incidents of robbery of tourists walking to visit Pascual Abaj, so the best plan is to join with others and go in a large group.

You don't really need a juvenile guide to find Pascual Abaj. Walk down the hill on 5a Avenida from the Santo Tomás church, turn right onto 9a Calle and continue downhill along this unpaved road, which bends to the left. At the bottom of the hill, when the road turns sharply to the right, bear left and follow a path through the cornfields, keeping the ditch on your left. Signs mark the way. Walk to the buildings just ahead, which include a farmhouse and a *morería*, a workshop where masks are made. Greet the family here. If the children are not in school, you may be invited to see them perform a local dance in full costume on your return from Pascual Abaj (a tip is expected).

Walk through the farm buildings to the hill behind, and follow the switchback path to the top and along the ridge of the hill, called Turukaj, to a clearing in which you will see the idol in its rocky shrine. The idol looks like something from Easter Island. The squat stone crosses near it have many

levels of significance for the Maya, only one of which pertains to Christ. The area of the shrine is littered with past offerings; the bark of nearby pines has been stripped away in places to be used as fuel in the incense fires.

Places to Stay

Chichi does not have a lot of accommodations, and most places are in the higher price range. As rooms are scarce, it's a good idea to arrive early on Wednesday or Saturday if you want to secure a room for the Thursday and Sunday markets. Safe car parking is available in the courtyard of most hotels.

Places to Stay – budget

Hotel Girón (☎ 756-1156, fax 756-1226), 6a Calle 4-52, Zona 1, is a pleasant, clean hotel, a good value for the money. Singles/doubles are US$6/10 with shared bath, US$9.15/15 with private bath, or US$11/19 with private bath and cable TV.

Hotel Pascual Abaj (☎ 756-1055), 5a Avenida Arco Gucumatz 3-38, Zona 1, is a clean little place one long block north downhill from the Arco Gucumatz, an arched bridge over the road on the north of town. Rooms with bath cost US$7.50/10 for a single/double.

Of the cheap hotels, *Hospedaje Salvador* (☎ 756-1329), 5a Avenida 10-09, Zona 1, two blocks southwest of the Santo Tomás church, is the biggest. This large, mazelike, white-and-yellow building has 48 rooms on three floors. Singles/doubles/triples are US$4.15/6.65/10 with shared bath, or US$5/10/15 with private bath. You can get a discount if you come on your own, without children bringing you.

Hotel Posada Belén (☎ /fax 756-1244), 12a Calle 5-55, Zona 1, is up on a hill with a fine view. Rooms here are US$5/8.35/12.50 for a single/double/triple with shared bath, US$8.35/12/15 with private bath. You can pay US$1.65 more to get cable TV, and there's laundry service. Upstairs is the *Cafetería New York*; the owner is a Guatemalan who spent 14 years in New York and speaks English.

Posada El Arco (☎ 756-1255), 4a Calle 4-36 near the Arco Gucumatz, is a pleasant guesthouse where travelers are made to feel at home with the family. You can sit in the lawn chairs in the rear garden and enjoy a great view northwards toward the mountains of Quiché. All five rooms are spotless and have attractive decor. The three rooms with shared bath are US$10 for one or two people (US$7.50 if you stay two nights or more); two larger with private bath are US$14/17 for two/three people. The friendly owners, Emilsa and Pedro Macario, speak English and Spanish.

Places to Stay – middle

Hotel Chugüilá (☎ 756-1134, fax 756-1279), 5a Avenida 5-24, is charming. Most of the 36 colonial-style rooms have private bath, some have a fireplace, and there are even a few two-room suites and a restaurant. For what you get, the price is very reasonable – US$15/19/24 for a single/double/triple without bath, US$31/36/41 with private bath.

Maya Lodge (☎ 756-1167), in the main plaza, has 10 rather dark rooms with clean add-on showers in the very midst of the market. Fairly plain despite some colonial touches, it is comfortable nonetheless, though overpriced. Rooms with shared bath are US$17/27 for a single/double; with private bath they are US$24/32.

Places to Stay – top end

The best hotel in town is one of the most pleasant in Guatemala. It's the lovely old *Mayan Inn* (☎ 756-1176, fax 756-1212), 8a Calle A and 3a Avenida, on a quiet street one long block southwest of the plaza. Founded in 1932 by Alfred S Clark of Clark Tours, it has grown to include several restored colonial houses, their courtyards planted with exuberant tropical gardens and their walls festooned with brilliantly colored indigenous textiles. The 30 rooms, all with fireplaces, are quite charming, with antique furnishings including carved wooden bedsteads, headboards painted with country scenes, heavily carved armoires and rough-hewn tables. The private bathrooms (many with tubs) may be old-fashioned, but they are decently maintained. A staff member in traditional costume is assigned to help you carry your bags, answer any questions and even serve at your table in the dining room, as well as to look after your room – there are no door locks. Rates are US$78/90/108 for a single/double/triple.

Hotel Santo Tomás (☎ 756-1316, fax 756-1306, hst@guate.net), 7a Avenida 5-32, two blocks east of the plaza, is colonial in architecture and decoration but modern in construction and facilities, and it is thus a favorite with bus-tour operators. Each of the 43 rooms has private bath (with tub) and fireplace; all the rooms are grouped around pretty courtyards with colonial fountains. There's a swimming pool, Jacuzzi and a good bar and dining room. Rates are US$66/78/96 for a single/double/triple.

Hotel Villa Grande (☎ 756-1053, 756-1236, fax 756-1140), one km south of Chichi's main square along the road into town, is a resort and convention center with 75 modern rooms and suites in low tile-roofed buildings set into a hillside. It has fine views, a swimming pool and a restaurant. The regular rooms are rather stark, but the suites all have fireplaces and patios with a view. Singles/doubles are US$72/80 in the regular rooms, US$105/112 in the suites. The pleasant walk to the center takes about 10 minutes.

Places to Eat – budget

On Sunday and Thursday, eat where the marketers do – at the cookshops set up in the center of the market. These are the cheapest in town. On other days, look for the little comedores near the post office and Guatel office on the road into town (7a Avenida).

Restaurant La Fonda del Tzijolaj, upstairs in the Centro Comercial Santo Tomás on the north side of the plaza, has everything: good views, nice decor, decent food and reasonable prices – US$2 to US$3 for breakfast, twice that for lunch or dinner. It's closed Tuesday. There are several other restaurants with portico tables in the Centro Comercial. At *La Villa de los Cofrades* you can while away the hours with checkers (draughts), backgammon and the best coffee in town. It's a popular place, with breakfast for around US$2.50, lunch or dinner around US$4.

The inner courtyard of the Centro Comercial Santo Tomás is a vegetable market on market days, a basketball court the rest of the time. Upstairs inside the courtyard, overlooking the vegetable market, *Cafetería Buenaventura* is clean, pleasant and one of the most economical places in town.

La Villa de los Cofrades No 2, upstairs overlooking the street at the corner of 6a Calle and 5a Avenida (enter from 6a Calle), has tables out on the balcony, overlooking the market street, as well as inside. It's run by the same owners as the original La Villa de los Cofrades, has the same good coffee and serves delicious food. An ample lunch or dinner with several courses and big portions costs around US$4 to US$6; simpler meals cost less.

Restaurant Tziguan Tinamit, at the corner of 6 Calle and 5a Avenida, takes its name from the Quiché Maya name for Chichicastenango. It's popular with locals and foreigners and is open all day every day.

Restaurant La Parrilla, at the corner of 5a Avenida Arco Gucumatz and 10a Calle, catty-corner from Hospedaje Salvador, is a good, economical little restaurant specializing in charcoal-grilled meats. Hearty meals of your choice of meat, served with rice, salad, soup and bread or tortillas are US$3 to US$5; breakfasts are cheaper. Half a block away, *Restaurant La Casa del Pueblo*, at 5a Avenida Arco Gucumatz 9-81, is another popular little restaurant.

Pensión Chugüilá (see Places to Stay) is one of the most pleasant places to eat, and there are always a few other travelers to talk with about life on the road. Main-course plates are priced at US$5.

Places to Eat – middle

The three dining rooms at the *Mayan Inn*, 8a Calle A and 3a Avenida on a quiet street one long block southwest of the plaza, have pale yellow walls, beamed ceilings, red-tiled floors, stocky colonial-style tables and chairs and decorations of colorful local cloth. Waiters wear traditional costumes,

which evolved from the dress of Spanish farmers of the colonial era: colorful headdress, sash, black tunic with colored embroidery, half-length trousers and squeaky leather sandals called *caïtes*. The daily set-price meals are the best way to order here; they cost US$6 for breakfast and US$12 for lunch or dinner, plus drinks and tip.

The *Hotel Santo Tomás*, 7a Avenida 5-32, two blocks east of the plaza, has a good dining room, but it's often crowded with tour groups. Try to get one of the pleasant courtyard tables, where you can enjoy the sun and the marimba band, which plays at lunchtime on market days.

Getting There & Away

Bus Chichi has no bus station. Buses heading south to Guatemala City, Panajachel, Quetzaltenango and all other points reached from the Interamericana arrive and depart from 5a Calle at the corner of 5a Avenida Arco Gucumatz, Zona 1, one block south of the arch. Buses heading north to Santa Cruz del Quiché arrive and depart from around the corner on 5a Avenida Arco Gucumatz. Any bus heading south can drop you at Los Encuentros, where you can catch a bus to your final destination.

Antigua – 170 km, 3½ hours; take any bus heading for Guatemala City and change buses at Chimaltenango

Guatemala City – 144 km, 3½ hours, US$2.50; buses every 20 minutes, 3:30 am to 6 pm

Los Encuentros – 17 km, 30 minutes, US$0.50; take any bus heading for Guatemala City, Panajachel, Quetzaltenango and so on

Nebaj – 103 km, 4½ hours, US$2.50; two buses daily, or take a bus to Santa Cruz del Quiché and change buses there

Panajachel – 37 km, 1½ hours, US$1.65; 11 buses daily (approximately hourly), 4:30 am to 2:30 pm; or take any bus heading south and change buses at Los Encuentros

Quetzaltenango – 94 km, three hours, US$6; seven buses daily, mostly in the morning; or take any bus heading south and change at Los Encuentros

Santa Cruz del Quiché – 19 km, 30 minutes, US$0.50; buses every 20 minutes, 6 am to 9 pm

Shuttle Minibus On market days, shuttle buses arrive *en masse*, bringing tourists from Panajachel, Antigua, Guatemala City and Quetzaltenango. The shuttles arrive around midmorning, park in front of the Hotel Santo Tomás and depart for the return trip around 2 pm. If you're in Chichi, you can usually catch a ride out on one of these.

Two shuttle bus companies in Chichi offer shuttle services to these same places: Chichi-Tours (☎ 756-1134, 756-1008), at the corner of 5a Calle and 5a Avenida Arco Gucumatz, Zona 1, and K'umarcaaj Tours (☎ 756-1226), 6a Calle 5-70, Local 1, Zona 1. With a minimum of three passengers (or an equivalent payment), Chichi-Tours will make trips to anyplace else you have in mind, including the ruins at K'umarcaaj (near Santa Cruz del Quiché).

SANTA CRUZ DEL QUICHÉ
Population 13,000

The capital of the department of Quiché (2020 meters) is 19 km north of Chichicastenango. As you leave Chichi heading north along 5a Avenida, you'll pass beneath Arco Gucumatz, an arched bridge built in 1932 and named for the founder of K'umarcaaj.

Without the bustle of the big market and the big tourism buses, Santa Cruz – which is usually called 'El Quiché' or simply 'Quiché' – is quieter and more typical of the Guatemalan countryside than is Chichi. The town is small and easy to navigate. There aren't many tourists here, but those who do come are treated well; the locals are friendly and will direct you anywhere you need to go.

Travelers who come to Quiché usually do so as a side trip from Chichi, or on their way to or from more remote places in the highlands (such as Nebaj, or the remote mountain route between Huehuetenango and Cobán), or to visit the ruins of K'umarcaaj (Utatlán). A visit to the ruins is best done early in the morning, as you may have to walk to the ruins and back (or taxi from town).

Orientation
Everything you need is within a few short blocks of the church, which is on the east side of the central plaza, called Parque Central. The bus station is about five blocks south and two blocks east of the church. The open-air market is one block east of the church.

On the northwest corner of the plaza, Banco Industrial changes US dollars travelers' checks and cash and gives advances on Visa and MasterCard.

K'umarcaaj
The ruins of the ancient Quiché Maya capital are three km west of El Quiché along an unpaved road. Start out of town along 10a Calle and ask the way frequently. No signs mark the way and there is no regular transport, unless you hire a taxi in town. Consider yourself very lucky if you succeed in hitching a ride with other travelers who have their own vehicle. Admission to the site costs a few pennies.

The kingdom of Quiché was established in Late Postclassic times (about the 14th century) from a mixture of indigenous people and Mexican invaders. Around 1400, King Gucumatz founded his capital at K'umarcaaj and conquered many neighboring cities. During the long reign of his successor Q'uikab (1425-75), the kingdom of Quiché extended its borders to Huehuetenango, Sacapulas, Rabinal and Cobán, even coming to influence the peoples of the Soconusco region in Mexico.

The Cakchiquel, a vassal people who once fought alongside the Quiché, broke away from their former overlords and established their capital at Iximché during the 15th century.

Pedro de Alvarado led his Spanish conquistadors into Guatemala in 1524, and it was the Quiché, under their king, Tecún Umán, who organized the defense of the country. In the decisive battle fought near Quetzaltenango on February 12, 1524, Alvarado and Tecún locked in mortal combat. Alvarado won. The defeated Quiché invited the victorious Alvarado to

GUATEMALA

visit their capital, where they secretly planned to kill him. Smelling a rat, Alvarado enlisted the aid of his Mexican auxiliaries and the anti-Quiché Cakchiquel, and together they captured the Quiché leaders, burnt them alive and destroyed K'umarcaaj (called Utatlán by his Mexican allies).

The history is more interesting than the ruined city, of which little remains but a few grass-covered mounds. Of the hundred or so large structures identified by archaeologists, only half a dozen are somewhat recognizable, and these are uninspiring. The site itself is a beautiful place for a picnic, shaded by tall trees and surrounded by defensive ravines, which failed to save the city from the conquistadors. Local prayer-men keep the fires of ancient Quiché burning, so to speak, by using ruined K'umarcaaj as a ritual site. A long *cueva* (tunnel) beneath the plaza is a favorite spot for prayers and chicken sacrifices.

Places to Stay & Eat

Hotel San Pascual (☎ 755-1107), 7a Calle 0-43, Zona 1, a block south of the church, is a pleasant, clean hotel run by a dynamo señora who also runs a typing school for local children in a room off the lobby. It's a friendly place, with guests gathering to watch TV in the evening. Rooms are US$4/6/8 for a single/double/triple with shared bath, or US$6/10/14 with private bath.

The clean, modern *Hotel Rey K'iche*, 8a Calle 0-39, Zona 5, is between the bus station and the plaza, about two blocks from each. New in 1996, it has five rooms with shared bath for US$6.65 per person, and 20 rooms with private bath (some with color TV) for US$10 per person.

Comedor Fliper, 1a Avenida 7-31, 1½ blocks south of the church, is inexpensive, pleasant, small, clean and friendly. Guests from the Hotel San Pascual often walk around the corner to eat here. It's open every day, 7 am to 9 pm.

Restaurante El Torito Steak House, on 4a Calle half a block west of the plaza, serves breakfast for US$2; burgers or sandwiches are the same. The house specialty, filet mignon, is US$4.50 for breakfast, US$6 for

a full dinner with soup and more. It's open every day. *La Casona*, on 2a Calle between 4a and 5a Avenidas, a few blocks northwest of the church, is another popular restaurant.

Getting There & Away

Many buses from Guatemala City to Chichicastenango continue to El Quiché (look for 'El Quiché' or just 'Quiché' on the signboard). The last bus from El Quiché headed south to Chichicastenango and Los Encuentros leaves mid-afternoon, so don't tarry too long here unless you want to spend the night.

El Quiché is the transport point for the sparsely populated and somewhat remote reaches of northern Quiché, which extends all the way to the Mexican border.

The bus station is about five blocks south and two blocks east of the plaza. Buses include:

Chichicastenango – 19 km, 30 minutes, US$0.50; take any bus heading for Guatemala City

Guatemala City – 163 km, 3½ hours, US$1.65; buses every 20 minutes, 3 am to 8 pm

Nebaj – 84 km, four hours, US$1.65; buses at 8 and 10 am, 12:30, 1 and 3:30 pm. Or take a bus to Sacapulas and change there

Sacapulas – 50 km, 1½ hours, US$1.15; hourly buses, 9 am to 4 pm; or take any bus heading for Nebaj or Uspantán

Uspantán – 90 km, six hours, US$2; buses at 10 and 11 am, noon and 1 pm. Or take a bus to Sacapulas and change there

NEBAJ
Population 9000

High among the Cuchumatanes lie the Ixil Maya village of Nebaj and its neighboring villages of Chajul and Cotzal. The scenery is breathtakingly beautiful, and the local people, remote from the cultural influences of TV and modern urbanity, proudly preserve their ancient way of life. Nebaj women wear very beautiful huipiles, and they make excellent handicrafts, mostly textiles.

Nebaj's location in this mountain fastness has been both a blessing and a curse. The Spaniards found it difficult to conquer and laid waste to the inhabitants when they did. In recent years guerrilla forces made the area a base of operations, and the army took strong measures to dislodge them. Many small villages were destroyed and their surviving inhabitants were herded into 'strategic hamlets', as in the Vietnam War.

Travelers come to Nebaj for the scenery, local culture, excellent handicrafts, market (Thursday and Sunday) and, during the second week in August, the annual festival.

If you're in Nebaj, consider taking this pleasant walk. Leave Nebaj on the road heading to Chajul. After walking 10 or 15 minutes, you'll reach a bridge over a small river. Just before the bridge, turn left onto a gravel road and follow the river. Walking downriver for 45 minutes to an hour, you'll pass several small waterfalls before reaching a larger waterfall about 25 meters high.

Places to Stay & Eat

Pensión Las Tres Hermanas is the best-known lodging, charging US$1 for a bed and the same price for a meal. There's no sign, but local children will bring you here from the bus. The *Hospedaje de la Esperanza* charges US$2.50 per night, but they also charge extra for bathroom tissue, hot water and so on. A new hotel in Nebaj is more expensive but very pleasant. Other alternatives include the *Pensión Las Gemelitas* and the *Hotel Ixil*.

Getting There & Away

Buses come to Nebaj from Santa Cruz del Quiché, Huehuetenango, Sacapulas and Cobán. Pickup trucks also provide transport at a fare equivalent to that of the bus.

Coming from the Cobán side, you have to change buses several times – it's about five hours from Cobán to Uspantán, three hours from Uspantán to Sacapulas, and 2½ hours from Sacapulas to Nebaj. It's easier to reach Nebaj from Huehuetenango or from Santa Cruz del Quiché, going via Sacapulas, as buses are more frequent.

USPANTÁN
Population 2800

Uspantán is a small village on the road between Sacapulas and Cobán. Rigoberta Menchú, the 1992 Nobel Peace Prize laureate, grew up in the mountains around Uspantán; travelers who have read her works might be interested to spend some time here. If you travel this way by bus, you may find yourself spending the night here.

Pensión Galindo, about three blocks from the church and the plaza, charges US$2.50 and is a fine place to stay. On the same street, *Comedor Central* is basic but good.

Two buses a day leave Uspantán for Sacapulas, at 3 am and 9 pm. It's a bad road, and it will three hours to cover about 40 km between the two towns.

Western Highlands

The departments of Quetzaltenango, Totonicapán and Huehuetenango are more mountainous and less frequented by tourists than regions closer to Guatemala City. The scenery here is just as beautiful and the indigenous culture just as colorful and fascinating. Travelers going to and from the border post at La Mesilla find these towns welcome breaks from long hours of travel, and there are some interesting possibilities for excursions as well.

Highlights of a visit to this area include Quetzaltenango, Guatemala's second-largest city; the pretty nearby town of Zunil, with its Fuentes Georginas hot springs; Totonicapán, a department capital noted for its handicrafts; the Friday market at San Francisco El Alto; the blanket-makers of Momostenango; and the restored Maya city of Zaculeu near Huehuetenango. Quetzaltenango is achieving a reputation for its Spanish-language schools, which attract students from around the world.

CUATRO CAMINOS

Following the Interamericana westward from Los Encuentros, the road twists and turns ever higher into the mountains, bringing still more dramatic scenery and cooler temperatures. After 58 km you come to another important highway junction known as Cuatro Caminos (Four Roads). The road east leads to Totonicapán (12 km), west to Quetzaltenango (13 km) and north (straight on) to Huehuetenango (77 km). Buses pass through Cuatro Caminos, shuttling to/from Totonicapán and Quetzaltenango, about every half hour from 6 am to 6 pm.

TOTONICAPÁN
Population 9000

If you want to visit a pleasant, pretty Guatemalan highland town with few other tourists in sight, San Miguel Totonicapán (2500 meters) is the place to go. Buses shuttle into the center of town from Quetzaltenango (passing through Cuatro Caminos) frequently throughout the day.

The ride from Cuatro Caminos is along a beautiful pine-studded valley. As you approach the town you pass a large hospital on the left. Turn around the enormous Minerva fountain and enter town along 17a Avenida.

Totonicapán's main plaza has the requisite large colonial church as well as a municipal theater, built in 1924 in the neoclassical style and recently restored. Buses go directly to the parque (as the plaza is called) and drop you there.

Market days are Tuesday and Saturday; it's a locals' market, not a tourist market, and it winds down by late morning.

Two km from the parque are the Agua Caliente hot springs, a popular bathing place for local people.

Casa de la Cultura Totonicapense
This cultural center (☎ /fax 766-1575), 8a Avenida 2-17, Zona 1, to the left of the Hospedaje San Miguel, has displays of indigenous culture and crafts. The museum administers a wonderful 'Meet the Artisans' program to introduce tourists to artisans and local families.

In 1991 artisans of the local Quiché community proposed to Sr Carlos Umberto Molino, director of the Casa de la Cultura Totonicapense, a program to interest tourists in visiting local handicrafts workshops. The program is now the most interesting activity in town. Starting at 10 am and lasting till about 4 pm, you

meet local artisans, toy makers, potters, carvers of wooden masks and musical instruments, weavers and musicians – watch them work, listen to their music, see their dances, experience their living conditions and eat a homecooked lunch. Cost for the program depends on the number of people in the group, with prices ranging from US$42 per person for four people to US$20 per person for 15 people or more, and the money goes directly to the artisans and musicians involved. An extended program includes a one-night stay with a local family for US$15 per person including meals.

The Casa de la Cultura also offers other, less expensive but equally interesting and worthwhile programs, including a tour of Totonicapán town (US$4 to US$8 per person) and a rural tour of the local Quiché region (US$5 to US$12.50 per person, depending on the number of people in the group).

Special Events
Totonicapán celebrates the Fiesta de Esquipulas on January 15 in Cantón Chotacaj, three km from the parque.

The festival of the Apparition of the Archangel Michael is on May 8, with fireworks and traditional dances. More dances follow on the last Sunday in June, with the Festival of Traditional Dance held in the Plaza Central from 9 am to 2 pm. There's also the Feria Titular de San Miguel Arcángel (Name-Day Festival of the Archangel Saint Michael) from September 24 to 30, with the principal celebration being on the 29th.

Places to Stay
On the way into town, one block before the parque, the *Hospedaje San Miguel* (☎ 766-1452) is on the left at 3a Calle 7-49, Zona 1. It's a tidy place – not what you'd call Swiss-clean, but good for the price. Singles/doubles are US$5/10 with shared bath, or US$6/11 with private bath. The rooms with private bath tend to be larger, with three beds. Flash heaters provide the hot water, which is thus fairly dependable.

QUETZALTENANGO
Population 90,000

Quetzaltenango is called Xelajú or simply Xela (SHAY-lah) by its Quiché Maya citizens, who still use the original Quiché name for the site where the Spanish conquistadors built their town. Quetzaltenango (2335 meters) is the commercial center of southwestern Guatemala. It is Guatemala's second-largest city and the center of the Quiché Maya people. Towering over the city to the south is the 3772-meter Santa María volcano, with the active 2488-meter Santiaguito volcano on its southwestern flank.

Xela's good selection of hotels in all price ranges makes it an excellent base for excursions to the nearby towns and villages, which are noted for their handicrafts and hot springs. In recent years, Xela has built a good, worldwide reputation for its Spanish-language schools.

History
Quetzaltenango came under the sway of the Quiché Maya of K'umarcaaj when they began their great expansion in the 14th century. Before that it had been a Mam Maya town. For the story of Tecún Umán, the powerful leader of the Quiché, and Pedro de Alvarado, see the K'umarcaaj section of Santa Cruz del Quiché.

When the Federation of Central America was founded in the mid-19th century, Quetzaltenango initially decided on federation with Chiapas and Mexico instead of with Central America. Later, the city switched alliances and joined the Central American Federation, becoming an integral part of Guatemala in 1840.

With the late 19th-century coffee boom, Quetzaltenango's wealth increased. Finca owners came to the city to buy supplies, and the coffee brokers opened warehouses. Things went along fine, the city getting richer and richer, until a dual calamity – an earthquake and a volcanic eruption – brought mass destruction and an end to the boom.

Still, the city's position at the intersection of the roads to the Pacific Slope, Mexico and Guatemala City guaranteed it some degree of prosperity. Today it's again busy with commerce, both Indian and ladino.

Orientation
The heart of Xela is the Parque Centroamérica, shaded by old trees, graced with neoclassical monuments and surrounded by the town's important buildings. Most of the town's lodging places are within a couple of blocks of the parque.

Quetzaltenango has several bus stations. The largest and busiest is the 2nd-class Terminal Minerva, on the western outskirts near the Parque Minerva on 6a Calle in Zona 3, next to the market. City buses Nos 2 and 6 run between the terminal and Parque Centroamérica – look for 'Terminal' and 'Parque' signs in the front windows of the buses.

First-class bus lines have their own terminals. For locations, see Getting There & Away, later in this section.

Information
Tourist Offices The INGUAT tourist office (☎ 761-4931) is in the right-hand wing of the Casa de la Cultura (also called the Museo de Historia Natural), at the lower (southern) end of the Parque Centroamérica. It's open Monday to Friday from 8 am to 1 pm and 2 to 5 pm, Saturday 8 am to noon (closed Sunday). It offers free maps and information about the town and the area, in Spanish and English.

Consulate There's a Mexican Consulate (☎ 763-1312/3/4/5) at 9a Avenida 6-19, Zona 1. It's open Monday to Friday from 8 to 11 am and 2 to 3 pm.

Money Parque Centroamérica is the place to go if you are looking for banks. Banco de Occidente, in the beautiful building on the north side of the plaza, and Construbanco, on the east side of the plaza, both change US dollars cash and travelers' checks and give cash advances on Visa cards. Banco Industrial, on the east side of the plaza, has a 24-hour ATM machine where you can get cash advances with a Visa card 24 hours a day.

GUATEMALA

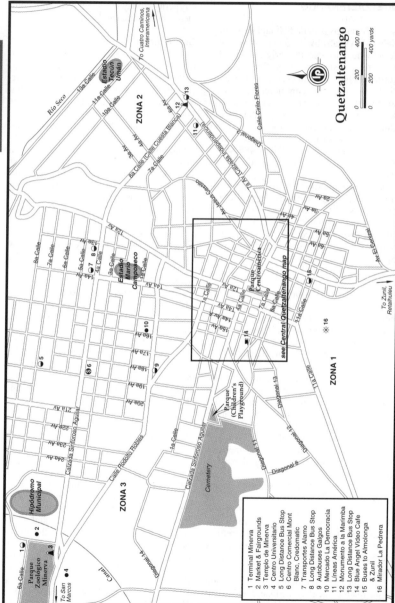

Quetzaltenango

ZONA 2

ZONA 1

ZONA 3

Estadio Tecún Umán

Río Seco

To Cuatro Caminos, Interamericana

Estadio Mario Camposeco

Parque Centroamérica

see Central Quetzaltenango map

Parque (Children's Playground)

Cemetery

Hipódromo Municipal

Parque Zoológico Minerva

To San Marcos

To Zunil, Retalhuleu

0   200   400 m
0   200   400 yards

1   Terminal Minerva
2   Market & Fairgrounds
3   Templo de Minerva
4   Centro Universitario
5   Long Distance Bus Stop
6   Centro Comercial Mont Blanc, Credomatic
7   Transportes Alamo
8   Long Distance Bus Stop
9   Autobuses Galgos
10 Mercado La Democracia
11 Líneas América
12 Monumento a la Marimba
13 Long Distance Bus Stop
14 Blue Angel Video Cafe
15 Buses to Almolonga & Zunil
16 Mirador La Pedrera

Credomatic (☎ 763-5722), in the Centro Comercial Mont Blanc, 4a Calle 18-01, Zona 3, gives cash advances on both Visa and MasterCard.

Post & Communications The post office is at 4a Calle 15-07, Zona 1. The Guatel telephone office is nearby, upstairs in the little shopping center at the corner of 15a Avenida and 4a Calle. It's open daily.

Several other places offer international telephone and fax services, as well as email and Internet connections. They include:

Alfa Internacional, 15a Avenida 3-51, Zona 1

Alternativos, 16a Avenida 3-35, Parque Benito Juárez, Zona 3

Arytex, below Casa de la Cultura, Parque Centroamérica, Zona 1

International Speed Calls, 15a Avenida 5-22, Zona 1

Maya Communications, Bar/Salon Tecún, Pasaje Enriquez, just off Parque Centroamérica, Zona 1

The Green House, 12a Avenida 1-40, Zona 1

Bookstores Check out the Vrisa Bookshop, 15a Avenida 0-67, Zona 1, which has a good variety of quality used books in English. They may move soon; if they have, ask around for the new location. The Blue Angel Video Cafe (see Places to Eat) sells international books, magazines and postcards.

Laundry Lavandería Mini-Max, 14a Avenida C47 at 1a Calle, faces the neoclassical Teatro Municipal. Lavandería El Centro is at 15a Avenida 3-51, Zona 1. Or there's Lavandería Pronto, 7a Calle 13-25A, Zona 1. One load costs US$1 to wash and US$1 to dry at each of these places.

Parque Centroamérica
The parque and the buildings surrounding it are pretty much what there is to see in Xela. Start your tour at the southern (lower) end and walk around the square counter-clockwise. The Casa de la Cultura holds the **Museo de Historia Natural**, which has exhibits on the Maya, the Liberal revolution in Central American politics and the Estado de Los Altos, of which Quetzaltenango was the capital. Marimbas, the weaving industry, stuffed birds and animals and other local lore also claim places here. It's fascinating because it's funky. It's open Monday to Friday, from 8 am to noon and 2 to 6 pm, Saturday from 9 am to 1 pm; admission is US$1.

Just off the southeastern corner of the parque is a small **market** devoted largely to handicrafts and daily necessities, a convenient spot for a little shopping.

The once-crumbling **cathedral** has been rebuilt in the last few decades. The facade of the colonial building was preserved, and a modern sanctuary built behind it.

The city's **Municipalidad** (Town Hall), next to Pensión Bonifaz at the northeastern end of the parque, follows the grandiose neoclassical style so favored as a symbol of culture and refinement in this wild mountain country.

On the west side of the parque between 4a and 5a Calles is the palatial **Pasaje Enriquez**, built to be lined with elegant shops, but as Quetzaltenango has few elegant shoppers, it has suffered decline.

At the southwest corner of the parque, on the corner of 12a Avenida and 7a Calle, is the **Museo del Ferrocarril de los Altos**, a museum focusing on the railroad that once connected Xela and Retalhuleu. Upstairs is an art museum, with mostly modern art, and schools of art, dance and marimba. Hours and admission are the same as at the Museo de Historia Natural.

Other Sights
Walk north on 14a Avenida to 1a Calle to see the impressive neoclassical **Teatro Municipal**, which holds regular performances. Inside are three tiers of seating, the lower two of which have private boxes for prominent families; each is equipped with a vanity.

Mercado La Democracia, in Zona 3, is about 10 blocks northwest of the Parque Centroamérica. To get there, walk along 14a Avenida to 1a Calle (to the Teatro Municipal), turn left, turn right onto 16a Avenida, cross the major street called Calle

Rodolfo Robles, and the market is on your right. It's an authentic Guatemalan city market with fresh produce and meat, foodstuffs and necessities for city dweller and villager alike.

Less than a km west of the Parque Centroamérica, near the Terminal Minerva, is the **Parque Minerva** with its neoclassical Templo de Minerva, built to honor the classical goddess of education and to inspire Guatemalan youth to new heights of learning.

Near the Templo de Minerva is the Parque Zoológico Minerva, a zoo with a children's playground and carnival rides; it's open Tuesday to Sunday, 9 am to 5 pm. A large outdoor market is also nearby.

The Mirador La Pedrera, a 15-minute walk from the center, offers a fine view over the city.

Courses

Language Studies In recent years, Xela has built a good reputation for its Spanish-language schools, which attract students from around the world. Unlike Antigua, which has had a similar reputation for quite a bit longer, Xela is not overrun with foreigners; there is a small student social scene.

Most of the Spanish schools here in Xela are somehow involved in social action programs working with the local Quiché Maya people, providing opportunities to get involved. Prices for the schools vary a little, but not by much; the standard price is US\$100/110/120 per week for four/five/six hours of instruction per day, Monday to Friday, including room and board with a local family, or around US\$85 per week without homestay. Reputable schools (there are more!) include:

Academia Latinoamericana Mayanse (ALM), 15a Avenida 6-75, Zona 1 (Apdo Postal 375) (☎ 761-2877); in the USA, write c/o Max Kintner and Mary Pliska, 3314 Sherwood Lane, Wichita Falls, TX 76308 (☎ (817) 696-3319)

Casa Internacional, 3a Calle 10-24, Zona 1 (☎ 761-2660, estrella@c.net.gt)

Centro Bilingüe Amerindia (CBA), 7a Avenida 9-05, Zona 1 (Apdo Postal 381) (☎ /fax 761-8773); in the USA, write c/o Martha Holden, 37 Run Hill Rd, Brewster MA (☎ (508) 896-7589)

Centro de Estudios de Español Pop Wuj, 1a Calle 17-22, Zona 1 (Apdo Postal 68) (☎ /fax 761-8286, popwujxel@pronet .net.gt); in the USA, PO Box 158, Sandstone, WV 25985-0158 (☎ (304) 466-2685, popwuj@aol.com)

Desarrollo del Pueblo (Progress of the People; a good, small school), 20a Avenida 0-65, Zona 1 (☎ 761-2932, 763-1190, ☎ /fax 761-6754)

English Club International Language School, Diagonal 4 9-71, Zona 9 (☎ 763-2198); classes in Spanish, Quiché and Mam

Escuela de Español Sakribal, 10a Calle 7-17, Zona 1 (Apdo Postal 164) (☎ /fax 761-5211, sakribal@aol.com); in the USA, write c/o 550 Ferncroft Ct, Danville, CA 94526 (☎ (510) 820-3632, fax (510) 820-6658)

Guatemalensis Spanish School, 19a Avenida 2-14, Zona 1 (fax 763-2198); in the USA, write c/o Elizabeth Oudens, 644 33rd Ave, San Francisco, CA 94121 (☎ (415) 221-8965)

Instituto de Estudios de Español y Participación en Ayuda Social (INEPAS), 15a Avenida 4-59 at 5a Calle, Zona 1 (☎ /fax 765-2584, 765-1308); in the USA, write c/o Bob Roughton, 180 Tower Rd, Belgrade, MT 59714 (☎ (406) 388-1919). English, French and Spanish are spoken

Juan Sisay Spanish School, 15a Avenida 8-38, Zona 1 (Apdo Postal 392) (fax 763-1684, bufetej@pronet.net.gt); in the USA, write c/o Jean Totzke, 3465 Cedar Valley Ct, Smyrna, GA 30080 (☎ (770) 436-6283, fax (770) 432-8793)

Kie-Balam Spanish School, Diagonal 12 4-46, Zona 1 (☎ 761-1636, fax 761-0391); in the USA, write c/o Martha Mora, 1007 Duncan Ave, Elgin, IL 60120 (☎ (847) 888-2514)

Proyecto Lingüístico Santa María, 14a Avenida A 1-26 and 1-27, Zona 1 (Apdo Postal 230) (☎ 761-2570, fax 761-8281)

Utatlán Spanish School, 12a Avenida 4-32, Zona 1, Pasaje Enriquez (☎ 763-0446)

GUATEMALA

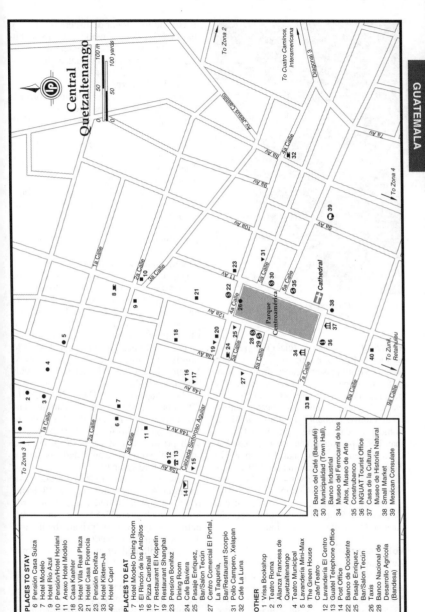

Central Quetzaltenango

PLACES TO STAY
6 Pensión Casa Suiza
7 Hotel Modelo
9 Hotel Río Azul
10 Pensión/Hotel Horiani
11 Anexo Hotel Modelo
18 Casa Kaehler
20 Hotel Villa Real Plaza
21 Hotel Casa Florencia
23 Pensión Bonifaz
33 Hotel Kiktem-Ja
40 Hotel Capri

PLACES TO EAT
7 Hotel Modelo Dining Room
15 El Rincón de los Antojitos
16 Pizza Cardinali
17 Restaurant El Kopetín
19 Restaurant Shanghai
23 Pensión Bonifaz
    Dining Room
24 Cafe Baviera
25 Pasaje Enríquez,
    Bar/Salon Tecún
27 Centro Comercial El Portal,
    La Taquería,
    Bar/Restaurant Scorpio
31 Pollo Campero, Xelapan
32 Cafe La Luna

OTHER
1 Vrisa Bookshop
2 Teatro Roma
3 Alianza Francesa de
    Quetzaltenango
4 Teatro Municipal
5 Lavandería Mini-Max
8 The Green House
    Cafe/Teatro
12 Lavandería El Centro
13 Guatel Telephone Office
14 Post Office
22 Banco de Occidente
25 Pasaje Enríquez,
    Bar/Salon Tecún
26 Taxis
28 Banco Nacional de
    Desarrollo Agrícola
    (Bandesa)
29 Banco del Café (Bancafé)
30 Municipalidad (Town Hall),
    Banco Industrial
34 Museo del Ferrocarril de los
    Altos, Museo de Arte
35 Construbanco
36 INGUAT Tourist Office
37 Casa de la Cultura,
    Museo de Historia Natural
38 Small Market
39 Mexican Consulate

CRAIG LOVELL

Weaving on a traditional
backstrap loom, Guatemala

Weaving La Escuela de Tejer (The Weaving School) offers the opportunity to learn weaving from master weavers from various different cooperatives. Classes are two hours per day; cost is US$50 per week. If you want, they can arrange a homestay with a local family, probably a traditional Maya home in which weaving is practiced, for less than US$5 per night. The school is based at Casa Argentina, Diagonal 12, No 8-37, Zona 1. For further information call Bethania in Guatemala City (☎ 361-2470) or Mark Camp in the USA (☎ (508) 433-9831).

Weaving lessons are also offered at the Cooperativa Santa Ana in Zunil; see the Around Quetzaltenango section.

Volunteering

Xela has several social organizations that work with the local Quiché Maya people and take volunteers. The Asociación Hogar Nuevos Horizontes (☎ 761-2608, fax 761-4328), 13a Avenida 8-34, Zona 1, works with women and children in situations of

need, and the Hogar de Esperanza, Diagonal 11 7-38, Zona 1, works with street children. Many of the Spanish-language schools also work with volunteer programs.

Organized Tours

Thierry Roquet, the Frenchman-turned-Guatemalan who runs the restaurant El Rincón de los Antojitos (see Places to Eat), organizes a variety of tours around the region. Contact him at the restaurant, or at the INEPAS language school, for details. The folks at the Casa Kaehler (see Places to Stay) also offer tours.

Two-day weekend climbs up Volcán Tajumulco – at 4220 meters, the highest volcano (and indeed the highest point) in Central America – are organized by the Casa Argentina, Diagonal 12, No 8-37, Zona 1.

Places to Stay – budget

Cheap hostelries are concentrated at the northern end of the Parque Centroamérica along 12a Avenida and south of the parque more or less behind the Casa de la Cultura.

Pensión/Hotel Horiani (☎ 763-0815), officially at 12a Avenida 2-23 though you enter on 2a Calle, is a simple but clean little family-run hospedaje with six rooms. Singles/doubles are US$3.35/4.20 with shared hot bath.

Hotel Capri (☎ 761-4111), 8a Calle 11-39, Zona 1, a block from the Parque Centroamérica and behind the Casa de la Cultura, has rooms for US$4.20 per person with private bath. It's a basic place, and some of the rooms are quite dark; ask to see a room before you pay.

Pensión Casa Suiza (☎ 763-0242), 14a Avenida A 2-36, Zona 1, has 18 basic rooms grouped around a big courtyard. Singles/doubles are US$5/7.50 with shared bath, US$11/13 with private bath, and there's a cheap comedor. Some readers have complained of noise and brusque management.

Casa Kaehler (☎ 761-2091), 13a Avenida 3-33, Zona 1, is an old-fashioned European-style family pension with seven rooms of various shapes and sizes. Room 7, with private bath, is the most comfortable;

it's US$8/10 for one/two people. Otherwise, rooms with shared bath are US$7/8/9 for a single/double/triple. This is an excellent, safe place for women travelers; ring the bell to gain entry. Ask them about tours in the region. Avoid the *Hotel Radar 99*, next door, which has many problems.

El Rincón de los Antojitos (see Places to Eat) has a room in the rear with private bath and cable TV for US$5/6, or US$6/9.35 with breakfast. They also rent two spacious apartments, about a 10-minute walk from the town center, for US$8.35/59/200 by the day/week/month; each has two bedrooms, fully equipped kitchen, living room, courtyard and cable TV. They also arrange homestays with local families and provide tours and other services for travelers. French, English and Spanish are spoken.

Southwest of the parque is the huge old *Hotel Kiktem-Ja* (☎ 761-4304), in the Edificio Fuentes, a colonial-style building at 13a Avenida 7-18, Zona 1. The 20 rooms, all with private bath and eight with fireplace, are on two levels around the courtyard, which also serves as a car park. Rooms hold one to eight people; singles/doubles are US$10/13.35.

Hotel Río Azul (☎ /fax 763-0654), 2a Calle 12-15, Zona 1, offers luxury compared to its neighbors. All rooms have private bath, and some have color TV. Prices are good for what you get: US$11/14/16 for a single/double/triple. Breakfast and dinner are served, and there's a car park.

Places to Stay – middle
If you want to spend a little more for a lot more comfort, head straight for the family-run *Hotel Modelo* (☎ 761-2529, 763-0216, fax 763-1376), 14a Avenida A 2-31, Zona 1. Pleasant small rooms with bath, cable TV and phone are US$28/32 in the main hotel (three rooms with fireplace are the same price), US$18/22 in the equally comfortable annex. The hotel's good dining room serves breakfast (7:15 to 9:30 am), lunch (noon to 2 pm) and dinner (6 to 9 pm) daily.

Hotel Casa Florencia (☎ 761-2326), 12a Avenida 3-61, Zona 1, just a few steps from the plaza, is run by a pleasant señora who keeps everything spotless. The nine spacious rooms, all with bath, cable TV and carpet, are US$21/25/30 for a single/double/triple. Breakfast is served in the dining room, and there's parking.

Hotel Villa Real Plaza (☎ 761-4045, 761-6270, fax 761-6780), 4a Calle 12-22, Zona 1, half a block west of the parque, is quite comfortable. The 60 large, airy rooms, all with bath, cable TV and phone, are US$42/48 for a single/double. There's a restaurant, bar, sauna and parking.

The four-star *Pensión Bonifaz* (☎ 761-2182, 761-2279, fax 761-2850), 4a Calle 10-50, Zona 1, near the northeast corner of Parque Centroamérica, is Xela's best hotel, a long-standing favorite for Guatemalans and foreigners alike. The 73 comfortably old-fashioned rooms all have private bath, some with tubs, cable TV and phone. Rooms in the original colonial-style building (the one you enter) are preferable to those in the adjoining modernized building. The hotel has a good dining room, a cheery bar and a car park. Singles/doubles are US$51/57.

The *Hotel del Campo* (☎ 761-8082, fax 763-0074), Km 224, Camino a Cantel, is Xela's largest and most modern hotel. Its 84 rooms have showers and TV and are decorated in natural wood and red brick, and there's an all-weather swimming pool. Rooms on the lowest floor can be dark, so get a room numbered in the 50s. Prices are reasonable: US$20/31 for a single/double. The hotel is 4.5 km (a 10-minute drive) east of the town center, a short distance off the main road between Quetzaltenango and Cuatro Caminos; watch for signs for the hotel and for the road to Cantel.

Places to Eat
As with hotels, Quetzaltenango has a good selection of places to eat in all price ranges. Cheapest are the food stalls in and around the small market to the left of the Casa de la Cultura, where snacks and substantial main-course plates are sold for US$1 or less.

Cafe Baviera, at the corner of 13a Avenida and 5a Calle, is a pleasant European-style cafe. It has good coffee and is a great place for breakfast. Other meals, pastries, snacks and alcoholic beverages are also served. It's open every day.

A popular spot with good food is the tiny *El Rincón de los Antojitos*, 15a Avenida at 5a Calle, Zona 1. The menu is mostly Guatemalan, with a few concessions to international tastes and a variety of vegetarian dishes. The specialty of the house is pepian (chicken in a special sesame sauce), a typical indigenous Guatemalan dish, for US$5. English, Spanish and French are spoken.

Cafe La Luna, at the corner of 8a Avenida and 4a Calle, Zona 1, is a pleasant little place to hang out, drink coffee, write letters and socialize with friends.

Blue Angel Video Cafe, 7a Calle 15-22, Zona 1, is popular with Spanish-language students. Prices are very economical, and there's a good variety of excellent, healthy foods to choose from. All the salads and veggies are sterilized. Alcohol is served. It's open every day, 2 to 11:30 pm (see Entertainment).

The *Bar/Salon Tecún* in Pasaje Enriquez, on the west side of the parque, is another popular spot for foreigners to gather in the evening. Good Italian food is served, and there's plenty of drinking and socializing. It's open every day, noon to 3 pm and 5 pm to 1 am.

Pizza Cardinali, 14a Avenida 3-41, Zona 1, serves tasty pizza and pasta dishes. In the same block, *Restaurant El Kopetin*, at No 3-51, has red tablecloths, natural wood, a family atmosphere and a long and varied menu ranging from Cuban-style sandwiches to filet mignon. An average full meal costs around US$5; alcohol is served. Both are open every day.

A couple of other pleasant restaurants are in the Centro Comercial El Portal, 13a Avenida 5-38, Zona 1. *La Taquería* is a bright, cheerful Mexican restaurant with excellent prices: full meals are US$2 to US$4. *Bar/Restaurant Scorpio* has lunch specials or burgers for US$2.65, main dishes for US$4. The big fireplace is pleasant in the evening. Both have tables inside and out on the patio.

Restaurant Shanghai, 4a Calle 12-22, Zona 1, is convenient to the parque. The cuisine is Guatemalan Chinese: pato (duck), camarones (shrimp) and other Chinese specialties for about US$3.35 to US$5 per plate.

Pollo Campero, 5a Calle half a block east of the parque, serves inexpensive fried chicken, burgers and breakfast every day. Next door, *Xelapan* is a decent bakery open every day from 5:15 am to 8 pm.

The dining room of the *Hotel Modelo*, 14a Avenida A 2-31, serves breakfast and has good set-price lunches and dinners (US$5.50).

The dining room of the *Pensión Bonifaz*, (☎ 761-2182, 761-2279, fax 761-2850), 4a Calle 10-50, Zona 1, at the northeast corner of the parque, is the best in town. This is where the local social set comes to dine and be seen. Food is good, and prices, though high by Guatemalan standards, are low when compared to those even in Mexico. Soup, main course, dessert and drink can run to US$12, but you can spend about half that much if you order only a sandwich and a beer.

Entertainment
It gets chilly when the sun goes down, so you won't want to sit out in the Parque Centroamérica enjoying the balmy breezes – there aren't any. Nevertheless, it's softly lit and still a pleasant place for an evening stroll.

The *Green House Cafe/Teatro* (☎ /fax 763-0271), 12a Avenida 1-40, Zona 1, is a pleasant venue for concerts, live theater, poetry readings, films, open-mike nights and other evening activities. It also has billiards, chess, backgammon and other games and a restaurant/bar. It's open Tuesday to Saturday, 4 pm until around midnight.

Performances and cultural events are also presented at the beautiful Teatro Municipal on 1a Calle, and at the Casa de la Cultura (☎ 761-6427) on the south side of the parque. The *Teatro Roma* (on 14a Avenida A, facing the Teatro Municipal) sometimes plays interesting movies.

The *Alianza Francesa de Quetzaltenango* (☎ 761-4076), 14a Avenida A, No

A-20, Zona 1, opposite the Teatro Municipal, offers free French films with Spanish subtitles once a week and other activities.

Videos are shown every night at 8 pm at the *Blue Angel Video Cafe* (see Places to Eat); the US$0.85 admission includes a bowl of popcorn. The video schedule is posted on the door, or you can choose a video from the list on the back of the menu and play it before 6 pm. The cafe here is popular for socializing in the evening, as is the *Bar/Salon Tecún* in Pasaje Enriquez (see Places to Eat).

The bar at the four-star *Pensión Bonifaz* (see Places to Eat) is the place for more high-brow socializing.

Getting There & Away

Bus For 2nd-class buses, head out to the Terminal Minerva, on the western outskirts near the Parque Minerva, on 6a Calle in Zona 3, next to the market. City bus Nos 2 and 6 run between the terminal and Parque Centroamérica (look for 'Terminal' and 'Parque' signs in the front window of the bus). You can catch the city bus (US$0.10) to the terminal from 8a Calle at 12a Avenida or 14a Avenida in the town center. The busy Terminal Minerva has almost hourly buses to many highland destinations.

Buses that depart from Terminal Minerva and head for the Interamericana pick up passengers at bus stops at the corner of 20a Avenida and 7a Calle, at the corner of 14a Avenida and 4a Calle, and at the corner of 7a Avenida (Calzada Independencia) and 8a Calle (Calle Cuesta Blanca) as they head out of town. You can board them at any of these stops, though you may have a better chance of getting a seat if you board at the terminal.

Transportes Alamo, Líneas América and Autobuses Galgos, three 1st-class lines operating buses between Guatemala City and Quetzaltenango, each have their own terminals. Transportes Alamo (☎ 761-2964) is at 14a Avenida 3-60, Zona 3. Líneas América (☎ 761-2063, 761-4587) is at 7a Avenida 13-33, Zona 2. Autobuses Galgos (☎ 761-2248) is at Calle Rodolfo Robles 17-83, Zona 1.

All of the following buses depart from Terminal Minerva, unless otherwise noted.

Almolonga (for Los Vahos) – six km, 10 minutes, US$0.35; buses every 15 minutes from 5:30 am to 5 pm, departing from Terminal Minerva, with a possible stop for additional passengers in Zona 4 southeast of the parque

Chichicastenango – 94 km, 2½ hours, US$1.35; buses at 6, 8:30, 9:30, 10:15 and 11 am, 12:30, 1:30, 2:30 and 4 pm. If you don't get one of these, change at Los Encuentros.

Ciudad Tecún Umán (Mexican border) – 129 km, 2½ hours, US$1.65; buses every half hour, 5:30 am to 4:30 pm

El Carmen/Talismán (Mexican border) – take a bus to Coatepeque, and change there to a direct bus to El Carmen. From Coatepeque it's two hours to El Carmen (US$1.65).

Guatemala City – 206 km, four hours, US$4.20; 1st-class buses with Transportes Alamo three or four times daily, with Líneas América six times daily and with Autobuses Galgos six times daily, each departing from their own terminals (see above). First-class buses stop at Totonicapán, Los Encuentros (change for Chichicastenango or Panajachel) and Chimaltenango (change for Antigua). Second-class buses depart from Terminal Minerva every half hour, 3 am to 4:30 pm, but they make many stops on the way, so they take longer to get there.

Huehuetenango – 90 km, two hours, US$1; buses every half hour, 5:30 am to 5:30 pm

La Mesilla (Mexican border) – 170 km, 3½ hours, US$3.35; uses every half hour, 5:30 am to 5:30 pm. Or bus to Huehuetenango and change there.

Momostenango – 35 km, 1½ hours, US$0.50; hourly buses, 6:30 am to 5 pm

Panajachel – 99 km, 2½ hours, US$2; buses at 5:30, 6:30, 8 and 10 am, noon, 1, 2 and 4 pm. Or take any bus bound for Guatemala City and change at Los Encuentros.

Retalhuleu – 67 km, one hour, US$0.85; buses every 20 minutes, 4:30 am to 6 pm. (Look for 'Reu' on the bus, 'Retalhuleu' won't be spelled out.)

San Francisco El Alto – 17 km, one hour, US$0.50; buses every 15 minutes, 6 am to 6 pm

Totonicapán – 30 km, one hour, US$0.35; buses every 15 minutes, 6 am to 5 pm, departing from the Parque Central Rotonda

Zunil – 10 km, 15 minutes, US$0.25; buses every half hour, 7 am to 7 pm, departing from Terminal Minerva, with a possible additional pick-up in Zona 4, southeast of the parque

Shuttle Minibus Pana Tours (☎ /fax 765-1209, 763-0606), 12a Avenida 7-12, offers shuttle service to Guatemala City, Antigua, Chichicastenango, Panajachel and other places around Guatemala, including nearby places such as Fuentes Georginas, Zunil and so on.

Car Rental car companies in Xela include Geo Rental (☎ 763-0267), 13a Avenida 5-38, Zona 1, Comercial El Portal, and Tabarini (☎ 763-0418), 9a Calle 9-21, Zona 1.

Getting Around

Quetzaltenango is served by a system of city buses, including those between Parque Centroamérica and Terminal Minerva mentioned in the previous section. The tourist office has information on city bus routes. There's a taxi stand on the north end of Parque Centroamérica.

AROUND QUETZALTENANGO

The beautiful volcanic countryside around Quetzaltenango has numerous possibilities for outings. The natural steam baths at Los Vahos are very primitive, but an outing into the hills surrounding the city can be fascinating whether you take a steam bath or not. The steam baths at Almolonga are basic but also cheap and accessible. The hot springs at Fuentes Georginas are idyllic.

Take note of the market days: Sunday in Momostenango, Monday in Zunil, Tuesday and Saturday in Totonicapán and Friday in San Francisco El Alto.

Buses from Quetzaltenango to Almolonga, Los Baños and Zunil depart several times per hour from Terminal Minerva; some buses stop at the corner of 9a Avenida and 10a Calle, Zona 1, to take on more passengers.

Los Vahos

If you're a hiker and the weather is good, you might enjoy a trip to the rough-and-ready sauna/steam baths at Los Vahos (The Vapors), 3.5 km from Parque Centroamérica. Take a bus headed for Almolonga and ask to get out at the road to Los Vahos, which is marked with a small sign reading 'A Los Vahos'. From here it's a 2.3-km uphill walk to Los Vahos. Views of the city on a clear day are remarkable.

If you're driving, follow 12a Avenida south from the parque to its end, turn left, go two blocks and turn right up the hill; this turn is 1.2 km from the parque. The remaining 2.3 km of unpaved road is steep and rutted, with a thick carpet of dust in the dry season, mud in the rainy season (when you may want a 4WD vehicle). Take the first turn along the dirt road (it's an unmarked sharp right). At the second bear left (this is badly marked).

The road ends at Los Vahos, where you can have a sauna/steam bath for only a few quetzals and (if you've brought food with you) a picnic. Los Vahos is open every day, 8 am to 6 pm; admission is US$1.

Zunil
Population 6000

Zunil (2076 meters) is a pretty agricultural and market town in a lush valley framed by steep hills and dominated by a towering volcano. As you approach it along the road from Quetzaltenango, you will see it framed as if in a picture, with its white colonial church gleaming above the red-tiled and rusted tin roofs of the low houses.

On the way to Zunil the road passes **Almolonga**, a vegetable-growing town four km from Quetzaltenango. Just over a km beyond Almolonga, on the left side of the road, is **Los Baños**, an area with natural hot sulfur springs. Several little places along here have bath installations; most are quite decrepit, but if a hot bath at low cost is your desire, you may want to stop. Tomblike enclosed concrete tubs rent for a few quetzals per hour. (Thierry, the Frenchman at the El Rincón de los Antojitos restaurant, likes El Manantial the best.)

Winding down the hill from Los Baños, the road skirts Zunil and its fertile gardens on the right side before intersecting the Cantel to El Zarco road. A bridge crosses a stream to lead into the town; it's one km from the bridge to the plaza.

Zunil, founded in 1529 as Santa Catarina Zunil, is a typical Guatemalan country town. The things that make it so beautiful are its setting in the mountains and the indigenous agriculture practiced here. The agricultural plots, divided by stone fences, are irrigated by canals; you'll see the farmers scooping up water from the canals with a shovel-like instrument and throwing it over their plants. Women wash their clothes near the river bridge, in pools of hot water that come out of the rocks.

Things to See & Do Another attraction of Zunil is its particularly pretty **church**. Its ornate facade, with eight pairs of serpentine columns, is echoed inside by a richly worked altar of silver. On market day (Monday) the plaza in front of the church is bright with the predominantly red traditional garb of the local Quiché Maya people buying and selling.

Half a block downhill from the church plaza, the **Cooperativa Santa Ana** is a handicrafts cooperative in which over 500 local women participate. Handicrafts are displayed and sold here, and weaving lessons are offered. It's open Monday to Saturday from 8:30 am to 5 pm, Sunday 2 to 5 pm.

While you're in Zunil, visit the image of San Simón, an effigy of a local Maya hero venerated as a saint (though not of the church) by the local people, who bring him offerings of rum, cigarettes, flowers and candles. The effigy, propped up in a chair, is moved each year to a different house; ask any local where to find San Simón, everyone will know (local children will take you for a small tip). You'll be charged a couple of quetzals to see him.

The festival day of San Simón is held each year on October 28, after which he moves to a new house. The festival of Santa Catarina Alejandrí, official patron saint of Zunil, is celebrated on November 25. Almolonga celebrates its annual fair on June 27.

Getting There & Away From Zunil, which is 10 km from Quetzaltenango, you can continue to Fuentes Georginas (nine km), return to Quetzaltenango via the Cantel road (16 km), or alternately, take the

jungle-bound toll road down the mountainside to El Zarco junction and the Carretera al Pacífico. Buses depart every 10 minutes, 6 am to 6:30 pm, for the return trip to Quetzaltenango (one hour, US$0.25).

Fuentes Georginas

Imagine a steep, high wall of tropical verdure – huge green leaves, ganglions of vines, giant ferns, spongy moss and profusions of tropical flowers – at the upper end of a lush mountain valley. At the base of this wall of greenery is a limpid pool of naturally warm mineral water. A pure white statue of a Greek goddess gazes benevolently across the misty water as families happily splash and play, clambering out for a drink or a snack at a rustic restaurant right at the pool's edge. This is Fuentes Georginas, the prettiest spa in Guatemala. Though the setting is intensely tropical, the mountain air currents keep it deliciously cool all day.

Besides the restaurant, there are three sheltered picnic tables with cooking grills (bring your own fuel). Down the valley a few dozen meters are seven rustic but pleasant cottages for US$7/9/11 for a single/double/triple. Each cottage has a shower, a BBQ area and a fireplace to ward off the mountain chill at night (wood and matches are provided).

Trails here lead to two nearby volcanoes: Volcán Zunil (three hours, one way) and Volcán Santo Tomás (five hours, one way). Going with a guide is essential, so you don't get lost. Guides are available (ask at the restaurant) for US$10 for either trip, whatever the number of people in the group.

Fuentes Georginas is open every day from 8 am to 6 pm; admission is US$1. Bring a bathing suit, which is required.

Getting There & Away Take any bus to Zunil, where pickup trucks wait to give rides the eight km up the hill to the springs, a half-hour ride. Negotiate the price for the ride. It's very likely they'll tell you it's US$4 roundtrip, and when you arrive at the top, tell you it's US$4 *each way* – this is an irritating game the pickup drivers play. If there are many people in the group, they may charge US$1 per person. Unless you want to walk back down the hill, arrange a time for the pickup driver to return to pick you up.

You can walk from Zunil to Fuentes Georginas in about two hours. If you're the mountain goat type, you may enjoy this; it's a strenuous eight-km climb.

Hitchhiking is not good on the Fuentes Georginas access road, as there are few cars and they are often filled to capacity with large Guatemalan families. The best days to try for a ride are Saturday and Sunday, when the baths are busiest.

If you're driving, walking or hitching, go uphill from Zunil's plaza to the Cantel road (about 60 meters), turn right and go downhill 100 meters to an unpaved road on the left marked 'Turicentro Fuentes Georginas, 8 km'. (This road is near the bus stop on the Quetzaltenango-Retalhuleu road – note that there are three different bus stops in Zunil.) This unpaved road heads off into the mountains; the baths are nine km from Zunil's plaza.

You'll know you're approaching the baths when you smell the sulfur in the air.

San Francisco El Alto
Population 3000

High on a hilltop (2610 meters) overlooking Quetzaltenango (17 km away) stands the market town of San Francisco El Alto. Six days a week it's a sleepy sort of place, but on Friday it explodes with activity. The large plaza, surrounded by the requisite church and Municipalidad and centered on a cupola-like *mirador* (lookout), is covered in country goods. Stalls spill into neighboring streets, and the press of traffic is so great that a special system of one-way roads is established to avoid monumental traffic jams. Vehicles entering the town on market day must pay a small fee.

San Francisco's market is not heavy with handicrafts as are those in Chichicastenango and Antigua. (One reader asked us to pass on the tip, beware of pickpockets in the market!)

Great views can be had from the roof of the church. The caretaker will let you go up.

The annual festival day is October 5.

Places to Stay & Eat Most people come to San Francisco as a day trip from Quetzaltenango. This is just as well, since the lodging and eating situation in San Francisco is dire. If you're in need of a bed, you'll have to suffer the *Hotel y Cafetería Vista Hermosa*, 3a Avenida 2-22, Zona 1. Its 25 rooms are ill-kept (though a few on the front enjoy good views), service is nonexistent and the cafeteria rarely has any food to serve. Doubles cost US$4 with shared bath, US$5.50 to US$7.50 with private shower.

As for eating, *Comedor San Cristóbal*, near the Hospedaje San Francisco de Assis, may be your best bet, but that's not saying too much.

Momostenango
Population 7500

Beyond San Francisco El Alto, 22 km from Cuatro Caminos (35 km from Quetzaltenango) along a fairly rough unpaved country road, this village in a pretty mountain valley is Guatemala's famous center for the making of *chamarras*, thick, heavy woolen blankets. The villagers also make ponchos and other woolen garments. As you enter the village square after an hour of bashing over the bad road, you will see signs inviting you to watch the blankets being made and to purchase the finished products. The best time to do this is on Sunday, which is market day; haggle like mad. A basic good blanket costs around US$10, perhaps twice as much for an extra-heavy 'matrimonial'.

You might also want to hike three km north to the hot springs of Pala Chiquito, where the blankets are washed and the dyes fixed. It has a cool water swimming pool and private hot bath rooms; admission is US$1 or less.

Momostenango is also noted for its adherence to the ancient Maya calendar and for observance of traditional rites. Hills about two km west of the plaza are the scene of these ceremonies, coordinated with the important dates of the calendar round (see Facts about the Region for details on the Maya calendar). Unfortunately, it's not as easy to witness these rites as it is to visit the Shrine of Pascual Abaj at Chichicastenango.

Picturesque diablo (devil) dances are held here in the plaza a few times a year, notably on Christmas Eve and New Year's Eve. The homemade devil costumes can get quite elaborate: all have masks and cardboard wings, and some go whole hog with fake fur suits, heavily sequined outfits and more. Dance groups gather in the plaza and dance to a five- to 13-piece band, drinking alcoholic refreshments during the breaks. For entertainment sake, they are at their best around 3 pm, but the festivities go on late into the night.

The annual fair, Octava de Santiago, is celebrated from July 28 to August 2.

Courses The Kuinik Ta'ik Language School (momos@guate.net) offers instruction in the Quiché (sometimes spelled K'iche') language; US$75 a week covers 12 hours of instruction, room and board with a local Quiché family and a weekly day trip. Their office is in the Hotel Ixchel.

The Teklib'al Maya Cultural School offers classes in the Maya calendar and culture. Its director, Rigoberto Itzep Chanchavac, is a day-keeper and traditional Sacerdote Maya (Maya priest), which involves advising the community on special days of the Maya calendar and natural medicine. Class size is limited to three or four, and a solid knowledge of Spanish is required. The office is on 2a Calle (also called Calle Morazán), about 300 meters east of Hotel Paclom. Neither school has a telephone. If you need to call them, you might try to contact them through the ADIFAM office.

Volunteering ADIFAM, a nongovernmental agency, works with educating the local Quiché children in 46 communities within the municipality of Momostenango. Most of these children are seasonal laborers, and thus they cannot attend normal school on a regular basis. Volunteers of any nationality are welcome to help out, especially anyone who has experience working with children or with organic gardening. The villagers are quite enthusiastic about ADIFAM, and it's a meaningful volunteer effort. The ADIFAM office (☎ /fax 736-5036, momos@guate.net) is located in the Hotel Ixchel. UNICEF does projects here as well.

Places to Stay & Eat New in 1997, the *Hotel Ixchel*, 1a Calle 4-15, Zona 1, has eight rooms sharing two large communal bathrooms for US$2.50 per room, plus two large rooms with private bath (one with a shower, the other a tub) for US$3.50 per room. It's 150 meters west of the Hotel Paclom on the same street, across the river.

Other places to stay in Momostenango are none too pleasant. *Casa de Huéspedes Paclom* charges US$5 for a bare double room; water to the toilets is shut off at night, there is no shower in the hotel and the food is no treat. *Hospedaje Roxana*, on the plaza, charges US$1, which may be too much. There are several basic comedores on the plaza.

Getting There & Away Catch an early bus from Quetzaltenango's Terminal Minerva, or at Cuatro Caminos, or at San Francisco El Alto. There are five or six buses daily, the last one returning from Momostenango by about 2:30 pm.

Another bus route departs from the west side of the plaza and goes through Pologua, which might be an advantage to travelers heading for Huehuetenango or La Mesilla. The road is basically in the same condition; same bumps, different scenery.

HUEHUETENANGO
Population 20,000

Separated from the capital by mountains and a twisting road, Huehuetenango (1902 meters) has that self-sufficient air exuded by many mountain towns. Coffee growing, mining, sheep raising, light manufacturing and agriculture are the main activities in this region.

The lively Indian market is filled daily with traders who come down from the Sierra de los Cuchumatanes, the mountain range (highest in Central America) that dominates the department of Huehuetenango. Surprisingly, the market area is about the only place you'll see colorful traditional costumes in this town, as most of its citizens are ladinos who wear modern clothes.

For travelers, Huehuetenango is usually a stage on the journey to or from Mexico. After leaving San Cristóbal de las Casas or Comitán in Mexico, and then crossing the border, Huehuetenango is the logical place to spend your first night in Guatemala. It's also a good introduction to Guatemalan highland life.

History

Huehuetenango was a Mam Maya region until the 15th century, when the Quiché, expanding from their capital at K'umarcaaj near present-day Santa Cruz del Quiché, pushed them out. Many Mam fled into neighboring Chiapas, which still has a large Mam-speaking population near its border with Guatemala. In the late 15th century the weakness of Quiché rule brought about civil war, which engulfed the highlands and provided a chance for Mam independence. The troubles lasted for decades, coming to an end in the summer of 1525 after the

PLACES TO STAY
1 Hotel Zaculeu
2 Hotel Central
4 Hospedaje El Viajero
8 Hotel Mary
10 Hotel Vásquez
11 Hotel Lerri Colonial
20 Mansión El Paraíso
21 Hotel Casa Blanca

PLACES TO EAT
1 Hotel Zaculeu
3 Especialidades Doña Estercita Cafetería y Pastelería
6 Steak House/Restaurante Las Brasas
7 Panadería Pan Delis
8 Cafatería Mary
12 Pizzería/Restaurante La Fonda de Don Juan
15 Los Pollos
21 Casa Blanca Restaurants
26 Pan del Trigo

OTHER
5 Banco G&T
9 Buses to Zaculeu
13 Municipalidad (Town Hall)
14 Banco del Café (Bancafé)
16 Servicios Sanitarios (Toilets)
17 Gobernación Departamental
18 Guatel Telephone Office
19 Post Office
22 Corpobanco
23 Cine Lili
24 Taxis
25 Church
27 Servicios Sanitarios (Toilets)
28 Banco Agrícola Mercantil
29 Mexican Consulate, Farmacia del Cid
30 Shuttle buses to Bus Terminal, Chiantla

arrival of Gonzalo de Alvarado, brother of Pedro, who conquered the Mam capital of Zaculeu for the king of Spain.

Orientation

The town center is five km north of the Interamericana. The bus station and new market are three km from the highway along the road to the town center (6a Calle), on the east side.

Almost every service of interest to tourists is in Zona 1 within a few blocks of the plaza. The old market, bordered by 1a and 2a Avenidas and 3a and 4a Calles in Zona 1, is still the busy one, especially on Wednesday, which is market day. Four blocks west of the market on 5a Avenida between 2a and 3a Calles is the main plaza, called the parque, the very center of town and the reference point for finding any other address. Hotels and restaurants are mostly near the parque, except for one or two small hotels near the bus station and one motel out on the Interamericana.

Information

The post office is at 2a Calle 3-54, next to the Guatel telephone office opposite the Hotel Mary, half a block east of the plaza. If you don't find the Guatel office here, look for it at 4a Avenida 6-54, four blocks south of the Parque Central; this is its temporary address while their regular office is being remodeled.

There is a Mexican consulate on 5a Avenida 4-11, near the corner of 4a Calle, in the same building as the Farmacia Del Cid; it's open Monday to Friday, 9 am to noon and 3 to 5 pm.

Town-operated *servicios sanitarios* (toilets) are on 3a Calle between 5a and 6a Avenida, only a few steps west of the plaza. *Farmacias* (chemists) and banks are dotted around the center.

Parque Central

Huehuetenango's main plaza is shaded by nice old trees and surrounded by the town's imposing buildings: the Municipalidad (with its band shell on the upper floor) and the huge colonial church. The plaza has its own little relief map of the department of Huehuetenango.

Zaculeu

Surrounded by natural barriers – ravines and a river – on three sides, the late Postclassic religious center of Zaculeu occupies a strategic defensive location that served its Mam Maya inhabitants well. It only failed in 1525 when Gonzalo de Alvarado and his conquistadors laid siege to the site. Good natural defenses are no protection against starvation, and it was this that defeated the Mam. Its name means 'tierra blanca' ('white earth') in the Mam language.

Visitors accustomed to seeing ruddy bare stones and grass-covered mounds rather than the tidiness of Zaculeu may find this place unsettling. Restoration has left its pyramids, ball courts and ceremonial platforms covered in a thick coat of graying plaster. It's rather stark and clean. Some of the construction methods used in the restoration were not authentic to the buildings, but the work goes farther than others in making the site look like it might have to the eyes of Mam priests and worshipers when it was still an active religious center.

When Zaculeu flourished, its buildings were coated with plaster, as they are now. What is missing is the painted decoration, which must have been applied to the wet plaster. The buildings show a great deal of Mexican influence and were probably designed and built originally with little innovation.

The parklike archaeological zone of Zaculeu is four km north of Huehuetenango's main plaza. It's open daily from 8 am to 6 pm; admission is US$0.20. Cold soft drinks are available. You're allowed to climb on the restored structures, but it's forbidden to climb the grassy mounds that await excavation.

From the Parque Central, you can reach Zaculeu by several routes. Jitney trucks and vans depart from in front of the school, on 2a Calle near the corner of 7a Avenida; they depart every 30 minutes (or possibly hourly), 7:30 am to 7:30 pm, and cost US$0.10 for the 20-minute ride to the ruins.

Or you can take a taxi from the central plaza for US$5 roundtrip, with a half hour to spend at the ruins. To walk all the way from the main plaza takes about 45 minutes.

Special Events
Special events include the Fiestas Julias (July 13 to 20), held in honor of La Virgen del Carmen, Huehue's patron saint, and the Fiestas de Concepción (December 5 and 6) honoring the Virgen de Concepción. The Carrera Maratón Ascenso Los Cuchumatanes, a 12-km marathon run from Huehue's central plaza up into the mountains to El Mirador, overlooking the town, is held around October or November each year and attracts hundreds of runners.

Courses
The Xinabajul Spanish Academy (☎ /fax 964-1518), 6a Avenida 0-69, offers one-to-one Spanish courses and room and board with local families.

Places to Stay
Huehuetenango has a useful selection of places to stay. Your first explorations should be along 2a Calle between 3a and 7a Avenida, just off the plaza; there are four little hotels and six eating places in this three-block stretch, and two more hotels half a block off 2a Calle.

Hotel Central (☎ 764-1202), 5a Avenida 1-33, facing the Hotel Zaculeu half a block northwest of the plaza, has 11 largish, simple and well-used rooms with shared bath. One or two people pay US$4; some rooms have three and four beds. The hotel's comedor provides cheap meals (US$1.70) every day except Sunday. It opens for breakfast at 7 am, which is earlier than most other places in town.

Hotel Lerri Colonial (☎ 764-1526), 2a Calle 5-49, half a block west of the plaza, is another tidy place in a convenient location, with 21 rooms around a courtyard. Rooms for one or two people are US$2.50/3.35 per person with shared/private bath. In the courtyard is a comedor and parking.

Across the street, *Hospedaje El Viajero*, 2a Calle 5-30, is not as good, but it's cheap,

with rooms for US$1.65 per person sharing bathrooms with cold showers. The *Mansión El Paraíso* (☎ 764-1827), 3a Avenida 2-41, is a similar place with the same prices.

Hotel Mary (☎ 764-1618, fax 764-1228), 2a Calle 3-52, is a block east of the plaza facing Guatel. It's a cut above the other places: the 25 small rooms have bedspreads and other nice touches. The ground-floor Cafetería Mary is handy, as is the Panadería Pan Delis bakery/cafe next door. Rooms for one or two people are US$6/7.50 with shared bath, or US$12 with private bath and cable TV.

Hotel Vásquez (☎ 764-1338), 2a Calle 6-67, has a car park in the front and 20 small, fairly cheerless but very clean rooms at the back. Rates for singles/doubles/triples are US$3.50/5.70/7.50 with shared bath, or US$4.20/6.65/9.30 with private bath.

Hotel Zaculeu (☎ 764-1086, fax 764-1575), 5a Avenida 1-14, half a block northwest of the plaza, is a colonial-style place with a lovely garden courtyard, a good dining room, laundry service and 37 rooms, all with private bath and cable TV. In the older downstairs section, rooms near the hotel entrance open onto the courtyard and are preferable to those at the back of the hotel; these are US$15/24/32 for singles/doubles/triples. Rooms in the newer upstairs section are US$31/40 for singles/doubles.

Hotel Casa Blanca (☎ /fax 764-2586), 7a Avenida 3-41, is such a bright, pleasant hotel that it's tempting to say it's the best place in town. The 15 rooms, all with private bath and cable TV, are US$18/26 for singles/doubles. There's private parking, too, and two lovely restaurants are open daily from 6 am to 10 pm.

On the Interamericana, two km northwest of the turnoff to Huehuetenango and about seven or eight km from the center of town, are several hotels.

Places to Eat
Especialidades Doña Estercita Cafetería y Pastelería, on 2a Calle a block west of the plaza, is a tidy, cheerful place serving pastries as well as more standard dishes. The

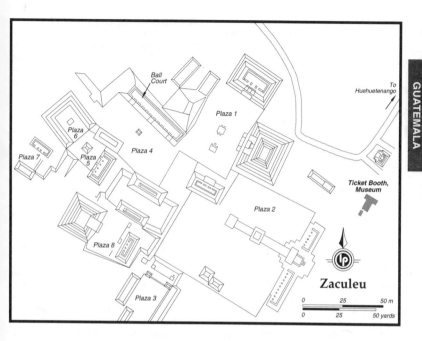

Zaculeu

Cafetería Mary and *Panadería Pan Delis* are next to the Hotel Mary, at 2a Calle 3-52. Another good bakery is the *Pan del Trigo*, 4a Calle 3-24, which usually has whole-grain breads; the cafeteria here, open every day, offers economical breakfasts and dinners for US$2.

The *Pizzería/Restaurante La Fonda de Don Juan*, 2a Calle 5-35, a few steps from the Parque Central, is a clean, pleasant place serving pizza and a variety of other dishes. It's open every day.

Los Pollos, 3a Calle between 5a and 6a Avenida, half a block west of the plaza, is open 24 hours a day. Two pieces of chicken with salad, chips and a soft drink cost US$2.85. Burgers and smaller chicken meals are even cheaper.

One of Huehue's best restaurants is the *Steak House/Restaurante Las Brasas*, on 4a Avenida just off 2a Calle, half a block from the Parque Central, where a full meal of Chinese food or steak (the spe-cialties here) should cost no more than US$7 or so. Alcohol is served, and it's open every day.

For lovely surroundings, you can't beat the two restaurants at the *Hotel Casa Blanca* (see Places to Stay), one inside and another outdoors in the garden. Breakfasts are around US$3.35, burgers or sandwiches no more than US$1.65, and steaks (try filet mignon or cordon bleu) are under US$6. Both restaurants are open every day from 6 am to 10 pm.

Getting There & Away

Bus The bus terminal is in Zona 4, two km southeast of the plaza along 6a Calle. Buses serving this terminal include:

Cuatro Caminos – 74 km, 1¾ to two hours, US$1; take any bus heading for Guatemala City or Quetzaltenango

Guatemala City – 270 km, five hours, US$4.20; buses at 2, 3, 8:30, 9:30 and 10 am

La Mesilla (Mexican border) – 84 km, 1½ to two hours, US$1; buses every half hour, 6 am to 5 pm

Quetzaltenango – 90 km, two hours, US$1; hourly buses, 4 am to 6 pm

Sacapulas – 62 km, four hours, US$2; buses at 11:30 am and 1 pm

Todos Santos Cuchumatán – 40 km, 2½ hours, US$1.20; 11:30 am, 12:30, 1 and 4 pm

Buses between the bus terminal and the center of town depart from 4a Calle at the corner of 4a Avenida from 2 am to 11 pm, running every five minutes in daytime, every half hour at night; cost is US$0.10. A taxi between the bus terminal and the center of town costs US$1.65.

Car Tabarini Rent A Car (☎ 764-1951) has an office here.

AROUND HUEHUETENANGO

El Mirador is a lookout point up in the Cuchumatanes, overlooking Huehuetenango, 12 km from town. On a sunny day it offers a great view of the entire region and its many volcanoes. A beautiful poem, *A Los Cuchumatanes*, is mounted on plaques here. This is the destination for annual marathon races (see Special Events in Huehuetenango). Getting to El Mirador is easiest with a private vehicle; a taxi from town costs around US$30 roundtrip.

LA MESILLA

There is a distance of four km between the Mexican and Guatemalan immigration posts at La Mesilla/Ciudad Cuauhtémoc, and you must take a collective taxi (US$1). There is no bank on either the Guatemalan or Mexican side, but money-changers will do the deal – at a good rate if you're changing dollars, a terrible one for pesos or quetzales.

There are good onward connections from Huehuetenango and Comitán, so just take the next bus from the border post to either of these cities.

TODOS SANTOS CUCHUMATÁN
Population 2000

If you're up for a trek into the Cuchumatanes, four buses per day depart from Huehuetenango on the 40-km ride to Todos Santos Cuchumatán. The road is rough, the mountain air chilly and the journey slow, but the scenery is spectacular.

The picturesque town of Todos Santos Cuchumatán (2450 meters) is one of the few in which the traditional Maya tzolkin calendar is still remembered and (partially) observed, and where both men and women still wear their traditional clothing. Saturday is market day, with a smaller market on Wednesday.

It's possible to take some vigorous treks from the town into the mountains and to rejuvenate in the traditional Mam sauna. From Todos Santos you can ride a horse or walk (all day) to San Juan Atitán village.

Todos Santos is famous for the annual horse races held on the morning of November 1, which culminate a week of festivities and an all-night drinking spree the night before. Traditional foods are served throughout the day, and there are mask dances. Christmas posadas are held on each of the 10 days leading up to Christmas, with locals making processions through the streets, re-creating the peregrinations of Joseph and Mary, leading up to the birth of Jesus.

If you're coming to Todos Santos in winter, bring warm clothes, as it's cold at this high altitude, especially at night.

Courses
La Hermandad Educativa, Proyecto Lingüístico offers Spanish classes for US$100 per week, including room and board with a local family. You can just show up, or contact them in the USA (PO Box 205-337, Sunset Park, NY 11220-0006).

Places to Stay & Eat
Hospedaje Casa Familiar, 30 meters south of the plaza, was built in 1995. It's clean but rustic, and there's hot water and a

sauna. The rooms have plenty of blankets, windows and a fine view; cost is US$2.50 per person. Breakfast is available. It's upstairs over a handicrafts shop, which is next door to the Comedor Katy. Todos Santos is very cold in winter, so you'll need those blankets.

Otherwise, accommodations consist of two primitive, cheap hospedajes: *Tres Olguitas* and *La Paz*. There are also rooms in private homes. People with rooms to rent will probably solicit your business as you descend from your bus and charge US$1 per person. Try the house attached to the cafe and shop *Ruinas de Tecumanchun*.

A few small comedores provide food; *Comedor Katy* is perhaps the best. Another comedor, on the plaza, is cheaper than the Katy and is also good.

Getting There & Away
Buses operate between Huehuetenango and Todos Santos four times daily (40 km, 2½ hours, US$1.20). Buses, which are run to take villagers into Huehue for shopping and then home again, start early in the morning, around 4 am, and the last bus of the day departs in early afternoon. Ride on the top of the bus, if you like – the bus goes slow and the views are spectacular.

Guatemala's Pacific Slope

A lush, humid region of tropical verdure, Guatemala's Pacific Slope is the southeasterly extension of Mexico's Soconusco. The rich volcanic soil is good for growing coffee at the higher elevations and palm oil seeds and sugar cane at the lower. Vast fincas exploit the land's economic potential, drawing seasonal workers from the highland towns and villages, where work is scarce. Along the Pacific shore are endless stretches of beaches of dark volcanic sand. The temperature and humidity along the shore are always uncomfortably high, day and night, rainy season and dry. The few small resorts attract mostly local – not foreign – beachgoers.

A fast highway, the Carretera al Pacífico (CA-2), runs from the border crossings at Ciudad Hidalgo/Tecún Umán and Talismán/El Carmen to Guatemala City. The 275 km between the Mexican border at Tecún Umán and Guatemala City can be covered in about four hours by car, five by bus – much less than the 342 km of the Interamericana through the western highlands between La Mesilla and Guatemala City, which takes seven hours. If speed is your goal, the Pacific Slope is your route.

Most of the towns along the Carretera al Pacífico are muggy, somewhat chaotic and hold little of interest for travelers. The beach villages are worse – unpleasantly hot, muggy and dilapidated. There are exceptions, though. Retalhuleu, a logical stopping place if you're coming from the Mexican border, is pleasant and fun to visit. Nearby is the active archaeological dig at Abaj Takalik. The pre-Olmec stone carvings at Santa Lucía Cotzumalguapa, eight km west of Siquinalá, and those at La Democracia, nine km south of Siquinalá, are unique.

The small beach resort village of Monterrico, with its nature reserve and wildlife preservation project, is becoming popular with foreigners, who come from Antigua and Guatemala City on weekends. Other-

wise, the port town of Iztapa and its beach resort of Likín are fine if you simply must get to the beach. South of Guatemala City, Lago de Amatitlán is the citified version of the more beautiful Lago de Atitlán.

CIUDAD TECÚN UMÁN

This is the preferable and busier of the two Pacific Slope border-crossings, with a bridge linking Ciudad Tecún Umán (Guatemala) with Ciudad Hidalgo (Mexico). The border posts are open 24 hours a day. Basic hotels and restaurants are available, but you'll want to get through the border and on your way as soon as possible.

Minibuses and buses run frequently between Ciudad Hidalgo and Tapachula, 38 km to the north (see the Soconusco section in the Chiapas chapter for details). From Ciudad Tecún Umán there are frequent buses heading east along the Carretera al Pacífico, stopping at Coatepeque, Retalhuleu, Mazatenango and Escuintla before climbing into the mountains to Guatemala City. If you don't find a bus to your destination, take any bus to Coatepeque or, preferably, Retalhuleu, and change buses there.

EL CARMEN

Though you can cross at El Carmen, you will encounter much less hassle and expense if you cross at Tecún Umán.

A toll bridge across the Río Suchiate connects Talismán (Mexico) and El Carmen (Guatemala). The border-crossing posts are open 24 hours every day. Minibuses and trucks run frequently between Talismán and Tapachula, a half-hour (20 km) away.

There are few services at El Carmen, and those that exist are very basic. There is good bus service from El Carmen to Malacatán, on the San Marcos-Quetzaltenango road, and to Ciudad Tecún Umán, 39 km to the south. Fairly frequent 1st-class buses run to Guatemala City along the Carretera al Pacífico (278 km, five to six hours,

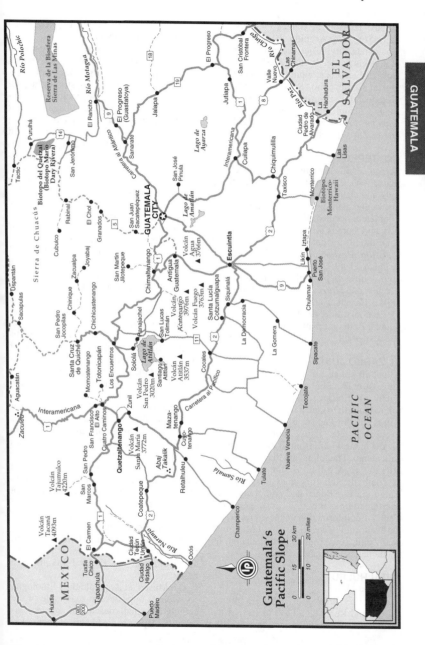

Guatemala's Pacific Slope

US$6). Transportes Galgos (☎ 232-3661, 253-4868), 7a Avenida 19-44, Zona 1, Guatemala City, is one company operating along this route. It runs five buses daily from El Carmen, stopping at Ciudad Tecún Umán, Coatepeque, Retalhuleu, Mazatenango and Escuintla (change for Santa Lucía Cotzumalguapa). Rutas Lima has a daily bus to Quetzaltenango via Retalhuleu and El Zarco junction.

COATEPEQUE

Set on a hill surrounded by lush coffee plantations, Coatepeque is a brash, fairly ugly and chaotic commercial center, noisy and humid at all times. The town is several kilometers north of the Carretera al Pacífico, and there is no reason to stop here.

Of the town's hotels, the 39-room *Hotel Mansión Residencial* (☎ 775-2018), 0 Avenida 11-49, Zona 2, is about the best, with double rooms with bath for US$8.35 per person. *Hotel Virginia* (☎ /fax 775-1801), Carretera al Pacífico Km 220, has 15 air-con rooms for US$30/40 a single/double. Both places have a swimming pool and restaurant.

EL ZARCO JUNCTION

About 40 km east of Coatepeque and nine km east of Retalhuleu on the Carretera al Pacífico is El Zarco, the junction with the toll road north to Quetzaltenango. The road winds up the Pacific Slope, carpeted in tropical jungle, rising more than 2000 meters in the 47 km from El Zarco to Quetzaltenango. The toll is less than US$1. Just after the upper toll booth, the road divides at Zunil: the left fork goes to Quetzaltenango via Los Baños and Almolonga (the shorter route); the right fork goes via Cantel. For information on these places and the beautiful Fuentes Georginas hot springs near Zunil, see Around Quetzaltenango in Guatemala's Highlands chapter.

RETALHULEU

Population 40,000

The Pacific Slope is a rich agricultural region, and Retalhuleu (240 meters) is its clean, attractive capital – and proud of it.

Most Guatemalans refer to Retalhuleu simply as Reu (RAY-oo).

If Coatepeque is where the coffee traders conduct business, Retalhuleu is where they come to relax, splashing in the pool at the Posada de Don José and sipping a cool drink in the bar. You'll see their big, expensive 4WD vehicles parked outside. The rest of the citizens get their kicks strolling through the plaza between the whitewashed colonial church and the wedding-cake government buildings, shaded by royal palms.

The balmy tropical air and laid-back attitude are restful. Tourists are something of a curiosity in Reu and are treated very well.

Orientation & Information

The town center is four km southwest of the Carretera al Pacífico along a grand boulevard lined with towering palm trees. The bus station is on 10a Calle between 7a and 8a Avenidas, Zona 1, northeast of the plaza. To find the plaza, look for the twin church towers and walk toward them.

Most services you may need are within two blocks of the plaza. There is no official tourist office, but people in the Municipalidad, on 6a Avenida facing the east side of the church, will do their best to help.

The post office is on 6a Avenida between 5a and 6a Calles. Guatel, at 5a Calle 4-50, is half a block from the parque.

Banco Occidente, 6a Calle at the corner of 6a Avenida, and Banco Industrial, 6a Calle at the corner of 5a Avenida, both change US dollars cash or travelers' checks and give cash advances on Visa cards. Banco del Agro, on 5a Avenida facing the parque, changes US dollars cash and travelers' checks and gives cash advances on MasterCard.

Things to See & Do

There's little to see in Retalhuleu proper, but about 30 km to the west is the active archaeological dig at Abaj Takalik (see below).

The Museo de Arqueología y Etnología, 6a Avenida opposite the south side of the church, is a small museum of archaeological relics. Upstairs are historical photos and

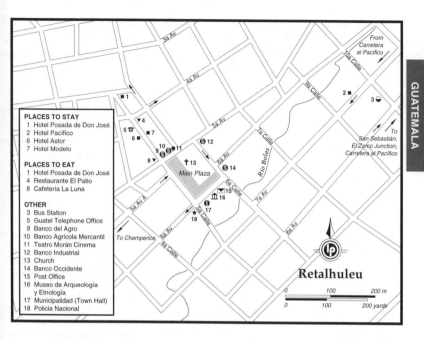

PLACES TO STAY
1 Hotel Posada de Don José
2 Hotel Pacífico
6 Hotel Astor
7 Hotel Modelo

PLACES TO EAT
1 Hotel Posada de Don José
4 Restaurante El Patio
8 Cafetería La Luna

OTHER
3 Bus Station
5 Guatel Telephone Office
9 Banco del Agro
10 Banco Agrícola Mercantil
11 Teatro Morán Cinema
12 Banco Industrial
13 Church
14 Banco Occidente
15 Post Office
16 Museo de Arqueología
   y Etnología
17 Municipalidad (Town Hall)
18 Policía Nacional

Retalhuleu

a mural showing locations of 33 archaeological sites in the department of Retalhuleu. It's open Tuesday to Sunday, 9 am to 1 pm and 2 to 5 pm; admission US$0.15.

You can swim in the pools at the Siboney and Colonial hotels (see Places to Stay) even if you're not staying there. Cost is US$0.65 at the Siboney, US$1.65 at the Colonial, where there's also a poolside bar and food service.

Places to Stay

There are budget places to stay in Reu and several low-priced, central hotels. Two of the most convenient are just half a block west of the plaza. The better of the two is the *Hotel Astor* (☎ 771-2562, fax 771-2564), 5a Calle 4-60, Zona 1, with a pretty courtyard and 15 well-kept rooms, each with ceiling fan, private bath and color cable TV. Singles/doubles are US$10/20, and there's private parking.

Hotel Modelo (☎ 771-0256), 5a Calle 4-53, Zona 1, opposite the Hotel Astor, is a similar place with seven clean rooms on two floors around a central courtyard. The rooms are of different sizes, with ceiling fans and private bath; singles/doubles are US$8/12 and there's private parking.

For a real cheapie, you could try the very basic *Hotel Pacífico*, 7a Avenida 9-29, around the corner from the bus station. Rooms are US$2.50 per person, with shared bath.

The nicest place in town is the *Hotel Posada de Don José* (☎ 771-0963, 771-0841, ☎ /fax 771-1179), 5a Calle 3-67, Zona 1, across the street from the railway station and two blocks northwest of the plaza. On weekends the Don José is often filled with finca owners in town for relaxation; at other times you can get an air-con room with color cable TV, telephone and private bath for US$23/30/36 a single/double/triple; reductions may be offered. The 23 rooms are on two levels overlooking the swimming pool, and the cafe and restaurant tables are beneath an arcade surrounding the pool.

Out on the Carretera al Pacífico are several other hotels. These tend to be 'tropical motels' by design, with bungalows, swimming pool and restaurant. *Hotel Siboney* (☎ 771-0149, fax 771-0711), Cuatro Caminos, San Sebastian, is four km east of town where Calzada Las Palmas meets the Carretera al Pacífico. The 25 rooms, all with air-con, color cable TV, telephone and private bath are US$34/37/40 for singles/doubles/triples. *Hotel La Colonia* (☎ 771-0038, fax 771-0191), Carretera al Pacífico Km 178, is one km east of the Siboney. It has a fairly luxurious layout, with 42 rooms with the same amenities for US$22/30 for singles/doubles, in bungalows around the swimming pool.

Places to Eat

Several little restaurants facing the plaza provide meals at low prices (under US$3). The *Cafetería La Luna* on the corner of 5a Calle and 5a Avenida, opposite the west corner of the plaza, is a town favorite; it's open every day. The *Restaurante El Patio* on the corner of 5a Calle and 4a Avenida is similar. Also around the plaza are several ice cream shops.

For the best meal in town, head for the *Posada de Don José* (see Places to Stay), where the pleasant restaurant offers beef and chicken plates for US$4 to US$6 and a big, full meal can be had for US$7 to US$10. Breakfast is served here as well.

Getting There & Away

Bus As Reu is the most important town on the Carretera al Pacífico, transport is easy. Most buses traveling along the highway stop at the city's bus station, on 10a Calle between 7a and 8a Avenidas, Zona 1, about 400 meters northeast of the plaza. Long-distance buses include:

Ciudad Tecún Umán – 78 km, 1½ hours, US$1.65; buses every 20 minutes, 5 am to 10 pm

Guatemala City – 186 km, 3½ to four hours, US$4.15; buses every 15 minutes, 2 am to 8:30 pm

Quetzaltenango – 67 km, one hour, US$0.85; buses every 15 minutes, 3 am to 7 pm

Local buses depart for Champerico and El Asintal (for Abaj Takalik).

Car Tabarini Rent A Car (☎ 771-1025) has an office here.

ABAJ TAKALIK

About 30 km west of Retalhuleu is the active archaeological dig at Abaj Takalik (ah-BAH tah-kah-LEEK). Large 'Olmecoid' stone heads have been discovered, along with many other objects, which date the site as one of the earliest in all of the Mayan realm. The site has yet to be restored and prettified for tourists, so don't expect a Chichén Itzá or Tikal. But if you're truly fascinated with archaeology and want to see it as it's done, pay a visit.

It's easiest to reach Abaj Takalik with your own vehicle, but it can be done by private transport. Catch a bus to El Asintal, about 15 km west along the Carretera al Pacífico and then five km down a road heading off to the right. Otherwise, early in the morning take any bus heading west towards Coatepeque, go about 15 km west along the Carretera al Pacífico and get out at the road, on the right, to El Asintal. From here it's five km to El Asintal (you may have some luck hitching). Pickups at El Asintal provide transport to Abaj Takalik, four km away.

CHAMPERICO

Built as a shipping point for coffee during the boom of the late 19th century, Champerico, 38 km southwest of Retalhuleu, is a tawdry, sweltering, dilapidated place that sees few tourists. Nevertheless, it's the only ocean beach easily accessible on a day trip by bus from Quetzaltenango. Most beachgoers come only to spend the day, but there are several cheap hotels and restaurants.

When you get to the beach, walk to the right, go under a pier and keep walking for five more minutes until you get to an estuary. Swimming is pleasant in the warm water at the river mouth, and you'll probably see only a few local families. Swimming can be dangerous in the sea, due to fierce waves and an undertow.

If you're just passing through, you'll probably prefer to reserve your seaside time for more attractive parts of La Ruta Maya.

MAZATENANGO
Population 38,000

East of Retalhuleu, about 26 km along the Carretera al Pacífico, Mazatenango (370 meters) is the capital of the department of Suchitepéquez. It's a center for farmers, traders and shippers of the Pacific Slope's agricultural produce. There are a few serviceable hotels if you need to stop in an emergency.

SANTA LUCÍA COTZUMALGUAPA
Population 24,000

Another 71 km eastward from Mazatenango brings you to Santa Lucía Cotzumalguapa (356 meters), an important stop for anyone interested in Mayan art and culture. In the sugar cane fields and fincas near the town stand great stone heads carved with grotesque faces and fine relief scenes in stone. The question of who carved these ritual objects, and why, remains a mystery.

The town itself, though pleasant, is unexciting. The people in town and in the surrounding countryside are descended from the Pipil, an Indian culture known to have historic, linguistic and cultural links with the Nahuatl-speaking peoples of central Mexico. In Early Classic times, the Pipil who lived here grew cacao, the 'money' of the time. They were obsessed with the Mayan/Aztec ball game and with the rites and mysteries of death. Pipil art, unlike the flowery and almost romantic style of the true Maya, is cold, grotesque and severe, but still very finely done. What were these 'Mexicans' doing in the midst of Mayan territory? How did they get here and where did they come from? Archaeologists do not have many answers. There are other concentrations of Pipils, notably in the Motagua Valley of southeastern Guatemala, and in western El Salvador. Today these people share a common lifestyle with Guatemala's other indigenous groups, except for their mysterious history.

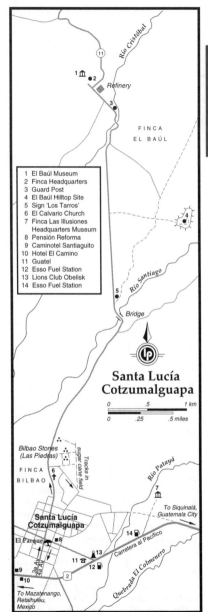

1 El Baúl Museum
2 Finca Headquarters
3 Guard Post
4 El Baúl Hilltop Site
5 Sign 'Los Tarros'
6 El Calvario Church
7 Finca Las Illusiones Headquarters Museum
8 Pensión Reforma
9 Caminotel Santiaguito
10 Hotel El Camino
11 Guatel
12 Esso Fuel Station
13 Lions Club Obelisk
14 Esso Fuel Station

Santa Lucía Cotzumalguapa

A visit to Santa Lucía Cotzumalguapa allows you to examine this unique 'lost culture' by visiting a number of its carved stones. Though the sites are accessible to travelers without their own transport, a car certainly simplifies matters. In your explorations you may get to see a Guatemalan sugar cane finca in full operation.

Orientation

Santa Lucía Cotzumalguapa is northwest of the Carretera al Pacífico. In its main square (El Parque), several blocks from the highway, are copies of some of the famous carved stones found in the region.

There are three main archaeological sites to visit: Bilbao, a finca right on the outskirts of Santa Lucía; Finca El Baúl, a large plantation farther from town, at which there are two sites (a hilltop site and the finca headquarters); and Finca Las Ilusiones, which has collected most of its findings into a museum near the finca headquarters. Of these sites, Bilbao and the hilltop site at El Baúl are by far the most interesting. If time and energy are short, head for these.

If you don't have a car and you want to see the sites in a day, haggle with a taxi driver in Santa Lucía's main square for a visit to the sites. It's hot and muggy, and the sites are several kilometers apart, so you will really be glad you rode at least part of the way. If you do it all on foot and by bus, pack a lunch so you won't have to return to town. The hilltop site at El Baúl is a perfect place for a picnic.

Bilbao

This site, no doubt a large ceremonial center, flourished about 600 AD. Plows have unearthed (and damaged) hundreds of stones during the last few centuries; thieves have carted off many others. In 1880 many of the best stones were removed to museums abroad, including nine stones to the Dahlem Museum in Berlin.

Known locally as simply *las piedras* (the stones), this site actually consists of several separate sites deep within tall stands of sugar cane. The fields come right to the edge of the town. From Santa

Lucía's main square, go north uphill on 3a Avenida to the outskirts of town. Pass El Calvario church on your right, and shortly thereafter turn sharp right. A hundred meters along, the road veers to the right but an unpaved road continues straight on; follow the unpaved road. The cane fields are on your left, and you will soon see a path cut into the high cane.

At times when the cane is high, finding your way around would be very difficult if it weren't for the swarms of local boys that coalesce and follow you as you make your way along the edge of the cane fields. At the first sign of bewilderment or indecision they'll yell: *'¿Las piedras? ¿Las piedras?'* You answer *'¡Sí!'* and they'll lead you without hesitation into the sea of waving cane along a maze of paths to each site. A tip is expected, of course, but it needn't be large and it needn't be given to every one of the multitude of guides. The boys are in school many days but are dependably at the ready on weekends, holidays and during school vacation time.

One stone is flat with three figures carved in low relief; the middle figure's ribs show prominently, as though he were starving. A predatory bird is in the upper left-hand corner. Holes in the middle-right part of the stone show that thieves attempted to cut the stone.

Another is an elaborate relief showing players in a ball game, fruit, birds, animals and cacao bean pods, for which this area was famous and which made it rich.

Although some of the other stones are badly weathered and worn, others bear Mexican-style circular date glyphs and other mysterious patterns that resemble closely those used by people along the Gulf Coast of Mexico near Villahermosa.

To continue on to El Baúl, you can save time by backtracking to the point where you turned sharp right just beyond El Calvario church. Buses heading out to El Baúl pass this point every few hours, or you can hitchhike. If you're driving, you'll have to return to the center along 4a Avenida and come back out on 3a Avenida, as these roads are one way.

A reader wrote the following about his experience finding the stones:

I had a hell of a time finding Las Piedras (the Bilbao stones) – the schoolboy guides must have been at school at 9:30 on a Tuesday. Having found them all (with the help of a local), I wrote these instructions:

From the unpaved road in your instructions, continue as far as the blue house (about 100 meters). Opposite this there is a path in the sugar cane (you need to climb through the fence) – the first glyph is just up on the left. From there, continue north, and take the second right – the arch-shaped glyph is on the top of the hill. Continue to the end of the path (about 20 meters), turn left, and left again after 50 meters up a small path to a very large glyph.

Returning to the previous path and following to the end, take a left turn. Eventually you'll come to the road to Finca El Baúl, cutting the corner.

Of course, these may not be the stones you were describing!

Finca El Baúl

Just as interesting as las piedras is the hilltop site at El Baúl, which has the additional fascination of being an active place of pagan worship for local people. This is an excellent place for a picnic. Some distance from the hilltop site on another road, next to the finca headquarters, is the finca's private museum of stones uncovered on the property.

The hilltop site at El Baúl is 4.2 km northwest of El Calvario church. From the church (or the intersection just beyond it), go 2.7 km to a fork in the road just beyond a bridge; the fork is marked by a sign reading Los Tarros. Take the right-hand fork (an unpaved road). From the Los Tarros sign it's 1.5 km to the point where a dirt track crosses the road; on your right is a tree-covered 'hill' in the midst of otherwise flat fields. The 'hill' is actually a great ruined temple platform that has not been restored. Make your way across the field and around the south side of the hill, following the track to the top. If you have a car, you can drive to within 50 meters of the top.

If you visit on a weekend, you may find several worshippers paying their respects to the idols here. They will not mind if you visit as well, and are usually happy to pose with the idols for photographs, in exchange for a small 'contribution'.

Of the two stones here, the great grotesque half-buried head is the most striking. The elaborate headdress, 'blind' eyes with big bags beneath them, beak-like nose and 'have a nice day' grin seem at odds with the blackened face and its position, half-buried in the ancient soil. The head is stained with wax from candles, with liquor and other drinks, and with the smoke and ashes of incense fires built before it, all part of worship. People have been coming here to pay homage for over 1400 years.

The other stone is a relief carving of a figure surrounded by circular motifs that may be date glyphs. A copy of this stone may be seen in the main square of Santa Lucía Cotzumalguapa.

From the hilltop site, retrace your steps 1.5 km to the fork with the Los Tarros sign. Take the other fork this time (what would be the left fork as you come from Santa Lucía), and follow the paved road three km to the headquarters of Finca El Baúl. (If you're on foot, you can walk from the hilltop site back to the unpaved road and straight across it, continuing on the dirt track. This will eventually bring you to the asphalt road that leads to the finca headquarters. When you reach the road, turn right.) Buses trundle along this road every few hours, shuttling workers between the refinery and the town center.

Approaching the finca headquarters (six km from Santa Lucía's main square), you cross a narrow bridge at a curve; continue uphill and you will see the entrance on the left, marked by a machine-gun pillbox. Beyond this daunting entrance you pass workers' houses and a sugar refinery on the right and finally come to the headquarters building, guarded by several men with rifles. The smell of molasses is everywhere. Ask permission to visit the museum and a guard will unlock the gate just past the headquarters building.

Within the gates, sheltered by a palapa, are numerous sculpted figures and reliefs found on the plantation, some of which are very fine. Unfortunately, nothing is labeled.

Finca Las Ilusiones

The third site is very close to Bilbao – indeed, this is the finca that controls the Bilbao cane fields – but, paradoxically, access is more difficult. Your reward is the chance to view hundreds of objects, large and small, that have been collected from the finca's fields over the centuries.

Leave the town center by heading east along Calzada 15 de Septiembre, the boulevard that joins the highway at an Esso fuel station. Go northeast for a short distance, and just past another Esso station on the left is an unpaved road that leads, after a little over one km, to Finca Las Ilusiones and its museum. If the person who holds the museum key is not to be found, you must be satisfied with the many stones collected around the outside of the museum.

Places to Stay & Eat

Pensión Reforma, Calzada 15 de Septiembre at 4a Avenida, is certainly not beautiful, but will do for a night. Rooms cost US$4/6 a single/double.

Just a few hundred meters west of the town, the *Caminotel Santiaguito* (☎ 882-5435/6/7), Km 90.4, Carretera al Pacífico, is fairly lavish for Guatemala's Pacific Slope, with spacious tree-shaded grounds, a nice swimming pool and a decent restaurant. The pool is open to nonguests for a small fee. Motel-style air-con rooms with private bath cost US$32/39. They're likely to be full on weekends, as the hotel is something of a resort for local people. In the spacious restaurant cooled by ceiling fans, you can order a cheeseburger, fruit salad and soft drink for US$4, or an even bigger meal for US$6.50 to US$8.

Across the highway from the Caminotel is the *Hotel El Camino* (☎ 882-5316), with rooms that are hot and somewhat noisy because of highway traffic. Singles/doubles are US$10/14.

Getting There & Away

Esmeralda 2nd-class buses shuttle between Santa Lucía Cotzumalguapa and Guatemala City (4a Avenida and 2a Calle, Zona 9) every half-hour or so between 6 am and 5 pm, charging US$1.50 for the 90-km, two-hour ride. You can also catch any bus traveling along the Carretera al Pacífico between Guatemala City and such points as Mazatenango, Retalhuleu or the Mexican border.

To travel between La Democracia and Santa Lucía, catch a bus running along the Carretera al Pacífico toward Siquinalá (eight km) and change there for a bus to La Democracia.

Between Santa Lucía and Lago de Atitlán you will probably have to change buses at Cocales junction, 23 km west of Santa Lucía and 58 km south of Panajachel.

LA DEMOCRACIA
Population 4200

South of Siquinalá, 9.5 km along the road to Puerto San José, is La Democracia (165 meters), a nondescript Pacific Slope town that's hot day and night, rainy season and dry. Like Santa Lucía Cotzumalguapa, La Democracia is in the midst of a region populated from early times – according to some archaeologists – by cultures with mysterious connections to Mexico's Gulf Coast.

At the archaeological site called Monte Alto, on the outskirts of the town, huge basalt heads have been found. Though cruder, the heads resemble those carved by the Olmecs near Veracruz several thousand years ago.

Today these great Olmecoid heads are arranged around La Democracia's main plaza. As you come into town from the highway, follow signs to the museo, which will cause you to bear left, then turn left, then turn left again.

Facing the plaza, along with the church and the modest Palacio Municipal, is the small, modern Museo Rubén Chevez Van Dorne, with other fascinating archaeological finds. The star of the show is an exquisite jade mask. Smaller figures, 'yokes' used in the ball game, relief carvings and other objects make up the rest of this important small collection. On the walls are overly dramatic paintings of Olmecoid scenes. A rear room has more dramatic paintings and lots of potsherds only an archaeologist could love. The museum is open from 8 am to noon and 2 to 5 pm; admission costs US$0.50.

Places to Stay & Eat

La Democracia has no places to stay and few places to eat. The eateries are very basic and ill-supplied; it's best to bring your own food and buy drinks at a place facing the plaza. *Café Maritza*, right next to the museum, is a picture-perfect hot-tropics hangout with a *rockola* (jukebox) blasting music, and a small crew of semisomnolent locals sipping and sweltering.

Getting There & Away

Chatia Gomerana, Muelle Central, Terminal de Buses, Zona 4, Guatemala City, has buses every half-hour from 6 am to 4:30 pm on the 92-km, two-hour ride between the capital and La Democracia. Buses stop at Escuintla, Siquinalá (change for Santa Lucía Cotzumalguapa), La Democracia, La Gomera and Sipacate. The fare is US$1.

AROUND LA DEMOCRACIA

The road south from La Democracia continues 42 km to **Sipacate**, a small and very basic beach town. The beach is on the other side of the Canal de Chiquimulilla, an intracoastal waterway. Though there are a few scruffy, very basic places to stay, you'd be better off saving your beach time for Puerto San José, 35 km to the east, reached via the road from Escuintla.

ESCUINTLA

Surrounded by lush tropical verdure, Escuintla should be an idyllic place where people swing languidly in hammocks and concoct pungent meals of readily available exotic fruit and vegetables. But it's not.

Escuintla is a hot, dingy, dilapidated commercial and industrial city that's very important to the Pacific Slope's economy but not at all important to travelers. It is an old town, inhabited by Pipils before the conquest but now solidly ladino. It has some fairly dingy hotels and restaurants.

You might have to change buses in Escuintla. The main bus station is in the southern part of town; this is where you catch buses to Puerto San José. For Guatemala City, you can catch very frequent buses in the main plaza.

Near Escuintla, Autosafari Chapin is a drive-through African wild animal park that's a popular outing for families from Guatemala City.

Buses come here; see Buses under Guatemala City.

PUERTO SAN JOSÉ, LIKÍN & IZTAPA

Guatemala's most important seaside resort leaves a lot to be desired, even when compared to Mexico's smaller, seedier places. But if you're eager to get into the Pacific surf, head south from Escuintla 50 km to Puerto San José and neighboring settlements.

Puerto San José (population 14,000) was Guatemala's most important Pacific port in the latter half of the 19th century and well into the 20th. Now superseded by the more modern Puerto Quetzal to the east, Puerto San José languishes and slumbers; its inhabitants languish, slumber, play loud music and drink. The beach, inconveniently located across the Canal de Chiquimulilla, is reached by boat.

It's smarter to head west along the coast five km (by taxi or car) to Balneario Chulamar, which has a nicer beach and also a suitable hotel or two.

About five km to the east of Puerto San José is Balneario Likín, Guatemala's only up-market Pacific resort. Likín is much beloved by well-to-do families from Guatemala City who have seaside houses on the tidy streets and canals of this planned development.

About 12 km east of Puerto San José is Iztapa, Guatemala's first Pacific port, first used by none other than Pedro de Alvarado in the 16th century. When Puerto San José was built in 1853, Iztapa's reign as the port of the capital city came to an end, and it relaxed into a tropical torpor from which it has yet to emerge. Having lain fallow for almost a century and a half, it has not suffered the degradation of Puerto San José. Iztapa is comparatively pleasant, with several small, easily affordable hotels and restaurants on the beach. The bonus here is that you can catch a Transportes Pacífico bus from the market in Zona 4 in Guatemala City all the way to Iztapa (four hours), or pick it up at Escuintla or Puerto San José to take you to Iztapa.

A Race to the Sea

From September to December a delightful ritual takes place every Saturday at sunset in front of Monterrico's beachfront hotels. Workers from the Tortugario Monterrico walk out on the beach carrying big plastic tubs and two long ropes. They lay one rope out along the beach at a certain distance from the waterline, and tourists from the beach hotels gather around. Come up to see what's going on and you'll find out the plastic tubs are full of baby sea turtles!

Pick a likely looking turtle out of the tub, make a small donation (less than US$2) to support the tortugario (turtle hatchery) and line up behind the rope farthest from the waves. It's an amazing feeling, to hold the baby sea turtle in your hand. When everyone is ready, on the count of three, everyone releases their sea turtles, which make a frantic scramble towards the sea. Keep an eye on your turtle; if yours is the first to reach the rope closer to the waves, you'll win a free meal for two at one of the Monterrico hotels. Eventually, all the turtles reach the water and are washed away by the waves, as the sun is sinking.

The race is not only a fun chance to win a free dinner, it's also poignant, as you consider the fate of 'your' little sea turtle as you hold it in your hand. All the turtles were hatched within the past two to three days. They're released in a group to give them a better chance of survival. Scientists say that on their race across the sand to the sea, the tiny turtles are being imprinted with the information about their place of birth (the components of the sand, the water, etc) that will enable them to return from the sea to this exact spot to lay eggs when they are adults. Most of them won't make it to adulthood. But the efforts of conservation groups such as this one are giving this endangered species a better chance. ■

MONTERRICO

Similar in many ways to the rest of Guatemala's Pacific Coast, Monterrico is a coastal village with a few small, inexpensive hotels right on the beach, a large wildlife reserve and a center for the hatching and release of sea turtles. The beach here is dramatic, where surf crashes onto black volcanic sand. Behind the beach, on the other side of town, is a large network of mangrove swamps and canals, part of the 190-km Canal de Chiquimulilla.

Monterrico is a good spot for a weekend break at the beach, if you're staying in Antigua or Guatemala City. It's becoming popular with foreigners. On weekdays it's very quiet.

Things to See & Do

Besides the beach, Monterrico's biggest attraction is the Biotopo Monterrico-Hawaii, a 20-km-long nature reserve of coast and coastal mangrove swamps filled with bird and aquatic life. Its most famous denizens are perhaps the endangered leatherback and Ridley turtles, who lay their eggs on the beach in many places along the coast. The mangrove swamps are a network of 25 lagoons, all connected by mangrove canals.

Boat tours of the reserve, going through the mangrove swamps and visiting several lagoons, take around 1½ to two hours and cost US$8.35 for one to three passengers. It's best to go early in the morning, when you can see the most wildlife. Bring binoculars for bird watching, if you have them. To arrange a boat tour of the canal, stop by the Tortugario Monterrico, on the beach. Other villagers also do boat tours, but the guides who work here are particularly concerned with wildlife. Or ask at your hotel.

The Tortugario Monterrico is just a short walk east down the beach from the Monterrico hotels (left, if you're facing the sea). Several endangered species of animals are raised here, including three species of sea turtles.

The Reserva Natural Hawaii is a nature reserve operated by the Asociación de

Rescate y Conservación de Vida Silvestre (ARCAS; Association to Rescue and Conserve Wildlife), which has a sea turtle hatchery eight km east along the beach from Monterrico. Volunteers are welcome all year round, but real sea turtle season is from June to November, with August and September being the peak months. See the Work section in the Guatemala Facts for the Visitor chapter for more about ARCAS.

Courses

For studying Spanish, the ALM Language School, based in Antigua and Quetzaltenango, has a branch here in Monterrico.

Places to Stay & Eat

Monterrico has four simple beachfront hotels, all with restaurants and all very near one another. From where you alight from the boat that has brought you over from La Avellana, it's about a 15-minute walk through the village to reach the beach and the hotels. If you've brought a vehicle across on a car ferry, you can park it at any of the hotels; all have parking areas.

All the hotels are similar, but the *Hotel Baule Beach* (☎ 473-6196), a cozy 17-room hotel run by former Peace Corps Volunteer Nancy Garver, is probably the best deal. Not only is it the cheapest, but it's also very pleasant; it's friendly and lots of young international travelers stay here. Rooms with private bath, right on the beach, cost US$3.60 to US$7.50 per person, depending on how many people share a room; rooms hold one to six people. Meals are reasonably priced as well. Current schedules for every type of transport serving Monterrico are posted here.

Hotel Pez de Oro (☎ 331-5620) is the most attractive hotel of the four. It has nine clean, pleasant bungalows, each with fan, mosquito nets, private bath and a hammock on the porch. Cost is US$29/40/50 for two/three/four people (singles pay the same as doubles). There's also a swimming pool, and the restaurant is operated by Italians.

Kaiman Inn (☎ 202-6513, 369-1258) has eight rooms, each with fan, mosquito nets

and private bath, for US$10 per person, with rooms holding two to five people. The restaurant, right on the beach, serves excellent Italian cuisine and seafood.

Johnny's Place (☎ 337-4191, fax 365-8072) has rooms for US$6/12.50 per person on weekdays/weekends. It also has seven bungalows, each with two bedrooms, living room, private bath and fully equipped kitchen for US$60 for four people (US$30 on weekdays if only two people stay). Two bungalows share a BBQ and small swimming pool. Also here is a swimming pool and restaurant.

Another hotel or two are set back from the beach.

All the beachfront hotels have their own restaurants. Or there's the *Pig Pen Pub*, an open-air beachfront bar a short walk down the beach. It's open from 8 pm 'until you're done drinking'.

Getting There & Away

Getting to Monterrico involves first getting to La Avellana, from where *lanchas* (small passenger boats) and car ferries depart for Monterrico. Direct buses operate between Guatemala City and La Avellana about 10 times daily (124 km, four hours, US$2.10). Or you can change buses at Taxisco, on CA-2 – buses operate hourly between Guatemala City and Taxisco (106 km, 3½ hours, US$1.65) and hourly between Taxisco and La Avellana (18 km, 20 minutes, US$0.40).

Shuttle buses also serve La Avellana. You can take a shuttle bus roundtrip from Antigua, coming on one day and returning on the next, for US$25, or one-way for US$12. From Antigua it's a 2½ hour trip. The Adventure Travel Center in Antigua (see the Antigua section) comes over every Saturday and returns every Sunday; other shuttle services also make the trip. Shuttle services depart from La Avellana for Antigua at 2 pm on Saturdays and Sundays (US$12) and for Guatemala City on Monday morning at 9 am (US$7). Phone the Hotel Baule Beach in Monterrico to check the current schedule for buses and shuttles, if you need to know in advance.

From Avellana, catch a passenger boat or car ferry to Monterrico. The *colectivo* passenger boats charge US$0.40 per passenger for the half-hour trip along the Canal de Chiquimulilla, a long mangrove canal.

LAGO DE AMATITLÁN

A placid lake backed by a looming volcano, situated a mere 25 km south of Guatemala City – that's Amatitlán. It should be a pretty and peaceful resort, but unfortunately it's not. The hourglass-shaped lake is divided by a railway line, and the lakeshore is lined with industry at some points. On weekends people from Guatemala City come to row boats on the lake (its waters are too polluted for swimming) or to rent a private hot tub for a dip. Many people from the capital own second homes here.

There's little reason for you to spend time here. If you really want to have a look, head for the town of Amatitlán, just off the main Escuintla-Guatemala City highway. Amatitlán has a scruffy public beach area. If you have a car and some spare time, a drive around the lake offers some pretty scenery. Perhaps the lake will one day be restored to its naturally beautiful state.

Central & Eastern Guatemala

North and east of Guatemala City is a land of varied topography, from the misty, pine-covered mountains of Alta Verapaz to the hot, dry-tropic climate of the Río Motagua valley. The Carretera al Atlántico (CA-9) heads northeast from the capital and soon descends from the relative cool of the mountains to the dry heat of a valley where dinosaurs once roamed.

Along this highway are many interesting destinations, including the beautiful highland scenery around Cobán; the paleontology museum at Estanzuela; the great basilica at Esquipulas, famous throughout Central America; the first-rate Mayan ruins at Copán, just across the border in Honduras; the marvelous Mayan stelae and zoomorphs at Quiriguá; and the tropical lake of Izabal and jungle waterway of Río Dulce. The Carretera al Atlántico ends at Puerto Barrios, Guatemala's Caribbean port, from which you can take a boat to Lívingston, a laid-back hideaway peopled by the Garifuna.

In the time before the Spanish conquest, the mountainous highland regions of the departments of Baja Verapaz and Alta Verapaz were peopled by the Rabinal Maya, noted for their warlike habits and merciless victories. They battled the powerful Quiché Maya for a century but were never conquered.

When the conquistadores arrived, they too had trouble defeating the Rabinals. It was Fray Bartolomé de las Casas who convinced the Spanish authorities to try peace where war had failed. Armed with an edict that forbade Spanish soldiers from entering the region for five years, the friar and his brethren pursued their religious mission and succeeded in pacifying and converting the Rabinals. It was renamed Verapaz (True Peace) and is now divided into Baja Verapaz, with its capital at Salamá, and Alta Verapaz, centered on Cobán.

The two departmental capitals are easily accessible along a smooth, fast, asphalt road that winds up from the hot, dry valley through wonderful scenery into the mountains, through long stretches of coffee-growing country. Along the way to Cobán is one of Guatemala's premier nature reserves, the Biotopo del Quetzal. Beyond Cobán, along rough unpaved roads, are the country's most famous caverns.

SALAMÁ
Population 11,000

Highway 17, also marked CA-14, leaves the Carretera al Atlántico at El Rancho, 84 km from Guatemala City. It heads west through a dry, desert-like lowland area, then turns north and starts climbing up into the forested hills. After 47 km you come to the turnoff for Salamá. Descending the other side of the ridge, the road winds down into the broad valley of the Río Salamá, and enters the capital of the department of Baja Verapaz, 17 km from the Carretera.

Salamá (940 meters) is an attractive town with some reminders of colonial rule. The main plaza boasts an ornate colonial church with many old gold-painted altars. If you arrive on a Sunday, you'll find the market bustling with activity.

Places to Stay & Eat
Should you want to stay the night, *Hospedaje Juárez* (☎ 940-0055), 10a Avenida 15-55, Zona 1, in the block directly behind the church, is a good, clean, friendly place to stay. All 15 rooms have private hot bath and cost US$6/8.50 a single/double. There's no sign out front.

The *Hotel Tezulutlán* (☎ /fax 940-0141), just off the main square behind the Texaco fuel station, has 15 rooms arranged around a pleasant garden courtyard. All have cable TV and all but two have private bath (four rooms have hot water); they cost US$13/18 a single/double. The two rooms with general bath are US$5/8. Across the street, *Hotel San Ignacio* (☎ 940-0186) is a clean family-run

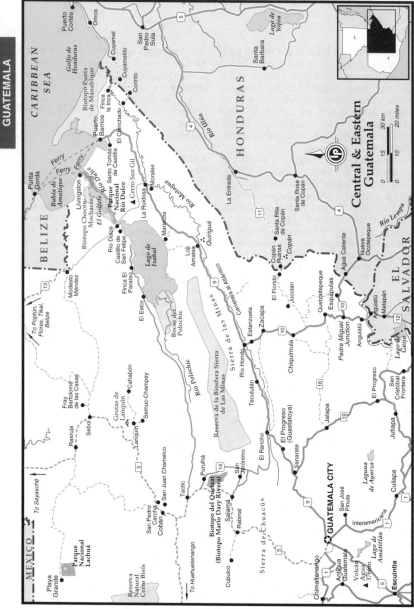

Central & Eastern Guatemala

place where singles/doubles are US$4/5 with shared bath, US$5/7 with private cold bath; the *Cafetería Apolo XI* is in the same building.

All of these places have parking available.

Near the plaza there are many places to eat. A few doors from the plaza, *Cafe Deli-Donas* is a clean, pleasant coffee shop serving light meals and sweets; it's open every day. At the *Restaurante El Ganadero*, a half-block off the main square on the road out of town, a lunch might cost US$4 to US$6, a sandwich much less. *Restaurante Caña Vieja* on the plaza is also an option.

Getting There & Away

As this is a departmental capital, there are frequent buses to and from Guatemala City, arriving and departing from a small bus station half a block from the central plaza. Buses bound for Guatemala City depart hourly, 2:30 am to 4 pm (151 km, three hours, US$2). Buses coming from Guatemala City continue west from Salamá to Rabinal (19 km, one hour, US$1) and then 15 km farther along to Cubulco.

In Guatemala City, buses to Salamá depart hourly, 5 am to 5 pm, from the office of Transporte Dulce María, 9a Avenida 19-20, Zona 1 (☎ 250-0082).

AROUND SALAMÁ

Ten km along the road to Salamá from the Cobán highway, you come to the turnoff for **San Jerónimo**, which is five km north of Hwy 5. Behind the town's beautiful church is an old sugar mill now used as a museum. On the plaza are some large stones that were carved in ancient times.

Nine km west of Salamá along Hwy 5 is the village of **San Miguel Chicaj**, known for its weaving. Continue along the same road for another 10 km to reach the colonial town of **Rabinal**, founded in 1537 by Fray Bartolomé de las Casas as a base for his proselytizing. Rabinal has gained fame as a pottery-making center (look especially

Guatemala's national bird, the quetzal

at the hand-painted chocolate cups), and for its citrus fruit harvest (November and December). Market day here is Sunday. Two small hotels, the *Pensión Motagua* and the *Hospedaje Caballeros*, can put you up.

It's possible to continue on from Rabinal another 15 km to the village of **Cubulco**. Or, from Rabinal you can follow Hwy 5 all the way to Guatemala City, a trip of about 100 km on which you pass through several small villages. It's best to traverse this remote route only with a 4WD vehicle. Buses do ply this route, albeit very slowly. Along the way you could visit the **ruins of Mixco Viejo** near **San Juan Sacatepéquez**, about 25 km from Guatemala City.

BIOTOPO DEL QUETZAL

Along the main highway (CA-14) 34 km beyond the turnoff for Salamá you reach the Biotopo Mario Dary Rivera nature reserve, commonly called the Biotopo del Quetzal, at Km 161, just east of the village of Purulhá (no services).

If you stop here intent on seeing a quetzal, Guatemala's national bird, you may be disappointed – the birds are rare and elusive. You have the best chance of seeing them from February to September.

Even if you never see a quetzal, though, it's still well worth a visit to explore and enjoy the lush high-altitude cloud forest ecosystem that is the quetzal's natural habitat.

Trail guide maps in English and Spanish may be purchased for US$0.50. They contain a checklist of 87 birds commonly seen here. Other animals include spider monkeys and *tigrillos*, which are similar to ocelots.

Two excellent, well-maintained nature trails wind through the reserve: the 1800-meter Sendero los Helechos (Fern Trail) and the Sendero los Musgos (Moss Trail), which is twice as long. As you wander through the dense growth, treading on the rich, dense, spongy humus and leaf-mold, you'll see many varieties of epiphytes (air plants), which thrive in the humid jungle atmosphere.

Both trails pass by waterfalls, most of which fall into small pools where you can take a dip; innumerable streams have their headwaters here. The Río Colorado cascades through the forest along a geological fault. Deep in the forest is Xiu Ua Li Che (Grandfather Tree), some 450 years old, which was alive when the conquistadors fought the Rabinals in these mountains.

The reserve is open every day from 7 am to 4 pm (you must be in by 4 pm, but you can stay longer); admission costs US$5.

There's a visitors' center, and drinks (but no food) are available at the site.

Places to Stay

Camping, once permitted here, is no longer allowed.

There are two lodging places within a short distance of the reserve. Just beyond it, another 200 meters up the hill toward Purulhá and Cobán, is the *Hotel y Comedor Ranchito del Quetzal* (☎ 331-3579 in Guatemala City), a rustic hospedaje. Rustic rooms with shared bath are US$5/8/11 a single/double/triple; rooms with private hot bath are US$8/11/14. Meals are US$1.35 for breakfast, US$2.50 for lunch or dinner (US$1.65 for vegetarian meals).

The more comfortable *Posada Montaña del Quetzal* (☎ 335-1805 in Guatemala City), Carretera a Cobán Km 156.5, Purulhá, Baja Verapaz, is five km back along the road toward the Carretera al Atlántico. This attractive hostelry has 18 white stucco, tile-roofed bungalow cabins, each with a sitting room and fireplace, a bedroom with three beds and a private hot bath, for US$20/26 a single/double; larger two-bedroom bungalows are US$28/35. The complex has a restaurant, a large swimming pool and a smaller children's pool. You can usually catch a bus to shuttle you between the Biotopo and the posada, or hitch a ride.

COBÁN

Population 20,000

The asphalt road between the Biotopo and Cobán is good, smooth and fast, though curvy, with light traffic. As you ascend into the evergreen forests, tropical flowers are still visible here and there. As you enter Cobán, a sign says 'Bienvenidos a Cobán, Ciudad Imperial', referring to the charter granted in 1538 by Emperor Charles V. About 126 km from the Carretera al Atlántico, you reach Cobán's main plaza.

The town now called Cobán (1320 meters) was once the center of Tezulutlán (Tierra de Guerra in Spanish, the Land of War), a stronghold of the Rabinal Maya.

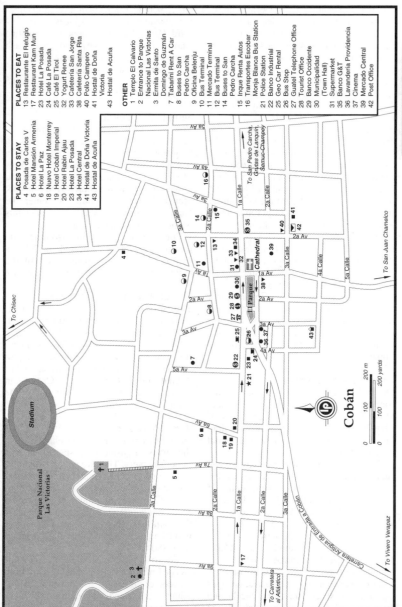

PLACES TO STAY
4 Posada de Carlos V
5 Hotel Mansión Armenia
6 Hotel La Paz
18 Nuevo Hotel Monterrey
19 Hotel Cobán Imperial
20 Hotel Rabin Ajau
23 Hotel La Posada
34 Hotel Central
41 Hostal de Doña Victoria
43 Hostal de Acuña

PLACES TO EAT
13 Restaurante El Refugio
17 Restaurant Kam Mun
23 Hotel La Posada
24 Café La Posada
25 Café El Tirol
32 Yogurt Renee
33 Cafetería San Jorge
38 Cafetería Santa Rita
40 Pollo Campero
41 Hostal de Doña Victoria
43 Hostal de Acuña

OTHER
1 Templo El Calvario
2 Entrance to Parque Nacional Las Victorias
3 Ermita de Santo Domingo de Guzmán
7 Tabarini Rent A Car
8 Buses to San Pedro Carcha
9 Oficina Belenju
10 Bus Terminal
11 Mercado Terminal
12 Bus Terminal
14 Buses to San Pedro Carcha
15 Inque Renta Autos
16 Transportes Escobar Monja Blanca Bus Station
21 Police Station
22 Banco Industrial
25 Geo Car Rental
26 Bus Stop
27 Guatel Telephone Office
28 Tourist Office
29 Banco Occidente
30 Municipalidad (Town Hall)
31 Supermarket
35 Banco G&T
36 Lavandería Providencia
37 Cinema
39 Mercado Central
42 Post Office

Cobán

In the 19th century, when German immigrants moved in and founded vast coffee fincas, Cobán took on the aspect of a German mountain town as the finca owners built town residences. The era of German cultural and economic domination ended during WWII, when the USA prevailed upon the Guatemalan government to deport the powerful finca owners, many of whom actively supported the Nazis.

Today Cobán can be a pleasant town to visit, though much depends upon the season. Most of the year it is either rainy or overcast, dank and chill. You can count on sunny days in Cobán for only about three weeks in April. In the midst of the 'dry' season (January to March) it can be misty and sometimes rainy, or bright and sunny with marvelous clear mountain air.

Guatemala's most impressive festival of Indian traditions, the folkloric festival of Rabin Ajau with its traditional dance of the Paabanc, takes place in the latter part of July or the first week of August.

There is not a lot to do in Cobán except enjoy the local color and the mountain scenery, but the town as a good base for visits to the Grutas de Lanquín and Cuevas Semuc-Champey nearby (see Around Cobán below).

Orientation & Information

The main plaza *(el parque)* features a disconcertingly modern concrete bandstand. Most of the services you'll need are within a few blocks of the plaza and the cathedral. The shopping district is around and behind the cathedral.

The tourist office, on the plaza near the Guatel office, has posted office hours, but you may or may not find it functioning. If you need information, the Hostal de Acuña or the Hostal de Doña Victoria (see Places to Stay) are good places to ask.

The post office is a block from the plaza on the corner of 2a Avenida and 3a Calle. The Guatel telephone office is on the plaza; public coin phones are outside the office.

Banco Occidente, on the plaza, changes US dollars cash and travelers' checks and gives cash advances on Visa cards. Banco

G&T, behind the cathedral, also changes money and gives cash advances on Master-Card. Banco Industrial, opposite the police station, changes money and gives cash advances on Visa at its 24-hour ATM.

Laundry service is available from Lavandería Providencia on the plaza or from Hostal de Acuña.

Templo El Calvario

You can get a fine view over the town from the Templo El Calvario, a church atop a long flight of stairs at the north end of 7a Avenida. Indigenous people leave offerings of natural elements at outdoor shrines and crosses in front of the church. You can walk around behind the church to enter the Parque Nacional Las Victorias, though this is not the park's main entrance.

The Ermita de Santo Domingo de Guzmán, a chapel dedicated to Cobán's patron saint, is 150 meters west of the bottom of the stairs leading to El Calvario.

Parque Nacional Las Victorias

This forested 82-hectare national park, right in town, has several trails, ponds, BBQ and picnic areas, children's play areas, a lookout point and free camping. It's open every day from 8 am to 4:30 pm; admission is free. The entrance is at 11a Avenida and 3a Calle, Zona 1. Or you can enter by walking around to the rear of the Templo El Calvario.

Vívero Verapaz

Orchid lovers mustn't miss a chance to see the many thousands of species at this famous nursery. The rare *monja blanca*, or white nun orchid, Guatemala's national flower, can be seen here; there are also hundreds of species of miniature orchids, so small that you'll need the magnifying glass they will loan you to see them. The owners will take you on a tour to see all the species for US$0.85.

Vívero Verapaz is on the Carretera Antigua de Entrada a Cobán, about two km from the center of town. It's a beautiful 20-minute walk from the plaza. It's open Monday to Saturday, 9 am to noon and 2 to 5 pm.

Organized Tours

The Hostal de Acuña and the Hostal de Doña Victoria both operate tour companies with trips to Semuc-Champey, the Grutas de Lanquín and other places further afield.

Places to Stay

There's free camping at the Parque Nacional Las Victorias, right in town. Water and toilets are available, but no showers.

Hostal de Acuña (☎ /fax 952-1547, fax 952-1268), 4a Calle 3-11, Zona 2, is a clean, very pleasant European-style hostel. Cost is US$4.15 per bunk, in rooms with two or four beds. Also here is a good restaurant, a sitting room, gift shop, laundry service and reasonably priced local tours.

Hotel Cobán Imperial (☎ 952-1131), 6a Avenida 1-12, Zona 1, 250 meters from the plaza, is administered along with the adjoining *Nuevo Hotel Monterrey*. It's old but clean, popular with Guatemalan families, and has parking in the courtyard. Singles/doubles are US$2.50/5 with shared cold bath, US$3.35/6.65 with private cold bath or US$7.50/15 with private hot bath and TV.

Hotel La Paz (☎ 952-1358), 6a Avenida 2-19, Zona 1, 1½ blocks north of the plaza, is cheerful, clean and an excellent deal for the price: singles/doubles are US$4/8 with shared bath, US$5/8 with private bath. It has many flowers, parking in the courtyard, and a cafeteria next door.

The old-fashioned *Hotel Rabin Ajau* (☎ 952-2296), 1a Calle 5-37, Zona 1, is well located and fairly plain; its disco is noisy. There's a restaurant and parking. Rooms with private bath are US$11/14/17 a single/double/triple.

The *Hotel Central* (☎ 951-1442), 1a Calle 1-79, Zona 4, is tidy, with rooms-with-bath arranged around a flowered courtyard. Singles/doubles/triples are US$8/10/12 for remodeled rooms, US$6/8/10 for those yet to be remodeled. The Cafetería San Jorge is also here.

Hotel Mansión Armenia (☎ 952-2284), 7a Avenida 2-18, Zona 1, one block from Templo El Calvario, is a comfortable place, new, clean, quiet and modern, with courtyard parking and a cafeteria. Rooms with

private bath and cable TV are US$14/19 a single/double. Even newer is the *Posada de Carlos V* (☎ /fax 952-1780), 1a Avenida 3-44, Zona 1, with singles/doubles/triples with private bath and cable TV are US$14/24/31.

Hotel Oxib Peck (☎ 952-1039, ☎ /fax 951-3224), 1a Calle 12-11, Zona 1, is 12 blocks (750 meters) west of the plaza on the road out of town. The rooms are clean and pleasant, and there's a dining room, laundry service and parking. Singles/doubles/triples with private bath and cable TV are US$15/22/29.

Hostal de Doña Victoria (☎ 952-2213/4), 3a Calle 2-38, Zona 3, is in a restored mansion over 400 years old. Comfortable rooms with private bath surround a central courtyard with plants and a restaurant/bar. Prices are US$17/26/34/39 for one to four people.

Best in town is the *Hotel La Posada* (☎ / fax 952-1495), 1a Calle 4-12, Zona 2, just off the plaza in the very center of town. Colonial in style, its colonnaded porches are festooned with tropical flowers and furnished with easy chairs and hammocks to enjoy the mountain views. The rooms have nice old furniture, fireplaces and wall hangings of local weaving; they rent for US$26/32/39 a single/double/triple with private bath.

The *Park Hotel* (☎ /fax 950-4539), in Santa Cruz Verapaz at Km 196.5, 14 km from Cobán on the highway to Guatemala City, has modern little bungalows and a restaurant amid tropical forest in park-like grounds. The 54 regular rooms in prefabricated duplex bungalows cost US$16/26/34 a single/double/triple. The suites are more attractive, with living room, fireplace and cable TV; these are US$42/55 a single/double.

Places to Eat

Most of Cobán's hotels have their own restaurants. The one at the *Hostal de Acuña* is one of the best in town, with good, reasonably priced Italian and other European-style dishes served in an attractive setting. Dinners are around US$5. The restaurant at the *Hostal de Doña Victoria* is also pleasant.

GUATEMALA

Café El Tirol, near the Hotel La Posada, advertises 'the best coffee' and several types of hot chocolate in four languages. It's a cozy little place in which to enjoy pastries and coffee for US$1 to US$2. Breakfast and light meals are served as well. It's closed on Monday.

Café La Posada on the west end of the plaza has tables on a verandah overlooking the plaza, and a comfortable sitting room inside with couches, coffee tables and a fireplace. All the usual cafe fare is served. In the same building, *Hotel La Posada* has a pleasant dining room with good food but slow service.

Cafetería Santa Rita, also facing the main square, is small, tidy and popular with locals. Good breakfasts, lunches and dinners go for around US$2.

Cafetería San Jorge, 1a Calle between 1a and 2a Avenidas, near the cathedral, has a varied menu and a dining room with views through large windows. Substantial meat dishes are offered (US$3), along with a variety of sandwiches (US$1 to US$2). Next door, *Yogurt Renee* makes delicious fruit yogurts and ice cream.

Pollo Campero has an outlet across from the post office on 2a Avenida at 2a Calle.

Restaurante El Refugio, at the corner of 2a Avenida and 2a Calle, Zona 4, has rustic wooden decor and a menu with lots of meat dishes (grilled steaks are US$3 to US$8), Mexican dishes and burgers, hot dogs and the like.

Almost 500 meters from the plaza the *Restaurant Kam Mun*, 1a Calle 8-12, Zona 2, is on the road out of town. Its Chinese fare, served in a pleasant, clean place, costs US$5 to US$8 for a full meal.

In the evening, food trucks (kitchens on wheels) park around the plaza and offer some of the cheapest dining in town. Some serve safe food, others don't.

Getting There & Away

Bus The highway connecting Cobán with Guatemala City and the Carretera al Atlántico is the most traveled route connecting Cobán with the outside world, but there are a few other off-the-beaten-track routes, all of which are served by buses. (If you're traveling by private vehicle, cut the bus times in half.)

From Cobán you can bus to Fray Bartolomé de las Casas in about six hours; from there, you can continue another seven hours to Poptún, south of Flores. There's a hospedaje in Fray Bartolomé de las Casas, if you need to spend the night. From Fray Bartolomé de las Casas it's also possible to take a pickup truck to Raxrujá, 20 km away. From Raxrujá you can catch a bus to Sayaxché (four hours), from where there are buses to Flores. (See Sayaxché in the El Petén section.) There's a place to stay overnight in Raxrujá.

Another route is from Cobán to Uspantán, about an eight hour trip by bus. There are places to stay in Uspantán. You can continue by bus from Uspantán to Huehuetenango in about six hours, or from Uspantán to Santa Cruz del Quiché in about six hours. In Santa Cruz del Quiché there are frequent connections to Chichicastenango and Guatemala City.

Another off-the-beaten-track route is from Cobán to El Estor, on Lago de Izabal, a nine-hour bus trip. From El Estor you can take a boat to Mariscos, from where it's a short bus ride to the Carretera al Atlántico.

Most buses depart from Cobán's bus terminal (☎ 951-3043), a rather large spread-out area on either side of 3a Calle, between 1a and 2a Avenida. Buses to Guatemala City depart from a different station. From Cobán, buses include:

Biotopo del Quetzal – 58 km, one hour, US$1; any bus heading for Guatemala City will drop you at the entrance to the Biotopo.

Cahabón – 85 km, 4½ hours, US$2; same buses as to Lanquín

El Estor – 168 km, nine hours, US$4; Brenda Mercedes and Valenciana buses depart from the bus terminal several times daily.

Fray Bartolomé de las Casas – 110 km, six hours, US$3; several buses daily

Guatemala City – 219 km, four hours, US$2 to US$3; Transportes Escobar Monja Blanca (☎ 952-1536, 952-1952), 2a Calle 3-77, Zona 4, has buses leaving for Guatemala City every half hour from 2 to 6 am, then hourly from 6 am to 4 pm.

Lanquín – 61 km, three hours, US$1.15; buses depart at 6 am, noon, 1 and 3 pm from Oficina Belenju on 3a Calle. The return buses depart from Lanquín at 5 am, 7 am and 3 pm.

San Pedro Carcha – six km, 20 minutes, US$0.10; buses every 10 minutes, 6 am to 7 pm

Uspantán – 94 km, eight hours, US$4; two buses daily

Car Because it is a good base for exploring the surrounding mountains, Cobán now has several places that rent cars. All of these companies are small and may not have every type of vehicle available at every moment. It's a good idea to reserve one in advance. If you want to go to the Grutas de Lanquín or Semuc-Champey, you'll need a vehicle with 4WD.

Rental car companies include:

Geo Rental, 1a Calle 3-13, Zona 1, in the same building as the Cafe El Tirol, in the rear right corner of the courtyard (☎ 952-2059)

Inque Renta Autos, 3a Avenida 1-18, Zona 4 (☎ 952-1994, 952-1172)

Ochoch Pec Renta Autos, opposite La Carrita el Viaje at the entrance to town (☎ 951-3474, 951-3214)

Tabarini Rent A Car, 5a Avenida 2-43, Zona 1 (☎ /fax 951-3282)

AROUND COBÁN

Cobán is becoming an established base for organized excursions to sites in the surrounding mountains. Several small companies have been founded just for this purpose. For example, Marcio and Ashley Acuña of the Hostal de Acuña run ecotours from Cobán to the Grutas de Lanquín, Semuc-Champey and also to many Mayan jungle sites such as La Candelaria, Ceibal, Aguateca, Dos Pilas, Yaxchilán, Yaxhá, Nakun, Tikal, Uaxactún and Río Azul, and rafting tours on the Río Cahabón. The Hostal de Doña Victoria runs similar tours. No doubt other operators will start up by the time you visit Cobán.

Balneario Las Islas

At the town of San Pedro Carcha, six km east of Cobán on the way to Lanquín, is the Balneario Las Islas, with a river coming down past rocks and into a natural pool great for swimming. It's a five- to 10-minute walk from the bus stop in Carcha; anyone can point the way. Buses operate frequently between Cobán and Carcha; the trip takes 20 minutes.

San Juan Chamelco

About 16 km southeast of Cobán is the village of San Juan Chamelco, with swimming at the Balneario Chio. In Aldea Chajaneb, Jerry Makransky (everyone knows him as 'Don Jeronimo') rents comfortable, simple bungalows for US$15 per person (US$25 per couple) per day, which includes three ample, delicious vegetarian meals fresh from the garden and many activities: tours to caves, to the mountains, inner tubing on the Río Sotzil and more. Jerry dotes on his guests, and the atmosphere is friendly.

To get there, take a bus from Cobán to San Juan Chamelco. From there, take a bus or pickup towards Chamil and ask the driver to let you off at Don Jeronimo's. Take the footpath to the left for 300 meters, cross the bridge and it's the first house on the right.

Grutas de Lanquín

If you don't mind bumping over bad and/or busy roads, the best excursion to make from Cobán is to the caves near Lanquín, a pretty village 61 km to the east.

The Grutas de Lanquín are a short distance northwest of the town, and extend for several kilometers into the earth. You must first stop at the police station in the Municipalidad (Town Hall) in Lanquín, pay the US$2 admission fee and ask them to open the cave for you; there is no attendant at the cave otherwise. The cave has lights, but bring along a powerful flashlight anyway. You'll also need shoes with good traction, as it's slippery inside.

Though the first few hundred meters of cavern has been equipped with a walkway and is lit by diesel-powered electric lights, most of this subterranean system is untouched. If you are not an experienced

---

Cardamom

The world's coffee drinkers know that high-quality coffee is important to Guatemala's export trade, but few know that Guatemala is the world's largest exporter of cardamom. In Alta Verapaz, cardamom is more important to the local economy than coffee, providing livelihood for some 200,000 people.

Cardamom *(Elettaria cardamomum)*, an herbaceous perennial of the ginger family native to the Malabar Coast of India, was brought to Alta Verapaz by German coffee-finca owners. The plants grow to a height of between five and 20 feet and have coarse leaves up to 30 inches long that are hairy on the underside. The flowers are white, and the fruit is a green, three-sided oval capsule holding 15 to 20 dark, hard, reddish-brown to brownish-black seeds.

Though the cardamom plants grow readily, it is difficult to cultivate, pick and sort the best grades, so fragrant cardamom commands a high price. That does not seem to bother the people of Saudi Arabia and the Arabian Gulf states, who purchase over 80% of the world supply. They pulverise the seeds and add the powder to the thick, syrupy, pungent coffee that is a social and personal necessity in that part of the world. ■

---

spelunker, you should think twice about wandering too far into the caves.

If you have camping equipment you can spend the night near the cave entrance. Otherwise, there are two places to stay at Lanquín. In town, *La Divina Providencia* has simple rooms for about US$2 to US$3 per person. *El Recreo*, between the town and the caves, is more attractive and more expensive, with singles/doubles for US$14/25. The *Comedor Shalom* is good for a meal.

Semuc-Champey

Ten km south of Lanquín along a rough, bumpy, slow road is Semuc-Champey, famed for a natural wonder: a great limestone bridge 300 meters long, on top of which is a series of pools of cool, flowing river water good for swimming. The water is from the Río Cahabón, and most of it passes beneath the bridge underground. Though this bit of paradise is difficult to reach, the beauty of its setting and the perfection of the pools, ranging from turquoise to emerald green, make it all worth it. Some people consider this the most beautiful spot in all Guatemala.

It's possible to camp at Semuc-Champey, but be sure to camp only in the upper areas, as flash floods are common down below. It's risky to leave anything unattended, though, as it might get stolen.

Tours to the Grutas de Lanquín and Semuc-Champey, offered in Cobán, are the easiest way to visit these places. On your own, if you're driving, you'll need a 4WD vehicle.

Buses operate several times daily between Cobán and Lanquín, continuing to Cahabón. Buses leave Lanquín to return to Cobán at 5am, 7 am and 3 pm. Since the last return bus departs so early, you should probably plan to stay the night. There are occasional buses and trucks from Lanquín to Semuc-Champey. Otherwise, it's a long, hot walk unless you have your own vehicle, in which case it's a slow, bumpy drive.

RÍO HONDO

Río Hondo lies along CA-9 southeast of Cobán, 42 km from El Rancho Junction (126 km from Guatemala City). Beyond Chiquimula are turnoffs to Copán, just across the Honduran border; to Esquipulas and on to Nueva Ocotepeque (Honduras); and a remote border crossing between Guatemala and El Salvador at Anguiatú, 12 km north of Metapán (El Salvador).

The town of Río Hondo (Deep River) is northeast of the junction, but lodging places hereabouts list their address as Río Hondo, Santa Cruz Río Hondo or Santa Cruz Teculután – it's all the same place. Nine km west of the junction are several attractive motels right on CA-9, which provide a good base for explorations of this region if you have your own vehicle. By car, it's an hour from here to Quiriguá, half an hour to Chiquimula or 1½ hours to Esquipulas.

Another big attraction of Río Hondo is the Valle Dorado aquatic park and tourist center (see Places to Stay).

Places to Stay & Eat

Note that the Río Hondo motels are looked upon as weekend resorts by locals and residents of Guatemala City, so they may be heavily booked on weekends. They're popular as bases for visits to the area in general, to the Valle Dorado aquatic park in particular, and also in their own right – all of them are modern, pleasant places, with well-equipped bungalows (all have color cable TV and private bath), spacious grounds, good restaurants, and all except the Hotel Santa Cruz have giant swimming pools. On weekdays they provide lodging for people who work in the area.

The following four motels are all near one another at Km 126 on the Carretera al Atlántico, 126 km from Guatemala City.

Cheapest of the four is the *Hotel Santa Cruz* (☎ 934-7112, ☎ /fax 934-7075), where rooms in duplex bungalows are US$8.35/10 a single/double with fan, US$10/20 with air-con. The popular restaurant here is cheaper than some of the others. Four new apartments with kitchen are also available.

Hotel El Atlántico (☎ 934-7160, fax 934-7041), Carretera al Atlántico Km 126, is probably the most attractive of the four, with a large swimming pool, beautiful spacious grounds and a good restaurant. Large, well-equipped bungalows are US$20/36/46 a single/double/triple. It's also probably the most popular; reservations are wise.

Across the highway, on the north side, the *Hotel Nuevo Pasabién* (☎ /fax 934-7201, 934-7073, 934-7074) has older, slightly more rustic rooms for US$10/20 a single/double, and newer, larger rooms for US$13/25 with fan, US$15/29 with air-con.

Opposite the Hotel Santa Cruz and behind the 24-hour Shell gas station, *Hotel Longarone* (☎ 934-7126, fax 934-7035) is the old standard in this area. Some rooms are in a long row, others are in duplex bungalows. Simple rooms are US$18/24/30 a single/double/triple, or US$24/30/36 with cable TV and fridge; all have air-con. It has two large swimming pools, two smaller ones for children and a tennis court.

The restaurants at all of these hotels are open every day from around 6 am to 10 pm. Along the highway are various other smaller, cheaper eateries.

Nine km east of these places, right at the junction with CA-10, the road heading south to Chiquimula and Esquipulas, is the *Hotel Río* (☎ 941-1267), Carretera al Atlántico Km 135. It's very beat-up. Rooms with private bath are US$6/7 with two/three beds.

Valle Dorado (☎ 941-2542, fax 941-2543), on the Carretera al Atlántico at Km 149, 14 km past the CA-10 junction and 23 km from the other Río Hondo hotels, is an enormous complex that includes an aquatic park with giant pools, waterslides, toboggans and other entertainment. Rooms are US$46 for one to three people, US$55 for four or US$78 for six. Make reservations on weekends, when it fills up with families.

Many people prefer to stay at one of the other Río Hondo hotels and come to Valle Dorado for the day. Day use costs US$6/5 for adults/children on weekends, US$4/3 during the week. The park is open for day use every day from 8 am to sunset.

ESTANZUELA

Population 10,000

Traveling south from Río Hondo along CA-10 you are in the midst of the Río Motagua valley, a hot expanse of what is known as 'dry tropic', which once supported a great number and variety of dinosaurs. Three km south of the Carretera al Atlántico you'll see a small monument on the right-hand (west) side of the road commemorating the terrible earthquake of February 4, 1976.

Less than two km south of the earthquake monument is the small town of Estanzuela, with its *Museo de Paleontología, Arqueología y Geología Ing Roberto Woolfolk Sarvia*, an interesting museum filled with dinosaur bones. The museum is open every day from 8 am to noon and from 1 to 5 pm; admission is free. To find the museum, go west from the highway directly through the town for one km, following the small blue signs pointing to the *museo*; anyone you see can help point the way. Next door to the museum is a small shop selling cold drinks and snacks.

Within the museum are most of the bones of three big dinosaurs, including those of a giant ground sloth some 30,000 years old and a prehistoric whale. Other exhibits include early Mayan artifacts.

ZACAPA
Population 18,000

Capital of the department of the same name, Zacapa (230 meters) is several kilometers east of the highway. It offers little to travelers, though the locals do make cheese, cigars and superb rum. The few hotels in town are basic and will do in an emergency; better accommodations are available in Río Hondo and Esquipulas.

CHIQUIMULA
Population 24,000

Another departmental capital set in a mining and tobacco-growing region, Chiquimula (370 meters) is on CA-10, 32 km south of the Carretera al Atlántico. It is a major market town for all of eastern Guatemala, with lots of buying and selling activity every day. It's also a transportation point and overnight stop for those making their way to Copán in Honduras; this is the only reason that most travelers stop here. Among other things, Chiquimula is famous for its hot climate.

Orientation & Information

Chiquimula is easy to get around on foot.

The post office, on 10a Avenida between 1a and 2a Calle, is in the dirt alley, around to the side of the building opposite the bus station. The Guatel telephone office is on 3a Calle, a few doors downhill from the plaza; coin phones are outside. The Hotel Hernández (near the plaza) and the Hotel Victoria (near the bus station) also offer domestic and international telephone services. The busy mercado is in the same block as Guatel.

Many banks will change US dollars cash and travelers' checks. Banco G&T, half a block from the plaza at 7a Avenida 4-75, Zona 1, changes both and also gives cash advances on Visa and MasterCard; it's open Monday to Friday from 9 am to 8 pm, Saturday 10 am to 2 pm. These hours are typical for most of the banks in town. Banoro at 3a Calle 8-30 has longer Saturday hours, from 9 am to 6 pm.

Places to Stay

Hotel Chiquimulja (☎ 942-0387), 3a Calle 6-51, is on the north side of the plaza. The rooms have fluorescent green walls; other than that, they're about average. All have private bath, and the ones on the street side have wide balconies overlooking the plaza. Rooms with fan are US$4/6 a single/double, or US$12/16 with air-con and cable TV. It has parking, too, as do most of the hotels here.

A block east of the Chiquimulja, downhill on the same street, are several other hotels. *Hotel Hernández* (☎ /fax 942-0708), 3a Calle 7-41, Zona 1, is clean, pleasant and friendly; the owner speaks English, Spanish and a little French. There's a swimming pool, parking, telephone service, and the rooms all have fans and good beds. Singles/doubles with shared bath are US$4/6.65; with private bath and cable TV they are US$8/12, or US$15 with air-con.

In the same block, just downhill, the *Pensión España*, 3a Calle 7-81, Zona 1, is more basic, with closet-like rooms, but it has gardens and it's cheaper, with singles/doubles for US$2.50/3.35. *Hospedaje Río Jordan* (☎ 942-0887), 3a Calle 8-91, Zona 1, a block farther downhill, has parking in the courtyard and charges US$2/4 per person in rooms with shared/private bath – probably better for the price than the España. *Antojitos Jordan*, also here, is a simple place for meals and snacks.

Hotel Victoria (☎ 942-2179), 2a Calle at 10a Avenida, is convenient to the bus

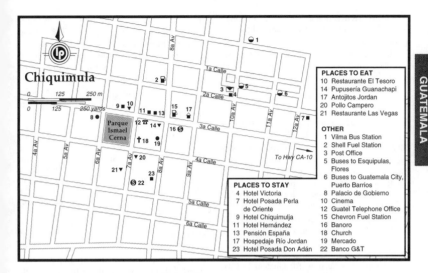

GUATEMALA

Chiquimula

0   125   250 m
0   125   250 yards

PLACES TO EAT
10 Restaurante El Tesoro
14 Pupusería Guanachapi
17 Antojitos Jordan
20 Pollo Campero
21 Restaurante Las Vegas

OTHER
1   Vilma Bus Station
2   Shell Fuel Station
3   Post Office
5   Buses to Esquipulas,
    Flores
6   Buses to Guatemala City,
    Puerto Barrios
8   Palacio de Gobierno
10 Cinema
12 Guatel Telephone Office
15 Chevron Fuel Station
16 Banoro
18 Church
19 Mercado
22 Banco G&T

PLACES TO STAY
4   Hotel Victoria
7   Hotel Posada Perla
    de Oriente
9   Hotel Chiquimulja
11 Hotel Hernández
13 Pensión España
17 Hospedaje Río Jordan
23 Hotel Posada Don Adán

station, which is probably the only reason to stay here. Small rooms with fan, cable TV, telephone and private bath are US$6/10/14/19 a single/double/triple/quad. The restaurant is good and cheap, with big breakfasts for US$2, and they also have telephone service.

Hotel Posada Perla de Oriente (☎ 942-0014, fax 942-0534), 12a Avenida 2-30, Zona 1, has a small swimming pool, a children's play area and a restaurant. Rooms are simple, with private bath, fan and cable TV, and cost US$10/15 a single/double.

Hotel Posada Don Adán (☎ 942-0549), 8a Avenida 4-30, Zona 1, is new and spotless. It's run by a friendly, efficient señora who charges US$17/23/29 a single/double/triple for rooms with private bath, telephone, cable TV, fan and air-con.

Places to Eat
Eating in Chiquimula is easy, as there are lots of cheap little places. Try the *Pupusería Guanachapi*, opposite the Pensión España. You can fill up for only a few quetzales.

Restaurante El Tesoro, on the main plaza, serves Chinese food at reasonable prices.

Near the southeast corner of the plaza, *Pollo Campero*, 7a Avenida at 4a Calle, serves up fried chicken, burgers and breakfasts. It's open every day, and its air-con is a treat.

For a step up in quality, try the *Restaurante Las Vegas*, 7a Avenida 4-40, half a block from the plaza. It's perhaps Chiquimula's best, with fancy plants, jazzy music, a well-stocked bar and full meals for around US$6 (sandwiches less). It's open every day from 7 am to midnight.

Getting There & Away
Chiquimula is not a destination but a transit point. Your goal is no doubt the fabulous Mayan ruins at Copán in Honduras, just across the border from El Florido.

Several companies operate buses to Guatemala City and Puerto Barrios; all of them arrive and depart from the bus station area on 11a Avenida, between 1a and 2a Calles. Buses to Esquipulas and Flores arrive and depart from the bus station area a block away, on 10a Avenida between 1a and 2a Calles. Vilma (☎ 942-2253), which operates buses to El Florido, the border crossing on the way to Copán, has its own bus station a couple of blocks north.

Anguiatú (El Salvador border) – 54 km, one hour, US$1; frequent minibuses, 5 am to 4 pm

El Florido (Honduras border) – 58 km, 2½ hours, US$1.20; buses depart from the Vilma bus station at 6, 9, 10:30 and 11:30 am, 12:30, 1:30, 2:30 and 3:30 pm. Coming in the opposite direction, they depart from El Florido at 5:30, 6:15, 7:15, 8:30 and 10:30 am, noon, 1:30 and 3:30 pm

Esquipulas – 52 km, one hour, US$1; minibuses every 10 minutes, 4 am to 8 pm

Flores – 385 km, 12 hours, US$10; Transportes María Elena buses depart at 6 am and 2:30 pm

Guatemala City – 169 km, three hours, US$2.50; Rutas Orientales, Transportes Guerra and Guatesqui operate buses departing every half hour, 5:30 am to 2 pm

Puerto Barrios – 192 km, 4½ hours, US$2.50; buses every 15 minutes, 4 am to 3 pm

Río Hondo – 32 km, 35 minutes, US$1; minibuses every half hour, 5 am to 6 pm. Or take any bus heading for Guatemala City, Flores or Puerto Barrios.

PADRE MIGUEL JUNCTION & ANGUIATÚ

Between Chiquimula and Esquipulas, 35 km from Chiquimula and 14 km from Esquipulas, Padre Miguel Junction is the turnoff for Anguiatú, the border of El Salvador, which is 19 km away. It takes half an hour to reach the border from this junction. Minibuses come by frequently, coming from Chiquimula, Quezaltepeque and Esquipulas. There's nothing much here at the crossroads, only a guard house and a bus stop shelter.

The border at Anguiatú is open every day from 6 am to 6 pm, though you might be able to get through on 'extraordinary service' until 9 pm. Across the border there are hourly buses to San Salvador, passing through Metapán, 12 km from the border, and Santa Ana, 47 km farther along.

ESQUIPULAS

From Chiquimula, CA-10 goes south into the mountains, where it's cooler and a bit more comfortable. After an hour's ride through pretty country, the highway descends into a valley ringed by mountains. Halfway down the slope, about a kilometer from the center of town, there is a mirador from which to get a good view. The reason for a trip to Esquipulas is evident as soon as you catch sight of the place: the great Basílica de Esquipulas that towers above the town, its whiteness shining in the sun. The view has changed little in the more than a century and a half since explorer John L Stephens saw it:

Descending, the clouds were lifted, and I looked down upon an almost boundless plain, running from the foot of the Sierra, and afar off saw, standing alone in the wilderness, the great church of Esquipulas, like the Church of the Holy Sepulchre in Jerusalem, and the Caaba in Mecca, the holiest of temples . . . I had a long and magnificent descent to the foot of the Sierra.

History

This town may have been a place of pilgrimage even before the Spaniards' conquest. Legend has it that the town takes its name from a noble Mayan lord who ruled this region when the Spanish arrived, and who received them in peace.

With the arrival of the friars, a church was built, and in 1595 an image of Christ carved from black wood was installed in it. The steady flow of pilgrims to Esquipulas became a flood after 1737, when Pedro Pardo de Figueroa, Archbishop of Guatemala, came here on pilgrimage and went away cured of a chronic ailment. Delighted with this development, the prelate commissioned a huge new church to be built on the site. It was finished in 1758, and the pilgrimage trade has been the town's livelihood ever since.

Orientation & Information

The church is the center of everything. Most of the good cheap hotels are within a block or two of it, as are numerous small restaurants. The town's only luxury hotel is on the outskirts, along the road back to Chiquimula. The highway does not enter town; 11a Calle, also sometimes called Doble Vía Quirio Cataño, comes in from the highway and is the town's 'main drag'.

The post office is at 6a Avenida 2-15, about 10 blocks north of the center. The

Guatel telephone office, 5a Avenida at the corner of 9a Calle, is open every day; coin phones are outside on the sidewalk.

A number of banks change US dollars cash and travelers' checks. Banco del Café, 3a Avenida 6-68, Zona 1, changes both, gives cash advances on Visa and MasterCard, and is the town's American Express agent.

There's a Honduran consulate (☎ 943-2027, 943-1547, fax 943-1371) in the Hotel Payaquí, facing the park. It's open Monday to Saturday, 8:30 am to noon and 2 to 5 pm.

Basilica

A massive pile of stone that has resisted the power of earthquakes for almost 2½ centuries, the basilica is approached through a pretty park and up a flight of steps. The impressive facade and towers are floodlit at night.

Inside, the devout approach El Cristo Negro with great reverence, many on their knees. Incense, the murmur of prayers and the shuffle of sandaled feet fills the air. To get a close view of the famous Black Christ you must enter the church from the side. Shuffling along quickly, you may get a good glimpse or two before being shoved onwards by the press of the crowd behind you. On Sundays, religious holidays and (especially) during the festival around January 15, the press of devotees is intense.

When you leave the church and descend the steps through the park, notice the vendors selling straw hats that are decorated with artificial flowers and stitched with the name 'Esquipulas', perfect for pilgrims who want everyone to know they've made the trip.

Cueva de las Minas

The Centro Turístico Cueva de las Minas has a 50-meter-deep cave (bring your own light), grassy play and picnic areas, and the Río El Milagro, where people come for a dip and say it's miraculous. The cave and river are half a kilometer from the entrance gate, which is behind the Basilica's cemetery, 300 meters south of the turnoff into town on the

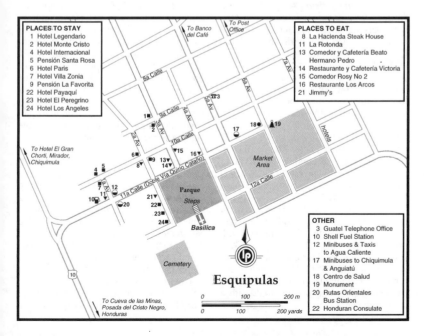

PLACES TO STAY
1 Hotel Legendario
2 Hotel Monte Cristo
4 Hotel Internacional
5 Pensión Santa Rosa
6 Hotel Paris
7 Hotel Villa Zonia
9 Pensión La Favorita
22 Hotel Payaquí
23 Hotel El Peregrino
24 Hotel Los Angeles

PLACES TO EAT
8 La Hacienda Steak House
11 La Rotonda
13 Comedor y Cafetería Beato Hermano Pedro
14 Restaurante y Cafetería Victoria
15 Comedor Rosy No 2
16 Restaurante Los Arcos
21 Jimmy's

OTHER
3 Guatel Telephone Office
10 Shell Fuel Station
12 Minibuses & Taxis to Agua Caliente
17 Minibuses to Chiquimula & Anguiatú
18 Centro de Salud
19 Monument
20 Rutas Orientales Bus Station
22 Honduran Consulate

To Banco del Café
To Post Office
To Hotel El Gran Chortí, Mirador, Chiquimula
Market Area
Parque
Steps
Basilica
Cemetery
To Cueva de las Minas, Posada del Cristo Negro, Honduras

Esquipulas

0   100   200 m
0   100   200 yards

road heading towards Honduras. It's open every day, 6:30 am to 4 pm; admission is US$0.35. Refreshments are available.

Places to Stay

Esquipulas has a great abundance of places to stay. On holidays and during the annual festival, every hotel in town is filled, whatever the price; weekends are fairly busy as well, with prices substantially higher. On weekdays when there is no festival, ask for a *descuento* (discount) and you'll probably get it.

Budget The best place to search for a cheap room is in the streets to the north of the basilica.

The family-run *Pensión Santa Rosa* (☎ 943-2908), 10a Calle at 1a Avenida, Zona 1, is typical of the small back-street places, charging US$5/7 for rooms with shared/private bath. The *Hotel Paris* next door is similar, as is the *Pensión La Favorita*, and there are several others on this street.

Hotel Monte Cristo (☎ 943-1256), 3a Avenida 9-12, Zona 1, is clean and OK, with parking and a restaurant. Singles/doubles are US$7/9 with shared bath, US$17/21 with private bath.

Hotel El Peregrino (☎ 943-1054, 943-1859), 2a Avenida 11-94, Zona 1, on the southwest corner of the park, has simple rooms with private bath for US$7/14, plus a new section in the rear where larger, fancier rooms with cable TV are US$13/25. Next door, the *Hotel Los Angeles* (☎ 943-1254), 2a Avenida 11-94, Zona 1, has 20 rooms arranged around a bright inner courtyard, all with private bath, fan and cable TV, for US$9/17. Both places have restaurants and parking.

In the same block, *Hotel Payaquí* (☎ 943-2025, fax 943-1371) is a large, attractive hotel with 55 rooms, all with private bath, cable TV, telephone and fridge. Rooms are the same price, with or without air-con: US$12/24 a single/double. It has two restaurants, one in the rear by the swimming pool and one in front, with a view of the park.

Hotel Villa Zonia (☎ 943-1304), 1a Avenida at the corner of 10a Calle, Zona 1, is a bright, new hotel with 15 rooms, all with private bath and cable TV. Rooms are US$17/25 with one/two double beds, and there's parking.

Middle *Hotel Internacional* (☎ 943-1131, 943-1530), 10a Calle 0-85, Zona 1, is new, clean and pleasant, with a small swimming pool, sauna, restaurant and parking. The 49 rooms, all with private bath, cable TV and phone, are US$25 with fan, US$37.50 with air-con.

Hotel Legendario (☎ 943-1824/5, ☎ /fax 943-1022), at the corner of 3a Avenida and 8a Calle, Zona 1, is new, modern and quite comfortable. The 40 rooms all have private bath, fan, cable TV and large windows opening onto a pleasant grassy courtyard with a swimming pool; singles/doubles are US$25/42. There's a restaurant and parking.

Hotel Posada del Cristo Negro (☎ 943-1482, fax 943-1829), Carretera Internacional a Honduras Km 224, is two km from the church, out of town on the way to Honduras. Broad green lawns, a pretty swimming pool, a large dining room and other services make it elaborate. In the 1960s, this might have been Guatemala's best country-club resort. Comfortable rooms with private bath, fridge and TV cost US$18/26/34/42 a single/double/triple/quad. Two or three children (up to age eight) are free in each room.

Top End *Hotel El Gran Chortí* (☎ 943-1148, 943-1560, fax 943-1551), Km 222, is one km west of the church on the road to Chiquimula. The lobby floor is a hectare of black marble; behind it a serpentine swimming pool is set between umbrella-shaded cafe tables, lawns and gardens. There's a game room for the children and, of course, a good restaurant, bar and cafeteria. The rooms have all the comforts, and the rates reflect it: US$45/60 a single/double, US$80 for a junior suite (sleeps four) and US$110 for a master suite (sleeps six).

Places to Eat

Restaurants all are more expensive here than in other parts of Guatemala. Low-budget restaurants are clustered at the north end of the park, where hungry pilgrims can find them readily. It is very important to ask in advance the price of each food item you order, and to add up your bill carefully.

3a Avenida, the street running north opposite the church, has many small eateries. *Comedor Rosy No 2* is tidy and cheerful, with meals for around US$2.50 and big bottles of pickled chiles on the tables. *Restaurante y Cafetería Victoria* across the street is a bit fancier, with tablecloths and plants, but prices are higher.

In the same block, *Comedor y Cafetería Beato Hermano Pedro* advertises *'¡Coma bien y pague menos!'* ('Eat well and pay less!'). Set prices for full meals are around US$2.

On the west side of the park, *Jimmy's* is a pleasant, bright and clean cafeteria with big windows looking out onto the park. Prices are reasonable, and there's a good selection. Roast chicken is one of the specialties here; you can get a whole chicken 'to go' for US$6, or a quarter chicken with fries, salad and tortillas for US$2.

La Rotonda, on 11a Calle opposite the Rutas Orientales bus station, is a round building with chairs around a round open-air counter under a big awning. It's a pleasant place, clean and fresh. The menu of the day, with soup, a meat main course, rice, vegetables, dessert, tortillas and coffee or lemonade is US$4, and there are plenty of other selections to choose from, including pizza, pasta and burgers.

All of these places are open every day from around 6 or 6:30 am until 9 or 10 pm.

The more expensive *La Hacienda Steak House*, 2a Avenida at the corner of 10a Calle, is an enjoyable place for grilled steaks, chicken and seafood; it's open every day from 8 am to 10 pm. *Restaurante Los Arcos*, on 11a Calle opposite the park, is another more upscale restaurant, open every day from 7 am to 10 pm.

All of the mid-range and top-end hotels have their own dining rooms.

Getting There & Away

Buses to Guatemala City arrive and depart from the Rutas Orientales bus station (☎ 943-1366) on 11a Calle at 1a Avenida, near the entrance to town. Minibuses to Agua Caliente arrive and depart across the street; taxis also wait here, charging the same as the minibuses, once they have five passengers.

Minibuses to Chiquimula and to Anguiatú depart from the east end of 11a Calle; you may see them hawking for passengers along the main street. Transportes María Elena operates buses to Flores.

Agua Caliente (Honduras border) – 10 km, 30 minutes, US$0.70; minibuses every half hour, 6 am to 5 pm

Anguiatú (El Salvador border) – 33 km, one hour, US$1; minibuses every half hour, 6 am to 4 pm

Chiquimula – 52 km, one hour, US$1; minibuses every 10 minutes, 5 am to 5 pm

Flores – 437 km, 14 hours, US$12; Transportes María Elena buses depart at 4:30 am and 1 pm

Guatemala City – 222 km, four hours, US$3.50; Rutas Orientales' *servicio especial* buses depart at 6:30 and 7:30 am, 1:30 and 3:30 pm; ordinary buses depart at 3:30, 5, 8:15 and 11:30 am, 1, 3 and 5:30 pm.

COPÁN ARCHAEOLOGICAL SITE (HONDURAS)

The ancient city of Copán, 13 km from the Guatemalan border in Honduras, is one of the most outstanding Mayan achievements, ranking with Tikal, Chichén Itzá and Uxmal in splendor. To fully appreciate Mayan art and culture, you must visit Copán. This can be done on a long day trip by private car, public bus or organized tour, but it's better to take at least two days, staying the night in the town of Copán Ruinas. In fact, you might decide to spend a few days at Copán.

There are two Copáns: the town and the ruins. The town is about 12 km east of the Guatemala-Honduras border. Confusingly,

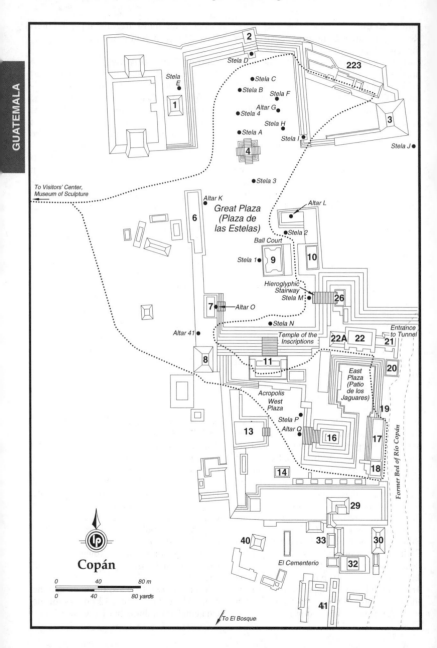

To Visitors' Center,
Museum of Sculpture

Stela E

Stela D

2

223

Stela C

Stela B

Stela F

Altar G

Stela 4

Stela H

Stela A

Stela I

1

3

Stela J

4

Stela 3

Great Plaza
(Plaza de
las Estelas)

Altar K

6

Altar L

Stela 2

Ball Court

10

Stela 1

9

Hieroglyphic
Stairway

Stela M

26

7

Altar O

Stela N

Altar 41

Temple of the
Inscriptions

22A

22

21

Entrance
to Tunnel

8

20

11

East
Plaza
(Patio
de los
Jaguares)

19

Acropolis
West
Plaza

Stela P

Altar Q

13

16

17

18

Former Bed of Río Copán

14

29

40

33

30

Copán

El Cementerio

32

0   40   80 m

0   40   80 yards

41

To El Bosque

the town is named Copán Ruinas, though the actual ruins are just over one km east of the town. Pickup trucks coming from the border will usually take you on to the ruins after a stop in the town. If not, the *sendero peatonal* (footpath) alongside the road makes for a pretty walk, passing several stelae and unexcavated mounds along the way to Las Sepulturas archaeological site a couple of kilometers farther.

History

Pre-Columbian People have been living in the Copán valley since at least around 1200 BC and probably before that; ceramic evidence has been found from around that date. Copán must have had significant commercial activity since early times; graves showing significant Olmec influence have been dated to around 900 to 600 BC.

Around 426 AD one royal family came to rule Copán, led by a mysterious king named Mah K'ina Yax K'uk' Mo' (Great Sun Lord Quetzal Macaw), who ruled from 426 to 435 AD. Archaeological evidence indicates that he was a great shaman; later kings revered him as the semidivine founder of the city. The dynasty ruled throughout Copán's florescence during the Classic period (250-900 AD).

Of the early kings who ruled from about 435 to 628 we know little. Only some of their names have been deciphered: Mat Head, the second king; Cu Ix, the fourth king; Waterlily Jaguar, the seventh; Moon Jaguar, the 10th; and Butz' Chan, the 11th.

Among the greatest of Copán's kings was Smoke Imix (Smoke Jaguar), the 12th king, who ruled from 628 to 695. Smoke Imix built Copán into a major military and commercial power in the region. He may have taken over the nearby princedom of Quiriguá, as one of the famous stelae there bears his name and image. By the time he died in 695, Copán's population had grown significantly.

Smoke Imix was succeeded by Uaxaclahun Ubak K'awil (18 Rabbit) (695-738), the 13th king, who willingly took the reins of power and pursued further military conquest. In a war with his neighbor, King Cauac Sky, 18 Rabbit was captured and beheaded, to be succeeded by Smoke Monkey (738-749), the 14th king. Smoke Monkey's short reign left little mark on Copán.

In 749, Smoke Monkey was succeeded by his son Smoke Shell (749-763), one of Copán's greatest builders. He commissioned the construction of the city's most famous and important monument, the great Hieroglyphic Stairway, which immortalizes the achievements of the dynasty from its establishment until 755, when the stairway was dedicated. It is the longest such inscription ever discovered in the Maya lands.

Yax Pac (Sunrise or First Dawn; 763-820), Smoke Shell's successor and the 16th king of Copán, continued the beautification of Copán. The final aspirant to the throne, U Cit Tok', became ruler in 822, but it is not known when he died.

Until recently, the collapse of the civilization at Copán has been a mystery. Now, archaeologists have begun to surmise that near the end of Copán's heyday, the population grew at an unprecedented rate, straining agricultural resources; in the end, Copán was no longer agriculturally self-sufficient and had to import food from other areas. The urban core expanded in the fertile lowlands in the center of the valley, forcing both agriculture and residential areas to spread onto the steep slopes surrounding the valley. Wide areas were deforested, resulting in massive erosion that further decimated agricultural production and resulted in flooding during rainy seasons. Skeletal remains of people who died during the final years of Copán's heyday show marked evidence of malnutrition and infectious diseases, as well as decreased lifespans.

The Copán valley was not abandoned overnight – agriculturists probably continued to live in the ecologically devastated valley for maybe another one or two hundred years. But by the year 1200 or thereabouts even the farmers had departed, and the royal city of Copán was reclaimed by the jungle.

European Discovery The first known European to see the ruins was a representative of Spanish King Felipe II, Diego

García de Palacios, who lived in Guatemala and traveled through the region. On March 8, 1576, he wrote to the king about the ruins he found here. Only about five families were living here then, and they knew nothing of the history of the ruins. The discovery was not pursued, and almost three centuries went by until another Spaniard, Coronel Juan Galindo, visited the ruins and made the first map of them.

It was Galindo's report that stimulated John L Stephens and Frederick Catherwood to come to Copán on their Central American journey in 1839. When Stephens published the book *Incidents of Travel in Central America, Chiapas, and Yucatán* in 1841, illustrated by Catherwood, the ruins first became known to the world at large.

Today The history of the ruins continues to unfold today. The remains of 3450 structures have been found in the 24 sq km surrounding the Principal Group, most of them within about half a kilometer of it. In a wider zone, 4509 structures have been detected in 1420 sites within 135 sq km of the ruins. These discoveries indicate that at the peak of civilization here, around the end of the 8th century AD, the valley of Copán had over 20,000 inhabitants – a population not reached again until the 1980s.

In addition to examining the area around the Principal Group, archaeologists are continuing to explore the Principal Group itself and making new discoveries. Five separate phases of building on this site have been identified; the final phase, dating from 650 to 820 AD, is what we see today. But buried underneath the visible ruins are layers of other ruins, which archaeologists are exploring by means of underground tunnels. This is how the Rosalila temple was found, a replica of which is now in the Museum of Sculpture; below Rosalila is yet another, earlier temple, Margarita.

Archaeologists are currently working on opening one such underground tunnel to the public. It will begin at the Archaeological Court and go right under Temple 22, emerging in the Patio de los Jaguares. Archaeologists also continue to decipher

more of the hieroglyphs and to get greater understanding of the early Maya.

Visiting the Ruins

The archaeological site is open every day from 8 am to 5 pm. The Museum of Sculpture, also at the site, closes an hour earlier, at 4 pm. Admission to the ruins costs US$10 and includes entry to the Las Sepulturas site. Admission to the museum costs US$5.

The visitors' center *(centro de visitantes)* at the entrance to the ruins houses the ticket seller and a small exhibition about the site and its excavation. Nearby are a cafeteria and souvenir and handicrafts shops. Cheaper food is available across the road at the *Comedor Mayapán*. There's a picnic area along the path to the Principal Group of ruins. A nature trail *(sendero natural)* entering the forest several hundred meters from the visitors' center passes by a small ball court.

Pickup a copy of the booklet *History Carved in Stone: A guide to the archaeological park of the ruins of Copán* by William L Fash and Ricardo Agurcia Fasquelle, available at the visitors' center for US$1.65. It will help you to understand and appreciate the ruins. It's also a good idea to go with a guide, who can help to explain the ruins and bring them to life.

The Principal Group

The Principal Group of ruins is about 400 meters beyond the visitors' center across well-kept lawns, through a gate in a strong fence and down shady avenues of trees.

Stelae of the Great Plaza The path leads to the Great Plaza and the huge, intricately carved stelae portraying the rulers of Copán. Most of Copán's best stelae date from 613 to 738 AD. All seem to have originally been painted; a few traces of red paint survive on Stela C. Many stelae had vaults beneath or beside them in which sacrifices and offerings could be placed.

Many of the stelae on the Great Plaza portray King 18 Rabbit, including Stelae A, B, C, D, F, H and 4. Perhaps the most beautiful stela in the Great Plaza is Stela A

(731 AD); the original has been moved inside the Museum of Sculpture, and the one outdoors is a reproduction. Nearby and almost equal in beauty are Stela 4 (731); Stela B (731), depicting 18 Rabbit upon his accession to the throne; and Stela C (782) with a turtle-shaped altar in front. This last stela has figures on both sides. Stela E (614), erected on top of Structure 1 on the west side of the Great Plaza, is among the oldest.

At the northern end of the Great Plaza at the base of Structure 2, Stela D (736) also portrays King 18 Rabbit. On its back are two columns of hieroglyphs; at its base is an altar with fearsome representations of Chac, the rain god. In front of the altar is the burial place of Dr John Owen, an archaeologist with the expedition from Harvard's Peabody Museum who died during the work in 1893.

On the east side of the plaza is Stela F (721), which has a more lyrical design, with the robes of the main figure flowing around to the other side of the stone, where there are glyphs. Altar G (800), showing twin serpent heads, is among the last monuments carved at Copán. Stela H (730) may depict a queen or princess rather than a king. Stela 1 (692), on the structure that runs along the east side of the plaza, is of a person wearing a mask. Stela J, farther off to the east, resembles the stelae of Quiriguá in that it is covered in glyphs, not human figures.

Ball Court South of the Great Plaza, across what is known as the Central Plaza, is the Juego de Pelota, or ball court (731), the second largest in Central America. The one you see is the third one on this site; the other two smaller courts were buried by this construction. Note the macaw heads carved atop the sloping walls. The central marker in the court is the work of King 18 Rabbit.

Hieroglyphic Stairway South of the ball court is Copán's most famous monument, the Hieroglyphic Stairway (743), the work of King Smoke Shell. Today it's protected from the elements by a roof. The flight of 63 steps bears a history – in several thou-

Glyphs from stelae at Copán

sand glyphs – of the royal house of Copán; the steps are bordered by ramps inscribed with more reliefs and glyphs. The story inscribed on the steps is still not completely understood because the stairway was partially ruined and the stones jumbled.

At the base of the Hieroglyphic Stairway is Stela M (756), bearing a figure (probably King Smoke Shell) in a feathered cloak; glyphs tell of the solar eclipse in that year. The altar in front shows a plumed serpent with a human head emerging from its jaws.

Beside the stairway, a tunnel leads to the tomb of a nobleman, a royal scribe who may have been the son of King Smoke Imix. The tomb, discovered in June 1989, held a treasure trove of painted pottery and beautiful carved jade objects that are now in Honduran museums.

Acropolis The lofty flight of steps to the south of the Hieroglyphic Stairway is called the Temple of the Inscriptions. On top of the stairway, the walls are carved with groups of hieroglyphs. On the south side of the Temple of the Inscriptions are the East Plaza and West Plaza. In the West Plaza, be sure to see Altar Q (776), among the most famous sculptures here; the original is inside the Museum of Sculpture. Around its sides, carved in superb relief, are the 16 great kings of Copán, ending with its creator, Yax Pac. Behind the altar was a sacrificial vault in which archaeologists discovered the bones of 15 jaguars and several macaws that were probably sacrificed to the glory of Yax Pac and his ancestors.

The East Plaza also contains evidence of Yax Pac – his tomb, beneath Structure 18. Unfortunately, the tomb was discovered and looted long before archaeologists arrived. Both the East and West Plazas hold a variety of fascinating stelae and sculptured heads of humans and animals. To see the most elaborate relief carving, climb Structure 22 on the northern side of the East Plaza. Excavation and restoration is still under way.

Museum of Sculpture

Copán is unique in the Maya world for its sculpture. The newest addition to the ruins at Copán is this magnificent museum, opened in August 1996. Entering the museum is an impressive experience all by itself: entering through the mouth of a serpent, you wind through the entrails of the beast, then suddenly emerge into a fantastic world of sculpture and light.

Highlight of the museum is a true-scale replica of the Rosalila temple, discovered in nearly perfect condition by archaeologists in 1989 by means of a tunnel dug into Structure 16, the central building of the Acropolis. Rosalila, dedicated in 571 AD by Copán's 10th ruler, Moon Jaguar, was apparently so sacred that when Structure 16 was built over it, Rosalila was not destroyed but was left completely intact.

The original Rosalila temple is still in the core of Structure 16. Under it are a still earlier temple, Margarita, built 150 years before, as well as other earlier platforms and tombs.

The other displays in the museum are stone carvings, brought here for protection from the elements. Eventually, all the important stelae may be housed here, with detailed reproductions placed outdoors to show where the stelae originally stood. So far, Altar Q and Stelae A, N, P and 2 have

been brought into the museum, and the ones you see outdoors are reproductions.

El Bosque & Las Sepulturas

Excavations at El Bosque and Las Sepulturas have shed light on the daily life of the Maya of Copán during its golden age.

Las Sepulturas, once connected to the Great Plaza by a causeway, may have been the residential area where rich and powerful nobles lived. One huge, luxurious residential compound seems to have housed some 250 people in 40 or 50 buildings arranged around 11 courtyards. The principal structure, called the House of the Bacabs (officials), had outer walls carved with the full-size figures of 10 males in fancy feathered headdresses; inside was a huge hieroglyphic bench.

To get to the site you have to go back to the main road, turn right, then right again at the sign (two km).

COPÁN RUINAS
Population 6000

The town of Copán Ruinas, also sometimes simply called Copán, is just over one km from the famous Maya ruins of the same name. It is a beautiful little village with cobblestone streets, white adobe buildings with red-tile roofs and a lovely colonial church on the plaza. This valley was inhabited by the Maya for around two thousand years, and an aura of timeless peace fills the air. Copán has become a primary tourist destination, but this hasn't disrupted the town's peacefulness to the extent one might expect.

The town's annual festival is from March 15 to 20. The annual artisans' fair with handicrafts and cultural presentations runs from December 15 to 21.

Orientation

Parque Central, with the church on one side, is the heart of town. The town is very small, and everything is within a few blocks of the plaza. The ruins are two km outside of town, on the road to La Entrada. Las Sepulturas archaeological site is a few kilometers farther along.

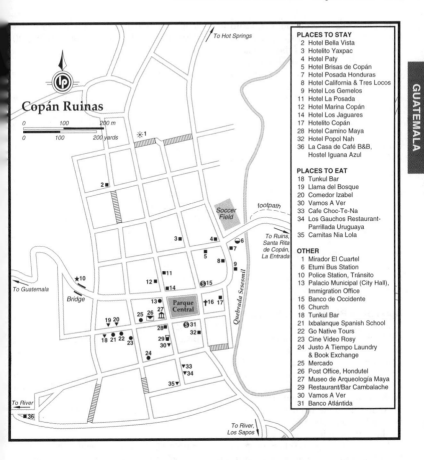

Copán Ruinas

0   100   200 m
0   100   200 yards

To Hot Springs

To Guatemala

Bridge

To River

Soccer Field

footpath

To Ruins,
Santa Rita
de Copán,
La Entrada

Quebrada Sesesmil

Parque
Central

To River,
Los Sapos

PLACES TO STAY
2 Hotel Bella Vista
3 Hotelito Yaxpac
4 Hotel Paty
5 Hotel Brisas de Copán
7 Hotel Posada Honduras
8 Hotel California & Tres Locos
9 Hotel Los Gemelos
11 Hotel La Posada
12 Hotel Marina Copán
14 Hotel Los Jaguares
17 Hotelito Copán
28 Hotel Camino Maya
32 Hotel Popol Nah
36 La Casa de Café B&B,
    Hostel Iguana Azul

PLACES TO EAT
18 Tunkul Bar
19 Llama del Bosque
20 Comedor Izabel
30 Vamos A Ver
33 Cafe Choc-Te-Na
34 Los Gauchos Restaurant-
    Parrillada Uruguaya
35 Carnitas Nia Lola

OTHER
1 Mirador El Cuartel
6 Etumi Bus Station
10 Police Station, Tránsito
13 Palacio Municipal (City Hall),
    Immigration Office
15 Banco de Occidente
16 Church
18 Tunkul Bar
21 Ixbalanque Spanish School
22 Go Native Tours
23 Cine Video Rosy
24 Justo A Tiempo Laundry
    & Book Exchange
25 Mercado
26 Post Office, Hondutel
27 Museo de Arqueología Maya
29 Restaurant/Bar Cambalache
30 Vamos A Ver
31 Banco Atlántida

Information

Banco de Occidente on the plaza changes US dollars and travelers' checks, Guatemalan quetzales and Salvadoran colones, and it gives cash advances on Visa and MasterCard. Banco Atlántida, also on the plaza, changes US dollars and travelers' checks and gives cash advances on Visa cards. For US dollars, both banks give a better rate than the moneychangers at the border but slightly less than banks elsewhere in Honduras. Both banks are open Monday to Friday from 8 am to noon and 2 to 4:30 pm, Saturday 8 to 11:30 am.

The post office and Hondutel are side by side, a few doors from the plaza.

The Justo A Tiempo laundry offers an expensive laundry service and English-language book exchange. The family at Hotel Los Gemelos operates a less expensive laundry service.

Things to See & Do

Of course, the main attraction of the Copán region is the archaeological site. There are, however, other fine places to visit in the area and these are covered in the Around Copán Ruinas section.

In town, the **Museo de Arqueología Maya** (☎ 98-3437) on the plaza is well worth a visit. It contains the original Stela B, portraying King 18 Rabbit. Other exhibits of painted pottery, carved jade, Maya glyphs and a calendar round are also interesting and informative, as is the 'Tumba del Brujo', the tomb of a shaman or priest who died around 700 AD and was buried with many items under the east corner of the Plaza de los Jaguares. The museum is open every day from 8 am to 4 pm; admission is US$2.

About four blocks north of the plaza is the **Mirador El Cuartel**, the old jail, with a magnificent view over town. The building is now used as a school; you can still go up there to enjoy the view.

A pleasant, easy walk on the road on the south side of town provides a fine view over the corn and tobacco fields surrounding Copán. It's also a pleasant walk to the river, also on the south side of town.

Horseback Riding & Los Sapos

You can rent a horse in Copán Ruinas to go out to the ruins or make other excursions. Rides can be arranged by either of the town's tour companies or by most hotels. There's also a horse operation just outside town on the way to the ruins. Or you could probably find a horse if you just ask around town and do some bargaining. The Hotel Hacienda El Jaral (see Places to Stay) also has horseback riding.

A popular horseback-riding excursion is to **Los Sapos**, five km from town in the Aldea de San Lucas. The *sapos* (toads) are old Mayan stone carvings in a spot with a beautiful view over town; you can get there by horseback in about half an hour or walk in about 45 minutes, all uphill. From Los Sapos you can walk to a stela.

Courses

The Ixbalanque Spanish School (☎ 98-3432, fax 98-0004, 57-6215) in the same block as the Tunkul Bar offers 20 hours weekly of one-on-one instruction in Spanish for US$150 per week, including

homestay with a local family that provides three meals a day. Instruction only, for 20 hours a week, costs US$95.

Organized Tours

Go Native Tours (☎ 98-3432, fax 57-6215), with an office in the same block as the Tunkul Bar, offers both local tours and ecological tours farther afield. It also organizes bird-watching tours to the Lago de Yojoa.

Xukpi Tours (☎ 98-3435, evening 98-3503), operated by Jorge Barraza, also offers a number of ecological tours both locally and farther afield. His ruins and bird-watching tours are justly famous. He offers ecological tours to all parts of Honduras and to Quiriguá (Guatemala).

Places to Stay – budget

Camping Attractive campsites are available at the *Hotel Hacienda El Jaral*, an ecotourism resort 11 km from town (see Around Copán Ruinas, below).

Hostel *Hostel Iguana Azul* (☎ 52-7274, fax 52-0523) is next door to La Casa de Café B&B (see below) and operated by the same friendly people. New in 1997, it contains 24 dorm-style bunk beds (US$4 per person) in four rooms with shared hot bath in a colonial-style ranch home. There's a pleasant garden, and the common area has books, magazines, travel guides and lots of travel information.

Hotels The *Hotel Los Gemelos* (☎ 98-3077), a block behind the plaza, is a longtime favorite with budget travelers. Operated by a very friendly family, it has a garden patio, a place to wash your clothes (or a laundry service if you prefer) and enclosed parking; coffee is always available. Singles/doubles with shared cold bath are US$4.15/5.

Across the street, *Hotel California & Tres Locos* (☎ 98-3515), new in 1996, has four attractive rooms decorated with lots of bamboo and woven mats, all sharing a hot bath, for US$8.35 per room.

In the same block, *Hotel Posada Honduras* (☎ 98-3082) has 13 simple rooms encircling a courtyard full of mango, mamey, lemon and coconut trees, with enclosed parking out back. Single/double rooms with shared cold bath are US$2.50/5; with private cold bath they are US$5/5.85. Also on the same street, the simple *Hotelito Copán* (☎ 98-3411) has single/double/triple rooms with shared bath for US$3.35/5/6.25, or with private cold bath for US$5/6.65/8.35.

Other simple places include *Hotelito Yaxpac* (☎ 98-3025) with just four plain rooms, all with private hot bath, for US$6/5.85. The *Hotel La Posada* (☎ 98-3070, 98-3072), half a block from the plaza, has rooms with shared cold bath for US$3.35/5.

Hotel Popol Nah (☎ 98-3095) is a clean, new place with seven rooms for US$15, all with private hot bath; it will soon have 12 rooms, some with air-con. The *Hotel Paty* (☎ 98-3021), near the entrance to town, has rooms around a courtyard, all with private hot bath, for US$11.65.

Places to Stay – middle

Copán also has a number of more upmarket places. One of the most attractive is *Hotel Brisas de Copán* (☎ 98-3018), near the entrance to town. Attractive upper rooms with cable TV, shared terraces and plenty of light are US$20.85; larger rooms with two double beds but no TV are US$16.65. They also have lower rooms for US$10 each, but these are darker and not as good. All the rooms come with private hot bath.

Also new in 1996, *Hotel Bella Vista* (☎ 98-3502) is up on a hill overlooking town, four blocks from the plaza. It has a beautiful view; large, comfortable rooms for US$13.35 with private hot bath, cable TV and phone; and parking in the courtyard.

For B&B accommodations there's the *La Casa de Café* (☎ 52-7274, fax 52-0523), four blocks from the plaza. It's a beautiful place in a beautiful setting; an outdoor area with tables and hammocks has a view over cornfields to the mountains of Guatemala. Five rooms with private hot bath are US$38 for one or two people; three rooms with

shared hot bath are US$20/28. All prices include a hearty breakfast.

Other more expensive places in town include *Hotel Los Jaguares* (☎ 98-3451), with singles/doubles for US$30/34; *Hotel Camino Maya* (☎ 98-3446, 98-3517, fax 39-3056), with singles/doubles for US$35/44; and the large *Hotel Marina Copán* (☎ 98-3070, 98-3071), with singles/doubles for US$70/81, including a swimming pool and restaurant/bar. All of these places are beautiful, luxurious and right on the plaza.

Hotel Hacienda El Jaral is a beautiful ecotourism resort with many activities, 11 km from town on the way to La Entrada (see Around Copán Ruinas, below).

Places to Eat

The *Tunkul Bar*, two blocks from the plaza, is the main gathering spot in town. It's an attractive covered-patio bar/restaurant with good food, good music, good company and a book exchange. A variety of meat and vegetarian meals all cost around US$2.50. The Tunkul is open every day from 7 am to 11 pm or midnight; happy hour runs from 7 to 8 pm for beer, 8 to 9 pm for mixed drinks.

Across the street, the *Llama del Bosque* is another popular place to eat, offering a good selection of meals and snacks; their *anafre* (fondue) is especially tasty. In the same block, *Comedor Izabel* is a cheap, typical comedor with decent food. Both are open every day from 6:30 am to 9 pm.

Another pleasant spot is the *Vamos A Ver* cafeteria/restaurant/cinema, half a block from the plaza. It's a pleasant little covered-patio place with good, inexpensive foods that you don't always see while traveling in Central America: good homemade breads, a variety of international cheeses, good soups, fruit or vegetable salads, good coffee, fruit licuados, a wide variety of teas and always something for vegetarians. It's open every day from 7 am to 10 pm; movies are shown every night at 7 pm.

In the next block, the *Cafe Choc-Te-Na* is another simple little cafe with a pleasant ambiance.

Farther along, *Carnitas Nia Lola* is an open-air restaurant with a beautiful view over corn and tobacco fields toward the mountains. It's a relaxing place with simple and economical food; the specialties are charcoal-grilled chicken and beef. It's open every day from 7 am to 10 pm.

Los Gauchos Restaurant-Parrillada Uruguaya is the fancy restaurant in town – come here for a splurge. It's great for meat-eaters; meat and seafood main courses are around US$6.25 to US$11, or you can get the giant Parrillada Especial for four people for US$20. There's a fine view from the tables outside on the verandah and beautiful decor inside.

Entertainment

The *Tunkul Bar* is the happening spot in the evening. Video movies (often in English) are shown at the *Vamos a Ver* cafe every night at 7 pm. *Cine Video Rosy*, a block from the plaza, also shows video movies. Next door to Vamos a Ver, the *Cambalache* restaurant/bar is another popular spot.

Getting There & Away

If you need a Honduran visa in advance, you can obtain it at the Honduran consulate in Esquipulas or Guatemala City.

Several Antigua travel agencies offer weekend trips to Copán, which may also include visits to other places, including the ruins at Quiriguá. Check with the agencies in Antigua for details.

Bus It's 280 km (seven hours) from Guatemala City to El Florido, the Guatemalan village on the Honduran border. Buses from Guatemala City take you to Chiquimula, where you must change buses and continue on to the border. See the Guatemala City and Chiquimula sections for further details about these routes.

If you're coming from Esquipulas, you can get off the bus at Vado Hondo, the junction of CA-10 and the road to El Florido, and wait for a bus there; but as the bus may fill up before departure, it may be just as well to go the extra eight km into Chiquimula and secure your seat before the bus pulls out.

Car If you travel by organized tour or private car, it's faster than going by bus. You could conceivably visit the ruins as a day trip from Guatemala City, but it's exhausting and far too rushed. Starting from Río Hondo, Chiquimula or Esquipulas, it still takes a full day to get to Copán, tour the ruins and return, but it's easier. Still, it's better to spend at least one night at Copán if you can.

Drive south from Chiquimula 10 km, north from Esquipulas 48 km, and turn eastward at Vado Hondo (Km 178.5 on CA-10). There's a small motel just opposite the turning, which will do if you need a bed. A sign reading 'Vado Hondo Ruinas de Copán' marks the way on the two-hour, 50-km drive from this junction to El Florido.

The road, though unpaved, is usually in good condition (you can average 40 km/h). Twenty km northeast of Vado Hondo are the Chortí Maya villages of Jocotán and Camotán, set amid mountainous tropical countryside dotted with thatched huts in lush green valleys. Jocotán has a small Centro de Salud (medical clinic) and the *Hotel/Pension Ramírez*, a half-block north of the hilltop church and main square. Rooms with private bath are US$4 per person; rooms with shared bath cost less. There's a small restaurant as well.

Along the road you may have to ford several small streams. This causes no problem unless there has been an unusual amount of rain during previous days.

Crossing the Border The village of El Florido, which has no services beyond a few soft-drink stands, is 1.2 km west of the border. At the border crossing are a few snack stands and the very basic *Hospedaje Las Rosas*, which can put you up in an emergency. The border crossing is open daily from 7 am to 6 pm.

Moneychangers will approach you on both sides of the border willing to change Guatemalan quetzals for Honduran lempiras or either for US dollars. Sometimes they offer a very poor rate; find out what the current rate of exchange should be, before you arrive at the border. Though quetzals and US dollars may be accepted at a few establishments in Copán Ruinas, you're best to change some money into Honduran currency. Banks in Copán Ruinas offer a better rate of exchange than the moneychangers at the border, so don't change too much at the border if you can make it to the bank.

You must present your passport and tourist card to the Guatemalan immigration and customs authorities, pay fees (some of which are unauthorized) of US$6, then cross the border and do the same thing with the Honduran authorities. If you just want a short-term permit to enter Honduras and plan to go only as far as Copán, tell this to the Honduran immigration officer and he will charge you a fee of US$3. With such a permit you cannot go farther than the ruins and you must leave Honduras by the same route. If you want to travel farther in Honduras, you'll probably need a tourist card, which costs US$10 and may take a bit more time.

When you return through this border point, you must again pass through both sets of immigration and customs and pay fees (lower this time). The Guatemalan immigration officer should give you your old tourist card back without charging the full fee for a new one.

If you are driving a rented car, you will have to present the Guatemalan customs authorities at the border with a special letter of permission to enter Honduras, written on the rental company's letterhead and signed and sealed by the appropriate company official. If you do not have such a letter, you'll have to leave your rental car at El Florido and continue to Copán by minibus.

On the Honduran side of the border are several little cookshacks where you can get simple food and cool drinks while waiting for a pickup truck to leave. Pickup trucks depart from the border every 40 minutes throughout the day. They should charge around US$1.25 for the 14-km, 45-minute ride to Copán Ruinas.

Last time we were in Copán, however, there had been a racket going on for many months, with the pickup drivers overcharging tourists on the ride from the border to Copán. Bus service had been suspended when the road between Copán and the border had fallen into disrepair, and though the road had been improved (still not paved, but in excellent shape), the bus service had still not resumed. If there is still no bus, stand your ground with the pickup drivers and demand to pay a fair price. Often the pickup drivers begin by asking for a ridiculous sum, but will eventually relent if they see you won't pay more than a reasonable price.

Copán Ruinas to Guatemala All the buses and pickup trucks serving Copán Ruinas depart from the tiny Etumi bus station at the entrance to town (except for the GAMA express bus to San Pedro Sula, which departs from the Hotel Paty).

Pickup trucks depart for the border from the Etumi bus station every 40 minutes, 6 am to 6 pm, and charge around US$1.25. Make sure you are charged the correct price – ask around beforehand to find out what the price should be. On the Guatemala side, buses to Chiquimula (58 km, 2½ hours, US$1.20) depart from the border at 5:30, 6:15, 7:15, 8:30 and 10:30 am, noon, 1:30 and 3:30 pm.

AROUND COPÁN RUINAS
Hacienda El Jaral
The *Hotel Hacienda El Jaral* (☎ 52-4457, ☎ /fax 52-4891), on the highway 11 km from town heading toward La Entrada, is an ecotourism resort offering many activities, including bird watching in a bird sanctuary-lagoon (thousands of herons reside here from November to May), horseback riding, bicycling, hiking, river swimming, inner tubing, canoeing and 'soft rafting' on the Río Copán. Also on the grounds are a swimming pool, a children's play area and two restaurants.

Guests and nonguests alike are welcome to use all the facilities (the exception is the swimming pool, which is for hotel guests only). If you want to stay over, luxurious rooms with air-con, private hot bath, cable TV and fridge, all in duplex cabins with outdoor terraces, are

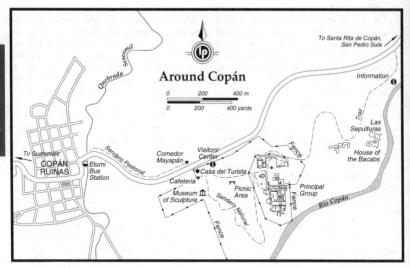

Around Copán

US$55/60 for singles/doubles, with larger rooms available. Or there are campsites with access to the river, champas and bathrooms for US$6.25 per site.

Santa Rita de Copán & El Rubí Waterfall

A few kilometers from town (20 minutes by bus) on the road toward La Entrada, Santa Rita de Copán is a lovely village built at the confluence of two rivers. Just outside Santa Rita is El Rubí waterfall, with a pleasant swimming hole. It's about a half-hour uphill walk on a trail departing from opposite the Esso gas station beside the bridge on the highway; ask people along the way how to get there.

QUIRIGUÁ

From Copán it is only some 50 km to Quiriguá as the crow flies, but the lay of the land, the international border and the condition of the roads makes it a journey of 175 km. Like Copán, Quiriguá is famed for its intricately carved stelae. Unlike Copán, the gigantic brown sandstone stelae at Quiriguá rise as high as 10.5 meters, like sentinels in a quiet tropical park.

A visit to Quiriguá is easy if you have your own transport; it's more difficult but certainly not impossible if you're traveling by bus. From Río Hondo junction it's 67 km along the Carretera al Atlántico to the village of Los Amates, where there are a couple of hotels and a restaurant. The village of Quiriguá is 1.5 km east of Los Amates, and the turn-off to the ruins is another 1.5 km to the east. Following the access road south from the Carretera al Atlántico, it's 3.4 km through banana groves to the archaeological site.

History

Quiriguá's history parallels that of Copán, of which it was a dependency during much of the Classic period. Of the three sites in this area, only the present archaeological park is of interest.

The location lent itself to the carving of giant stelae. Beds of brown sandstone in the nearby Río Motagua had cleavage planes suitable for cutting large pieces. Though soft when first cut, the sandstone dried hard in the air. With Copán's expert artisans nearby for guidance, Quiriguá's stonecarvers were ready for greatness. All they needed was a great leader to inspire them – and to pay for the carving of the huge stelae.

That leader was Cauac Sky (725-84), who decided that Quiriguá should no longer be under the control of Copán. In a war with his former suzerain, Cauac Sky took King 18 Rabbit of Copán prisoner in 737 and later had him beheaded. Independent at last, Cauac Sky commissioned his stonecutters to go to work, and for the next 38 years they turned out giant stelae and zoomorphs dedicated to the glory of King Cauac Sky.

Cauac Sky was followed by his son Sky Xul (784-800), who lost his throne to a usurper, Jade Sky. This last great king of Quiriguá continued the building boom initiated by Cauac Sky, reconstructing Quiriguá's Acropolis on a grander scale.

Quiriguá remained unknown to Europeans until John L Stephens arrived in 1840. Impressed by its great monuments, he lamented the world's lack of interest in them:

Of one thing there is no doubt: a large city once stood there; its name is lost, its history unknown; and . . . no account of its existence has ever before been published. For centuries it has lain as completely buried as if covered with the lava of Vesuvius. Every traveler from Yzabal to Guatimala has passed within three hours of it; we ourselves had done the same; and yet there it lay, like the rock-built city of Edom, unvisited, unsought, and utterly unknown.

Stephens tried to buy the ruined city in order to have its stelae shipped to New York, but the owner, Sr Payes, assumed that Stephens, being a diplomat, was negotiating on behalf of the US government and that the government would pay. Payes quoted an extravagant price, and the deal was never made.

Between 1881 and 1894, excavations were carried out by Alfred P Maudslay. In the early 1900s all the land around Quiriguá was sold to the United Fruit Company and turned into banana groves. The company is gone, but the bananas and Quiriguá remain. Restoration of the site was carried out by the University of Pennsylvania in the 1930s.

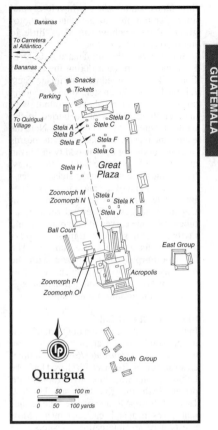

Ruins

The beautiful park-like archaeological zone is open every day from 7:30 am to 5 pm; admission costs US$0.20. A small stand near the entrance sells cold drinks and snacks, but you'd do better to bring your own picnic.

Despite the sticky heat and (sometimes) bothersome mosquitoes, Quiriguá is a wonderful place. The giant stelae on the Great Plaza are all much more worn than those at Copán. To impede their further deterioration, each has been covered by a thatched roof. The roofs cast shadows that make it difficult to examine the carving closely and almost impossible to get a good photograph. But somehow this does little to inhibit one's sense of awe.

Seven of the stelae, designated A, C, D, E, F, H and J, were built during the reign of Cauac Sky and carved with his image. Stela E is the largest Mayan stela known, standing some eight meters above ground, with another three meters or so buried in the earth. It weighs almost 60,000 kg. Note the exuberant, elaborate headdresses; the beards on some of the figures (an oddity in Mayan art); the staffs of office held in the kings' hands; and the glyphs on the stelae's sides.

At the far end of the plaza is the Acropolis, far less impressive than the one at Copán. At its base are several zoomorphs, blocks of stone carved to resemble real and mythic creatures. Frogs, tortoises, jaguars and serpents were favorite subjects. The low zoomorphs can't compete with the towering stelae in impressiveness, but as works of art, imagination and mythic significance, the zoomorphs are superb.

Places to Stay & Eat

In the center of the village of Quiriguá, 700 meters south of the Carretera al Atlántico, the *Hotel y Restaurante Royal* is simple, clean and quiet. Rooms with shared bath are US$4/6 a single/double; larger rooms with private bath and five beds are US$6/9/13/17/20 for one to five people. The restaurant serves meat and vegetarian meals. Most guests here are international visitors who have come to visit the archaeological site.

At Los Amates, on the Carretera al Atlántico three km west of Quiriguá village, is a 24-hour Texaco fuel station. Behind the Texaco station, the *Hotel y Restaurante Santa Mónica* has rooms with private bath for US$6/12/18 a single/double/triple. About 100 meters east of the Texaco station is the *Ranchón Chileño*, the best restaurant in the area, where you can get good, filling meals for about US$6 and light meals for half that much.

Comedor y Hospedaje Doña María, Carretera al Atlántico Km 181, is at the east end of the Doña María bridge, 20 km west

of Los Amates. The 10 rooms here, all with private bath, rent for US$6 per person; they are old but clean, lined up along an open-air walkway beside the river. Across the river there's a large, grassy parklike camping area with coconut palms and fruit trees, covered picnic tables and campsites for US$4 per group, vehicle or tent. Ask at the hotel, and they'll open the gate for you. The open-air restaurant, open every day from 6 am to 9 pm, has a great view of the river, and there's good swimming here. You're welcome to go across the footbridge for a picnic, just ask permission first.

Getting There & Away

The turnoff to Quiriguá is 205 km (four hours) northeast of Guatemala City, 70 km northeast of the Río Hondo junction, 43 km southwest of the road to Flores in El Petén, and 90 km southwest of Puerto Barrios.

Buses running Guatemala City-Puerto Barrios, Guatemala City-Flores, Esquipulas-Flores or Chiquimula-Flores will drop you off or pick you up here. They'll drop you at the turnoff to the archaeological site if you ask.

The transportation center in this area is Morales, about 40 km northeast of Quiriguá. This is where it's easiest to catch a bus for Río Dulce.

Getting Around

From the turnoff on the highway it's 3.4 km to the archaeological site. Buses and pickups provide transport between the turnoff and the site for US$0.15 each way. If you don't see one, don't fret; it's a pleasant walk on a dirt road running through banana plantations to get there.

If you're staying in the village of Quiriguá or Los Amates and walking to and from the archaeological site, you can take a short cut along the railway branch line that goes from the village through the banana fields, crossing the access road very near the entrance to the archaeological site.

LAGO DE IZABAL

This large lake to the northwest of the Carretera al Atlántico is just starting to be developed for tourism. Most visitors who stay here stay at Río Dulce, the village on the north side of the bridge where CA-13, the road heading north to Flores and Tikal, crosses the east end of the lake. East of this bridge are El Golfete and the beautiful Río Dulce, which meets the Caribbean at Lívingston; river trips are a highlight of a visit to eastern Guatemala. Other places to stay around the lake include San Felipe, Mariscos, El Estor and Finca Paraíso.

Other highlights of the lake include El Castillo de San Felipe (an old Spanish fortress), the Cerro San Gil wildlife refuge and the Bocas del Polochic river delta.

Río Dulce

Head northwest from Morales and La Ruidosa junction (Carretera al Atlántico Km 245) along the road to Flores in El Petén, and after 34 km you reach the village of Río Dulce, also sometimes called El Relleno or Fronteras. Río Dulce (Fronteras) is the village on the north side of the bridge over the lake, El Relleno is the village on the south side. In addition to the locals, Río Dulce has a sizable population of foreign yachties.

Get off the bus on the north side of the bridge. It stops on the highway, just uphill from the Hollymar Restaurant, which serves as Río Dulce's visitor information center, dining room, lounge, and dock for motorboats making trips down the Río Dulce. You can also rent canoes and kayaks, ask about boat and inner tube trips on the Río Ciénega, and generally hang out. If you need to change money or travelers' checks, there are two banks in town.

The minute you alight from the bus, young men will approach you and try to put you on a motorboat to Lívingston. This may be exactly what you want to do. However, you can spend some relaxing days around the lake if you're so inclined. For details of the Río Dulce boat trip, see the Lívingston section.

Places to Stay & Eat *Hacienda Tijax* (☎ 902-7825), a 500-acre hacienda a two-minute boat ride across the cove from the

Hollymar Restaurant, is a special place to stay. Activities include horseback riding, hiking, bird watching, boat trips and tours around the rubber plantation. Dorm beds in open-air upstairs Thai-style thatch-roofed houses with downstairs kitchens are US$5 per person (US$25 to have the whole house to yourself). Small private rooms over the hacienda's restaurant are US$3.35 per person or US$1.65 per person in hammocks (yours or theirs). There's also a camping area, where camping costs US$1.65 per tent or US$3.35 per vehicle. Access is by boat from the Hollymar or by road from the highway about one km north of the village. The owner, Eugene, speaks Spanish, English, French and Italian. There's a restaurant open in high season.

Other places to stay in the village include the *Riverside Motel*, a simple place on the highway, with simple rooms with shared bath and fan for US$4/5 a single/double. *Hotel Don Paco*, a yellow building with no sign, is another simple place; rooms with shared bath are US$4/7. *Hotel Portal del Río* is the best of the hotels in the village, with rooms with private bath for US$9/13.

For dining you can't beat the *Hollymar* (hollymarg@aol.com), with an open-air deck over the lake, just on the north side of the bridge. The food here is delicious and cheap, and it has a relaxed international ambiance.

Nearby, *Bruno's*, another open-air place right beside the water, is a restaurant/sports bar with satellite TV and video; its floating dock makes it popular with yachties. *Cafetería La Carreta*, off the highway on the road towards San Felipe, is often recommended by locals. *Hacienda Tijax* has a restaurant open in high season.

Several more expensive places to stay are on the waterfront farther from town. All have their own restaurants and are accessible only by boat. *Hotel Catamaran* (☎ 361-1937 in Guatemala City, fax 331-8450) is an upmarket place with rooms for US$36/41, bungalows for US$44/51 and a fancy restaurant and sports bar. Also on the lakeshore, *Mario's Marina* has good food; it's a popular hangout for yachties.

Getting There & Away Buses head north along a very bad road to Poptún (95 km, 3½ to four hours, US$2.50) and Flores (208 km, seven hours, US$5). In the other direction, buses go to Guatemala City (488 km, five hours, US$6). To bus to Puerto Barrios, take any bus heading for Guatemala City and change buses at La Ruidosa. The Atitlán Shuttle minibus operates from an office on the highway, near the Hollymar.

Colectivo motorboats go down the Río Dulce to Lívingston whenever a minimum of six to eight people want to go. With plenty of stops, the trip takes about three hours and costs around US$12.50 per person (bargain for a fair price). Boats usually leave in the morning, but they may leave throughout the day.

San Felipe & El Castillo de San Felipe

The fortress and castle of San Felipe de Lara, about three km west of the bridge, was built in 1652 to keep pirates from looting the villages and commercial caravans of Izabal. Though it deterred the buccaneers a bit, a pirate force captured and burned the fortress in 1686. By the end of the next century, pirates had disappeared from the Caribbean and the fort's sturdy walls served as a prison. Eventually, though, the fortress was abandoned and became a ruin. The present fort was reconstructed in 1956.

Today the castle is protected as a park and is one of the lake's principal tourist attractions. In addition to the fort itself, there's a large grassy park grounds, BBQ and picnic areas and swimming in the lake. It's open every day, 8 am to 5 pm; admission is US$1.

Places to Stay & Eat Near the Castillo, the *Hotel Don Humberto* can put you up for US$6/11/16 a single/double/triple in simple but clean rooms with private bath. There's also a restaurant here, or you could try the *Cafetería Selva Tropical*. Nearby, *Viñas del Lago* is a fancier, more expensive hotel.

On the lakeshore, about a 10-minute walk from El Castillo, the *Rancho Escondido* (☎ /fax 369-2681 in Guatemala City) is a pleasant little hotel and restaurant. Downstairs rooms with shared bath are US$5/9 a single/double; more attractive upstairs rooms with private bath are US$7/13, or you can stay in a hammock for US$2.50 per night. There's laundry service, good food, swimming in the lake and other activities. The owners will come to pick you up when you arrive in Río Dulce; ask at the Hollymar and they'll radio for you.

Getting There & Away San Felipe is on the lakeshore, three km west of Río Dulce. It's a beautiful 45-minute walk between the two towns. A colectivo pickup truck provides transport between the two towns for US$0.35, running about every half-hour. In Río Dulce it stops on the corner of the highway and the San Felipe road (see map); in San Felipe it stops in front of the Hotel Don Humberto, at the entrance to El Castillo.

Boats coming from Lívingston will drop you in San Felipe if you ask them to. The Río Dulce boat trips usually come to El Castillo, allowing you to get out and visit the castle if you like. Or you can come over from Río Dulce by private launch for US$5.

Finca El Paraíso & Río Agua Caliente

On the north side of the lake, between San Felipe and El Estor, the Finca El Paraíso is a popular destination for day trips coming from Río Dulce and other places around the lake. At the finca, which is a working ranch, you can walk to an incredibly beautiful spot in the jungle where a wide, hot waterfall drops 30 or 40 feet into a clear, deep pool. You can bathe in the hot water, swim in the cool pool or duck under an overhanging promontory and enjoy a jungle-style sauna. Also on the finca are a number of interesting caves and good hiking.

El Estor

The major settlement on the northwestern shore is El Estor. Once a nickel-mining town, it is now growing in popularity as a way station for intrepid travelers on the Cobán-Lago de Izabal route through the beautiful Panzós valley.

Places to Stay & Eat Overlooking the lake as its name implies, the *Hotel Vista al Lago* (☎ 949-7205), 6a Avenida 1-13, Zona 1, is pleasant and clean. Built between 1825 and 1830, the building was once a general store owned by an Englishman and a Dutchman; 'the store' gave the town of El Estor its name. The 21 rooms here, each with private bath and fan, are US$8/10/15 a single/double/triple.

Hotel Santa Clara, 5a Avenida 2-11, also has clean rooms with private bath. *Hotel Villela*, 6a Avenida 2-06, is another pleasant place to stay.

Ask at *Hugo's Restaurant* about tours around the lake and cabañas on the Río Sauce.

Getting There & Away Buses operate between El Estor and Cobán, a nine-hour journey. The route, a dirt road in good condition, is slow going but very beautiful. Buses also connect El Estor and Guatemala City.

The link from El Estor to the Carretera al Atlántico is completed by the El Estor-Mariscos ferry, which leaves El Estor every day at 6 am and departs from Mariscos for the return journey at noon. The trip across the lake takes one hour. Buses run from Mariscos down to the highway.

Mariscos

Mariscos is the principal town on the lake's south side. *Denny's Beach*, 10 minutes by boat from the town, offers cabañas, tours, hiking and swimming, and a full moon party. It's operated by Dennis Gulck and his wife, Lupe. When you arrive in Mariscos, you can radio them on VHF channel 9 – many people and businesses in Mariscos use radios, so it isn't hard to find one – and they'll come to pick you up. *Karlinda's* and *Marinita* are other places to stay in Mariscos; both have restaurants and offer lake tours. For transport information, see El Estor, above.

THE ROAD TO FLORES

North across the bridge is the road into El Petén, Guatemala's vast jungle province. It's 208 km to Santa Elena and Flores, and another 65 km to Tikal.

The road from the Carretera al Atlántico to Modesto Méndez is not bad, but from Méndez to Santa Elena it's in terrible condition. It's a bone-jangling ride of at least six hours to Flores.

The forest here is disappearing at an alarming rate, falling to the machetes of subsistence farmers. Sections of forest are felled and burned off, crops are grown for a few seasons until the fragile jungle soil is exhausted and then the farmer moves deeper into the forest to slash and burn new fields. Cattle ranchers, slashing and burning the forest to make pasture, have also contributed to the damage.

POPTÚN

Population 8000

The small town of Poptún (540 meters) is about halfway between Río Dulce and Flores. The reason most travelers come here is to visit Finca Ixobel. There are also a couple of other places to stay and eat. Otherwise, there's not much reason to stop in Poptún.

Places to Stay & Eat

The best facilities are at the 400-acre *Finca Ixobel* (☎ /fax 927-7363). For several decades Carole DeVine has offered travelers tent sites, palapas for hanging hammocks, beds and good homemade meals, with or without meat. Finca Ixobel is a special place, famous for its camaraderie – it's friendly and relaxed, a great place for meeting other travelers from around the world. It's also famous for its food and its activities. Horseback riding, camping trips, inner-tubing on the river and a famous cave trip are all organized on a daily basis, for a reasonable charge.

Camping costs US$2 to US$3 per person. Beds are US$4 in dormitories or tree houses, or pay US$6/8 for a single/double private room, or US$12.50 for a bungalow with private bath. Meals offer excellent value, right up to the eat-all-you-like buffet dinner for US$5. Or you can cook in the campground; if you do, you must bring all your own food, as there is no store on the finca.

GUATEMALA

The turnoff for the finca is marked on the highway, five km south of town. In the daytime, you can ask the bus driver to let you off there; it's a 15-minute walk to the finca. At night, or if you don't feel like making the walk, get off the bus in town and go to the Fonda Ixobel II restaurant, near the bus stop. They will radio for a taxi, which costs US$1.50 per person to the finca. It's important not to walk to the finca at night, as it's an isolated spot and robberies have been known to occur on the way.

There are also a couple of other places to stay in Poptún. *Camping Cocay*, seven km north of town and then 700 meters from the highway, is a very primitive campground in the jungle beside the river, good for swimming, inner tubing and fishing. The prices of US$2.50 per person in a tent or hammock, US$3.35 in a dorm, include breakfast; dinner

is available for US$2.50. They, too, offer activities in the area. This place is primitive, remote and right in the jungle. Bring plenty of mosquito repellent; you'll need it.

The more upmarket *Hotel Ecológico Villa de los Castellanos* (☎ 927-7222, 927-7518, fax 927-7365) is just off the highway, seven km north of Poptún. It, too, is right beside the river and is great for swimming and inner tubing. Thatch-roofed cabins with electricity, private hot bath and two or three double beds are US$20/30/40 a single/double/triple. There's a restaurant here and acres of gardens with many edible and/or medicinal plants.

Getting There & Away
Bus All the Guatemala City-Flores buses stop in Poptún; see the sections on Flores and Guatemala City for bus details.

United Fruit Company
As late as 1870, the first year that bananas were imported to the USA, few Americans had ever seen a banana, let alone tasted one. By 1898 they were eating 16 million bunches annually.

In 1899 the Boston Fruit Company merged with the interests of the Brooklyn-born Central American railroad baron Minor C Keith to form the United Fruit Company. The aim was to own and cultivate large areas of Central American land by well-organized modern methods, providing predictable harvests of bananas that Keith, who controlled virtually all of the railroads in Central America, would then carry to the coast for shipment to the USA.

Central American governments readily granted United Fruit rights, at low prices, to large tracts of undeveloped jungle, for which they had no other use. The company provided access to the land by road and/or rail, cleared and cultivated it, built extensive port facilities for the export of fruit and offered employment to large numbers of local workers.

By 1930, United Fruit was capitalized at US$215 million and was the largest employer in Central America. The company's Great White Fleet of transport ships was one of the largest private navies in the world. By controlling Puerto Barrios and the railroads serving it, all of which it had built, United Fruit effectively controlled all of Guatemala's international commerce, banana or otherwise.

The company soon came to be referred to as *El Pulpo*, The Octopus, by local journalists, who accused it of corrupting government officials, exploiting workers and, in general, exercising influence far beyond its role as a foreign company in Guatemala.

United Fruit's treatment of its workers was paternalistic. Though they worked long and hard for low wages, the workers' wages were higher than those of other farmworkers, and they received housing, medical care and in some cases schooling for their children. Still, indigenous Guatemalans were required to 'give right of way to whites and remove their hats when talking to them'. And the company took out of the country far more in profits than it put in: between 1942 and 1952 the company paid stockholders almost 62 cents in dividends for every dollar invested.

The US government, responding to its rich and powerful constituents, saw its role as one of support for United Fruit and defense of its interests.

Buses also travel the remote route between Poptún and Fray Bartolomé de las Casas (usually called simply Las Casas), on the way to Cobán. From Poptún it's six hours to Las Casas, where there's a pensión where you can spend the night, and then a further five hours to Cobán.

Flores – 113 km, 4½ to five hours, US$2.50; several buses daily

Fray Bartolomé de las Casas – 100 km, six hours, US$4.20; one or two buses daily

Guatemala City – 393 km, seven to nine hours, US$10; several buses daily

Río Dulce – 95 km, 3½ to four hours, US$2.50; take any bus heading for Guatemala City

Car If you're driving, fill your fuel tank before leaving Flores or Río Dulce, take some food and drink and a spare tire, and get an early start. The road is not good in either direction; the excessive ruts mean you'll have to drive slowly. A normal car can make it, albeit slowly; a 4WD is better but not essential.

PUERTO BARRIOS
Population 35,000

Heading eastward from La Ruidosa junction, the country becomes even more lush, tropical and humid until you arrive at Puerto Barrios.

The powerful United Fruit Company owned vast plantations in the Río Motagua valley and many other parts of the country. The company built railways to ship its produce to the coast, and it built Puerto Barrios early in the 20th century to put that produce onto ships sailing for New Orleans and New York. Laid out as a company town,

On October 20, 1944, a liberal military coup paved the way for Guatemala's first-ever free elections. The winner and new president was Dr Juan José Arévalo Bermejo, a professor who, inspired by the New Deal policies of Franklin Roosevelt, sought to remake Guatemala into a democratic, liberal nation guided by 'spiritual socialism'. His successor, Jacobo Arbenz, was even more vigorous in pressing the reform program. Among Arbenz's many supporters was Guatemala's small Communist party.

Free at last from the repression of past military dictators, labor unions clamored for better conditions, with almost constant actions against *la Frutera*, United Fruit. The Guatemalan government, no longer willing to be bought off, demanded more equitable tax payments from the company and divestiture of large tracts of its unused land.

Alarm bells sounded in the company's Boston headquarters and in Washington, where powerful members of Congress and the Eisenhower administration – including Secretary of State John Foster Dulles – were convinced that Arbenz was intent on turning Guatemala communist. Several high-ranking US officials had close ties to United Fruit, and others were persuaded by the company's effective and expensive public relations and lobbying campaign that Arbenz was a threat.

During the summer of 1954, the CIA planned and carried out an invasion from Honduras by 'anti-communist' Guatemalan exiles, which resulted in Arbenz's resignation and exile. The CIA's hand-picked 'liberator' was Carlos Castillo Armas, a military man of the old caste, who returned Guatemala to rightist military dictatorship. The tremendous power of the United Fruit Company had set back democratic development in Guatemala by at least half a century.

A few years after the coup, the US Department of Justice brought suit against United Fruit for operating monopolistically in restraint of trade. In 1958 the company signed a consent decree, and in the years following it surrendered some of its trade in Guatemala to local companies and some of its land to local owners. It yielded its monopoly on the railroads as well.

Caught up in the 'merger mania' of the 1960s, United Fruit merged with United Brands, which collapsed as the financial climate worsened in the early 1970s. In 1972 the company sold all of its remaining land in Guatemala to the Del Monte corporation. ∎

GUATEMALA

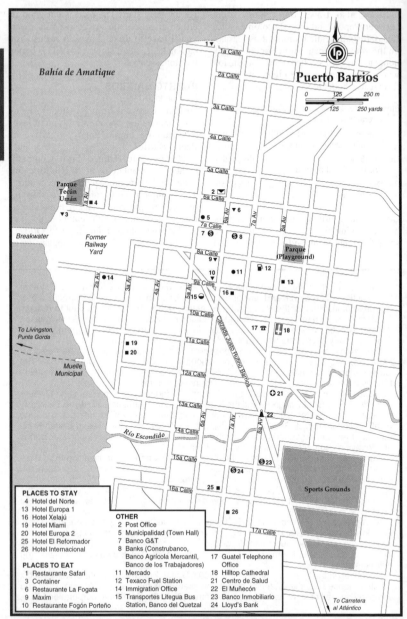

Bahía de Amatique

Puerto Barrios

0   125   250 m
0   125   250 yards

Parque
Tecún
Umán

Breakwater

Former
Railway
Yard

Parque
(Playground)

To Livingston,
Punta Gorda

Muelle
Municipal

Río Escondido

Calzada Justo Rufino Barrios

Sports Grounds

To Carretera
al Atlántico

PLACES TO STAY
4   Hotel del Norte
13 Hotel Europa 1
16 Hotel Xelajú
19 Hotel Miami
20 Hotel Europa 2
25 Hotel El Reformador
26 Hotel Internacional

PLACES TO EAT
1   Restaurante Safari
3   Container
6   Restaurante La Fogata
9   Maxim
10 Restaurante Fogón Porteño

OTHER
2   Post Office
5   Municipalidad (Town Hall)
7   Banco G&T
8   Banks (Construbanco,
    Banco Agrícola Mercantil,
    Banco de los Trabajadores)
11 Mercado
12 Texaco Fuel Station
14 Immigration Office
15 Transportes Litegua Bus
    Station, Banco del Quetzal

17 Guatel Telephone
    Office
18 Hilltop Cathedral
21 Centro de Salud
22 El Muñecón
23 Banco Inmobiliario
24 Lloyd's Bank

Puerto Barrios has wide streets arranged neatly on a grid plan and lots of Caribbean-style wood-frame houses, many on stilts.

When United Fruit's power and influence declined in the 1960s, the Del Monte company became successor to its interests. But the heyday of the imperial foreign firms was past, as was that of Puerto Barrios. A new, modern, efficient port was built a few km to the southwest, at Santo Tomás de Castilla, and Puerto Barrios settled into tropical torpor.

For foreign visitors, Puerto Barrios is little more than the jumping-off point for boats to Punta Gorda (Belize) or for a visit to Lívingston, the fascinating Garifuna enclave on the northwestern shore of the Río Dulce. As the boats for Lívingston leave at odd hours, you may find yourself staying the night in Puerto Barrios.

Orientation & Information

Because of its spacious layout, you must walk or ride farther in Puerto Barrios to get from place to place. For instance, it's 800 meters from the bus terminal by the market to the Muelle Municipal (Municipal Boat Dock) at the foot of 12a Calle, from which boats depart for Lívingston and Punta Gorda. You are liable to be in town just to take a boat, so you may want to select a hotel near the dock.

El Muñecón, at the intersection of 8a Avenida, 14a Calle and the Calzada Justo Rufino Barrios, is a statue of a *bananero* (banana worker); it's a favorite monument in the town.

The post office is on the corner of 6a Calle and 6a Avenida. Guatel is on 8a Avenida near 10a Calle.

Many banks change US dollars cash and travelers' checks. Banco G&T, 7a Calle between 5a and 6a Avenidas, changes both and gives cash advances on MasterCard and Visa; it's open Monday to Friday from 9 am to 8 pm, Saturday 10 am to 2 pm. The Banco de Quetzal is upstairs over the Litegua bus station.

The immigration office (☎ 948-0802, 948-0327) is at 9a Calle and 2a Avenida, a couple of blocks from the dock. Be sure to get your entry or exit stamp if you're entering or leaving the country.

In the evening, the noisy bars and brothels along 9a Calle really get going.

Places to Stay

A couple of good, clean hotels are on 3a Avenida between 11a and 12a Calles, one block from the dock. Both have clean rooms with private bath and fan arranged around a central courtyard used as a car park. *Hotel Europa 2* (☎ 948-1292), perhaps the slightly more attractive, has singles/doubles for US$6/10; at the *Hotel Miami* (☎ 948-0537) they are US$9/13, or US$15 with air-con. If you're driving and need a safe place to leave your car while you visit Lívingston, you can park in the courtyard of either place for US$2.50 per day.

The original *Hotel Europa 1* (☎ 948-0127), on 8a Avenida between 8a and 9a Calles, is 1½ blocks from the cathedral and Guatel telephone office (look for the open-work cross on top of the steeple, and the Guatel signal tower). Fairly clean, pleasant and quiet, it has singles/doubles with bath for US$6/12.

Hotel Xelajú (☎ 948-0482), nearby on 9a Calle between 6a and 7a Avenidas, is a cheaper, more basic place but it's OK; singles/doubles/triples with shared bath are US$4/6/8. Parking in the courtyard costs US$1.65 extra.

In a class by itself, the old *Hotel del Norte* (☎ 948-2116, ☎ /fax 948-0087), 7a Calle at 1a Avenida, is at the waterfront end of 7a Calle, 1.2 km from the dock (you must walk around the railway yard). In its airy dining room overlooking the Bahía de Amatique, you can almost hear the echoing conversation of turn-of-the-century banana moguls and smell their pungent cigars. Spare, simple and agreeably dilapidated, this is a real museum piece. Rooms with sea view and private bath are US$17/25/31/37 a single/double/triple/quad; interior rooms with shared bath are US$11/17/23/27. Meals are served in the dining room; there's also a bar, and two swimming pools beside the sea. Service is refined, careful and elegantly old-fashioned, but the food can be otherwise.

East of the stream bed and south of the main road, Calzada Justo Rufino Barrios, are two fancier, more comfortable hotels. The 48-room *Hotel El Reformador* (☎ 948-0533), 16a Calle and 7a Avenida No 159, is a modern building offering rooms with fan, TV and private bath for US$17/33/44, or US$30/38/48 with air-con. It has its own restaurant.

Around the corner, *Hotel Internacional* (☎ /fax 948-0367) on 7a Avenida between 16a and 17a Calles has a swimming pool, restaurant and parking. Singles/doubles with private bath and TV are US$9/14 with fan, US$14/25 with air-con.

Puerto Barrios' fanciest is the *Hotel Puerto Libre* (☎ 948-3066, fax 948-3513), at the junction of the Carretera al Atlántico, the road into Puerto Barrios, and the road to Santo Tomás de Castilla, five km from the boat dock. Rebuilt after a fire in 1992, its 44 rooms come with private bath, air-con, cable TV and phone. It also has a swimming pool, restaurant and parking. Rates are US$46/53 a single/double.

Places to Eat

The town's most enjoyable restaurant is *Restaurante Safari*, on a thatch-roofed, open-air dock right over the water at the west end of 5a Avenida, about a kilometer from the center of town. Locals and visitors alike love to eat here, catching the fresh sea breezes while mariachis stroll from table to table. Seafood meals of all kinds are the specialty, and they go for around US$6 to US$10; burgers, sandwiches and chicken are also served. It's open every day, 10 am to 9 pm.

Restaurante La Fogata, 6a Avenida between 6a and 7a Calle, is another fancy place, specializing in charcoal-grilled steaks and seafood. There's live music most nights, and a meal of the day for US$3.50 at lunchtime.

Simpler places include the *Restaurante Fogón Porteño*, opposite the bus station, which features charcoal-grilled chicken, steak and seafood. *Maxim* is a funky Chinese place at the corner of 6a Avenida and 8a Calle.

Perhaps the oddest eatery in town is *Container*, a cafe and drinks stand at the foot of 7a Calle, near the Hotel del Norte. It's made of two steel shipping containers, and the chairs and tables set out in the street afford a fine view of the bay.

Getting There & Away

Bus The Transportes Litegua bus station (☎ 948-1172, 948-1002) is near the corner of 6a Avenida and 9a Calle. Express buses to Guatemala City (307 km, five hours, US$6) leave at 1, 1:30, 3, 7:30 and 10 am, noon and 4 pm. Ordinary buses (not express) take several hours longer.

You can store your luggage at the terminal for about US$0.20 per day.

Boat Boats depart from the Muelle Municipal at the foot of 12a Calle. Get to the dock at least 30 or 45 minutes prior to departure for a decent seat; otherwise, you could end up standing.

A ferry departs for Lívingston every day at 10:30 am and 5 pm; the trip takes 1½ hours and costs US$1.35. On the Lívingston side, it departs for Puerto Barrios every day at 5 am and 2 pm. *Colectivo lanchas* (collective launches) depart from both sides whenever there are 12 people ready to go; they take 45 minutes and cost US$2.50.

Most of the movement is from Lívingston to Puerto Barrios in the morning, returning in the afternoon. From Lívingston, your last chance of the day to come by boat may be on the 2 pm ferry. After that, it might be the next morning before 12 people get together for the colectivo. The ferry arrives in Puerto Barrios at 3:30 pm and the last express bus to Guatemala City leaves at 4 pm, so you'll have to rush from the dock to the bus station.

A 100-passenger boat leaves Puerto Barrios for Punta Gorda (Belize, see that chapter) on Tuesday and Friday at 7 am; it departs Punta Gorda for the return trip at noon. The trip takes 2½ hours and costs US$5.50. Smaller *lanchas* depart from Punta Gorda every day around 8:30 or 9 am, and depart from Puerto Barrios for the return trip at around 1 or 2 pm; these take 50 minutes and charge US$9.

The boats to Punta Gorda no longer stop in Lívingston. If you take one of these boats, you must pass through Guatemalan customs and immigration before boarding the boat. Allow some time, and have your passport and tourist card handy.

Overland Route – Puerto Barrios to Puerto Cortés (Honduras)

Information on this route is based on letters sent to us by Camille Geels and Anja Boye (Denmark), Peter Kügerl (Austria) and Matthew Willson (UK).

This trip takes about six hours, so get an early start. The first thing you need to do is to get your Guatemalan exit stamp from the immigration office in Puerto Barrios. You may want to get it the day before, so you don't have to spend the time on the day of travel.

Take the bus from the mercado in Puerto Barrios to Finca La Inca, the last station on the bus line; the buses depart hourly, starting at 7 am. Just before you get to Finca La Inca, get off the bus and walk a few minutes to the Río Motagua, where you take a small boat to El Límite (US$3), at the border. From El Límite, take another boat through marsh and jungle to the small village of Cuyamelito (45 minutes, US$1.50). From Cuyamelito, walk about 30 minutes (or hitch a lift) to the highway, where you can catch a bus or truck going to Puerto Cortés. Be sure to get your Honduran entrance stamp entered into your passport at the first opportunity (Puerto Cortés and Omoa both have immigration offices).

Presumably, the same thing can be done in reverse if you're coming to Guatemala from the Honduras side.

LÍVINGSTON

Population 5500

As you come ashore in Lívingston, you will be surprised to meet black Guatemalans who speak Spanish as well as their traditional Garifuna language; some also speak the musical English of Belize and the islands. The town of Lívingston is an interesting anomaly, with a laid-back, very Belizean way of life, groves of coconut palms, gaily painted wooden buildings, and an economy based on fishing and tourism.

The Garifuna (Garinagu, or Black Carib) people of Lívingston and southern Belize are the descendants of Africans brought to the New World as slaves. They trace their roots to the Honduran island of Roatán, where they were settled by the British after the Garifuna revolt of 1795 on the Caribbean island of St Vincent. From Roatán the Garifuna people have spread out along the Caribbean Coast of Central America all the way from Belize to Nicaragua. Intermarrying with Carib Indians in St Vincent as well as with the indigenous inhabitants (in Guatemala, the Maya) and shipwrecked sailors of other races after arriving in Central America, they have developed a distinctive culture and language incorporating African, Indian and European elements.

Other people in Lívingston include the indigenous Kekchi Maya, who have their own community a kilometer or so upriver from the main dock, ladinos and a smattering of international travelers.

Beaches in Lívingston are mostly disappointing, as the jungle comes right down to the water's edge in most places. Those beaches that do exist are often clogged with vegetation and are unsafe for swimming due to contaminated water. Safe swimming can be had at Las Siete Altares; see Around Lívingston, below.

Orientation & Information

After being in Lívingston for half an hour, you'll know where everything is. Walk up the hill from the dock along the town's main street. The fancy Hotel Tucán Dugú is on your right, with several small restaurants on your left. The street off to the left at the base of the hill goes to the Casa Rosada and several other hotels, and continues on to a Kekchi Maya community. At the top of the hill another street goes left to several hotels and restaurants.

There's no tourist information office in Lívingston, but Exotic Travel (☎ 902-7109), based at the Bahía Azul restaurant on the main street in the center of town,

GUATEMALA

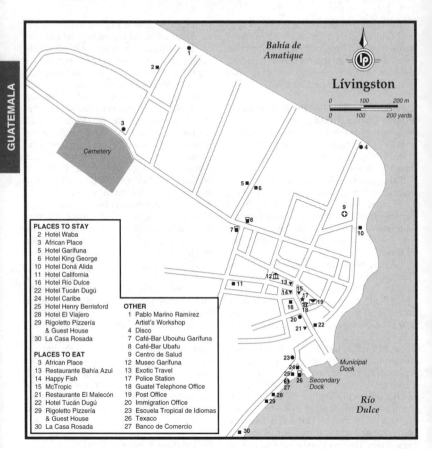

PLACES TO STAY
2 Hotel Waba
3 African Place
5 Hotel Garífuna
6 Hotel King George
10 Hotel Doná Alida
11 Hotel California
16 Hotel Río Dulce
22 Hotel Tucán Dugú
24 Hotel Caribe
25 Hotel Henry Berrisford
28 Hotel El Viajero
29 Rigoletto Pizzería
   & Guest House
30 La Casa Rosada

PLACES TO EAT
3 African Place
13 Restaurante Bahía Azul
14 Happy Fish
15 McTropic
21 Restaurante El Malecón
22 Hotel Tucán Dugú
29 Rigoletto Pizzería
   & Guest House
30 La Casa Rosada

OTHER
1 Pablo Marino Ramírez
   Artist's Workshop
4 Disco
7 Café-Bar Ubouhu Garífuna
8 Café-Bar Ubafu
9 Centro de Salud
12 Museo Garífuna
13 Exotic Travel
17 Police Station
18 Guatel Telephone Office
19 Post Office
20 Immigration Office
23 Escuela Tropical de Idiomas
26 Texaco
27 Banco de Comercio

hands out free town maps and is a good source of information about the town and the things to do in the area (see Organized Tours).

The post office is half a block off the main road. Guatel is next door.

The Banco de Comercio changes US dollars cash and travelers' checks. Several private businesses do too, including the Restaurante Bahía Azul, which also changes the currencies of Belize and Honduras.

Laundry service is available at the Rigo-letto Pizzería & Guest House (more economical) and at the Hotel La Casa Rosada.

The immigration office is on the main street coming up from the dock. It's open every day, 7 am to 9 pm.

Use mosquito repellent and other sensible precautions, especially if you go out into the jungle; remember that the mosquitoes here on the coast carry both malaria and dengue fever.

Museo Garifuna

The Museo Garifuna displays arts and implements of Garifuna daily life, with notes in English and Spanish, and has a small variety of Garifuna handicrafts and music cassettes on sale.

Pablo Marino Ramírez has a workshop by the sea where he makes Garifuna drums and woodcarvings. You're welcome to visit.

Courses

Escuela Tropical de Idiomas (☎ /fax 948-1544) offers Spanish language classes. If you like, they can also arrange homestays with local families for US$50 per week, meals included.

Special Events

Lívingston is packed with holiday-makers during Semana Santa. The day of San Isidro Labrador, who was a cultivator, is celebrated on May 15 with people bringing their agricultural products to a mass in the morning, followed by a procession through the streets with an image of the saint. The national day of the Garifuna is celebrated on November 26 with a variety of Garifuna cultural events. The day of the Virgin of Guadalupe, Mexico's patron saint, is celebrated on December 12.

Organized Tours

Exotic Travel, based at the Restaurante Bahía Azul, offers various tours enabling you to get out and see the natural wonders around the area. Their Ecological Tour takes you for a walk through town, up to a lookout spot and on to the Río Quequeche, where you take a half-hour canoe trip down the river and then a jungle walk to Las Siete Altares (the Seven Altars, see below). From there you walk down to the beach, hang out for a while, then walk down the beach back to Lívingston. The trip leaves from the Bahía Azul restaurant every day at 9 am and arrives back around 4 pm; the cost is US$6.65. This is a great way to see the area, and the friendly local guides also give you a good introduction to the Garifuna people who live here.

The Playa Blanca tour goes by boat first to the Seven Altars, then to the Río Cocolí where you can swim, and then on to Playa Blanca, for two or three hours at the best

beach in the area. The trip goes with a minimum of six people and costs US$8.50. The Casa Rosada hotel offers the same trip for US$12.50, including a picnic lunch.

Exotic Travel also offers day trips to the Cayos Sapodillas, well off the coast in southern Belize, where there is great snorkeling and fishing. Cost is split among the number of people going (if eight people go, it's US$19 each), plus US$10 to enter the cayes.

Exotic Travel also offers trips to the Punta de Manabique biological reserve (US$12.50).

Tours are also organized to the Finca Paraíso on Lago de Izabal (see the Lago de Izabal section). It's a long day trip from Lívingston, leaving at around 6 am and returning by around 7 pm. Hotel La Casa Rosada offers this trip for US$25, lunch included.

All of the above trips are also organized by the Happy Fish restaurant (☎ 902-7143), but not on any fixed schedule.

Places to Stay

When you arrive by boat, you may be met by local boys who will offer take you to a hotel, helping you carry your luggage if you like (there are no taxis in Lívingston). They'll take you to one place after another until you find one you like. They'll expect a small tip from you and also get a commission from the hotel.

Don't sleep on the beach in Lívingston – it isn't safe.

Budget Several places to stay are right beside the river, to the left of the boat dock. *Hotel Caribe*, a minute's walk along the shore, is one of the cheapest places in town: singles/doubles are US$2.50/4 with shared bath or US$5.50 with private bath. Look before you rent. *Hotel El Viajero* is another basic place along here, with rooms for US$4/5 with shared/private bath.

Hotel Río Dulce, an authentic Caribbean two-story wood-frame place up the hill from the dock on the main street, is another cheapie. Upstairs rooms are US$3.35, with shared bathrooms out in the back yard; three rooms with private bath are US$6.65. The rooms here are none too clean, and you may hear mice at night. Still, many shoestring travelers like this funky old place. The wide balcony overlooking the street catches the breeze and is great for people watching.

Hotel California is a clean, fine place with 10 simple rooms with private bath for US$5/8 a single/double.

A few blocks from the center of town, the *Hotel King George* is a new hotel, simple but clean and pleasant. Singles/doubles are US$4/7 with shared bath, or US$6/8 with private bath. Across the street, the *Hotel Garifuna* (☎ /fax 948-1581) is similar, with rooms with private bath for US$6/8/13/15 a single/double/triple/quad.

The *African Place*, a large white building with Moorish arches, is an old favorite in Lívingston. The 25 rooms are clean and pleasant, and there's a big garden in the rear with lots of space and flowers. Rooms with shared bath are US$4/6/8 a single/double/triple; with private bath they are US$8.50 a single, US$12.50 a double or triple, US$20 for four or five people. There's also a good restaurant here.

The African Place does have some problems, though. It's a longish walk from town (10 or 15 minutes), the road is unlit and there have been many robberies at night along here. There have also been mixed reports on personal security at the hotel, and some travelers have had items stolen from their rooms.

Turn right at the African Place and you come to the *Hotel Waba* (reservations ☎ 948-2065, 948-1367), new in 1996, where clean rooms with private bath are US$7/10 a single/double. The balcony has a sea view, and there's an open-air palapa restaurant in the yard.

For homey, friendly atmosphere, you can't beat the *Rigoletto Pizzería & Guest House*, beside the river 300 meters to the left of the dock. Two clean, pleasant guestrooms sharing a clean bathroom are US$7/11 a single/double. All three meals are served (the owner is a great cook), there's laundry service, and a rear garden with tables and chairs right beside the river. Boats will drop you off here if you ask.

Hotel Henry Berrisford (☎ /fax 948-1568) beside the river has clean, comfortable rooms with private bath and TV. Beware, though: it often runs out of water, and the swimming pool is not always clean. Rooms with fan are US$7.50 per person, or US$10 per person with breakfast; with air-con and breakfast they are US$14 per person.

Hotel Doña Alida (☎ 948-1567), beside the sea a few blocks from the center of town, has a beautiful beach, a restaurant and terraces with a sea view. Singles/doubles are US$14 with shared bath, US$24 with private bath, some with a sea view. A double bungalow is US$29, and extra-large triple rooms are US$49.

La Casa Rosada (fax at Guatel 948-2395) is probably Lívingston's most attractive place to stay. It's right on the river, 800 meters to the left of the dock; boats will drop you here if you ask. Ample riverside gardens, a dock with a gazebo and refreshments available anytime all contribute to the relaxed, friendly ambiance. For US$16 a night you can enjoy ten pleasant, free-standing, thatch-roofed bungalows with fans, screens and mosquito nets that share three clean bathrooms. Also available are a laundry service, daily trips and tours and one of the best restaurants in town.

Top End Among all these laid-back, low-priced Caribbean lodgings, the 45-room *Hotel Tucán Dugú* (☎ /fax 948-1588, in Guatemala City 334-7813, fax 334-5242), just up the hill from the dock, is a luxurious anomaly. Modern but still definitely Caribbean in style, it has many conveniences and comforts, including tropical gardens, a swimming pool and a jungle bar where you might expect to see Hemingway or Bogart. Rooms are fairly large, with modern bathrooms, ceiling fans and little balconies overlooking the pool and gardens. Singles/doubles are US$78/84.

Places to Eat

Food in Lívingston is a bit more expensive than in the rest of Guatemala because most of it (except fish and coconuts) must be brought across from Puerto Barrios. *Tapado*, a rich stew made from fish, shrimp, crab and other seafood, coconut, plantain, banana and spiced with coriander, is the special local dish.

The main street is lined with little comedores, *tiendas* (shops) and *almacenes* (stores). Your best plan may be to choose the place that is currently the most popular.

On our last visit, the *Restaurante Bahía Azul* was all the rage, a popular gathering spot with pleasant surroundings, good food for good prices and live music some evenings. It's open every day, 7 am to 10 pm.

Other popular places on the main street include the *Restaurante El Malecón*, just up the hill from the dock, on the left. It's airy and rustic, with a loyal local clientele and good views of the water; a full meal of Caribbean-inspired fare can be had for US$4 to US$7. A bit farther up the hill, the *McTropic*, on the right-hand side, is half restaurant and half shop; it's favored by the thriftiest crowd. The *Happy Fish* on the main street is also good.

The *African Place*, a few blocks from the center of town (see Places to Stay), serves a variety of exotic and local dishes. Full meals, including tapado, are available for US$6 or less.

On the road beside the river are a couple of other good restaurants. The *Rigoletto Pizzería* (see Places to Stay), operated by the talented cook María who has lived in several countries, has an international menu of Italian, east Indian, Chinese and other dishes, with many meat and vegetarian selections.

Farther along, the restaurant at *La Casa Rosada* is another very enjoyable riverside spot. All three meals are served, with good, ample dinners for around US$6 to US$8; dinner reservations are advisable. The coffee here is probably the best in town.

The dining room of the *Hotel Tucán Dugú* is the most expensive spot in town; a good, complete dinner with drinks goes for around US$10 to US$15.

Entertainment

Garifuna people have a distinctive form of music and dance. The traditional Garifuna band is composed of three large drums, a turtle shell, some maracas and a big conch shell, producing throbbing, haunting rhythms and melodies. The chanted words are like a litany, with responses often taken up by the audience. The dance is the *punta*, a Garifuna dance with a lot of hip movement.

Lívingston is about the only place in Guatemala where Garifuna music and dance are easily accessible for visitors. The *Restaurante Bahía Azul* has live Garifuna music on weekends and sometimes on other evenings. The *Café-Bar Ubafu* has live Garifuna music and dancing most evenings; it's liveliest on weekends. Across the street, the *Café-Bar Ubouhu Garifuna* is another popular night spot.

The disco by the sea on the north side of town is open on weekends. Several locals told us that problems had recently occurred there and that it might not be the most recommendable place for travelers.

Some nights of the week, the busiest place in town with the loudest music, is the Templo Evangélico Iglesia del Nazareno (Evangelical Church of the Nazarene).

Getting There & Away

The only way to get to Lívingston is by boat. Frequent boats come downriver from Río Dulce and across the bay from Puerto Barrios; see those sections for details. There are also international boats coming from Honduras and Belize.

Exotic Travel (☎ 902-7109, in Guatemala City ☎ 477-4090), based at the Restaurante Bahía Azul, operates a couple of international boat routes, to Omoa (Honduras) and Punta Gorda (Belize). They run on a schedule, but will also go at any other time there are a minimum of six people. Be sure to get your entry and exit stamps entered into your passport at the immigration offices on both ends of the journey.

The boats to Omoa depart from Lívingston at 7:30 am on Tuesdays and Fridays, arriving at about 10 am. In Omoa, the boat docks near the bus stop where you can catch a bus to Puerto Cortés and on to San Pedro Sula. The boat leaves Omoa for the return trip around noon or 1 pm, arriv-

GUATEMALA

ing back in Lívingston around 3:30 pm. Cost is US$30 from Lívingston to Omoa, US$25 from Omoa to Lívingston. The captain will take you to get your passport exit and entry stamps on both ends of the journey.

The boats to Punta Gorda (Belize) also leave Lívingston at 7:30 am on Tuesdays and Fridays. This is a shorter trip, taking just 45 minutes; cost is US$12 each way. The boats depart Punta Gorda for the return trip at 10:30 am. Get your own exit stamp from the immigration office in Lívingston; the captain will take you to get your entry stamp in Punta Gorda.

Trips to Punta Gorda, Omoa and other places can also be arranged at the Happy Fish restaurant (☎ 902-7143).

The sailboat *Osprey* makes a trip from Utila (one of Honduras's Bay Islands) to Lívingston twice a month or so. Cost to Lívingston is US$96 per person, with a maximum of 12 passengers. Travel agents in Lívingston should have information about it, but they may not. In Utila, information is available from Gunter's Dive Shop (☎ /fax (504) 45-3350).

AROUND LÍVINGSTON
Río Dulce Cruises
Lívingston is the starting point for boat rides on the Río Dulce. Passengers enjoy the tropical jungle scenery, have a swim and a picnic and explore the Biotopo Chocón-Machacas, 12 km west along the river.

There are several ways to make the voyage up the Río Dulce. Almost anyone in Lívingston can tell you who's currently organizing trips up the river. Exotic Travel, based at the Restaurante Bahía Azul, makes trips daily, as do the Hotel La Casa Rosada and the Happy Fish restaurant. Or you can simply walk down to the dock and arrange a trip – many local boatmen are there, and it's good to support them.

Shortly after you leave Lívingston, the river enters a steep-walled gorge, its walls hung with great tangles of jungle foliage and bromeliads and the humid air noisy with the cries of tropical birds. A thermal spring forces sulfurous water out at the base of the cliff, providing a delightful place for a swim.

Emerging from the gorge, the river eventually widens into **El Golfete**, a lake-like body of water that presages the even vaster expanse of Lago de Izabal.

On the northern shore of El Golfete is the **Biotopo Chocón-Machacas**, a 7600-hectare reserve established to protect the beautiful river landscape, the valuable mangrove swamps and, especially, the manatees that inhabit the waters (both salt and fresh). A network of 'water trails' (boat routes around several jungle lagoons) provide ways to see the bird, animal and plant life of the reserve. A nature trail begins at the visitors' center and winds its way through forests of mahogany, palms and rich tropical foliage. Jaguars and tapirs live in the reserve, though your chances of seeing one are slight. The walrus-like manatees are even more elusive. These huge mammals can weigh up to a ton, yet they glide effortlessly beneath the calm surface of the river.

From El Golfete and the nature reserve, the boats continue upriver to the village of Río Dulce, where the road into El Petén crosses the river, and to the Castillo de San Felipe on Lago de Izabal (see the Lago de Izabal section).

The trip is also offered from Río Dulce; ask at the Restaurant Hollymar.

From whichever end you begin, you can make it a one-way (US$8) or roundtrip (US$12.50) between Lívingston and Río Dulce. (Trips organized by the Hotel La Casa Rosada, which include a picnic lunch and stop at more places, cost a bit more.)

Las Siete Altares
The Seven Altars is a series of freshwater falls and pools about five km (1½-hour walk) northwest of Lívingston along the shore of the Bahía de Amatique. It's a pleasant goal for a walk along the beach and a good place for a picnic and a swim. Follow the shore northwards to the mouth of a river. Ford the river and follow the path

into the woods all the way to the falls. If you'd rather not do the ford, boats at the mouth of the river will ferry you across for a few quetzals.

Boat trips go to the Seven Altars, but locals say it's better to walk there, because you get to see the pure nature and also the Garifuna people who live along the way. Unfortunately, robberies have been known to happen along the beach here, so don't take valuables with you. Locals say the walk is still worth doing, as long as you take this precaution.

El Petén

In the dense jungle cover of Guatemala's vast northeastern department of El Petén, you may hear the squawk of parrots, the chatter of monkeys and the rustlings of strange animals moving through the bush. The landscape here is utterly different from that of Guatemala's cool mountainous highlands or its steamy Pacific Slope.

The monumental ceremonial center at Tikal is among the most impressive of the Mayan archaeological sites. The ruins of Uaxactún and Ceibal, though not so easily accessible, are perhaps more exciting to visit for that reason. Several dozen other great cities lie hidden in El Petén's jungles, accessible only to archaeologists with aircraft (or to artifact poachers).

In 1990 the Guatemalan government established the one million-hectare Maya biosphere reserve, which includes most of

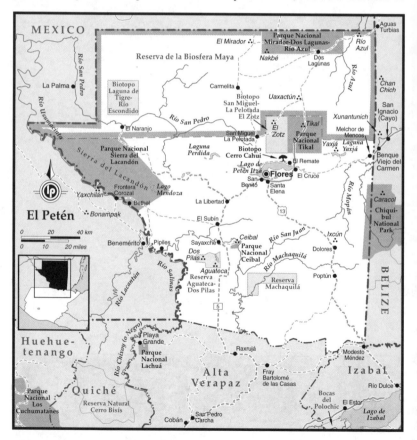

246

northern El Petén. The Guatemalan reserve adjoins the vast Calakmul biosphere reserve in Mexico and the Río Bravo Conservation Area in Belize, forming a huge multinational reserve of over two million hectares.

There are three reasons travelers want to penetrate the forests of El Petén: first to visit Tikal, the greatest Mayan religious center yet discovered; second to enjoy the great variety of birdlife; and third to see the Guatemala of small farming villages and jungle hamlets, without paved roads or colonial architecture.

Though it is possible to visit Tikal on a single-day excursion by plane from Guatemala City, I encourage you to stay over at least one night, whether in Flores, El Remate or Tikal itself. There is a great deal to see and experience, and a day trip simply cannot do it justice.

Getting Around

The roads leading into El Petén – from the Carretera al Pacífico and from Belize – have been left in a state of disrepair, partly due to lack of funds and partly because better roads would encourage migration of farmers and ranchers from other areas of the country. With El Petén's forests already falling to the machete at an alarming rate, good new roads might prove disastrous. Thus road transport in El Petén is slow, bumpy, uncomfortable and sometimes unsafe. There have been several incidents of robbery of buses traveling along the roads between Río Dulce and Flores and the Belizean border at Melchor de Mencos/Benque Viejo del Carmen. For current information on the safety of traveling these roads, contact your embassy or consulate in Guatemala City.

The only exception is the road connecting Flores/Santa Elena and Tikal, a good, fast asphalt road built so that tourists arriving by air in Santa Elena can proceed quickly and comfortably to Tikal, 71 km to the northeast. The Guatemalan government long ago decided to develop the adjoining towns of Flores, Santa Elena and San Benito, on the shores of Lago de Petén Itzá, into the region's tourism base. The airport,

hotels and other services are here. Though there are a few small hotels and restaurants at Tikal, other services will remain limited.

FLORES & SANTA ELENA

The town of Flores (population 2000) is built on an island on Lago de Petén Itzá. A 500-meter causeway connects Flores to her sister town of Santa Elena (110 meters, population 17,000) on the lakeshore. Adjoining Santa Elena to the west is the town of San Benito (population 22,000).

Flores, the departmental capital, is more dignified, with its church, small government building and municipal basketball court arranged around the main plaza atop the hill in the center of the island. The narrow streets, paved in cement blocks, hold numerous small hotels and restaurants.

Santa Elena is a disorganized town of dusty unpaved streets, with many small hotels and restaurants. San Benito is even more disorganized, but its honky-tonk bars keep it lively.

The three towns actually form one large settlement, usually referred to simply as Flores.

History

Flores was founded on an island *(petén)* by the Itzaes after their expulsion from Chichén Itzá, and it was named Tayasal. Cortés dropped in on King Canek of Tayasal in 1524 while on his way to Honduras, but the meeting was peaceable. Only in March 1697 did the Spaniards finally bring the Maya of Tayasal forcibly under their control.

At the time of its conquest, Flores was perhaps the last major functioning Mayan ceremonial center, covered in pyramids and temples, with idols everywhere. The God-fearing Spanish soldiers destroyed these 'pagan' buildings. Today when you visit Flores you will see not a trace of them, although the modern town is doubtless built on the ruins and foundations of Mayan Tayasal.

Tayasal's Mayan citizens fled into the jungle, giving rise to the myth of a 'lost' Mayan city.

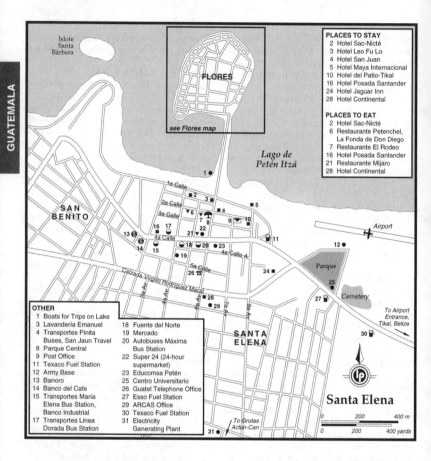

PLACES TO STAY
2   Hotel Sac-Nicté
3   Hotel Leo Fu Lo
4   Hotel San Juan
5   Hotel Maya Internacional
10 Hotel del Patio-Tikal
16 Hotel Posada Santander
24 Hotel Jaguar Inn
28 Hotel Continental

PLACES TO EAT
2   Hotel Sac-Nicté
6   Restaurante Petenchel,
    La Fonda de Don Diego
7   Restaurante El Rodeo
16 Hotel Posada Santander
21 Restaurante Mijaro
28 Hotel Continental

Lago de
Petén Itzá

OTHER
1   Boats for Trips on Lake
3   Lavandería Emanuel
4   Transportes Pinita
    Buses, San Jaun Travel
8   Parque Central
9   Post Office
11 Texaco Fuel Station
12 Army Base
13 Banoro
14 Banco del Cafe
15 Transportes María
    Elena Bus Station,
    Banco Industrial
17 Transportes Linea
    Dorada Bus Station
18 Fuente del Norte
19 Mercado
20 Autobuses Máxima
    Bus Station
22 Super 24 (24-hour
    supermarket)
23 Educomsa Petén
25 Centro Universitario
26 Guatel Telephone Office
27 Esso Fuel Station
29 ARCAS Office
30 Texaco Fuel Station
31 Electricity
    Generating Plant

Santa Elena

0   200   400 m
0   200   400 yards

Orientation

The airport is on the eastern outskirts of Santa Elena, two km from the causeway connecting Santa Elena and Flores. Each bus company has its own terminal.

4a Calle is Santa Elena's 'main drag'. All the important hotels, restaurants and banks are on this street or just off it.

Information

Tourist Offices INGUAT has a tourist information desk at the airport (☎ 926-0533). They are open every day from 7:30 to 10 am and from 3 to 6 pm.

Money None of the banks in Flores will change money, but have no fear, as all the banks in Santa Elena do.

In Flores, cash and travelers' checks can be changed at any of several travel agencies.

Banks in Santa Elena are on 4a Calle. Banco Industrial has a 24-hour ATM and gives cash advances on Visa cards. Banco del Cafe changes cash, travelers' checks and gives cash advances on Visa cards. It's open Monday to Friday, 8:30 am to 7 pm, Saturday 9 am to 1 pm. Banoro changes cash and travelers' checks. It's open weekdays 8:30 am to 8 pm, Saturday 9 am to

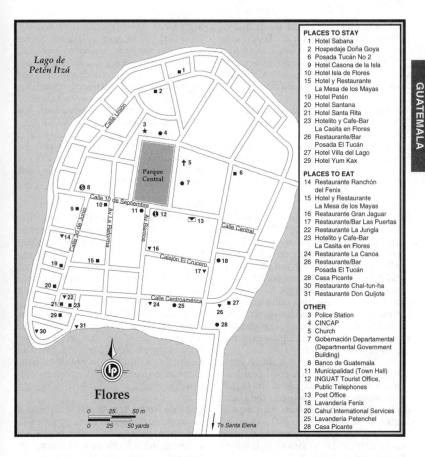

PLACES TO STAY
1 Hotel Sabana
2 Hospedaje Doña Goya
6 Posada Tucán No 2
9 Hotel Casona de la Isla
10 Hotel Isla de Flores
15 Hotel y Restaurante
   La Mesa de los Mayas
19 Hotel Petén
20 Hotel Santana
21 Hotel Santa Rita
23 Hotelito y Cafe-Bar
   La Casita en Flores
26 Restaurante/Bar
   Posada El Tucán
27 Hotel Villa del Lago
29 Hotel Yum Kax

PLACES TO EAT
14 Restaurante Ranchón
   del Fenix
15 Hotel y Restaurante
   La Mesa de los Mayas
16 Restaurante Gran Jaguar
17 Restaurante/Bar Las Puertas
22 Restaurante La Jungla
23 Hotelito y Cafe-Bar
   La Casita en Flores
24 Restaurante La Canoa
26 Restaurante/Bar
   Posada El Tucán
28 Casa Picante
30 Restaurante Chal-tun-ha
31 Restaurante Don Quijote

OTHER
3 Police Station
4 CINCAP
5 Church
7 Gobernación Departamental
   (Departmental Government
   Building)
8 Banco de Guatemala
11 Municipalidad (Town Hall)
12 INGUAT Tourist Office,
   Public Telephones
13 Post Office
18 Lavandería Fenix
20 Cahuí International Services
25 Lavandería Petenchel
28 Casa Picante

Flores

Lago de
Petén Itzá

Parque
Central

To Santa Elena

4 pm. San Juan Travel at the San Juan
Hotel gives cash advances on Visa, Master-
Card and American Express cards.

Currencies of the USA, Mexico and
Belize can be changed at the airport.

Post & Communications In Flores, the
post office is just off the plaza. Martsam
Travel Agency and Cahuí International
Services offer domestic and international
telephone and fax services. Casa Picante
offers telephone, fax, email and computer
services and also has a multi-language
book exchange and library.

In Santa Elena, the post office is on the
corner of 2a Calle and 7a Avenida. The
Guatel telephone office is open every day.
Educomsa Petén (☎ 926-0765), 4a Calle 6-
76, Local B, Zona 1, offers email and computer services.

Travel Agencies Several travel agencies
in Flores offer a range of services for visitors. Casa Picante, facing the causeway, has
information on the area's attractions and
affordable tours; it also operates a pizzería,
bookstore/book exchange and telephone,
fax and email services.

Also in Flores, Martsam Travel Agency (☎ /fax 926-0493), next to the Hotel Petén, and Cahuí International Services (☎ /fax 926-0494), next to the Hotel Santana, offer travel agency and telephone/fax services, tours, currency exchange and bicycle rental.

Laundry In Flores, try Lavandería Fenix or Lavandería Petenchel, open Monday to Saturday 8 am to 8 pm, Sunday 10 am to 6 pm. In Santa Elena, Lavandería Emanuel on 6a Avenida near the causeway does a good job and the laundry is ready in an hour. It's open Monday to Saturday, 8 am to 7 pm.

Grutas Actun-Can
The caves of Actun-Can, also called La Cueva de la Serpiente (The Cave of the Serpent), are of standard limestone. No serpents are in evidence, but the cave-keeper will turn on the lights for you after you've paid the US$1.15 admission fee (8 am to 5 pm daily) and may give you the rundown on the cave formations, which suggest animals, humans and various scenes. Bring a flashlight if you have one and adequate shoes – it can be slippery. Explorations take about 30 to 45 minutes.

At the cave entrance is a shady picnic area. Actun-Can makes a good goal for a long walk from Santa Elena. To find it, walk south on 6a Avenida past the Guatel office. About one km from the center of Santa Elena, turn left, go 300 meters and turn right at the electricity generating plant. Go another one km to the site. A taxi from Santa Elena costs US$2.

Useful Organizations
CINCAP The Centro de Información sobre la Naturaleza, Cultura y Artesanía del Petén, on the north side of the plaza in Flores, sells handicrafts of the region and has exhibits on the natural resources and forest conservation of the Petén.

ARCAS The Asociación de Rescate y Conservación de Vida Silvestre has a wildlife rescue center about two km from the Hotel Villa Maya, which is about 10 km east of

Santa Elena. Animals here include macaws, green and yellow parrots, jaguars, howler and spider monkeys, kinkajous and coatimundis that have been rescued from smugglers and the illegal pet trade. At the center the animals are rehabilitated for release back into the wild. You are welcome to visit, but you should ask permission first (☎ /fax in Guatemala City 591-4731).

Volunteers are welcome to stay here, paying per week for room and board and volunteering any amount of time. Contact ARCAS (see Work in the Guatemala Facts for the Visitor chapter) for further details.

Organized Tours
Land Tours Travel agencies in Flores offer a number of interesting tours around the remote parts of the Petén region. Ask about the Scarlet Macaw Trail, visiting Centro Campesino, El Eprú, Paso Caballos, Buena Vista, El Cruce a Dos Aguadas, San Andrés and Tikal. It takes six days to do the whole tour, but you can also do parts of it.

Monkey Eco Tours (☎ 928-8132, fax 928-8113), based at the Hotel Ni'tún on the northwest side of the lake, and Epiphyte Adventures (☎ /fax 926-0775), based in Flores, do this and a variety of other tours. These are both professional operations with bilingual guides.

Lago de Petén Itzá As you stroll around town, particularly in Flores, locals will present themselves and offer boat rides around the lake. Many are freelance agents who get a commission; it's better to talk with the boat owner directly. You should bargain over the price, and inspect the boat. Or ask at the Restaurante/Bar Las Puertas in Flores; Carlos, the owner, offers boat trips around the lake and across to the other side, where he has land and a private dock for swimming and sunning. The travel agencies may also be able to arrange boat trips.

There's good bird watching on the Río Ixpop, which runs into the east side of the lake. Boat trips start from El Remate, on the east side of the lake.

Places to Stay – budget

Santa Elena *Hotel Posada Santander* (☎ 926-0574) on 4a Calle is a simple but spotless and friendly family-run hostelry in a convenient location. Ample rooms with private bath and two good double beds are US$6.65/8.35 a single/double. An open-air restaurant upstairs serves all meals. The family also operates Transportes Inter Petén, with economical minibus service to Tikal and other places.

Nearer the lake, *Hotel Sac-Nicté* (☎ 926-0092) has clean, large upstairs rooms with private bath, balcony and views across the lake to Flores for US$12. Downstairs rooms have no view and cost US$8.35. They have a restaurant, parking and transportation service and are planning to build a swimming pool.

Hotel Continental (☎ 926-0095) on 6a Avenida at Calle Virgilio Rodríguez Macal is a large hotel built in 1995. Rooms are US$2.50 per person with shared bath, or US$5/8.35 a single/double with private bath. There's a restaurant here, and parking in the courtyard.

Santa Elena has other cheap but less attractive hotels, including the *Hotel Fu Lo* (US$2.50 per person) and the *Hotel San Juan* (US$4/6 with shared bath, US$10/12 with private bath).

Flores The cheerful, family-run *Hotel Villa del Lago* (☎ 926-0629/0508) beside the lake is a clean, pleasant place to stay, much nicer inside than its appearance would suggest. Five rooms sharing three clean bathrooms are US$6.65/8.35 a single/double; rooms with private bath are US$17. Next door, *Restaurante/Bar Posada El Tucán* has forgettable rooms with shared bath for US$7. These are off to one side of the restaurant.

Hotelito y Cafe-Bar La Casita en Flores, near the larger Hotel Yum Kax, is another simple, clean and friendly place, operated by a German-Guatemalan family. Four rooms, each with private bath, go for US$6.65/13.35 a single/double. Up on the rooftop is a grill restaurant with a view across the lake to Santa Elena.

Hospedaje Doña Goya is a good economical choice, with rooms with shared/private bath for US$3.35/4.20 per person.

The simple but clean *Posada Tucán No 2* (☎ 926-1467) is OK. Singles/doubles are US$6/7 with shared bath, US$8.35/11 with private bath. Some rooms have lake views.

Hotel Santa Rita (☎ 926-0710) is clean and family-run; it's an excellent value at US$9/12 a single/double with private bath.

Hotel Yum Kax (☎ /fax 926-0686) is to the left as you arrive on the island along the causeway. Rooms are US$15/20/25 per single/double/triple with fan, US$5 more with air-con.

Hotel y Restaurante La Mesa de los Mayas (☎ /fax 926-1240) is a lovely place, very clean and well-kept. Rooms with private bath and fan are US$15/22/24 per double/triple/quad, a little more with air-con.

Places to Stay – middle

Santa Elena The *Hotel Jaguar Inn* (☎ 926-0002), Calzada Rodríguez Macal 8-79, Zona 1, is comfortable without being fancy, but slightly inconveniently located 150 meters off the main road near the airport. It's good if you have a vehicle. Rooms with private bath are US$18/24 a single/double with fan, US$24/30 with air-con. *Hotel Maya Internacional* (☎ 926-1276, fax 926-0087), right beside the water, has singles/doubles/triples for US$30/36/42.

Flores *Hotel Sabana* (☎ /fax 926-1248), on the north side of the island, has a restaurant and sun deck over the water. Rooms with private bath, fan, air-con and cable TV are US$20/25/30 a single/double/triple.

Hotel Casona de la Isla (☎ 926-0523, fax 926-0593) is a romantic place with a lakeside swimming pool with a waterfall and an open-air lakeside bar/restaurant. All 27 rooms have private bath, cable TV, air-con and chairs on the balcony outside the room. Singles/doubles/triples are US$25/30/40.

Hotel Petén (☎ 926-0692, fax 926-0593) has a small courtyard with tropical plants, a pleasant lakeside terrace and restaurant and an indoor swimming pool. The 19 comfy-if-plain rooms, all with private bath, air-con and fan, are US$20/30/40 a single/double/triple. Try to get a room on the top floor with a view of the lake.

At the *Hotel Santana* (☎ 926-0491, ☎ / fax 926-0662), most of the rooms have a great view over the lake, with large private balconies with chairs. They also have private bath, cable TV, air-con and fan. Singles/doubles/triples are US$30/45/50. There's a restaurant with a lakeside terrace.

Hotel Isla de Flores (☎ 926-0614, in Guatemala City ☎ 476-8775, fax 476-0294), new in 1996, is clean and attractive. The rooms are large and well-equipped, with cable TV, air-con, ceiling fan, telephone and private bath with tub. Many have private balconies with a view of the lake. Singles/doubles/triples are US$35/40/45.

Places to Stay – top end

In Santa Elena, *Hotel del Patio-Tikal* (☎ / fax 926-0104, 926-1229, in Guatemala City 331-5720) looks severe from the outside but is actually a nice colonial-style hotel with a pretty central courtyard. The 22 rooms, all with air-con and ceiling fan, cable TV, telephone and private bath, are US$40/50 a single/double.

Hotel Villa Maya (☎ /fax 926-0086, in Guatemala City 334-8136), on Laguna Petenchel about 10 km east of Santa Elena, has 40 double rooms in bungalows with private bath, ceiling fan, hot water, beautiful views of the lake and blissful quiet. There's a patio restaurant, three tennis courts, two swimming pools, two private lagoons and a wildlife refuge. Prices are US$93/99 a single/double.

Places to Eat

As with hotels, the restaurants in Santa Elena tend to be cheaper than those in Flores. All are fairly simple and are open all the time. Beer, drinks and sometimes even wine are served. Also on the menu at most places are a variety of local game, including tepezcuintle (a rabbit-sized jungle rodent), venado (deer), armadillo, pavo silvestre (wild turkey) and pescado blanco (white fish).

Santa Elena Hotel Posada Santander, Hotel Sac-Nicté and the Hotel Continental have restaurants.

Restaurante El Rodeo at the corner of 2a Calle and 5a Avenida is often recommended by locals. It's open every day from 11 am to 9 pm. In the same block, *Super 24* is a 24-hour supermarket. In the next block of 2a Calle, *Restaurante Petenchel* and *La Fonda de Don Diego* are also popular. *Restaurante Mijaro*, a simple comedor on the main road, is another place recommended by locals; it's open every day, 7 am to 9 pm.

Flores *Restaurante/Bar Las Puertas* is a popular restaurant/bar with good food, and it's a good spot for friendly conversation as well – this is the hangout for an interesting mixture of people. There's live music on weekends. It's open Monday to Saturday, 8 am to 1 am. *Casa Picante*, a pizzeria and travelers' resource center near the causeway, is another popular place.

Restaurante Chal-tun-ha is small and pleasant, with an open and fresh decor, a terrace right over the water and a fine view across the lake. The menu offers a good selection of inexpensive dishes. It's open every day, 9 am to 7:30 pm. *Restaurante Don Quijote*, another pleasant little place, is on a small boat docked near the Hotel Yum Kax.

Restaurante/Bar Posada El Tucán, next to the Villa del Lago, has a thatched roof and a lakeside terrace that catches any breezes. Set breakfasts cost US$2 to US$3, lunches and dinners US$5 to US$8. *Restaurante Ranchón del Fenix*, next to the Hotel Casona de la Isla, is another pleasant restaurant with a lakeside terrace.

Restaurante La Canoa is cheaper and plainer, but its dark, high-ceilinged dining room appeals to budget travelers, as does the decent food at low prices. *Restaurante La Jungla* has a tiny streetside terrace.

Hotel y Restaurante La Mesa de los Mayas is a popular restaurant serving good traditional foods as well as local game. A mixed plate goes for US$9, a vegetarian plate is US$5 and chicken costs even less. It's open every day, 7 am to 11 pm.

The *Restaurante Gran Jaguar* is often recommended by locals. It has a good variety of inexpensive dishes, attractive decor and bar service. It's open Monday to Saturday, 11 am to 10 pm.

Getting There & Away

Air The airport at Santa Elena (usually called 'the airport at Flores') is quite busy these days. International flights include those to/from Belize City with Tropic Air, Island Air and Aerovías; flights to/from Palenque, Chetumal and Cancún with Aerocaribe; and a flight to/from Cancún four times a week with Aviateca.

There's quite a variation in price flights between Flores and Guatemala City, ranging from around US$60 to US$90. Package tours including airfare and accommodations may work out to be cheaper and are available at many travel agencies. See the Tikal section, below, for more on this.

More regional airlines will be opening up routes to and from Flores in the near future. Ask at travel agencies in Cancún, Mérida, Belize City and Guatemala City. Your travel agent at home may not be able to get up-to-date information on some of these small regional carriers. And travel agents in Flores and Santa Elena may charge more for a ticket than you would pay by buying it at the airport.

When you arrive at the airport in Flores you may be subjected to a cursory customs and immigration check, as this is a special customs and immigration district.

Bus Travel by bus to or from Flores is slow and uncomfortable, with the exception of the road to Tikal. Each bus company has its own bus station. Transportes Pinita buses depart from the Hotel San Juan in Santa Elena (☎ 926-0041/2). Transportes María Elena buses go from the Hotel Santander in Santa Elena (☎ 926-0574). Other bus companies in Santa Elena include Fuente del Norte (☎ 926-0517), Linea Dorada (☎ 926-0070), Autobuses Máxima (☎ 926-0676) and Transportes Rosío.

Belize City – 222 km, 5½ hours, US$20; 1st class buses depart from the Hotel San Juan and Hotel Continental in Santa Elena every day at 5 am, arriving in Belize City around 10:30 am, connecting with the boat to Caye Caulker and San Pedro, Ambergris Caye.

Bethel (Mexico border) – 127 km, four hours, US$3; Transportes Pinita buses, 5 am and 1 pm

Ceibal – see Sayaxché

Chetumal (Mexico) – 350 km, nine hours, US$35; a special direct 1st-class Servicio San Juan bus departs from the Hotel San Juan and Hotel Continental in Santa Elena every day at 5 am, bypasses Belize City and goes straight to Chetumal. At Chetumal it connects with a 2 pm ADO bus heading north along the coast to Tulum, Playa del Carmen and Cancún. In the opposite direction, the bus to Flores departs from the main bus terminal in Chetumal at 2:30 pm.

El Naranjo – see From El Petén to Chiapas, later in the chapter.

El Remate/Puente Ixlú – 35 km, 45 minutes; Tikal-bound buses and minibuses (see Tikal) will drop you here. Buses to/from Melchor de Mencos will drop you at Puente Ixlú/El Cruce, less than two km south of El Remate.

Guatemala City – 506 km, 11 to 12 hours, US$12 to US$15; Fuente del Norte (☎ 926-0517) operates Especial buses at 9:30 and 11:30 am, 1:30 and 3:30 pm, and Pullman buses at 5, 7 and 8 pm. Linea Dorada (☎ 926-0070) luxury buses (US$18.35) depart at 8 pm. Autobuses Máxima (☎ 926-0676) runs Pullman buses at 7 and 8 pm.

La Ruidosa (crossroads to Puerto Barrios) – 242 km, eight hours, US$6; take any bus bound for Guatemala City.

Melchor de Mencos (Belize border) – 101 km, three hours, US$2; 2nd-class Transportes Pinita buses at 5, 8 and 10 am. Rosita buses at 5, 7, 9:30 and 11 am, 2, 3 and 6 pm. On the Belize side, buses (US$0.50) and share-taxis (US$2) take you to Benque Viejo and San Ignacio every hour or so.

Palenque (Mexico) – see From El Petén to Chiapas, later in the chapter.

Poptún – 113 km, 4½ to five hours, US$2.50; take any bus heading for Guatemala City.

Río Dulce – 208 km, seven hours, US$5; take any bus heading for Guatemala City.

GUATEMALA

San Andrés (around the lake) – 20 km, 40 minutes, US$0.65; Transportes Pinita buses, 5:30 am and noon. They depart San Andrés for the return trip at 7 am and 1:30 pm. Boats also make this trip, departing from San Benito, on the west side of Santa Elena.

Sayaxché – 61 km, two hours; 2nd-class Transportes Pinita buses (US$2) at 6, 9 and 10 am, 1 and 4 pm. There are also tours from Santa Elena via Sayaxché to the Mayan ruins at Ceibal, departing from Hotel San Juan and Hotel Continental at 8:15 am and returning to Santa Elena at 4 pm (US$30).

Tikal – 71 km, 2½ hours, US$2.50; Transportes Pinita bus daily at 1 pm, continuing on to Uaxactún. It departs Tikal for the return trip at 6 am. It's quicker and more convenient to take a shuttle minibus to Tikal (see below).

Uaxactún – 96 km, three hours, US$2.50; Transportes Pinita, 1 pm. It departs from Uaxactún for the return trip at 5 am.

Shuttle Minibus Minibuses bound for Tikal depart each morning from various hotels in Santa Elena and Flores (4, 6, 8 and 10 am) and from the airport (meeting all flights). Any hotel can arrange a trip for you. The fare is US$3.35 per person one way, double for roundtrip; the trip takes one to 1½ hours.

Return trips depart from Tikal at 2, 4 and 5 pm. Your driver will anticipate that you'll want to return to Flores that same afternoon; if you know which return trip you plan to be on, they'll hold a seat for you or arrange a seat in a colleague's minibus. If you stay overnight in Tikal and want to take a minibus to Flores, it's a good idea to reserve a seat with one of the minibus drivers when they arrive in the morning. Don't wait until departure time and expect to find a seat.

A taxi (for up to four people) from Flores/Santa Elena or the airport to Tikal costs US$40 roundtrip.

Getting Around
Bus Buses and minibuses bound for the small villages around the lake and in the immediate vicinity depart from the market area in Santa Elena.

Car Several hotels, car rental companies and travel agencies offer rentals, including cars, 4WDs, pickup trucks and minibuses. Rental car companies are in the arrivals hall at Flores airport. They include:

Garrido	☎ 926-0092
Hertz	☎ 926-0332, 926-0415
Koka	☎ 926-0526, 926-1233
Los Compadres	☎ 926-0444
Los Jades	☎ 926-0734
Nesa	☎ 926-0082

A basic car with unlimited *kilometraje* (distance allowance) costs a minimum of around US$50 per day. The travel agency at the Hotel San Juan in Santa Elena (☎ /fax 926-0041/2) also has rental cars.

Bicycle Cahuí International Services in Flores (☎ /fax 926-0494) rents bicycles for US$0.85 per hour or US$6.65 per day. *Casa Roja* (☎ 926-0269, in Antigua ☎ 832-0162) rents mountain bikes.

Boat Motor launches making cruises and tours on Lago de Petén Itzá depart from the Santa Elena end of the causeway (see map). Colectivo boats to San Andrés and San José, villages across the lake, depart from San Benito, on the west side of Santa Elena; or, bargain for a private boat.

EL REMATE
Once little more than a few thatched huts 35 km northeast of Santa Elena on the Tikal road, the village of El Remate has recently grown into a small town, thanks to the tourist trade. Right on the lakeshore, El Remate is becoming a secondary tourist center between Flores and Tikal. Halfway between the two places, it allows you to be closer to Tikal but still be on the lake.

El Remate is known for its wood carving. Several handicrafts shops on the lakeshore opposite La Mansión del Pájaro Serpiente sell local handicrafts and rent canoes, rafts and kayaks.

From El Remate an unpaved road snakes its way around the northeast shore of the lake to the Biotopo Cerro Cahuí, the luxury Hotel Camino Real Tikal and on to the villages of San José and San Andrés, on the northwest side of the lake. It's possible to go all the way around the lake by road.

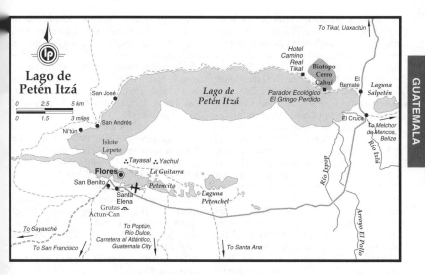

With their newfound prosperity, Remate-cos have built a *balneario municipal* (municipal beach) just off the highway and have opened several cheap pensions and small hotels.

Biotopo Cerro Cahuí

At the northeast end of Lago de Petén Itzá, about 43 km from Santa Elena and three km from the Flores-Tikal road, the Biotopo Cerro Cahuí covers 651 hectares of hot, humid, subtropical forest. Within the reserve are mahogany, cedar, ramón, broom, sapodilla and cohune palm trees, as well as many species of lianas (climbing plants) and epiphytes (air plants), including bromeliads, ferns and orchids. The hard wood of the sapodilla was used in temple door lintels, which have survived from the Classic period to our own time.

Animals in the reserve include spider and howler monkeys, ocelots, white-tailed deer, raccoons, armadillos and some 21 other species. In the water are 24 species of fish, turtles and snakes, as well as the *Crocodylus moreletti*, the Petén crocodile. The birdlife, of course, is rich and varied. Depending upon the season and migration patterns, you might see kingfishers, ducks,

herons, hawks, parrots, toucans, wood-peckers and the famous ocellated (or Petén) turkey, a beautiful big bird resembling a peacock.

A network of loop trails starts at the road and goes up the hill, affording a view of the whole lake and of Laguna Salpetén and Laguna Petenchel. A trail map is at the entrance.

When we visited, the reserve was always open and admission was free. However, a ranger told us there was a plan to start charging US$5 per person. You may find the gate always open, or it may be open only from 7 am to 4 pm (once in, you can stay as late as you like). If you want to enter earlier and find the gate closed, go to the administration center and they'll let you in.

Places to Stay & Eat

El Remate has several small hotels and pensions, and more are opening all the time.

La Casa de Don David (message ☎ 926-0227), on the lakeshore about 10 meters from the Flores-Tikal road, is operated by American-born David Kuhn (the original 'gringo perdido') and his friendly Guatemalan wife. Rooms with shared bath are US$5 per person or US$7.50 per person for free-standing bungalows with private bath. Economical meals are served on the wide upstairs terrace overlooking the lake. There's horseback riding, and in the early evenings they do a two- or three-hour boat ride, crossing the lake and entering the Río Ixpop to see the crocodiles, birds and other wildlife.

Across the Flores-Tikal road from the lake are a couple of other pleasant places with great lake views. At the *Mirador del Duende* (☎ 926-0269, fax 926-0397) you can camp with your own hammock or tent for US$2.50/4.20 a single/double, sleep in a shelter (like a permanent tent) for US$3.35 per person or stay in a bungalow for US$4.20 per person. Healthy, economical vegetarian food is served. The pleasant owner boasts that this is a 'mosquito-free zone', due to the breezes blowing off the lake. Forest hiking tours are offered.

Next door, *La Mansión del Pájaro Serpiente* (☎ /fax 926-0065) has 10 very attractive rooms with private hot bath for US$75, plus lovely gardens, a swimming pool and a reasonably priced restaurant/bar.

A couple of other good places are about three km west of El Remate on the road around the north side of the lake, near the Biotopo Cerro Cahuí. The *Parador Ecológico El Gringo Perdido* (The Lost Gringo Ecological Inn; ☎ /fax in Guatemala City 236-3683) is right on the lakeshore. Shady, rustic hillside gardens hold a restaurant, a bucolic camping area, and simple but pleasant bungalows and dormitories. Rates are US$3 per person for a campsite, US$6 per person for a camping bungalow with roof, beds and mosquito netting, US$10 per person for a dorm bunk, and US$14 per person for rooms with private bath. Four-person bungalows, each with its own patio with hammocks and chairs and a small private dock for swimming and sunning on the lake, are US$25 per person, breakfast and dinner included. Two luxury bungalows with air-con are US$50. Overall cost is cheaper if you get a room-and-meals package. Activities include swimming, fishing, windsurfing, volleyball, basketball, boat trips on the lake, and bicycling.

Nearby, *Casa Roja* (☎ 926-0269, in Antigua ☎ 832-0162), across the road from the lake, has simple camping bungalows with outside bathrooms for US$7/12/15 a single/double/triple. It's cheaper if you get meals here: US$13 per person covers accommodations, dinner and breakfast. A swimming dock is in front, and they rent mountain bikes.

Farther around the lake is the luxury *Hotel Camino Real Tikal* (☎ 926-0206), the fanciest hotel in the Petén. Located within the Biotopo Cerro Cahuí five km west of El Remate, the Camino Real has 120 air-con rooms with all the comforts. Two restaurants and two bars keep guests happy, as do tennis courts, swimming pools, water sports on the lake and all the other top-class services. Rates are US$100/110 a single/double, meals extra. (This hotel is rather remote, especially if you don't have your own wheels.)

Getting There & Away

Any bus or minibus going north from Santa Elena to Tikal can drop you at El Remate. Taxis from Santa Elena or the airport will take you for US$20. Once you are in El Remate, you can hail any passing bus or minibus on the Flores-Tikal road to take you to Tikal or Flores.

AROUND THE LAKE

San Andrés, a small town on the northwest side of the lake, has the Eco-Escuela de Español (☎ 928-8106, 926-1370, in the USA (202) 973-2264), a Spanish language school often recommended by those who have studied there. Cost is US$60/70/80/95 per week for four/five/six/seven hours of instruction daily, plus US$50 per week for room and board with a local family.

A few kilometers further west, *Hotel Ni'tún* (☎ 928-8132, fax 928-8113) is a beautiful place on the lakeshore with 30 hectares of grounds. Four spacious, attractive houses, each with three double beds, thatched roof, stone walls and private patio, are US$40 single or double, US$50 triple. The restaurant here is also very beautiful; a package of accommodations, three meals a day and open

Top: Main plaza in La Democracia, with Olmecoid basalt heads, Guatemala (TB)
Bottom: Bas-relief from the Cotzumalguapa culture, Santa Lucía Cotzulmalguapa, Guatemala (TB)

Top: The basilica of Esquipulas, Guatemala (TB)
Left: Workers building a protective palapa above a stela at Quiriguá (TB)
Right: Ceibal Ruins, El Petén, Guatemala (TB)

bar costs US$79 per person. A daily boat trip to Flores is included in the price. Bernie, who built and operates the hotel, is an adventurer who also operates Monkey Eco Tours (see Organized Tours under Flores).

TIKAL

Towering pyramids rise above the jungle's green canopy to catch the sun. Howler monkeys swing noisily through the branches of ancient trees as brightly colored parrots and toucans dart, squawking, from perch to perch. When the complex warbling song of some mysterious jungle bird tapers off, the buzz of tree frogs provides background noise.

Certainly the most striking feature of Tikal is its steep-sided temples, rising to heights of more than 44 meters. But Tikal is different from Chichén Itzá, Uxmal, Copán and most other great Mayan sites because it is deep in the jungle. Its many plazas have been cleared of trees and vines, its temples uncovered and partially restored, but as you walk from one building to another you pass beneath the dense canopy of the rain forest. Rich smells of earth and vegetation, peacefulness and animal noises all contribute to an experience not offered by any other major Mayan site.

If you visit from December to February, expect some cool nights and mornings. March and April are the hottest and driest months. The rains begin in May or June, and with them come the mosquitoes – bring rain gear, repellent and, for camping, a mosquito net. July to September is muggy and buggy. October and November see the end of the occasional rains and a return to cooler temperatures.

Day trips by air from Guatemala City to Tikal (landing in Flores/Santa Elena) are popular, as they allow you to get a glimpse of this spectacular site in the shortest possible time. Still, Tikal is so big that you need at least two days to see even the major parts thoroughly.

History

Tikal is set on a low hill, which becomes evident as you walk up to the Great Plaza from the entry road. The hill, affording relief from the surrounding low-lying swampy ground, may be why the Maya settled here around 700 BC. Another reason was the abundance of flint, the valuable stone used by the ancients to make clubs, spearpoints, arrowheads and knives. The wealth of flint meant good tools could be made, and flint could be exported in exchange for other goods. Within 200 years the Maya of Tikal had begun to build stone ceremonial structures, and by 200 BC there was a complex of buildings on the site of the North Acropolis.

Classic Period The Great Plaza was beginning to assume its present shape and extent by the time of Christ. By the dawn of the Early Classic period about 250 AD, Tikal had become an important religious, cultural and commercial city with a large population. King Yax Moch Xoc, who ruled about 230 AD, is looked upon as the founder of the dynasty that ruled Tikal thereafter.

Under Yax Moch Xoc's successor, King Great Jaguar Paw, who ruled in the mid-4th century, Tikal adopted a new and brutal method of warfare used by the rulers of Teotihuacán in central Mexico. Rather than meeting their adversaries on the plain of battle in hand-to-hand combat, the army of Tikal used auxiliary units to encircle the enemy and, by throwing spears, to kill them at a distance. This first use of 'air power' among the Maya of Petén enabled Smoking Frog, the Tikal general, to conquer the army of Uaxactún; thus Tikal became the dominant kingdom in Petén.

By the middle of the Classic period, in the mid-6th century, Tikal's military prowess and its alliance with Teotihuacán allowed it to grow until it sprawled over 30 sq km and had a population of perhaps 100,000. In 553, Lord Water came to the throne of Caracol (in southwestern Belize), and by 562, using the same warfare methods learned from Tikal, had conquered Tikal's king and sacrificed him. Tikal and other Petén kingdoms suffered under Caracol's rule until the late 7th century.

GUATEMALA

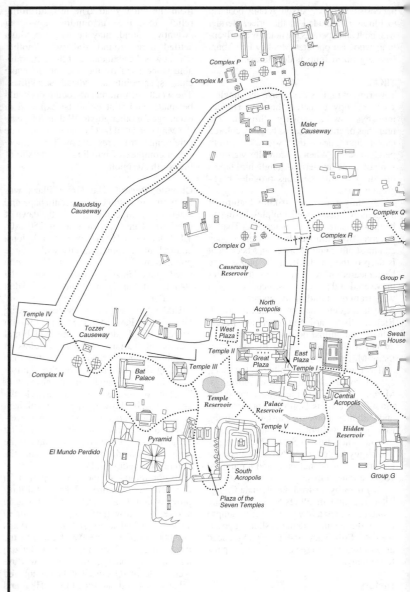

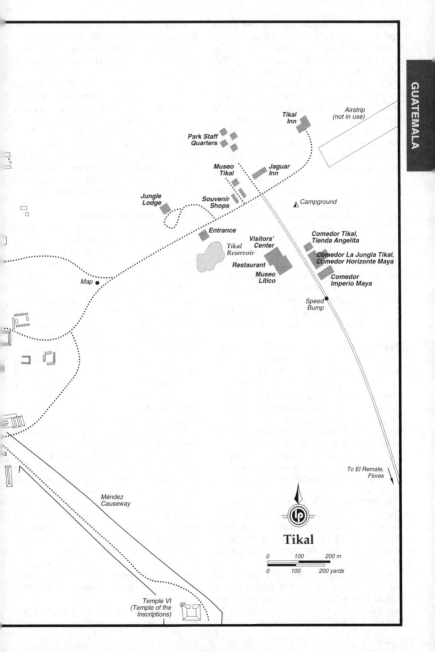

GUATEMALA

Tikal

0   100   200 m
0   100   200 yards

Tikal's Renaissance Around 700 a new and powerful king named Moon Double Comb (682-734), also called Ah Cacau (Lord Chocolate), 26th successor of Yax Moch Xoc, ascended the throne of Tikal. He restored not only the military strength of Tikal, but also its primacy as the most resplendent city in the Mayan world. He and his successors were responsible for building most of the great temples around the Great Plaza that survive today. King Moon Double Comb was buried beneath the staggering height of Temple I.

The greatness of Tikal waned around 900, but it was not alone in its downfall, which was part of the mysterious general collapse of lowland Mayan civilization.

No doubt the Itzaes, who occupied Tayasal (now Flores), knew of Tikal in the Late Postclassic period (1200 to 1530). Perhaps they even came here to worship at the shrines of their old gods. Spanish missionary friars who moved through El Petén after the conquest left brief references to these junglebound structures, but these writings moldered in libraries for centuries.

Rediscovery It wasn't until 1848 that the Guatemalan government sent out an expedition, under the leadership of Modesto Méndez and Ambrosio Tut, to visit the site. This may have been inspired by John L Stephens' bestselling accounts of fabulous Mayan ruins, published in 1841 and 1843 (though Stephens never visited Tikal). Like Stephens, Méndez and Tut took an artist, Eusebio Lara, to record their archaeological discoveries. An account of their findings was published by the Berlin Academy of Science.

In 1877 the Swiss Dr Gustav Bernoulli visited Tikal. His explorations resulted in the removal of carved wooden lintels from Temples I and IV and their shipment to Basel, where they are still on view in the Museum für Völkerkunde.

Scientific exploration of Tikal began with the arrival of English archaeologist Alfred P Maudslay in 1881; others continued his work: Teobert Maler, Alfred M Tozzer and RE Merwin. Tozzer worked tirelessly at Tikal on and off from the beginning of the century until his death in 1954. The inscriptions at Tikal were studied and deciphered by Sylvanus G Morley.

Since 1956, archaeological research and restoration has been carried out by the University Museum of the University of Pennsylvania and the Guatemalan Instituto de Antropología y Historia. In the mid-1950s an airstrip was built at Tikal to make access easier. In the early 1980s the road between Tikal and Flores was improved and paved, and direct flights to Tikal were abandoned (flights now land in Flores/Santa Elena).

Orientation & Information

Tikal is located in the vast Tikal national park, a 575-sq-km preserve containing thousands of separate ruined structures. The central area of the city occupied about 16 sq km, with more than 4000 structures.

The road from Flores enters the national park boundaries about 15 km south of the ruins. When you enter the park you must pay a fee of US$5 for the day; if you enter after about 3 pm, you can have your ticket validated for the following day as well.

The area around the visitors' center includes three hotels, a camping area, three small comedores, a tiny post office, a police post, two museums and a disused airstrip. From the visitors' center it's a 20- to 30-minute walk southwest to the Great Plaza.

The walk from the Great Plaza to the Temple of the Inscriptions is over one km; from the Great Plaza to Complex P, it's one km in the opposite direction. To visit all of the major building complexes you must walk at least 10 km, probably more.

For complete information on the monuments at Tikal, pick up a copy of *Tikal – A Handbook of the Ancient Maya Ruins*, by William R Coe. The guide is widely available and on sale in Flores and at Tikal. *The Birds of Tikal* by Frank B Smithe (Natural History Press, 1966), available at the Tikal museums, is a good resource for bird watchers.

The ruins are open from 5 am to 5 pm. You may be able to get permission to stay until 8 pm by applying to the Inspectorería to the west of the visitors' center. Carry a flashlight if you stay after sunset.

Great Plaza

Follow the signs to reach the Great Plaza. The path comes into the Great Plaza around Temple I, the Temple of the Grand Jaguar. This was built to honor – and to bury – King Moon Double Comb. The king may have worked out the plans for the building himself, but it was erected above his tomb by his son, who succeeded to the throne in 734. The king's rich burial goods included 180 beautiful jade objects, 90 pieces of bone carved with hieroglyphs, pearls and stingray spines, which were used for ritual bloodletting. At the top of the 44-meter-high temple is a small enclosure of three rooms covered by a corbelled arch. The zapote-wood lintels over the doors were richly carved; one of them is now in a Basel museum. The lofty roofcomb that crowned the temple was originally adorned with reliefs and bright paint. It may have symbolized the 13 realms of the Mayan heaven.

The climb up is dangerous (at least two people have tumbled to their deaths so far), but the view from the top is magnificent.

Temple II, directly across the plaza from Temple I, was once almost as high, but now measures 38 meters without its roofcomb. This one seems a bit easier to climb and the view is just as stupendous.

The North Acropolis, while not as immediately impressive as the twin temples, is of great significance. Archaeologists have uncovered about 100 different structures, the oldest of which dates from before the time of Christ, with evidence of occupation as far back as 400 BC. The Maya built and rebuilt on top of older structures, and the many layers, combined with the elaborate burials, added sanctity and power to their temples. Look for the two huge wall masks, uncovered from an earlier structure and now protected by roofs. The final version of the Acropolis, as it stood around 800 AD, had more than 12 temples atop a vast platform, many of them the work of King Moon Double Comb.

On the plaza side of the North Acropolis are two rows of stelae. Though hardly as impressive as the magnificent stelae at Copán or Quiriguá, these served the same purpose: to record the great deeds of the kings of Tikal, to sanctify their memory and to add 'power' to the temples and plazas that surrounded them.

Central Acropolis

On the south side of the Great Plaza, this maze of courtyards, little rooms and small temples is thought by many to have been a palace where Tikal's nobles lived. Others think the tiny rooms may have been used for sacred rites and ceremonies, as graffiti found within them suggest. Over the centuries the configuration of the rooms was repeatedly changed, suggesting perhaps that this 'palace' was in fact a noble or royal family's residence changed to accommodate different groups of relatives. A hundred years ago, one part of the acropolis, called Maler's Palace, provided lodgings for archaeologist Teobert Maler when he worked at Tikal.

West Plaza

The West Plaza is north of Temple II. On its north side is a large Late Classic temple. To the south, across the Tozzer Causeway, is Temple III, 55 meters high. Yet to be uncovered, it allows you to see a temple the way the last Tikal Maya and first white explorers saw them. The causeway leading to Temple IV was one of several sacred ways built among the temple complexes of Tikal, no doubt for astronomical as well as aesthetic reasons.

South Acropolis & Temple V

Due south of the Great Plaza is the South Acropolis. Excavation has hardly even begun on this huge mass of masonry covering two hectares. The palaces on top are from Late Classic times (the time of King Moon Double Comb), but earlier constructions probably go back 1000 years.

Temple V, just east of the South Acropolis, is 58 meters high and was built around 700 AD. Unlike the other great temples, this one has rounded corners, and one very tiny room at the top. The room is less than a meter deep, but its walls are up to 4½ meters thick. The view (as usual) is wonderful, giving you a 'profile' the temples on the Great Plaza.

Plaza of the Seven Temples

On the other side of the South Acropolis is the Plaza of the Seven Temples. The little temples, all quite close together, were built in Late Classic times, though the structures beneath must go back at least a millennium. Note the skull and crossbones on the central temple (the one with the stela and altar in front). On the north side of the plaza is an unusual triple ball court; another, larger version in the same design stands just south of Temple I.

El Mundo Perdido

About 400 meters southwest of the Great Plaza is El Mundo Perdido (the Lost World), a large complex of 38 structures with a huge pyramid in its midst. Unlike the rest of Tikal, where Late Classic construction overlays work of earlier periods, El Mundo Perdido exhibits buildings of many different periods: the large pyramid is thought to be essentially Preclassic (with some later repairs and renovations); the Talud-Tablero Temple (or Temple of the Three Rooms), Early Classic; and the Temple of the Skulls, Late Classic.

The pyramid, 32 meters high and 80 meters along the base, has a stairway on each side, and had huge masks flanking each stairway, but no temple structure at its top. Each side of the pyramid displays a slightly different architectural style. Tunnels dug into the pyramid by archaeologists reveal four similar pyramids beneath the outer face; the earliest (Structure 5C-54 Sub 2B) dates from 700 BC, making the pyramid the oldest Mayan structure at Tikal.

Temple IV & Complex N

Complex N, near Temple IV, is an example of the 'twin-temple' complexes popular among Tikal's rulers during the Late Classic period. These complexes are thought to have commemorated the completion of a katun,

or 20-year cycle in the Mayan calendar. This one was built in 711 by King Moon Double Comb to mark the 14th katun of Baktun 9. The king himself is portrayed on Stela 16, one of the finest stelae at Tikal.

Temple IV, at 64 meters, is the highest building at Tikal and the highest pre-Columbian building known in the Western Hemisphere. It was completed about 741, in the reign of King Moon Double Comb's son. From the base it looks like a steep little hill. Clamber up the path, holding onto trees and roots, to reach the metal ladder that will take you to the top. Another metal ladder, around to the side, lets you climb to the base of the roofcomb. The view is almost as good as from a helicopter – a panorama across the jungle canopy. If you stay up here for the sunset, climb down immediately thereafter, as it gets dark on the path very quickly.

Temple of the Inscriptions (Temple VI)

Compared to Copán or Quiriguá, there are relatively few inscriptions on buildings at Tikal. The exception is this temple, 1.2 km southeast of the Great Plaza. On the rear of the 12-meter-high roofcomb is a long inscription; the sides and cornice of the roofcomb bear glyphs as well. The inscriptions give us the date 766 AD. Stela 21 and Altar 9, standing before the temple, date from 736. The stela had been badly damaged (part of it was converted into a *metate* for grinding corn!) but has now been repaired.

Warning Note that the Temple of the Inscriptions is remote from the other complexes, and there have been incidents of robbery and rape of single travelers and couples. Ask a guard before you make the trek out here, or come in a group.

Northern Complexes

About one km north of the Great Plaza is Complex P. Like Complex N, it's a Late Classic twin-temple complex that probably commemorated the end of a katun. Complex M, next to it, was partially torn down by the Late Classic Maya to provide building materials for a causeway now named after Alfred Maudslay, which runs southwest to Temple IV. Group H had some interesting graffiti within its temples.

Complexes Q and R, about 300 meters due north of the Great Plaza, are very Late Classic twin-pyramid complexes with stelae and altars standing before the temples. Complex Q is perhaps the best example of the twin-temple type, as it has been mostly restored. Stela 22 and Altar 10 are excellent examples of Late Classic Tikal relief carving, dated 771.

Complex O, due west of these complexes on the western side of the Maler Causeway, has an uncarved stela and altar in its north enclosure. An uncarved stela? The whole point of stelae was to record great happenings. Why did this one remain uncarved?

Trails

The Sendero Benilj'a'a, a three-km trail with three sections, begins in front of the Jungle Lodge. Ruta Monte Medio (one hour) and Ruta Monte Medio Alto (two hours) are accessible all year round. Ruta Monte Bajo (35 minutes) is accessible only in summer.

Museums

Tikal has two museums. **Museo Lítico**, the larger museum, is in the visitors' center. It houses a number of stelae and carved stones from the ruins. Outside is a large relief map showing how Tikal would have looked during the Late Classic period, around 800 AD. Admission is free.

The **Museo Tikal**, which is smaller, is near the Jungle Lodge. It has some fascinating exhibits, including the burial goods of King Moon Double Comb, carved jade, inscribed bones, shells, stelae, ceramics and other items recovered from the excavations. Admission is US$1.65.

Both museums are open Monday to Friday from 9 am to 5 pm, Saturday and Sunday 9 am to 4 pm.

Organized Tours

All the hotels can arrange guided tours of the ruins, and tours to other places in the region such as Uaxactún, Ceibal, Yaxha,

Nakum. The Jungle Lodge is a good place to ask about this.

Places to Stay

Some intrepid visitors sleep atop Temple IV, convincing the guards to overlook this illegal activity for a consideration of US$5 per person, but this is not to be recommended. Safety is a major concern.

Otherwise, there are only four places to stay at Tikal. Most are booked in advance by tour groups, even though most groups (and individuals as well) stay near Lago de Petén Itzá and shuttle up to Tikal for the day. In recent years I have heard numerous complaints of price gouging, unacceptable accommodations and 'lost' reservations at these hotels. It may be best to stay in Flores or El Remate and visit Tikal on day trips.

On the other hand, staying at Tikal enables you to relax and savor the dawn and dusk, when most of the jungle birds and animals can be seen. If you'd like the thrill of staying overnight at Tikal, the easiest way is to forget about making reservations (which can be frustrating) and take a tour. Any travel agency can arrange one including lodging, a meal or two, a guided tour of the ruins and airfare. The Adventure Travel Center (☎ /fax 832-0162, viareal@guate.net), 5a Avenida Norte No 25-B, near the arch in Antigua, is one, and there are plenty of others. There's no need to make reservations if you just want to camp in the camping area.

Camping Cheapest of Tikal's lodgings is the official camping area by the entrance road and the disused airstrip. Set in a large, open lawn of green grass with some trees for shade, it has tent spaces on the grass and also on concrete platforms under palapa roofs. Water for the toilets and showers is more dependable now than it has been in previous years, since it's now brought in. Camping is US$5 per person.

The Jaguar Inn (see below) has a smaller camping area with bathroom and shower facilities. Camping is US$4.20 per person with your own tent or hammock, or you can rent camping gear; cost is US$6.65 for a hammock with mosquito net, US$10/16.65 a single/double for a tent with sheets, pillow and pad.

Hotels Largest and most attractive of the hotels is the *Jungle Lodge* (☎ in Guatemala City 476-8775, 477-0754, fax 476-0294), built originally to house the archaeologists excavating and restoring Tikal. It has 34 pleasant rooms in duplex bungalows, each room with private hot bath and two double beds, for US$48/60/70/80 a single/double/triple/quad. In an older section are 12 much less attractive rooms with shared bath for US$20/25 a single/double. There's a swimming pool, a large garden grounds, and a restaurant/bar with breakfast for US$5, lunch or dinner for US$10.

Tikal Inn (fax 926-0065), past the Jaguar Inn as you walk away from the small museum down towards the old airstrip, is the next more attractive. It has 17 rooms in the main building, as well as bungalows, which are slightly nicer, plus gardens, a swimming pool and restaurant. The rooms are quite simple and clean, all with private hot bath and ceiling fan, but have walls that extend only partway up to the roof and thus afford little conversational privacy. Singles/doubles are US$25/35 in the main building, US$45/55 in the bungalows. The electricity operates only from 11 am to 10 pm.

The *Jaguar Inn* (☎ 926-0002), to the right of the museum as you approach on the access road, has nine bungalow rooms with private bath and ceiling fan for US$30/48/66/78 a single/double/triple/quad. The restaurant serves breakfast for US$3, lunch and dinner for US$6.

Places to Eat
As you arrive in Tikal, look on the right-hand side of the road to find the three little comedores: *Comedor Imperio Maya, Comedor La Jungla Tikal, Comedor Tikal* and *Tienda Angelita*. The Comedor Imperio Maya, first on the way into the site, seems to be the favored one. You can buy cold drinks and snacks in the adjoining shop. All three comedores are similar in their lack of comfort and style, all rustic

and pleasant, all are run by local people and all serve huge plates of fairly tasty food at low prices. The meal of the day is almost always a piece of roast chicken, rice, salad, fruit and a soft drink for US$4. All of these places are open every day from around 5 am to 9 pm.

Picnic tables beneath shelters are located just off Tikal's Great Plaza, with itinerant soft-drink peddlers standing by, but no food is sold. If you want to spend all day at the ruins without having to make the 20- to 30-minute walk back to the comedores, carry food with you.

The restaurant in the visitors' center, across the street from the comedores, serves fancier food at fancier prices. Lomito (tenderloin of beef) is featured, as are other steaks, at US$10 a portion. Plates of fruit cost less. All the hotels also have restaurants.

Getting There & Away
For details of transport to and from Flores/Santa Elena, see that section. Coming from Belize, you can get off the bus at El Cruce/Puente Ixlú. Wait for a northbound bus or minibus – or hitch a ride with an obliging tourist – to take you the remaining 35 km to Tikal. Note that there is very little northbound traffic after lunch. If you come to Puente Ixlú in the afternoon, it's probably best to continue to Flores or El Remate for the night rather than risk being stranded at El Cruce.

You don't need a car to get to Tikal, but a 4WD vehicle of your own can be useful for visiting Uaxactún. If you're driving, fill your fuel tank in Flores; there is no fuel available at Tikal or Uaxactún.

UAXACTÚN
Uaxactún (pronounced wah-shahk-TOON), 25 km north of Tikal along a poor, unpaved road through the jungle, was Tikal's political and military rival in Late Preclassic times. It was conquered by Tikal's King Great Jaguar Paw in the mid-4th century, and was subservient to its great sister to the south for centuries thereafter.

When you arrive at Uaxactún, sign your name in the register at the guard's hut (at the edge of the disused airstrip, which now serves as pasture for cattle). About halfway down the airstrip, roads go off to the left and to the right to the ruins.

Villagers in Uaxactún live in houses lined up on either side of the disused airstrip, making a living by collecting chicle, *pimienta* (allspice) and *xate* in the surrounding forest.

Ruins

The pyramids at Uaxactún were uncovered and put in a stabilized condition so that no further deterioration would result; they were not restored. White mortar is the mark of the repair crews, who patched cracks in the stone to prevent water and roots from entering. Much of the work on the famous Temple E-VII-Sub was done by Earthwatch volunteers in 1974; among them was Jane A Fisher, a Uaxactún-lover who later married Tom Brosnahan, co-author of this guidebook.

Turn right from the airstrip to reach Group E and Group H, a 10- to 15-minute walk. Perhaps the most significant temple here is E-VII-Sub, among the earliest intact temples excavated, with foundations going back perhaps to 2000 BC. It lay beneath much larger structures, which have been

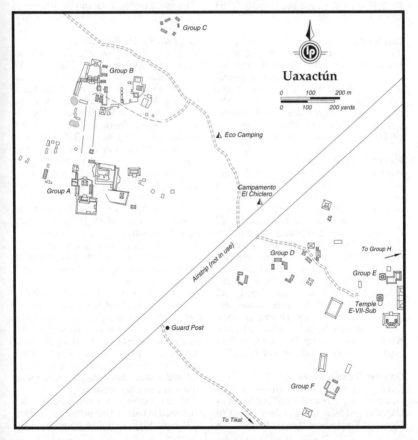

Uaxactún

0   100   200 m
0   100   200 yards

Group C

Group B

Group A

Eco Camping

Campamento El Chiclero

Airstrip (not in use)

Group D

To Group H

Group E

Temple E-VII-Sub

Guard Post

Group F

To Tikal

stripped away. On its flat top are holes, or sockets, for the poles that would have supported a wood-and-thatch temple.

About a 20-minute walk to the northwest of the runway are Group A and Group B. At Group A, early excavators sponsored by Andrew Carnegie simply cut into the sides of the temples indiscriminately, looking for graves. Sometimes they used dynamite. This unfortunate work destroyed many of the temples, which are now in the process of being reconstructed.

The ruins are always open and accessible, and no admission is charged. However, the turnoff onto the Uaxactún road is inside the gate to Tikal, so you must pay the US$5 admission fee there.

Organized Tours

Tours to Uaxactún can be arranged at the hotels in Tikal. The Jungle Lodge, for example, offers a trip to Uaxactún departing daily at 8 am and returning at 1 pm, in time to meet the 2 pm buses back to Flores. The trip costs US$60 for one to four people, split among the number of people going, or US$15 per person for over four people.

Places to Stay & Eat

If you have your own camping gear, there are plenty of places to camp. *Eco Camping*, at the entrance to the larger group of ruins, is an organized camping ground with basic cabins. *Posada y Restaurante Campamento El Chiclero*, on the left side of the airstrip, is a primitive place with seven musty thatch-roofed rooms with walls going only part way up, and screen the rest of the way. Singles/doubles are US$6.65/9, or you can pitch a tent. Bathrooms are shared, and there's no electricity. It's a 10-minute walk from the ruins. Trips can be arranged here to other places in the area, including Parque Nacional El Mirador-Dos Lagunas-Río Azul, La Muralla, Nakbé and Manantial.

Getting There & Away

During the rainy season (from May to October), you may find it difficult to get to Uaxactún. At other times of the year, ask in Flores or Tikal about the condition of the

road. You may be advised to make the hour-long drive only in a 4WD vehicle.

A bus operates daily between Santa Elena and Uaxactún, stopping at Tikal on the way. The cost is US$2.50 for the three-hour ride from Santa Elena, or US$1 for the one-hour ride from Tikal. The bus departs Uaxactún daily at 5 am and departs Santa Elena at 1 pm for the return trip.

If you're driving, fill your fuel tank in Flores; there is no fuel available at Tikal or Uaxactún. You might also want to pack some food and drink, though drinks and a few snacks are available in the village at Uaxactún.

From Uaxactún it's a further 104 km to the Río Azul ruins, or 88 km to San Andrés.

EASTWARD TO BELIZE

It's 101 km from Flores/Santa Elena eastwards to Melchor de Mencos, the Guatemalan town on the border with Belize. You can take a bus from Santa Elena to Melchor de Mencos, where you can transfer to the Belizean side. Alternatively, there's a Transportes Pinita bus at 5 am that goes all the way to Belize City and connects with the boat to Caye Caulker and Ambergris Caye. This bus enables travelers to avoid spending the night in Belize City. See the Flores/Santa Elena section for details on buses.

The road from Flores to El Cruce/Puente Ixlú is good, fast asphalt. If you're coming from Tikal, start early in the morning and get off at El Cruce to catch a bus or hitch a ride eastward. For the fastest, most reliable service, however, it's best to be on that 5 am bus.

East of El Cruce the road reverts to what's usual in El Petén – unpaved mud in bad repair. The trip to Melchor de Mencos takes three or four hours. There has been guerrilla and bandit activity along this road, and there's a remote chance that your bus could be stopped and its passengers relieved of their valuables. (It's been a long time since this has happened.)

At the border you must hand in your Guatemalan tourist card before proceeding to Benque Viejo in Belize, about three km from the border. See the section on Benque Viejo for transport information to Benque Viejo, San Ignacio, Belmopan and Belize City. If you arrive in Benque Viejo early enough in the day, you may have sufficient time to visit the Mayan ruins of Xunantunich on your way to San Ignacio.

FROM EL PETÉN TO CHIAPAS (MEXICO)

There are currently three routes through the jungle from Flores (Guatemala) to Palenque (Mexico). Whichever way you go, make sure you clear customs and get your exit and entry stamps in your passport on both sides of the border.

Via El Naranjo & La Palma

The traditional route is via bus to El Naranjo, then by boat down the Río San Pedro to La Palma, then by colectivo and bus to Tenosique and Palenque.

Transportes Pinita buses to El Naranjo (on the Río San Pedro) depart from the Hotel San Juan in Santa Elena daily at 5, 8 and 11 am, 1 and 2 pm; cost is US$3 for the rough, bumpy, 125-km, five-hour ride. Rosío buses depart for the same trip at 4:45, 8 and 10:30 am and at 1:30 pm.

El Naranjo is a hamlet with a few thatched huts, large military barracks, an immigration post and a few basic lodging places. From El Naranjo you must catch a boat on the river around midday for the four-hour cruise to the border town of La Palma (US$24). From La Palma you can go by colectivo or bus to Tenosique (1½ hours), then by bus or combi to Emiliano Zapata (40 km, one hour), and from there by bus or combi to Palenque.

Going in the reverse direction, travel agencies in Palenque offer to get you from Palenque to La Palma by minibus in time to catch the boat to El Naranjo, which departs between 8 and 9 am. You then catch the bus for the dreadful five-hour ride to Flores, arriving there around 7 pm the same day. The cost is about US$55 per person. However, you can do it yourself by taking the 4:30 am bus from the ADO terminal to Tenosique, then a taxi (US$10) to La Plama

to catch the 8 am-ish boat. If you catch a later bus, there are basic, cheap hotels in Tenosique, or you can find a place to hang your hammock and rough it in La Palma.

Via Bethel & Frontera Corozal

A faster route is by early morning bus from Flores via La Libertad and the El Subín crossroads to the co-op hamlet of Bethel (four hours, US$3), on the Río Usumacinta, which forms the border between Guatemala and Mexico.

The early bus should get you to Bethel before noon, but if you're stuck you can spend the night at the *Posada Maya*, beside the river in the tropical forest one km from Bethel. Lodging and meals are available here, and it's not expensive; you can take a cabin, or sleep in a hammock. Food is grown in the organic garden. Activities include swimming in the river and tours to nearby places such as Yaxchilán, a natural spring and a lookout point. The owners are friendly and helpful to travelers, and they can arrange transport including boats and horses.

Frequent boats make the half-hour trip downriver from Bethel to Frontera Corozal on the Mexico side, charging from US$4 to US$12 for the voyage, depending to some extent on your bargaining power.

At Frontera Corozal (formerly Frontera Echeverría) there's a restaurant and primitive accommodations, but you're better off taking one of the colectivos (shared taxi-minibuses) that wait for passengers to Palenque. The last colectivo tends to leave around 2 or 3 pm.

From Frontera Corozal, a chartered boat to the Yaxchilán archaeological site might cost US$60, but sometimes you can hitch a ride with a group for US$10 or so. Buses from Frontera Corozal take four to 4½ hours to reach Palenque; the fare is US$5.

Coming from Palenque, you can bus to Frontera Corozal (two or three hours, US$4), take a boat upstream (25 minutes to the Posada Maya, 35 minutes to the village of Bethel), and either stay overnight at the Posada Maya or continue on the bus to Flores.

In Palenque, travel agencies may insist that you can't do the trip on your own, that you must sign up for their US$30 trip, and that there is no place to stay overnight at the border. Not so! These organized trips save you some hassle, but you can do the same thing yourself for half the price. Just be sure to hit the road as early as possible in the morning.

Via Sayaxché, Pipiles & Benemerito

From Sayaxché, you can negotiate a ride on one of the cargo boats for the eight-hour trip (US$8) down the Río de la Pasión via Pipiles (the Guatemalan border post) to Benemerito, in Chiapas. From Benemerito, proceed by bus or boat to the ruins at Yaxchilán and Bonampak, and then onward to Palenque. There are also buses that run directly between Benemerito and Palenque (10 hours, US$12).

SAYAXCHÉ & CEIBAL

The town of Sayaxché, 61 km south of Flores through the jungle, is the closest settlement to a half-dozen Mayan archaeological sites, including Aguateca, Altar de Sacrificios, Ceibal, Dos Pilas, El Caribe, Itzán, La Amelia and Tamarindito. Of these, Ceibal is currently the best restored and most interesting, partly because of its Mayan monuments and partly because of the river voyage and jungle walk necessary to reach it.

Dos Pilas, presently under excavation, is not equipped to receive visitors without their own camping gear. From Dos Pilas, the minor sites of Tamarindito and Aguateca may be reached on foot and by boat, but they are unrestored, covered in jungle and of interest only to the very intrepid.

Sayaxché itself is of little interest, but its few basic services allow you to eat and to stay overnight in this region.

Orientation

The bus from Santa Elena drops you on the north bank of the Río de la Pasión. The main part of the town is on the south bank. Frequent ferries carry you over the river for a minimal fare.

Ceibal

Unimportant during the Classic Period, Ceibal grew rapidly thereafter, attaining a population of perhaps 10,000 by 900 AD. Much of the population growth may have been due to immigration from what is now Chiapas, in Mexico, because the art and culture of Ceibal seems to have changed markedly during the same period. The Postclassic Period saw the decline of Ceibal, after which its low ruined temples were quickly covered by a thick carpet of jungle.

Today, Ceibal is not one of the most impressive of Mayan sites, but the journey to Ceibal is among the most memorable. A two-hour voyage on the jungle-bound Río de la Pasión brings you to a primitive dock. After landing, you clamber up a narrow, rocky path beneath gigantic ceiba trees and ganglions of jungle vines to reach the archaeological zone.

Smallish temples, many of them still (or again) covered with jungle, surround two principal plazas. In front of a few temples, and standing seemingly alone on paths deeply shaded by the jungle canopy, are magnificent stelae, their intricate carvings still in excellent condition.

Places to Stay & Eat

Hotel Guayacan (☎ 926-6111), just up from the dock on the south side of the river in Sayaxché, is basic and serviceable. A double costs around US$8/10 with shared/private bath. The *Hotel Mayapan*, up the street to the left, has cell-like rooms for US$5 a double. The *Hotel Ecológico Posada Caribe* (☎ /fax 928-6114, in Guatemala City ☎ /fax 230-6588) is more expensive.

Restaurant Yaxkin is typical of the few eateries in town: basic, family-run and inexpensive.

Getting There & Away

Day trips to Ceibal are organized by various agencies and drivers in Santa Elena, Flores and Tikal for about US$30 per person roundtrip. It can be done cheaper on your own, but this is significantly less convenient.

Transportes Pinita buses depart from Santa Elena at 6, 9 and 10 am, 1 and 4 pm for Sayaxché (two hours, US$2.50), where you must strike a deal with a boat owner to ferry you up the river – a two-hour voyage – and back. The boat may cost anywhere from US$30 to US$60, depending upon its size and capacity. From the river, it's less than 30 minutes' walk to the site. You should hire a guide to see the site, as some of the finest stelae are off the plazas in the jungle.

Facts about Belize

This English-speaking tropical country with its highly unlikely mixture of peoples and cultures is being 'discovered', and it is changing fast.

Belize is tiny: The population of the entire country is only about 250,000 (the size of a small city in Mexico, Europe or the USA), and its 23,300-sq-km area is only slightly larger than that of Wales or Massachusetts.

Those who say that the political scene here is turbulent are referring to the purple rhetoric and high emotions of its politics. Belize is a democracy and has never had a military coup; indeed, it does not have an army, only the tiny Belize Defense Force.

Belize is friendly, laid-back, beautiful, proud, poor and hopeful for the future. It's difficult not to love the place, but it happens. If a visitor is disappointed, usually it is because of unrealistic expectations. A few points must be kept in mind:

Belize is not yet fully prepared to receive lots of visitors. Services in some areas are few, far between, basic and comparatively expensive. The country has a small number of hotels, most simple, but these may be full when you arrive, leaving you little choice of accommodations. There are only a few paved roads in the whole country, so transport can be slow. Public transport is either by small airplane or used schoolbus, so many hotels and lodges operate their own tour minibuses to allow guests to take excursions with some level of convenience.

More than half of the tourists who visit Belize go straight to the cayes (islands). Some spend their whole time there; others use island hotels as bases for excursions to other parts of the country and to Tikal (Guatemala). Likewise, many visitors to the mountains of western Belize go straight from the airport to their reserved rooms at small forest lodges or resorts. When they want to make excursions, they sign up for guided tours operated by the lodges. These tours, like the lodges, are small, convenient and personal, and often priced higher than mass-market excursions.

If you expect convenience, comfort and ultracheapness while traveling independently, you may not think the best of Belize. But if you are adaptable and adventurous, you'll find travel in Belize to be a singular experience.

HISTORY
Colonial Times

In the opinion of its Spanish conquerors, Belize was a backwater good only for cutting logwood to be used for dye. It had no obvious riches to exploit, and no great population to convert for the glory of God and the profit of the conquerors. Far from being profitable, it was dangerous, because the barrier reef tended to tear the keels from Spanish ships attempting to approach the shore.

Though Spain 'owned' Belize, it did little to rule it, as there was little to rule. The lack of effective government and the safety afforded by the barrier reef attracted English and Scottish pirates to Belizean waters during the 17th century. They operated mostly without serious hindrance, capturing Spanish galleons heavily laden with the gold and other riches taken from Spain's American empire. In 1670, however, Spain convinced the British government to clamp down on the pirates' activities. The pirates, now unemployed, mostly went into the logwood business, becoming lumberjacks instead of buccaneers.

By today's standards, the erstwhile pirates made bad timber managers, cutting logwood indiscriminately and doing damage to the jungle ecosystem.

During the 18th century the Spanish wanted the British loggers out of Belize, but with little control over the country and more important things to attend to in other parts of its empire, Spain mostly ignored Belize.

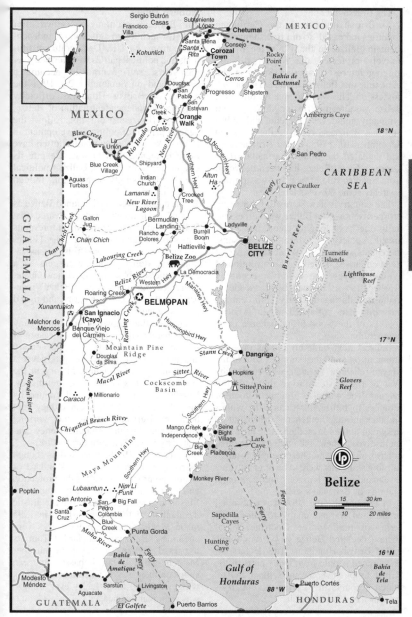

BELIZE

The British did not.

As British interests in the Caribbean countries increased, so did British involvement in Belize. In the 1780s the British actively protected the former pirates' logging interests, assuring Spain at the same time that Belize was indeed a Spanish possession. This was a fiction. By this time, Belize was already British by tradition and sympathy, and it was with relief and jubilation that Belizeans received the news, on September 10, 1798, that a British force had defeated the Spanish armada off St George's Caye. Belize had been delivered from Spanish rule, a fact that was ratified by treaty some 60 years later.

The country's new status did not bring prosperity, however. Belize was still essentially one large logging camp, not a balanced society of farmers, artisans, merchants and traders. When the logwood trade collapsed, killed by the invention of synthetic dyes, the colony's economy crashed. It was revived by the trade in mahogany during the early 19th century, but this also collapsed when African sources of the wood brought fierce price competition.

Belize's next trade boom was in arms, ammunition and other supplies sold to the Mayan rebels in Yucatán, who fought the War of the Castes during the mid-19th century. The war also brought a flood of refugees to Belize. First came the whites and their mestizo lieutenants, driven out by the wrath of the Maya; then came the Maya themselves when the whites regained control of Yucatán. These people brought farming skills that were to be of great value in expanding the horizons and economic viability of Belizean society.

In 1862, while the USA was embroiled in the Civil War and unable to enforce the terms of the Monroe Doctrine, Great Britain declared Belize to be its colony, called British Honduras. The declaration encouraged people from many parts of the British Empire to come and settle in Belize, which accounts in part for the country's present-day ethnic diversity.

Modern Times

The Belizean economy worsened after WWII, which led to agitation for independence from the UK. Democratic institutions and political parties were formed over the years, self-government became a reality, and on September 21, 1981 the colony of British Honduras officially became the independent nation of Belize. Luckily, Belizeans did not follow the general pattern of political development in Central America, where bullets often have more influence than ballots. Despite its establishment by pirates, Belize's political life is surprisingly nonviolent, though hardly incorrupt.

Guatemala, which had claimed Belize as part of its national territory, feared that Belizean independence would kill forever its hopes of reclaiming Belize. The Guatemalans threatened war, but British troops stationed in Belize kept the dispute to a diplomatic squabble. In 1992 a new Guatemalan government recognized Belize's independence and territorial integrity, and signed a treaty relinquishing its claim.

Though the logwood and mahogany trades had brought some small measure of prosperity to Belize in the late 18th century and early 19th century, this was never a rich country. Its economic history in the 20th century has been one of getting by, benefiting from economic aid granted by the UK and the USA, from money sent home by Belizeans living and working abroad, and from the foreign currency generated by its small agricultural sector.

In the early 1990s, it looked as though tourism might raise Belize's standard of living and provide funds for the protection and restoration of its many important Mayan archaeological sites. But the drastic devaluation of the Mexican peso in 1995 made Mexican goods and services very cheap by Belizean standards. Tourists bypassed Belize to travel in cheaper Mexico, and Belizeans bypassed Belizean shops on their way to Chetumal (Mexico), where clothing, food, fuel – everything – was significantly cheaper.

Top: Belize City from the roof of Fort George Hotel, Belize (TB)
Bottom: Beach and jetty, Caye Caulker, Belize (TB)

Top: Tropical Paradise Hotel, Caye Caulkler, Belize (TB)
Bottom: Small hotel, Placencia, Belize (TB)

Then budget-balancing concerns in the USA substantially decreased US foreign aid to Belize.

It was at this delicate moment (1996) that the Belizean government, in its wisdom, decided to increase substantially the value-added tax (15%) and to levy high new taxes on tourist services. Though the taxes were later moderated, the damage was done.

GEOGRAPHY

Belize, like Yucatán, is mostly tropical lowland. The limestone bedrock extends eastwards offshore for several kilometers, covered by about a five-meter depth of sea-water. At the eastern extent of the shelf is the famous barrier reef, longest in the Western Hemisphere and second in the world only to Australia's. The Belizean coastline is mostly swampy mangrove, indistinctly defining the line between land and sea. Many of the offshore islands, called cayes, are also surrounded by mangrove, with little in the way of sand beach.

Northern Belize is low tropical country, very swampy along the shore.

In the western and southern parts of the country, the Maya Mountains rise to almost 1000 meters. Even here the forest is lush and well watered, humid even in the dry season but more pleasant than the lowlands.

CLIMATE

It is comfortably warm during the day in the Maya Mountains, cooling off a bit at night. The rest of the country is hot and humid day and night for most of the year. Rainfall is lightest in the north, heaviest in the south. In the rain forests of southern Belize, the humidity is very high because of the large amount of rainfall (almost four meters per year). Out on the cayes, tropical breezes waft constantly through the shady palm trees, providing natural air-conditioning; on the mainland, you swelter.

GOVERNMENT & POLITICS

British colonial rule left Belize with a tradition of representative democracy that

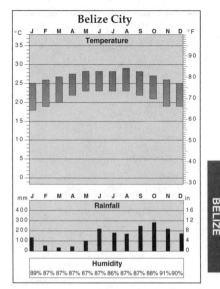

continued after independence. The British monarch is Belize's head of state, represented on Belizean soil by the governor-general, who is appointed by the monarch with the advice of the Belizean prime minister. The Belizean legislature is bicameral, with a popularly elected House of Representatives, and a nominated Senate similar in function to the British House of Lords.

The prime minister is the actual political head of Belize, and since independence the prime minister has usually been George Price, a founder of the People's United Party (PUP). The PUP was born in the 1950s during the early movement for independence. For the first decade of its existence, the PUP was seen as anti-British, and its leaders were harassed by the colonial authorities. But by 1961 the British government saw that Belizean independence was the wave of the future. Price went from being considered a thorn in the British side to being the prospective leader of a fledgling nation.

Districts of Belize

1989 held a surprise: PUP took 15 seats in the House of Representatives while the UDP took only 13. The venerable George Price changed places with Manuel Esquivel, taking the prime minister's seat while Esquivel resumed his old seat at the head of the opposition.

In 1993 the PUP called early elections, secure in its popularity and intent on extending its mandate for an additional three years. To most Belizeans, a PUP victory was a foregone conclusion. Many PUP adherents didn't bother to vote, but UDP supporters did, and the UDP squeaked to victory by the slimmest of margins – a single vote in some districts. Manuel Esquivel became prime minister again, while PUP supporters looked on in disbelief.

In 1996 the venerable George Price announced his retirement as head of PUP, opening the way to a noisy power struggle among his lieutenants. Said Musa won the struggle, and led PUP to a stunning sweep of town board seats in the March 1997 by-elections. Every town is now governed by PUP, and it hopes to regain complete power in the 1998 general elections.

In 1964 Belize got a new constitution for self-government, and the PUP, led by Price, won the elections of 1965, 1969, 1974 and 1979. The PUP was the leading force for full independence, achieved in 1981. Despite this success, the party did not fulfill Belizeans' dreams of a more prosperous economy, a failure due in part to world market conditions beyond its control. The party was also seen as having been in power too long; there were charges of complacency and corruption.

The PUP's main opposition, the multi-party coalition later named the United Democratic Party (UDP), won the elections of 1984 under the slogan 'It's time for a change', and Manuel Esquivel replaced George Price as prime minister. Priding itself on its handling of the economy, the UDP gained more ground in municipal elections held at the end of the decade. But the early national election of September

ECONOMY

Cattle ranching and farming of maize (corn), fruits (especially citrus, for orange juice concentrate) and vegetables are important in the lands west and south of Belize City, as is forestry in the Maya Mountains. In the north are large sugar cane plantations and processing plants. The cayes offshore depend on tourism and fishing for their income, but these two pursuits are sometimes in conflict. The spiny lobster and some types of fish have been seriously overexploited.

With many small, remote airstrips, a weak naval force and a sufficient number of compliant persons in official positions, Belize has also become a transshipment point for illicit drugs. Marijuana is said to be grown in industrial quantities near Orange Walk, and a certain amount of it obviously makes its way onto the streets of Belize City, along with some crack cocaine.

POPULATION & PEOPLE

The peoples of Mexico and Guatemala, however diverse and interesting, are easily outdone by the fabulous, improbable ethnic diversity of little Belize, with a population of about 250,000.

The Maya of Belize are of three linguistic groups. In the north, near the border with Yucatán, they speak Yucatec and also probably Spanish. Use of the Mayan language is decreasing, that of Spanish is increasing, and English – the official language of Belize – is making inroads into both. The Mopan Maya live in Cayo District in western Belize near the border town of Benque Viejo del Carmen; the Kekchi live in far southern Belize in and around Punta Gorda. The Maya make up only about 10% of Belize's population, while fully one-third of Belize's people are mestizos, some of whom immigrated from Yucatán during the 19th century. In recent years, political refugees from Guatemala and El Salvador have been added to Belize's Mayan population.

The largest segment of Belizeans is Creole, descendants of the African slaves and British pirates who first settled here to exploit the country's forest riches. Racially mixed and proud of it, Creoles speak a fascinating, unique dialect of English which, though it sounds familiar at first, is not easily intelligible to a speaker of standard English. Most of the people you meet and deal with in Belize City and Belmopan are Creole.

Southern Belize is the home of the Garifunas (or Garinagus, also called Black Caribs), who account for less than 10% of the population. The Garifunas are of South American Indian and African descent. They look more African than Indian, but they speak a language that's much more Indian than African, and their unique culture combines aspects of both peoples.

Besides the Maya, mestizos, the Creoles and Garifunas, Belize has small populations

BELIZE

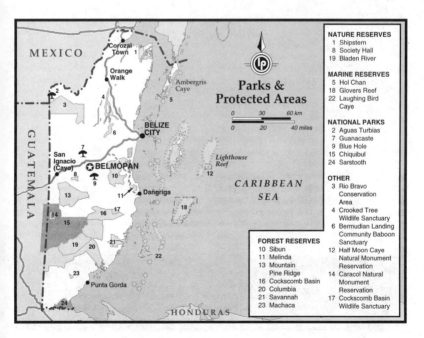

MEXICO

Corozal Town 1

Orange Walk

Ambergris Caye

Parks & Protected Areas

0   30   60 km
0   20   40 miles

BELIZE CITY

San Ignacio (Cayo)

BELMOPAN

Dangriga

Lighthouse Reef

CARIBBEAN SEA

Punta Gorda

HONDURAS

NATURE RESERVES
1 Shipstern
8 Society Hall
19 Bladen River

MARINE RESERVES
5 Hol Chan
18 Glovers Reef
22 Laughing Bird Caye

NATIONAL PARKS
2 Aguas Turbias
7 Guanacaste
9 Blue Hole
15 Chiquibul
24 Sarstooth

OTHER
3 Rio Bravo Conservation Area
4 Crooked Tree Wildlife Sanctuary
6 Bermudian Landing Community Baboon Sanctuary
12 Half Moon Caye Natural Monument Reservation
14 Caracol Natural Monument Reservation
17 Cockscomb Basin Wildlife Sanctuary

FOREST RESERVES
10 Sibun
11 Melinda
13 Mountain Pine Ridge
16 Cockscomb Basin
20 Columbia
21 Savannah
23 Machaca

of Chinese restaurateurs and merchants, Lebanese traders, German-Swiss farmers, Indian merchants from the Asian subcontinent, Europeans and North Americans.

RELIGION

Belize's mixture of religions follows its ethnic heritage. There are Anglican, Buddhist, Catholic, Hindu, Muslim, Mennonite and evangelical Protestant communities as well as those that still observe some traditional Mayan rites.

LANGUAGE

Belize is English-speaking, officially. But the Creoles, its largest ethnic group (over half of the population), speak their own colorful creole dialect as well as standard English, and when they speak standard English it is with the musical lilt of the Caribbean. Spanish is the first language in the north and in some towns in the west. You may also hear Mayan, Chinese, Mennonite German, Lebanese Arabic, Hindi and Garifuna.

BELIZE

Facts for the Visitor

PLANNING
When to Go
The busy winter season is from mid-December to April. As with the rest of the Ruta Maya area, the dry season (November to May) is the better time to travel, but prices are lower and lodgings on the cayes easier to find in summer (July to November). If you do visit in summer, be aware that this is hurricane season. Belize City was badly damaged by hurricanes, with heavy loss of life, in 1931, 1961 and 1978.

TOURIST OFFICES
Besides several useful websites (see the Online Services sidebar in the Facts for the Visitor chapter), Belize maintains the following offices abroad:

Cancún, Quintana Roo, Mexico
Belize Tourist Board, Hotel Parador Lobby, Avenida Tulum 26, Supermanzana 5, Cancún

Mérida, Yucatán, Mexico
Belize Tourist Board, Calle 58 No 488-B at Calle 43, Mérida 97000

New York, NY, USA
Belize Tourist Board, 421 7th Ave, New York, NY 10001
(☎ (212) 563-6011, (800) 624-0686)

Stuttgart, Germany
Belize Tourist Board, Bopserwaldstrasse 40-G, D-70184 Stuttgart (☎ (711) 233-947)

Within Belize, there are two tourist offices in Belize City (see that chapter).

VISAS & DOCUMENTS
Belizean Visitor's Permit
British subjects and citizens of Commonwealth countries, citizens of the USA, and citizens of Belgium, Denmark, Finland, Germany, Greece, Holland, Mexico, Norway, Panama, Sweden, Switzerland, Tunisia, Turkey and Uruguay who have a valid passport and an onward or roundtrip airline ticket from Belize do not need to obtain a Belizean visa in advance. The stamp made in your passport by the Belizean immigration official at the border or at the airport is your visitor's permit. If you look young and shabby or poverty-stricken, the immigration officer may demand to see your airline ticket out and/or a sizable quantity of money or travelers' checks before you're admitted.

EMBASSIES & CONSULATES
Belizean Embassies & Consulates Abroad
Because Belize is a small country and far from rich, its diplomatic affairs overseas are usually handled by the British embassies and consulates.

Some of the consulates mentioned below are actually honorary consuls or consular agencies. These posts can usually issue visas, but they refer more complicated matters to the nearest full consulate or to the Belizean embassy's consular section.

The following are Belize's diplomatic posts abroad:

Canada
Honorary Consul, 1080 Beaver Hall Hill, Suite 1720, Montréal, QC H2Z 1S8
(☎ (514) 871-4741, fax (514) 397-0816)
Honorary Consul, Suite 3800, South Tower, Royal Bank Plaza, Toronto, ON M5J 2J7,
(☎ (416) 865-7000, fax (416) 865-7048)

Germany
Honorary Consul, Lindenstrasse 46-48, 74321 Beitigheim, Bissingen
(☎ (71) 423-925, fax (71) 423-225)

Guatemala
Embassy, Avenida La Reforma 1-50, Zona 9, Edificio El Reformador, Suite 803
(☎ 334-5531, 331-1137, fax 334-5536)

Mexico
Embassy, Calle Bernardo de Gálvez 215, Colonia Lomas de Chapultepec, Mexico, DF 11000
(☎ (5) 520-1274, fax (5) 520-6089)

UK
> Belize High Commission to London,
> 22 Harcourt House, 19 Cavendish Square,
> London W1M 9AD, England
> (☎ (0171) 499-9728, fax (0171) 491-4139)

USA
> Embassy, 2535 Massachusetts Ave NW,
> Washington, DC 20008
> (☎ (202) 332-9636, fax (202) 332-6888)
> Consulate General, 5825 Sunset Blvd,
> Suite 206, Hollywood, CA 90028
> (☎ (213) 469-7343, fax (213) 469-7346)

Embassies & Consulates in Belize

Nearly all of Belize's embassies and consulates are located in Belize City; see that section.

CUSTOMS

Customs inspection is usually cursory. Don't bring in firearms or illegal drugs. The agent or the sniffer dog will find you out.

MONEY
Costs

Though a poor country, Belize is more expensive than you might anticipate. A small domestic economy and a large proportion of imports keep prices high. That fried-chicken dinner which costs US$3 in Guatemala costs US$5 in Belize, and is no better. That very basic, waterless pension room, cheap in Guatemala and Mexico, costs US$7 to US$9 per person on Caye Caulker. You will find it difficult to live for less than US$15 per day for a room and three meals in Belize; US$20 is a more realistic bottom-end figure, and US$25 makes life a lot easier.

Credit Cards & ATMs

Major credit cards such as Visa and MasterCard (or Eurocard and Access) are accepted at all airline and car-rental companies and at the larger hotels and restaurants everywhere; American Express is often accepted at the fancier and larger places, and at some smaller ones. Smaller establishments which accept credit cards may add a surcharge (usually 5%) to your bill when doing so.

Cash (ATM) cards, used to obtain cash from automated teller machines (ATMs), are just coming into use in Belize. There are few ATMs, and so far these work only with cards issued in Belize by the bank providing the machine. If you depend upon your ATM card for money, stock up on cash in Mexico or Guatemala before entering Belize!

Currency

The Belizean dollar (BZ$) bears the portrait of Queen Elizabeth II and is divided into 100 cents. Coins come in denominations of one, five, 10, 25 and 50 cents, and one dollar; bills (notes) are all of the same size but differ in color, and come in denominations of one, two, five, 10, 20, 50 and 100 dollars.

The Belizean dollar's value has been fixed for many years at US$1=BZ$2.

Prices are generally quoted in Belizean dollars, written as '$30 BZE', though you will also occasionally see '$15 US'. You must make sure that you know whether the dollars are US or Belizean; otherwise you might end up being surprised with a bill twice as high as you had anticipated. Often people will quote prices as '20 dollars Belize, 10 dollars US' just to make it clear.

Currency Exchange

Most businesses accept US currency in cash without question. They usually give change in Belizean dollars, though they may return US change if you ask and if they have it. Many also accept US-dollar travelers' checks. Belizean ATMs do not yet accept foreign ATM cards (see above).

Moneychangers around border-crossing points and in downtown business areas will change your US cash for Belizean dollars legally at the standard rate of US$1=BZ$2. If you change money or travelers' checks at a bank, you may get only US$1=BZ$1.97; they may also charge a fee of BZ$5 (US$2.50) to change a travelers' check.

Canadian dollars (CN$1=BZ$1.46) and UK pounds sterling (UK£1=BZ$3.22) are exchangeable at any bank. It is difficult if not impossible to exchange other foreign currencies in Belize.

Taxes & Refunds

Belize levies a 15% value-added tax (VAT), as well as a 7% tax on hotel rooms, meals and drinks. If you stay in a small hotel or guesthouse just one night and don't insist on a receipt, you may not be charged the tax. There are no refund plans for the VAT.

POST & COMMUNICATIONS
Post

An airmail postcard (BZ$0.30) or letter (BZ$0.60) sent to Canada or the USA may take anywhere from four to 14 days to arrive. An airmail postcard (BZ$0.40) or letter (BZ$0.75) sent to Europe will take one to three weeks to arrive.

Address poste restante (general delivery) mail to: (name), c/o Poste Restante, (town), Belize. To claim poste restante mail, present a passport or other identification; there's no charge.

Telephone

The telephone system is operated by Belize Telecommunications Ltd (BTL), with offices (open Monday to Friday from 8 am to noon and from 1 to 4 pm, and Saturday from 8 am to noon) in major towns.

Local calls cost BZ$0.25 (about US$0.13). Telephone debit cards are sold in denominations of BZ$10, BZ$20 and BZ$50.

To call one part of Belize from another, dial 0 (zero), then the one- or two-digit area code, then the four- or five-digit local number.

Here are Belize's area codes:

Ambergris Caye	26
Belize City	2
Belmopan/Spanish Lookout	8
Benque Viejo del Carmen	93
Burrell Boom	28
Caye Caulker	22
Corozal	4
Dangriga	5
Independence/Placencia	6
Ladyville	25
Orange Walk	3
Punta Gorda	7
San Ignacio	92

Calls dialed direct (no operator) from Belize to other Western Hemisphere countries cost BZ$3.20 (US$1.60) per minute; to Europe, BZ$6 (US$3) per minute; to all other countries, BZ$8 (US$4) per minute. The best plan for calling internationally from Belize is to dial your call direct from a telephone office; or you can call collect from your hotel. Be sure to ask before you call what the charges (and any hotel surcharges) may be. Here are some useful numbers:

Directory assistance	113
Local & regional operator	114
Long-distance (trunk) operator	110
International operator	115
Fire & ambulance	90
Police	911

To place a collect call, dial the international operator (115), give the number you want to call and the number you're calling from, and the operator will place the call and ring you back when it goes through. Rates for operator-assisted calls are the same as those for direct-dial calls, but the minimum initial calling period is three minutes.

The large American long-distance companies provide international service as well. Their rates may not be much different than BTL's, however. To reach AT&T's USADirect and WorldConnect services, dial 555 from your hotel or dial 815 and ask the operator for AT&T Direct. For Sprint Express, dial 556 from your hotel or 812 from pay phones. For MCI World-Phone service, dial 557 from hotels or 815 from pay phones.

Fax, Internet & Email

Fax service is available at many hotels and businesses.

BTL provides Internet access to local residents with accounts. If your hotel has Internet access, they may be willing to send and receive email messages for a fee. CompuServe and America Online do not have nodes in Belize at this writing.

For several Belize-specific websites, see the Online Services sidebar in the Facts for the Visitor chapter at the start of the book.

BELIZE

NEWSPAPERS & MAGAZINES

Belizean newspapers are small in size, circulation and interest. Most are supported by one political party or another, so much space is devoted to political diatribe.

Foreign newspapers such as the *Miami Herald* are difficult to find. Few newsstands – even those in the luxury hotels and resorts – carry current foreign periodicals.

RADIO & TV

Radio Belize provides local news and rap music on the AM (middle wave) and FM bands.

There are two local television stations. Programming consists mainly of rebroadcasted US satellite feeds and a few hours of local content such as local news, ceremonies and special sports events. Most hotels with TVs in their guestrooms provide cable service with several dozen channels including CNN, NBC, CBS, Discovery, Showtime and curiosities such as TV Asia and the channel from Dubai in the Arabian Gulf.

BUSINESS HOURS

Banking hours depend upon the individual bank, but most are open Monday to Thursday from 8 am to 1:30 pm and Friday from 8 am to 4:30 pm. Most banks and many businesses and shops are closed on Wednesday afternoon. Shops are usually open Monday to Saturday from 8 am to noon and Monday, Tuesday, Thursday and Friday from from 1 to 4 pm. Some shops have evening hours from 7 to 9 pm on those days as well. Most businesses, offices and city restaurants are closed on Sunday.

FOOD

Cooking in Belize is mostly borrowed – from the UK, from the Caribbean, from Mexico, from the USA. Being a young, small, somewhat isolated and relatively poor country, Belize never developed an elaborate native cuisine. Each community has its own local favorites, but Garifuna and Mayan dishes and traditional favorites such as *boil-up* rarely appear on restaurant menus. Even so, there is some good food to be had.

As a Belizean wag described it to me on my first visit years ago, 'We eat a lot of rice and beans in Belize, and when we get tired of that, we eat beans and rice'.

The mixed rice and red beans usually come with other ingredients – chicken, pork, beef, fish, vegetables, even lobster – plus some spices and condiments like coconut milk. 'Stew beans with rice' is stewed beans on one side of the plate, boiled rice on the other side and chicken, beef or pork on top. For garnish, sometimes you'll get slices of fried plantain.

More exotic traditional foods include armadillo, venison and gibnut (also called paca), a small, brown-spotted rodent similar to a guinea pig. These are served more as curiosities than as staples of the diet.

Getting There & Around

Getting There & Away

AIR

American Airlines flies to Belize from Miami, Continental from Houston and TACA (the Costa Rican airline) from Los Angeles. International air routes to Belize City all go through these gateways. Continental has perhaps the best service, flying to every capital city in Central America, with a nonstop from Houston to Belize City.

American Airlines, New Rd at Queen St
(PO Box 1680), Belize City
(☎ (2) 32522, fax (2) 31730)

Continental, 32 Albert St, Belize City,
in a little Hindu-esque 'temple'
(☎ (2) 78309, (2) 78463, fax (2) 78114)

TACA, 41 Albert St
(Belize Global Travel), Belize City
(☎ (2) 77363, (2) 77185, fax (2) 75213)

In the past there has been service by small regional airlines between Cancún and Belize City, and though there is currently no service operating on this route, it may be revived in the future as traffic increases.

Several small airlines fly between Flores (near Tikal in Guatemala) and Belize City, with connections to and from Guatemala City. Tropic Air has tours by air from San Pedro on Ambergris Caye (US$200) Monday to Friday at 8 am and 2 pm, stopping at Belize City's Goldson International Airport (US$155 roundtrip) at 8:30 am and 2:30 pm, returning from Flores Monday to Friday at 9:30 am and 3:30 pm. The tour price includes airfare, ground transport to Tikal, lunch, and a guided tour of the archaeological site at Tikal; departure taxes are extra.

Departure taxes and airport fees of BZ$30 (US$15) are levied on non-Belizean travelers departing Belize City's Goldson International Airport for foreign destinations.

LAND

Several companies, including Batty Brothers and Venus, operate direct buses from Chetumal (Mexico) to Belize City. Companies including Batty Brothers, Novelo's and Shaw's run between Belize City and Benque Viejo del Carmen on the Guatemalan border, connecting with Guatemalan buses headed for Flores. Some of these lines arrange connections so that you can travel between Flores and Chetumal directly, with only brief stops in Belize to change buses. For details see under Chetumal in the Yucatán section and under Flores in the Guatemala section. For information on Belizean buses, see Getting Around, below.

Exit tax at Belizean land border-crossing points is BZ$7.50 (US$3.75).

BOAT

Scheduled and occasional small passenger boats ply the waters between Punta Gorda in southern Belize and Lívingston and Puerto Barrios in eastern Guatemala. Another service runs from Punta Gorda to Puerto Cortés (Honduras), and yet another connects Dangriga in central Belize with Roatán (Honduras). Refer to the Southern Belize chapter for details.

These boats can usually be hired for special trips between countries, and if there are enough passengers to split the cost, it can be reasonable.

Getting Around

Belize is a small country with a few basic transportation routes. Here is information for traveling to most destinations in the country.

AIR

With few paved roads, Belize depends greatly on small airplanes (de Havilland

Twin Otters, Cessnas, etc) for fast, reliable transport within the country.

Belize City has two airports. Philip SW Goldson International Airport (BZE) at Ladyville, 16 km northwest of the city center, handles all international flights. The Municipal Airport (TZA) is 2.5 km north of the city center, on the shore. Most local flights will stop and pick you up at either airport, but fares are almost always lower from Municipal, so if you have a choice, use that one.

There are two main domestic air routes which the small airplanes follow from Belize City: Belize City-Caye Chapel-Caye Caulker-San Pedro-Corozal, returning along the reverse route; and Belize City-Dangriga-Placencia/Big Creek-Punta Gorda, returning along the reverse route. Often the planes do not stop at a particular airport if they have no passengers to put down or reservations for passengers to pick up, so be sure to reserve your seat in advance whenever possible.

Airlines

The following are the main Belizean airline companies:

Aerovías – the Guatemalan regional airline, operates several flights per week between Belize City's Goldson International Airport and Flores (Guatemala) (US$70 one way), with onwards connections to Guatemala City. For details, see Flores in the El Petén chapter of the Guatemala section. (☎ (2) 75445)

Island Air – flies between Belize City and San Pedro via Caye Chapel and Caye Caulker. They also fly twice daily between Corozal and San Pedro. (☎ (2) 31140, in San Pedro on Ambergris Caye (26) 2435)

Maya Airways – has a similar schedule of flights to points in Belize. 6 Fort St (PO Box 458), Belize City (☎ (2) 77215, (2) 72313, fax (2) 30585, in the USA (800) 552-3419, mayair@btl.net)

Tropic Air – is the largest and most active of Belize's small airline companies. PO Box 20, San Pedro, Ambergris Caye (☎ (26) 2012, (26) 2117, (26) 2029, fax (26) 2338, in Belize City (2) 45671); in the USA PO Box 42808-236, Houston, TX 77242 (☎ (800) 422-3435).

Flights

Here is information on flights from Belize City to various points. Fares are one way from Municipal/Goldson International airports:

Big Creek; BGK – see Placencia

Caye Caulker; CLK/CKR – 10 minutes, US$22/39; flights to San Pedro stop at Caye Caulker on request; see San Pedro.

Caye Chapel; CYC – 10 minutes, US$22/39; flights to San Pedro stop at Caye Chapel on request; see San Pedro.

Corozal; CZL – one to 1½ hours, US$52/69; Tropic Air's 8:30 am and 2:30 pm flights from Belize City to Caye Chapel, Caye Caulker and San Pedro continue to Corozal, then return to Belize City from Corozal at 10:30 am and 3:30 pm via San Pedro, Caye Caulker and Caye Chapel. Maya Airways has flights from San Pedro to Corozal (and back) at 7:15 am and 3:30 pm.

Dangriga; DGA – 20 minutes, US$28/41; Maya Airways flies to Dangriga from Belize City at 8:30 and 10:30 am, noon and 2 and 4:30 pm; Tropic Air has four daily flights as well.

Flores (Guatemala) – one hour, US$85; Tropic Air has flights from Goldson International Airport daily at 8:30 am and 2:30 pm.

Placencia; PLA – 25 to 35 minutes, US$51/61; there are three airstrips in the vicinity of Placencia: Placencia (PLA), on the Placencia peninsula two km north of Placencia village; Big Creek, on the west side of the Placencia lagoon just south of Independence; and Savannah, five km inland west of Big Creek. Transport from Savannah and Big Creek to Placencia can be expensive and difficult, even impossible, especially in the afternoon and evening. Make sure your flight lands right at Placencia, on the peninsula just south of the Rum Point Inn. Maya Airways operates five flights daily (only one on Sunday) from Belize City via Dangriga; Tropic Air has flights from Belize City at 8:30 and 11 am and 1:30 and 4:30 pm, returning to Belize City at 7:20 and 9:50 am and 2:50 pm.

Punta Gorda; PND – 55 minutes, US$66/77; departures from Belize City are the same as for Placencia. Tropic Air has four flights per day and Maya Airways has two. Return flights on Tropic Air depart from Punta Gorda for Belize City at 7 and 9:30 am, noon and 2:30 pm; on Sunday, they depart only at 7 am and noon; return flights on Maya Airways leave Punta Gorda at 9:55 am and 3:35 pm.

BELIZE

San Pedro, Ambergris Caye; SPR – 20 minutes, US$22/39; Tropic Air flies every hour on the half-hour from 7:30 am to 5 pm, stopping at Caye Chapel and Caye Caulker on request. The 8:30 am and 2:30 pm flights continue from San Pedro to Corozal. Island Air has nine, and Maya Airways has six flights daily between Belize City and San Pedro.

BUS

Most Belizean buses are used US school-buses. The larger companies operate frequent buses along the country's three major roads. Smaller village lines tend to be run on marketeers' schedules: buses run from a smaller town to a larger town in the morning and return in the afternoon. Trucks willing to take on passengers go to some remote sites, traveling on rough roads which are sometimes impassable after heavy rains.

Each major bus company has its own terminals. Belize City's bus terminals are near the Pound Yard Bridge, along or near the Collett Canal on West Collett Canal St, East Collett Canal St, or neighboring streets. This is a rundown area not good for walking at night; take a taxi.

Batty Brothers Bus Service – operates buses along the Northern Hwy to Orange Walk, Corozal and Chetumal (Mexico) and also runs a few buses westwards to San Ignacio and Benque Viejo del Carmen. 54 East Collett Canal St (☎ (2) 77146)

Novelo's Bus Service – is the line to take to Belmopan, San Ignacio, Xunantunich, Benque Viejo del Carmen and Melchor de Mencos on the Guatemalan border. 19 West Collett Canal St (☎ (2) 77372)

Shaw's Bus Service – based in San Ignacio, Shaw's runs buses between that town and Belize City via Belmopan.

Urbina's Bus Service and Escalante's Bus Service – based in Orange Walk, both run between Belize City and Corozal via Orange Walk.

Venus Bus Lines – operates buses between Belize City and Chetumal as well. Magazine Rd (☎ (2) 73354, (2) 77390)

Z-Line Bus Service – runs buses south to Dangriga, Big Creek, Placencia and Punta Gorda, operating from the Venus Bus Lines terminal on Magazine Rd in Belize City. (☎ (2) 73937)

Pilferage of luggage is a problem, particularly on the Punta Gorda route. Give your luggage only to the bus driver or conductor, and watch as it is stored. Be there when the bus is unloaded to retrieve your luggage at once.

Here are the details on buses from Belize City to major destinations. Travel times are approximate, as the length of a ride depends upon how many times the driver stops to pick up and put down passengers along the way:

Belmopan – 84 km, 1¼ hours, US$1.75; see Benque Viejo del Carmen

Benque Viejo del Carmen – 131 km, three hours, US$3; Novelo's operates daily buses from Belize City to Belmopan, San Ignacio and Benque Viejo del Carmen at 11 am, noon, 1, 2, 3, 4, 5 and 7 pm (at noon, 1, 2, 3, 4 and 5 pm on Sunday). Batty Brothers operates nine morning buses westwards between 5 and 10:15 am daily. Several of these go all the way to Melchor de Mencos (Guatemala). Returning from Benque/Melchor, buses to San Ignacio, Belmopan and Belize City start at noon; the last bus leaves at 4 pm.

Chetumal (Mexico) – 160 km, four hours, US$5; express three hours, US$6; Batty Brothers runs 12 northbound buses from Belize City to Chetumal's Nuevo Mercado via Orange Walk and Corozal from 4 am to 11:15 am; 12 southbound buses from Chetumal's Nuevo Mercado run from 10:30 am and 6:30 pm. Venus Bus Lines has buses departing from Belize City for Chetumal every hour on the hour from noon to 7 pm; departures from Chetumal for Belize City are hourly from 4 to 10 am.

Corozal – 155 km, three hours, US$4; virtually all Batty Brothers and Venus buses to and from Chetumal stop in Corozal, and there are also several additional buses stopping in the town. There are frequent southbound buses in the morning but few in the afternoon; almost all northbound buses depart from Belize City in the afternoon.

Dangriga – 170 km, 2½ or four hours, US$3.50 to US$5.50; Z-Line runs five buses daily (four on Sunday) to Dangriga, at least one of which takes the cheaper, faster Coastal (Manatee) Hwy. Most buses go via Belmopan and the Hummingbird Hwy.

BELIZE

Flores (Guatemala) – 235 km, five hours, US$20; take a bus to Melchor de Mencos (see Benque Viejo del Carmen) and transfer to a Guatemalan bus. Some hotels and tour companies organize minibus trips which are more expensive but much faster and more comfortable.

Independence – 242 km, seven hours, US$7; buses bound for Punta Gorda stop at Independence, whence you may be able to find a boat over to Placencia (see Punta Gorda listing below).

Melchor de Mencos (Guatemala) – 135 km, 3¼ hours, US$3; see Benque Viejo del Carmen

Orange Walk – 94 km, two hours, US$3; same schedule as for Chetumal

Placencia – 260 km, four hours, US$9; take a morning Z-Line bus to Dangriga, then another Z-Line bus to Placencia. A bus returns from Placencia to Dangriga at 6 am; there may be others as well, depending upon the number of customers.

Punta Gorda – 339 km, eight hours, US$11; Z-Line runs three buses daily, at 8 am, noon and 3 pm. Return buses from Punta Gorda to Belize City via Independence depart at 5 and 9 am and at noon; on Friday and Sunday there's also a 3:30 pm bus.

San Ignacio – 116 km, 2¾ hours, US$2.50; see Benque Viejo del Carmen

CAR

Belize has two good asphalt-paved two-lane roads: the Northern Hwy between the Mexican border near Corozal and Belize City, and the Western Hwy between Belize City and the Guatemalan border at Benque Viejo del Carmen. The Hummingbird Hwy from Belmopan to Dangriga is unpaved for the first 29 km south and east of Belmopan, then paved for the following 58 km to Dangriga. Most other roads are narrow one- or two-lane dirt roads; many are impassable after heavy rains.

Anyone who drives a lot in Belize has a 4WD vehicle: a Jeep, Land Rover, Samurai, Sidekick, Trooper or high-clearance pickup truck. If you bring your own vehicle or rent one in Belize, keep in mind that sites off the main roads may be accessible only by 4WD vehicles, especially between May and November.

Indeed, they may not be accessible at all. Forget the glossy television advertisements showing these 4WD vehicles going anywhere and everywhere without problems. In Belize, after heavy rains, you can get profoundly stuck in floodwaters or mud even with 4WD, and getting winched out is discouragingly expensive.

Fuel stations are found in the larger towns and along the major roads. Leaded gasoline/petrol is usually sold by the US gallon (3.79 liters) for about US$2.50; that's US$0.66 per liter. Unleaded fuel is currently unavailable in Belize.

Highway signs and mileposts record distances in miles and speed limits in miles per hour, even though most vehicles have odometers and speedometers calibrated in kilometers.

Seat belts are required. If you are caught not wearing yours, the fine is US$12.50.

Rental

Generally, renters must be at least 25 old, have a valid driver's license and pay by credit card or leave a large cash deposit. Cars may not be driven out of Belize except by special arrangement (best done in advance of rental).

Most car-rental companies have representatives at Belize City's Goldson International Airport; many will also deliver or take return of cars at Belize City's Municipal Airport.

The best rental rates and service are at Budget Rent-a-Car (☎ (2) 32435, (2) 33986, fax (2) 30237), 771 Bella Vista (PO Box 863), Belize City, opposite the Belize Biltmore Plaza Hotel on the Northern Hwy, 4.5 km north of central Belize City. Most of its Suzuki and Vitara cars have 4WD, AM-FM radios and air-con, and they are priced from US$78 to US$113 per day (US$469 to US$676 per week), 15% tax included, with unlimited kilometrage. A Loss Damage Waiver (LDW) costs an additional US$14 per day, tax included; even with the LDW, you're liable for the first US$750 of damage to the vehicle.

National (☎ (2) 31587, (2) 31650, fax (2) 31586), 12 North Front St, Belize City, has offices at Goldson airport and at the Belize Biltmore Plaza Hotel.

Tour Belize Auto Rental (☎ (2) 71271,

fax (2) 71421, tourbelize@btl.net), Central American Blvd at Fabers Rd, Belize City, is also worth trying.

Note that there is no need to rent a car for travel on any of the cayes. Bicycles, motorcycles and electric golf carts are for rent in San Pedro on Ambergris Caye and Caye Caulker, and these are sufficient.

Insurance

Liability insurance is required in Belize, and you must have it for the customs officer to approve the temporary importation of your car into Belize. It can usually be bought at booths just across the border in Belize for about US$1 per day. Note that the booths are generally closed on Sunday, meaning no insurance is sold that day and no temporary import permits are issued. If you're crossing the border with a car, try to do it on a weekday morning.

Driving in Belize

Except in Cayo District in western Belize, there are few mileage or directional signs pointing the way to towns or villages. One-way streets are often unmarked as such.

BOAT

Fast motor launches zoom between Belize City, Caye Chapel, Caye Caulker and Ambergris Caye frequently every day.

Preparations

This boat trip is usually fast, windy and bumpy; it is not particularly comfortable. You will be in an open boat with no shade for at least 45 minutes, so provide yourself with

sunscreen, a hat and/or clothing to protect you from the sun and the spray. If you sit in the bow, there's less spray, but you bang down harder when the boat goes over a wave. Sitting in the stern gives a smoother ride, but you may get dampened by spray. If it rains, the mate will drag out a plastic tarp that passengers may hold above their heads. But – surprise! – the tarp is not waterproof.

Schedules

The Belize Marine Terminal (☎ (2) 31969), on North Front St at the northern end of the Swing Bridge in Belize City, is the main dock for boats to the northern cayes. It has a small Marine Museum, open from 8 am to 5 pm (closed Monday).

Boats depart the Marine Terminal for Caye Caulker at 9 and 11 am and 1, 3 and 5:15 pm, and charge US$7.50 one way, US$12.50 for a same-day roundtrip. They stop at Caye Chapel on request. The trip against the wind takes 40 minutes to one hour, depending upon the speed of the boat. Boats return from Caye Caulker at 6:45, 8 and 10 am and 3 pm.

For San Pedro on Ambergris Caye, boats depart the Marine Terminal at 9 am; the return trip departs San Pedro at 2:30 pm. The fare is US$15 one way, US$25 same-day roundtrip for the 1¼-hour to 1½-hour voyage.

Triple J Boating Service (☎ (2) 33464, fax (2) 44375), 5182 Baymen Ave, Belize City, runs good, big, fast boats to Caye Caulker and San Pedro from the Court House Wharf behind the Supreme Court building at slightly cheaper fares.

Belize City

Population 80,000

Ramshackle, colorful, fascinating, daunting, homely – these are only a few of the words that describe the country's biggest city and former capital. Tropical storms, which periodically razed the town in the 19th and early 20th centuries, still arrive to do damage to its aging wooden buildings, but they also flush out the open drainage canals, redolent with pollution, that crisscross the town. When there's no storm, Belize City bustles and swelters.

Few people come to Belize City on vacation; most people pass through while changing buses or planes. But if you need a hospital, a spare part for a car or a new sleeping bag, you'll come to Belize City to get it.

ORIENTATION

Haulover Creek, a branch of the Belize River, runs through the middle of the city, separating the commercial center (Albert, Regent, King and Orange Sts) from the slightly more genteel residential and hotel district of Fort George to the northeast. Hotels and guesthouses are found on both sides of the Swing Bridge over the creek.

Albert St (in the center) and Queen St (running through the Fort George and King's Park neighborhoods) are joined by the Swing Bridge. It seems as though everything and everybody in Belize City crosses the Swing Bridge at least once a day. The bridge, a product of Liverpool's ironworks (1923), is swung open daily at 5:30 am and 5:30 pm to let tall-masted boats through. When the Swing Bridge is open, virtually all vehicular traffic in the center of the city grinds to a halt in hopeless gridlock.

The Belize Marine Terminal, used by motor launches traveling to Caye Caulker and Ambergris Caye, is at the northern end of the Swing Bridge.

Each of Belize's bus companies has its own terminal. Most are on the west side of West Collett Canal St near Cemetery Rd. See the prior chapter, Getting There & Around, for details.

INFORMATION

Tourist Offices

The Belize Tourist Board (☎ (2) 77213, (2) 73255, fax (2) 77490, btb@btl.net), 83 North Front St (PO Box 325), just a few steps south of the post office, is open Monday to Friday from 8 am to noon and 1 to 5 pm (until 4:30 pm on Friday); it's closed on weekends.

The Belize Tourism Industry Association (☎ (2) 75717, (2) 78709, fax (2) 78710, btia@btl.net), 10 North Park St (PO Box 62), on the north side of Memorial Park in the Fort George district, can provide information about its members, which include most of the country's hotels, restaurants, tour operators and other travel-related businesses. Hours are Monday to Friday from 8:30 am to noon and 1 to 4:30 pm (until 4 pm on Friday).

Embassies & Consulates

A few countries have ambassadors resident in Belize. Many others appoint nonresident ambassadors who handle Belizean affairs from their home countries. Embassies and consulates tend to be open Monday to Friday from about 9 am to noon. Unless otherwise mentioned, all the offices listed below are in Belize City.

Belgium
    Consular Representative, Marelco Ltd,
    Queen St (☎ (2) 45769, fax (2) 31946)

Cuba
    Consulate-General, 6048 Manatee Drive
    (☎ (2) 35345, fax (2) 31105)

Denmark
    Consulate, 13 Southern Foreshore
    (☎ (2) 72172, fax (2) 77280)

European Union
    Commission of the European Union, Eyre
    St at Hutson St (☎ (2) 72785, (2) 32070)

France
Honorary Consul, 9 Barracks Rd
(☎ (2) 32708, fax (2) 32416)

Germany
Honorary Consul, 8 Princess Margaret
Drive (☎ (2) 35940, fax (2) 35413)

Guatemala
Embassy, 6A St Matthew's St
(☎ (2) 33150, (2) 33314, fax (2) 35140),
near Municipal Airport, open Monday to
Friday from 9 am to 1 pm

Honduras
Embassy, 91 North Front St
(☎ (2) 45889, fax (2) 30562)

Israel
Honorary Consul, 4 Albert St
(☎ (2) 73991, fax (2) 30463)

Italy
Honorary Consul, 18 Albert St
(☎ (2) 78449, fax (2) 73056)

Mexico
20 North Park St (☎ (2) 30194, (2) 31388,
fax (2) 78742); there is also a Mexican
embassy in Belmopan

Netherlands
Honorary Consul, 14 Central American
Blvd (☎ (2) 75663, fax (2) 75936)

Nicaragua
Honorary Consul, 50 Vernon St
(☎ (2) 70621)

Norway
Honorary Consul, 1 King St
(☎ (2) 77031, fax (2) 77062)

Panama
Consulate, 5481 Princess Margaret Drive
(☎ (2) 34282, fax (2) 30653)

Sweden
Honorary Consul General, 11 Princess
Margaret Drive (☎ (2) 30623)

UK
British High Commission, Embassy Square,
Belmopan (☎ (8) 22146, fax (8) 22761)

USA
Embassy, 29 Gabourel Lane
(☎ (2) 77161, fax (2) 30802)

Money
The Bank of Nova Scotia (ScotiaBank,
☎ (2) 77027), on Albert St at Bishop St, is
open Monday to Friday from 8 am to 1 pm
and Friday afternoon from 3 to 6 pm.

Nearby, the Atlantic Bank Limited (☎ (2)
77124, atlantic@btl.net), 6 Albert St at King
St, is open Monday, Tuesday and Thursday
from 8 am to noon and 1 to 3 pm, Wednesday
from 8 am to 1 pm and Friday from 8 am to
4:30 pm.

Also on Albert St is the prominent Belize
Bank (☎ (2) 77132, bbankisd@btl.net), 60
Market Square (facing the Swing Bridge),
and Barclay's Bank (☎ (2) 77211), 21
Albert St.

Post & Communications
The main post office is at the northern
end of the Swing Bridge, at the intersection of Queen and North Front Sts. Hours
are 8 am to noon and 1 to 5 pm Monday
through Saturday. If you want to pick up
mail at the American Express office, it's
at Belize Global Travel Service (☎ (2)
77185, fax (2) 75213), 41 Albert St (PO
Box 244).

Belize Telecommunications Ltd, or BTL
(☎ (2) 77085), 1 Church St near the Bliss
Institute, runs all of Belize's telephones, and
does it pretty well, though very expensively.
They have a public fax machine (fax (2)
45211). The office is open Monday to Friday
from 8 am to 5 pm.

Travel Agencies
Belize Global Travel Service (☎ (2) 77257,
fax (2) 75213, bzeadventure@btl.net), 41
Albert St, is an experienced agency which
works with the major airlines. You might
also try Belize Air Travel Service (☎ (2)
73174), 28 Regent St, and Belize International Travel Services (☎ (2) 71701, fax (2)
71700), 18 Bishop St.

Laundry
Try the Belize Laundromat (☎ (2) 31117),
7 Craig St near Marin's Travelodge, open
Monday to Saturday from 8 am to 5:15 pm
(closed on Sunday). A wash costs US$5
per load; detergent, fabric softener, bleach
and drying are included. A similar establishment is Carry's Laundry, 41 Hydes
Lane, open Monday to Saturday from 8 am
to 5:30 pm (closed on Sunday).

BELIZE

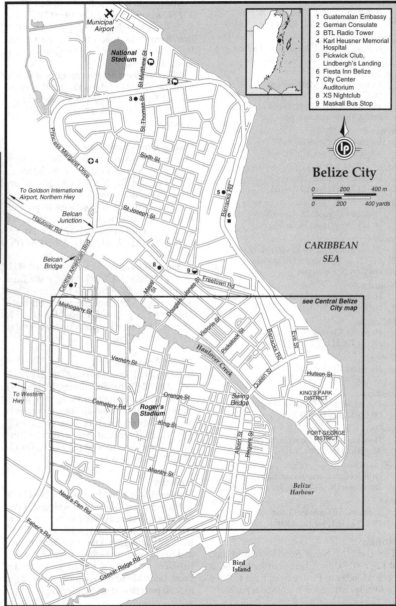

1 Guatemalan Embassy
2 German Consulate
3 BTL Radio Tower
4 Karl Heusner Memorial Hospital
5 Pickwick Club, Lindbergh's Landing
6 Fiesta Inn Belize
7 City Center Auditorium
8 XS Nightclub
9 Maskall Bus Stop

Belize City

0   200   400 m
0   200   400 yards

CARIBBEAN SEA

Medical Services

Karl Heusner Memorial Hospital (☎ (2) 31548) is on Princess Margaret Drive in the northern part of town. Many Belizeans with medical problems travel to Chetumal or Mérida (both in Mexico) for treatment. A modern, private clinic is the Clinica de Chetumal (☎ (983) 26508), Avenida Juárez, Chetumal, near the old market and the city's other hospitals. For serious illnesses, Belizeans fly to Houston, Miami or New Orleans.

Business Hours

Note that some shops and businesses close early on Wednesday or Thursday, and many close on Saturday afternoon. Most establishments close on Sunday, when transport schedules may also differ from the rest of the week.

Dangers & Annoyances

There is petty crime in Belize City, so follow some commonsense rules. Don't flash wads of cash, expensive camera equipment or other signs of wealth. Don't change money on the street – not because it's illegal, but because changing money forces you to expose where you keep your cash. Muggers will offer to change money, then just grab your cash and run off. Don't leave valuables in your hotel room. Don't use or deal in illicit drugs.

Don't walk alone at night. It's better to walk in pairs or groups and to stick to major streets in the city center, Fort George and King's Park. Especially avoid walking along Front St south and east of the Swing Bridge; this is a favorite area for muggers.

WALKING TOUR
City Center

One does not come to Belize City to see the sights, but anyone who comes to Belize City does enjoy a walk around – in one or two hours, you can see everything there is to see.

If you prefer to ride, BLASTours (Belize Land Air Sea Tours Ltd, ☎ (1) 48777, fax (2) 73897), 27 Dean St, operates a two-hour, open-air bus tour of the city daily.

Start – of course – at the Swing Bridge. The **Maritime Museum** (☎ (2) 31969) in the Belize Marine Terminal is open Monday to Saturday from 8 am to 5 pm (closed Sunday); admission costs US$3 (US$2 for students, US$0.50 for children under 12).

From the Marine Terminal, cross the Swing Bridge and walk south along Regent St, one block inland from the shore. The large, modern **Commercial Center** to the left, just off the Swing Bridge, replaced a ramshackle market dating from 1820. The ground floor holds a food market; offices and shops are above.

As you start down Regent St, you can't miss the prominent **Court House**, built in 1926 as the headquarters of Belize's colonial administrators. It still serves administrative and judicial functions.

Battlefield Park is on the right just past the Court House. Always busy with vendors, loungers, con men and other slice-of-life segments of Belize City society, the park offers welcome shade in the sweltering midday heat.

Turn left just past the Court House and walk one long block to the waterfront street, called Southern Foreshore, to find the **Bliss Institute**. Baron Bliss was an Englishman with a happy name and a Portuguese title who came to Belize on his yacht to fish. He seems to have fallen in love with Belize without ever having set foot on shore. When he died – not too long after his arrival – he left the bulk of his wealth in trust to the people of Belize. Income from the trust has paid for roads, market buildings, schools, cultural centers and many other worthwhile projects over the years.

The Bliss Institute (☎ (2) 77267) is open Monday to Friday from 8:30 am to noon and 2 to 8 pm and Saturday from 8 am to noon (closed on Sunday). Belize City's prime cultural institution, it is home to the National Arts Council, which stages periodic exhibits, concerts and theatrical works. There's a small display of artifacts from the Mayan archaeological site at Caracol. The **National Library** is upstairs.

BELIZE

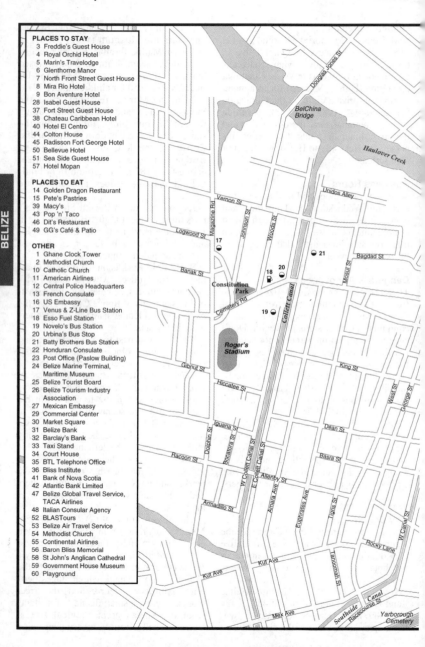

PLACES TO STAY
3 Freddie's Guest House
4 Royal Orchid Hotel
5 Marin's Travelodge
6 Glenthorne Manor
7 North Front Street Guest House
8 Mira Rio Hotel
9 Bon Aventure Hotel
28 Isabel Guest House
37 Fort Street Guest House
38 Chateau Caribbean Hotel
40 Hotel El Centro
44 Colton House
45 Radisson Fort George Hotel
50 Bellevue Hotel
51 Sea Side Guest House
57 Hotel Mopan

PLACES TO EAT
14 Golden Dragon Restaurant
15 Pete's Pastries
39 Macy's
43 Pop 'n' Taco
46 Dit's Restaurant
49 GG's Café & Patio

OTHER
1 Ghane Clock Tower
2 Methodist Church
10 Catholic Church
11 American Airlines
12 Central Police Headquarters
13 French Consulate
16 US Embassy
17 Venus & Z-Line Bus Station
18 Esso Fuel Station
19 Novelo's Bus Station
20 Urbina's Bus Stop
21 Batty Brothers Bus Station
22 Honduran Consulate
23 Post Office (Paslow Building)
24 Belize Marine Terminal,
     Maritime Museum
25 Belize Tourist Board
26 Belize Tourism Industry
     Association
27 Mexican Embassy
29 Commercial Center
30 Market Square
31 Belize Bank
32 Barclay's Bank
33 Taxi Stand
34 Court House
35 BTL Telephone Office
36 Bliss Institute
41 Bank of Nova Scotia
42 Atlantic Bank Limited
47 Belize Global Travel Service,
     TACA Airlines
48 Italian Consular Agency
52 BLASTours
53 Belize Air Travel Service
54 Methodist Church
55 Continental Airlines
56 Baron Bliss Memorial
58 St John's Anglican Cathedral
59 Government House Museum
60 Playground

BELIZE

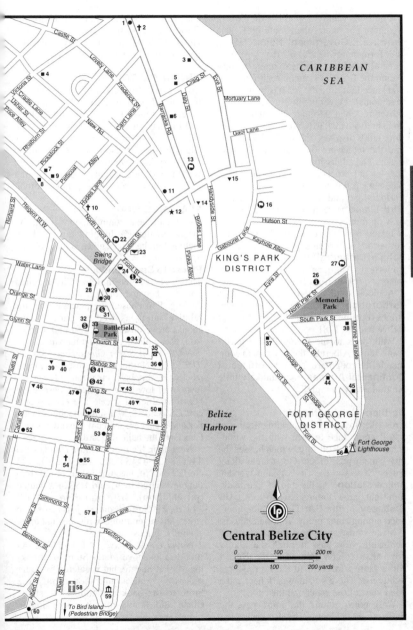

CARIBBEAN
SEA

Mortuary Lane

Gaol Lane

KING'S PARK
DISTRICT

Memorial
Park

Belize
Harbour

FORT GEORGE
DISTRICT

Fort George
Lighthouse

Swing
Bridge

Battlefield
Park

Central Belize City

0   100   200 m

0   100   200 yards

To Bird Island
(Pedestrian Bridge)

Continue walking south to the end of Southern Foreshore, then south on Regent St to reach **Government House** (1814), the former residence of the governor-general. Belize attained independence within the British Commonwealth in 1981, and since that time the job has been purely ceremonial. Government House is now a museum, open Monday through Friday from 8:30 am to 4:30 pm for US$5. The first floor holds displays of historic photographs and the tableware once used at the residence. The admission price is a bit steep to look at old crockery, but you can have a pleasant stroll in the grounds for free.

Down beyond Government House is **Bird Island**, a recreation area accessible only on foot.

Inland from Government House, at the corner of Albert and Regent Sts, is **St John's Cathedral**, the oldest and most important Anglican church in Central America, dating from 1847.

A block southwest of the cathedral is **Yarborough Cemetery**, whose gravestones outline the turbulent history of Belize back to 1781.

Walk back to the Swing Bridge northwards along Albert St, the city's main commercial thoroughfare. Note the **offices of Continental Airlines** in an unlikely little Hindu fantasy 'temple'.

Northern Neighborhoods

Cross the Swing Bridge heading north and you'll come face to face with the woodframe **Paslow Building**, which houses the city's main post office. Go straight along Queen St to see the city's quaint wooden **police station**. At the end of Queen St, turn right onto Gabourel Lane to see the **US Embassy** in the Fort George neighborhood among some pretty Victorian houses.

Make your way to the southern tip of the peninsula. You pass through the luxury hotel district and emerge at the **Baron Bliss Memorial**, next to the Fort George lighthouse. There's a small park here and a good view of the water and the city.

Walk north around the point, pass the Radisson Fort George Hotel on your left

and walk up Marine Parade to **Memorial Park**, between the Chateau Caribbean Hotel and the Mexican Embassy. The park's patch of green lawn is a welcome sight.

ORGANIZED TOURS

You can use Belize City as your base for tours to all parts of Belize. Most middle-range and top-end hotels can arrange half- and full-day guided tours to Altun Ha, the Baboon Sanctuary, the Belize Zoo, Caracol, the Cockscomb Basin Wildlife Sanctuary (also called the Jaguar Reserve), Xunantunich, etc, usually at prices ranging from US$60 to US$150 per person per tour.

PLACES TO STAY

As with all the accommodations listings in the book, the 7% lodging tax has been included in the prices given below.

Places to Stay – budget

The cheapest hotels in Belize City are often not safe because of break-ins and drug dealing. I've chosen the places below for relative safety as well as price. If one should prove unsafe or if you find a good, safe, cheap place, please let me know.

North Front Street Guest House (☎ (2) 77595), 124 North Front St, just east of Pickstock St, is very basic but clean and secure, a favorite of low-budget travelers despite the heavily trafficked street. The eight rooms cost US$8.50/13.50 a single/double. Breakfast and dinner are served if you order ahead. Check out the bulletin board.

Next door, the *Bon Aventure Hotel* (☎ (2) 44248, (2) 44134, fax (2) 31134), 122 North Front St, has nine rooms at US$14 a double (shared bath) and US$24 a double (private bath). *Mira Rio Hotel* (☎ (2) 44970), 59 North Front St, just across the street, has seven rooms with sink and toilet at similar prices.

Isabel Guest House (☎ (2) 73139), PO Box 362, is above Matus Store, overlooking Market Square, but is entered by a rear stairway – walk around the Central Drug Store to the back and follow the signs. Clean and family-run, it offers double rooms with shower for US$24.

Freddie and Tona Griffith keep *Freddie's Guest House* (☎ (2) 44396), 86 Eve St, among the tidiest in Belize. Two rooms share one bath and cost US$21 a double; the room with private bath costs US$23. The showers gleam and shine.

Sea Side Guest House (☎ (2) 78339), 3 Prince St, between Southern Foreshore and Regent St, is operated by Friends Services International, a Quaker service organization. The six clean, simple rooms share baths and rent for US$16.50/24 a single/double. Breakfast is available, as is information on Friends social, educational and environmental projects in Belize.

Marin's Travelodge (☎ (2) 45166), 6 Craig St, is on the upper floor of a fairly well-kept yellow wooden Caribbean house with a comfy swing on the verandah and seven rooms for rent. Shared showers are clean, and the price for the plain rooms is right – US$8/12 a single/double.

Places to Stay – middle

Belize City's prettiest guesthouse is undoubtedly *Colton House* (☎ (2) 44666, fax (2) 30451, coltonhse@btl.net), 9 Cork St, near the Radisson Fort George Hotel. The gracious old wooden colonial house (1928) has been beautifully restored by Alan and Ondina Colton. Large, airy, cheerful, immaculate rooms with fan and private bath cost US$40/48/56 a single/double/triple; add US$5 for air-con. Morning coffee is served, but no meals. A garden apartment with kitchen rents for slightly more.

Just up the street, the *Fort Street Guest House* (☎ (2) 30116, fax (2) 78808, fortst@btl.net), 4 Fort St, is renowned more for its restaurant than for its six guestrooms with fan and shared bath, but the rooms are comfortable enough and priced at US$65, breakfast included.

Glenthorne Manor (☎ (2) 44212), 27 Barracks Rd (PO Box 1278), is a nice Victorian house with a small garden, high ceilings and eclectic furnishings. There are only four rooms, all with breakfast included: US$35/45/50 for a single/double/triple. Get the suite with its own verandah if it's available.

Hotel El Centro (☎ (2) 75077, (2) 77739, fax (2) 74553), 4 Bishop St (PO Box 2267), has a marble facade and 12 small, tidy, modern double guestrooms with cable TV, phone and air-con for US$45.

Hotel Mopan (☎ (2) 73356, (2) 77351, fax (2) 75383), 55 Regent St, is a big old Caribbean-style wood-frame place. The very basic rooms cost US$30/40/45/50 a single/double/triple/quad with only a fan, US$40/50/60/70 with air-con, and the ambiance is pure Belize. Meals are served, and there's a congenial bar.

Royal Orchid Hotel (☎ (2) 32783, fax (2) 32789), New Rd at Victoria St, is a modern hotel without the homey feel of the city's guesthouses, but with 22 air-conditioned rooms equipped with private bath, cable TV and fans. There's a restaurant and bar. Rooms cost US$50/60 a single/double.

Chateau Caribbean Hotel (☎ (2) 30800, fax (2) 30900), 6 Marine Parade (PO Box 947), by Memorial Park, was once a gracious old Belizean mansion, and then a hospital; it's now a comfortable if simple hotel with 25 air-conditioned guestrooms and a dining room. Rates are US$74/84/95/102 a single/double/triple/quad, tax included.

The 35-room *Bellevue Hotel* (☎ (2) 77051, fax (2) 73253, fins@btl.net), 5 Southern Foreshore (PO Box 428), near King St, is in the city center not far from the Bliss Institute. The hotel's unimpressive facade hides a tidy, modern interior with 35 comfortable, air-conditioned, TV-equipped rooms (US$84/88 per single/double). There's a restaurant and bar.

Places to Stay – top end

The city's longtime favorite is the *Radisson Fort George Hotel* (☎ (2) 33333, (2) 77400, fax (2) 73820), 2 Marine Parade (PO Box 321). Its 76 air-conditioned rooms have all the comforts; those in the Club Section are larger. Besides a swimming pool, a good restaurant and a bar, the Fort George has its own boat dock for cruise and fishing craft. Rooms cost US$149 to US$181 a single, US$11 more for a double. For reservations in the USA call ☎ (800) 333-3333, in the UK (0800) 89-1999.

The 120-room *Fiesta Inn Belize* (☎ (2) 32670, fax (2) 32660), Barracks Rd, Kings Park, northeast of the city center, was formerly the Ramada Royal Reef Hotel. It has a swimming pool and a marina, and rates are US$85 to US$105. For reservations in the USA call ☎ (800) 343-7821, in the UK (0171) 734-9354.

Belize Biltmore Plaza (☎ (2) 32302, fax (2) 32301), Mile 3, Northern Hwy, is in the Bella Vista section, 4.5 km north of the city center on the way to Ladyville and Goldson International Airport. The 90 aircon rooms have no sea views and thus offer a good value for the money at US$77 to US$88 a single or double. The Victorian Room's cuisine is among the tastiest in the city, and the bar is often astir with karaoke or live music.

PLACES TO EAT

Belize City is not noted for its cuisine, but there is some decent food. Unless otherwise noted, all restaurants are closed on Sunday.

GG's Café & Patio (☎ (2) 74378), 2-B King St, may be the tidiest little eatery in the city. Arched windows and a tiled floor give it a modern feel, and the pretty patio to the left of the cafe is the place to eat in good weather. 'The best hamburgers in town' cost around US$3 or US$4; big plates of rice and beans with beef, chicken or pork are about the same. GG's is open from 11:30 am to 2:30 pm and 5:30 to 9 pm (until 10 pm on Friday and Saturday).

Macy's (☎ (2) 73419), 18 Bishop St, has consistently good Caribbean Creole cooking, friendly service and decent prices. Fish fillet with rice and beans costs about US$4, armadillo or wild boar a bit more. Hours are 11:30 am to 10 pm.

Dit's Restaurant (☎ (2) 33330), 50 King St, is a homey place with powerful fans and a loyal local clientele who come for huge portions and low prices. Rice and beans with beef, pork or chicken costs US$3, and burgers are a mere US$1.50. Cakes and

pies make a good dessert at US$1 per slice. Dit's is open from 8 am to 9 pm every day.

Pete's Pastries (☎ (2) 44974), 41 Queen St (near Handyside St), serves good cakes, tarts, and pies of fruit or meat. A slice and a soft drink costs US$1; my favorite is the raisin pie. You might try Pete's famous cowfoot soup, served on Saturday only (US$1.75) or a ham and cheese sandwich (US$1.50). Pete's is open from 8:30 am to 7 pm (8 am to 6 pm on Sunday).

Golden Dragon Chinese Restaurant (☎ (2) 72817), in a cul-de-sac off Queen St, is one of the city's several Chinese restaurants, with a long menu heavy on chow mein and chop suey, wonton soup and sweet-and-sour dishes. Full meals cost US$6 to US$14.

Pop 'n' Taco, at the corner of King and Regent Sts, serves simple Belizean, Chinese and Mexican food at low prices, and is open on Sunday.

Fort Street Restaurant (☎ (2) 30116), 4 Fort St, is a nice old house with dining tables set up in its 1st-floor rooms and on its wraparound verandah. The cuisine is nouvelle, with California inspiration and strengths in Belizean seafood. Prices are not low – a full dinner with wine or beer might cost US$30 to US$40 per person – but this is perhaps the most pleasant and romantic dining experience to be had in Belize City. Breakfast is served every day; lunch and dinner are served daily except Sunday.

The dining room at the *Radisson Fort George Hotel* (tel (2) 77400) has perhaps the most genteel service in the city, and good food at moderate prices. For a hearty burger and a beer (US$12), try the adjoining *Paddles* lounge. You might also try the dining rooms at the *Bellevue* and *Chateau Caribbean* hotels, also open seven days a week.

ENTERTAINMENT

There's lots of interesting action at night in Belize City. The problem is that much of it is illegal or dangerous.

Be judicious in your choice of nightspots. Clubs and bars that look like dives probably are. If drugs are in evidence, there's lots of room for trouble, and as a foreigner you'll have a hard time blending into the background.

The lounges at the upmarket hotels – *Radisson Fort George, Fiesta Inn Belize* – are sedate, respectable and safe. The *Belize Biltmore Plaza Hotel* has karaoke many nights, live music on others.

XS, Freetown Rd at Mapp St, is the latest hot nightspot. Locals laud it for its lack of violence and its safe parking as well as its music and drinks. Try also *Lindbergh's Landing*, next to the Pickwick Club in King's Park across from the Fiesta Inn Belize. The longtime local favorite is the *Lumba Yaad*, 300 meters northwest of Belcan Junction, just northwest of a real lumber yard.

GETTING THERE & AWAY
Buses, boats and planes take you from Belize City to any other part of the country. See Getting Around in the Belize Getting There & Around chapter for details.

GETTING AROUND
Belize City is not large, and most people get around on foot.

To/From the Airports
The taxi fare to or from the international airport is US$15. You might want to approach other passengers about sharing a cab to the city center.

It takes about half an hour to walk from the air terminal three km out the access road to the Northern Hwy; from here it's easy to catch a bus going either north or south.

Going to Municipal Airport, normal city taxi fares apply (see below).

Taxi
Trips by taxi within Belize City (including to and from Municipal Airport) cost US$2.50 for one person, US$6 for two or three and US$8 for four.

Car & Motorcycle
See Getting Around in the Belize Getting There & Around chapter for rental details.

BELIZE

The Cayes

Belize's 290-km-long barrier reef, the longest in the Western Hemisphere, is the eastern edge of the limestone shelf which underlies most of the Mayan lands. To the west of the reef the sea is very shallow – usually not much more than four or five meters deep – which allows numerous islands called cayes (pronounced 'keys') to bask in warm waters.

Of the dozens of cayes, large and small, which dot the blue waters of the Caribbean off the Belizean coast, the two most popular with travelers are Caye Caulker and Ambergris Caye. Caulker is commonly thought of as the low-budget island, where hotels and restaurants are less expensive than on resort-conscious Ambergris, though with Caulker's booming popularity this distinction is blurring.

Both islands have an appealing, laid-back Belizean atmosphere. No one's in a hurry here. Stress doesn't figure in the lives of many islanders. Pedestrian traffic on the sandy, unpaved streets moves at an easy tropical pace. The fastest vehicle is a kid on a bicycle. Motor vehicles are few and mostly parked.

Island residents include Creoles, mestizos and a few transplanted North Americans and Europeans. They run lobster- and conch-fishing boats, hotels and pensions, little eateries and island businesses which supply the few things necessary in a benevolent tropical climate.

CAYE CAULKER
Population 800

Approaching Caye Caulker on the boat from Belize City, you glide along the eastern shore, which is overhung with palm trees. Dozens of wooden docks jut out from the shore to give moorings to boats. Off to the east, about two km away, the barrier reef is marked by a thin white line of surf.

Caye Caulker (called Hicaco in Spanish, sometimes Corker in English) lies some 33 km north of Belize City and 24 km south of Ambergris Caye. The island is about seven km long from north to south, and is only about 600 meters wide at its widest point. Mangrove covers much of the shore and coconut palms provide shade. The village is on the southern portion of the island. Actually Caulker is now two islands, since Hurricane Hattie split the island just north of the village. The split is called, simply, The Split (or The Cut). It has a tiny beach, with swift currents running through it. North of The Split – now crossable by a small ferry – is mostly undeveloped land, but that won't last long.

You disembark and wander ashore to find a place of sandy unpaved 'streets' which are actually more like paths. The government has carefully placed 'Go Slow' and 'Stop' signs at the appropriate places, even though there are no vehicles in sight and everyone on Caulker naturally goes slow and stops frequently. The stops are often to get a beer – most right hands spend much of the day wrapped around a cold one. Virtually constant sea breezes keep the island comfortable even in Belize's sultry heat. If the wind dies, the heat immediately becomes noticeable, as do the sandflies and mosquitoes.

Many gardens and paths on the island have borders of conch shells, and every house has its 'catchment', or large cistern, to catch rainwater for drinking.

Orientation & Information

The village has two principal streets: Front St to the east and Back St to the west. The distance from The Split in the north to Shirley's Guest House at the southern edge of the village is little more than one km.

The BTL telephone office is open Monday to Friday from 8 am to noon and 1 to 4 pm and Saturday from 8 am to noon (closed on Sunday). The BTL office fax (fax (22) 2239) serves the whole island.

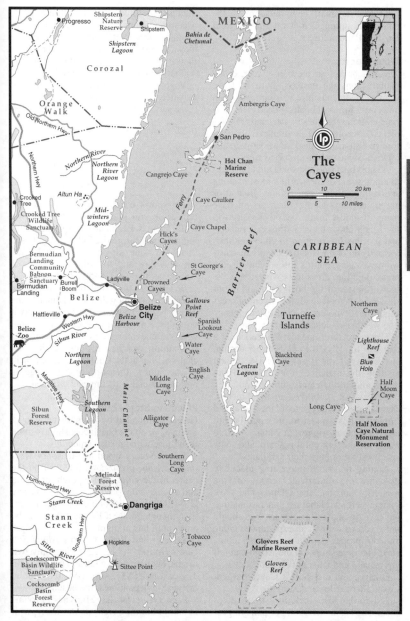

BELIZE

There's a small new museum in the Island Shopping Center on Barrier Reef Drive at Pelican Street.

Water Sports

The surf breaks on the barrier reef, easily visible from the eastern shore of Caye Caulker. Don't attempt to swim out to it, however – the local boaters speed their powerful craft through these waters and are completely heedless of swimmers. Several foreign visitors have died from boat-propeller injuries. Swim only in protected areas.

A short boat ride takes you out to the reef to enjoy some of the world's most exciting snorkeling, diving and fishing. Boat trips are big business on the island, so you have many to choose from. Ask other visitors to the island about their boating experiences, and use this information to choose a boat. Virtually all of the island residents are trustworthy boaters, but it's still good to discuss price, duration, areas to be visited and the seaworthiness of the boat. Boat and motor should be in good condition. Even sailboats should have motors in case of emergency (the weather can change quickly here).

There are three standard excursions: a reef trip for US$10 to US$30 per person, Hol Chan Marine Reserve for US$25 and visiting the manatees for US$30. Tours depart midmorning and return around 5 pm.

Underwater visibility is up to 60 meters. The variety of underwater plants, coral and tropical fish is wonderful. Be careful not to touch the coral, to prevent damage both to it and to yourself; coral is sharp, and some species sting or burn their assailants.

Among the more interesting places to dive are the underwater caves off the western shore of the island. The cave system here is elaborate and fascinating, but cave diving is a special art. You should not go down without an experienced guide and the proper equipment (strong lights, etc). The dive shops on the island can tell you what – and what not – to do.

Other goals are Goff's Caye, Sargent Caye, Shark Alley and Stingray Alley.

A one-day trip including three dives costs US$175 to US$200 per person, gear

included. A three-day trip with meals and accommodations costs US$325 to US$350. Compare prices at several dive shops as they can vary significantly. For more information on dive sites, see the section on Ambergris Caye in this chapter.

Voyages for diving, snorkeling or manatee watching can be arranged through these services:

Belize Diving Service	(☎ (22) 2143, fax (22) 2217)
Carlos Ayala	At Cindy's Café
Chocolate's	(☎ (22) 22151)
Frenchie's Diving	(☎ (22) 2234, fax (22) 2074)

Water-sports equipment is available for rent at several places in town, including Pattie's Bar & Beach at The Split. Snorkeling gear costs around US$5 per day, beach floats the same, sit-on sea kayaks US$20 per half-day and a Hobie Cat sailboat US$20 per hour or US$50 a half-day.

Beachgoers will find the water warm, clear and blue, but will not find much in the way of beach. Though there's lots of sand, it doesn't seem to arrange itself in nice, long, wide stretches along the shore. Most of your sunbathing will be on docks or in deck chairs at your hotel. Caulker's public beach, at The Split to the north of the village, is nothing special – it's tiny and crowded.

Places to Stay – budget

Hotels surrounded by trees, or with some grounds, or on the beach cost slightly more than those without such amenities.

The two-story wood-and-masonry *Martinez Caribbean Inn* (☎ (22) 2113) at the center of the village has a porch for sitting and rooms with private shower. You pay US$12/20 a single/double for a good location, though the Reef Bar next door can be noisy until late at night.

Sylvano and Kathy Canto's *Island Sun Guest House* (☎ (22) 2215) has only two rooms, but both have a fan and private bath. The cost is US$17.50 or US$20 a double. It's neat, quiet and near the beach.

Lena's Hotel (☎ (22) 2106) has 11 rooms in an old building right on the water, with

BELIZE

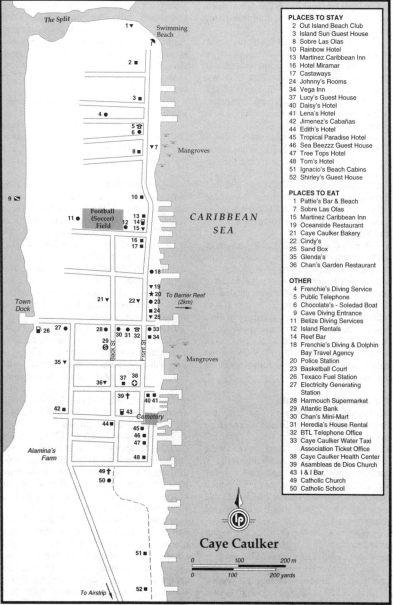

PLACES TO STAY
2   Out Island Beach Club
3   Island Sun Guest House
8   Sobre Las Olas
10 Rainbow Hotel
13 Martinez Caribbean Inn
16 Hotel Miramar
17 Castaways
24 Johnny's Rooms
34 Vega Inn
37 Lucy's Guest House
40 Daisy's Hotel
41 Lena's Hotel
42 Jimenez's Cabañas
44 Edith's Hotel
45 Tropical Paradise Hotel
46 Sea Beezzz Guest House
47 Tree Tops Hotel
48 Tom's Hotel
51 Ignacio's Beach Cabins
52 Shirley's Guest House

PLACES TO EAT
1   Pattie's Bar & Beach
7   Sobre Las Olas
15 Martinez Caribbean Inn
19 Oceanside Restaurant
21 Caye Caulker Bakery
22 Cindy's
25 Sand Box
35 Glenda's
36 Chan's Garden Restaurant

OTHER
4   Frenchie's Diving Service
5   Public Telephone
6   Chocolate's - Soledad Boat
9   Cave Diving Entrance
11 Belize Diving Services
12 Island Rentals
14 Reef Bar
18 Frenchie's Diving & Dolphin
    Bay Travel Agency
20 Police Station
23 Basketball Court
26 Texaco Fuel Station
27 Electricity Generating
    Station
28 Harmouch Supermarket
29 Atlantic Bank
30 Chan's Mini-Mart
31 Heredia's House Rental
32 BTL Telephone Office
33 Caye Caulker Water Taxi
    Association Ticket Office
38 Caye Caulker Health Center
39 Asambleas de Dios Church
43 I & I Bar
49 Catholic Church
50 Catholic School

Caye Caulker

no grounds to speak of. Rates are high for what you get: US$20/30 a double without/ with private shower.

Daisy's Hotel (☎ (22) 2123) has 11 rooms in several blue-and-white buildings which get full sun most of the day. Rooms with table or floor fan and shared bath cost US$14 a double; with private shower the rate is US$21.

Edith's Hotel is tidy and proper, with tiny rooms, each with a private shower; they're priced at US$18 a single, US$21 a double (one bed) or US$23 a double (two beds).

Hotel Miramar (☎ (22) 2157) has rooms on two floors in a building facing the sea. Rooms with private bath cost US$25.

Castaways (☎ (22) 2294) has six rooms. They're quite clean and cost a reasonable US$12/16 a single/double. There's a decent restaurant (main courses for around US$8) and bar as well.

Johnny's Rooms (☎ (22) 2149) has clean hotel rooms for US$18 a double and cabañas with private bath for US$26.

Ignacio's Beach Cabins is a collection of very simple thatched cottages shaded by dozens of palms. Ignacio is the island eccentric, defending his territory with a machete and refusing to spray against sand fleas. But the beachfront location is good, as are the prices: US$15 to US$25 per hut with private shower, depending upon the hut and the season.

Places to Stay – middle

My favorite place has got to be Terry and Doris Creasey's tidy, friendly *Tree Tops Hotel* (☎ (22) 2008, fax (22) 2115), PO Box 1648, Belize City. Terry served in the British army here, and decided to retire in paradise. Five bright rooms have a fridge and TV, share baths and cost US$22.50 a double without sea view, US$25 a double with sea view; one room with private shower goes for US$30.

Jimenez's Cabañas (☎ (22) 2175) has little thatched huts with walls of sticks, each with a private shower. The place is quaint, quiet, relaxing, atmospheric and family-run, and constitutes a very good value at US$22 to US$30 a double, US$32 a triple and US$36 a quad.

Lucy's Guest House is not on the shore, but it has some trees and gardens, and porches off the bungalows for hanging hammocks. Prices are good: a double with shared bath costs US$15 in summer, US$22 in winter; a double with private shower costs US$25 in summer, US$32 in winter.

Tom's Hotel (☎ (22) 2102) has nice, tidy, white buildings on the beach. The 20 cheapest, very simple, waterless rooms cost US$10/12 a single/double; bigger rooms in the newer building go for US$19/22; and the comfortable cabins with private shower cost US$30.

Sobre Las Olas (☎ /fax (22) 2243) is mostly a restaurant and bar, but there are a few good rooms for rent: US$33 for a double with fan and shower and US$50 for a triple with air-con and shower.

The *Out Island Beach Club* (☎ (22) 2156) is a group of cabins and a more modern hotel building just south of The Split. The cabins rent for US$30 and have the advantage of being only steps from The Split's safe swimming beach. The hotel rooms are more expensive.

Tropical Paradise Hotel (☎ (22) 2124, fax (22) 2225) has six tidy, paneled rooms in a long wooden building (US$28/32 a single/double with private shower and ceiling fan) and an equal number of individual yellow cabins with ceiling fan and private bath (some with tub) for US$36/42. There's a decent restaurant and bar and a big dock for boats or sunning.

Shirley's Guest House (☎ (22) 2145, fax (22) 2264), along the southeastern shore, has nice bungalows with four rooms (two upstairs, two down) boasting mahogany floors, good ventilation and fans. Each pair of rooms shares a bath. Rates are US$36 a single and US$40 to US$50 a double.

Sea Beezzz Guest House (☎ (22) 2176) is a solid, two-story house on the shore with a nice patio garden in front. Safe, secure and comfortable, with hot water in the private showers and a dining-room service for all three meals, its only disadvantage is that it closes down for the summer. Rates are US$40 to US$60 per room.

Rainbow Hotel (☎ (22) 2123, fax (22) 2172), just north of the boat docks, is a two-story concrete building. Plain, clean, somewhat cell-like rooms go for US$35 (ground floor) or US$40 (upper floor) a double with tiled private shower and air-con.

Vega Inn (☎ (22) 2142, fax (22) 2269), owned by the congenial Vega family – Antonio ('Tony'), Lidia and Maria – has several tidy, waterless rooms upstairs in a wooden house, with clean showers down the hall; these go for US$20/25 a single/double. Other, much bigger rooms with private shower are in a concrete building and cost US$50/60. All rooms have wall fans; there's some shady space in front of the house for sitting. An adjoining shady camping area is just the place to pitch your tent, for US$7.50 per person. The Vegas rent snorkeling equipment and little sailboats (Sunfish), and can sign you up for snorkeling or sportfishing trips. For reservations, write to them at PO Box 701, Belize City.

Heredia's House Rental (☎ (22) 2132) can arrange room or house rentals for two days or longer. Call, or write to PO Box 1018, Belize City.

Places to Eat

Though they serve such 'luxury' items as lobster and conch, there are no fancy restaurants on Caulker. Even so, prices are not dirt cheap because much must be brought from the mainland.

Do your part to avoid illegal lobster fishing: don't order lobster off-season (mid-March to mid-July), and complain if they serve you a 'short' (a lobster below the legal size for harvest).

Glenda's, on the west side of the island, is favored for breakfast (7 to 10 am): eggs, bacon or ham, bread and coffee for US$3. A big glass of fresh-squeezed orange juice goes for US$1. Lunch is served from noon to 3 pm. Another good place for breakfast and good coffee is *Cindy's Café*, opposite the basketball court on Front St.

The *Caye Caulker Bakery* on Back St is the place to pick up fresh bread, rolls and similar goodies. Other picnic supplies are available at the *Harmouch Supermarket* and *Chan's Mini-Mart*.

Sobre Las Olas (☎ /fax 2243), north of the center, on the water, is a tidy open-air place with a wooden dock, a bar and umbrella-topped tables and Belgian managers. Belizean and continental fare is served from 7 am to 10 pm every day but Monday. Expect to pay US$8 to US$12 for a full meal.

The *Sand Box* is perhaps the island's most popular place to dine and drink. All three meals (and lots of Belikin) are served. For dinner, try the fish with spicy banana chutney (US$6) or barbecued chicken for less. Pasta plates (including vegetarian lasagna) cost about the same.

Pattie's Bar & Beach at The Split serves a surprisingly extensive menu of burgers, fajitas, vegetable soups and so forth to swimmers and hangers-about. A substantial lunch can be had for US$5 to US$8. The faithful stay here until long after dark.

The *Martinez Caribbean Inn* restaurant serves sandwiches, burgers and antojitos (garnaches, tacos, panuchos, etc), as well as rice and beans with chicken or lobster. For breakfast, a coffee and a fruit plate costs less than US$4. Lunch or dinner can cost US$4 to US$10. They concoct a tasty rum punch here, sold by the bottle or the glass.

Chan's Garden Restaurant has reasonably authentic Chinese food (the owner is from Hong Kong) at moderate prices.

The *Oceanside Restaurant* features daily specials, posted on its blackboard menu.

The restaurant at the *Tropical Paradise Hotel* is busy all day because it serves the island's most consistently good food in big portions at decent prices. In the light, cheerful dining room, breakfast is served from 8 am to noon, lunch from 11:30 am to 2 pm and dinner from 6 to 10 pm. You can order curried shrimp or lobster for US$12 or many other things for less.

Entertainment

After one evening on the island, you'll know what there is to do after the sun goes down. The *Reef Bar*, by the Martinez Caribbean Hotel, has a sand floor and tables that have clusters of bottles (mostly beer) as their

BELIZE

semipermanent centerpiece. This is the gathering, sipping and talking place for the locals. *I & I* is a bit classier, with reggae playing nonstop, setting the proper island mood.

Getting There & Away

Air Most flights between Belize City (Goldson and Municipal airports) and San Pedro on Ambergris Caye stop at Caye Caulker on request. See the Belize Getting There & Around chapter for details.

Boat The Caye Caulker Water Taxi Association runs boats from Caulker to Belize City at 6:45, 8 and 10 am and 3 pm for US$7.50 one way; children five to 10 pay half fare; children under five ride free. Another water taxi goes from Caulker to San Pedro on Ambergris Caye at 10 am (US$7.50), returning from San Pedro at 2:30 pm.

Getting Around

Caulker is so small that most people walk everywhere. There are a few bicycles, and locals with things to carry use electric golf carts. Besides, this is an island – all serious transport is done by boat.

AMBERGRIS CAYE & SAN PEDRO
Population 2000

The largest of Belize's cayes, Ambergris (pronounced am-BER-griss) lies 58 km north of Belize City. It's over 40 km long, and on its northern side almost adjoins Mexican territory.

Most of the island's population lives in the town of San Pedro, near the southern tip. The barrier reef is only one km east of San Pedro. In the morning, before the workday noises begin, stand on one of the docks on the town's eastern side – you can hear the low bass roar of the surf breaking over the reef.

San Pedro started life as a fishing town but is now Belize's prime tourist destination. More than half of the tourists who visit Belize fly straight to San Pedro and use it as their base for excursions elsewhere. Even so, San Pedro is certainly no Cancún, though there has been some small-scale development in recent years.

Like Caye Caulker, Ambergris has an engaging, laid-back atmosphere. A sign in a local restaurant has it right: 'No shirt, no shoes – *no problem!*' San Pedro is sandy streets with little traffic, lots of Caribbean-style wooden buildings (some on stilts), and few people who bother to wear shoes. Everyone is friendly and every visitor is looked upon not as a tourist nor a simple source of dollars, but as a person.

Orientation

It's about one km from the Paradise Resort Hotel (in the northern part of town) to the airport (in the south), so everything is within easy walking distance unless you're burdened with lots of luggage. You'll want a taxi only to reach the few resort hotels which lie several kilometers south of the airport.

San Pedro has three main north-south streets, which used to be called Front St (to the east), Middle St and Back St (to the west). Now these streets have tourist-class names: Barrier Reef Drive, Pescador Drive and Angel Coral Drive, but some islanders might still use the old names.

Information

Ambergris Caye has its own website: www.ambergriscaye.com.

Money You can change money easily in San Pedro, and US cash and travelers' checks are accepted in most establishments.

Atlantic Bank Limited (☎ (26) 2195), on Barrier Reef Drive, is open Monday, Tuesday and Thursday from 8 am to noon and 1 to 3 pm, Wednesday from 8 am to 1 pm, Friday from 8 am to 1 pm and 3 to 6 pm and Saturday from 8:30 am to noon. Nearby, the Belize Bank is open Monday to Thursday from 8 am to 3 pm, Friday from 8 am to 1 pm and 3 to 6 pm and Saturday from 8:30 am to noon.

Post & Communications The post office is on Bucaneer St off Barrier Reef Drive beside the Alijua Hotel Suites. Hours are 8 am to noon and 1 to 5 pm on weekdays (until 4:30 pm on Friday). It's closed on Saturday and Sunday.

BELIZE

San Pedro
(Ambergris Caye)

| 0 | 75 | 150 m |
| 0 | 75 | 150 yards |

PLACES TO STAY
2 Rock's Inn
6 Paradise Resort Hotel
7 Milo's Hotel
11 Hotel San Pedrano
13 Tomas Hotel
14 Lily's Caribbean Lodge
15 Mayan Princess Resort
   Hotel
18 Hotel Casablanca
22 Martha's Hotel & Food
   Shop
24 Barrier Reef Hotel
   & Restaurant
31 Alijua Hotel Suites
42 Coral Beach Hotel
43 Spindrift Hotel
55 Ruby's (Rubie's) Hotel
56 San Pedro
   Holiday Hotel

59 Ramon's Village
61 Sun Breeze Beach
   Hotel

PLACES TO EAT
14 Lily's Restaurant
17 Island Style Food Palace
18 Lagoon Restaurant
19 Ambergris Delight
21 Elvi's Kitchen
24 Barrier Reef Hotel
   & Restaurant
33 Estel's Dine by the Sea
37 Panadería El Centro
39 Casa de Café
43 Little Italy Restaurant
55 Rubie's Caffe
56 Celi's Restaurant,
   The Deli
60 Tropical Take-Out

OTHER
1 Statue
3 BTL Telephone Office
4 Electricity Generating Plant
5 Sandals Bar
8 Polo's EZ-Go Rentals
9 Cemetery
10 San Carlos Medical Clinic
12 Amigos del Mar Dive Shop
16 Andrea & Triple J Boats
   to Belize City
20 Fido's Courtyard
23 Tarzan Club & Cheetah's Bar
25 Basketball Court
26 Mayan Statue
27 Public Telephone
28 Catholic Church
29 Big Daddy's Disco
30 Post Office
32 Atlantic Bank

34 Marinos Bar
35 J's Laundromat
36 Rock's Store
38 Belize Laundry & Dry Cleaning
40 Belize Bank
41 Amigo Travel
44 Municipality, Police Station
45 Aqua Fresh Drinking Water
46 Adventures in Water Sports
47 Tackle Box Bar
48 Hyperbaric Chamber
49 Island Air
50 Lion's Club Medical Clinic
51 Maya Airways, Ramon's
   Wheel Rentals
52 Travel & Tour Belize
53 Hustler Tours
54 Catholic Primary School
55 Rental Center
58 Tropic Air Terminal

The BTL telephone office, up north on Pescador Drive, is open Monday to Friday from 8 am to noon and 1 to 4 pm and Saturday from 8 am to noon (closed on Sunday).

Laundry There are several laundromats at the southern end of Pescador Drive, including J's Laundromat and Belize Laundry & Dry Cleaning.

Medical Services San Carlos Medical Clinic, Pharmacy & Pathology Lab (☎ (26) 2918, (26) 3649, in emergencies (014) 9251), on Pescador just south of Caribeña, treats ailments and does blood tests.

The Lion's Club Medical Clinic is across the street from the Island Air terminal at the airport. Right next door to it is the island's hyperbaric chamber for diving accidents.

Travel & Dive Agencies Most hotels, travel agencies and dive shops in San Pedro can arrange for a day's snorkeling or scuba diving, or for excursions to the mainland lasting one to several days. Here are some of the leading agencies:

Adventures in Watersports – offers all sorts of water sports (including PADI diving certification courses) and inland trips as well. Barrier Reef Drive at Black Coral St (☎ (26) 3706, fax (26) 3707, in the USA (800) 648-8990, advwtrspts@btl.net)

Amigo Travel – is a travel agency which can arrange flights and guided tours inland. Barrier Reef Drive (☎ (26) 2180, fax (26) 2192, amigotrav@btl.net)

Amigos del Mar Dive Shop – rents scuba and snorkeling gear and runs diving and fishing trips. On the dock, east of Lili's Restaurant (☎ (26) 2706, (26) 3239, fax (26) 2648)

Belize Dive Connection – offers diving and snorkeling tours. Coconut Drive, PO Box 66 (☎ (26) 2797, fax (26) 2892)

Blue Hole Dive Center – offers a variety of snorkeling and diving trips, including overnight excursions, and is known for the competence and professionalism of its staff. At the Spindrift Hotel on Barrier Reef Drive (☎ (26) 2982, bluehole@btl.net)

Coral Beach Hotel & Dive Club – arranges a variety of trips, including overnight boat excursions, and gets high marks from experienced divers. (☎ (26) 2013, fax (26) 2864, forman@btl.net)

Travel & Tour Belize – is a travel agency. PO Box 42, Barrier Reef Drive at Bucaneer St, in the Alijua Hotel Suites building (☎ (26) 2535, fax (26) 2185)

Water Sports

Ambergris is good for all water sports: scuba diving, snorkeling, sailboarding, boating, swimming, deep-sea fishing and sunbathing. Many island hotels have their own dive shops which rent equipment, provide instruction and organize diving excursions. In fact, just about any local can put you in touch with someone organizing water-sports trips.

Hire a fishing boat for US$135 a day (deep-sea fishing for US$350 a day), or a boat and guide for a two-tank dive (US$45, plus equipment rental costs of about US$36). Take a full diving certification course (US$350) or just sign up for a full-day barbecue beach picnic on a remote beach (US$40, lunch included). Rent a canoe (US$30 a day) or a snorkel, mask and fins (US$8). You could also take a bird watching cruise (US$20) or go sailing and snorkeling for the day (US$35, drinks included).

Among the favorite seafaring destinations near and far are:

- Blue Hole – a deep sinkhole of vivid blue water where you can dive to 40 meters, observing the cave with diving lights

- Caye Caulker North Island – the relatively uninhabited northern part of Caulker, with good snorkeling, swimming and places for a beach barbecue

- Glover's Reef – about 50 km east of Dangriga, one of only three coral atolls in the Western Hemisphere

- Half Moon Caye – a small island on Lighthouse Reef, 113 km east of Belize City, with a lighthouse, excellent beaches and spectacular submerged walls teeming with marine flora and fauna (underwater visibility can extend more than 60 meters); the caye is a bird sanctuary and home to the rare pink-footed booby

- Hol Chan Marine Reserve – with submerged canyons 30 meters deep, busy with large fish; the canyon walls are covered with colorful sponges

- Lighthouse Reef (which includes Half Moon Caye) – another of the three coral atolls in the Western Hemisphere, lying 100 km east of Belize City

- Mexico Cave – filled with colorful sponges, lobsters and shrimp

- Palmetto Reef – with lots of canyons, surge channels and many varieties of coral (hard and soft), sponges and fish

- Punta Arena – an area of underwater canyons and sea caves teeming with fish, rays, turtles, sponges and coral

- San Pedro Cut – the large break in the barrier reef, the cut is used by the larger fishing and pleasure boats

- Tres Cocos Cut – a natural break in the barrier reef that attracts a variety of marine life

- Turneffe Islands – the Western Hemisphere's third coral atoll, 30 km east of Belize City, teeming with coral and alive with fish and large rays

Swimming is best off the pier at the Paradise Resort Hotel. All beaches are public, and you can probably use their lounge chairs if it's a slow day. At Ramon's Village there is a thatched cabaña for sunset watching at the end of the pier.

Organized Tours
Tours by Boat Several boats run trips to the best diving spots. *Off-Shore Express* is a boat with sleeping and dining facilities for dive trips to the Blue Hole, Half Moon Caye and the Turneffe Islands. The 55-foot *Manta IV* has similar itineraries, as does the 38-foot *Blue Hole Express*. Reserve space through the Blue Hole Dive Center or the Coral Beach Hotel & Dive Club (see above).

The *Winnie Estelle* (☎ (26) 2394, fax (26) 2576), 15 Barrier Reef Drive, a 66-foot island trader moored at the Paradise Resort Hotel pier, goes out on daily snorkeling trips to Caye Caulker.

The *Reef Seeker* glass-bottom boat, based at the San Pedro Holiday Hotel, makes daily

reef trips for US$12.50 per adult (half price for kids), and occasional trips upriver to the Altun Ha ruins (US$60 per person).

Mainland Tours Many visitors to Belize fly to Ambergris and make it their base for excursions by plane or boat to other parts of this small country. Tours are available to the Mayan ruins at Altun Ha and Xunantunich, to the Belize Zoo, Crooked Tree Bird Sanctuary, the Baboon Sanctuary, Mountain Pine Ridge and even to Tikal (Guatemala). Any hotel or travel agency can fill you in on tours.

Places to Stay – budget
Wherever you stay, you'll never be more than a minute's walk from the water. All but the cheapest hotels accept major credit cards. Prices below include 7% tax.

Ruby's (or *Rubie's*) *Hotel* (☎ (26) 2063, fax (26) 2434), PO Box 56, at the south end of Barrier Reef Drive, is close to the airport and right on the water. Five of the nine rooms here have a private shower; not all of the rooms overlook the sea. Rates are US$15/20 a single/double with shared bath and US$29 to US$38 a double with private bath.

Tomas Hotel (☎ (26) 2061), Barrier Reef Drive, offers a very good value for your money. This family-run place charges US$21 (summer) or US$28 (winter) for eight light, airy double rooms with private bath (some with tub). Two rooms have double beds; the others have a double and a single, making them good for families.

Milo's Hotel (☎ (26) 2033), PO Box 21, on Barrier Reef Drive on the north side of town, has nine small, dark, fairly dismal rooms above a shop in a blue-and-white Caribbean-style building. It's quiet and cheap, and often full for those reasons. Rooms with shared shower go for US$11/14/19 a single/double/triple. Newer rooms with private shower and air-con cost US$22.

Martha's Hotel (☎ (26) 2053, fax (26) 2589), Ambergris St at Pescador Drive, has 16 rooms. All have a private bath, and sometimes the sink is in the room because the bathroom is so small. Rooms 11 and 12 are lighter and airier than the rest. Rates are US$24/35/47/59 a single/double/triple/quad from November through April and slightly cheaper in summer.

Hotel San Pedrano (☎ (26) 2054, fax (26) 2093), Barrier Reef Drive at Caribeña St, has one apartment and seven rooms, all with fan and private bath. Though most rooms don't have ocean views, there's a wraparound porch. The rooms rent for US$29/35/43/49 a single/ double/triple/quad in winter; summer prices are about 17% to 20% lower. Add US$10 per room for air-con.

Lily's Caribbean Lodge (☎ (26) 2059), off the eastern end of Caribeña St and facing the sea, has 10 clean, pleasant rooms; several (especially those on the top floor) have good sea views. Air-con doubles the winter cost of US$35 to US$40. There's a tidy restaurant on the ground floor.

Places to Stay – middle
Many of these hotels cater to divers, who are often willing to pay more for a room – any room – if the diving's good. Note that some of these hotels charge 10% or 15% for service in addition to the 7% government room tax. I've included both of these extra charges in the rates quoted below.

The *Barrier Reef Hotel* (☎ (26) 2075, fax (26) 2719, barriereef@btl.net), on Barrier Reef Drive in the center of town, is a landmark, its attractive Caribbean wood-frame construction captured by countless tourist cameras daily. Most of the 10 rooms are not in this structure, however, but in a newer and less charming concrete-block addition at the back. The bonus here is air-con – good on sticky, hot days. Winter rates are US$52/70/80 a single/double/triple.

Spindrift Hotel (☎ (26) 2018, (26) 2174, fax (26) 2251, in the USA (800) 688-0161), Bucaneer St at Barrier Reef Drive, has a good location right in the center of town on the beach. It's a modern concrete building with 30 rooms ranging from small ones with one double bed, ceiling fan and a view of the street (US$53 a double) to ones with two double beds, air-con and a view of the sea (US$93 a double). There are also several apartments (US$123 to US$186).

Hotel Casablanca (☎ (26) 2327, fax (26) 2992), on Pescador Drive above the Lagoon Restaurant, charges US$25 for a small double with fan and shared bath and US$50 for a large double with air-con and breakfast.

San Pedro Holiday Hotel (☎ (26) 2014, fax (26) 2295), PO Box 1140, Belize City, is on Barrier Reef Drive in the southern part of town. It's a comfortable modern building on the beach, with a full list of services. Rates are US$95 to US$140 for air-con double rooms, bungalows and apartments, many with refrigerator.

Changes in Latitude B&B (☎ /fax (26) 2986) is a trim two-story guesthouse south of the airport on Coconut Drive, just north of the Belize Yacht Club, offering six ground-floor rooms with private bath for US$65 with fan, US$10 more with air-con. Here you're a short block inland from the beach. The *Seychelles Guest House* (☎ (26) 3817), across the road, is a bit simpler and cheaper.

Coral Beach Hotel (☎ (26) 2013, fax (26) 2864), PO Box 16, on Barrier Reef Drive, is a simple diver's hotel charging US$53/76/90 a single/double/triple for air-con rooms.

Places to Stay – top end
Ambergris has many resort hotels, but they aren't huge, Cancún-style high-rises. On Ambergris, a resort is often a collection of thatched bungalows which can house upwards of two dozen people. All rooms mentioned below have a private bath; most have air-con as well. Many top-end hotels offer free taxi shuttle from the airport.

Sun Breeze Beach Hotel (☎ (26) 2191, fax (26) 2346), PO Box 14, at the southern end of Barrier Reef Drive not far from the airport, is a Mexican-style two-story concrete building with a sandy inner court opening towards the beach. Shady tiled porticos set with easy chairs are great for lounging and watching nothing happen. The 34 air-conditioned rooms each have two double beds, cable TV and a private bath. Prices are US$101 to US$140 a single, US$115 to US$150 a double and US$125 to US$160 a triple in winter.

Rock's Inn (☎ (26) 2326, fax (26) 2358), PO Box 50, is a small three-story all-suite hotel on the beach at the northern end of town. Suites include fully furnished kitchen and cost US$111 to US$146 a double, up to US$170 for four persons in the best suite.

Alijua Hotel Suites (☎ (26) 2791, fax (26) 2362), 41 Barrier Reef Drive, is in the center a short block from the beach, with similar suite accommodations priced at US$88/105/117/129 a single/double/triple/quad.

Mayan Princess Resort Hotel (☎ (26) 2778, fax (26) 2784, mayanprin@btl.net), PO Box 1, is an up-to-date condominium building right in the town center, on the beach. When suites (with kitchenette) are not occupied by their owners, they are rented to travelers for US$135/146/158/170 a single/double/triple/quad.

Ramon's Village (☎ (26) 2071, fax (26) 2214, in the USA (601) 649-1990, fax (601) 649-1996), on Coconut Drive south of the Tropic Air terminal, has 60 rooms in two-story cabañas, thatched Tahitian-style, facing a good beach. A dive shop, boats for excursions, jet skis, sailboards, lounge chairs for sunbathing, a swimming pool with bar surrounded by coconut palms . . . it's got everything, and it's very well-kept. Some cabañas have sea views, many have porches for sitting, and all come with at least a king-size bed or two double beds. Rates range from US$143 to US$200 a double. This is among the island's best places to stay.

Victoria House (☎ (26) 2067, fax (26) 2429, in the USA (800) 247-5159), PO Box 22, is an idyllic small resort hotel three km south of the airport, on the beach. The beach, the lawns and the 31 rooms are beautifully kept; there's a dining room, bar and dive shop. Here you're away from it all, but San Pedro is a quick 10-minute (free) bike, shuttle van or (rentable) golf cart ride away. You pay US$150 to US$230 a double from mid-December to mid-April, and lower rates at other times.

Paradise Resort Hotel (☎ (26) 2083, fax (26) 2232, in the USA (800) 451-8017), at the northern end of Barrier Reef Drive, has 25 rooms, cabañas and villas (some with kitchenette), all large, airy and comfortable, plus its own dock and dive shop. Winter rates range from US$60 to US$125 a double.

The *Belize Yacht Club* (☎ (26) 2777, fax (26) 2768), on Coconut Drive less than one km south of the airport, has several Spanish-style two-story buildings arranged around a swimming pool amid lawns stretching to the beach. Accommodations are in air-conditioned one- to three-bedroom suites with full kitchen, and cost US$175 to US$375 per night in the winter.

Places to Eat

Several small cafes in the town center serve cheap, simple meals and good java.

Casa de Café, on Barrier Reef Drive just north of the Belize Bank, serves pastries and light meals to go with its high-quality coffee.

Ruby's Caffe, next to Ruby's Hotel on Barrier Reef Drive, is a tiny place with good cakes and pastries but unpredictable opening hours. For simpler take-out pastries and bread, try the *Panadería El Centro* on Bucaneer at Pescador.

The Deli, on Barrier Reef Drive just north of the San Pedro Holiday Hotel, serves food to go: fried chicken, sandwiches and their own banana bread for US$1.50 to US$5.

Tropical Take-Out, across the street from the Tropic Air terminal at the airport, has daily specials as well as the usual list of sandwiches and light meals.

Elvi's Kitchen (☎ (26) 2176, fax (26) 3056), on Pescador Drive near Ambergris St, the old reliable, has gone upscale in recent years. The floors are still covered in sand, but the waiters now wear black and white and speak in breathy tones. The menu has been expanded from fish and chips (US$7) and rice and beans with fish (US$5), but the daily specials are unabashed nouvelle cuisine. You can spend as little as US$2.50 for a ham and cheese sandwich or as much as US$30 for a full lobster dinner with wine. Try their licuados of banana, melon, papaya, pineapple, soursap or watermelon. Lunch and dinner are served daily except Sunday.

Celi's Restaurant (☎ (26) 2014), next to the San Pedro Holiday Hotel, has a beachfront screened dining room, a long breakfast menu (try the homemade cinnamon rolls or banana bread, US$1.75) and seafood main courses for lunch or dinner priced from US$10 to US$17. The shrimp dejonghe is a favorite.

Estel's Dine by the Sea, on the beach east of the Alijua Hotel Suites, is not particularly cheap, but it has an eclectic menu and a great location. Rice and beans goes for US$7, a Mexican plate for US$14. It's closed on Tuesday.

Jade Garden (☎ (26) 2126), on Coconut Drive a 10-minute walk south of the airport, is San Pedro's best Chinese restaurant, with a long menu and moderate prices. Fried rice and chow mein dishes cost US$5 to US$9, sweet-and-sour US$7 to US$10, steaks and fish US$10 to US$18. Food can be packed to take away. It's open daily from 11 am to 2 pm and 6 to 10 pm.

Lily's (☎ (26) 2059), in Lily's Caribbean Lodge, off the eastern end of Caribeña St, is a family-run place specializing in seafood. A seafood lunch or dinner might cost US$12 to US$18; breakfasts are served for about US$5.

The *Barrier Reef Hotel*, on Barrier Reef Drive, has a small restaurant on its ground floor, specializing in pizza: nine-, 12- and 16-inch pizzas priced from US$9 to US$22, depending upon ingredients. They also serve shrimp cocktails, a few sandwiches and nachos. It's closed Monday off-season.

Island Style Food Palace, on Pescador north of Ambergris, is a homey eatery with lunch and dinner 'burgers' of beef, chicken, shrimp or lobster for US$2 to US$5 and fish and chips for a bit more.

Little Italy Restaurant (☎ (26) 2866), in the Spindrift Hotel, is a step up in comfort and quality, with indoor, patio and beachside dining. Spaghetti plates and Italian main courses cost US$6 to US$20; sandwiches are less. It's closed from 2 to 5:30 pm.

The *Lagoon Restaurant*, on Pescador in the Hotel Casablanca, has a versatile chef who can cook anything from Thai pork satay to coq au vin and chayote Maya to vegetarian black-bean lasagna. For the quality and variety offered, it's very reasonable – about US$16 to US$22 for a full dinner. In season, breakfast and lunch are

served as well. The rooftop Sunset Bar is a prime place for watching the daily solar disappearance.

Ambergris Delight, on Pescador Drive near Pelican, serves fried chicken, burgers and pies, as well as the inevitable rice and beans, at moderate prices daily except Wednesday.

Entertainment

Sipping, sitting, talking and dancing are parts of everyday life on Ambergris. Many hotels have comfortable bars, often with sand floors, thatched roofs and reggae music.

The *Tackle Box Bar*, on a wharf at the eastern end of Black Coral Drive, is a San Pedro institution. Very popular with divers and boat owners, it's a good place to get the latest information on diving trips and conditions, boat rentals and excursions.

Fido's Courtyard, on Barrier Reef Drive near Pelican St, is the landlubbers' favorite. *Sandals*, near the north end of Barrier Reef Drive, is an alternative.

Big Daddy's Disco, located right next to San Pedro's church, is the town's hot nightspot, often featuring live reggae, especially during the winter. Across Barrier Reef Drive, the *Tarzan Club & Cheetah's Bar* is often closed off-season, but it rocks in the winter.

To drink with the locals in a real cantina at lower prices, head for *Marinos* on Pescador Drive at Bucaneer St. Don't expect a beautiful place; this is a real Mexican-style cantina, and women may not find the atmosphere welcoming or comfortable.

Getting There & Away

Triple J sails from San Pedro to Caye Caulker daily at 3 pm for US$6 per person, and to Belize City for US$10. The *Banana Boat* departs the Wahoo! dock (near the Hustler dock at the northern end of town) Monday through Friday at 8 am for Belize City; it departs Belize City on the return trip to San Pedro at 4 pm. For further details on getting to and from Ambergris Caye, see the Belize Getting There & Around chapter.

Endangered Turtles

There are eight species of sea turtles, three of which inhabit the coasts of Belize, all of which are endangered species.

The green turtle *(Chelonia mydas)*, named for the greenish color of its fat, is prized as food and is the main ingredient in turtle soup. In the wild, it can grow to be more than four feet in length and over 600 pounds. Green turtles are now an endangered species, their numbers having been decimated by hunters and by the destruction of seagrass, their main food source.

The loggerhead *(Caretta caretta)* has a large head, short neck and heart-shaped shell colored red to brown. Females return faithfully to nest on the beach where they themselves were born, usually in June, July or August. They crawl slowly up the beach to a spot above the high tide line, dig a pit and lay up to 100 white eggs. After covering the eggs with sand, they returns to the sea, leaving the eggs to their fate, which may include being eaten by animals, stolen by poachers or stepped on by humans. The eggs that survive these perils hatch after about two months, scratch their way to the surface, wait until nightfall, then crawl down into the sea. Many are eaten by birds, crabs and lizards before reaching the water or by fish afterwards. Only about 5% survive from egg to reproductive age.

The hawksbill *(Eretmochelys imbricata)* has a narrow bill and a sharp pointed beak. Its shell is not solid, but is made up of bony overlapping scales in beautiful colors of orange, brown and gold. Its beauty is the reason it is endangered: sea hunters capture hawksbills to be stuffed and displayed as trophies or to strip their scales to make tortoise shell combs, jewelry, eyeglass frames and other items.

What can you do to help turtles survive?

• Don't approach or otherwise disturb or frighten a sea turtle on the beach during nesting season (June through August).

• Don't eat turtle eggs, turtle soup or any other dish made with turtles.

• Don't buy or use any product made from real turtle shell.

• Don't litter the beach or seabed with plastic bags.

• Encourage efforts to preserve turtle nesting beaches as natural reserves, avoiding resort development. ■

Getting Around

It's no more than a 10-minute walk to any place in town from the airport, less from the boat docks. If your luggage is heavy, you can take a taxi from the airport to any place in town for US$3, or to hotels south of town for US$6.

San Pedranos get around on foot or by bicycle, golf cart or pickup truck. You can rent bicycles, motorcycles and golf carts at several locations, including *Polo's EZ-Go Rentals* (☎ (26) 2080, (26) 3542) at the northern end of Barrier Reef Drive and the *Rental Center* and *Ramon's Wheel Rentals*

(☎ (26) 2790, fax (26) 3236) on Coconut Drive just south of the Tropic Air terminal at the airport. Bikes rent for around US$2.50 per hour, US$9 for four hours or US$14 for eight hours. Golf carts go for US$10 per hour, US$30 for four hours, US$40 for eight hours, US$60 for 24 hours or US$250 per week.

OTHER CAYES

Though Ambergris and Caulker are the most easily accessible and popular cayes, it is possible to arrange visits to others. Serious divers are the usual customers at

BELIZE

camps and resorts on the smaller cayes. Often a special flight or boat charter is necessary to reach these cayes, and this can be arranged when you book your lodgings. Most booking offices are in Belize City, as the smaller cayes have infrequent mail service and no telephones (only radios).

Caye Chapel

Just south of Caye Caulker, Caye Chapel is the site of the *Pyramid Island Resort* (☎ (2) 44409, fax (2) 32405), PO Box 192, Belize City.

St George's Caye

Fourteen km east of Belize City, St George's Caye was the first capital of the Belize settlement, between 1650 and 1784, and saw the decisive battle of 1798 between the British settlers and a Spanish invasion force.

Today it holds *St George's Lodge* (☎ (2) 44190, fax (2) 30461), PO Box 625, Belize City, a 16-room, moderately priced resort. For reservations in the USA call ☎ (800) 678-6871. There is also the *Cottage Colony Resort* (☎ (2) 77051, fax (2) 73253), PO Box 428, Belize City.

Spanish Lookout Caye

Spanish Bay Resort (☎ (2) 77288, (2) 72725, fax (2) 72797), 71 North Front St (PO Box 35), Belize City, is on Spanish Lookout Caye, between Belize City and the Turneffe Islands. It's a five-cabaña, family-run place where you can really get away from it all.

Turneffe Islands

A coral atoll about 30 km east of Belize City, the Turneffe Islands hold numerous lodgings, from low-budget camps like the six-room *Turneffe Flats* (☎ (2) 45634), 56 Eve St, Belize City, to the luxury *Turneffe Islands Lodge* (☎ (1) 49564, fax (03) 0276, in the USA (770) 536-3922, fax (770) 536-8365), PO Box 480, Belize City.

Half Moon Caye

This caye is in Lighthouse Reef, and is protected as the Half Moon Caye Natural Monument. Standing less than three meters above sea level, the caye's 18 hectares hold two distinct ecosystems. To the west is lush vegetation fertilized by the droppings of thousands of seabirds, including some 4000 red-footed boobies, the wonderfully named magnificent frigatebird and some 98 other species of birds; to the east, there is less vegetation but more coconut palms. Loggerhead and hawksbill turtles, both endangered, lay their eggs on the southern beaches. There are no accommodations, but camping is allowed in designated areas. Organized boat trips stop at Half Moon Caye and the nearby Blue Hole.

Gallows Point Caye

Just off Belize City, Gallows Point Caye has the six-room guesthouse called *The Wave* (☎ (2) 73054), 9 Regent St, Belize City.

Southern Cayes

For details on cayes off the southern Belizean coast, see the Southern Belize chapter.

Northern Belize

Low-lying, often swampy and cut by rivers and lagoons, northern Belize has a varied topography of broadleaf forest, pine forest and savanna and tropical riparian forest filled with vines and epiphytes. The shoreline in the north is often vague – a wide band of marshy land edged with dense mangrove.

This is also farming country. Sugar cane is a primary crop, but many farmers are branching out to different crops to avoid being held hostage to the fluctuations of the commodities markets.

The north has several significant biosphere reserves. Largest and most significant is the Río Bravo Conservation Area, more than 1000 sq km of tropical forests, rivers, ponds and Mayan archaeological sites in the western part of Orange Walk District. Spread along the Mexican and Guatemalan borders, the Río Bravo reserve joins the

Maya biosphere reserve in Guatemala and the Calakmul reserve in Mexico to form a vast multinational reserve.

Other reserves include the Shipstern Nature Reserve, south of Sarteneja on the large peninsula to the southeast of Corozal. Shipstern is an excellent place for bird watching, as is the Crooked Tree Wildlife Sanctuary, midway between Orange Walk and Belize City. The Bermudian Landing Community Baboon Sanctuary, west of Belize City, protects the black howler monkey.

The ancient Maya prospered in northern Belize, scooping up the rich soil and piling it onto raised fields, and at the same time creating drainage canals. These *chinampas* (raised growing-beds surrounded by water) supported many rich coastal trading towns.

At Cerros, across the bay from Corozal, a small Mayan fishing settlement became a powerful kingdom in Late Preclassic times. At least a dozen other powerful Mayan cities flourished here, but like Cerros their

howler monkey

ruins are somewhat difficult to reach, and their largely unrestored temples do not seem particularly impressive to eyes that have seen Tikal, Chichén Itzá or even Tulum. Not so Lamanai, which is one of the best sites to visit in Belize.

BERMUDIAN LANDING COMMUNITY BABOON SANCTUARY

There are no real baboons in Belize, but locally the black howler monkey is given that name. Though there are howler monkeys throughout the Mayan areas, the black howler, an endangered species, exists only in Belize, and like so much wildlife in the rapidly developing Mayan lands, its existence is threatened.

In 1985 local farmers were organized to help preserve the black howler and to protect its habitat by harmonizing its needs with their own. Care is taken to maintain the forests along the banks of the Belize River where the black howler feeds, sleeps and – at dawn and dusk – howls (loudly and unmistakably). You can learn all about the black howler and the other 200 kinds of animals and birds to be found in the reserve at the Visitors' Center (☎ (2) 44405) in the village of Bermudian Landing.

Black howlers are vegetarians and spend most of the daylight hours cruising the tree-tops in groups of four to eight, led by a dominant male. Various fruits, flowers, leaves and other tidbits keep them happy, and they don't seem to mind visitors lurking below.

You must tour the sanctuary with a guide (US$4 per hour, US$12 per half-day). For further information about the sanctuary, check with the Belize Audubon Society (☎ (2) 35004, fax (2) 34985, base@btl.net), 12 Fort St (PO Box 1001), Belize City. For full ecological information, buy a copy of the field guide to the sanctuary (US$15).

Places to Stay & Eat

Camping (US$5 per person) is allowed at the *Visitors' Center* and at the *Jungle Drift Lodge* in Bermudian Landing village (☎ (2) 32842, fax (2) 78160), PO Box 1442, Belize City. The lodge has five cabins priced at US$22 a double. Inexpensive meals are served, canoes and kayaks are for rent and tours are offered.

Getting There & Away

Russells buses leave the corner of Orange St and Euphrates Ave in Belize City at 12:30 pm (noon on Saturday); there are no buses on Thursday or Sunday. The hour-long ride to Bermudian Landing costs US$2. Departures from Bermudian Landing for Belize City are at 5:30 am, meaning that if you take the bus, you must plan to stay the night. The roundtrip fare is US$3.50.

ALTUN HA

Northern Belize's most famous Mayan ruin is at Altun Ha, 55 km north of Belize City along the Old Northern Hwy, near the village of Rockstone Pond, 16 km south of Maskall.

The Northern Hwy divides at the town of Sand Hill, with the new highway going northwest and the old one heading northeast. The old road is narrow, potholed and broken in places, passing through jungle and the occasional hamlet. The ruins are a few minutes' walk west of the highway.

Altun Ha (Mayan for 'Rockstone Pond') was undoubtedly a small (population about 3000) but rich and important Mayan trading town, with agriculture also playing an important role in its economy. Altun Ha had formed as a community by at least 600 BC, perhaps several centuries earlier, and the town flourished until the mysterious collapse of Classic Mayan civilization around 900 AD. Most of the temples you will see in Altun Ha date from Late Classic times, though burials indicate that Altun Ha's merchants were trading with Teotihuacán in Preclassic times.

Altun Ha is open daily from 9 am to 5 pm; admission costs US$5. There are modern toilets and a drinks shop at the site, but no accommodations.

Of the grass-covered temples arranged around the two plazas here, the largest and most important is the Temple of the Masonry Altars (Structure B-4), in Plaza B. The restored structure you see dates from

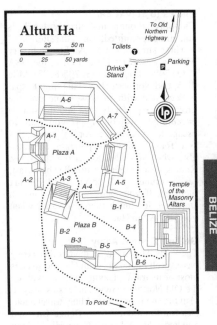

the first half of the 7th century AD and takes its name from altars on which copal resin was burnt and beautifully carved jade pieces were smashed in sacrifice. Excavation of the structure in 1968 revealed many burials of important officials. Most sites had been looted or desecrated, but two were intact. Among the jade objects found in one of these was a unique mask sculpture portraying Kinich Ahau, the Mayan sun god, the largest known well-carved jade object from the Mayan area.

In Plaza A, Structure A-1 is sometimes called the Temple of the Green Tomb. Deep within it was discovered the tomb of a priest/king dating from around 600 AD. Tropical humidity had destroyed the king's garments and the paper of the Mayan 'painted book' that was buried with him, but many riches were intact: shell necklaces, pottery, pearls, stingray spines used in bloodletting rites, jade beads and pendants and ceremonial flints.

BELIZE

Places to Stay & Eat

Camping, though not strictly legal, is sometimes permitted; ask at the site.

Three km north of Maskall is the luxury Maruba Resort (☎ (3) 22199, in the USA (713) 799-2031, fax (713) 795-8573), Mile 40.5, Old Northern Hwy. This 'jungle spa' is decorated with an artist's fine eye; the grounds are perfectly kept and the staff is exceedingly welcoming. If you want to escape to an oasis in a tropical jungle, this is it. Tours of the country's sights are available when you want to get out for a day. Rooms cost US$266 a double, breakfast, lunch, dinner, 15% service and 7% tax included. If your budget allows, you can stop here for lunch (about US$20) when you visit Altun Ha.

Getting There & Away

The 'New Alignment' of the Northern Hwy passes well inland of Altun Ha, and so does most of its traffic, leaving little activity on the Old Northern Hwy. The easiest way to visit the site is on a tour. Many travel agencies run tours daily from Belize City and San Pedro on Ambergris Caye. Hitchhiking is usually disappointing, but there are buses departing from Douglas Jones St (see Belize City map) for the town of Maskall, north of Altun Ha.

CROOKED TREE WILDLIFE SANCTUARY

Midway between Belize City and Orange Walk, 5.5 km west of the Northern Hwy, lies the fishing and farming village of Crooked Tree. In 1984 the Belize Audubon Society succeeded in having 12 sq km around the village declared a wildlife sanctuary, principally because of the wealth of birdlife. Migrating birds flock to the rivers, swamps and lagoons here each year during the dry season (November to May, which is winter up north). Seventy species of birds are regularly seen here, including various species of herons, ducks, kites, egrets, ospreys, kingfishers and hawks.

Among Crooked Tree's most famous winter visitors is a large group of jabiru storks, which come here to nest. With a wingspan of 2.5 meters, the jabiru is the largest flying bird in the Western Hemisphere. Black howler monkeys, Morelet's crocodiles, coatimundis, iguanas and turtles also have habitats among the mango and cashew trees at Crooked Tree.

For details about the sanctuary, check with the Belize Audubon Society (☎ (2) 77369, base@btl.net), 49 Southern Foreshore (PO Box 1001), Belize City.

Places to Stay & Eat

Cheapest accommodations are at *Molly's Rooms*, where very basic, simple waterless rooms go for US$10/15 a single/double. *Sam Tillett's Hotel* (☎ (2) 44333) charges a bit more for its three rooms with private bath.

Bird's Eye View Lodge (☎ (2) 44101), PO Box 1976, Belize City, is in Crooked Tree village near the lagoon. Four of the five rooms in the concrete building have two double beds; the other has one double bed. All have private bath. Rooms cost US$60/75 a single/double. Meals are available, as are sites for camping.

Also in the village is the *Paradise Inn* (☎ (25) 2535, fax (25) 2534), renting simple cabañas for US$38/50 a single/double. They have a restaurant as well.

Getting There & Away

Jex Bus, at 34 Regent St in Belize City, runs three buses daily from Crooked Tree village to Belize City early in the morning, returning midmorning and late afternoon. Thus you must spend the night at Crooked Tree to take advantage of these buses.

If you start early from Belize City, Corozal or Orange Walk, you can bus to Crooked Tree Junction, walk the 5.5 km to the village (about an hour), learn about the reserve's flora and fauna at the Visitors' Center, spend some time bird watching and head out again.

It's a good idea to ask at the Belize Audubon Society about any more recent transportation developments.

A faster, more comfortable but more expensive alternative is to take a day-long tour from Belize City. Several travel agencies organize these for about US$75 per person.

CHAN CHICH LODGE

Chan Chich Lodge (☎ (2) 75634, fax (2) 76961, info@chanchich.com), 1 King St (PO Box 37), Belize City, is among the most luxurious of Belize's jungle lodges. Its setting is incredible: thatched cabañas fill the central plaza of a Mayan archaeological site! Resident ornithologists have identified more than 260 species of birds here. Each of the 12 cabañas has private bath, fan, two queen-size beds and a verandah. Rooms cost US$169/231 a single/double, all meals and tax included. For information and reservations in the USA call ☎ (800) 343-8009.

Chan Chich is located in Orange Walk District between the settlement of Gallon Jug and the Guatemalan border, and is best reached by chartered plane from Belize City, though there is an all-weather road (210 km, 3½ hours from Belize City).

LAMANAI

By far the most impressive site in this part of the country is Lamanai, in its own archaeological reserve on the New River Lagoon near the settlement of Indian Church. Though much of the site remains unexcavated and unrestored, the trip to Lamanai, by motorboat up the New River, is an adventure in itself.

Figuring 1½ hours' boat travel each way and somewhat over two hours at the site, the excursion to Lamanai takes most of a day.

History

As with most sites in northern Belize, Lamanai ('Submerged Crocodile', the original Mayan name of the place) was occupied as early as 1500 BC, with the first stone buildings appearing between 800 and 600 BC. Lamanai flourished in Late Preclassic times, growing into a major ceremonial center with immense temples long before most other Mayan sites.

Unlike many other sites, Maya lived here until the coming of the Spanish in the 16th century. The ruined Indian church (actually two of them) nearby attests to the fact that there were Maya here for the Spanish friars to convert. Convert them

they did, but by 1640 the Maya had reverted to their ancient forms of worship. British interests later built a sugar mill, now in ruins, at Indian Church. The archaeological site was excavated by David Pendergast in the 1970s and '80s.

New River Voyage

You motor for 1½ hours up the New River from the Tower Hill toll bridge south of Orange Walk, between river banks crowded with dense jungle vegetation. Along the way, your boatman/guide points out many local birds and will almost certainly spot a crocodile or two. Along the way you pass the Mennonite community at Shipyard. Finally the river opens out into the New River Lagoon, a broad and very long expanse of water which can be choppy during the frequent rainshowers.

Touring Lamanai

Landing at Lamanai (open from 9 am to 5 pm daily), you'll sign the visitors' book, pay the admission fee (US$5) and wander into the dense jungle, past gigantic guanacaste, ceiba and *ramón* (breadnut) trees, strangler figs, allspice, epiphytes and black orchids, Belize's national flower. In the canopy overhead you may see one of the five groups of howler monkeys resident in the archaeological zone.

A tour of the ruins takes 90 minutes minimum, more comfortably two or three hours.

Of the 60 significant structures identified here, the grandest is Structure N10-43, a huge Late Preclassic building rising more than 34 meters above the jungle canopy. Other buildings along La Ruta Maya are taller, but this one was built well before the others. It's been partially uncovered and restored.

Not far from N10-43 is Lamanai's ball court, a smallish one, partially uncovered.

To the north along a path in the jungle is Structure P9-56, built several centuries later, with a huge stylized mask of a man in a crocodile-mouth headdress four meters high emblazoned on its southwest face. Archaeologists have dug deep into this structure (from the platform level high on the east side) to look for burials and to document the several earlier structures which lie beneath.

Near this structure is a small temple and a very fine ruined stela. The tall stela of fine limestone once stood on the front face of the temple. Apparently some worshippers built a fire at the base of the stela and later doused it with water. The hot stone stela, cooled too quickly by the water, broke and toppled. The low-relief carving of a majestic figure is extremely fine.

There is a small museum near the boat landing, with quite interesting figurative pottery and some large flint tools.

Places to Stay & Eat

Lamanai Outpost Lodge (☎ /fax (2) 33578), PO Box 63, Belize City, is a five-minute boat ride (a 15-minute walk) south of the archaeological zone. Situated on a hillside sloping down to the lagoon, the well-kept modern lodge buildings enjoy panoramic views. Guests stay in modern bungalows with fan and private bath. Meals are available at moderate prices in the cheerful dining room (lunch costs US$8), and there's a bar. Rooms cost US$94/115 a single/double, tax and service included. Meals cost US$7 for breakfast, US$10 for lunch and US$18 for dinner. Two- and three-night tour packages, including transfers to and from Belize City or Goldson International Airport, river excursions, wildlife walks and tours of Lamanai are available.

In the nearby village of Indian Church, *Doña Blanca* (☎ (3) 23369) rents serviceable cabins for US$25 a double, breakfast included.

Getting There & Away

Lamanai can be reached by road (58 km) from Orange Walk via Yo Creek and San Felipe. The bus service from Orange Walk – departing on Tuesday at 3 pm and Thursday at 4 pm – is only of use to village people coming to the big city for marketing. For travelers, the river voyage is much more convenient and enjoyable.

Take a sun hat, sun block cream, insect repellent, shoes (rather than sandals), lunch and a beverage (unless you plan to take a tour which includes lunch). From May to October, a raincoat or parka is useful to ward off an afternoon shower.

The main base for river departures is the Tower Hill toll bridge, seven km south of Orange Walk on the Northern Hwy. Several guide services operate boat tours on the river.

The Novelo brothers (Antonio and Herminio) run Jungle River Tours (☎ (3) 22293, fax (3) 23749), 20 Lovers' Lane (PO Box 95), Orange Walk, and have excellent reputations as guides and naturalists. Contact them at the bridge or at their office near the southeastern corner of the central park in Orange Walk or make a reservation by phone or fax. Be at their boat dock, on the northwestern side of the Tower Hill toll bridge, by 9 am for the day-long trip (you'll be back by 4 pm), which includes lunch, beverages and the guided tour along the river and at Lamanai (US$50 per person, with a minimum of four persons).

Reyes & Sons (☎ (3) 23327) run tours from Jim's Cool Pool, just north of the toll bridge (by Novelo's), at 9 am daily (be there by 8:30 am) for the river tour to Lamanai. The boat ride and guided tour costs US$30 per person; a boxed lunch is another US$8.

Donald 'Jack' Rhaburn, who runs Crocodile Jack's Jungle River Adventures (☎ (3) 22142), is one of the most experienced guides on the river. He runs tours from his cabin on the west side of the Northern Hwy a short distance south of the Tower Hill toll bridge. He'll give you the best river tour available, but his age doesn't allow him to guide you around the site at Lamanai. He charges US$50 per person (no lunch).

It's possible to take the 6 am Batty Brothers bus from Belize City to Orange Walk, get out at the Tower Hill toll bridge, and be in time for the 9 am departure of the boats for Lamanai. Boats return to the bridge before 4 pm, allowing you to catch the 4 pm Batty's bus southwards to Belize City.

ORANGE WALK
Population 10,000

The agricultural and social center of northern Belize is this town 94 km north of Belize City. It's important to the farmers (including many Mennonites) who till the soil of the region, raising sugar cane and citrus fruits. Another important crop is said to be marijuana. Orange Walk is not very important to visitors unless you're bound for one of the archaeological sites or wildlife reserves nearby, in which case its modest hotels and Chinese restaurants are useful.

The center of town is the shady central park on the east side of the main road, called Queen Victoria Ave. The town hospital is in the northern outskirts, readily visible on the west side of the Northern Hwy.

Cuello & Nohmul Archaeological Sites
Near Orange Walk is Cuello, a Mayan site with a 3000-year history but little to show for it. Archaeologists have found plenty here, but only Structure 350, a nine-tiered stepped pyramid, will draw your interest. The site is on private property, that of the Cuello Brothers Distillery (☎ (3) 22141),

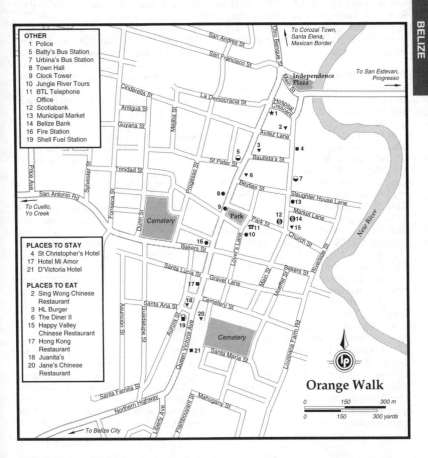

Orange Walk

four km west of Orange Walk along San Antonio (Yo Creek) Rd. The distillery, on the left-hand (southern) side of the road, is unmarked; the site is through and beyond it. Ask permission at the distillery gate.

Nohmul ('Great Mound' in Mayan), 12 km north of Orange Walk and two km west of the village of San Pablo, was a much more important site. Structure 2, the tallest building at the site, marks a lofty acropolis looming over the surrounding countryside. Though it is a vast site covering more than 18 sq km, most of it is now overgrown by grass and sugar cane. The site is owned by Estevan Itzab, who lives in the northern part of San Pablo village, opposite the water tower. Stop at Itzab's house for permission to visit; a guide will be sent with you.

Places to Stay

Orange Walk has several hotels, none of them very grand, and several of them sullied by nuclear-powered discos on their ground floor.

St Christopher's Hotel (☎ (3) 21064), 10 Main St, is simple, relatively quiet and decently priced. Rooms with shower cost US$25/28/33/38 a single/double/triple/quad with fan or US$40/45/54 with air-con.

Hotel Mi Amor (☎ (3) 22031, fax (3) 23462), 19 Queen Victoria Ave (PO Box 117), is simple and clean, but the disco is deafening. Its double rooms cost US$25 with fan, US$38 with TV and air-con.

D'Victoria Hotel (☎ (3) 22518, fax (3) 22847), 40 Queen Victoria Ave (PO Box 74), has the same disco noise problem, and guestrooms priced at US$22 to US$25 with private bath, US$38 to US$55 with air-con.

New River Park Hotel (☎ (3) 23987), PO Box 34, Orange Walk, on the eastern side of the Northern Hwy seven km south of Orange Walk, just north of the Tower Hill toll bridge, is a great place to stay before and/or after your boat trip to Lamanai. Double rooms cost US$32 with fan, US$52 with air-con. There's a restaurant, bar, game room and convenience store.

Places to Eat

Locals favor *Juanita's*, on Santa Ana St near the Shell fuel station, a simple place with local fare at low prices.

HL Burger, three blocks north of the central park on the main road, has good, cheap burgers (US$2), rice and bean plates and ice cream.

When it comes to Chinese restaurants, Orange Walk has them. *Happy Valley* (☎ (3) 22554), 38 Main St at Church, and *Sing Wong*, Main St at Avilez Lane, are about the nicest, along with the *Hong Kong*, right next to the Hotel Mi Amor, and *Jane's Chinese Restaurant*, about three blocks farther south.

The Diner (☎ (3) 22424), 37 Clark St, is the favorite local hangout for breakfast, lunch and dinner, but it's somewhat difficult to access without a car. Go north and turn left just before the hospital, then bear right (follow the signs) and go 400 meters. *The Diner II*, however, is conveniently located just a block north of the central park.

Getting There & Away

Four bus lines compete for the traffic on the route between Orange Walk and Belize City: Batty Brothers, Venus, Escalante's and Urbina's. The latter two lines are based in Orange Walk.

Southbound buses pass through town at least every hour (usually on the hour, and sometimes on the half-hour as well) from 4:30 am to about 12:30 pm, with a few later buses. Northbound buses pass through at 15 minutes before the hour from 1:45 pm to 8:45 pm. It's 61 km to Corozal (1½ hours, US$2) and 94 km to Belize City (two hours, US$2.50).

COROZAL
Population 9000

Corozal is a farming town. Several decades ago the countryside was given over completely to sugar cane (there's a refinery south of the town). Today, though sugar is still important, crops are more diversified. The land is fertile, the climate is good for agriculture and the town is prosperous.

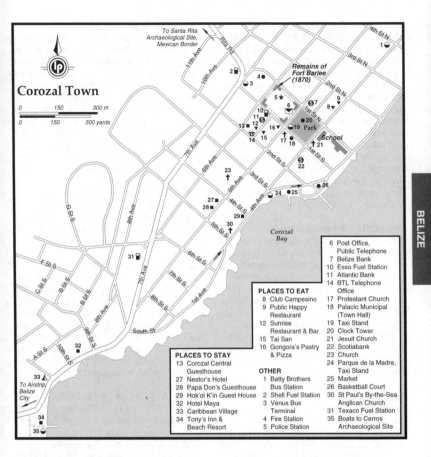

Corozal Town

0   150   300 m
0   150   300 yards

To Santa Rita
Archaeological Site,
Mexican Border

Remains of
Fort Barlee
(1870)

Corozal
Bay

School

Park

To Airstrip,
Belize
City

6   Post Office,
    Public Telephone
7   Belize Bank
10 Esso Fuel Station
11 Atlantic Bank
14 BTL Telephone
    Office

PLACES TO EAT
8   Club Campesino
9   Public Happy
    Restaurant
12 Sunrise
    Restaurant & Bar
15 Tai San
16 Gongora's Pastry
    & Pizza

PLACES TO STAY
13 Corozal Central
    Guesthouse
27 Nestor's Hotel
28 Papa Don's Guesthouse
29 Hok'ol K'in Guest House
32 Hotel Maya
33 Caribbean Village
34 Tony's Inn &
    Beach Resort

OTHER
1   Batty Brothers
    Bus Station
2   Shell Fuel Station
3   Venus Bus
    Terminal
4   Fire Station
5   Police Station

17 Protestant Church
18 Palacio Municipal
    (Town Hall)
19 Taxi Stand
20 Clock Tower
21 Jesuit Church
22 Scotiabank
23 Church
24 Parque de la Madre,
    Taxi Stand
25 Market
26 Basketball Court
30 St Paul's By-the-Sea
    Anglican Church
31 Texaco Fuel Station
35 Boats to Cerros
    Archaeological Site

BELIZE

Many of those who do not farm commute to Orange Walk or Belize City to work.

Corozaleños, most of whom speak Spanish as their first language, are pleasant folks, and you may find that people greet you on the street or at least offer a smile. There is a small North American expatriate community, with retirement developments in Consejo Shores resembling comfortable gringo ghettos.

History

Corozal's Mayan history is long and important. On the northern outskirts of the town are the ruins of a Mayan ceremonial center once called Chetumal, now called Santa Rita. Across the bay at Cerros is one of the most important Late Preclassic sites yet discovered.

Maya have been living around Corozal since 1500 BC. Modern Corozal dates from only 1849, however. In that year, refugees from the War of the Castes in Yucatán fled across the border to safe haven in British-controlled Belize. They founded a town and named it after the cohune palm, a symbol of fertility. For years it had the look of a typical Caribbean town, until Hurricane Janet roared through in 1955 and blew away many of the old wooden buildings on stilts. Much of Corozal's cinderblock architecture dates from the late 1950s.

As recently as the 1970s, when Belize's Northern Hwy was a potholed moonscape negotiated only by trucks, Corozal enjoyed a prosperous if small tourist trade. Travelers would cross the border from Mexico and relax on the shores of Corozal before taking the punishing trip southwards in the back of a truck. Now that the highway is improved and is served regularly by buses, most travelers zip straight through Corozal to Belize City or beyond.

Orientation & Information
Though founded by the Maya, Corozal now resembles a Mexican town, with its plaza, its Palacio Municipal and its large church. The chimes of the clock tower keep everyone on schedule. You can walk easily to any place in town. Even Tony's Inn & Beach Resort, on the southwestern outskirts, is only a 20-minute walk (1.75 km) from the plaza.

The Belize Bank on the north side of the plaza is open for currency exchange Monday to Friday from 8 am to 1 pm and Friday afternoon from 3 to 6 pm.

Santa Rita Archaeological Site
Santa Rita is a small, nicely kept park with one small restored Mayan temple, located just over one km northwest of the Venus bus terminal in Corozal. Go north on the main highway; after 700 meters bear right, just before the statue. After another 100 meters turn left at the Restaurant Hennessy and go straight for 300 meters to the site. The 'hill' on the right is actually a temple. The site is open during daylight hours, for free.

The Santa Rita site was discovered almost a century ago by amateur archaeologist Thomas Gann, Corozal's town physician. Called Chetumal by the Maya, this city sat astride important riverine trade routes and had its share of wealth. The jade and pottery artifacts found here have been dispersed to museums and the important frescoes destroyed.

Cerros Archaeological Site
Cerros is an oddity in that it flourished in Late Preclassic times, and was not extensively overbuilt during the Classic and Post-Classic periods. The site has thus given archaeologists important insights into Mayan Preclassic architecture.

There is more to see at Cerros (also called Cerro Maya) than at Santa Rita: namely Structure 4, a temple more than 20 meters high. Though the site is still mostly a mass of grass-covered mounds, the center has been cleared and consolidated, though not extensively restored.

The best way to get to Cerros, three km across the water from Corozal, is by boat chartered at the dock of Tony's Inn & Beach Resort. The boat trip takes about 15 minutes; then you walk 10 minutes to the site.

Places to Stay – budget
Camping *Caribbean Village* (☎ (4) 22045, (4) 22752), PO Box 55, 1.5 km south of the plaza, has large swaths of lush grass shaded by coconut palms. Amenities include usable toilets, moldy showers and all hookups. Rates are US$4 per person for a tent, US$8 per person for a camper van (RV). The park is marked only by a sign reading 'Hailey's Restaurant'.

Hotels *Hotel Maya* (☎ (4) 22082, fax (4) 22827), PO Box 112, on 7th Ave (the main road) about 400 meters south of the plaza, is the longtime budget favorite. The 17 aged but clean rooms with private shower cost US$22 a double with fan or US$30 with air-con. Good, cheap meals are served in the adjoining eatery.

Corozal Central Guesthouse (☎ (4) 22784, vince@btl.net), 22 6th Ave, a short walk from the plaza, is simpler and cheaper, with waterless rooms going for US$15, single or double. Bonuses include a cooking area, two clean communal showers and email service.

Nestor's Hotel (☎ (4) 22354), 125 5th Ave South, makes most of its money from its restaurant-bar and video machines. Rooms are cheap at US$13 a single, US$16 to US$22 a double, but may suffer from bar noise. Hot water is solar heated.

On the south side of Nestor's, *Papa Don's Guesthouse* (☎ (4) 22666), 125 Fifth Ave South, is simpler, quieter and cheaper, at US$8/10 single/double in a waterless room. The walls are thin here, so beware of noisy or smoky neighbors.

Places to Stay – middle
Newest among Corozal's accommodations is *Hok'ol K'in Guest House* (☎ (4) 23329, fax (4) 23569), 4th St at 4th Ave (PO Box 145), a small modern hotel with a nice dining room and patio, and comfortable rooms on the upper level. Each has two double beds, bathroom and cable TV, for US$32/44 a single/double. This is the best value in town.

About one km south of the plaza on the shore road is *Tony's Inn & Beach Resort* (☎ (4) 22055, fax (4) 22829), PO Box 12, an attractive holiday enclave with land-scaped grounds and lawn chairs set to enjoy the view of the bay. It has its own swimming lagoon, satellite TV, and an air-conditioned restaurant and bar. The 26 rooms on two floors come with fan or air-con and cost from US$60 to US$84 per double in winter (about 20% cheaper in summer).

Places to Eat
The *Hok'ol K'in Guest House, Hotel Maya* and *Tony's Inn & Beach Resort* have decent restaurants. Other restaurants are much less dependable.

There are many small Chinese restaurants, such as the *Public Happy Restaurant* on 4th Ave at 2nd St North. Chow mein, chop suey, lobster or fish with rice and many other items are listed on the menu. Portions cost US$1.75 to US$5, depending upon the ingredients and the size of the portion. Other choices are *Chang Fa* just east of the plaza and *Tai San* to the north-west. *Sunrise Restaurant & Bar*, across from Tai San, serves Belizean rather than Chinese food.

The *Club Campesino* has grilled meats, chicken, etc, but opens only at 6:30 pm for dinner, drinks and late-night socializing. For fresh bread and pastries, check out *Gongora's Pastry & Pizza*, off the western corner of the plaza.

Getting There & Away
Air Corozal has its own little airstrip (code CZL) several kilometers south of the town center, reached by taxi (US$4 – you can share the cost with other passengers). It is only an airstrip – there's no shelter and not even so much as a vendor selling soft drinks, so there's no point in arriving too early for your flight. If it's raining, you'll wait in the rain. There are taxis at the airstrip to meet all incoming flights.

Tropic Air (☎ (26) 2542, (26) 2012 in San Pedro on Ambergris Caye) has two flights daily between Corozal and San Pedro (20 minutes, US$30 one way). You can connect at San Pedro with flights to Belize City, and from Belize City connect to other parts of the country. For information and tickets, apply to Hailey's Restaurant (☎ (4) 22725) at the Caribbean Village near the southern end of Corozal.

Island Air (☎ (26) 2435 in San Pedro) has a morning and a midafternoon flight between San Pedro and Corozal. The Island Air agency in Corozal is at the Hotel Maya (☎ (4) 22082).

Bus Venus Bus Lines (☎ (4) 22132) and Batty Brothers Bus Service (☎ (2) 77146 in Belize City) operate frequent buses between Chetumal (Mexico) and Belize City, stopping at Corozal. For details, see Chetumal (in the Yucatán Caribbean Coast chapter) and also the Belize Getting There & Around chapter.

Buses leave Corozal and head south via Orange Walk for Belize City at least every hour from 3:30 am to 11:30 am, with extra buses on the half-hour during busy times. There's virtually no southbound traffic in the afternoon. All buses stop at Orange Walk. From Belize City to Corozal, departures are on the hour between noon and 7 pm.

Belize City – 155 km, 2¼ to 2¾ hours, US$4

Chetumal – 30 km, one hour with border formalities, US$1

Orange Walk – 61 km, 1¼ hours, US$1.50

BELIZE

NORTH TO MEXICO

Corozal is 13 km south of the border-crossing point at Santa Elena/Subteniente López. Most of the Venus and Batty Brothers buses traveling between Chetumal and Belize City stop at Corozal. Otherwise, hitch a ride or hire a taxi (expensive at US$12) to get to Santa Elena. From Subteniente López, minibuses shuttle the 12 km to Chetumal's Minibus Terminal frequently all day.

Santa Elena border station has nothing more than the requisite government offices and one or two very basic restaurants.

Southern Belize

Southern Belize is perhaps the most remote stretch of La Ruta Maya. The roads are long and usually in bad condition, the towns are small and access to sites requires time, energy and – sometimes – money. But if you want to explore off the tourist track, southern Belize is the place to do it.

Among the places to visit are Dangriga, the main town of Stann Creek District and center of the Black Carib/Garifuna (or Garinagu) culture; Blue Hole National Park and Cockscomb Basin Wildlife Sanctuary; Placencia, where the laid-back life is similar to that on the cayes; and Punta Gorda, near several unrestored Mayan sites. From Punta Gorda there are boats across the bay to Guatemala and Honduras.

Both roads to southern Belize are reached via the Western Hwy. The mostly unpaved Coastal (or Manatee) Hwy goes

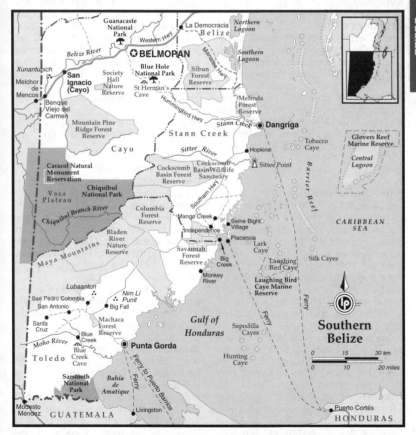

southeast from the Western Hwy at the village of La Democracia, a short distance past the Belize Zoo. Though the countryside is lush, there's nothing to stop for, and during the rainy summer months it's often flooded and impassable. The Hummingbird Hwy is the all-weather route.

HUMMINGBIRD HIGHWAY

Heading south from Belmopan, the Hummingbird Hwy is unpaved for the first 29 km south and east of Belmopan, then paved for the following 58 km to Dangriga. The unpaved portion may be paved by the time you arrive.

St Herman's Cave

About 18 km south of Belmopan, a trail on the right-hand (southern) side of the road leads 400 meters south to St Herman's Cave, a large cavern once used by the Maya during the Classic period. The cave entrance is a 60-meter-wide sinkhole which narrows towards the cave entrance. Within the cave it's cool and dark – bring a flashlight.

A rugged nature trail leads from the cave site 2.5 km east to the Blue Hole (see below). Midway along the trail, a path goes north about 1.5 km to the Hummingbird Hwy.

Blue Hole National Park

Just under 20 km south of Belmopan is the visitors' center of the Blue Hole National Park, where underground tributaries of the Sibun River bubble to the surface and fill a deep limestone sinkhole about 33 meters deep and 100 meters in diameter. After running out of the sinkhole and down a short distance, the stream cascades into a domed cavern. Deliciously cool on the hottest days, the cavern makes an excellent swimming hole.

The park is open daily from 8 am to 4 pm. There's another approach trail to the Blue Hole two km southeast of the visitors' center, but parking is not as secure; there have been car break-ins.

Between the two entrances, a road on the left (east) leads to *Ian Anderson's Caves Branch Adventure Company & Jungle Camp* (☎ /fax (8) 22800), PO Box 356,

Belmopan, a rustic jungle camp featuring tours to nearby points of interest and rooms for US$35 a double.

Over the Top & Five Blues National Park

About 29 km southeast of Belmopan, the unpaved Hummingbird Hwy crosses a bridge and becomes paved.

Thirty-six km south of Belmopan is *Over the Top* (☎ (8) 12005), a cafe/restaurant good for a snack or a meal. Nearby, a road goes east about 6.5 km to Five Blues National Park, a primitive reserve surrounding five blue lakes. About 400 meters northwest of Over the Top is *Camping Souci*, and three km southeast of Over the Top is *Palacio's Mountain Retreat* (☎ (2) 52761, jlinker@btl.net), with a natural swimming pool, restaurant and rustic cabañas for rent.

Onwards to Dangriga, the road crosses several rivers emptying out of the Maya Mountains to the south and passes through plantations of cacao, bananas and citrus before coming to the junction of the Southern Hwy and the road into Dangriga.

DANGRIGA

Population 10,000

Once called Stann Creek Town, Dangriga is the largest town in southern Belize. It's much smaller than Belize City, but friendlier and quieter. B Nicholas, Belize's most famous painter, lives and works in Dangriga near the Bonefish Hotel. His paintings are displayed in banks, hotel lobbies and public buildings throughout the country. Stop in at his studio and have a look.

There's not much to do here except spend the night and head onwards – unless it's November 19 (see the sidebar on the Garifuna people).

Orientation & Information

North Stann Creek (also called the Gumaragu River) empties into the Gulf of Honduras at the center of town. Dangriga's main street is called St Vincent St south of the creek and Commerce St to the north. The bus station is at the southern end of St Vincent St just north of the Shell fuel

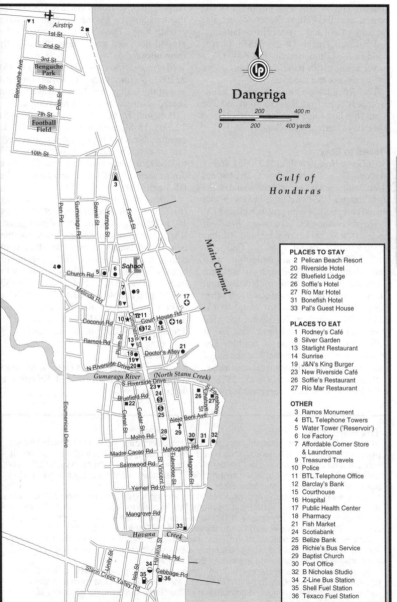

Dangriga

0   200   400 m

0   200   400 yards

Gulf of Honduras

Main Channel

Gumaragu River (North Stann Creek)

Havana Creek

PLACES TO STAY
2 Pelican Beach Resort
20 Riverside Hotel
22 Bluefield Lodge
26 Soffie's Hotel
27 Río Mar Hotel
31 Bonefish Hotel
33 Pal's Guest House

PLACES TO EAT
1 Rodney's Café
8 Silver Garden
13 Starlight Restaurant
14 Sunrise
19 J&N's King Burger
23 New Riverside Café
26 Soffie's Restaurant
27 Río Mar Restaurant

OTHER
3 Ramos Monument
4 BTL Telephone Towers
5 Water Tower ('Reservoir')
6 Ice Factory
7 Affordable Corner Store & Laundromat
9 Treasured Travels
10 Police
11 BTL Telephone Office
12 Barclay's Bank
15 Courthouse
16 Hospital
17 Public Health Center
18 Pharmacy
21 Fish Market
24 Scotiabank
25 Belize Bank
28 Richie's Bus Service
29 Baptist Church
30 Post Office
32 B Nicholas Studio
34 Z-Line Bus Station
35 Shell Fuel Station
36 Texaco Fuel Station

station. The airstrip, two km north of the center, near the Pelican Beach Resort, has Rodney's Café and a small airline building.

Treasured Travels (☎ (5) 22578, fax (5) 23481), 64 Commerce St (PO Box 43), a travel agency, can handle questions about airline tickets and the like.

The Affordable Corner Store & Laundromat is open from 9 am to noon and 2 to 8 pm (the last wash is at 5 pm). It's closed Thursday afternoon and Sunday.

Places to Stay

Pal's Guest House (☎ /fax (5) 22095), 868-A Magoon St, is the best choice, spartan but clean, with a sea breeze and the sound of the surf. You pay US$18 a double in a room with shared bath, US$24 with private bath and TV.

The recommended family-run *Bluefield Lodge* (☎ (5) 22742), 6 Bluefield Rd, has seven tidy rooms with fan for US$12.50/14.50 a single/double with shared bath or US$17.50 with private bath.

On the southern bank of North Stann Creek, at the creek's mouth, are two other cheap choices. The *Río Mar Hotel* (☎ (5) 22201), 977 Southern Foreshore, has nine rooms, all with bath and most with TV, at US$18 to US$28, single or double. The upstairs rooms are preferable. The restaurant and bar serve good, cheap meals and drinks.

Nearby is *Soffie's Hotel* (☎ (5) 22789), 970 Chatuye St, with 10 serviceable rooms ranging in price from US$22 to US$33, the most expensive having air-con; all have private bath. There's a restaurant on the ground floor and good views of the water from upstairs.

Riverside Hotel (☎ (5) 22168, fax (5) 22296), 5 Commerce St, at the northern end of the bridge, has 12 rooms with clean shared showers for US$11 per person.

Bonefish Hotel (☎ (5) 22165, fax (5) 22296), 15 Mahogany St (PO Box 21), is comfortable – the 10 big, clean rooms have fan, air-con, TV and private bath for US$53 to US$75 a double with air-con. There's a dining room as well. For reservations in the USA call ☎ (800) 798-1558.

Pelican Beach Resort (☎ (5) 22044, fax (5) 22570, pelicanbeach@btl.net), PO Box 14, is Dangriga's upmarket lodging place. It's at the northern end of town, on the beach, and boasts a restaurant, bar, sand beach, boat dock and a full program of tours to sites in the area. Simple rooms with bath cost US$45 to US$64 a single, US$60 to US$80 a double and US$73 to US$93 a triple. The Pelican also has cottages on South Water Caye (US$151 to US$171 double per day, three meals included).

Places to Eat

Río Mar Hotel and *Soffie's Hotel* have cheap restaurants. The *Bonefish* and *Pelican* are the upmarket places.

The Garifunas

Southern Belize is the home of the Garifunas (or Garinagus, also called Black Caribs), people of mixed South American Indian and African blood, who inhabited the island of St Vincent as a free people in the 17th century. By the end of the 18th century, British colonizers had brought the independent-minded Garifunas under their control and transported them from one island to another in an effort to subdue them.

In the early 19th century, oppression and wandering finally brought many of the Garifunas to southern Belize. The most memorable migration took place late in 1832, when on November 19 a large number of Garifunas reached Belize from Honduras in dugout canoes. The event is celebrated annually in Belize as Garifuna Settlement Day.

The Garifunas, who account for less than 10% of Belize's population, look more African than Indian, but they speak a language that's much more Indian than African, and their unique culture combines aspects of both peoples.

Most of the citizens of Dangriga, chief town of the Stann Creek District, are Garifunas. Dangriga is the place to be on Garifuna Settlement Day as the town explodes in a frenzy of dancing, drinking and celebration of the Garifuna/Garinagu heritage. ■

The *New Riverside Café* on Riverside Drive (also called Waight's St) 50 meters east of the North Stann Creek Bridge, is run by an expatriate Englishman named Jim, who serves up three tasty meals daily at budget to moderate prices. This is a good place to ask about fishing and snorkeling trips out to the cayes or treks inland.

Otherwise, the locals favor *J & N's King Burger*, a tidy lunchroom on Commerce St with a long and varied menu, from burgers to fish fillets to chicken. Their breakfast special of eggs, refried beans, toast and coffee is good at US$2.75.

Most of the other restaurants along Commerce St are Chinese: the *Sunrise*, *Starlight* and *Silver Garden* serve full meals for about US$6.

Getting There & Away
Air Maya Airways and Tropic Air serve Dangriga. For details, see the Belize Getting There & Around chapter.

Bus Z-Line has five buses daily from Belize City (via Hummingbird Hwy, 170 km, four hours, US$7; via Coastal Hwy, 79 km, three hours, US$5). Return buses leave Dangriga for Belize City at 5, 6 and 9 am; on Sunday departures are at 10 am and 3 pm.

Two Z-Line buses (12:15 and 4:30 pm) continue southwards to Placencia (85 km, two to 3½ hours, US$4). Richie's Bus Service also has a bus at 5 pm.

Z-Line buses depart Dangriga for Punta Gorda (169 km, six hours, US$5.50) at noon and 7 pm (on Sunday, at 2 pm only).

Boat A motor launch departs Roatán (Honduras) Wednesday and Saturday at 8 am, arriving in Dangriga at the bridge over North Stann Creek around 12:30 pm and departing for the return trip to Roatán shortly thereafter. The fare is US$35 one way.

SOUTHERN CAYES
Several cayes are accessed from Dangriga.

Tobacco Caye's lodging possibilities include *Island Camps* (☎ (2) 72109, (5) 22201), 51 Regent St, Belize City; *Reef End Lodge*, PO Box 10, Dangriga; and

---

Glover's Atoll Resort,
Glover's Atoll Resort (☎ (1) 48351, (5) 23048), PO Box 563, Belize City, offers an adventurous budget living experience on the cayes of Glover's Atoll.

Participants help to load and sail the boat, which departs Sittee River village near Hopkins (south of Dangriga) each Sunday morning at 8 am on the five-km, three- to four-hour voyage to the island. You stay on the island in simple beachfront cabañas – equipped with candles for light, rainwater to drink, outhouse, etc.

Make a reservation by phone or mail, buy some supplies (food, towels, etc), then on Saturday take the 8 am Z-Line bus from Belize City to Sittee River, the 12:15 pm Z-Line bus from Dangriga to Sittee River or another bus to the Sittee River junction, then hitch to the village and the Glover's Atoll Resort.

You must take some supplies to the island, as this is a very simple place, but there's lots of water-sports equipment for rent, excellent diving and very few other people to disturb the tranquillity.

The basic cost is US$102 per person per week for lodging in a beach cabin or tent or US$86 for a camping spot, including roundtrip boat transportation between Sittee River and the island (including an average amount of luggage and your small box of supplies) and use of the cooking area. Any other services (drinking water, meals, phone calls, equipment rentals, etc) are at extra cost. ■

Fairweather & Friends, PO Box 240, Belize City.

Dangriga's *Pelican Beach Resort* (see the Dangriga Places to Stay section) has cottages on South Water Caye.

SOUTHERN HIGHWAY
The Southern Hwy, south of Dangriga, is unpaved and can be rough, especially in the rainy months, but along the way are some good opportunities for experiencing untouristy Belize. Some southern reaches of the highway, near Punta Gorda, are being paved.

Hopkins
Population 1100

The farming and fishing village of Hopkins is seven km east of the Southern Hwy, on the coast. Most of its people are Garifunas, living as the coastal inhabitants of Belize have lived for centuries.

If you're interested in simple living and Garifuna culture, visit Hopkins and stay at the *Sandy Beach Lodge* (☎ (5) 22023), at the southern end of the village. The lodge, owned and operated by the Sandy Beach Women's Cooperative, has six simple thatched rooms renting for US$13/20 a single/double with shared bath, US$20/27 with private bath. Meals cost US$5 for breakfast or dinner, US$7 for lunch. There's also *Jungle Jeanie's* beach huts. The *Swinging Armadillo* has two rooms for rent as well, but they're right next to the bar, and thus noisy.

More expensive accommodations are at the *Jaguar Reef Lodge* (☎ /fax (2) 12041), with 14 rooms in cabañas right on the beach.

Sittee River
Another small coastal village where you can get away from it all is Sittee River. *Prospect Cool Spot Guest House & Camp Site* (☎ (5) 22006, (5) 22389; ask for Isaac Kelly Sr) will put you up in adequate simplicity for US$10/15 a single/double or US$2.50 in a tent. Simple, inexpensive meals are served.

Cockscomb Basin Wildlife Sanctuary
Almost halfway between Dangriga and Independence is the village of Maya Centre, where a track goes 10 km west to the Cockscomb Basin Wildlife Sanctuary, sometimes called the Jaguar Reserve.

Created in 1984, the sanctuary now covers more than 40,000 hectares. The varied topography and lush tropical forest make this an excellent place to observe Belizean wildlife. Within the reserve are found wild cats including jaguars, pumas, ocelots, margays and jaguarundis. Other animals, many the prey of the cats, include agoutis, anteaters, armadillos, Baird's tapirs, brocket deer, coatis, kinkajous,

otters, pacas, peccaries and the weasel-like tayras. Reptiles, some of which are deadly poisonous, include the boa constrictor and the fer-de-lance. There are birds galore.

There's no public transport to the reserve, but the walk through the lush forest is a pretty one. At the reserve is a campsite (US$2 per person), several simple shared rental cabins with solar electricity (US$15 per person, kitchen use US$1 per person), a visitors' center and numerous hiking trails. Though you cannot be assured of seeing a jaguar (though this is their preferred habitat), you will certainly enjoy seeing many of the hundreds of other species of birds, plants and animals in this rich environment.

For information, contact the Belize Audubon Society (☎ (2) 35004, fax (2) 34985, base@btl.net), 12 Fort St (PO Box 1001), Belize City, or the Cockscomb Basin Wildlife Sanctuary, PO Box 90, Dangriga.

PLACENCIA
Population 600

Perched at the southern tip of a long, narrow, sandy peninsula, Placencia is 'the caye you can drive to'. Not too long ago, the only practical way to get here was by boat from the mainland at Independence/ Big Creek. Now there is a road all the way down the peninsula and an airstrip just north of the town. But Placencia still has the wonderful laid-back ambiance of the cayes, along with beaches, varied accommodations and friendly local people. Activities here are the same as on the cayes: swimming, sunbathing, lazing, water sports and excursions to cayes and to points inland. Unfortunately, the village is littered; the Belize Tourism Industry Association (BTIA) *Bettah no litta* campaign has yet to have an effect.

Orientation & Information
The town owes its layout to years gone by, when all commerce and activity was carried out by boat and there was little use for streets. Thus, the village's main north-south 'street' is actually a narrow concrete footpath less than a meter wide which threads

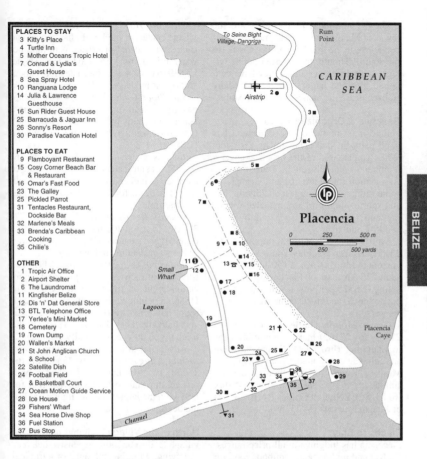

PLACES TO STAY
3 Kitty's Place
4 Turtle Inn
5 Mother Oceans Tropic Hotel
7 Conrad & Lydia's
   Guest House
8 Sea Spray Hotel
10 Ranguana Lodge
14 Julia & Lawrence
   Guesthouse
16 Sun Rider Guest House
25 Barracuda & Jaguar Inn
26 Sonny's Resort
30 Paradise Vacation Hotel

PLACES TO EAT
9 Flamboyant Restaurant
15 Cosy Corner Beach Bar
   & Restaurant
16 Omar's Fast Food
23 The Galley
25 Pickled Parrot
31 Tentacles Restaurant,
   Dockside Bar
32 Marlene's Meals
33 Brenda's Caribbean
   Cooking
35 Chilie's

OTHER
1 Tropic Air Office
2 Airport Shelter
6 The Laundromat
11 Kingfisher Belize
12 Dis 'n' Dat General Store
13 BTL Telephone Office
17 Yerlee's Mini Market
18 Cemetery
19 Town Dump
20 Wallen's Market
21 St John Anglican Church
   & School
22 Satellite Dish
24 Football Field
   & Basketball Court
27 Ocean Motion Guide Service
28 Ice House
29 Fishers' Wharf
34 Sea Horse Dive Shop
36 Fuel Station
37 Bus Stop

CARIBBEAN SEA

To Seine Bight Village, Dangriga

Rum Point

Airstrip

Placencia

Small Wharf

Lagoon

Channel

Placencia Caye

0   250   500 m
0   250   500 yards

BELIZE

its way among simple wood-frame houses (some on stilts) and beachfront lodges.

An easy walk takes you anywhere. From the airstrip it's one km south to the northern limit of the village, then 1.5 km to the southern tip of the peninsula. Various resorts are scattered along the coast north of Placencia.

An unpaved road skirts the town to the west, ending at the peninsula's southern tip, which is the bus stop.

There is no central landmark in the village and no town square. At the southern end you'll find the wharf, the fuel station, the bus stop and the ice house. Midway to

the north, the Flamboyant Restaurant gives about as much civic focus as one gets (or wants) in Placencia.

Placencia has no bank, but you can change travelers' checks at Wallen's Market if and when they have enough cash; try in the afternoon.

There are public telephones at the BTL office, at Sonny's Resort and at the gas station at the southern end of the village.

Laundry service is available at several places, including The Laundromat (☎ (6) 23123) in the northern part of the village, open from 8 am to 6 pm every day.

On the mainland to the west are the towns of Mango Creek (to the north), Independence (in the middle) and Big Creek (to the south). Though they started out as villages with different names, they have coalesced into one larger settled area. Many Belizeans use the names interchangeably.

Beaches & Organized Tours

Unlike most of the cayes, Placencia has good palm-lined beaches on its east side. When you're tired of the beach, contact a member of the Placencia Tourist Guide Association (there are 16) and arrange for some sailing, snorkeling, scuba diving, fly- and sportfishing, bird and manatee watching and trips to the Cockscomb Basin Wildlife Sanctuary.

Morris Caye Adventure Camping (☎ (6) 23152; ask for Douglas Young) will take you out to Morris Caye, a 150-by-40-meter island 13 km east of Placencia, for snorkeling (US$25 per person with equipment, but no lunch) and rustic camping (US$7.50 per person).

Ocean Motion Guide Service (☎ (6) 23363, (6) 23162) makes snorkeling trips to Laughing Bird Caye, Ranguana Caye and Silk Caye, and nature boat trips up the Monkey River. Many other guides do similar trips. Try Placencia Tours (☎ /fax (6) 23186), Southern Guides (☎ (6) 23277) or Jaguar Tours (☎ (6) 23139).

Places to Stay

Placencia has lodgings in all price ranges. Budget and midrange accommodations are in the village; top-end places are several kilometers to the north along the beach.

Village Center *Conrad & Lydia's Guest House* (☎ (6) 23117, fax (6) 23354) has simple rooms (shared bath) for US$19 on the lower floor or US$22 on the upper floor. They also have a house for rent.

Paradise Vacation Hotel is a tidy white board structure at the southern end of the village. Rooms (single or double) sharing bath rent for US$14; with private bath they're US$22 to US$25.

Sea Spray Hotel (☎ (6) 23148), right in the village center on the beach, has rooms and cabins with shared or private bath (and hot water) priced from US$14 to US$38 a single, US$19 to US$44 a double. The more expensive rooms are larger and have sea views.

Sun Rider Guest House (☎ (6) 23236) has good, clean rooms with bath, facing a beach with shady palms (US$23 a double). One room has two beds and a kitchenette (US$39).

Julia & Lawrence Guesthouse (☎ (6) 23185) is central and clean enough, but not as cheap as it once was. Its four rooms with shared bath go for US$12/16/21 a single/double/triple.

Sonny's Resort (☎ (6) 23103, fax (2) 32819), to the south, has expensive rooms (US$44) and cabañas (US$58) with shower. There's a restaurant and bar as well.

Ranguana Lodge (☎ /fax (6) 23112) has tidy and attractive, if simple, mahogany cabins right on the beach for US$50 to US$60 a double with private shower. Each room has a fan, refrigerator, coffeemaker and balcony. They knock US$10 off the price if you do your own daily cleaning.

Wende Bryan and Anton Holmes' *Barracuda & Jaguar Inn* (☎ (6) 23330, fax (6) 23250) has two hardwood cabañas with refrigerator and coffeemaker that rent for US$45 in the winter season, light breakfast included.

North of the Village Lodgings north of the village tend to be more expensive but very satisfying, with the ambiance of a tropical isle. All offer various water sports, activities and excursions.

Kitty's Place (☎ (6) 23227, fax (6) 23226, kittys@btl.net), 2.5 km north of the village, is a Caribbean Victorian beachfront lodge with rooms (US$88/98 a single/double) and cabins (US$123/138). This is perhaps Placencia's best place to stay.

Turtle Inn (☎ (6) 23244, fax (6) 23245), a short walk south of Placencia's airstrip, has the perfect atmosphere: thatched cabañas of bamboo, each with hammocks swinging lazily on its front porch, and a palm-lined white-sand beach bordering the azure Caribbean. Cabañas with private bath and fan cost US$95/120/150/170 a single/double/triple/quad, including breakfast, tax and service. For lunch and dinner, add about US$30 per person.

Mother Oceans Tropic Hotel (☎ (6) 23223, fax (6) 23224, in the USA (800) 662-3091), PO Box 7, has six cabins with kitchenette for US$98 a double. The restaurant is open from mid-December through mid-April. Clent Whitehead, the owner, has been here for most of two decades and brought the first motor vehicles to the peninsula.

Nautical Inn (☎ /fax (6) 22310) is a small modern resort in Seine Bight, an unspoiled Belizean fishing village north of Placencia. Ben and Janie Ruoti are equipped for all adventures, renting motorcycles, running diving and coastal tours, etc. The 12 comfortable modern rooms cost US$135/180 a single/double, tax, service and three meals included.

Places to Eat

A social center of the village is the *Flamboyant Restaurant*, with indoor and outdoor tables and the usual list of sandwiches, rice and beans and fish dishes for US$3 to US$6. Happy hour is from 7 to 9 pm. Say 'Hi!' to Maureen, the friendly manager.

Omar's Fast Food, in the Sun Rider Guest House, has homemade food and low prices, with views of the beach. Try the cheap, good burritos or, if you can afford it, the conch steak for US$7.50.

Brenda's Caribbean Cooking is a cozy thatched eatery down on the southern shore, with cheap, delicious daily specials of creative Belizean cuisine for US$3 to US$5. A few meters to the west is *Marlene's Meals*, run by Brenda's sister, who specializes in snacks and baked goods.

Right by the gas station on the beach is *Chilie's*, a snack stand hangout popular with local boaters. The menu is verbal; a sign boasts 'All you can eat – $5000'.

The *Cosy Corner Beach Bar & Restaurant* is open for lunch and dinner daily, and goes on with drinks until 2 am. Another good place to hang out late is the *Pickled Parrot*, the restaurant and bar at the Barracuda & Jaguar Inn. Try the enormous pizza for US$15.

The Galley, west of the main part of the village, is a favorite for long dinners with good conversation. A full meal with drinks costs about US$10 to US$15.

Tentacles Restaurant is another evening favorite – a breezy, atmospheric place with its popular *Dockside Bar* built on a wharf out in the water. It may be closed off-season.

Getting There & Away

Air Maya Airways and Tropic Air serve Placencia with daily flights. For details, see the Belize Getting There & Around chapter. The village begins one km to the south of the airstrip; a taxi meets most flights. If you're staying at one of the pricier resorts, ask to be picked up.

Bus Two daily Z-Line buses from Belize City via Dangriga continue to Placencia (3½ hours); there's a Richie's Bus Service bus as well. From Placencia, Z-Line buses depart for Dangriga and Belize City at 5:30 and 5:45 am; the Richie's bus departs at 6 am.

You can also take one of the three daily Z-Line buses which stop at Independence, and get a boat over to Placencia, though the price of the boat can be high if you can't share it with other travelers.

Boat Daily except Sunday, the *Hokey Pokey Water Taxi* (US$5) departs Placencia at 10 am for Mango Creek, returning to Placencia from Mango Creek at 2:30 pm. The water taxi departs Placencia again at 4 pm. Many boats will do a charter run to/from Mango Creek for US$20 for up to six persons.

A boat runs each Monday at 8 am from Placencia to Puerto Cortés (Honduras), a two-hour voyage costing US$40. For tickets and current information, contact Kingfisher Belize (☎ (6) 23323).

BELIZE

PUNTA GORDA
Population 3000

At the end of the Southern Hwy is Punta Gorda. Rainfall and humidity are at their highest and the jungle at its lushest in the Toledo District, which surrounds Punta Gorda, the southernmost town in Belize. Punta Gordians endure more than four meters of rain per year – prepare yourself for at least a short downpour almost every day.

Known throughout Belize simply as 'PG', this sleepy town was founded for the Garifunas who emigrated from Honduras in 1832. In 1866, after the US Civil War, some Confederate veterans received land grants from the British government and founded a settlement here, but it didn't endure.

Though still predominantly Garifuna, it is also home to the usual bewildering variety of Belizean citizenry: Americans, British, Canadians, Chinese, Creoles, East Indians, Lebanese and Kekchi Maya.

Fishing was the major livelihood for almost two centuries, but now farming is important as well. There is also an incipient tourist trade, as PG is the base for excursions inland to the Mayan archaeological sites at Lubaantun and Nim Li Punit, the

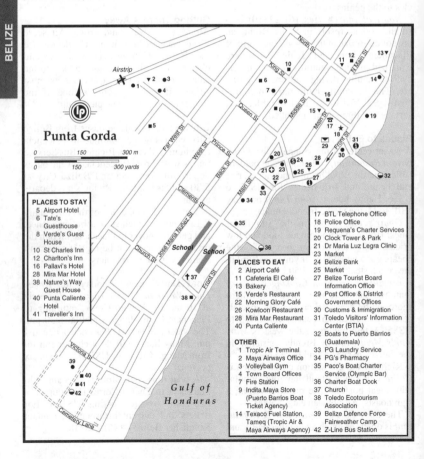

Punta Gorda

Gulf of Honduras

PLACES TO STAY
5 Airport Hotel
6 Tate's Guesthouse
8 Verde's Guest House
10 St Charles Inn
12 Charlton's Inn
16 Pallavi's Hotel
28 Mira Mar Hotel
38 Nature's Way Guest House
40 Punta Caliente Hotel
41 Traveller's Inn

PLACES TO EAT
2 Airport Café
11 Cafeteria El Café
13 Bakery
15 Verde's Restaurant
22 Morning Glory Café
26 Kowloon Restaurant
28 Mira Mar Restaurant
40 Punta Caliente

OTHER
1 Tropic Air Terminal
2 Maya Airways Office
3 Volleyball Gym
4 Town Board Offices
7 Fire Station
9 Indita Maya Store (Puerto Barrios Boat Ticket Agency)
14 Texaco Fuel Station, Tameq (Tropic Air & Maya Airways Agency)
17 BTL Telephone Office
18 Police Office
19 Requena's Charter Services
20 Clock Tower & Park
21 Dr Maria Luz Legra Clinic
23 Market
24 Belize Bank
25 Market
27 Belize Tourist Board Information Office
29 Post Office & District Government Offices
30 Customs & Immigration
31 Toledo Visitors' Information Center (BTIA)
32 Boats to Puerto Barrios (Guatemala)
33 PG Laundry Service
34 PG's Pharmacy
35 Paco's Boat Charter Service (Olympic Bar)
36 Charter Boat Dock
37 Church
38 Toledo Ecotourism Association
39 Belize Defence Force Fairweather Camp
42 Z-Line Bus Station

Mayan villages of San Pedro Colombia and San Antonio and the Blue Creek Cave.

Late in February each year, Punta Gorda celebrates the International Rainforest Festival, which pursues an ecological theme.

Orientation & Information

The town center is the triangular park with a bandstand and the distinctive blue-and-white clock tower. The airstrip is 350 meters to the northwest, and the dock for boats to and from Guatemala is even closer.

The Belize Tourist Board (☎ (7) 22531) office is on Front St, open every day from 9 am to 5 pm. At the boat dock, the Toledo Visitors' Information Center (☎ (7) 22470), PO Box 73, run by the BTIA, is open daily except Thursday and Sunday from 9 am to 1 pm.

Places to Stay

Punta Gorda's lodging is resolutely budget-class, with only a few places rising above basic shelter.

Nature's Way Guest House (☎ (7) 22119), 65 North Front St, is the intrepid travelers' gathering place. This converted house charges US$9/14/18 a single/double/triple in rooms with clean shared showers (no heated water). Trips by minibus and boat can be arranged to all points of interest around PG.

The sleepy *Airport Hotel*, near the airstrip, is quiet, and identical in price.

St Charles Inn (☎ (7) 22149), 23 King St, offers a good value for the money. Clean and well-kept (for PG), it has rooms with private bath and fan for US$17/23 a single/double. Small groups sometimes fill it.

Tate's Guesthouse (☎ (7) 22196), 34 José María Nuñez St (enter on West St), is clean and family-run, with good rooms for US$13 to US$23 a single, US$15 to US$25 a double or US$35 a double with air-con; the more expensive rooms have private bath.

Punta Caliente Hotel (☎ (7) 22561), 108 José María Nuñez St near the Z-Line bus station, has a good restaurant on the ground floor and rooms above. Each room has good ventilation as well as fan and private bath. Prices are good: US$22 to US$28 a double.

Charlton's Inn (☎ (7) 22197, fax (7) 22471), 9 North Main St, has serviceable

rooms with shower for US$17/23 a single/double.

The town's other budget hotels are cheap, and rightly so, offering shelter but little comfort. *Mira Mar Hotel* (☎ (7) 22033), 95 Front St, has a Chinese restaurant occupying the ground floor and a porch for watching passersby. Rooms can be simple, at US$14/26 a single/double with private bath, or more elaborate (US$59 with bath, TV and air-con). *Verde's Guest House* (☎ (7) 22069), on José María Nuñez St, is the standard frame barracks construction – OK at US$11 a double in a waterless room. *Pallavi's Hotel*, on North Main St, is similar.

For real comfort you must step up to the *Traveller's Inn* (☎ (7) 22568, fax (7) 22814), at the southern end of José María Nuñez St, next to the Z-Line bus station. For US$53/67/75 a single/double/triple you get a modern air-conditioned room with private bath and cable TV, breakfast included. There's secured parking as well.

Places to Eat

Morning Glory Café, at Front and Prince Sts, is a standard Belizean restaurant/bar, more attractive than most. Hours are 7 am to 2 pm and 6:30 to 11 pm (closed on Monday off-season).

Punta Caliente serves stew pork, fish fillet, beans and rice with chicken and similar dishes for US$3.50 to US$5, and it's all good. *Mira Mar* and *Kowloon* are the places to go for Chinese food at only slightly higher prices.

Cafeteria El Café is a tidy place open for breakfast and lunch. *Verde's Restaurant* has standard Belizean family cooking.

The *Airport Café* has good, big plates of rice, beans, cabbage and red snapper for US$3.75. It's a good place to meet other travelers.

Getting There & Away

Air Punta Gorda is served daily by Maya Airways and Tropic Air. For details see the Belize Getting There & Around chapter. Tameq, behind the Texaco fuel station, sells Tropic Air and Maya Airways tickets.

BELIZE

There are ticket offices at the airport as well. If you plan to fly out of PG, be at the airstrip at least 15 minutes before departure time, as the planes sometimes leave early.

Bus Z-Line buses (☎ (7) 22165) roll down the Southern Hwy from Belize City (8 am, noon and 3 pm), Belmopan, Dangriga and Independence (for Placencia, US$4.50) to Punta Gorda for US$11, returning northwards at 5 and 9 am and noon. On Friday and Sunday, there's also a 3:30 pm bus northwards.

Boat Boats connect Punta Gorda with several points in Guatemala and Honduras. Requena's Charter Services (☎ (7) 22070), 12 Front St (PO Box 18), operates the *Mariestela*, departing Punta Gorda at 9 am for Puerto Barrios (Guatemala), and departing Puerto Barrios' public pier at 2 pm for the return to PG. Tickets cost US$10 one way.

On Tuesday and Friday, the traditional mail boat run by the Agencia de Lineas Maritimas Puerto Santo Tomás de Castilla, Izabal (Guatemala), also runs between Punta Gorda and Puerto Barrios. It arrives from Puerto Barrios at 9 am and departs Punta Gorda at noon for the return to Puerto Barrios. Adults pay US$10, children US$7. Buy your tickets at the Indita Maya Store (☎ (7) 22065) on José María Nuñez St.

Paco's Boat goes to Lívingston (Guatemala) most days, charging US$12.50 one way. Ask for details at the Olympic Bar on Clements St.

There are occasional boats to points in Honduras as well. I expect that in the next few years this will develop into regular service. Contact the Belize Tourist Board office for the latest information.

AROUND PUNTA GORDA

Two organizations can help you get a close-up-and-personal look at traditional village life in the Toledo District.

Toledo Ecotourism Association

The Toledo Ecotourism Association (☎ (7) 22119, fax (7) 22199, ttea@btl.net) at

Nature's Way Guest House, 65 North Front St (PO Box 75), Punta Gorda, runs a Village Guesthouse and Ecotrail Program which takes participants to any of 13 traditional Mopan Maya, Kekchi Maya, Creole and Garifuna villages.

The basic village guesthouse tour gives visitors overnight lodging in a village home, three meals (each at a different village home) and two nature tours for US$43. The full tour adds music, dancing and storytelling for US$88.

These prices cover your village stay and activities, but not transportation. Local buses run between the villages and Punta Gorda on Wednesday and Saturday for US$5; special charter trips are very expensive – around US$80 – so plan accordingly.

Canoe trips, horseback riding, camping, kayaking, fishing and lessons in traditional arts and crafts (backstrap weaving, embroidery, jipijapa basketry) are available by special arrangement.

More than 85% of what you pay stays in the village with the villagers, helping them to achieve a sustainable, ecologically advantageous economy as an alternative to traditional slash-and-burn agriculture.

Dem Dats Doin

Dem Dats Doin (☎ (7) 22470), PO Box 73, Punta Gorda, is an innovative ecological farm founded by Antonio and Yvonne Villoria. Photovoltaic cells for electricity, biogas methane for light and refrigeration, natural insect repellents and fertilizers in place of chemicals – the farm is a showcase of what determined, sensitive and knowledgeable people can do to promote appropriate technology and sustainable farming.

A tour of the farm costs US$5 and takes between one and two hours. Bed and breakfast is sometimes available; check in advance.

The Villorias also supervise a program for home stays with Mayan families, called The Indigenous Experience. They will put you in touch with a village family who will welcome you into their home, provide you with a hammock and meals and also let you share in their traditional way of life. No special allowances are made for you, so you should be fully prepared for very simple living conditions. In return for roughing it, you'll learn a lot and will provide valuable cash income to help the family get by.

Hammock rent is US$4 per night; meals cost US$1.50 each. The Villorias ask a US$5 fee for putting you in touch with a family. You should inquire in advance by mail if possible, and enclose US$2 to pay for postage and printing.

Home stays are customarily in San Pedro Columbia, a Kekchi Maya village 41 km northwest of Punta Gorda, whose founders fled the tedious life of the coffee fincas in Alta Verapaz (Guatemala) to find freedom in Belize. Their Guatemalan highland customs, traditions and dress have been preserved to a remarkable degree and differ markedly from those of the lowland Mopan or 'Belizean' Maya.

Lubaantun

The Mayan ruins at Lubaantun, two km northwest of San Pedro Columbia village, are aptly named. Lubaantun ('Fallen Stones') has been excavated to some extent, but not restored. The many temples are still mostly covered with jungle, so you will have to use your imagination to envisage the great city (covering over three sq km) which once thrived here.

Archaeologists have found evidence that Lubaantun flourished until the late 8th century AD, after which little was built. In its heyday, the merchants of Lubaantun traded with people on the cayes, in Mexico and Guatemala and perhaps beyond.

Of its 18 plazas, only the three most important (plazas III through V) have been cleared. Plaza IV, the most important, is built along a ridge of hills and surrounded by the site's most impressive buildings: structures 10, 12 and 33.

Getting There & Away San Pedro Columbia is 41 km northwest of Punta Gorda off the Southern Hwy. A bus can drop you at the fuel station on the highway; from here it's a walk of almost six km to the village.

If you catch a San Antonio bus from the main plaza in Punta Gorda, it will get you 2.5 km closer to San Pedro Columbia.

Nim Li Punit

About 38 km northwest of Punta Gorda, just north of Big Falls and less than one km west of the Southern Hwy, stand the ruins of Nim Li Punit, a less impressive site than Lubaantun. Nim Li Punit ('Big Hat'), named for the headgear worn by the richly clad figure on Stela 14, may in fact have been a tributary city to larger, more powerful Lubaantun.

Discovered by oil prospectors in 1976, it was looted within several years by antiquities thieves. In 1983 proper archaeological work was begun, resulting in some excavation and preliminary studies but little restoration or stabilization.

The South Group of structures was the city's ceremonial center, and is of the most interest. The plaza has been cleared, but the structures surrounding it are largely unrestored. Have a look at the stelae, especially Stela 14, at almost 10 meters the longest Mayan stela yet discovered, and Stela 15, dating from 721 AD, the earliest dated work recovered here.

San Antonio & Blue Creek

The Mopan Maya of San Antonio are descended from former inhabitants of the Guatemalan village of San Luis Petén, just across the border. The San Antonians fled oppression in their home country to find freedom in Belize. They brought their ancient customs with them, however, and you can observe a traditional lowland Mayan village on a short visit here. If you are here during a festival, your visit will be much more memorable.

About six km west of San Antonio, near the village of Santa Cruz, is the archaeological site of Uxbenka, which has numerous carved stelae.

About 20 km south of San Antonio lies the village of Blue Creek, and beyond it the nature reserve of Blue Creek Cave. Hike into the site (less than one km) along the marked trail and enjoy the rain forest

BELIZE

around you and the pools, channels, caves and refreshingly cool waters of the creek system.

Places to Stay There is one small hotel in San Antonio: *Bol's Hilltop Hotel*, with beds for US$5. If you'd prefer not to stay the night, arrange a day excursion from Punta Gorda.

Getting There & Away The San Antonio bus runs for the convenience of San Antonio villagers going into the big city, departing from the village each morning at 5 am for Punta Gorda and returning from Punta Gorda at 4 pm. The best way to get around this area is on a tour organized by the Toledo Ecotourism Association (see earlier in this section).

Western Belize

Western Belize is the country's highlands, with peaks rising above 300 meters. The land is beautiful. What has been cleared is cultivated by diligent farmers who produce most of Belize's fresh fruits and vegetables.

Some travelers pass through Cayo District, stopping for a few days in San Ignacio in order to take a short excursion into the forests of Mountain Pine Ridge. Others come for a week or so, staying at one of the many forest lodges that provide simple accommodations, meals and the opportunity to explore the area by canoe, mountain bike or 4WD vehicle, on horseback or on foot.

Most lodges are well away from the towns (which is the point), but this means you will probably eat most of your meals at the lodges. Figure in this cost when you plan your budget.

Head west from Belize City along Cemetery Rd (right through Lords Ridge Cemetery), which continues westwards as the Western Hwy. Along the way you'll pass Hattieville, founded in 1961 after Hurricane Hattie wreaked destruction on Belize City. Many residents sought refuge from the storm's violence in this inland spot. Some decided to stay, and Hattieville was born.

BELIZE ZOO

The Belize Zoo & Tropical Education Centre (☎ (9) 23310), PO Box 474, Belize City, is home to a variety of indigenous Belizean cats and other animals, kept in natural surroundings. The zoo's terrain, 46 km west of Belize City (Mile 29 on the Western Hwy), hasn't been cleared; it's as if cages just appeared from nowhere and then paths were built for tourists. A sign marks the turnoff for the zoo, on the northern side of the road; the entrance is less than one km off the highway. Hours are 9 am to 4:30 pm daily; admission costs US$6.50, and it goes

to a worthy cause. The zoo is closed on major Belizean holidays.

The Belize Zoo had an odd beginning. In 1983 Sharon Matola was in charge of 17 Belizean animals during the shooting of a wildlife film entitled *Path of the Raingods*. By the time filming was over, her animals were partly tame, and thus might not have survived in the wild. With the movie budget exhausted, there were no funds to support the animals, so Matola founded the Belize Zoo. In 1991 the zoo was substantially enhanced with spacious natural enclosures for the inhabitants and a modern visitors' center.

Take a map leaflet and follow the marked trails through the zoo, a microcosm of Belize's ecological wealth. The self-guided tour takes 45 minutes to an hour. You'll see Baird's tapir (Belize's national animal) and the gibnut or paca *(tepezcuintle)*, a sort of rodent that appears on some Belizean dinner tables. Jaguar, ocelot, howler monkey, peccary, vulture, stork and even a crocodile appear during the fascinating tour. People spend a lot of money at Disneyland to see hokey mechanical replicas of such wild creatures; here they're all real and right at home.

Places to Eat

JB's Watering Hole (☎ (1) 48098), at Mile 32 on the Western Hwy, is a traditional stopping-place for food and drink. The original, eponymous JB is long gone, his place currently being held by a European couple who serve surprisingly good continental and Central American cuisine at moderate prices.

Getting There & Away

See the Belize Getting There & Around chapter for details on buses running along the Western Hwy; ask to get out at the Belize Zoo. Look at your watch when you get out; the next bus will come by in about an hour.

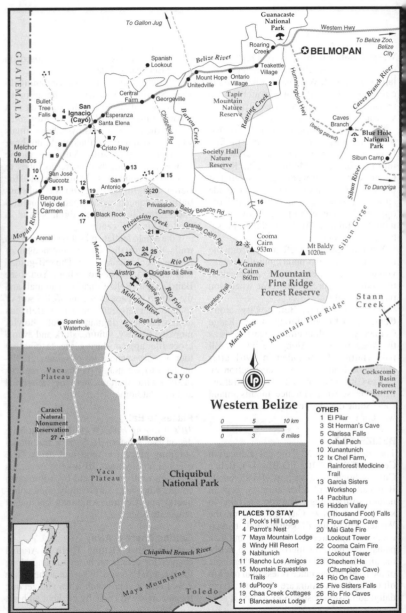

Western Belize

OTHER
1 El Pilar
3 St Herman's Cave
5 Clarissa Falls
6 Cahal Pech
10 Xunantunich
12 Ix Chel Farm,
   Rainforest Medicine
   Trail
13 Garcia Sisters
   Workshop
14 Pacbitun
16 Hidden Valley
   (Thousand Foot) Falls
17 Flour Camp Cave
20 Mai Gate Fire
   Lookout Tower
22 Cooma Cairn Fire
   Lookout Tower
23 Chechem Ha
   (Chumpiate Cave)
24 Río On Cave
25 Five Sisters Falls
26 Río Frio Caves
27 Caracol

PLACES TO STAY
2 Pook's Hill Lodge
4 Parrot's Nest
7 Maya Mountain Lodge
8 Windy Hill Resort
9 Nabitunich
11 Rancho Los Amigos
15 Mountain Equestrian
   Trails
18 duPlooy's
19 Chaa Creek Cottages
21 Blancaneaux Lodge

GUANACASTE NATIONAL PARK

Almost four km east of Belmopan, a few meters north of the junction of the Western and Hummingbird Hwys, is Guanacaste National Park. This small (21-hectare) nature reserve at the confluence of Roaring Creek and the Belize River holds a giant guanacaste tree which survived the axes of canoe makers and still rises majestically in its jungle habitat. The great tree supports a whole ecosystem of its own, festooned with bromeliads, epiphytes, ferns and dozens of other varieties of plants. Wild orchids flourish in the spongy soil among the ferns and mosses, and several species of 'exotic' animals pass through. Birdlife is abundant and colorful.

Admission is free (donations are accepted). The reserve is open every day from 8 am to 4:30 pm. Stop at the information booth to learn about the short nature trails in the park. If you're in Belize City when you read this, you can get more information from the Belize Audubon Society (☎ (2) 77369, base@btl.net), 49 Southern Foreshore (PO Box 1001), Belize City.

Just west of the highway junction, across the bridge, is the village of Roaring Creek, with several small restaurants.

BELMOPAN

Population 4000

In 1961, Hurricane Hattie all but destroyed Belize City. Many people were skeptical when in 1970 the government of Belize declared its intention to build a model capital city in the geographic center of the country, but certain that killer hurricanes would come again and that Belize City could never be properly defended from them, the government decided to move.

During its first decade Belmopan was a lonely place. Weeds grew through cracks in the streets, a few bureaucrats dozed in new offices and insects provided most of the town's traffic. But more than a quarter of a century after its founding, Belmopan has begun to come to life. Its population is growing slowly, some embassies have moved here and when, inevitably, the next killer hurricane arrives, the new capital will no doubt get a population boost.

Orientation & Information

Belmopan, just under four km south of the Western Hwy, is a small place easily negotiated on foot (unless your luggage is heavy). The bus stops are at Market Square, near the post office, police station, market and telephone office. Unless you need to visit the British High Commission (☎ (8) 22146, fax (8) 22761), 34-36 Half Moon Ave, you'll probably only stay long enough to have a snack or a meal at one of the restaurants near the bus stops. Most of the town's few hotels, unfortunately, are a 10-minute walk from the bus stops.

Archaeology Department

If you're excited about Mayan ruins, examine the archaeological treasures preserved in the vault at the Archaeology Department (☎ (8) 22106). There is no museum yet, but if you call and make an appointment for a visit on Monday, Wednesday or Friday afternoon from 1:30 to 4:30 pm, you can see many of the artifacts recovered from Belize's rich Mayan sites. The vault is only a few minutes' walk from the bus stops.

Places to Stay

Belmopan is a bureaucrats' and diplomats' town, not one for budget travelers.

The 14-room *Circle A Lodge* (☎ (8) 22296, fax (8) 23616), 35-37 Half Moon Ave, is perhaps the town's oldest hotel, but it's still serviceable at US$25 a double with fan or US$30 with air-con.

The neighboring *Bull Frog Inn* (☎ (8) 22111, fax (8) 23155), 25 Half Moon Ave (PO Box 28), also with 14 rooms, is Belmopan's nicest place to stay. Its cheerful air-conditioned rooms cost US$50/67 a single/double, and there's a restaurant.

A few blocks northwest, the *Hotel El Rey* (☎ (8) 23438), 23 Moho St, is cheapest of all, but cheerless and basic. Rates are US$20/25 a single/double with bath and ceiling fan.

The *Belmopan Hotel* (☎ (8) 22130, (8) 22340, fax (8) 23066), 2 Bliss Parade (PO Box 237), is the most convenient to the bus stops. Guests pay US$44/50 a single/double for one of its 20 air-conditioned, bath-equipped rooms.

BELIZE

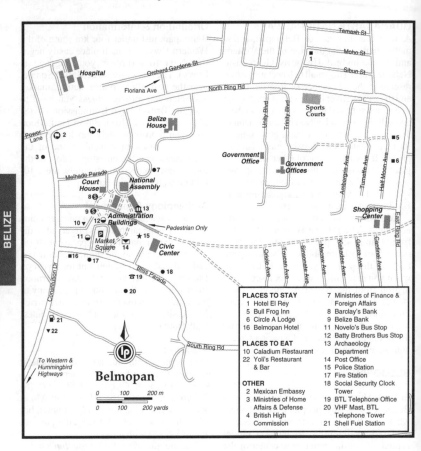

Belmopan

0	100	200 m
0	100	200 yards

To Western &
Hummingbird
Highways

PLACES TO STAY
1 Hotel El Rey
5 Bull Frog Inn
6 Circle A Lodge
16 Belmopan Hotel

PLACES TO EAT
10 Caladium Restaurant
22 Yoli's Restaurant
& Bar

OTHER
2 Mexican Embassy
3 Ministries of Home
Affairs & Defense
4 British High
Commission
7 Ministries of Finance &
Foreign Affairs
8 Barclay's Bank
9 Belize Bank
11 Novelo's Bus Stop
12 Batty Brothers Bus Stop
13 Archaeology
Department
14 Post Office
15 Police Station
17 Fire Station
18 Social Security Clock
Tower
19 BTL Telephone Office
20 VHF Mast, BTL
Telephone Tower
21 Shell Fuel Station

About 20 km southwest of Belmopan is
Ray and Vicki Snaddon's *Pook's Hill*
(☎ (8) 12017, fax (8) 22948), a 120-
hectare estate bordering the Tapir Mountain Nature Reserve. The main lodge
surrounds a small Mayan plaza and the
thatched cabins have insect screens, handicraft decorations and private bath. Rates
are US$72/90/110 a single/double/triple,
breakfast included. Lunch costs US$9,
dinner US$15. River swimming and forest
hiking are free, and there are reasonable
charges for horseback riding, river tubing
and mountain biking.

Places to Eat
The *Caladium Restaurant* (☎ (8) 22754), on
Market Square just opposite the Novelo's
bus station, is your best bet in the center of
town. Daily special plates cost US$4. *Yoli's*,
next to the Shell fuel station on the road into
town, is a less convenient alternative.

Getting There & Away
Bus Virtually all buses which stop in Bel-
mopan are on their way to somewhere else:
Belize City, San Ignacio, Dangriga, etc.
See the Belize Getting There & Around
chapter for details.

CENTRAL FARM

The Western Hwy continues westwards through Cayo District, climbing slowly to higher altitudes through lush farming country. Tidy country towns with odd names such as Teakettle Village, Ontario Village, Mount Hope and Unitedville appear along the way. Near the town of Central Farm, a road heads south towards San Antonio in Mountain Pine Ridge. Signs along the Western Hwy point the way to various guest ranches and lodges.

Riverwalk B&B (☎ (9) 23026), at Mile 62 (Km 100), is a ranch house high on a hill with panoramic views. Two comfortable rooms here go for US$55/66/77 a single/double/triple, breakfast included. A half-day's horseback riding costs US$25 per person.

Just across the road is *Caesar's Place* (☎ (9) 22341), PO Box 48, San Ignacio. It offers guestrooms, camping and campervan (RV) sites with hookups, as well as horseback riding and tours.

Mountain Equestrian Trails (☎ (8) 23310, fax (8) 23505), Mile 8 (Km 13), Mountain Pine Ridge Rd, Central Farm PO, Cayo District, is a four-room jungle lodge specializing in horseback riding. More than 100 km of forest trails have been laid out since the lodge opened in 1986, and the personnel are experts at matching riders (with or without horseback experience) to their well-behaved mounts. Accommodations in cabañas with private bath and kerosene (paraffin) lamps – there's no electricity – cost US$64/75/86 a single/double/triple; meals cost US$5/10/12 per person for breakfast/lunch/dinner.

SAN IGNACIO (CAYO)

Population 8000

San Ignacio, also called Cayo, is a prosperous farming and holiday center in the lovely, tropical Macal River valley. Though the chief town of Cayo District, it's a quiet place of about 8000 people (counting the population of neighboring Santa Elena, on the eastern side of the river). At night the quiet disappears and the jungle rocks to music from the town's bars, and restaurants which sometimes serve as bars.

Market day is Saturday, with the marketeers setting up behind the New Belmoral Hotel, at the bus station. The small market building beneath Hawkesworth Bridge, built through the largesse of Baron Bliss, has some vegetables and fruits on sale every day.

There's nothing much to do in town, but San Ignacio is a good base from which to explore the natural beauties of Mountain Pine Ridge. Horseback treks, canoe trips on the rivers and creeks, spelunking in the caves, bird watching, touring the Mayan ruins of Cahal Pech, Xunantunich and Caracol and hiking in the tropical forests are all popular ways to spend time. This is the district of macaws, mahogany, mangoes, jaguars and orchids.

San Ignacio, with its selection of hotels and restaurants, is also the logical place to spend the night before or after you cross the Guatemalan border. The Belizean town on the border, Benque Viejo del Carmen, has fewer facilities, so stay in San Ignacio if you can.

Orientation

San Ignacio is west of the river; Santa Elena is to the east. The two are joined by the one-lane Hawkesworth Bridge, San Ignacio's landmark suspension bridge. As you come off the western end of the bridge, turn right and you'll be on Burns Ave, the town's main street. Almost everything in town is accessible on foot.

Information

Tourist Office The town's traditional information exchange is Eva's Restaurant & Bar (see Places to Eat, below). The Belize Tourism Industry Association (BTIA) office in a row of shops off West St is not always open.

Money Belize Bank, on Burns Ave, is open Monday to Friday from 8 am to 1 pm (also Friday afternoon from 3 to 6 pm) for money exchange. The Atlantic Bank is on Burns Ave as well, and many freelance money-changers will approach you on the street to give you Belizean cash for US dollars.

BELIZE

BELIZE

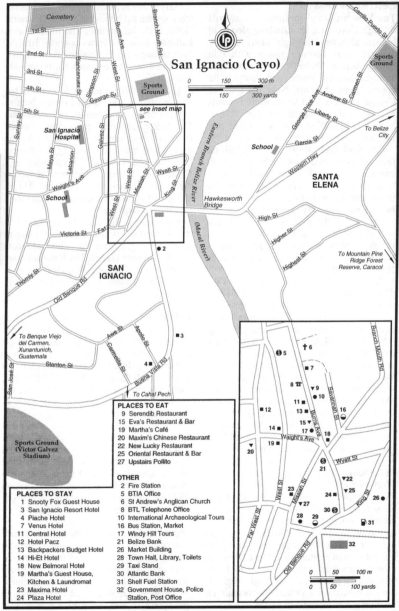

San Ignacio (Cayo)

PLACES TO EAT
9   Serendib Restaurant
15 Eva's Restaurant & Bar
19 Martha's Café
20 Maxim's Chinese Restaurant
22 New Lucky Restaurant
25 Oriental Restaurant & Bar
27 Upstairs Pollito

OTHER
2   Fire Station
5   BTIA Office
6   St Andrew's Anglican Church
8   BTL Telephone Office
10 International Archaeological Tours
16 Bus Station, Market
17 Windy Hill Tours
21 Belize Bank
26 Market Building
28 Town Hall, Library, Toilets
29 Taxi Stand
30 Atlantic Bank
31 Shell Fuel Station
32 Government House, Police
     Station, Post Office

PLACES TO STAY
1   Snooty Fox Guest House
3   San Ignacio Resort Hotel
4   Piache Hotel
7   Venus Hotel
11 Central Hotel
12 Hotel Pacz
13 Backpackers Budget Hotel
14 Hi-Et Hotel
18 New Belmoral Hotel
19 Martha's Guest House,
     Kitchen & Laundromat
23 Maxima Hotel
24 Plaza Hotel

Post & Communications San Ignacio's post office is on the upper floor of Government House, near the bridge. It's open Monday to Friday from 8 am to noon and 1 to 5 pm and Saturday from 8 am to 1 pm.

BTL has an office on Burns Ave north of Eva's, in the Cano's Gift Shop building. Hours are Monday to Friday from 8 am to noon and 1 to 4 pm and Saturday from 8 am to noon (closed on Sunday).

Medical Services The very simple, basic San Ignacio Hospital (☎ (9) 22066) is up the hill off Waight's Ave, to the west of the center. Across the river in Santa Elena is the Hospital La Loma Luz (☎ (9) 22087, fax (9) 22674), an Adventist hospital and clinic.

Cahal Pech
Cahal Pech ('Tick City' – not its original name) was a Mayan city of some importance from 900 BC through 800 AD. It flourished in the Late Preclassic and the Middle and Late Classic periods, when it was perhaps the chief city of the region.

Though the site was known to archaeologists by the 1950s, little work was done until after looters had pillaged it between 1970 and 1985. Fearing more damage, local authorities organized an archaeological mission led by Jaime Awe and Mark D Campbell in 1988.

The site is open from 9 am to 4:30 pm; admission costs US$5. You might want to bring a picnic lunch and enjoy the views from this hilltop site.

Cahal Pech's 34 buildings are spread over 2.5 hectares and grouped around seven plazas. It's 150 meters from the museum building and parking area to Plaza B, the largest and, surrounded by some of the most significant buildings, the most impressive. Plaza A is also worth seeing, as Structure A-1 is the tallest pyramid at the site.

The site is less than two km uphill from Hawkesworth Bridge. Follow the Buena Vista Rd south for one km, uphill and past the San Ignacio Resort and Piache hotels, until you see a radio antenna and Cahal Pech Village, a hotel with a large thatched main building and 14 thatched cabins (see Places

to Stay in this section). Turn left and follow the signs uphill to the archaeological site.

Organized Tours
Lodges in Cayo District operate their own tours and excursions on foot, by canoe and on horseback. But you can also take similar excursions using a cheap hotel in San Ignacio as your base. Every hotel and most restaurants in town will want to sign you up. Compare offerings, shop around and talk to other travelers before making your choice. Most of the trips offered give a good value for your money.

Many guides and tour operators advertise their services at Eva's Restaurant & Bar (☎ /fax (9) 22267, evas@btl.net) or at nearby shops on Burns Ave. Drop by and see what's available.

Among the favorite trips are:

- Voyages by boat or canoe along the Macal, Mopan and Belize rivers; a favorite goal on the Macal River is the Rainforest Medicine Trail at Ix Chel Farm

- A visit to a Mennonite community, usually combined with a tour of the Hershey chocolate company's cacao plantation

- A picnic and swim in the pools at Río On

- A walk to the 300-meter waterfall at Hidden Valley (which is less than spectacular at dry times of the year)

- An overland trip to the Mayan ruins at Caracol

- A stop at the Tanah Maya Art Museum and Mayan slate-carving workshop of the Garcia sisters, just north of San Antonio

- A trip to Chechem Ha's Mayan ceremonial cave and a picnic at Vaca Falls

- Tubing through caves along the Chiquibul River

- An excursion to Tikal (Guatemala), either for the day or overnight

Easy Rider (☎ (9) 23310, pager (17) 5197), a stable on the outskirts, will pick you up in San Ignacio and take you on a horseback excursion into the jungle for US$30 per person, lunch included. Shorter rides can be had for US$20.

Bob Jones at Eva's Restaurant can arrange a day trip to Tikal for less than US$60 per person, lunch included.

BELIZE

BELIZE

Places to Stay – budget

Martha's Guest House, Kitchen & Laundromat (☎ (9) 23647), 10 West St, is a modern home offering rooms with shared bath and fan for US$15 a double, good cooking in the ground-floor cafe (see Places to Eat later in this section) and even a laundromat, all in a family atmosphere.

Hotel Pacz (☎ (9) 22110), 2 Far West St, is fairly tidy, charging US$15/17/20 a single/double/triple for rooms with shared showers.

Hi-Et Hotel (☎ (9) 22828), 12 West St at Waight's Ave, is a simple old house with lots of family atmosphere, clean beds and low rates of US$10/15 for a room with shared bath.

Plaza Hotel (☎ (9) 23332), 4-A Burns Ave, is a good choice, with clean modern rooms with bath for US$20/25 a single/double or US$38/45 with air-con.

New Belmoral Hotel (☎ (9) 22024), 17 Burns Ave at Waight's Ave, has 15 serviceable rooms with bath and cable TV for US$15/20 a single/double with fan or US$30/40 with air-con.

Maxima Hotel (☎ (9) 23993), on Missiah St, is clean, good and reasonably priced at US$25 a double with private bath and fan or US$5 more with air-con.

Central Hotel (☎ (9) 22253), 24 Burns Ave, is among the town's cheapest hotels, a bargain at US$9/12/14 a single/double/triple in rooms without running water. The neighboring *Backpackers Budget Hotel* competes fiercely for the same clientele.

Venus Hotel (☎ (9) 23203, fax (9) 22186, daniels@btl.net), 29 Burns Ave, has 25 rooms – some better than others – with ceiling fan. Most share cramped showers and cost US$14/18 a single/double. Rooms with private shower cost US$20/23. Rooms 10 and 16 have good views of the football field and river.

Midas Eco-Resort (☎ (9) 23172, fax (9) 23845, evas@btl.net, ATTN: Midas), on Branch Mouth Rd, 700 meters from the bus station, has six thatched bungalows with private bath for US$22/25/30 a single/double/triple. Camping is available at US$3.30/5 for one/two persons.

The tidy *Snooty Fox Guest House* (☎ (9) 22150, fax (9) 23556), 64 George Price Ave, Santa Elena, has clean rooms with bath, TV and stereo for US$22 a double, cabins for US$38 and an apartment with two bedrooms and kitchen for US$60. A long stairway leads down to the river, where you can rent a canoe. Walk east over Hawkesworth Bridge and follow the main road to the left. At a fork, continue left (the main road is to the right); the guesthouse is 500 meters along on the left-hand side.

Rose's Guesthouse (☎ /fax (9) 22282), 1178 Cahal Pech Hill, is almost two km from the center, but quiet and homey, with fine views. The five rooms share baths and rent for US$35/43 a single/double, breakfast included.

Places to Stay – middle

San Ignacio Resort Hotel (☎ (9) 22034, fax (9) 22134, sanighot@btl.net), PO Box 33, on Buena Vista Rd about one km uphill from Government House, enjoys magnificent views of the jungle and river from its swimming pool and balconies. Its 25 rooms, priced at US$51/59/70 a single/double/triple or about US$25 more per room for deluxe air-con accommodations, are often full, especially on weekends. The hotel has a restaurant, bar and disco.

Piache Hotel (☎ (9) 22032, fax (9) 22685), 18 Buena Vista Rd, around the corner from the San Ignacio Resort Hotel, has 11 rooms in a series of thatched buildings set on emerald lawns. With fan, rooms are US$26/34/40 a single/double/triple; with air-con, US$50 a double. The setting is fine, and Cahal Pech is only one km away.

Cahal Pech Village (☎ (9) 23740, fax (9) 22225, daniels@btl.net), about two km uphill from the town center, has a large thatched main building surrounded by 14 small thatched cabins with bath priced at US$38 to US$48 a double. Perched atop Cahal Pech Hill, the cabins enjoy fine views of the town and valley, but without a car the walk to and from town can get tedious. You can make reservations at the Venus Hotel on Burns Ave, which is under the same ownership.

For other ranches near San Ignacio, see Exploring Cayo District, later in this chapter.

Places to Eat

Eva's Restaurant & Bar (☎ /fax (9) 22267, evas@btl.net), on Burns Ave, is the information and social center of the expatriate set – temporary and permanent – in San Ignacio. Daily special plates at US$4 to US$6 are the best value, but there's also chilmoles (black bean soup), chicken curry, beef soup, sandwiches, burgers and many other dishes. A beer garden out back is for those who want to drink more than to eat. Note that Eva's has fax and email service (sending and receiving).

The terrace cafe at *Martha's*, 10 West St, is popular for all three meals, freshly prepared. Breakfasts cost US$4 to US$5, pizzas US$9 to US$11 and sandwiches US$1.50 to US$2.50.

Upstairs Pollito, on Missiah St, is another popular spot for cheap, good eats.

Maxim's Chinese Restaurant, at Far West St and Waight's Ave, serves fried rice, sweet-and-sour dishes and vegetarian plates which range in price from US$2.50 to US$5. The restaurant is small and dark, and open from 11:30 am to 2:30 pm and 5 pm until midnight. Other choices for Chinese food are the *Oriental* and *New Lucky* on Burns Ave.

Across Burns Ave and a few meters north of Eva's is the *Serendib Restaurant*, serving – of all things – Sri Lankan dishes, here in the Belizean jungle. Service is friendly, the food is good and prices are not bad, ranging from US$3.50 for the simpler dishes up to US$10 for steak or lobster. Lunch is served from 9:30 am to 3 pm, dinner from 6:30 to 11 pm.

Getting There & Away

Buses run to and from Belize City (116 km, 2½ hours, US$2.50), Belmopan (32 km, 45 minutes, US$2) and Benque Viejo del Carmen (15 km, 20 minutes, US$0.75). For details, see the Belize Getting There & Around chapter.

The Cayo Taxi Drivers Association (☎ (9) 22196) stand is on the traffic circle opposite Government House. Rates can be surprisingly high for short trips out of town (a trip of a few kilometers can easily cost US$5 to US$10), but a jitney cab ride to Benque Viejo del Carmen costs only US$1.50.

EXPLORING CAYO DISTRICT

Western Belize has lots of beautiful, unspoiled mountain country dotted with waterfalls and teeming with wild orchids, parrots, keel-billed toucans and other exotic flora and fauna. Almost 800 sq km to the south and east of San Ignacio has been set aside as the Mountain Pine Ridge Forest Reserve.

Though there is now an unpaved but graded road as far south as the Caracol archaeological site, roads in the reserve are still sometimes impassable from May through October. Relative inaccessibility is one of Mountain Pine Ridge's assets, for it keeps this beautiful land in its natural state for visitors willing to see it by 4WD vehicle, on horseback, on foot or along its rivers in canoes. Always check with tour operators in San Ignacio about road conditions; otherwise you may drive deep into the jungle only to be turned back at a forest ranger guardpost. Day tours of Mountain Pine Ridge cost between US$53 and US$79.

Access roads into the Mountain Pine Ridge Forest Reserve go south from the Western Hwy in Santa Elena (across the river from San Ignacio) and near Georgeville (about nine km east of San Ignacio).

El Pilar

About 19 km northwest of San Ignacio, 11 km northwest of Bullet Tree Falls, the Mayan archaeological site of El Pilar is perched 275 meters above the Belize River. El Pilar was occupied for 15 centuries, from the Middle Preclassic (about 500 BC) through the Late Classic (about 1000 AD) periods.

With 25 plazas, the city was more than three times the size of Xunantunich. It's now within the El Pilar Archaeological Reserve for Maya Flora and Fauna. Unlike other major Mayan sites, El Pilar has been left largely uncleared, with five archaeological

BELIZE

and nature trails meandering among the jungle-covered mounds. Interesting bits of various structures have been uncovered and consolidated to exhibit the archaeological and architectural variety of the site.

Rainforest Medicine Trail

Formerly called the Pantí Medicine Trail, this herbal-cure research center is at Ix Chel Farm (fax (9) 22267), located right next to Chaa Creek Cottages (see Places to Stay later in this section), 13 km southwest of San Ignacio.

Dr Eligio Pantí, who died in 1996, was a healer in San Antonio village who used traditional Mayan herb cures. As he died at age 103, he seems to have known what he was doing.

Dr Rosita Arvigo, an American, studied medicinal plants with Dr Pantí, then began several projects to spread the wisdom of traditional healing methods and to preserve the rain forest habitats, which harbor an incredible 4000 species of plants.

Chicle & Chewing Gum

Chicle, a pinkish to reddish-brown gum, is actually the coagulated milky sap, or latex, of the sapodilla tree *(Achras zapota)*, a tropical evergreen native to the Yucatán Peninsula and Central America. *Chicleros* (chicle-workers) enter the forests and cut large gashes in the sapodillas' trunks, making a pattern of V-shaped cuts as high as 30 feet. The sap runs from the wounds and down the trunk to be collected in a container at the base. After being boiled, it is shaped into blocks for shipping. The cuts often kill the tree, and chicle harvesting has often resulted in the serious depletion of sapodilla forests.

First used as a substitute for natural rubber (to which the sapodilla is related), by about 1890 chicle was best known as the main ingredient in chewing gum.

As a result of war research for a rubber substitute during the 1940s, synthetic substitutes were developed for chicle. Now chewing gum is made mostly from these synthetic substitutes. ■

One of her projects was the establishment of the Rainforest Medicine Trail, a self-guiding path among the jungle's natural cures. Admission costs US$5; it's open every day from 8 am to noon and 1 to 5 pm.

At the farm's shop you can buy Rainforest Remedies, herbal cures drawn from the farm's resources and marketed by the Ix Chel Tropical Research Foundation. Profits from sales support the work of the foundation, which carries out the Belize Ethnobotany Project in association with the New York Botanical Garden.

In 1993, working through the Belize Association of Traditional Healers, Belize's traditional healers succeeded in convincing the government to transfer control of 2500 hectares of old-growth forest, renamed Terra Nova, to the association for the careful preservation of its flora.

Pacbitun

This small Mayan archaeological site, 20 km south of San Ignacio near San Antonio, seems to have been occupied continuously through most of Mayan history, from 900 BC to 900 AD. Today only lofty Plaza A has been uncovered and partially consolidated. Structures 1 and 2, on the eastern and western sides of the plaza, are worth a look. Within them archaeologists discovered the graves of noble Mayan women buried with a variety of musical instruments, perhaps played at their funerals.

Caves

Several caves are open to exploration in the Black Rock Canyon region, including Flour Camp Cave, reached after an uphill hike, and Waterhole Cavern. Barton Creek Cave is best reached by canoe.

Farther south near Vaca Falls, Chechem Ha (Chumpiate Cave) is a Mayan cave complete with ceremonial pots. Members of the Morales family, who discovered the cave, act as guides, leading you up the steep slope to the cave mouth, then down inside, walking and sometimes crouching, to see what the Maya left. A fee of US$25 pays for one to three people. Take water and a flashlight. You can also camp at

Chechem Ha or sleep in one of the simple bunks. Tours often visit the cave.

Río Frio Caves, not far from the forest station called Douglas da Silva (formerly Augustine), are the region's most famous and visited caverns, usually included on Mountain Pine Ridge tours.

Pools & Waterfalls

Most Mountain Pine Ridge tours stop for a swim at the Río On and/or Five Sisters Falls pools, but the aquatic highlight of the region is Hidden Valley (or Thousand Foot) Falls, southeast of San Antonio.

Caracol

South of San Ignacio (86 km via the Chiquibul Rd) lies Caracol, a vast Mayan city hidden in the jungle. The site encompasses some 88 sq km, with 36,000 structures marked so far. A University of Central Florida team under the direction of Drs Arlen F and Diane Z Chase is studying, consolidating and partially restoring some of the major buildings and artifacts. During the digging season (mid-February to early June, with a 10-day break at Eastertime), archaeologists take visitors on two- to four-hour tours at 10:30 am and 1 pm; donations to the archaeological work are gratefully accepted.

Caracol was occupied in the Postclassic period from around 300 BC until 1150 AD. At its height, between 650 and 700 AD, Caracol is thought to have had a population of 150,000 – not much less than the entire population of Belize today.

Highlights of the site include Caana ('Sky-Palace') in Plaza B, Caracol's tallest structure at 42 meters; the Temple of the Wooden Lintel, dating from 50 AD, in Plaza A; the ball court with a marker commemorating Caracol's defeat of rivals Tikal in 562 AD and Naranjo in 631 AD; and the Central Acropolis, containing a royal tomb. The South Acropolis, Barrio residential area, Aguada (reservoir) and causeway are also worth a look.

Caracol can be reached on a long day trip in a good 4WD vehicle. The best way is to sign up for a tour in San Ignacio or at one of the lodges for US$53 to US$79 per person.

There are no services available at the site, so bring your own food, water and motor fuel.

Places to Stay

The forests and mountains surrounding San Ignacio are dotted with small inns, lodges and ranches offering accommodations, meals, hiking, horseback trips, spelunking, swimming, bird watching and similar outdoor activities. Most of the lodges below have full programs of hikes, horseback rides, excursions and activities. Some of them are profiled on the website www.belize.com.

Only a few of these lodges are for the budget traveler; the rest are more expensive, though they offer a good value for the money. I've given simple room rates here, but at most of the lodges you can take advantage of package arrangements which include lodging, meals and tours; these can save you money.

Though you can sometimes show up unannounced and find a room, these are small, popular places, so it's best to write or call for reservations as far in advance as possible. When you do, ask for information on activities as well.

Among the inexpensive places is *Rancho Los Amigos* (☎ (9) 32483; leave a message), almost two km south of the highway from San José Succotz over an atrocious road. It's a good place to get away from it all on a budget. Ed and Virginia Jenkins did just that when they moved here from Los Angeles, California. They've built four cool, thatch-roofed stone cabins for guests and charge US$25 per person, including all three meals. Lighting is by kerosene (paraffin) lamps; bath and toilet facilities are shared. Vegetarian meals are available.

Parrot's Nest (☎ (9) 23702), at the edge of the wilderness in Bullet Tree Falls, northwest of San Ignacio, is aptly named: guests stay in treehouse-like thatched cabins built high on stilts. Baths are shared, but there's electricity all the time and the price is right: US$20 a double. Three meals cost US$13 per person. The site is beautiful, surrounded by the river on three sides. Besides hiking and canoeing, there's horseback riding for only US$18 per day. You

BELIZE

can reach Bullet Tree Falls by taxi (US$15) or bus from San Ignacio. This is the best of the budget places.

Maya Mountain Lodge (☎ (9) 22164, fax (9) 22029, maya_mt@btl.net), 9 Cristo Rey Rd (PO Box 46), San Ignacio, Cayo, is the closest lodge to San Ignacio, just over two km from the center. (Follow the signs from near the Esso fuel station in Santa Elena.) The thatched cottages have fan and private shower with hot water. Meals are served in the verandah restaurant. Tours to most destinations in Mountain Pine Ridge and beyond can be arranged; mountain bikes and canoes are available for rent. Bart and Suzi Mickler, the owners, are walking encyclopedias of Belizean jungle lore and educate others through their Educational Field Station and Rainforest Institute. The 14 rooms and cottages are priced at US$47 to US$82 a single or double. Homestyle meals cost US$7/6/15 for breakfast/lunch/dinner.

Several other lodges (Chaa Creek Cottages, duPlooys', Black Rock River Lodge) are reached by a common, rough road that goes south from the Western Hwy at a point eight km west of San Ignacio, three km east of Benque Viejo del Carmen.

Chaa Creek Cottages (☎ (9) 22037, fax (9) 22501, chaacreek@btl.net), PO Box 53, San Ignacio, Cayo, is on the bank of the Macal River right next to Ix Chel Farm and the Rainforest Medicine Trail. The 16 thatch-roofed cottages set in tropical gardens are beautifully kept and richly decorated with Mayan textiles and local crafts; all have fan and private bath. Rates are US$107/129/154 a single/double/triple, tax and service included. Lunch costs US$7 to US$10 and dinner is US$22. This is the most pristine of the Maya Mountain lodges. Chaa Creek Cottages is five km south of the Western Hwy over a very rough, slow road.

There are three levels of accommodations at *duPlooys'* (☎ (9) 23101, fax (9) 23301, judy@btl.net), Big Eddy, San Ignacio, Cayo: Rooms in the Pink House have fan and shared bath and cost US$42/53/64 a single/double/triple, breakfast included. Bungalows and rooms in the Jungle Lodge

have fan and private bath and cost US$123 to US$165 a single, US$156 to US$210 a double and US$210 to US$255 a triple, three meals included. Besides the normal array of Mountain Pine Ridge activities, duPlooys' offers you a white, sandy beach for sunbathing, and swimming in the Macal River. To find duPlooys', take the same road that leads to Chaa Creek Cottages; after four km, you'll see the duPlooys' sign and turn right. The lodge is just under three km farther along this rough road.

Also take the Chaa Creek/duPlooys' turnoff from the Western Hwy to reach *Black Rock River Lodge* (☎ (9) 22341, fax (9) 23449, evas@btl.net, ATTN: Black Rock), PO Box 48, San Ignacio, Cayo, a simpler place with thatch-topped tent cottages, solar electricity generation and solar-heated hot water. Rates are US$40/46/51/56 a single/double/triple/quad with shared bath or US$61/72/78/84 with private bath. Black Rock is more than 11 km off the highway, a drive of about 35 minutes. For details, ask at Caesar's Place, described earlier in this chapter under Central Farm.

Nabitunich (☎ /fax (9) 22096, fax (9) 33096), on San Lorenzo Farm, San Ignacio, Cayo, is another attractive collection of thatched cottages on a hillside sloping down to the river. In this case, the towering ruins of Xunantunich are right on the opposite bank of the river. Theresa Graham and family host you, preparing plentiful four-course meals after days of swimming or canoeing on the river, horseback riding or touring. You pay US$75/91 a single/double for a cabaña with bath and fan, breakfast and dinner included; the room alone costs US$43/54. Nabitunich ('stone house' in Mayan) is two km east of Benque Viejo del Carmen, then one km north downhill toward the river.

Windy Hill Resort (☎ (9) 22017, fax (9) 23080, in the USA (800) 946-3995), at Graceland Ranch, San Ignacio, Cayo, has all the facilities: swimming pool, riding horses, nature trail, canoes ready for a paddle on the Mopan River and a full program of optional tours. Accommodations in cabañas with private bath and ceiling fan cost US$48/64/80 a single/double/triple without meals. To find it, go west 2.5 km from San Ignacio and look for the signs for the road going north.

Blancaneaux Lodge (☎ (9) 23878, fax (9) 23919, in the USA (800) 746-3743, evas@btl.net, ATTN: Blancaneaux), PO Box B, Central Farm, Cayo, offers 14 rooms in thatched cabins and luxury villas overlooking waterfalls deep in Mountain Pine Ridge. The restaurant serves Italian cuisine, following the culinary preference of the resort's owner, cinema director Francis Ford Coppola. Rooms (including light breakfast) cost US$88/112 a single/double, cabins US$159/188/218 a single/double/triple, villas (which have two bedrooms and two baths) even more.

By the way, the famous *Chan Chich Lodge*, at Gallon Jug, near the Guatemalan border north of Spanish Lookout, is accessible by road from Orange Walk. See the Northern Belize chapter for details.

Getting There & Away

Unless you have your own transport, you'll have to depend on taxis or the hospitality of your Mountain Pine Ridge lodge hosts to transport you between San Ignacio and the lodges. Sometimes the lodges will shuttle you at no extra cost; sometimes they'll arrange a taxi for you.

XUNANTUNICH

Xunantunich (pronounced soo-NAHN-too-neech) is Belize's most accessible Mayan site of significance. Set on a leveled hilltop overlooking the Mopan River, Xunantunich ('Stone Maiden') controlled the riverside track which led from the hinterlands of Tikal down to the Caribbean. During the Classic period, a ceremonial center flourished here. Other than that, not too much is known. The kings of Xunantunich erected a few beautiful stelae inscribed with dates, but we have no full history of their reigns as we have at Tikal, Copán and other sites.

Archaeologists have uncovered evidence that an earthquake damaged the city badly about 900 AD, after which the place may

have been largely abandoned. Archaeological work is continuing under the guidance of Dr Richard Leventhal of the University of California at Los Angeles.

Though it is an interesting site and its tallest building – El Castillo – is impressive as it rises some 40 meters above the jungle floor, Xunantunich will perhaps disappoint you after you've seen Tikal, Chichén Itzá, Uxmal, Palenque or even Lamanai. It has not been extensively restored, as those sites have been, and the jungle has grown around and over the excavated temples. But the walk from the ferry beneath arches of palm fronds, the tropical plants and animals and the lack of crowds at the site are compensations.

Xunantunich is open from 9 am to 5 pm; admission costs US$5. In the rainy season (June to October) bugs can be a problem; you may need your repellent. There are no facilities at Xunantunich except picnic tables, pit toilets and a cistern of murky rainwater for drinking, so bring water and perhaps a picnic or snacks.

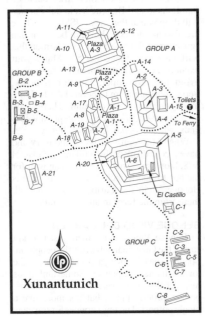

Xunantunich

The path from the guardian's hut leads to Plaza A-2, surrounded by low, bush-covered buildings, and then on to Plaza A-1, dominated by Structure A-6: El Castillo. A thatched pavilion near El Castillo provides shelter from the sun or rain. On the edges of the grassy plazas, hummingbirds hover in the humid air, sucking nectar from brilliantly colored tropical flowers. The stairway on the northern side of El Castillo – the side you approach from the courtyard – goes only as far as the temple building. To climb to the roofcomb you must go around to the southern side and use a separate set of steps. On the eastern side of the temple, a few of the masks which once surrounded this structure have been restored.

Getting There & Away

The ferry to Xunantunich is opposite the village of San José Succotz, on the Western Hwy 8.5 km west of San Ignacio, 1.5 km east of Benque Viejo del Carmen. From the ferry it's a walk of two km uphill to the ruins.

Novelo's buses on their way between San Ignacio and Benque Viejo del Carmen will drop you at the ferry (US$0.75). There are also jitney taxis shuttling between San Ignacio and Benque Viejo del Carmen that will take you for US$1.50. Make your excursion to Xunantunich in the morning to avoid the ferry operator's lunch break. Ferry hours are 8 am to noon and 1 to 5 pm; the ferry crosses on demand. There is no fee for passengers or cars, except on weekends, when cars pay US$1 each way.

When you return, cross on the ferry and have a cold drink at the Xunantunich Hotel & Saloon across the road. You can wait for the bus to San Ignacio here. If your goal is Benque Viejo del Carmen, you can walk there from the ferry in about 15 minutes.

BENQUE VIEJO DEL CARMEN

In Benque Viejo del Carmen, just two km east of the Guatemalan border, the people are Spanish-speaking Maya or ladinos; even the town's name is Spanish. Some ambitious maps of the town make it look like a prosperous, orderly place, but it's more like a jungle outpost. The few services for travelers

are cheap, as well they should be, but you're better off eating and sleeping in San Ignacio.

Benque Viejo del Carmen stirs from its normal tropical somnolence in mid-July, when the Benque Festival brings three days of music and revelry. Then it's back to sleep.

Places to Stay & Eat

Maya Hotel y Restaurante (☎ (9) 32116), 11 George St, is a dreary family-run lodging near the bus terminal. The 10 rooms have lots of bunks; most have no running water (there are communal showers). The restaurant serves all three meals. Rates are US$8/12 a single/double without bath or US$14/19 with private shower.

Next best is the *Hospedaje Roxy*, on St Joseph St at the southwestern end of town. It's family-run and charges US$7 per person.

The *Da Xin* Chinese restaurant is a local favorite for both eating and drinking. *Oki's New Restaurant* is the fanciest place in town, which isn't saying much.

Getting There & Away

There are frequent jitney taxis (US$1.50) and hourly buses (US$0.75) between San Ignacio and Benque Viejo del Carmen. A few buses go all the way to Melchor de Mencos (Guatemala). From Benque Viejo del Carmen, taxis shuttle back and forth from the border, charging a high US$4 for the three-km ride, so you might want to make the 35-minute walk instead.

WEST TO GUATEMALA

Cross early in the morning to have the best chance of catching buses onwards. Get your passport (and, if applicable, your car papers) stamped at the Belizean station, then cross into Guatemala. The border station is supposedly open 24 hours a day, but officers are usually only on duty from 6 am to midnight. If you need a Guatemalan visa (see the Visas & Documents and Embassies & Consulates sections in the Guatemala Facts for the Visitor chapter), as citizens of most British Commonwealth countries do, you should obtain it before you reach the border. Guatemalan tourist cards (US$5) are obtainable at the border.

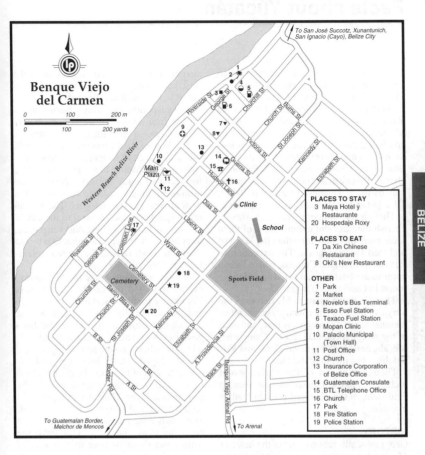

Benque Viejo del Carmen

To San José Succotz, Xunantunich, San Ignacio (Cayo), Belize City

0   100   200 m
0   100   200 yards

Western Branch Belize River

Main Plaza

Clinic

School

Sports Field

Cemetery

To Guatemalan Border, Melchor de Mencos

To Arenal

PLACES TO STAY
3 Maya Hotel y Restaurante
20 Hospedaje Roxy

PLACES TO EAT
7 Da Xin Chinese Restaurant
8 Oki's New Restaurant

OTHER
1 Park
2 Market
4 Novelo's Bus Terminal
5 Esso Fuel Station
6 Texaco Fuel Station
9 Mopan Clinic
10 Palacio Municipal (Town Hall)
11 Post Office
12 Church
13 Insurance Corporation of Belize Office
14 Guatemalan Consulate
15 BTL Telephone Office
16 Church
17 Park
18 Fire Station
19 Police Station

BELIZE

There are two banks at the border for changing money, but the itinerant money-changers often give you a better deal – for US cash. The rates for exchanging Belizean dollars to Guatemalan quetzals and vice versa are very poor. Use up your local currency before you get to the border, then change hard foreign currency, preferably US dollars.

The Guatemalan town of Melchor de Mencos has cheap hotels and restaurants.

Both Transportes Pinita and Transportes Rosalita buses westwards to Santa Elena (Guatemala) depart early in the morning (3, 4, 5 and 8:30 am) for US$1.50. Sometimes there are more comfortable – and expensive – minibuses (US$10 per person) as well; many travelers feel it is money well spent.

To go on to Tikal, get off the bus at El Cruce (Puente Ixlu), 36 km east of Flores, and wait for another bus, minibus or obliging car or truck to take you the final 35 km north to Tikal. Note that the flow of traffic from El Cruce to Tikal drops dramatically after lunch.

Facts about Yucatán

The largest, most populous and most developed region of the Mayan world is in Mexico. The southeastern states of Campeche, Chiapas, Quintana Roo, Tabasco and Yucatán together boast more and bigger Mayan archaeological sites than Guatemala and Belize combined. The peninsula is said to have some 1400 sites. The ruins of Bonampak, Chichén Itzá, Cobá, Palenque, Uxmal, Yaxchilán and other sites are equaled only by the great cities of Caracol in Belize, Tikal in Guatemala and Copán in Honduras.

Though the 'modern' Maya of Mexico cherish their ancient culture, most of them seem more distant from it than the Maya of highland Guatemala do. The exception to this rule is highland Chiapas, where Indian cultures are basically an extension of those found in Guatemala's highlands.

There is much more to Mexico than the Maya, of course. The country's prime international resort – Cancún – is here, and each of the region's colonial cities – Campeche, Mérida, San Cristóbal de las Casas and Valladolid – has its particular charm.

Though this part of the Mayan world includes Chiapas, Tabasco and the Yucatán Peninsula, in this chapter I refer to it all as Yucatán.

HISTORY

Geographically removed from the heart of Mexico, the colonists of the Yucatán Peninsula participated little in Mexico's War of Independence. Even though Yucatán joined liberated Mexico, the peninsula's long isolation gave it a strong sense of independence, and this Mayan region desired little subsequent interference from Mexico City.

War of the Castes

Not long after independence, the Yucatecan ruling classes were again dreaming of independence, this time from Mexico, and perhaps union with the USA. With these goals in mind, and in anticipation of an invasion from Mexico, the *hacendados* made the mistake of arming and training their Mayan peons as local militias. Trained to use European weaponry, the Maya envisioned a release from their own misery and boldly rebelled against their Yucatecan masters.

The War of the Castes of 1847 began in Valladolid, a city known for its particularly strict and oppressive laws: The Maya were forbidden to enjoy the main plaza or the prominent streets and had to keep to the back streets and the outskirts. The Mayan rebels quickly gained control of the city in an orgy of killing, looting and vengeance. Supplied with arms and ammunition by the British through Belize, they spread relentlessly across Yucatán.

In little more than a year the Mayan revolutionaries had driven their oppressors from every part of Yucatán except Mérida and the walled city of Campeche. Seeing the whites' cause as hopeless, Yucatán's governor was about to abandon Mérida when the rebels saw the annual appearance of the winged ant. In Mayan mythology, corn (the staff of life) must be planted at the first sighting of the winged ant. If the sowing is delayed, Chac, the rain god, will be affronted and respond with a drought. The rebels abandoned the attack and went home to plant the corn. This gave the whites and mestizos time to regroup and receive aid from their erstwhile adversary, the government in Mexico City.

The Talking Cross

The counterrevolution against the Maya was without quarter and vicious in the extreme. Between 1848 and 1855 the Indian population of Yucatán was halved. Some Mayan combatants sought refuge in the jungles of southern Quintana Roo. There they were inspired to continue fighting by a religious leader working with a ventriloquist, who in 1850 at Chan Santa Cruz made a sacred cross 'talk' (the cross

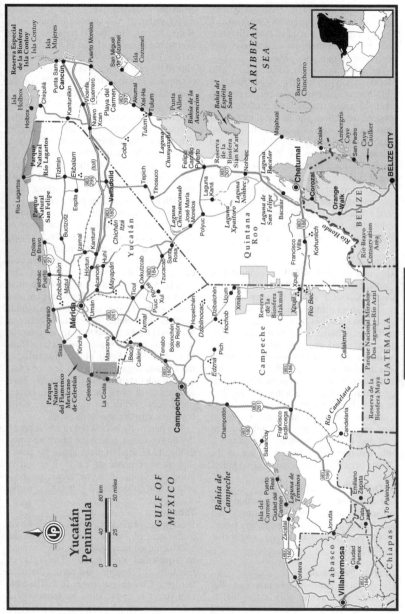

Yucatán Peninsula

was an important Mayan religious symbol long before the coming of Christianity). The talking cross convinced them that their gods had made them invincible, and they continued to fight until 1866.

The governments in Mexico City and Mérida largely ignored the Mayan rebels of Chan Santa Cruz until the turn of the century, when Mexican troops with modern arms subdued the region. The shrine of the talking cross at Chan Santa Cruz was destroyed, and the town was renamed Felipe Carrillo Puerto in honor of a progressive Yucatecan governor, but the local Maya were allowed a good deal of autonomy. The region was declared a Mexican 'territory' only in 1936 and did not become a state until 1974. Today, if you visit Felipe Carrillo Puerto, you can visit the restored shrine of the talking cross above a cenote in what is now a city park.

Yucatán Today

Although the post-WWII development of synthetic fibers led to the decline of the henequen (sisal rope) industry, it still employs about a third of the peninsula's work force. The slack has been more than picked up by the oil boom in Tabasco and Chiapas, the fishing and canning industries of the peninsula and the rapid growth of tourism over the past decade. Though the power elite is still largely of Spanish or mestizo parentage, Yucatán's Maya are better off today than they have been for centuries.

A good number of Maya till the soil as their ancestors did, growing staples such as corn and beans. Subsistence agriculture is little different from the way it was in the Classic period, with minimal mechanization.

GEOGRAPHY & GEOLOGY

The Mexican Mayan lands include cool pine-clad volcanic mountain country, hot and dry tropical forest, dense jungly forest, broad grassy savannas and sweltering coastal plains.

Yucatán Peninsula

The Yucatán Peninsula is one vast, flat limestone shelf rising only a few meters above sea level. The shelf extends outward

from the shoreline for several kilometers under water. If you approach Yucatán or Belize by air, you should have no trouble seeing the barrier reef that marks the limit of the limestone shelf. On the landward side of the reef the water is shallow, usually no more than five or 10 meters deep; on the seaward side the water is deeper.

The underwater shelf makes Yucatán's coastline wonderful for aquatic sports, keeping the waters warm and the marine life (fish, crabs, lobsters, tourists) abundant, but it makes life difficult for traders: At Progreso, north of Mérida, the *muelle* (wharf) must extend 6.5 km from dry land across the shallow water to reach water deep enough to receive ocean-going vessels.

The only anomaly in the flat terrain of the Yucatán Peninsula is the low range of the Puuc Hills, near Uxmal, which attains heights of several hundred meters.

Because of their geology, northern and central Yucatán have no rivers or lakes. The people there have traditionally drawn their fresh water from *cenotes*, limestone caverns with collapsed roofs, which serve as natural cisterns. Rainwater, which falls between May and October, collects in the cenotes for use during the dry season, which lasts from October to May. South of the Puuc Hills, in the Chenes region, there are few cenotes, and the inhabitants there traditionally have resorted to drawing water from limestone pools deep within the earth. These wells *(chenes)* give the region its name.

The peninsula is covered in a blanket of dry thorny forest, which the Maya have traditionally cleared to make space for planting crops or pasturing cattle. The soil is good for crops in some areas, poor in others, and cultivating it is hot, hard work.

Tabasco

West of the peninsula along the Gulf Coast is the state of Tabasco, low, well-watered and humid country that is mostly covered in equatorial rain forest. The relative humidity at Palenque (just across the state border in Chiapas) averages 78%. The lush rain forest is endangered by farmers and cattle ranchers who slash and burn it to make way for more crops and cattle, which in this climate are guaranteed to thrive.

Besides its agricultural wealth, Tabasco is one of Mexico's most important regions of petroleum production.

Chiapas

Chiapas is a huge state comprising several distinct topographical areas. The northern part of the state is lowland with low hills similar to those of Tabasco, and is well watered, sparsely populated and dotted with important Mayan cities such as Palenque, Toniná, Bonampak and Yaxchilán.

The central and south-central area is mountainous and volcanic, rising from several hundred meters in the west to more than 3900 meters in the southeast, near the Guatemalan border. Annual rainfall varies from less than 40 cm at Tuxtla Gutiérrez, the state capital, to more than 200 cm on the mountain slopes facing the Pacific Ocean. The high country around San Cristóbal de las Casas is known locally as the *tierra fría*, (cold country), because of its altitude and many cloudy days. The mountains in this area are covered in forests of oak and pine.

The Continental Divide follows the ridge of the Sierra Madre, which towers above the Pacific littoral. South and west of the ridge is the Pacific Slope of the mountains and the coastal plain, which is known as the Soconusco. Rainfall there is abundant, as the weather arrives from the west and the wet clouds dump their loads as they ascend the high mountains. Cotton is the choice crop on the plain, but on the mountain slopes (up to 1400 meters) it's cacao and coffee.

CLIMATE
Yucatán Peninsula

The temperature is always hot in Yucatán, often reaching as high as 40°C (100°F) in the heat of the day. From May to October, the rainy season makes the air hot and humid. From October to May it is hot and dry, though there are occasional showers even in the dry season. Violent but brief storms called *nortes* can roll in on any afternoon, their black clouds, high winds

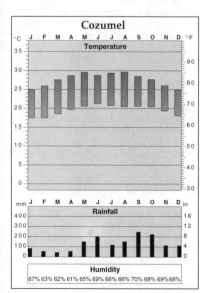

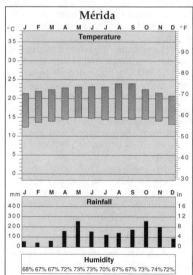

and torrents of rain followed within an hour by bright sun and utterly blue sky.

Tabasco & Chiapas

The low-lying state of Tabasco is always hot and muggy, but it's more pleasant in the dry season (October to May) than the rainy season. As in Yucatán, it's always hot there; unlike Yucatán, the area is not seasonally crowded with tourists.

Mountainous central Chiapas can get lots of rain in summer, but at least it's cool at the higher altitudes. In winter the air is cool most of the time, warming up considerably on sunny days, though many days are overcast. In the tierra fría around San Cristóbal de las Casas, mornings and evenings are usually chilly (a thrill after the sticky heat of Palenque!) and the nights downright cold (though frost is rare), especially if it's raining, which it often is from May to October.

The Soconusco is hot and humid all the time and frequently rainy in summer.

GOVERNMENT & POLITICS

In theory the United Mexican States (Estados Unidos Mexicanos) is a multiparty democracy with an elected president, a bicameral legislature and an independent judiciary.

In practice the gigantic, authoritarian Partido Revolucionario Institucional, or PRI ('el PREE'), controlled all aspects of political life and society, including the government, the labor movement, the press and most of the small 'opposition' parties, since its foundation in the 1930s.

However, the municipal and congressional elections of July 6, 1997, may have changed all that.

Widely condemned for corruption, mishandling of the economy, and election fraud, the PRI was on the defensive. President Ernesto Zedillo was pressured to make the July elections fairer than any in Mexican history. The result was a revolution in Mexican politics. Instead of its normal absolute majority, the PRI claimed less than 40% of the vote. The right-of-center National Action Party (PAN) gar-

nered 27%, the Party of the Democratic Revolution (PRD) 26%, with another 10% going to splinter parties. The PRI lost 12 seats in the Senate and was forced to share power in the Chamber of Deputies, the lower house of Congress, which determines the country's budget.

The most symbolic opposition gains were in Mexico City. In earlier years the mayor of the capital had been appointed by the president, but in the first elections ever for the post, the mayoralty was won by the PRD's standard-bearer, Cuauhtémoc Cárdenas, son of the late president Lázaro Cárdenas.

Lázaro Cárdenas, a young army general, was elected president of Mexico in 1934. He embarked on a vigorous, far-reaching program of reforms that included giving Mexico's peasants greater rights in the land they cultivated and greatly reducing the power and influence of foreign corporations in Mexico's economy – especially in the petroleum industry. He also shaped the PRI to be the organ of control over all of Mexican society.

His son, named for the last Aztec emperor, was raised in the PRI and advanced to leadership positions easily. Uncomfortable with the authoritarian nature of the party, he attempted reforms from within, but finally broke with the PRI and began an opposition political movement during the 1980s.

In 1988 Cuauhtémoc Cárdenas challenged the PRI's handpicked presidential candidate, Carlos Salinas de Gortari, for the nation's highest office, but 'lost' when the PRI-controlled election computers mysteriously broke down during vote-counting. With his victory in the Mexico City mayoralty race, Cárdenas is well positioned to run for the presidency at the end of Zedillo's term in the year 2000.

Cárdenas and his party, the PRD, have revived many of Lázaro Cárdenas' political themes, including empowerment of workers and a hard line toward foreign economic interests with influence in Mexico. But without the authoritarian powers of past presidents – including his revered father –

Cuauhtémoc Cárdenas will have to pursue his intentions through the normally messy, compromise-clouded organs of democracy.

ECONOMY

Because it lacks plentiful water resources, the Yucatán Peninsula has minimal agriculture, with some cattle ranches. The important exception is the cultivation of henequen, the plant from which sisal rope is made.

The export economy based on henequen thrived in the latter half of the 19th century. By WWI it was said that Mérida had more millionaires per capita than any other city in the world. The plantation owners were a de facto Yucatecan aristocracy and built opulent mansions along Mérida's Paseo de Montejo, many of which still stand. They decorated their homes with the artistic treasures of the world and sent their children off to the best schools of Europe.

With the invention of synthetic fibers such as nylon, henequen lost much of its importance, but it is still a significant part of Yucatán's agriculture.

Besides henequen, Yucatán has some pig and chicken farms, and light industry around Mérida and Chetumal. Tourism is very important in the states of Yucatán and neighboring Quintana Roo.

Campeche is an important fishing port for lobster, shrimp and fish, much of the catch being for export. Towns along the northern coast of the peninsula also depend on fishing.

By far the richest sector of the Mexican economy is petroleum. The deposits beneath Tabasco and Veracruz are among the richest in the world. Campeche has petroleum reserves as well.

Farming, mining, forestry and oil exploration are important in Chiapas, as is tourism. Tuxtla Gutiérrez, the Chiapan capital, is one of Mexico's main coffee-producing regions. The cattle ranches in Chiapas and along the Gulf Coast in Tabasco are expanding into the rain forest, threatening the tropical ecosystem and triggering revolts by indigenous peoples who are being swept from their traditional lands.

POPULATION & PEOPLE

Over millennia, the Maya of Yucatán and Chiapas have intermarried with neighboring peoples, especially those of central Mexico with whom they had diplomatic and commercial relations and the occasional invasion and conquest. During the 20th century they also have intermarried, to some degree, with the descendants of the conquering Spanish. People of mixed Mayan and Spanish blood are called mestizos. Most of Mexico's population is mestizo, but the Yucatán Peninsula has an especially high proportion of pure-blooded Maya. In many areas of Yucatán and Chiapas, Mayan languages prevail over Spanish, or Spanish may not be spoken at all. In remote jungle villages some modern cultural practices descend directly from those of ancient Mayan civilization.

Thanks to the continuation of their unique cultural identity, the Maya of Yucatán are proud without being arrogant, confident without the machismo seen so frequently elsewhere in Mexico, and kind without being servile. And with the exception of those who have become jaded by the tourist hordes of Cancún, many Maya retain a sense of humor.

YUCATÁN

Facts for the Visitor

PLANNING
When to Go
The dry season is generally preferred for travel in Yucatán because you needn't dodge the raindrops, the heat is not as muggy and, most important, it's winter in most of North America and Europe! November and early December are perhaps the best times, as there are fewer tourists and prices are low.

From mid-December to April is the busy winter tourism season, when premium prices prevail (with surcharges around Christmas, New Year's and Easter). May, the end of the dry season, and June, when the rains begin, are the hottest and muggiest months. If you have a choice of months, don't choose them. July and August are hot, not too rainy, and busy with the summer travel crowd. September and October are pretty good for travel, as the traffic decreases markedly and so do the rains.

TOURIST OFFICES
All large cities and resorts have tourist offices, which may be run by the city, state or federal government. There are also the following tourist offices abroad:

Canada
> *British Columbia*
> 999 West Hastings Street, Suite 1610,
> Vancouver, BC V6C 2W2
> (☎ (604) 669-2845)
> *Ontario*
> 2 Bloor Street West, Suite 1801,
> Toronto, Ontario M4W 3E2
> (☎ (416) 925-0704)
> *Québec*
> 1 Place Ville Marie, Suite 1526, Montréal,
> Québec H3B 2B5 (☎ (514) 871-1052)

France
> 4 rue Notre Dame des Victoires, 75002
> Paris (☎ 01.42.86.56.30)

Germany
> Wiesenhüttenplatz 26, D60329
> Frankfurt-am-Main (☎ 069-252-413)

Italy
> Via Barberini 3, 00187 Rome
> (☎ 06-487-2182)

Spain
> Calle Velázquez 126, Madrid 28006
> (☎ 91-561-3520)

UK
> 60-61 Trafalgar Square, 3rd floor,
> London WC2N 5DS (☎ (0171) 734-1058)

USA
> *California*
> 1801 Century Park East, Suite 1080,
> Los Angeles, CA 90067 (☎ (310) 203-8191)
> *Florida*
> 2333 Ponce de Leon Blvd, Suite 710,
> Coral Gables, FL 33134 (☎ (305) 443-9160
> *Illinois*
> 70 East Lake Street, Suite 1413,
> Chicago, IL 60601 (☎ (312) 606-9015)
> *New York*
> 405 Park Ave, Suite 1401,
> New York, NY 10022 (☎ (212) 755-7261)
> *Texas*
> 5075 Westheimer Blvd, Suite 975W,
> Houston, TX 77056 (☎ (713) 629-1611)
> *Washington, DC*
> 1911 Pennsylvania Ave NW, Washington,
> DC 20006 (☎ (202) 728-1750)

VISAS & DOCUMENTS
Mexican Tourist Card
The Mexican tourist card (it's actually a multicopy paper form) costs US$5. As you present your card to the immigration official upon entering Mexico, say that you want to stay 90 days, or you're liable to get less time.

Don't lose your tourist card, as obtaining another one from the Migración (Immigration) officials is a long, frustrating, time-consuming process.

When you leave Mexico, you're supposed to turn in your tourist card.

Parent & Child
If you are an adult traveling with a child under 18 years of age, the Mexican immigration officer will require you to show a

notarized affidavit from the child's other parent permitting you to take the child into Mexico. This is to prevent separated, divorcing or divorced parents from absconding to Mexico with a child against the wishes – or legal actions – of the other parent. In the case of divorced parents, a custody document may be needed as well as the notarized consent form. If one or both parents is dead, or the traveler has only one legal parent, a notarized statement saying so may be required. These rules are aimed primarily at North Americans but apparently apply to all nationalities. If both parents are traveling together with the child or children, there's no problem and no affidavit is needed.

If you have any questions about this procedure, talk them over in advance of your trip with a Mexican diplomatic representative to find out exactly what you need to do. Don't wait until you're at the border or airport without an affidavit and the immigration officer refuses to permit you and the child to enter the country!

EMBASSIES & CONSULATES
Mexican Embassies & Consulates Abroad
Some of the consulates mentioned here are actually honorary consuls or consular agencies. These posts can issue tourist cards and visas, but they refer more complicated matters to the nearest full consulate or to the embassy's consular section.

Australia
Embassy, 14 Perth Ave, Yarralumla, Canberra ACT 2600 (☎ 02-6273-3905)
Consulate, Level 1, 135-153 New South Head Rd, Edgecliff, Sydney, NSW 2027 (☎ 02-9326-1311)

Austria
Embassy, Turkenstrasse 15, 1090 Vienna (☎ 0222-310-7383)

Belgium
Embassy, Av Franklin Roosevelt 94, 1050 Brussels (☎ 02-629-0711)

Belize
Embassy, 20 North Park St, Fort George Area, Belize City (☎ 02-30-193/194)

Canada
Embassy Consular Section, 45 O'Connor St, Suite 1500, Ottawa, ON K1P 1A4 (☎ (613) 233-8988/6665)
Consulates:
British Columbia
810-1130 West Pender St, Vancouver, BC V6E 4A4 (☎ (604) 684-3547/1859)
Ontario
Commerce Court West, 199 Bay St, Suite 4440, Toronto, ON M5L 1E9 (☎ (416) 368-2875/1847)
Québec
2000 rue Mansfield, Suite 1015, Montréal, QC H3A 2Z7 (☎ (514) 288-2502/2707)

Costa Rica
Embassy, Av 7a No 1371, San José (☎ 257-0633, 225-4430)

El Salvador
Embassy, Av Circunvalación and Pasaje 12, Colonia San Benito, San Salvador (☎ 243-3458/3190)

France
Embassy, 9 rue de Longchamp, 75116 Paris (☎ 01.45.53.99.34, 01.45.53.76.43)
Consulate, 4 rue Notre Dame des Victoires, 75002 Paris (☎ 01.42.61.51.80)

Germany
Embassy, Adenauerallee 100, 53113 Bonn (☎ 0228-914-8620)
Consulates:
Berlin
Kurfurstendamm 72, 10709 Berlin (☎ 030-324-9047)
Frankfurt-am-Main
Hochstrasse 35-37, 60330 Frankfurt-am-Main (☎ 069-299-8750)

Guatemala
Embassy, Edificio Central Ejecutivo, Nivel 7th floor, 15 Calle 3-20, Zona 10, Guatemala City (☎ 333-72-54)
Consulates:
Guatemala City
13a Calle 7-30, Zona 9, Guatemala City (☎ 331-81-65, 332-52-49)
Quetzaltenango
9a Av 6-19, Zona 1, Quetzaltenango (☎ 763-13-12/13/14/15

Honduras
Embassy, Av República de México 2907, Colonia Palmira, Tegucigalpa (☎ 32-64-71, 32-40-39)

Israel
Embassy, Bograshov 3, 63808 Tel Aviv (☎ 03-523-0367/68/69)

Italy
    Embassy, Via Lazzaro Spallanzani 16,
    00161 Rome (☎ 06-440-2309/4404)
    Consulate, Via Cappuccini 4, Milan
    (☎ 02-7602-0541)

Japan
    Embassy, 2-15-1, Nagata-cho, Chiyoda-ku,
    Tokyo 100 (☎ 3-3580-2961/62,
    3-3581-1131/32/33/34/45)

Netherlands
    Embassy, Nassauplein 17, 2585 EB The
    Hague (☎ 070-360-2900, 070-345-2569)

New Zealand
    8th Floor, 111-115 Customhouse Quay,
    Wellington (☎ 04-472-5555/56)

Nicaragua
    Embassy, Carretera a Masaya Km 4.5, 25
    Varas Arriba (next to Optica Matamoros),
    Altamira, Managua (☎ 02-75-1859)

Panama
    Embassy, Calle 50 at Calle San José,
    Edificio Plaza Bancomer, 5th floor, Panama
    City (☎ 263-5021)

Spain
    Embassy, Carrera de San Jerónimo 46,
    Madrid 28014 (☎ 91-369-4781/2814)
    Consulates:
    Barcelona
    Avenida Diagonal Sur 626, 4th floor,
    Barcelona 08021 (☎ 93-201-1822)
    Seville
    Calle San Roque 6, Seville 41001
    (☎ 95-456-3944)

Sweden
    Embassy, Grevgatan 3, 11453 Stockholm
    (☎ 08-661-2213, 08-663-5170)

Switzerland
    Embassy, Bernestrasse 57, 3005 Bern
    (☎ 031-351-4060/1814)

UK
    Embassy, 8 Halkin St, London SW1X 7DW
    (☎ (0171) 235-6393)

USA
    Embassy, 1911 Pennsylvania Ave NW,
    Washington, DC 20006
    (☎ 202-728-1633/36/94)
    There are consulates in the following cities:
    Arizona: Nogales, Phoenix, Tucson
    California: Calexico, Fresno, Los Angeles,
    Sacramento, San Bernardino, San Diego,
    San Francisco, San Jose
    Colorado: Denver
    Florida: Miami, Orlando

Georgia: Atlanta
Illinois: Chicago
Louisiana: New Orleans
Massachusetts: Boston
Michigan: Detroit
Missouri: St Louis
New Mexico: Albuquerque
New York: New York
Pennsylvania: Philadelphia
Texas: Austin, Brownsville, Corpus Christi,
Dallas, Del Rio, Eagle Pass, El Paso,
Houston, Laredo, McAllen, Midland, San
Antonio
Utah: Salt Lake City
Washington: Seattle

Embassies & Consulates in Mexico
Embassies are in Mexico City. Cancún has
many consulates, Mérida has fewer. All are
mentioned in the text.

CUSTOMS
When entering Mexico (especially by air),
customs agents may indicate a button for
you to push on what looks like a traffic
signal. If you get a green light, you go right
through without inspection. If you get a red
light, your luggage will be inspected,
usually quickly and courteously. This
system was instituted to discourage the
former system, whereby the tediousness of
the inspection was inversely proportional to
the size of the 'tip' (actually, a bribe) you
paid the customs official.

MONEY
Costs
At this writing, Mexico is the cheapest
country in the Mayan region.

Cancún and Cozumel are the two most
expensive places in the country, far more
expensive than Mexico City or even Acapulco. Small towns such as Tizimin and
Izamal, not being heavily touristed, are much
cheaper. Cities such as Mérida and San
Cristóbal de las Casas offer a good range of
prices, with good values for your money.

A single traveler staying in budget or
lower-middle-range accommodations and
eating two meals a day in restaurants may
pay US$10 to US$25 per day, on average,
for those basics. Add in the other costs of

travel (snacks, purified water, soft drinks, admission to archaeological sites etc, plus roughly US$2 per hour on long-distance buses), and you may find yourself spending more like US$17 to US$35 per day.

If there are two or more of you sharing accommodations, costs per person come down considerably. Double rooms are often only a few dollars more than singles, and triples or quadruples are only very slightly more expensive than doubles.

Travelers on middle-range budgets find excellent value for their money in Mexico, with good hotel rooms with private bath and air conditioning costing US$25 to US$50 and full meals in good restaurants costing US$8 to US$15.

At the top end, airfares, car rental rates and prices for luxury hotels and meals are usually lower than in Canada, Europe or the USA, but not by much.

Credit Cards & ATMs

Major credit cards such as Visa, Master-Card, Eurocard, and Access are accepted at all airline and car rental companies and at the larger hotels and restaurants; American Express cards are often accepted at the fancier and larger places and at some smaller ones.

Many smaller establishments will readily accept your credit card, even for charges as little as US$5 or US$10. Cancún, for example, lives on credit cards and even has some telephones that accept them for long-distance (trunk) calls.

For information on ATMs, see the Currency Exchange section.

Currency

The Mexican unit of currency is the New Peso (N$), which is further divided into 100 centavos. Mexican coins come in denominations of one, five, 10, 20 and 50 centavos, and one peso. Bills (notes) are in denominations of one, five, 10, 50, 100 and 500 New Pesos.

You may see prices written as '$100 m.n.', meaning *moneda nacional,* or Mexican pesos, to distinguish it from '$100 dlls.' (US dollars).

Currency Exchange

The peso is exchanged freely, so there is no black market.

Though banks and *casas de cambio* (exchange houses) exchange offices change most major currencies, US dollars are always easiest. Bank automated teller machines (ATMs) give the best service (24 hours a day) and rates. Look for locations on our town and city maps.

In such heavily touristed areas as Cancún and Cozumel you can often spend US dollars as easily as pesos at hotels, restaurants and shops. Most of the time you won't get as good an exchange rate as if you had changed your dollars for pesos at a bank – sometimes the rates in hotels, restaurants and shops will be downright outrageous. However, in other establishments dollars are accepted at an exchange rate as good as or better than that of the banks to induce you to spend your money there.

Australia	A$1	=	N$5.78
Canada	CN$1	=	N$5.62
France	FFr1	=	N$1.33
Germany	DM1	=	N$4.43
Guatemala	Q1	=	N$1.31
Italy	IL1000	=	N$4.54
Japan	J¥100	=	N$6.94
New Zealand	NZ$1	=	N$5.24
UK	UK£1	=	N$13.17
USA	US$1	=	N$7.89

Taxes

Mexico has a value-added tax called the Impuesto de Valor Agregado (IVA), usually referred to as *el IVA* (ehl EE-bah). By law the tax must be *included* in virtually any price quoted to you; it should not be added afterward. Signs in shops and notices on restaurant menus usually reiterate this fact as *incluye el IVA* or *IVA incluido.* When asking prices, it's still not a bad idea to confirm that the tax will not be added to the price later.

Airport usage taxes are levied on every passenger on every flight. The tax on international flights departing Mexico is equivalent to approximately US$12; domestic departure taxes cost less.

YUCATÁN

Student Discounts

Discounts for foreign students are virtually unknown. A few places offer small discounts on admission fees to students under 26.

POST & COMMUNICATIONS

Almost every city and town (but not village) has an Oficina de Correos (Post Office), where you can buy postage stamps and send or receive.

Sending Mail

If you are sending something by airmail from Mexico, be sure to clearly mark it with the words 'Por Avión'. An airmail letter sent to Canada or the USA may take anywhere from four to 14 days. Airmail letters to Europe can take anywhere from one to three weeks.

Receiving Mail

Receiving mail in Mexico can be tricky. You can send or receive letters and packages care of a post office if they're addressed as follows:

Jane SMITH (surname should be in capitals)
a/c Lista de Correos
Mérida, Yucatán
(numerical postal code if possible) MEXICO

When the letter arrives at the post office, the name of the addressee is placed on an alphabetical list called the Lista de Correos, which is updated daily. If you can, check the list yourself, because the letter might be listed under your first name instead of your surname.

To claim your mail, present your passport or other identification; there's no charge. The snag is that many post offices hold Lista mail only for 10 days before returning it to the sender. If you think you're going to pick mail up more than 10 days after it has arrived, have it sent to you at Poste Restante, Correo Central, Town/ City, State, Mexico. Poste Restante holds mail for up to a month, but no list of what has been received is posted. Again, there's no charge for collection.

Telephone

Teléfonos de México (TelMex), once government owned, now privatized, is still the major telephone company, but competition is growing in the telecommunications market, promising better service at lower prices, both of which are sorely needed.

Telephone numbers in Mexico have different numbers of digits for different cities and towns. You must dial seven digits in Mexico City, but only six in Mérida, and only five in Palenque, etc. Expect this to change as Mexico modernizes its telecommunications system. No doubt Mexico will soon switch to a US-style system, with three-digit area codes and seven-digit local numbers.

Local calls are inexpensive and easy to place from public telephones (call boxes) and *casetas de teléfonos* (telephone call stations in shops). Long-distance (trunk) calls within Mexico are still quite expensive, and international calls are among the most expensive in the world.

Long-Distance Calls You may see the abbreviation *Lada* in connection with long-distance calls; it's short for *larga distancia* (long distance). Domestic and international long-distance (trunk) calls are exorbitantly taxed. Be warned! A 15-minute operator-assisted call to the USA can easily cost US$60, much more to Europe or Australia.

Tolls for calls placed from the USA or Canada to Mexico are much cheaper than for the same call placed from Mexico to Canada or the USA. Use a short call from Mexico to advise the call's recipient of your hotel telephone number in Mexico, and agree on a time for them to call you back (don't forget time zone differences).

From a *caseta de larga distancia* (long-distance call station), an operator will connect your number. Calls may cost anywhere from US$1 to US$2 per minute within Mexico, or US$2 to US$5 per minute to the USA or Canada, or even more for countries farther away. Ask before you call.

A collect/reverse charge call *(llamada por cobrar)* is usually much cheaper than a normal operator-assisted call, but you may end up paying one or two dollars for the privilege of discovering that the party you're calling collect is not at home.

It is now possible to use direct foreign telephone services. Dial (95-800) 462-4240 for AT&T, or (95-800) 674-7000 for MCI, to be connected with an operator in the USA. In my experience these services do not work from all Ladatel phones (see next section). You may have to keep trying different phones. Those directly in front of TelMex offices seem to work best.

Ladatel Phones TelMex Ladatel call stations have blue handsets and small liquid-crystal displays, and are clearly marked with the word *Ladatel*. Calling instructions are posted on Ladatel phones in Spanish, English and French. From a Ladatel phone you can dial long-distance calls directly to any place in the world at prices much lower than for operator-connected calls.

You must be well supplied with peso coins, Ladatel tokens or debit cards.

To call San Francisco, press 95 + 415 + the local number; for Toronto, 95 + 519 + the local number; for London press 98 + 44 + 171 + the local number; for Melbourne press 98 + 61 + 3 + the local number.

NEWSPAPERS & MAGAZINES

The English-language *Mexico City News* is distributed throughout Mexico wherever tourists gather. Price varies with location, but is usually about US$1.

Mexico has a thriving local Spanish-language press as well as national newspapers. Even small cities often have two or three newspapers of their own. In Mérida it's *El Diario de Yucatán*. Chiapas has its own excellent independent magazine, *Perfil del Sureste*, which comes out every two months and covers many issues that the authorities would prefer to keep quiet.

For those interested in a non-establishment view of events, *La Jornada* is a good national daily with a mainly left-wing viewpoint; it covers a lot of stories that other papers don't. *Proceso* is a weekly news magazine with a similar approach.

BUSINESS HOURS

Banks are open from 9 am to 1:30 pm, Monday to Friday. Businesses are generally open from 9 am to 2 pm and 4 to 7 pm, Monday to Friday; various sorts of shops are open on Saturday as well. Shops and offices close for siesta from roughly 1 or 2 to 4 or 5 pm, then open again until 7 or 8 pm.

FOOD

It's tantalizing to consider that some of the dishes prepared in Yucatán's kitchens today may be very similar to ones served in ancient times to Mayan royalty. Many often-used ingredients such as *pavo* (turkey), *venado* (venison) and *pescado* (fish) were available in ancient times, as they are today.

Yucatán's resident chile is the habanero, and my own personal anthropological theory holds that in the old days the victims of human sacrifice were given a choice: munch a habanero or have your heart carved out. Most thought the heart option offered a less painful end. If you go after a habanero chile, you had better be equipped with a steel tongue.

Despite its reputation as a fissionable material in vegetable form, the habanero is an important ingredient in *achiote*, the popular Yucatecan sauce, which also includes chopped onions, the juice of sour Seville oranges, cilantro (fresh coriander leaf) and salt. You'll see a bowl of achiote on most restaurant tables in Yucatán. Put it on your food – or ignore it – as you like.

One local hearty breakfast favorite is *huevos motuleños*, or eggs in the style of the town of Motul, east of Mérida. Fresh tortillas are spread with refried beans, then topped with an egg or two, then garnished with chopped ham, green peas and shredded cheese, with a few slices of fried banana on the side. It can be slightly picante or muy picante, depending on the cook.

An authentic Yucatecan lunch or supper might begin with *sopa de lima* (lime soup), a chicken stock containing shreds of chicken meat, bits of tortilla and lime juice. It's tangy and delicious if made well; made badly, it's greasy.

For a main course you might order *pollo pibil*, chicken marinated in achiote sauce, sour Seville-orange juice, garlic, black pepper, cumin and salt, then wrapped in banana leaves and baked. There are no nuclear chiles to blow your head off. A variant is *cochinita pibil*, made with suckling pig instead of chicken.

The restaurant named Los Almendros in Ticul, Yucatán, claims to have created *poc-chuc*, slices of pork marinated in sour orange juice, cooked and served with a tangy sauce and pickled onions. A more traditional pork dish is *frijol con puerco*, the Mayan version of pork-and-beans, with black beans, tomato sauce and rice.

Another hearty dish is *puchero*, a stew made with chicken, pork, carrots, cabbage, squash (marrow) and sweet potato.

The turkey is native to Yucatán and has been used as food for millennia. *Pavo relleno negro*, or dark stuffed turkey, is slices of turkey over a 'filling' made with pork and beef, all topped by a rich dark sauce.

Venison, also native to Yucatán, is perhaps best as a *pipián de venado*, steamed in banana leaves a la pibil and topped with a sauce made with ground squash (marrow) seeds.

Among the lighter traditional dishes, *papadzules* are tortillas sprinkled with chopped hard-boiled eggs, rolled up and topped with a sauce that is made with squash or pumpkin seeds. *Salbutes* are the native tacos: fried corn tortillas topped with shredded turkey meat, avocado and pickled onions. *Panuchos* are similar, but are made with refried beans.

As for seafood, the all-time favorite is *pescado frito*, simple fried fish, but there's also *langosta* (lobster), usually just the tail. The most interesting seafood concoctions are the ceviches, cocktails made of raw or parboiled seafood in a marinade of lime juice, tomato sauce, chopped onion and cilantro. Cheapest is the *ceviche de pescado* made with whatever fish is in season and cheap in the markets. Other choices include *ceviche de camarones* (with shrimp) and *ceviche de ostiones* (with oysters).

At the open-air markets and cookshops you'll need to know some Spanish to read the menus: *higado encebollado* is liver and onions, *longaniza* is a spicy sausage, *pollo asado o frito* is roasted or fried chicken, *bistec de res/puerco* is a beef or pork steak, *puerco empanizado* is a crumbed pork chop and *bistec a la Mexicana* is bits of beef sautéed with chopped tomatoes and hot peppers.

Getting There & Around

Following is general information for the Yucatán region. For specific information on each town or city, see the individual sections. For detailed information on flights to and from Cancún, see the introductory Getting There & Away chapter.

AIR

Cancún
Cancún's international airport is unquestionably the busiest airport in the region, with the most regional and international flights.

Aerocaribe (in Cancún ☎ (98) 86-01-62, fax (98) 86-00-83), Mexicana's regional airline, covers destinations in the Yucatán Peninsula and beyond in small and medium-sized planes.

Cozumel
Some domestic and international flights to or from Cancún stop at Cozumel as well, giving it excellent air service.

Mérida
Most international flights to Mérida are connections through Mexico City or Cancún; there is no nonstop international service, except for Aeromexico's two daily flights from Miami.

Domestic service includes half a dozen Aerocaribe/Mexicana flights daily from Mexico City to Mérida, and one or two by Aeromexico as well. Bonanza flies to Cancún, Mérida, Palenque, Tuxtla Gutiérrez and Villahermosa.

Palenque
The small town of Palenque now receives scheduled flights by Aerocaribe and Bonanza from Villahermosa, Tuxtla Gutiérrez, Cancún and Mérida.

Tuxtla Gutiérrez
Aviacsa, the Chiapan regional airline, has several daily nonstop flights to and from Mexico City and also a daily nonstop to

MARIO GALLOTTA
Baroque facade of Templo de Santo Domingo, San Cristóbal de las Casas

Tapachula. Bonanza flies to and from Palenque. The major airport for the region, however, is at the Tabascan capital of Villahermosa.

Villahermosa
Because of its oil wealth, Villahermosa has good domestic air links to Mérida, Cancún, Tuxtla Gutiérrez and Mexico City.

Departure Tax
A departure tax equal to about US$12 is levied on international travelers departing Mexico by air.

LAND
Mexico can be entered by land from the USA at 24 points. For details, refer to Lonely Planet's *Mexico*.

The most popular and easily accessible entry points to Mexico from Guatemala are at Tecún Umán/Ciudad Hidalgo, entering the Soconusco region of Chiapas from Guatemala's Pacific Slope, and at La Mesilla/Ciudad Cuauhtémoc, entering highland Chiapas from the southwestern highlands of Guatemala. More adventurous routes take you by country bus and riverboat from El Petén down the Río Usumacinta or the Río de la Pasión to Palenque in lowland Chiapas. For information on these routes, see the chapter on El Petén, in the Guatemala section.

Bus
In Mexico the buses range from luxury-class air-conditioned cruisers to shabby but serviceable village buses. The various companies offer different levels of comfort and service, usually determined by price: the more you pay, the more comfortable the bus and the faster the trip. Luxury service is available on the busiest long-haul routes.

There are as yet no international bus lines; you take one company to the border, then change to another company's. The exception is Chetumal, which receives buses from Belize, and the special fast service from Flores (Guatemala), near Tikal.

Car
Insurance Though not strictly required in Mexico, it is foolish to travel without Mexican liability insurance. If there is an accident and you cannot show a valid insurance policy, you will be arrested and not permitted to leave the locale of the accident until all claims are settled, which could be weeks or months. Mexico's legal system follows the Napoleonic model, in which all persons involved in an incident are required to prove their innocence; trial is by a court of three judges, not by a jury. Your embassy can do little to help you in such a situation, except to tell you how stupid you were to drive without local insurance.

Mexican insurance is sold in US, Guatemalan and Belizean towns near the Mexican border. Approaching the border from the USA you will see billboards advertising offices selling Mexican policies. At the busiest border-crossing points (Tijuana, Mexicali, Nogales, Agua Prieta, Ciudad Juárez, Nuevo Laredo and Matamoros), there are insurance offices open 24 hours a day.

Prices for Mexican policies are set by law in Mexico, so bargain-hunting isn't easy. Instead of discounts (which cannot be offered), insurance offices offer incentives such as free guidebooks and/or maps, connections to automobile clubs and other treats.

Mexican motor-vehicle insurance policies are priced so as to penalize the short-term buyer with extremely high rates. You may pay almost as much for a one-month policy (which is approximately US$200, on average) as you would for a full year's policy.

Rental The cost of car rentals ranges, on average, from US$30 to US$45 per day. For information on rental agencies, see the Getting Around sections of the Mérida and Tabasco chapters, or under San Cristóbal de las Casas in the Chiapas chapter.

Cancún & Isla Mujeres

In the 1970s Mexico's ambitious tourism planners decided to outdo Acapulco with a brand new, world-class resort in Yucatán. The place they chose was a deserted sand spit offshore from the little fishing village of Puerto Juárez, on Yucatán's eastern shore. The island sand spit was shaped like a lucky 7. The name of the place was Cancún.

As Cancún was discovered by the world, so was nearby Isla Mujeres. This tropical island had earlier been a haven for local mariners and adventurous young travelers in search of the simple life at low prices. Though Isla Mujeres retains some of its earlier allure, it is now also a day-trip destination for boatloads of Cancúnites.

Cancún

Population 400,000

In the last two decades Cancún has grown from a tiny jungle village into one of the world's best-known holiday resorts. The Mexican government built the resort as an investment in the tourism business. Vast sums were sunk into landscaping and infrastructure, yielding straight, well-paved roads, potable tap water (so they say) and great swaths of sandy beach. Cancún's raison d'être is to shelter planeloads of tourists who fly in (usually on a weekend) to spend one or two weeks in a resort hotel before flying home again (usually on a weekend).

During their stay they can get by with speaking only English, spending only dollars and eating only familiar food. During the day, group tourists enjoy the beaches, rent a car or board a bus for an excursion to Chichén Itzá or Tulum, or browse in an air-conditioned shopping mall straight out of Dallas. At night they dance and drink in clubs and discos to music that's

the same all over the world. They have a good time. This is the business of tourism.

ORIENTATION

Cancún is actually two places in one.

On the mainland lies Ciudad Cancún, a planned city founded as the service center of the resort. The main north-south thoroughfare is Avenida Tulum, a one-km-long tree-shaded boulevard lined with banks, shopping centers, restaurants and touts selling time-share condominiums. On the east side of the boulevard in the city center is the City Hall, marked 'Ayuntamiento Benito Juárez'.

Those who are content to trundle out to the beach by bus or taxi can save pots of money by staying in Ciudad Cancún in one of the smaller, low- to medium-priced

367

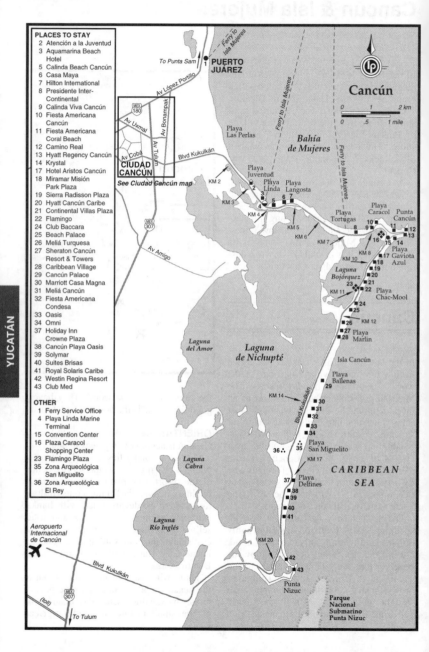

PLACES TO STAY
2 Atención a la Juventud
3 Aquamarina Beach Hotel
5 Calinda Beach Cancún
6 Casa Maya
7 Hilton International
8 Presidente Inter-Continental
9 Calinda Viva Cancún
10 Fiesta Americana Cancún
11 Fiesta Americana Coral Beach
12 Camino Real
13 Hyatt Regency Cancún
14 Krystal
17 Hotel Aristos Cancún
18 Miramar Misión Park Plaza
19 Sierra Radisson Plaza
20 Hyatt Cancún Caribe
21 Continental Villas Plaza
22 Flamingo
24 Club Baccara
25 Beach Palace
26 Meliá Turquesa
27 Sheraton Cancún Resort & Towers
28 Caribbean Village
29 Cancún Palace
30 Marriott Casa Magna
31 Meliá Cancún
32 Fiesta Americana Condesa
33 Oasis
34 Omni
37 Holiday Inn Crowne Plaza
38 Cancún Playa Oasis
39 Solymar
40 Suites Brisas
41 Royal Solaris Caribe
42 Westin Regina Resort
43 Club Med

OTHER
1 Ferry Service Office
4 Playa Linda Marine Terminal
15 Convention Center
16 Plaza Caracol Shopping Center
23 Flamingo Plaza
35 Zona Arqueológica San Miguelito
36 Zona Arqueológica El Rey

YUCATÁN

Cancún

To Punta Sam
PUERTO JUÁREZ
Av López Portillo
MEX 180
Av Uxmal
Av Bonampak
Av Tulum
Av Cobá
CIUDAD CANCÚN
See Ciudad Cancún map
MEX 307
Av Amigo
Playa Las Perlas
Bahía de Mujeres
Ferry to Isla Mujeres
Blvd Kukulkán
Playa Juventud
KM 2
Playa Linda
Playa Langosta
KM 3
KM 4
KM 5
KM 6
KM 7
Playa Tortugas
Playa Caracol
Punta Cancún
KM 8
KM 10
Playa Gaviota Azul
Laguna Bojórquez
KM 11
Playa Chac-Mool
KM 12
Playa Marlin
Isla Cancún
Laguna del Amor
Laguna de Nichupté
Playa Ballenas
KM 14
Blvd Kukulkán
Playa San Miguelito
KM 17
CARIBBEAN SEA
Laguna Cabra
Playa Delfines
KM 20
Laguna Río Inglés
Aeropuerto Internacional de Cancún
Blvd Kukulkán
MEX 307 (toll)
To Tulum
Punta Nizuc
Parque Nacional Submarino Punta Nizuc

0   1   2 km
0   .5   1 mile

hotels, many of which have swimming pools. Restaurants in the city center range from ultra-Mexican taco joints to fairly smooth and expensive salons where the package-tour people come to have a 'real' Mexican experience.

The 23-km-long sandy island, Isla Cancún, is known as the Zona Hotelera or Zona Turística. Boulevard Kukulcán, a four-lane divided avenue, leaves Ciudad Cancún and goes westward out on the island nine km past the smaller, older, moderately priced hotels and some larger ones to Punta Cancún and the Centro de Convenciones. The boulevard then heads south for 14 km, past dozens of mammoth hotels, shopping centers, restaurants and bars, to Punta Nizuc, where it turns eastward, rejoins the mainland, and heads inland to the airport.

With the exception of the overpriced youth hostel, there are no budget hotels in the Zona Hotelera.

Cancún International Airport is about eight km south of the city center. Puerto Juárez, the port for passenger ferries to Isla Mujeres, is about three km north of the center. Punta Sam, the dock for the slower car ferries to Isla Mujeres, is about five km north of the center.

INFORMATION
Tourist Office

The State Tourism Office for Quintana Roo (☎ (98) 84-04-37), 26 Avenida Tulum, is next to the Multibanco Comermex, to the left (north) of the municipalidad.

Consulates

If your consulate or agent is not listed here, call your consulate in Mérida or your embassy in Mexico City.

Belize
    Calle Rosas 22, SM 22
    (☎ (98) 84-65-98, 84-85-46)

Canada
    Avenida Tulum 200, Plaza México 312, 2nd floor (☎ (98) 84-37-16, fax (98) 87-67-16); Canadian Embassy in Mexico City (☎ (5) 724-7900)

France
    Instituto de Idiomas de Cancún, Avenida Xel-ha 113
    (☎ (98) 84-60-78, fax (98) 87-33-62)

Germany
    Punta Conoco 36, SM 24 (☎ (98) 84-18-98)

Italy
    Calle Alcatraces 39
    (☎ (98) 83-12-61, fax (98) 84-54-15)

Netherlands
    Hotel President Inter-Continental
    (☎ (98) 83-02-00, fax (98) 83-25-15)

Spain
    Oasis Building, Blvd Kukulcán Km 6.5
    (☎ (98) 83-24-66, fax (98) 83-28-70)

UK
    At the Royal Caribbean in the Zona Hotelera (☎ (98) 85-11-66 ext 462, fax (98) 85-12-25)

USA
    Plaza Caracol shopping center, 3rd floor, in the Zona Hotelera (☎ (98) 83-02-72); or call the US Consulate General in Mérida (☎ (99) 25-50-11, open 7:30 am to 3:30 pm weekdays) or, after hours, the Mérida duty officer (☎ (99) 25-54-09). It is said that the Consulate General will soon move from Mérida to Cancún.

Money

Banks on Avenida Tulum are open from 9 am to 1:30 pm, but some limit foreign exchange transactions to between 10 am and noon. Casas de cambio usually are open from 8 or 9 am to 1 pm and again from 4 or 5 pm till 7 or 8 pm; some casas are open seven days a week. Bank ATMs (cash machines) are numerous throughout Ciudad Cancún and the Zona Hotelera.

Post & Communications

The main post office (Oficina de Correos, Cancún, Quintana Roo 77500) is at the western end of Avenida Sunyaxchén. Hours for buying stamps and picking up Lista de Correos (poste restante) mail are 8 am to 7 pm Monday to Friday and 9 am to 1 pm Saturday and holidays, closed Sunday. For international money orders and registered mail, hours are 8 am to 6 pm Monday to Friday, 9 am to noon Saturday and holidays, closed Sunday.

YUCATÁN

Now that Mexico has opened its telephone system up to competition, the phone situation is in flux. TelMex Ladatel phones are numerous, to be found on street corners and in large public buildings, as are other sorts of phones aimed at foreigners, especially North Americans. Before you call, check the rates; they can be very high – up to US$6 per minute.

Travel Agencies

Any travel agent can book or change a flight for you. Most of the big hotels and many of the smaller, moderately priced hotels have travel agencies of their own.

Bookstores

A store with periodicals and books in several languages is Fama Cancún, Avenida Tulum 105, near the southern end of Tulipanes.

Laundry

Several shops offer these services. The Lavandería María de Lourdes, near the hotel of the same name, is on Calle Orquideas off Avenida Yaxchilán. You might also try the Lavandería y Tintorería Cox-Boh, Avenida Tankah 26, Supermanzana 24. Walk toward the post office along Avenida Sunyaxchén; in front of the post office, bear right onto Avenida Tankah, and Cox-Boh is on the right-hand side of the street.

Laundry costs US$3.50 per kilogram for bulk service. To have a pair of trousers washed and ironed costs US$3.50, or $6.50 for dry cleaning. Washing and ironing a shirt costs US$2.25. Cox-Boh is open every day except Sunday.

Medical Services

Cancún's hospitals include:

IMSS (Social Security), Avenida Cobá at Avenida Tulum (☎ (98) 84-23-42)

Cruz Roja (Red Cross), Avenida Labná 1 (☎ (98) 84-16-16)

Hospital Americano, Calle Viento 15 (☎ (98) 84-64-30, 84-60-68)

Hospital Total Assist, Calle Claveles 22, next to the Hotel Antillano, just off Avenida Tulum (☎ (98) 84-10-92, 84-81-16)

MAYAN RUINS

There are Mayan ruins in Cancún, and while they are not particularly impressive they are worth a look if you have lots of time. Most extensive are the ruins in the Zona Arqueológica El Rey, south of the Sheraton and Conrad hotels. Heading south along Blvd Kukulcán from Punta Cancún, watch for the marker for Km 17. Just past the marker there's an unpaved road on the right, which leads to the ruins. They are open from 8 am to 5 pm every day; admission costs US$2. El Rey consists of a small temple and several ceremonial platforms.

If you've seen larger ruins, you may want to take just a quick glimpse at El Rey. If so, continue on Blvd Kukulcán 700 meters past the Km 17 marker and up the hill. At the top of the hill, just past the restaurant La Prosperidad de Cancún, you can survey the ruins without hiking in or paying the admission charge.

The tiny Mayan structure and chac-mool statue set in the beautifully kept grounds of the Sheraton Hotel are actually authentic ruins found on the spot.

ARCHAEOLOGICAL MUSEUM

The Museo de Antropología y Historia, next to the Centro de Convenciones in the Zona Hotelera, has a limited collection of Mayan artifacts. Although most of the items are from the Postclassic period (1200-1500 AD) – including jewelry, masks and skull deformers – there is a Classic-period hieroglyphic staircase inscribed with dates from the 6th century, as well as the stucco head that gave the local archaeological zone its name of El Rey (The King).

Hours are Tuesday to Saturday 9 am to 7 pm, Sunday 10 am to 5 pm, closed Monday. Admission costs US$1.50. But on my last visit the museum was closed, and there was no indication of when – or if – it might reopen.

BEACHES

All of Cancún's beaches are open to you, because all Mexican beaches are public property. Several of the resort's beaches have particularly easy public access, but you should know that you have the right to walk and swim on any beach at all. In practice it may be difficult to approach certain stretches of beach without going through a hotel's property, but few hotels will notice you walking through to the beach.

Starting at Ciudad Cancún and heading out to Isla Cancún, all the beaches are on the left-hand side of the road as you go (the lagoon is on your right). They are: Playa Las Perlas, Playa Linda, Playa Langosta, Playa Tortugas, Playa Caracol, and then Punta Cancún, the corner point of the 7. South from Punta Cancún are Playa Gaviota Azul and Playa Marlin, then the long stretches of Playa Chac-Mool, Playa Ballenas (Km 15), and Playa Delfines (Km 18).

Beach Safety
Cancún's Rescate 911 ambulance crews respond to as many as a dozen near-drownings per week. The most dangerous beaches seem to be Playa Delfines and Playa Chac-Mool.

As any experienced swimmer knows, a beach fronting on open sea can be deadly dangerous, and Cancún's eastern beaches are no exception. Though the surf is usually gentle, undertow is a possibility and sudden storms (called *nortes*) can blacken the sky and sweep in at any time without warning. The local authorities have devised a system of colored pennants to warn beachgoers of potential dangers. Look for the pennants on the beaches where you swim:

Blue	Normal, safe conditions
Yellow	Use caution, changeable conditions
Red	Unsafe conditions; use a swimming pool instead

Getting There & Away
To reach the beaches, catch any bus marked 'Hoteles' or 'Zona Hotelera' going south along Avenida Tulum or east along Avenida Cobá. The cost of a taxi depends on how far you travel. For details, see Getting Around at the end of the Cancún section.

SNORKELING
Most snorkelers who wish to explore reefs pay a visit to nearby Isla Mujeres – see that

---

Air-Conditioned Sand
The dazzling white sand of Cancún's beaches is light in weight and cool underfoot even in the blazing sun. That's because it's composed not of silica, but of microscopic, star-shaped fossils of a plankton called Discoaster. The coolness of the sand has not been lost on Cancún's ingenious promoters, who have dubbed the sand 'air-conditioned'. Combined with the crystalline azure waters of the Caribbean Sea, it makes for beaches that are pure delight. ■

---

section for information. If you just want to see the sparser aquatic life off Cancún's beaches, you can rent snorkeling equipment for about US$8 from most luxury hotels.

The bigger hotels and travel agencies can also book you on day-cruise boats that take snorkelers to La Bandera, Los Manchones, Cuevones and Chital reefs.

SCUBA DIVING
This expensive sport is all the pricier in equipment rental and boat transport from Cancún. Veteran divers might prefer nearby Palancar Reef, accessible from Cozumel and Playa del Carmen. Nonetheless, agencies and hotels rent gear and provide passage to some fine reefs in the vicinity. Los Manchones and Cuevones reefs, situated between Cancún and Isla Mujeres, afford diving depths of 10 to 15 meters.

FISHING
Deep-sea fishing excursions can be booked through a travel agent or one of the large hotels.

OTHER WATER SPORTS
Numerous dive shops and water sports marinas offer rentals of waterskis, sailboats, sailboards, Jet Skis and scuba and snorkeling gear. Many of the larger hotels have water sports shops with similar rentals.

PLACES TO STAY
Even though there are more than 20,000 hotel rooms in Cancún, this resort offers

YUCATÁN

the low-budget traveler the worst selection of cheap accommodations at the highest prices of any place in Mexico.

Places to Stay – budget

To make your room search as easy as possible, I've arranged my hotel recommendations on walking itineraries starting from the bus station. If you arrive by air and take a minibus into town (see Getting Around), your minibus driver should drop you at your chosen hotel at no extra charge.

In general, bottom-end rooms range from US$14 to US$38 a double, tax included, in the busy winter season. Prices drop 15% to 20% in the less busy summer months. Except for the cheapest places, this gets you a room with private bathroom, fan and probably air-conditioning, and the hotel might even have a small swimming pool.

Youth Hostel Four km from the bus station, the local youth hostel is called *Atención a la Juventud* (☎ (98) 83-13-37), Blvd Kukulcán Km 3.2, on the left-hand (north) side of the road just past the Km 3 marker as you come from Ciudad Cancún.

Built decades ago as a modern 600-bed complex in honor of youth, it is now sadly dilapidated, though still functioning. Though the staff is friendly, the place is overpriced for what you get: a single-sex dorm bed for US$11 (plus a US$7 deposit). (Two people can usually find a decent hotel room with bath in Ciudad Cancún for the same US$22 – or less.) Camping on the beach costs US$6 per person, with a locker and use of the hostel's facilities, as there are none for the camping area itself. The beach there is silty and shallow.

Avenida Uxmal All of Cancún's cheap hotels are in Ciudad Cancún, and many are within a few blocks of the bus station. Go northwest on Avenida Uxmal and you'll come to the following cheap lodgings.

Hotel El Alux (☎ (98) 84-06-62, 84-05-56), Avenida Uxmal 21, is only a block from the bus station. Air-con rooms with shower go for US$15 to US$20 a single,

US$20 to US$25 a double. An *alux*, by the way, is the Mayan version of a leprechaun.

Across Uxmal on the south side is the 38-room *Hotel Cotty* (☎ (98) 84-13-19, 84-05-50), Avenida Uxmal 44, a motel-style place that's more or less quiet. It has seen better days, but it's certainly cheap: rooms with shower and air-con cost US$15/20/25 a single/double/triple or quad. It also has off-street parking.

A few steps farther along Uxmal is Calle Palmera and the *Hotel María Isabel* (☎ (98) 84-90-15), Palmera 59, a tiny, clean place with a quieter location. Rooms with private shower and air-con cost US$18/22 a single/double. This is perhaps the best value close to the bus station.

From Avenida Uxmal, walk south along Avenida Yaxchilán and turn right after one block at Calle Punta Allen to find the quiet *Casa de Huéspedes Punta Allen* (☎ (98) 84-02-25, 84-10-01), Punta Allen 8. This family-run guesthouse has several double rooms with bath and air-con for US$18 to US$22, light breakfast included.

Farther west along Uxmal, on the left-hand side just before the corner with Avenida Chichén Itzá, stands the *Hotel Uxmal* (☎ (98) 84-22-66, 84-23-55), Uxmal 111, a clean, family-run hostelry where US$24 will buy you a double room with fan and/or air-con, TV and off-street parking.

Avenidas Sunyaxchén & Tankah Staying here puts you close to the post office and Mercado 28, with its good, cheap eateries.

Just off Avenida Yaxchilán stands the *Hotel Hacienda Cancún* (☎ (98) 84-36-72, fax (98) 84-12-08), Sunyaxchén 39-40, on the right-hand (north) side. It's popular with Mexican tour groups. For US$25 to US$32 (single or double) you get an air-con room with color TV and private bath, use of the hotel's pretty swimming pool and patio and a good location.

Continue along Sunyaxchén to the post office and bear right onto Avenida Tankah. Watch on the right-hand side of the street for the *Hotel Tankah* (☎ (98) 84-44-46, 84-48-44), Tankah 69, charging US$18 for a double with fan, US$7 more with air-con.

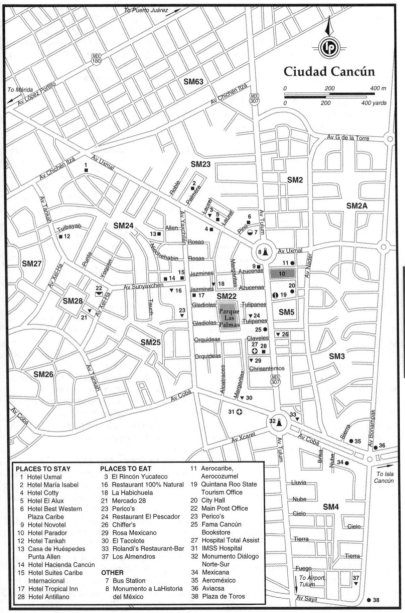

Ciudad Cancún

To Puerto Juárez

To Mérida

To Isla Cancún

To Airport, Tulum

YUCATÁN

PLACES TO STAY
1 Hotel Uxmal
2 Hotel María Isabel
4 Hotel Cotty
5 Hotel El Alux
6 Hotel Best Western
  Plaza Caribe
9 Hotel Novotel
10 Hotel Parador
12 Hotel Tankah
13 Casa de Huéspedes
   Punta Allen
14 Hotel Hacienda Cancún
15 Hotel Suites Caribe
   Internacional
17 Hotel Tropical Inn
28 Hotel Antillano

PLACES TO EAT
3 El Rincón Yucateco
16 Restaurant 100% Natural
18 La Habichuela
21 Mercado 28
23 Perico's
24 Restaurant El Pescador
26 Chiffer's
29 Rosa Mexicano
30 El Tacolote
33 Rolandi's Restaurant-Bar
37 Los Almendros

OTHER
7 Bus Station
8 Monumento a LaHistoria
  del México

11 Aerocaribe,
   Aerocozumel
19 Quintana Roo State
   Tourism Office
20 City Hall
22 Main Post Office
23 Perico's
25 Fama Cancún
   Bookstore
27 Hospital Total Assist
31 IMSS Hospital
32 Monumento Diálogo
   Norte-Sur
34 Mexicana
35 Aeroméxico
36 Aviacsa
38 Plaza de Toros

Farther North Several cheap hotels are hidden away on quiet residential streets 1200 meters north of the bus terminal. Go north on Avenida Tulum past the large San Francisco de Asis store (on the right/east side), and just after the road narrows turn right on Calle 6 Oriente. (If you take a bus, get off opposite the big Plaza Cancún 2000 shopping center, which is on the left/west side of the street.) Go three short blocks east, then turn left onto Calle 7 Oriente, and the *Hotel Piña Hermanos* (☎ (98) 84-21-50) is on the right-hand side. Rooms with fan and private bath on this quiet street cost US$10/14 a single/double. If it's full, look at the similarly priced *Hotel Mary Tere* (☎ (98) 84-04-96) nearby.

Places to Stay – middle

Middle-range hotel rooms cost from US$50 to US$95 in the busy winter season, somewhat less during the summer. During the very slow times (late May to early June, October to mid-December), prices may be only half those quoted here, particularly if you haggle a bit. These hotels offer air-con rooms with private bath and color cable TV, a swimming pool, restaurant and perhaps some other amenities such as a bar, elevators (lifts) and shuttle vans from the hotel to the beach.

Near the Bus Station Directly across from the bus station is the *Hotel Best Western Plaza Caribe* (☎ (98) 84-13-77, fax (98) 84-63-52, in the USA (800) 528-1234), offering very comfortable air-con rooms and all the amenities for US$60 a double in summer, US$85 in winter.

Avenida Tulum Around the corner from the bus station on Avenida Tulum is the *Hotel Novotel* (☎ (98) 84-29-99, fax 84-31-62), Avenida Tulum 75 (Apdo Postal 70). Rooms in the main building have air-con and cost US$30 to US$38, single or double; front rooms can be noisy. Rooms in cabañas behind the main building around the pool have fans only, are quiet, and cost US$22 to US$28. They have triples and quad rooms as well.

Across Avenida Tulum from the Novotel is the *Hotel Parador* (☎ (98) 84-13-10, fax (98) 84-97-12), Avenida Tulum 26, a modern building with 66 rooms, each with two double beds, costing US$30 to US$45 a single/double.

The *Hotel Antillano* (☎ (98) 84-15-32, fax (98) 84-18-78), Calle Claveles just off Avenida Tulum, has 48 good guestrooms and all the mid-range services for US$35/50/65 a single/double/triple in winter.

Avenida Yaxchilán *Hotel Tropical Inn* (☎ (98) 84-30-78, fax (98) 84-34-78), Avenida Yaxchilán 31, corner of Jazmines, has 87 nice rooms with two double beds each, priced at US$35/50/65 a single/double/triple in winter. It's popular with foreign tour groups.

Across Yaxchilán from the Tropical Inn is the *Hotel Suites Caribe Internacional* (☎ (98) 84-39-99, fax (98) 84-19-93), Sunyaxchén 36 at Avenida Yaxchilán. The 80 rooms here include normal double rooms, but also junior suites with two beds, sofa, kitchenette with range and refrigerator and a living room. Prices for doubles are similar to the Tropical Inn, with the suites a bit higher.

Zona Hotelera The *Aquamarina Beach Hotel* (☎ (98) 83-14-25, fax (98) 83-17-51), Blvd Kulkulcán Km 4.5 (Apdo Postal 751), was built with tour goups of young-adult sun lovers in mind. Rooms, single or double, go for under US$100 in summer, US$135 in winter. Some rooms have kitchenettes and refrigerators.

Places to Stay – top end

Cancún's top places range from comfortable but boring to luxurious full-service hostelries of an international standard. Prices range from US$150 to US$250 and more for a double room in winter. All the top places are located on the beach, many have vast grounds with rolling lawns of manicured grass, tropical gardens, swimming pools (virtually all with swim-up bars – a Cancún necessity) and facilities for sports such as tennis, handball, waterskiing and sailboarding. Some are constructed in whimsical fantasy styles with turrets, bulbous domes, minarets, dramatic glass canopies and other architectural megalomania. Guestrooms have air-con and are equipped with minibar and TV linked to satellite receivers for US programs.

To get the most advantageous price at any of these luxury hotels, sign up for an inclusive tour package, which includes lodging.If you have not come with a group, you can find the best value for your money at the following hotels.

Km 4 *Calinda Beach Cancún* (☎ (98) 83-16-00, fax (98) 83-18-57, in Mexico (91-800) 90-000, in the USA (800) 221-2222) facing the Playa Linda Marine Terminal, has a decor of red tiles, white stucco and modern muted colors, all with a light, airy feel. Rooms cost US$110 in summer, US$155 in winter.

Km 8 *Calinda Viva Cancún* (☎ (98) 83-08-00, fax (98) 83-20-87, in Mexico (91-800) 90-000, in the USA (800) 221-2222) has 210 rooms and rates very similar to those at the aforementioned Calinda Beach Cancún.

Km 8.5 *Fiesta Americana Cancún* (☎ (98) 83-14-00, in the USA (800) 343-7821) is an oddity, resembling nothing so much as an old-city streetscape: it's an appealing jumble of windows, balconies, roofs and other features. Rooms cost US$165 to US$225 in summer, US$185 to US$265 in winter.

Just past the Fiesta Americana Cancún is the *Hyatt Regency Cancún* (☎ (98) 83-12-34, fax (98) 83-16-94, in the USA (800) 233-1234, hyattreg@cancun.rce.com.mx), a gigantic cylinder with a lofty open court at its core and 300 guestrooms arranged around it. Situated right on Punta Cancún by the Centro de Convenciones, virtually all of its rooms have excellent views. The beach is right outside the building. Rates in winter are US$185 to US$245, in summer US$160 to US$205, the higher rates being for Regency Club rooms.

Km 9 *Hotel Aristos Cancún* (☎ (98) 83-00-11, fax (98) 83-00-78, in the USA (800) 527-4786) has about the best rates in the neighborhood: US$90 a double in summer, US$130 in winter, lunch and tax included.

Km 11.5 *Hyatt Cancún Caribe* (☎ (98) 83-00-44, fax (98) 83-15-14, in the USA (800) 233-1234) has a good variety of accommodations. Its 198 rooms and suites include ground-level rooms with private terraces, upper-level rooms with fine sea views, and Regency Club villas surrounding their own clubhouse with private pool and Jacuzzi. Rooms and villas cost US$205 to US$242 in summer, US$286 to US$331 in winter.

Km 14 *Cancún Palace* (☎ (98) 85-05-33, fax (98) 85-15-93, in the USA (800) 346-8225), works extra hard to offer a good value to guests. The 421 rooms and suites have all the amenities and services you'd expect, plus balconies with water views.

PLACES TO EAT

Nowhere in Mexico have I found more mediocre food at higher prices than in Cancún. Don't expect too much from Cancún's restaurants, and when you get a memorable meal (and you will have at least a few) you'll be pleasantly surprised.

Places to Eat – budget

As usual, market eateries provide the biggest portions at the lowest prices. Ciudad Cancún's market, near the post office, is a building set back from the street and emblazoned with the name Mercado Municipal Artículo 115 Constitucional. Called simply *Mercado 28* (that's 'mercado veintiocho') by the locals, it has shops selling fresh vegetables, fruits and prepared meals.

In the second courtyard in from the street are the eateries: *Restaurant Margely*, *Cocina Familiar Económica Chulum*, *Cocina La Chaya*, etc. These are pleasant, simple eateries with tables beneath awnings and industrious señoras cooking away behind the counters. Most are open for breakfast, lunch and dinner and all offer full meals (comidas corridas) for as little as US$2.50, and sandwiches for less.

YUCATÁN

El Rincón Yucateco, Avenida Uxmal 24, across from the Hotel Cotty, serves good Yucatecan food. Service is from 7 am to 10 pm every day. Main courses cost US$2.50 to US$4.

El Tacolote, on Avenida Cobá across from the big red IMSS hospital, is brightly lit and attractive, with dark wood benches. Tacos – a dozen types – are priced from US$1 to US$3. El Tacolote (the name is a pun on taco and *tecolote*, owl) is open from 7 to 11:30 am for breakfast, then till 10 pm for tacos.

Chiffer's, in the big San Francisco de Asis department store on the east side of Avenida Tulum, has welcome air-conditioning. You can spend as much as US$13 for a full, heavy meal with dessert and drink, but most people keep their bill below US$6. It's open from 7 am to 11 pm daily.

Places to Eat – middle

Most of the moderately priced restaurants are located in the city center. If you're willing to spend between US$12 and US$20 for dinner, you can eat fairly well in Cancún.

The *Restaurant El Pescador* (☎ (98) 84-26-73), Tulipanes 28, has been serving dependably good meals since the early days of Cancún. The menu lists sopa de lima and fish ceviche for starters, then charcoal-grilled fish, red snapper in garlic sauce and beef shish kebab. El Pescador is open for lunch and dinner (closed Monday).

Rolandi's Restaurant-Bar (☎ (98) 84-40-47), Avenida Cobá 12, between Tulum and Nader just off the southern roundabout, is an attractive Italian eatery open every day. It serves elaborate one-person pizzas (US$5 to US$10), spaghetti plates and more substantial dishes of veal and chicken. Watch out for the high drink prices. Hours are 1 pm to midnight (Sunday, 4 pm to midnight).

Every visitor to Cancún makes the pilgrimage to *Los Almendros* (☎ (98) 87-13-32), Avenida Bonampak at Avenida Sayil, across from the bullring, the local incarnation of Yucatán's most famous restaurant. Started in Ticul in 1962, Los Almendros set out to serve *platillos campesinos para los dzules* (country food for the bourgeoisie, or townfolk). The chefs at Los Almendros (the almond trees) claim to have created poc-chuc, a dish of succulent pork cooked with onion and served in a tangy sauce of sour orange or lime. If you don't know what to order, try the *combinado yucateco* (Yucatecan combination plate). A full meal costs about US$16 per person. Come any day for lunch or dinner.

Restaurant 100% Natural (☎ (98) 84-36-17), Avenida Sunyaxchén at Yaxchilán, is an airy cafe. Though the menu lists several natural food items, such as fruit salads and juices, green salads and yogurt, it also includes hamburgers, enchiladas, wine and beer at moderate prices. There are branches in the Plaza Terramar (☎ (98) 83-11-80) and Kukulcán Plaza (☎ (98) 85-29-04) shopping centers in the Zona Hotelera.

Perico's (☎ /fax (98) 84-31-52), Avenida Yaxchilán 71 at Calle Marañón, is quintessential Cancún, a huge thatched structure stuffed with stereotypical Mexican icons: saddles, enormous sombreros, baskets, bullwhips, etc. An army of señors and señoritas dressed in Hollywood-Mexican costumes doesn't serve so much as 'dramatize your dining experience'. Oh well. But if you're in the mood for dinner a la Disney, Perico's will do. The menu is heavy with the macho fare most popular with group tourists: filet mignon, jumbo shrimp, lobster, barbecued spareribs. After the show, fork over US$20 to US$30 per person to pay your bill. It's supposedly open from noon to 2 am, but may in fact serve only dinner.

Places to Eat – top end

Traditionally, Mexican restaurants have followed the European scheme of simple decor and elaborate food. Cancún, however, caters mostly to those who prefer simple, familiar food served in elaborate surroundings. Thus half the menus in town are composed of such grill-me items as steak, jumbo shrimp, fish fillet and lobster tail, and Cancún's expensive restaurants feature rhapsodic menu prose, lots of tropical gardens, mirrors, waterfalls, paraphernalia, even fish tanks and aviaries of exotic birds. The food can be good, forgettable or execrable. If the last, at least you'll have pleasant music and something to look at as you gnaw and gag.

The exceptional places are listed below.

Ciudad Cancún A long-standing favorite is *Rosa Mexicano* (☎ (98) 84-63-13), Calle Claveles 4, the place to go for unusual Mexican dishes in a pleasant hacienda decor. There are some concessions to Cancún, such as tortilla soup and filete tampiqueña, but also squid sautéed with three chilies, garlic and scallions and shrimp in a pipían sauce (made of ground pumpkin seeds and spices). Dinner, served daily from 5 to 11 pm, goes for US$20 to US$30.

Another dependable favorite (since 1977) is *La Habichuela* (☎ (98) 84-31-58), Margaritas 25, just off Parque Las Palmas in a residential neighborhood. The menu tends toward dishes easily comprehended and easily perceived as elegant: shish kebab flambé, lobster in champagne sauce, jumbo shrimp and beef tampiqueña: US$25 to US$38 per person for dinner. Hours are 1 pm to about 11 pm, every day of the year. La Habichuela (LAH-b'CHWEH-lah) means The Stringbean.

ENTERTAINMENT
Most of the nightlife is loud and bibulous, as befits a supercharged beach resort. If the theme restaurants, bars and discos don't do it for you, take a dinner cruise on a mock pirate ship.

The local *Ballet Folklorico* performs some evenings at various halls for about US$40 per person, which includes dinner. The dancers come on at 8:30 pm. Don't expect the finesse and precision of the performances in Mexico City.

Bullfights (four bulls) are held each Wednesday afternoon at 3:30 pm in the Plaza de Toros, at the southern end of Avenida Bonampak, across the street from the Restaurant Los Almendros, about one km from the center of town. Tickets cost about US$15 and can be purchased from any travel agency.

THINGS TO BUY
Gift shops and touts are everywhere in Cancún, with crafts from all over Mexico, often at exorbitant prices. Save your shopping for other Mexican destinations. If you hanker for a hammock, buy it in Mérida. Still, window-shopping in Cancún's air-conditioned and luxurious shopping centers can be good fun.

GETTING THERE & AWAY
Air
Airport Cancún's international airport is the busiest in southeastern Mexico. Upon arrival, don't change money until after you've passed through Customs and Immigration, as the rate of exchange is terrible. Then, if you really want the best rate, walk two minutes to the *departures* area and look for exchange windows hidden in the back corners – they have the best rates.

The arrivals area has lockers big enough for a briefcase or small suitcase, but not for a stuffed backpack; they cost US$3 for 24 hours.

Airlines For fares and departure points from North America, see the introductory Getting There & Away chapter. Be sure to ask your travel agent about charter and group flights, which can be quite cheap, especially in summer.

Aerocaribe is a regional airline owned by Mexicana; it offers a special fare deal called the Mayapass, good for a series of flights at reduced prices. Aerocaribe has flights to points in Yucatán and beyond, in small and medium-sized planes, at the following prices (one way): Chetumal US$60, Cozumel US$30, Mérida US$50, Mexico City US$120 and Villahermosa US$90. Excursion fares offer better deals than these one-way fares.

Aviacsa is a regional carrier based in Tuxtla Gutiérrez, Chiapas, with flights from Cancún to Mérida, Mexico City, Oaxaca, Tapachula, Tuxtla Gutiérrez, Villahermosa and points in Guatemala.

Aviateca, Guatemala's national airline, runs flights from Cancún to Flores, El Petén (for Tikal), and onward to Guatemala

YUCATÁN

City on Monday, Wednesday, Saturday and Sunday, returning on Tuesday, Friday, Saturday and Sunday.

Airline contact addresses are:

Aerocancún, Oasis building, Blvd Kukulcán (☎ (98) 83-24-75)

Aerocaribe/Aerocozumel, Avenida Tulum 29, Plaza América, at the roundabout intersection with Avenida Uxmal (☎ (98) 84-20-00; at the airport ☎ /fax (98) 86-00-83)

Aeromexico, Avenida Cobá 80, between Tulum and Bonampak (☎ (98) 84-35-71, fax 84-70-05)

American Airlines, at Cancún airport (☎ (98) 86-00-55, fax (98) 86-01-64, in Mexico (91-800) 9-04-60)

Aviacsa, Avenida Cobá 37 (☎ (98) 87-42-14, fax (98) 84-65-99)

Aviateca, Plaza México, Avenida Tulum 200 (☎ (98) 84-39-38, fax (98) 84-33-28)

Continental, at Cancún airport (☎ (98) 86-00-06, fax (98) 86-00-07, in Mexico (91-800) 9-00-50)

LACSA, Edificio Atlantis, Avenida Bonampak at Avenida Cobá (☎ (98) 87-31-01)

Mexicana, Avenida Cobá 39 (☎ (98) 87-44-44)

Northwest, at Cancún airport (☎ (98) 86-00-46)

Taesa, Avenida Yaxchilán 31 (☎ (98) 87-43-14, fax 87-33-28)

Bus

The confusing bus station on Avenida Uxmal just west of Avenida Tulum has two separate parts under the same roof; look in both. Companies include Autobuses de Oriente (ADO), Autotransportes de Oriente (Oriente), Transportes de Lujo Linea Dorada (Linea Dorada, a 2nd-class line despite its pompous name), Autotransportes del Sur (ATS), Autobuses del Noroeste and Autobuses del Centro. Services are 2nd-class, 1st-class or any of several luxury flavors.

Across from the bus station entrance is the ticket office of Playa Express, which runs shuttle buses down the Caribbean Coast to Tulum and Felipe Carrillo Puerto at least every 30 minutes all day, stopping

at major towns and points of interest along the way.

Here are some major routes (daily):

Chetumal – 382 km, six hours, US$10 to US$14; 23 buses

Chichén Itzá – 205 km, two to 3½ hours, US$4.50 to US$7; 10 buses

Mérida – 320 km, four to six hours, US$7 to US$12; buses at least every half hour; Super Expresso buses make the run in under four hours

Mexico City – 1772 km, 22 hours, US$45 to US$55; six buses

Playa del Carmen – 65 km, one hour, US$1.75; Playa Express buses every 30 minutes; others 12 times daily

Puerto Morelos – 36 km, 40 minutes, US$1; Playa Express buses every 30 minutes; others 12 times daily

Ticul – 395 km, six to eight hours, US$10; five buses by Linea Dorada

Tizimin – 212 km, three hours, US$4; six buses via Valladolid

Tulum – 132 km, two hours, US$3 to US$4; Playa Express buses every 30 minutes; other buses about every two hours

Valladolid – 160 km, 1½ to two hours, US$4 to US$8; same as Mérida

Villahermosa – 915 km, 11 hours, US$28; three by ADO

GETTING AROUND
To/From the Airport

Orange-and-beige airport vans (Transporte Terrestre, US$7.50) monopolize the trade, charging taxi fare for a van ride with other travelers. If you want taxi service (that is, if you want the van or car to yourself, direct to your hotel), the cost is an outrageous US$25 (just a bit less than airfare to Cozumel). A taxi back to the airport from Ciudad Cancún costs about US$8.

The route into town is invariably via Punta Nizuc and north up Isla Cancún along Blvd Kukulcán, passing all of the luxury beachfront hotels before reaching the youth hostel and Ciudad Cancún. If your hotel is in Ciudad Cancún, the ride to your hotel may take as long as 45 minutes.

If you walk out of the airport and follow the access road, you can often flag down a taxi that will take you for less because the driver is no longer subject to the expensive regulated airport fares. Walk the two km to the highway and you can flag down a passing bus, which is very cheap.

To return to the airport you must take a taxi or hop off a southbound bus at the airport junction and walk the two km to the terminal.

Bus

Although it's possible to walk most everywhere in Ciudad Cancún, to get to the Zona Hotelera, catch a Ruta 1 'Hoteles-Downtown' local bus heading southward along Avenida Tulum. The fare depends on distance and ranges from US$0.50 to US$1.25.

To reach Puerto Juárez and the Isla Mujeres ferries, take a Ruta 13 ('Pto Juárez' or 'Punta Sam') bus.

Taxi

Cancún's taxis do not have meters, so you must haggle over fares. Generally, the fare between Ciudad Cancún and Punta Cancún (where the Hyatt, Camino Real and Krystal hotels and the Centro de Convenciones are) is US$4 or US$5. To the airport costs US$8 (from Ciudad Cancún) to US$12 (from Punta Cancún). To Puerto Juárez you'll pay about US$3.

Ferry

There are frequent passenger ferries from Puerto Juárez to Isla Mujeres (see Getting Around in the next section for details). Local buses (Ruta 13, US$0.55) take about 20 minutes from stops on Avenida Tulum to the Puerto Juárez ferry dock. Taxis cost about US$3.

Car

There are dozens of places to rent cars in Cancún, from the big international companies to small local ones. Assume you will pay a total of US$40 to US$60 per day (tax, insurance and gas included) for the cheapest car offered, usually a bottom-of-the-line Volkswagen or Nissan.

Isla Mujeres

Population 13,500

Isla Mujeres (Island of Women), has a reputation as a backpackers' Cancún, a place where one can escape the megaresorts for the laid-back life of a tropical isle – at bargain prices. Though that was true for many years, it is less so today.

The chief attribute of Isla Mujeres is its relaxed social life in a tropical setting, with surrounding waters that are turquoise blue and bathtub warm. If you have been doing some hard traveling through Mexico, you will find many travelers you met along the way taking it easy here. Others make Isla Mujeres the site of their one- to two-week holiday. Many visitors have a hard time tearing themselves away.

The principal beach is rather small, however, and the island as a whole not all that attractive. Most of the palm trees were killed by a blight, the rest swept away by Hurricane Gilbert in 1988 and the part of the island not built up consists of Yucatán scrub bush. The ballyhooed snorkeling at Garrafón National Park is overrated, because of overcrowding.

Cancún makes itself felt each morning as boatload after boatload of package tourists arrives on Isla Mujeres for a day's excursion. Every year, ever more restaurants and nightclubs close and T-shirt shops and moped-rental agencies open, highlighting the shift from local tourism to that supplied in bulk from Cancún.

HISTORY

Although it is said by some that the Island of Women got its name because Spanish buccaneers kept their lovers there while they plundered galleons and pillaged ports, a less romantic but still intriguing explanation is probably more accurate: In 1519 a chronicler sailing with Hernández de Córdoba's expedition wrote that when the conquistadors' ships were forced by high winds into the island's harbor, the crew reconnoitered. What they found

YUCATÁN

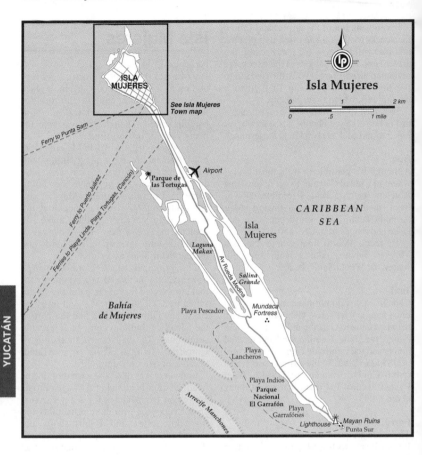

onshore was a Mayan ceremonial site filled with clay figurines of females. Today some archaeologists believe that the island was a stopover for the Maya en route to worship their goddess of fertility, Ixchel, on the island of Cozumel. The clay idols are thought to represent the goddess.

ORIENTATION

The island is about eight km long and anywhere from 300 to 800 meters wide. The good snorkeling and some of the better swimming beaches are on the southern part of the island along the western shore; the eastern shore is washed by the open sea, and the surf there is dangerous. The ferry docks, the town and the most popular sand beach (Playa Norte) are at the northern tip of the island.

INFORMATION
Tourist Office

The Delegación Estatal de Turismo (State Tourism Department, ☎ (987) 7-03-16) faces the basketball court in the main plaza.

Money

The island's Banco del Atlántico, at Juárez 5, and Banco Serfin, at Juárez 3, are so packed during the two hours a day (10 am to noon, Monday to Friday) when foreign currency may be exchanged that many travelers change money at a lower rate at a grocery store, their hotel or at the tourist office.

Post & Communications

The post office, next to the market, is open Monday to Friday from 8 am to 7 pm, Saturday and Sunday from 9 am to 1 pm. For information about telephones, see this section under Cancún.

Laundry

Lavandería Automática Tim Phó, Avenida Juárez at Abasolo, is modern and busy. They'll wash, dry and fold four kilos of laundry for US$3.50.

GARRAFÓN NATIONAL PARK

Although the waters are translucent and the fish abundant, Garrafón is perhaps a bit overrated. Hordes of day trippers from Cancún fill the water during the middle of the day, so you are more often ogling fellow snorkelers than you are aquatic life. Furthermore, the reef is virtually dead, which makes it less likely to inflict cuts but also reduces its color and the intricacy of its formations.

The water can be extremely choppy, sweeping you into jagged areas. When the water is running fast – not an unusual occurrence – snorkeling is a hassle and can even be dangerous. Those without strong swimming skills should be advised that the bottom falls off steeply quite close to shore; if you are having trouble, you might not be noticed amid all those bobbing heads.

Garrafón is open daily from 8 am to 5 pm, and the earlier you get there (see the Getting Around section at the end of this chapter), the more time you will have free of the milling mobs from Cancún. Admission to the park costs US$4. There are lockers for your valuables – recommended

as a safeguard. Snorkeling equipment can be rented for the day at Garrafón US$8. Garrafón also has a small aquarium and museum.

PLAYA NORTE

Walk west along Calles Hidalgo or Guerrero to reach Playa Norte, sometimes called Playa Los Cocos or Cocoteros, the town's principal beach. The slope of the beach is gradual, and the transparent and calm waters are only chest-high even far from shore. However, the beach is relatively small for the number of sun seekers who flock to it.

PLAYA LANCHEROS

Five km south of the town and 1.5 km north of Garrafón is Playa Lancheros, the southernmost point served by local buses. The beach is less attractive than Playa Norte, but it has free festivities on Sundays and you might want to go to enjoy the music.

MAYAN RUINS

At the southern tip of the island, just past Garrafón National Park, are the badly ruined remains of a temple to Ixchel, Mayan goddess of the moon, fertility and other worthy causes. Observed by Hernández de Córdoba when his ships were forced by high winds into the island's coastal waters in 1519, the temple has been crumbling ever since. Hurricane Gilbert almost finished it off in 1988. There's really little left to see other than a fine sea view and, in the distance, Cancún. The clay female figurines were pilfered long ago, and a couple of the walls were washed into the Caribbean.

You can walk to the ruins, beyond the lighthouse at the south end of the island, from Garrafón.

MUNDACA FORTRESS

The story behind the ruins of this house and fort are more intriguing than what remains of them. A slave-trading pirate, Fermin Antonio Mundaca de Marechaja, fell in love with a visiting Spanish beauty. To win her, the rogue built a two-story mansion

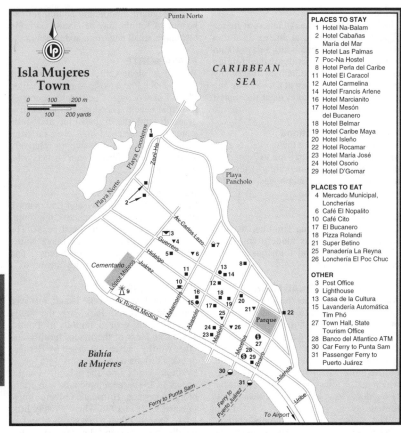

PLACES TO STAY
1 Hotel Na-Balam
2 Hotel Cabañas
  María del Mar
5 Hotel Las Palmas
7 Poc-Na Hostel
8 Hotel Perla del Caribe
11 Hotel El Caracol
12 Autel Carmelina
14 Hotel Francis Arlene
16 Hotel Marcianito
17 Hotel Mesón
  del Bucanero
18 Hotel Belmar
19 Hotel Caribe Maya
20 Hotel Isleño
22 Hotel Rocamar
23 Hotel María José
24 Hotel Osorio
29 Hotel D'Gomar

PLACES TO EAT
4 Mercado Municipal,
  Loncherías
6 Café El Nopalito
10 Café Cito
17 El Bucanero
18 Pizza Rolandi
21 Super Betino
25 Panadería La Reyna
26 Lonchería El Poc Chuc

OTHER
3 Post Office
9 Lighthouse
13 Casa de la Cultura
15 Lavandería Automática
  Tim Phó
27 Town Hall, State
  Tourism Office
28 Banco del Atlantico ATM
30 Car Ferry to Punta Sam
31 Passenger Ferry to
  Puerto Juárez

complete with gardens and graceful archways, as well as a small fortress to defend it. While Mundaca built the house, the object of his affection's ardor cooled and she married another islander. Brokenhearted, Mundaca died, and his house, fortress and garden fell into disrepair.

The Mundaca Fortress is east of the main road near Playa Lancheros, about six km south of the town. Watch for signs.

SCUBA DIVING

Diving to see sunken ships and beautiful reefs in the crystalline waters of the Caribbean is a memorable way to pass time on Isla Mujeres. If you're a qualified diver, you'll need a license, rental equipment and a boat to take you to the good spots. Arrangements made at any of the island's several dive shops range from US$50 to US$100, depending on how many tanks you use up.

A regular stop on the dive boat's route is the Sleeping Shark Caves, about five km north of the island and at 23 meters' depth, where the otherwise dangerous creatures are alleged to be lethargically nonlethal because of the low oxygen content of the caves' waters. Veteran divers say it's foolish to test the theory: you could become shark bait. It's far better to explore the fine reefs off the island, such as Los Manchones, La Bandera, Cuevones or Chital.

PLACES TO STAY

During the busy seasons (mid-December to March and midsummer), many island hotels are booked solid by midday; at these times prices are also highest (as given here).

Places to Stay – budget

Poc-Na (☎ (987) 7-00-90), on Matamoros at Carlos Lazo, is a privately run youth hostel. The fan-cooled dormitories take both men and women together. The charge for a bunk and bedding is US$2.50; you must put down a deposit on the bedding.

Hotel Caribe Maya (☎ (987) 7-01-90), Madero 9, between Guerrero and Hidalgo, charges US$16 a double with fan, US$21 with air-con – a bargain.

Hotel El Caracol (☎ (987) 7-01-50, fax 7-05-47), Matamoros 5, between Hidalgo and Guerrero, is run by a smiling and efficient señora. The tidy restaurant off the lobby serves meals at decent prices. Rooms have insect screens, ceiling fans and clean tiled bathrooms, and many have two double beds. You pay US$26/32 a double with fan/air-con. Watch out for disco noise from across the street.

Hotel Osorio (☎ (987) 7-00-18), Madero at Juárez, has an older section with huge, clean rooms with fan and bath for US$18 a double and a newer, tidier section for US$26. It may be closed in summer. If so, try the nearby *Hotel María José*.

Autel Carmelina (☎ (987) 7-00-06), Guerrero 4, also has OK cheap rooms: US$14/17/24 for one/two/three beds per room.

Hotel Las Palmas (☎ (987) 7-04-16), Guerrero 20, across from the Mercado Municipal, offers dreary but cheap rooms with fan and bath for US$12/15 a single/double.

Hotel Marcianito (☎ (987) 7-01-11), Abasolo 10, between Juárez and Hidalgo, with double rooms for US$12, is cheap, clean and offers a good value.

Hotel Isleño (☎ (987) 7-03-02), Madero 8 at the corner of Guerrero, has rooms with ceiling fans and good cross-ventilation, without/with bath for US$14/20 a double. There's a shared bathroom for every three guestrooms. Get a room on the upper floor if you can.

Places to Stay – middle

Moderately priced rooms have private baths and usually (but not always) air-con, a balcony and/or a nice sea view, restaurant, bar and swimming pool.

The *Hotel Perla del Caribe* (☎ (987) 7-04-44, fax (987) 7-00-11, in the USA (800) 258-6454), on Madero a block north of Guerrero right on the eastern beach, has 63 rooms on three floors, most with balconies, many with wonderful sea views and good cross-ventilation, for US$48 to US$65 a double, depending on view; the most expensive rooms have air-con.

The *Hotel Rocamar* (☎ (987) 7-05-87, fax (987) 7-01-01), at the eastern end of Guerrero, was the town's first real hotel, built decades ago. It has been updated and charges US$35/40/45/55 a single/double/triple/quad for its rooms, some with fine views.

Hotel Belmar (☎ (987) 7-04-30, fax (987) 7-04-29), Hidalgo between Abasolo and Madero, is right above the Pizza Rolandi restaurant and is run by the same family. Rooms are comfy, well kept and well priced, at US$35 a double.

Hotel Francis Arlene (☎ /fax (987) 7-03-10), Guerrero 7, is new and particularly comfortable. Many rooms have refrigerators, kitchenettes and balconies with sea views and rent for US$28/34, including fan/air-con.

Hotel D'Gomar (☎ /fax (987) 7-01-42), Rueda Medina 150, above a boutique and facing the ferry dock, has four floors of double-bedded rooms that rent for US$32 a double.

Hotel Mesón del Bucanero (☎ (987) 7-02-10, fax (987) 7-01-26), Hidalgo 11, between Abasolo and Madero, is above the restaurant of the same name. Rooms are pleasant enough, at US$25 to US$28 a double.

YUCATÁN

Places to Stay – top end

Hotel Na Balam (☎ (987) 7-02-79, fax (987) 7-05-93, nabalam@cancun.rce.com.mx), Calle Zazil-Ha 118, at the northern tip of the island, faces Playa Norte. Most of the 12 spacious junior suites have fabulous sea views. There are numerous nice touches, such as bathroom vanities made of colorful travertine. Prices for suites with a balcony are US$105 to US$120 a double in season, US$85 to US$105 off season.

Near Na Balam is *Hotel Cabañas María del Mar* (☎ (987) 7-01-79, fax (987) 7-02-13, in the USA (800) 223-5695), on both sides of Avenida Carlos Lazo, also right on the beach. The 12 cabañas and 51 hotel rooms are priced from US$55 to US$61 a double in low season, US$83 to US$90 in the winter season, light breakfast included. There are many other services, such as a restaurant and swimming pool.

PLACES TO EAT

Beside the market are several *cocinas económicas* (economical kitchens) serving simple but tasty and filling meals at the best prices on the island. Prices are not marked, so ask before you order. Hours are usually (and approximately) 7 am to 6 pm.

Another cocina económica is *Lonchería El Poc Chuc*, a tiny hole-in-the-wall eatery on Juárez at Madero, offering a ham-and-eggs breakfast for a mere US$2, poc-chuc and other meals for US$2.75.

Super Betino, the food store on the plaza, has a little cafeteria serving tacos and fruit plates for US$0.75, and sometimes cheap breakfasts.

Panadería La Reyna, on Madero at Juárez, is the place for breakfast buns, picnic breads and snacks.

Most of the island's restaurants fall into the middle category. Depending on what you order, breakfast goes for US$2.50 to US$4, lunch or dinner for US$7 to US$15 per person, unless you order lobster.

Café Cito, a small place at Juárez and Matamoros, has a New Age menu printed in English and German: croissants, fruit, 10 varieties of crepes and the best coffee in town. Come for breakfast (8 am to noon, about US$5), or supper (6 to 10 pm, about US$10).

Café El Nopalito, on Guerrero near Matamoros, serves delicious set breakfasts from 8 am to noon and daily special plates for US$5 to US$7, specializing in healthful but fancy food.

El Bucanero (☎ (987) 7-02-36), Avenida Hidalgo 11 between Abasolo and Madero, has a long menu: ham and cheese breakfast omelets (US$3.50), fried chicken or fish (US$5) and Mexican traditional foods (enchiladas, tacos etc) for about the same. Besides the usual, they also serve offbeat dishes such as asparagus au gratin with wholemeal bread.

Pizza Rolandi (☎ (987) 7-04-30), across the street from El Bucanero, serves pizzas and calzones cooked in a wood-fired oven and pastas with various sauces for US$5 to US$9 per person. The menu includes fresh salads, fish and some Italian specialties. Hours are 1 pm to midnight daily (6 pm to midnight on Sunday).

ENTERTAINMENT

The first place to go is the *main plaza*, where there's always something to watch (a football match, a basketball or volleyball game, an impromptu concert or serenade) and lots of somebodies watching it.

As for discos, *Tequila Video Bar* (☎ (987) 7-00-19), at the corner of Matamoros and Hidalgo, is a favorite with locals, but draws a respectable number of foreigners as well. Hours are 9 pm to 3 am every day except Monday.

GETTING THERE & AWAY
Ferry

There are four points of embarkation by ferry from the mainland or Isla Cancún to Isla Mujeres, which is 11 km off the coast.

Puerto Juárez In Ciudad Cancún take a Ruta 13 bus heading north on Avenida Tulum (US$0.30) or a taxi (US$2.50) to Puerto Juárez, about three km north of the city center.

Transportes Marítimos Magaña operates boats every 30 minutes from 6 to 8:30 am and every 15 minutes from 8:30 am to 8:30 pm for a fare of US$2.25 per person in either direction.

The boats *Sultana del Mar* and *Blanca Beatriz* run about every hour from 7 am to 5:30 pm, taking 45 minutes to reach Isla, for US$1 per person.

Punta Sam Car ferries (which also take passengers) depart from Punta Sam, about five km north of the city center and 3.5 km north of Puerto Juárez. The car ferry is more stable but less frequent and slower than the other ferries, taking 45 minutes to an hour to reach the island.

Ferries leave Punta Sam at 8 and 11 am and 2:45, 5:30 and 8:15 pm. Departures from Isla Mujeres are at 6:30 and 9:30 am and 12:45, 4:15 and 7:15 pm. Passengers pay US$1.50; a car costs US$6 to US$8. If you're taking a car, be sure to get to the dock an hour or so before departure time. Put your car in line and buy your ticket early.

Playa Linda Terminal Four times daily, *The Shuttle* (☎ (98) 84-63-33, 84-66-56) departs from Playa Linda on Isla Cancún for Isla Mujeres. Voyages are at 9 and 11:15 am and 4 and 7 pm from Playa Linda; return voyages depart Isla Mujeres at 10 am and 12:30, 5 and 8 pm. The roundtrip fare is US$14, but it includes free beer and soft drinks on board.

Show up at the Playa Linda Marine Terminal – Blvd Kukulcán Km 5 on Isla Cancún, just west of the bridge, between the Aquamarina Beach and Calinda Cancún hotels – at least 30 minutes before departure so you'll have time to buy your ticket and get a good seat on the boat.

Playa Tortugas *Isla Mujeres Shuttle* (☎ (98) 83-34-48) departs Isla Cancún from Fat Tuesday's on Playa Tortugas beach at 9:15 and 11:30 am and 1:45 and 3:45 pm, returning from Isla Mujeres at 10 am and 12:30, 2:30 and 5 pm, for US$10 per person each way.

GETTING AROUND
Bus
By local bus from the market or dock, you can get within 1.5 km of Garrafón; the terminus is Playa Lancheros. The personnel at Poc-Na Youth Hostel can give you an idea of the bus's erratic schedule. Locals in league with taxi drivers may tell you the bus doesn't exist.

If you walk to Garrafón from town, bring some water – it's a hot, two-hour, six-km walk. By taxi it costs about US$2 to Garrafón, just over US$1 to Playa Lancheros. Rates are set by the municipal government and are posted at the ferry dock, though the sign is frequently defaced by the taxi drivers.

Bicycle & Moped
Bicycles can be rented from a number of shops on the island, including Sport Bike, on the corner of Juárez and Morelos, a block from the ferry docks. Before you rent, compare prices and the condition of the bikes in a few shops, then arrive early in the day to get one of the better bikes. Costs are US$3 to US$5 for four hours, only a bit more for a full day; you'll be asked to plunk down a deposit of US$8 or so.

Everybody and his/her grandmother is prepared to rent you a moped on Isla Mujeres. Shop around, compare prices and look for these things: new or newer machines in good condition, full gas tanks and reasonable deposits. Cost per hour is usually US$5 or US$6 with a two-hour minimum, US$22 all day, or even cheaper by the week. Shops away from the busiest streets tend to have better prices, but not necessarily better equipment. Many places also rent motorized golf carts, which seat four, at a higher price.

When driving, remember that far more people are seriously injured on motorcycles than in cars. Your enemies are inexperience, speed, sand, wet or oily roads and other people on motorcycles. Don't forget to slather yourself with sunblock before you take off. Be sure to do your hands, feet, face and neck thoroughly.

AROUND ISLA MUJERES
Isla Contoy Bird Sanctuary

You can take an excursion by boat to tiny Isla Contoy, a national bird sanctuary about 25 km north of Isla Mujeres. It's a treasure trove for birdwatchers, with an abundance of brown pelicans, olive cormorants and red-pouched frigates, as well as frequent visits by flamingos and herons. There is good snorkeling both en route to and just off Contoy.

Getting There & Away For a one-day excursion (about US$30 per person), ask at the Sociedad Cooperativa Transporte Turística Isla Mujeres (☎ (987) 7-02-74), on Avenida Rueda Medina to the north of the ferry docks.

Central & Northern Yucatán

VALLADOLID
Population 80,000

Small and manageable, with an easy pace of life, graced with many handsome colonial buildings and provided with a few hotels and restaurants, Valladolid is a good place to stop, spend the night and get to know the real Yucatán. It can also be your base from which to visit the important Mayan ruins at Chichén Itzá, 40 km farther west.

Heading west from Cancún takes you through the town of Nuevo Xcan, where the road from Cobá and Tulum meets the Cancún-Mérida highway. Nuevo Xcan has a few little restaurants.

If you're driving, beware of the new toll highway (cuota). Huge signs south and west of Cancún direct you to take the cuota, which is expensive - US$18 to Mérida. You

may want to leave Cancún along Avenida López Portillo and follow the old road (libra, free). It is not as smooth or fast as the cuota, but it costs nothing. The highway signs are expressly designed to catch and fool tourists driving rental cars from Cancún to Chichén Itzá and Mérida. Few Mexicans take the toll highway, and all know about the old road.

Valladolid, 160 km (about two hours) west of Cancún, has no sights of stop-the-car immediacy, but those tourists more interested in the country stop to enjoy its colonial charm.

History
The Mayan ceremonial center of Zací was here long before the Spanish arrived to lay out a new city on the classic colonial plan.

YUCATÁN

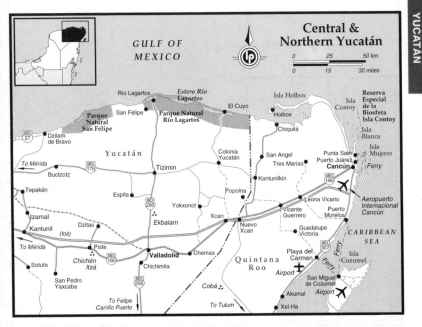

YUCATÁN

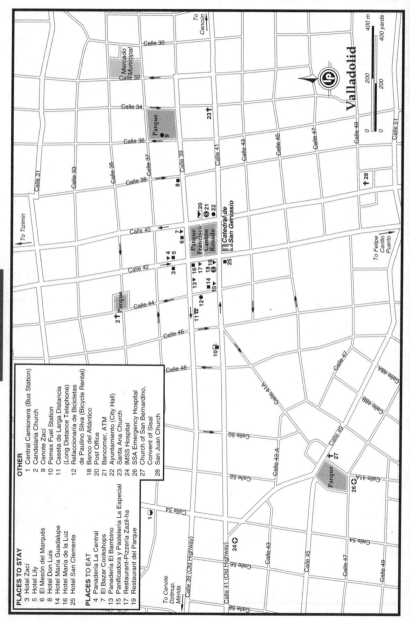

PLACES TO STAY
3 Hotel Zací
5 Hotel Lily
6 El Mesón del Marqués
8 Hotel Don Luis
14 Hotel María Guadalupe
16 Hotel María de la Luz
25 Hotel San Clemente

PLACES TO EAT
4 Panadería La Central
7 El Bazar Cookshops
13 Panadería El Bambino
15 Panificadora y Pastelería La Especial
17 Restaurant-Pizzeria Zazil-ha
19 Restaurant del Parque

OTHER
1 Central Camionera (Bus Station)
2 Candelaria Church
9 Cenote Zací
10 Pemex Fuel Station
11 Caseta de Larga Distancia
   (Long Distance Telephone)
12 Refaccionaria de Bicicletas
   de Paulino Silva (Bicycle Rental)
18 Banco del Atlántico
20 Post Office
21 Bancomer, ATM
22 Ayuntamiento (City Hall)
23 Santa Ana Church
24 IMSS Hospital
26 SSA Emergency Hospital
27 Church of San Bernardino,
   Convent of Sisal
28 San Juan Church

The initial attempt at conquest in 1543 by the conquistador Francisco de Montejo, nephew of Montejo El Adelantado, was thwarted by fierce Mayan resistance, but El Adelantado's son Montejo El Mozo ultimately conquered the Indians and appropriated the town.

During much of the succeeding colonial era, Valladolid's distance from Mérida and its humidity and surrounding forests kept it isolated and thus relatively autonomous of royal rule. With the French and American revolutions as a catalyst, local Mayan leaders plotted a rebellion in 1809 that was discovered and quashed. Nonetheless, the seeds of future unrest were sown, and Valladolid would play an important role in the next uprising.

Brutally exploited and banned along with the mestizos from even entering this town of pure-blooded Spaniards, the Maya rebelled and in the War of the Castes of 1847 they made Valladolid their first point of attack. Besieged for two months, Valladolid's Spanish defenders were finally overcome; many of the citizens fled to the safety of Mérida and the rest were slaughtered by the Mayan forces.

Today Valladolid is the principal city of the peninsula's midsection and a prosperous seat of agrarian commerce, with some light industry as well. Its hotels and restaurants offer exceptional value, especially after the depredations Cancún will inflict on your wallet.

Orientation & Information

The old highway goes right through the center of town, though all signs will direct you to the toll highway north of town. To follow the old highway eastbound, follow Calle 41; westbound, Calle 39 or 35. The bus terminal is on Calle 37 between Calles 54 and 56, eight blocks from the plaza.

Recommended hotels are on the main plaza, called the Parque Francisco Cantón Rosado, or just a block or two away from it.

The post office is on the east side of the main plaza at Calle 40 No 195-A. Hours are Monday to Friday from 8 am to 6 pm, Saturday 9 am to 1 pm.

Church of San Bernardino de Siena & Convent of Sisal

Although Valladolid has a number of interesting colonial churches, the Church of San Bernardino de Siena and the Convent of Sisal, one km southwest of the plaza along Calle 41A, are said to be the oldest Christian structures in Yucatán. Constructed in 1552, the complex was designed to serve a dual function as fortress and church, given the enmity of the Indians for the Spaniards.

If you venture inside, apart from the miracle-working Virgin of Guadalupe on the altar, the church is relatively bare. During the uprisings of 1847 and 1910, angry Indians responded to the clergy's links with landowners by stripping the church of its ornamentation.

Cenote Zací

Cenotes, those vast underground wells formed of limestone, were the Maya's most dependable source of water. The Spaniards depended on them also, and the Spanish town of Valladolid benefited in its early years from several cenotes in the area. The Cenote Zací, Calle 36 between Calles 39 and 37, a three-block walk from the plaza, is perhaps the most famous.

It's set in a pretty park that also holds the town's museum exhibits, an open-air amphitheater and traditional stone-walled thatched houses. The cenote itself, at the end of a flight of slippery stairs, is vast, dark and formidable. If this is your first cenote, you'll be impressed; if you don't think you'll get the chance to see another, by all means make the short walk to this one. It's open daily from 8 am to 8 pm; admission costs US$2 for adults, half-price for children.

Cenote Dzitnup (Xkakah)

More impressive and beautiful, but less easily accessible, Cenote Dzitnup is also called Cenote Xkakah, seven km west of Valladolid's main plaza. Follow the old highway west toward Mérida for five km; you'll pass a Coca-Cola bottling plant on the right-hand side. Turn left (south) at the sign for Dzitnup and go two km to the site, on the left. A taxi from Valladolid's main plaza charges US$10 for the excursion there and back, with half an hour's wait.

Another way to reach the cenote is on a bicycle rented from the Refaccionaría de Bicicletas de Paulino Silva on Calle 44 between Calles 39 and 41, facing Hotel María Guadalupe; look for the sign 'Alquiler y Venta de Bicicletas'. Rental costs US$2 per hour. Check out your bike carefully before putting money down. They rent some wrecks here, and you don't want yours to break down miles from nowhere. The first five km out to Dzitnup are not particularly pleasant because of the traffic, but the last two are on a quiet country road. It should take you only 20 minutes to pedal to the cenote.

Another way to get there is to hop aboard a westbound bus, ask the driver to let you off at the Dzitnup turning, then walk the final two km (20 minutes) to the site.

Cenote Dzitnup is open from 7 am to 5 pm daily. Admission costs US$1.50. There's a restaurant and a drinks stand. If you've brought a bathing suit and towel you can go for a swim.

Places to Stay - budget

Hotel María Guadalupe (☎ (985) 6-20-68), Calle 44 No 188, between Calles 39 and 41, is a study in modernity in this colonial town. The simple rooms go for US$7/9/13 a single/double/triple with private shower and fan.

The well-kept *Hotel Zací* (☎ (985) 6-21-67, fax (985) 6-25-94), Calle 44 No 191, between Calles 37 and 39, has rooms built around a quiet, long-and-narrow courtyard with a swimming pool. You may choose from rooms with fan (US$15/22/28 a single/double/triple) or with air-con (US$18/25/32).

Across the street and a few doors south is the *Hotel Lily* (☎ (985) 6-21-63), Calle 44 No 190. Rooms are cheaper and very basic: US$8 to US$12 a double with bath and fan.

Hotel Don Luis (☎ (985) 6-20-08), Calle 39 No 191, at the corner of Calle 38, is a motel-style structure with a palm-shaded patio, murky swimming pool and acceptable rooms priced as low as US$8/11/14 for a single/double/triple with fan, or US$10/13/15 with air-con.

Places to Stay - middle

If you're willing to spend more money, the rest of the town's hotel choices are open to you. All have swimming pools, restaurants and secure parking facilities.

The best is *El Mesón del Marqués* (☎ (985) 6-20-73, fax (985) 6-22-80), Calle 39 No 203, on the north side of the main plaza. It has two beautiful colonial courtyards and modernized guestrooms with both air-con and ceiling fans. Rates are US$45 to US$58 a single, US$50 to US$70 a double.

Next best is the *Hotel María de la Luz* (☎ (985) 6-20-70, fax (985) 6-20-71), on Calle 42 near Calle 39, at the northwest corner of the plaza. Boasting one of the more popular restaurants on the square, it also has serviceable air-con rooms for US$16 to US$20.

Hotel San Clemente (☎ (985) 6-22-08, fax (985) 6-35-14), Calle 42 No 206 at the corner of Calle 41, is at the southwest corner of the main plaza. Colonial decoration abounds, and the 64 double rooms have private baths and fans for US$16 to US$22, or air-con for US$20 to US$28.

Places to Eat - budget

El Bazar is a collection of little open-air market-style cookshops at the corner of Calles 39 and 40 (northeast corner of the plaza). This is my favorite place for a big cheap breakfast. At lunch and dinnertime, comidas corridas of soup, main course and drink cost less than US$4 - if you ask for the prices before you order. There are a dozen eateries here - Doña Mary, El Amigo Panfilo, Sergio's Pizza, La Rancherita, El Amigo Casiano, etc - open from 6:30 am to 2 pm and from 6 to about 9 or 10 pm.

For a bit more you can dine at the breezy tables in the *Hotel María de la Luz*, overlooking the plaza. The breakfast buffet costs only US$3, a luncheon comida corrida the same.

The comida costs even less at the old-fashioned, high-ceilinged *Restaurant del Parque*.

Restaurant-Pizzería Zazil-ha, Calle 42 on the west side of the plaza, has been fixed up and now offers good, cheap pizza, as well as rock music at ear-splitting volume.

Valladolid has several good bakeries, including *Panificadora y Pastelería La Especial*, on Calle 41 less than a block west of the plaza, and *Panadería El Bambino* on Calle 39 a half-block west of the plaza. There's also *Panadería La Central* next door to the Hotel Lily on Calle 44.

Places to Eat - middle

Best is the *Hostería del Marques*, the dining room of the Hotel El Mesón del Marqués, Calle 39 No 203, on the north side of the main plaza. Start with gazpacho, continue with pork loin Valladolid style (in a tomato sauce) or grilled pork steak and finish up with a slice of cake, all for US$7 to US$11 per person.

Getting There & Away

Bus The bus terminal is on Calle 37 between Calles 54 and 56, eight blocks from the plaza. It has a long-distance telephone station with fax service. Main companies are Autotransportes de Oriente Mérida-Puerto Juárez and Expresso de Oriente. Most buses are *de paso*, meaning that they start their routes somewhere else and take on passengers at Valladolid only if there are seats available. Here are daily departures:

Cancún - 160 km, 1 1/2 to two hours, US$4 to US$8; seven local buses (originating here), hourly de paso buses from 6 am to 9 pm

Chichén Itzá - 42 km, 30 to 45 minutes, US$1; 10 buses

Chiquilá (for Isla Holbox) - 155 km, 2 1/2 hours, US$5; at least one bus daily

Cobá - 106 km, two hours, US$3; one bus runs at 2:30 pm

Izamal - 115 km, two hours, US$3; Autobuses del Centro del Estado de Yucatán operates five buses

Mérida - 160 km, three hours, US$5; seven local buses (originating here), hourly de paso buses from 6 am to 9 pm

Motul - 156 km, three hours, US$5; Autobuses del Noreste runs five buses via Dzitas, Tunkas, Izamal and Tixcocob

Playa del Carmen - 213 km, 3 1/2 hours, US$7; Autobuses de Oriente (ADO) runs five buses (US$6), Autotransportes del Sur (ATS) runs four buses (US$5)

Río Lagartos - 103 km, two hours, US$3.50; the 10 am bus to Tizimin continues to Río Lagartos, or change buses at Tizimin

Tizimin - 51 km, one hour, US$2; Autobuses del Noreste en Yucatán operates hourly buses

Tulum - 156 km, three hours, US$7; one bus at 2:30 pm

Taxi A quicker, more comfortable but more expensive way to Cancún is by taking one of the shared taxis parked outside the bus station, which leave as soon as all seats are filled. The trip costs approximately twice the bus fare.

EKBALAM

Midway from Valladolid to Tizimin, turn right (east) following signs to Santa Rita and Ekbalam to find the Ekbalam archaeological site, 10.5 km along butterfly-busy roads through fields of corn and beans.

The site is open during daylight hours for US$1.50 (plus a tip if you follow the guide).

The temple mounds are still largely covered by jungle, as is the great plaza, but the guide, Sr Anastasio Vaas, will show you cisterns, a subterranean entry, a *sacbé* (ancient ceremonial road, paved with limestone), several stelae with high relief carving, and other features. From the top of the main pyramid, the tedious flatness of the landscape is broken only by a few small tree-covered 'hills' on the horizon - which are not hills at all, but other tree-covered pyramids marking other once-great Mayan cities.

Excavation continues annually from May to July under the auspices of the National Geographic Society (USA), the Middle American Research Institute, Tulane University and Davidson College.

YUCATÁN

TIZIMIN

Many travelers bound for Río Lagartos will change buses in Tizimin (Place of Many Horses), a farming center of note (cattle ranches, beehives and citrus groves make the wealth here). There is little to warrant an overnight stay, so Tizimin is relatively free of tourists.

The main plaza is pleasant. Two great colonial structures, the Convento de los Tres Reyes Magos (Monastery of the Three Wise Kings) and the Convento de San Francisco de Assis (Monastery of Saint Francis of Assisi) are worth a look. Five lengthy blocks from the plaza, northwest on Calle 51, is a modest zoo, the Parque Zoológico de la Reina.

The Banco del Atlántico, next to the Hotel San Jorge on the south side of the plaza, will change money for you between 10 am and noon Monday to Friday.

Places to Stay

Hotel San Jorge (☎ (986) 3-20-37), Calle 53 No 411, has basic but serviceable rooms with private bath for US$15/20 for a double with fan/air-con. *Hotel San Carlos* (☎ (986) 3-20-94), Calle 54 No 407, is built like a motel and charges prices identical to those at San Jorge.

Posada María Antonia (☎ (986) 3-23-84), Calle 50 No 408, on the east side of the Parque de la Madre, also has comfy rooms at these prices. Doubles with air-con cost US$22. The reception desk is also a long-distance telephone station.

Places to Eat

The market, a block northwest of the bus station, has the usual cheap eateries. *Panificadora La Especial* is on Calle 55, down a little pedestrian lane from the plaza.

Restaurant Los Tres Reyes (☎ (986) 3-21-06), on the corner of Calles 52 and 53, opens early for breakfast and is a favorite with town notables who take their second cup of coffee around 9 am. Lunch or dinner costs US$3 to US$5 and is well worth it.

Facing the plaza are several simple places good for a quick, cheap bite, including *Los Portales, La Parrilla, Tortas Económicas La Especial,* and the *Cocina Económica Ameli.*

Pizzería Cesar's, at the corner of Calles 50 and 53, serves pizza and pasta (US$2.50

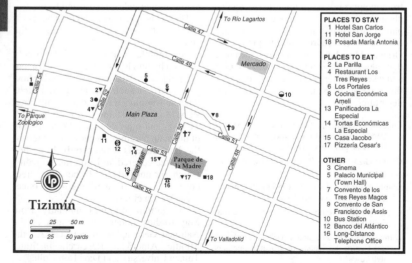

PLACES TO STAY
1 Hotel San Carlos
11 Hotel San Jorge
18 Posada María Antonia

PLACES TO EAT
2 La Parilla
4 Restaurant Los Tres Reyes
6 Los Portales
8 Cocina Económica Ameli
13 Panificadora La Especial
14 Tortas Económicas La Especial
15 Casa Jacobo
17 Pizzería Cesar's

OTHER
3 Cinema
5 Palacio Municipal (Town Hall)
7 Convento de los Tres Reyes Magos
9 Convento de San Francisco de Assis
10 Bus Station
12 Banco del Atlántico
16 Long-Distance Telephone Office

Tizimín

to US$5) in air-conditioned comfort from 5:30 to 11 pm.

Getting There & Away

Autobuses del Noreste en Yucatán operates hourly buses from Valladolid to Tizimin (51 km, one hour, US$2). From Cancún and Puerto Juárez there are several direct buses to Tizimin (212 km, three hours, US$4). There are several daily 1st- and 2nd-class buses between Tizimin and Mérida (210 km, four hours, US$3.75) via Valladolid. For Río Lagartos there are three daily 1st-class departures and five daily 2nd-class buses that continue to San Felipe.

RÍO LAGARTOS

If you're interested in seeing the most spectacular flamingo colony in Mexico, it is worth going out of your way to this little fishing village 103 km north of Valladolid and 52 km north of Tizimin. In addition to harboring thousands of flamingos, the estuaries are home to snowy egrets, red egrets, great white herons and snowy white ibis. Although Río Lagartos (Alligator River) was named after the once-substantial alligator population, don't expect to see any of those reptiles today, as hunting has virtually wiped them out.

The town of Río Lagartos itself, with its narrow streets and multihued houses, has little charm, though the panorama of the boats and the bay is pleasant. Were it not for the flamingos, you would have little reason to come here. Although the state government has been making noises about developing the area for tourism, that has not happened yet.

At the center of town is a small triangular plaza, the Presidencia Municipal (Town Hall) and the Conasupo store.

Flamingos

The sight of a foreigner in Río Lagartos provokes in any local citizen a Pavlovian response: the mouth opens, the larynx tenses, the lungs compress and out come the words ¡Los flamingos! ¡A la playa! The

response from the foreigner is equally automatic: ¡Sí!

Your first encounter with a Lagartan thus highlights your first duty here: to find a reliable boat-owner and a good price for the trip to see the flamingos or to swim at the beach nearby.

The Spanish word flamenco, which means 'flaming', makes sense in terms of the bird's name as you approach a horizon of hundreds of brilliantly hued, red-pink birds. When the flock takes flight, the sight of the suddenly fiery horizon makes the long hours on the bus to get here all worthwhile. However, in the interests of the flamingos' well-being, convince your local guide not to frighten the birds into flight. Being frightened away from their habitat several times a day can't be good for them, however good it may be for the guide's business.

Bird Watching by Boat Everybody in town will offer to set you up with a boat. Haggling over price is essential. In general, a short trip (two to three hours) to see a few nearby local flamingos and to have a swim at the beach costs US$20 to US$30 for a five-seat boat. The much longer voyage to the flamingos' favorite haunts (four to six hours) costs US$60 or so for the boat, or about US$12 per person for a full load.

Places to Stay & Eat

The forlorn Hotel María Nefertiti, Calle 14 No 123, is currently closed for lack of trade. The cavernous palapa-shaded Restaurant Los Flamingos, at the back, is equally empty most of the time. The Restaurant Familiar Isla Contoy, just down from Los Flamingos on the water, is perhaps a better bet. To find the hotel, walk from the triangular plaza, keeping the Presidencia Municipal on your left. Pass Conasupo on your right, and at the next corner turn left and walk 100 meters to the hotel.

If the hotel's restaurant is empty, you might do better by grabbing a bite at the Restaurant La Económica, directly across the street from it. There's also the Restaurant Los Negritos facing a little park with a

YUCATÁN

statue of Benito Juárez, two blocks inland from the main square.

It is sometimes possible to rent a bed or a pair of hammock hooks in a local house, which brings the cost of sleeping down considerably.

Getting There & Away

Autobuses del Noreste en Yucatán operates hourly buses from Valladolid to Tizimin, and several of them go on to Río Lagartos (103 km, two hours, US$4). There is also one direct Autotransportes del Noroeste bus daily between Mérida and Tizimin (211 km, four hours, US$9), from where you can continue to Río Lagartos.

SAN FELIPE

Population 400

This tiny, unspoiled fishing village of traditional brightly painted wooden fishing cabins on narrow streets makes a nice day trip from Río Lagartos, 12 km to the east. While the waters are not Caribbean turquoise and there's little shade, in spring and summer scores of visitors come here to camp. Other than lying on the beach, bird watching is the main attraction, as just across the estuary at Punta Holohit is abundant bird life.

Places to Stay & Eat

The proprietor of the Floresita grocery store near the pier can rent you a spartan room above the Cinema Marrufo. Campers are ferried across the estuary to islands, where they pitch tents or set up hammocks.

Otherwise, there's the new *Hotel San Felipe de Jesús* (☎ (98) 63-37-38), Calle 9 between 14 and 16 which rents quite nice rooms for US$15. It has a good restaurant as well.

For cheap seafood, try *El Payaso*. Even cheaper eats, such as chicken and turkey soups and tacos, can be purchased from vendors.

Getting There & Away

Some buses from Tizimin to Río Lagartos continue to San Felipe and return. The 12-km ride takes about 20 minutes.

ISLA HOLBOX

Fed up with the tourist hordes of Cancún, Isla Mujeres and Cozumel? Want to find a beach site virtually devoid of gringos? In that case Isla Holbox (pronounced HOHL-bosh) might appeal to you. But before you make haste for the island note that the most basic facilities are in short supply and the beaches are not Cancún-perfect strips of clean, air-conditioned sand. To enjoy Isla Holbox, you must be willing to rough it.

The island, 25 km by three km, has sands that run on and on, as well as tranquil waters where you can wade out quite a distance before the sea reaches shoulder level. Moreover, Isla Holbox is absolutely magic for shell collectors, with a galaxy of shapes and colors. The fishing families of the island are friendly - unjaded by encounters with exotic tourists or the frenetic pace of the urban mainland. There are even flamingos here.

As to drawbacks, the water is not the translucent turquoise of the Quintana Roo beach sites, because here the Caribbean waters mingle with those of the darker Gulf. Seaweed can create silty waters near shore at some parts of the beach.

Places to Stay & Eat

While there are big plans to develop Isla Holbox one day, at the time of this writing there was only one modest hotel, the aptly named *Hotel Flamingo* (with doubles for US$12), and a few snack shops. Most travelers camp or stay in spartan rooms rented from locals.

Getting There & Away

To reach Isla Holbox, take the ferry from the unappealing port village of Chiquilá. If you are going from Isla Mujeres or Cancún to Isla Holbox, catch a direct bus from Puerto Juárez or Cancún to Chiquilá. There are also buses three times a day from Valladolid to Chiquilá (155 km, 2½ hours, US$5), and in theory the ferry is supposed to wait for them. However, it may not wait for a delayed bus or may even leave early (!) should the captain feel so inclined.

It is therefore recommended that you reach Chiquilá as early as possible. The ferry is supposed to depart for the island at 8 am and 3 pm and make the trip in about an hour. Ferries return to Chiquilá at 2 and 5 pm. The cost is US$2.50.

Try not to get stuck in Chiquilá, as it is a tiny hole of a port with no hotels, no decent camping and disappointing food.

CHICHÉN ITZÁ

The most famous and best restored of Yucatán's Mayan sites, Chichén Itzá will awe the most jaded of ruins visitors. Many mysteries of the Mayan astronomical calendar are made clear when one understands the design of the 'time temples' here. But one astronomical mystery remains: why do most people come here from Mérida and Cancún on day trips, arriving at 11 am, when the blazing sun is getting to its hottest point, and departing around 3 pm, when the heat finally begins to abate? Climbing El Castillo at midday in the heat and humidity is sheer torture.

I strongly recommend that you stay the night nearby and do your exploration of the site either early in the morning, late in the afternoon, or both. Should you have the good fortune to visit Chichén Itzá on the vernal equinox (March 20 to 21) or autumnal equinox (September 21 to 22), you can witness the light-and-shadow illusion of the serpent ascending or descending the side of the staircase of El Castillo. The illusion is almost as good in the week preceding and the week following each equinox.

History

Most archaeologists agree that Chichén Itzá (The Mouth of the Well of the Itzaes) was first settled during the Late Classic period between 550 and 900 AD and was pure Mayan. In about the 10th century the city was largely abandoned for reasons now unknown.

The city was resettled about 1100 AD. Shortly thereafter, Chichén was invaded by the Toltecs, who had moved down from their central-highlands capital of Tula, north of present-day Mexico City. The Toltecs fused their culture with that of the Maya, incorporating the cult of Quetzalcóatl (Kukulcán in Mayan).

Quetzalcóatl, the plumed serpent, was a blond king with great powers who was supposedly cast out of his kingdom and exiled from the central highlands to Mexico's southeast. Legend had it that he would reappear someday and bring a great era with him. That legend would ultimately help pave the way for Cortés in his conquest of Mexico.

In Chichén Itzá you will see images of Quetzalcóatl and Chac, the Mayan rain god, throughout the city. However, because there appears to be evidence of Toltec influence long before the supposed Toltec invasion, some speculate that Tula had once been a colony of Chichén and that Toltec influence thus filtered back to the Yucatán from there.

The warlike Toltecs contributed more than their architectural skills to the Maya. They elevated human sacrifice to a near obsession, and there are numerous carvings of the bloody ritual in Chichén to prove it. After a Toltec leader moved his political capital to Mayapán, while keeping Chichén as his religious capital, Chichén Itzá fell into decline. Why it was subsequently abandoned in the 14th century is a mystery, but the once-great city remained the site of Mayan pilgrimages for years afterward.

Orientation

Highway 180 skirts the archaeological site to the east and north. Coming from Cancún, you approach Chichén Itzá from the south along an access road formed by the old highway. It's 1.5 km from Hwy 180 to the eastern entrance to the ruins. On the way you pass the Villa Arqueológica, Hacienda Chichén and Mayaland luxury hotels. The moderately priced Hotel Dolores Alba is 3.1 km east of the eastern entrance to the ruins, on the highway to Cancún.

Except for those hotels, Chichén's lodgings, restaurants and services are ranged along one km of highway in the village of Piste (PEESS-teh), to the west (or Mérida) side of the ruins. It's 1.5 km from the

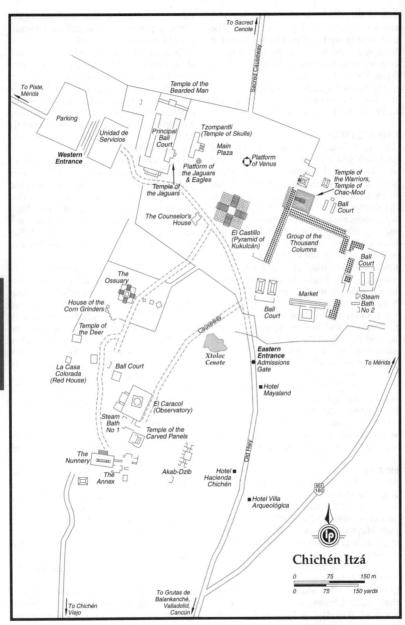

To Sacred Cenote

Sacred Causeway

To Piste, Mérida

Parking

Unidad de Servicios

Western Entrance

Temple of the Bearded Man

Principal Ball Court

Tzompantli (Temple of Skulls)

Main Plaza

Platform of the Jaguars & Eagles

Platform of Venus

Temple of the Jaguars

The Counselor's House

El Castillo (Pyramid of Kukulcán)

Temple of the Warriors, Temple of Chac-Mool

Ball Court

Group of the Thousand Columns

Ball Court

The Ossuary

House of the Corn Grinders

Temple of the Deer

Market

Steam Bath No 2

Ball Court

Ball Court

La Casa Colorada (Red House)

Causeway

Xtoloc Cenote

Eastern Entrance • Admissions Gate

To Mérida

El Caracol (Observatory)

Steam Bath No 1

Temple of the Carved Panels

■ Hotel Mayaland

The Nunnery

The Annex

Akab-Dzib

Hotel ■ Hacienda Chichén

Old Hwy

MEX 180

■ Hotel Villa Arqueológica

YUCATÁN

Chichén Itzá

0   75   150 m
0   75   150 yards

To Chichén Viejo

To Grutas de Balankanché, Valladolid, Cancún

western entrance of the ruins to the first hotel in Piste (Pirámide Inn), or 2.5 km from the ruins to the village square (actually a triangle), which is shaded by a huge tree. Buses generally stop at the square; you can make the hot walk to or from the ruins in 20 to 30 minutes.

Chichén's little airstrip is north of the ruins, on the north side of the highway.

Information

You can change money in the Unidad de Servicios, at the western entrance to the ruins, or at your hotel. There are several telephone stations (casetas) in Piste. Look for the signs.

Archaeological Zone Chichén Itzá is open every day from 8 am to 5 pm; the interior passageway in El Castillo is open only from 11 am to 1 pm and from 4 to 5 pm. Admission to the site costs US$5; US$10 extra for your video camera and US$5 extra if you use a tripod with your camera. Admission is free to children under 12 and to all on Sunday. Parking costs US$0.75. Explanatory plaques are in Spanish, English and French.

The main entrance to the ruins is the western one, with a large parking lot and a big, modern entrance building called the Unidad de Servicios, open 8 am to 10 pm. The Unidad has a small but worthwhile museum (open 8 am to 5 pm) with sculptures, reliefs and artifacts.

The Chilam Balam Auditorio, next to the museum, has audio-visual shows about Chichén in English at noon and 4 pm.

In the central space of the Unidad stands a scale model of the archaeological site, and off toward the toilets is an exhibit on Thompson's excavations of the sacred cenote in 1923. There's also a souvenir and book shop, currency exchange desk (open 9 am to 1 pm) and a *guardarropa* at the main ticket desk, where you can leave your belongings (US$0.35) while you explore the site.

A sound-and-light show lasting 45 minutes begins each evening in Spanish at 7 pm in summer and 8 pm in winter (US$3.75). The English version (US$5) starts at 9 pm year round.

El Castillo The first temple here was pre-Toltec, built around 800 AD. But the present 25-meter-high structure, built over the old one, has the plumed serpent sculpted along the stairways and Toltec warriors represented in the doorway carvings of the temple at the top.

The pyramid is actually the Mayan calendar formed in stone. Each of El Castillo's nine levels is divided in two by a staircase, making eighteen separate terraces that commemorate the eighteen 20-day months of the Vague Year. The four stairways have 91 steps each; add the top platform and the total is 365, the number of days in the year. On each facade of the pyramid are 52 flat panels, which are reminders of the 52 years in the Calendar Round.

Most amazing of all, during the spring and autumn equinoxes (around March 21 and September 21), light and shadow form a series of triangles on the side of the north staircase that mimic the creep of a serpent (note the serpent's head at the bottom of the staircase). The serpent appears to ascend in March and descend in September. This illusion lasts three hours and 22 minutes and was all arranged by the brilliant Mayan architects and astronomers who designed El Castillo.

The older pyramid *inside* El Castillo boasts a brilliant red jaguar throne with inlaid eyes and spots of shimmering jade. The inner sanctum also holds a Toltec chacmool figure.

The inner pyramid is open only from 11 am to 1 pm and 4 to 5 pm. The dank air inside can make climbing the stairs a sweltering, slippery, claustrophobic experience.

Principal Ball Court This is only one of the city's eight courts, but it's the best preserved and largest ball court in all of Mexico. The field is flanked by temples at either end and bounded by towering parallel walls with stone rings cemented up high.

YUCATÁN

Jaguar chomping on a human heart

Carvings show players with padding on their elbows and knees. It is thought that they played a soccerlike game with a hard rubber ball, forbidding the use of hands. Other carvings show players wielding bats; it appears that if a player hit the ball through one of the stone hoops, his team was declared the winner. It may be that during the Toltec period the losing captain, and perhaps his teammates as well, were sacrificed.

Along the walls of the ball court are some fine stone reliefs, including scenes of decapitations of players. Acoustically the court is amazing - a conversation at one end can be heard 135 meters away at the other end, and if you clap, you hear a resounding echo.

Temple of the Bearded Man & Temple of the Jaguars The structure at the northern end of the ball court, called the Temple of the Bearded Man after a carving inside it, has some finely sculpted pillars and reliefs of flowers, birds and trees. The Temple of the Jaguars, to the southeast, has some rattlesnake-carved columns and jaguar-etched tablets. Inside are faded mural fragments depicting a battle.

Tzompantli (Temple of Skulls) The Tzompantli, a Toltec term for Temple of Skulls, is between the Temple of the

Jaguars and El Castillo. You can't mistake it, because the T-shaped platform is festooned with carved skulls and eagles tearing open the chests of men to eat their hearts. In ancient days this platform held the heads of sacrificial victims.

Platform of the Jaguars & Eagles Adjacent to the Temple of Skulls, this platform has carvings depicting jaguars and eagles gruesomely grabbing human hearts in their claws. It is thought that the platform was part of a temple dedicated to the military legions responsible for capturing sacrificial victims.

Platform of Venus The Toltec Venus is a feathered serpent bearing a human head between its jaws. The platform is decked with feathered snake figures.

Sacred Cenote The Sacred Cenote, 300 meters (a five-minute walk) north of the Platform of Venus along a crushed-stone road, is an awesome natural well some 60 meters in diameter and 35 meters deep. There are ruins of a small steam bath next to the cenote, as well as a modern drinks stand with toilets.

Around the turn of the century Edward Thompson, a Harvard professor and US Consul to the Yucatán, bought a hacienda that included Chichén for US$75. He had the cenote dredged, and artifacts, gold and jade jewelry from all parts of Mexico were recovered, along with the skeletons of men, women and - mostly - children. These objects were given to Harvard's Peabody Museum, which later returned many of them.

The artifacts' origins show the far-flung contact the Maya had; some items are from as far away as Colombia.

Subsequent diving expeditions in 1923 and in the 1960s, sponsored by the US National Geographic Society, brought up hundreds more artifacts.

Group of the Thousand Columns Comprising the Temple of the Warriors, Temple of Chac-Mool and Sweat House or Steam Bath, this group takes its name from the forest of pillars in front.

The platformed temple greets you with a statue of the reclining god, Chac, as well as stucco and stone-carved animal deities. The temple's roof, once supported by columns entwined with serpents, disappeared long ago.

Archaeological work in 1926 revealed a Temple of Chac-Mool beneath the Temple of the Warriors. You may enter via a stairway on the north side. The walls inside have badly deteriorated murals of what is thought to be the Toltecs' defeat of the Maya.

Just east of the Temple of the Warriors lies the rubble of a Mayan sweathouse, with an underground oven and drains for the water. The sweathouses were regularly used for ritual purification.

Ossuary The Ossuary, otherwise known as the Bonehouse or the High Priest's Grave, has recently been restored. As with most of the buildings in this southern section, the architecture is more Puuc than Toltec.

La Casa Colorada La Casa Colorada, or The Red House, was named by the Spaniards for the red paint of the mural on its doorway. This building has little Toltec influence; its design shows largely a pure Puuc-Mayan style. Referring to the stone latticework at the roof facade, the Maya named this building Chichán-Chob, or House of Small Holes.

El Caracol Called El Caracol (The Giant Conch Snail) by the Spaniards for its interior spiral staircase, the observatory is one of the most fascinating and important of all of Chichén Itzá's buildings. Its circular design resembles some central-highlands structures, although, surprisingly, not those of Toltec Tula. In a fusion of architectural styles and religious imagery, there are Mayan Chac masks over four external doors facing the cardinal directions.

The windows in the observatory's dome are aligned with the appearance of certain stars at specific dates. From the dome the priests decreed the times for rituals, celebrations, corn-planting and harvests.

Nunnery & Annex Thought by archaeologists to have been a palace for Mayan royalty, the Nunnery, with its myriad rooms, resembled a European convent to the conquistadors, hence their name for the building. The Nunnery's dimensions are imposing: its base is 60 meters long, 30 meters wide and 20 meters high. The construction is Mayan rather than Toltec, although a Toltec sacrificial stone stands in front. A small building added on to the west side is known as the Annex. These buildings are in the Puuc-Chenes style, particularly evident in the lower jaw of the Chac mask at the opening of the Annex.

Akab-Dzib On the path east of the Nunnery, the Akab-Dzib is thought by some archaeologists to be the most ancient structure excavated here. The central chambers date from the 2nd century. Akab-Dzib means Obscure Writing in Mayan and refers to the south-side Annex door, whose lintel depicts a priest with a vase etched with hieroglyphics. The writing has never been translated, hence the name. Note the red fingerprints on the ceiling, thought to symbolize the deity Itzamná, the sun god from whom the Maya sought wisdom.

Chichén Viejo Chichén Viejo, or Old Chichén, comprises largely unrestored, basically Mayan ruins, though some have Toltec additions. Here you'll see a pristine part of Chichén, one without much archaeological restoration.

Grutas de Balankanché In 1959 a guide to the Chichén ruins was exploring a cave on his day off. Pushing against a cavern wall, he broke through into a larger subterranean opening. Archaeological exploration revealed a path that runs some 300 meters past carved stalactites and stalagmites, terminating at an underground pool.

The Grutas de Balankanché (Balankanché Caves) are six km east of the ruins of Chichén Itzá and two km east of the Hotel Dolores Alba on the highway to Cancún. Second-class buses heading east from Piste toward Valladolid and Cancún

YUCATÁN

will drop you at the Balankanché road. The entrance to the caves is 350 meters north of the highway.

The cave entrance is surrounded by a pretty botanical garden displaying many of Yucatán's native flora, including many species of cactus. In the entrance building is a little museum, a shop selling cold drinks and souvenirs and a ticket booth. Plan your visit for an hour when the compulsory tour and Light & Color Show will be given in a language you can understand: the 40-minute show (minimum six persons, maximum 30) is given in the cave at 11 am and 1 and 3 pm in English, at 9 am, noon and 2 and 4 pm in Spanish and at 10 am in French. Tickets are available between 9 am to 4 pm (last show) daily. Admission costs US$5 (US$2.50 Sunday).

Places to Stay

Most of the lodgings convenient to Chichén are in the middle and top-end price brackets. No matter what you plan to spend on a bed, be prepared to haggle off-season (May, June, September and October), when prices should be lower at every hotel.

Places to Stay - budget

Camping There's camping at the *Pirámide Inn* (see below). For US$4 per person you can pitch a tent, enjoy the Pirámide Inn's pool and watch satellite TV in the lobby. There are hot showers and clean shared toilet facilities. Those in vehicles pay US$12 for two for full hookups.

Hotels *Posada Olalde*, two blocks south of the highway by Artesanías Guayacan, is the best of Piste's small pensions: clean, quiet and attractive, but a little bit more expensive at US$19/28 a double/triple.

Posada Chac-Mool, just east of Hotel Misión Chichén on the opposite (south) side of the highway in Piste, charges US$12 for a double with shower and fan. *Posada Novelo*, on the west side of the Pirámide Inn, charges the same for similar basic accommodations, but you can use the Pirámide's pool.

Hotel Posada Maya, a few dozen meters north of the highway (look for the sign) also charges US$12 for double rooms with shower and fan, but only US$4 to hang your hammock. It's a bit quieter, but drab. *Posada Poxil*, at the western end of town, charges the same for relatively clean, quiet rooms.

Places to Stay - middle

Hotel Dolores Alba (☎ in Mérida (99) 21-37-45), Carretera Km 122, is just over three km east of the eastern entrance to the ruins and two km west of the road to Balankanché, on the highway to Cancún. (Ask the bus driver to stop here.) It has more than a dozen rooms surrounding a small swimming pool. The dining room is good (breakfasts US$3 to US$4, dinner US$10), which is important, as there is no other eating facility nearby. The hotel will transport you to the ruins, but you must walk or take a taxi or bus back. Single/double/triple rooms with shower and air-con cost US$22/25/28.

Stardust Inn (☎ /fax (985) 1-01-22), next to the Pirámide Inn in Piste and less than two km west of the ruins, is an attractive place with two tiers of rooms surrounding a palm-shaded swimming pool and restaurant. Air-con rooms with TV cost US$38 a single or double.

Next door, *Pirámide Inn* (☎ /fax (985) 1-01-14) has been here for years. Its gardens therefore have had years to mature, and its swimming pool is a blessing on a hot day. There's a selection of different rooms, some older, some newer (look before you buy), all priced at US$25/30/40/50 per air-con single/double/triple/quad. This is as close as you can get to the archaeological zone's western entrance.

Places to Stay - top end

All of the following hotels have beautiful swimming pools, restaurants, bars, well-kept tropical gardens, comfortable guest rooms and tour groups coming and going. Several are very close to the ruins. If you splurge on just one expensive hotel in Mexico, this is a good place to do it.

Hotel Mayaland (☎ in Mérida (99) 25-21-22, fax (99) 25-70-22, in the USA (800) 235-4079), a mere 200 meters from the

Henequen

Henequen *(Agave fourcroydes)*, also called sisal, is a common plant in Yucatán and indeed in most of Mexico. Its stalk grows almost two meters high in the wild, about one meter high in cultivation, and has lance-shaped leaves up to two meters long and 10 to 15 cm wide, edged with thorns. The plant's evil-smelling flowers are borne on a central stalk, which grows straight up to heights of six meters. Agaves flower periodically but infrequently, some species only once in a century.

A cultivated henequen plant yields about 25 leaves annually from the fifth to the sixteenth year after planting. The leaves are cut off by a worker with a machete, taken to a factory, and crushed between heavy rollers. The pulpy vegetable matter is scraped away to reveal fiber strands up to 1.5 meters in length, which are slightly stretchable and resistant to marine organisms.

Around Izamal and en route from Chichén Itzá to Mérida you pass through the henequen fields that gave rise to Yucatán's affluence in the 19th century. Prosperity in these parts reached its high point during WWI, when the demand for rope was great and synthetic fibers had not yet been invented.

Sometimes you can smell the grayish, spike-leafed henequen plants before you can see them, as they emit a putrid, excremental odor. Once planted, henequen can grow virtually untended for seven years. Thereafter, the plants are annually stripped for fiber. A plant may be productive for upwards of two decades.

Although growing henequen for rope is still economically viable, synthetic fibers have greatly diminished the profits. This decline has not been all that devastating for Maya, as the crop never employed a great many laborers to begin with, and those who worked during henequen's heyday on the haciendas were badly exploited. ■

eastern entrance to the archaeological zone, is the oldest (built in 1923) and most gracious at Chichén. From the lobby you look through the main portal to see El Caracol framed as if in a photograph. Rooms are priced at US$88/100 a single/double.

Hotel Hacienda Chichén (☎ in Mérida (99) 24-21-50, fax (99) 24-50-11, in the USA (800) 624-8451), a few hundred meters farther from the ruins on the same eastern access road, was the hacienda where the archaeologists lived when excavating Chichén. Their bungalows have been refurbished and new ones have been built. Rooms in the garden bungalows, priced at US$60 a single or double, US$70 a triple, have ceiling fans, air-con and private baths, but no TVs or phones. The dining room serves simple meals at moderate prices.

The *Hotel Villa Arqueológica* (☎ (985) 6-28-30), Apdo Postal 495, Mérida, is a few hundred meters east of the Mayaland and Hacienda Chichén on the eastern access road to the ruins. Run by Club Med, it's a modern layout with a good restaurant, tennis courts and a swimming pool. Rooms are fairly small but comfortable and air-

conditioned and priced at US$55/60/75 a single/double/triple.

On the western side of Chichén, in the village of Piste, the *Hotel Misión Chichén* (☎ (985) 1-00-22, fax (985) 1-00-23, in the USA (800) 648-7818) is comfortable without being distinguished. Its pool is refreshing, its vast restaurant often filled with bus tours. Air-conditioned rooms cost US$75 a single or double.

Places to Eat

The cafeteria in the *Unidad de Servicios*, at the western entrance to the archaeological zone, serves mediocre food at high prices in pleasant surroundings.

The highway through Piste is lined with more than 20 little restaurants. The cheapest places are the entirely unatmospheric little market eateries on the main square opposite the huge tree. The others, ranged along the highway from the square to the Pirámide Inn, are fairly well tarted up in a Mayan villager's conception of what foreign tourists expect to see. *Los Pajaros* and *Cocina Económica Chichén Itzá* are among the cheapest ones, serving sandwiches, omelets, enchiladas and quesadillas for around US$2.50. *Restaurant Sayil*, facing the Hotel Misión Chichén, offers a good value: bistec, cochinita or pollo pibil for US$2. Another simple little eatery with wooden benches and tables is the *Restaurant Parador*.

Prices are higher at the larger, more atmospheric restaurants, such as the *Pueblo Maya, Carrousel* and *Fiesta. Restaurant Ruinas* serves big plates of fruit for US$1.50, tuna salad with mango for US$4, and hamburgers, sandwiches, fried chicken, and spaghetti plates for around US$4.

The big *Restaurant Xaybe*, opposite the Hotel Misión Chichén, has decent food and prices, about US$10 per person. Customers of the restaurant get to use its swimming pool free, but even if you don't eat here, you can still swim for about US$2.

The luxury hotels all have restaurants, with the Club Med-run *Villa Arqueológica* serving particularly distinguished cuisine. If you try its French-inspired Mexican-Mayan restaurant, it'll cost you about US$15 per person for a four-course comida corrida, and almost twice that much if you order a la carte - but the food is good.

Getting There & Away
Air Aerocaribe runs one-day excursions by air from Cancún to Chichén Itzá in little planes, charging US$99 for the flight. Aerocozumel performs a similar service from Cozumel to Chichén Itzá for US$109.

Bus The fastest buses between Mérida, Valladolid and Cancún travel by the cuota (toll highway) and do not stop at Chichén Itzá.

Autotransportes de Oriente has a ticket desk right in the souvenir shop in Chichén's Unidad de Servicios. The Oriente bus station is a small building just west of the Pirámide Inn.

Here are some bus routes daily from Piste:

Cancún - 205 km, two to 3½ hours, US$4.50 to US$7; 10 buses

Cobá - 148 km, 2½ hours, US$4; one bus

Izamal - 95 km, 2 hours, US$3.50; change buses at Hóctun

Mérida - 116 km, 2½ hours, US$2.75 to US$3.50; 10 buses; those by Oriente stop right at the Chichén ruins. A special roundtrip excursion bus by Oriente (US$6.75) departs from Mérida at 8:45 am and returns from Chichén Itzá at 3 pm.

Playa del Carmen - 272 km, four hours, US$6 to US$9; five buses

Tulum - 402 km, 6½ hours, US$5; one bus

Valladolid - 42 km, 30 to 45 minutes, US$1; 10 buses

Getting Around
Be prepared for walking at Chichén Itzá: from your hotel to the ruins, around the ruins and back to your hotel, all in the hot sun and humidity. For the Grutas de Balankanché, you can set out to walk early in the morning, when it's cooler (it's eight km from Piste, less if you're staying on the eastern side of the ruins), and then hope to hitch a ride or catch a bus for the return.

A few taxis are available in Piste and sometimes at the Unidad de Servicios parking lot at Chichén Itzá, but you cannot depend on finding one unless you've made arrangements in advance.

IZAMAL
Population 40,000
In ancient times Izamal was a center for the worship of the supreme Mayan god Itzamná and the sun god Kinich Kakmó. A dozen temple pyramids in the town were devoted to those or other gods. Perhaps this Mayan religiosity is why the Spanish colonists chose Izamal as the site for an enormous and very impressive Franciscan monastery. As site of the monastery's main church, the planners selected the platform of one of the major Mayan temples.

Today Izamal is a quiet provincial town with the atmosphere of life in another century. The occasional horse-drawn carriage clip-clopping through town reinforces that feeling. The town's two principal squares are surrounded by impressive arcades and dominated by the gargantuan bulk of the monastery.

Convento de San Antonio de Padua

When the Spaniards conquered Izamal they destroyed the major Mayan temple, the Popul-Chac pyramid, and in 1533 they began to build from its stones one of the first monasteries in the hemisphere. The work was finished in 1561.

As you enter the center of town you can't miss the monastery, which dominates everything. An architectural feature both useful and beautiful - the arcade - was used abundantly by Izamal's colonial designers in the monastery, in the Palacio Municipal, in the small market and in many other town buildings. The traditional yellow you see everywhere gives the town its nickname of Ciudad Amarilla (Yellow City).

The monastery's principal church is the Santuario de la Virgen de Izamal, accessed by a ramp from the main square. Walk up the ramp and through a gallery to the atrium, a spacious arcaded courtyard in which the fiesta of the Virgin of Izamal takes place each August 15. Across the atrium is the 12-meter-high church, which is very simple in design, without much decoration. A miraculous portrait of the Virgin of Izamal, patron saint of Yucatán, hangs in the church. The original of the portrait was brought here from Guatemala in 1558, but was destroyed by fire in 1829 and replaced with a copy.

The monastery and church were restored and spruced up for the papal visit of John Paul II in August 1993. Entry to the church is free. The best time to visit the monastery is in the morning, as it may be closed during the afternoon siesta.

In various parts of the town are remnants of the other 11 Mayan pyramids. The largest is the temple of Kinich Kakmó; all are unrestored piles of rubble.

Places to Stay & Eat

Few travelers stay the night in Izamal. The small *Hotel Kabul* (☎ (995) 4-00-08), on Calle 31 facing the main plaza, will put you up in simple but fairly clean rooms without private bath for US$12 in one bed (one or two persons), or US$15 in two beds. Next door to the hotel is the *Cocina Económica La Reina Itzalana*, where the food is cheap and filling. Directly across the square are more cheap little loncherías and also the small market area.

Organized Tours

On Sundays at 8 am you can board a special train at Mérida's railroad station for a day excursion to Izamal, arriving in the Yellow City at 9:50 am. You then have a city tour (in Spanish), lunch and a folklore show before reboarding the train at 3 pm, arriving back in Mérida at 5 pm.

There's also a minibus tour from Mérida every Tuesday, Thursday and Saturday, departing Mérida's Parque de Santa Lucia at 9 am, returning by 5 pm.

Most travel agencies can reserve you a place, or you can call Cultur (☎ (99) 24-96-77), the cultural department of the Yucatán state government, which sponsors the excursions.

Getting There & Away

Oriente runs 20 buses daily between Mérida and Izamal (72 km, 1½ hours, US$1) from its terminal in Mérida on Calle 50 between 65 and 67; there are buses from Valladolid (155 km, two hours, US$3) as well. Coming from Chichén Itzá, you must change buses at Hóctun. If you're driving from the east, turn north at Kantunil.

Mérida

Population 600,000

The capital of the state of Yucatán is a charming city of narrow streets, colonial buildings, shady parks and Mayan pride. It has been the center of Mayan culture in Yucatán since before the conquistadors arrived; today it is the peninsula's center of commerce as well. If Cancún is Yucatán's cash register, Mérida is Yucatán's heart and soul.

Though it is the largest city in southeastern Mexico, the commercial Mérida of furniture factories, breweries, flour mills, auto dealerships and warehouses filled with sisal products, fruit, timber, tobacco and beef is mostly on the outskirts. At the city's heart is a colonial street grid dotted with old mansions and churches. There are lots of hotels and restaurants of every class and price range and good transportation services to any part of the peninsula and the country. Mérida can be your base for numerous excursions into the Mayan countryside that surrounds it.

If Mérida has drawbacks, they are pollution and heat. Noisy buses pump clouds of noxious fumes into the air. It's unpleasant but bearable. And Yucatán's high temperatures seem even higher in this city. Many buildings catch the heat and hold it well into the evening. But even those sensory assaults will do little to dampen your enjoyment of this interesting city, however.

Mérida seems busiest with tourists in high summer (July and August) and winter (mid-December through March).

HISTORY

The Spaniards had to work hard to conquer Yucatán. Mayan forces put up such fierce resistance to the advance of Francisco de Montejo's conquistadors in the early 1530s that Montejo returned to his base in central Mexico utterly discouraged. But his son, also named Francisco de Montejo, took up the struggle and returned to found a

Spanish colony at Campeche in 1540. From this base he and his army were able to take advantage of political dissension among the Maya, conquering Tihó (now Mérida) in 1542. By the end of the decade Yucatán was mostly under Spanish colonial rule.

When Montejo's conquistadors entered defeated Tihó they found a major Mayan settlement of lime-mortared stone, which reminded them of the Roman architectural legacies in Mérida, Spain. They promptly renamed the city after its Spanish likeness and proceeded to build it into the colonial capital and center of control. Mérida took its colonial orders directly from Spain, not from Mexico City, and Yucatán has had a distinct cultural and political identity ever since.

With the conquest of Yucatán, the indigenous people became little more than slaves. With religious redemption as their rationale, the colonial governors and church leaders built their own little empires on the backs of the Indians. Their harsh rule created resentments that would later explode.

When the Mexican War of Independence ended in 1821 the Spanish colonial governor of Yucatán resigned his post and the peninsula enjoyed a brief two years as an independent nation before it finally threw in its lot with Mexico, joining the union of Mexican states in 1823.

Spanish control, harsh as it was, had prevented certain abuses of power from becoming too much of a problem in Yucatán. With colonial rule removed, local potentates were free to build vast estates, or haciendas, based on the newly introduced cultivation of sugar cane and henequen, and the lot of the indigenous peoples got even worse. Though the Indians were nominally free citizens in a new republic, their hacienda bosses kept them in debt peonage.

As the hacendados grew in power and wealth they began to fear that outside forces (the government in central Mexico, or the USA) might covet their prosperity.

So the Méridan government organized armed forces and issued weapons to the soldiers, who were the same Indians being oppressed on the haciendas. Given the power to achieve their freedom, the Indians rebelled in 1847, beginning the War of the Castes.

Only Mérida and Campeche were able to hold out against the rebel forces; the rest of Yucatán came under Indian control. On the brink of surrender, the ruling class in Mérida was saved by reinforcements sent from central Mexico in exchange for Mérida's agreeing to take orders from Mexico City.

Though Yucatán is certainly part of Mexico, there is still a strong feeling of local pride in Mérida, a feeling that the Mayab (Mayan lands) are a special realm set apart from the rest of the country.

ORIENTATION

The Plaza Mayor, or main square, has been the center of Mérida since Mayan times. Most of the services you want are within five blocks of the square; the rest are on the broad, tree-lined boulevard named Paseo de Montejo.

Be advised that house numbers may progress very slowly; you cannot know whether Calle 57 No 481 and Calle 56 No 544 are one block or 10 blocks apart. Perhaps for this reason, addresses are usually given in this form: Calle 57 No 481 x 56 y 58 (between Calles 56 and 58).

INFORMATION
Tourist Offices

There are information booths of minimal usefulness at the airport and the bus station.

Your best bet for information is the Tourist Information Center (☎ (99) 24-92-90, 24-93-89), at the corner of Calles 60 and 57, in the southwest corner of the huge Teatro Peón Contreras, less than two blocks north of the Plaza Mayor.

The city government (Ayuntamiento de Mérida) has a tourism office one block west of the Parque Hidalgo along Calle 59 at the corner of 62.

Consulates

A number of countries have consulates in Mérida:

Belgium
  Calle 25 No 159, between Calles 28 and 30 (☎ (99) 25-29-39)

Denmark
  Calle 32 No 198 at Calle 17, Colonia Garcia Ginerés (☎ (99) 25-44-88, 25-45-27)

France
  Calle 33-B No 528, between Calles 62 and 64 (☎ (99) 25-22-91, fax (99) 25-70-09)

Germany
  Calle 7 No 217, between Calles 20 and 20-A, Colonia Chuburna de Hidalgo (☎ (99) 81-29-76)

Honduras
  Calle 54 No 280, Fraccionamiento del Norte (☎ (99) 27-44-74)

Netherlands
  Calle 64 No 418, between Calles 47 and 49 (☎ (99) 24-31-22, 24-41-47)

Spain
  Calle 3 No 237, Fraccionamiento Campestre (☎ (99) 27-15-20, fax (99) 23-00-55)

UK
  Calle 53 No 489, at Calle 58, Fraccionamiento del Norte (☎ (99) 28-29-62, fax (99) 28-39-62); you can get information about travel in Belize at the British Vice-Consulate weekday mornings from 9:30 am to noon.

USA
  Paseo de Montejo 453, at Avenida Colón (☎ (99) 25-54-09, fax (99) 25-62-19); it is rumored that this consulate-general will soon be downgraded and a new Consulate General opened in Cancún.

Money

Casas de cambio, though they may charge a fee for changing money, offer faster, better service than banks. Try the Money Marketing Centro Cambiario to the left of the Gran Hotel on Parque Hidalgo; Finex (☎ (99) 24-18-42), Calle 59 No 498-K, to the left of the Hotel Caribe; or Cambio La Peninsular, on the east side of Calle 60 between Calles 55 and 57.

YUCATÁN

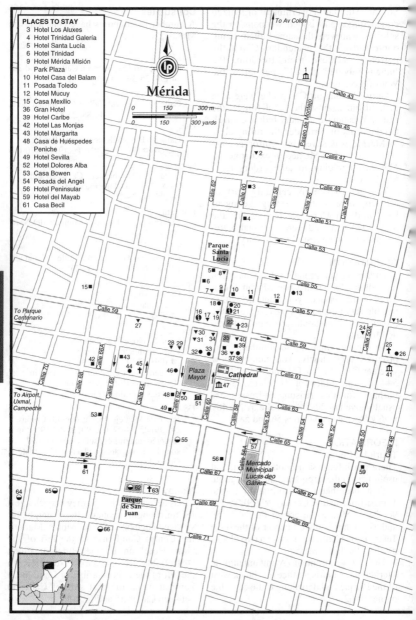

PLACES TO STAY
3   Hotel Los Aluxes
4   Hotel Trinidad Galería
5   Hotel Santa Lucía
6   Hotel Trinidad
9   Hotel Mérida Misión
    Park Plaza
10 Hotel Casa del Balam
11 Posada Toledo
12 Hotel Mucuy
15 Casa Mexilio
36 Gran Hotel
39 Hotel Caribe
42 Hotel Las Monjas
43 Hotel Margarita
48 Casa de Huéspedes
    Peniche
49 Hotel Sevilla
52 Hotel Dolores Alba
53 Casa Bowen
54 Posada del Angel
56 Hotel Peninsular
59 Hotel del Mayab
61 Casa Becil

Mérida

PLACES TO EAT
2 La Casona
7 Pop Cafetería,
   Restaurante Portico
   del Peregrino
8 Restaurant Santa Lucia
14 Gran Almendros
17 Amaro
19 La Bella Epoca
21 Café Peón Contreras
24 Los Almendros
27 Lonchería Mily
28 Kükis by Maru
29 El Louvre
30 Pizzería de Vito Corleone
31 Panificadora El Retorno
34 Café-Restaurant Express
37 Giorgio's Pizza & Pasta
39 Cafetería El Rincón
40 Tiano's
50 Panificadora Montejo

OTHER
1 Anthropology Museum
   (Palacio Cantón)
13 Alianza Francesa
   (Alliance Française)
16 City Tourism Office
18 Universidad de Yucatán
   del Estado
20 Teatro Peón Contreras
21 Tourist Information Center
22 Parque de la Madre
23 Iglesia de Jesús,
   Pinacoteca del Estado
25 Ex-Convento de
   la Mejorada
26 Centro Cultural de
   los Pueblos Mayas
32 Pasaje Picheta
33 Palacio de Gobierno
35 Parque Hidalgo
38 Cine Fantasio
41 Museo Regional
   de Artesanías
44 Casa de los Artesanías
45 Ex-Convento de
   las Monjas
46 Palacio Municipal
47 MACAY (Contemporary
   Art Museum)
51 Casa de Montejo
   (Banamex)
55 Progreso Bus Station
57 Correos (Main
   Post Office)
58 Oriente & Noroeste
   Bus Station
60 Autobuses del Noreste
   en Yucatán Bus Station
62 Minibus to Dzibilchaltún
63 Iglesia de San Juan
64 Terminal CAME
65 Old Terminal
   de Autobuses
66 Celestún Bus Station

Train
Station

To Acanceh,
Mayapán

To Chichén
Itzá

YUCATÁN

In addition, there are lots of banks along Calle 65 between Calles 60 and 62, the street one block behind Banamex/Casa de Montejo (that is, one block south of the Plaza Mayor). Banking hours are generally 9:30 am to 1:30 pm, Monday to Friday.

Post & Communications

Mail The main post office (Correos; ☎ (99) 21-25-61) is in the market area on Calle 65 between Calles 56 and 56A, open Monday to Friday from 8 am to 7 pm and Saturday from 9 am to 1 pm. There are postal service booths at the airport and the bus station, open on weekdays.

Telephone Ladatel phones for national and international calls are found on the Plaza Mayor, in Parque Hidalgo and at the airport, the bus station, at the corner of Calles 59 and 62 or Calles 64 and 57, or on Calle 60 between Calles 53 and 55. Yucatán is not served by a sufficient number of circuits, and you may have problems getting a line.

CDC, a private telephone company, has phones in many transport terminals, hotels and pensions. Before you make a call find out what it will cost.

Travel Agencies

Most middle-range hotels have lobby travel agencies, the most convenient of which is perhaps the one in the lobby of the Hotel Caribe, on Parque Hidalgo. There are others on Calle 60 north of Calle 57. Tour prices vary from one to the next, so shop around.

Bookstores

Librería Dante Peón (☎ (99) 24-95-22), in the Teatro Peón Contreras, at the corner of Calles 60 and 57 two blocks north of the main plaza, has a few English, French and German books as well as Spanish ones. It's open seven days a week. There's another branch at the northeast corner of the Parque Hidalgo.

Laundry

Lavamática La Fe, Calle 61 No 520, at Calle 64, can deal with your washing.

Medical Services

Hospital O'Horan (☎ (99) 24-41-00) is near the Parque Centenario on Avenida de los Itzaes. For the Red Cross, call ☎ (99) 24-98-13.

Dangers & Annoyances

Guard against pickpockets, bag-snatchers and bag-slashers in the market district and in any crowd, such as at a performance. They see you, but you won't see them.

PLAZA MAYOR

The most logical place to start a tour of Mérida is in the main plaza, Plaza Mayor. This was the religious and social center of ancient Tihó. Under the Spaniards it was the Plaza de Armas, or parade ground, laid out by Francisco de Montejo the Younger. Surrounded by harmonious colonial buildings, its carefully pruned laurel trees provide welcome shade for those who come here to relax or socialize. On Sunday the main plaza's adjoining roadways are off limits to traffic, and hundreds of Méridans take their paseo in the park.

Cathedral

On the east side of the plaza, on the site of a Mayan temple, is Mérida's, hulking, severe cathedral, begun in 1561 and completed in 1598. Some of the stone from the Mayan temple was used in the cathedral's construction.

Walk through one of the three doors in the baroque facade and into the sanctuary. The great crucifix at the east end of the nave is Cristo de la Unidad (Christ of Unity), a symbol of reconciliation between those of Spanish and those of Mayan stock. To your right over the south door is a painting of Tutul Xiú, *cacique* (local ruler) of the town of Maní, paying his respects to his ally Francisco de Montejo at Tihó (Montejo and Xiú jointly defeated the Cocoms; Xiú converted to Christianity and his descendants still live in Mérida).

Look in the small chapel to the left (north) of the principal altar for Mérida's most famous religious artifact, a statue of Jesus called Cristo de las Ampollas (Christ

of the Blisters). Local legend has it that this statue was carved from a tree in the town of Ichmul. The tree, hit by lightning, supposedly burned for an entire night yet showed no sign of fire. The statue carved from the tree was placed in the local church, where it alone is said to have survived the fiery destruction of the building, though it was blackened and blistered from the heat. It was moved to the Mérida cathedral in 1645.

The rest of the church's interior is plain, its rich decoration having been stripped by angry peasants at the height of anticlerical feeling during the Mexican Revolution.

Museo de Arte Contemporáneo

On the south side of the cathedral, housed in the former archbishop's palace, is the Museo de Arte Contemporáneo Ateneo de Yucatán (MACAY, ☎ (99) 28-32-58), at Pasaje de la Revolución 1907. The attractive museum holds permanent exhibits of Yucatán's most famous painters and sculptors, as well as changing exhibits by local artists and artisans.

MACAY is open daily except Tuesday from 10 am to 6 pm; Mexicans pay US$0.75 for admission, non-Mexicans pay US$3; students, teachers, workers, campesinos and seniors may enter free. On Sunday admission is free to all. There's a cafeteria inside.

Palacio de Gobierno

On the north side of the plaza, the Palacio de Gobierno houses the state of Yucatán's executive government offices; it was built in 1892 on the site of the palace of the colonial governors. Make your way past the armed guards to see the historical murals painted by local artist Fernando Castro Pacheco. The murals, completed in 1978 after 25 years of work, were restored in 1993.

In vivid colors the murals portray a symbolic history of the Maya and their interaction with the Spaniards. Over the stairwell is a painting of Mayan sacred corn, the 'ray of sun from the gods'. Overall, the murals suggest that despite the oppressive intrusion of the Europeans, the spirit of Mayan culture lives on. The palace is open every day from 8 am to 8 pm.

On Sunday at 11 am, there's usually a concert (jazz, classical pops, traditional Yucatecan) in the Salón de la Historia of the Palacio de Gobierno.

Palacio Municipal

Facing the cathedral across the square, the Palacio Municipal (Town Hall) is topped by a clock tower. Originally built in 1542, it has twice been refurbished, once in the 1730s and again in the 1850s. Today the building also serves as the venue for performances of Yucatecan dances (especially the jarana) and music at the weekly *Vaquería Regional*, a regional festival held to celebrate the branding of the cattle on haciendas. Performances are on Monday evenings at 9 pm.

Every Sunday at 1 pm the city sponsors a reenactment of a colorful mestizo wedding at the Palacio Municipal.

Casa de Montejo

From its construction in 1549 until the 1970s, the mansion on the south side of the plaza was occupied by the Montejo family. Sometimes called the Palacio de Montejo, it was built at the command of the conqueror of Mérida, Francisco de Montejo the Younger.

These days the great house shelters a branch of Banamex, and you can look around inside whenever the bank is open (usually from 9 am to 1:30 pm, Monday to Friday). If the bank is closed, content yourself with a close look at the plateresque facade, where triumphant conquistadors with halberds hold their feet on the necks of generic barbarians (who are not Maya, but the association is inescapable). Also gazing across the plaza from the facade are busts of Montejo the Elder, his wife and his daughter. The armorial shields are those of the Montejo family.

CALLE 60

A walk north from the Plaza Mayor along Calle 60 takes you past many of Mérida's churches, parks, hotels and restaurants and brings you toward the beginning of Paseo de Montejo.

Parque Hidalgo

A block north of the main plaza is the shady refuge of the Parque Hidalgo (sometimes called the Parque Cepeda Peraza, after a 19th-century general who collected a significant library).

At the far end of the park several restaurants, including Café El Mesón and Tiano's, offer alfresco sipping and dining. Tiano's often has a marimba band in the evening, enjoyable whether you eat there or just sit nearby. The city sponsors free marimba concerts here on Sunday mornings at 11:30 as well.

Iglesia de Jesús

Just to the north of the park rises the 17th-century Iglesia de Jesús, also called the Iglesia El Tercer Orden. Built by the Jesuits in 1618, it is the surviving edifice in a complex of Jesuit buildings that once filled the entire city block. Always interested in education, the Jesuits founded schools that later gave birth to the Universidad de Yucatán, just a few steps farther to the north. General Cepeda Peraza's library of 15,000 volumes is housed in a building behind the church.

In the church opposite the northeast corner of the Parque Hidalgo is the entrance to the Pinacoteca del Estado, the state painting gallery. Local and Mexican artists are featured; it's open from 8 am to 8 pm (Sunday 8 am to 2 pm), closed Monday.

Parque de la Madre

Directly in front of the Iglesia de Jesús and across from the Parque Hidalgo is the little Parque de la Madre, sometimes called the Parque Morelos. The modern Madonna and Child statue, which is a common fixture of town squares in this nation of high birth rates, is a copy of a statue by Lenoir that stands in the Jardín du Luxembourg in Paris.

Teatro Peón Contreras

Just north of the Parque de la Madre you confront the enormous bulk of the great Teatro Peón Contreras, built from 1900 to 1908, during Mérida's henequen heyday. Designed by Italian architect Enrico Deserti, it boasts a main staircase of Carrara marble, a dome with frescos by Italian artists and the Tourist Information Center, in its southwest corner.

The main entrance to the theater is at the corner of Calles 60 and 57. A gallery inside the entrance often holds exhibits by local painters and photographers; its hours are usually 9 am to 2 pm and 5 to 9 pm Monday to Friday, 9 am to 2 pm Saturday and Sunday. To see the grand theater itself, you'll have to attend a performance. Perhaps the best and most interesting performance to attend is Yucatán y sus Raices (Yucatán and Its Roots), a *ballet folklórico* show sponsored by the university and held each evening at 9 pm.

Universidad de Yucatán

Across Calle 60 from the Teatro Peón Contreras is the entrance to the main building of the Universidad de Yucatán. Though the Jesuits provided education to Yucatán's youth for centuries, the modern university was not established until the 19th century, when the job was done by Governor Felipe Carrillo Puerto and General Manuel Cepeda Peraza. The story of the university's founding is rendered graphically in a mural done in 1961 by Manuel Lizama. Walk in and ask for directions to the mural.

The central courtyard of the university building is the scene of concerts and folk performances every Tuesday or Friday evening at 9 pm (check with the Tourist Information Center for performance dates and times).

Parque Santa Lucia

A block north of the university, at the intersection of Calles 60 and 55, is the Parque Santa Lucia, with arcades on the north and west sides. When Mérida was a lot smaller, this was where travelers would get into or out of the stagecoaches that bumped over the rough roads of the peninsula, linking towns and villages with the provincial capital.

Today the park is the venue for orchestral performances of Yucatecan music on Thursday evenings at 9 and Sunday morn-

ings at 11. Also here on Sunday at 11 am is the Bazar de Artesanías, the local handicrafts market.

PASEO DE MONTEJO

To reach the Paseo de Montejo, walk 3½ blocks north along Calle 60 from the Parque Santa Lucia to Calle 47. Turn right on Calle 47 and walk two blocks to the paseo, on your left.

The Paseo de Montejo was an attempt by Mérida's 19th-century city planners to create a wide European-style grand boulevard, similar to Mexico City's Paseo de la Reforma or Paris's Avenue des Champs-Elysées. Since this is Mérida, not Paris, the boulevard is more modest, but it is still a beautiful swath of green and open space in an urban conglomeration of stone and concrete.

As Yucatán has always looked on itself as distinct from the rest of Mexico, the peninsula's powerful hacendados and commercial barons maintained good business and social contacts with Europe, concentrating on them to balance the necessary relations with Mexico City. Europe's architectural and social influence can be seen along the paseo in the surviving fine mansions built by wealthy families around the turn of the century.

Many other mansions have been torn down to make way for the banks, hotels and other high-visibility establishments that always want prime places on the grand boulevards of the world. Most of the remaining ones are north of Calle 37, which is three blocks north of the anthropology museum. Sidewalk cafes and restaurants south of Calle 39 can provide sustenance during your stroll along the avenue.

Two and a half blocks north along the paseo from Calle 47 brings you to the splendid white Palacio Cantón, home of Mérida's anthropology museum.

Museo Regional de Antropología

The great white palace at the corner of Paseo de Montejo and Calle 43 is the Museo Regional de Antropología de Yucatán, housed in the Palacio Cantón. The great mansion was designed by Enrico Deserti, who also was responsible for the Teatro Peón Contreras. Construction took place from 1909 to 1911. When it was completed the mansion's owner, General Francisco Cantón Rosado (1833-1917), moved in and lived there for a brief six years before he headed off to that great mansion in the sky.

After General Cantón's death his palace served as a school, as the official residence of the governors of the state of Yucatán and now as the anthropology museum. No building in Mérida exceeds it in splendor or pretension.

Admission to the museum costs US$5, free Sunday. It's open Monday to Saturday from 8 am to 8 pm, Sunday from 8 am to 2 pm. The museum shop is open from 8 am to 3 pm (2 pm on Sunday).

Exhibits on Mayan culture include explanations of the forehead-flattening which was done to beautify babies, and other practices, such as sharpening teeth and implanting them with tiny jewels. If you plan to visit archaeological sites near Mérida, you can study the many exhibits here. Lavishly illustrated with plans and photographs, they cover the great Mayan cities of Mayapán, Uxmal and Chichén Itzá, as well as lesser sites. However, labels on the exhibits are in Spanish only.

AVENIDA COLÓN
For more mansion viewing, turn left (west) onto Avenida Colón. The first block west of Paseo de Montejo is Mérida's posh entertainment and shopping district, serving the big hotels: Holiday Inn, Fiesta Americana, and Hyatt. Beyond the hotels are several splendid turn-of-the-century mansions.

PARQUE CENTENARIO
About 12 blocks west of the Plaza Mayor lies the large, verdant Parque Centenario, bordered by Avenida de los Itzaes, which is also Hwy 180, the highway to the airport and Campeche. There's a zoo in the park that specializes in exhibiting the fauna of Yucatán. To get there, take a bus westward along Calle 61 or 65. The park is open daily (except Monday) from 6 am to 6 pm, the zoo from 8 am to 5 pm. Admission to both is free.

MAYAN CULTURAL CENTER
The Centro Cultural de los Pueblos Mayas, on Calle 59 between 48 and 50, six blocks east of the Plaza Mayor, holds displays of the best of indigenous arts and crafts. Located behind the ancient ex-Convento de la Mejorada, it will satisfy your curiosity about the weaving of colorful huipiles, the carving of ceremonial masks, the weaving of hammocks and hats, and the turning of pottery. It's open daily (except Monday) from 8 am to 8 pm, Sunday from 9 am to 2 pm.

SPECIAL EVENTS
Prior to Lent in February or March, Carnaval features colorful costumes and nonstop festivities. It is celebrated with greater vigor in Mérida than anywhere else in Yucatán. During the first two weeks of October the Cristo de las Ampollas statue in the cathedral is venerated with processions.

ORGANIZED TOURS
You can choose from many group tours to sights around Mérida: Chichén Itzá (US$17), Chichén with drop-off in Cancún (US$29), Uxmal and Kabah (US$17), Uxmal sound-and-light (US$17), Puuc Route (US$32) and Izamal (US$14). All prices are per person. Ask at your hotel reception desk, in a fancier hotel or at any of the travel agencies on Calle 60.

PLACES TO STAY
Most of the budget and middle-range hotels are within about six blocks of the plaza; the largest concentration of luxury hotels is along the Paseo de Montejo and Avenida Colón, 12 to 16 long blocks from the plaza.

If you arrive by bus into CAME, the main bus terminal, check at the tourism desk for flyers announcing discounted hotel rooms. Some of the sponsoring hotels are among those recommended in this guide. Put the flyer in your pocket, ask the price at the hotel, and if the flyer price is lower, whip it out and claim your discount.

YUCATÁN

Places to Stay – budget

Prices for basic, suitable rooms in Mérida range from about US$9 to US$15 for a small but clean double room with fan and private shower and only a short walk from the plaza. All hotels should provide purified drinking water, usually at no extra charge. (The water bottles are not always readily evident, so ask for *agua purificada*.)

Hotel Las Monjas (☎ (99) 28-66-32), Calle 66A No 509, at Calle 63, is one of the best deals in town. All 28 rooms in this little place have ceiling fans and sinks or private baths with hot and cold water. Doubles with one bed cost US$10, with two beds US$12. One room has air-con and goes for a dollar more. Rooms are tiny and most are dark, but all are clean. Room No 12 is the best.

Hotel Margarita (☎ (99) 23-72-36), Calle 66 No 506, between Calles 61 and 63, offers low standards for low prices, but a convenient location. Its small, fairly grubby rooms with fan and running water cost US$7/8/10/11 a single/double/triple/quad. Air-con is in some rooms for a few dollars more.

Casa de Huéspedes Peniche (☎ (99) 28-55-18), Calle 62 No 507, between Calles 63 and 65, is in terrible condition, but right off the Plaza Mayor, and single/double rooms without running water cost as little as US$5/6, or US$7 a double with shower. If you're really broke, look at it.

Hotel Mucuy (☎ (99) 28-51-93, fax (99) 23-78-01), Calle 57 No 481, between Calles 56 and 58, has been serving thrifty travelers for more than a decade. It's a family-run place with 26 tidy rooms on two floors facing a long, narrow garden courtyard. Sra Ofelia Comin and her daughter Ofelia speak English; Sr Alfredo Comin understands it. Rooms with ceiling fan and private shower cost US$11/13/16 a single/double/triple.

Casa Bowen (☎ (99) 28-61-09), Calle 66 No 521-B, near Calle 65, is a large old Mérida house converted to a hotel. The narrow courtyard has a welcome swath of green grass. Rooms are simple, even bare, and some are dark and soiled, but all have

fans and showers for US$9/11 a single/double, US$19 with air-con. The staff tends to be sullen. *Café Terraza*, across the street, provides quick, cheap meals.

Casa Becil (☎ (99) 24-67-64), Calle 67 No 550-C, between Calles 66 and 68 near the bus station, is a house with a high-ceilinged sitting room/lobby and small, sometimes hot, guestrooms at the back. With private shower and fan, the price is US$11 to US$14 a double.

Hotel Sevilla (☎ (99) 23-83-60), Calle 62 No 511, at the corner of Calle 65, offers a whisper of faded elegance, but most rooms are musty and dark. The price is not too bad: US$8/10/13 for a single/double/triple.

If you don't mind walking or busing a few extra blocks and you want to really save money, try the *Hotel del Mayab* (☎ (99) 28-51-74, fax (99) 28-60-47), Calle 50 No 536-A, between Calles 65 and 67. Street-side rooms can be noisy, but interior rooms with shower are quiet, and there's a swimming pool, all for US$8 a double with fan, US$11 with air-con.

Hotel Santa Lucia (☎ (99) 28-26-72, 28-26-62), Calle 55 No 508, between Calles 60 and 62 and facing the Parque Santa Lucia, has 51 decent, well-located double rooms for US$18 with fan or US$20 with air-con.

Hotel Trinidad (☎ (99) 23-20-33), Calle 62 No 464, between Calles 55 and 57, is run by artists and can be funky or quirky, depending on your perspective. Modern Mexican paintings draw your eye from the peeling paint on the walls. The guestrooms, priced from US$12 to US$13 double, are all different and exhibit both charm and squalor.

The Trinidad's sister hotel, *Hotel Trinidad Galería* (☎ (99) 23-24-63, fax (99) 24-23-19), Calle 60 No 456, at the corner of Calle 51, was once an appliance showroom. It has a small swimming pool, bar, art gallery and antique shop, as well as presentable rooms with fans and private showers renting for rates similar to those at the Trinidad.

Hotel Peninsular (☎ (99) 23-69-96), Calle 58 No 519, between Calles 65 and 67, is in the midst of the market district. You enter down a long corridor to find a neat restaurant and a maze of rooms, most with windows opening onto the interior spaces. It costs US$9/11/15 per single/double/triple with private bath and fan; add a few dollars for air-con.

The neocolonial *Posada del Angel* (☎ (99) 23-27-54), Calle 67 No 535 between Calles 66 and 68, is three blocks northeast of Terminal CAME and is quieter than most other hotels in this neighborhood. It's convenient and priced at US$11 to US$13 a double, US$17 with air-con.

Places to Stay – middle

Mérida's middle-range places provide surprising levels of comfort for what you pay. Most charge US$20 to US$50 for a double with air-con, ceiling fan and private shower, and most have restaurants, bars and little swimming pools.

Hotel Dolores Alba (☎ (99) 21-37-45), Calle 63 No 464, between Calles 52 and 54, 3½ blocks east of the plaza, is one of the top choices in Mérida because of its pleasant courtyard, beautiful swimming pool and clean, comfortable rooms for US$22/25/28 a single/double/triple with shower, fan and air-con.

Hotel Caribe (☎ (99) 24-90-22, fax (99) 24-87-33, in Mexico (91-800) 20003, in the USA (800) 826-6842), Calle 59 No 500, at the corner of Calle 60 on the Parque Hidalgo, is a favorite with visiting foreigners because of its central location, its rooftop pool and its two restaurants. Most rooms have air-con and range in price from US$20 for a small single with fan to US$40 for a large double with air-con.

Gran Hotel (☎ (99) 24-77-30, fax (99) 24-76-22), Calle 60 No 496, between Calles 59 and 61, is on the southern side of the Parque Hidalgo. Corinthian columns support terraces on three levels around the verdant central courtyard, and fancy wrought-iron and carved-wood decorations evoke a past age. All 28 rooms have air-con and cost US$30/40/50 a single/double/triple.

Casa Mexilio (☎ /fax (99) 28-25-05, in

the USA (800) 538-6802), Calle 68 No 495, between Calles 59 and 57, is Mérida's most charming pension, a well-preserved and decorated house with a small pool and quiet, comfortable rooms for US$28 to US$50 a double, breakfast included.

Posada Toledo (☎ (99) 23-16-90, fax (99) 23-22-56), Calle 58 No 487, at Calle 57, three blocks northeast of the main plaza, is a colonial mansion with rooms arranged on two floors around a classic courtyard. It has a dining room straight out of the 19th century and small, modernized double rooms with fan or air-con for US$20 on the ground floor or US$26 on the upper floor.

Places to Stay – top end

Top-end hotels charge between US$70 and US$150 for a double room with air-con. Each hotel has a restaurant, bar, swimming pool and probably other services, such as a newsstand, hairdresser, travel agency and nightclub.

If you reserve your top-end room through your travel agent at home, you're likely to pay typical international-class rates for these hotels. But if you walk in and ask about *promociones* (promotional rates) or – even better – look through local newspapers and handouts for special rates aimed at a local clientele, you can lower your lodging bill substantially.

Mérida's newest and most luxurious hotel is the 17-story, 300-room *Hyatt Regency Mérida* (☎ (99) 42-12-34, fax (99) 25-70-02), Avenida Colón and Calle 60, 100 meters west of Paseo de Montejo and about two km north of the Plaza Mayor. Rooms with all the comforts cost US$95 to US$135, but promotional deals can bring those prices down.

Holiday Inn Mérida (☎ (99) 25-68-77, fax (99) 25-77-55, in the USA (800) 465-4329), Avenida Colón 498, at Calle 60, half a block off the Paseo de Montejo behind the US Consulate General, is one of Mérida's most luxurious establishments. Its 213 air-con rooms cost US$65 to US$85.

Across Avenida Colón from the Hyatt and Holiday Inn is a large multipurpose building within which you'll find the *Fiesta Americana Mérida* (☎ (99) 42-11-11, fax (99) 42-11-12, in Mexico (91-800) 50450, in the USA (800) 343-7821), a new neo-colonial luxury hotel charging US$105 to US$125 for its very comfortable rooms and junior suites.

Hotel Casa del Balam (☎ (99) 24-88-44, fax (99) 24-50-11, in the USA (800) 624-8451), Calle 60 No 488, at Calle 57, has numerous advantages: agreeable colonial decor, modern rooms and services, a central location and a price of US$75 per room, with discounts offered when it's not busy.

For all-around quality, convenience and price, try the *Hotel Los Aluxes* (☎ (99) 24-21-99, fax (99) 23-38-58, in the USA (800) 782-8395), Calle 60 No 444, at Calle 49. This 109-room hotel, popular with tour groups, has all the services, plus modern architecture and an intriguing name: *aluxes* (ah-LOO-shess) are the Mayan equivalent of leprechauns. Rates are US$65 a single/double, US$85 a triple.

The *Hotel Mérida Misión Park Plaza* (☎ (99) 23-95-00, fax (99) 23-76-65), Calle 60 No 491, at Calle 57, is half modern and half colonial in decor and comfortable without being particularly charming. Rates for the 150 air-con rooms are US$75 a single or double.

PLACES TO EAT

Mérida's restaurants are less numerous than Cancún's, but they are also less hyped, less expensive and more varied in cuisine. In Cancún it's expected that you want expensive lobster and shrimp at every meal; in Mérida you can order from a variety of Yucatecan, Mexican, American, Italian, French, even Lebanese dishes. The best restaurants are only moderately priced, and the market eateries are cheap and good.

Places to Eat – budget

Walk two blocks south from the Plaza Mayor to Calle 67, turn left (east) and walk another two or three blocks to the market. Continue straight up the flight of steps at the end of Calle 67. As you ascend you'll pass the touristy Bazar de Artesanías on your left.

At the top of the ramp turn left, and you'll see a row of family-run eateries with names like *El Chimecito, La Temaxeña, Saby, Mimi, Saby y El Palon, La Socorrito, Reina Beatriz* and so forth. Comidas corridas here are priced from US$1 to US$2. Big main-course platters of beef, fish or chicken with vegetables and rice or potatoes go for US$1.25 to US$2.50. The market eateries are open from the early morning until early evening – some as late as 8 or 8:30 pm – every day.

El Louvre (☎ (99) 21-32-71), Calle 62 No 499, corner of Calle 61 at the northwest corner of the Plaza Mayor, is grubby but has a loyal local clientele who come for the daily US$1.50 comida corrida, though it's hardly a gourmet treat. Breakfast costs the same.

Cafeteria Erick's, Cafe Los Amigos, Chicken Express and *El Trapiche*, up Calle 62 from El Louvre, offer nearly as cheap food in more attractive surroundings.

Lonchería Mily, Calle 59 No 520, between Calles 64 and 66, opens at 7:30 am and serves cheap breakfasts (US$1), a two-course comida corrida (US$2) and cheap sandwiches. It closes at 5 pm and is closed all day Sunday.

For take-out food, try the *Pizzería de Vito Corleone* (☎ (99) 23-68-46), Calle 59 No 508, at Calle 62. This tiny eatery suffers from loud street noise, so many customers take their pizzas to the Parque Hidalgo instead. Pizzas are priced from US$2 to US$8, depending on size and ingredients. Vegetarian varieties are available.

The best cheap breakfasts can be had by picking up a selection of *pan dulces* (sweet rolls and breads) from one of Mérida's several *panificadoras* (bakeries). A convenient one is the *Panificadora Montejo*, at the corner of Calles 62 and 63, at the southwest corner of the main plaza. Pick up a metal tray and tongs, select the pastries you want and hand the tray to a clerk, who will bag them and quote a price, usually US$2 or so for a full bag. *Panificadora El Retorno*, on Calle 62 just north of 61, is a tiny, mod-ish version of the same.

Kükis by Maru, Calle 61 between Calles

62 and 64, a few doors west of El Louvre, serves fresh-baked cookies ('kükis') and cappuccino (even iced!) for less than US$2. More substantial fare, such as scones with ham and cheese and sandwiches made with whole-grain bread, cost even less.

Places to Eat – middle

Those willing to spend a bit more money can enjoy the pleasant restaurants of the Parque Hidalgo at the corner of Calles 59 and 60.

The least expensive, yet one of the most pleasant, restaurants here is the *Cafetería El Rincón* (the stained-glass sign above the door reads El Mesón; ☎ (99) 21-92-32) in the Hotel Caribe. Meat, fish and chicken dishes are priced from US$4 to US$7, but sandwiches and burgers cost less. El Rincón is open from 7 am to 10:30 pm.

Perhaps the most popular spot on the Parque Hidalgo is *Giorgio's Pizza & Pasta*, to the left of the Gran Hotel. This is the center of action in the park. Come and carbo-load plates of spaghetti for US$4, or pizzas for US$3.50 (small) to US$7 (large).

Right next to El Rincón is *Tiano's* (☎ (99) 23-71-18), Calle 59 No 498, which hires a marimba group each evening to entertain its patrons and the dozens of hangers-on in the square. The menu bears the cheerful warning 'Please avoid ambulant sellers, touching money during meals unhygienic, or you can choke.' Have sopa de lima, puntas de filete, dessert and a drink and your bill might be US$13. It's a bit expensive for the quality of the food.

Across Calle 60, facing the Parque Hidalgo, is an old Mérida standard, the *Café-Restaurant Express* (☎ (99) 21-37-38), Calle 60 No 502, south of Calle 59. With a loyal crowd of regulars and foreigners, Express is a bustling and noisy meeting place, and prices are just a bit too high, but the food is okay and service is fast. Hours are 7 am to midnight daily.

Amaro (☎ (99) 28-24-51), Calle 59 No 507, between Calles 60 and 62, specializes in Yucatecan food and beer and also offers vegetarian dishes and pizzas. It's open daily from 9 am to 10 pm. The setting,

complete with strolling troubadour, is the courtyard of the house in which Andrés Quintana Roo – poet, statesman and drafter of Mexico's Declaration of Independence – was born in 1787.

A few steps north along Calle 60 from the Parque de la Madre is the *Cafe Peón Contreras*, attractive for its outdoor sidewalk tables. The menu is long, varied and moderately priced, with breakfasts for US$2.50 to US$4, pizzas for around US$5 and a combination plate of Yucatecan specialties for US$10.

Restaurant Santa Lucia (☎ (99) 28-59-57), Calle 60 No 479, at Calle 55, is cozy and atmospheric, with low lights and a strolling guitarist. The Yucatecan combination plate, including sopa de lima, costs US$5, though other main courses may go as high as US$13. Service is slow, and some dishes are bland.

Pop Cafetería (☎ (99) 28-61-63), Calle 57 between Calles 60 and 62, is plain, modern, bright, air-conditioned and named for the first month of the 18-month Mayan calendar. Though the menu includes hamburgers, spaghetti, chicken and other maincourse platters for US$2.50 to US$5, most people come for breakfast (US$2 to US$4), coffee, fruit plates or pastries. It's open daily from 7 am to midnight.

Places to Eat – top end

The secret to enjoying a dinner at *La Bella Epoca* (☎ (99) 28-19-28), Calle 60 between Calles 57 and 59, opposite the Parque de la Madre, is to get there early enough to get one of the five little two-person tables set out on the 2nd-floor balconies. Have an appetizer, pollo pibil, dessert and a beer for US$14 per person. It's open from 7 am to 11 pm daily.

Restaurante Portico del Peregrino (☎ 28-61-63), Calle 57 No 501, between Calles 60 and 62 right next to Pop, is a 'Pilgrim's Refuge' of several pleasant, almost elegant traditional dining rooms (some are air-conditioned) arranged around a small courtyard replete with colonial artifacts. Yucatecan dishes are the forte, but you'll find many continental dishes as well. Lunch (noon to 3 pm) and dinner (6 to 11 pm) are served every day, and your bill for a full meal might be US$12 to US$20 per person.

La Casona (☎ (99) 23-83-48), Calle 60 No 434, between Calles 47 and 49, is a fine old city house with tables set out on a portico next to a small but lush garden; dim lighting lends an air of romance. Italian dishes crowd the menu, with a few concessions to local cuisine. Plan to spend anywhere from US$9 to US$17 per person. La Casona is open every evening for dinner; on weekends you might want to make reservations.

Los Almendros (☎ (99) 28-54-59), Calle 50A No 493, between Calles 57 and 59, facing the Plaza de Mejorada, specializes in authentic Yucatecan country cuisine such as pavo relleno negro (grilled turkey with hot-peppered pork stuffing), papadzul (tacos filled with egg and smothered in a fiery sauce), sopa de lima (chicken broth with lime and tortillas) or Los Almendros's most famous dish, the zingy onion-and-tomato pork dish pocchuc. Full meals cost US$9 to US$15. Some people come away disappointed with Los Almendros because they go expecting delicacies; this is hearty food.

Mérida boasts two other Los Almendros locations, one of which is the fancier *Gran Almendros* (☎ (99) 23-81-35), Calle 57 at Calle 50.

ENTERTAINMENT

Watching the daily people-circus in the Plaza Mayor or Parque Hidalgo is among Mérida's most amusing pastimes. But there are lots of traditional entertainments as well.

Concerts & Folklore

Proud of its cultural legacy and attuned to the benefits of tourism, the city of Mérida offers nightly folkloric and musical events in parks and historic buildings, put on by local performers of considerable skill. Admission is free to city-sponsored events.

Monday – *Vaquerías* (traditional dances) are performed on the west side of the Palacio Municipal at 9 pm.

Tuesday – At the Teatro Peón Contreras, the University stages Yucatán's Ballet Folklórico at 9 pm (tickets on sale at the theater).

Wednesday – Classical music is performed in the Casa de las Artesanías, Calle 63 and 64, at 9 pm.

Thursday – Traditional Yucatecan serenades in the Parque Santa Lucía, Calles 55 and 60, at 9 pm.

Friday – Traditional Yucatecan serenades are sung in the courtyard of the Universidad Autónoma de Yucatán, Calles 57 and 60, at 9 pm; also, *Estampas Yucatecas* (regional folk dances) are performed in the shop-lined Pasaje Picheta, on the west side of the Palacio de Gobierno, from 8 to 9 pm.

Sunday – Mérida en Domingo, a series of concerts and special events, takes place in the Plaza Mayor and other plazas.

Cinemas

Many English-language films, some of fairly recent release, are screened in Mérida with Spanish subtitles. Buy your tickets (usually about US$2) before showtime and well in advance on weekends. The popular *Cine Fantasio*, Calle 59 at 60, facing the Parque Hidalgo and between the Gran Hotel and Hotel Caribe, is convenient. There's also the *Cinema 59*, Calle 59 between Calles 68 and 70, and the *Plaza Cine Internacional*, Calle 58 between Calles 57 and 59.

THINGS TO BUY

From standard shirts and blouses to Mayan exotica, Mérida is *the* place on the peninsula to shop. Purchases you might want to consider include traditional Mayan clothing (such as the colorful women's embroidered blouse called a *huipil*), a Panama hat woven from palm fibers, local craft items and of course the wonderfully comfortable Yucatecan hammock, which holds you gently in a comfortable cotton web.

Guard your valuables extra carefully in the market area. Watch for pickpockets, purse-snatchers and slash-and-grab thieves.

Mérida's main market, the Mercado Municipal Lucas do Gálvez, is bound by Calles 56 and 56A at Calle 67, four blocks southeast of the Plaza Mayor. The market building is more or less next door to the city's main post office (Correos) and telegraph office, which is at the corner of Calles 65 and 56. The surrounding streets are all part of the large market district, lined with shops selling everything one might need.

The Bazar de Artesanías, Calle 67 at the corner of Calle 56A, is set up to attract tourists and their dollars. You should have a look at the stuff here, then compare the goods and prices with independent shops outside the Bazar.

Handicrafts

The place to go for high-quality craft and art items is the Casa de las Artesanías Estado de Yucatán, on Calle 63 between Calles 64 and 66; look for the doorway marked 'Dirección de Desarrollo Artesanal DIF Yucatán'. It's open Monday to Friday from 8 am to 8 pm, Saturday from 8 am to 6 pm, closed Sunday. This is a government-supported marketing effort for local artisans. The selection of crafts is very good, the quality usually high and the prices reasonable.

You can also check out locally made crafts at the Museo Regional de Artesanías, on Calle 59 between Calles 50 and 48. The work on display is superlative, but the items for sale are not as good. Admission is free and it's open Tuesday to Saturday 8 am to 8 pm and Sunday 9 am to 2 pm, closed Monday.

Panama Hats

Panama hats are woven from jipijapa palm leaves in caves and workshops in which the temperature and humidity are carefully controlled, as humid conditions keep the fibers pliable when the hat is being made. Once blocked and exposed to the relatively drier air outside, the hat is surprisingly resilient and resistant to crushing. The Campeche town of Becal is the center of the hat-weaving trade, but you can buy

---

Hammocks

In the sticky heat of Yucatán most locals prefer sleeping in a hammock, where the air can circulate around them, rather than in a bed. The fine strings of Yucatecan hammocks make them supremely comfortable. Yucatecan hammocks are normally woven from strong nylon or cotton string and dyed various colors, though there also are natural, undyed versions.

Yucatán hammocks come in several widths. From smallest to largest, the names generally used to describe them are *sencillo* (about 50 pairs of end strings, US$12), *doble* (100 pairs, US$15 to US$25), *matrimonial* (about 150 pairs, US$25 to US$35) and *matrimonial especial* or *quatro cajas* (175 pairs or more, US$35 and up). You must check to be sure that you're really getting the width that you are paying for.

Peddlers who approach you on the street may quote low prices, but the quality of street-sold hammocks is mediocre at best. Check the hammock very carefully. Look closely at the string; it should be sturdy and tightly and evenly spun. Check the end loops; they should be fairly large and tightly wrapped in string. Many hammocks are made for sleepers of Mayan stature (that is, short). To make sure you get a hammock long enough for you, hold the hammock at the point where the end strings join the main body of the hammock and raise your hand as high as your head; the other end of the body of the hammock should extend at least to the ground. In other words, the body of the hammock (not counting the end strings) should be as long as you are tall.

Open the hammock and look at the weave; it should be even, with few mistakes. Watch out for dirty patches and stains. Check the width. Any hammock looks very wide at first glance, but a matrimonial especial should be truly enormous, at least as wide as it is long, and probably wider.

If you intend to sleep in a place without insect protection, be sure to buy one of the long, tube-shaped mosquito nets to hang around your hammock. ■

good examples of the hat maker's art here in Mérida.

The best-quality hats have a fine, close weave of slender fibers. The coarser the weave, the lower the price should be. Prices range from a few dollars for a hat of basic quality to US$20 or more for top quality.

Hammocks

You will be approached by peddlers on the street wanting to sell you hammocks about every hour throughout your stay in Mérida (every five minutes in Parque Hidalgo). Check the quality of the hammocks on offer carefully. (See the hammocks sidebar for more information).

You can save yourself a lot of trouble by shopping at a hammock store with a good reputation. I've been able to recommend La Poblana (☎ (99) 21-65-03), at Calle 65 No 492, between Calles 58 and 60, for decades. Some travelers report slightly cheaper prices for good quality at El Aguacate, Calle 58 No 604, at the corner of Calle 73. El Campesino, at Calle 58 No 548, between Calles 69 and 71, is farther from the city center.

It's interesting to venture out to the nearby village of Tixcocob to watch hammocks being woven. The bus runs regularly from the Progreso bus station, south of the main plaza at Calle 62 No 524, between Calles 65 and 67.

GETTING THERE & AWAY
Air

Mérida's modern airport is a 10-km, 20-minute ride southwest of the Plaza Mayor off Hwy 180 (Avenida de los Itzaes). The airport has car rental desks and a tourism office that can help with hotel reservations.

Most international flights to Mérida are connections through Mexico City or Cancún. The only nonstop international services are Aeromexico's two daily flights from Miami and Aviateca's flights to and from Guatemala City. Domestic flights are operated mostly by smaller regional airlines, with a few flights by Aeromexico and Mexicana.

Aerocaribe – flies between Mérida and Cancún (morning and evening flights; US$55 one way, US$100 roundtrip excursion), Chetumal, Mexico City, Oaxaca, Tuxtla Gutiérrez (for San Cristóbal de las Casas), Veracruz and Villahermosa. Paseo de Montejo 476-A (☎ (99) 24-95-00, 23-00-02)

Aerolineas Bonanza – flies roundtrips daily from Mérida to Cancún, Chetumal and Palenque. Calle 56A No 579, between Calles 67 and 69 (☎ (99) 26-06-09, fax (99) 27-79-99)

Aeromexico – has a few flights as well. Paseo de Montejo 460 (☎ (99) 27-95-66, 27-92-77)

Aviacsa – flies nonstop to Cancún, Villahermosa and Mexico City. At the airport (☎ (99) 26-32-53, 26-39-54, fax (99) 26-90-87)

Aviateca – flies to Tikal and Guatemala City several times a week. At the airport (☎ (99) 24-43-54)

Litoral – flies to Ciudad del Carmen, Veracruz and Monterrey. Based in Veracruz (☎ in Mexico (91-800) 2-90-20)

Mexicana – has nonstop flights to and from Havana, Cancún and Mexico City. Calle 58 No 500 (☎ (99) 24-66-33)

Bus

Mérida is the bus transport hub of the Yucatán peninsula, with several bus stations.

Terminal CAME Mérida's main bus terminal, seven blocks southwest of the Plaza Mayor at Calle 70 No 555, between Calles 69 and 71, is known as Terminal CAME (KAH-meh). It handles ticketing and departures for ADO (Autobuses de Oriente), one of Mexico's biggest bus companies. Come here if you're headed for Campeche, Palenque, Villahermosa, Tuxtla Gutiérrez, San Cristóbal de las Casas or points in the rest of Mexico.

Buses run by Linea Dorada and UNO depart from CAME, but their ticket counters are in the old Terminal de Autobuses, around the corner.

CAME has Ladatel long-distance telephones and a hotel desk. Look through the flyers offering hotel room discounts (see Places to Stay).

Terminal de Autobuses The old bus terminal, around the corner from CAME on

Calle 69, between Calles 68 and 70, has ticket counters for Linea Dorada, UNO, ADO, Autotransportes del Sur, Omnitur del Caribe and Transportes Mayab; see Bus Companies, below, for points served. Come here for buses to points in the state and peninsula of Yucatán and some beyond.

Parque de San Juan The Parque de San Juan, on Calle 69 between Calles 64 and 66, is the terminus for Volkswagen minibuses going to Dzibilchaltún Ruinas (US$0.55), Muna, Oxkutzcab, Peto, Sacalum, Tekax and Ticul (US$1.75).

Oriente & Noroeste Autotransportes de Oriente and Autotransportes del Noroeste en Yucatán share a terminal at Calle 50 No 527-A, between Calles 65 and 67, and another one right across the street. Oriente serves routes to Cancún via Chichén Itzá and Valladolid and to Cobá, Playa del Carmen and Tulum; some of these buses depart from the old Terminal de Autobuses as well. Noroeste serves many small towns in the northeastern part of the peninsula, including Tizimin (US$3.50) and Río Lagartos (two buses daily, US$4.50).

Autotransportes del Sur Though most Autotransportes del Sur buses depart from the old Terminal de Autobuses, the company also runs buses to Celestún from its own old terminal, at Calle 50 No 531, at Calle 67.

Progreso The separate bus terminal for Progreso is at Calle 62 No 524, between Calles 65 and 67.

Bus Companies Here's a quick rundown on the companies and the destinations they serve:

Autobuses de Oriente (ADO) – long-haul 1st-class routes to Campeche, Palenque, Villa-hermosa, Veracruz, Mexico City and beyond

Autotransportes de Oriente (Oriente) – buses every hour from 5:15 am until 12:15 am between Mérida and Cancún, stopping at Chichén Itzá and Valladolid; buses between Mérida and Cobá, Izamal, Playa del Carmen and Tulum

Autotransportes del Sur (ATS) – hourly buses to Cancún and buses every 20 to 40 minutes to Campeche; also runs buses to Bolonchén de Rejón, Cancún, Celestún, Chiquilá, Ciudad del Carmen, Emiliano Zapata, Hecelchakan, Hopelchén, Izamal, Ocosingo, Palenque, Playa del Carmen, San Cristóbal de las Casas, Tizimin, Tulum and Valladolid. Special buses serve the Ruta Puuc, and Uxmal for the evening sound-and-light show; see Uxmal, in Bus Routes, below, for details.

Omnitur del Caribe (Caribe) – luxury service between Mérida and Chetumal via Felipe Carrillo Puerto; ticket counter in the old Terminal de Autobuses

Transportes Mayab (Mayab) – buses to Cancún, Chetumal, Felipe Carrillo Puerto, Peto and Ticul; ticket counters and departures in the old Terminal de Autobuses

Transportes de Lujo Linea Dorada (LD) – luxury service to Felipe Carrillo Puerto and Chetu-mal; ticket counter in the old Terminal de Autobuses, departures from Terminal CAME

Bus Routes Here's information on daily trips to and from Mérida:

Campeche – 1.95 km (short route via Becal), 2½ to three hours; 250 km (long route via Uxmal), four hours; ATS has buses every 20 to 30 minutes (US$3 to US$3.50); ADO has 33 around the clock (US$6).

Cancún – 320 km, four to six hours; Oriente has hourly buses from 5:15 am to 12:15 am (US$7); ATS runs buses hourly from 4 am to midnight (US$7); ADO has 21 luxury buses daily (US$8.75); and UNO has morning and evening super-luxury buses for US$11.

Celestún – 95 km, 1½ to two hours, US$1.75; 12 buses from 5 am to 8 pm, departing from the Unión de Camioneros de Yucatán terminal, on Calle 71 between Calles 62 and 64, then stopping at the Autotrans-portes del Sur terminal at Calle 50 No 531, at Calle 67.

Chetumal – 456 km, eight hours; luxury Caribe has buses at 12:30, 9 and 10:30 pm (US$13); LD and Mayab have buses for less.

Chichén Itzá – 116 km, 2½ hours, US$2.75 to US$3.50, 10 buses; those by Oriente stop right at the Chichén ruins. A special roundtrip excursion bus by Oriente (US$6.75) departs from Mérida at 8:45 am and returns from Chichén Itzá at 3 pm.

YUCATÁN

Dzibilchaltún – 15 km, 30 minutes, US$0.55; minibuses and jitney taxis depart when full from the Parque de San Juan (see listing, above), on Calle 69 between Calles 62 and 64, and go all the way to the ruins; the alternative is a bus from the Progreso terminal that drops you on the highway at the Dzibilchaltún access road, five km west of the ruins.

Felipe Carrillo Puerto – 310 km, 5½ to six hours; Caribe, LD and Mayab run buses (US$6.50 to US$8); see Chetumal, above.

Izamal – 72 km, 1½ hours, US$1; 20 Oriente runs buses from its terminal at Calle 50 between Calles 65 and 67.

Kabah -101 km, two hours, US$2; buses on the 'Chenes', or inland, route between Mérida and Campeche may stop at Kabah on request.

Mexico City – 1550 km, 20 hours; ADO runs five buses (US$45).

Palenque – 556 km, nine or 10 hours; two each (morning and evening) by ATS (US$15) and ADO (US$16.50) go directly to Palenque; many more drop you at Catazajá, the main highway junction 27 km north of Palenque town. From Catazajá you can hitchhike or catch a bus or jitney to Palenque.

Playa del Carmen – 385 km, seven hours; ADO runs nine buses (US$10 to US$11.75); ATS runs several others (US$8), as does Mayab (US$10).

Progreso – 33 km, 45 minutes, US$0.70; Autoprogreso buses run every six minutes from 5 am to 9:45 pm from the Progreso bus terminal, at Calle 62 No 524, between Calles 65 and 67, 1½ blocks south of the Plaza Mayor.

Ticul – 85 km, 1½ hours, US$2; Mayab runs frequent buses, or you can take a minibus from the Parque de San Juan (see listing, above).

Tizimin – 210 km, four hours, US$3.75; Oriente and ATS have a few buses daily, or take a bus to Valladolid and change there for Tizimin.

Tulum – 320 km, five hours via Cobá or seven hours via Cancún; Oriente (US$7) and ADO (US$8.25) have a few buses.

Tuxtla Gutiérrez – 995 km, 14 hours; Colón runs three buses (US$25), or change at Palenque or Villahermosa.

Uxmal – 80 km, 1½ hours; six by ATS, including two special excursions. The Ruta Puuc excursion (US$4.50) departs from Mérida's old Terminal de Autobuses at 8 am and goes to Uxmal, Kabah and several other sites, departing Uxmal on the return journey to

Mérida at 2:30 pm. The sound-and-light excursion (US$3.75) departs Mérida at 6:15 pm and Uxmal at 10 pm.

Valladolid – 160 km, three hours, US$5; ADO, Oriente and ATS, as well as other companies, run many buses; see the Cancún listing.

Villahermosa – 700 km, nine hours; ADO (US$20) runs 10 buses, UNO (US$32) one; ATS (US$16) has several buses as well.

If you take an all-night bus, don't put anything valuable in the overhead racks, as there have been several reports of gear being stolen at night.

Train
Buses are preferable to trains, because they are faster and safer. Rail robberies in some areas (between Mérida, Campeche and Palenque in particular) have reached epidemic proportions. There are no *dormitorios* (sleeping compartments) to lock on trains traveling this route – just vulnerable 1st- and 2nd-class seating.

If you really want to ride a Yucatecan train, sign up for the special excursion by train from Mérida to Izamal; see the Izamal section in the previous chapter for details.

If you still want to get between Mérida and other points by rail, a train with no diner departs at midnight for Campeche, Palenque and ultimately Mexico City (two days' journey). The station is on Calle 55 between Calles 46 and 48, about nine blocks northeast of the main plaza. Tickets should be bought several hours in advance.

Car
Rental car is the optimal way to tour the many archeological sites south of Mérida, especially if you have two or more people to share costs.

Assume you will pay a total of US$40 to US$60 per day (tax, insurance and gas included) for the cheapest car offered, usually a bottom-of-the-line Volkswagen or Nissan.

Mexico Rent a Car (☎ /fax (99) 27-49-16, 23-36-37), Calle 62 No 483-E, between Calles 59 and 57, owned and operated by Alvaro and Teresa Alonzo and their children, offers good service and value. The Alonzos also have a desk on Calle 60 at the parking lot entrance next to the Hotel del Parque, just north of the Parque Hidalgo. Several friends of mine have rented from them for years with no complaints.

Several other car rental companies have offices on Calle 60 just north of the Teatro Peón Contreras:

Dollar Rent A Car, Calle 60 No 491, between Calles 55 and 57 (☎ (99) 28-67-59, in Mexico (91-800) 90010, fax (99) 25-01-55)

Hertz Rent a Car, Calle 60 No 486-D, between Calles 55 and 57 (☎ (99) 24-28-34, in Mexico (95-800) 654-3030, fax (99) 84-01-14)

National Car Rental, Calle 60 No 486-F, between Calles 55 and 57 (☎ (99) 28-63-08, in Mexico (91-800) 00395)

GETTING AROUND
To/From the Airport

Bus 79 ('Aviación') travels infrequently between the airport and city center for US$0.40. Most arriving travelers use the Transporte Terrestre taxis to go from the airport to the center (US$9.50). A normal taxi from the Plaza Mayor to the airport costs US$6.50.

Bus

Most parts of Mérida that you'll want to visit are within five or six blocks of the Plaza Mayor and are thus accessible on foot. Given the slow speed of city traffic, particularly in the market areas, travel on foot is also the fastest way to get around.

City buses are cheap, at US$0.20 per ride (US$0.25 in a minibus), but routes are confusing. Most routes start in suburban neighborhoods, meander through the city center, and terminate in another distant suburban neighborhood.

To travel between the Plaza Mayor and the upscale neighborhoods to the north along Paseo de Montejo, catch a 'Tecnológico' bus or minibus on Calle 60 and get out at Avenida Colón; to return to the city center, catch almost any bus – such as the López Mateos or Chedraui – along Paseo de Montejo.

The bus system is supplemented by minibus jitneys, which are easier to use, as they run shorter and more comprehensible routes. The minibus (colectivo) you're liable to find most useful is the Ruta 10 (US$0.35), which departs from the corner of Calles 58 and 59, half a block east of the Parque Hidalgo, and travels along the Paseo de Montejo to Itzamná.

To walk from CAME to the Plaza Mayor, exit the terminal, turn left, then right onto Calle 69; the old Terminal de Autobuses will be on your right. Walk straight along Calle 69 for four blocks, passing the Church of San Juan de Dios and a park, to Calle 62. Turn left on Calle 62 and walk the remaining three blocks north to the plaza.

Taxi

Most taxi rides within the city center, including from the CAME bus terminal to the Plaza Mayor and from the Plaza Mayor to the Holiday Inn or Hyatt, off Paseo de Montejo, should cost around US$1.50 to US$2. A taxi to the airport costs US$6.50.

Around Mérida

The region around Mérida is the heartland of late Mayan civilization, abounding in ancient ruins, colonial towns, traditional crafts and even some beaches. Using Mérida as your base you can see many of the wonders of Yucatán on day trips, or you can stay the night at most of the sites worth visiting.

Mérida's heat can be oppressive, even in the winter. When it gets too hot, and especially on hot weekends, Mérida's citizens flock to the beaches at Progreso, 33 km north of the city. Along the way you might want to stop at the ruined city of Dzibilchaltún. Besides an interesting ruin or two, the site boasts a cool, clear cenote for swimming.

DZIBILCHALTÚN

This was the longest continuously used Mayan administrative and ceremonial city,

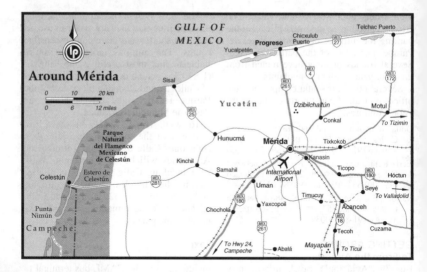

serving the Maya from 1500 BC or earlier until the European conquest in the 1540s. At the height of its greatness Dzibilchaltún covered 80 sq km. Archaeological research in the 1960s mapped 31 sq km of the city, revealing some 8500 structures.

Though the site itself is far less exciting today than Chichén Itzá or Uxmal is, there is a fine museum, the interesting little Temple of the Seven Dolls, and the cenote swimming pool.

Dzibilchaltún (Place of Inscribed Flat Stones) is a large site, open from 8 am to 5 pm every day for US$3, but the museum is closed Monday. Parking costs US$0.75; there's a US$4 fee for use of a video camera.

You enter the site along a nature trail that terminates at the modern, air-conditioned Museo del Pueblo Maya, featuring artifacts from throughout the Mexican-Mayan region. Exhibits explaining Mayan daily life and beliefs from ancient times until the present are in Spanish and English.

Beyond the museum, a path leads to the central plaza, where stands an open chapel dating from the time of the conquistadors (1590-1600).

The Temple of the Seven Dolls, which

got its name from seven grotesque dolls discovered here during excavations, is a one-km walk from the central plaza. As you approach the temple take note, while you're still a good distance away, that you can see right through the building's doors and windows on the east-west axis, but when you move closer this view is lost. The temple's construction is such that you can't see through from north to south at all. The rising and setting sun of the equinoxes 'lit up' the temple's windows and doors, making them blaze like beacons and signaling those important turning points in the year. Thus the temple is impressive not for its size or beauty, but for its precise astronomical orientation and its function in the Great Mayan Time Machine.

The Cenote Xlacah, now a public swimming pool, is over 40 meters deep. In 1958 an expedition sponsored by the US National Geographic Society sent divers down and recovered some 30,000 Mayan artifacts, many of ritual significance. The most interesting of them are displayed in the site's small but good museum. But enough history – plunge in and cool off!

Getting There & Away

Minibuses and jitney taxis depart frequently from Mérida's Parque de San Juan, on Calle 69 between Calles 62 and 64, for the village of Dzibilchaltún Ruinas (15 km, 30 minutes, US$0.55), only a little over one km from the museum.

Buses depart every 15 minutes from the Progreso bus terminal in Mérida, at Calle 62 No 524, between Calles 65 and 67, 1½ blocks south of the Plaza Mayor. These Progreso-bound buses drop you on the right (east) side of the highway, five km from the entrance to the archaeological site. From the site entrance, it's another 700 meters to the museum.

PROGRESO

Population 40,000

This is a seafarers' town, the port for Mérida and northwestern Yucatán. The Yucatecan limestone shelf declines so gradually into the sea here that a *muelle* (pier) 6.5 km long had to be built to reach the deep water and its ocean-going ships.

This same gradual slope of land into water affects Progreso's long beach: the waters are shallow, warm and safe from such dangers as rip tide and undertow, though usually murky with seaweed and swirling sand. The beach is nearly shadeless, having lost its palm trees to hurricanes. The few diminutive shelters are inadequate for the crowds, so you bake and burn. The beach at Yucalpetén, a 10-minute bus ride west, is much better.

Progreso is normally a sleepy town, but on weekends, especially in summer, it seems as if all of Mérida is here.

History

After the founding of Mérida, the conquistador Francisco de Montejo advised his son that a road should be built to the coast, facilitating the export of goods. The port of Sisal, southwest of Progreso, served that function until the middle of the 19th century, when its shallow harbor and distance from Mérida proved inadequate for the needs of the growing henequen industry.

In 1840 local leaders suggested the site of Progreso, but the War of the Castes delayed the project until 1872, when Progreso was established as a village. During the heyday of the henequen boom Progreso prospered as Yucatán's most prominent port. A new harbor is scheduled for construction in the hope that cruise ships will dock here and Progreso will once again prosper from sea trade, this time in live tourists.

Orientation

Progreso is long and narrow, stretched out along the seashore. If you want to move around the town and you don't have your own vehicle, you'll find yourself fighting the distances.

Though Progreso has an apparently logical street grid, it illogically is subject to two numbering systems that are 50 numbers apart. One system has the city center's streets numbered in the 60s, 70s and 80s, another has them in the 10s, 20s and 30s. Thus you might see a street sign on Calle 30 calling it Calle 80, or on a map Calle 10 might also be referred to as Calle 60. I've included both systems on the map.

The bus stations are near the main square. It's six short blocks from the main square to the waterfront boulevard, known as the Malecón, and the muelle.

Places to Stay

Progreso is looked on as a resort, if a modest one, so rooms here tend to be a bit more expensive than in other Yucatecan towns. On Sundays in July and August even the cheapest hotels fill up.

Hotel Miralmar (☎ (993) 5-05-52), Calle 77 No 124, at the corner of Calle 76, offers rooms with private shower, fan and one double bed for US$11, and with two beds for US$14. Rooms on the upper floor are preferable – they're not as dungeonlike as the ground-floor rooms.

Three blocks east, at the corner of Malecón and Calle 70, are two more hotels. *Tropical Suites* (☎ (993) 5-12-63) has tidy rooms with showers and fans going for US$18 to US$35 a double. Some rooms have sea views. *Hotel Real del Mar* (☎ (993) 5-07-98), between Calles 70 and 72 behind

GULF OF MEXICO

Progreso

PLACES TO STAY		OTHER	
2	Hotel Carismar	5	Centro de Salud
7	Hotel Real del Mar		(Medical Center)
8	Tropical Suites	10	Lighthouse, Park
15	Hotel Miralmar	11	Mercado Municipal
		13	IMSS Hospital
		14	Mérida Bus Station
PLACES TO EAT		17	TelMex Tower,
1	Sol y Mar		Ladatel Phones
3	Saint Bonnet	18	Local Bus Station
4	Las Rocas	19	Palacio Municipal
6	Restaurant	20	Iglesia de la Purísima
	Los Pelícanos		Concepción
9	Capitán Marisco	21	Post Office
12	Restaurant	22	Centro Médico
	Mary Doly		Americano
16	Restaurant	23	Tourism Office
	El Cordóbes		

the Restaurant Los Pelícanos, is an older hostelry that looks its age sometimes but is still a good deal, as it's right on the Malecón. Rooms with shower and fan cost US$11 a single, US$14 a double in one bed, US$15 a double in two beds, and US$18 a double with sea view.

Hotel Carismar (☎ (993) 5-29-07), Calle 71 No 151, between Calles 78 and 80, has cheap, uninspiring rooms for US$11/14 a single/double with bath.

Places to Eat

Seafood is the strong point on the menus of Progreso's restaurants. Note that if you come on a day trip to Progreso, you can often change clothes at the *vestidores* (changing cubicles) attached to most beachfront restaurants.

An all-purpose inexpensive eatery on the north side of the main square is *Restaurant El Cordóbes*, at the corner of Calles 81 and 80, open from early morning until late at night. Standard fare –

tacos, enchiladas, sandwiches, chicken, etc – is served cheap.

For cheap seafood you must avoid the Malecón and seek out the *Restaurant Mary Doly*, Calle 75 No 150, between Calles 74 and 76, a homey place with no sea view, but good food and low prices.

About the best prices you can find at an eatery on the Malecón are at *Las Rocas*, on the Malecón at Calle 78, a homey eatery where you can get a full fish dinner for about US$9, everything included. The popular *Sol y Mar* and *Saint Bonnet* are more upscale.

Moving eastward along the Malecón restaurant prices rise. *Restaurant Los Pelícanos*, on the Malecón at Calle 70 by the Hotel Real del Mar, is appealing, with its shady terrace, sea views and good menu at moderate prices.

At the eastern end of the Malecón between Calles 62 and 60, almost one km from the muelle, stands *Capitán Marisco* (☎ (993) 5-06-39), perhaps Progreso's fanciest seafood restaurant and certainly one of its most pleasant.

Getting There & Away

A fast four-lane highway continues north from Mérida's Paseo de Montejo to the Dzibilchaltún intersection (15 km, 30 minutes) and Progreso (33 km, 45 minutes).

Autoprogreso buses depart the Progreso bus terminal, 1½ blocks south of the main plaza in Mérida at Calle 62 No 524, between Calles 65 and 67, every six minutes from 5 am to 9:45 pm. The fare is US$0.70 one way, US$1.25 roundtrip.

CELESTÚN

Famed as a bird sanctuary, Celestún makes a good beach-and-bird day trip from Mérida. Although this region abounds in anhingas and egrets, most bird watchers come here to see the flamingos.

The town is on a spit of land between the Río Esperanza and the Gulf of Mexico and is cooled by brisk westerly sea breezes on most days. The white-sand beach is appealing, but on some days fierce afternoon winds swirl clouds of choking dust through town. The wind makes the sea surfy and silty and therefore unpleasant for swimming in the afternoon. Row upon row of fishing boats outfitted with twin long poles line the shore.

Given the winds, the best time to see birds is in the morning. You can hire a *lancha* (boat) from the bridge on the highway one km east of the town or from the beach 200 meters west of the main square and bus station. The rental should run to about US$20; a boat may take up to eight people at high tide, but perhaps only four at low tide, lest it run aground. The voyage to the flamingo area takes about 30 minutes; after another 30 minutes of viewing, the boat begins the voyage back to Celestún. Don't attempt to make the birds fly or let your boat approach too close to them.

Orientation

You come into town along Calle 11, past the marketplace and church (on your left/south) to Calle 12, the waterfront street.

Death of the Dinosaurs

North of Progreso, beneath the emerald-green water, lies the crater of Chicxulub (CHIK-shoo-LOOB).

In 1980 Nobel Prize laureate Luis Alvarez and some colleagues put forth the theory that the tremendous impact caused by an asteroid or small comet hitting the earth about 65 million years ago caused climatic changes so severe that they resulted in the extinction of the dinosaurs. In 1991 the huge Chicxulub crater – some 200 km in diameter, the largest yet discovered on Earth – was identified as the most likely candidate for the site of impact.

Numerous scientific expeditions have added to the evidence. Some scientists now believe that the celestial missile came in from the southwest at a low angle – about 30 degrees. If that is true, North American flora and fauna would have suffered the most from the impact.

In 1996 scientists found what they believe to be tiny pieces of the original meteor or comet. Work continues and will no doubt lend support to the contentions of many out-of-work nuclear-bomb-makers that the world needs a massive, well-funded effort to develop an enormous nuke to vaporize the next meteor that threatens to smack our planet. ■

Places to Stay

Hotels are few, and filled on weekends. A day trip from Mérida is the best way to visit, but you can try for a room at these places:

Turn left (south) along Calle 12 from Calle 11 to find the *Hotel Gutiérrez* (☎ (99) 28-04-19, 28-69-78), Calle 12 No 22, at Calle 13, the best budget choice, with well-kept rooms with fan and bath costing US$15. *Hotel María del Carmen*, just south of it, is similar; enter from Calle 15.

Turn right (north) from Calle 11 along Calle 12 to find the *Hotel San Julio* (☎ (99) 1-85-89), Calle 12 No 92, at Calle 9, where singles with fan and bath cost US$9 and doubles US$12.

Places to Eat

Celestún's specialty is crab claws and of

course fresh fish. The junction of Calles 11 and 12 has many small restaurants, including the *Celestún*, *Playita*, *Boya* and *Avila*, most with sea views. Locals in the know favor *La Palapa* (☎ (99) 62-004). The cheaper eateries, as always, are inland.

Getting There & Away

Buses start 12 times daily between 5 am and 8 pm from Mérida's Unión de Camioneros de Yucatán terminal, on Calle 71 between Calles 62 and 64, then stop at the Autotransportes del Sur station, on Calle 50 No 531, at Calle 67. To be assured of a seat, get on board at the terminal on Calle 71. The 95-km trip takes about 1½ to two hours and costs US$1.75.

Cultur (☎ (99) 24-96-77), the cultural department of the Yucatán state government, organizes minibus tours to Celestún every Wednesday, Friday and Sunday, departing Mérida's Parque de Santa Lucia at 9 am, returning by 4:30 pm. Ask at your hotel or any travel agency.

Hacienda Teya

The *casa principal* (main house) at the Hacienda San Ildefonso Teya (☎ (99) 28-50-00, fax (99) 28-18-89), 13 km east of Mérida on the Chichén Itzá road, was built in 1683 with its own chapel. More than three centuries have passed, and the grand house and lush gardens look better than ever.

The elegant Casa de Maquinas (Machinery House), facing the main house, was built in 1905 to harbor the high-tech of its day: an oily assemblage of engines, gears, pulleys and belts, which worked harder than the hacienda's oppressed peasantry at processing henequen.

Today the ground floor of the Hacienda Teya houses the elegant *Restaurant La Cava*, serving Yucatecan cuisine from noon to 6 pm daily. The specialty is a stone platter bearing an assortment of Yucatecan specialties for US$10.

Upstairs are a handful of period rooms for guests, updated with air-con, whirlpool baths and minibars and priced at US$50 to US$65 double.

Another fine old hacienda, the Hacienda Katanchel, near San Bernardino on the Mérida-Chichén Itzá road, is also being restored and may be open by the time you arrive.

Uxmal & the Puuc Route

La Ruta Maya runs southward from Mérida, penetrating a region rich in ancient Mayan sites that have been restored and made accessible to the public. The towns of this region - Acanceh, Ticul and Oxkutzcab - provide views of how the Maya live today.

You cannot possibly visit all of these towns and ruins in a day trip from Mérida. Uxmal alone deserves most of a day, the Puuc Route sites another day. If time is short, go to Uxmal and Kabah. Otherwise, plan to stay overnight for at least one or two nights along the way. Lodgings at Uxmal are expensive; those in Ticul are not.

Ticul is well known as the place to get excellent local handicrafts, as well as being a good stopover on the way to Campeche.

After exploring the archaeological wealth of this area head south past Bolonchén de Rejón and Hopelchén to Cayal and the

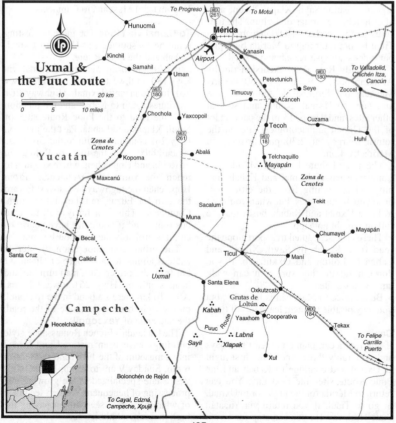

turnoff for the ruins of Edzná and finally to Campeche. If your goal is the Caribbean Coast, go southeast from Ticul and Oxkutzcab to Felipe Carrillo Puerto, then north to the coast or south to Chetumal and Belize. Alternatively, take the road, now fully paved, south from Hopelchén to Xpujil.

GETTING AROUND
Bus
Though hardly ideal, there is some bus service to Puuc Route sites.

Cultur (☎ (99) 24-96-77), the cultural department of the Yucatán state government, organizes Puuc Route tours every day, departing Mérida's Parque Santa Lucia at 9 am, visiting Sayil, Xlapak, Labná and, after lunch, the Grutas de Loltún. The tour stops at the market in Oxkutzcab and in Ticul before returning to Mérida by 7 pm, but it does not visit Kabah and Uxmal.

The daily Ruta Puuc excursion run by Autotransportes del Sur (US$4.50) departs Mérida's old Terminal de Autobuses at 8 am, goes to Uxmal, Kabah and several other sites, and departs from the parking lot of the Uxmal archaeological site on the return journey at 2:30 pm, arriving in Mérida by 4 pm.

The inland route between Mérida and Campeche passes Uxmal and Kabah, and most buses coming from the cities will drop you at those sites; but when you want to leave Uxmal and Kabah, buses may be full and might not stop.

There is no scheduled transport along the road from Kabah by Sayil, Xlapak and Labná to Loltún and Oxkutzcab. If you don't mind the hot sun, you can walk among those sites.

Bus service to Mayapán is irregular, but you may be able to hitch; leave lots of time.

Car
If you rent a car, plan on at least two days and preferably three. Spend the first night at Uxmal and continue to Kabah and the Puuc Route sites the next day. You can return to Mérida for the night, or to Uxmal, or go to Ticul. If you return via Yucatán State Highway 18, you can stop for a visit

to the ruins of Mayapán and a look at the pyramid in Acanceh. Those going directly to Campeche should take the shorter, faster route via Hwy 180.

There are three routes between Mérida and Campeche: the fastest and westernmost route, straight to Campeche on Hwy 180; the central route, which takes you to the Uxmal ruins via the town of Muna; and the easternmost route, which takes you to the ruins at Mayapán via the town of Acanceh.

Fast Road to Campeche The westernmost route leaves Mérida by Avenida de los Itzaes, passes the airport and travels through the towns of Uman, Chochola, Kopoma and Maxcaná to Campeche.

To Uxmal via Muna The more interesting route heads southeast at Uman to Uxmal, Kabah and the Puuc Route.

It's 78 km from Mérida to Uxmal via Hwy 180 southwest to Uman and then Hwy 261 to Muna and Uxmal. Highway 261 continues south to Kabah and the junction with the road to the Puuc Route sites of Sayil, Xlapak and Labná. Past the junction Hwy 261 continues south to the Grutas de Xtacumbilxunaan, the town of Bolonchén de Rejón and Hopelchén, where you turn to reach the ruins of Dzibalchén. From Hopelchén the highway heads west toward the turn for Edzná and, beyond the turn, Campeche. This is a fairly well-traveled bus route, and if you don't have your own car, it is probably the way you'll come.

The urban conglomeration of Mérida extends almost to the suburb of Uman, 17 km from the center. At Uman turn left and head south on Hwy 261 toward Muna. After 16 km there's a bend in the road and, on the right-hand (west) side of the road, the hacienda of **Yaxcopoil**.

The hacienda's French Renaissance-style buildings have been restored and turned into a museum of the 17th century (8 am to 6 pm, Sunday 9 am to 1 pm, US$5). This vast estate specialized in the growing and processing of henequen. You can see much of what there is to see without paying the high museum admission fee.

Twenty-nine km south of Yaxcopoil is **Muna**, an old town with several interesting colonial churches, including the former Convento de la Asunción and the churches of Santa María, San Mateo and San Andrés. Another 16 km south of Muna is Uxmal; the highway passes the Hotel Misión Uxmal on the right and comes to the Hotel Hacienda Uxmal. Just across the highway from the hotel is the short entrance road (400 meters) to the ruins.

To Ticul via Acanceh The third, eastern-most route south goes via Acanceh and the ruins of the old Mayan capital city of Mayapán before reaching Ticul. Take Yucatán State Highway 18 southeast via Kanasin, Acanceh and Tecoh to Mayapán, then on to the provincial town of Ticul, which has several inexpensive hotels. From Ticul you can go directly to Uxmal via Muna or go southeast to Oxkutzcab, then west to the Grutas de Loltún and the Puuc Route sites of Labná, Xlapak, Sayil and Kabah before heading north and west to Uxmal. Transport on this route is much more difficult without your own car. It might take the better part of a day to get from Mérida via the ruins of Mayapán to Ticul by bus. If you take this route you miss a visit to the hacienda of Yaxcopoil, but you get to see the ruins at Acanceh and Mayapán instead.

UXMAL

In 1840 the American explorer John L Stephens stood atop the Pyramid of the Magician at Uxmal (oosh-MAHL) and surveyed the ruins:

From its front doorway I counted sixteen elevations, with broken walls and mounds of stones and vast, magnificent edifices, which at that distance seemed untouched by time and defying ruin. I stood in the doorway when the sun went down, throwing from the buildings a prodigious breadth of shadow, darkening the terraces on which they stood and presenting a scene strange enough for a work of enchantment.

He later wrote about them in his book *Incidents of Travel in Central America, Chiapas & Yucatan*. Only Chichén Itzá and Tikal present as magnificent a picture as Uxmal.

History

Set in the Puuc Hills, which lent their name to the architectural patterns in this region, Uxmal was an important city during the Late Classic period (600-900 AD) of a region that encompassed the satellite towns of Sayil, Kabah, Xlapak and Labná. Although Uxmal means 'Thrice Built' in Mayan, it was actually reconstructed five times.

That a sizable population flourished at all in this area is a mystery, as there is precious little water in the region. The Maya built a series of reservoirs and cisterns *(chultunes)* lined with lime mortar to catch and hold water during the dry season, and they must have been adequate.

First occupied in about 600 AD, Uxmal was influenced by highland Mexico in its architecture, most likely through contact fostered by trade. This influence is reflected in the town's serpent imagery, phallic symbols and columns. The well-proportioned Puuc architecture, with its intricate, geometric mosaics sweeping across the upper parts of elongated facades, is unique to this region.

Given the scarcity of water in the Puuc Hills, Chac, the rain god or sky serpent, was of great significance. His image is ubiquitous here in the form of monsterlike stucco masks protruding from facades and cornices.

There is much speculation as to why Uxmal was abandoned in about 900 AD. Drought conditions may have reached such proportions that the inhabitants had to relocate. One widely held theory suggests that the rise to greatness of Chichén Itzá drew people away from the Puuc Hills.

The first written account of Uxmal by a European came from the quill of the priest López de Cogullado in the 16th century. Thinking of Spanish convents, he referred to one building as the residence of Mayan virgins or nuns. The temple to this day is called the Nunnery Quadrangle.

The next influential European account of the site was written by Count de Waldeck in 1836 (see Palenque, in the Chiapas chapter). In the hope of selling his work,

YUCATÁN

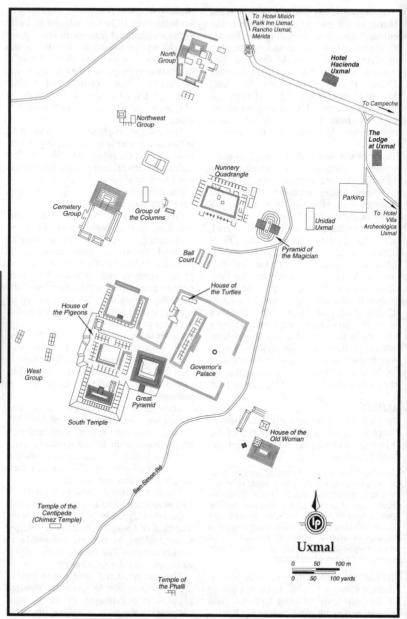

YUCATÁN

Uxmal

| 0 | 50 | 100 m |
| 0 | 50 | 100 yards |

the Count made Uxmal sound like a Mediterranean ruin. Fortunately, misconceptions generated by Count de Waldeck were corrected by the great American archaeologist John L Stephens and his British illustrator, Frederick Catherwood, who wrote about and drew the site with accuracy.

Uxmal was excavated in 1929 by Frans Blom. His was the first modern excavation and paved the way for others. Although much has been restored, there is still a good deal to discover.

Orientation & Information

As you come into the site from the highway the big new hotel called Lodge at Uxmal is on the left, with the Hotel Villa Arqueológica beyond it; the site parking lot is to the right (US$0.75 per car).

You enter the site through the modern Unidad Uxmal building, which holds the air-conditioned Restaurant Yax-Beh. Also in the Unidad Uxmal are a small museum, shops selling souvenirs and crafts, the auditorium Kit Bolon Tun and the bathrooms. The Librería Dante has a good selection of travel and archaeological guides in English, Spanish, German and French, though imported books are very expensive.

The archaeological site at Uxmal is open daily from 8 am to 5 pm; admission costs US$5, free on Sunday. The Unidad Uxmal building stays open till 10 pm because of the 45-minute Luz y Sonido (Light & Sound) show, held each evening in English at 9 pm (US$5.50) and in Spanish at 8 pm (US$4).

If you come for the day and want to stay for the evening sound-and-light show, plan to have dinner and a swim at one of the restaurants; most hotels allow restaurant patrons to use their pools.

As you pass through the turnstile and climb the slope to the ruins, the rear of the Pyramid of the Magician comes into view.

Pyramid of the Magician

This tall temple, 39 meters high, was built on an oval base. The smoothly sloping sides have been restored; they date from the

temple's fifth incarnation. The four earlier temples were covered in the rebuilding, except for the high doorway on the west side, which remains from the fourth temple. Decorated in elaborate Chenes style (which originated farther south and takes its name from the many natural wells there), the doorway proper takes the form of the mouth of a gigantic Chac mask.

The ascent to the doorway and the top is best done from the west side. Heavy chains serve as handrails to help you up the steep steps. Queen Elizabeth II ascended this way in 1974, during a rainstorm. The plucky British monarch seemed to have no trouble getting to the top - an attendant held an umbrella for her as she climbed.

At this point in every guidebook covering Uxmal it is customary to recount the legend of the pyramid's construction and how it got its other name, the House of the Dwarf, so here goes:

There was a childless old woman who lived in a hut on the very spot now occupied by the pyramid. In her distress she took an egg, covered it with a cloth and laid it away carefully. Every day she went to look at it, until one morning she found the egg hatched and a creature born. The old woman called it her son and took good care of it, so that in one year it walked and talked like a man, but it also had stopped growing. The old woman was more delighted than ever and said he would be a great lord or king.

One day she told him to go to the governor and challenge him to a trial of strength. Any feat of strength the governor performed, the dwarf did just as well, striking a blow to the governor's manhood. In exasperation the governor ordered the dwarf to build a house higher than any other and to do it in one night, or else the dwarf would be put to death. The dwarf complied and the pyramid was the result. In a last test of strength the governor and the dwarf beat one another over the head with heavy clubs. Guess who won and became the new governor?

So there's the legend, adapted from John L Stephens, who wrote, 'I received it from the lips of an Indian'.

From the top of the pyramid, survey the rest of the archaeological site. Directly west of the pyramid is the Nunnery Quadrangle. On the south side of the quadrangle,

YUCATÁN

down a short slope, is a ruined ball court. Further south stands the great artificial terrace holding the Governor's Palace; between the palace and the ball court is the small House of the Turtles. Beyond the Governor's Palace and not really visible from the pyramid are remains of the Great Pyramid, and next to that are the House of the Pigeons and the South Temple. There are many other structures at Uxmal, but most have been recaptured by the jungle and are now just verdant mounds.

Nunnery Quadrangle

Archaeologists have not yet deciphered what this 74-room quadrangle was used for, but they guess that it might have been a military academy, royal school or palace complex. The long-nosed face of Chac appears everywhere on the facades of the four separate temples that form the quadrangle. The northern temple, grandest of the four, was built first, followed by the southern, then the eastern and then the western.

Several decorative elements on the facades show signs of Mexican, perhaps Totonac, influence. The feathered serpent (Quetzalcóatl) motif along the top of the west temple's facade is one of them. Note also the stylized depictions of the *na* (Mayan thatched hut) over some of the doorways in the northern building. The na motif alternates with stacks of Chac masks over the doors. Similar na depictions are over the doors of the southern building as well.

Ball Court

Pass through the corbeled arch in the middle of the south building of the quadrangle and continue down the slope to the ball court, which is much less impressive than the great ball court at Chichén Itzá.

House of the Turtles

Climb the steep slope up to the artificial terrace on which stands the Governor's Palace. At the top of the climb, on the right, is the House of the Turtles, which takes its name from the turtles carved on the cornice. The frieze of short columns, or

'rolled mats', that runs around the top of the temple is characteristic of the Puuc style. Turtles were associated by the Maya with the rain god, Chac. According to Mayan myth, when the people suffered from drought so did the turtles, and both prayed to Chac to send rain.

Governor's Palace

When Stephens laid eyes on the Governor's Palace he wrote:

There is no rudeness or barbarity in the design or proportions; on the contrary, the whole wears an air of architectural symmetry and grandeur; and as the stranger ascends the steps and casts a bewildered eye along its open and desolate doors, it is hard to believe that he sees before him the work of a race in whose epitaph, as written by historians, they are called ignorant of art . . . If it stood . . . in Hyde Park or the Garden of the Tuileries, it would form a new order . . . not unworthy to stand side by side with the remains of Egyptian, Grecian and Roman art.

The magnificent facade of the palace, nearly 100 meters long, has been called 'the finest structure at Uxmal and the culmination of the Puuc style' by Mayanist Michael D Coe. Buildings in Puuc style have walls filled with rubble, faced with cement and then covered in a thin veneer of limestone squares; the lower part of the facade is plain, the upper part festooned with stylized Chac faces and geometric designs, often latticelike or fretted. Other elements of Puuc style are decorated cornices, rows of half-columns (as in the House of the Turtles) and round columns in doorways (as in the palace at Sayil). The stones forming the corbeled vaults in Puuc style are shaped like boots.

Great Pyramid

Adjacent to the Governor's Palace, this 32-meter mound has been restored only on the northern side. There is a quadrangle at the top which archaeologists theorize was largely destroyed in order to construct another pyramid above it. That work, for reasons unknown, was never completed. At the top are some stucco carvings of Chac, birds and flowers.

Top: Cancún, Yucatán, Mexico (TB)
Left: Ferry to Isla Mujeres, Yucatán, Mexico (GE)
Right: Chichén Itzá, Yucatán, Mexico (GE)

Top: Convento de San Antonio de Padua, Izamal, Yucatán, Mexico (TB)
Left: Colonial House, Mérida, Yucatán, Mexico (GE)
Right: Religious wares, Mérida, Yucatán, Mexico (GE)

House of the Pigeons

West of the great pyramid sits a structure whose roofcomb is latticed with a pigeon-hole pattern - hence the building's name. The nine honeycombed triangular belfries sit on top of a building that was once part of a quadrangle. The base is so eroded that it is hard for archaeologists to guess its function.

Places to Stay - budget

As there is no town, not even a village, at Uxmal - only the archaeological site and several top-end hotels - you cannot depend on finding cheap food or lodging.

Campers can pitch their tents five km north of the ruins on Hwy 261, the road to Mérida, at *Rancho Uxmal* (☎ (99) 47-80-21) for US$2.50 per person. The *Parador Turístico Cana Nah*, next door, has a 'trailer park' camping lot as well.

Rancho Uxmal has 28 basic, serviceable guestrooms with shower and fan for US$25 a double - expensive for what you get, but this is Uxmal. It also has a restaurant. It may take you 45 to 55 minutes to walk there from the ruins - in the hot sun - but there's some possibility of hitching a ride.

Other than the Rancho Uxmal, there's no cheap lodging in the area. If you don't want to return to Mérida for the night, make your way to Ticul.

Places to Stay - top end

Mayaland Resorts' *Hotel Hacienda Uxmal* (☎ (99) 23-02-75, fax (99) 23-47-44, in the USA (800) 235-4079), 500 meters from the ruins across the highway, originally housed the archaeologists who explored and restored Uxmal. High ceilings with fans, good cross-ventilation and wide, tiled verandahs set with rocking chairs make this an exceptionally pleasant and comfortable place to stay. The beautiful swimming pool is a dream come true on a sweltering day.

Simple rooms in the annex cost US$38 a single or double; the nicer rooms in the main building range from US$50 to US$90 a single, US$60 to US$100 a double. You supposedly can make reservations in Mérida at the Mérida Travel Service in the Hotel Casa del Balam (☎ (99) 24-88-44), at the corner of Calles 60 and 57, but they seem not to know the correct room prices and have always told me the hotel is full, even if it isn't.

The Lodge at Uxmal (☎ (99) 23-02-75, fax (99) 23-47-44, in the USA (800) 235-4079), another Mayaland Resort, just opposite the entrance to the Unidad Uxmal and the archaeological site, is Uxmal's newest, most luxurious hotel and the closest one to the ruins. Air-con rooms with all the comforts cost US$94/111 a single/double.

Chac mask on corner of building, Uxmal

Hotel Villa Arqueológica Uxmal (in Mérida ☎ /fax (99) 28-06-44, Apdo Postal 449), run by Club Med, is an attractive modern hotel with swimming pool, tennis courts and air-con guestrooms for US$45/55/65 a single/double/triple.

The *Hotel Misión Park Inn Uxmal* (☎ / fax (99) 24-73-08) is set on a hilltop two km north of the turnoff to the ruins. Many rooms have balcony views of Uxmal, but they are overpriced at US$75 a single or double.

Places to Eat
The *Salon Nicté-Ha*, just across the highway from the road to the ruins, on the grounds of the Hotel Hacienda Uxmal, is an informal air-con restaurant open from 1 to 8:30 pm daily, offering sandwiches (US$3.75 to US$4.50), fruit salads and similar fare at prices higher than those at the Yax-Beh, the restaurant in the Unidad Uxmal building. The beer is cold. There's a swimming pool for restaurant patrons.

The *Hotel Hacienda Uxmal* itself serves unremarkable, moderately priced meals. The restaurant at Club Med's *Hotel Villa Arqueológica Uxmal* serves good, French-inspired meals.

Getting There & Away
Air An airstrip is under construction near Uxmal. When it is finished routes from Cancún will be developed, making it possible for Cancúnites to visit Uxmal on a day excursion.

Bus From Mérida it's 80 km (1½ hours) to Uxmal. See Bus Routes in the Getting There & Away section of the Mérida chapter for details.

If you're going to Ticul, hop on a bus heading north, get off at Muna and get another bus eastward to Ticul.

For buses to Kabah, the Puuc Route turnoff and points on the road to Campeche, flag down a bus on Hwy 261 at the turnoff to the ruins.

Tour agencies in Mérida operate guided tours to Uxmal and Kabah for US$20 to US$25 per person; evening excursions for the sound-and-light show cost the same.

PUUC ROUTE
The ruins at Kabah, Sayil, Xlapak, Labná and the Grutas de Loltún offer a deeper acquaintance with the Puuc Mayan civilization. The Palace of Masks at Kabah and El Palacio at Sayil are really worth seeing, and if you're not prepared to make the rounds of all the Puuc sites I'd suggest that you visit at least these two. The Grutas de Loltún (Loltún Caves) are also impressive, especially if you enjoy visiting cool caves. You can then continue to Oxkutzcab and Ticul if you like.

See the Kabah and Uxmal entries under Bus Routes in Getting There & Away in the Mérida chapter for details on transportation. If you make this excursion on Sunday, you will enjoy free admission to the archaeological sites.

Kabah
Heading southeast from Uxmal on Hwy 261, 15 km brings you to Santa Elena, with its huge church on a hill looming over the village. The highway turns south here, and another 3.5 km brings you to the Zona Arqueológica Puuc and the ruins of Kabah. The highway passes right through the middle of the site, which is open from 8 am to 5 pm. Admission costs US$2, free on Sunday.

The temples here are under restoration, which will make them doubly impressive. Cold drinks and snacks are available.

Palace of Masks The Palace of Masks, set on its own high terrace, is truly an amazing sight, its facade covered with nearly 300 masks of Chac. Unlike other Puuc buildings, the lower part of this facade is not severely plain; the decoration of masks extends from the base of the building all the way to the top. So Chacified is the facade that you enter some of the rooms by stepping on a Chac mask's hooked nose! Each of these mosaic masks consists of more than two dozen carved stones. The temple is unusual in having several series of rooms with both front and back chambers.

At the back of the palace is a restored doorway surmounted by two Atlantean figures. The roofcomb has also been restored.

The temple's Mayan name, Codz Pop (Rolled Mat), is explained in various ways by archaeologists and travel writers, none of them convincing. John L Stephens wrote:

To many of these structures the Indians have given names stupid, senseless and unmeaning, having no reference to history or tradition. This one they call Xcocpoop, which means in Spanish petato doblado, or a straw hat doubled up; the name having reference to the crushed and flattened condition of the facade and the prostration of the rear wall of the building.

Other Kabah Ruins To the north of the Palace of Masks is a small pyramid. Behind and to the left of the Palace of Masks is **El Palacio**, with a broad facade having several doorways; in the center of each doorway is a column, a characteristic of the Puuc architectural style. El Palacio at Sayil is somewhat similar in design, but much larger and grander.

Walk around the northern side of El Palacio and follow a path to the **Temple of Columns**, called by John L Stephens the Tercera Casa, famous for the rows of semi-columns on the upper part of its facade. The effect is similar to that on the House of the Turtles at Uxmal, but this temple is much larger and grander, with lots more columns.

Cross the highway, walk up the slope and on your right you'll pass a high mound of stones that was once the **Gran Teocalli** (Great Temple). Continue straight on to the *sacbé,* (cobbled elevated ceremonial road) and look to the right to see a monumental arch with the Mayan corbeled vault (two straight stone surfaces leaned against one another, meeting at the top). This arch is ruined; the one at Labná is in much better condition. It is said that the sacbé here runs past the arch and through the jungle all the way to Uxmal, terminating at a smaller

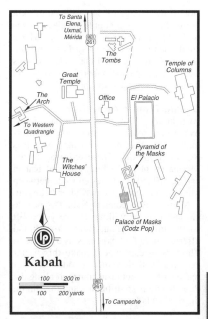

Kabah

0   100   200 m
0   100   200 yards

To Campeche

YUCATÁN

arch; in the other direction it went to Labná. Once all of Yucatán was connected by these marvelous 'white roads' of rough limestone.

Beyond the sacbé, about 600 meters farther from the road, are several other complexes of buildings, none as impressive as what you've already seen. The **Cuadrángulo del Oeste** (Western Quadrangle) has some decoration of columns and masks. North of the quadrangle are the **Temple of the Key Patterns** and the **Temple of Lintels**; the latter had intricately carved lintels of tough sapodilla wood. John L Stephens had them removed and shipped to New York for 'safekeeping', where they were destroyed in a fire shortly after their arrival. Luckily, Stephens' assistant, Frederick Catherwood, had made detailed drawings of the lintels before they were shipped.

Places to Stay   The quiet, well-kept *Camping Sacbé* (no phone), on the south side of the village of Santa Elena, 3.5 km north of Kabah, has simple but clean rooms with shared bath for US$8 to US$10 a single or double; one room has a private shower. Camping amid the orchards costs US$2.50 per person. Good breakfasts and dinners are served at low prices.

Getting There & Away Kabah is 101 km (two hours, US$2) from Mérida, or just over 18 km south of Uxmal. For bus information, see Kabah and Uxmal under Bus Routes in Getting There & Away in the Mérida chapter. Catching buses at Kabah can be difficult, as buses en route between Mérida and Campeche may already be full.

Many visitors come to Kabah by private car and may be willing to give you a lift southward on the Puuc Route. You should offer to share fuel expenses as a courtesy. Those with cars would make this writer very happy if they offered rides to other readers of this guide, as transport along the Puuc Route is so difficult - and the sun on the road so hot.

Sayil
Five km south of Kabah on Hwy 261 a road turns east: this is the Puuc Route. Despite the interesting archaeological sites along this route, there is not much traffic, and hitchhiking can be difficult. The ruins of Sayil are 4.5 km from the junction of the Puuc Route with Hwy 261, on the south side of the road. Sayil is open from 8 am to 5 pm daily; admission costs US$2, free on Sunday.

El Palacio Sayil is best known for El Palacio, the huge three-tiered building with a facade some 85 meters long that makes one think of the Minoan palaces on Crete. The distinctive columns of Puuc architecture are used here over and over as supports for the lintels, as decoration between doorways and as a frieze above the doorways, alternating with huge stylized Chac masks and 'descending gods'.

Climb to the top level of the Palacio and look to the north to see several chultunes

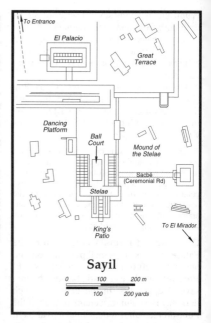

Sayil

(cisterns), in which precious rainwater was collected and stored for use during the dry season. Some of these chultunes can hold more than 30,000 liters.

If you visit the Palacio just before Easter, you can test a local superstition. John L Stephens, after his visit to Sayil (which he called Zayi), wrote that the Indians 'believed that the ancient buildings were haunted and, as in the remote region of Santa Cruz del Quiché, they said that on Good Friday of every year music was heard sounding among the ruins'.

El Mirador If you take the path southward from the palace for about 400 meters, you come to the temple named El Mirador, with its interesting roosterlike roofcomb once painted a bright red. About 100 meters beyond El Mirador by the path to the left is a stela beneath a protective palapa that bears a relief of a phallic god, now badly weathered.

Xlapak

From the entrance gate at Sayil it's six km to the entrance gate at Xlapak (shla-PAK). The name means Old Walls in Mayan and was a general term among local people for ancient ruins, about which they knew little. The site is open from 8 am to 5 pm; admission is US$1.50, free on Sunday.

The ornate palace at Xlapak is smaller than those at Kabah and Sayil, measuring only about 20 meters in length. It's decorated with the inevitable Chac masks, columns and colonnettes and fretted geometric latticework of the Puuc style. Immediately to the right is the rubble of what were once two smaller buildings.

If you hike along the remnant of an old 4WD road behind the palace, you may be rewarded with the sight of some brilliantly colored tropical birds. The long-tailed motmot, or clock bird, is here in good number.

Labná

From the entrance gate at Xlapak, it's 3.5 km to the gate at Labná. The site here is open from 8 am to 5 pm; admission costs US$2.

El Arco Labná is best known for its magnificent arch, once part of a building which separated two quadrangular courtyards. It now appears to be a gate joining two small plazas. The corbeled structure, three meters wide and six meters high, is well preserved and stands close to the entrance of Labná. The mosaic reliefs decorating the upper facade are exuberantly Puuc in style.

If you look at the ornate work on the northeastern side of the arch, you will make out mosaics of Mayan huts. At the base of either side of the arch are rooms of the adjoining building, now ruined, including upper lattice patterns constructed atop a serpentine design. Archaeologists believe a high roofcomb once sat over the fine arch and its flanking rooms.

El Mirador Standing on the opposite side of the arch and separated from it by the limestone-paved sacbé is a pyramid called

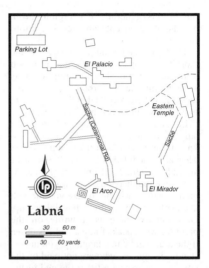

El Mirador, topped by a temple. The pyramid itself is poorly preserved, largely stone rubble. The temple, with its five-meter-high roofcomb, true to its name, looks like a watchtower. When John L Stephens saw El Mirador in 1840 it had a row of death's heads along the top and two lines of human figures beneath; over the center doorway was a colossal seated figure in high relief.

El Palacio The palace, the first edifice you come to at Labná, is connected by a sacbé to El Mirador and the arch. Though it is one of the longest buildings in the Puuc Hills, its design is not as impressive as that of its counterpart at Sayil. There's a relief in the eastern corner on the upper level of a serpent gripping a human head between its jaws. Close to this carving is a well-preserved Chac mask. At Labná's peak there were some 60 chultunes in and around the city.

Grutas de Loltún

From Labná it's 15 km eastward to the village of Yaaxhom, which is surrounded by lush orchards and palm groves, surprising in this generally dry region. From Yaaxhom a road goes another four km to Loltún.

The Grutas de Loltún (Loltún Caves), the most interesting caves in Yucatán, provided a treasure trove of data for archaeologists studying the Maya. Carbon dating of artifacts found here reveals that the caves were first used by humans some 2500 years ago.

Loltún is open from 9 am to 5 pm daily; admission costs US$4. To explore the 1.5-km labyrinth, you must take a guided tour. They are scheduled to begin at 9:30 and 11 am and at 12:30, 2 and 3 pm but may depart early if enough people are waiting. The guides may be willing to take you through at other hours if you offer a few dollars' tip. Occasionally there is a guide on the premises who speaks English - check to see if the tour will be in a language you understand. The guides, who are not paid by the government, expect a tip at the end of the hourlong tour.

For refreshments there's the *Restaurant El Guerrero* near the exit of the caves, a walk of eight to 10 minutes (600 meters) along a marked path from the far side of the parking lot near the cave entrance. Their comida corrida costs about US$7. Icy-cold drinks are served at high prices.

Getting There & Away Loltún is on a country road leading to Oxkutzcab (eight km away), and there is usually some transport along the road. Try hitchhiking, or catch a paying ride in one of the colectivos - often a pickup truck or *camión* - that ply this route, charging about US$0.50 for the ride. A taxi from Oxkutzcab may charge US$6 or so, one way, for the eight-km ride.

Buses run frequently every day between Mérida and Oxkutzcab via Ticul.

If you're driving from Loltún to the Puuc Route site of Labná, drive out of the Loltún parking lot, turn right and take the next road on the right, which passes the access road to the restaurant. Do not take the road marked for Xul. After four km you'll come to the village of Yaaxhom, where you turn right to join the Puuc Route westward.

UXMAL TO CAMPECHE
South of Uxmal and Kabah Hwy 261 leaves the Puuc Hills and heads straight for the border with the neighboring state of Campeche. There is little except jungle until, 31 km south of Uxmal, you pass beneath the great arch over the roadway that marks the border between the two Mexican states. For details on Bolonchén de Rejón, Hopelchén, Edzná and other points along the road to Campeche, see the Campeche chapter.

TICUL
Ticul, is a center for weaving of fine *huipiles*, traditional Mayan dresses with embroidered bodices. While you are here you can pay homage to the best Yucatecan cooking by dining at the original Restaurant Los Almendros, which has branches in Mérida and Cancún.

Ticul's main street is Calle 23, sometimes called the Calle Principal, going from the highway northeast past the market and the town's best restaurants to the main plaza.

Places to Stay - budget
Hotel Sierra Sosa (☎ (997) 2-00-08, fax (997) 2-02-82), Calle 26 No 199-A, half a block northwest of the plaza, has very basic rooms for US$9 a single/double with fan, US$12 with air-con. A few rooms at the back have windows, but most are dark and dungeonlike. Be sure the ceiling fan works.

Similarly basic but even cheaper is the *Hotel San Miguel* (☎ (997) 2-03-82), Calle 28 No 195, near Calle 23 and the market. Singles at the San Miguel cost US$5 with fan and bath, doubles US$6 to US$7.

Places to Stay - middle
Ticul's better hotels don't really offer too much more in the way of comfort, and both are on the highway on the outskirts of town, an inconvenient two-km walk from the center, but fine if you have a car.

Best in town is the *Hotel Las Bougambillias* (☎ (997) 2-07-61), Calle 23 No 291-A, near the junction of the western end of Calle 25 and the highway to Muna and

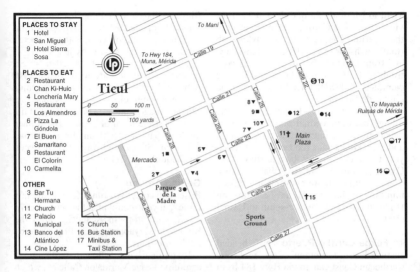

PLACES TO STAY
1 Hotel
  San Miguel
9 Hotel Sierra
  Sosa

PLACES TO EAT
2 Restaurant
  Chan Ki-Huic
4 Lonchería Mary
5 Restaurant
  Los Almendros
6 Pizza La
  Góndola
7 El Buen
  Samaritano
8 Restaurant
  El Colorín
10 Carmelita

OTHER
3 Bar Tu
  Hermana
11 Church
12 Palacio
  Municipal
13 Banco del
  Atlántico
14 Cine López
15 Church
16 Bus Station
17 Minibus &
  Taxi Station

Mérida. The darkish rooms are simple but newer and far cleaner than the competition's. Prices are US$8 for two in one bed, US$12 for two in two beds.

A hundred meters northwest of the Bougambillias on the opposite side of the highway is the older *Hotel-Motel Cerro Inn*. Set in more spacious, shady grounds, the Cerro Inn has nine well-used rooms with private shower and ceiling fan for US$8 to US$10 a double.

Places to Eat

Ticul's lively market provides all the ingredients for picnics and snacks. It also has lots of those wonderful market eateries where the food is good, the portions generous and the prices low. For variety, try out some of the loncherías along Calle 23 between Calles 26 and 30.

For bread and sweet rolls, there's *El Buen Samaritano*, on Calle 23 west of Calle 26.

Should you want a sit-down meal, there's the cheap *Restaurant El Colorín* (☎ (997) 2-03-14), Calle 26 No 199-B, close to the Hotel Sierra Sosa half a block northwest of the plaza. Have a look at the *Carmelita*, on the opposite side of the Hotel Sierra Sosa, as well.

Pizza La Góndola, Calle 23 at Calle 26A, is tidy, with two-person pizzas cooked to order for US$5 to US$8. *Restaurant Chan Ki-Huic*, on Calle 23 west of Calle 28, is new, bright and clean. The *Lonchería Mary*, on Calle 23 east of Calle 28, is a clean, family-run place.

Restaurant Los Almendros (☎ (997) 2-00-21), Calle 23 No 207, between 26A and 28, is set up in a fortresslike townhouse with a large courtyard and portico. The air-conditioned restaurant, open every day from 10 am to 9 pm, is fairly plain, but the food is authentically Yucatecan. The *combinado yucateco* (Yucatecan combination plate) with a soft drink or beer costs less than US$7.

Getting There & Away

Ticul's bus station is behind the massive church off the main square. Autotransportes del Mayab makes the 85 km, 1½-hour run between Mérida and Ticul for US$2. There are also three buses to Felipe Carrillo Puerto (US$7), frequent ones to Oxkutzcab (US$1), and nine a day to Chetumal (6½ hours, US$7).

You can catch a *combi* (minibus) from the intersection of Calles 23 and 28 in

YUCATÁN

Ticul to Mérida's Parque de San Juan (or vice-versa - see Getting There & Away in the Mérida chapter), or to Oxkutzcab (that's osh-kootz-KAHB), 16 km away, and from Oxkutzcab a minibus or pickup truck to Loltún (eight km); ask for the camión to Xul (SHOOL), but get off at the Grutas de Loltún.

Minibuses to Santa Elena (15 km), the village between Uxmal and Kabah, also depart from the intersection of Calles 23 and 28, taking a back road and then leaving you to catch another bus northwest to Uxmal (15 km) or south to Kabah (3.5 km). You may find it more convenient to take a minibus or bus to Muna (22 km) on Highway 261 and another south to Uxmal (16 km).

To Felipe Carrillo Puerto Those headed eastward to Quintana Roo and the Caribbean Coast can go via Hwy 184 from Muna and Ticul via Oxkutzcab to Tekax, Tzucacab and Peto. At Polguc, 130 km from Ticul, a road turns left (east), ending after 80 km in Felipe Carrillo Puerto, 210 km from Ticul, where there are hotels, restaurants, fuel stations, banks and other services. The right fork of the road goes south to the region of Lago de Bacalar.

From Oxkutzcab to Felipe Carrillo Puerto or Bacalar there are few services: very few places to eat (those that exist are rock-bottom basic), no hotels and few fuel stations. Mostly you see small, typical Yucatecan villages with their *topes* (speed bumps), traditional Mayan *na* (thatched houses) and agricultural activity.

Getting Around

For getting around Ticul, the local method is to hail a three-wheeled cycle, Ticul's answer to the ricksha - you'll see them on Calle 23 just up from the market. The fare is around US$0.50 for a short trip.

MÉRIDA TO TICUL VIA ACANCEH & MAYAPÁN

The route south from Mérida via Acanceh and the ruins of Mayapán to Ticul and Oxkutzcab reveals a landscape of small

Mayan villages, crumbling haciendas surrounded by henequen fields, a ruined Mayan capital city and of course the expected expanses of limitless scrubby jungle.

Those taking this route, whether by car or bus, should be careful to distinguish between the Ruinas de Mayapán - the ruins of the ancient city - and Mayapán - a Mayan village some 40 km southeast of the ruins, past the town of Teabo. The Ruinas de Mayapán are right on the main road (Yucatán State Highway 18) between Telchaquillo and Tekit.

Getting Around

Buses and colectivos run fitfully along this route, but you should plan the better part of a day, with stops in Acanceh and at the Ruinas de Mayapán, to travel the route by public transport.

If you're driving, follow these directions carefully: Leave Mérida on Calle 59, which runs one-way eastward. When you reach a four-lane boulevard with railroad tracks running in its center you've reached Circuito Colonias. Turn right onto this boulevard and go south until you reach a traffic circle with a fountain. Go three-quarters of the way around (you enter at 6 o'clock and exit at 9 o'clock) and head due east on the road marked for Kanasin, Acanceh and Tecoh.

Acanceh

The road enters Acanceh and goes to the main plaza, flanked by a shady park and the church. To the left of the church is a partially restored pyramid (admission US$1.50), and to the right of the church are market loncherías, if you're in need of a snack. In the park note the statue of the smiling deer; the name Acanceh means 'Pond of the Deer'. Another local sight of interest is the cantina *Aqui Me Quedo* (I'm Staying Here), a ready-made answer for husbands whose wives come to the cantina to urge them homeward.

Ruinas de Mayapán

One or two km past Telchaquillo (about 48 km from Mérida), look for a sign on the right-hand (west) side of the road indicating the Ruinas de Mayapán.

At the entrance, 100 meters west of the road, pay the admission fee of US$1.50 and enter the site any day between 8 am and 5 pm.

History Mayapán was supposedly founded by Kukulcán (Quetzalcóatl) in 1007, shortly after the former ruler of Tula arrived in Yucatán. His dynasty, the Cocom, organized a confederation of city-states that included Uxmal, Chichén Itzá and many other notable cities. Despite their alliance, animosity arose between the Cocoms of Mayapán and the Itzaes of Chichén Itzá during the late the late 12th century and the Cocoms stormed Chichén Itzá, forcing the Itzá rulers into exile. The Cocom dynasty under Hunac Ceel Canuch emerged supreme in all of northern Yucatán and obliged the other rulers to pay tribute in cotton clothing, fowl, cacao and incense resin.

Cocom supremacy lasted for almost 2½ centuries, until the ruler of Uxmal, Ah Xupán Xiú, led a rebellion of the oppressed city-states and overthrew Cocom hegemony. Every member of the Cocom dynasty was massacred, except for one prince who had the good fortune to be away on business in Honduras. The great capital of Mayapán was utterly destroyed and remained uninhabited ever after.

The Xiú victors founded a new capital at Maní, which remained the strongest Mayan city until the arrival of the conquistadors. But there was no peace in Yucatán after the Xiú victory. The Cocom dynasty recovered and marshaled its forces, and struggles for power erupted frequently until 1542, when Francisco de Montejo the Younger founded Mérida. At that point the current lord of Maní and ruler of the Xiú people, Ah Kukum Xiú, offered to submit his forces to Montejo's control in exchange for a military alliance against the Cocoms, his ancient rivals. Montejo willingly agreed, and Ah Kukum Xiú was baptized as a Christian, taking the unoriginal name of Francisco de Montejo Xiú. The Cocoms

were defeated and - too late - the Xiú rulers realized that they had willingly signed the death warrant of Mayan independence.

Orientation The city of Mayapán was huge, with a population estimated to be around 12,000; its ruins cover several square kilometers, all surrounded by a great defensive wall. Over 3500 buildings, 20 cenotes and traces of the city wall were mapped by archaeologists working in the 1950s and in 1962. The workmanship was inferior to the great age of Mayan art; though the Cocom rulers of Mayapán tried to revive the past glories of Mayan civilization, they succeeded only in part.

Jungle has returned to cover many of the buildings, though you can visit several cenotes (including Itzmal Chen, a main Mayan religious sanctuary) and make out the large piles of stones that were once the Temple of Kukulcán and the circular Caracol.

Getting There & Away After visiting the ruins, head south again to Tekit, about eight km from the ruins (67 km from Mérida). Turn right and go through the town square to find the road marked for Oxkutzcab. Another seven km brings you to Mama, with its particularly fortresslike church. At Mama the road forks: straight on to Oxkutzcab (27 km), right to Chapab and Ticul (25 km).

MÉRIDA TO CAMPECHE - SHORT ROUTE (HIGHWAY 180)

The short route from Mérida to Campeche is the fast way to go, and if you simply buy a bus ticket from Mérida to Campeche, this is the route your bus will follow. If you'd prefer to go the long way via Uxmal and Kabah, you must ask for a seat on one of the less frequent long-route buses. If you'd like to stop at one of the towns along the short route, catch a 2nd-class bus.

Becal, Calkini & Hecelchakan

Becal, 85 km southwest of Mérida and just across the boundary in the state of Campeche, is a center of Yucatán's Panama hat trade. The soft, pliable hats, called *jipi-japa* by the locals, have been woven by townsfolk from the fibers of the huano palm tree in humid limestone caves since the mid-19th century. The caves provide just the right atmosphere for shaping the fibers, keeping them pliable and minimizing breakage. So devoted to hat making is Becal that the sculpture in the main square is composed of several enormous concrete hats tipped up against one another. As soon as you descend from your bus someone is sure to approach you and ask if you want to see the hats being made; the guide expects a tip of course.

Jipi hats are of three general quality grades, judged by the pliability and fineness of the fibers and closeness of the weave. The coarse, open weave of large fibers is the cheapest grade and should cost only a few dollars. Middle-grade hats have a finer, closer weave of good fibers and cost about US$20. Truly beautiful hats of the finest, closest weave may cost twice that amount.

Eight km south of Becal you pass through Calkini, site of the 17th-century Church of San Luis de Tolosa, with a plateresque portal and lots of baroque decoration. Each year the Festival of San Luis is celebrated on August 19.

Another 24 km brings you to Hecelchakan, home of the Museo Arqueológico del Camino Real, where you will find some burial artifacts from the island of Jaina, as well as ceramics and jewelry from other sites. The museum is open from Monday to Saturday from 9 am to 6 pm, closed Sunday. The Church of San Francisco is the center of festivities on the saint's day, October 4. From August 9 to 18, a popular festival called the Novenario is held, with bullfights, dancing and refreshments.

From Hecelchakan it's another 77 easy km to the city of Campeche.

Campeche

The impressive walled city of Campeche, with its ancient *baluartes* (fortresses), propels the visitor back to the days of the buccaneers. Those who explore the region's ancient Mayan Chenes-style ruins of Edzná could find they have the sites all to themselves. With so much of interest, why is Campeche the least-visited state in the Yucatán peninsula?

For all its attractiveness, Campeche is not particularly tourist-friendly. Hotels are few, often disappointing and expensive for what you get. The fine regional museum charges a very high admission price. The beaches, such as they are, can be less than clean, and transport to Edzná can be haphazard.

Even so, the state has its attractions, and you should enjoy a short stay here.

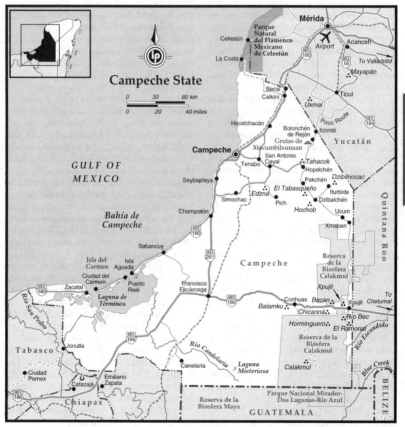

CAMPECHE
Population 170,000

Filled with historic buildings, the center of Campeche is quite appealing. Local people make their living fishing for shrimp or digging for oil, and the prosperity brought by those two activities is apparent in the town.

History
Once a Mayan trading village called Ah Kim Pech (Lord Sun Sheep-Tick), Campeche was invaded by the conquistadors in 1517. The Maya resisted and for nearly a quarter of a century the Spaniards were unable to fully conquer the region. Campeche was founded in 1531 but later abandoned because of Mayan hostility. Finally, by 1540 the conquistadors had gained sufficient control, under the leadership of Francisco de Montejo the Younger, to found a settlement here that survived. They named it the Villa de San Francisco de Campeche.

The settlement soon flourished as the major port of Yucatán. Locally grown timber, *chicle* (the sap of the sapodilla tree) and dyewoods were exported to Europe, as were gold and silver mined from other regions and shipped via Campeche. Such wealth did not escape the notice of pirates, who began their attacks only six years after the town was founded.

For two centuries the depredations of pirates terrorized Campeche. Not only were ships attacked, but the port itself was invaded, its citizens robbed, its women raped and its buildings burned. In their most gruesome of assaults, in early 1663, the various pirate hordes set aside their jealousies to converge on the city as a single flotilla, massacring many of Campeche's citizens in the process.

It took this tragedy to make the Spanish monarchy take preventive action, but not until five years later. Starting in 1668, 3.5-meter-thick ramparts were built. After 18 years of construction, a 2.5-km hexagon incorporating eight strategically placed baluartes surrounded the city.

Originally part of the state of Yucatán, Campeche became an autonomous state of Mexico in 1863. In the 19th century it fell into an economic decline brought on by the demise of mineral shipments to Spain. Independence, the freeing of Indians from plantation slavery, the devastation wrought by the War of the Castes and overall isolation put the port into a protracted decline.

Today the hardwood timber and fishing industries are thriving, and the discovery of offshore oil has led to a miniboom in the city of Campeche.

Orientation
The old part of Campeche, enclosed by fragments of the sturdy walls, is where you'll spend most of your time. Though the baluartes stand, most of the walls themselves have been razed and replaced by a street, which rings the city center just as the walls once did. This is the Avenida Circuito Baluartes (Circuit Avenue of the Bulwarks).

Besides the modern Plaza Moch-Cuouh, Campeche has its Parque Principal, also called the Plaza de la Independencia, the standard Spanish colonial park, with the cathedral on one side and former Palacio de Gobierno on another. Band concerts take place here on Sunday evenings.

According to the compass Campeche is oriented with its waterfront to the northwest, but tradition and convenience hold that the water is to the west, inland is east.

The ADO bus terminal is 1.7 km northeast of Plaza Moch-Cuouh along Avenida Gobernadores (Hwy 180).

The railroad station is three km east of the center, south of Avenida Gobernadores on Avenida Héroes de Nacozari in the district called Colonia Cuatro Caminos.

The airport is east of the railroad station at the northern end of Avenida López Portillo. To reach the air terminal you must go east to Avenida Central, which turns into Avenida López Portillo, then north to the terminal, 3.5 km from Plaza Moch-Cuouh.

The central market, Mercado Pedro Sainz de Baranda, is at the junction of Calle 53 and Avenida Circuito Baluartes Este, just inland from the old city.

Information

Tourist Offices The Coordinación General de Turismo (☎ (981) 6-60-68, 6-67-67) is at Calle 12 No 153, at Calle 53. The staff is very friendly and available Monday to Saturday from 8 am to 2:30 pm and 4 to 8:30 pm; closed Sunday.

The city maintains the Coordinación Municipal de Turismo, on Calle 55 at Calle 8, just west of the cathedral, facing the Parque Principal.

Money Banks are open Monday to Friday from 9 am to 1 pm. See the map for bank and ATM locations.

Post The central post office (☎ (981) 6-21-34), at the corner of Avenida 16 de Septiembre and Calle 53, is in the Edificio Federal. Hours are Monday to Friday 8 am to 7 pm, Saturday 8 am to 1 pm and Sunday 8 am to 2 pm.

Walking Tour

Seven bulwarks still stand; four of them are of interest. You can see them all by following the Avenida Circuito Baluartes around the city on a two-km walk.

Because of traffic, some of the walk is not very pleasant, so you might want to limit your excursion to the first three or four baluartes described below, which house museums and gardens. If you'd rather have a guided tour, you can sign up for a city tour at either the Ramada Inn or Hotel Baluartes for about US$18. We'll start at the southwestern end of the Plaza Moch-Cuouh.

Close to the modern Palacio de Gobierno, at Circuito Baluartes and Avenida Justo Sierra, near the intersection of Calles 8 and 65 and a ziggurat fountain, is the **Baluarte de San Carlos**. The interior of the bulwark is now arranged as the **Sala de las Fortificaciones**, or Chamber of Fortifications, with some interesting scale models of the city's fortifications in the 18th century. You can also visit the dungeon and look out over the sea from the roof. Baluarte de San Carlos is open from 9 am to 1 pm and 5 to 7:30 pm daily, and admission is free.

Next, head north along Calle 8. At the intersection with Calle 59, notice the **Puerta del Mar**, or Sea Gate, which provided access to the city from the sea before the area to the northwest was filled in. The gate was demolished in 1893 but rebuilt in 1957, when its historical value was realized.

The **Baluarte de la Soledad**, on the north side of the Plaza Moch-Cuouh, close to the intersection of Calles 8 and 57, is the setting for the **Museo de Estelas Maya**. Many of the Mayan artifacts here are badly weathered, but the precise line drawing next to each stone shows you what the designs once looked like. The bulwark also has an interesting exhibition of colonial Campeche. Among the antiquities are 17th- and 18th-century seafaring equipment and armaments used to battle pirate invaders. The museum is open 9 am to 2 pm and 3 to 8 pm Tuesday to Saturday, 9 am to 1 pm on Sunday, closed Monday. Admission costs US$0.50.

Just across the street from the baluarte is the **Parque Principal**, Campeche's favorite park. Whereas the sterile, modernistic, shadeless Plaza Moch-Cuouh was built to glorify its government builders, the Parque Principal (Plaza de la Independencia) is the pleasant place where locals go to sit and think, chat, smooch, plot, snooze, stroll, cool off after the heat of the day or have their shoes shined. Come for the band concerts on Sunday evenings.

Construction was begun on the **Catedral de la Concepción**, on the north side of the plaza, in the mid-1500s, shortly after the conquistadors established the town, but it wasn't finished until 1705.

The attractive, arcaded former **Palacio de Gobierno** (or Palacio Municipal) dates only from the 19th century.

Continue north along Calle 8 for several blocks to the **Baluarte de Santiago**, at the intersection of Calles 8 and 51. It houses a minuscule yet lovely tropical garden, the **Jardín Botánico Xmuch Haltun**, with 250 species of tropical plants set around a lovely courtyard of fountains. Tours of the garden are given from Monday through Friday between 5 and 6 pm. The garden is

YUCATÁN

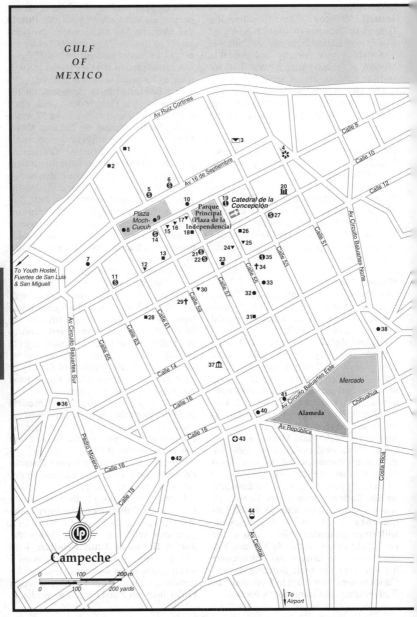

GULF
OF
MEXICO

Av Ruiz Cortines

■1

■2

6 ●
5 ●
Ⓢ

Av 16 de Septiembre

✉ 3

4 ✳

Calle 5

Calle 10

Calle 12

10 ●

19 ⓘ   **Catedral de la Concepción**

20 �🏛

Plaza
Moch-
Cuouh

9 ●

Parque
Principal
(Plaza de la
Independencia)

Ⓢ 27

Calle 51

Av Círculo Baluartes Norte

●8

Ⓢ
14

15 ▼ 17 ▼
16

18 ■

■26

▼25

Calle 53

7 ●

13 ■

12 ▼

21 Ⓢ
22 Ⓢ

24 ▼

23 ■

ⓘ35

✝34

Calle 55

11 Ⓢ

▼30

29 ✝

Calle 59

32 ●

33 ●

31 ■

Calle 57

●38

■28

Calle 63

Calle 61

To Youth Hostel,
Fuertes de San Luis
& San Miguell

Av Círculo Baluartes Sur

Calle 14

37 🏛

Mercado

Chihuahua

●36

Calle 16

41
●

Av Círculo Baluartes Este

Alameda

●40

Calle 18

Av República

●42

✛43

Pedro Moreno

Calle 16

Calle 18

Av Central

44
●

Costa Rica

Campeche

0   100   200 m
0   100   200 yards

To
Airport

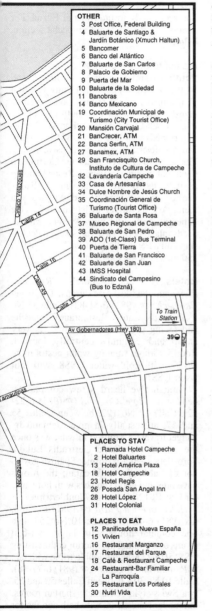

To Train
Station

Av Gobernadores (Hwy 180)

39

open weekdays from 8 am to 3 pm and 6 to 8:30 pm, Saturday from 9 am to 1 pm and 6 to 8 pm, Sunday from 9 am to 1 pm. Admission is free.

From the Baluarte de Santiago, walk east (inland) along Calle 51 to Calle 18, where you'll come to the **Baluarte de San Pedro**, in the middle of a complex traffic intersection that marks the beginning of the Avenida Gobernadores. Within the bulwark is the **Exposición Permanente de Artesanías**, a regional crafts sales center, open Monday to Friday from 9 am to 2 pm and 5 to 8 pm. Admission is free.

To make the entire circuit, head south from the Baluarte de San Pedro along the Avenida Circuito Baluartes to the **Baluarte de San Francisco**, at Calle 57, and, a block farther along at Calle 59, the **Puerta de Tierra**, or Land Gate. The **Baluarte de San Juan**, at Calles 18 and 65, marks the southwesternmost point of the old city walls. From here bear right (southwest) along Calle 67 (Avenida Circuito Baluartes) to the intersection of Calles 14 and 67 and the **Baluarte de Santa Rosa**.

Museo Regional de Campeche

The Regional Museum (☎ (981) 6-91-11) is set up in the former mansion of the Teniente del Rey (King's Lieutenant), at Calle 59 No 36, between Calles 14 and 16. Architecture, hydrology, commerce, art, religion and Mayan science are all dealt with in interesting and revealing displays.

Hours are Tuesday to Saturday 8 am to 2 pm and 2:30 to 8 pm, Sunday 9 am to 1 pm, closed Monday. Admission is an unreasonable US$3.

Mansión Carvajal

The Mansión Carvajal, Calle 10 between Calles 51 and 53, started its eventful history as the city residence of Don Fernando Carvajal Estrada and his wife, Sra María Iavalle de Carvajal. Don Fernando was among Campeche's richest *hacendados* (hacienda owners). Sometimes the building is open and you can take a quick walk around. The monogram you see throughout the building, 'RCY', is that of

Rafael Carvajal Ytorralde, Don Fernando's father and founder of the fortune.

Other Sights

Walk through Campeche's streets – especially Calles 55, 57 and 59 – looking for more beautiful houses. The Casa de Artesanías (see Things to Buy) is a fine one. The walk is best done in the evening, when the sun is not blasting down and when the lights from inside illuminate the courtyards, salons and alleys.

Forts

Four km south of the Plaza Moch-Cuouh along the coast road stands the Fuerte de San Luis, an 18th-century fortress of which only a few battlements remain.

Near the San Luis, a road off to the left (southeast) climbs the hill one km to the Fuerte de San Miguel, a restored fortress now used as a museum for artifacts discovered in the excavations at Calakmul, in the southern reaches of the state. The museum is open daily except Monday from 8 am to 8 pm, admission US$1. The view of the city and the sea is beautiful, but the walk uphill is a killer.

To reach the Fuerte de San Luis, take a Lerma or Playa Bonita bus southwest along the coastal highway (toward Villahermosa); the youth hostel is out this way as well (see below).

Beaches

Campeche's beaches are not particularly inviting. The Balneario Popular, four km south of the Plaza Moch-Cuouh along the coastal road just past the Fuerte de San Luis, should be avoided. A few km farther along is Playa Bonita, with some facilities (restaurant, lockers, toilets) but water of questionable cleanliness and, on the weekends, wall-to-wall people.

If you're really hard up for a swim, head southwest to the town of Seybaplaya, 33 km from Plaza Moch-Cuouh. The highway skirts narrow, pure-white beaches dotted with fishing shacks, where the water is much cleaner but there are no facilities. The best beach here is called Payucan.

Edzná Ruins

Tours run daily to the ruins at Edzná. For details, see the Eastern Campeche section, below.

Places to Stay – budget

Youth Hostel Campeche's *youth hostel* (☎ (981) 6-18-02) is in the Centro Cultural y Deportivo Universitario on Avenida Agustín Melgar, 3.5 km southwest of the Plaza Moch-Cuouh, off the shore road. Dormitory beds cost less than US$4 per night, and a cafeteria serves inexpensive meals. The shore road is Avenida Ruiz Cortines in town, but becomes Avenida Resurgimiento as it heads toward Villahermosa. Buses marked 'Avenida Universidad' will take you there. Ask the driver to let you off at the Albergue de la Juventud. Avenida Melgar heads inland between a Volkswagen dealership and a Pemex fuel station. The hostel is 150 meters up on the right.

Hotels The cheapest hotels – *Reforma, Roma* and the like – are dumps. The *Hotel Campeche* (☎ (981) 6-51-83), Calle 57 No 2, above the Café y Restaurant Campeche and facing the Parque Principal, is very cheap and certainly centrally located. Rooms without running water cost a mere US$6, with cold water US$8, with hot water US$10.

Though I've heard a few complaints, beds at the *Hotel Colonial* (☎ (981) 6-22-22), Calle 14 No 122, between Calles 55 and 57, are usually in great demand by budget travelers. Housed in what was once the mansion of Doña Gertrudis Eulalia Torostieta y Zagasti, former Spanish governor of Tabasco and Yucatán, the rooms have fans and good showers with hot water for US$10/12/15 a single/double/triple.

Hotel América Plaza (☎ (981) 6-45-88, fax (981) 6-45-76), Calle 10 No 252, is a fine colonial house with large, not-bad rooms overlooking the interior court costing US$15/19/22 a single/double/triple with fan.

Posada San Angel Inn (☎ (981) 6-77-18), Calle 10 No 307, between Calles 53 and 55, is a Swiss-style cell block: spartan rooms, but modern and clean, with bath and fan for

Top: Swimming in the Cenote Xlacah, Dzibilchaltún archeological site, Mexico (TB)
Left: Pyramid of the Magician, Uxmal, Yucatán, Mexico (TB)
Right: Tulum Ruins, Quintana Roo, Mexico (TB)

Top: Waterfall at Agua Azul, Chiapas, Mexico (JL)
Bottom: Cañón del Sumidero, Chiapas, Mexico (PW)

US$12/15/17/20 per single/double/triple/quad, US$3 more with air-con.

Places to Stay – middle

Hotel Regis (☎ (981) 6-31-75), Calle 12 No 148, between 55 and 57, is conveniently located and serviceable, with adequate air-con rooms for US$12/18/24/28 a single/double/triple/quad.

Hotel López (☎ (981) 6-33-44, fax (981) 6-24-88), Calle 12 No 189, between Calles 61 and 63, is somewhat more expensive and not quite as nice as the Regis, charging US$14/15/19/25 a single/double/triple/quad with fan, though you do get a color TV. Air-con rooms cost a few dollars more.

Places to Stay – top end

The best hotel in town is the 119-room *Ramada Hotel Campeche* (☎ (981) 6-22-33, fax (981) 1-16-18), Avenida Ruiz Cortines No 51. Prices range from US$85 a single or double for a standard room to US$125 for a master suite.

Just south of the Ramada is its competition, the older but still comfortable *Hotel Baluartes* (☎ (981) 6-39-11, fax (981) 6-24-10). The Baluartes' well-used rooms are air-conditioned and comfortable, with sea views, and are cheaper, at US$35/40 a single/double.

Places to Eat

Among the best eateries is the *Restaurant Marganzo* (☎ (981) 6-23-28), Calle 8 No 265, between Calles 57 and 59, facing the sea and the Baluarte de la Soledad. Breakfast costs US$2 to US$3, regional specialties US$3 to US$5; the seafood menu, priced up to US$8, includes lots of shrimp.

The *Café y Restaurant Campeche* (☎ (981) 6-21-28), Calle 57 No 2, opposite Parque Principal, is in the building that saw the birth of Justo Sierra, founder of Mexico's national university, but the restaurant is very simple, bright with fluorescent light bulbs and loud with a blaring TV set. The *platillo del día* usually costs less than US$3.

On the same block, facing the plaza, is the *Restaurant del Parque* (☎ (981) 6-02-40), Calle 57 No 8, a cheerful little place serving fish, meat and shrimp for around US$3 a platter. It opens early for breakfast and is open on Sunday.

If you'd just like to pick up some sweet rolls, biscuits, bread or cakes, head for the *Panificadora Nueva España*, Calle 10 at the corner of Calle 61, which has a large assortment of fresh baked goods at very low prices.

Every now and then a brave entrepreneur opens a natural-foods restaurant in Campeche, only to close soon after. I hope the latest effort, the *Vivien*, beneath the Hotel Reforma at Calle 8 No 263, survives. Another place to look for whole food and vegetarian fare is *Nutri Vida*, Calle 12 No 167.

Perhaps the best-known restaurant in town is the *Restaurant-Bar Familiar La Parroquía* (☎ (981) 6-18-29), Calle 55 between 10 and 12. The complete family restaurant-cafe-hangout, La Parroquía serves breakfasts priced at US$2.25 to US$3.50 from 7 to 10 am Monday to Friday and substantial lunch and dinner fare such as chuleta de cerdo (pork chop), filete a la tampiqueña, shrimp cocktail or shrimp salad and even fresh pampano, for US$5 to US$9. It's open every day for all three meals.

Entertainment

On Friday evenings at 8 pm from September to May (weather permitting) the state tourism authorities sponsor *Estampas Turísticas*, performances of folk music and dancing, in the Plaza Moch-Cuouh. Other performances, sponsored by the city government, take place in the Parque Principal on Thursday, Friday, Saturday and Sunday evenings around 7 pm.

Things to Buy

The Casa de Artesanías (☎ (981) 6-90-88), Calle 55 No 25, between 12 and 14, is run by the state government. Crafts are on sale from 9 am to 2 pm and 5 to 8 pm. (See also the Baluarte de San Pedro under Walking Tour.)

Getting There & Away

Air The airport is east of the railroad station at the end of Avenida López Portillo (Avenida Central), across the tracks and about 800 meters away, or 3.5 km from Plaza Moch-Cuouh. You must take a taxi (US$4) to the city center.

Bus Campeche's 1st-class ADO bus terminal is on Avenida Gobernadores, 1.7 km from Plaza Moch-Cuouh, or about 1.5 km from most hotels. The 2nd-class terminal is directly behind it.

Here's information on daily buses from Campeche:

Cancún – 512 km, nine hours, US$12 to US$15; change at Mérida

Chetumal – 422 km, seven hours, US$11 to US$14; three buses

Edzná – 66 km, 1½ hours, US$1.50; catch bus to Pich or Hool from the Sindicato del Campesino, on Avenida Central, or take a faster bus to San Antonio Cayal (45 km) and hitch south from there.

Hopelchén – 86 km, two hours, US$1.50; a dozen 2nd-class buses by Camioneros de Campeche

Iturbide (Vicente Guerrero) – 155 km, three hours, US$2.50; five 2nd-class buses by Camioneros de Campeche

Mérida – 195 km (short route via Becal), 2½ to three hours; 250 km (long route via Uxmal), four hours; 33 buses by ADO around the clock (US$6); buses every 20 or 30 minutes by ATS (US$3 to US$3.50)

Mexico City – 1360 km, 20 hours, US$50; two buses by ADO

Palenque – 362 km, five hours; one bus by ADO (US$12), two by Colón (US$12), two by ATS (US$10); many others drop you at Catazajá (Palenque turnoff), 27 km north of Palenque village

San Cristóbal de las Casas – 820 km, 14 hours; three buses by ADO (US$15 to US$18), one by ATS (US$14)

Villahermosa – 450 km, six hours, US$14 to US$17; 15 buses (they'll drop you at Catazajá, the Palenque junction, if you like)

Xpujil – 306 km, six hours, US$8; four buses by ATS

Eastern Campeche

If you're approaching the city of Campeche from Uxmal, you'll pass several interesting places along the way.

After passing beneath the arch that marks the border between the states of Yucatán and Campeche, the road heads southwest for Bolonchén de Rejón. Three km north of Bolonchén, just off the highway, is the archaeological zone of **Itzimté**, with its many unrestored buildings in the Puuc style. This is the southernmost limit of the style; south of this point the ancient Mayan buildings are more elaborately decorated in the style known as Chenes, named for the many natural wells in the region. The suffix *-chén* is often found at the end of town names hereabouts.

BOLONCHÉN DE REJÓN & XTACUMBILXUNAAN

Bolonchén ('Nine Wells', for the *chultunes*, or cisterns, in the town square) is noted mostly as the town near the Grutas de Xtacumbilxunaan (or Xtacumbinxuna, as it's sometimes spelled), about three km south of town. Follow Hwy 261 south and watch on the right (west) for a small sign indicating the caves, which are 800 meters off the highway.

These Caves of the Hidden Girl get their unpronounceable Mayan name from a legend (of course) in which a girl was stolen from her mother by her lover and hidden in the cave. If that is true, the lovers left no trace of their tryst. In former centuries the Nine Wells would fail each year during the dry season, and the local inhabitants would make their way to this cave and descend several hundred meters into the earth through a narrow, claustrophobic system of tunnels to fill their small water jars.

Today you can visit the cavern by taking a 30- to 45-minute tour with the guide/caretaker for the price of a tip. The cave is open whenever the caretaker is around, which is most of the time during daylight hours.

HOPELCHÉN & TAHACOK

Hopelchén (population 7000) is a tidy town with topiary linden trees shading its main plaza and the hopefully named Ladies Bar to one side. A few small eateries provide sustenance for travelers, and the *Hotel Los Arcos* (☎ (982) 2-00-37), on Calle 23 just off the plaza, offers basic, inexpensive lodging. Now that the road south to Xpujil has been improved, Hopelchén's hotels and restaurants will probably improve and proliferate. (See the Southern Campeche section for details on Xpujil.)

Hopelchén has a few banks. They did not offer foreign exchange functions at this writing, but they may do so soon.

Two km west of Hopelchén on the Campeche road are the ruins of Tahacok (or Tohkok). The one ruined structure here, dating from Late Classic times, is on the north side of the highway. Its decoration is a blend of Puuc and Chenes styles.

EL TABASQUEÑO, HOCHOB & DZIBILNOCAC

Three minor Mayan sites are fairly easy of access if you're on your way between Hopelchén and Xpujil in your own vehicle. Admission to all is free.

El Tabasqueño

Northwest of Dzibalchén, El Tabasqueño boasts a temple-palace (Structure 1) with a striking monster-mouth doorway flanked by Chac masks. The doorway is similar to the one atop the Pyramid of the Magician at Uxmal, though in Chenes style. Structure 2 is a solid freestanding tower, an oddity in Mayan architecture. To reach El Tabasqueño, go south from Hopelchén 30 km, turn right (south) to the village of Pakchén and follow an unpaved road another four km to the site.

Hochob

Five km south of Chencoh is Hochob, the most rewarding of these sites. Though small, it is among the most beautiful and impressive of Chenes-style sites. The Principal Palace (Structure 2) is faced with an amazingly elaborate Chenes monster-mouth doorway in surprisingly good condition. Structure 1 is similar, though in worse condition. Structure 5, on the east side of the plaza, retains part of its roofcomb. Structure 6, to the west, is in ruins. To reach Hochob, turn right (south) about a half-km west of Dzibalchén and drive the nine km to Chencoh on a rocky road, then the remaining five km on a rough dirt road.

Dzibilnocac

Though relatively easy to reach, Dzibilnocac is the least interesting of these three Chenes sites. There is really only one building to see, the Temple-Palace (Structure A1). Its eastern tower, with Chenes-style monster-mask decoration on all four sides, has been consolidated. Within its vaulted rooms are traces of paint that were once murals, though it's virtually impossible to make much out now.

Dzibilnocac was a large city in late Preclassic and Late Classic times. Ruins of seven pyramids – now mere piles of rubble – can be found near Structure A1. The structure is 700 meters beyond the basketball court on the main square of the town of Iturbide (population 3,000), sometimes called Vicente Guerrero. Coming into the main square from Dzibalchén (21 km), drive to the basketball court and turn right, keeping the Centro de Salud on your left, and proceed straight to the site.

EDZNÁ

Continuing west on Highway 261 from Hopelchén brings you, after 40 km, to the village of San Antonio Cayal and the junction with the road south to Edzná (20 km).

Edzná, meaning House of Grimaces or House of Echoes, may well have been host to both, as there has been a settlement here since about 800 BC. Most of the carvings are of a much later date: 550 to 810 AD. Though a long way from the Puuc Hills, some of the architecture here is similar to Puuc style, but with local variations in design.

The refreshments stand to the left as you enter has icy-cold bottled drinks, which you will probably want in the intense heat. The site is open from 8 am to 5 pm daily, admission US$4.

Though the archaeological zone covers two sq km, the thing to see here is the main plaza, 160 meters long and 100 meters wide, surrounded by temples. Every Mayan site has huge masses of stone, but at Edzná there are cascades of it, terrace upon terrace of bleached limestone.

The major temple here, the 30-meter-high Temple of Five Levels, is to the left as you enter the plaza from the ticket kiosk. Built on a vast platform, it rises five levels from base to roofcomb, with rooms and some weathered decoration (masks, serpents and jaguars' heads) on each level. A great central staircase of 65 steps goes right to the top. On the opposite (right) side of the plaza as you enter is a monumental staircase 100 meters wide, which once led up to the Temple of the Moon. At the far end of the plaza is a ruined temple that could well have been the priests' quarters.

Organized Tours
Picazh Servicios Turísticos (☎ (981) 6-44-26, fax (981) 6-27-60), Calle 16 No 348, between 57 and 59 in Campeche, runs tours from Campeche to Edzná. For US$10 per person they'll drive two or more people to the Edzná ruins and back. For another US$5 per person they'll give you a guided tour in Spanish and/or English. Entry to the site is not included in these prices. Join the tour at the plaza next to the Puerta de Tierra, at the eastern end of Calle 59 (see map). Tours depart daily at 9 am and 2 pm.

Getting There & Away
The Picazh tours (see preceding section) are worth the money for convenience, but you can do it even cheaper by bus. Catch a 2nd-class village bus early in the morning headed for Edzná (66 km) from near the Sindicato del Campesino, on Avenida Central south of the Circuito Baluartes; it may be a bus going to Pich, 15 km southeast of Edzná, or to Hool, 25 km southwest. Either bus will drop you at the access road to the site.

Coming from the north and east, get off at San Antonio Cayal and hitch or catch a bus 20 km south to Edzná.

A sign just north of the junction says 'Edzná 2 km', but the ruins are just 500 meters beyond the sign, only about 400 meters off the highway.

When you leave you'll have to depend on hitchhiking or buses to get you to San Antonio Cayal, from which you can hitch or catch a bus west back to Campeche or east and north to Hopelchén, Bolonchén and ultimately Uxmal.

Southern Campeche

XPUJIL & VICINITY
The southeastern corner of Campeche state boasts many important Mayan archaeological sites, with more being discovered every year.

Orientation
The hamlet of Xpujil, at the junction of the east-west and northern highways, is growing into a village, but services are still few and basic.

The Xpujil ruins are 1.5 km west of the junction, Becan is eight km west, Chicanná is 11.5 km west, and Balamku is 60 km west. There are no services (drinks, snacks, toilets, etc) as yet at any of these sites.

Xpujil Ruins
Xpujil, 'Place of the Cattails' in Mayan, flourished during the Late Classic period from 400 to 900 AD, though there was a settlement here much earlier. The site, 200 meters north of the highway, is open from 8 am to 5 pm for US$1.50.

Structure I in Group I, built about 760 AD, is a fine example of the Río Bec architectural style, with its lofty towers. The three towers (rather than the usual two) have traces of the impractically steep ornamental stairways reaching nearly to their tops, and several fierce jaguar masks (go around to the back of the tower to see the best one). About 60 meters to the east is Structure II, an elite residence.

Xpujil is a far larger site than may be imagined from these two buildings. Three other structure groups have been identified, but it may be decades before they are restored.

Becan

Becan, sitting atop a rock outcrop, means 'Path of the Snake' in Mayan. It is well named, as a two-km fosse (dry moat; 'becan' in Mayan) snakes its way around the entire city to protect it from attack. Seven causeways crossed the fosse, providing access to the city. Becan was occupied from 550 BC until 1000 AD. Today the site, 400 meters north of the highway, is open from 8 am to 5 pm for US$1.50.

This is among the largest and most elaborate sites in the area. The first building you reach, Structure I on the Southeast Plaza, has the two towers typical of Río Bec style. Climb a stairway on the east side of the building to get to the Southeast Plaza, surrounded by four large temples, with a circular altar (Structure III-a) on the east side.

Arrows direct you to a path that leaves the plaza at its northeast corner and descends a flight of stairs, then turns left (west) and passes along a rock-walled walk and beneath a corbeled arch. At the end of the path is a huge twin-towered temple with cylindrical columns at the top of a flight of stairs. This is Structure VIII, dating from about 600 to 730 AD. The view from the top of this temple is good in all directions.

Northwest of Structure VIII is the Central Plaza, surrounded by the 30-meter-high Structure IX, tallest building at the site, and the better-looking Structure X.

Lots more ruins await you in the jungle. The West Plaza, west of Structure X, is surrounded by low buildings, one of which is a ball court.

Chicanná

Almost 12 km west of Xpujil junction and 800 meters south of the highway, Chicanná is a mixture of Chenes and Río Bec architectural styles buried in the jungle. The city flourished from about 660 to 680 AD; today it is open from 8 am to 5 pm for US$1.50.

Enter through the modern palapa admission building, then follow the rock paths through the jungle to Group D and Structure XX (750 to 830 AD), which boasts not one but two monster-mouth doorways, one above the other, the pair topped by a roofcomb.

A five-minute walk along the jungle path brings you to Group C, with two low buildings (Structures X and XI) on a raised platform; the temples bear a few fragments of decoration.

The buildings in Group B have some intact decoration as well, and a good roofcomb on Structure VI.

At the end of the path is Chicanná's most famous building, Structure II (750 to 770 AD) in Group A, with its gigantic Chenes-style monster-mouth doorway. (If you've been to Hochob, this will look familiar.) If you photograph nothing else here, you'll want a picture of this, best taken in the afternoon.

Balamku

Discovered only in 1990, Balamku (also called Chunhabil) is famous for the facade of one building: It is decorated with a well-preserved stucco bas relief stylized figure of a jaguar flanked by two large mask designs and topped with designs of other animals and humans. This elaborate, unusual design bears little resemblance to any of the known decorative elements in the Chenes and Río Bec styles and has mystified archaeologists.

Balamku is 60 km west of Xpujil junction (less than three km west of Conhuas), then just under three km north of the highway along a rough unpaved road. There are no services.

Calakmul

Most Mayanists agree that Calakmul is a very important site, but at this writing little of its vast expanse – larger than Tikal – had been cleared and few of its 6500 buildings consolidated, let alone restored. Access can

YUCATÁN

be difficult or practically impossible during the rainy summer season, as the site is 118 km southwest of Xpujil junction over very rough roads and tracks. See Organized Tours, below.

Beneath Structure VII archaeologists discovered a burial crypt and a funerary offering of some 2000 pieces of jade. Other jade offerings were found beneath other structures. Calakmul also has a surprising number of carved stelae, many eroded.

Hormiguero

Hormiguero (Spanish for 'anthill') is an old site, with some buildings dating from 50 to 250 AD, though it flourished during the Late Classic period.

Located 22 km southwest of Xpujil junction (six km beyond the village of Carrizal), Hormiguero has one of the most impressive buildings in the region. The 50-meter-long Structure II has a huge Chenesstyle monster-mouth doorway with much of its decoration in good condition. Though similar to the huge monster mouths at Hochob and Chicanná, Hormiguero's is even bigger and bolder. You'll also want to see Structure V, 60 meters to the north, and Structure E-1, in the East Group.

Río Bec

Río Bec is the designation for an agglomeration of small sites, 17 at last count, in a 50-sq-km area southeast of Xpujil. Of these many sites, the most interesting is certainly Group B, followed by Groups I and N. These sites were difficult to reach at this writing and required a guide. See Organized Tours, below.

Río Bec gave its name to the prevalent architectural style of the region characterized by long, low buildings that look as though they're divided into sections, each with a huge serpent-mouth for a door. The facades are decorated with smaller masks, geometric designs and columns. At the corners of the buildings are tall, solid towers with extremely small, steep, nonfunctional steps and topped by small temples. Many of these towers have roofcombs as well.

The best example is Structure I at Group B, a Late Classic building dating from around 700 AD. Though not restored, Structure I has been consolidated and is in a condition certainly good enough to allow appreciation of its former glory.

At Group I look for Structures XVII and XI. At Group N, Structure I is quite similar to the grand one at Group B.

El Raminal

The entrance to the collective farm Ejido 20 de Noviembre is 10 km east of Xpujil junction. Follow the unpaved ejido road south for five km to reach the collective itself and its **U'lu'um Chac Yuk Nature Reserve**. As you come into the spartan village, with its free-roaming livestock and thatched huts, look for the 'museum', the fourth building on the right-hand side of the road. Ask here for guides to show you the sights of El Raminal, the fairly impressive ruins within walking distance of the settlement.

Guides from the ejido can also show you the various sites of Río Bec, about 13 km away.

The people of the ejido are building tourist bungalows with solar-heated hot water and other ecologically sensitive features, so when you arrive there should even be accommodations.

Organized Tours

Xpujil's guides have formed an association, and with a 4WD vehicle they can show you the more remote sites, such as Calakmul, Hormiguero and Río Bec, for about US$30 per person. One place to book is at El Mirador Maya restaurant, from which tours depart at 8 am. Book at least a day in advance.

Places to Stay & Eat

The best choice for budget travelers is *El Mirador Maya* (no phone), one km west of Xpujil junction. Rooms with shared baths go for US$14 a single or double. The little palapa-covered restaurant serves decent meals at decent prices, and there's even a little swimming pool. You can sign up for tours here (see Organized Tours, above). This is currently the intrepid travelers' gathering place.

About 350 meters west of Xpujil junction, the *Restaurant-Hotel Calakmul* has slightly cheaper rooms with shared bath, but also a few rooms with private shower for US$19 a double.

Near the junction and the ADO bus station (just east of the junction) are a few very basic eateries. I expect this area will develop rapidly, so there should be other sleeping and eating options available by the time you arrive.

Incredibly, Xpujil has luxury accommodations, in the form of the *Ramada Chicanná Ecovillage Resort* (☎ /fax (981) 6-22-33), Hwy 186 Km 144, 12 km west of Xpujil junction, then 500 meters north of the highway. Large, airy rooms with private baths and ceiling fans are grouped four to a bungalow and set amid well-tended grass lawns, an odd sight here in the jungle. The small dining room and bar serves decent meals at fairly high prices, but the ambiance here means this is the only place you'll find such a meal anywhere within 100 km of Xpujil. Rates are US$75 to US$95 a double. As this is the only luxury hotel here, you should reserve your room in advance.

Getting There & Away
Xpujil is 220 km south of Hopelchén, 153 km east of Escárcega and 120 km west of Chetumal. There are four buses daily between Xpujil and Campeche, and more between Escárcega and Chetumal. No buses originate in Xpujil, so you must hope to find a vacant seat on one passing through. The bus station is 100 meters east of the highway junction in Xpujil on the north side of the highway.

There is a Pemex fuel station dispensing both leaded and unleaded fuel five km east of Xpujil junction. Make sure you don't get overcharged.

Getting Around
Xpujil Ruins are within walking distance of Xpujil junction. You may be able to hitch a ride to the access roads for Becan and Chicanná, but for other sites you will need to join a tour (see below).

Your own wheels will get you to the sites along the highway, but you may want to abandon them and join a tour to Calakmul or Hormiguero, relying on the guide's 4WD vehicle to get you there and back.

ESCÁRCEGA
Population 18,000

Most buses passing through Escárcega stop here to give passengers a refreshments break, but there is no other reason to stop in this town at the junction of Hwys 186 and 261, 150 km south of Campeche and 301 km from Villahermosa.

The town is spread out along two km of Hwy 186 toward Chetumal. It's 1.7 km between the ADO and Autobuses del Sur bus stations. Most hotels are nearer to the Autobuses del Sur bus station than to the ADO; most of the better restaurants are near the ADO bus station.

Among the better hotels is the *Hotel El Yucateco* (☎ (981) 4-00-65), Calle 50 No 42-A, charging US$13 a double for a room with fan and private shower, a bit more with air-con.

There's also the *Hotel María Isabel* (☎ (981) 4-00-45), Avenida Justo Sierra No 127, 450 meters from Autobuses del Sur, 1200 meters from ADO. Rates are similar to El Yucateco

Hotel Escárcega (☎ (981) 4-01-86/7/8), on the main street, is the best place in town, one km from Autobuses del Sur, 550 meters from ADO.

ESCÁRCEGA TO PALENQUE
The 212-km ride from Escárcega to Palenque is unremarkable and very hot. Upon leaving Escárcega and heading southwest, the fast, straight Highway 186 passes through regions aptly known as El Tormento (Torment) and Sal Si Puedes (Get Out if You Can).

YUCATÁN

By the time you reach Río Champon (or Chumpan), the traditional Mayan *na* with thatched roofs and walls of sticks, wattle-and-daub or stone, have given way to board shacks with roofs of corrugated steel. As you enter the region of the Río Usumacinta the landscape becomes lush, the rich greenery a pleasant surprise after the semiarid, riverless limestone shelf of Yucatán. But along with the lushness comes high humidity and hot temperatures.

About 184 km southwest of Escárcega you come to Catazajá, the junction with the road to Palenque, Ocosingo and San Cristóbal de las Casas. Turn left (south) for Palenque, 27 km south of the highway junction. If your goal is Villahermosa, then continue straight on along Hwy 186.

Yucatán's Caribbean Coast

The coast of Quintana Roo is among the fastest developing areas in Mexico. Because of the raging success of Cancún, developers are rushing to build more leisure palaces along the beaches of what is known rather romantically as the 'Cancún-Tulum Corridor'. A new, wider highway is planned to run along the corridor, inland from the old highway. When finished it will bring the bustle of the city to this otherwise laid-back coast.

For the time being, however, there are still many places to enjoy. Small hotels stand alone on some stretches of beach. The Sian Ka'an Biosphere Reserve, south of Tulum, is protected from development. And it will be a few more years before Playa del Carmen, now a delightful, laid-back town, achieves the uptight money-grubbing fervor of Cancún.

GETTING AROUND

Playa Express runs shuttle buses up and down the coast between Cancún and Tulum every 20 minutes, stopping at major towns and tourist attractions along the way. The fare depends on the distance traveled. There are also regular intercity buses – see the Cancún chapter for details.

Distances shown in this chapter ('Km 328', etc) are as measured from the center of Chetumal, capital of the state of Quintana Roo, down south near the Belizean border.

PUERTO MORELOS (Km 328)

Puerto Morelos, 32 km south of Cancún, is a sleepy fishing village known principally for its car ferry to Cozumel, though a burgeoning industrial park may soon be its claim to fame. There are a few good hotels, and travelers who have reason to spend the night here find it refreshingly free of tourists. A handful of scuba divers come to explore the splendid reef 600 meters offshore, reachable by boat.

Only a few km north of the town, just off the highway, the Jardín Botánico Dr

Alfredo Barrera gives you a look at the flora of Yucatán (and also some fauna) for US$3 per person between 9 am and 5 pm daily.

Places to Stay & Eat

The *Posada Amor* (☎ (987) 1-00-33, fax (987) 1-01-78), Apdo Postal 806, 77580 Cancún, south of the center, is the longtime lodging here. Rooms with fan, shared bathroom and a double bed are expensive, at US$22 or US$28 with two beds, single or double. Meals are served.

Hotel Hacienda Morelos (☎ /fax (987) 1-00-15), 150 meters south of the plaza, on the waterfront, has nice sea-view, sea-breeze rooms for US$50, single or double, and a decent restaurant called *El Mesón* as well. Right next door is *Las Palmeras*, another good restaurant choice, though the best is *Los Pelícanos*, just off the southeast corner of the plaza.

Farther to the south, beyond the ferry terminal, *Rancho Libertad* (☎ (987) 1-01-81, in Mexico (95-800) 730-4322, in the USA (800) 305-5225) has several small, two-story thatched bungalows with a guestroom on each floor. Upstairs rooms are priced at US$65, downstairs US$55, for a single or double, all with private bath, buffet breakfast included. Lower rates are offered when it's not busy. Scuba diving and snorkeling gear is available for rent, as are bicycles.

The *Caribbean Reef Club* (☎ (987) 1-01-91, fax (987) 1-01-90, in the USA (800) 322-6286), right next to the Rancho Libertad, is a beautiful, very comfortable, quiet resort hotel right on the beach. Lots of water sports and activities and helpful owners are the bonuses when you pay the rates: US$110 to US$140 from mid-December to late April, about 30% cheaper in summer.

Getting There & Away

Playa Express buses running between Cancún and Playa del Carmen drop you on the highway, two km west of the center of

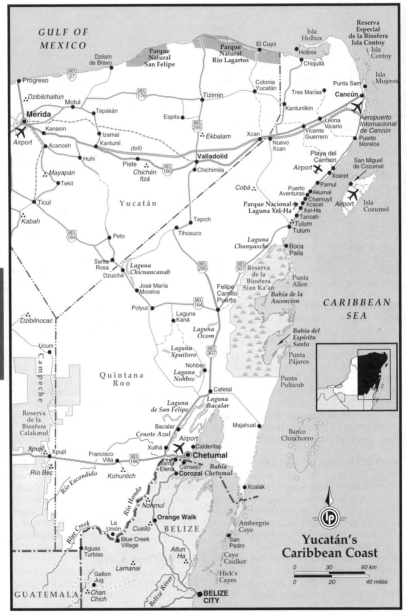

GULF OF MEXICO

Reserva Especial de la Biosfera Isla Contoy

Isla Holbox
Holbox
Chiquilá
Isla Contoy

El Cuyo

Dzilam de Bravo

Parque Natural San Felipe

Parque Natural Río Lagartos

Colonia Yucatán

Punta Sam

Isla Mujeres

Progreso

Tres Marías

Cancún

Dzibilchaltún

Motul

Tizimín

Kantunilkin

Aeropuerto Internacional de Cancún

Mérida

Tepakán

Espita

Ekbalam

Xcan

Leona Vicario

Vicente Guerrero

Puerto Morelos

Airport

Kanasin

Izamal

Kantunil

Nuevo Xcan

Playa del Carmen

San Miguel de Cozumel

Acanceh

Huhi

(toll)

Valladolid

Airport

Xcaret

Pamul

Piste

Chichén Itzá

Chichimila

Cobá

Akumal

Puerto Aventuras

Chemuyil

Xcacel

Airport

Mayapán

Tekit

Parque Nacional Laguna Xel-Ha

Xel-Ha

Tancah

Isla Cozumel

Ticul

Yucatán

Kabah

Tepich

Tulum
Tulum

Peto

Tihosuco

Laguna Chunyaxche

Boca Paila

MEX 184

Santa Rosa

Laguna Chicnancanab

MEX 295

Felipe Carrillo Puerto

Reserva de la Biosfera Sian Ka'an

Punta Allen

CARIBBEAN SEA

Dzuiché

José María Morelos

Polyuc

Laguna Kaná

MEX 184

Bahía de la Ascención

Dzibilnocac

Laguna Ocom

Ucum

MEX 307

Bahía del Espíritu Santo

Laguna Xpaitoro

Punta Pájaros

Campeche

Quintana Roo

Nohbec

Laguna Nohbec

Cafetal

Punta Pulticub

Reserva de la Biosfera Calakmul

Laguna de San Felipe

Laguna Bacalar

Majahual

Banco Chinchorro

Xpujil

Xpujil

Bacalar

Cenote Azul

Airport

Calderitas

Francisco Villa

MEX 186

Xulhá

Chetumal

Río Bec

Santa Elena

Consejo

Bahía Chetumal

Río Escondido

Kohunlich

Corozal

Xcalak

Río Hondo

Nohmul

La Unión

Cuello

Orange Walk

Ambergris Caye

Blue Creek

Blue Creek Village

BELIZE

San Pedro

Aguas Turbias

Altun Ha

Caye Caulker

Gallon Jug

Lamanai

Hick's Cayes

GUATEMALA

Chan Chich

Belize River

BELIZE CITY

Yucatán's Caribbean Coast

0   30   60 km

0   20   40 miles

Puerto Morelos. All 2nd-class and many 1st-class buses stop at Puerto Morelos coming from, or en route to, Cancún, 36 km (45 minutes) away.

The *transbordador* (car ferry, in Cozumel ☎ (987) 2-09-50, 2-09-50) to Cozumel leaves Puerto Morelos at noon on Tuesday, at 8 am on Monday and Wednesday, and at 6 am on other days. Departure times are subject to change from season to season and according to the weather.

Unless you plan to stay for a while on Cozumel, it's hardly worth shipping your vehicle: You must get in line up to 12 hours before departure time and hope there's enough space on the ferry for you. Fare for the 2½- to four-hour voyage is US$30 per car, US$4.50 per person.

Departure from Cozumel is from the dock in front of the Hotel Sol Caribe, south of town along the shore road.

PLAYA DEL CARMEN

For decades Playa del Carmen was just a simple fishing village on the coast opposite Cozumel. With the construction of Cancún, however, the number of travelers roaming this part of Yucatán increased exponentially. Now Playa del Carmen has taken over from Cozumel as the preferred resort town in the area. Playa's beaches are better and the nightlife groovier than Cozumel's, and the reef diving is just as good. On the beaches tops are optional everywhere; nudity is optional about a kilometer north of the Playa del Carmen town center.

What's to do in Playa? Hang out. Swim. Dive. Stroll the beach. Get some sun. Catch the Playa Express shuttle to other points along the coast. In the evening Avenida Quinta, the pedestrian mall, is the place to sit and have a meal or a drink or stroll and watch others having meals and drinks. Early evening happy hour (5 to 7 pm), with two drinks for the price of one, is an ironclad rule. I found it impossible to order a single beer. The waiter automatically brought two.

Places to Stay

Playa del Carmen is developing and changing so fast that almost anything written about it is obsolete by the time it's printed. Expect many new hotels by the time you arrive, and many changes in the old ones. The room prices given below are for the busy winter season. Prices are substantially lower at other times.

Places to Stay – budget

The youth hostel, or *Villa Deportiva Juvenil* (no phone), 1.2 km from the ferry docks, is a modern establishment offering the cheapest clean lodging in town, but it's quite a walk to the beach and you sleep in single-sex dorm bunks. On the positive side, the hostel is quite cheap, at US$3 per bunk.

Camping-Cabañas La Ruina (☎ (987) 2-14-74, fax (987) 2-15-98), on Calle 2 just off the beach, offers several cheap ways to sleep. Pitch your own tent for US$3 per person or hang your hammock beneath their palapa for slightly more; rent a hammock from them, or a simple cabaña with two cots and ceiling fan for US$8 to US$11, or a more comfortable cabaña with private bath for US$15 to US$40. Be careful to secure your stuff from roaming thieves. La Ruina rents lockers, but it's best to have your own sturdy lock.

Posada Lily, on Avenida Juárez (Avenida Principal) just a block inland from the main square, offers clean rooms with private shower and fan for US$16 a double.

Posada Yumil-Kin (no phone), Calle 1 between Avenidas Quinta and 10, is simple, clean, convenient and cheap, at US$15 a double with fan.

At *Cabañas Nuevo Amanecer* (☎ (987) 3-00-30), Calle 4 between Avenidas 5 and 10, each cabaña has a shady little porch complete with hammock. The cabañas go for US$18 with shared bath, US$26 with private bath.

Tour groups sometimes fill the *Hotel Mar Caribe* (☎ (987) 3-02-07), Calle 1 and Avenida 15, but if you can get a room it'll be clean, if simple, and cost about US$30 with private bath, a good price for what you get.

Places to Stay – middle

Hotel Costa del Mar (☎ (987) 3-00-58, fax (987) 2-02-31) has clean, attractive rooms

YUCATÁN

PLACES TO STAY
2   Villa Deportiva Juvenil
     (Youth Hostel)
3   Hotel Mayan Paradise
4   Quinta Mija
5   Hotel Da Gabi
7   Hotel Maya Bric
9   Copa Cabaña
10 Hotel Casablanca
11 Hotel Costa del Mar
16 Cabañas Nuevo Amanecer
25 Camping-Cabañas La Ruina
29 Hotel Mar Caribe
33 Posada Lily
34 Posada Yumil-Kin
42 Hotel Continental Plaza

PLACES TO EAT
5   Restaurant Da Gabi
8   Apple Café
13 Restaurant El Chino
17 Panadería del Carmen
18 Restaurant Limones
22 Karen's Grill & Pizza
23 Panificadora Aguilar
26 Restaurant La Tarraya
36 Restaurant Playa Caribe
38 Restaurant Máscaras
40 Las Piñatas

OTHER
1   Pemex
6   Lavandería Aventuras
12 Blue Parrot Inn
14 Municipal Market, Comedores
15 Lavandería Yee
19 Bancomer, ATM
20 Post Office
21 Town Hall
24 Maya Laundry
27 Small Mayan Ruin
28 Aero Cozumel Ticket Office
30 Centro de Salud
31 School
32 Banco del Atlántico
35 Bus Terminal
37 Tourist Information Booth
39 Church
41 Cozumel Ferry Ticket Booths

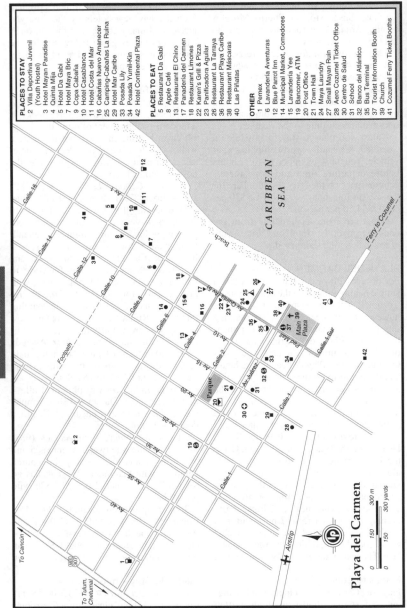

Playa del Carmen

To Cancún

To Tulum,
Chetumal

Airstrip

CARIBBEAN
SEA

Ferry to Cozumel

Parque

Main
Plaza

Beach

Ped Mall

0   150   300 m
0   150   300 yards

YUCATÁN

on the beach off Avenida Quinta at Calle 10 for US$55/75 a double with fan/air-con. The simpler cabañas are considerably cheaper but have no air-con.

Across the street, the *Hotel Casablanca* (☎ (987) 3-00-57), Avenida 1 between Calles 10 and 12, is new, nice, clean and neat, with a palapa restaurant-bar perched above the street. Double rooms cost US$32 with one bed, US$40 with two, US$50 with air-con.

Copa Cabaña (☎ (987) 3-02-18), Avenida 5 between Calles 10 and 12, boasts comfortable fan-cooled rooms with private showers arranged around a particularly lush courtyard; macaws in a cage add color. You pay US$40 for a double with one or two beds.

Even more posh and atmospheric is *Quinta Mija* (☎ /fax (987) 3-01-11), Avenida 5 at Calle 14, where the lush tropical courtyard features a quiet bar as well. Rooms with double beds go for US$50 with one bed or US$70 with two.

Hotel Maya Bric (☎ /fax (987) 3-00-11), on Avenida Quinta between Calles 8 and 10, is a small hotel with big rooms set around a swimming pool amid flowering shrubs and coconut trees. Rates vary with the seasons, ranging from US$30 in summer to US$45 in winter for a double with bath.

Hotel Da Gabi (☎ (987) 3-00-48, fax (987) 3-01-98), Calle 12 south of Avenida Quinta, is much less fancy than its adjoining *ristorante* (see below). Serviceable (though far from fancy) rooms with private shower and ceiling fan cost US$35.

Hotel Mayan Paradise (☎ (987) 3-09-33, in the USA ☎ (800) 217-2192, fax (904) 824-5284), Avenida 10 at Calle 12, is among the best values in town. Beautifully kept two-and three-story wooden thatch-roofed bungalows house large, comfortable, modern rooms complete with bath, kitchenette, cable TV, fans and air-con. The pool is surrounded by fine, if small, tropical gardens. With a light breakfast, you pay US$65/75/85/95 a single/double/triple/quad.

Places to Stay – top end

Those seeking international-class luxury lodging will find the *Hotel Continental*

Plaza (☎ (987) 3-01-00, fax (987) 3-01-05, in the USA (800) 882-6684) to their liking at US$140 to US$200 per room.

Places to Eat

It was inevitable: As Playa del Carmen became more popular, souvenir and jewelry shops pushed out the cheap restaurants along Avenida Quinta. Prices are now higher for meals here, but this is where the action is. The best plan is to stroll along the avenue, look for a busy restaurant, peruse the menu, ask the drink prices, and decide whether or not to settle in.

For value, look inland several blocks, where the locals dine. The cheapest eateries, as always, are the little *comedores* right next to the Municipal Market. Another good place to look is Calle 1 Sur just northwest of the plaza, a short street with several restaurants.

For make-your-own breakfasts and picnics, there's the *Panadería del Carmen*, on Avenida Quinta southwest of Calle 6, and *Panificadora Aguilar*, one block farther southwest.

Restaurant La Tarraya, at the southern end of Calle 2, has guacamole for US$1.50, fried fish for US$2.50 and *pulpo* (octopus) for US$3.25 – good prices, and it's right on the beach.

The *Apple Café* is a tidy, German-run place serving crepes, quesadillas, burgers, waffles and other light meals for moderate prices. A hamburger and a glass of fresh orange juice costs US$4.50.

Restaurant Da Gabi is fancier than the adjoining hotel of the same name, but prices are moderate and the quiet atmosphere soothed by jazz is more refined than that of Avenida Quinta. Pasta plates and huge pizzas sell for US$5 to US$8, grilled meat and fish for US$7 to US$12. They even have a few imported wines.

Because it's farther from the beach and Avenida Quinta, *Restaurant El Chino*, Calle 4 between Avenidas 10 and 15, has lower prices and better food, as well as a pleasant setting and decent service. A full meal of soup, ceviche or grilled fish and dessert might cost US$10 or US$12, drinks and tip included.

YUCATÁN

Of the more expensive places, the *Restaurant Máscaras*, on the main plaza, is the most famous and long-lived. The pizzas (US$4 to US$7) are dependably good, the more complex dishes less so, but it's the company you come for. Drinks are expensive. *Las Piñatas*, downhill from Máscaras, has the best sea view.

A better choice as far as the food is concerned is the *Restaurant Limones*, Avenida Quinta at Calle 6, where the atmosphere is more sedate than jolly. Though you can pay up to US$19 for their 'Symphony of Seafood', with lobster, shrimp and conch, most fish dishes cost around US$5, and filet mignon costs US$12.

Restaurant Playa Caribe, on Avenida Quinta, seems to be a bit cheaper than the other places. A big, varied Mexican combination plate costs US$7.50.

Entertainment

The evening happy hour is more certain than death and taxes in Playa. When the sun goes down the sound of beer bottles being opened is louder than the crash of surf. Avenida Quinta is the epicenter. *Karen's Grill & Pizza* often has marimba music in the evenings, and the *Red & Black Bar* at Restaurant Limones features live jazz, but the bar at the *Blue Parrot Inn* is among the cooler places, with an international clientele.

Getting There & Away

Air Playa's little airstrip handles mostly small charter, tour and air taxi flights. Aero Cozumel (☎ (987) 3-03-50), part of Mexicana Inter, has an office next to Playa's airstrip, as does Aero Saab. They'll fly you to Cozumel for US$70 (up to five people), or roundtrip to Chichén Itzá for US$120 per person.

Bus ADO, ATS, Cristóbal Colón, Mayab and Oriente serve Playa's bus terminal, at the corner of Avenida Juárez and Avenida Quinta. Playa Express buses run up and down the coast every 20 minutes, charging US$1.75 from Playa to either Tulum or Cancún.

Cancún – 65 km, one hour, US$1.75; frequent buses by ADO, Playa Express and Oriente

Chetumal – 315 km, five hours; seven buses by ADO (US$10 to US$12), one by Colón (US$10) and three by Mayab (US$6.50)

Chichén Itzá – 272 km, four hours, US$6 to US$9; five buses

Cobá – 113 km, two hours; four buses by Oriente (US$2.50) and one by ATS (US$2.75)

Mérida – 385 km, seven hours; nine buses by ADO (US$10 to US$11.75), several others by ATS (US$8) and Mayab (US$10)

Palenque – 800 km, 12 hours; one bus each by ADO (US$27), Colón (US$25) and ATS (US$20)

San Cristóbal de las Casas – 990 km, 18 hours; one each by ADO (US$30), Colón (US$27) and ATS (US$24)

Tulum – 63 km, one hour; Playa Express every 20 minutes (US$2.25) and four buses by (US$1.50)

Valladolid – 213 km, 3½ hours; five buses by ADO (US$6) four by ATS (US$5); many buses going to Mérida via Cancún stop at Valladolid, but it's faster to go on the *ruta corta* ('short route') via Tulum and Cobá (see Cobá).

Boats to Cozumel Approach the dock and you can't miss the ticket booths for *México, México II* and *México III*, charging US$4 one way to Cozumel. Together they make a dozen runs daily on the 30-minute voyage.

ISLA COZUMEL

Population 175,000

Cozumel (Place of the Swallows) floats in the midst of the Caribbean's crystalline waters 71 km south of Cancún. Measuring 53 km long and 14 km wide, it is the largest of Mexico's islands. Cozumel's legendary Palancar Reef was made famous by Jacques Cousteau and is a lure for divers from all over the world.

Though it has that beautiful offshore reef, Cozumel does not have many good swimming beaches. The western shore is mostly sharp, weathered limestone and coral, and the eastern beaches are too often pounded by dangerous surf.

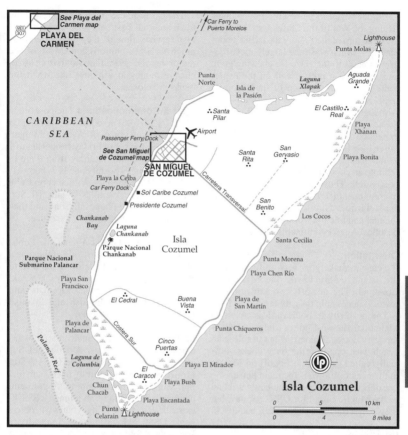

Isla Cozumel

History

Mayan settlement here dates from 300 AD. During the Postclassic period, Cozumel flourished both as a commercial center and as a major ceremonial site. Maya sailed here on pilgrimages to shrines dedicated to Ixchel, the goddess of fertility and the moon.

Although the first Spanish contact with Cozumel in 1518 by Juan de Grijalva was peaceful, it was followed by the Cortés expedition in 1519. Cortés, en route to his conquest of the mainland, laid waste to Cozumel's Mayan shrines. The Maya offered staunch military resistance until they were conquered in 1545. The coming of the Spaniards brought smallpox to this otherwise disease-free place. Within a generation after the conquest, the island's population had dwindled to only 300 souls, Mayan and Spanish.

While the island remained virtually deserted into the late 17th century, its coves provided sanctuary and headquarters for several notorious pirates, including Jean Lafitte and Henry Morgan. Pirate brutality led the remaining populace to move to the mainland, and it wasn't until 1848 that

Cozumel began to be resettled by Indians fleeing the War of the Castes.

At the turn of the century the island's population – which was now largely mestizo – grew, thanks to the craze for chewing gum. Cozumel was a port of call on the export route for *chicle* (the sap of the sapodilla tree), and locals harvested it on the island. Although chicle was later replaced by synthetic gum, Cozumel's economic base expanded with the building of a US Air Force base here during WWII.

When the US military departed, the island fell into an economic slump and many of its people left. Those who stayed fished for a livelihood until 1961, when underwater scientist Jacques Cousteau arrived, explored the reef and told the world about Cozumel's beauties. A resort destination was born.

Orientation

It's easy to make your way on foot around the island's only town, San Miguel de Cozumel. The airport, two km north of town, is accessible only by taxi or on foot.

The waterfront boulevard is Avenida Melgar; on the west side of Melgar, south of the ferry docks, is a narrow but usable sand beach. Just opposite the ferry docks (officially called the Muelle Fiscal) on Melgar in the center of town is the main plaza.

Lockers are for rent at the landward end of the Muelle Fiscal for US$2 per day, but they're not big enough for a full backpack.

Information

Tourist Office The local tourist office (☎ (987) 2-09-72) is on the 2nd floor of a building facing the main square to the north of the Bancomer. Hours are Monday to Friday 9 am to 3 pm and 6 to 8 pm.

Money For currency exchange, Banamex and Banca Serfin (see map) have ATMs. Bancomer and Banco del Atlántico, off the main plaza, change money only from 10 am to 12:30 pm, Monday to Friday, and the queues are long. Banpaís, facing the ferry docks, will change your travelers' checks Monday to Friday from 9 am to 1:30 pm for a 1% commission.

The casas de cambio located around the town are your best bets for long hours and fast service, though they may charge as much as 3.5% commission. Most of the major hotels, restaurants and stores will change money at a higher rate when the banks are closed.

Post & Communications The post office (☎ (987) 2-01-06) is south of Calle 7 Sur on the waterfront, just off Avenida Melgar. Hours are Monday to Friday from 9 am to 1 pm and 3 to 6 pm, Saturday from 9 am to noon. Cozumel's postal code is 77600.

The TelMex telephone office is on Calle Salas between Avenidas 5 and 10 Sur. There are Ladatel phones in front, and they sell telephone debit cards in the office.

Bookstore The Gracia Agencia de Publicaciones, on the southeast side of the plaza, 40 meters from the clock tower and next to Bancomer, is open seven days a week, selling English, French, German and Spanish books and English and Spanish magazines and newspapers.

Laundry Margarita Laundromat (Lavandería de Autoservicio), Avenida 20 Sur 285, between Calle Salas and Calle 3 Sur, is open Monday to Saturday from 7 am to 9 pm, Sunday from 9 am to 5 pm, and charges US$1.50 to wash a load (US$0.40 extra if you don't bring your own detergent), US$0.70 for 10 minutes in the dryer. Ironing and folding cost extra. There's also the Lavandería Express, Calle Salas at Avenida 10 Sur.

Island Museum

The Museo de la Isla de Cozumel, Avenida Melgar between Calles 4 and 6 Norte, has nautical exhibits covering the history of the island. It's open daily from 10 am to 6 pm (closed Saturday); admission is US$3.

Activities

Scuba Diving For equipment rental, instruction and/or boat reservations, there are numerous dive shops on Avenida Melgar along San Miguel's waterfront.

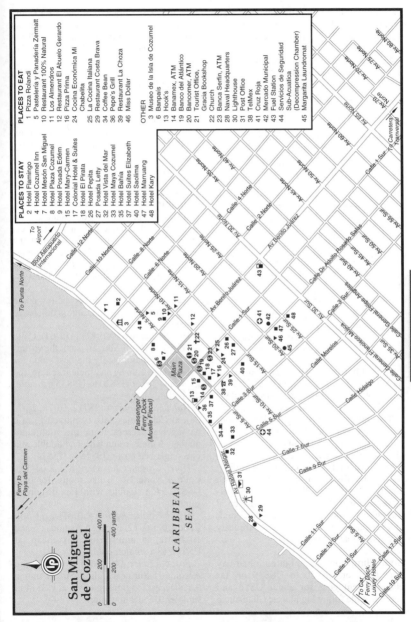

San Miguel de Cozumel

0   200   400 m
0   200   400 yards

To Airport
To Punta Norte
Ferry to Playa del Carmen
CARIBBEAN SEA
Passenger Ferry Dock (Muelle Fiscal)
To Car Ferry Dock Luxury Hotels
To Carretera Transversal

PLACES TO STAY
2   Hotel Flamingo
4   Hotel Cozumel Inn
7   Hotel Mesón San Miguel
8   Hotel Plaza Cozumel
9   Hotel Posada Edém
15   Hotel Mary-Carmen
17   Colonial Hotel & Suites
18   Hotel El Pirata
26   Hotel Pepita
27   Posada Letty
32   Hotel Vista del Mar
33   Hotel Maya Cozumel
35   Hotel Bahía
37   Hotel Suites Elizabeth
40   Hotel Saolima
47   Hotel Marruang
48   Hotel Kary

PLACES TO EAT
1   Pizza Rolandi
5   Pastelería y Panadería Zermatt
10   Restaurant 100% Natural
11   Los Almendros
12   Restaurant El Abuelo Gerardo
16   Pizza Prima
24   Cocina Económica Mi Chabelita
25   La Cocina Italiana
29   Restaurant Costa Brava
34   Coffee Bean
36   Pepe's Grill
39   Restaurant La Choza
46   Miss Dollar

OTHER
3   Museo de la Isla de Cozumel
6   Banpais
13   Hook's
14   Banamex, ATM
19   Banco del Atlántico
20   Bancomer, ATM
21   Tourist Office;
     Gracia Bookshop
22   Church
23   Banca Serfin, ATM
28   Naval Headquarters
30   Lighthouse
31   Post Office
38   TelMex
41   Cruz Roja
42   Mercado Municipal
43   Fuel Station
44   Servicios de Seguridad Sub-Acuatica (Decompression Chamber)
45   Margarita Laundromat

YUCATÁN

Generally, a two-tank, full-day scuba trip will cost US$50 to US$65, an introductory scuba course US$60 and a full certification course US$300.

Cozumel has over 60 dive shops. Here are a few names and addresses:

Black Shark Dive Shop, Avenida 5 Sur
between Calle Salas and Calle 3 Sur
(987) 2-03-96, fax 2-56-57)

Blue Bubble Divers, Avenida 5 Sur and
Calle 3 Sur (☎ /fax (987) 2-18-65)

Caballito del Caribe, Avenida 10 Sur No 124-B
(☎ (987) 2-14-49)

Caribbean Divers, Avenida Melgar at
Calle 5 Sur (☎ (987) 2-10-80)

Dive Paradise (Paraíso del Buceo),
Avenida Melgar 601
(☎ (987) 2-10-07, (987) fax 2-10-61)

Pascual's Scuba Center, Calle Salas 176
(☎ /fax (987) 2-54-54)

Pro Dive, Calle Salas 198, at Avenida 5 Sur
(☎ /fax (987) 2-41-23)

Yucatech Expeditions, Avenida 15 Sur
between Salas and Calle 1 Sur
(☎ (987) 2-46-18, 4-78-35); Yucatech
specializes in diving Yucatán's cenotes.

The local hyperbaric chamber is Servicios de Seguridad Sub-Acuatica (☎ (987) 2-23-87, 2-14-30, fax (987) 2-18-48), Calle 5 Sur No 21-B, open 24 hours.

The most prominent scuba destinations are the five-km-long Palancar Reef, where stunning coral formations and a 'horse-shoe' of coral heads in 70-meter visibility offer some of the world's finest diving; Maracaibo Reef, where the current and aquatic life offer experienced divers a challenge; Paraíso Reef, famous for its coral formations, especially brain and star coral; and Yocab Reef, shallow yet vibrantly alive and great for beginners.

Snorkeling You can go out on a half-day boat tour for US$20 to US$30 or, far cheaper, rent gear for about US$8 and snorkel at the following places: Chankanab Bay, Playa San Francisco, Playa La Ceiba (near the car ferry dock, where a plane was purposely sunk for the film *Survive)*, Presidente Cozumel Hotel and Palancar.

Glass-Bottom Boat You can enjoy the coral formations and aquatic life by taking a tour by glass-bottom boat on the *Palapa Marina* (☎ (987) 2-05-39), Calle 1 Sur No 177, between Avenidas 5 and 10. The boat departs the Sol Caribe pier, south of San Miguel, near the car ferry dock, daily at 9 am and 1 pm. The fare is US$15 per person.

Places to Stay – budget
Camping To camp anywhere on the island, you'll need a permit from the island's naval authorities, obtainable 24 hours a day, free, from the naval headquarters, south of the post office on Avenida Melgar. The best camping places are along the relatively unpopulated eastern shore of the island.

Hotels All rooms described below come with private bath and fan, unless otherwise noted.

Hotel Flamingo (☎ (987) 2-12-64), Calle 6 Norte No 81, off Melgar, is not the cheapest, but it's undoubtedly the best value for your money. Run by an efficient señora, the 21 rooms go for US$20 to US$35 a double, depending on the season.

Hotel Marruang (☎ (987) 2-16-78, 2-02-08), at Calle Salas 440, is entered from a passageway across from the municipal market. A clean room with one double and one single bed costs US$16 to US$24.

Hotel Cozumel Inn (☎ (987) 2-03-14), Calle 4 Norte No 3, has rooms for only US$20/24 a double with fan/air-con in summer.

Hotel Posada Edém (☎ (987) 2-11-66), Calle 2 Norte 12, between Avenidas 5 and 10 Norte, is uninspiring but cheap, at US$12/18 a single/double.

Posada Letty (☎ (987) 2-02-57), on Avenida 15 Sur near Calle 1 Sur, is among the cheapest lodgings in town, at US$14 in summer, US$19 in winter.

Hotel Saolima (☎ (987) 2-08-86), Calle Salas 268, between Avenidas 10 and 15 Sur, has clean, pleasant rooms in a quiet locale for US$14/18 a double/triple in summer.

Hotel Kary (☎ (987) 2-20-11), Calle Salas at Avenida 25 Sur, is five blocks east of the plaza and thus a bit out of the way. They charge US$17 for a double with fan and US$24 with air-con. There's even a pool.

Places to Stay – middle
Most middle-range hostelries offer air-conditioning and swimming pools. All have private bathrooms.

Hotel Vista del Mar (☎ (987) 2-05-45, fax (987) 2-04-45), Avenida Melgar 45, at Calle 5 Sur, has a small swimming pool, restaurant, liquor store and rental car and travel agency. Some rooms have balconies with sea views. The price in summer is US$40 a double, rising to US$50 in winter.

Tried and true, clean, comfortable lodgings are yours at the *Hotel Mary-Carmen* (☎ (987) 2-05-81), Avenida 5 Sur 4, half a block south of the plaza. The 27 tidy air-con rooms cost US$28 a double in summer, US$40 in winter. Equally pleasant and even cheaper is the *Hotel Suites Elizabeth* (☎ (987) 2-03-30), Calle Salas 44. Air-con bedrooms have kitchenettes here.

Hotel Pepita (☎ (987) 2-00-98, fax (987) 2-02-01), Avenida 15 Sur No 120, corner of Calle 1 Sur, has well-maintained rooms around a delightful garden for US$25 in summer, US$35 in winter. Most rooms have two double beds, insect screens, little refrigerators and fans, as well as the air-con, and there's free morning coffee.

Colonial Hotel & Suites (☎ (987) 2-40-34, fax (987) 2-13-87), Avenida 5 Sur No 9, has studios and one-bedroom suites (some of which can sleep up to four people) with kitchenette, air-con and pretensions to decor for US$42 to US$52 a double.

The similar *Hotel Bahía* (☎ (987) 2-02-09, fax (987) 2-13-87), facing the sea on Avenida Melgar at Calle 3 Sur, under the same management, charges slightly more.

Hotel El Pirata (☎ (987) 2-00-51), Avenida 5 Sur 121, offers decent rooms with private bath and fan for US$19 a double in summer, US$28 with air-con.

Hotel Maya Cozumel (☎ (987) 2-00-11, fax (987) 2-07-18), Calle 5 Sur No 4, has good TV-equipped rooms and a pool surrounded by grass and bougainvillea for US$35/40/45 a single/double/triple in winter, about US$5 less per room in summer.

Hotel Plaza Cozumel (☎ (987) 2-27-11, fax (987) 2-00-66), Calle 2 Norte 3, just off Avenida Melgar a block north of the plaza, is a modern hotel with a rooftop swimming pool, color TV and prices of US$50 in summer, US$75 in winter.

Hotel Mesón San Miguel (☎ (987) 2-03-23, fax (987) 2-18-20), Avenida Juárez 2-B, on the north side of the plaza, has a little pool, blissful air-con, a restaurant, and 100 rooms with balconies. There's also a separate beach club with water sports facilities seven blocks from the hotel, on the water. Rates are US$55/80 a double in summer/winter.

Places to Stay – top end
Several km south of town are the big luxury resort hotels of an international standard, which charge US$150 to US$300 for a room during the winter season. North of town along the western shore of the island are numerous smaller, more modest resort hotels, usually cheaper than the big places, but catering mostly to package tour groups.

South of town, the *Presidente Cozumel* (☎ (987) 2-03-22, fax (987) 2-13-60), Carretera a Chankanab Km 6.5, is hard to miss, with its 259 rooms, many with sea views, set amid tropical gardens.

Sol Caribe Cozumel (☎ (987) 2-07-00, fax (987) 2-13-01), Playa Paraíso Km 3.5 (Apdo Postal 259, Cozumel, Quintana Roo 77600), has 321 luxurious rooms and a lavish layout, with a tropical swimming pool complete with a large 'island'. For reservations at both of the above hotels, call ☎ (800) 343-7821 in the USA.

Paradisus Cozumel (☎ (987) 2-04-11, fax (987) 2-15-99), Playa Santa Pilar, is a 200-room Meliá resort with a full list of water sports equipment. Another Meliá hotel right nearby, the *Sol Cabañas del Caribe* (☎ (987) 2-01-61, 2-00-17, fax (987) 2-15-99) caters mostly to divers. For reservations, call ☎ (800) 336-3542 in the USA.

Places to Eat – budget
Cheapest of all eating places, with fairly tasty food, are the market loncherías, located next to the Mercado Municipal on Calle Salas between Avenidas 20 and 25 Sur. All these little eateries offer soup and a main course for less than US$3, with a large selection of dishes available. Hours are 6:30 am to 6:30 pm daily.

Restaurant Costa Brava, on Avenida Melgar just south of the post office, is among the more interesting places to dine on the island. Cheap breakfasts (US$2 to US$3) and such filling dishes as chicken tacos, grilled steak and fried fish or chicken (US$3 to US$7) are served daily from 6:30 am to 11:30 pm.

Restaurant La Choza, Calle Salas 198, specializes in authentic Mexican traditional cuisine, which is not all tacos and enchiladas. Have the pozole, a filling, spicy meat-and-hominy stew. With a soft drink, you pay US$6 for a huge bowl.

The *Cocina Económica Mi Chabelita*, Avenida 10 Sur between Calle 1 Sur and Calle Salas, is a tiny, fairly cheap eatery run by a señora who serves up decent portions of decent food for US$3 or less. It opens for breakfast at 7 am and closes at 7 pm.

The forthrightly named *Miss Dollar* earns its money by providing meals to take out. The *Coffee Bean*, Calle 3 Sur just off Avenida Melgar, serves up the latest trendy java recipes.

Restaurant 100% Natural, Calle 2 Norte at Avenida 10 Norte, serves meals for as little as US$6 – and they're all natural.

For pastries, try the *Pastelería y Panadería Zermatt*, Avenida 5 Norte and Calle 4 Norte.

Places to Eat – middle
My favorite is *Pizza Prima* (☎ (987) 2-42-42), Calle Salas 109 between Avenidas 5

and 10 Sur, open from 1 to 11 pm (closed Wednesday). The American owners produce homemade pasta and fresh pizza (US$5 to US$12), as well as excellent Italian specialties (US$8 to US$15). Dine streetside or upstairs on the patio.

Pizza Rolandi, Avenida Melgar between Calles 6 and 8 Norte, serves good one-person pizzas (20 cm in diameter) for US$7 to US$9. It's open from 11:30 am to 11:30 pm; closed Sunday.

Restaurant El Abuelo Gerardo (☎ (987) 2-10-12), Avenida 10 Norte No 21, is attractive, with locally made crafts for decoration and lively salsa music. The menu is extensive, and prices moderate: US$3 for chicken, US$6 for beef, US$5 to US$9 for seafood. The guacamole and chips are on the house.

La Cocina Italiana, Avenida 10 Sur No 121, at Calle 1 Sur, has rustic wooden tables and rustic pizzas and pastas, but prices straight out of central Roma: US$6 to US$8 for pizzas, US$10 to US$13 for meat or fish.

Los Almendros, the famous Yucatecan restaurant that originated in Ticul, has branches in Mérida, Cancún and now Cozumel, at Avenida 10 Norte and Calle 2 Norte. Come here for authentic Yucatecan dishes at moderate prices.

Places to Eat – top end
Cozumel's traditional place to dine well and richly is *Pepe's Grill* (☎ (987) 2-02-13), Avenida Melgar at Calle Salas. Flaming shrimp, grilled lobster, caesar salad and other top-end items can take your bill to the lofty heights of US$25 to US$40 per person.

Entertainment
Nightlife in Cozumel is pricey, but if you want to dance, the most popular disco is *Neptuno Dance Club*, five blocks south of the post office, on Avenida Melgar at Calle 11 Sur. Cover charge is US$5, with drinks (even Mexican beer) for US$3 and up. Another hot spot, similarly priced, is *Hook's*, at the intersection of Avenida

Melgar and Calle Salas. For Latin salsa music, try *Los Quetzales*, Avenida 10 Sur at Calle 1 Sur, a block from the plaza. It's open every evening from 6 pm.

Getting There & Away

Air Cozumel has a surprisingly busy international airport, with numerous direct flights from other parts of Mexico and the USA. Flights from Europe are usually routed via the USA or Mexico City. There are direct flights on Continental (☎ (987) 2-02-51) and American (☎ (987) 2-08-99) from their hubs at Dallas, Houston and Raleigh-Durham, with many direct flights from other US cities via these hubs. Mexicana (☎ (987) 2-02-63) has nonstops from Miami and direct flights from Mérida and Mexico City.

Aero Cozumel (☎ (987) 2-09-28, 2-05-03), with offices at Cozumel airport, operates flights between Cancún and Cozumel about every two hours throughout the day for US$50 one way. Reserve in advance.

Ferry Passenger ferries run from Playa del Carmen, car ferries from Puerto Morelos. See those sections for details.

Getting Around

To/From the Airport The airport is about two km north of town. You can take a minibus from the airport into town for less than US$2, slightly more to the hotels south of town, but you'll have to take a taxi (US$4) to return to the airport.

Bus & Taxi Cozumel's taxi drivers have a lock on the local transport market, defeating any proposal for convenient bus service. Fares in and around town are US$3 per ride; from the town to Laguna Chankanab it's US$7.

Car & Motorcycle Rates for rental cars are upwards of US$40 to $55 per day, all inclusive. You could probably haggle with a taxi driver to take you on a tour of the island, drop you at a beach and come back and pick you up, and still save money;

keep this shocking fact in mind when you consider renting a car. If you do rent, observe the law on vehicle occupancy: Usually only five people are allowed in a vehicle (say, a Jeep). If you carry more, the police will fine you.

The island has one fuel station, on Avenida Juárez five blocks east of the main square.

Rented mopeds are popular with those who want to tour the island on their own. It seems that every citizen and business in San Miguel – hotels, restaurants, gift shops, morticians – rents mopeds, generally for US$25 to US$32 per day (24 hours), though some rent from 8 am to 5 pm for US$18. Insurance and tax are included in those prices. It's amusing that a 24-hour rental of two mopeds (for two people) almost equals the cost of renting a car (for up to four people) for the same period of time.

You must have a valid driver's license, and you must use a credit card to rent, or put down a hefty deposit (around US$50).

The best time to rent is first thing in the morning, when all the machines are there. Choose a good one, with a working horn, brakes, lights, starter, rear-view mirrors, and a full tank of fuel; remember that the price asked will be the same whether you rent the newest, pristine machine or the oldest, most beat-up rattletrap. (If you want to trust your life to a second-rate moped, at least haggle the price down significantly.) You should get a helmet and a lock and chain with the moped; the law requires that you wear a helmet.

Don't plan to circumnavigate the island with two people on one moped. The well-used and ill-maintained machine may well break down under the load, stranding you a long way from civilization with no way to get help.

When riding keep in mind that you will be as exposed to sunshine on a moped as you would be if you were roasting on a beach. Slather yourself with sun block (especially the backs of your hands, feet and neck and your face), or cover up, or

YUCATÁN

suffer the consequences. Also, be aware of the dangers involved: Of all motor vehicle operators, the inexperienced moped driver on unfamiliar roads in a foreign country has the highest statistical chance of having an accident, especially when faced with lots of other inexperienced moped drivers. Drive carefully.

TOURING ISLA COZUMEL

In order to see most of the island (except for Chankanab Bay, which you can walk to) you will have to rent a moped or bicycle or take a taxi (see Getting Around in the previous section). The following route will take you south from the town of San Miguel, then counterclockwise around the island.

Chankanab Bay Beach

This bay of clear water and fabulously colored fish is the most popular on the island. It is nine km south of the town.

You used to be able to swim in the adjoining lagoon, but so many tourists were fouling the water and damaging the coral that Laguna Chankanab was made a national park and put off limits to swimmers. Don't despair – you can still snorkel in the sea here, and the lagoon has been saved from destruction.

Snorkeling equipment can be rented for about US$7 per day. Divers will be interested in a reef offshore; there is a dive shop at the beach, and scuba instruction is offered.

If you get hungry, there is a restaurant and snack shop on the premises. The beach has dressing rooms, lockers and showers, which are included in the US$3 admission price to the national park, open 9 am to 5 pm daily. The park also has a botanical garden containing 400 species of tropical plants.

San Francisco & Palancar Beaches

Playa San Francisco, 14 km from San Miguel, and Playa Palancar, a few km to the south, are the nicest of the island's beaches. San Francisco's white sands run

for more than three km, and rather expensive food is served at its restaurant. If you want to scuba or snorkel at Palancar Reef, you will have to sign on for a day cruise or charter a boat.

El Cedral

To see these small Mayan ruins, the oldest on the island, go 3.5 km down a paved road a short distance south of Playa San Francisco. Although El Cedral was thought to be an important ceremonial site, its minor remnants are not well preserved. The surrounding area is the agricultural heart of Cozumel.

Punta Celarain

The southern tip of the island has a picturesque lighthouse, accessible via a dirt track, four km from the highway. To enjoy truly isolated beaches, climb over the sand dunes. There's a fine view of the island from the top of the lighthouse.

East Coast Drive

The wildest part of the island, the eastern shoreline, is highly recommended for beautiful panoramas of rocky coast, though lately some views are sullied by rubbish. Unfortunately, except for Punta Chiqueros, Chen Río and Punta Morena, swimming is dangerous on Cozumel's east coast because of potentially lethal rip tides and undertow. Be careful! Swim only in coves protected from the open surf by headlands or breakwaters. There are small eateries at both Punta Morena and Punta Chiqueros and a hotel at Punta Morena. Some travelers camp at Chen Río.

El Castillo Real & San Gervasio Ruins

Beyond where the east coast highway meets the Carretera Transversal (cross-island road) that runs to town, intrepid travelers may take the sand track about 17 km from the junction to the Mayan ruins known as El Castillo Real. They are not very well preserved, and you'll need luck or a 4WD vehicle to navigate the sandy road.

There is another, equally unimpressive ruin off the carretera called San Gervasio. Vehicles with 4WD can reach it from a track heading northeast off the Carretera Transversal, but most rental-car insurance policies do not cover unpaved roads such as this. The jungle en route is more interesting than the ruins.

Punta Molas Lighthouse
There are some fairly good beaches and minor Mayan ruins in the vicinity of the island's northeast point, accessible only by 4WD vehicle or foot.

BEACHES ALONG THE COAST
Some of the world's most beautiful beaches lie between Cancún and Tulum.

Xcaret (Km 290)
Once a communal turkey farm, Xcaret (sh-KAH-ret) (☎ (98) 83-31-43, fax (98) 83-33-24), 'Nature's Sacred Paradise,' has been heavily Disneyfied. The beautiful *caleta* (inlet), filled with tropical marine life, is surrounded by several minor Mayan ruins and has a cenote for swimming, a restaurant and an evening show of 'ancient Mayan ceremonies' worthy of Las Vegas. Package tourists from Cancún fill the place every day, arriving in a caravan of special Xcaret buses and happily paying the US$25 admission fee, plus supplemental fees for many attractions and activities, such as swimming with dolphins (US$50). It is typical of our time that such an overdeveloped, hyper-commercialized amusement can be called an 'eco-archaeological park'.

Pamul (Km 274)
Although Pamul's small rocky beach does not have long stretches of white sand like some of its Caribbean cousins, the palm-fringed surroundings are inviting. If you walk only about two km north of Pamul, you will find an alabaster sand beach to call your own. The least rocky section is the southern end, but watch out for spiked sea urchins in the shallows offshore.

Giant sea turtles come ashore here at night in July and August to lay their eggs. Why they return to the same beach every year is a mystery. If you run across a turtle during your evening stroll along the beach, keep a good distance from it and don't use a light, as that will scare it. Do your part to contribute to the survival of the turtles, which are endangered: Let them lay their eggs in peace.

Places to Stay & Eat *Hotel Pamul* offers basic but acceptable rooms with fan and bath for US$16 a single and US$26 a double. There is electricity in the evenings until 10 pm. The fee for camping is US$6 for two people per site. There are showers and toilets.

The friendly family that runs this somewhat scruffy hotel and campsite also serves breakfasts and seafood at the little restaurant.

Puerto Aventuras (Km 269.5)
The Cancún lifestyle spreads inexorably southward, dotting this recently pristine coast with yet more sybaritic resort hideaways. One such is the *Puerto Aventuras Resort* (☎ (987) 2-22-11), Apdo 186, Playa del Carmen, Quintana Roo 77600, a modern luxury complex of hotel rooms, swimming pools, beach facilities and other costly comforts.

Xpu-ha (Km 264)
Xpu-ha (shpoo-HAH) offers camping and moderately priced cabañas on a beautiful stretch of beach just north of the Club Robinson resort and accessed by an unpaved road. Bonanza Beach has the best camping – that is, until the developers drive us out. Walk 15 minutes north to find Laguna Tin-ha and Cenote Manatee.

Laguna Yal-Ku (Km 256.5)
Laguna Yal-Ku, once a well-kept secret of snorkeling enthusiasts, has been discovered. Access is now by taxi from the northernmost of the Akumal hotels, thus providing rich income for local drivers. Bring your own refreshments and snorkeling gear.

YUCATÁN

Akumal (Km 255)

Famous for its beautiful beach, Akumal (Place of the Turtles) does indeed see giant turtles come ashore to lay their eggs during the summer.

Activities There are two dive shops here where you can rent snorkeling gear. The best snorkeling is at the north end of the bay, or try Laguna Yal-Ku, 1.5 km north of Akumal.

World-class divers come here to explore the Spanish galleon *Mantancero*, which sank in 1741. You can see artifacts from the galleon at the museum at nearby Xel-Ha. The dive shops will arrange all your scuba excursion needs. Beginners' scuba instruction can be provided for less than US$120; if you want certification, the dive shops offer three-day courses. They will also arrange deep-sea fishing excursions.

Places to Stay Lodgings at Akumal can be reserved via a toll-free phone number in the USA: ☎ (800) 448-7137.

The least expensive hotel is the *Hotel-Club Akumal Caribe Villas Maya*, where basic two-person air-con cabañas with bath and the amenities of tennis and basketball courts cost US$90 to US$125 a double.

The *Hotel Akumal Caribe*, on the south end of the beach, is an attractive two-story modern lodge with swimming pool, boat rental and night tennis. Spacious air-con rooms equipped with refrigerators cost US$110. They can sleep six.

On the north side of the beach you will find the cabañas of *Las Casitas Akumal* (☎ (987) 2-25-54), consisting of a living room, kitchen, two bedrooms and two bathrooms. Bungalows cost US$160 in the busy winter season, US$110 in summer.

Places to Eat Even the shade-huts near the beach are expensive for light lunches and snacks, considering what you get. Just outside the walled entrance of Akumal is a grocery store patronized largely by the resort workers; if you are day-tripping here, this is your sole inexpensive source of food. The store also sells tacos.

Las Aventuras (Km 250)

Developers got the first chance at Las Aventuras, which now has a planned community of condominiums, villas and the beautiful *Aventuras Akumal Hotel*, which has double rooms for about US$115.

Chemuyil (Km 248)

Here there's a beautiful sand beach shaded by coconut palms and good snorkeling in calm waters with exceptional visibility. Admission costs US$2.

Chemuyil is being developed, with some condos already built. During winter's high season there are a fair number of campers here (US$3.75 per person).

The cheap accommodations are spartan, screened shade huts with hammock hooks. Inquire about availability at the bar; huts cost US$20, and showers and toilets are communal.

Local fare is prepared at the bar, including some seafood.

Xcacel (Km 247)

Xcacel (shkah-CELL) has no lodging other than camping (US$2.50 per person), no electricity and only a small restaurant stall. You can enjoy this patch of paradise for a day-use charge of US$1.50.

For fine fishing and snorkeling, try the waters north of the campground. The rocky point leads to seas for snorkeling, and the sandy outcropping is said to be a good place to fish from. Swimming, like snorkeling, is best from the rocky point to the north end of the beach.

Xcacel offers good pickings for shell collectors, including that aquatic collector, the hermit crab. There are also some colorful and intricate coral pieces to be found. When beachcombing here, wear footgear.

Take the old dirt track that runs two km north to Chemuyil and three km south to Xel-Ha, and you may spy parrots, finches or the clockbird (mot-mot), with its long tail.

Parque Nacional Laguna Xel-Ha (Km 245)

Once a pristine natural lagoon brimming with iridescent tropical fish, Xel-Ha

(SHELL-hah) is now a Mexican national park with landscaped grounds, changing rooms, restaurant and bar. The fish are regularly driven off by the dozens of busloads of day-trippers who come to swim (and shed sun block) in the pretty lagoon.

Should you visit Xel-Ha? Sure, so long as you come off-season (in the summer) or, in winter, either very early or very late in the day to avoid the tour buses. Bring your own lunch, as the little restaurant here is overpriced. Entry to the lagoon area costs US$12 (US$7 for children under 12); it's open from 8 am to 6 pm daily. You can rent snorkeling gear, but the price is high and the equipment may be leaky.

Xel-Ha Ruins There is a small archaeological site on the west side of the highway 500 meters south of the lagoon entry road. The ruins, which are not all that impressive, date from Classic and Postclassic periods and include El Palacio and the Templo de los Pájaros. It's open from 8 am to 5 pm for US$1.50.

TULUM

Don't come to Tulum, expecting majestic pyramids like those at Chichén Itzá and Uxmal. The buildings here, decidedly Toltec in influence, were the product of a Mayan civilization in decline.

Tulum ('City of the Dawn' or 'City of Renewal'), though well preserved, would hardly merit rave notices if it weren't for its setting. The gray-black buildings of the past sit on a palm-fringed beach, lapped by the turquoise waters of the Caribbean.

Tulum is open from 8 am to 5 pm. Because the site is so close to Cancún, it is constantly crowded. The press of crowds threatened to damage the temples, so it is now not permitted to approach them closely or to climb atop them.

Recent development has turned the site into a money-sucking machine: You pay to park your car (US$1.50), then pass through a warren of shops to get to the minitrain (US$1.30) that takes you the 800 meters to the site entrance (US$3). Inside

the site the buildings aren't marked, so you'll need a guide (US$15 to US$22). The cost for a couple to tour Tulum can thus mount to around US$30 – and this for a second-rate site in which you can't even get close to the buildings.

History

Most archaeologists believe that Tulum was settled in the Early Postclassic period (900 to 1200), with its walls dating from 1200 to 1450. When Juan de Grijalva's expedition sailed past Tulum in 1518, Grijalva was amazed by the sight of this walled city, with its buildings painted a gleaming red, blue and white and a ceremonial fire flaming atop its seaside watchtower.

The ramparts that surround three sides of Tulum (the fourth side being the sea) leave little question as to its strategic function as a fortress. Averaging nearly seven meters in thickness and standing three to five meters high, the walls protected the city during a period of considerable strife between Mayan city-states.

The city was abandoned about three-quarters of a century after the Spanish conquest. Mayan pilgrims continued to visit over the years, and Indian refugees from the War of the Castes took shelter here from time to time.

In 1842 John L Stephens and Frederick Catherwood visited Tulum by boat. They made substantial drawings and notes, which aroused the curiosity of the outside world when published in 1848. Subsequent expeditions were mounted, the most important being the 1916-22 investigations by the Carnegie Institute.

Orientation

There are many Tulums: Tulum Crucero is the junction with Hwy 307 and the old access road to the ruins (the new entrance is 400 meters south of Tulum Crucero); Tulum Ruinas is the ruins, 800 meters southeast of Tulum Crucero; Tulum Pueblo is the modern settlement 3.5 km south of Tulum Crucero; and Tulum Zona Hotelera is the assortment of beach cabañas from one

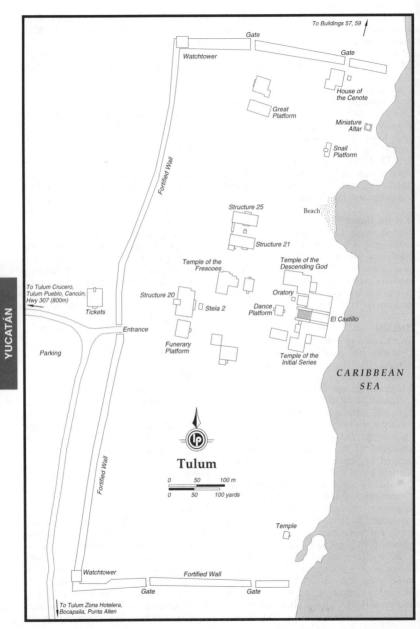

To Buildings 57, 59

Gate

Watchtower

Gate

House of
the Cenote

Great
Platform

Miniature
Altar

Snail
Platform

Fortified Wall

Structure 25

Beach

Structure 21

Temple of the
Frescoes

Temple of the
Descending God

Structure 20

Oratory

To Tulum Crucero,
Tulum Pueblo, Cancún,
Hwy 307 (800m)

Tickets

Stela 2

Dance
Platform

El Castillo

Entrance

Parking

Funerary
Platform

Temple of the
Initial Series

CARIBBEAN
SEA

YUCATÁN

Tulum

0   50   100 m

0   50   100 yards

Temple

Watchtower

Fortified Wall

Gate

Gate

To Tulum Zona Hotelera,
Bocapaila, Punta Allen

to seven km south of the ruins. The Zona Hotelera is reached by an access road two km south of Tulum Crucero (1.5 km north of Tulum Pueblo), opposite the Cobá road.

South of the Zona Hotelera the unpaved road enters the Sian Ka'an Biosphere Reserve and continues for some 50 km past Boca Paila to Punta Allen.

El Castillo
Tulum's tallest building (Structure 1) is a watchtower fortress overlooking the Caribbean, appropriately named El Castillo by the Spaniards. Note the Toltec-style serpent columns at the temple's entrance, echoing those at Chichén Itzá.

Temple of the Descending God
The Temple of the Descending (or Diving) God is named for the relief figure above the door, a diving figure, partly human, that may be related to reverence for bees. This figure appears at several other east coast sites and at Cobá.

Temple of the Frescoes
This two-story building (Structure 16) was constructed in several stages sometime between 1400 and 1450. Its decoration was among the more elaborate examples at Tulum, including the diving god, relief masks, and colored murals on an inner wall. The murals, painted in three levels, show the three realms of the Mayan universe: the dark underworld of the deceased, the middle order of the living and the heavenly home of the creator and rain gods.

Great Palace
Smaller than El Castillo, this largely deteriorated site (Structure 25) contains a fine stucco carving of a diving god.

Temple of the Initial Series
This restored temple is named for Stela 1, now in the British Museum, which was inscribed with the Mayan date corresponding to 564 AD. At first that confused archaeologists, who believed Tulum to have been settled several hundred years later than this date. It's now believed that

Stela 1 was brought to Tulum from Tankah, four km to the north, a settlement dating from the Classic period.

Structures 57 & 59
These two small temples are north of the city wall. Structure 57, about 500 meters north of the wall, is a one-room shrine in good condition. Structure 59, another 500 meters to the north, is another one-room temple, with remains of a roofcomb, the only one found at Tulum.

Places to Stay & Eat
El Crucero Right at the junction of Hwy 307 and the old Tulum access road are several hotels and restaurants, including the basic, well-used *Motel El Crucero*, expensive at US$8 to US$11 a double with shower and fan. More useful are the restaurant and shop selling ice, meals, drinks and souvenirs. A chicken dinner costs US$5.

Facing the Motel El Crucero across the access road are the *Hotel Acuario*, with air-con rooms overpriced at US$30 to US$45 double (and you must pay in advance) and its *Restaurant El Faisan y El Venado*.

Zona Hotelera South of the archaeological zone is a paradise of palm-shaded white beach dotted with collections of cabañas, little thatched huts of greater or lesser comfort, and simple wooden or concrete bungalows. Most of these places have little eateries at which you can eat your meals, and some have electric generators that provide light for several hours each evening.

The cheapest way to sleep here is to have your own hammock, preferably with one of those tubelike mosquito nets to cover it; if you don't carry your own, several of the cheaper places will rent you what you need. If you have candles or a flashlight, they'll come in handy here. In the cheapest places you'll have to supply your own towel and soap.

I'll start by describing the places closest to the Tulum ruins, then head south to describe the places farther and farther away.

YUCATÁN

Closest to the ruins are *Cabañas El Mirador* and *Cabañas Santa Fe*, on the beach about 600 meters south of the Tulum ruins parking lot. The Santa Fe is preferable, though a bit more expensive, charging US$3 per person for a campsite, US$8 to hang your hammock in a cabin, or US$10 to US$12 and up to US$18 per person for beds. At El Mirador a cabaña sleeping up to four people is yours for US$9 a double with hammocks.

Cabañas Don Armando, just south of Santa Fe, is the most famous of the bottom-end cabaña places. For US$14 to US$18 (single or double) you get one of 17 cabins built on concrete slabs and outfitted with lockable doors, hammocks or beds (you pay a deposit for sheets and pillows), mosquito netting, good showers and a good, cheap restaurant. Smaller, less comfy cabañas rent for US$9 to US$12. Lighting in the rooms is by candles. This place is fun, right on the beach, and still only a 10-minute walk to the ruins.

The *Hotel El Paraíso* (☎ (987) 1-21-42, fax (987) 1-20-07), 1.5 km south of the ruins, approaches a conventional hotel in its services. The newer rooms, with two double beds and private bath, cost US$38, the nicer cabañas US$55. There's a restaurant with sea view, and electricity until 10 pm. *Gato's Cabañas*, 700 meters south, charges slightly less.

A kilometer south of the junction of the access road from and Hwy 307 is a cluster of lodgings. *La Conchita* is simple and cheap, as is *Punta Piedra*, with cabañas for US$12.

Cabañas Nohoch Tunich, just south of Punta Piedra, has older but still serviceable cabañas for US$10 to US$18 and comfortable modern ones for US$40 to US$55. *La Perla*, Apdo Postal 77, Tulum, Quintana Roo 77780, has quite good rooms for US$35 to US$45; some are newer than others, so look at several if possible.

Zamas, Apdo Postal 49, Tulum, Quintana Roo 77780 (☎ in the USA (800)

Tulum Cabañas

The cabañas south of Tulum are famous as a little bit of paradise. Here's what you need to know to pass through the pearly gates safely and thriftily:

1. All of the cabañas are full by 10 or 11 am every day during the winter season (mid-December through March) and in July and August. You must get here very early to get one, or make a reservation the night before. If you have your own hammock and mosquito net, you'll be able to find some place to sleep without too much problem.

2. If you take an afternoon or evening bus to the Tulum Crucero or zona arqueológica entrance, then a taxi to the cabañas, the taxi driver will know that there are no rooms available, but he won't tell you that, because he doesn't want to lose the fare. Besides, having discovered that there are no rooms, you'll give him another fare to taking you back to the highway.

3. There is great variety in the cabañas: comfortable, secure ones; ramshackle ones; some with hammocks provided, others for which you must bring your own hammock or rent one; some with sea views and good beds, others with neither. Most will be full when you arrive, so you'll have to take whatever's vacant, at least for the first night or two.

4. Cheapest are the rustic cabañas made of sticks and provided with hammocks. They are about one km south of the Tulum ruins along the old road and include the Cabañas El Mirador, Santa Fe and Don Armando's.

5. Supposedly, you can reserve cabañas in advance, but reservations are dependable only with the more expensive ones.

6. Security is a big problem here. Few of the flimsy, primitive cabañas can be reliably secured. Thieves lift the poles in the walls to gain entrance, or they burrow beneath through the sand or jimmy the locks. You may even have your beach towel stolen from a drying line. Consider security carefully when you choose a place to stay. ■

538-6802) fronts on a beach accented by dramatic rock formations. Rooms range from US$25 for a double with shared bath to US$50 for one with two double beds and private bath.

Piedra Escondida (☎ /fax (987) 1-20-92), Apdo Postal 128, Tulum, Quintana Roo 77780, is the nicest accommodation in the area, with modern, stylish two-story thatched cabañas renting for US$60 to US$80 with one or two double beds. The management is Italian.

Just south of this cluster the paved road gives way to a good sand track.

Osho Oasis Retreat (☎ (987) 4-27-72, in the USA ☎ /fax (707) 778-1320), Apdo Postal 99, Tulum, Quintana Roo 77780, is a resort for plain living and high thinking. There's a meditation hall and facilities for yoga, Zen, kundalini and massage, as well as the beach. Cabañas cost US$50 to US$70 a double in high season; meals are US$7/6/14 for breakfast/lunch/dinner.

Los Arrecifes, south of Osho, has fairly rustic cabañas (some of sticks, others of cinder block) for US$28, single or double. About 3.5 km south of the access road intersection (seven km south of the ruins), *Cabañas de Ana y José* (☎ (98) 80-60-22, fax (98) 80-60-21), has older bungalows for US$40 or newer ones for US$50 a double, and a sand-floor restaurant/bar.

Just south is *Cabañas Tulum* (☎ (99) 25-82-95), Apdo Postal 63, Tulum, Quintana Roo 77780, where older concrete bungalows look out through palms to the sea and the beach. The rate is US$36 per night, single or double, in summer, US$40 in winter. There's a restaurant and bar. The electric generator runs (if it's working) from dusk to 10 pm each evening.

Getting There & Away
You can walk from Tulum Crucero to the ruins (800 meters), or take the minitrain for US$1.30.

Reaching the cabañas is more difficult. The closest are one km from Tulum Crucero on foot, or at least six km by taxi, and there is no public transport except taxis. Though

you may occasionally be able to hitch a ride, you can depend only on your own two feet or a taxi to get you to your lodgings and from your lodgings to the ruins.

There is a small ADO bus station at the southern end of Tulum Pueblo. When leaving Tulum you can wait at Tulum Crucero for a Playa Express or regular intercity bus. Here are some distances and travel times:

Cancún – 132 km, two hours, US$3 to US$4

Chetumal – 251 km, four hours, US$5 to US$7

Chichén Itzá – 402 km, 6½ hours, US$5; one bus

Cobá – 45 km, one hour

Felipe Carrillo Puerto – 98 km, 1¾ hours

Mérida – 320 km, five hours via Cobá or seven hours via Cancún; Oriente (US$7) and ADO (US$8.25) have a few buses

Palenque – 738 km, 11 hours; two by Colón (US$20)

Playa del Carmen – 63 km, one hour

Punta Allen – 57 km, 1½ hours

Valladolid – 156 km, three hours, US$7

TULUM TO BOCA PAILA & PUNTA ALLEN
The scenery on the 50-km stretch from Tulum Ruinas past Boca Paila to Punta Allen is the typically monotonous flat Yucatecan terrain, but the land, rich with wildlife, is protected as the Sian Ka'an Biosphere Reserve. The surfy beaches aren't spectacular, but there's plenty of privacy.

A minivan makes the trip from Tulum Pueblo to Punta Allen more or less daily, taking anywhere from two to four hours for the trip, depending on the condition of the road.

It's important to have plenty of fuel before heading south from Tulum, as there is no fuel available on the Tulum-Punta Allen road.

Sian Ka'an Biosphere Reserve
Over 5000 sq km of tropical jungle, marsh, mangrove and islands on Quintana Roo's coast have been set aside by the Mexican

government as a large biosphere reserve. In 1987 the United Nations appointed it a World Heritage Site – an irreplaceable natural treasure.

A trip into Sian Ka'an ('Where the Sky Begins') reveals thousands of butterflies, as well as varied fauna: howler monkeys, foxes, ocelots, pumas, vultures, caimans (crocodiles), eagles, raccoons, giant land crabs and – if you're very lucky – a jaguar. Unrestored Mayan ruins are everywhere. Though they are small and mostly unimpressive, it's still a thrill to visit one of these quiet sites, which have lain here unheeded for centuries.

Treks into the reserve are run from Cancún and Playa del Carmen. For details on the reserve, contact Amigos de Sian Ka'an (☎ (98) 84-95-83, 87-30-80), Plaza América, Avenida Cobá 5, 3rd floor, Suites 48-50, Cancún, Quintana Roo 77500.

Boca Paila

Boca Paila is 25 km south of Tulum. One of the two hotels on the road to Punta Allen is *La Villa de Boca Paila*, where luxury cabañas complete with kitchens cost about US$90 per double, including two meals. The clientele is predominantly affluent American sport fishers. For reservations, write to Apdo Postal 159, Mérida, Yucatán.

Ten km south of Boca Paila you cross a rickety wooden bridge. Beyond it is *El Retiro Cabañas*, where you can camp or hang hammocks for a few dollars.

Punta Allen

Once a pocket of wealthy lobster fishers in a vast wilderness, Punta Allen suffered considerable damage from the ferocious winds of Hurricane Gilbert in 1988. The hurricane and overfishing have depleted the lobster stocks, but a laid-back ambiance reminiscent of the Belizean cayes gives hope for a touristed future.

Punta Allen does have some rustic lodgings. The *Cruzan Inn* (fax (983) 4-03-83) has cabañas with hammocks for about US$25 a double. The couple who run it prepare breakfast and lunch at a

cost of US$6.50 per person and charge US$14 for dinner. They can arrange snorkeling and fishing expeditions or visits to the offshore island of Cayo Colibri, known for its bird life. To write for reservations, the address is Cruzan Inn, c/o Sonia Lillvik, Apdo Postal 703, Cancún, Quintana Roo 77500.

The *Bonefishing Club of Ascension Bay*, run by Jan Persson, specializes in guided fishing expeditions but also has two rooms for rent in the house that is its headquarters. Family-style meals are served.

Let It Be Inn has three thatched cabañas with comforts such as private bath (with hot water) and sea-view porches hung with hammocks. For reservations write to Rick Montgomery, Let It Be Inn, Apdo Postal 74, Tulum, Quintana Roo 77780.

If you wish to camp on Punta Allen's beach, simply ask the Maya in front of whose house you would be sleeping for permission.

COBÁ

Perhaps the largest of all Mayan cities, Cobá, 50 km northwest of Tulum, offers the chance to explore mostly unrestored antiquities set deep in tropical jungles.

History

Cobá was settled earlier than Chichén Itzá or Tulum, its heyday dating from 600 AD until the site was mysteriously abandoned, about 900 AD. Archaeologists believe that this city once covered 50 square km and held 40,000 Maya.

Cobá's architecture is a mystery; its towering pyramids and stelae resemble the architecture of Tikal, several hundred km away, rather than that of Chichén Itzá and other sites of northern Yucatán, a quarter of that distance away.

Some archaeologists theorize that an alliance with Tikal was made through marriage to facilitate trade between the Guatemalan and Yucatecan Maya. Stelae appear to depict female rulers from Tikal holding ceremonial bars and flaunting their power by standing on captives. These Tikal

The first excavation was by the Austrian archaeologist Teobert Maler. Hearing rumors of a fabled lost city, he came to Cobá alone in 1891. There was little subsequent investigation until 1926, when the Carnegie Institute financed the first of two expeditions led by J Eric S Thompson and Harry Pollock. After their 1930 expedition not much happened until 1973, when the Mexican government began to finance excavation. Archaeologists now estimate that Cobá contains some 6500 structures, of which just a few have been excavated and restored.

Orientation

The small village of Cobá, 2.5 km west of the Tulum-Nuevo Xcan road, has several small, simple, cheap lodging and eating places. At the lake turn left for the ruins, right for the upscale Villa Arqueológica Cobá hotel.

Cobá archaeological site is open from 8 am to 5 pm; admission costs US$2.50 (free on Sunday).

Be prepared to do quite a bit of walking – at least five to seven km – on jungle paths. Dress for heat and humidity and bring insect repellent. It's also a good idea to bring a canteen of water; it's hot and there are no drinks stands within the site, only at the entrance. Avoid the midday heat if possible. A visit to the site takes two to four hours.

Cobá Group

Less than 100 meters along the main path from the entrance brings you to the Temple of the Churches, on your right, the most prominent structure in the Cobá Group. It's an enormous pyramid, from the top of which there is a fine view of the Nohoch Mul pyramid to the north and shimmering lakes to the east and southwest.

Back on the main path you pass through the Juego de Pelota, or ball court, 30 meters farther along. It's now badly ruined.

Macanxoc Group

About 500 meters beyond the Juego de

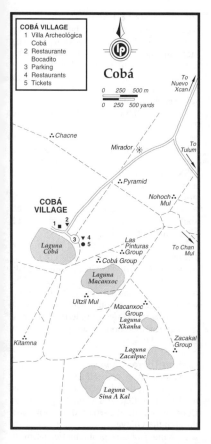

COBÁ VILLAGE
1 Villa Archeológica Cobá
2 Restaurante Bocadito
3 Parking
4 Restaurants
5 Tickets

Cobá

0   250   500 m
0   250   500 yards

To Nuevo Xcan

∴Chacne

Mirador

To Tulum

∴Pyramid

COBÁ VILLAGE

Nohoch ∴ Mul

Laguna Cobá

Las Pinturas ∴Group
∴ Cobá Group

To Chan Mul

Laguna Macanxoc

Uitzil Mul

Macanxoc Group
Laguna Xkanha

Kitamna

Zacakal Group

Laguna Zacalpuc ∴

Laguna Sina A Kal

YUCATÁN

royal women, when married to Cobá's royalty, may have brought architects and artisans with them.

Archaeologists are also baffled by the network of extensive *sacbeob* (stone-paved avenues) in this region, with Cobá as the hub. The longest runs nearly 100 km from the base of Cobá's great pyramid, Nohoch Mul, to the Mayan settlement of Yaxuna. In all, some 40 sacbeob passed through Cobá. The sacbeob were parts of the huge astronomical 'time machine' that was evident in every Mayan city.

Pelota is the turn (right) for the Grupo Macanxoc, a group of stelae that bore reliefs of royal women thought to have come from Tikal.

Las Pinturas Group

One hundred meters beyond the Macanxoc turn a sign points left toward the Conjunto de las Pinturas, or the Temple of Paintings. It bears easily recognizable traces of glyphs and frescoes above the door and traces of richly colored plaster inside.

You approached the Temple of Paintings from the southwest. Leave by the trail at the northwest (opposite the temple steps) to see several stelae. The first of them is 20 meters along, beneath a palapa. A regal figure stands over two others, one of them kneeling with his hands bound behind him. Sacrificial captives lie beneath the feet of a ruler at the base. Continue along the path past another badly weathered stela to the Nohoch Mul path and turn right.

Nohoch Mul – The Great Pyramid

It's a walk of 800 meters to Nohoch Mul. Along the way, just before the track bends sharply to the left, a narrow path on the right leads to a group of badly weathered stelae. Farther along the track bends between piles of stones – obviously a ruined temple – before passing Temple 10 and Stela 20. The exquisitely carved stela bears a picture of a ruler standing imperiously over two captives. Eighty meters beyond the stela stands the Great Pyramid.

At 42 meters high, the huge Great Pyramid is the tallest of all Mayan structures in the Yucatán Peninsula. Climb the 120 steps, observing that the Maya carved shell-like forms on which to put your feet.

There are two diving gods carved over the doorway of the Nohoch Mul temple at the top, similar to the sculptures at Tulum. The view is spectacular.

From Nohoch Mul it's a 1.4-km, 30-minute walk back to the site entrance.

Places to Stay & Eat

There are several small restaurants among the souvenir shops by the parking lot. The staff at the drinks stand right by the entrance tends to be surly, so buy your drinks at either the *Restaurant El Faisan* or the *Restaurant El Caracol*, both of which serve cheap meals.

In the village of Cobá *Restaurant Lagoon* is nearest the lake, with good views and friendly service. The *Restaurant Isabel* and *Restaurant Bocadito* are also popular.

The Bocadito rents rooms with bath for US$8/12 a single/double, though I've had a complaint of fleas. Meals are overpriced.

As for camping, there's no organized spot, though you can try finding a place along the shore of the lake.

For upscale lodging and dining the choice is easy: there's only the *Villa Arqueológica Cobá* (☎ in Cancún (98) 84-25-74, in the USA (800) 528-3100). The pleasant hotel has a swimming pool and a good restaurant. Rooms with air-con cost US$50/65/75 a single/double/triple. Lunch or dinner in the good restaurant might cost US$12 to US$20.

Getting There & Away

Numerous buses trace the route between Tulum and Valladolid. Be sure to mention to the driver that you want to get out at Cobá junction; the road does not pass through the village.

Leaving Cobá is problematic, as most buses are full when they pass here. If you're willing to stand for the 50-km ride to Tulum or to Nuevo Xcan (120 km to Valladolid), you have a better chance of getting a ride.

A more comfortable and dependable but expensive way to reach Cobá is a day trip by taxi from Tulum Crucero. Find some other travelers interested in the trip and split the cost, about US$18 to US$25 roundtrip, including two hours (haggle for three) at the site.

By the way, many maps show a road from Cobá to Chemax, but this road is impassable.

FELIPE CARRILLO PUERTO
Population 17,000

Now named for a progressive governor of Yucatán, this town was once known as Chan Santa Cruz, the dreaded rebel headquarters during the War of the Castes.

History

In 1849 the War of the Castes went against the Maya of northern Yucatán, who made their way to this town seeking refuge. Regrouping their forces, they were ready to sally forth again in 1850 when a 'miracle' occurred. A wooden cross erected at a cenote on the western edge of the town began to 'talk', telling the Maya they were the chosen people, exhorting them to continue the struggle against the whites and promising the Maya forces victory. The talking was done by a ventriloquist who used sound chambers, but the people nonetheless looked upon it as the authentic voice of their aspirations.

The oracular cross guided the Maya in battle for eight years, until their great victory in conquering the fortress at Bacalar. For the latter part of the 19th century, the Maya in and around Chan Santa Cruz were virtually independent of the governments in Mexico City and Mérida. In the 1920s a boom in the chicle market brought prosperity to the region, and the Maya decided to come to terms with Mexico City, which they did in 1929. Some of the Maya, unwilling to give up the cult of the talking cross, left Chan Santa Cruz to take up residence at small villages deep in the jungle, where they still revere the talking cross to this day. You may see some of them visiting the site where the cross spoke, now a little city park, especially on May 3, the day of the Holy Cross.

To visit the **Sanctuario del Cruz Parlante**, start at the Pemex fuel station on the main street (called Avenida Juárez, Calle

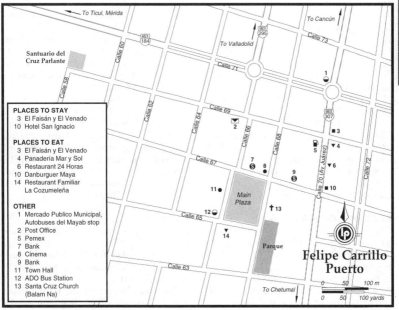

PLACES TO STAY
3 El Faisán y El Venado
10 Hotel San Ignacio

PLACES TO EAT
3 El Faisán y El Venado
4 Panadería Mar y Sol
6 Restaurant 24 Horas
10 Danburguer Maya
14 Restaurant Familiar
    La Cozumeleña

OTHER
1 Mercado Publico Municipal,
   Autobuses del Mayab stop
2 Post Office
5 Pemex
7 Bank
8 Cinema
9 Bank
11 Town Hall
12 ADO Bus Station
13 Santa Cruz Church
   (Balam Na)

Santuario del Cruz Parlante

To Ticul, Mérida

To Cancún

To Valladolid

Main Plaza

Parque

Felipe Carrillo Puerto

To Chetumal

0   50   100 m
0   50   100 yards

YUCATÁN

70, and Hwy 307) in the commercial center of town and walk five blocks west. There's little to see in the park besides the cenote and a stone shelter, though the place reverberates with history.

Places to Stay & Eat

El Faisán y El Venado (☎ (983) 4-07-02), Calle 70 No 81, across from the Pemex station, has 13 air-con rooms with private shower and ceiling fan for US$8/16/18 a single/double/triple. They have a restaurant with good food and service, too.

Just a few dozen meters to the south is the *Restaurant 24 Horas*, which is a bit cheaper.

South of the 24 Horas is the *Hotel San Ignacio*, with air-con rooms for US$12 to US$16 and an air-con restaurant with the odd name of *Danburguer Maya*.

Restaurant Familiar La Cozumeleña is a tidy family-run place, cheaper than the others.

For breads and pastries, try the *Panadería Mar y Sol*.

Getting There & Away

Buses running between Cancún (230 km, four hours, US$8) and Chetumal (155 km, three hours, US$4 to US$6) stop here, as do buses traveling from Chetumal to Valladolid (160 km, three hours, US$6) and Mérida (310 km, 5½ to six hours, US$6.50 to US$8). There are also a few buses between Felipe Carrillo Puerto and Ticul (200 km, 3½ hours, US$8); change at Ticul or Muna for Uxmal. Bus fare between FCP and Tulum is US$3.75.

Note that there are very few hotels, restaurants or fuel stations between Felipe Carrillo Puerto and Ticul.

XCALAK & COSTA MAYA

The coast south of Sian Ka'an Biosphere Reserve to the small fishing village of Xcalak (shka-LAK, population 200) is known as the Costa Maya. Unknown and difficult to access until 1981, it is now drawing handfuls of adventurous travelers in search of that fast-disappearing natural asset, the undeveloped stretch of coastline.

Travel services along the Costa Maya are few, and accommodations are often full. Unless you have advance reservations, be prepared to pitch your own tent, hang your own hammock or return on the same bus that brought you. There are no banks, and currently the local economy runs on cash US dollars, not pesos, though this must change soon.

Several dive shops offer instruction and certification for scuba divers, rent snorkeling and scuba gear, and provide boat transportation to Chinchorro Reef.

Places to Stay & Eat

The six-room *Hotel Caracol* is currently the village's only cheap place to stay, offering cold-water rooms with fan for US$7/9 a single/double. Look for the owner next door to the hotel. No doubt these prices will rise and new, small lodging-places will open as word of Xcalak's beauties spreads around the world.

Costa de Cocos (☎ in the USA (800) 538-6802), Apdo Postal 62, Chetumal, Quintana Roo 77000, 1.5 km north of Xcalak, has eight thatched cabañas with private bath, solar hot water, and 24-hour electricity. There's a restaurant-bar, and the Xcalak Dive Center (fax (909) 839-1003, in the USA ☎ (510) 490-5597).

Villa Caracol (☎ (983) 8-18-72), Km 45, Carretera Majahual-Xcalak, has six comfortable air-con rooms and two cabañas, each with two queen-size beds, purified water, private bath and 24-hour electricity.

Several small restaurants – *Capitan Caribe*, *Conchitas* and *El Caracol* – serve cheap, good seafood dinners.

Getting There & Away

From Hwy 307, turn east at Cafetal, 68 km south of Felipe Carrillo Puerto and 46 km north of Bacalar, for Majahual (58 km). South of Majahual is an all-weather road to Xcalak (58 km).

Sociedad Cooperativa del Caribe buses depart Chetumal's main bus terminal for

Majahual and Xcalak (200 km, five hours, US$3) daily at 6 am and 3:30 pm. There are also minibuses from Chetumal, departing from the corner of Avenida 16 de Septiembre and Mahatma Gandhi, near the Restaurant Pantoja, at 7 am and departing from Xcalak at 1 pm.

There are plans for a daily ferry service to link Chetumal, Xcalak and San Pedro, Ambergris Caye, Belize.

LAGUNA BACALAR

Nature has set a turquoise jewel in the midst of the scrubby Yucatecan jungle – Laguna Bacalar. A large, clear freshwater lake with a bottom of gleaming white sand, Bacalar comes as a surprise in this region of tortured limestone.

The small, sleepy town of Bacalar, just east of the highway some 125 km south of Felipe Carrillo Puerto, is the only settlement of any size on the lake. It's noted mostly for its old fortress and its swimming facilities.

The fortress was built over the lagoon to protect citizens from raids by pirates and Indians. It served as an important outpost for the whites in the War of the Castes. In 1859 it was seized by Mayan rebels, who held the fort until Quintana Roo was finally conquered by Mexican troops in 1901. Today, with formidable cannon still on its ramparts, the fortress remains an imposing sight. It houses a museum exhibiting colonial armaments and uniforms from the 17th and 18th centuries, open daily from 8 am to 1 pm for US$1.

A divided avenue runs between the fortress and the lakeshore northward a few hundred meters to the *balneario* (bathing facilities). Small restaurants line the avenue and surround the balneario, which is very busy on weekends.

Costera Bacalar & Cenote Azul

The road that winds southward along the lakeshore from Bacalar town to Hwy 307 at Cenote Azul is called the Costera Bacalar. It passes a few lodging and camping places along the way.

Hotel Laguna (in Chetumal ☎ (983) 2-35-17), 3.3 km south of Bacalar town along the Costera, is only 150 meters east of Highway 307, so you can ask a bus driver to stop here for you. Clean, cool and hospitable, it boasts a wonderful view of the lake, a swimming pool, a breezy terrace restaurant and a bar. Rooms cost US$20 to US$30 a single or double with fan, good cross-ventilation and private bath.

Only 700 meters past the Hotel Laguna along the Costera is *Los Coquitos* camping area, on the shore and run by a family that lives in a shack on the premises. You can camp in the dense shade of the palm trees, enjoy the view of the lake from the palapas, and swim from the grassy banks, all for US$4 per couple. Bring your own food and drinking water, as the nearest supplier is the restaurant at the Hotel Laguna.

The Cenote Azul is a 90-meter-deep natural pool on the southwestern shore of Laguna Bacalar, 200 meters east of Hwy 307. (If you're approaching from the north by bus, get the driver to stop and let you off here.) Because it's a cenote there's no beach, just a few steps leading down to the water from the vast palapa that shelters the restaurant. You might pay US$8 to US$12 for the average meal here. A small sign purveys Mayan wisdom: 'Don't go in the cenote if you can't swim'.

Getting There & Away

Coming from the north, have the bus drop you in Bacalar town, at the Hotel Laguna or at Cenote Azul, as you wish; check before you buy your ticket to see if the driver will stop.

Heading west out of Chetumal, you turn north onto Hwy 307; 15.5 km north of this highway junction is a turn on the right marked for the Cenote Azul and Costera Bacalar.

Catch a minibus from Chetumal's minibus terminal, on Primo de Verdad at Hidalgo. Departures are about every 20 minutes from 5 am to 7 pm for the 39-km (40 minutes, US$2) run to the town of Bacalar; some northbound buses departing from the Chetumal bus terminal (US$1.25) will also drop you near the town of Bacalar. Along the way the minibuses pass Laguna Milagros (14 km), Xul-ha (22 km) and the Cenote Azul (33 km), and all four of these places afford visitors a chance to swim in fresh water. The lakes are beautiful, framed by palm trees, with crystal-clear water and soft, white limestone-sand bottoms.

CHETUMAL
Population 130,000

Before the conquest Chetumal was a Mayan port for shipping gold, feathers, cacao and copper from this region and Guatemala to northern Yucatán. The modern town was founded in 1898 to put a stop to the illegal trade in arms and lumber carried on by the descendants of the War of the Castes rebels. Dubbed Payo Obispo, the town's name was changed to Chetumal in 1936.

In 1955 Hurricane Janet virtually obliterated Chetumal. During the rebuilding the city planners laid out the new town on a grand scale with a grid of wide boulevards. In times BC (Before Cancún) the sparsely populated territory of Quintana Roo could not support such a grand city, even though Quintana Roo was upgraded from a territory to a state in 1974. But the boom at Cancún brought prosperity to all, and the vast spaces between boulevards are finally being filled in with buildings worthy of an important state capital.

Chetumal is also the gateway to Belize. With the peso so low and Belize so expensive, Belize nearly empties out on weekends with shoppers coming to Chetumal's markets.

Orientation

Despite Chetumal's sprawling layout the city center is easily manageable on foot. Once you find the all-important intersection of Avenida de los Héroes and Avenida Alvaro Obregón, you're within 50 meters of several inexpensive hotels and restaurants. The best hotels are only four or five blocks from this intersection.

Information

Tourist Office A tourist information kiosk (☎ (983) 2-36-63) on Avenida de los Héroes at the eastern end of Aguilar can answer questions. Hours are 8 am to 1 pm and 5 to 8 pm.

Consulates The Guatemalan Consulate (☎ (983) 2-85-85) is at Avenida Héroes de Chapultepec 354, nine blocks (just over one km) west of Avenida de los Héroes. Look for the blue-and-white flag on the left (south) side of the street. It's open Monday to Friday from 9 am to 2 pm and offers quick visa service.

The Belizean Consulate (☎ (983) 2-01-00), Avenida Obregón 226-A, between Juárez and Independencia, is open Monday to Friday from 9 am to 2 pm and 5 to 8 pm, Saturday from 9:30 am to 2 pm, closed Sunday. Last time I visited, telephone service had been cut off for nonpayment.

Money See the map for locations of currency exchange offices and banks with ATMs.

Post The post office (☎ (983) 2-00-57) is at Plutarco Elias Calles 2-A. The postal code for Chetumal is 77000.

Museo de la Cultura Maya

This dramatic museum is the city's claim to cultural fame, a bold, block-long air-conditioned showpiece designed to draw visitors from as far away as Cancún. It's open from 9 am to 7 pm (closed Monday) for US$2.50, half-price for children.

The exhibits cover all of the Mayab (lands of the Maya), not just Quintana Roo or Mexico, and seek to explain the Mayan way of life, thought and belief. There are beautiful scale models of the great Mayan buildings as they may have appeared; replicas of stelae from Copán (Honduras); and reproductions of the murals found in Room 1 at Bonampak (in Chiapas), as well as artifacts discovered at sites in Quintana Roo.

The museum is divided into three levels, as is Mayan cosmogony, which is based on the 'World Tree': The main floor represents this world, the upper floor the heavens and the lower floor Xibalba, the underworld. All exhibits are labeled in Spanish and English.

Places to Stay – budget

Instituto Quintanarroense de la Juventud y El Deporte (☎ (983) 2-05-25), the youth hostel, on Calzada Veracruz near the corner with Obregón, is the cheapest place in town. It has a few drawbacks: single-sex dorms, 11 pm curfew and a location five blocks east of the intersection of Héroes and Obregón. The cost is US$5 for a bunk in a room with four or six beds and shared bath, or US$2.50 per person to camp. Breakfast costs US$1.75 and lunch or dinner US$2.50 in the cafeteria.

Hotel María Dolores (☎ (983) 2-05-08), Obregón 206 west of Héroes, above the Restaurant Sosilmar, is the best for the price, with tiny, stuffy rooms for US$7/9/11/13 a single/double/triple/quad with fan and private bath. Some rooms sleep up to six.

Hotel Ucum (☎ (983) 2-07-11), Avenida M Gandhi 167, is a large place with lots of rooms around a bare central courtyard and a good, cheap little restaurant. Plain rooms with fan and shower cost US$8/10/12 a single/double/triple, or US$11 a double with air-con.

Hotel Cristal (☎ (983) 2-38-78), Cristóbal Colón 207, between Juárez and Belice, is run by an energetic woman who offers clean rooms for US$7/9/11 a single/double/triple with fan, and US$14 a double with air-con.

Want a very clean, quiet room with good cross-ventilation, fan, air-con, TV and private bath for only US$14? Then find your way to the *Posada Pantoja* (☎ (983) 2-17-81), Lucio Blanco 95, one km northeast of the tourist information kiosk in a peaceful residential area. Ask at the Restaurant Pantoja for directions.

Hotel El Cedro (☎ (983) 2-68-78), on Héroes between Calles and Cárdenas, has acceptable rooms for US$19 a double with air-con, TV and private baths.

The quiet *Hotel Caribe Princess* (☎ (983) 2-09-00), Obregón 168, has lots of marble and good air-con rooms for US$18/20/23 a single/double/triple.

Two blocks (200 meters) south of the Nuevo Mercado and buses to Belize the *Hotel Nachancan* (☎ (983) 2-32-32), Calzada Veracruz 379, offers decent, more or less quiet rooms with air-con and TV for US$15/18/21 a single/double/triple. The *Hotel Posada Rosas del Mar*, Calzada Veracruz 407, is directly across from the market and is cheap, at US$8 double, but is nothing special.

One km north of the Museo Maya on the way to the bus terminal, the *Hotel Principe* (☎ (983) 2-47-99, fax (983) 2-51-91), Héroes 326, has decent rooms, a restaurant and even a small swimming pool. Rooms cost US$20 a double with air-con.

Places to Stay – middle

Hotel Los Cocos (☎ (983) 2-05-44, fax (983) 2-09-20), Avenida Héroes at Chapultepec, has a nice swimming pool set in grassy lawns, a guarded parking lot and a popular sidewalk restaurant. Air-con rooms with TV, rich in nubby white stucco, cost US$38 to US$55 a single or double.

Two blocks north of Los Cocos, along Héroes near the tourist information kiosk, is the *Holiday Inn Chetumal Puerta Maya* (☎ (983) 2-11-00, 2-10-80, fax (983) 2-16-76, in the USA (800) 465-4329), Héroes 171. Its comfortable rooms overlook a small courtyard with a swimming pool set amid tropical gardens; there's a restaurant and bar. Rates are US$66 a single or double. This is the best in town.

Places to Eat

Across from the Holiday Inn and the tourist information kiosk is the Mercado Ignacio Manuel Altamirano and its row of small, simple market eateries purveying full meals for US$2 or US$3.

Restaurant Sosilmar, on Obregón below the Hotel María Dolores, is bright and simple, with prices listed prominently. Filling platters of fish or meat go for US$3 to US$5.

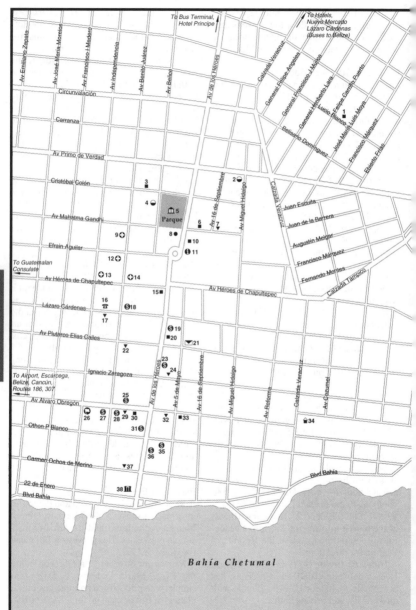

Bahía Chetumal

Chetumal

0 100 200 m
0 100 200 yards

YUCATÁN

Next door is the *Panadería La Muralla*, providing fresh baked goods for bus trips, picnics, and make-your-own breakfasts. An even grander pastry shop is the *Panadería y Pastelería La Invencible*, on Carmen Ochoa de Merino west of Héroes.

West of the Sosilmar is *Pollo Brujo*, where a roasted half chicken is yours for US$2.50. Take it with you or dine in their air-conditioned salon.

Restaurant Vegetariano La Fuente, Avenida Cárdenas 222 between Independencia and Juárez, is a tidy meatless restaurant next to a homeopathic pharmacy. Healthy meals cost US$4 or less.

Café-Restaurant Los Milagros, on Zaragoza between Héroes and 5 de Mayo, serves meals for US$3 to US$4 indoors or outdoors, and there's a book exchange with numerous English titles. It's a favorite place for Chetumal's student and intellectual set.

The family-owned *Restaurant Pantoja* (☎ (983) 2-39-57), Avenida M Gandhi 181 at 16 de Septiembre, is a neighborhood favorite that opens for breakfast early and later provides a comida corrida for US$2.50, enchiladas for US$2, and meat plates such as bistec or higado encebollado (liver and onions) for US$3. The nearby *Restaurant Ucum*, in the Hotel Ucum, also provides good cheap meals.

To sample the typical traditional food of Quintana Roo, head for the *Restaurant Típico El Taquito*, Avenida Plutarco Elias Calles 220 at Juárez. You enter past the cooks, hard at work, to an airy, simple dining room where good, cheap food is served. Tacos cost US$0.50 each, slightly more with cheese. There's a daily comida corrida for US$2.75. This is a good place to go with a jolly group of friends.

Maria's (☎ (983) 2-04-91) and *Sergio's Pizzas* (☎ (983) 2-23-55), Obregón 182, a block east of Héroes, are actually the same full-service restaurant with two wood-paneled, air-con dining rooms open from 1 pm to midnight daily. Look for the stained glass windows, enter to low lights and soft classical music. In Maria's order one of the many wines offered, then any of the Mexican or continental dishes, such as seafood or beef cordon bleu (US$7), finishing up with a slice of sacher torte. In Sergio's order a cold beer in a frosted mug and select a pizza priced from US$3 (small, plain) to US$14 (large, fancy).

For people-watching (especially in the evening), try the sidewalk cafe at the Hotel Los Cocos, where a full lunch or dinner is yours for US$6 to US$12. Drinks are expensive here.

Getting There & Away

Air Chetumal's small airport is less than two km northwest of the city center along Obregón and Revolución.

Mexicana's regional carrier, Aerocaribe, (☎ /fax (983) 2-66-75), Avenida Héroes 125, Plaza Baroudi Local 13, operates flights between Chetumal and Cancún, Cozumel, Flores (Petén, Guatemala) and Palenque.

Aviacsa (☎ (983) 2-76-76, fax (983) 2-76-54, at the airport (983) 2-77-87, fax (983) 2-76-98) flies nonstop to Villahermosa and direct to Mexico City.

For flights to Belize City (and on to Tikal) or to Belize's cayes, cross the border into Belize and fly from Corozal.

Bus The Terminal de Autobuses de Chetumal is three km north of the Museo de la Cultura Maya, at the intersection of Avenida de los Insurgentes and Avenida Belice. ADO, Autotransportes del Sur, Cristóbal Colón, Omnitur del Caribe, Linea Dorada and Unimaya provide service. The terminal has lockers, a tourist information kiosk, a bookstore, a newsstand, a post office, international phone and fax services, and shops. Next to the terminal is a huge San Francisco de Asis department store.

You can buy ADO tickets in the city center on Avenida Belice just west of the Museo de la Cultura Maya.

Many local buses, and those bound for Belize, depart from the Nuevo Mercado Lázaro Cárdenas, on Calzada Veracruz at Regundo, 10 blocks (1.5 km) north of the Museo Maya along Héroes, then turn at the Jeep dealership and go three blocks east.

The minibus terminal, at the corner of Avenida Primo de Verdad and Hidalgo, has minibuses to Bacalar and other nearby destinations.

Bacalar – 39 km, 45 minutes; minibuses from the minibus terminal (US$2); nine 2nd-class buses from the bus terminal (US$2.50)

Belize City – 160 km, four hours, US$5; express three hours, US$6; Batty's runs 12 northbound buses from Belize City via Orange Walk and Corozal to Chetumal's Nuevo Mercado from 4 am to 11:15 am; 12 southbound buses from Chetumal's Nuevo Mercado run from 10:30 am to 6:30 pm. Venus Bus Lines has buses departing from Belize City every hour on the hour from noon to 7 pm; departures from Chetumal are hourly from 4 to 10 am

Campeche – 422 km, seven hours; three buses (US$11 to US$14)

Cancún – 382 km, six hours; 23 buses (US$10 to US$14)

Corozal (Belize) – 30 km, one hour with border formalities, US$1.75; see Belize City schedule, above.

Felipe Carrillo Puerto – 155 km, three hours; 23 buses (US$4 to US$6)

Flores (Guatemala) – 350 km, nine hours, US$35; Servicio San Juan operates a bus at 2:30 pm daily from Chetumal's main bus terminal to Flores and Tikal.

Kohunlich – 67 km, 1¼ hours; take a bus heading west to Xpujil or Escárcega. Get off just before the village of Francisco Villa and walk nine km (1¾ hours) to site.

Mérida – 456 km, eight hours; 12 buses (US$9 to US$13)

Orange Walk (Belize) – 91 km, 2¼ hours; Urbina's and Chell's each run one bus daily (US$4), departing Chetumal's Nuevo Mercado around lunchtime; see also Belize City.

Palenque – 425 km, seven hours; one by ADO at 10:20 pm (US$15), two by Colón (US$15), one by ATS (US$12) at 8:15 pm; see also Villahermosa.

Playa del Carmen – 315 km, five hours; seven by ADO (US$10 to US$12), one by Colón (US$10), three by Mayab (US$6.50)

San Cristóbal de las Casas – 700 km, 11 hours; two by Colón (US$21 to US$24), two by ATS (US$18), plus several ADO buses de paso (US$22)

Ticul – 352 km, 6½ hours; nine buses (US$7)

Tikal (Guatemala) – 351 km, 11 hours, US$40; see Flores.

Tulum – 251 km, four hours; at least 12 buses (US$5 to US$7)

Villahermosa – 575 km, eight hours; eight buses (US$18); get off at Catazajá for Palenque.

Xcalak – 200 km, five hours; Sociedad Cooperativa del Caribe runs buses at 6 am and 3:30 pm (US$3).

Xpujil – 120 km, two hours; eight buses (US$3 to US$4)

Getting Around
Official taxis from the bus terminal to the center overcharge. Rather, walk out of the terminal to the main road, turn left, walk to the traffic circle, and catch a regular cab.

AROUND CHETUMAL
West of Chetumal along Hwy 186 is rich sugar cane and cattle country; logging is still important here, as it was during the 17th and 18th centuries.

Kohunlich Ruins
The archaeological site of Kohunlich is only partly excavated, with many of its nearly 200 mounds still covered in vegetation. The surrounding jungle is thick, but the archaeological site itself has been cleared selectively and is now a delightful forest park. Admission to the site costs US$1.50; it's open from 8 am to 5 pm daily. Drinks are sometimes sold at the site. The toilets are usually locked and 'under repair'.

These ruins, dating from the late Preclassic (100-200 AD) and Early Classic (250-600 AD) periods, are famous for the great Pyramid of the Masks: A central stairway is flanked by huge, three-meter-high stucco masks of the sun god. The thick lips and prominent features are reminiscent of Olmec sculpture. Though there were once eight masks, only two remain after the ravages of looters. The masks themselves are impressive, but the large thatch coverings that have been erected to protect them from further weathering also obscure the view; you can see the masks only from

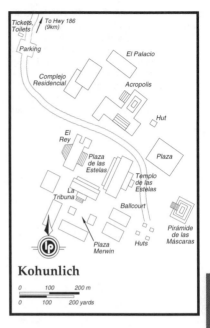

Kohunlich

close up. Try to imagine what the pyramid and its masks must have looked like in the old days as the Maya approached them from across the sunken courtyard at the front.

The hydraulic engineering used at the site was a great achievement; nine of the site's 21 hectares were cut to channel rainwater into Kohunlich's once enormous reservoir.

Getting There & Away At the time of this writing, there was no public transportation running directly to Kohunlich. To visit the ruins without your own vehicle, start early in the morning and take a bus heading west from Chetumal to Xpujil or Escárcega, then watch for the village of Nachi-Cocom, some 50 km from Chetumal. About 9.5 km past Nachi-Cocom, just before the village of Francisco Villa, is a road on the left (south) that covers the nine km to the archaeological site. Have the bus driver stop and let you off here; plan to walk and hope to hitch a ride from tourists in a car – hold up this guidebook for the driver to see.

Developers plan to build a luxury hotel on the Kohunlich access road, which may result in better public transportation.

To return to Chetumal or head westward to Xpujil or Escárcega, you must hope to flag down a bus on the highway; not all buses will stop.

SOUTH TO BELIZE

Corozal, 18 km south of the Mexican-Belizean border, is a pleasant, sleepy, laid-back farming and fishing town and an appropriate introduction to Belize. For details, see the Belize section.

For details on bus service to Corozal, Orange Walk and Belize City, as well as Flores and Tikal in Guatemala, see Getting There & Away in the Chetumal section.

YUCATÁN

Tabasco

The state of Tabasco is one big swampy river delta watered by the huge rivers – Usumacinta, San Pedro, Grijalva, Tonalá – that slice through the state on their way to the Gulf of Mexico.

Unlike Chiapas, to the south, which has a varied topography and climate, Tabasco is mostly low, wet, hot and humid. Rainfall averages 150 cm annually. It was in this unlikely territory that the Olmecs developed Mesoamerica's first great civilization. The greatest relics of the Olmecs are now on view in the excellent museums of the state's capital city, Villahermosa.

Besides its cultural wealth, Tabasco is noted for its mineral riches, particularly petroleum, which have brought great prosperity in recent years.

History
The religion, art, astronomy and architecture of the Olmecs (1200 to 400 BC) deeply influenced the later civilizations of the Aztecs, Mayas, Totonacs, Zapotecs and others. The Olmec capital, La Venta, was situated in the western part of Tabasco state. The Chontal Maya, who followed the Olmecs, built a great ceremonial city called Comalcalco outside present-day Villahermosa. By the time the Spaniards landed, Comalcalco had already been long abandoned and lost in the jungle.

Cortés, who disembarked on the Gulf Coast near present-day Villahermosa in 1519, initially defeated the Maya and founded a settlement called Santa María de la Victoria. The Maya regrouped and offered stern resistance until they were defeated by Francisco de Montejo, who pacified the region by 1540. This tranquillity was short-lived, however, as the depredations of pirates forced the original settlement to be moved inland from the coast and renamed Villahermosa de San Juan Bautista.

After Mexico won its independence from Spain local land barons asserted their power over the area, causing considerable strife. The French intrusion under Maximilian of

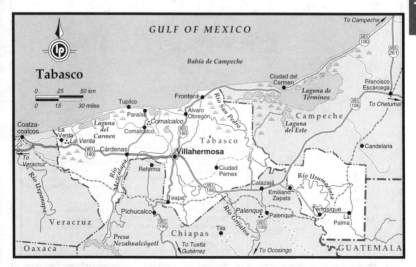

491

Hapsburg in 1863 met firm resistance here and thus promoted regional solidarity and political stability. Nonetheless, the region's economy languished until after the Mexican Revolution of 1910-17, when exports of cacao, bananas and coconuts began to increase. In the 1930s oil was discovered, and Tabasco's forward-looking socialist governor, Tomás Garrido Canabal, put forward progressive labor laws. But it took the oil crisis of the 1970s to show the importance – and lead to the exploitation of – Tabasco's vast reserves of oil. The oil boom catapulted Tabasco to the forefront of the Mexican economy and made this once-backward state into one of the richest in Mexico.

VILLAHERMOSA
Population 250,000

Courtesy of the Tabasco oil boom, Villahermosa is a beautiful city of wide, tree-shaded boulevards, sprawling parks, fancy hotels (for the oilies) and excellent cultural institutions.

The Parque-Museo La Venta is one of Mexico's great archaeological exhibits and will take up most of a morning. The excellent Regional Archaeological Museum

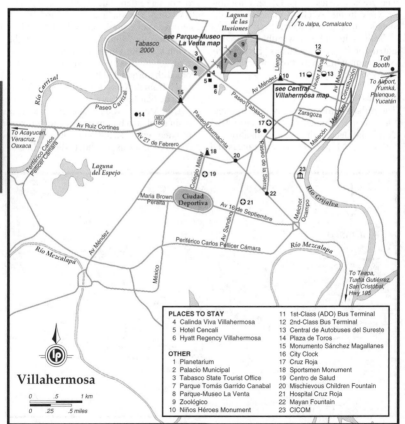

Villahermosa

0   .5   1 km
0   .25   .5 miles

PLACES TO STAY
4 Calinda Viva Villahermosa
5 Hotel Cencali
6 Hyatt Regency Villahermosa

OTHER
1 Planetarium
2 Palacio Municipal
3 Tabasco State Tourist Office
7 Parque Tomás Garrido Canabal
8 Parque-Museo La Venta
9 Zoológico
10 Niños Héroes Monument

11 1st-Class (ADO) Bus Terminal
12 2nd-Class Bus Terminal
13 Central de Autobuses del Sureste
14 Plaza de Toros
15 Monumento Sánchez Magallanes
16 City Clock
17 Cruz Roja
18 Sportsmen Monument
19 Centro de Salud
20 Mischievous Children Fountain
21 Hospital Cruz Roja
22 Mayan Fountain
23 CICOM

deserves at least an hour or two. Half a day can be enjoyed viewing wildlife at Yumká's nature interpretive center. The ruins of ancient Comalcalco are a short bus ride from the city center.

Plan to stay at least one night, though in a pinch you could leave your stuff at the bus terminal, see the sights during the day, and get to Palenque by nightfall.

With even more time you can relax at beach sites like El Paraíso, El Limón, Pico de Oro and Frontera. Although not on the Caribbean Sea, these beaches are pleasant enough and nearly free of tourists. The town of Teapa, an hour (60 km) south of Villahermosa, offers cave exploration, river swimming and a sulfur spa.

Orientation

Villahermosa is a sprawling city, and you will find yourself walking some considerable distances – in the sticky heat – and occasionally hopping on a *combi* (minibus or microbus, US$0.25) or taking a taxi (US$1.25 to US$2).

Budget and middle-range hotel and restaurant choices are mostly in the older commercial center of the city, known as the Zona Luz (Zone of Lights), which stretches from the Plaza de Armas, between Independencia and Guerrero, to Parque Juárez, bounded by streets named Zaragoza, Madero and Juárez. The zona is a lively place, busy with shoppers.

Top-end hotels are located on and off Avenida Ruiz Cortines, the main highway, which passes through the city. The Parque-Museo La Venta is also on Ruiz Cortines, 500 meters northwest of Paseo Tabasco.

The Central Camionera de Primera Clase (1st-class bus station), usually called the ADO terminal (☎ (93) 12-89-00) is on Javier Mina, three long blocks south of Ruiz Cortines and about 12 blocks north of the Zona Luz. The Central de Autobuses de Tabasco (2nd-class bus station) is right on Ruiz Cortines, one block east of Javier Mina, four long blocks north of the 1st-class station, and about 16 long blocks from the center.

Villahermosa's Rovirosa Airport (☎ (93) 12-75-55) is 13 km east of the Zona Luz on Hwy 180.

Information

Tourist Offices There's a small, often unstaffed tourist office next to the ticket window at the Parque-Museo La Venta and a more reliably staffed desk at Rovirosa Airport.

The administrative staff at the Tabasco state tourist office (☎ (93) 16-28-89, fax (93) 16-28-90), Paseo Tabasco 1504, in the governmental development known as Tabasco 2000, 500 meters northwest of Avenida Ruiz Cortines, does its best to answer travelers' questions. Hours are 8:30 am to 4 pm Monday to Friday. Go northwest along Paseo Tabasco from Ruiz Cortines to the first huge building on the right (northeast) side. Walk along the building's monumental central corridor, down the steps, and look for the office on the right-hand side.

Travel Agencies Viajes Villahermosa Travel Agency (☎ (93) 12-54-56, fax (93) 14-37-21), at 27 de Febrero 207 and Madero 422, sells international and domestic tickets; the staff speaks English and can arrange excursions. Hours are Monday to Friday 9 am to 7 pm, Saturday 9 am to 1 pm.

Turismo Nieves (☎ (93) 14-18-88), Sarlat 202, at the corner of Fidencia, is the American Express representative.

Turismo Creativo (☎ (93) 12-79-73, fax (93) 12-85-82) is at Mina 1011, corner of Paseo Tabasco.

Viajes Tabasco (☎ (93) 12-53-18, fax (93) 14-27-80) is at Madero 718 and also in the Hyatt Regency Villahermosa.

Money There are at least eight banks within the Zona Luz (see the Central Villahermosa map). Banking hours are generally 9 am to 1:30 pm, Monday through Friday. Banamex (☎ (93) 12-89-94), at the corner of Madero and Reforma, has an ATM, as does Bancomer (☎ (93) 12-37-00), at Zaragoza and Juárez.

YUCATÁN

Post The main post office (☎ (93) 12-10-40), is in the Zona Luz at Saenz 131, at the corner of Lerdo de Tejada. Hours are Monday to Friday 8 am to 5:30 pm, Saturday 9 am to noon, closed Sunday.

Medical Services The hospital of the Cruz Roja Mexicana (Red Cross; ☎ (93) 15-55-55) is on Avenida Sandino north of Avenida 16 de Septiembre in Colonia Primera, a short ride southwest of the Zona Luz. Unidad Medico Guerrero Urgencias (☎ (93) 14-56-97/98), on 5 de Mayo 44, at Lerdo de Tejada, is open 24 hours.

Laundry Super Lavandería Rex (☎ (93) 12-08-15), Madero 705 at Méndez, is open 8 am to 8 pm Monday to Saturday. A three-kg load costs US$8 for three-hour service.

Acua Lavandería (☎ (93) 14-37-65), next to the river on the corner of Constitución and Reforma, is open every day but Sunday; they charge US$1 per kg for two-day service, US$1.50 per kg for same-day service and have no self-service.

Parque-Museo La Venta

The Olmec city of La Venta, built on an island where the Río Tonalá runs into the

Parque-Museo La Venta
Not to Scale

ZOOLÓGICO
1 Nocturnal Animals
2 Tourist Office
3 Tickets
4 Entrance
5 Snakes
6 Aviary
7 Small Mammals
8 Museo de la Historia Natural
9 Spider Monkeys
10 Small Felines
11 Big Mammals
12 Museo de los Olmecas de la Venta
13 Turtles, Crocodiles
14 Cafeteria
15 Giant Cieba Tree
16 Big Felines

PARQUE-MUSEO LA VENTA
17 El Viejo (Old Warrior)
18 El Joven Guerrero (Young Warrior)
19 Estacada de Columnas Naturales (Palisade of Natural Basalt Columns)
20 Tumba (Tomb)
21 Mosaico-Mascarón (Large Mask)
22 La Abuela (Grandmother)
23 El Hombre Barbado (Bearded Man)
24 El Trono (Throne)
25 El Caminante (Walker)
26 Diosa Joven (Young Goddess)
27 Cabeza Inconclus (Unfinished Head)
28 Altar Cuadrangular (Quadrangular Altar)
29 Altar de los Niños (Altar of the Children)
30 Altar Triunfal (Triumpal Altar)
31 Personaje con Estandarte (Figure with Standard)
32 Cabeza Hendida (Cloven Head)
33 La Silueta (Silhouette)
34 Altar del Diálogo (Dialogue Altar)
35 Lápida con Incisione (Stone with Incisions)
36 Altar Erosionado (Eroded Altar)
37 Altar de los Tecolote (Altar of the Owls)
38 Altar Felino (Feline Altar)
39 El Gobernante (Governor)
40 Fragmentos (Fragments)
41 Cabeza Tatudo (Tattooed Head)
42 Mosaico-Mascarón (Mask)
43 Estela del Rey (Royal Stele)
44 Cabeza del Guerrero (Warrior's Head)
45 Jaguars
46 Altar del Jaguar (Jaguar Altar)
47 El Contorsionista (Contortionist)
48 Jaguar Niño (Jaguar Child)
49 El Delfín (Dolphin)
50 Mono Mirando El Cielo (Monkey Looking at the Sky)

Parque de Convivencia Infantil

Zoológico

Laguna de las Ilusiones

Plaza de Artesanas

Parque Tomás Garrido Canabal

Toilets
Shelters

Av. Ruiz Cortines

YUCATÁN

gulf, some 129 km west of Villahermosa, was originally constructed in about 1500 BC and flourished from 800 BC to 200 AD. Danish archaeologist Frans Blom did the initial excavations in 1925, and work was continued by Tulane University and the University of California. MW Sterling is credited with having discovered, in the early 1940s, five colossal Olmec heads sculpted from basalt. The largest weighs over 24 tons and stands more than two meters tall. It is a mystery how the Olmecs managed to move these massive basalt heads and other weighty religious statues some 100 km without the use of the wheel.

When petroleum excavation threatened the site of La Venta, the most significant finds – including three of the massive Olmec heads – were moved to Villahermosa and arranged as the Parque-Museo La Venta, a fascinating combination indoor-outdoor museum, nature preserve, sculpture park and tropical zoo.

Admission Parque-Museo La Venta (☎ (93) 15-22-28) is open every day from 8 am to 5 pm (last tickets sold at 4 pm); the zoo is closed Monday 'to give the animals a rest'. Admission costs US$2.50. Indoor (air-con) and outdoor snack stands provide sustenance. Plan at least two hours for your visit, and preferably three.

Museum & Nature Trail As you enter the park, detour to the spider monkeys on the left, then follow the purple tiles set in the pavement and proceed through the zoo to the well-done **Museo de las Olmecas de La Venta**, which explains Olmec history and culture using statuary, scale models, pottery and photos; signs are in Spanish and English.

On the other side of the museum is a giant ceiba, sacred tree of the Olmecs and Maya, which marks the starting point of the *recorrido* (nature trail) through lush tropical verdure past the 33 Olmec sculpture exhibits. The trail is 1050 meters long and takes at least an hour to walk if you spend a few minutes at each exhibit. Along the way, many trees bear signs giving their names and species. Keep an eye out for the cacao

tree just past the crocodile pool on the way to Monument 19: see how the cacao beans (from which chocolate is made) grow right out of its trunk and branches. Everybody wants to be photographed with Monument 26, the finest example of the great Olmec basalt heads.

Zoo Animals from Tabasco and nearby regions live in habitats grouped near the entrance to the park and at several places along the nature trail. Colorful macaws and toucans, pumas and jaguars (including black jaguars), white-tailed deer, crocodiles, boa constrictors and peccaries show Tabasco's diversity of fauna. Several animals that pose little danger to humans, such as coati and agouti, roam freely throughout the jungle habitat.

Getting There & Away Parque-Museo La Venta is three km from the Zona Luz. Catch any bus or combi heading northwest along Paseo Tabasco, get out before the intersection with Ruiz Cortines, and walk northeast through the sprawling Parque Tomás Garrido Canabal, a larger park that actually surrounds Parque-Museo La Venta. A taxi from the Zona Luz costs US$1.50.

Other Parks & Museums
Right next to the entrance to Parque-Museo La Venta is Tabasco's **Museo de Historia Natural**, open from 9 am to 4 pm (closed Monday); admission costs US$0.75 per adult, US$0.35 per child.

To the northeast is the **Parque de Convivencia Infantil**, the city's children's park. Playgrounds, a small zoo and aviary keep the kids happy here from 9 am to 5 pm any day except Monday, when it's closed. Admission costs US$0.50 for adults, free for children under 12.

Behind Parque-Museo La Venta you can stroll along the Laguna de las Ilusiones in **Tomás Garrido Canabal Park** or climb the 200 steps of the circular stairway to the modern lookout tower.

The **Museo de la Historia** (☎ (93) 12-49-96), at the corner of Juárand 27 de Febrero in the historic Casa de Azulejos

(House of Tiles), houses an eclectic assortment of artifacts from Tabasco's past, on view from 9 am to 5 pm daily for US$0.75.

CICOM & Regional Museum of Anthropology

The Center for Investigation of the Cultures of the Olmecs & Maya (CICOM) is a complex of buildings on the bank of the Río Grijalva one km south of the Zona Luz. The centerpiece of the complex is the Museo Regional de Antropología Carlos Pellicer Cámara, which is dedicated to the scholar and poet responsible for the preservation of the Olmec artifacts in the Parque-Museo La Venta. Besides the museum, the complex holds a theater, research center, an arts center and other buildings.

The anthropology museum (☎ (93) 12-32-02) is open 10 am to 5 pm every day; admission is US$1.75.

Just inside the front door you're greeted by the timeless gaze and regal expression of a massive Olmec head, one of those wonders from La Venta. The best way to proceed with your tour of the museum is to turn left, take the elevator to the 2nd (top) floor (3rd floor, US-style) and work your way down. Although the museum's explanations are all in Spanish, they are often accompanied by photos, maps and diagrams.

On the top floor, exhibits outline Mesoamerica's many civilizations, from the oldest Stone Age inhabitants to the more familiar cultures of our millennium. Don't miss the codices by the window on the north side. They are copies of the famous painted books of the Maya; the originals are in repositories outside Mexico. The window here, by the way, offers a nice view of the river and Villahermosa's cathedral.

After you've brushed up on the broad picture descend one flight to the 1st (middle) floor, where the exhibits concentrate on the Olmec and Mayan cultures. Especially intriguing are the displays concerning Comalcalco, the ruined Mayan city not far from Villahermosa, which you may want to visit (see the end of the chapter).

Finally, the ground floor of the museum holds various changing and traveling exhibits.

The house of Carlos Pellicer Cámara is now the **Casa Museo Carlos Pellicer**, Calle Saenz 203, in the Zona Luz. It's open daily from 9 am to 6 pm; admission is free.

Getting There & Away CICOM is one km south of the Zona Luz, or 600 meters south of the intersection of Malecón Madrazo and Paseo Tabasco. You can walk there in 12 to 15 minutes or catch any bus or colectivo (CICOM or No 1) traveling south along Madrazo; just say 'CICOM?' before you get in.

Tabasco 2000 & Parque La Choca

The ultramodern Tabasco 2000 complex is a monument to the prosperity the oil boom brought to Villahermosa. There are huge state and city government buildings, the high-rise Hotel Casa Real, chic boutiques in a gleaming mall, a convention center, a floral clock and pretty fountains. Coming from the Zona Luz, take a Tabasco 2000 bus along Paseo Tabasco.

Parque La Choca, 600 meters northwest of the Tabasco 2000 complex, is the site of a state fair, complete with livestock exhibitions and a crafts festival, in late April. It is a pleasant place to picnic, has a swimming pool and is open Monday to Saturday from 7 am to 9 pm.

Yumká

Yumká (☎ /fax (93) 13-23-90), 18 km east of the city (northeast of the airport), is Villahermosa's tribute to ecotourism, a one-sq-km nature interpretive center boasting spider monkeys, antelope, wildebeests, zebras, giraffes, elephants, white rhinos, water buffalo, ostriches, camels, caged jaguars and maybe a crocodile. Though some metal fences partition the park, most animals are free to roam.

Named for the legendary dwarf who looks after the jungle, the Yumká reserve is split into three sections: you begin with a half-hour stroll through the jungle, followed by an Asian and African Savannah tour by tractor-pulled trolley and finish up with a boat trip on the large lagoon. The obligatory guided tour takes 1½ to two hours. It's hardly a Kenya game drive, but if you fancy a dose of open space, greenery and a glimpse of the animal kingdom, go.

Yumká is open every day from 9 am to 5:30 pm. Admission costs US$5. Drinks and snacks are available at the front gate.

Getting There & Away On weekends shuttle buses run between the Parque-Museo La Venta parking lot and Yumká every 30 minutes from 10 am to 4 pm. On weekdays there are supposedly combis to Yumká from Parque La Paz on Madero, but I could find only taxis, which were charging US$13 for the ride.

Places to Stay – budget
Youth Hostel & Camping There is an *albergue de la juventud* (youth hostel) in the *Ciudad Deportiva* in the southern part of the city, but it is decrepit, inconvenient, and not particularly economical. You're better off staying at a bottom-end hotel in the Zona Luz.

It's sometimes possible to set up a tent or RV at the Ciudad Deportiva. Ask at the field house adjacent to the Olympic Stadium during the day. The Tamolte bus runs out here.

Zona Luz The Zona Luz has the best selection of inexpensive hotels. Try to keep street noise in mind when you are choosing accommodations.

On Lerdo de Tejada between Juárez and Madero are three small, plain, cheap hotels all in a row. *Hotel San Miguel* (☎ (93) 12-15-00), Lerdo 315, is perhaps the best of the lot, renting its plain rooms with fan for US$7/9/11 a single/double/triple or US$15 for a double with air-con. *Hotel Oviedo* (☎ (93) 12-14-55), Lerdo 303, the worst of the lot, charges the same prices. *Hotel Tabasco* (☎ (93) 12-00-77), Lerdo 317, is a step down from the neighboring San Miguel but charges even less. *Hotel Oriente* (☎ (93) 12-01-21), around the corner at Madero 425, is marginally better, though the front rooms are noisier.

Hotel San Francisco (☎ (93) 12-31-98), at Madero 604, between Marmol and Carmen Sanchez, is considerably better for just a little more money. An elevator does away with the sweaty hike upstairs, where you'll find rooms with ceiling fan or air-con for only about US$2 more.

Hotel Madero (☎ (93) 12-05-16), Madero 301, between Reforma and 27 de Febrero, is in an old building with some character. The rooms are among the best at this price in the city, US$8/10/12 a single/double/triple with ceiling fan and private shower. Air-con costs US$2.50 more. *Hotel Palma de Mallorca* (☎ (93) 12-01-44/5), Madero 516, between Lerdo de Tejada and Zaragoza, costs about the same but is not as nice.

Even cheaper? Try the *Hotel San Rafael* (☎ (93) 12-01-66), Constitución 240 at Lerdo de Tejada, where two people sharing a double bed in a room with shower and fan pay only US$7, though many rooms are noisy. *Hotel Santa Lucia* (☎ (93) 12-24-99), on Madero next door (south) to the Hotel Don Carlos, charges a bit more.

Posada Brondo (☎ (93) 12-59-61), on Pino Suárez 411, between Carmen Sánchez and Mármol, has bright, clean double rooms with TV and shower for US$10. For US$14 you get a room with a small couch, refrigerator and perhaps a balcony (with street noise).

Near the ADO Bus Station *Hotel Palomino Palace* (☎ (93) 12-84-31), Javier Mina at Pedro Fuentes, is directly across from the main entrance to the ADO (1st-class) bus station. Its location lets it get away with charging US$16 for a basic room (with fan and shower). It's often noisy, and you may be put on the 4th or 5th floor (stairs only). Even including taxi fare to and from the ADO bus station, Zona Luz hotels are cheaper.

Places to Stay – middle
Most middle-range hotels are also in the Zona Luz. The 64-room *Hotel Miraflores* (☎ (93) 12-00-22, fax (93) 12-04-86), Reforma 304 just west of Madero, is conveniently located and relatively quiet and offers nicely appointed air-con rooms with bath for US$27/29/32 a single/double/triple.

YUCATÁN

YUCATÁN

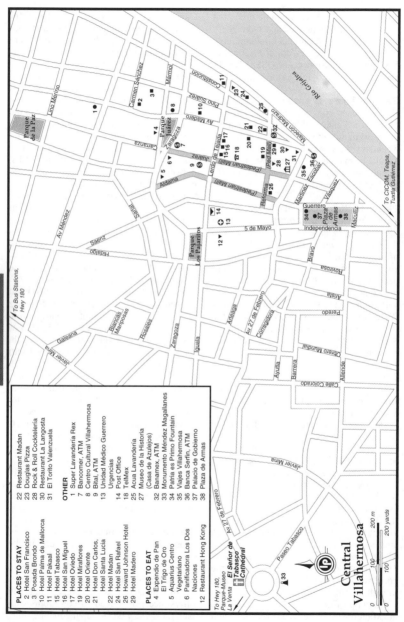

PLACES TO STAY
2 Hotel San Francisco
3 Posada Brondo
10 Hotel Palma de Mallorca
11 Hotel Pakaal
15 Hotel Tabasco
16 Hotel San Miguel
17 Hotel Oviedo
19 Hotel Miraflores
20 Hotel Oriente
21 Hotel Don Carlos,
    Hotel Santa Lucia
22 Hotel Madan
24 Hotel San Rafael
26 Howard Johnson Hotel
29 Hotel Madero

PLACES TO EAT
4 Expendio de Pan
    El Trigo de Oro
5 Aquarius Centro
    Vegetariano
6 Panificadora Los Dos
    Naciones
12 Restaurant Hong Kong

22 Restaurant Madan
23 Douglas Pizza
28 Rock & Roll Cocktelería
30 Restaurant La Langosta
31 El Torito Valenzuela

OTHER
1 Super Lavandería Rex
7 Bancomer, ATM
8 Centro Cultural Villahermosa
9 Bital, ATM
13 Unidad Medico Guerrero
    Urgencias
14 Post Office
18 TelMex
25 Acua Lavandería
27 Museo de la Historia
    (Casa de Azulejos)
32 Banamex, ATM
33 Monumento Méndez Magallanes
34 Patria es Primo Fountain
35 Viajes Villahermosa
36 Banca Serfin, ATM
37 Palacio de Gobierno
38 Plaza de Armas

Hotel Madan (☎ (93) 12-16-50), Madero 408, has 20 modern air-con rooms with bath right in the center for US$23 to US$25, single or double. *Hotel Pakaal* (☎ (93) 12-45-01, fax (93) 14-46-48), Lerdo de Tejada 106 at Constitución, is newer but charges even less for air-con rooms with bath and TV. *Hotel Don Carlos* (☎ (93) 12-24-99, fax (93) 12-46-22), Madero 422 between Reforma and Lerdo, charges more for its older air-con rooms.

Howard Johnson Hotel (☎ /fax (93) 14-46-45, hotel@mail.inforedmx.com.mx), Aldama 404 at Reforma, has small but comfortable rooms right in the midst of the Zona Luz's pedestrian streets for US$34 a single or double in one bed, US$38 in two beds.

Places to Stay – top end

As an oil boom town, Villahermosa has no shortage of luxury lodgings. Three of the best hotels are located near the intersection of Paseo Tabasco and Avenida Ruiz Cortines (Hwy 180), a pleasant 10-minute walk from Parque-Museo La Venta.

Poshest is the *Hyatt Regency Villahermosa* (☎ (93) 15-12-34, fax (93) 15-58-08, toll-free fax (91-800) 23-234), Calle Juárez, Colonia Lindavista, near the intersection of Avenida Ruiz Cortines and Paseo Tabasco. It has all the expected luxury services, including swimming pool and tennis courts, for US$85 a single or double. The food in the restaurants is particularly good here. Note that this Calle Juárez is a different street from the one in the Zona Luz, three km away.

Hotel Cencali (☎ (93)15-19-99, (93) fax 15-66-00) is on Calle Juárez, Colonia Lindavista, off Paseo Tabasco, next to the Hyatt. The hotel's setting, away from noisy streets amid tropical greenery, is excellent, yet modern air-con rooms cost only US$60 a single or double. There's even a swimming pool.

Calinda Viva Villahermosa (☎ (93) 15-00-00, fax (93) 15 30 73, in Mexico (91-800) 90-000, in the USA (800) 221-2222), next to the two aforementioned hotels, is a two-story motel-style white stucco building surround-ing a large swimming pool. Comfortable rooms cost US$65 a single or double.

Places to Eat – budget

Avenida Madero and the pedestrian streets of the Zona Luz (Lerdo, Juárez, Reforma, Aldama) have lots of snack and fast-food shops. Coffee drinkers beware! Most cheap places give you a cup of lukewarm water and a jar of instant coffee (sometimes decaf). If you need a quick early-morning shot of the good stuff, try KFC, at Juárez 420, near Reforma.

El Torito Valenzuela, 27 de Febrero 202 at Madero, next to the Hotel Madero is the most popular and convenient taquería, open from 8 am to midnight. Tacos made with various ingredients cost US$0.30 to US$0.60 apiece. More substantial platters range from US$3.75 to US$6, but the daily comida corrida costs less than US$3.50 for four courses.

The neighboring *Restaurant La Langosta*, despite its name, specializes in rotisserie chicken, charging US$2 for half a bird. Other dishes are good and cheap as well.

Douglas Pizza, Lerdo de Tejada 107, at Constitución and opposite the Hotel Pakaal, offers a wide assortment of two-person pizzas for US$4 to US$5.50 and *grandes* for US$6 to US$7.50.

Near Parque Juárez, *Aquarius Centro Vegetariano*, Zaragoza 513, between Aldama and Juárez, is open from 9 am to 9 pm; closed Sunday. Try the granola, yogurt and honey (US$1), a soyaburger (US$1) or the special sandwich (alfalfa, tomatoes, onions, avocado, cheese and beans on whole-grain bread (US$1.50). They also sell whole-wheat baked goods and vitamins.

Always packed in the late afternoon is *Rock & Roll Cocktelería*, on Reforma just east of Juárez. Here you may sample a cocktel (fish, tomato sauce, lettuce, onions and a lemon squeeze) with crackers for US$4.

At the Parque Los Pajaritos, between Zaragoza and 5 de Mayo, are two antojito stands, where tacos are US$0.20 and tortas US$0.60. The food is OK, but it's the natural shade of the big trees and the enormous cage of colorful birds that make this park a relaxing snack stop. Somehow the breeze finds its way here, and the fountain's quiet roar drowns out most city sounds.

If you're eating or drinking on the run, try *Jugos*, next to the Hotel San Miguel on Lerdo, for licuados or heaping fruit platters (US$0.70), or the *Expendio de Pan El Trigo de Oro*, on Mármol facing the Parque Juárez, for sweet rolls, bread and pastries. Another useful bakery is the *Panificadora Los Dos Naciones*, at the corner of Juárez and Zaragoza.

Places to Eat – middle

There's not much in the Zona Luz. *Restaurant Madan*, on Madero just north of Reforma, is bright, modern and air-conditioned, with a genuine espresso machine hissing in one corner. But the regulars come to chat and sip coffee, not to eat, so the food suffers from lack of patronage.

Restaurant Hong Kong, 5 de Mayo 433, just off the Parque Los Pajaritos, is a Chinese restaurant on an upper floor with a six-page menu. A full meal, from won ton soup through steamed duck to fortune cookie, costs between US$6 and US$11.

You may want to coordinate a visit to the Museo Regional de Antropología with lunch at the *Restaurant Los Tulipanes*, in the CICOM complex, open from noon to 8 pm every day. Seafood and steaks are the specialties and cost between US$6.50 and US$11. There is a pianist every afternoon and a Sunday buffet for US$12.

Entertainment

Teatro Esperanza Iris, at the CICOM complex, frequently hosts folkloric dance, theater, comedy and music performances. For information on cultural goings-on, call the Instituto de la Cultura (☎ (93) 12-75-30) or ask at the tourist office or your hotel. The *Centro Cultural Villahermosa*, on Madero between Mármol and Zaragoza, east of Parque Juárez, sponsors films, musical performances and changing art and cultural exhibits. It's open from 10 am to 9 pm, and admission is free.

Live music is featured at bars in the Calinda Viva, Hyatt and Cencali hotels, open every evening except Sunday and Monday from about 10 pm. The *'Ku' Disco*, near the junction of Sandino and Paseo Usumacinta, has a good reputation. Cover charge at any of these bars is around US$7.

Getting There & Away

Air Villahermosa's Rovirosa Airport (☎ (93) 12-75-55) is 13 km east of the center on Hwy 180, a 20-minute ride. There are nonstop or one-stop direct flights between Villahermosa (VSA) and:

Chetumal – Aviacsa, daily except Saturday

Ciudad del Carmen – Aerocaribe, four days per week

Mérida – Aerocaribe, Aeromexico, and Aviacsa, daily

Mexico City – Aerocaribe, Aeromexico, and Aviacsa, daily

Oaxaca – Aerocaribe, three days per week (daily with one stop); Aeromexico, daily

Palenque – Aerocaribe, three days weekly

Tuxtla Gutiérrez – Aerocaribe, twice daily; Aeromexico, daily

Veracruz – Aeromexico, daily

Aerocaribe (☎ (93) 16-50-46, fax (93) 16-50-47), operated by Mexicana, has its ticket office in the Centro Comercial Plaza de Atocha, Avenida Vía 3, No 20, Tabasco 2000.

Aeromexico (☎ (93) 12-15-28, in Mexico (91-800) 3-62-02), is at Periférico Carlos Pellicer 511-2, in the CICOM complex.

Aviacsa (☎ (93) 14-57-70, fax (93) 12-57-74, toll-free in Mexico (91-800) 2-30-80) is at Francisco Javier Mina 1025-D.

1st-Class Bus The 1st-class (ADO) bus station, Javier Mina 297, has a luggage room (US$0.15 per hour) and a selection of little eating places.

The two main 1st-class companies are ADO and Cristóbal Colón; UNO, the luxury line, has buses to central Mexico. Villahermosa is an important transportation point, but many buses serving it are de paso (they take passengers in Villahermosa only if they have room), so buy your onward ticket as far in advance as possible.

The following listings are for daily 1st- or luxury-class buses that start their runs in Villahermosa; there are many more de paso buses. Prices are for 1st class; the few luxury ADO GL and Maya de Oro buses cost about 15% more.

Campeche – 450 km, six hours, US$14 to US$17; 15 by ADO

Cancún – 915 km, 11 hours, US$28; three by ADO in the evening

Catazajá – 116 km, two hours, US$4; 10 by ADO

Chetumal – 575 km, eight hours, US$18; eight by ADO

Comalcalco – 53 km, 1½ hours, US$3; three by ADO, at 12:30 pm and later

Mérida – 700 km, nine hours; 10 by ADO (US$20), one evening UNO (US$32), several by ATS (US$16)

Mexico City – 820 km, 14 hours; 11 by ADO (US$30), three by UNO in the evening (US$43)

Oaxaca – 700 km, 13 hours, US$32; three by ADO

Palenque – 150 km, 2½ hours; 10 ADO by (US$5), one by Colón (US$5)

Playa del Carmen – 848 km, 14 hours, US$26; two by ADO nightly

San Cristóbal de las Casas – 300 km, eight hours, US$10; one by Colón, or go via Tuxtla Gutiérrez

Tapachula – 735 km, 13 hours, US$24; one by Colón

Teapa – 60 km, one hour, US$2; five by Colón

Tenosique – 290 km, four hours, US$6; nine by ADO

Tuxtla Gutiérrez – 294 km, six hours; 10 by Colón (US$9), three by ATG (US$6.50)

Veracruz – 475 km, eight hours; 10 by ADO (US$16), one evening UNO (US$24)

2nd-Class Bus The 2nd-class bus station, Central de Autobuses de Tabasco, is on the north side of Avenida Ruiz Cortines (Hwy 180) just east of the intersection with Javier Mina, about five blocks north of the 1st-class bus station. Use the pedestrian overpass just east of the station to cross the highway.

A number of smaller companies serve local destinations within the state of Tabasco, but most of the buses you'll want depart from the 1st-class ADO station.

Car Most car rental companies have desks at Rovirosa Airport. Here are the city offices:

Avis, at the airport (☎ (93) 12-92-14, in Mexico (91-800) 7-07-77)

Budget, Malecón Madrazo 761 (☎ /fax (93) 14-37-90)

Dollar Rent A Car, Paseo Tabasco 600, next to the cathedral (☎ (93) 13-68-35, fax (93) 13-35-84)

Hertz, in the Hotel Casa Real, Paseo Tabasco Prolongación 1407, Tabasco 2000 (☎ (93) 16-44-00, toll-free (91-800) 7-00-16)

National, Reforma 304, also in the Hyatt Regency Villahermosa (☎ (93) 15-12-34)

Getting Around

To/From the Airport Transporte Terrestre minibuses charge US$3 per person for the trip into town; a taxi costs US$8. The 13-km trip takes about 20 minutes to the Zona Luz and 25 minutes to the top-end hotels. Buy your tickets from a counter in the terminal. From town to the airport a taxi is your only choice (US$8).

Bus Stations From the 1st-class ADO bus station, it's a 15- to 20-minute walk to the Zona Luz. Colectivo taxis depart from just outside the main entrance for the Zona Luz (US$0.40). Regular taxis charge US$1.25 to US$2 for a ride to any point in the city.

For buses and minibuses, go out the main (east) door of the ADO station, turn left, and walk two blocks north to the corner of Mina and Zozaya, where minibuses and combis stop en route to the Zona Luz and Madero, the main thoroughfare; look for 'Centro' on the windshield.

To walk to the Zona Luz, go out the side (south) door, turn left onto Lino Merino and walk five blocks to Parque de la Paz, then turn right on Madero.

Bus & Minibus A dozen municipal bus routes link the Zona Luz with outlying areas of the city; VW combi minibuses are useful as well (US$0.20). These vehicles travel tortuous routes that are summarized by cryptic words scrawled in their windshields: landmarks, major streets and distant *colonias* (neighborhoods). Here are some translations:

2000 – Tabasco 2000 government complex

Centro – Zona Luz

Chedraui – big department store near ADO bus station

CICOM – Anthropology Museum

Deportes – Ciudad Deportiva

Palacio Mpal – Palacio Municipal in Tabasco 2000 complex

Reloj – clock at 27 de Febrero and Calle 1, southwest of Paseo Tabasco

Tabasco – Paseo Tabasco

Terminal – ADO bus station

X 27 – via Calle 27 de Febrero

COMALCALCO RUINS

Comalcalco flourished during the Mayan Late Classic period between 500 and 900 AD, when the region's agricultural productivity prompted population expansion. The principal crop that brought Indian peasants from Palenque to this region was the cacao bean, which the Comalcalcans traded with other Mayan settlements. It is still the area's chief cash crop.

Comalcalco is open daily from 9 am to 5 pm; admission costs US$1.75.

Resembling Palenque in architecture and sculpture, Comalcalco is unique because it is built of bricks made from clay, sand and – ingeniously – oyster shells. Mortar was provided with lime obtained from the oyster shells.

As you enter the ruins the substantial structure to your left may surprise you, because the pyramid's bricks look remarkably like those used in construction today. Look on the right-hand side for remains of the stucco sculptures that once covered the pyramid. In the northern section of the acropolis are remains of fine stucco carvings.

Although the west side of the acropolis once held a crypt comparable to that of Palenque's Pakal, the tomb was vandalized centuries ago and the sarcophagus stolen. Continue up the hill to the Palace, and from this elevation enjoy the breeze while you gaze down on unexcavated mounds.

Getting There & Away

The 55-km journey takes about an hour. ADO runs buses at 12:30, 4:45 and 8:30 pm daily for US$2.75. Ask the driver to get you to *las ruinas*.

If you want to get an earlier start (and you should), walk along the colectivo taxi ranks on the north side of the ADO bus station in the morning. The Comalcalco colectivo leaves when all seats are filled and charges US$4 for the ride. A private taxi trip to Comalcalco and back, with an hour's waiting time, costs US$24.

Chiapas

Chiapas is southeastern Mexico's huge, naturally beautiful, potentially rich, politically troubled frontier. It is among the most varied and fascinating places in the country and has been a Mayan stronghold for centuries, with long-time, continuing links to the neighboring Mayan highlands of Guatemala.

For the traveler, Chiapas can be divided into three parts.

Lowland Chiapas, the northern portion of the state, shares the Río Usumacinta floodplain with the state of Tabasco. Its steamy tropical climate encouraged a flourishing of ancient Mayan culture, which survives in the graceful buildings of Palenque and, farther up the Usumacinta, the jungle-bound ruins of Bonampak and Yaxchilán.

At the center of Chiapas are the highlands, a cool, cloudy, mountainous region with

503

peaks reaching nearly 3000 meters. The cultural center of the highlands is San Cristóbal de las Casas, a tranquil hill-country colonial town surrounded by mysterious, very traditional Indian villages. Two hours' drive west – and nearly 1600 meters lower – the surprisingly modern state capital, Tuxtla Gutiérrez, has probably Mexico's best zoo, devoted entirely to Chiapas's varied fauna. Only a few kilometers from Tuxtla is the 1000-meter-deep Sumidero Canyon, through which you can take an awesome boat ride. Three hours' drive southeast of San Cristóbal, near the border with Guatemala, is the lovely Montebello Lakes region.

Chiapas's third region is the Soconusco, the state's steamy, agriculturally rich Pacific coast. Puerto Arista, near Tonalá, is a very laid-back beach spot, and Tapachula is a logical stop on the road to Guatemala, but in general southern Chiapas is the least interesting of the state's three regions, unless you are easily enthralled by coffee and banana plantations.

HISTORY

Pre-Hispanic civilizations straddled the Chiapas-Guatemala border, and for most of the colonial era Chiapas was governed from Guatemala.

Pre-Hispanic

Central and coastal Chiapas came under the influence of the Olmecs, who flourished on the Gulf Coast from about 1200 to 400 BC. Izapa, in the southern corner of Chiapas near Tapachula, was the center of a culture that peaked around 200 BC to 200 AD and is thought to be a link between the Olmecs and the Maya.

During the Classic era (approximately 300 to 900 AD) coastal and central Chiapas were relative backwaters, but low-lying, jungle-covered eastern Chiapas gave rise to two important Mayan city-states, Palenque and Yaxchilán, which both flourished in the 7th and 8th centuries. Toniná and Chinkultic were lesser Mayan centers.

After the Classic Mayan collapse highland Chiapas and Guatemala came to be divided among a number of often warring kingdoms,

many with cultures descended from the Maya but some also with rulers claiming central Mexican Toltec ancestry. Coastal Chiapas, a rich source of cacao, from which chocolate is made, was conquered by the Aztecs at the end of the 15th century and became their most distant province, under the name Xoconochco (from which its present name, Soconusco, is derived).

Spanish Era

Central Chiapas didn't come under effective Spanish control until the 1528 expedition of Diego de Mazariegos, who defeated the dominant, warlike Chiapa Indians, many of whom jumped to their death in Sumidero Canyon rather than be captured. Outlying areas of Chiapas were subdued in the 1530s and 1540s, though the Spaniards never gained control of the Lacandón forest, which remained a Mayan refuge.

Soconusco and inland Chiapas were administered separately, both from Guatemala, for most of the Spanish era, which meant that they lacked supervision for long periods and there was little check on colonists' excesses against the Indians. New diseases were brought by the Spaniards, and one epidemic in 1544 killed about half the Indians of Chiapas.

The only light in the Indians' darkness was the work of some Spanish church figures, among them the Dominican monks. Preeminent was Bartolomé de las Casas (1474-1566), appointed the first bishop of Chiapas in 1545. Las Casas had come to the Caribbean as an ordinary colonist, but in 1510 he entered the Dominican order and spent the rest of his life fighting for Indian rights in the new colonies. His achievements, including partly observed laws reducing compulsory labor (1543) and banning Indian (but not black) slavery (1550), earned him the hostility of the colonists but the affection of the Indians.

19th & 20th Centuries

In 1821, with the end of Spanish rule over Mexico and Central America, Mexico's new emperor, Agustín Iturbide, invited Spain's former Central American provinces (including Chiapas) to unite with Mexico. But Iturbide was soon overthrown, and when the Mexican congress was dissolved in 1823 the United Provinces of Central America declared their independence. A small military force under General Vicente Filísola, sent from Mexico City by Iturbide to preserve order in Guatemala City, returned home by way of Chiapas. Filísola used his power to bring Chiapas into the Mexican union, which it joined in 1824 after holding a referendum.

Permanent union with Mexico has not solved Chiapas's problems, however. Though quite rich in natural resources and economic potential, a succession of governors sent out from Mexico City, along with local landowners, has maintained an almost feudal control over the state – particularly in the highlands. Periodic uprisings and protests by the local indigenous peoples have borne witness to bad government, but the world took little notice until January 1, 1994, when a group calling itself the Zapatista National Liberation Army briefly occupied San Cristóbal de las Casas and nearby towns by military force. With world press attention riveted on Chiapas, the Mexican government was forced to take vigorous measures to restore order and to meet the rebels' demands. Whether the Zapatista rebellion is the one that will bring Chiapas better government and better times, or is just another in the state's long history of rebellions, remains to be seen.

GEOGRAPHY & CLIMATE

Chiapas's 74,000 sq km fall into five distinct bands, all roughly parallel to the Pacific Coast. The highest rainfall in all of them occurs from May to October.

The hot, fertile coastal plain, 15- to 35-km wide, called the Soconusco, receives heavy rainfall from June to October, especially in July and August.

Rising from the Soconusco is the mountain range called the Sierra Madre de Chiapas, mostly between 1000 and 2500 meters but higher in the south, where the Tacaná volcano on the Guatemalan border reaches 4092 meters. The Sierra Madre continues into Guatemala, throwing up several more volcanoes.

Inland from the Sierra Madre is the wide, warm, fairly dry Río Grijalva valley, also called the Central Depression of Chiapas, 500 to 1000 meters high. The state capital, Tuxtla Gutiérrez, lies in the west of this valley.

Next come the Chiapas highlands, known to locals simply as Los Altos, mostly 2000 to 3000 meters high and stretching into Guatemala. San Cristóbal de las Casas, in the small Jovel valley in the middle of these uplands, is cool, with temperatures between the high single figures and the low 20s Celsius year round. Rainfall in San Cristóbal is negligible from November to April, but about 110 cm fall in the other half of the year. The Chichonal volcano, at the northwest end of these highlands, erupted in 1981.

The northern and eastern parts of the state include one of Mexico's few remaining areas of tropical rain forest, shrinking but still extensive at around 10,000 sq km. Its eastern portion is known as the Selva Lacandona.

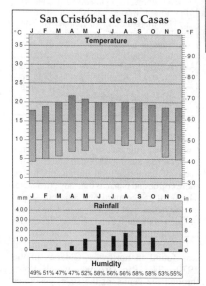

San Cristóbal de las Casas climate chart showing Temperature, Rainfall, and Humidity graphs. Humidity: 49% 51% 47% 47% 52% 58% 56% 56% 58% 58% 53% 55%

YUCATÁN

Chiapas Indians

The Indian people whom travelers are most likely to contact are the 296,000 or so Tzotzils around San Cristóbal de las Casas. Tzotzil textiles are among the most varied, colorful and elaborately worked in Mexico. You may also encounter the Tzeltals, another strongly traditional people, about 334,000 strong, who inhabit the region just east of San Cristóbal.

Other Chiapas Indians include about 80,000 Chols on the north side of the Chiapas highlands and the low-lying areas beyond, east and west of Palenque; an estimated 20,000 Mexican Mames near the Guatemalan border between Tapachula and Ciudad Cuauhtémoc, including some on the slopes of Tacaná (many more Mames – around 300,000 – are Guatemalans); and the Zoques, some 25,000 of whom used to inhabit western Chiapas but were dispersed by the 1981 Chichonal eruption. Some have moved back to the area, and there are hopes that the damage is not irreversible.

There are still a few hundred Lacandóns, the last true inheritors of ancient Mayan traditions, in the eastern Chiapas rain forest, who speak a language they call Maya, related to Yucatán Maya. The past four decades have wrought more changes in Lacandón life than the four centuries that preceded them: 100,000 land-hungry settlers have arrived in the forest, and North American missionaries have succeeded in converting some Lacandóns to Christianity. ■

ECONOMY

Chiapas has little industry but is second only to Veracruz among Mexican states in the value of its agricultural output, producing more coffee and bananas than any other state. The fertile Soconusco and adjacent slopes are the richest part of Chiapas and the source of much of the coffee and bananas. Tapachula is the commercial hub of the Soconusco.

Chiapas has other sources of wealth. Oil was found in northwest Chiapas in the 1970s. The Río Grijalva, which flows through the center of the state, generates more electricity than any other river in Mexico at huge dams such as La Angostura, Chicoasén and Nezahualcóyotl. Most Chiapans, however, are very poor, and wealth is concentrated in a small oligarchy. Ironically, in this electricity-rich state, fewer than half the homes have electricity.

PEOPLE

Of Chiapas's approximately 3.2 million people, an estimated 700,000 are Indians, descendants of the peoples who were here before the Spaniards came, including outlying Mayan groups. The Indians are 2nd-class citizens in economic and political terms, living on the least productive land in the state. Some have emigrated into the eastern jungle to clear new land, or to cities further afield in search of jobs.

Despite these problems, traditional festivals, costumes, crafts, religious practices and separate languages help Indian self-respect survive. Indians remain suspicious of outsiders and are often resentful of interference – especially in their religious practices. Many particularly dislike having their photos taken, so ask if you're in any doubt. Nevertheless, if you treat them with due respect, Indians may also be friendly. Keep in mind that Spanish is no more than a second language to them.

Lowland Chiapas

Much like neighboring Tabasco in climate and terrain, northern and eastern Chiapas boast some of La Ruta Maya's finest ancient cities. After visiting the graceful Mayan city of Palenque, use the nearby modern town as a base for excursions to the ruins at Bonampak and Yaxchilán or the waterfalls at Agua Azul and Misol-Ha.

PALENQUE

Population 20,000

Set on a series of foothills, watered by rushing streams and surrounded by emerald jungle, Palenque (elevation 80 meters) is the most atmospheric and romantic of the great Mayan sites. Its setting, architecture and decoration are superb.

History

Palenque means 'Palisade' in Spanish and has no relation to the ancient city's real name, which may have been Nachan, Chocan, Culhuacán, Xhembobel Moyos, Huehuetlapalla or Otolum.

Evidence from pottery fragments indicates that Palenque was first occupied more than 1500 years ago. It flourished from 600 to 800 AD, and what a glorious two centuries they were! The city rose to prominence under Pakal, a clubfooted king who reigned from 615 to 683 AD, and who lived to a ripe old age, possibly 80 to 100 years. In Mayan hieroglyphs he is represented by the signs for 'sun' and 'shield'.

During its golden age the city grew to some 20 sq km and included many handsome buildings characterized by mansard roofs and fine stucco bas-reliefs. Pakal's reign saw the construction of many of Palenque's finest plazas and buildings, including the superlative Temple of Inscriptions.

Pakal was succeeded by his son Chan-Balum, symbolized in hieroglyphs by the jaguar and the serpent. Chan-Balum continued Palenque's political and economic expansion, as well as the development of its art and architecture. He completed his father's crypt in the Temple of Inscriptions and presided over the construction of the Plaza of the Sun temples, placing sizable narrative stone stelae within each. One can see the influence of Palenque's architecture in the ruins of the Mayan city of Tikal in Guatemala's Petén region and in the pyramids of Comalcalco, near Villahermosa.

Not long after Chan-Balum's death Palenque started on a precipitous decline, due perhaps to ecological catastrophe, civil strife or invasion. After the 10th century Palenque was largely abandoned, its great buildings reclaimed by the fast-growing jungle.

Rediscovery of Palenque

It is said that Hernán Cortés came within 40 km of the ruins without any awareness of them. In 1773 Mayan hunters told a Spanish priest that stone palaces lay in the jungle. Father Ordoñez y Aguilar led an expedition to Palenque and wrote a book claiming that the city was the capital of an Atlantis-like civilization.

An expedition led by Captain Antonio del Río set out in 1787 to explore Palenque. Although his report was then locked up in the Guatemalan archives, a translation of it was made by a British resident of Guatemala who was sufficiently intrigued to have it published in England in 1822. This led a host of adventurers to brave malaria in their search for the hidden city.

Among the most colorful of them was the eccentric Count de Waldeck, who, in his 60s, lived atop one of the pyramids for two years (1831-33). He wrote a book complete with fraudulent drawings that made the city resemble great Mediterranean civilizations, causing all the more interest in Palenque. In Europe, Palenque's fame grew, and it was mythologized as a lost Atlantis or an extension of ancient Egypt.

Finally, in 1837 John L Stephens reached Palenque with artist Frederick Catherwood. Stephens wrote insightfully about the city's aqueduct system, and the six pyramids he examined in detail. His was the first truly scientific investigation, and it paved the way for serious research by others.

Orientation

There are two Palenques, the town and the archaeological zone, 6.5 km apart. Most visitors to the area arrive either via Villahermosa or Campeche or from San Cristóbal de las Casas, in highland Chiapas.

Coming south from Hwy 186 at Catazajá it's 20 km to the village of Pakal-na, which has the Palenque train station, and several more kilometers, passing the airport, to the town of Palenque itself. Buses and minibuses run between Catazajá and Palenque town frequently in the morning and afternoon. A taxi between Catazajá and Palenque costs US$7.50 for the 25-minute ride.

Coming northeast from Tuxtla Gutiérrez, San Cristóbal and Agua Azul you pass the Calinda Hotel Nututún and, shortly after,

YUCATÁN

join the town-to-ruins road. Turn right for the town.

As you approach Palenque there is a fork in the road marked by the huge, dramatic statue of a Maya head (it may be King Pakal). East of the statue is the wooded area known as La Cañada. Go east from the statue to Palenque town (one km) or west for the ruins (5.5 km), within the national park.

Most hotels and restaurants are in the town center; the camping areas and several top-end hotels are located along the road to the ruins. There are also hotels and restaurants in La Cañada.

Though relatively low in population, Palenque town spreads for two km, with the Maya head statue at the western limit and the Hotel Misión Park Plaza at the eastern end. Most of the bus stations are clustered a few hundred meters east of the Maya head statue on the way into town; the walk to most hotels is 800 meters or less. The main road from the Maya head statue into town is Avenida Juárez, the main commercial street, which holds most of the services you may want, including banks, hotels, telephone casetas, restaurants, travel agencies, pharmacies, bakeries, grocery stores and

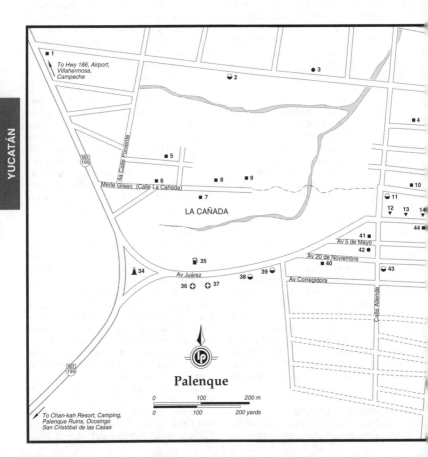

Palenque

drink shops, etc. Juárez ends at the town's main square, known simply as el parque (the park). The Iglesia de Santo Domingo (church) is east of the park. Avenida Velasco Suárez, north of the center, is the market street, with nary a tourist in sight.

With an average humidity of 78%, it's always sweltering in Palenque, and there's rarely any breeze.

Information

Tourist Office Located in the Mercado de Artesanías building on Juárez, the tourist office (☎ (934) 5-08-28) has an English-speaking staff, reliable town and transit information and a few maps. Office doors are open every day from 8:30 am to 8:30 pm.

Money Bancomer, 1½ blocks west of the park on Juárez, changes money between 10 and 11:30 am Monday to Friday. Banamex, 2½ blocks west of the park, does the exchange from 10:30 am to noon Monday to Friday. Both banks have ATMs. Some hotels, restaurants, travel agents and exchange shops in town will also change money, though at less favorable rates.

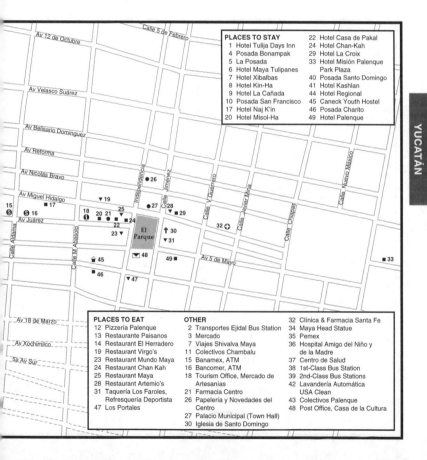

YUCATÁN

PLACES TO STAY
1 Hotel Tulija Days Inn
4 Posada Bonampak
5 La Posada
6 Hotel Maya Tulipanes
7 Hotel Xibalbas
8 Hotel Kin-Ha
9 Hotel La Cañada
10 Posada San Francisco
17 Hotel Naj K'in
20 Hotel Misol-Ha
22 Hotel Casa de Pakal
24 Hotel Chan-Kah
29 Hotel La Croix
33 Hotel Misión Palenque Park Plaza
40 Posada Santo Domingo
41 Hotel Kashlan
44 Hotel Regional
45 Caneck Youth Hostel
46 Posada Charito
49 Hotel Palenque

PLACES TO EAT
12 Pizzería Palenque
13 Restaurante Paisanos
14 Restaurant El Herradero
19 Restaurant Virgo's
23 Restaurant Mundo Maya
24 Restaurant Chan Kah
25 Restaurant Maya
28 Restaurant Artemio's
31 Taquería Los Faroles, Refresquería Deportista
47 Los Portales

OTHER
2 Transportes Ejidal Bus Station
3 Mercado
7 Viajes Shivalva Maya
11 Colectivos Chambalu
15 Banamex, ATM
16 Bancomer, ATM
18 Tourism Office, Mercado de Artesanías
21 Farmacia Centro
26 Papelería y Novedades del Centro
27 Palacio Municipal (Town Hall)
30 Iglesia de Santo Domingo

32 Clínica & Farmacia Santa Fe
34 Maya Head Statue
35 Pemex
36 Hospital Amigo del Niño y de la Madre
37 Centro de Salud
38 1st-Class Bus Station
39 2nd-Class Bus Stations
42 Lavandería Automática USA Clean
43 Colectivos Palenque
48 Post Office, Casa de la Cultura

Post & Communications The post office, in the Casa de la Cultura, on the south side of the park, is open Monday to Friday from 9 am to 1 pm and 3 to 6 pm, and Saturday from 9 am to 1 pm (closed Sunday).

You can place long-distance calls from the ADO bus station. There also are several telephone shops on Juárez. Calls within Mexico cost about US$0.50 per minute, to the USA and Canada US$1.75 per minute, and to the rest of the world US$2.85 per minute.

Bookstores Papelería y Novedades del Centro (☎ (943) 5-07-77), at Independencia 18 and Nicolás, is a small bookstore attached to a cafe. Shelves hold a few English guidebooks, some Mayan literature and maps of Chiapas.

Laundry Lavandería Automática USA Clean is on Avenida 5 de Mayo across from the Hotel Kashlan.

Medical Services The Hospital Amigo del Niño y de la Madre, across from the Pemex station near the Maya statue, treats all ailments, not just those of children and mothers. There's also a Centro de Salud Urbano

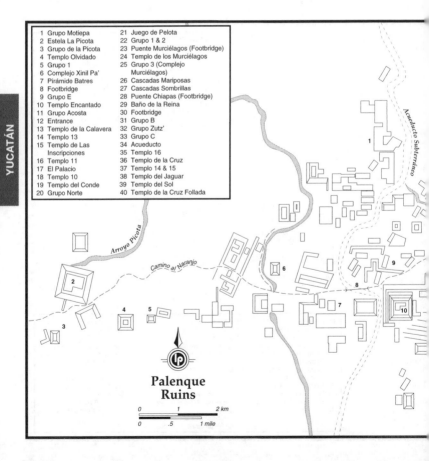

1	Grupo Motiepa
2	Estela La Picota
3	Grupo de la Picota
4	Templo Olvidado
5	Grupo 1
6	Complejo Xinil Pa'
7	Pirámide Batres
8	Footbridge
9	Grupo E
10	Templo Encantado
11	Grupo Acosta
12	Entrance
13	Templo de la Calavera
14	Templo 13
15	Templo de Las Inscripciones
16	Templo 11
17	El Palacio
18	Templo 10
19	Templo del Conde
20	Grupo Norte
21	Juego de Pelota
22	Grupo 1 & 2
23	Puente Murciélagos (Footbridge)
24	Templo de los Murciélagos
25	Grupo 3 (Complejo Murciélagos)
26	Cascadas Mariposas
27	Cascadas Sombrillas
28	Puente Chiapas (Footbridge)
29	Baño de la Reina
30	Footbridge
31	Grupo B
32	Grupo Zutz'
33	Grupo C
34	Acueducto
35	Templo 16
36	Templo de la Cruz
37	Templo 14 & 15
38	Templo del Jaguar
39	Templo del Sol
40	Templo de la Cruz Follada

Palenque
Ruins

0   1   2 km
0   .5   1 mile

(Urban Health Center) next door to the hospital, as well as various other clinics and pharmacies (see map).

Palenque Ruins

Only a few dozen of Palenque's nearly 500 buildings have been excavated. Everything you see here was built without metal tools, pack animals or the wheel. As you explore the ruins try to picture the gray stone edifices as they would have been at the peak of Palenque's power: painted bright red.

The best way to visit is to take a bus, minibus or taxi to the main (upper) entrance, visit the main plaza, then walk downhill through the jungle along the Arroyo Otolum, visiting minor ruins all the way to the museum. From the museum you can catch a minibus back to town.

The best time to visit is when the site opens, as the morning mist rises and wraps the ancient temples in a picturesque haze. The effect is best in the winter, when the days are shorter. If you visit between May and October, be sure to have mosquito repellent.

The archaeological site is open from 8 am to 4:45 pm; the crypt in the Temple of Inscriptions – not to be missed – is open only

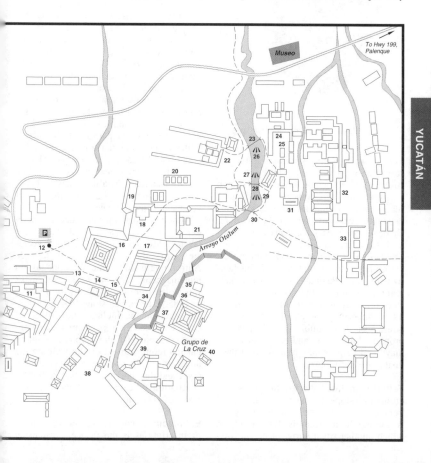

YUCATÁN

Bust of Mayan ruler, Palenque, Chiapas

from 10 am to 4 pm. Admission to the site costs US$3; parking in the lot by the gate costs US$0.50. There is no additional charge for entry to the crypt or the museum. Drinks, snacks and souvenirs are for sale in stands facing the car park, and at the museum. Guide service is available at an extra (negotiated) fee at the entrance. The ruins are not well labeled, the better to support the guides.

Compared to the flat sites of Chichén-Itzá or Uxmal, Palenque is physically challenging: Jungle paths go up and down steep hillsides of slippery limestone, made more slippery by carpets of wet leaves. If you're fit and nimble you'll have no problem, but seniors and the handicapped may need help or may have to limit their visit to the main plaza.

Templo de las Inscripciones As you climb the slope to the ruins, the grand Temple of Inscriptions comes into view. Adjoining to its right is Temple 13, in which another royal burial place was dis-

covered in 1993, and to the right of that, the Templo de la Calavera (Temple of the Skull). Right by the path, to the north of this complex, is the tomb of Alberto Ruz Lhuillier, the tireless archaeologist who began work here in 1945 and who revealed many of Palenque's mysteries – including Pakal's secret crypt in 1952.

The magnificent Temple of Inscriptions is the tallest and most prominent of Palenque's buildings. Constructed on eight levels, it has a central staircase rising some 23 meters to a series of small rooms; the tall roofcomb that once crowned it is long gone. Between the doorways are stucco panels with reliefs of noble figures. On the temple's interior rear wall are the reason Ruz Lhuillier gave the temple its name: three panels with a long inscription in Mayan hieroglyphs. The inscription, dedicated in 692 AD, recounts the history of Palenque and of the temple.

Ascend the 69 steep steps to the top for access to stairs down to the tomb of Pakal (open 10 am to 4 pm). If you cannot climb these stairs, take the path around to the side of the temple and into the jungle, emerging high up at the back of the temple. Though still difficult, this back way is easier than the front staircase. You'll still have to negotiate the slippery steps down to the crypt if you want to see it, however.

Although Pakal's jewel-bedecked skeleton and his jade mosaic death mask were taken to Mexico City and the tomb recreated in the Museo Nacional de Antropología, the stone sarcophagus lid remains here. (The priceless death mask was stolen from the Mexico City museum in 1985.) The carved stone slab protecting the sarcophagus includes the image of Pakal encircled by serpents, mythical monsters, the sun god and glyphs recounting Pakal's reign. Carved on the wall are the nine lords of the underworld. Between the crypt and the staircase a snakelike hollow ventilation tube connected Pakal to the realm of the living.

El Palacio Diagonally opposite the Temple of Inscriptions is the Palace, an unusual structure harboring a maze of courtyards, corridors and rooms. The tower, restored in 1955, has fine stucco reliefs on its walls, but it is no longer open to visitors.

Archaeologists and astronomers believe that the tower was constructed so that Mayan royalty and the priest class could observe the sun falling directly into the Temple of Inscriptions during the December 22 winter solstice.

Templo del Jaguar On the east side of Temple of Inscriptions a steep, uphill, somewhat difficult path leads south into the jungle to the small, ruined Temple of the Jaguar. It has been partly reclaimed from the jungle verdure and clings romantically to a steep hillside next to a great ceiba tree. The facade of this small temple has fallen away, down the hillside toward the rushing Arroyo Otolum, exposing the interior, which bears mold-covered traces of colored murals. The large pyramid behind the Temple of the Jaguar is still a mere hill of rubble engulfed in jungle.

Grupo de la Cruz Although Pakal had only the Temple of Inscriptions dedicated to him during his 68-year reign, Chan-Balum had four buildings dedicated to him, known today as the Grupo de la Cruz (Group of the Cross).

The Templo del Sol (Temple of the Sun), with the best-preserved roofcomb at Palenque, bears narrative inscriptions dating from 642, replete with scenes of offerings to Pakal, the sun-shield king.

The smaller, less well preserved Temple 14 also has tablets showing ritual offerings – a common scene in Palenque.

The Templo de la Cruz (Temple of the Cross), largest in this group, was restored in 1990 and also has narrative stones within.

On the Templo del Cruz Follada (Temple of the Foliated Cross) the arches are fully exposed, revealing how Palenque's architects designed these buildings. A well-preserved inscribed tablet shows a king (most likely Pakal) with a sun-shield emblazoned on his chest, corn growing from his shoulder blades and the sacred quetzal bird atop his head.

Templo del Conde North of the Palace are the ruined Juego de Pelota (ball court) and several unrestored temples, one of which is the Templo del Conde (Temple of the Count). Constructed in 647 AD, during the reign of Pakal, it is where crazy Count de Waldeck lived during his time here.

Arroyo Otolum Continue east past the Templo del Conde and Grupo Norte to the Arroyo Otolum (Otolum Stream). Cross the stream, turn left (north) and continue into the jungle. You have a better chance of seeing wildlife here – including howler monkeys – than around the main plaza.

A flight of steep steps by the Cascada Motiepa waterfall brings you to the Complejo Murciélagos (Bat Complex) and Puente Chiapas. The ruins, thought to have been residential, are not spectacular, but the jungle setting by the waterfalls (the other is called the Baño de la Reina, or Queen's Bath) certainly is.

Farther along the Otolum is Group B, a central plaza surrounded by five elongated buildings rising from terraces built between the Otolum and Bat rivers. Also residential, these buildings were thought to have been occupied around 770 to 850 AD; tombs were found beneath them.

Continue along the river to the Grupo de los Murciélagos (Bat Group), another residential quarter. Descend the stairway to the Puente Murciélago (Bat Bridge), a suspension footbridge across the Otolum offering grand views of the waterfalls. If you've brought your bathing suit, this is where to use it, though you should be discreet.

Across the bridge and downstream a path goes west to Groups 1 & 2, a few minutes' walk uphill. These ruins, only partially uncovered and restored, are at least in a beautiful jungle setting.

Back to the river and the bridge, the main path continues north along the west bank of the river to the museum and visitor center.

Getting There & Away A paved footpath, shaded in some parts, runs beside the road from the Maya head statue all the way to the museum, almost six km.

Several companies, including Colectivos Chambalu and Colectivos Palenque, operate minibuses between Palenque town and the ruins. Service is every 15 minutes (or when seats are full) from 6 am to 6 pm daily. The minibuses will stop to pick you up anywhere along the town-to-ruins road, making it especially handy for campers. Fare is US$0.50.

Organized Tours
Several companies in Palenque town operate transport and tour services to Palenque ruins, Agua Azul and Misol-Ha, Bonampak and Yaxchilán, and La Palma (see El Petén, under Guatemala), usually offering similar features at similar prices. (See each of those destinations for details.) Here are the agencies:

Colectivos Chambalu, at the corner of Hidalgo and Allende (☎ (934) 5-08-67)

Colectivos Palenque, at the corner of Allende and 20 de Noviembre

Viajes Misol-Ha, on Avenida Juárez 48 at Aldama (☎ (934) 5-09-11, fax (934) 5-04-88)

Viajes Pakal-Kin, 5 de Mayo 7, half a block west of the park (☎ (934) 5-11-80)

Viajes Shivalva, Merle Green 9, La Cañada (☎ (934) 5-04-11, fax (934) 5-03-92)

Viajes Toniná, Juárez 105, near Allende (☎ (934) 5-03-84)

Viajes Yax-ha, Juárez 123, next to Banamex (☎ (934) 5-07-98, fax (934) 5-07-67)

Places to Stay – budget
Camping Despite sullen management, *Camping Mayabell*, less than 300 meters east of the museum at Palenque ruins, is the best and most convenient place to camp. For US$1.75 per person you get toilets, showers, some shade, full hookups and snacks and drinks for sale. They rent cabañas as well, for US$17 for up to three

people. *Camping El Panchan*, another 500 meters east, is an alternative.

Hotels *Posada Charito* (☎ (934) 5-01-21), 20 de Noviembre 15, one block west of the park, is quiet, well kept, and run by a friendly family. For US$7.50 you get a double with shower, clean sheets, ceiling fan and a Gideon Bible (in Spanish) on your pillow.

Across the street, the *Caneck Youth Hostel* is not an official hostel, but it offers big, bright rooms with two to three beds each, wooden lockers big enough for the biggest backpack, and a private toilet and sink. All three floors have separate-sex showers. Dorm beds go for US$3, doubles for US$8.50, triples for US$11, quads for US$14.

On the same street but nearer to the bus stations is *Posada Santo Domingo* (☎ (934) 5-01-36), 20 de Noviembre 119, with clean double rooms (private shower and fan) going for US$8.50.

The *Hotel La Croix* (☎ (934) 5-00-14), Hidalgo 10, on the north side of the park, has a pretty courtyard with potted tropical plants and adequate rooms with fan and shower for US$13 a double. La Croix is usually full by mid-afternoon.

Best of the rock-bottom places is the *Posada Bonampak* (☎ (934) 5-09-25), Avenida Belisario Dominguez 33, five blocks northwest of the park. No frills here, but rooms are well kept, bathrooms are nicely tiled, and prices are only US$6 a single or double with one bed, US$8 with two beds.

Other rock-bottom options are on Hidalgo, west of the park. The *Posada San Francisco* is basic and dingy at US$6 to US$8 per double. Across the street, the Posada San Vicente is similar. Much nicer and only slightly more expensive is *Hotel Naj K'in*, Hidalgo 72, a family-run place with middling rooms, nice bathrooms, hot water and fans for US$8.50/12/15/18 a single/double/triple/quad.

The well-located *Hotel Kashlan* (☎ (934) 5-02-97, fax (934) 5-03-09), Avenida 5 de

Mayo 105 at Allende, has decent rooms with private baths for US$16/20 a single/double with fan, US$10 more with air-con. A laundry is just across the street.

The *Hotel Regional* (☎ (934) 5-01-83), Juárez at Aldama, has adequate rooms with shower and fan around a small plant-filled courtyard priced at US$10/14/18. The *Hotel Misol-Ha* (☎ (934) 5-00-92), Av Juárez between Abasolo and Independencia, is priced similarly.

La Posada (☎ (934) 5-04-37), behind Hotel Maya Tulipanes in La Cañada, is a quiet backpackers' hangout with a grassy courtyard, table tennis and a lobby wall covered with messages of peace, passion and travel. Average rooms with bath cost US$10/13 a single/double.

Places to Stay – middle

The *Hotel Palenque* (☎ (934) 5-01-88, fax (934) 5-00-39), Avenida 5 de Mayo 15 at Jiménez, the town's oldest hotel, has been spruced up and now offers a good value. Its rooms, priced at US$17/18/20 a single/double/triple with private bath and fan, are arranged around a pretty garden courtyard that boasts a small and sometimes presentably clean swimming pool. Rooms with air-con cost US$10 more.

Hotel Chan-Kah (☎ (934) 5-03-18, fax (934) 5-04-89), above the restaurant of the same name, is at the corner of Juárez and Independencia, overlooking the park. There are lots of extras here: a lift, insect screens, two double beds and a TV in each room, little balconies and air-con, all for US$30 a double.

Around the corner, near the park on Juárez, the *Hotel Casa de Pakal* has 14 small double rooms with air-con and private bath for US$22.

In La Cañada walk northeast from the Mayan head statue to find the *Hotel Maya Tulipanes* (☎ (934) 5-02-01, fax (934) 5-10-04), Calle La Cañada 6, the most comfortable lodging on the street. Air-con rooms go for US$35/42 a single/double; there is a small pool and nice restaurant.

Next along the street, and under the same management as the Maya Tulipanes, is the cheaper *Hotel Kin-Ha* (☎ (934) 5-04-46), with large air-con rooms going for US$23/29 a single/double.

Across the road is Hotel Xibalbas (☎ (934) 5-04-11, fax (934) 5-03-92, which has attractive rooms above the Viajes Shivalva travel agency and in the modern A-frame next door, priced at US$20/23 a single/double.

Hotel La Cañada (☎ (934) 5-01-02) is a group of cottages at the eastern end of the street, many with huge ceramic bathtubs. This was once a favorite with archaeologists working at the ruins. Rates are US$20/23 a single/double with fan, slightly more for air-con.

On the road to the ruins is *Villas Solymar Kin-Ha*, with cabañas for US$25 to US$29 with fan, US$10 more with air-con.

Places to Stay – top end

The most attractive and interesting lodgings in Palenque are at *Chan-Kah Resort Village* (☎ (934) 5-03-18, fax (934) 5-04-89), three km west of town and two km east of the ruins. The palapa-topped restaurant, enormous stone-bound swimming pool, lush jungle gardens and other accouterments enhance the handsome wood and stone cottages with Mayan traditional accents, private baths, ceiling fans and air-con, all for US$60 a double.

South of town, 3.5 km on the road to San Cristóbal, is the *Calinda Nututum Palenque* (☎ (934) 5-01-00, fax (934) 5-01-61). The modern motel-style buildings are set in spacious jungle gardens shaded by palm trees. Large air-con rooms with bath cost US$60 a double.

The *Hotel Misión Palenque Park Plaza* (☎ (934) 5-02-41, fax (934) 5-03-00), at the far eastern end of town along Avenida Hidalgo, has gardens, a pool, a restaurant and a bar but is inconveniently located and overpriced, at US$75 a double, sometimes without air-con.

Other hotels are north of the Maya head statue, but none are conveniently located or distinguished in their services.

The *Hotel Tulija Days Inn* (☎ (934) 5-01-04, fax (934) 5-01-63) is closest to the Maya head statue. Doubles cost US$62. The *Best Western Plaza Palenque* (☎ (934) 5-05-55, fax (934) 5-03-95), 500 meters farther north, charges the same for its 100 air-con rooms surrounding a garden and swimming pool; there's a disco, bar and restaurant. Even farther north, the 72-room *Hotel Ciudad Real Palenque* (☎ /fax (934) 5-12-85, 5-13-15) has three-story motel-style lodgings around a central swimming pool and restaurant/bar.

Places to Eat

Cheapest fare in Palenque is at the taquerías along the eastern side of the park, in front of the church. Try *Los Faroles* or *Refresquería Deportista* for a plate of tacos at US$2 to US$3.

Restaurant Maya, at the corner of Independencia and Hidalgo on the northwest corner of the park, is the long-standing favorite 'since 1958', or so the menu says. The food is típico and the hours long (7 am to 11 pm). Prices range from US$3 to US$7 for a full meal; the comida corrida costs US$3.50.

Next most popular is *Los Portales*, at 20 de Noviembre and Independencia, offering breakfasts for US$1.75 to US$2.50, set-priced meals for US$3 to US$3.75, and – some evenings – special two-for-one prices on drinks.

Restaurant Virgo's (☎ (934) 5-08-83), Hidalgo 5, offers 2nd-story open-air dining one block west of the park. White pillars, a red tile roof, plants and occasional live marimba music set the scene. Try the burritos al aguacate (US$2.25) or one of their pasta plates for about the same. Meat dishes cost around US$4. They serve wine here, as well as beer.

Also good is *Restaurant Mundo Maya*, on Avenida Juárez a half block west of the park, with rustic decor and numerous set-price menus.

Restaurant Artemio's is a family-run place facing the park. Everything on the menu seems to cost between US$2.25 and US$4.50, whether it be filete, chicken or traditional Mexican antojitos.

Several good, cheap eateries are to be found along Avenida Juárez west of the park. *Restaurante Paisanos* is a tidy, cheap workers' place where everything seems to cost about US$2.25. The nearby *Restaurant El Herradero* is similar.

Pizzería Palenque, on Juárez at Allende, has surprisingly good pizzas, ranging in price from a small cheese (US$3.25) to a large combination (US$9).

Restaurant Chan-Kah, facing the park at the corner of Independencia and Juárez, offers a Mexican variety plate with an assortment of antojitos for US$4. Sometimes there's live music in the upstairs bar.

Getting There & Away

Air Palenque's airport terminal is little more than a shack, but Aerocaribe (☎ (934) 5-06-18, 5-06-19) runs flights between Palenque (PQM) and Villahermosa daily except Thursday (US$50); Tuxtla Gutiérrez daily except Monday (US$45); Cancún on Monday, Wednesday and Friday (US$135); and Flores, Guatemala (for Tikal) on Monday, Wednesday and Friday (US$85).

Aerolineas Bonanza (☎ in Mexico (91-800) 0-30-62) runs flights on Monday, Wednesday and Friday between Palenque and Tuxtla Gutiérrez, Mérida and Cancún.

Bus Some bus passengers have reported goods stolen on trips to or from Palenque. Don't leave anything of value in the overhead rack, and stay alert. Your gear is probably safest in the luggage compartment under the bus, but watch as it is stowed and removed.

Autobuses de Oriente (ADO), Cristóbal Colón and Autotransportes del Sur (ATS) share the 1st-class bus station; the 2nd-class Autotransportes Tuxtla Gutiérrez (ATG), Figueroa and Transportes Lacandonia bus stations are nearby, all on Juárez. The 1st-class terminal has a baggage check (left luggage) room for US$1 per piece per day.

It's a good idea to buy your onward ticket from Palenque a day in advance if possible. Here are some distances, times and prices:

Agua Azul crucero – 60 km, 1½ hours; numerous 2nd-class buses by ATG, Figueroa and Lacandonia (US$1.60). These buses go on to Ocosingo, San Cristóbal and Tuxtla Gutiérrez; seats are sold to those passengers first. Tickets to Agua Azul go on sale 30 minutes before departure, and if all seats are sold, you must stand all the way to the Agua Azul turnoff. It is easier to take a combi (see the Getting Around section).

Bonampak – 152 km, four hours, US$4.50; Autobuses Lagos de Montebello runs buses at 3 am, 9 am, 6 pm, 8 pm

Campeche – 362 km, five hours; one bus by ADO at 8 am (US$12), others by Colón at 1:45 and 9 pm (US$12), and two by ATS (US$10)

Cancún – 869 km, 13 hours; one bus by ADO at 8 pm (US$26), others by Colón at 6:50 and 10:30 pm (US$28)

Catazajá – 27 km, 30 minutes, US$1; six buses by ADO, many more local

Chetumal – 425 km, seven hours; one bus by ADO at 8 pm (US$15), others by Colón at 6:50 and 10:30 pm (US$15), and one by ATS (US$12)

Flores, Petén (Guatemala) – for details on three routes between Palenque and Flores that can be done in a day or overnight, see Flores in the El Petén chapter of the Guatemala section.

Mérida – 556 km, nine or 10 hours; one bus by ADO at 8 am (US$18), others by Colón at 1:45 and 9 pm (US$18), and several by ATS

Misol-Ha – 47 km, one hour; see Agua Azul crucero, above

Mexico City – 1,020 km, 16 hours, US$35; one bus by ADO at 6 pm

Oaxaca – 850 km, 15 hours, US$27; one bus by ADO at 5:30 pm

Ocosingo – 85 km, two hours; at least a dozen buses daily: four by Colón (US$3.75), more by Figueroa and Lacandonia (US$2.25 to US$3.75)

Playa del Carmen – 800 km, 12 hours; one bus by ADO at 8 pm (US$27), others by Colón at 6:50 and 10:30 pm (US$25) and by ATS (US$20)

San Cristóbal de las Casas – 190 km, 4½ hours; eight buses by Colón (US$6), seven by Figueroa (US$6), others by ATG, ATS and Lacandonia

Tulum – 738 km, 11 hours, US$20; buses by Colón at 6:50 and 10:30 pm

Tuxtla Gutiérrez – 275 km, six hours; more than a dozen buses: six by Colón (US$9), seven by Figueroa (US$8), others by ATG and Oriente de Chiapas

Villahermosa – 150 km, 2½ hours, US$5; 10 buses by ADO, one by Colón at 11:10 pm

Getting Around
Taxis wait at the park and the bus stations. Minibuses (US$0.50) shuttle between Palenque town and ruins about every 15 minutes until 6 pm. The airport is less than one km north of the Maya head statue along the road to Catazajá. The train station is at Pakal-na, six km north of Palenque town on the road to Catazajá, though the trains should be avoided.

Travel and colectivo agencies operate excursions to Agua Azul and Misol-Ha, departing daily about 9 am, returning about 4 pm, and charging between US$6 and US$8 per person. Taking the organized tours, though more expensive than the bus, eliminates standing for hours on crowded buses and walking (perhaps with all your luggage) the 1.5 km in from the highway to (and back out from) Misol-Ha, and the 4.5 km walk downhill from the highway to Agua Azul proper – and then back uphill when it comes time to leave.

RÍO USUMACINTA
The mighty Río Usumacinta snakes its way northwestward along the border between Mexico and Guatemala. A journey along the river reveals dense rain forest, thrilling bird and animal life and ruined cities such as Bonampak and Yaxchilán. You can also use tributaries of the Usumacinta as your waterways into El Petén, Guatemala's vast jungle province, with its stupendous ruins at Tikal. For details on three routes, see the El Petén chapter in the Guatemala section.

YUCATÁN

BONAMPAK & YAXCHILÁN

The ruins of Bonampak – famous for frescoes – and the ancient city of Yaxchilán are accessible by bus, on organized camping excursions from Palenque, or by chartered small plane.

Bonampak and Yaxchilán have neither food nor water, so make certain you are well supplied; also bring insect repellent and a flashlight (torch). Don't leave your gear unattended, as thefts have been reported.

Bonampak

Bonampak, 155 km southeast of Palenque near the Guatemalan frontier, was hidden from the outside world by dense jungle until 1946. A young WWII conscientious objector named Charles Frey fled the US draft and somehow wound up in the Lacandón rain forest. Local Indians showed him the ruins, which they used as a sacred site. Frey told Mexican officials about the ruins, and archaeological expeditions were mounted. Frey died in 1949 trying to save an expedition member from drowning in the turbulent Usumacinta.

The ruins of Bonampak lie around a rectangular plaza. Only the southern edifices are preserved. It was the frescoes of Building 1 that excited Frey: three rooms covered with paintings depicting ancient Mayan ceremonies and customs.

Unfortunately, 12 centuries of weather-induced deterioration were accelerated when the first expedition attempted to clean the murals with kerosene. On the positive side, some restoration has been undertaken and reproductions installed for comparison.

Yaxchilán

Set above the jungled banks of the Usumacinta, Yaxchilán was first inhabited about 200 AD, though the earliest hieroglyphs found have been dated from 514 to 807 AD. Although not as well restored as Palenque, the ruins here cover a greater extent, and further excavation may yield even more significant finds.

Yaxchilán rose to the peak of its prominence in the 8th century under a king whose name in hieroglyphs was translated as Shield Jaguar. His shield-and-jaguar symbol appears on many of the site's buildings and stelae. The city's power expanded under Shield Jaguar's son, Parrot Jaguar (752-70). His hieroglyph consists of a small jungle cat with feathers on its back and a bird superimposed on the head. Building 33, on the southwestern side of the plaza, has some fine religious carvings over the northern doorways and a roofcomb that retains most of its original beauty.

The central plaza holds statues of crocodiles and jaguars. Building 20 has a lintel showing a dead man's spirit emerging from the mouth of a man speaking about him and stelae of Maya making offerings to the gods.

Be certain to walk to Yaxchilán's highest temples, which are still covered with trees and are not visible from the plaza. Building 41 is the tallest of them, and the view from its top is one of the highlights of a visit to Yaxchilán. Some tour guides do not want to make the effort to show you Building 41 – insist on it!

Getting There & Away

The road from Palenque to Bonampak is being improved, and access will soon be easier and faster. At this writing, travel

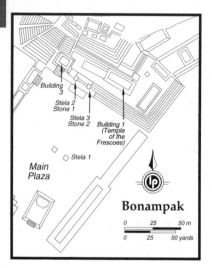

Building 3
Stela 2
Stone 1
Stela 3
Stone 2
Building 1
(Temple of the Frescoes)
Stela 1
Main Plaza
Bonampak
0   25   50 m
0   25   50 yards

YUCATÁN

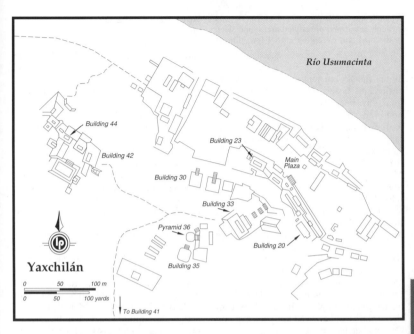

Río Usumacinta

Building 44

Building 42

Building 23

Main Plaza

Building 30

Building 33

Pyramid 36

Building 20

Yaxchilán

Building 35

0   50   100 m
0   50   100 yards

To Building 41

agencies in Palenque were running two-day road and river tours to Bonampak and Yaxchilán (see Organized Tours under Palenque for phone numbers). A minivan takes you within seven km of Bonampak, and you walk the rest of the way. (By the time you take your trip the improved road may reach closer to the ruins.) Tents are provided for overnight. The next morning you are driven to the Río Usumacinta, where a motor boat takes you through the jungle to Yaxchilán. The rate is US$80 to US$100 per person for the two-day venture, including transportation and all meals.

There are also one-day trips offered to Bonampak or Yaxchilán. Most travel agents charge US$50 to US$70 for a one-day excursion.

It doesn't much matter which agency you sign up with; you'll probably end up in the same vehicle with others booked by other agencies.

If you have camping gear and are on a tight budget, you can do the same trip by yourself on jungle buses for about half the price. Take a Lagos de Montebello bus to Frontera Corozal (about 4½ hours). Register at the Migración office; it's sometimes possible to bed down here for the night. Renting a boat to cruise down the Usumacinta to Yaxchilán is fairly easy. The bus from Frontera to Palenque leaves early in the morning; you can make the trek to Bonampak from the road turnoff, if you care to.

PALENQUE TO SAN CRISTÓBAL

According to Captain Dupaix, a French citizen who trekked along La Ruta Maya in 1807:

Palenque is eight days' march from Ocosingo. The journey is very fatiguing. The roads, if they can be so called, are only narrow and difficult paths, which wind across mountains and precipices, and which one must follow sometimes on mules, sometimes on foot, sometimes on the shoulders of Indians and sometimes in hammocks. In some places it is necessary to pass on bridges or, rather, trunks of trees badly secured, and over lands covered with wood, and through desert and unpeopled areas, and sleep in the open air, excepting a very few villages and huts.

Today the 85-km journey is considerably easier and faster, taking only about two hours by bus. It may take you longer, however, because the entire 190-km journey from Palenque to San Cristóbal de las Casas is dotted with interesting stopovers. Only 20 km from Palenque is the spellbinding tropical waterfall park Misol-Ha, and another 36 km into the mountains are the many rapids and waterfalls at Agua Azul.

Ocosingo, 30 km beyond Agua Azul, is the nearest town to the seldom-visited Mayan ruins at Toniná, 14 km east of the town on a side road. From Ocosingo you will wind your way higher into the mountains another 92 km, past the Tzotzil and Tzeltal Mayan villages of Huixtán and Oxchuc, to the Interamericana (Hwy 190), meandering through the Jovel Valley. Turn right (north) and after 12 km you're in San Cristóbal de las Casas.

Misol-Ha Cascade

About 20 km south of Palenque a waterfall plummets nearly 35 meters into a beautiful, wide pool safe for swimming. The Misol-Ha cascade and its jungle surroundings are spectacular enough to be the setting for an Arnold Schwarzenegger epic.

The waterfall is 1.5 km west by dirt road off Hwy 199, and the turnoff is signposted. A fee of US$1 is charged.

Places to Stay & Eat You can set up a tent or hammock near the falls for US$5 or stay in one of the eight newly renovated cabins. Cabins are clean and comfortable, with dark wood interiors, large bathrooms, hot water and furnished kitchenettes. Cabins with one double bed are US$16 to US$30, with two double beds US$30 to US$48. Rates vary with the seasons.

There is a small cafe near the entrance, but you're better off bringing food from Palenque.

Agua Azul Cascades

Just 50 km south of Palenque and 4.5 km off the highway, scores of dazzling turquoise waterfalls tumble over white limestone surrounded by jungle. Beyond the rapids numerous pools of tranquil water offer a refreshing respite from the rain forest's sticky humidity.

On holidays the site is thronged with local families; at other times you will have few companions. Admission is US$1.50 per car, US$0.75 per person on foot.

The temptation to swim is great, but take extreme care. The current is deceptively fast, especially during the rainy season, when the 'turquoise' waters, brown with silt, reduce underwater visibility to zero and submerged trees and rocks are impossible to see. Use your judgment to identify slower, safer areas. Drownings are all too common here, as the crosses in the upper cascades show.

The falls stretch some distance up- and downstream. Upstream a trail takes you over some swaying, less-than-stable foot bridges and up through the jungle to much better swimming spots, but beware of robbers (and even rapists) who may lurk in the jungle here.

Places to Stay & Eat There are a few spots to hang your hammock or pitch a tent, but if you are looking for a decent bed, go back to Palenque. *Camping Agua Azul*, near the entrance, and *Restaurant Agua Azul*, next to the car park, rent hammocks and hammock space for a few dollars. You can leave your backpacks at Restaurant Agua Azul for US$1 per day. You'll find more solace and scenery if you camp upstream. Follow the trail up the left bank.

A five- to ten-minute walk will bring you to *Camping Casablanca*. It's far from elegant, but you can hang your hammock (US$2) or rent one (US$3) in its big hollow barn. Owner Geronimo guides three-hour, five-km hikes around the cascades for US$5 per person.

If you can gather another five minutes of walking energy, you'll find more pleasant camping at *José Antonio's*. It's the yellow house with the white furniture and a Coca-

Cola sign in front, a stone's throw from the water. There's a grassy lawn for tents, a palapa for hammocks, palm trees for atmosphere, and you're just steps from safe swimming. A night here will cost you US$2.

There are several restaurants and food stalls next to the car park, but the food is overpriced and average. You would be much better off packing a picnic from Palenque.

Getting There & Away The Agua Azul *crucero* (junction) on Hwy 199 is 45 km south of Palenque, 40 km north of Ocosingo, and 248 km northeast of San Cristóbal (3½ hours by bus). The 4.5-km walk from the crucero to the falls is OK on the way down, but the sweltering heat makes it hard on the uphill trip back out. If you want to take the risk, hitchhiking is possible, but don't rely on it.

An easy way of visiting Agua Azul and Misol-Ha is a day trip from Palenque. Several travel agents in Palenque offer such trips, lasting about seven hours, with typically three hours at Agua Azul and half an hour at Misol-Ha, for US$8 per person, including entrance fees. Colectivos Chambalu and Colectivos Palenque in Palenque charge US$6 for the 6½-hour trip. (For a list of Palenque travel agents, see Organized Tours under Palenque.)

You also can travel by 2nd-class bus to the crucero and trust your legs and luck from there. Any 2nd-class bus between Palenque and San Cristóbal or Ocosingo will drop you there; 1st-class buses might not stop. The crucero is about four hours from San Cristóbal (US$4), one hour from Ocosingo (US$1) and 1½ hours from Palenque (US$1.60). Try to book ahead on these buses, unless you want to stand. Catching a bus from the crucero when you leave almost certainly means standing, to start with at least. Again, hitchhiking is possible, but don't count on it.

Over the years I've received occasional reports from travelers who have been robbed along the Palenque-San Cristóbal road in the vicinity of Ocosingo. Thieves stop buses, cars and cyclists and relieve them of their valuables.

Ocosingo
Population 20,000

Ocosingo is a small mestizo and Tzeltal valley town on the Palenque-San Cristóbal road. It's friendly but of no particular interest except as an access point for the Mayan ruins of Toniná, 14 km east.

Orientation & Information Ocosingo spreads downhill to the east of Hwy 199. Avenida Central runs straight from the main road to the plaza. Most of the bus stations are on Avenida 1 Norte, parallel to Avenida Central, a block north.

To orient yourself on the main plaza, remember that the church is on the east side and the Hotel Central on the north side. The large market is three blocks east along Avenida 1 Sur Oriente from the church.

None of the banks in town will change dollars or travelers' checks, but this may change as Ocosingo edges into the tourist milieu.

Places to Stay The *Hotel Central* (☎ (967) 3-00-39), Avenida Central 1, just northwest of the plaza, has simple, clean rooms with fan and bath for US$8/12/15 a single/double/triple.

Hotel Margarita (☎ (967) 3-02-80) on Calle 1 Poniente Norte, one block northwest of Hotel Central, charges US$20 a double. It's nothing elaborate but nicer than most hotels in town; rooms have fan and bath, and there is a comfortable lobby downstairs and a restaurant upstairs.

Posada Agua Azul, at Calle 1 Oriente Sur 127, two blocks south of the church, has medium-size, average rooms around a courtyard that harbors a few tightly caged anteaters, hawks and macaws. Rooms are US$9/13.

At the really cheap end you'll find *Hospedaje La Palma*, on the corner of Calle 2 Poniente Norte and Avenida 1 Norte Poniente, just down the hill from the ATG bus station. It's a clean, family-run place where singles/doubles are US$4/8 with shared bathrooms. *Hotel San Jacinto*, at Avenida Central 13, around the corner from the church, charges US$4/9 for drab

YUCATÁN

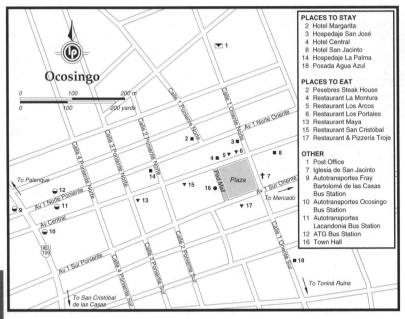

Ocosingo

PLACES TO STAY
2 Hotel Margarita
3 Hospedaje San José
4 Hotel Central
8 Hotel San Jacinto
14 Hospedaje La Palma
18 Posada Agua Azul

PLACES TO EAT
2 Pesebres Steak House
4 Restaurant La Montura
5 Restaurant Los Arcos
6 Restaurant Los Portales
13 Restaurant Maya
15 Restaurant San Cristóbal
17 Restaurant & Pizzería Troje

OTHER
1 Post Office
7 Iglesia de San Jacinto
9 Autotransportes Fray
    Bartolomé de las Casas
    Bus Station
10 Autotransportes Ocosingo
    Bus Station
11 Autotransportes
    Lacandonía Bus Station
12 ATG Bus Station
16 Town Hall

rooms with a shared bath. *Hospedaje San José* (☎ (967) 3-00-39), Calle 1 Oriente Norte 6, half a block north of the northeast corner of the plaza, has small, dark, but clean rooms for US$6/10 a single/double.

Places to Eat Ocosingo is famous for its queso amarillo (yellow cheese), which comes in three-layered one-kg balls. The two outside layers are like chewy Gruyère, the middle is creamy.

Restaurant La Montura has a prime location on the north side of the plaza, with tables on the Hotel Central's verandah. It's good for breakfast (fruit, eggs, bread and coffee for US$2.50), as well as lunch or dinner (comida corrida for US$5 or a plate of tacos for US$2). They'll build you some sandwiches if you want to take a picnic to Toniná ruins.

Restaurant Los Portales, Avenida Central 19, facing the northeast corner of the plaza, is a homey, old-fashioned place. Several matronly señoras will mother you here,

offering traditional meals for US$2 to US$5. The Portales proves an interesting contrast to the neighboring *Restaurant Los Arcos*, which is more modern, but not nearly so pleasant. On the opposite side of the plaza, *Restaurant & Pizzería Troje* features the famous queso amarillo. Quesadillas are cheap (US$1.25), and pizzas of different sizes and sorts go for US$2.50 to US$7.

Restaurant Maya, two blocks west of the plaza on Avenida Central, is a tidy, bright little eatery featuring platos fuertes (main-course lunch or dinner platters) for US$2.50; fruit salads and antojitos are less. The *Restaurant San Cristóbal*, Avenida Central 22, near the Town Hall, is a simple lonchería where nothing on the menu is more than US$3.

Pesebres Steak House, on Calle 1 Poniente Norte above Hotel Margarita, has a nice breeze, super views and good prime rib or filet mignon for US$6.50; Mexican dishes and salads will run you less than US$3.

Getting There & Away All buses are 2nd-class. The Autotransportes Tuxtla Gutiérrez (ATG) terminal is on Avenida 1 Norte Poniente, one block from Hwy 199. Autotransportes Lacandonia is on the same street a little higher up.

Autotransportes Fray Bartolomé de las Casas (in between the previous two companies for price and comfort) is on the far side of the main road, at the top of Avenida 1 Norte Poniente. They have a mixture of modern microbuses and decrepit big buses. Autotransportes Ocosingo is at the corner of Avenida Central and the main road. Quickest are the combis, which shuttle to Palenque and San Cristóbal. They leave when full from the intersection of Hwy 199 and Avenida Central and charge US$2.50.

Palenque – 82 km, 1½ hours; five buses by ATG (US$2.80), two by Autotransportes Fray Bartolomé de las Casas (US$3)

San Cristóbal – 108 km, 2½ hours; six buses by ATG (US$2), six by Autotransportes Lacandonia (US$1.75), five by Autotransportes Fray Bartolomé de las Casas (US$2.30)

Tuxtla Gutiérrez – 193 km, 4½ hours; seven buses by ATG (US$4), two morning buses by Autotransportes Lacandonia (US$3), five buses by Autotransportes Ocosingo (US$2)

Villahermosa – 232 km, six hours, US$3; two morning buses by Autotransportes Lacandonia

Toniná Ruins

Toniná was probably a city-state independent of both Palenque and Yaxchilán, though it declined when they did, around 800 AD. Dates found at the site range from 500 to 800 AD.

Toniná doesn't compare with Palenque for beauty or importance, but that may change, as major excavations are under way that may uncover more significant structures. The ruins are open every day for US$2.50.

The track into the site goes past the small museum, which holds quite a number of good stone carvings – statues, bas-reliefs, altars and calendar stones. Continue past the museum, over a stream and up to a flat area from which rises the terraced hill supporting the main structures. As you face this hillside, behind you are an outlying pyramid and the main ball court. The flat area contains a small ball court and fragments of limestone carvings. Some appear to show prisoners holding out offerings, with glyphs on the reverse sides.

The most interesting area of the terraced hillside is the right-hand end of its third and fourth levels. The stone facing of the wall rising from the third to the fourth level here has a zigzag X shape, which may represent Quetzalcóatl and also forms flights of steps. To the right of its base are the remains of a tomb, with steps leading up to an altar. Behind and above the tomb and altar is a rambling complex of chambers, passageways and stairways, believed to have been Toniná's administrative hub.

One level higher than the top of the Quetzalcóatl wall is a tomb, covered in tin sheeting, thought to be of a ruler, buried with two others; lift the sheet to see the stone coffin beneath. To the left on the same level is a shrine to Chac, the rain god.

Getting There & Away The 14-km track from Ocosingo is unpaved and rough in spots, but crosses pleasant ranch land with lots of colorful birds.

If you have your own vehicle, follow Calle 1 Oriente Sur south from the Ocosingo church. Before long it curves left and you pass a cemetery on the right. At the fork a couple of kilometers farther on go left. At the next fork the site is signposted to the right. Finally a sign marks the entry track to Toniná at Rancho Guadalupe, on the left. From here it's another kilometer to the site itself.

Without your own vehicle you have the option of a taxi (about US$20 roundtrip, with a one-hour wait at the ruins), hitchhiking (maybe six vehicles an hour pass Toniná), trying to pick up one of the passenger trucks from the Ocosingo market, or a Carga Mixta Ocosingo bus from the company's yard near the market. There appear to be two or three buses to Guadalupe (near the ruins) and back each day. The trip costs US$1 and takes about 45 minutes. The Rancho Guadalupe sometimes puts people up for the night or allows them to camp.

YUCATÁN

Highland Chiapas

Beautiful, rugged, backward, impoverished and rich in potential – that's highland Chiapas. Much of the land is still farmed using traditional Mayan methods. But the Maya are being pushed off their traditional lands by developers, oil prospectors and rich cattle ranchers from central Mexico.

Fearful of the adverse economic effects that might come with NAFTA (the North American Free Trade Agreement), highland Chiapas's Indians revolted in January 1994. Armed rebels of a group calling itself the Zapatista National Liberation Army (EZLN) seized several towns and villages briefly, kidnapped government officials and destroyed government offices. Upwards of 100 people were killed in the fighting. The revolt underlines Chiapans' traditional resentment against the powers that be in Mexico City.

VILLAHERMOSA TO TUXTLA GUTIÉRREZ

Highway 195, the road into the Chiapan mountains, leaves Villahermosa to the southeast, passing CICOM, following Avenida Melchor Ocampo, then heading out of the city to pass through vast banana groves. The road is fairly fast, with wide bends.

At Teapa, 60 km from Villahermosa, bear right toward Pichucalco rather than enter the town of Teapa proper. Five km past the Teapa turnoff, on the left-hand side, is Balneario El Azufre (Sulfur Bath), as you can tell when you descend into the valley to cross a stream and the stink of sulfur rises to meet you.

Just past the bridge over the stream a large sign announces your entry into the state of Chiapas, 'Siempre México, Siempre Mexicano' (Always Part of Mexico, Always Mexican). The sign and the sentiment may have more to do with the central government in Mexico City than with the Chiapan people, who have been ambivalent throughout history about their links with the lands to the west of the Isthmus of Tehuantepec.

Upon entering Chiapas, the road climbs into the mountains through lush forests. It's still hot and muggy here, with typical tropical scenes on every side: gigantic ceiba trees, banana groves, Brahma cattle grazing contentedly, and jungle verdure everywhere.

The road passes through a beautiful *cañón* (river gorge). After passing through the village of Ixhuapan you'll notice that the air is definitely lighter, cooler and less humid.

About 150 km from Villahermosa is the small mountain town of Rayón (population 8500), which has a very basic eatery for travelers and a spartan hostelry for emergencies. Ten km past Rayón is a *mirador* (lookout) named El Caminero. The view would be beautiful but for the mist and fog.

At Rincón Chamula it is clear by the local people's dress that you've entered Maya country. Besides wearing traditional clothing, the villagers sell it to travelers at little open-air stands by the roadside.

Pueblo Nuevo (population 10,000) is at 1200 meters in altitude, deep in the beautiful mountain country, but still the road climbs. Past the junction with the road to Simojovel the countryside becomes drier, but it's still mountainous.

The village of Bochil (population 13,000), 215 km from Villahermosa at an altitude of 1272 meters, is inhabited by Tzotzil Maya. It has two hotels: the tidy *Hotel Juárez*, on the main road, and the more modest *Hotel María Isabel*, set back a bit from the road. There's also a Pemex fuel station, the only one for many kilometers.

After traveling 264 km from Villahermosa on Hwy 195 you come to the junction with Hwy 190. Turn left to go directly to San Cristóbal de las Casas (34 km), or right to go to Tuxtla Gutiérrez (50 km).

Heading toward Tuxtla Gutiérrez, after a few kilometers the road rounds a bend to reveal a breathtaking panorama: You are clinging to a mountainside with a broad valley spread out below. The highway descends the steep slope by a series of switchbacks, then strikes out dead straight across the wide, warm, dry Río Grijalva valley, also called the Central Depression of Chiapas, at 500 to 1000 meters in alti-

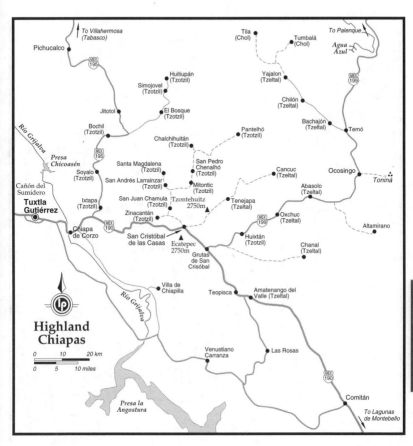

Highland Chiapas

0   10   20 km
0   5   10 miles

tude. Next stop is Tuxtla, the capital of Chiapas, 294 km south of Villahermosa.

TUXTLA GUTIÉRREZ
Population 300,000

Tuxtla Gutiérrez is toward the west end of Chiapas's hot, humid central valley at an elevation of 532 meters. Many travelers simply change buses in Chiapas's state capital as they head straight through to San Cristóbal de las Casas. But if you're not in a hurry, this clean, surprisingly lively and prosperous modern city has several things worth stopping for – among them probably

Mexico's best zoo (devoted solely to the fauna of Chiapas) and easy access to motorboat trips through the 1000-meter-deep Cañón del Sumidero.

History

The name Tuxtla Gutiérrez comes from the Nahuatl word *tuchtlán*, meaning 'where rabbits abound'. The conquistadors pronounced tuchtlán as Tuxtla (TOOSHT-lah), and in the 19th century the family name of Joaquín Miguel Gutiérrez was added. Gutiérrez was a liberal politician, governor of Chiapas, and leading light in

YUCATÁN

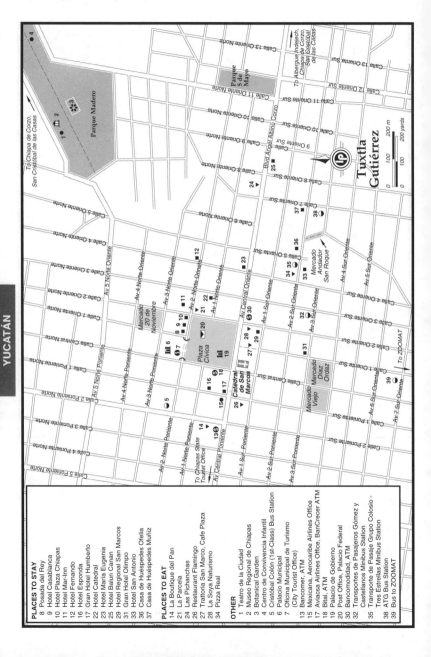

PLACES TO STAY
8   Posada del Rey
9   Hotel Casablanca
10 Hotel Plaza Chiapas
11 Hotel Mar-Inn
12 Hotel Fernando
16 Hotel Esponda
17 Gran Hotel Humberto
22 Hotel Catedral
23 Hotel Maria Eugenia
25 Hotel Balun Canan
29 Hotel Regional San Marcos
31 Gran Hotel Olimpo
33 Hotel San Antonio
36 Casa de Huéspedes Ofelia
37 Casa de Huéspedes Muñiz

PLACES TO EAT
14 La Boutique del Pan
21 La Parcela
24 Las Pichanchas
26 Restaurant Flamingo
27 Trattoria San Marco, Cafe Plaza
28 La Soya Naturismo
34 Pizza Real

OTHER
1   Teatro de la Ciudad
2   Museo Regional de Chiapas
3   Botanical Garden
4   Centro de Convivencia Infantil
5   Cristóbal Colón (1st-Class) Bus Station
6   Palacio Municipal
7   Oficina Municipal de Turismo
      (City Tourist Office)
13 Bancomer, ATM
15 Mexicana, Aerocaribe Airlines Office
17 Aviacsa Airlines Office, BanCrecer ATM
18 Bital, ATM
19 Palacio de Gobierno
20 Post Office, Palacio Federal
30 Bancomodidad, ATM
32 Transportes de Pasajeros Gómez y
      Castellanos Minibus Station
35 Transporte de Pasaje Grupo Colosio -
      Tres Estrellas Minibus Station
38 ATG Bus Station
39 Bus to ZOOMAT

Chiapas's early-19th-century campaign not to be part of Guatemala.

San Cristóbal was capital of the state until 1892, when the title went to Tuxtla Gutiérrez – apparently because of hostility in San Cristóbal toward Mexico's dictator Porfirio Díaz.

Orientation

The center of Tuxtla Gutiérrez is the large Plaza Cívica, with the cathedral on its south side. The city's main east-west artery, here called Avenida Central, runs across the main plaza in front of the cathedral. As it enters the city from the west the same road is Blvd Dr Belisario Domínguez; to the east it becomes Blvd Ángel Albino Corzo.

The Cristóbal Colón 1st-class bus station is two blocks west of the main plaza's northwest corner. The main 2nd-class bus station, Autotransportes Tuxtla Gutiérrez (ATG), is on Avenida 3 Sur Oriente just west of Calle 7 Oriente Sur.

Street Numbering System The central point for Tuxtla's street-numbering system is the corner of Calle Central and Avenida Central beside the cathedral. East-west streets are called Avenidas – 1 Sur, 2 Sur, etc as you move south from Avenida Central, and 1 Norte, 2 Norte, etc moving north. North-south streets are called Calles – 1 Poniente, 2 Poniente and so on going west of Calle Central; 1 Oriente, 2 Oriente, etc to the east.

It all gets a bit complicated with the addition (sometimes) of secondary names: each Avenida is divided into a Poniente part (west of Calle Central) and an Oriente part (east of Calle Central) – thus 1 Sur Oriente is the eastern half of Avenida 1 Sur. Likewise, Calles have Norte and Sur parts: 1 Poniente Norte is the northern half of Calle 1 Poniente.

Information

Tourist Offices The Oficina Municipal de Turismo (city tourism office) is at Calle Central Norte and Avenida 2 Norte Poniente, in the auto underpass beneath the modern Palacio Municipal at the northern end of the Plaza Cívica. The Chiapas state tourist office (☎ (961) 2-55-09, 3-30-28, fax (961) 2-45-35), Blvd Dr Belisario Domínguez 950, is 1.75 km west of the main plaza, on the ground floor of the Edificio Plaza de las Instituciones, the building beside Bancomer. The office is open from 9 am to 8 pm every day.

Money Bancomer, at the corner of Avenida Central Poniente and Calle 2 Poniente, does foreign exchange Monday to Friday 10 am to noon. Bital, on Calle Central Norte on the west side of the main plaza, will exchange money during all banking hours at a snail-like pace. Many banks in the center have ATMs. See the map for some locations.

Post & Communications The post office, on a pedestrian-only block of Avenida 1 Norte Oriente just off the east side of the main plaza, is open from 8 am to 6 pm Monday to Saturday for all services, and 9 am to 1 pm on Sunday for stamps only; Tuxtla's postal code is 29000. Ladatel phones are easily found around the plaza.

Laundry Gaily II Central de Lavado, at Avenida 1 Sur Poniente 575, between Calles 4 and 5 Poniente Sur, charges US$2 for a four-kg load if you wash, US$4 if they wash. Hours are 8 am 2 pm and 4 pm to 8 pm Monday to Saturday.

Plaza Cívica

Tuxtla's lively main plaza, the Plaza Cívica, occupies two blocks, with San Marcos cathedral facing it across Avenida Central at the south end. Be sure to visit on the hour, when clockwork statues of the 12 apostles parade high above the cathedral's main door to bell music that changes with every procession.

Zoo

Chiapas, with its huge range of environments, claims the highest concentration of animal species in North America – among them several varieties of big cats, 1200 types of butterflies and 641 bird species.

You can see a good number of them in Tuxtla's excellent Zoológico Miguel Alvárez del Toro (ZOOMAT), where they're kept in relatively spacious enclosures in a hillside woodland area just south of the city.

Among the creatures you'll see are ocelot, jaguar, puma, tapir, red macaw, boa constrictor, the monkey-eating *aguila arpia* (harpy eagle) and some mean-looking scorpions and spiders.

The zoo is open 8 am to 5:30 pm daily except Monday, and entry is free. It has a bookstore. To get there take a bus marked Cerro Hueco (US$0.20) from the corner of Calle 1 Oriente Sur and Avenida 7 Sur Oriente. They leave about every 20 minutes for the 20-minute trip. A taxi – easy to pick up in either direction – costs US$1.

Parque Madero

This museum-theater-park area is 1.25 km northeast of the city center. If you don't want to walk, take a colectivo along Avenida Central to Parque 5 de Mayo, at the corner of Calle 11 Oriente, then another north along Calle 11 Oriente Norte.

The **Museo Regional de Chiapas** has splendid archaeological exhibits, colonial history and costume and craft collections, all from Chiapas, plus interesting changing exhibitions. Hours are 9 am to 4 pm daily except Monday. Next door is the 1200-seat **Teatro de la Ciudad**. Nearby there's a shady **botanical garden**, with many species labeled, open 9 am to 6 pm daily except Monday; entry is free.

Also in Parque Madero are a public swimming pool (US$0.25) and an open-air children's park, the **Centro de Convivencia Infantil**, which adults may enjoy too. It has models and exhibits on history and prehistory, a minirailway, miniature golf and pony and boat rides.

Places to Stay – budget

Camping *La Hacienda Hotel & Trailer Park* (☎ (961) 2-79-86), Blvd Belisario Domínguez 1197, on the west edge of town beside a roundabout, has a pool, cafeteria and all hookups for US$6 a double. The *Hotel Bonampak* (☎ (967) 8-16-21, fax (967)

8-16-22), on the highway at the western edge of town, has a trailer park as well.

Hotels Tap water in the cheaper hotels is 'al tiempo' (not heated) but since this is a hot town, it is not cold either.

The *Villa Juvenil – Albergue INDEJECH* (☎ (961) 3-34-05) at Blvd Ángel Albino Corzo 1800, just under two km (17 blocks) east of the main plaza, is Tuxtla's youth hostel, though you need no hostel card to stay here. For a bed in a small, clean separate-sex dormitory you pay US$4 (plus a US$2 deposit for sheets), which is not really any cheaper than you'd pay for a private room in a cheap hotel or pension. Breakfast costs US$1.75, lunch or dinner US$2. From the main plaza take a Ruta 1 colectivo east along Avenida Central to the statue of Albino Corzo, beneath a yellow pedestrian overpass.

Closest to the ATG bus station is the *Casa de Huéspedes Muñiz*, at Avenida 2 Sur Oriente 733 (across from the north end of the bus yard). Rooms are bearable, bathrooms are shared; singles/doubles are US$5.50/8. On the same block, at Avenida 2 Sur Oriente 643, the *Casa de Huéspedes Ofelia* (☎ (961) 2-73-46) has no sign, but '643' is visible above its doorway in the black stone facade with silver pointing. Rooms have no fan but are clean and cost US$5.50/8 a single/double. Note that Señora Ofelia goes to bed around 10 pm, so you must be in before then.

Closer to the Plaza Cívica and slightly more expensive are the many hotels on Avenida 2 Norte Oriente, near the northeast corner of the main plaza. *Hotel Casablanca* (☎ (961) 1-03-05), half a block off the main plaza, at Avenida 2 Norte Oriente 251, is bare and basic, but exceptionally clean for the price. Rooms with fan and shower are US$7.50/10/15 single/double/triple; with TV, air-con and twin beds, two pay US$18, or US$28 with two double beds.

The glitzy mirrored lobby of the *Hotel Plaza Chiapas* (☎ (961) 3-83-65), Avenida 2 Norte Oriente 229, at Calle 2 Oriente Norte, is deceptive, because the rooms are no fancier and actually are a bit cheaper than other hotels on this block.

The *Hotel Fernando* (☎ (961) 3-17-40), Avenida 2 Norte Oriente 515, has spacious, decent rooms with big windows for only US$8, about the best deal on the street.

The *Hotel San Antonio* (☎ (961) 2-27-13) at Avenida 2 Sur Oriente 540, is an amicable place, a modern building with a small courtyard and clean rooms for US$5.50/8. Surprisingly, the rambling *Gran Hotel Olimpo* (☎ (961) 2-02-95) at Avenida 3 Sur Oriente 215, charges the same rates for small, muggy rooms, but they're clean and come with bath.

For the traveling foursome that enjoys space, check out the *Hotel Catedral* (☎ (961) 3-08-24), at Avenida 1 Norte Oriente 367, between Calle 3 Oriente Sur Norte and the post office. They have enormous quadruples – two large rooms with a double bed in each are partitioned by a hallway. Bathroom, fans, hot water and cleanliness are included for US$9/10/13/17 a single/double/triple/quad.

The *Hotel Mar-Inn* (☎ (961) 2-10-54, fax (961) 2-49-09), at Avenida 2 Norte Oriente 347, has 60 decent rooms, wide, plant-lined walkways and a roof that seems to trap in humidity, but a double costs only US$12.

Places to Stay – middle

The bright, clean *Hotel Regional San Marcos* (☎ (961) 3-19-40, fax (961) 3-18-87), Calle 2 Oriente Sur 176, at Avenida 1 Sur Oriente, one block from the main plaza, is the best value in this group, at US$18/22/25 for mid-size rooms with tile baths.

Hotel Balun Canan (☎ (961) 2-30-48, fax (961) 2-82-49), Avenida Central Oriente 944, has good rooms for good prices – US$18/23/25/28 a single/double/triple/quad, but get one at the back, not on the noisy street.

The 51-room *Hotel Esponda* (☎ (961) 2-00-80, fax (961) 2-97-71), Calle 1 Poniente Norte 142, a block west of the main plaza, has middling fan-cooled rooms with big bathrooms for US$14/17/21. Its sister hotel around the corner, the aging but clean 105-room *Gran Hotel Humberto* (☎ (961) 2-25-04, fax (961) 2-97-71), Avenida Central Poniente 180, at Calle 1 Poniente Norte,

charges more – too much – for its rooms with air-con, TV, phone and vast showers.

The most elaborate and comfortable downtown hotel is the *Hotel María Eugenia* (☎ (961) 3-37-67, fax (961) 3-28-60), Avenida Central Oriente 507, at Calle 4 Oriente, three blocks east of the main plaza. The hotel has a good restaurant and attractive air-con rooms with TV and bath for US$32/37/40/44 a single/double/triple/quad.

Places to Stay – top end

Tuxtla's most luxurious hostelry is the five-star, 210-room *Camino Real Hotel Tuxtla* (☎ (961) 7-77-77, fax (961) 7-77-71), Belisario Domínguez 1195, four km west of the main plaza. Very comfortable rooms cost US$65 to US$85 a single or double. The town's other top-end hotels – the *Arecas* (☎ (961) 5-11-22, fax (961) 5-11-21) and the *Flamboyant* (☎ (961) 5-09-99, fax (961) 5-00-87) are nearby.

Places to Eat

The cheapest quick bite you'll find is at one of cook shops in the Mercado Andador San Roque, a pedestrian alley just west of the ATG bus station. The going rate is US$0.30 a taco, but the fumes may inspire vegetarian thinking. Other cheap eateries are clustered near the market at the corner of Avenida 3 Sur Poniente and Calle 1 Oriente Sur.

The city's fanciest bakery is *La Boutique del Pan*, Calle 2 Poniente Norte 173, two blocks west and around a corner from the main plaza.

If you want a bag of granola, swing by *La Soya Naturismo*, at Calle 3 Oriente Sur 132, just off Avenida Central. They sell vitamins, healthy snacks and health care products.

There's a row of popular restaurants on the east side of the cathedral along Callejon 1 Oriente Sur in the Edificio Plaza. At the *Trattoria San Marco* (☎ (961) 2-69-74) enjoy 20 varieties of pizza (US$2 to US$7), or sandwiches on baguettes (US$1.50 to US$3), or salads and papas relleñas (potatoes with filling) or savory crepas. It's open from 7 am to midnight. Next door, *Cafe Plaza* has a simpler menu, but good breakfasts (yogurt, fruit, cereal and coffee) for around US$2.

YUCATÁN

If you're looking for a big meal at a little price, try *Pizza Real*, Avenida 2 Sur Oriente 557, across from the Hotel San Antonio, where a comida corrida costs only US$1.75. *La Parcela*, on Calle 2 Oriente Norte behind the post office, serves hotcakes, huevos or seven tacos for under US$2 or a four-course comida corrida for US$1.75.

It's worth making the short trek six blocks east to *Las Pichanchas* (☎ (961) 2-53-51), Avenida Central Oriente 857. This plant-filled courtyard restaurant has a long menu of local specialties. Try the chipilín, a cheese-and-cream soup with a maize base, and for dessert, chimbos, made from egg yolks and cinnamon. In between, have tamales, vegetarian salads (beets and carrots), or carne asada. A full dinner might cost US$5 to US$10. There's music and folk dancing nightly except Monday.

The *Restaurant Flamingo*, down a passage at Calle 1 Poniente Sur 17, is a quiet, slightly superior place with air-con. A full hotcakes breakfast is yours for US$2.50, an order of luncheon tacos or enchiladas for about the same. Meat and fish dishes cost US$3.50 to US$7.

As for a good comida corrida, one of the best for the money (US$5) is served in the dining room of the *Hotel María Eugenia*, on Avenida Central Oriente, three blocks east of the main plaza.

Entertainment

There's live music in the *Plaza Cívica* on Sunday evenings.

Cinemas Gemelos, next to the Trattoria San Marco on the east side of the cathedral, has first-run movies.

If it's dancing you're after, Tuxtla's best disco is *Colors*, in the Hotel Arecas at Belisario Domínguez 1080, just west of the Hotel Flamboyant. Friday is the busiest – entry costs about US$5 and drinks US$1. The mosquelike *Disco Sheik* (get it?), at the Hotel Flamboyant, is reputed to be fun, as is the singles bar in the *Hotel Bonampak*, on Avenida Central Poniente at the western edge of the city. The teen and 20s crowd fills the *Tropicana Salon*, Calle 2 Oriente

Sur, south of Avenida Central Oriente, more or less opposite the Hotel Regional San Marcos.

Getting There & Away

Air Aviacsa flies nonstop to Mexico City (US$110) and Tapachula. Aerocaribe/Mexicana flies nonstop to Mexico City, Oaxaca, Palenque and Villahermosa.

Aviacsa (☎ (961) 2-80-81, 2-49-99, fax (961) 3-50-29, 2-88-84) is at Avenida Central Poniente 160, a block west of the Plaza Cívica, beneath the Gran Hotel Humberto. Mexicana/Aerocaribe (☎ (961) 2-20-53, fax (961) 1-17-61), Avenida Central Poniente 206, is two blocks west of the main plaza.

Tuxtla has two airports. Aeropuerto Llano San Juan, 28 km west of the city, handles the jets and bigger aircraft, while Aeropuerto Francisco Sarabia (also called Aeropuerto Terán) (☎ (961) 2-29-20), two km south of Hwy 190 from a signposted turnoff, about five km west of the main plaza, takes some of the smaller planes.

Bus Omnibus Cristóbal Colón, at the corner of Avenida 2 Norte Oriente and Calle 2 Poniente Norte, two blocks northwest of the main plaza, is the city's 1st-class bus terminal. ADO operates from this terminal as well. The terminal has no baggage checkroom, but there are private ones nearby. Exit the terminal onto Avenida 2 Norte Poniente and look right for the sign 'We Keep Your Objet'.

Many 2nd-class bus companies have offices on Avenida 3 Sur Oriente west of Calle 7 Oriente Sur, chief of which is Autotransportes Tuxtla Gutiérrez (ATG), at 3 Sur Oriente 712. Other companies on this street include Autotransportes Rápidos de San Cristóbal and Oriente de Chiapas.

Transporte de Pasaje Grupo Colosio – Tres Estrellas (Colosio) runs minibuses to San Cristóbal de las Casas from its Tuxtla terminus, at Avenida 2 Sur Oriente, opposite the Hotel San Antonio.

Transportes de Pasajeros Gómez y Castellanos (Gómez) runs minibuses from its Tuxtla terminal, at Calle 3 Oriente Sur 380, to Cahuare and Chiapa de Corzo every 20 or 25 minutes from 5 am to 10 pm for US$0.50.

Cancún – 1100 km, 16 hours, US$35; one 1st-class bus by Colón

Chiapa de Corzo – 12 km, 20 minutes, US$0.50; see above; frequent Chiapa-Tuxtla and Gómez minibuses stop at Cahuare and Chiapa

Ciudad Cuauhtémoc (Guatemalan border) – 255 km, four hours; two buses by Cristóbal Colón (US$6), one by ATG (US$5.50)

Comitán – 168 km, 3½ hours; five buses by Cristóbal Colón (US$5), hourly buses by ATG (US$2.75)

Mérida – 995 km, 14 hours, US$25; three buses by Cristóbal Colón

Mexico City – 1000 km, 17 hours, US$37; three afternoon buses by Cristóbal Colón, two evening buses by ADO

Oaxaca – 550 km, 10 hours, US$16; two buses by Cristóbal Colón

Palenque – 275 km, six hours; six buses by Cristóbal Colón (US$9), several by ATG (US$7) and several by Oriente de Chiapas (US$6)

San Cristóbal de las Casas – 85 km, two hours; hourly buses by Cristóbal Colón (US$2.50), ATG (US$1.50) and Oriente de Chiapas (US$1.50); frequent shared taxis by Auto-transportes Rápidos de San Cristóbal (US$3.75 to US$4.50 per person)

Tapachula – 400 km, seven hours; five buses by Cristóbal Colón (US$12), six by ATG (US$10)

Villahermosa – 294 km, six hours; six buses by Cristóbal Colón (US$8.75), three by ATG (US$6.50)

Car Rental companies include:

Budget, Blvd Belisario Domínguez 2510 (☎ (961) 5-06-72, fax (961) 5-09-71; in Mexico (91-800) 7-00-17)

Dollar, Avenida 5 Norte Poniente 2260 (☎ (961) 2-52-61, fax (961) 2-89-32; in Mexico (91-800) 9-00-10)

Gabriel Rent-a-Car, Belisario Domínguez 780 (☎ (961) 2-07-57, fax (961) 2-24-51)

Getting Around

Airports Transporte Terrestre (☎ (961) 2-15-54) runs taxis (US$10) and minibuses (US$5) from Aeropuerto Llano San Juan to the city center. Minibuses depart from the airline offices for the Aeropuerto Llano San Juan two hours before flight time. For Aeropuerto Terán, use a taxi (US$2).

Local Transport All colectivos (US$0.30) on Belisario Domínguez-Avenida Central-Blvd Albino Corzo run at least as far as the tourist offices and the Hotel Bonampak to the west, and Calle 11 Oriente to the east. Official stops are marked by the blue 'Ascenso/Decenso' signs, but they'll sometimes stop for you elsewhere. Taxis are abundant, and rides within the city usually cost around US$1.

AROUND TUXTLA GUTIÉRREZ
Cañón del Sumidero

The Cañón del Sumidero is a daunting fissure in the countryside a few kilometers east of Tuxtla Gutiérrez, with the Río Grijalva (or Río Grande de Chiapas) flowing northward through it. In 1981 the Chicoasén Dam was completed at the canyon's northern end, and the canyon became a narrow, 35-km-long reservoir.

Touring the Canyon Fast passenger launches speed up the Cañón del Sumidero between sheer walls rising to heights of 1200 meters. Renting an entire boat (one to seven persons) for the two- to three-hour voyage to see Chiapas's most awesome scenery costs US$55 to US$60; in a colectivo boat with eight to 12 persons the fare is US$7 or US$8.

Highway 190, going east from Tuxtla Gutiérrez, crosses the canyon mouth at Cahuare, about 10 km from central Tuxtla. Just east of the bridge and about 500 meters off the highway is Cahuare embarcadero. You can board one of the fast, open-air fiberglass launches here, or at another embarcadero in Chiapa de Corzo, between roughly 8 am and 4 pm.

If you don't have enough people to fill a boat, relax; even on weekdays you should

YUCATÁN

the **Museo de la Laca** (closed Monday), which features the lacquered gourds that are the local artistic specialty.

Bital, at 21 de Octubre and 5 de Febrero, has an ATM.

Places to Eat By the embarcadero are eight restaurants with almost identical menus and deafening music. All are equally overpriced, though the view of the river is certainly nice.

Near the municipal market on Calle Coronel Urbina, across from the Museo de la Laca, are the standard ultracheap market eateries.

More appealing is the friendly *Restaurant Jardines de Chiapa*, in a garden off Calle F Madero, one block west of the plaza.

Ristorante Italiano, on the west side of the plaza, serves cheap pizza and more elaborate, moderately priced Italian-style dishes.

Restaurant Los Corredores, on Madero at 5 de Febrero, has good cheap breakfasts and plenty of reasonably priced fish plates for lunch or dinner.

Getting There & Away See Getting There & Away, Bus, in the Tuxtla section.

SAN CRISTÓBAL DE LAS CASAS
Population 90,000

San Cristóbal (cris-TOH-bal; 'Jovel' to the locals), a tranquil colonial town in a temperate, pine-clad mountain valley (elevation 2100 meters), doesn't have many major postcard-type 'sights', but it rewards generously those who have the time to get acquainted with it. The area is endlessly intriguing to explore, surrounded by Indian villages and endowed with abundant good-value accommodations, food to suit all tastes and easy-to-find good company.

In the early weeks of January 1994 world attention was riveted on San Cristóbal as the Zapatista National Liberation Army representing Mexico's (and especially Chiapas's) oppressed Indians, seized the town by force of arms. Though the rebellion was suppressed by the Mexican army within a matter of weeks, it sent shock waves through the country and attracted increased

not have to wait more than a half-hour or so. Noontime is the busiest. Bring a layer or two of warm clothing and something to shield you from the sun.

Chiapa de Corzo
Minibuses from Tuxtla to Chiapa de Corzo (population 50,000) stop along Calle 21 de Octubre, on the north side of the spacious plaza named for General Ángel Albino Corzo. Impressive arcades frame three sides of the plaza, a statue of General Corzo rises on the west side, and an elaborate castlelike brick fountain said to resemble the Spanish crown stands in the southeastern corner.

Chiapa's **embarcadero** for boat trips through the Cañón del Sumidero is two blocks south of the plaza, along Calle 5 de Febrero, the street on the plaza's west side.

The town's ancient church, the **Templo de Santo Domingo de Guzmán**, one block south of the plaza, was built in 1572 by the Dominican order. Its adjoining convent is now the Centro Cultural, holding attention to the plight of Mexico's oppressed indigenous peoples. At the time of this writing an uneasy peace had returned to the region. The Mexican government has promised redress of grievances and the Zapatistas and the local Indians are waiting, restlessly, to see those promises fulfilled.

The numbers of visitors, hotels, restaurants and glossy shops have all risen sharply in recent years. Nevertheless, the highland light retains its unrivaled clarity, the Tzotzil and Tzeltal Indians from nearby villages still brighten the streets with their pink, turquoise, black or white clothing, and on cool evenings wood smoke still lingers calmly over the town.

History

The Maya ancestors of the Tzotzils and Tzeltals moved to these highlands after the collapse of lowland Maya civilization. The Spaniards arrived in 1524, and Diego de Mazariegos founded San Cristóbal as their regional headquarters four years later.

For most of the colonial era San Cristóbal's Spanish citizens made their fortunes – usually from wheat – at the cost of the Indians, who lost their lands and suffered diseases, taxes and forced labor. Early on, the church gave the Indians some protection against colonist excesses. Dominican monks arrived in Chiapas in 1545 and made San Cristóbal their main base. Bartolomé de las Casas (after whom the town is now named), appointed bishop of Chiapas that year, and Juan de Zapata y Sandoval, bishop from 1613 to 1621, are both fondly remembered.

San Cristóbal was the state capital from 1824, when Chiapas joined independent Mexico, to 1892, when Tuxtla Gutiérrez took over. The road from Tuxtla Gutiérrez wasn't paved until the 1940s.

Orientation

San Cristóbal is easy to walk around, with straight streets rambling up and down several gentle hills. The Interamericana (Hwy 190), passes along the south side of town. Officially named the Boulevard Juan Sabines Gutiérrez, it's called 'El Bulevar' by locals.

From the bus terminals on the highway, walk north (slightly uphill) to the main plaza (Plaza 31 de Marzo), also called the Parque Central, which has the cathedral on its north side. From the Cristóbal Colón terminal it's just six blocks up Insurgentes to the main plaza; from ATG it's five blocks up Allende, then two to the right (east) along Mazariegos.

Places to stay and eat are scattered all around town, but there are concentrations on Insurgentes, and east of the plaza on Madero and Real de Guadalupe. Real de Guadalupe is the 'foreigners' street', with boutiques, lodgings, currency exchange offices, public telephones and other travel necessities.

Information

Tourist Offices San Cristóbal's helpful tourist office (☎ (967) 8-04-14) is in the north end of the Palacio Municipal, on the west side of the main plaza. Hours are 8 am to 8 pm Monday to Saturday, 9 am to 2 pm Sunday. The notice board in front is plastered with flyers of the current happenings; there's a message board inside, and they will hold mail.

The Secretaría de Desarrollo Turístico (SEDETUR, ☎ /fax (967) 8-65-70) has an information office at Hidalgo 2 at Mazariegos, just north of La Galería.

There is also a little tourist information kiosk in front of the Cristóbal Colón bus station that is staffed – so it seems – on sunny days.

Money Banamex, on the main plaza, is the most efficient at currency exchange, but it's still quicker and easier to use bank ATMs (see map) or to change cash or travelers' checks at a casa de cambio. Casa de Cambio Lacantún (☎ (967) 8-25-87), Real de Guadalupe 12-A, half a block from the main plaza, offers rates not much worse than at the banks. The minimum transaction is US$50, and hours are Monday to Saturday 8:30 am to 2 pm and 4 to 8 pm, Sunday 9 am to 1 pm. There are many others, so shop around. The Posada Margarita (see Places to Stay) changes money at good rates without charging commission.

YUCATÁN

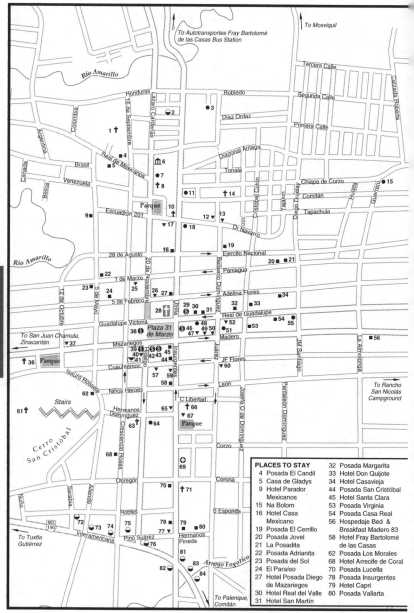

PLACES TO STAY
4 Posada El Candil
5 Casa de Gladys
9 Hotel Parador Mexicanos
15 Na Bolom
16 Hotel Casa Mexicano
19 Posada El Cerrillo
20 Posada Jovel
21 La Posadita
22 Posada Adrianita
23 Posada del Sol
24 El Paraíso
27 Hotel Posada Diego de Mazariegos
30 Hotel Real del Valle
31 Hotel San Martín
32 Posada Margarita
33 Hotel Don Quijote
34 Hotel Casavieja
44 Posada San Cristóbal
45 Hotel Santa Clara
53 Posada Virginia
54 Posada Casa Real
56 Hospedaje Bed & Breakfast Madero 83
58 Hotel Fray Bartolomé de las Casas
62 Posada Los Morales
68 Hotel Arrecife de Coral
70 Posada Lucella
78 Posada Insurgentes
79 Hotel Capri
80 Posada Vallarta

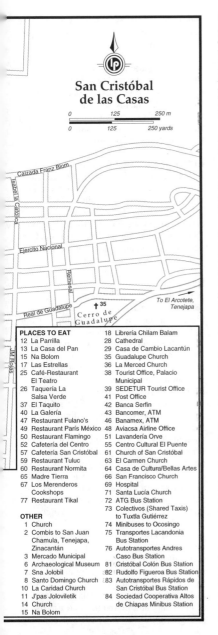

**San Cristóbal
de las Casas**

PLACES TO EAT		18	Librería Chilam Balam
12	La Parrilla	28	Cathedral
13	La Casa del Pan	29	Casa de Cambio Lacantún
15	Na Bolom	35	Guadalupe Church
17	Las Estrellas	36	La Merced Church
25	Café-Restaurant	38	Tourist Office, Palacio
	El Teatro		Municipal
26	Taquería La	39	SEDETUR Tourist Office
	Salsa Verde	41	Post Office
37	El Taquito	42	Banca Serfin
40	La Galería	43	Bancomer, ATM
47	Restaurant Fulano's	46	Banamex, ATM
49	Restaurant París México	48	Aviacsa Airline Office
50	Restaurant Flamingo	51	Lavandería Orve
52	Cafetería del Centro	55	Centro Cultural El Puente
57	Cafetería San Cristóbal	61	Church of San Cristóbal
59	Restaurant Tuluc	63	El Carmen Church
60	Restaurant Normita	64	Casa de Cultura/Bellas Artes
65	Madre Tierra	66	San Francisco Church
67	Los Merenderos	69	Hospital
	Cookshops	71	Santa Lucía Church
77	Restaurant Tikal	72	ATG Bus Station
		73	Colectivos (Shared Taxis)
OTHER			to Tuxtla Gutiérrez
1	Church	74	Minibuses to Ocosingo
2	Combis to San Juan	75	Transportes Lacandonia
	Chamula, Tenejapa,		Bus Station
	Zinacantán	76	Autotransportes Andres
3	Mercado Municipal		Caso Bus Station
6	Archaeological Museum	81	Cristóbal Colón Bus Station
7	Sna Jolobil	82	Rudolfo Figueroa Bus Station
8	Santo Domingo Church	83	Autotransportes Rápidos de
10	La Caridad Church		San Cristóbal Bus Station
11	J'pas Joloviletik	84	Sociedad Cooperativa Altos
14	Church		de Chiapas Minibus Station
15	Na Bolom		

Post & Communications The post office
(☎ (967) 8-07-65) is on the corner of
Cuauhtémoc and Crescencio Rosas, one
block west and one south of the main plaza.
It's open Monday to Friday 8 am to 7 pm,
Saturday, Sunday and holidays 9 am to 1
pm. San Cristóbal's postal code is 29200.
For telegrams, go to Mazariegos 29, 2½
blocks west of the main plaza.

There are Ladatel phones on the west
side of the main plaza and in the Cristóbal
Colón and ATG bus stations.

Bookstores & Library La Pared, next to
the Centro Cultural El Puente on Real de
Guadalupe, has used books in English and
Spanish.

Librería Chilam Balam has a good selection of history and anthropology books,
and some novels and guidebooks in
English, German and French. Their larger
shop is on Utrilla 33 at Dr Navarro (diagonally opposite La Caridad Church); a
smaller shop is on Insurgentes 18 at León.
Libros Soluna, at Real de Guadalupe 13-B,
less than a block east of the main plaza, has
a decent English section.

The 14,000 books at Na Bolom, at the
corner of Guerrero and Chiapa de Corzo,
constitute one of the world's biggest collections on the Maya and their lands. Those
interested can use the library Tuesday to
Saturday from 9 am to 1 pm.

Laundry Lavandería Orve (☎ (967) 8-18-
02), Belisario Domínguez 5, at Real de
Guadalupe, run by the Posada Margarita,
offers same-day service from 8 am to 8 pm.

Lavasor has a drop-off/pickup shop at
Real de Guadalupe 26, between Utrilla and
Belisario Domínguez. Same-day service
costs US$3 for four kg; hours are 8 am to
10 pm daily.

Plaza 31 de Marzo
Officially called Plaza 31 de Marzo, the
main plaza was used for markets until the
early 1900s. Today it is a fine place to sit
and watch the town life happen around
you or enjoy a drink or a snack in the
central kiosk.

YUCATÁN

The cathedral, on the north side, was begun in 1528 but was completely rebuilt in 1693. Its gold-leaf interior has a baroque pulpit and altarpiece.

The Hotel Santa Clara, on the southeastern corner, was the house of Diego de Mazariegos, the Spanish conqueror of Chiapas. It's one of the few nonecclesiastical examples of the plateresque style in Mexico.

Santo Domingo Church

Northwest of the center, opposite the corner of Lázaro Cárdenas and Real de Mexicanos, Santo Domingo is the most beautiful of San Cristóbal's many churches – especially when its pink facade is floodlit at night. The church and the adjoining monastery were under construction from 1547 to 1560. The church's baroque facade was added in the 17th century. There's plenty of gold inside, especially on the ornate pulpit. Chamulan women conduct a daily crafts market around Santo Domingo and La Caridad Church (1712) immediately to its south.

Weavers' Cooperatives

Each Chiapas highland village has its own distinctive woven or embroidered dress. Most of the seemingly abstract designs are in fact stylized snakes, frogs, butterflies, dog paw prints, birds, people or saints.

Cooperatives of village weavers were founded to foster this important folk art for income and to preserve Indian identity and tradition. The weavers aim to revive forgotten techniques and designs and to continue to develop dyes from plants, soil, tree bark and other natural sources.

At Lázaro Cárdenas 42, by Santo Domingo Church, is **Sna Jolobil**, a Tzotzil name meaning Weavers' House (☎ /fax (967) 8-26-46). Open from 9 am to 2 pm and 4 to 6 pm daily except Sunday, it represents 800 women; in its showrooms you can see huipiles, shawls, sashes, ponchos, hats and other craft items. Prices range from a few dollars for small items up to US$500 for the finest huipiles and ceremonial garments.

Nearby at Utrilla 43, just past La Caridad Church, is **J'pas Joloviletik**, which represents about 850 weavers from 20 Tzotzil

and Tzeltal villages. It's open Monday to Saturday 9 am to 1 pm and 4 to 7 pm, Sunday 9 am to 1 pm.

Archaeological Museum

The Museo de Arqueología, Etnografía, Historia y Arte, located next to Santo Domingo Church, deals mainly with the history of San Cristóbal. It's open daily except Monday from 10 am to 5 pm for US$2. All explanatory material is in Spanish.

El Carmen Church & Casa de Cultura

El Carmen Church stands at the corner of Hidalgo and Hermanos Domínguez. Formerly part of a nunnery (built in 1597), it has a distinctive tower (1680) resting on an arch, erected to replace one destroyed by floods 28 years earlier. Across the street is the Casa de Cultura, containing an art gallery, library and the Bellas Artes auditorium.

Na Bolom

A visit to Na Bolom, a house on Guerrero 33 at the corner of Chiapa de Corzo, six blocks north of Real de Guadalupe, is one of San Cristóbal's most fascinating experiences. For many years it was the home of Danish archaeologist Frans Blom, who died in 1963, and his wife, Swiss anthropologist and photographer Gertrude (Trudy) Duby-Blom, who died in 1993 at age 92.

The couple shared a passion for Chiapas and particularly for its Indians. While Frans explored, surveyed and dug at ancient Mayan sites, including Toniná, Chinkultic and Moxviquil, Trudy devoted much of her life to studying the tiny Lacandón Indian population of eastern Chiapas. She worked for the Lacandóns' well-being, but also attracted criticism for shielding the Lacandóns too zealously from change.

The house, whose name is Tzotzil for 'Jaguar House' as well as a play on the owners' name, is full of photographs, archaeological and anthropological relics and books, a treasure-trove for anyone with an interest in Chiapas. Visits are by informal guided tour, conducted daily in Spanish at 11:30 am, and in Spanish and English at 4:30 pm, for US$2.50. No tours on Monday.

Following the tour, a film is shown on the Lacandón and Trudy Blom's work.

Na Bolom also offers meals and lodging (see Places to Stay).

Centro Cultural El Puente

El Puente (☎/fax (967) 8-22-50), on Real de Guadalupe 55, 2½ blocks east of the main plaza, is an information and cultural center buzzing with locals, artists and interested travelers, open every day but Sunday from 8 am to 10 pm. El Puente has a gallery with changing exhibitions and a media room busy nightly with films, lectures, music or theater (English or Spanish). The Centro's *Café El Puente* serves food, including vegetarian.

For information on Spanish courses at Centro Bilingüe, see the Language Courses section.

Mercado Municipal

The flavor of outlying Indian villages can be sampled at San Cristóbal's busy municipal market, between Utrilla and Belisario Domínguez, eight blocks north of the main plaza, open till late afternoon daily except Sunday. Many of the traders are Indian villagers for whom buying and selling is the main reason to come to town.

The Indians generally keep their distance from the mestizo population, the result of centuries of exploitation. But they can be friendly and good-humored (and hard bargainers!).

San Cristóbal & Guadalupe Hills

The most prominent of the several small hills over which San Cristóbal undulates are the Cerro (Hill) de San Cristóbal, in the southwest quarter of town, reached by steps up from Allende, and the Cerro de Guadalupe, seven blocks east of the main plaza along Real de Guadalupe. Both are crowned by churches and afford good views, but there have been reports of attempted rapes here, too.

Grutas de San Cristóbal

The *grutas* (caves) are in fact a single long cavern nine km southeast of San Cristóbal. The entrance is among lovely pine woods a five-minute walk south of the Interamericana

in the midst of a huge army encampment set up since the EZLN rebellion in 1994.

The first 350 meters or so of the cave have a wooden walkway and are lit. You can enter for US$0.50 from 7 am to 5 pm daily. To get there take a minibus east along the Interamericana and ask for 'Las Grutas' (US$0.30). Camping is allowed, and there are horses for hire.

Huitepec Ecological Reserve & Pro-Natura

The Reserva Ecológica Huitepec is a two-km interpretive nature trail on the slopes of Cerro Huitepec, about 3.5 km out of San Cristóbal on the Chamula road. The ascent, rising through various vegetation types to rare cloud forests, takes about 45 minutes. It's open from 9 am to 4 pm daily except Monday.

Pro-Natura, an independent organization staffed by volunteers and funded by donations, offers tours for US$2. Its office is at María Adelina Flores 2 (☎ (967) 8-40-69).

Activities

Horseback Riding Various travel agents and hotels can arrange rides to surrounding villages or the caves. Try to find out about the animals before you commit yourself: are they horses or just ponies, fiery or docile, fast or slow? Will there be a guide?

Posada Margarita, Posada Jovel and Posada Del Sol charge about US$10 for a three- to five-hour ride. The rates are cheaper at José Hernández (☎ (967) 8-10-65), at Elías Calles 10 (a dirt road two blocks northwest of Na Bolom, off Huixtla, just north of Chiapa de Corzo) – US$7 a ride. The Rancho San Nicolás campground (☎ (967) 8-18-73) also provides mounts.

Bicycle Rentals Los Pinguinos (☎ (967) 8-02-02, fax (967) 8-66-38), Avenida 5 de Mayo 10-B, rents bikes for US$1 per hour, US$7.50 per day, including a lock, a map and a water bottle. They also lead half-day bike tours for US$7 to US$11, full-day tours for US$12.50. It's a good way to explore the city and surrounding country. The guides speak English, Spanish, German and Romansh.

Also check out Bicirent, Belisario Domínguez 5-B, open 9 am to 8 pm daily, which makes similar arrangements.

Courses

Centro Bilingüe (☎ (967) 8-41-57, fax (967) 8-37-23, fax in the USA (800) 303-4983), a language school, has two offices. Spanish classes are given in Centro Cultural El Puente (☎ /fax (967) 8-22-50), at Real de Guadalupe 55, and English is taught at Insurgentes 57 (☎ (967) 8-41-57).

One-on-one lessons are about US$3 per hour, three-on-one lessons are about US$2.25 per person per hour.

Home-stay programs offer 15 hours of instruction (three hours per day, five days a week), at least three hours of homework every day, home stay for a full week (seven days, double occupancy) and three meals a day (every day except Sunday). A home stay with one-on-one instruction is US$76; three-on-one is about US$60 per week. If you study for more than one week, it's a bit cheaper. For US$47.50 you can sign up for 'lunch/breakfast with Spanish', a five-day program that includes a meal and three hours of lessons each day.

Organized Tours

For many years, Mercedes Hernández Gómez, a fluent English speaker who grew up in San Juan Chamula, has been leading fascinating tours to the villages. You can find Mercedes at 9 am near the kiosk in the main plaza, twirling a colorful umbrella. Tours are US$8 and generally last five to six hours, traveling by minibus and on foot.

Readers of this guide have also enjoyed the tours led by Alex and Raúl (☎ (967) 8-37-41), whom you can find in front of the cathedral on the main plaza daily at 9:30 am. They offer similar tours at similar prices and also give city tours.

Travel agents in San Cristóbal offer day trips further afield for those who are short of time. Average prices (per person, minimum four people) are: Indian Villages (five hours, US$12), Cañón del Sumidero (eight hours, US$22), Lagunas de Montebello/Chincultik ruins/Amatenango Del

Valle (nine hours, US$20), Palenque ruins/Agua Azul/Misol-Ha (13 hours, US$26) and Toniná (six hours, US$18).

Several travel agents are:

Viajes Kanan-Ku – specializes in ecological study tours to organic farms, herbolaria, butterfly breeding areas and the jungle. In Centro Cultural El Puente, Real de Guadalupe 55, 2½ blocks east of the main plaza (☎ /fax (967) 8-41-57)

Viajes Chincultik – can arrange almost any budget trip on horseback or by car, bus or plane. Real de Guadalupe 34 in the Posada Margarita (☎ /fax (967) 8-09-57)

Viajes Pakal -Cuauhtémoc 6 at Hidalgo (☎ /fax (967) 8-28-19)

Special Events

In spring, Semana Santa (Holy Week, before Easter), with processions on Good Friday and the burning of 'Judas' figures on Holy Saturday, is followed by the Feria de la Primavera y de la Paz (Spring & Peace Fair) with more parades, bullfights and so on. Sometimes the celebrations for the anniversary of the town's founding (March 31) fall in the midst of it all too!

Also look out for events marking the feast of San Cristóbal (July 17 to 25), the anniversary of Chiapas joining Mexico in 1824 (September 14), National Independence Day (September 15 and 16), the Day of the Dead (November 2), the Feast of the Virgin of Guadalupe (December 10 to 12) and preparations for Christmas (December 16 to 24).

Places to Stay – budget

Camping The *Rancho San Nicolás* campground and trailer park (☎ (967) 8-00-57) is two km east of the main plaza: go east along León for a km after it becomes a dirt track. It's a friendly place with a grassy lawn, apple trees, horses grazing and hot showers. Cost is US$2 per person in a tent, US$5 in a cabin, US$4 to US$6 per person in a camper or trailer with full hookups.

Hotels & Casas de Huéspedes Several cheap hostelries are on and just off Insurgentes, the street leading from the Cristóbal Colón bus station to the main plaza.

Casas de huéspedes (guesthouses) don't post their prices in this town. Don't be afraid to haggle a bit.

Insurgentes A block and a half up from the Cristóbal Colón bus station, *Hotel Capri* (☎ (967) 8-30-13, fax (967) 8-00-15), Insurgentes 54, has modern, clean and fairly quiet rooms around a narrow, flowery courtyard for US$11/13. Across the street, *Posada Insurgentes* (☎ (967) 8-24-35), Insurgentes 73, is even newer, with similar prices.

Posada Lucella (☎ (967) 8-09-56), Insurgentes 55, directly across from the Santa Lucia Church, has OK doubles for US$9, US$12 with private bath.

The nice *Posada San Cristóbal* (☎ (967) 8-68-81), at Insurgentes 3, near the main plaza, has airy, colorful rooms set around a pleasant courtyard for US$15/19/23 a single/double/triple.

The colonial *Hotel Fray Bartolomé de las Casas* (☎ (967) 8-09-32), Niños Héroes 2 at Insurgentes, two blocks south of the main plaza, has cleanliness, character and a variety of rooms for US$15/18/22.

Posada Vallarta (☎ (967) 8-04-65), half a block east off Insurgentes at Hermanos Pineda 10 (the first street to the right as you go up Insurgentes), has clean and modernish rooms with private bath and balcony for US$11/12/14 – a good value.

Real de Guadalupe One and a half blocks east of the main plaza *Posada Margarita* (☎ (967) 8-09-57), Real de Guadalupe 34, has long been a popular budget travelers' halt and a good meeting place. A *dormitorio* bed is US$5, a clean double with shared bath US$10; there are triples and quads as well, though all rooms tend to be small and airless. The Margarita has a good cheap restaurant, a travel agency, laundry facilities, bike rentals and will hold mail for you.

The tidy *Posada Virginia* (☎ (967) 8-11-16), Cristóbal Colón 1, between Real de Guadalupe and Madero, is run by a friendly, efficient woman who even provides a few parking spaces. Doubles with shower cost US$13.

On Real de Guadalupe next to El Puente is *Posada Casa Real*. It is humble, clean and cheap, at US$4 a bed.

Hotel Real del Valle (☎ (967) 8-06-80, fax (967) 8-39-55), Real de Guadalupe 14, is good, clean and central, with a nice courtyard and 36 rooms costing US$12/15/19 a single/double/triple. The neighboring *Hotel San Martín* (☎ /fax (967) 8-05-33), Real de Guadalupe 16, is similarly priced and pleasant.

Elsewhere Undoubtedly the best deal in town is at *Hospedaje Bed and Breakfast Madero 83* (☎ (967) 8-04-40), Madero 83, five blocks east of the main plaza. Clean dorm beds (US$3.25), singles (US$4.50), and rooms with private baths (US$7.50 to US$11) all include a breakfast of eggs, beans, tortillas and coffee. For a few pesos you can use the kitchen. This place fills up.

The tidy *Posada Jovel* (☎ (967) 8-17-34), at Paniagua 28 between Cristóbal Colón and Santiago, attracts backpackers with its friendly owners, good atmosphere and good prices – US$6.75/10 a single/double with shared bath, US$8.50/12.50 with private bath. They rent bikes, too. If it's full, try *La Posadita*, next door at Paniagua 30.

Posada Del Sol (☎ (967) 8-04-95), on 1 de Marzo 22 at 5 de Mayo, three blocks west of the main plaza, has caged birds, '70s decor and great prices: US$8/10/14/15 with shared bath, slightly more with private bath.

For a hint of the '60s, try the easygoing *Casa de Gladys* at Real de Mexicanos 16, a colonial house with a purplish courtyard, hanging hammocks and peace posters. Doubles with shared bath cost US$10; coffee and purified water are free. The nearby *Posada El Candil* (☎ (967) 8-27-55), Real de Mexicanos 7, has starkly bright, clean, simple, rooms with shared bath for US$7/11.

Posada El Cerrillo, Belisario Domínguez 27, just north of Ejercito Nacional, has a beautiful flowered courtyard and big guest rooms for US$15 a double with shower. *Posada Adrianita* (☎ (967) 8-12-83), 1 de Marzo 29 at 5 de Mayo, is similar.

Places to Stay – middle

You can stay at the research institute of *Na Bolom* (tel (967) 8-14-18, fax (967) 8-55-86), Guerrero 33, for US$27/30/35 a single/double/triple, with reductions when it's not busy.

Back in the 16th century the *Hotel Santa Clara* (☎ (967) 8-08-71, fax (967) 8-10-41), Avenida Insurgentes 1 (the southeast corner of the main plaza) was home to Diego de Mazariegos, the Spanish conqueror of Chiapas. Amenities here include sizable, comfortable rooms, a pleasant courtyard brightened by caged red macaws, a restaurant, a bar/lounge and a heated pool. Singles/doubles/triples/quads are US$20/22/26/30.

El Paraíso (☎ (967) 8-00-85, fax (967) 8-51-68), 5 de Febrero 19, 2½ blocks northwest of the main plaza, has a cheery, flower-filled courtyard with leather sun chairs. The comfortable rooms cost US$25/29/34 a single/double/triple. The restaurant serves Swiss and Mexican dishes.

Hotel Parador Mexicanos (☎ (967) 8-00-55), at 5 de Mayo 38, just south of Escuadrón 201, has big comfortable rooms flanking its garden-cum-drive, at the end of which is a tennis court. A lobby lounge, restaurant and pleasant verandahs make it a fair value at US$15/23/28.

Posada Los Morales (☎ (967) 8-14-72), at Allende 17, has a dozen bare, whitewashed two-person bungalows in a maze of gardens on a slope five blocks southwest of the plaza. Each has a fireplace, bathroom and gas stove and rents for US$20. Some are cleaner and brighter than others, so check out a few.

Hotel Don Quijote (☎ (967) 8-09-20, fax (967) 8-03-46), Cristóbal Colón 7, between Real de Guadalupe and Adelina Flores, is among the brightest and newest in the area. Colorful maps and traditional costumes embellish the walls; rooms (US$15/18/22/25) and the upstairs restaurant are pleasing, and it has a laundry, travel service and free morning coffee.

Hotel Arrecife de Coral (☎ (967) 8-21-25, fax (967) 8-20-98), Crescencio Rosas 29, between Hermanos Domínguez and Obregón, reminds one of an American motel, with its several buildings set amid grassy lawns. The 50 quiet, modern rooms on two floors have baths, TVs and phones and offer a great value, at US$23/28/32/36 a single/double/triple/quad.

Hotel Casavieja (☎ (967) 8-03-85, fax (967) 8-52-23), Adelina Flores 27, between Colón and Dujelay, is new but colonial in style, attractive and comfortable, with very friendly management. Rooms are arranged around grassy, flowered courtyards; there's a tidy restaurant. Rates are US$30/38/42 a single/double/triple.

Places to Stay – top end

Hotel Casa Mexicano (☎ (967) 8-06-98, fax (967) 8-26-27), 28 de Agusto at Utrilla, with its skylighted garden, fountains, plants, and traditional art and sculptures, exudes colonial charm. Rooms are agreeable, have views of the courtyard and cost US$38/42/47; suites with whirlpool bath cost US$65.

The *Hotel Posada Diego de Mazariegos* (☎ (967) 8-18-25, fax (967) 8-08-27), 5 de Febrero 1, occupies two fine buildings on Utrilla one block north of the main plaza. Rooms (US$38/45/54 a single/double/triple) are tastefully furnished, and most have fireplace and TV. There's a restaurant and a nightclub with live entertainment.

Places to Eat

The cheapest meals are from the cook shops in a complex called *Los Merenderos*, just south of the Templo de San Francisco on Insurgentes. To be safe, pick items that look fresh and hot. A full meal can be had for little over US$1.50.

A perennially popular eatery is *Restaurant Tuluc*, at Insurgentes 5, 1½ blocks south of the plaza. The Tuluc scores with its opening time for early breakfasts (6:15 am), efficient service, good food and good prices. Most main courses cost US$2.50 to US$4.50.

Madre Tierra (Mother Earth), Insurgentes 19 at Hermanos Domínguez, is a vegetarian oasis in the land of carnes and aves. The menu is eclectic and appetizing, with filling soups, whole-meal sandwiches, brown rice dishes, pasta, pizzas and salads.

Most everything on the menu is between US$1.75 and US$4, and the daily set menu costs US$6. Excellent whole-grain bread is served with all meals. The *Panadería Madre Tierra* next door is a whole-food bakery selling breads, muffins, cookies, cakes, quiches, pizzas and frozen yogurt.

La Casa del Pan, at Dr Navarro 10, one long block east of Utrilla, serves a 'feel-great breakfast' of fruit, granola, yogurt, muffins and organic coffee, and a veggie comida corrida of soup, rice, beans, quesadilla, beverage and dessert, each for US$4. There's lunch and dinner as well. You may dine in the calming courtyard or the dining room, where they sell whole-grain breads, bagels, brownies and cookies. Hours are 7 am to 10 pm daily, closed Monday.

Probably the best coffee in town, and good cakes too, are served in the little *Cafetería San Cristóbal*, on Cuauhtémoc just off Insurgentes. The clientele is mainly Mexican men who bring along chess sets and newspapers to relax.

The walls of *Las Estrellas*, at Escuadrón 201 6-B, across from La Caridad park, are covered with beautiful batiks (for sale, of course). Its menu includes pesto dishes, veggie quiches and rice plates for US$2, and pasta with garlic bread or pizza for US$2.75. Service is friendly and fast.

Restaurant París México at Madero 20, one block east of the main plaza, is an artsy little cafe serving French and Mexican specials daily for US$4, crepas for US$2 and great coffee.

For local cooking, try the *Restaurant Normita*, JF Flores at Juárez. A big bowl of pozole, a soup of maize, cabbage, pork, radishes and onions, costs US$2 and a plato típico Coleto, a local mixed grill with pork sausage, chops, frijoles and guacamole, goes for US$4, but there is plainer, cheaper fare as well.

Cafetería del Centro, Real de Guadalupe 15, has cheap breakfasts: less than US$2 for the works – eggs, toast, butter, jam, juice and coffee. On the upper level at Hidalgo 3, *La Galería* serves pizza at popular prices.

At humble *El Taquito*, on the corner of Mazariegos and 12 de Octubre, tacos are cheap and good. You can also enjoy filete al queso a la parrilla (grilled meat filet with a cheese topping) or fruit cocktail with granola and honey.

Speaking of tacos, *Taquería La Salsa Verde*, 20 de Noviembre north of 5 de Febrero, has an open kitchen with señoras hard at work making them by hand. They're good and not expensive, at about US$1.50 a plate.

La Parrilla, on the corner of Belisario Domínguez and Dr Navarro and open daily except Saturday from 6:30 pm to midnight, serves excellent carnes and quesos al carbón (charbroiled meats and cheese). A dinner, drink and dessert will cost about US$7.

Restaurant Tikal, a block north of the Cristóbal Colón bus terminal on Insurgentes, serves generous spaghettis (such as Genovesa, with cheese, nutmeg and spinach) and good guacamole with totopos for US$2.50. Meat dishes and burgers cost a bit more.

Café-Restaurant El Teatro, upstairs at 1 de Marzo 8, near 16 de Septiembre, is among the few upscale restaurants in town. The menu, based on French and Italian cuisine, lists Chateaubriand, crepes, fresh pasta, pizzas and desserts. Expect to spend US$6 to US$12 for a full dinner here.

Restaurant Flamingo and *Restaurant Fulano's*, on Madero, are respectable if unremarkable, with similar menus and prices: spaghetti and salads are about US$2, pizzas and main dishes are twice that.

You must reserve about two hours ahead for lunch (1:30 pm) or dinner (7 pm) at *Na Bolom*, Guerrero 33, at the corner of Chiapa de Corzo, but breakfast is served anytime from 7:30 to 10 am. Meals are somewhat expensive, but the ambiance is unique.

Entertainment

San Cristóbal is an early-to-bed town, and conversation in cafes, restaurants or rooms will most likely occupy many of your evenings. However, there are films, cultural events, concerts and rowdy music scenes to be relished, if you are so motivated. Check the notice boards in front of the tourist office and in El Puente for scheduled events.

YUCATÁN

Centro Cultural El Puente, on Real de Guadalupe 55, has cultural programs, films, concerts or conferences nightly.

There are fairly regular musical and theatrical performances at the *Casa de Cultura/Bellas Artes*, at the corner of Hidalgo and Hermanos Domínguez.

Things to Buy

Chiapas's Indian crafts are justifiably famous, and there are now hosts of shops in San Cristóbal selling them. The heaviest concentrations are along Real de Guadalupe (where prices go down the farther you get from the main plaza) and Utrilla (toward the market end). La Galería, at Hidalgo 3, has beautiful and expensive crafts.

Textiles – huipiles, rebozos, blankets – are the outstanding items, for Tzotzil weavers are some of the most skilled and inventive in Mexico (see the Weaving Cooperatives section). Indian women also sell textiles in the park around Santo Domingo. You'll also find some Guatemalan Indian textiles and plenty of the appealing and inexpensive pottery from Amatenango del Valle (animals, pots, jugs, etc) in San Cristóbal. Leather is another local specialty.

You can even buy black ski-mask hooded Subcommandante Marcos dolls (Marcos is the popular leader of the Zapatista Liberation Army, or EZLN).

You're expected to bargain, unless prices are labeled (though there's no harm in trying even then). The first price quoted is traditionally much more than the going rate for the item.

There's a vegetable-and-fruit street market on Dujelay between Real de Guadalupe and Madero on Wednesdays.

Getting There & Away

Air Scheduled flights come no nearer than Tuxtla Gutiérrez. Aviacsa (☎ (967) 8-44-41, fax (967) 8-43-84) is at Real de Guadalupe 7, Pasaje Mazariegos 16. Travel agencies can make bookings on other airlines.

Chevy Suburban vans shuttle between Tuxtla Gutiérrez's Aeropuerto Llano San Juan and San Cristóbal for US$7 per person. Buy your ticket at the Aviacsa office.

Bus A new Central de Autobuses is planned for the south of the town, but for the moment each company has its own terminal.

Each bus company serving San Cristóbal has various classes of service, which it may call 2nd, 1st or deluxe, or by proprietary names. Usually price is a surer determinant of comfort and speed than class: the more you pay, the higher the comfort and the quicker the trip.

Omnibus Cristóbal Colón is at the junction of Insurgentes and the Interamericana (Hwy 190), and shares the 1st-class terminal with Autobuses del Sur. There is no place to leave your luggage, but shops nearby on Insurgentes will hold it for a small fee. Look for signs reading 'Se Reciben Equipaje', or words to that effect.

Autotransportes Tuxtla Gutiérrez is on Allende half a block north of the Interamericana. The terminal is not visible from the highway; walk up the little street opposite the Chevrolet dealership, northwest of the Supermercado Jovel, southeast of the Policia Federal de Caminos.

Autotransportes Andrés Caso is on the Interamericana at Hidalgo (a block west of Cristóbal Colón); Autotransportes Rápidos de San Cristóbal is on the Interamericana half a block east of the Cristóbal Colón station; and Transportes Fray Bartolomé de las Casas is on Avenida Salomon González Blanco, the continuation of Utrilla, 300 meters north of the market.

Sociedad Cooperativa Altos de Chiapas runs minibuses up and down the Interamericana; you can catch them anywhere along the route.

Bus departures from San Cristóbal include:

Chetumal – 700 km, 11 hours; Colón Maya de Oro (deluxe) buses at 9:30 am and 4:35 pm (US$24), which continue to Cancún (US$33 from San Cristóbal); others by Colón (US$21) at 2:30 pm and Sur (US$18) at 12:30 pm

Chiapa de Corzo – 70 km, 1½ hours; ATG buses (US$1.50) every half-hour, which may or may not stop at Chiapa; Altos de Chiapas minibuses or shared-taxi colectivos are a better bet (see map)

Ciudad Cuauhtémoc (Guatemalan border) – 165 km, three hours; seven buses by Colón (US$3.75), nine by ATG (US$3), others by Andrés Caso and Altos de Chiapas. Take an early bus if you hope to get any distance into Guatemala the same day.

Comitán – 83 km, 1½ hours; seven buses by Colón (US$1.75) from 7 am to 10 pm; many cheaper ones by other companies

Mérida – 770 km, 15 hours; one evening Colón deluxe (US$26) and a normal (US$22) at 5:30 pm, one ATG Plus (deluxe) at 6 pm (US$21)

Mexico City (TAPO, or Terminal Oriente) – 1085 km, 19 hours, US$33 to US$43; five buses by Colón, more by ATG

Oaxaca – 718 km, 12 hours, US$18 to US$22; two buses by Colón

Ocosingo – 108 km, 1½ hours, US$2.50; eight buses by Colón; most other lines run this route as well, and there are frequent minibuses (see map)

Palenque – 190 km, 4¼ to five hours; eight buses by Colón (US$6); seven by Figueroa (US$5), more by ATG, ATS and Lacandonia (US$5)

Tapachula – 350 km, eight hours; five buses by Colón (US$11), more by ATG and Andrés Caso (US$6)

Tuxtla Gutiérrez – 85 km, two hours; hourly buses by Colón (US$2.50), ATG (US$1.50) and Oriente de Chiapas (US$1.50); frequent shared taxis by Autotransportes Rápidos de San Cristóbal (US$3.75 to US$4.50 per person) – see map

Villahermosa – 300 km, eight hours; one bus by Colón (US$10), or go via Tuxtla Gutiérrez

Getting Around

Bus & Taxi For buses to the Indian villages near San Cristóbal, see Around San Cristóbal. Taxis are fairly plentiful. One stand is on the north side of the main plaza. A typical trip within the city costs US$1.

Car Budget Rent-a-Car (☎ (967) 8-18-71) is at Auto Rentas Yaxchilán, at Mazariegos 36, 2½ blocks from the plaza. Hours are from 8 am to 2 pm and 3 to 8 pm Monday to Saturday, from 8 am to noon and 5 to 7 pm Sunday. At busy periods you may need to

Subcomandante Marcos, leader of the Zapatista National Liberation Army

book your car a few days in advance. The cheapest, a VW sedan, is around US$40 a day, taxes included.

AROUND SAN CRISTÓBAL

There are many interesting villages to visit near San Cristóbal. Note that it can be dangerous to walk between villages, because of robbers. Play it safe and ride. The best way to get to the villages is on a tour with Mercedes or Alex and Raúl; see Organized Tours in the San Cristóbal section for details.

San Juan Chamula

The Chamulans have always defended their independence fiercely: they put up strong resistance to the Spaniards in 1524 and launched a famous rebellion in 1869. Today they are one of the most numerous of the Tzotzil groups – 40,000 strong – and their village, 10 km northwest of San Cristóbal, is the center for some unique religious practices. A big sign at the entrance to the village says it is strictly forbidden to take photos in the church or anywhere rituals are being performed.

A sign on the church door tells visitors to ask at the 'tourist office', also on the plaza, for tickets (US$1) to enter. If the sense that you are intruding doesn't overwhelm you, the atmosphere inside is extraordinary. The rows of burning candles, the thick clouds of incense, the chanting worshippers kneeling with their faces on the pine-needle-carpeted floor – all are as reminiscent of an Asian temple as of anywhere else. Among the candles stand Pepsi and Coke bottles – offerings to the spirits of the ancestors buried nearby.

Next to the church, the Museo de Chamula (open 9 am to 6 pm, US$1) preserves the traditional way of life in its exhibit of handicrafts and wattle-and-daub construction.

The Chamulans believe that Christ rose from the cross to become the sun. Christian festivals are interwoven with older ones: the pre-Lent Carnaval celebrations, which are among the most important and last several days in February or March, also mark the five 'lost' days *(uayeb)* of the ancient Mayan Long Count calendar (see the Vague Year section in the Facts about the Region chapter). Other festivals include ceremonies for San Sebastián (mid to late January); Semana Santa; San Juan, the village's patron saint (June 22 to 25); and the annual change of village leadership posts (December 30 to January 1).

Zinacantán

This Tzotzil village, center for roughly 15,000 Zinacantecos, is 11 km northwest of San Cristóbal. The road to it forks left off the Chamula road, then down into the valley. Zinacantán has two churches (entry US$0.50), in which photography is not allowed.

The men wear distinctive red-and-white striped tunics (which appear pink) and flat, round, beribboned palm hats. Unmarried men's hats have longer, wider ribbons. A market is usually held only at

---

Photography Around San Cristóbal

In some villages, particularly those nearest San Cristóbal, you may be greeted with wariness, the result of centuries of oppression and the desire to preserve traditions from interference. Cameras are at best tolerated – and sometimes not even that. The San Cristóbal tourist office displays a sign stating that photography is banned in the church and during festivals at San Juan Chamula, and banned completely at Zinacantán. For years a tale circulated that two tourists were killed for taking photos in the Chamula church. Whether or not that's true, it's certainly evidence of the hostility that can be aroused by insensitive behavior. If in any doubt at all, ask before taking a picture. ■

---

fiesta times. The most important celebrations are for the patron saint, San Lorenzo, between August 8 and 11, and for San Sebastián in January.

Zinacantecos venerate the geranium, which, along with pine branches, is offered in rituals to bring a wide range of benefits. The crosses dotting the Zinacantán countryside mostly mark entrances to the abodes of the important ancestor gods or of the Señor de la Tierra (Earth Lord), all of whom must be kept happy with offerings at appropriate times.

If you walk a few hundred meters along the road past the San Lorenzo church, you'll come to the **Museo Ik'al Ojov**, a private entity dedicated to the Earth Lord. The thatched buildings hold exhibits showing Zinacantán's traditional way of life.

Tenejapa

Tenejapa is a Tzeltal village 28 km northeast of San Cristóbal, set in a pretty valley with a river running through it. There are about 20,000 Tenejapecos in the surrounding area. Early on Sunday mornings a busy market fills the main street (behind the church). More interesting than what's on sale in the market is the people's clothing.

Tenejapa has a few comedores on the main street and one basic posada, the *Hotel*

Molina, but it's not always open. The main festival is for the village's patron saint, San Ildefonso, on January 23.

Amatenango del Valle
The women of this Tzeltal village, 37 km southeast of San Cristóbal down the Interamericana, are renowned potters. Amatenango pottery is still fired by the pre-Hispanic method of burning a wood fire around the pieces, rather than putting them in a kiln.

San Francisco, Amatenango's patron saint, is feted on October 4.

Other Villages
Intrepid Mayaphiles might want to make visits to some more remote villages.

San Andrés Larráinzar is a hilltop Tzotzil and mestizo village 28 km northwest of San Cristóbal (18 km beyond San Juan Chamula). A turnoff uphill to the left, 10 km past San Juan Chamula, leads through spectacular mountain scenery to the village. San Andrés was the setting for negotiations between the EZLN rebels and government officials during 1996. The patron saint's day is November 30. A weekly Sunday market is held, and the people seem less reserved toward outsiders than those of other villages. People from Santa Magdalena, another Tzotzil village a few kilometers north, attend the San Andrés market; their ceremonial huipiles are among the finest of all Chiapas Indian garments.

The plaza at **Mitontic**, a small Tzotzil village a few hundred meters left of the Chenalhó road and 23 km beyond San Juan Chamula, has both a picturesque ruined 16th-century church and a more modern working one. The patron saint, San Miguel, is honored from May 5 to 8.

San Pedro Chenalhó is a Tzotzil village in a valley with a stream running through it; it's 1500 meters high, 27 km beyond and quite a descent from Chamula. It's the center for about 14,000 people in the surrounding area. There's a weekly Sunday market. The main fiestas are for San Pedro (June 27 to 30), San Sebastián (January 16 to 22) and Carnaval.

Huixtán, 32 km from San Cristóbal and the center for roughly 12,000 Tzotzils, was one of the main pre-Hispanic Tzotzil centers. Huixtán has a 16th-century church. **Oxchuc**, 20 km beyond Huixtán, is a small Tzeltal and mestizo town dominated by the large colonial church of San Tomás.

Getting There & Away
There are paved roads to San Juan Chamula, Zinacantán, Amatenango del Valle and most of the way to Tenejapa. Reaching the other villages mentioned involves long stretches of pretty rough dirt track, but buses make it along them and so can a VW sedan (slowly).

Bus and colectivo schedules are geared toward getting villagers into town early for shopping and back home not too late; they are not optimal for getting you there from the city and back in the same day.

Combis for San Juan Chamula and Zinacantán depart from the northwest corner of the San Cristóbal market every 20 minutes or so (US$0.75). For Tenejapa they leave about every half-hour; the hour ride costs US$1. Return services from Tenejapa start getting scarce after noon. To Amatenango del Valle, take a Comitán bus (see San Cristóbal – Getting There & Away); the fare is US$1.

Transportes Fray Bartolomé de las Casas (see San Cristóbal – Getting There & Away) runs buses to Chenalhó (2½ hours, US$1.50), and to San Andrés Larraínzar (2½ hours, US$1.25).

Mayaspeak
Nine languages are commonly spoken in Chiapas. Spanish is the language of commerce, education and government in the cities. In the countryside the Mayan dialects Chol, Chuj, Lacandón, Mam, Tojolabal, Tzeltal, Tzotzil and Zoque can be heard, depending on which area you visit. Although they're all derived from the ancient Mayan language, these dialects are mutually unintelligible, so local inhabitants use Tzeltal or Spanish to communicate with members of other linguistic groups. ■

COMITÁN
Population 84,000

Comitán (elevation 1635 meters) is a pleasant town, the jumping-off point to the Lagunas de Montebello and the last place of any size before the Guatemalan border post at Ciudad Cuauhtémoc.

The first Spanish settlement in the area, San Cristóbal de los Llanos, was established in 1527. Today the town is officially called Comitán de Domínguez, after Belisario Domínguez, a local doctor who was also a national senator during the presidency of Victoriano Huerta. Domínguez had the cheek to speak out in 1913 against Huerta's record of political murders and was himself murdered for his pains.

Orientation
Comitán is set amid hills, so you'll find yourself walking up and down, down and up – with your gear.

The wide and attractive main plaza is bounded by Avenida Central on its west side and Calle 1 Sur Poniente on the south. The street numbering scheme resembles that of Tuxtla Gutiérrez in its complexity.

The 1st-class Cristóbal Colón bus station is on the Interamericana, here named the Boulevard Dr Belisario Domínguez and called simply 'El Bulevar'. It passes through the western part of town, about 20 minutes' walk from the main plaza. To reach the plaza, cross El Bulevar in front of the bus station and catch any minibus with 'Centro' in its window.

Taxis outside the terminal charge US$1 for the short trip to the main plaza.

The 2nd-class Autotransportes Tuxtla Gutiérrez (ATG) bus station is several blocks north of the Colón station.

Linea Comitán-Montebello serves Lagunas de Montebello; they go from Avenida 2 Poniente Sur 17-B, between Calles 2 and 3 Sur Poniente, two blocks west and 1½ blocks south of the main plaza.

Information
Tourist Office There's a helpful tourist office (☎ (963) 2-40-47) in the Palacio Municipal, on the north side of the main plaza, open 9 am to 8 pm Monday to Saturday, 9 am to 2 pm Sunday. The tall iron gates to the palacio may be closed to keep out terrorists; just ask the soldiers to open them and go inside to the left.

Consulate The Guatemalan Consulate (☎ (963) 2-26-69) is at the corner of Avenida 2 Poniente Sur and Calle 1 Sur Poniente, open 8 am to 1 pm and 2:30 to 4:30 pm Monday to Friday.

Money See the map for banks and ATMs.

Post & Communications The post office is on Avenida Central Sur between Calles 2 and 3 Sur, 1½ blocks south of main plaza. Hours are Monday to Friday 8 am to 7 pm, Saturday 8 am to 1 pm. There's a Ladatel phone at the southwest corner of the main plaza, and a Lada caseta on Calle 2 Sur Poniente, half a block west of Avenida Central Sur.

Things to See
On the east side of the main plaza, **Santo Domingo church** dates from the 16th century. The adjacent **Casa de la Cultura**, on the southeastern corner of the main plaza, includes an exhibition gallery, auditorium and museum. Just east of it is Comitán's small **archaeological museum**.

Casa Museo Dr Belisario Domínguez, the family home of the martyr-hero, has been turned into a museum that provides fascinating insights into the medical practices and the life of the professional classes in turn-of-the-century Comitán. The museum is at Avenida Central Sur 29, half a block south of the main plaza. It's open daily from 10 am to 6:45 pm (Sunday 9 am to 12:45 pm), closed Monday. Admission costs only a peso.

Places to Stay
Comitán has several cheap posadas with small, often dingy and severely plain rooms, most of them OK for a night. *Posada Primavera*, Calle Central Poniente 4, only a few steps west of the main plaza, charges US$3.25 per bed for rooms with sinks, but without bath or windows. The *Hospedaje*

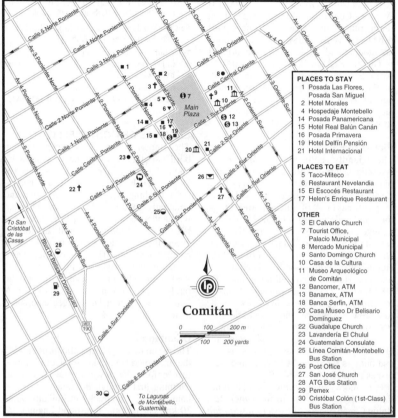

PLACES TO STAY
1 Posada Las Flores,
   Posada San Miguel
2 Hotel Morales
4 Hospedaje Montebello
14 Posada Panamericana
15 Hotel Real Balún Canán
16 Posada Primavera
19 Hotel Delfín Pensión
21 Hotel Internacional

PLACES TO EAT
5 Taco-Miteco
6 Restaurant Nevelandia
15 El Escocés Restaurant
17 Helen's Enrique Restaurant

OTHER
3 El Calvario Church
7 Tourist Office,
   Palacio Municipal
8 Mercado Municipal
9 Santo Domingo Church
10 Casa de la Cultura
11 Museo Arqueológico
   de Comitán
12 Bancomer, ATM
13 Banamex, ATM
18 Banca Serfín, ATM
20 Casa Museo Dr Belisario
   Domínguez
22 Guadalupe Church
23 Lavandería El Chulul
24 Guatemalan Consulate
25 Línea Comitán-Montebello
   Bus Station
26 Post Office
27 San José Church
28 ATG Bus Station
29 Pemex
30 Cristóbal Colón (1st-Class)
   Bus Station

Comitán

0   100   200 m

0   100   200 yards

Montebello (☎ (963) 2-17-70), a block away at Calle 1 Norte Poniente 10, has equally basic rooms around a courtyard for US$4 per person. *Posada Panamericana*, at the corner of Calle Central Poniente and Avenida 1 Poniente Norte, has dark downstairs cubicles for US$3 and brighter, breezier rooms upstairs for US$6.50.

Posada Las Flores (☎ (963) 2-33-34), Avenida 1 Poniente Norte 15, half a block north of Calle 2 Norte Poniente, is better, with rooms around a quiet courtyard and doubles for US$5. Its neighbor, *Posada San Miguel*, is less comfortable.

About the best value is the *Hotel Internacional* (☎ (963) 2-01-10), Avenida Central Sur, 16 at Calle 2 Sur Oriente, a block south of the plaza, with older rooms for US$14/16/19 a single/double/triple, or renovated rooms for US$18/22/26.

Comitán's most polished place is *Hotel Real Balún Canán* (☎ (963) 2-10-94), a block west of the main plaza at Avenida 1 Poniente Sur 7. Prints of Frederick Catherwood's 1844 drawings of Mayan ruins decorate the stairs, and the small rooms are comfortable, with TV and phone. Rates are US$18/22/25.

Hotel Delfín Pensión (☎ (963) 2-00-13), Avenida Central on the west side of the main plaza, has spacious rooms with private baths for US$12/15. Back rooms are modern and overlook a leafy courtyard.

The *Hotel Morales* (☎ (963) 2-04-36), Avenida Central Norte 8, 1½ blocks north of the main plaza, resembles an aircraft hangar, with small rooms perched around an upstairs walkway, but it's clean, and rooms with baths cost US$13.

Places to Eat

The friendly, colorful *Taco-Miteco*, on Avenida Central Norte 5, near the main plaza, serves 13 varieties of tacos for US$0.35 each, quesadillas for US$2, and a 'super-breakfast' of juice, coffee, eggs, toast and chilaquiles for US$2.25.

Several reasonable cafes line the west side of the main plaza. Prime among them is *Helen's Enrique Restaurant*, in front of the Hotel Delfín. With a porch and pretensions to decor, Helen's serves all three meals for US$2.50 to US$6. *Restaurant Acuario*, *Restaurant Yuly* and *Restaurant Vicks*, in the same row, are cheaper and more basic.

Restaurant Nevelandia, on the northwest corner of the main plaza, has tacos for US$0.30 to US$0.65, antojitos, spaghetti and burgers for around US$2.25, and meat dishes typically for US$4.50.

For a more expensive meal amid international surroundings, go to the Hotel Real Balún Canán, where *El Escocés Restaurant* is open until 11 pm and the *Disco Tzisquirin* until 1 am.

Getting There & Away

Comitán is 85 km southeast down the Interamericana from San Cristóbal and 80 km north of Ciudad Cuauhtémoc. Buses are regularly stopped for document checks by immigration and army officials both north and south of Comitán, so keep your passport handy.

Departures include:

Ciudad Cuauhtémoc (Guatemalan border) – 80 km, 1½ hours; seven buses by Cristóbal Colón (US$2.50), six by ATG (US$1.75)

Mexico City – 1168 km, 20 hours; two buses by Cristóbal Colón (US$40 or US$46)

San Cristóbal de las Casas – 83 km, 1½ hours; two dozen buses (US$1.25 to US$1.75)

Tapachula – 260 km, seven hours (via Motozintla); seven buses by Colón (US$8), more by ATG (US$6.50)

Tuxtla Gutiérrez – 170 km, 3½ hours; 16 buses by Colón (US$4.75 to US$6), others by ATG (US$4)

LAGUNAS DE MONTEBELLO

The temperate forest along the Guatemalan border southeast of Comitán is dotted with about 60 small lakes – the Lagunas (or Lagos) de Montebello. The area is beautiful, refreshing, not hard to reach, quiet and eminently good for hiking. Some Mexican weekenders come down here in their cars, but the rest of the time you'll see nobody except the few resident villagers and a small handful of visitors. There are two very basic hostelries, a campground and a restaurant. And at one edge of the lake district are the rarely visited Mayan ruins of Chinkultic. A number of Guatemalan refugee camps are in and around the lakes area.

Orientation

The paved road to Montebello turns east off the Interamericana 16 km south of Comitán, just before the town of La Trinitaria. Running first through flat ranch and *ejido* land, it passes the track to Chinkultic after 30 km, entering the forest and Lagunas de Montebello National Park five km further on. At the park entrance (no fee) the road splits. The paved section continues four km ahead to the Lagunas de Colores, where it dead-ends at two small houses 50 meters from Laguna Bosque Azul. To the right (east) from the park entrance a dirt road leads past tracks to several more lakes, then to the village and lake of Tziscao (nine km).

Chinkultic

These dramatically sited ruins lie two km along a track leading north off La Trinitaria-Montebello road, 27 km from the Interamericana at the village of Hidalgo. A sign, 'Chinkultic 3', marks the turnoff.

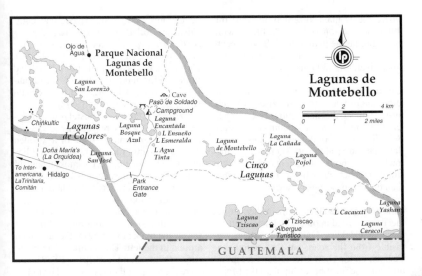

Lagunas de Montebello

Doña María at La Orquidea restaurant, half a kilometer further along the road, has a map and book on Chinkultic.

Chinkultic was on the extreme western edge of the ancient Mayan area. Dates carved here extend from 591 to 897 AD – the last of which is nearly a century after the latest dates at Palenque, Yaxchilán and Toniná. These years no doubt span Chinkultic's peak period, but occupation is thought to have started in the late Preclassic period (around 200 AD) and continued until after 900. Of the 200 mounds scattered over a wide area, few parts have been cleared, but still it's worth the effort.

The track from the road brings you first to a gate with a hut on the left. Here take the path to the left, which curves around to the right. On the overgrown hill to the right of this path stands one of Chinkultic's major structures, called simply E23. The path leads to a long ball court, where several stelae lie on their sides under thatched shelters. Other stelae – some carved with Mayan-looking human figures – lie in the vicinity.

Follow the track back to the hut and turn left, passing what could be a parking lot,

soon after which you can spot a few stone mounds in the undergrowth to the right. The hillside ahead of you shortly comes into full view, and on it is the partly restored temple called El Mirador. The path goes over a stream and steeply up to El Mirador, from which there are good views of the surrounding lakes and down into a big 50-meter-deep cenote.

Lakes

Lagunas de Colores The paved road straight on from the park entrance leads through the Lagunas de Colores, so called because their colors range from turquoise to deep green. The first of these, on the right after about two km, is Laguna Agua Tinta. Then on the left come Laguna Esmeralda and Laguna Encantada, with Laguna Ensueño on the right opposite Encantada. The fifth and biggest of the Lagunas de Colores is Laguna Bosque Azul, on the left where the road ends. One of the two small houses here sells drinks and food, and there's a lakeside campsite.

Two paths lead on from the end of the road. Proceeding straight on for 800 meters brings you to the gruta – a cave shrine

YUCATÁN

where locals make offerings to ward off illness and so on (take a flashlight with you). Taking the path to the left, you reach Paso de Soldado, a picnic site beside a small river, after 300 meters.

Laguna de Montebello About three km along the dirt road toward Tziscao (which turns right at the park entrance), a track leads 200 meters left to Laguna de Montebello. This is one of the bigger lakes, with a flat, open area along its shore where the track ends. About 150 meters to the left is a stony area, which is better for swimming than the muddy fringes elsewhere.

Cinco Lagunas Three km farther along the Tziscao road another track leads left to these 'five lakes'. Only four of them are visible from the road, but the second, La Cañada, on the right after about 1.5 km, is probably the most beautiful of all the Montebello Lakes – it's nearly bisected by two rocky outcrops. The track eventually reaches the village of San Antonio and, amazingly, is a bus route.

Laguna Pojoj Another km farther along the Tziscao road, a track to the left leads to this lake, one km off the road.

Laguna Tziscao This comes into view on the right a further km along the road. Continue on to the junction for Tziscao village on the right. The village has pleasant grassy streets, friendly people and a hostel.

Places to Stay & Eat

Half a kilometer past the Chinkultic turnoff you can camp or rent a cabin at *La Orquidea*, a small restaurant to the left of the road. The owner, Señora María Domínguez de Castellanos, better known as Doña María, has helped Guatemalan refugees by buying a nearby farm and turning it over to them. For the cabins, which have electric lights but no running water, you pay US$3; meals are a bit less.

Inside the national park camping is officially allowed only at Laguna Bosque Azul (no fee), the last and biggest of the Lagunas

de Colores, where the paved road ends. There are toilets and water here. *Bosque Azul Restaurant*, at the Laguna Bosque Azul parking lot, serves eggs (US$2), chiles rellenos or meaty dishes (US$4) and drinks, chips and fruit. Outside the restaurant local cowboys wait, eager to guide you (by horse) to the caves (US$3).

Tziscao village has a hostel – the *Albergue Turístico* – where you pay US$3 per person for a dormitory bunk or a wooden cabaña, or camp for US$1. The hostel lies on the shore of one of the most beautiful lakes – you can rent a rowboat – and Guatemala is just a few hundred meters away. Entering the village, turn right beside a corner store soon after you come level with a small church on the hill, and follow the track down toward the lake, then around to the left. The señora will cook up eggs, frijoles and tortillas (US$2) and there's a fridge full of refrescos. The toilets seem to be in permanent desperate need of a good cleaning.

Getting There & Away

It's possible to make a whirlwind tour of Chinkultic and the lakes in a day from San Cristóbal – either by public transport or tour – but if you prefer a pace that enables you to absorb something of your surroundings, it's better to stay at the lakes or at least at Comitán.

Buses and combis to the Lagos de Montebello go from the yard of Línea Comitán-Montebello in Comitán. One or the other leaves every 20 or 30 minutes up till about 5 pm. Vehicles have a number of different destinations, so make sure you get one that's going your way.

Most people head initially for Chinkultic, Doña María's (La Orquidea), Lagunas de Colores, Laguna de Montebello or Tziscao. The last vehicle to Tziscao (1¼ hours, US$2) leaves Comitán at about 2 pm. By combi it's 45 minutes to Doña María's; a local bus can take up to 1½ hours (US$1.75). It's the same fare to get off at the Chinkultic turnoff or Lagunas de Colores.

Returning to Comitán, the last bus leaves Lagunas de Colores at 4:30 pm.

MOTOZINTLA

The small town of Motozintla lies in a deep valley in the Sierra Madre 70 km southwest of Ciudad Cuauhtémoc. A good road leads to it from the Interamericana a few km north of Ciudad Cuauhtémoc, then continues down to Huixtla near the Chiapas coast near Tapachula – a spectacular, unusual trip. Have your passport handy for identity checks.

GUATEMALAN BORDER – CIUDAD CUAUHTÉMOC

Ciudad Cuauhtémoc is just the Mexican border post, a few houses and a comedor or two, but it's the last/first place in Mexico on the Interamericana (Hwy 190). Comitán is 80 km away, San Cristóbal 165 km away. The Guatemalan border post is three km south, at La Mesilla. If your bus from Comitán or San Cristóbal isn't going on to La Mesilla, there are taxis (US$2), combis (US$0.50) and trucks (US$0.50) to take you across the border.

If yours is a passport that requires only a tourist card to visit Guatemala (see Facts for the Visitor), you can get it at the border. If you need a visa, obtain it in advance at the Guatemalan Consulate in Comitán.

There's no bank at this border. Individual money changers operate here, but they give you fewer quetzals than a bank would.

Getting There and Away

Many buses and minibuses shuttle between Ciudad Cuauhtémoc, Comitán and San Cristóbal all day. See those two cities' sections for details.

Guatemalan buses depart La Mesilla every half hour from 8 am to 8 pm for main points inside Guatemala such as Huehuetenango (84 km, 1½ to two hours, US$1), Quetzaltenango (also known as Xela, 170 km, 3½ hours, US$3.35) and Guatemala City (380 km, seven hours, US$4.50). Lago de Atitlán (245 km, five hours) and Chichicastenango (244 km, five hours) both lie a few kilometers off the Interamericana. Before boarding a bus at La Mesilla, try to find out when it's leaving and when it reaches your destination. That could save you several hours of sitting in a stationary bus.

Pacific Chiapas

Along the Pacific coast of southwestern Chiapas is the hot, fertile plain known as the Soconusco, which is 15 to 35 km wide and has quite heavy rainfall from June to October, especially in July and August. Inland and parallel to the coast is the range of the Sierra Madre de Chiapas, mostly between 1000 and 2500 meters but higher in the south, where the Tacaná volcano on the Guatemalan border reaches 4092 meters.

Because it was a rich source of highly valued cacao, this littoral was conquered by the Aztecs at the end of the 15th century and became their empire's most distant province, under the name Xoconochco. Soconusco was the first part of Chiapas to be subdued by the Spaniards, lying as it did on Pedro de Alvarado's route to conquer Guatemala in 1524.

ARRIAGA

Arriaga, where the Juchitán-Tapachula road meets the Tuxtla Gutiérrez-Tapachula road, has a few suitable lodgings and restaurants, but no good reason for you to stop.

For some reason, quite a few buses end their runs in Arriaga. Happily, the same number start their runs here. The new Centro de Autobuses houses all the 1st- and 2nd-class buses that serve Arriaga. Departures include:

Juchitán – 135 km, two hours; three buses by Colón (US$3.30), many by Sur and Fletes y Pasajes/Transportes Oaxaca-Istmo

Mexico City (TAPO) – 900 km, 16 hours; one afternoon Cristóbal Colón bus (US$34), a Plus at 6:30 pm (US$43), 2nd-class buses daily by Fletes y Pasajes/Transportes Oaxaca-Istmo

Oaxaca – 400 km, seven hours; a 10 pm bus by Colón (US$13), a few 2nd-class buses daily by Sur and Fletes y Pasajes/Transportes Oaxaca-Istmo

Salina Cruz – 175 km, three hours, US$6.25; several buses daily by Colón and Sur

San Cristóbal de las Casas – 240 km, five hours; buses every 30 minutes (via Tuxtla) by Colón (US$6.50), several by ATG (US$6)

Tapachula – 245 km, 3½ hours, US$8; seven buses by Colón, and by Sur and ATG

Tonalá – 23 km, 30 minutes; Transportes Arriaga-Tonalá minibuses every few minutes (US$0.75)

Tuxtla Gutiérrez – 155 km, three hours, US$4.50; buses every hour by Colón, others by ATG

TONALÁ

Twenty-three km southeast of Arriaga on Hwy 200, Tonalá has only marginally more intrinsic appeal than Arriaga but is the jumping-off point for the laid-back beach spot of Puerto Arista. A tall pre-Hispanic stela in the Tonalá main plaza appears to depict Tláloc, the central Mexican rain god. There's also a small regional museum at Hidalgo 77, with some archaeological pieces found in the region.

The tourist office (☎ (966) 3-01-01) is on the ground floor of the Palacio Municipal (look for its clock), on the Hidalgo side of the main plaza. It's open 9 am to 3 pm and 6 to 8 pm Monday to Friday, 9 am to 2 pm Saturday.

Tonalá has no great deals on accommodations. If you're heading for Puerto Arista, go straight there if you can.

PUERTO ARISTA

Puerto Arista, 18 km southwest of Tonalá, is a half-km collection of palm shacks and a few more substantial buildings in the middle of a 30-km gray beach. The food's mostly fish, you get through a lot of refrescos, and nothing else happens except the crashing of the Pacific waves . . . until the weekend, when a few hundred Chiapanecos cruise into town, or until Semana Santa and Christmas, when they come in the thousands and the residents of Puerto Arista make their money for the year.

Usually the most action you'll see is when an occasional fishing boat puts out to sea or a piglet breaks into a trot if a dog gathers the energy to bark at it. Mosquitoes and sand fleas seem to be the only relentlessly energetic beings in town. The temperature's usually sweltering if you stray more than a few yards from shore, and it's humid in summer.

The sea is clean here, but don't go far from the beach: there's an undertow, and rip tides known as *canales* can sweep you a long way out in a short time.

TAPACHULA
Population 250,000

Most travelers come to Mexico's southernmost city only because it's a gateway to Guatemala, though for ruins buffs, Izapa, 11 km east, is worth a visit.

Tapachula is a busy commercial center, overlooked by the 4092-meter Tacaná volcano to its northeast, the first of a chain of volcanoes stretching down into Guatemala.

Orientation

The Parque Hidalgo (or Parque Central) is the main plaza, with the SEDETUR tourist office, banks and the Casa de la Cultura, formerly the Palacio Municipal.

For bus station locations, see Getting There & Away, below.

Information
Tourist Offices The city tourist office (☎ (962) 6-54-70, fax (962) 6-55-22) is at Avenida 4 Norte 35 on the 3rd floor, a few doors northwest of Hospedaje Colonial, and has few customers. The SEDETUR office (☎ (962) 6-87-55, fax (962) 6-35-02) is at Avenida 8 Norte at Calle 3 Poniente, on the main plaza.

Consulate The Guatemalan Consulate (☎ (962) 6-12-52) is on Avenida 9 Norte just south of Calle Central Oriente. It's open 8 am to 4 pm Monday to Friday. Visas are issued quickly.

Money There are banks with ATMs around the main plaza, including Banamex on the east side and BanCrecer on the west. The Casa de Cambio Tapachula, at the corner of Calle 3 Poniente and Avenida 4 Norte, open 7:30 am to 7:30 pm Monday to Saturday and 7 am to 2 pm Sunday, is another option.

Post & Communications The post office is nine blocks southeast of the plaza, at the corner of Calle 1 Oriente and Avenida 9 Norte, and is open 8 am to 6 pm Monday to Friday, 8 am to noon Saturday. Tapachula's postal code is 30700.

There are Lada casetas on Calle 17 Oriente, 1½ blocks west of the Cristóbal Colón bus station, and in the Farmacia Monaco, across from Hotel Don Miguel on Calle 1 Poniente.

Soconusco Regional Museum
The Museo Regional del Soconusco, on the west side of the Parque Hidalgo, has some archaeological and folklore exhibits, including some finds from Izapa. Entry costs US$2.

Places to Stay – budget
The friendly *Hospedaje Las Américas* (☎ (962) 6-27-57), at Avenida 10 Norte 47, north of the main plaza, has singles with fans and private bathroom for US$4.50/7 a single/double.

The *Hospedaje Colonial* (☎ (962) 6-20-52), at Avenida 4 Norte 31, half a block north of Calle 3 Poniente, has clean, bright rooms with private bath along a balcony for US$5.50 per person. Ring the bell to enter.

Around the corner (one block west) from the Cristóbal Colón bus station is the *Hospedaje Chelito* (☎ (962) 6-24-28), at Avenida 1 Norte 107, between Calles 15 and 17 Poniente. Rooms with black & white TV, fan and private bathroom cost US$11; for US$17 you get a color TV and air-con. Attached is a small cafe.

Places to Stay – middle
The *Hotel Santa Julia* (☎ (962) 6-31-40), Calle 17 Oriente 5, next door to the Cristóbal Colón 1st-class bus station, has clean singles/doubles with TV, telephone and private bath for US$18/26.

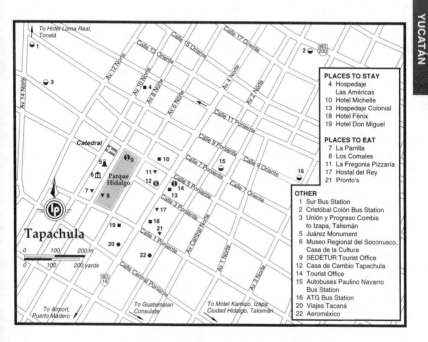

Tapachula

PLACES TO STAY
4 Hospedaje Las Américas
10 Hotel Michelle
13 Hospedaje Colonial
18 Hotel Fénix
19 Hotel Don Miguel

PLACES TO EAT
7 La Parrilla
8 Los Comales
11 La Fregonia Pizzaría
17 Hostal del Rey
21 Pronto's

OTHER
1 Sur Bus Station
2 Cristóbal Colón Bus Station
3 Unión y Progreso Combis to Izapa, Talismán
5 Juárez Monument
6 Museo Regional del Soconusco, Casa de la Cultura
9 SEDETUR Tourist Office
12 Casa de Cambio Tapachula
14 Tourist Office
15 Autobuses Paulino Navarro Bus Station
16 ATG Bus Station
20 Viajes Tacaná
22 Aeroméxico

Hotel Fénix (☎ (962) 5-07-55), Avenida 4 Norte 19, near the corner of Calle 1 Poniente a block west of the main plaza, has an encouraging lobby and room service but a mixed bag of medium-size rooms within. Some fan-cooled ones at US$18 are less dilapidated than some air-con ones at US$24.

The nearby modern and pricier *Hotel Don Miguel* (☎ (962) 6-11-43), at Calle 1 Poniente 18, is probably the best city center hotel. Rooms are clean and bright, with air-con and TV for US$28/38. There's a good little restaurant here too.

A half-block east of the main plaza, at Calle 5 Poniente 23, the *Hotel Michelle* (☎ (962) 6-88-74, 5-26-40) has comely 2nd- and 3rd-story rooms with air-con, TV, big closets and desks for US$24/32 a single/double.

Places to Stay – top end

The town's two top hotels, both with air-con rooms and swimming pools, are the *Motel Kamico* (☎ (962) 6-26-40), on Hwy 200 east of the city (singles/doubles US$45/57), and the *Hotel Loma Real* (☎ (962) 6-14-40), just off Hwy 200 on the west side of town, where rooms are US$60.

Places to Eat

Several restaurants line the south side of the main plaza. *Los Comales* serves a filling comida corrida for US$3.75 and traditional antojitos for less. *La Parrilla*, across the street on Avenida 8 Norte, is probably a better value and is open 24 hours. *Pronto's*, on Calle 1 Poniente between Avenidas 4 and 2 Norte, is also open 24 hours but is pricier.

If the sun isn't glaring, you may want to sit at one of *La Fregonia Pizzaría*'s sidewalk tables on the pedestrian extension of Calle 5 Poniente, half a block west of the plaza. Pizzas, pastas, burgers and antojitos are all priced between US$2 and US$5.

Breakfast at *Hostal Del Rey*, Avenida 4 Norte 17, near Calle 3 Poniente, with its quiet music, waiters in pink bow ties and cummerbunds, and pretty decor, is a nice

way to begin the day. An early meal of hotcakes, fruit, eggs and coffee is US$3. Later in the day you may want soup and salad or antojitos for US$2.50, or aves or carne for US$4.50 to US$7.

Getting There & Away

Air Aviacsa (☎ (962) 6-14-39, fax (962) 6-31-59), Calle Central Norte 52-B, operates daily nonstop flights from Tapachula to Tuxtla Gutiérrez and twice daily to Mexico City.

Aeromexico (☎ (962) 6-20-50), Avenida 2 Norte 6, has a daily nonstop flight to and from Mexico City.

Viajes Tacaná (☎ (962) 6-87-95, fax (962) 6-35-02) on Avenida 4 Norte 8, between Calle 1 Poniente and Calle Central, sells Aviacsa, Aeromexico and Mexicana tickets.

Bus The Cristóbal Colón bus station is at Calle 17 Oriente and Avenida 3 Norte, five blocks east and six north of the main plaza. To reach the main plaza go west (left) along Calle 17 Oriente for two blocks, then six blocks south (left) down Avenida Central Norte and three west (right) along Calle 5 Poniente.

The main 2nd-class bus stations are Sur, at Calle 9 Poniente 63, a block west of Avenida 12 Norte; Autotransportes Tuxtla Gutiérrez (ATG), at the corner of Calle 9 Oriente and Avenida 3 Norte; and Autobuses Paulino Navarro, on Calle 7 Poniente 5, half a block west of Avenida Central Norte.

Buses to/from the Guatemalan border are covered in the Talisman & Ciudad Hidalgo section, below. Other departures include:

Arriaga – 245 km, 3½ hours; eight buses by Cristóbal Colón (US$9), three afternoon buses by ATG (US$6), buses every 30 minutes by Autobuses Paulino Navarro (US$6)

Comitán – 260 km, seven hours (via Motozintla); three buses by ATG (US$12), several by Paulino Navarro (US$13)

Juchitán – 380 km, six hours; three buses by ATG (US$12), several daily by Sur

Mexico City – 1150 km, 20 hours; six regular
Cristóbal Colón buses (US$43) and two
afternoon Plus buses (US $53)

Oaxaca – 650 km, 11 hours; two buses by Colón
(US$23), and one 2nd-class evening bus by
Sur

Salina Cruz – 420 km, seven hours, US$14; two
buses daily by ATG

San Cristóbal de las Casas – 350 km, eight hours;
five buses by Colón via Tuxtla (US$11),
more by ATG and Andrés Caso (US$6)

Tonalá – 220 km, three hours; eight buses by
Colón (US$7), three by ATG (US$5.50),
several by Sur

Tuxtla Gutiérrez – 400 km, seven hours; five
buses by Colón (US$12), six by ATG
(US$10)

Train The station lies just south of the intersection of Avenida Central Sur and Calle
14. Only masochists, the dull-witted and the
hopelessly adventurous take the train.

Getting Around
Tapachula's airport is 20 km south of the
city off the Puerto Madero road. Transporte
Terrestre (☎ (962) 6-12-87), at Avenida 2
Sur 40-A, charges US$3.25 to the airport
and will pick you up from any hotel in
Tapachula. A taxi is US$7.

AROUND TAPACHULA
Izapa Ruins
If this site were in a more visited part of
Mexico it would have a constant stream of
visitors, for it's not only important to
archaeologists as a link between the
Olmecs and the Maya but also interesting
to walk around. It flourished from approximately 200 BC to 200 AD. The Izapa
carving style – typically seen on stelae with
altars placed in front – is derived from the
Olmec style, and most of the gods shown
are the descendants of Olmec deities, with
their upper lips grotesquely lengthened.
Early Maya monuments from lowland
north Guatemala are similar.

Northern Area Most of this part of the site
has been cleared and some restoration has

been done. There are a number of platforms, a ball court, and several of the stelae
and altars whose carvings provide Izapa's
main interest for archaeologists. The platforms and ball court were probably built
some time after Izapa was at its peak.

Southern Area This area is less visited
than the northern area. Go back about 1.75
km along the road toward Tapachula and
take a dirt road to the left. Where the
vehicle track ends, a path leads to the right.
There are three areas of interest – you may
have to ask the caretaker to find and explain
them, as they are separated by foot trails
that are less than obvious. The first is a
plaza with several stelae under thatched
roofs. The second is a smaller plaza, with
more stelae and three big pillars topped
with curious stone balls. The third has just
one item – a carving of the jaws of a jaguar
holding a seemingly human figure.

Getting There & Away Izapa is 11 km
east of Tapachula on the road to Talismán.
You can reach it by the combis of Unión y
Progreso, which depart from Calle 5
Poniente, half a block west of Avenida 12
Norte in Tapachula. The main (northern)
part of the site is marked on the left of the
road. The second (southern) part lies less
than one km back toward Tapachula on the
other side of the road.

TALISMÁN & CIUDAD HIDALGO
(GUATEMALAN BORDER)
The road from Tapachula to Guatemala
heads 20 km east past the Izapa ruins to the
border at Talismán bridge, opposite El
Carmen (Guatemala). A branch south of
this road leads to another border crossing at
Ciudad Hidalgo (38 km from Tapachula),
opposite Ciudad Tecún Umán. Both of the
crossings are open 24 hours.

At the time of this writing it was possible to obtain Guatemalan visas and tourist
cards at the border, but check in advance.
There's a Guatemalan Consulate at
Oriente 10 in Ciudad Hidalgo, as well as
the one in Tapachula. The officials at the

Guatemalan border may make various small charges as you go through and insist that you pay for your tourist card in US dollars or quetzals, so get some before you leave Tapachula.

Getting There & Away

Combis of Unión y Progreso shuttle between Tapachula and Talismán every few minutes. The fare is US$0.75. A taxi from Tapachula to Talismán takes 20 minutes and costs US$3.

Autobuses Paulino Navarro makes the 45-minute journey between Tapachula and Ciudad Hidalgo every hour for US$1.

There are two daily Cristóbal Colón 1st-class buses from Talismán to Mexico City for US$43.

For information on the border crossing, see the Guatemala section.

Spanish Phrasebook

Groups of people in the region speak native Indian languages and dialects, but Spanish is the most commonly spoken language of the countries of La Ruta Maya. English is the official language of Belize, although both Spanish and a local creole are widely spoken.

For more Spanish words and phrases, get a copy of Lonely Planet's *Latin American Spanish phrasebook*.

For information on Spanish language courses, see Courses in the Facts for the Visitor chapter.

Pronunciation Most of the sounds in Spanish have equivalents in English, and written Spanish is mostly phonetic.

Stress Usually the stress is on the second to last syllable of a word. Words ending in an 'r' (usually verbs) have the stress on the last syllable. If there is an accent on any vowel, the stress is on that syllable.

amigo – a-MI-go
comer – com-ER
aquí – a-QUI

Greetings & Civilities Greetings are used frequently. The first three are often shortened to *buenos/as*.

Good morning.	*Buenos días.*
Good afternoon.	*Buenas tardes.*
Good evening/night.	*Buenas noches.*
Hello.	*Hola.*

How are you?
¿Cómo está? (formal)
¿Cómo estás? (informal)

How are things going?	*¿Qué tal?*
Well, thanks.	*Bien, gracias.*
Very well.	*Muy bien.*
Very badly.	*Muy mal.*
Goodbye.	*Adiós.*
	(rarely used)

Bye, see you soon.	*Hasta luego.*
	('*sta luego*')
Please.	*Por favor.*
Thank you.	*Gracias.*
Many thanks.	*Muchas gracias.*
You're welcome.	*De nada.*
Excuse me.	*Permiso.*
Sorry.	*Perdón.*
Excuse me/Forgive me.	*Disculpe,*
	Discúlpame.
Good luck!	*¡Buena suerte!*
Mister, Sir	*Señor* (formal)
Mrs, Madam	*Señora* (formal)
unmarried woman	*Señorita*
pal, friend	*compañero/a,*
	amigo/a

More Useful Words & Phrases The following brief guide should help you cope in the lands of the Maya.

I'd like to introduce you to ...
Le presento a ...

A pleasure (to meet you).
Mucho gusto.

What is your name?
¿Cómo se llama usted? (formal)
¿Cómo te llamas? (informal)

My name is ...   *Me llamo ...*

Where are you from?
¿De dónde es usted? (formal)
¿De dónde vienes? (familiar)

I am from ...	*Soy de ...*
Australia	*Australia*
Canada	*Canadá*
England	*Inglaterra*
France	*Francia*
Germany	*Alemania*
Israel	*Israel*
Italy	*Italia*
Japan	*Japón*
New Zealand	*Nueva Zelanda*
Norway	*Noruega*
Scotland	*Escocia*

South Africa	*África del Sur*
Sweden	*Suecia*
Switzerland	*Suiza*
the United States	*los Estados Unidos*

Can I take a photo?
¿Puedo sacar una foto?

Of course/Why not/Sure.
Por supuesto/Cómo no/Claro.

How old are you?
¿Cuántos años tiene?

Do you speak English?
¿Habla inglés?

I speak a little Spanish.
Hablo un poquito de español.

I don't understand.
No entiendo.

Could you repeat that?
¿Puede repetirlo?

Could you speak more slowly please?
¿Puede hablar más despacio por favor?

How does one say ...?
¿Cómo se dice ...?

What does ... mean?
¿Qué significa ...?

Where is ...?	*¿Dónde hay ...?*
a hotel	*un hotel*
a boarding house	*una pensión*
a guesthouse	*un hospedaje*

I am looking for ...
Estoy buscando ...

a cheap hotel	*un hotel barato*
a good hotel	*un hotel bueno*
a nearby hotel	*un hotel cercano*
a clean hotel	*un hotel limpio*

Are there any rooms available?
¿Hay habitaciones libres?

Where are the toilets?
¿Dónde están los servicios/baños?

I would like a ...	*Quisiera un ...*
single room	*cuarto sencillo*
double room	*cuarto doble*
room with a bath	*cuarto con baño*

Can I see it? — *¿Puedo verlo?*
Are there others? — *¿Hay otros?*
How much is it? — *¿Cuánto cuesta?*
It's too expensive. — *Es demasiado caro.*

your name	*su nombre*
your surname	*su apellido*
your room number	*el número de su cuarto*

Where is ...?	*¿Dónde está ...?*
the central bus station	*la estación central de autobuses*
the railway station	*la estación de trenes*
the airport	*el aeropuerto*
the ticket office	*la boletería*
bus	*autobús/camión*
bus (long distance)	*flota/bus*

When does the bus/train/plane leave?
¿Cuándo sale el autobus/tren/avión?

I want to go to ...
Quiero ir a ...

What time do they leave?
¿A qué hora salen?

Can you take me to ...?
¿Puede llevarme a ...?

Could you tell me where ... is?
¿Podría decirme dónde está ...?

Is it far?
¿Está lejos?

Is it close to here?
¿Está cerca de aquí?

I'm looking for ... — *Estoy buscando ...*

the post office	*el correo*
the ... embassy	*la embajada de ...*
the museum	*el museo*
the police	*la policía*
the market	*el mercado*
the bank	*el banco*
Stop!	*¡Pare!*
Wait!	*¡Espera!*

I want to change some money.
Quiero cambiar dinero.

I want to change travelers' checks.
Quiero cambiar cheques viajeros.

What is the exchange rate?
¿Cuál es el tipo de cambio?

How many colones/pesos/quetzales per dollar?
¿Cuántos colones/pesos/quetzales por dólar?

Is there an ATM around here?
¿Está una cajera automática cerca de aquí?

cashier	*caja*
automated teller machine (ATM)	*cajera automática*
credit card	*tarjeta de crédito*
the black market	*el mercado negro*
bank notes	*billetes de banco*
exchange houses	*casas de cambio*
Watch out!	*¡Cuidado!*
Help!	*¡Socorro! ¡Auxilio!*
Fire!	*¡Fuego!*
Thief!	*¡Ladrón!*
I've been robbed.	*Me han robado*
They took . . .	*Se llevaron . . .*
my money	*mi dinero*
my passport	*mi pasaporte*
my bag	*mi bolsa*
Where is . . . ?	*¿Dónde hay . . . ?*
a policeman	*un policía*
a doctor	*un doctor*
a hospital	*un hospital*
Leave me alone!	*¡Déjeme!*
Don't bother me!	*¡No me moleste!*
Get lost!	*¡Váyase!*
today	*hoy*
this morning	*esta mañana*
this afternoon	*esta tarde*
tonight	*esta noche*
yesterday	*ayer*
tomorrow	*mañana*
week/month/year	*semana/mes/año*
last week	*la semana pasada*
next month	*el próximo mes*
always	*siempre*
it's early/late	*es temprano/tarde*
now	*ahora*
before/after	*antes/después*
What time is it?	*¿Qué hora es?*
It is 1 o'clock.	*Es la una.*
It is 7 o'clock.	*Son las siete.*

Numbers

0	cero	10	*diez*
1	*uno*	11	*once*
2	*dos*	12	*doce*
3	*tres*	13	*trece*
4	*cuatro*	14	*catorce*
5	*cinco*	15	*quince*
6	*seis*	16	*dieciséis*
7	*siete*	17	*diecisiete*
8	*ocho*	18	*dieciocho*
9	*nueve*	19	*diecinueve*

20	*veinte*	40	*cuarenta*
21	*veintiuno*	50	*cincuenta*
22	*veintidós*	60	*sesenta*
		70	*setenta*
30	*treinta*	80	*ochenta*
31	*treinta y uno*	90	*noventa*

100	*cien, (ciento,* when followed by a noun*)*
101	*ciento uno*
102	*ciento dos*
200	*doscientos*
300	*trescientos*
500	*quinientos*
600	*seiscientos*
900	*novecientos*
1000	*mil*
2000	*dos mil*
100,000	*cien mil*
1,000,000	*un millón*
2,000,000	*dos millones*

Ordinals

first	*primero*
second	*segundo*
third	*tercero*
fourth	*cuarto*
fifth	*quinto*
sixth	*sexto*
seventh	*séptimo*
eighth	*octavo*
ninth	*noveno, nono*
tenth	*décimo*
eleventh	*undécimo*
twelfth	*duodécimo*
twentieth	*vigésimo*

PHRASEBOOK

Modern Mayan

Since the Classic period, the two ancient Mayan languages, Yucatecan and Cholan, have subdivided into 35 separate Mayan languages (Yucatec, Chol, Chorti, Tzeltal, Tzotzil, Lacandon, Mam, Quiché, Cakchiquel, etc), some of them unintelligible to speakers of others. Writing today is in the Latin alphabet brought by the conquistadors – what writing there is. Most literate Maya are literate in Spanish, the language of the government, the school, the church, radio, TV and the newspapers; they may not be literate in Mayan.

Pronunciation There are several rules to remember when pronouncing Mayan words and place names. Mayan vowels are pretty straightforward; it's the consonants that give problems. Remember:

c is always hard, like 'k'

j is always an aspirated 'h' sound. So *jipijapa* is pronounced HEE-pee-HAA-pah and *abaj* is pronounced ah-BAHH; to get the 'HH' sound, take the 'h' sound from 'half' and put it at the end of ah-BAHH

u is 'oo' except when it begins or ends a word, in which case it is like English 'w'. Thus *baktun* is 'bahk-TOON', but *Uaxactún* is 'wah-shahk-TOON' and *ahau* is 'ah-HAW'

x is like English 'sh', a shushing sound

Mayan glottalized consonants, those followed by an apostrophe (b', ch', k', p', t'), are similar to normal consonants, but pronounced more forcefully and 'explosively'. An apostrophe following a *vowel* signifies a glottal stop, *not* a more forceful vowel.

Another rule to remember is that in most Mayan words the stress falls on the last syllable. Sometimes this is indicated by an acute accent, sometimes not. Here are some pronunciation examples:

Abaj Takalik	ah-BAHH tah-kah LEEK
Acanceh	ah-kahn-KEH
Ahau	ah-HAW
Dzibilchaltún	dzee-beel-chahl-TOON
Kaminaljuyú	kah-mee-nahl-hoo-YOO
Oxcutzkab	ohsh-kootz-KAHB
Pacal	pah-KAHL
Pop	pope
Tikal	tee-KAHL
Uaxactún	wah-shahk-TOON
Xcaret	sh-kah-REHT
Yaxchilán	yahsh-chee-LAHN ∎

Menu Translator

Antojitos

Many traditional Mexican dishes are *antojitos* ('little whims'), savory or spicy concoctions that delight the palate.

burrito – any combination of beans, cheese, meat, chicken or seafood, seasoned with salsa or chile and wrapped in a flour tortilla

chilaquiles – scrambled eggs with chiles and bits of tortillas

chile relleno – *poblano* chile stuffed with cheese, meat or other foods, dipped in egg whites, fried and baked in sauce

enchilada – ingredients similar to those used in tacos and burritos wrapped in a corn tortilla, dipped in sauce and then baked or fried

machaca – cured, dried and shredded beef or pork mixed with eggs, onions, cilantro and chiles

papadzul – corn tortillas filled with hard-boiled eggs, cucumber or marrow seeds and covered in tomato sauce

quesadilla – flour tortilla topped or filled with cheese and occasionally other ingredients and then heated

queso relleno – 'stuffed cheese', a mild yellow cheese stuffed with minced meat and spices

taco – a soft or crisp corn tortilla wrapped or folded around the same filling as a burrito

tamale – steamed corn dough stuffed with meat, beans, chiles or nothing at all, wrapped in corn husks

tostada – flat, crisp tortilla topped with meat or cheese, tomatoes, beans and lettuce

Sopas (Soups)

birria – a spicy-hot soup of meat, onions, peppers and cilantro, served with tortillas

chipilín – cheese and cream soup on a maize base

gazpacho – chilled vegetable soup spiced with hot chiles

menudo – popular soup made with the spiced entrails (tripe) of various four-legged beasts

pozole – hominy soup with meat and vegetables (can be spicy)

sopa de arroz – not a soup at all but just a plate of rice; commonly served with lunch

sopa de lima – 'lime soup', chicken stock flavored with lime and filled with pieces of crisped corn tortilla

sopa de pollo – bits of chicken in a thin chicken broth

Huevos (Eggs)

huevos estrellados – fried eggs

huevos fritos – fried eggs

huevos motuleños – local dish of the Yucatecan town of Motul: fried eggs atop a tortilla spread with refried beans, garnished with diced ham, green peas, shredded cheese and tomato sauce, with fried bananas *(plátanos)* on the side

huevos rancheros – ranch-style eggs: fried, laid on a tortilla and smothered with spicy tomato sauce

huevos revueltos estilo mexicano – 'eggs scrambled Mexican-style' with tomatoes, onions, chiles and garlic

huevos revueltos – scrambled eggs; *con chorizo* (chor-REE-so) is served with spicy sausage, *con frijoles* is with beans

Pescado, Mariscos (Seafood)

The variety and quality of seafood from the coastal waters of Yucatán and Belize is excellent. Lobster is available on Mexico's Caribbean coast and in Belize, particularly on the cayes. Campeche (Mexico) is a major shrimping port, with much of its catch exported.

All of the following types of seafood are available in seafood restaurants most of the year. Clams, oysters, shrimp and prawns are also often available as *cocteles* (cocktails).

TRANSLATOR

abulón – abalone
almejas – clams
atún – tuna
cabrilla – sea bass
camarones gigantes – prawns
camarones – shrimp
cangrejo – large crab
ceviche – raw seafood marinated in lime juice and mixed with onions, chiles, garlic, tomatoes and *cilantro* (fresh coriander leaf)
dorado – dolphin
filete de pescado – fish fillet
huachinango – red snapper
jaiba – small crab
jurel – yellowtail
langosta – lobster
lenguado – flounder or sole
mariscos – shellfish
ostiones – oysters
pargo – red snapper
pescado al mojo de ajo – fish fried in butter and garlic
pescado – fish after it has been caught
pez espada – swordfish
pez – fish which is alive in the water
sierra – mackerel
tiburón – shark
tortuga or *caguama* – turtle
trucha de mar – sea trout

Carnes y Aves (Meat & Poultry)

asado – roast
barbacoa – literally 'barbecued', but by a process whereby the meat is covered and placed under hot coals
bistec – beefsteak; sometimes any cut of meat, fish or poultry
bistec de res – beefsteak
birria – barbecued on a spit
borrego – sheep
cabro – goat
carne al carbón – charcoal-grilled meat
carne asada – tough but tasty grilled beef
carnitas – deep-fried pork
chicharrones – deep-fried pork skin
chorizo – pork sausage
chuletas de puerco – pork chops
cochinita – suckling pig
codorniz, la chaquaca – quail
conejo – rabbit
cordero – lamb

costillas de puerco – pork ribs or chops
guajolote – turkey
hígado – liver
jamón – ham
milanesa de res – crumbed beefsteak
milanesa – crumbed, breaded
patas de puerco – pig's feet
pato – duck
pavo – turkey, a fowl native to Yucatán that figures prominently in Yucatecan cuisine
pibil – Yucatecan preparation: meat is flavored with *achiote* sauce, wrapped in banana leaves and baked in a pit oven, or *pib*
poc-chuc – slices of pork cooked in a tangy sauce of onion and sour oranges or lemons
pollo – chicken
pollo asado – grilled (not roast) chicken
pollo con arroz – chicken with rice
pollo frito – fried chicken
puerco – pork
tampiqueño, tampiqueña – 'in the style of Tampico', with spiced tomato sauce
tocino – bacon or salt pork
venado – venison

Frutas (Fruit)

coco – coconut
dátil – date
fresas – strawberries; any berries
guayaba – guava
higo – fig
limón – lime or lemon
mango – mango
melón – melon
naranja – orange
papaya – papaya
piña – pineapple
plátano – banana (suitable for cooking)
toronja – grapefruit
uva – grape

Legumbres, Verduras (Vegetables)

Vegetables are rarely served as separate dishes, but are often mixed into salads, soups and sauces.

aceitunas – olives
calabaza – squash, marrow or pumpkin
cebolla – onion
champiñones – mushrooms

chícharos – peas
ejotes – green beans
elote – corn on the cob; commonly served from steaming bins on street carts
jícama – a popular root vegetable that resembles a potato crossed with an apple; eaten fresh with a sprinkling of lime, chile and salt
lechuga – lettuce
papa – potato
tomate – tomato
zanahoria – carrot

Dulces (Desserts, Sweets)

flan – custard, crème caramel
helado – ice cream
nieve – Mexican equivalent of the American 'snow cone': flavored ice with the consistency of ice cream
paleta – flavored ice on a stick
pan dulce – sweet rolls, usually eaten for breakfast
pastel – cake
postre – dessert, after-meal sweet

Other Foods

achiote – a sauce of chopped tomato, onion, chiles and *cilantro* (fresh coriander leaf) used widely in Yucatán
azúcar – sugar
bolillo – French-style bread rolls
crema – cream
guacamole – mashed avocados mixed with onion, chile sauce, lemon, tomato and other ingredients
leche – milk
mantequilla – butter; intestinal upset from butter gone rancid in this hot climate has generated its jocular colloquial name 'meant-ta-kill-ya'

mole poblano – a popular hot sauce from Puebla, Mexico, made from more than 30 ingredients, including bitter chocolate, various chiles and many spices; often served over chicken or turkey
pimienta negra – black pepper
queso – cheese
salsa – sauce made with chiles, onion, tomato, lemon or lime juice and spices
sal – salt

Café (Coffee)

café sin azúcar – coffee without sugar. This keeps the waiter from adding heaps of sugar to your cup, but it doesn't mean your coffee won't taste sweet; sugar is often added to and processed with the beans.
café negro or *café americano* – black coffee with nothing added except sugar, unless it's made with sugar-coated coffee beans
café con leche – coffee with hot milk
café con crema – coffee with cream served separately
nescafé – instant coffee

At the Table

copa – glass
cuchara – spoon
cuchillo – knife
cuenta – bill
lista – menu (short for *lista de precios*); see *menú*
menú – fixed price meal, as in *menú del día*; sometimes menu; see *lista*
plato – plate
propina – the tip, 10 to 15% of the bill
servilleta – table napkin
taza – cup
tenedor – fork
vaso – drinking glass

TRANSLATOR

Glossary

abrazo – embrace, hug; in particular, the formal, ceremonial hug between political leaders

alux, aluxes – Mayan for gremlin, leprechaun, benevolent 'little people'

Apartado Postal – post office box, abbreviated *Apdo Postal*

Ayuntamiento – often seen as *H Ayuntamiento (Honorable Ayuntamiento)* on the front of Town Hall buildings, it translates as 'Municipal Government'

barrio – district, neighborhood

billete – bank note (unlike in Spain, where it's a ticket)

boleto – ticket (bus, train, museum, etc)

caballeros – literally 'horsemen', but corresponds to 'gentlemen' in English; look for it on toilet doors

cacique – Indian chief; also used to describe provincial warlord or strongman

cafetería – literally 'coffee-shop', it refers to any informal restaurant with waiter service; it is not usually a cafeteria in the American sense of a self-service restaurant

cajero automático – automated bank teller machine (ATM)

callejón – alley or small, narrow or very short street

camión – truck; bus

casa de cambio – currency exchange office; it offers exchange rates comparable to banks and is much faster to use

caseta de larga distancia – long-distance telephone station, often shortened to *caseta*

cazuela – clay cooking pot, usually sold in a nested set

cenote – large natural limestone cave used for water storage (or ceremonial purposes) in Yucatán

cerveza – beer

Chac – Mayan god of rain

chac-mool – Mayan sacrificial stone sculpture

chapín – a citizen of Guatemala; Guatemalan

charro – cowboy

chingar – literally 'to rape' but in practice a word with a wide range of colloquial meanings similar to the use of 'to screw' or 'to fuck' in English

chultún – artificial Mayan cistern found at Puuc archaeological sites south of Mérida

Churrigueresque – Spanish baroque architectural style of the early 18th century, with lavish ornamentation; named for architect José Churriguera

cigarro – cigarette

cocina – cookshop (literally 'kitchen'), a small, basic restaurant usually run by one woman, often located in or near a municipal market; also seen as *cocina económica* (economical kitchen) or *cocina familiar* (family kitchen); see also *lonchería*

colectivo – jitney taxi or minibus (usually a *combi*, or minibus) which picks up and drops off passengers along its route

completo – full up, a sign you may see on hotel desks in crowded cities

conquistador – Explorer-conqueror of Latin America from Spain

correos – post office

curandero – Indian traditional healer

damas – ladies, the usual sign on toilet doors

dzul, dzules – Mayan for foreigners or 'townfolk', that is, not Maya from the countryside

ejido – in Mexico, communally owned Indian land taken over by landowners but returned to the original owners under a program initiated by President Lázaro Cárdenas

encomienda – Spanish colonial practice of putting Indians under the 'guardianship' of landowners, practically akin to medieval serfdom

estación ferrocarril – train station

ferrocarril – railroad

galón, galones – US gallons (fluid measure of 3.79 liters; sometimes used in Belize and Guatemala)

gringo/a – a mild Mexican pejorative term applied to a male/female North American visitor; sometimes applied to any visitor of European heritage

gruta – cave

guayabera – man's thin fabric shirt with pockets and appliquéd designs on the front, over the shoulders and down the back; often worn in place of a jacket and tie at formal occasions

guardarropa – cloakroom, place to leave parcels when entering an establishment

hacienda – estate; also 'Treasury', as in *Departamento de Hacienda*, Treasury Department

hay – pronounced like 'eye', meaning 'there is', 'there are'. You're equally likely to hear *no hay*, 'there isn't' or 'there aren't'.

henequen – agave fiber used to make rope, grown particularly around Mérida in Yucatán

hombre/s – man/men

huipil – woven white dress from the Mayan regions with intricate, colorful embroidery

IMSS – Instituto Mexicana de Seguridad Social, the Mexican Social Security Institute; it operates many of Mexico's larger public hospitals. In Guatemala the corresponding institution is the IGSS.

IVA – the *impuesto al valor agregado* or 'ee-vah' is a value-added tax which can be as high as 15% and is added to many items in Mexico

Kukulcán – Mayan name for the Aztec-Toltec plumed serpent Quetzalcóatl

ladino – in Guatemala, a person of mixed Indian and European race; see also *mestizo*

larga distancia – long-distance telephone, abbreviated as Lada; see also caseta de larga distancia

lavandería – laundry; a *lavandería*

automática is a coin-operated laundry (laundromat)

leng – colloquial Mayan term for coins (Guatemalan highlands)

libras – pounds (weight measurement of 0.45 kilogram; sometimes used in Guatemala)

lista de correos – general delivery in Mexico; literally 'mail list,' the list of addressees for whom mail is being held, displayed in the post office

lonchería – from English *lunch*; a simple restaurant which may in fact serve meals all day (not just lunch). You often see loncherías near municipal markets.

lleno – full (fuel tank)

machismo – maleness, masculine virility; an ever-present aspect of Mexican society

malecon – waterfront boulevard

manzana – apple; also a city block. A *supermanzana* is a large group of city blocks bounded by major avenues. Ciudad Cancún uses manzana and supermanzana numbers as addresses.

mariachi – small ensemble of Mexican street musicians; strolling mariachi bands often perform in restaurants

mestizo – in Mexico, a person of mixed Indian and European blood; the word now more commonly means 'Mexican'; see also *ladino*

metate – flattish stone on which corn is ground with a cylindrical stone roller

millas – miles (distance of 1.61 km); sometimes used in Guatemala

Montezuma's revenge – Mexican version of 'Delhi-belly' or travelers' diarrhea

mordida – 'bite,' or small bribe that's usually paid to keep the wheels of bureaucracy turning. Giving a *mordida* to a traffic policeman may ensure that you won't have a bigger traffic fine to pay.

mudéjar – Moorish architectural style

mujer/es – woman/women

onza(s) – ounce(s) (weight of 28.35 grams); sometimes used in Guatemala

Palacio de Gobierno – building housing the executive offices of a state or regional government

Palacio Municipal – City Hall, seat of the corporation or municipal government

palapa – thatched palm-leaf roof shelter with open sides

parada – bus stop, usually for city buses

pie, pies – foot, feet (measure of 0.30 meters); sometimes used in Guatemala

pinchazo – automobile tire repair shop (Guatemala)

pisto – colloquial Mayan term for money, quetzals (Guatemalan highlands)

Plateresque – 'silversmith-like'; the architectural style of the Spanish renaissance (16th century), rich in decoration

PRI – Institutional Revolutionary Party, the controlling force in Mexican politics for more than half a century

propino, propina – a tip, different from a *mordida*, which is really a bribe

puro – cigar

Quetzalcóatl – plumed serpent god of the Aztecs and Toltecs

rebozo – long woolen or linen scarf covering the head or shoulders

retablo – ornate gilded, carved decoration of wood in a church

retorno – 'return'; in Cancún, a U-shaped street which starts from a major boulevard, loops around and 'returns' to the boulevard a block away

roofcomb – a decorative stonework lattice atop a Mayan pyramid or temple

rutelero – jitney

sacbé, sacbeob – ceremonial limestone avenue or path between great Mayan cities

sanatorio – hospital, particularly a small private one

sanitario – literally 'sanitary'; usually means toilet

serape – traditional woolen blanket

stela, stelae – standing stone monument(s), usually carved

supermercado – supermarket, ranging from a corner store to a large, American-style supermarket

taller – shop or workshop. A *taller mecánico* is a mechanic's shop, usually for cars. A *taller de llantas* is a tire-repair shop (Mexico).

teléfono monedero – coin-operated telephone (Guatemala)

templo – in Mexico, a church; anything from a wayside chapel to a cathedral

tequila – clear, distilled liquor produced, like pulque and mezcal, from the maguey cactus

Tex-Mex – Americanized version of Mexican food

típico – typical or characteristic of a region; particularly used to describe food

topes – speed bumps found in many Mexican towns, sometimes indicated by a highway sign bearing a row of little bumps

viajero – traveler

vulcanizadora – automobile tire repair shop (Mexico)

War of the Castes – bloody Mayan uprising in Yucatán during the mid-19th century

zócalo – Aztec for 'pedestal' or 'plinth', but used to refer to a town's main plaza (Mexico)

zotz – bat, the mammal, in many Mayan languages

Thanks to all the following travelers (and to any we've missed!) who took the time to write to us about their experiences along the Mayan Route.

Anders Aarkrog, Masoud Afarinkia, Paul Altomonte, Vicente Alvarez, Lotta Andersson, Brian Andreasen, James Andrick, Giuseppe Anzalone, Bianca Arens, Jörg Ausfelt, Jan Bailey, Myriam Baum, Taylor Beavers, Matthew K Belcher, Rob Bell, Steve Bell, Martin Belzile, Charles Bennett, Caryl Bergeron, Béatrice Blaise, Joel Bleskacek, Adam Blissett, Claire Bonnet, Nicole Boogaers, Theo Borst, Stephan Bössler, Annemarie Breeve, Peter Brennan, Heather Brown, James Brown, Ciara Browne, Steve Burton, Eric Calder, Elizabeth Canter, John Carlisle, Alexandre Chatin, Evelyne Chauis, Paula Cipolla, Michelle Clark, Jennifer Compton, David J Connor, Gianluigi Contin, Thomas P Coohill, Michelle Cooper, Elisabetta Corva, Francesc Costa, Jean-François Cousin, Colleen Coyle, Steve Creamer, Clare Cronan, Ingrid Dauh, Susanne de Raaij, Sylvia de Verga, Dean Desantis, Adolf Descalzi, Joseph-Ambroise Desrosiers, Elke Ditscheid-Göller, Bernard Dix, MG Dixon, Clement Djossen, Stéphane Doutriaux, J Winslow Dowson, Daniel Drazan, Annabella Dudziec, Linda A Dufresne, Roel Duijf, Kari Eloranta, Doron Ezra, Lisa Falloon, Daniel Finkbeiner, Jerry D Finley, Franesa Fiore, Artemis Fire, R Steve Fox, William F Frank, Lill Tove Fredriksen, Barbara Fricke, Eileen Fruggiero, Ulf Gäbler, Caroline & Mark Galanty, Rafael Jiménez García-Pascual, Elissa Gershon, Clive Giddings, Tracy R Glass, Ian Gleave, Javier Gonzalez-Ustes, Roberto Gotta, Emanuel Graef, Pamela Grist, Suzette Hafner, Susan Hall, Marion C Halmos, Mary Anne Hamer, Rhonda Hankins, Steve Harris, Colin Harvey, Ayman Hasson, Andrea Hazard, Michelle Hecht, KJ Herman, Matthias Herrlein, Gary Hickman, Allan Hindmarch, Dean R Hoge, Dorsey Holappa, Derek Hollinsworth, Paul Hopcraft, Camilla Hult, Nancy Hummel, Maury Hurt, Mary Ellen Jarvis, Tim Jeffries, Ginger Johnson, Tim Johnson, Jerven Jongkind, Tom Josephs, Tim San Jule, Alexander Jurk, Rikke Kamstrup, Tom Kegelman, David Kerkhoff, Hans Kerres, Samyra Keus, Zella King, Paul-Michael Klein, Esther Kobel, Raghu Krishnan, Randall R Krueger, Rainer Kugler, Louise La Valliére, Charles & Thelma L'Anson, Sean Lawson, Katalyne Lens, Steven Lidgey, Iris Lohrengel, Gaute Losnegård, To Man Mak, Yoshi Makino, Alessandro Marcolin, Anna Marron, Bob Mason, Christopher Mathis, Alexander Matskevich, Barrie McCormick, Stephanie Mills, Conrad Milne, Ramon Mireles, Alexis Morgan, Kat Morgenstern, Jennifer Morrissey, Julie Morse, Juraj Neidel, Michael Newton, Hugo Nielsen, Salena Noel, Karin Offer, Fernando Miguel Moreno Olmedo, Frank E Orgain, Louise Palmer, Ned Palmer, Eric Patrick, Patrik Paulis, Jane Anemærke Pedersen, Antonio Perez, Arnd Peterhoff, Karen Petersen, Ilse Pijl, David Plotz, Brigitte Poels, Andreas Poethen, Julio Puig, Jeannine Pulsfort, M Philippe Queriaux, Ben Radford, Hanna Ramberg, Laila Rasmussen, Ingrid Rauh , Bob Redlinger, Yolanda Ribas, Brane Ribic, Lisa Roberts, Paul Roberts, Stefan Roemer-Blum, Steve Rogowski, Geoffrey Rollins, Cheri Rosenthal, Hanna Rosin, Leo Ross, Fernando Sanchez Cuenca, Marietta Sander, David Schaffer, Jed Schlosberg, Stephen Schmidt, Emanuel Schnidrig, Wanda Schooley, Thomas Schwarz, Peter Schweitzer, Devin Scott, Kelly Shields, Elena Shtromberg, Aisha Siddiqi, Amy Sillman, Michael S Singer, Bo Sjoholm, Tijn Sleegers, Donald M Smith, Shirley Smith, Janne Solpark, Stan Spacey, Giulliame Stephane, Paul Steng, Jill Strudwick, Hilary Tempest, Dino ten Have, Tim C Thatcher, Lisette Thresh, Louri Lynn Throgmorton, Jason Throop, Cecile Tiano, Dogan Tirtiroglu, Thomas Todl, Sheila Tratt, Mike & Pauline Truman, Karena Ulede, Henk van der Berg, Joeke van Waesberghe, Michael Vestergaard, Joanne Viveash, Kathryn Wagner, Lidka Washington, Lindsey Webb, David Weinberg, Jim Whitaker, John T Widdowson, Geert Wijnhoven, Dave & Ann Williams, Bill Willoughby, Claudia Wink, Eva Wortman, Michael Wray, Iris Wüest, Susan Yanow, Camil Züloura

Index

TEXT

SIDEBARS

LONELY PLANET JOURNEYS

JOURNEYS is a unique collection of travel writing – published by the company that understands travel better than anyone else. It is a series for anyone who has ever experienced – or dreamed of – the magical moment when they encountered a strange culture or saw a place for the first time. They are tales to read while you're planning a trip, while you're on the road or while you're in an armchair, in front of a fire.

JOURNEYS books catch the spirit of a place, illuminate a culture, recount a crazy adventure, or introduce a fascinating way of life. They will always entertain, and always enrich the experience of travel.

'Idiosyncratic, entertainingly diverse and unexpected . . . from an international writership'

– The Australian

'Books which offer a closer look at the people and culture of a destination, and enrich travel experiences'
– American Bookseller

FULL CIRCLE
A South American Journey
Luis Sepúlveda

(translated by Chris Andrews)

Full Circle invites us to accompany Chilean writer Luis Sepúlveda on 'a journey without a fixed itinerary'. Whatever his subject - brutalities suffered under Pinochet's dictatorship, sleepy tropical towns visited in exile, or the landscapes of legendary Patagonia - Sepúlveda is an unflinchingly honest yet lyrical storyteller. Extravagant characters and extraordinary situations are memorably evoked: gauchos organizing a tournament of lies, a scheming heiress on the lookout for a husband, a pilot with a corpse on board his plane . . . Part autobiography, part travel memoir, *Full Circle* brings us the distinctive voice of one of South America's most compelling writers.

Luis Sepúlveda was born in Chile in 1949. Imprisoned by the Pinochet dictatorship for his socialist beliefs, he was for many years a political exile. He has written novels, short stories, plays and essays. His work has attracted many awards and has been translated into numerous languages.

'Detachment, humor and vibrant prose' – **El País**

'an absolute cracker' – **The Bookseller**

This project has been assisted by the Commonwealth Government through the Australian Council, its arts funding and advisory body.

LONELY PLANET PHRASEBOOKS

Building bridges,
Breaking barriers,
Beyond babble-on

Listen for the gems

Speak your own words

Ask your own questions

Master of your own image

- handy pocket-sized books

- easy to understand Pronunciation chapter

- clear and comprehensive Grammar chapter

- romanization alongside script to allow ease of pronunciation

- script throughout so users can point to phrases

- extensive vocabulary sections, words and phrases for every situation

- full of cultural information and tips for the traveler

'. . . vital for a real DIY spirit and attitude in language learning.' – Backpacker

'the phrasebooks have good cultural backgrounders and offer solid advice for challenging situations in remote locations'   – San Francisco Examiner

'. . . they are unbeatable for their coverage of the world's more obscure languages'
                          – The Geographical Magazine

Arabic (Egyptian)
Arabic (Moroccan)
Australian
 *Australian English,
 Aboriginal and Torres Strait
 languages*
Baltic States
 *Estonian, Latvian,
 Lithuanian*
Bengali
Brazilian
Burmese
Cantonese
Central Asian
Central Europe
 *Czech, French, German,
 Hungarian, Italian and Slovak*
Eastern Europe
Ethiopian Amharic
Fijian
French
German
Greek

Hindi/Urdu
Indonesian
Italian
Japanese
Korean
Lao
Latin American Spanish
Malay
Mandarin
Mediterranean Europe
 *Albanian, Croation, Greek,
 Italian, Macedonian, Maltese,
 Serbian, Slovene*
Mongolian
Nepali
Pidgin (Papua New Guinea)
Pilipino (Tagalog)
Quechua
Russian
Scandinavian Europe
 *Danish, Finnish, Icelandic,
 Norweign and Swedish*

South East Asia
 *Burmese, Indonesian, Khmer,
 Lao, Malay, Tagalog (Pilipino),
 Thai and Vietnamese*
Sri Lanka
Swahili
Thai
Thai Hill Tribes
Tibetan
Turkish
Ukrainian
USA
 *US English, Vernacular Talk,
 Native American languages and
 Hawaiian*
Vietnamese
Western Europe
 *Basque, Catalan, Dutch,
 French, German, Irish, Italian,
 Portuguese, Scottish, Gaelic,
 Spanish (Castilian) and Welsh*

LONELY PLANET TRAVEL ATLASES

Lonely Planet has long been famous for the number and quality of its guidebook maps. Now we've gone one step further and in conjunction with Steinhart Katzir Publishers produced a handy companion series: Lonely Planet travel atlases–maps of a country produced in book form.

Unlike other maps, which look good but lead travelers astray, our travel atlases have been researched on the road by Lonely Planet's experienced team of writers. All details are carefully checked to ensure the atlas corresponds with the equivalent Lonely Planet guidebook.

The handy atlas format means no holes, wrinkles, torn sections or constant folding and unfolding. These atlases can survive long periods on the road, unlike cumbersome fold-out maps. The comprehensive index ensures easy reference.

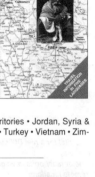

- full-color throughout
- maps researched and checked by Lonely Planet authors
- place names correspond with Lonely Planet guidebooks –no confusing spelling differences
- legend and traveling information in English, French, German, Japanese and Spanish
- size: 230 x 160 mm

Available now:
Chile & Easter Island • Egypt • India & Bangladesh • Israel & the Palestinian Territories • Jordan, Syria & Lebanon • Kenya • Laos • Portugal • South Africa, Lesotho & Swaziland • Thailand • Turkey • Vietnam • Zimbabwe, Botswana & Namibia

---

LONELY PLANET TV SERIES & VIDEOS

Lonely Planet travel guides have been brought to life on television screens around the world. Like our guides, the programs are based on the joy of independent travel, and look honestly at some of the most exciting, picturesque and frustrating places in the world. Each show is presented by one of three travelers from Australia, England or the USA and combines an innovative mixture of video, Super-8 film, atmospheric soundscapes and original music.

Videos of each episode–containing additional footage not shown on television–are available from good book and video shops, but the availability of individual videos varies with regional screening schedules.

Video destinations include: Alaska • American Rockies • Australia (Southeast) • Baja California • Brazil • Central Asia • Chile & Easter Island • Corsica, Sicily & Sardinia • East Africa, Tanzania & Zanzibar • Ecuador & the Galápagos Islands • France • Greenland & Iceland • Indonesia • Israel & the Sinai Desert • Jamaica • Japan • La Ruta Maya • Morocco • New York City • North India (Varanasi to the Himalayas) • Pacific Islands • South India • Southwest China • Turkey • Vietnam • West Africa • Zimbabwe, Botswana & Namibia

The Lonely Planet TV series is produced by:
Pilot Productions
Duke of Sussex Studios
44 Uxbridge St
London W8 7TG UK

Lonely Planet videos are distributed by:
IVN Communications Inc
2246 Camino Ramon
California 94583, USA

107 Power Road, Chiswick
London W4 5PL UK

Music from the TV series is available on CD & cassette.
For ordering information contact your nearest Lonely Planet office.

PLANET TALK

Lonely Planet's FREE quarterly newsletter

We love hearing from you and think you'd like to hear from us.
When... is the right time to see reindeer in Finland?
Where... can you hear the best palm-wine music in Ghana?
How... do you get from Asunción to Areguá by steam train?
What... is the best way to see India?

For the answer to these and many other questions read PLANET TALK.

Every issue is packed with up-to-date travel news and advice including:

- a letter from Lonely Planet founders Tony and Maureen Wheeler
- travel diary from a Lonely Planet author—find out what it's really like out on the road
- feature article on an important and topical travel issue
- a selection of recent letters from our readers
- the latest travel news from all over the world
- details on Lonely Planet's new and forthcoming releases

To join our mailing list contact any Lonely Planet office .

Also available: Lonely Planet T-shirts. 100% heavyweight cotton (S, M, L, XL)

LONELY PLANET ONLINE

Get the latest travel information before you leave or while you're on the road

Whether you've just begun planning your next trip, or you're chasing down specific info on currency regulations or visa requirements, check out Lonely Planet Online for up-to-the-minute travel information.

As well as travel profiles of your favorite destinations (including maps and photos), you'll find current reports from our researchers and other travelers, updates on health and visas, travel advisories, and discussion of the ecological and political issues you need to be aware of as you travel.

There's also an online travelers' forum where you can share your experience of life on the road, meet travel companions and ask other travelers for their recommendations and advice. We also have plenty of links to other online sites useful to independent travelers.

And of course we have a complete and up-to-date list of all Lonely Planet travel products including guides, phrasebooks, atlases, Journeys and videos and a simple online ordering facility if you can't find the book you want elsewhere.

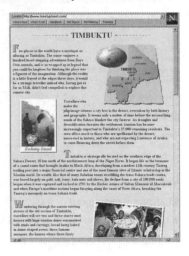

www.lonelyplanet.com or AOL keyword: lp

LONELY PLANET PRODUCTS

Lonely Planet is known worldwide for publishing practical, reliable and no-nonsense travel information in our guides and on our web site. The Lonely Planet list covers just about every accessible part of the world. Currently there are eight series: *travel guides, shoestring guides, walking guides, city guides, phrasebooks, audio packs, travel atlases* and *Journeys*–a unique collection of travel writing.

EUROPE

Amsterdam • Austria • Baltic States & Kaliningrad • Baltic States phrasebook • Britain • Central Europe on a shoestring • Central Europe phrasebook • Czech & Slovak Republics • Denmark • Dublin city guide • Eastern Europe on a shoestring • Eastern Europe phrasebook • Finland • France • Greece • Greek phrasebook • Hungary • Iceland, Greenland & the Faroe Islands • Ireland • Italy • Mediterranean Europe on a shoestring • Mediterranean Europe phrasebook • Paris city guide • Poland • Portugal • Portugal travel atlas • Prague city guide • Russia, Ukraine & Belarus • Russian phrasebook • Scandinavian & Baltic Europe on a shoestring • Scandinavian Europe phrasebook • Slovenia • Spain • St Petersburg city guide • Switzerland • Trekking in Greece • Trekking in Spain • Ukrainian phrasebook • Vienna city guide • Walking in Britain • Walking in Switzerland • Western Europe on a shoestring • Western Europe phrasebook

NORTH AMERICA

Alaska • Backpacking in Alaska • Baja California • Bermuda • California & Nevada • Canada • Florida • Hawaii • Honolulu city guide • Los Angeles city guide • Mexico • Miami city guide • New England • New Orleans city guide • New York City • New York, New Jersey & Pennsylvania • Pacific Northwest USA • Rocky Mountain States USA • San Francisco city guide • Southwest USA • USA phrasebook • Washington, DC & The Capital Region

CENTRAL AMERICA & THE CARIBBEAN

Central America on a shoestring • Costa Rica • Cuba • Eastern Caribbean • Guatemala, Belize & Yucatán: La Ruta Maya • Jamaica

SOUTH AMERICA

Argentina, Uruguay & Paraguay • Bolivia • Brazil • Brazilian phrasebook • Buenos Aires city guide • Chile & Easter Island • Chile travel atlas • Colombia • Ecuador & the Galápagos Islands • Latin American Spanish phrasebook • Peru • Quechua phrasebook • Rio de Janeiro city guide • South America on a shoestring • Trekking in the Patagonian Andes • Venezuela

Travel Literature: Full Circle: A South American Journey

AFRICA

Arabic (Moroccan) phrasebook • Africa on a shoestring • Africa The South • Cape Town city guide • Central Africa • East Africa • Egypt & the Sudan • Egypt travel atlas • Ethiopian (Amharic) phrasebook • Kenya • Kenya travel atlas • Malawi, Mozambique & Zambia • Morocco • North Africa • South Africa, Lesotho & Swaziland • South Africa travel atlas • Swahili phrasebook • Trekking in East Africa • West Africa • Zimbabwe, Botswana & Namibia • Zimbabwe, Botswana & Namibia travel atlas

Travel Literature: The Rainbird: A Central African Journey • Songs to an African Sunset: A Zimbabwean Story

ISLANDS OF THE INDIAN OCEAN

Madagascar & Comoros • Maldives & Islands of the East Indian Ocean • Mauritius, Réunion & Seychelles

Also Available: Travel with Children • Traveller's Tales

MAIL ORDER

Lonely Planet products are distributed worldwide. They are also available by mail order from Lonely Planet, so if you have difficulty finding a title please write to us. North American and South American residents should write to Embarcadero West, 155 Filbert St, Suite 251, Oakland CA 94607, USA; European and African residents should write to 10 Barley Mow Passage, Chiswick, London W4 4PH; and residents of other countries to PO Box 617, Hawthorn, Victoria 3122, Australia.

NORTH-EAST ASIA

Beijing city guide • Cantonese phrasebook • China • Hong Kong city guide • Hong Kong, Macau & Canton • Japan • Japanese phrasebook • Japanese audio pack • Korea • Korean phrasebook • Mandarin phrasebook • Mongolia • Mongolian phrasebook • North-East Asia on a shoestring • Seoul city guide • Taiwan • Tibet • Tibet phrasebook • Tokyo city guide

Travel Literature: Lost Japan

MIDDLE EAST & CENTRAL ASIA

Arab Gulf States • Arabic (Egyptian) phrasebook • Central Asia • Iran • Israel & the Palestinian Territories • Israel & the Palestinian Territories travel atlas • Istanbul city guide • Jerusalem city guide • Jordan & Syria • Jordan, Syria & Lebanon travel atlas • Middle East • Turkey • Turkey travel atlas • Turkish phrasebook • Trekking in Turkey • Yemen

Travel Literature: The Gates of Damascus • Kingdom of the Film Stars: Journey into Jordon

INDIAN SUBCONTINENT

Bengali phrasebook • Bangladesh • Delhi city guide • Hindi/Urdu phrasebook • India • India & Bangladesh travel atlas • Indian Himalaya • Karakoram Highway • Nepal • Nepali phrasebook • Pakistan • Rajasthan • Sri Lanka • Sri Lanka phrasebook • Trekking in the Indian Himalaya • Trekking in the Karakoram & Hindukush • Trekking in the Nepal Himalaya

Travel Literature: In Rajasthan • Shopping for Buddhas

SOUTH-EAST ASIA

Bali & Lombok • Bangkok city guide • Burmese phrasebook • Cambodia • Ho Chi Minh city guide • Indonesia • Indonesian phrasebook • Indonesian audio pack • Jakarta city guide • Java • Laos • Lao phrasebook • Laos travel atlas • Malay phrasebook • Malaysia, Singapore & Brunei • Myanmar (Burma) • Philippines • Pilipino phrasebook • Singapore city guide • South-East Asia on a shoestring • Thailand • Thai phrasebook • Thailand travel atlas • Thai audio pack • Thai Hill Tribes phrasebook • Vietnam • Vietnamese phrasebook • Vietnam travel atlas

ANTARCTICA

Antarctica

AUSTRALIA & THE PACIFIC

Australia • Australian phrasebook • Bushwalking in Australia • Bushwalking in Papua New Guinea • Fiji • Fijian phrasebook • Islands of Australia's Great Barrier Reef • Melbourne city guide • Micronesia • New Caledonia • New South Wales & the ACT • New Zealand • Northern Territory • Outback Australia • Papua New Guinea • Papua New Guinea phrasebook • Queensland • Rarotonga & the Cook Islands • Samoa • Solomon Islands • South Australia • Sydney city guide • Tahiti & French Polynesia • Tasmania • Tonga • Tramping in New Zealand • Vanuatu • Victoria • Western Australia

Travel Literature: Islands in the Clouds • Sean & David's Long Drive

THE LONELY PLANET STORY

Lonely Planet published its first book in 1973 in response to the numerous 'How did you do it?' questions Maureen and Tony Wheeler were asked after driving, bussing, hitching, sailing and railing their way from England to Australia.

Written at a kitchen table and hand collated, trimmed and stapled, *Across Asia on the Cheap* became an instant local best seller, inspiring thoughts of another book.

Eighteen months in South-East Asia resulted in their second guide, South-East Asia on a shoestring, which they put together in a backstreet Chinese hotel in Singapore in 1975. The 'yellow bible', as it quickly became known to backpackers around the world, soon became the guide to the region. It has sold well over half a million copies and is now in its 9th edition, still retaining its familiar yellow cover.

Today there are 240 titles, including travel guides, walking guides, language kits & phrasebooks, travel atlases and travel literature. The company is the largest independent travel publishers in the world. Although Lonely Planet initially specialized in guides to Asia, today there are few corners of the globe that have not been covered.

The emphasis continues to be on travel for independent travelers. Tony and Maureen still travel for several months of each year and play an active part in the writing, updating and quality control of Lonely Planet's guides.

They have been joined by over 70 authors and 170 staff at our offices in Melbourne (Australia), Oakland (USA), London (UK) and Paris (France). Travelers themselves also make a valuable contribution to the guides through the feedback we receive in thousands of letters each year and on our website.

The people at Lonely Planet strongly believe that travelers can make a positive contribution to the countries they visit, both through their appreciation of the countries' culture, wildlife and natural features, and through the money they spend. In addition, the company makes a direct contribution to the countries and regions it covers. Since 1986 a percentage of the income from each book has been donated to ventures such as famine relief in Africa; aid projects in India; agricultural projects in Central America; Greenpeace's efforts to halt French nuclear testing in the Pacific; and Amnesty International.

'I hope we send people out with the right attitude about travel. You realize when you travel that there are so many different perspectives about the world, so we hope these books will make people more interested in what they see. Guidebooks can't really guide people. All you can do is point them in the right direction.'

– Tony Wheeler

LONELY PLANET PUBLICATIONS

Australia
PO Box 617, Hawthorn 3122, Victoria
☎ (03) 9819 1877 fax (03) 9819 6459
e-mail talk2us@lonelyplanet.com.au

USA
Embarcadero West, 155 Filbert St, Suite 251
Oakland, California 94607
☎ (510) 893 8555, TOLL FREE (800) 275 8555
fax (510) 893 8563
e-mail info@lonelyplanet.com

UK
10 Barley Mow Passage, Chiswick,
London W4 4PH
☎ (0181) 742 3161 fax (0181) 742 2772
e-mail lonelyplanetuk@compuserve.com

France
71 bis rue du Cardinal Lemoine, 75005 Paris
☎ 1 44 32 06 20 fax 1 46 34 72 55
e-mail 100560.415@compuserve.com

World Wide Web: www.lonelyplanet.com